INTRODUCTION

TO

AMERICAN LAW.

DESIGNED AS A

FIRST BOOK FOR STUDENTS.

BY

TIMOTHY WALKER, LL.D.,

LATE PROFESSOR OF LAW IN THE CINCINNATI COLLEGE.

NINTH EDITION.

REVISED BY

CLEMENT BATES,

OF THE CINCINNATI BAR.

THE LAWBOOK EXCHANGE, LTD.
Union, New Jersey
2002

ISNB-13: 978-1-58477-214-9
ISBN-10: 1-58477-214-X

Second printing 2006

Printed in the United States of America on acid-free paper

THE LAWBOOK EXCHANGE, LTD.
33 Terminal Avenue
Clark, New Jersey 07066-1321

Please see our website for a selection of our other publications and fine facsimile reprints of classic works of legal history:
www.lawbookexchange.com

Library of Congress Cataloging-in-Publication Data

Walker, Timothy, 1802-1856.
Introduction to American law : designed as a first book for students / by Timothy Walker.— 9th ed. / rev, by Clement Bates.
p. cm.
Originally published: 9th ed. Boston: Little, Brown & Co., 1887.
Includes bibliographical references and index.
ISBN 1-58477-214-X (cloth: alk. paper)
1. Law—United States. I. Bates, Clement, 1845-1931. II. Title.

KF386 .W3 2001
349.73—dc21 2001038955

INTRODUCTION

TO

AMERICAN LAW.

DESIGNED AS A

FIRST BOOK FOR STUDENTS.

BY

TIMOTHY WALKER, LL.D.,

LATE PROFESSOR OF LAW IN THE CINCINNATI COLLEGE.

NINTH EDITION.

REVISED BY

CLEMENT BATES,

OF THE CINCINNATI BAR.

BOSTON:
LITTLE, BROWN, AND COMPANY.
1887.

UNIVERSITY PRESS:
JOHN WILSON AND SON, CAMBRIDGE.

TO THE

HONORABLE JOSEPH STORY,

WHO EQUALLY ADORNS AND ILLUSTRATES AMERICAN JURISPRUDENCE IN THE SEVERAL CAPACITIES OF

JUDGE, AUTHOR, AND TEACHER,

IN EACH OF WHICH HE HAS NO SUPERIOR, THE FOLLOWING HUMBLE EFFORT TO PREPARE THE WAY FOR MORE READILY APPRECIATING HIS VAST AND VARIOUS LABORS,

IS MOST RESPECTFULLY INSCRIBED,

BY ONE WHO HAS ENJOYED THE GOOD FORTUNE OF BEING HIS PUPIL AND FRIEND.

PREFACE

TO THE NINTH EDITION.

In the present edition the text where relating to statutory law, as in the chapter on Crimes and on Title by Descent, has been altered to conform to the present law, but otherwise remains untouched. The new notes, except when consisting of mere additions of late cases, are designated by brackets, and the index has been somewhat enlarged.

Of the preceding editions the first three were the work of the author himself; the fourth was by Mr. E. L. Pierce, author of the well-known Treatise on the Law of Railroads. The lamented Judge J. Bryant Walker prepared the sixth edition; and the seventh and eighth editions, in which for the first time English authorities were drawn upon, were prepared by Judge M. F. Force, of the Superior Court of Cincinnati.

CLEMENT BATES.

Cincinnati, *Feb.* 1, 1887.

PREFACE

TO THE EIGHTH EDITION.

THE first three editions, with the notes, were entirely the work of the author. Mr. E. L. PIERCE, author of a Treatise on the Law of Railroads, added notes to the fourth edition. Judge J. BRYANT WALKER, son of the author, made additional notes for the sixth edition; and I added more to the seventh. The text remains as it was left by the author.

The notes added by Mr. Pierce, Judge J. B. Walker, and myself, were enclosed in brackets of different forms, which distinguished the work of each. As those designating marks are omitted in this edition, I have felt at liberty to omit some of the older notes, supplying their place by new matter. Only American decisions were cited by the former editors. Although the work is entitled "Introduction to American Law," I have preferred to use also English decisions.

M. F. FORCE.

CINCINNATI, *September*, 1882.

PREFACE

TO THE FIRST EDITION.

ACCORDING to the custom of the times, a preface usually takes the form of an apology for adding to the multitude of books; and I shall so far comply with this custom as to explain my reason for making this publication.

While pursuing my legal studies, I found myself much in the condition of a mariner without chart or compass. I experienced at every step the want of a first book upon the law of this country. I felt that much time would have been saved if I could have commenced my course with a systematic outline of American instead of English law; for, as the two systems differ in nearly as many points as they correspond, and as I had no means of distinguishing between the applicable and the inapplicable, I necessarily acquired many false impressions, the more difficult to be subsequently corrected because they were first impressions. In a word, I came to the conclusion that fewer facilities have been provided for studying the elementary principles of American jurisprudence, than for perhaps any other branch of useful knowledge.

And these results of my experience as a student have acquired additional confirmation from my experience as a teacher. In the year 1833, I became connected with the Cincinnati Law School, at first a private institution, but afterwards a department of the Cincinnati College; and here I was hourly called upon to remove the doubts and difficulties which I had myself encountered. In order to do this in the most convenient and effectual manner, and without a thought of publication, I commenced the preparation of the following Lectures, which I read to the students, as an introduction or accompaniment to the usual course of legal study. Such being my object, I endeavored to be clear and simple, rather than to seem profound or erudite; and instead of attempting to give a complete exposition of any single branch of law, I sought to bring together all the various branches, and present them to view under a comprehensive but systematic outline, which would exhibit their general bearings and relations only, and not their particular details; but, at the same time, in connection with each successive topic, I mentioned the books containing more detailed information.

Such, briefly, were the views with which these Lectures were prepared; and I now publish them under a belief that they will be useful to two classes of persons; namely, first, those who are beginning a course of professional study, and require something in the nature of a guide-book; and, secondly, those who desire to obtain some general notions of the law, as an important part of practical education, but do not intend to pursue it as a profession. Whether this belief be well founded or not, experiment only can determine. If not, as my aim has been utility only, and not fame, so my failure will only occasion regret, and not mortification. I have, however, been induced to hope for a happier result, from the favorable opinion almost unanimously expressed by the students to whom these Lectures were read, and who may be presumed to be the best judges of what will satisfy their own wants; and also from the approbation expressed by several distinguished professional gentlemen, to whom I submitted the manuscript, and in whose judgment and candor I have the utmost confidence. I mention these facts to show that I have not acted rashly or unadvisedly; but not to make others responsible for my errors. If I have been guilty of adding one more to the catalogue of useless books, as mine has been the presumption, let the censure rest on me alone; and I will no further deprecate criticism, or implore mercy, than by asking those who may pass judgment upon my efforts to keep my purpose distinctly in view. Let it be remembered that I have written for beginners only, and not for adepts; that I have made no pretensions to deep professional lore; that this book does not propose to supersede other elementary books, but only to prepare the way for them; and that I seek no other praise than that of usefulness.

If an author may be allowed to express an opinion in his own case, I would say that the chief merits of this book will be found to consist in perspicuity and condensation. As to originality, unless it be in the arrangement and modes of illustration, it does not belong to such an undertaking; but it is proper to say, that I have quoted very sparingly the language of other writers, and never without giving credit. I have, moreover, scrupulously avoided giving long abstracts of cases, though this is a very convenient method of making or amplifying law-books. In a word, I have crowded as many general principles as I could into the smallest compass compatible with clearness; and, to this end, I have sought to use just such words and so many words as would express my meaning, and no more. Believing that the language of a law-book should be seen through rather than looked at, I have made no attempt at what is called fine writing, but have used as much plainness and familiarity of speech as the exceedingly technical character of the subject would permit. Indeed, what other fault soever may be found, professional pedantry will not be imputed to me.

But I have entitled this book an Introduction to American Law, and I may be called upon to vindicate the propriety of this title. I confess, then, that in some minor respects it may not be equally adapted to all parts of the Union; but my excuse is, that without being ten times as large as it is, it could not have been made so. If I had possessed the knowledge, I could not, within any reasonable compass, have referred to the local law of twenty-six different States; and yet local references were occasionally necessary, in order to exhibit an entire system. I was compelled, therefore, in such cases, to make choice of some particular State; and I naturally selected that State in which the Lectures were read. But these local references, in an outline so general as this, are not so frequent as to detract materially from the general adaptation of the book to students in other States; and, in case of diversity, the necessary corrections can be easily made. At all events, the diversity is less between the different States than between any one State and England; and therefore something is certainly gained even on the score of general adaptation.

And here let me anticipate an objection of another sort. It may be said, that, in attempting to teach what the law is, I have dwelt too much upon what I think it should be; or, in other words, that in a work professedly didactic, I have speculated too much upon projects of reform. To this objection I have two answers. In the first place, I have never undertaken to show what the law ought to be, without first stating what it is. While, therefore, the primary end of instruction is obtained, the mind of the student is at the same time excited to compare, examine, and discuss the principles in question; and thus impress them the more deeply upon his memory. And, in the second place, if the suggestions I have ventured to make be sound, they cannot be made too early, because bad laws are the very worst of bad things; and if these suggestions be not sound, they can do no harm, because the antidote accompanies the bane; nay, the provision complained of will inspire increased confidence in the mind of the student from having been unsuccessfully assailed. But I cannot help believing that many of the proposed alterations would be decided improvements; and, in that belief, I have been anxious to present them to minds unhackneyed by custom, and therefore the more fitted to examine them without prejudice. I confess myself sanguine on the subject of legal reform; but I trust that I have nowhere pressed such considerations in an improper spirit.

Such, then, are the prefatory explanations which I have deemed it proper to make. That a book like that which I have endeavored to furnish is very much wanted, all will agree. How far my execution has corresponded with my design, it is for my readers to decide. I cannot but wonder, as well as regret, that the task has not long since been performed by abler hands, for it is well worthy of the very ablest. Why has not some distinguished lawyer, after retiring from the more active labors of his profession, added one more laurel to his brilliant wreath, by embodying, in an enduring form, for the instruction of those who are to come after him, the matured results of wisdom and experience? A complete exposition of American Law, by such a man, whose very name would command respect and confidence, would be a glorious liquidation of that debt which every great lawyer is said to owe to his profession; but such a benefactor has not appeared. The American Blackstone is yet to be desired: otherwise, the author of the following pages, without the age, learning, or experience which qualify him to speak with authority, and wholly unknown to fame, would have had no apology for attempting to instruct even beginners in the noble science which so many illustrious men at this moment adorn.

CINCINNATI, *Feb.* 25, 1837.

PREFACE

TO THE SECOND EDITION.

My original purpose in publishing this book is fully explained in the former preface. In the present edition, I have made such alterations and additions as experience taught me to believe would increase the usefulness of the work. Upon some of the more important topics I have given, in the Notes, an abstract of the leading cases. Upon others, I have enlarged the text. In the department of Constitutional Law, I have availed myself of the new light derived from the Madison Papers. I have added two Lectures upon International Law. I have made the Law of Procedure more intelligible, by annexing the most approved forms. And I have thrown into the Appendix the text of our fundamental law, together with a catalogue of the most important books. The first edition was received with far more favor than I had a right to expect; and I think I may venture to assure the public that the second is a decided improvement upon the first.

T. WALKER.

CINCINNATI, *Oct.* 1, 1844.

PREFACE

TO THE THIRD EDITION.

IN this edition I have made such changes in the text as the progress of the age in Legislation and Jurisprudence made necessary, and have added one Lecture upon Admiralty Procedure. I have also added a large number of Notes upon some of the leading titles, especially upon the law of Real Property. And, in order that the volume might not be enlarged to an inconvenient size, I have omitted the Appendix altogether.

T. WALKER.

CINCINNATI, *Oct.* 1, 1855.

CONTENTS.

PART FIRST.

PRELIMINARY CONSIDERATIONS.

LECTURE I.

STUDY OF THE LAW.

LECTURE II.

PRINCIPLES OF POLITICAL ORGANIZATION.

LECTURE III.

HISTORICAL SUMMARY.

LECTURE IV.

DIVISIONS AND DEFINITIONS.

PART SECOND.

CONSTITUTIONAL LAW.

LECTURE V.

RELATIONS OF THE STATES.

LECTURE VI.

LEGISLATIVE DEPARTMENT.

LECTURE VII.

EXECUTIVE DEPARTMENT.

LECTURE VIII.

JUDICIAL DEPARTMENT.

LECTURE IX.

ENUMERATED POWERS.

LECTURE X.

INCIDENTAL POWERS.

LECTURE XI.

BILL OF RIGHTS.

PART THIRD.

THE LAW OF PERSONS.

LECTURE XII.

CORPORATIONS.

LECTURE XIII.

PARTNERSHIPS.

LECTURE XIV.

HUSBAND AND WIFE.

LECTURE XV.

PARENT AND CHILD.

LECTURE XVI.

GUARDIAN AND WARD.

LECTURE XVII.

MASTER AND SERVANT.

LECTURE XVIII.

EXECUTORS AND ADMINISTRATORS.

PART FOURTH.

THE LAW OF PROPERTY.

LECTURE XIX.

PRELIMINARY CONSIDERATIONS.

LECTURE XX.

INCORPOREAL HEREDITAMENTS, EASEMENTS, AND FIXTURES.

LECTURE XXI.

ESTATES WITH RESPECT TO DURATION.

LECTURE XXII.

ESTATES IN REVERSION AND REMAINDER.

LECTURE XXIII.

ESTATES IN COMMON.

LECTURE XXIV.

ESTATES UPON CONDITION.

LECTURE XXV.

MORTGAGES.

LECTURE XXVI.

EQUITABLE ESTATES.

LECTURE XXVII.

TITLE BY OCCUPANCY.

LECTURE XXVIII.

TITLE BY MARRIAGE.

LECTURE XXIX.

TITLE BY DESCENT.

LECTURE XXX.

TITLE BY DEVISE.

LECTURE XXXI.

TITLE BY PURCHASE.

LECTURE XXXII.

CONTRACTS IN GENERAL.

LECTURE XXXIII.

PARTICULAR CONTRACTS.

PART FIFTH.

THE LAW OF CRIMES.

LECTURE XXXIV.

CRIMES AND PUNISHMENTS IN GENERAL.

LECTURE XXXV.

CRIMES UNDER THE STATE LAW.

LECTURE XXXVI.

CRIMES UNDER THE LAW OF THE UNITED STATES.

PART SIXTH.

THE LAW OF PROCEDURE.

LECTURE XXXVII.

CIVIL PROCEEDINGS IN COURTS OF LAW.

LECTURE XXXVIII.

CHANCERY PROCEEDINGS.

LECTURE XXXIX.

ADMIRALTY PROCEEDINGS.

LECTURE XL.

CRIMINAL PROCEEDINGS.

PART SEVENTH.

INTERNATIONAL LAW.

LECTURE XLI.

PUBLIC INTERNATIONAL LAW.

LECTURE XLII.

PRIVATE INTERNATIONAL LAW.

LECTURE XLIII.

CONCLUDING REFLECTIONS.

INTRODUCTION TO AMERICAN LAW.

PART I.

PRELIMINARY CONSIDERATIONS.

LECTURE I.

STUDY OF THE LAW. (*a*)

§ 1. **Difficulties to be overcome.** The course of lectures to which this is introductory, is intended to comprehend the rudiments of American law. I say *rudiments*, because I am persuaded that nothing beyond principles strictly elementary, can be profitably presented in the form of lectures. The almost infinite variety of details into which this science runs, can only be learned by a laborious examination of books, and an assiduous attendance upon courts. The attempt to embrace them in lectures, would only confuse the memory of the hearers. To me the task would be endless; to you comparatively useless. I shall have accomplished all I propose to myself, if I can furnish you with a general chart of the long voyage upon which you are about to embark. Accordingly the views I shall present will always be general, and, sometimes, unavoidably superficial. They will be outlines merely for you to fill up by your own investigations. I shall endeavor to imbue you with the spirit and philosophy of law, as a science, consisting of principles arranged into a system. I shall commence and proceed throughout upon the supposition that you are beginners only, not adepts. I shall consider you as having one of two objects in view; either to make the law a regular profession, or to acquaint yourselves with its elements as a part of general education. It is matter of surprise as well as regret that the number of persons of the latter description is not greater. But I trust that public sentiment is changing on this subject. I think I perceive a manifest tendency towards a more general acquisition of

(*a*) See the first section of Blackstone's Introduction; Warren on the Study of the Law; Hoffman's Course of Legal Study; an Essay prefixed to Anthon's Blackstone: and a work entitled Law and Lawyers.

legal information among persons who never design to be professional lawyers; and I rejoice at the prospect; for there is no branch of knowledge so essential to the proper discharge of the various duties of a citizen. This is especially true with respect to American citizens, whose high prerogative it is, by virtue of the doctrine of universal suffrage, to have a direct and personal participation in all public affairs. Surely that man is not fit to be the maker or the guardian of laws, who has never been educated in their first principles. But apart from public and patriotic considerations, self-interest should induce every man to understand his own rights and obligations. This proposition is almost too clear to need enforcement. As the *subjects* of law, certainly, if not as the *makers*, all ought to know enough to avoid its penalties, and reap its benefits. Unquestionably, on the score of practical utility, no kind of knowledge can stand higher; for it comes into immediate application, almost every hour we live. And yet how little provision has hitherto been made, in our seminaries of learning, for this so important department of instruction! The reasons commonly assigned for its neglect, are chiefly predicated upon the difficulties of teaching law in an easy and popular manner. Some of these difficulties are worthy of a brief notice, because they apply equally to professional teaching. They have reference principally to the language of the law, to the want of suitable books, and to the peculiar nature of the science.

First, the language of the law is the subject of much complaint. (*a*) No doubt it is obnoxious to the charge of unnecessary technicality. But it shares this reproach in common with every science of ancient date. There has always been a disposition in the votaries of learning towards exclusiveness. They have sought to create a monopoly of their acquisitions, by employing a language not generally understood, nor easily acquired; and when a phraseology, however barbarous or inelegant, has been consecrated by time, it is very difficult to change it. The old law language was, in fact, a jargon compounded of three distinct languages. From the date of the Norman Conquest to 1363, legal proceedings were conducted, recorded, and reported in Norman French, (*b*) itself a mixture of French and Saxon. A statute of that year required them to be conducted in English, and recorded in Latin, (*c*) but for some time after they continued to be reported in French. With the exception of a few years during the protectorate of Cromwell, the records continued to be in Latin until 1730; when an act of Parliament required them to be in English. (*d*) Yet two years after, it was found necessary to enact that the *technical terms* of

(*a*) See 3 Black. Com. 317.

(*b*) There is a Dictionary of this language by *Kelham*.

(*c*) 36 Edward III. c. 15.

(*d*) Mr. Stephen maintains that, whatever may have been the ancient language of pleading, the *record* was, from the earliest period to which that document can be traced, in the Latin language. — Pleading, Appendix, note (14). The first reports published in English were by Style, in 1658.

the law might still remain in their original language, whether French, Latin, or Saxon; and so they have continued to this day. Some of them are indeed incapable of a convenient translation. But the number is very small, consisting chiefly of the names of legal proceedings; and it may be safely affirmed that one can become a profound lawyer, without a general acquaintance either with French or Latin. These will serve for embellishment, but our own mother tongue is all that is indispensable. It is time that this should be generally understood; and that efforts should be made on all hands, to simplify the language of the law so as to make it level to the comprehension of all. The same overpowering reasons which opened the Scriptures to the laity in their vernacular tongue, should operate to make human laws intelligible to every inquirer. There would then be no plausibility in the objection, that it takes so long to learn terms, that little time is left for principles. And in conformity to these views, I shall avoid foreign terms as much as possible. Indeed, it ought to be a maxim with every man, not only in reference to the law, but to every kind of knowledge, never to use a foreign word when a native one will express the idea as well.

Secondly, a serious impediment is found in the want of *American treatises* adapted to popular instruction. This is no small obstacle even to the professional student. There is no work on American law, at all suitable for a *first book;* and we are compelled, for want of such a work, to commence with Blackstone's Commentaries on *English law*, to learn the rudiments of *American law*. This admirable book was first published in 1765. Prior to that time, the elements of what we now call *Jurisprudence*, existed only in a rude and undigested mass. Some efforts had indeed been made to bring order out of this confusion; but with small success. Sir Matthew Hale had published his "Analysis of the Law," for the purpose of showing, to use his own words, "that it was not altogether impossible, by much attention and labor, to reduce the laws of England into at least a tolerable method." Thomas Wood had also published his "Institutes;" in which he speaks of the law as "a heap of good learning, which he hoped it would not be impossible to sort and put into some order." This very guarded manner, in which these pioneers in the great work venture to hint at the possibility of reducing the scattered elements of law to something like order, significantly indicates the wretched condition of the study at that time. But a more striking view is presented by the following abstract of Lord Chief Justice Reeve's direction for the first stage of legal inquiry. "Read Wood's Institutes cursorily, and for explanation of the same, Jacob's Law Dictionary. Next strike out what lights you can from Bohun's Institutio Legalis, and Jacob's Practising Attorney's Companion, and the like; helping yourself by indexes. Then read and consider Littleton's Tenures without notes, and abridge it. Then venture upon Coke's Commentaries. After reading it once, read it again, for it will require many readings. Abridge it; commonplace it; make it your own; apply to it all the faculties of your mind. Then read Sergeant Hawkins to throw light on Lord Coke. Then read Wood again to throw light on Sergeant Hawkins. And then read the Statutes at Large, to throw light on Wood." (a) When such were the miserable facilities for legal education, the scene all at once changed; and from a repulsive mass of disjointed fragments, the law suddenly became a connected and methodical science. This transformation was effected by the comprehensive knowledge, luminous method, and beautiful style of Sir William Blackstone. There is probably no branch of knowledge towards the perfecting of which a single mind has accomplished more. Sir William Jones justly pronounces the Commentaries "an incomparable work, and the most correct and beautiful outline that has ever been exhibited of any human science." But it is needless to multiply encomiums because there have never been two opinions on the subject. Time, which consigns so many works to oblivion, does but add to the reputation of this. As a *first book* on the law, as a philosophical outline, serving the same purpose in the study of law, as a general map does in the study of geography, it still remains without a rival. Yet this work, admirable as it is, was written for *English students;* and, of course, contains much that is inapplicable to this country. The American student, who reads it without a guide, obtains many erroneous impressions, and much useless learning. We have innovated upon the institutions of our English ancestors with an unsparing hand; and not merely in minute details, but also in fundamental principles. We cannot, therefore, find in Blackstone, an accurate outline of American law. Our great desideratum is, a work which would be to us precisely what that work is to the English. And that man would be a great public benefactor, who should *Americanize* Blackstone's Commentaries; that is, who should give this work with just such additions, omissions, and corrections, as would make it an accurate exposition of American law; or what were still better, who should equal the style and manner of Blackstone, in an original work, upon the laws of his own country. But among the various obstacles in the way of such an enterprise, there is one, which, if not insurmountable, is certainly formidable. I refer to the great diversity of State Laws. This renders it almost impossible to prepare a work of any reasonable compass, which shall be equally adapted to every part of the United States; and yet sufficiently full and complete, to answer the end proposed. On this account, the efforts hitherto made by Judge Swift, of Connecticut, in his *Digest* of the laws of that State; by Judge Tucker, of Virginia, in his *Notes to Blackstone;* and by Judge Wilson, of Pennsylvania, in his *Lectures*, have failed to be as generally useful as their great merit would otherwise make them. The works of Professor Hoffman, of Maryland, including

(a) See Quincy's Dedication Address at the Dane Law College, 9 Am. Jurist, 53.

his *Legal Outlines*, and his *Course of Legal Study*, form an exception to this remark, being very general in their character. So, too, the very learned Commentaries of Chancellor Kent, are almost equally applicable to all parts of the Union. But this book was not designed by its author for a first book. It presupposes some elementary knowledge both of terms and principles.

Thirdly, the two obstacles I have been describing, may, perhaps, be regarded as temporary in their character, and such as time will either greatly diminish, or wholly remove. But there is one permanent cause, which must ever render a thorough mastery of the law an arduous undertaking. And this is found in the nature of law as a study. I shall not here attempt to give you an accurate definition of law. Not less than twenty have been proposed, with each of which, hypercriticism might perhaps find some fault. (*a*) But thus much may be safely said — the term *law*, though used in a great variety of relations, always means an *established rule*. Thus, whether we speak of the laws of God or of man, of matter or of mind, we uniformly refer to those established rules of action or operation, which belong to the subject-matter in question. And it was in this comprehensive sense, that Hooker spoke of law, when he said, "Her seat is the bosom of God, and her voice the harmony of the world; all things in heaven and earth, do her homage; the very least as feeling her care, and the greatest as not exempted from her power." But our inquiries relate only to that class of laws which are denominated *municipal;* and which comprehend *the established regulations of political society*. And it was of law in this sense, that Burke spoke, when he called it "the pride of the human intellect, and the collected wisdom of ages; combining the principles of original justice, with the boundless variety of human concerns." Blackstone also describes it as "a science which distinguishes the criterions of right and wrong; which teaches to establish the one, and to prevent, punish, or redress the other; which employs in its theory the noblest faculties of the soul, and exerts in its practice the cardinal virtues of the heart; a science which is universal in its use and extent, accommodated to each individual, yet comprehending the whole community." Nor can such language be deemed extravagant; for municipal law is indeed the grand regulator of human affairs. Its functions may be appropriately compared to those of gravitation. If you could imagine even a momentary suspension of that great law which regulates the universe of matter, keeping the minutest particle, as well as the mightiest mass, in its proper condition, the stupendous confusion which would thence result, and which we designate by the fearful name of *chaos*, furnishes a strong but faithful illustration of that social disorder, which would as certainly result from the suspension of municipal law, and which we designate by the hardly less fearful name of *anarchy*. It is to be

(*a*) 1 Hoffman's Legal Outlines, 252.

remembered, also, that just in proportion as society advances in civilization, the importance of municipal law becomes greater, and its functions more complicated. Barbarians need few laws, because they have few interests to be regulated by law, but every step in the progress of improvement gives occasion for adding to the body of law some new provision, until the aggregate becomes formidable to the boldest mind. What could once be written upon ten or twelve tables, anon spreads over thousands; until the practice of law becomes a distinct avocation; and a thorough comprehension of all its infinite details requires the labor of a long and industrious life. Moreover, the *criterions* of law are not like those of other sciences. When the question is, what is the law regulating a given matter? it resolves itself into two others — who has the law-making power in reference to this matter? — and what has this power in fact ordained? Now you cannot, as in natural science, resolve these questions by analysis or induction. You cannot apply to them the principles of mathematical demonstration. They cannot be reached by reasoning *a priori.* Nor can you, as in ethics, appeal to the monitor within. Conscience may inform you what the moral law is, and what the municipal law ought to be; but it might greatly mislead you as to what the municipal law actually is. To determine this, you must search the voluminous records of law, until you find the positive regulation; in which constant searching chiefly consists the labor of a lawyer. And this leads me to speak of the sources from which our knowledge is to be obtained.

§ 2. **Sources of Legal Knowledge.** A stranger to our institutions might think that a knowledge of our law could be easily obtained by a diligent perusal of the *statutes.* Adverting to the beautiful theory of our social system, according to which a legislature is provided to make the laws necessary for our government, he might naturally conclude, that the acts of this legislature would comprise the entire body of our law, with the exception of what is embraced in our constitutions and treaties. Finding in these constitutions no other law-making power than the legislative department, the inference would be, that we have no other laws than our legislative acts. Were this the fact, the law would indeed be a simple study. Could our whole law be found in our statute books, we might dispense with law schools, and almost with lawyers. In ordinary cases every man might find for himself the law he wished to know, by a good index to the statute book. But what would that stranger say, if I should tell him, that although in our theory the legislature makes our laws, yet in fact, our legislative acts do not contain, perhaps, a fiftieth part of the law which governs us? I doubt not that he would be amazed at this discrepancy between our theory and practice. Yet, nevertheless, it exists. Nowhere in this country is there to be found anything approaching to a complete code of statute law. But, on the contrary, until very recently, those who have proposed measures for enlarging our codes, and thus gradually advancing them towards completion, have been sneered at, by the profession, as visionary schemers; and the consequence is, that, up to this moment, the people of the United States are contented to live under a system of law, only a small portion of which has ever received an express legislative sanction. Hence we have a science embracing such a vast compass of study; so much of doubt and uncertainty; such a singular mixture of formality and technicality; so many curious yet convenient fictions; and, at the same time, so many astonishing specimens of acute discrimination and profound logic; that when, by the persevering toil of years, we have at length climbed up into "the gladsome light of jurisprudence," we need feel no apprehension, lest every man should undertake to become his own lawyer. I would not of course be understood as saying that the most perfect code of statute law would render our profession entirely unnecessary; though it is quite evident, that, by rendering the acquisition of the law more simple and expeditious, it would tend to diminish the importance which at present attaches to this profession. But whence, then, comes the main body of our law? and where is it to be found? I will endeavor briefly to answer these questions.

First, there is what we call the *common law*. This is a vast collection of judicial precedents, commencing with the earliest glimmerings of English history, accumulating there up to the period of colonizing this country, brought over the ocean by the first colonists, and here again accumulating up to the present moment. These precedents are contained in hundreds of volumes of *Reports*, embracing the decisions of the English and American courts; which decisions have again been condensed, digested, abridged, and commented upon, in hundreds of volumes more, for the convenience of the profession.

Secondly, there is the system of *equity* or *chancery law*, which had its origin in the early deficiencies of the English statutory and common law. This, like the other, consists of judicial precedents, running through nearly the same lapse of time, and contained in similar, though not quite so many repositories. In round numbers, the books containing the common and chancery law, including *reports*, *digests*, *abridgments* and *commentaries*, may be set down at not less than fifteen hundred volumes. (*a*)

Now, even if all these precedents were of the same binding force as legislative acts, so that when you had once found a principle decided, you might rest upon it as unquestionable law, it would still be a Herculean labor to master the contents of so many

(*a*) On the subject of legal bibliography, see Hoffman's Course of Legal Study; Anthon's Preliminary Essay to Blackstone; the 22d and 23d Lectures of Kent's Marvin's Legal Bibliography; 12 American Jurist, p. 5, Article 8, by Charles Sumner, on Characters of Law Books and Judges; 8 id. 260, Article by Theron Metcalf, on Characters of Reports; The Reporters, by J. W. Wallace, who, in 1855, put the number of volumes of Reports at not far from two thousand volumes. (The Reporters, p. 25). The Reports — U. S., State, English, Irish, Scotch, and Canadian — now number about six thousand.

volumes. But this is not the fact. When you have found a precedent to suit your case, you must look downward through all subsequent reports, to ascertain whether it has not been overruled. For to avoid the evil of being bound absolutely by precedents settled some hundreds of years ago, under an entirely different state of society, judges have been under the necessity of treating prior decisions, rather as lights to inform their judgment, than as imperative rules to govern their decisions. And hence the proverbial uncertainty of the law. In the first place, you may not find the precedent you want. If you do find one, it may turn out to have been overruled. And if not yet overruled, you have no assurance that it will not be overruled in the very case before you. (*a*) To say nothing, then, of the imperfection of human language, which occasions ambiguity in written, as well as unwritten law; or of the thousand points where law and equity come in contact with each other, making it difficult to determine to which jurisdiction a given case belongs, there is enough in the very nature of common and chancery law, as above explained, to try the strength and task the patience of the strongest and most resolute mind. To most of the sciences you may discern some limits, some stage, at which the mind may repose upon its acquisitions as complete. But to jurisprudence, as at present constituted, I know not where the limits are. (*b*)

These things are not said to discourage you, but rather to excite your emulation at the prospect before you. Knowing what you have to go through you will the better nerve yourselves at the outset. You cannot expect to become accomplished lawyers in the short period usually assigned in this country to a legal novitiate. It is obvious, that, if you would be in any measure prepared, in so short a time, to begin the practice, you must confine your studies to the most practical subjects. You cannot indulge in black-letter lore. The antiquities of the science must be reserved for that future leisure which every young lawyer may be sure to find. It may well be doubted, whether a longer term of preparation would not, on the whole, be better for the profession. In the early days of Rome, we are told that all her youth were required to learn the twelve tables by heart, as an indispensable part of education. In later times, when the laws became more numerous, five years were devoted to their study. And this custom still prevails in all of the European universities, where the Roman or civil law is taught. As to the study of the English law, its history is briefly this. Up

(*a*) See Bigelow's Overruled Cases.

(*b*) Voluminous as the precedents have become, there are certain axioms or elementary principles expressed in sententious phrases, which are declared or assumed in nearly all of them. They lie at the basis of the law, and are called by Lord Coke, "The Conclusions of Reason." In the thorough knowledge of these maxims and of their right application, consists sound professional learning. The work of Mr. Broom, entitled, "A Selection of Legal Maxims Classified and Illustrated," is a valuable aid to the profession. These maxims are also collated in Bouvier's Law Dictionary, under the head of "Maxims."

to the twelfth century, the clergy were the only lawyers. But when the Great Charter made one of the principal courts stationary at Westminster, which had before followed the person of the king, an important change took place. Lawyers began to congregate in the vicinity of this court, and a strong spirit of association was the natural result. This was fostered by the resolute Saxon opposition to the influence of the Norman clergy, who had exerted themselves to fasten the Roman law upon the English people. The result was that the lovers of the English law united in purchasing for their accommodation several houses in the vicinity of the court, which, belonging to the nobility, were then called hotels or *inns.* In these inns they gradually formed themselves into collegiate bodies; and, though never incorporated, the old writers speak of them as judicial universities. They were of two sorts: *inns of chancery*, for the younger students; and *inns of court*, for those more advanced. The king took them under his protection, and prohibited instruction in the English law to be given anywhere else. In a short period, we are told that the number of students amounted to two thousand. The regulations of these inns were numerous and minute, embracing the diet, dress, and whole deportment of the students: and, although purely conventional, and without any legal sanctions, they were rigorously enforced, and singularly efficient. If you are at all curious on this subject, you may derive much amusement from reading *Dugdale's Origines Juridiciales*, or *Cunningham's Antiquities of the Inns of Court;* where you will find a full account of these regulations. (*a*) Suffice it for me to say, that the students were surrounded by a constant

(*a*) Also see article on the English Inns of Court, by George S. Hillard, in American Jurist for April, 1835. The old system of education at the Inns of Court began to lose its life and spirit and become matter of form in the middle part of the seventeenth century; and for the space of nearly two centuries the English students were left mainly to books and private tuition in offices. The attendance at the inns amounted merely to eating a certain number of dinners there, and the years were shortened. In the latter part of the eighteenth century some attempts were made at a legal education at the universities, one of the fruits of which was the Commentaries of Sir William Blackstone. In the first half of the present century, also, the different inns tried various measures independently. At length, in 1852, a joint system was established by which the superintendence of the instruction of students was committed to a board of eight members, two appointed by each inn, called the council of legal education. Five readerships were established, the subjects being: 1. Jurisprudence and Civil Law; 2. Real Property; 3. Common Law; 4. Equity; and 5. Constitutional Law and Legal History. Public written examinations were also to be held three times a year, and certificates of proficiency given to the students passing satisfactorily, with honors to those distinguishing themselves. These examinations were not, however, compulsory; the old road to the bar by attendance for a certain number of terms remaining open. In 1871 the examination was made compulsory upon students entering after January 1, 1872. Under this system no student can be examined until he has kept nine terms (something over two years), and has received a certificate of competency after passing an examination. {And the student must keep twelve terms (about three years) before he can be called to the bar.} Special honors are also granted to the most meritorious students. The subjects as now established are: 1. Jurisprudence, including International Law, Public and Private; 2. The Roman Civil Law; 3. Constitutional Law and Legal History; 4. Common Law; 5. Equity; 6. The Law of Real and Personal Property; 7. Criminal Law. Four examinations are held each year, one immediately before each term. {See also an article on The Legal Profession in England, 19 Am. Law Rev. 677.}

atmosphere of law for seven or eight years, at least, before they could be called to the bar. Their promotion was through several successive degrees not known in this country; and there was every thing to excite their emulation. In a word they enjoyed, in perfection, all the advantages of social, over solitary study. Even the most indolent could not reside there for the full period, and undergo the discipline of the place, without acquiring an immense amount of legal information. In this country we have no such institutions. The nearest approach to them is to be found in our *Law Schools*, the benefits of which are just beginning to be appreciated. And could we keep the students as long in these schools as they were kept in the English Inns, we might safely count upon making them accomplished lawyers by the time of graduation. But such are the opinions entertained of the law as a profession, that not only is it everywhere and at all times crowded in point of numbers, but those who have chosen it are always impatient to be reaping its fruits. (*a*)

§ 3. **Subdivisions of the Law.** The necessity for law grows out of man's social nature. It contemplates him, not as a single, solitary being, moving on alone to his final destination, but as making part of a vast multitude of similar beings, performing their earthly career in company, and, therefore, requiring numerous regulations to prevent confusion. These regulations constitute the science of law. If men were angels, no such regulations would be necessary. The eternal principles of right and wrong, emblazoned by a revelation from on high, and applied by a sleepless and unerring monitor within, would be all-sufficient for their government; and they might be safely left in that state of nature where their Creator left them. But, being men and not angels, they require, in addition to the restraints of religion and morality, the positive regulations of municipal law. Society dares not leave the human will in the same absolute freedom in which God has left it; but to the indirect sanctions of duty, has added the direct sanctions of law. And this consideration serves to designate the proper scope of the science of which I speak. It is not a part of religion or ethics, but is so much superadded to them both. They commit an egregious error, who consider jurisprudence as looking forward into eternity. It begins and ends with this world. It regards men only as members of civil society. It assists to conduct them from the cradle to the grave, as social beings; and there it leaves them to their final Judge. I would that this attribute of law were more generally appreciated. I say, then, that its proper scope would have been the same that it now is, had no voice from heaven, or from the depths of the human soul, proclaimed another world beyond the present. Religion and morality embrace both time and eternity in their mighty grasp; but human laws reach not beyond the boundaries of time. As immortal beings, they leave men to their conscience and their God. And though this consideration

(*a*) {For the requirements to admission to the bar in the United States, see article in 15 Am. Law Rev. 295.}

may seem, at first view, to detract from their dignity, I rejoice at it as a consequence of our absolute moral freedom. I rejoice, that in this country at least, government dares not interfere between man and his Creator. I know no higher subject of congratulation than the fact, that we have confined our legislators to their proper sphere; which is, to provide for our social welfare here on earth, and leave each to select his own pathway to immortality. But let me not be misunderstood. I do not say that human law has no concern with our moral condition; for it should do much to improve it. But why? Not because we are the subjects of future retribution; but because our social welfare, here on earth, is intimately connected with our moral condition. So far then as the dignity of the law depends upon the relation in which it contemplates man, I claim for it no more than it would have had, if death, instead of being the introduction to another life, had been an eternal sleep. Even then human laws would aim to make this brief existence as happy as possible; and this is all they now aim to do. Doubtless they succeed infinitely better now, from having the all-powerful aid of religion, which would then be wanting; but still their proper function remains the same. Such, then, being the general aspect in which the law contemplates man, let us consider some of the subjects which it presents for our study.

First, *International Law*. Beginning with the aggregate of human beings, spread over the whole surface of the earth, the law contemplates them as divided into distinct *nations;* each supreme within its own limits, and independent of every other, so long as there is ability to maintain this supremacy and independence. Yet these nations are not isolated and disconnected, like the inhabitants of different planets. They exist together on the same planet; and, therefore, like individuals, require established rules to regulate their intercourse. These rules constitute the *public law of nations*, which may be set down as the first and highest branch of jurisprudence. Passing over individuals, it deals only with sovereignties. It is, in fact, the gravitation of the social system, causing nations, like planets, to revolve in their proper orbits. What are the rights and duties of nations, in peace and in war, on the land and on the ocean? These are the grave and solemn questions, which it is the province of the law of nations to answer. But it may be asked, what power is there to ordain laws for nations, which acknowledge no common government? There is no great international legislature; no general congress of nations. Whence, then, comes this branch of law? I answer, that nations, like individuals, are bound to observe the immutable principles of natural justice; and these, accordingly, profess to form the basis of the international code. But as nations might not, in all cases, concur in the deductions to be drawn from these abstract principles, recourse is had to past usage; and the doctrine is, that nations are bound by what custom has settled. The law of nations, then, is a collection of usages and precedents, dating back from the earliest historical traditions, and gradually accumulating with the progress of ages, until the aggregate has become a comprehensive code of established law; the study of which is of the highest interest, as well with reference to the nature of its inquiries, as to the dignity of the parties concerned. The conquerers, and statesmen, and diplomatists, of all past time, come up in review before the student; and he scrutinizes their conduct amidst the lights which have been shed around it, first, by philosophical historians, and, afterwards, by the luminous minds of Grotius, Puffendorf, Vattel, Burlamaqui, Mackintosh, Wheaton, and other distinguished commentators on this branch of jurisprudence. Moreover, there is high moral sublimity in the very idea of associated millions, constituting the highest supremacy this side of heaven, yet bound by laws, the observance of which is invited by the public opinion of the whole civilized world, and the violation of which is sure to be punished by the countless horrors of war; for such are the awful sanctions which secure obedience to the law of nations. The assembled world is the court in which this law is adjudicated; and destroying armies are commissioned to carry its sentence into execution. Who, then, will question the dignity of this branch of legal study? Next to religion, I know not that the human mind can employ itself in contemplations more interesting or sublime; and if the law of nations be not as practical as the branches which follow, it certainly makes up in grandeur what it lacks in everyday utility.

But there is another division of international law of the highest practical importance, which is denominated *private*, to distinguish it from the preceding. It grows out of the *conflict of laws* between different nations; a subject upon which our distinguished jurist, the late Mr. Justice Story, has given us a most learned commentary. No two nations have precisely the same internal laws. On the contrary, the diversity is so great as almost to occasion a doubt whether there be any thing like immutable principles in jurisprudence. Now it results from the very nature of sovereignty, that each nation, without reference to extent, numbers, or situation, has unqualified supremacy within its own limits. Hence no law made in one nation can have force in another, without the consent of that other. Yet, in the close and constant intercourse of nations, it must often happen, that in deciding in one nation upon rights which originated under the law of another, complete justice cannot be done without recognizing the law of that other. Here, then, is opened to the student a field of research at once extensive and interesting. When the *lex loci* and *lex fori* come into conflict, in what cases shall the right of sovereignty yield to comity, and one nation recognize and enforce the law of another? If this be done in all cases, sovereignty is shorn of half its beams; if not done at all, the harmony of nations and the rights of individuals may be alike jeoparded. There must be, then, a system of general rules to determine when the law of the place of adjudication shall prevail, and when not. Such rules there are; and they are to be found in the treatises on the conflict of laws. What was originally an open question, addressed to the comity or good feeling of nations, is now settled by precedent; and when the citizens of one nation remove to or travel in another, and make contracts, acquire property, marry or die there, it is no longer a matter of doubt by which law their rights will be determined. Thus the conflict of laws forms the second important and interesting branch of legal study. The mind becomes elevated and expanded by the contemplation of great principles broadly applied. Human nature, too, presents itself under its most inviting aspect. The very idea that a branch of law has sprung up, from sacrificing the strict and imperative right of sovereignty to the accommodating principle of national comity, is in itself a subject of the most gratifying reflection. The ancient and barbarous notion that nations are natural enemies, and disposed, not merely to exact the last tittle of their rights, but also to do each other as much harm as possible, is shown to be a foul libel on the human race. The student finds, on the contrary, that the feelings of courtesy and benevolence are cherished with even greater constancy between neighboring nations than between neighboring individuals; and he leaves the study with a higher opinion of his species than he commenced with.

Secondly, Constitutional Law. Having explored these two divisions of international law, the course of study brings the student home to his own institutions. For the rest, he is to investigate that internal or domestic law, by which his own rights and the rights of his fellow-citizens are more particularly regulated. And here we begin with *constitutional law*, which, in this country, lies at the foundation of the social fabric. I say in this country, because it has been our glory to give the first example of a political organization based upon written constitutions. We hear much said, it is true, of the English constitution; but what is it? A mere collection of usages and precedents gathered up in the progress of some twenty centuries, and subject to be modified or abrogated by the omnipotent will of Parliament. Not so with the American idea of a constitution. We understand it to be a solemn written declaration of the sovereign will of the people, in their original capacity, as the highest earthly power, prescribing the form and limiting the powers of the government, which they have thus voluntarily created. And this idea is as simple, as it is new and grand. A sufficient number of people to form a nation, enter into a compact for that purpose, and reduce the terms to writing. That instrument is their constitution; in conformity with which, as their organic and fundamental law, all other laws are to be made, and all delegated powers executed. But this primary idea of a constitution acquires some complexity from the peculiar organization of our political system. The people of the United States might have agreed to form themselves into one consolidated government; and in that case, we should have had but a single constitution, but, for a variety of reasons, they preferred state governments, united under a federal government. This renders the department of constitutional law less simple than it would otherwise have been. For, in the first place, we have the federal constitution, which speaks the sovereign voice of all the people of the United States, and is supreme over the subjects to which it extends; and next, we have a constitution for each State, which is subordinate to the federal constitution, but supreme in all other respects. Notwithstanding, however, this double aspect of constitutional law, it is still very far from being a difficult study; illustrated as it has been by the most able commentators. And as to its dignity and importance, I presume there cannot be two opinions on the subject. Whatever may be said about subordinate branches, no American citizen can hesitate about this. He can but poorly appreciate the freedom he enjoys, who does not understand the great charter which secures it. I was about to go further, and say, that he does not deserve to be free, who will not inform himself in what his freedom consists. But when I consider how many of our citizens have no opportunity of studying our constitutions, for want of suitable provisions in our seminaries of learning, I forbear. In Rome, had Rome been blessed with a constitution instead of the law of the twelve tables, every citizen would have been required to know it by heart. And shall the many here, whose high prerogative it is to rule the few, leave the study of the constitution only to the few? Lawyers must study it, as the foundation of all other law; and shall not others study it as the foundation of their liberty? I trust this disgrace is not always to attach to our system of education.

Thirdly, the Law of Persons. Having mastered the principles of constitutional law, and thus laid firm and strong the foundations of the legal edifice, the student is prepared to commence the superstructure. He now understands the limits of delegated power. He has seen what laws may, and what laws may not be made; and how the permitted laws are made and administered. It remains, then, to inquire, what the existing laws do in fact provide? We may say, in general terms, that all the subjects of law resolve themselves into *rights* and *remedies*, connected with *persons* and *property;* and this may sound like a very simple matter. But if, from this generalization, we descend into particulars, we shall find that there is scarcely an individual relation or interest, which is not the subject of legal provision, and, therefore, of legal study. We take up, then, in the next place, *the law of persons*, which comprehends all the various relations which the members of society can sustain towards each other. Here we have natural and artificial persons, including corporations; public and private persons, including all who occupy official stations; citizens, aliens, and Indians; males and females, including the relation of husband and wife; infants and adults, including the relations of parent and child, and of guardian and ward; sane and insane persons; masters and servants, including slaves, apprentices, and agents; partners in business; and, lastly, executors and administrators, who come in to wind up affairs, when death has terminated all other relations.

Fourthly, the Law of Property. Here we have things in possession, and things in expectation, including all the various kinds of contracts; and things real, and things personal, including all the various distinctions between real and personal property. And when we have mastered these, we have yet to study their various modes of acquisition and transfer; by occupancy, marriage, descent, devise, and purchase, including the forms and properties of all the various instruments by which ownership is evidenced or transferred, and the numerous liens which may attach in the course of these operations.

Fifthly, the Law of Crimes. Here we shall be little aided by any American works. (*a*) Even Kent's Commentaries omit this subject altogether; and we have comparatively few reported criminal cases. In some of the States, as in Ohio, this branch of law is made exceedingly simple, by substituting a criminal code in place of the common law; and even where this is not the case, the spirit of humanity has occasioned numerous modifications, all tending to make this division of legal study, equally simple and interesting.

Sixthly, the Law of Procedure. The preceding subdivisions comprise what may be called the *theory* of the law; but the *practice* yet remains to be studied. It is one thing to learn what our legal rights are; but a very different thing to learn how remedies are administered, when these rights have been violated. *The law of procedure*, then, which is the only remaining division, is of great extent and intricacy. First, you have to acquaint yourself with *common-law proceedings*, including whatever belongs to the conduct of a suit through the courts, from its commencement in the lowest court, to its final determination in the court of last resort. This would be no short task, if there were but a single form of action. But when you consider that there are as many as nine (*b*) different actions, abounding in nice distinctions and cunning technicalities, you will realize that the labor must be multiplied as many fold. I know not that society bears, at present, one burden so unnecessary, as the cumbrous system of common-law proceedings. There would seem to be no more need of so many and such tedious forms of action, than there is of the exploded system of syllogistic reasoning. But this is not the place to enlarge upon such a topic. You turn, then, in the next place, to *chancery proceedings;* and

(*a*) The excellent treatises of Wharton on Criminal Law and on the Law of Homicide have appeared since the text was written. Still later treatises on the Criminal Law are referred to in the first note to Lecture XXXIV., *post.*

(*b*) How the code has since changed the system of pleading at common law will be seen hereafter.

here you find much greater simplicity. There is but one general form for all cases; and this is so perfect, as an instrument of litigation, that it might just as well be adapted to remedies at law, as in equity. It is, however, so entirely different in every particular, that it must be made a distinct study. Lastly, you have to acquaint yourself with *criminal proceedings*, which differ essentially from both the others. But here, again, there is but a single form, and this is, perhaps, as simple as it could be made, consistently with precision. I should, perhaps, be safe in saying, that it requires four times as much labor to become familiar with civil proceedings at common law, as with chancery and criminal proceedings both together.

§ 4. **Inducements to Legal Study.** My object thus far has been to illustrate the nature of legal study, by hasty references to the sources of information, and to the subjects with which the law is conversant. If I have at all succeeded in this object, I have verified the declaration of Blackstone, "that the law employs in its theory the noblest faculties of the soul." He further declares, "that it exerts in its practice the cardinal virtues of the heart;" and this is what I shall now endeavor to demonstrate. I do not intend to maintain that the legal profession is superior in respectability to all other professions; for I do not so believe. On the contrary, I consider all honest occupations as, in the abstract, equally respectable; because they are all equally necessary. If there be any difference, in this respect, it consists not so much in the profession itself, as in the manner in which its duties are discharged — "Act well your part: there all the honor lies." In this view, the world may be compared to a vast workshop, in which all varieties of business must be going on simultaneously, because the countless wants of mankind cannot be otherwise supplied; and in order that each kind of work may be performed well, this mass of labor is divided into an almost infinite number of branches, each workman attending exclusively to his own particular branch. If, then, all the laborers work equally well, they deserve to be accounted equally respectable. And yet between the employment of making heads for pins, and that of administering laws for a nation, there is certainly vast room for preference. Both are necessary, and both respectable; and yet every one feels that they differ immeasurably in point of dignity.

I begin, then, with the remark, that the employment of the lawyer is pre-eminently one of trust and confidence. The law itself so regards it; for it excuses the lawyer from revealing what his client has confided to him, while it compels a disclosure even from a religious confessor. (*a*) But what is still more to the purpose, men so regard it. The province of a lawyer is to vindicate rights and redress wrongs; and it is a high and holy function. Men come to him in their hours of trouble; not such trouble as religion

(*a*) {It not only excuses but forbids him without the client's consent; and the same is now true of the physician and the religious confessor. R. S. of Ohio, § 5241.}

can solace, or medicine cure; but the trouble arising from innocence accused, confidence betrayed, reputation slandered, liberty assailed, property invaded, promises broken, the domestic relations violated, or life endangered. The guilty and the innocent, the upright and the dishonest, the wronging and the wronged, the knave and the dupe, alike consult him, and with the same unreserved confidence. It is not given to man to see the human heart completely unveiled before him. But the lawyer perhaps comes more nearly to this, than any other; for there is no aspect in which the human character does not present itself, in his secret consultations. All the passions, all the vices, and all the virtues, are by turns subjected to his scrutiny. He has thus studied human nature in its least disguised appearances. He has watched it under all trials; in the light and in the shade, in ecstasy and in despair, in glory and in shame.

But let us leave his office, and pursue him to the forum. Here is his field of triumph and renown, or of defeat and shame. Here he meets his antagonist, in the sharp encounter of wit, reasoning, and persuasion. He has pledged his best exertions to his client; he has a liberal compensation in prospect or possession; and his reputation is at stake in the result of the cause. Here, then, is every incentive to eloquence, and every opportunity to display it. He is in the field where the great advocates who have gone before him, have won their laurels. He speaks indeed to convince the court, and persuade the jury. But a listening crowd are hanging upon his accents, and making up a verdict for or against himself. And, above all, his client is there, intently watching every word and motion, because on them are suspended all he holds dear.

At length we follow the successful lawyer, from the bar to the bench. The counsellor has at last become the judge. The topmost round of the ladder is now reached. And here all the high qualities of his nature are called into exercise. The sagacity which cannot be misled by sophistry; the integrity which nothing can shake or bribe; the stern impartiality, which forgets the parties and looks only at the cause; the dignified courtesy, which rebukes levity, while it wins respect; these are the qualities without which all the learning of a Coke would not make a worthy judge, and which nowhere shine so conspicuously as from the bench. Of the power which belongs to the judicial office, of the all-pervading influence exerted by a Mansfield or a Marshall, for example, I need not here speak. Such men live in their decisions, through all coming time; for these decisions go to swell the great aggregate of common law, and thus determine the rights of generations yet unborn.

Nor is it to the judicial office alone that the lawyer may aspire. His studies pre-eminently fit him for every civil office. In the halls of legislation he must ever occupy a conspicuous place, because no man is so well prepared to suggest and frame new laws, as he who knows what the existing laws contain. It is a well-known fact, that, from the days of the revolution down to the present time, no single class of the community has performed so much of the public service of the country, as the members of this profession. I do not mention this as a motive to study law, but as a proof of the estimation in which the profession has been held. As a motive, I should rather hold it in contempt. I know not a greater vice of the times, than the all-prevalent hankering after office. It is degrading alike to electors and elected. The old idea was, that office should seek the man; now the man seeks the office; and he descends to the most humiliating compliances in order to obtain it. Men seem to forget their self-respect, when they seek honor from office; as if that which is factitious could alter that which is inherent in the man. But this is a digression. I would hold up the legal profession, as an end in itself, not as a stepping-stone to something higher. In fact there is nothing higher. He who stands at the head of this profession, is on a level with the most elevated in the land; and instead of owing his eminence to the solicited suffrages of others, he has the proud satisfaction of having achieved it for himself. Nor is this all. If such be the influence of the profession, in calm and peaceful times, what must it not be, when the elements of society are thrown into unwonted commotion? Hitherto, indeed, since the formation of our government, the political horizon has been comparatively calm. There have been some threatening clouds now and then, but no destroying tempests. In the main, the fundamental rights of men have been scrupulously respected, and the laws duly observed and administered. A learned bench, and an upright bar, have quietly preserved the order of the system, while the busy and protected public have hardly felt their influence. But imagine a reverse; for it is at least possible, and the enemies of free government are loudly predicting it. We are trying the greatest political experiment the world ever witnessed; and the experience of all history warns us not to feel too secure. A voice from the tombs of all the departed republics, tells us that if our liberty is to be ultimately preserved, it is at the price of sleepless vigilance. I refer not to foreign aggression, for of this we have nothing to fear; our only foes are those of our own household. Domestic aggression may come from two quarters; from those who govern, or from those who are governed. On the one hand, power is always tending to augmentation. Those who have some, employ it to gain more; and if not seasonably withstood, become too strong to be resisted. And on the other hand, liberty is always tending toward licentiousness. The more men have, the more they are likely to want. Being free from many restraints, they would do away with all. Now when dangers threaten, from either of these quarters; when rulers would trample the law under their feet, or mobs would rise to overthrow it; who are the sentinels to give the alarm? Do I assume too much, in saying society looks with confidence to that class of men whose profession it is to watch over the law?

We have now followed the lawyer through his whole career of study, practice, and distinction. Rising with the dawn, and trimming assiduously the midnight lamp, we have seen him exploring the law of nations, constitutional law, the law of persons, the law of property, the law of crimes, and the law of procedure; and, for this purpose, ransacking the precedents of all ages, to supply the immense chasms in actual legislation. Having thus stored his mind with the vast and various lore of jurisprudence, we have seen him in secret consultation with his clients, contending at the bar, deciding from the bench, and filling the high places in his country's service. But perhaps it may be said, that one side only has been exhibited. I am well aware that there are prejudices against the profession. It is said to abound with pettifoggers, who pervert the law to the purposes of knavery; with quacks, who sacrifice their clients through their ignorance; and with needy hangers-on, who will foment lawsuits rather than not have them. Lawyers are said to delight in tricks, stratagems, and chicanery; to argue as strenuously for the wrong as for the right, for the guilty as for the innocent, and to hire out their conscience, as well as their skill, to any client who will pay the fee. What shall be said to these charges? I, for one, am willing to admit their truth, to some extent. Our profession abounds with opportunities and temptations to abuse its high functions; and it would be strange indeed, if it had not some unworthy members. We lay no claim to superhuman virtue. We see unworthy members in every other profession, and therefore take no shame to ourselves that they are sometimes to be found in ours. We also take refuge behind the maxim, that supply corresponds to demand. If there were no dishonest or knavish clients, there would be no dishonest or knavish lawyers. Our profession, therefore, does but adapt itself to the community in which it is exercised. From all these views, however the leading impression which I desire to leave upon your minds is, that lawyers must dearly earn all they obtain, whether of honor or emolument. Let no man enter the profession as a sinecure. Genius, without toil, may, to some extent, distinguish a man elsewhere; but here he must labor, or he cannot succeed. No quickness of invention can supply the place of patient investigation. A clear mind might determine at once what the law ought to be, but actual inspection alone can determine what the law is. Let those, therefore, who would prepare themselves "for untying the knots and solving the enigmas of jurisprudence," first of all make up their minds to hard work. Let them weigh well the fact, that "to scorn delights and live laborious days," is the indispensable condition of professional eminence. On somewhat easier terms they may prepare themselves "to prowl in courts of law for human prey;" but nothing short of resolute, emulous, persevering study, can raise them to that height which alone should satisfy a generous ambition.

It only remains that I announce the general plan of these lectures. As I am to treat only of the elements or first principles of law, I shall be very sparing in the citation of authorities. Particular references to volume and page, for each proposition I may advance, would consume much time and space to very little purpose. Unless, therefore, there be some special reason to the contrary, I shall merely name the authors who may be consulted on each subject; and request you to take my word for the truth of what I may advance. Moreover, while I shall endeavor to state correctly what the law is, I shall also take occasion sometimes to suggest how it may be improved. For highly as I estimate the dignity of the profession, I am not so much enamored of the law itself, as not to perceive that it has many imperfections. It is true that the common law comes to us with letters of commendation from a comparatively remote antiquity. Sage after sage, through a long lapse of time, has paid it the tribute of lofty panegyric. It has not only been said to embody "the gathered wisdom of a thousand years," but also to be in sober truth, "the perfection of reason." Americans are called upon especially to revere it, as the parent of modern liberty. Because it withstood, with genuine Saxon obstinacy, the early encroachments of Norman usurpation, we are expected to believe that it breathes throughout the very soul of indomitable freedom; and that, for this reason our ancestors brought it over to this country, on their first immigration, and cherished it as their most precious heritage. But to all such suggestions, it is sufficient here to reply, that if hoary antiquity and unbounded encomium had been permitted to preclude scrutiny, the philosophy of Aristotle would still enslave the human mind. The true ground to be assumed is, that neither the antiquity of our law, nor its present wide supremacy, proves any thing, one way or the other, as to its intrinsic excellence. Our ancestors adopted it from necessity, because they had no other, and we have been slowly modifying it to suit our condition. But numerous changes are yet required, before the system can be pronounced as perfect as it admits of being made. How, indeed, can it be otherwise? Admitting that mankind are improving from generation to generation, how is it possible that rules, and maxims, and usages, which grew out of, and were adapted to, the condition of ages comparatively dark and barbarous, should be adapted to our present condition? Will not a total change in the opinions, habits, manners, and political institutions of a people, make a corresponding change necessary in their municipal regulations? These questions will admit of but one answer; and therefore I regard the subject of *law reform*, as one of momentous importance. The laws by which we are governed, affect so intimately all our relations and interests, that a single defect, from the universality of its operation, swells into a vast evil; for its effect in a single instance, is to be multiplied by the crowding millions of our population, in order to estimate it rightly. If, then, there be defects in our system, let them be fearlessly exposed. He is no enlightened friend, but a blind bigot to the law, who will see no imperfections himself; or, seeing them, will endeavor to conceal them from others. I am not, however, a lover of innovation for its own sake. I know that the mere fact of novelty is no recommendation of itself; and that great respect is always due to the experience of past ages. I will also grant, that in the unparalleled mental activity of the present age, the tendency is to think too little, rather than too much, of present institutions. And when about to propose any radical reform, this fact should always be borne in mind; otherwise we may unintentionally give the wheel of reformation such an impetus that it will revolve too far. But, on the other hand, there may be such a thing as too much contentment with things as they are. That sluggish disposition of mind, which desires no change, is as much to be deprecated as its opposite. Let it become universal, and the progress of human improvement would cease; the world would come to a final pause; and a deep and hopeless lethargy would settle down upon the race of man. There is, however, a golden medium between these two extremes. It is that disposition of mind which neither reveres what is old, nor admires what is new, merely on account of its being old or new; but submits every question to the test of strict examination upon its intrinsic merits. And this is the disposition with which I hope to comment upon the various topics hereafter to be presented. (*a*)

LECTURE II.

PRINCIPLES OF POLITICAL ORGANIZATION.

§ 5. **Origin of Government.** In the preceding lecture, I stated that municipal law comprehends the established regulations of political society; hence the propriety of a preliminary inquiry into the fundamental principles of *political organization.* To this end, let us begin with man in that condition which is usually denominated *a state of nature.* In point of fact, this condition may not now exist; but it can be understood by imagining a sufficient number of persons to have been casually thrown together in a wilderness, beyond the control of any human government; and that we may not be embarrassed with tracing their slow progress from

(*a*) In harmony with these views is the language of an illustrious statesman and philanthropist, still spared to mankind: —

"It was the boast of Augustus, that he found Rome of brick and left it of marble. But how much nobler will be the sovereign's boast, when he shall have it to say, that he found law dear and left it cheap; found it a sealed book, left it a living letter; found it the patrimony of the rich, left it the inheritance of the poor; found it the two-edged sword of craft and oppression, left it the staff of honesty and the shield of innocence!" — Lord Brougham.

ignorance to intelligence, let them be supposed to have already attained to this condition. It is obvious, that upon first meeting, these persons would be subject to no other *laws* than those which belong originally and inseparably to their constitution, as *intellectual, moral*, and *physical* beings; and which are denominated the *laws of nature*. We need not now inquire how these laws are made and ascertained; it being sufficient for our purpose, that their universal existence and supremacy are admitted. By them, therefore, the *rights of nature*, or *natural rights*, are to be determined and regulated. The term *right* has many meanings, which need not here be discussed. As a quality of actions it means *consistent with law;* and therefore the rights of nature depend upon the laws of nature. *Wrong*, as a quality of action, is the opposite of right, and means, *inconsistent with law*. Both right and wrong, therefore, in a state of nature, are determined by the laws of nature; and *obligation*, or *duty*, is determined in the same way, for it corresponds to right. When we are subjected to any law, we are said to be under obligation to conform to it. This is implied in the very nature of law. The kind of obligation depends upon the nature of the law. If it be a physical law, the obligation is a matter of physical necessity; we cannot help obeying it. If not, the obligation is a matter of choice, and is determined by motives; and herein consists *natural liberty*, or the freedom of a state of nature. Individuals, in this condition, are under no other restraint, than that which results from an apprehension of the consequences which follow from conformity or non-conformity to the laws of nature; in other words, their conduct is regulated by a sense of *moral obligation* alone. Having as yet contracted no engagements with one another, each individual is in a state of complete *personal independence;* and since no one can as yet have acquired any rights which nature does not vouchsafe equally to all, it follows, that, in a state of nature, there is a perfect *equality of rights and obligations*. And this is the only equality that would exist: for we cannot suppose that any two individuals would be absolutely equal in point of fact, either physically or intellectually. The only equality that can exist among men is a *moral equality*, or an *equality of rights and obligations;* and this is a fundamental condition of the state of nature.

Such being the relations of men in a state of nature, we may safely conclude that they could not long continue in this primeval condition. A community of angels might need no other restraint upon their actions; but constituted as men are, the moral obligations of a state of nature would not be sufficient to maintain harmony and order. To hinder the strong from oppressing the weak, and prevent might from trampling upon right; in a word, to avoid the nameless evils of *anarchy*, something more than a *moral government* would be found indispensable. But a *civil government* could only be established in one of two ways; by *coercion or consent*. A government founded on coercion, is called *despotism* and exists whenever one or more individuals make their *will* the law for the rest of the community, and *compel* them to submit. Perhaps in the case supposed, some such attempt would be first made. But there being no moral obligation to submit to such usurped dominion, and a strong natural impulse in every bosom to resist it, a despotic government could have no hope of permanency. The first opportunity would be seized to throw it off. This could only be done by concert and co-operation among the disaffected and oppressed. Sooner or later this crisis must arrive; and then, if not at first, there would be a voluntary association, for the purpose of establishing a government by consent. This is what we understand by entering into the *social compact;* the result of which would be to exchange *natural* for *civil liberty.* Each member of the new community would relinquish some portion of his natural rights, to obtain better security for those reserved, which would now be called *civil rights.* For the reasons before given, the concessions made by each ought to be the same; and the aggregate of these individual concessions would measure and constitute the *powers* of the new government. As no unnecessary restraint would be voluntarily submitted to by rational men, the problem to be solved, in framing the terms of the compact, would be to construct such a system of government as would effectually secure the general welfare of the whole, at the least possible sacrifice of individual freedom. A government so constructed would be emphatically a *free government*, since it would derive all its powers from the consent of the governed. The nature and limits of these powers need not here be discussed in detail. It may be well, however, to glance at some of the more general principles by which they would be determined.

It is not improbable that the supposed community would set out with the experiment of holding all things in common, recognizing no separate individual property. If so, the powers of government would extend only to the regulation of the *personal rights* of the members. But this state of things would not long continue. Experience would soon demonstrate that the only efficient incentive to activity, is the hope of profit and accumulation, which results from the appropriation, to each individual, of the avails of his own labor. The *exclusive ownership of property* by individuals, therefore, would ultimately, if not at first, become the subject of regulation; and then the powers of government would extend to the regulation of the *proprietary* as well as *personal* rights of the members. And we may say, in general terms, that the regulation of these rights would be the whole aim and purpose of the compact creating the government. Such, then, being the *objects* to which the powers of government would extend, the following general rules ought to regulate their exercise: —

1. The powers of government should operate upon *conduct* only, and not upon *opinions.* And the reason is, that mere opinions, not carried into action, can affect neither the *persons* nor *property*

of others. Besides, the very attempt to regulate opinions would be preposterous; for though government may enforce outward conformity, it cannot, in the nature of things, reach the inward thoughts. Men could not renounce the freedom of opinion if they would; and they would not if they could.

2. They should operate upon *civil conduct* only, and not upon *moral conduct* apart from civil. I have touched upon this topic before. The reason is, that government has no concern with men, except in the capacity of *citizens*, or members of civil society. As *moral agents*, we are accountable to another and higher power. Human government cannot fix the standard of moral right and wrong; and it should not even attempt to enforce conformity to the standard established by the Creator, any further than the temporal welfare of society requires. Its province does not reach into eternity, but ends with time. This attribute of human power, which may be called its *worldiness*, depends upon the obvious consideration, that there can be no such thing as *merit* or *demerit*, without the liberty of choice. We cannot be good or bad upon compulsion. It is only as *free agents* that we can deserve praise or blame. Hence we must be careful to distinguish between *moral right and wrong* and *legal right and wrong*. Human power may determine the latter; but the former depends upon a superhuman power.

3. They should be revocable at pleasure, by the people who granted them. The reason is, that if one generation could bind its successors for any definite period, it might, on the same principle, bind them for ever; and thus make slaves of all posterity. Perpetual powers would be clearly incompatible with liberty. Each generation must have the option of dissenting from powers previously conferred; and then, from its omission to dissent, its continued assent may be presumed. How far this general principle has been departed from, in the case of *charters*, will be considered hereafter.

4. The system must be founded on a *perfect equality of rights*. The reason is, that an intelligent people would consent to no other arrangement. Enjoying this equality in the state of nature, we cannot doubt that they would insist upon retaining it under the compact. Sooner than voluntarily disfranchise themselves, by yielding up rights to be enjoyed by others having no better claim than themselves, they would undoubtedly refuse to join in the compact.

5. It must be agreed, that in all points of difference, *the majority shall prevail*. This would be a matter of necessity. Absolute unanimity on all subjects is out of the question. Concession therefore must come from some quarter, or compulsion would follow. If resort be had to physical force, the majority must of course prevail; and the only way to avoid this resort would be for the minority to submit without it. This would be the more readily agreed to, however, for another reason, there is always a

fair presumption, that of two sides of a question, that side on which the greatest number of free minds concur, is the right side. This indeed may not always be true, and therefore it might be expedient to provide, that certain very important measures should require the concurrence of something more than a bare majority. But still it must obviously be a preliminary condition to the first movement, that the majority shall prevail.

§ 6. **Idea of a Constitution.** Setting out, then, with the position that while all are to have equal rights, yet in cases of difference of opinion, the majority are to prevail; the question would now be, who shall exercise the functions of government? Or, in other words, where shall the supreme power or *sovereignty* of the community be lodged? Since all power belongs originally *to the people in mass*, it is probable that, in the first instance, arrangements would be made for exercising it personally; each member participating equally in all public affairs. This would constitute a *simple democracy*. But it would obviously be adapted only to a small and compact population. When the people should become numerous and widely diffused, they would find it inconvenient, if not impracticable, to assemble for public business, as often as occasion would require; and when assembled, there would be too many voices to act with energy and despatch. These considerations would suggest the adoption of some other scheme. And since we cannot suppose that a wise people would consent to give up the fundamental doctrine, that all power belongs of right to them, the problem would be to substitute some form of government, which would retain this great democratic principle, and at the same time obviate the necessity of a direct participation by each individual in all public affairs. This could only be done by adopting the principle of *representation*, whereby one person would be authorized to represent or act for any given number. In this way, the system might be adapted to any amount of population or extent of territory; while at the same time, the great body of the people could attend, with little interruption, to their private affairs. The *representatives*, to whom authority would thus be *delegated*, would be the *servants* and not the *masters* of their *constituents*, whose will it would be their office to execute; and the government would now be changed from a *simple*, to a *representative democracy*. But since representatives ought not to be trusted with *unlimited discretion*, some method must be devised for defining their powers. And as it would be difficult, if not impossible, to give them *special instructions* for each particular occasion, a set of *general and permanent instructions* would be provided to serve for all occasions. And this is what we understand by a *constitution*. In other words, a constitution is a written expression of the sovereign will of the people, in relation to the form and powers of government. Proceeding from the people in their supreme capacity, as the highest earthly power, it could be transcended or abrogated by them only; while to their representatives, it would be a supreme and inviolable law. In framing this constitution, one of the leading objects would manifestly be, to define with all possible accuracy the powers delegated to government. This might be done by *enumeration*, or by *prohibition*, or by a combination of both. First, all the powers to be exercised might be specifically enumerated; and thus all powers not specified, would, for that reason, be prohibited; because the grant would be special, and the prohibition general. But the difficulty of this method would be to make an enumeration so full and complete as to reach all the details of municipal regulation. Again, all powers not to be exercised might be specially prohibited, and thus all powers not thus prohibited, would, for that reason, be conferred; because here the prohibition would be special, and the grant general. This method would be less difficult than the other, because there are fewer things to be prohibited, than to be authorized. And the manner of prohibition might be twofold. Some things might be *directly* prohibited, by declaring in so many words that they shall not be done; while other things might be *indirectly* prohibited, by a declaration of certain fundamental rights of the people, which should never be infracted. But after all, absolute certainty could scarcely be attained in either way. And even when both should be combined, much, probably, would still remain to be deduced from the fundamental doctrines of the social compact.

§ 7. **Checks and Balances.** The definition of delegated powers by a written constitution, would thus be the first grand movement towards free government. But as yet, there would only be a government on parchment. To give directions is one thing; to insure obedience is a very different thing. These powers are to be exercised by men over men; and it would be necessary to take all possible precautions to secure their proper administration. The two principal qualities required in the officers of government, in order to insure a good administration, are *ability* and *fidelity*. Accordingly in constructing the machinery of the constitution, all efforts would be directed to these two points; and the results would constitute what are denominated the *checks* and *balances* of the government. On the nice adjustment of these, the experiment would mainly depend. For unless delegates can be prevented from abusing the trust committed to them, a representative government would be little better than a despotism. What, then, are the safeguards of delegated power? Some of the more important I will briefly describe.

1. *Mode of designating Officers.* Much would depend upon the mode of designating the public functionaries. They should not be designated *by lot*, because this would render their fitness a mere matter of chance; and the only other method which suggests itself, is by *suffrage*. As the right of suffrage would, on the principle of equality before mentioned, be *universal*, every individual would thus be enabled to exercise his *judgment* as to the qualifications of the candidates; and we may reasonably presume that the best men

would thus be elected. If not, it would be the fault of the voters, and not of the system. Whether the voting should be done openly, by oral declaration, or secretly, by written ballot, would be a subordinate question, upon which fair minds might reasonably differ, and which I shall not stop to discuss.(*a*)

2. *Tenure of Office.* This would be the next important point. Office should not be made *hereditary*, for the same reason that the first incumbents should not be designated by lot; namely, because this would render fitness a mere matter of chance; and also because the creation of a *privileged order* or *aristocracy*, born to rights not enjoyed by others, would conflict with the principle of equality. Should it then be for life, or for some shorter period? This question must be decided upon a comparison of advantages. On the one hand, a long term of service would furnish to the incumbent the strongest motive to qualify himself well, because he would hold the office long; it would afford opportunity for so doing, because in all things practice makes perfect; and it would give uniformity and stability to the administration of government, because the same men would be likely to continue the same policy. But, on the other hand, a short term would afford the best of all securities for fidelity, because it would allow no opportunity for any systematic plan of encroachment; and more especially, because it would render the responsibility of the incumbent to his constituents more immediate and certain. And, therefore, since the want of fidelity would be more to be dreaded than the want of ability, because the consequences would be more pernicious, a comparatively short term of service would, on the whole, be preferred, as a general rule; subject, however, to exceptions, depending upon the nature of the service.

3. *Number of Officers.* This would be another important matter. If all power should be delegated to a single person, which would constitute a *simple monarchy*, to say nothing of the impossibility that one man could personally manage all public affairs, the liability to abuse would manifestly be greater, than where several minds were required to concur. And on the other hand, if the number should be very large, their movements would be unwieldy, and the government expensive. A medium between these extremes

(*a*) The vote by ballot prevails in the United States, except in Virginia, Kentucky, and Missouri, where the *viva voce* mode is adhered to. It is the mode of exercising the right of suffrage in France and elsewhere on the continent of Europe. The *viva voce* mode is still adhered to in England, against repeated attempts in Parliament to substitute the ballot for it. The Romans practised the *viva voce* mode till, in the last half of the second century before Christ, the ballot was introduced.

The ballot or written vote has now been introduced in the English elections with modifications, one of which is that the paper, though the contents are unknown, bears a number, which is also affixed to the strip retained by the voter, so that in case of contest each man's vote can be ascertained. This does away with much of its privacy, and a similar device has lately been held unconstitutional in Indiana under a constitution requiring all voting to be by ballot. There the law required the inspector to place on the outside of each ballot the same number that was put to the voter's name on the poll book, and the court held this inconsistent with the nature of a ballot. Williams *v.* Stein, 38 Ind. 9.

would therefore be preferred; and the public functionaries would be sufficiently numerous to perform the public service well, and no more.

4. *Division of Powers.* This would be the next point of discussion. Should all delegated power be concentrated in a single body of men, thus constituting a *simple oligarchy;* or should it be distributed among different bodies, thus constituting a *mixed government?* There would be two reasons in favor of distribution. *First*, the liability to abuse would be less, because the different departments could not so readily cabal together; and *secondly*, the distribution would secure that increased ability, which, in all human affairs, results from a division of labor. These reasons would preponderate over the argument derived from the simplicity of a single body; and the powers of government would be distributed among distinct departments. But what should be the number of departments? This would be determined by an analysis of the powers to be distributed. Since no wise people would voluntarily subject themselves to the *transient commands* of any set of men, however instructed and controlled by a constitution, the public functionaries would be required *to govern by fixed laws;* and it follows, that the aggregate of power to be delegated, would be that which is necessary for making and administering a system of laws, founded on the constitution, as the paramount law. This admits of a threefold division, according to the functions naturally called into exercise. *First*, the laws must be made and promulgated; and the persons designated for this function, would constitute the *legislative department. Secondly*, the laws thus made must be expounded and applied to cases as they should arise; and the persons designated for this function, would constitute the *judicial department. Thirdly*, the laws thus made and adjudicated upon, must be carried into execution, and the persons designated for this function, would constitute the *executive department.* Accordingly, there would be a primary distribution of all delegated powers among three distinct departments, the legislative, judicial, and executive.

5. *Subdivision of Powers.* After this primary division of powers, a further *subdivision* might advantageously be made. The first desideratum would be a system of laws *good in themselves*, independently of their administration. This would depend upon the organization of the legislative department; and here the object would be, to insure a thorough knowledge of the wants of the community, and the most mature deliberation upon the measures proposed for supplying those wants. Now, all others things being equal, it requires no argument to show that a subdivision of the legislative department into *two distinct branches*, whose independent concurrence should be necessary to the enactment of every law, would furnish greater assurance of salutary legislation, than if the legislative power were all concentrated in one body. Again, the judicial power would, in like manner, admit of a beneficial subdivision. It is obvious, that in every case of an alleged violation of

law, two questions are submitted to judicial cognizance. First, what are the *facts* of the case? Secondly, the facts being ascertained, what is the *law* applying to them? These questions being entirely distinct, and security against abuse of power being more important than simplicity of organization, the power of deciding these two questions, instead of being committed to the same persons, might be advantageously divided between two distinct sets of persons. Thus there would be *jurors* to pronounce upon the facts, and *judges* to decide upon the law. Lastly, in regard to the executive department, although it must comprehend many individuals, yet as the nature of its functions requires energy, and despatch, to which unity is essential, this would be a sufficient reason for departing from the principle of division, and vesting the whole executive power primarily in a single person. He must, however, employ many subordinate agents; and to guard this power of appointment from being abused, his nominations might be made to require the confirmation of an independent body of men, before taking effect.

6. *Constitutionality of Laws.* In addition to the security thus provided that the laws would be well made and administered, a further safeguard would be found in the doctrine, that no law would be valid unless *conformable to the constitution.* Although the constitution could not specify in detail what laws should, and what laws should not be enacted, yet it might and should specify certain fundamental properties, without which no law should be valid, and these should serve as landmarks in legislation. But here the question would arise, who is to decide upon the *constitutionality* of laws? In the first instance, the *legislature* would express its opinion by enacting the law in question; hence it must of course suppose itself not to have transcended its powers. In the next place, it might be found expedient, for this and other purposes, to require the assent of the *executive* to the consummation of the law; and since an *absolute veto* might be dangerous, the executive discretion could be restricted to referring an objectionable law back to the legislature for *reconsideration.* But still there would be wanted some tribunal to settle the question of constitutionality in the last resort, whose decision should be final and conclusive; and this tribunal would of course be the *judiciary.* For when a law should come before this department for adjudication, its constitutionality would be the first question to be decided; since if it were unconstitutional it would not be a law, though it had the form; and it would accordingly be declared invalid.

7. *Other Safeguards.* The safeguards now enumerated, being provided for in the constitution, would form the principal securities for good government. Some minor precautions might indeed be taken, by so regulating the *compensation* of officers, as to remove all temptation to venality; by so securing the *freedom of speech and of the press,* that their conduct should be constantly open to public scrutiny and animadversion; and by providing such

means of *removal from office* by impeachment or otherwise, for official misbehavior, as would enable an unworthy incumbent to be displaced, even before his term of service expired. But without pursuing this course of inquiry into further details, suffice it to say, that when all this complicated machinery should be put into complete operation, the community thus organized would constitute one of those distinct political societies, which we denominate a *State* or *Nation*.

§ 8. **Idea of a Federal Government.** And now for the purpose of further illustration, let us suppose *several States or Nations* organized in a similar manner. It is obvious that these nations, however unequal in numbers or resources, would be entirely equal in their political rights. Having as yet contracted no mutual engagements of any kind, each would be in itself completely sovereign and independent. Their relative situation as nations, would be in all respects analogous to that of individuals, prior to entering into the social compact. There being no common power to legislate for them, their reciprocal rights and obligations must at first be deduced solely from the laws of nature applied to them as moral beings. In process of time, however, the principles of natural law, deduced from reason and revelation, and applied to cases as they should arise, would acquire the additional force of custom and usage, and in this way a system of rules for the government of national intercourse would be gradually formed, and would constitute their *jus gentium* or *law of Nations*. In addition to which, they might also enter into mutual engagements, under the name of *compacts or treaties*, and thus superadd their own positive stipulations to the moral and conventional code before mentioned. But howsoever complete might be the code of international law thus slowly matured, there would be no common judicial or executive power; and consequently the due observance of the laws thus acknowledged, must depend solely upon good faith. Each nation would still remain the exclusive judge of its own rights and duties; and in case of controversy, there being no common interpreter or umpire, with power to enforce his decisions, the only alternative would be war or submission. The weaker nation would thus lie at the mercy of the stronger, and right would be compelled to surrender to might. This state of things must continue so long as these nations should remain entirely distinct. Peace would thus be burdened with preparations for war, and war would bring on a train of evils which no words can adequately describe. These contiguous nations, therefore, would have almost the same motives for forming a common government, as individuals have for entering into the social compact. And now the problem would be, to construct a government adapted to the end proposed. On the one hand, a mere *league* or *alliance*, binding the several States only in their collective capacities, and not operating upon individuals, would hardly deserve the name of a government, since it would want the requisite strength and efficiency. Reliance must still be had upon the good faith of the members; since, if they should refuse to comply with the terms of the league, there would be no means of compulsion. Such a feeble union, therefore, would soon be dismembered. And on the other hand, an absolute *consolidation* of all the States into one, by completely annihilating their separate governments, and extending one universal government over the whole, would not be agreed to, because the people of the several States would naturally cling with fondness to their own particular governments; and also because such an arrangement, even if assented to, would be scarcely practicable, on account of the vast extent to which it would thus be necessary to carry the details of municipal regulation. For these reasons, a medium between a league and a consolidated government would probably be preferred; and this would be a *federal government*, in the strict sense of these words. The grand design of this government would be to unite the people of the *several States* into one nation for *national purposes* only; and accordingly for all *municipal purposes*, each State would still retain its former government, divested, however, of the attributes of complete national sovereignty. The powers conferred upon the federal government would extend to no other objects than these of the most public and general concern to all the members of the confederacy; and these powers would be carefully defined by a *federal constitution;* while all other powers would of course be reserved to the State governments, or to the people. With these qualifications, the structure of the federal government in all its departments, would resemble that of the State government already described: and consequently the particulars need not now be repeated. Suffice it to say, that each citizen would now owe obedience to two distinct governments, one *national* and the other *municipal;* and political organization would thus have reached the furthest limits to which it has yet been carried.

§ 9. **Legal Sanctions.** (*a*) This outline, however, would be incomplete, if I should dismiss it without adverting, for a moment, to the *sanctions* of law. By sanction is here meant the inducement or motive to obedience. *Legal sanctions* consist in the prospective pains or pleasures consequent upon violating or conforming to the laws. No doubt, the citizens of a free government are under a *moral obligation* to obey the laws on the principle of consent; but it is unnecessary to discuss this question, because obedience is not left to a sense of duty. If laws were merely *recommended* to the observance of the citizens as a system of salutary rules, and then left to invite obedience or not, according as their intrinsic importance should be felt, they would be in a great measure nugatory. The social compact would add little or nothing to the restraints of a state of nature. In order, then, to give the laws a requisite efficiency, there must be something more than a moral sanction; and, accordingly, there is annexed to every law a

(*a*) See 1 Hoffman's Legal Outlines, 279.

direct sanction, which consists in this, that when a violation is judicially ascertained, the legal consequences will be enforced by the whole power of the community. Legal sanctions, however, are of two kinds, *civil* and *penal*. When the injury which would result from the violation of a law, is such that it can be redressed by a mere *compensation* or *restitution* to the party injured, it is deemed sufficient to compel the aggressor to render this kind of satisfaction. And this is the case with respect to a large proportion of all the injuries, whether to the *person* or to *property*, which take place in society. Such injuries are denominated *civil;* and the sanction of the laws made to prevent or redress them, consists in the pledge of the public faith, that if the injured party take the proper steps to obtain redress, it will be enforced by the public arm. But there are other injuries, both to the *person* and to *property*, of so atrocious a character, that either they do not admit of any thing like compensation, or, for other reasons, the welfare of society requires a more efficient sanction, in order to prevent them. Such injuries are denominated *crimes*, *offences*, or *misdemeanors*. And to guard against them, in addition to the enforcement of restitution, where the case admits of it, the laws provide a *penalty* or *punishment*, in the case of transgression; which penalty or punishment is proportioned, not so much to the actual injury sustained in each particular case, as to the necessity of preventing a repetition of the act. Such, then, are the civil and penal sanctions which give efficacy to municipal laws. By entering into the social compact, the citizen has renounced the right of taking redress for injuries into his own hands; and in return for this, society has given him its pledge to redress them for him. Instead, therefore, of relying upon his own individual strength, as in a state of nature, every member of society may command, if necessary, the whole strength of that society to prevent or redress his wrongs.

For the sake of simplicity, I have presented this outline of political organization *hypothetically*; but I have, in fact, described the precise system under which it is our happiness to live; and I trust that this method of exhibiting it, while it traces government in general up to its elementary principles, will, at the same time, have the effect of demonstrating the entire conformity of our government to the principles of enlightened reason, as applied to the free nature of man. We did not, indeed, pass through the exact gradations I have supposed; and, probably, no nation has. But the consummation of our system is precisely such as I have endeavored to sketch; this will be abundantly proved in the sequel. In the mean time, it is sufficient to say, that when the British colonies in America declared their independence, they may be considered as returning for a moment to that state of nature to which I have referred. The people of each colony then established by general consent an independent State government; and, afterwards, the people of all the States became united, by like consent, under one federal government: so that, at this moment, the

United States exhibit a complete picture of that political organization of which I have only traced a very general and imperfect outline.

LECTURE III.

HISTORICAL SUMMARY.

§ 10. **Title of Great Britain.** (*a*) In the preceding lecture, I presented a *hypothetical* outline of the organization of civil society. I shall now offer a brief *historical* outline of the actual organization of our American society. Prior to the year 1492, this entire continent was in the exclusive possession of an uncivilized race of men called *Indians* or *Aborigines*, who had *occupied* it from time immemorial. Had the character of their occupancy been the same as that of civilized men, it is obvious that the Europeans could have obtained their title only by *purchase* or *conquest;* (*b*) since the right of *discovery* can manifestly attach only to unoccupied territory. But the occupancy of the Indians, who subsisted chiefly by hunting, was considered, by the various discovering nations, to be of too vague and undefined a character to confer an exclusive right to the vast regions over which they habitually roamed. The civilians of that day maintained the doctrine — whether correctly or not, I shall not stop to inquire — that it never could have been the design of the Creator that a few thousand savages should monopolize for hunting-grounds an extent of territory which, under the cultivation of civilized men, might be made to support perhaps ten times as many millions; and, accordingly, the European nations founded their respective claims upon *the right of discovery.* On this ground, the greater part of what is now the territory of the United States fell to the share of

(*a*) See the tenth lecture of Kent; 1 Story, Const.; Marshall's Life of Washington; Bancroft's History of the United States; Pitkin's History of the United States; Curtis's History of the Constitution.

The American doctrine on the subject of Indian title is briefly this: The Indians have no fee in the lands they occupy. The fee is in the government. They cannot of course alien them either to nations or individuals, the exclusive right of pre-emption being in the government. Yet they have a qualified right of occupancy which can only be extinguished by treaty, and upon fair compensation; until which they are entitled to be protected in their possession. See the third article of the Ordinance of 1787; Vattel, chap. 1, § 81, 209; 3 Kent. Com. 386; 1 Story, Const. § 7, 153; Johnson *v.* McIntosh, 8 Wheat. 543; Jackson *v.* Hudson, 3 Johns. 375; Cherokees *v.* Georgia, 5 Pet. 1; Worcester *v.* Georgia, 6 Pet. 515; Clark *v.* Smith, 13 Pet. 195; Chaffee *v.* Garrett, 6 Ohio, 421. {Beecher *v.* Wetherby, 5 Otto, 517. As said in United States *v.* Cook, 19 Wall. 591, they are life tenants and cannot cut timber except for improvement, for that is waste.} It will thus be seen that all valid individual title must be traced to some one of the governments for whom the discoveries were made, or who claim title under them. See 3 Kent, Com. 377; Jackson *v.* Ingraham, 4 Johns. 16; Jackson *v.* Waters, 12 Johns. 365.

(*b*) There is an interesting discussion of the rights gained by a nation by conquest in the United States *v.* Repentigny, 5 Wallace, 211.

Great Britain by virtue of the expedition of John Cabot, who, in 1495, under the auspices of Henry the Seventh, sailed along the eastern coast, from the 56th to the 38th degree of north latitude; and thereupon claimed for his sovereign the whole vast region from the Gulf of Mexico to the Northern Ocean, and from the Atlantic to the Pacific. It turned out that France and Spain had superior titles to some portions of this domain; but for the rest the claim of Great Britain was acquiesced in. No successful attempt, however, was made to establish *colonies* here until 1606, when James the First granted a charter to certain of his subjects, which laid the foundation of the colonies of Virginia and Massachusetts. From this period other colonies were successively established along the whole eastern coast, — the last being that of Georgia, in 1732.

§ 11. **The Revolution.** The colonies were now thirteen in number; and though distinguished by their original organization into *provincial*, *proprietary*, and *charter* governments, they did not differ very essentially from each other in their relations to the mother country. (*a*) As British subjects they all brought from the mother country the laws and institutions adapted to their condition. They all had local legislatures also; but being *dependent colonies*, and not independent States, they could make no laws repugnant to those of Parliament. The exact limits, however, of colonial dependency were never very precisely ascertained; and claims to supremacy asserted beyond the Atlantic were often rejected here. At length Parliament, by way of preamble to one of its acts, asserted the unqualified right to bind the colonies in all cases whatsoever. But the colonies, while they admitted the general authority of Parliament, most resolutely denied it in the case of *taxation*. They held it to be a fundamental principle of British law that taxation and representation go together; and, since they were not represented in Parliament, they could not be taxed by Parliament. And the controversy which began upon this question ended in the revolution which established our independence. But in order that three millions of people might resist, with any hope of success, a power upon whose dominions the sun never sets, it was necessary that they should act in perfect unison. The idea of co-operation had already been rendered familiar to the colonies by the New England alliance, in 1643, for protection against the Indians; by a convention at Albany, in 1754, to discuss a plan of union against the French and Indians; and by a congress of nine colonies at New York in 1765, to declare the rights of the colonies with reference to the mother country; but as yet there was nothing like a permanent and efficient union. When, however, the determination to resist was unalterably taken, the first step was to form a *revolutionary league*. Accordingly, in

(*a*) For the distinguishing features of these several forms of Colonial Government see 1 Story, Const. § 1-197.

1774, the people of all the colonies elected delegates to represent them in a general *Congress*, (*a*) which, from its universality, was dignified with the name of *Continental;* and which was the commencement of that glorious Union which we now enjoy. Passing over the earlier acts of this Continental Congress, the mind hastens at once to that sublime manifesto of the 4th of July, 1776, which fixes the birthday of our national existence. Upon the merits of the *Declaration of Independence*, (*b*) the highest terms of panegyric might be exhausted without extravagance; but this is not the proper occasion. The effect of declaring the "United Colonies" to be "free and independent States" was to make them so. For although it was not until the treaty of peace ratified on the 15th of April, 1783, that Great Britain "acknowledged the thirteen States to be free, sovereign, and independent," yet we universally regard the *declaration* and not the *recognition* of our independence as our true national era. From that moment, in the language of that instrument, "all political connection" between the colonies and the mother country was "totally dissolved;" and from dependent colonies they rose at once to the rank of independent States. But how far was this independence to extend? Were the States to be independent of each other, as well as of Great Britain? This was now an open question; for as yet there was no formal instrument of union. The bond of common danger would hold them together until the revolution should be consummated; but then it would be at their option to remain united or not. In a word, by dissolving their connection with Great Britain, they so far placed themselves in a state of nature

(*a*) For an account of the organization and doings of this Congress, see 1 Story, Const. § 198–206; 1 Pitkin's Hist. U. S. chap. 8 and 9, pages 282–383. It was called on the recommendation of Massachusetts, and assembled at Philadelphia on the 5th of September, 1774. All the colonies were represented except Georgia, which came in the next year. They sat with closed doors, and each colony had one vote. One of their first acts was to adopt a declaration of rights. 1 Pitkin, 285. The members also unanimously signed an agreement for non-intercourse, to which they pledged themselves and their constituents, "under the sacred ties of virtue, honor, and love of their country" — id. 289. They then prepared an address to the people of Great Britain — id. 291; another to the king — id. 293; and another to their constituents — id. 297. It was of this Congress, and of these their doings, that Lord Chatham said: "For genuine sagacity, for singular moderation, for solid wisdom, manly spirit, sublime sentiments, and simplicity of language, for everything respectable and honorable, the Congress of Philadelphia shine unrivalled. This wise people speak out. They do not hold the language of slaves; they tell you what they mean. They do not ask you to repeal your laws as a favor, they claim it as a right" — id. 309."

(*b*) On the 10th of May, 1776, Congress had adopted a significant resolution reported by Mr. Adams, recommending to all the colonies which had not already established governments for themselves to do so without delay. The resolution for independence was moved by Mr. Lee, of Virginia, on the 7th of June. The committee appointed to prepare the Declaration consisted of Messrs. Jefferson, Adams, Franklin, Sherman, and Livingston. It was drawn up by Mr. Jefferson, approved by the committee, and reported to Congress on the 28th of June. For a brief sketch of the debates by Mr. Jefferson, see Mad. Pap. 9; and for the original draft of the Declaration, with the alterations made by Congress, see id. 19. For a further account see 1 Story, Const. § 205; 1 Pitkin's Hist. U. S. chap. 9, pages 360–370. The most important alteration made by Congress was to strike out the entire clause reprobating the slave-trade. Mad. Pap. 24.

that they could enter into whatsoever kind of social compact should be most agreeable. (*a*) But, fortunately, this momentous question was settled before the common danger was removed. For on the 15th of November, 1777, the Continental Congress, after long debate, agreed upon the *Articles of Confederation*, (*b*) and recommended them to the States for ratification. So great, however, was the opposition that the ratification was not effected until the 1st of March, 1781. This formed the second stage in the progress of our Union. And without attempting a particular analysis of these "Articles," I will refer to some of their leading characteristics. The union thereby created, though declared to be *perpetual*, was professedly nothing but a *league*, having for its object, "the common defence and general welfare." In Congress, the States were represented *equally*, each having one vote. The subjects of jurisdiction were enumerated, and the determinations of Congress were declared to be binding on the States. There was, however, no regular *judiciary*, and nothing resembling an *executive*, except a "committee of the States," to act during the recess of Congress. The radical defect, therefore, was the total want of power to *execute* what Congress might *direct*. The acts of Congress were not *laws*, as we understand the term, but merely *ordinances* or *requisitions* operating upon the States, in their *collective* capacities, and not upon individuals. Obedience depended solely upon the good faith of the States, and was often refused with impunity. The consequence was that the moment peace took off the pressure of a common danger the Union was

(*a*) I am aware that this has always been a disputed point. There certainly was a national government *de facto* from the first meeting of the Continental Congress. And it is equally true that the Declaration of Independence was not the act of each colony separately, but of all united. Still, I think it clear that nothing more than a temporary union, dissoluble at the option of the States, can be considered as existing prior to the Articles of Confederation. But see 1 Story, Const. § 207–217.

(*b*) A plan of confederation had been submitted by Dr. Franklin, on the 21st of July, 1775, but was not acted upon. On the 11th of June, 1776, during the discussion of the question of independence, a committee of one from each State was appointed to prepare a plan. They reported, through Mr. Dickinson, on the 12th of July, 1776. Their plan was debated and amended from time to time until the 15th of November, 1777, when it was adopted by Congress. Mad. Pap. 688–9 ; 1 Story, Const. § 218–228 ; 2 Pitkin's Hist. U. S. chap. 11, pages 9–19. Of the debates on these Articles, we have no full report. Mr. Jefferson has preserved a sketch of the debate on the quotas of contribution among the States, and also on the equality of votes in Congress. Mad. Pap. 27–39. The Articles were submitted to the legislatures of the States for approval, in which case, they were to authorize their delegates in Congress to ratify them by signature. Much opposition was made in all the States, and the ratification, commenced on the 9th of July, 1778, was not completed until the 1st of March, 1781. The last three ratifications were, by New Jersey on the 25th of November, 1778, by Delaware on the 22d of February, 1779, and by Maryland on the 1st of March, 1781. The principal reason for this long delay was the claim made by some of the States to the vacant Western lands. And it is probable that Maryland never would have come into the Union, if this obstacle had not been removed by the relinquishment of these claims. 1 Story, Const. § 226–228 ; 2 Pitkin's Hist. U. S. chap. 11, pages 19–36. For a very clear analysis of these Articles, see 1 Story, Const. § 229–242. For a full exposition of the defects of this system, and a vivid description of the state of anarchy and despondency to which the country was reduced by it, see 1 Story, Const. § 243–271 ; 2 Marshall's Washington, chap. 4, pages 94–125 ; 2 Pitkin's Hist. U. S. chap. 16, pages 214–223.

found to be too feeble to answer its design; and every day increased the prospect of a fatal dismemberment.

§ 12. **Formation of the Federal Constitution.** (*a*) In this state of things, a universal feeling of danger turned the thoughts of all patriots towards the establishment of a more perfect union. In

(*a*) The convention at Annapolis was called for commercial purposes. The States represented were, Virginia, Delaware, Pennsylvania, New Jersey, and New York. For the report of their proceedings, see Mad. Pap. 698. Its most important feature is the recommendation of a general convention to meet at Philadelphia, for the purpose of revising the Articles of Confederation. The day assigned was May 14, 1787. A quorum of seven States did not appear until the 25th of May, when the convention was organized by the unanimous election of Washington for president. — Mad. Pap. 721, 722. New Hampshire was not represented until the 23d of July, and Rhode Island refused to take any part. The convention deliberated with closed doors. The yeas and nays could not be demanded. None but a member could inspect the journal, and he could not take a copy from it without leave. Nor could anything spoken in the house be published or communicated without leave. But the most important rule of all was, that the voting should be by States. That this should have been assented to without debate by the large States is a fact strikingly illustrative of the conciliatory temper with which those great men commenced their task — id. 724–8. On the 29th of May the business of the convention was opened by Mr. Randolph, of Virginia, who offered a series of resolutions agreed upon by his delegation which formed the groundwork of future debate — id. 728–35. Mr. C. Pinckney, of South Carolina, submitted a plan, but it was not acted upon — id. 735. Mr. Hamilton, of New York, prepared a plan, but did not submit it — id. App. No. 5. The debate proceeded in committee of the whole, upon Mr. Randolph's resolutions, until the 13th of June, when nineteen were reported to the house — id. 848. At this point, Mr. Patterson, of New Jersey, brought forward what was called the *federal plan*, proposing merely to amend the Articles of Confederation by adding new powers, but not to alter the basis of that system — id. 863. Both plans were referred to the committee of the whole, and after a warm debate, calling out a very full expression of opinion upon the merits of the two systems, the *national plan* of Mr. Randolph prevailed by a vote of seven to three — id. 904. The debate proceeded in the house until the 26th of July, when the resolutions thus far agreed upon were referred to a *committee of detail*, consisting of five members, who were to incorporate them into a constitution — id. 1220. The convention then adjourned to the 6th of August, when the committee of detail reported a constitution — id. 1226. This was discussed, section by section, until the 8th of September, when the whole was referred to a *committee of style*, consisting of five members, to revise and arrange what had now been agreed to — id. 1532. This committee, on the 12th of September, reported the constitution nearly in its present shape, together with a letter to accompany it — id. 1543–61. Alterations and additions were proposed and discussed until the 15th of September, when the constitution was agreed to and engrossed by a unanimous vote — id. 1595. Only one alteration was afterwards made, which was to change the ratio of representation from forty to thirty thousand. Washington expressed himself in favor of this change, and this was the only time he took any part in the discussions — id. 1599. On the 17th of September the closing scene took place. Great efforts were made to procure a unanimous signature by every member — id. 1596–1603. Of the fifty-five members, only forty-two were then present; and of these, thirty-nine did sign it. Messrs. Randolph, Mason, and Gerry alone refused — id. 1623–4. The journal and other papers of the convention were then deposited in the hands of the president, to be kept by him subject to the order of Congress, if ever formed under the constitution — id. 1604–5. By order of Congress this journal was published in 1821. But the only complete history of the doings of the convention is to be found in the Madison Papers, published by order of Congress, in 1840, from pages 721 to 1624, inclusive. For the circumstances under which this report of the debates was made, see pages 716–719. A very succinct account of the doings of this convention may be found in 2 Pitkin's Hist. U. S. chap. 18, pages 224–263. The Madison Papers now make up the fifth volume of Elliott's Debates on the Adoption of the Federal Constitution, — a compilation which, besides the debates in the convention and in the States, contains other very important documents illustrative of the constitution. Published by Lippincott and Co., Philadelphia, 1859.

1786, at the instance of Virginia, a convention of five States assembled at Annapolis, and, among other things, recommended a general convention to amend the Articles of Confederation. Congress afterwards made a similar recommendation. The result was that on the 14th of May, 1787, a convention of delegates appointed by the *legislatures* of all the States except Rhode Island, assembled at Philadelphia. It was obviously impracticable to *amend* the articles of Confederation so as to answer the purpose, because the evil to be cured lay at their very foundation. Something more than a *league* was necessary. Accordingly the convention gave up this project and proceeded to provide a substitute. The result was our present "Constitution of the United States," which was signed by the convention on the 17th of September, 1787. The formation of a constitution, at all times an arduous work, was peculiarly so in this case. So strong was the general feeling against an efficient federal government that the success of the undertaking is almost miraculous. It was agreed, at the outset, that the States should part with no more of their former powers than was absolutely necessary in order to perpetuate their union. And there were two difficulties which could only be overcome by a magnanimous compromise of opposing interests; I mean the inequality of the States in respect to *size*, and their inequality in respect to *slaves*. How admirably these differences were adjusted, in fixing the federal relations of the States, will be explained hereafter. The convention, having completed the constitution, recommended that it should "be submitted to a convention of delegates chosen in each State by the *people* thereof, under a recommendation of its legislature, for their assent and *ratification*." The constitution itself provided that "the *ratification* of the convention of *nine* States should be sufficient for its establishment, between the States so ratifying the same." (*a*) Conventions were accordingly called in all the States; and it is not easy to conceive of a severer ordeal than that to which this constitution was subjected in these conventions. In most of them divers *amendments* were recommended, of which ten were afterwards adopted. In the course of one year, however, all the States, except North Carolina and Rhode Island, had given in their ratifications "in

(*a*) The first proposition in the convention was that the ratification should be by convention, appointed by the people, which passed by a vote of six to three. Mad. Pap. 795, 846. After a subsequent warm debate, a proposition to refer it to the State legislatures was negatived by a vote of three to seven; a proposition to refer it to one general convention did not pass to a vote; and the original proposition was re-affirmed by a vote of nine to one — id. 1177–1185, 1468–74. In less than one year, the constitution had been ratified by eleven of the States. North Carolina gave her assent in November, 1789, and Rhode Island in May, 1790; 1 Story, Const. § 272–280; 2 Pitkin's Hist. U. S. chap. 18, pages 264–291. For a very full report of the debates in the conventions of several of the States, see Elliott's Debates. When the constitution was first submitted to the people, the chances seemed to be against its ratification; and perhaps we are indebted for this happy consummation mainly to that celebrated series of essays written by Messrs. Hamilton, Madison, and Jay, for the New York papers, and afterwards collected and published under the title of "The Federalist." See 2 Marshall's Washington, chap. 4, pages 126, 127.

the name of the people thereof;" and these two shortly afterwards came into the great measure. Accordingly, on the 4th of March, 1789, the new government established by the federal constitution went into operation.

§ 13. **The Public Domain.** (*a*) As yet the Union comprehended

(*a*) The conflicting claims to the vacant western territory formed one of the chief obstacles to a general union of the States under the Articles of Confederation. Those States whose colonial charters gave them no claim to any part of this territory insisted that the other States should surrender their claims, and thus throw the whole into a common fund. Maryland made this an indispensable condition of her accession to the Union. In February, 1780, New York made the first movement by a cession of her claims. In the latter part of the same year, Congress made an earnest recommendation to all the States to follow her example, promising that the territory so relinquished should be disposed of for the common benefit of the Union, and formed into republican States; and that the expenses incurred by any State in relation to such territory should be reimbursed. Virginia complied with this recommendation in January, 1781, and thereupon Maryland, on the first of March, 1781, without waiting for other cessions, ratified the Articles of Confederation. 2 Pitkin's Hist. U. S. chap. 11, pages 27-33.

It will be borne in mind that the text was written before the stupendous acquisitions of Texas, New Mexico, California, Oregon, or Alaska.

The original boundaries of the Virginia charter were: "From Point Comfort all along the sea-coast to the northward, two hundred miles; and from the said Point Comfort to the southward, two hundred miles; and all that space and circuit of land lying from the sea-coast of the precinct aforesaid, up into the land throughout from sea to sea, west and north-west." — Land Laws, U. S. 25. Under this grant Virginia claimed all that portion of the North-western Territory which lies between the forty-first parallel of latitude and the Ohio River, extending from Pennsylvania to the Mississippi River. The cession was authorized in 1783, and executed in 1784. One of the conditions was, that if the land reserved south of the Ohio (now Kentucky) should not be sufficient to pay the bounties promised to her troops, the deficiency should be made up from lands between the Scioto and Little Miami Rivers; pursuant to which some three millions of acres have been appropriated to that purpose, known as the Virginia Military District. See Parker *v.* Wallace, 3 Ohio, 490. {The unsurveyed parts of which District were granted by Congress to Ohio in 1871.}

The boundaries of the Connecticut charter were Narragansett Bay on the east, Massachusetts on the north, the sea on the south, "and in longitude as the line of the Massachusetts colony, running from east to west, that is to say, from the said Narragansett Bay on the east, to the south sea on the west." — Land Laws, U. S. 24. Under this grant Connecticut claimed between the forty-first and forty-second parallels from Pennsylvania to the Mississippi River. The cession was made in 1786, reserving a tract extending one hundred and twenty miles west from Pennsylvania, known as the *Western Reserve*, and containing over three millions of acres.

In the eastern division of Ohio the ranges are numbered from east to west, and the townships from north to south. In the western, the ranges are numbered from west to east, and the townships as before, except in Symmes' Purchase, where the ranges are numbered from south to north, and the townships from west to east. In the public lands generally, the sections are numbered progressively, beginning at the north-east corner of the township, and counting first west and then east alternately, fractions having the same number as if whole. But in the purchases of Symmes and of the Ohio Company, the sections begin at the south-east corner and are numbered north without alternation.

The federal scheme is perhaps the most simple and certain which could be framed. But the Virginia scheme has, of necessity, created quite an original system of land law in the whole of Kentucky, and in the Virginia Military District of Ohio. I shall note a few points decided in Ohio. The only mode of deriving a *legal* title from the United States is by *patent*. The *entry*, *survey*, and *certificate* of purchase, constitute only an *equitable* title. Roads *v.* Symmes, 1 Ohio, 281; Anderson *v.* Clark, 1 Peters, 628; Wilcox *v.* Jackson, 13 Peters, 516. Where land has been entered and surveyed by the ancestor, and the patent issues to the heir, he takes by descent, and not by purchase. Bond *v.* Swearingen, 1 Ohio, 395. The whole process of consummating a title, from the warrant to the patent, is to be regarded as one transaction, and the assignee, at any stage, takes the title as it then was in the assignor, with all his rights only the thirteen original States. But these occupy but a small portion of the territory now subject to the federal government. The entire surface of our country may be stated at fourteen hundred millions of acres; of which only about four hundred millions have as yet been appropriated; so that there are now about one thousand millions in the wild solitude of nature. (*a*) This vacant territory is the exclusive property of the United States, subject only to the *Indian rights*, to be explained hereafter, and constitutes our *public domain*. In whatever light it may be viewed, it is a subject of surpassing interest. Who can foresee the consequences which may result from the possession of a vacant territory more than twice as large as the whole organized portion of the Union? I shall consider the subject in two points of view; first, the acquisition and title; secondly, the scheme of survey and sale.

Acquisition of Title. The United States acquired their title to the public domain in three ways: *first*, by succession to Great Britain; *secondly*, by cessions from the different States; *thirdly*, by purchase from foreign governments. The effect of the revolu-

and obligations. M'Arthur *v.* Nevill, 3 Ohio, 178. A certificate of entry, not being within the statute of frauds, may be assigned by parol. Reed *v.* M'Grew, 5 Ohio, 375. A patent issued to an assignee stands upon the same footing as if issued to the original owner. Wallace *v.* Miner, 7 Ohio, 1 pt. 249. An entry and survey made in the name of an attorney in fact of a decedent is utterly void. Wallace *v.* Saunders, 7 Ohio, 1 pt. 173. A patent for land issuing from the government of the United States in the name of a deceased person is void, and the title thereto remains in the government. Wood *v.* Ferguson, 7 Ohio State, 288. Where the patent purports to issue to an assignee, he need not prove his purchase except in rebutting. M'Arthur *v.* Phœbus, 2 Ohio, 415, and see M'Arthur *v.* Gallaher, 8 Ohio, 512. Assignees of a claim may prosecute it for confirmation in the name of the original claimant. United States *v.* Sutter, 21 Howard, 170. A patent issued to the original beneficiary, who had previously sold his right, enures to the benefit of the purchaser. French *v.* Spencer, 21 Howard, 228. The court will not undertake to decide upon the evidence upon which a patent emanated. Milliken *v.* Starling, 16 Ohio, 61. When there is a discrepancy between the calls in the survey and patent, the survey must prevail. Wyckoff *v.* Stephenson, 14 Ohio, 13. There is no inflexible rule for running the open or lost lines of a survey, each case depending on its own circumstances. Bishop *v.* McMullen, 5 Ohio State, 19. As to the meaning of the term "due west," where the original survey was made by the magnetic or the true meridian, see McKinney *v.* McKinney, 8 Ohio State, 423. If a mistake made in the survey be continued in the patent, a Court of Equity cannot correct it, as against subsequent adjoining purchasers. Porter *v.* Robb, 7 Ohio 1 pt. 206. An entry which does not contain such calls as will enable a diligent inquirer to locate it is void; and the notoriety of the calls must be coeval with the entry. Kerr *v.* Mack, 1 Ohio, 161; Martin *v.* Boon, 2 Ohio, 237. The surveys must be limited to strict measure, notwithstanding an alleged custom to add five per cent. Houston *v.* M'Arthur, 7 Ohio, 2 pt. 54. A senior entry, surveyed and patented, will prevail in equity over a senior patent upon a junior entry. Parker *v.* Wallace, 3 Ohio, 490; Parker *v.* Dunn, 4 Ohio, 232; and see Hastings *v.* Stevenson, 2 Ohio, 8. Where two patents are issued for the same land, and the first is obtained fraudulently or against law, it does not carry the legal title. Stoddard *v.* Chambers, 2 Howard, 284. The common doctrine of notice does not apply when parties claim under distinct entries. Kerr *v.* Mack, 1 Ohio, 161. Roseberry *v.* Hollister, 4 Ohio State, 297. When the holder of a survey suffers the land to be sold for taxes, his whole interest passes. Wallace *v.* Seymour, 7 Ohio, 1 pt. 156.

(*a*) In the report of the census for 1860, the territorial area of the United States is stated to be, including the area covered by water, 3,250,000 square miles; excluding the area covered by water, 3,010,370 square miles. To this is now to be added the area of Russian America, lately ceded by treaty to the United States. This is stated in the pamphlet on Alaska by the Hon. Charles Sumner to be 557,390 square miles.

tion was to transfer to the United States all the rights which Great Britain had acquired by discovery or otherwise, and had not then parted with. Accordingly, in the treaty of peace, the king expressly relinquished, for himself and his successors, "all claims to the government, propriety, and territorial rights" of the thirteen States, and every part thereof. But so little was known of our topography when the grants were made to the different colonies that, besides being vague and often contradictory, some of them were highly extravagant in point of quantity. For example, the descriptive words in the grant to Virginia covered a tract four hundred miles in width, and extending in terms from the Atlantic to the Pacific Ocean. The grant to Connecticut was of a similar character, and the rest not greatly different. The consequence was that immediately after the Declaration of Independence, conflicting claims to territory were set up by the several States, which threatened to prevent the formation of a permanent union. Impoverished as the States then were, and overburdened with debts contracted for the general good of the whole, it was reasonably claimed by many that this vacant territory, so unequally distributed originally, ought to be made a common fund for defraying the expenses of the war; and in this state of things, Congress, in 1781, made an appeal to the patriotism and magnanimity of the favored States, which had its effect. New York had already set the first example, by ceding to the Union all her claims; and this was imitated, at successive intervals, by all the other States. By these cessions, the United States derived their title to all that portion of the public domain which lies north of Florida and east of the Mississippi River. Various conditions were attached to these cessions, but all agreed in this one, namely, that the territory thus ceded should be a *common fund* for the joint benefit of all the present and future members of the Union. This fact will serve to show the character of those claims which have been set up in some of the States to the exclusive ownership of all the public lands which happen to fall within their territorial limits. Should Congress ever acquiesce in these claims, it would be a virtual forfeiture of the whole grant, by a breach of the condition annexed to it. But another mode of acquisition was by *purchase*. Although Great Britain originally claimed the region west of the Mississippi, it was finally decided to belong to France, and took the name of Louisiana. It was afterwards, for a short time, owned by Spain, and then again by France, until it was finally purchased by the United States in 1803. In like manner, Florida, which originally fell to Spain, was purchased by the United States in 1817. The power to make these purchases is nowhere expressly conferred by the constitution; but the importance of these acquisitions, particularly that of Louisiana, including, as it does, the vast region beyond the Mississippi, together with the exclusive control of that mighty river, cannot be overrated.

Scheme of Survey and Sale. Some of the earliest sales were negotiated directly with the treasury department. This was the case with the first two sales within the present State of Ohio, namely, the *Ohio Company's purchase*, made in July, 1787, and including nearly one million of acres, about the mouth of the Muskingum; and *Symmes' purchase*, made in the autumn of the same year, and ultimately including about three hundred thousand acres between the two Miamis. Since then, however, the scheme has been entirely changed, and its present outline is as follows: In 1812, the department of *public lands* was made a distinct branch of the treasury department, and placed under the control of a chief officer entitled *commissioner of the General Land-Office.* (*a*) The public domain is divided into *districts*, in each of which there is a *register* and a *receiver of the public moneys.* In each convenient number of districts, there is a *surveyor-general.* The first step is to extinguish by treaty the Indian title, which is done through the Indian *agents.* The territory is then surveyed into *ranges, townships*, and *sections*, by means of lines always running with the cardinal points, but not including Indian reservations or navigable rivers. The townships are six miles square, and divided into thirty-six sections of one mile square. Thus a township contains twenty-three thousand and forty acres, and a section six hundred and forty. The sections are again subdivided into *halves, quarters, eighths.* The ranges, townships, and sections are progressively numbered, and fractions have the same numbers as if they were whole. By referring, therefore, to the meridian assumed for the survey, and giving the number of the range, township, and section, we have a brief and yet certain description of a given tract, and herein the scheme has immeasurably the advantage over that adopted by Virginia, in disposing of her reserved lands. There was no previous survey. *Warrants* were issued for certain quantities, to be *located* by the holders upon any tract not already occupied. These locations or *entries*, vaguely described, were *registered* and *surveyed.* The necessary result was extreme confusion, and uncertainty in the titles thus acquired. But under the federal scheme, no such evil can happen, because the land has been first surveyed. All things being now ready for sale, the land is first offered at auction for the *minimum* price of one dollar and a quarter per acre, and no credit. (*b*) If not sold, it remains open to

(*a*) By the Act of March 3, 1849, establishing the Department of the Interior, the General Land-Office was made a part of it.

(*b*) The settlement of the lands was much facilitated by what were known as the pre-emption laws. Laws had been several times passed, giving to actual settlers on the lands at specified times the preference in the purchase of the lands improved by them, and, in 1841, a general act was passed which, with some modifications and extensions, is still in force. It at first applied only to surveyed lands, but was in 1843 extended to unsurveyed lands also, and has generally been extended as fast as the Indian title was extinguished. The plan is to give any actual settler and cultivator a preference over any one else in the purchase of not to exceed one hundred and sixty acres, covering his improvements at the minimum government price. Indeed, under the homestead law of 1862, he may even acquire them for nothing, under certain restrictions, by cultivating them for five years. But it has been decided in the case private sale at the land-office in the district, on the same terms. On payment to the receiver, the purchaser obtains a certificate from the register, which is transmitted to the commissioner at Washington, and a *patent* issues to complete the title. Salt springs and lead mines are reserved to the United States. And in pursuance of a most liberal and enlightened policy, one section, numbered sixteen, in every township, making one thirty-sixth part of the whole, is appropriated by Congress for *education*. In the Ohio Company and Symmes' purchases, a section was also set apart for the support of *religion*, but this is not now done. Immense donations have likewise been made for colleges, and various internal improvements.

§ 14. **Territorial Governments.** — *Ordinance of* 1787. (*a*) When lands not lying within the limits of any State have been sold and settled, provision must be made for governing the inhabitants. This is done by creating territorial governments, dependent upon the federal government. The power to do this is contained in these words of the constitution: "The Congress shall have power to dispose of, and make all needful rules and regulations respecting the territory, and other property belonging to the United States; and nothing in this constitution shall be so construed as to prejudice any claims of the United States, or of any particular State." The first government of this kind was that of the "Territory north-west of the river Ohio," commonly called the North-western Territory, having for its southern boundary the northern side of the Ohio River at low-water mark. (*b*) This territory

of the celebrated Yosemite Valley, among others, that these laws do not confer vested rights until the entry is complete and the money paid, but that before that time Congress may at pleasure withdraw the land from entry and sale. Frisbie *v.* Whitney, 9 Wall. 187; Hutchins *v.* Low (Yosemite Valley Case), 15 Wall. 77.

(*a*) See 2 Story, Const. § 1318; Mad. Pap. 1456–1466.

(*b*) See the case of Handly *v.* Anthony, 5 Wheat. 374. The original act of cession offered by Virginia, January 2, 1781, ceding all right, title, and claim to the territory within the limits of the Virginia charter, situate, lying, and being to the north-west of the river Ohio, contained eight conditions. The eighth was "that all the territory south-east of the Ohio, included between the boundaries of Pennsylvania, Maryland, and North Carolina, to the Atlantic, should be guaranteed to Virginia by the United States." Congress declined to accept this cession, and recommended that the seventh and eighth sections be struck out. Virginia afterwards, on the 20th October, 1783, accordingly struck out those conditions, made the cession thus amended, and Congress accepted it.

The Supreme Courts of the United States, in Handly *v.* Anthony, 5 Wheat. 374; of Kentucky, in Fleming *v.* Kenney, 4 J. J. Marsh. 158, McFall *v.* Commonwealth, 2 Metc. 394; and of Indiana, Stinson *v.* Butler, 4 Blackf. 285, Cowden *v.* Kerr, 6 Blackf. 280, Carlisle *v.* The State, 32 Ind. 55, — assuming that Virginia owned the land to the north-west of the river, and assuming that the terms of the act of cession of 1783 alone determine the extent of the grant, — hold that the boundary between Kentucky on the one side, and Ohio and Indiana on the other, is low-water mark on the north-west shore of the river. The Supreme Court of Virginia, Garner's Case, 3 Grattan, 655, deciding that Virginia owned the land to the north-west of the river, and assuming that the terms of the act of cession of 1783 alone determine the extent of the cession, holds that the boundary between Ohio and Virginia is low-water mark on the north-west shore of the river. The Supreme Court of Ohio, Booth *v.* Hubbard's Admr., 8 Ohio State, 243, held the boundary of Ohio extends at least to the low-water mark on the north-west shore; apparently reserving an opinion, till a decision shall be necessary, included the present States of Ohio, Indiana, Illinois, and Michigan, and part of the territory of Wisconsin, — making a surface of about four hundred thousand square miles. It was embraced in the cessions of Virginia and Connecticut. The government of this territory was created by the celebrated *Ordinance of July* 13, 1787, (*a*) just prior to the adoption of the federal constitution.

upon two questions : 1. Whether Virginia in fact owned the territory north-west of the Ohio. 2. Whether the terms of the original act of cession do not fix the middle of the river as the boundary. And in the opinion of the Court in Covington Bridge Co. *v.* Mayer, 31 Ohio State, 327, 329, it is said, "The State of Ohio, I believe, has always claimed to own to the centre of the river." {See articles on the southern boundary of Ohio by F. M. Coppock, 9 Am. Law Record, pp. 449, 529, 577.}

Virginia, in its compact with Kentucky in 1789, consented that Kentucky should be erected into a State, upon several conditions. The seventh is, "The respective jurisdiction of this Commonwealth and of the proposed State on the river aforesaid shall be concurrent only with the States which may possess the opposite shore of said river." Hence each State bordering on the Ohio has exclusive jurisdiction over the river to low-water mark on its own side ; and has, between low-water mark on the two sides, concurrent jurisdiction with the State possessing the opposite shore. Carlisle *v.* The State, 32 Ind. 55; McFall *v.* The Commonwealth, 2 Metc. 394; opinion of Johnston, J., 3 Gratt. 721, in Garner's Case.

(*a*) For an account of this ordinance, see 2 Story, Const. § 1318–1325; 9 Dane's Abr. Appendix; {Escanaba Co. *v.* Chicago, 106 U. S. 678}. For judicial construction, see Hogg *v.* Zanesville Canal & Mfg. Co., 5 Ohio, 410 ; Hutchinson *v.* Thompson, 9 Ohio, 52 ; Spooner *v.* McConnel, 1 McLean's Rep. 337 ; La Plaisance *v.* Monroe, 1 Walker, Ch. Rep. (Mich.) 155. As to the effect of this ordinance now, opinions are conflicting. In the case of Hogg *v.* Zanesville Canal & Mfg. Co., 5 Ohio, 410, the court say: "This portion of the ordinance (the 4th article) of 1787, is as much obligatory upon the State of Ohio as our own constitution. In truth it is more so; for the constitution may be altered by the people of the State, while this cannot be altered without the assent both of the people of this State and of the United States, through their representatives. It is an article of compact, and until we assume the principle that the sovereign power of the State is not bound by compact, this clause must be considered obligatory." In the case of Hutchinson *v.* Thompson, 9 Ohio, 52, the court say: "The ordinance consists of two parts, first, of a constitution of government for the territory ; and secondly, of articles of compact, which were intended to look beyond the period when the people should emerge from their territorial condition, and become members of the Union. I have called this part a compact, because it is so termed in the instrument ; but if it were not for some things which have since taken place, there might be great difficulty in regarding it in that light. There was in reality but one party to it originally, and that was the general government. But when application for admission into the Union was made by the people inhabiting the eastern part of the territory, modifications in several parts of the ordinance were asked for ; and they were granted, by the United States as one party, to the State as another. This seems to show that the people of Ohio have, so far, treated the articles of compact as of perpetual obligation." In the case of La Plaisance *v.* Monroe, 1 Walker, Ch. Rep. (Mich.) 155, the court say : "The ordinance of 1787, in my opinion, is no part of the fundamental law of the State since its admission into the Union. It was then superseded by the State constitution ; and such parts of it as are not to be found in the federal or State constitutions were then annulled by mutual consent. The articles of confederation between the thirteen original States were entered into July 9th, 1778, and were afterwards superseded by the constitution of the United States in March, 1789. The ordinance was passed July 13th, 1787, one year and eight months before the constitution took effect, and two months before it came from the hands of the convention that framed it. The ordinance must consequently have been drawn with a view to the existing government under the articles of confederation. If the constitution had been in operation at that time, it can hardly be supposed that the ordinance would have been what it is ; for a new, and, in most respects a different, state of things exists under the constitution from what existed under the confederation." See Jones *v.* Van Zandt, 5 How. 230 ; {to the same effect, Duluth Lumber Co. *v.* St. Louis Boom, &c. Co., 17 Fed. Rep. 419 ; that the ordinance is subordinate to the federal constitution, Strader *v.* Graham, 10 How. 82}. When a State has adopted a constitution, and the government of the United

The whole region, with some trifling exceptions, was then one continuous solitude, upon which no laws had operated but the laws of nature. Here, then, was an unequalled opportunity for the establishment of an improved system of local law. No ancient rubbish was to be cleared away; no time-hallowed prejudices to be overcome. All was open and free as an unsullied sheet, to receive the best impressions of legislative wisdom. Under such auspices, this ordinance was drawn up, by the late Nathan Dane, of Massachusetts, almost word for word as it now stands; and for brevity, comprehension, and forecast, it has no superior in the annals of legislation. Being the model of all subsequent territorial governments, it deserves a brief analysis. 1. By a few sweeping provisions relating to the acquisition, descent, and transfer of property, it effectually excluded many of those feudal doctrines which still incumber the laws of the older States. 2. It provided two grades of territorial government. The first grade consisted of a governor, secretary, and three judges, appointed by Congress, and other inferior officers. The governor and judges, in addition to their ordinary functions, were empowered "to adopt and publish" such laws from "the original States" as they should think proper, Congress retaining a negative. This grade continued until 1799, when the second commenced. A legislature was now added, consisting of a house of representatives, and a legislative council of five, upon whose acts the governor had an absolute negative. The legislature chose one delegate to Congress, who had the privilege of debating, but not of voting. Thus far, this form has been substantially followed in all the subsequent territorial governments, until quite recently. 3. The most remarkable part of the ordinance is the six "articles of compact between the original States, and the people and States in the said territory;" which were designed "to fix and establish the fundamental principles of civil and religious liberty, as the basis of all future laws, constitutions, and governments;" and which were "forever to remain unalterable, except by common consent." These articles are worthy of a brief abstract. The *first* article asserts religious liberty in its widest extent. The *second*, after a series of declarations guarding personal liberty, contains the then new and original provision that no law should interfere with private contracts previously made; which has since been adopted into all the American constitutions. The *third* declares the encouragement of education to be a binding duty of legislators. The *fourth* provides that the future States shall always remain a part of the United States; shall never interfere with the primary disposal of the soil by Congress; shall not tax the lands owned by the United States, nor non-resident proprietors higher than residents; and that the navigable waters, and the carrying places

States has assented to it, and admitted the State to the Union, the provisions of the ordinance of 1787, so far as they conflict with this State constitution, are abrogated by common consent. Connecticut Insurance Co. *v.* Cross, 18 Wis. 109.

between them, shall forever remain public highways. The *fifth* article provides that not more than five nor less than three States shall be formed within the territory, whose constitutions shall be republican, and conformable to these articles. The *sixth* article forever prohibits slavery within the territory; but provides that fugitive slaves may be reclaimed from it. It is hoped that this abstract may be an inducement to examine this remarkable example of legislative wisdom.

§ 15. **Admission of New States into the Union.** (*a*) When territories have acquired the requisite amount of population, the next step is to admit them as States into the Union. The constitution declares that "new States may be admitted by the Congress into the Union; but no new State shall be formed or erected within the jurisdiction of any other State; nor any State be formed by the junction of two or more States, or parts of States, without the consent of the legislatures concerned, as well as of the Congress." By this provision the whole subject of admitting new States, where other States are not interfered with, is placed under the control of Congress, with the single restriction, contained in another clause, that their constitutions must be "*republican*." Pursuant to this power, thirteen new States have been already admitted, and there are other territories preparing for admission. (*b*) The result is that the centre of empire is rapidly moving westward, and the original States falling into a minority. For the sake of illustrating the action of Congress, I will describe the admission of Ohio. An Act of Congress was passed for this purpose, on the 30th of April, 1802, which, after specifying the boundaries, and providing for a convention to frame the constitution, submitted three *propositions* for the acceptance of the State. These, after some modifications, were adopted as follows: 1. One full thirty-sixth part of the entire surface of the State was to be vested in the legislature for the support of schools; and as the whole extent is about twenty-five millions of acres, this donation exceeds seven hundred thousand. It will be remembered that the present land scheme, which would have resulted in the same thing, was not then formed. 2. Cer-

(*a*) There was much diversity of opinion upon this subject in the convention. It was first resolved that provision ought to be made for admitting new States without requiring a unanimous vote of Congress. Mad. Pap. 861. But it was repeatedly proposed to restrict them as to their right of representation, so that they might never outvote the old States. It was said that they would be hostile to commerce, poor, uneducated, and wholly unfit to control the destinies of a great nation. Mad. Pap. 1034, 1053, 1070, 1095. It was then proposed that a majority of two-thirds should be required for their admission, but that they should be admitted on the same terms as the original States. Strenuous opposition was made to the equality of terms; but justice ultimately prevailed, and it was agreed that they should be admitted by a majority of votes, and upon an equality of terms. Mad. Pap. 1456–1466. And see 2 Story, Const. § 1314–1322.

(*b*) The number of new States organized out of territories since the adoption of the constitution is twenty-four, and in 1862 Virginia was divided into two States, the western portion being called West Virginia, thus making the whole number of the States thirty-eight. {There are eight organized territories, and two not organized, namely, Indian Territory and Alaska.}

tain salt springs which had been reserved by Congress were to be given to the State, "for the use of the people thereof," and one township, for a college, pursuant to the contract with Symmes. Two townships had been previously given for a similar purpose, in the contract with the Ohio Company. 3. Three per centum of the net proceeds of the sales of public lands within the State were to be appropriated to the construction of roads within the State, and under the direction of Congress. These three propositions were based upon the *condition* that the public lands within the State should be exempted from taxation for five years from the sale thereof. Such were the terms upon which Ohio came into the Union. The convention, after only three weeks of deliberation, signed the *constitution* (*a*) on the 29th of November, 1802. It was of necessity submitted to Congress for approval; but was not submitted to the people for ratification. It bears some marks of the haste with which it was framed; but still more of the spirit of the times. Public sentiment was then inclining against what is called a strong government. And this constitution, accordingly, aimed to govern as little through the medium of public agents, and as much through the immediate action of the people, in their primary capacity, as the nature of a representative government will admit. It may, in fact, be regarded as a fair experiment to ascertain the *minimum* of power necessary to be delegated to the people by their representatives.

It will thus be seen that the power to admit includes the power to prescribe the terms of admission; and this is equivalent to the power to refuse admission. When Missouri applied for admission, a large party in Congress were in favor of requiring slavery to be prohibited, as one of the conditions of admission; and there would seem to be no question of the power of Congress so to do; but in this instance, there was a majority the other way, and slavery was not prohibited. Again, Michigan was required to assent to the boundary line claimed by Ohio, as one of the conditions of her admission. From all which it appears that the people of a territory seeking admission into the Union are considered as asking a favor, rather than demanding a right. They indeed frame their own constitution, but it must meet the approbation of Congress. In a word, they are placed very much at the discretion of Congress.(*b*)

(*a*) The convention assembled at Chillicothe on the first of November, 1802. A large majority of the members belonged to the party friendly to the new administration of Mr. Jefferson. See preliminary sketch prefixed to 1 Chase's Ohio Statutes, 30–35. But this constitution gave way to a new one, bearing date the 10th of March, 1851, which, after being ratified by the people, took effect on the 1st of September following.

(*b*) In several instances, the people of a territory have formed a State constitution, and have been admitted under it into the Union without a previous enabling act of Congress. The constitution under which California was admitted into the Union, in 1850, was framed by a convention, the delegates to which were chosen under a proclamation of Gen. Riley, the military governor of the territory, acting under instructions from the President. Among other instances of irregularity in the preliminary

LECTURE IV.

DIVISIONS AND DEFINITIONS. (a)

§ 16. **Municipal Law. — Rights.** In the two preceding lectures we have taken a general survey of the organization of American society; and we have seen that all the powers which the people by their constitutions have conferred upon their respective governments, whether state or federal, have relation, directly or indirectly, to making, interpreting, and executing laws. Our future inquiries, therefore, will be directed to the following points: How are these laws made? How are they interpreted? How are they executed? What laws may, and what may not, be made? What do the existing laws in fact provide? When these questions shall have been answered, my task will be accomplished. But, before proceeding to answer them directly, there are various preliminary explanations, definitions, and divisions, by attending to which now we shall greatly facilitate the proposed inquiries. To that object, therefore, this lecture will be devoted. According to Blackstone, "municipal law is a rule of civil conduct, prescribed by the supreme power in a State, commanding what is right and prohibiting what is wrong." This definition is imperfect, because it does not clearly distinguish between *moral right and wrong* and *legal or civil right and wrong*. Every law either commands something to be done, or regulates the manner of doing it, or forbids it. If it so happen that religion or morality forbids the same thing which the law forbids, we call that thing *malum in se* or *wrong in itself;* otherwise, *malum prohibitum*, or *wrong because prohibited*. This very distinction shows that municipal law and moral law do not necessarily command or forbid the same things. In fact, many things are morally right which the law does not command; and many things are morally wrong which the law does not forbid. We have already seen that human government has nothing to do with moral conduct, apart from civil. It must, indeed, generally happen that these will correspond; and seldom that they will conflict with each other. But the former belongs to a treatise on ethics, and the latter only to a treatise on law. We say, then, in this view, that a thing is right or wrong, in a legal sense, because the law commands or forbids it; and it is to *rights and wrongs*, as thus explained, that our inquiries will be directed. But these

proceedings, see the cases of Tennessee and Michigan, Benton's Abridgment of the Debates of Congress, vol. i. p. 754; vol. xii. p. 748–750. The Act of Congress of February 22, 1872, declares that no State shall be admitted without the necessary population to entitle it to one representative in Congress.

(a) There are several works expressly devoted to definitions. See the Law Dictionaries of Bouvier, Burrill, Holt, Jacob, Tomlins, Abbott, Wharton, and Rapalje & Lawrence; Taylor's Law Glossary; Termes de la Ley; Kelham's Dictionary of Norman French. In general, the best definitions will be found in Blackstone.

again are correlative terms. A wrong always results from the violation of a right; so that by describing the one, you indicate the nature of its opposite. Again, *right* and *obligation* are reciprocal. The existence of a right in any person imposes on all others an obligation to respect it. This obligation the law will always enforce, if the proper steps be taken; for it is a fundamental maxim that for every right which the law recognizes, it provides a *remedy* in case of violation. A treatise, therefore, upon municipal law is, for the most part, a treatise upon rights and remedies, or upon wrongs and remedies, as one may choose to express it; and this suggests a remark upon Blackstone's primary division of legal subjects into rights of persons, rights of things, private wrongs, and public wrongs. These expressions do not on their face indicate that remedies are to enter into the discussion. Moreover, the phrase *rights of things, jura rerum*, by itself, conveys no definite idea, since all rights are the rights of persons; that is, they belong to persons, though they may have relation to things. There is a distinction sometimes made in the books between *natural rights*, or those which would have belonged to men in a state of nature, and *social rights*, or those which are created by the social compact. But this distinction is only a matter of speculative interest; since under the compact, both are equally legal rights. There is, however, a division of rights which, as citizens of a free and constitutional government, we should always bear in mind; I mean *those which are defined by the constitution*, and *those which are not.* The former may be designated as *fundamental;* since they are made the foundation of our social relations, and cannot be altered by delegated power. The people alone in their sovereign capacity can change them by changing the constitution. While the latter may be called *discretionary*, since they depend upon legislative action. The idea of a formal *declaration* or *bill of rights* (*a*) is not original in this country. England furnished the first example, in the celebrated *Magna Charta*, promulgated in 1225; since which epoch, the fundamental rights of her people have been several times solemnly declared; although they are still without a written constitution, as we understand the term. In this country the determination to have fundamental rights indubitably ascertained, so as to be beyond the possibility of cavil, has been at all times remarkable. We find it in the proceedings of the earliest colonial assemblies and congresses. In the Declaration of Independence, it appears in the most imposing form. The federal constitution was strongly objected to, because it did not contain a full and formal bill of rights; and though it did in fact contain many provisions of that nature, the first ten amendments were added to obviate this objection. In all the State constitutions, a like precaution has been taken. Our fundamental rights are thus imperatively declared, and placed beyond the usual

(*a*) See 1 Black. Com. 127; 2 Kent, Com. lec. 24; 2 Story, Const. ch. xliv.

fluctuations of opinion. What they are, will be explained in the sequel. It is sufficient here to say that they operate as so many limitations of delegated power; and that they are as efficient for this purpose as express prohibitions.

§ 17. **Written Law.** (*a*) Such being the general nature of municipal law, its various kinds form the next subject of inquiry. The most general division of law is into *written* and *unwritten law*. But these are again subdivided in this country as follows: *Written law* consists of *constitutions*, *treaties*, and *statutes*. *Unwritten law* consists of *common law* and *equity*. The general distinction between written and unwritten law is that the former is regularly enacted and promulgated by the proper authority; while the latter is made up of judicial decisions without any formal enactment. I shall explain each of the above subdivisions, beginning with those of written law.

Constitutions. By a constitution we understand a solemn written declaration of the sovereign will of the people, defining the form and powers of government. This idea has been already sufficiently developed. But this definition would not apply to what is called the British constitution; for that is a mere collection of immemorial customs and traditions, and properly belongs to the division of unwritten law. The history of the formation of the federal constitution, and also of that of Ohio, has been briefly traced; and their provisions will be examined in detail hereafter. Suffice it here to say that the federal constitution unites the people of all the States into one nation for all national purposes, in the same manner as a State constitution unites the people of one State for municipal purposes,— the one being a declaration of the sovereign will of all the people of the United States; and the other, of that portion of the same people constituting one State.

Treaties. (*b*) The making of treaties has not usually been considered as an act of legislative power. In England, the treaty-making power belongs to the king alone. And by the common definition, a treaty is regarded merely as a solemn *written compact*, entered into between independent nations, to regulate their intercourse. Were this the American definition, our Indian treaties would form a partial exception, since we do not recognize the Indian tribes as wholly independent. But there is a provision in the federal constitution, declaring treaties duly made to be a part of "the supreme law of the land." (*c*) Thus, instead of being

(*a*) See 1 Black. Com. 85; 1 Kent, Com. lec. 20.

(*b*) It was first proposed in the convention that the senate should have the treaty-making power, and that no treaty should be binding until ratified by law. Mad. Pap. 1412–15. When the power was conferred on the president, it was proposed that it should be with the consent of both houses; but the considerations of secrecy and despatch prevailed to vest the power in the hands of the president, with the advice of two-thirds of the senate. Id. 1518–20. See also Black. Com. 257; 2 Story, Const. § 1499–1518.

(*c*) A treaty {repeals inconsistent State laws. Hauenstein *v.* Lynham, 100 U. S. 483}. It is considered binding, when ratified, as between the respective governments, from the date of its signature. But as regards the rights of private parties which have merely compacts, binding the nation at large, treaties are here made binding, like other laws, upon every individual. In this view, therefore, treaties may be strictly called the *written law of nations.* The power to make treaties is vested in the president with the concurrence of two-thirds of the senate. The first object is to secure secrecy and despatch; and to this end treaties are framed by the president alone, through his appropriate ministers; but in order to guard this high power from abuse, the assent of two-thirds of the senate is made necessary to their consummation. It has been made a question whether the house of representatives have not an indirect negative power, by refusing to pass such laws as treaties may require; but in the discussions which have taken place in Congress, the prevailing opinion seems to be that by the ratification of a treaty the national faith is solemnly pledged to the enactment of every law necessary for giving it effect; and, therefore, that the house of representatives cannot properly refuse so to do. The making of treaties being one of the highest attributes of national sovereignty, the States are expressly prohibited from entering into "any treaty, alliance, or confederation;" because they are not, in this view, recognized as nations. But, with the assent of Congress, a State may enter into "an agreement or compact with another State or with a foreign power." This permission is understood to include nothing more than negotiations respecting matters of mere local concern, such as questions of boundary, and the like; and even these are invalid without the consent of Congress. The design is to take it out of the power of a single state to disturb, by its own act, the harmony of the Union. (*a*)

Statutes. (*b*) By a statute, we understand a law duly enacted by the legislature. The mode of enactment will be considered hereafter. Statutes are either *public* or *private.* The former embrace the whole community; the latter only certain individuals

vested between the signature and the ratification, the latter cannot be considered retroactive, and the treaty will take effect only from the exchange of ratifications Haver *v.* Yaker, 9 Wall. 32.

(*a*) {In an interesting article on the treaty-making power under the Constitution, 20 Am. Law Review, 513 (1886), Mr. S. G. Croswell concludes that the constitutional clause providing that Congress shall regulate commerce has no bearing on the treaty-making power of the president and senate, that the clause that all bills for raising revenue shall originate in the house does not apply to treaties, although the treaty may be upon the subject of imposts, and that the treaty-making power covers all the usual subjects of diplomacy, commercial or otherwise, regardless of prior statutes; but that the power of Congress to pass laws inconsistent with a treaty is not impaired. The clause stating that the treaties of the United States shall be the supreme law of the land was inserted to prevent State laws nullifying them, but creates no supremacy over the laws of Congress. In the case of The Cherokee Tobacco, 11 Wall. 616, it was said that a treaty might supersede a prior act of Congress, and an act of Congress might supersede a prior treaty. The consequences in such cases give rise to questions which must be met by the political department of the government, and are beyond the sphere of judicial cognizance. Although the latest expression of the legislative will may thus infringe on international obligations, the courts cannot declare it null.}

(*b*) See 1 Black. Com. 85; 1 Kent, Com. lec. 20; Smith's Commentaries; Dwarris on Statutes; Sedgwick on Statutory and Constitutional Law.

or associations. The only important distinction is that courts take notice of the former without special reference, but not of the latter. It is usual, however, to do away with this distinction, by inserting in private statutes a special clause declaring that they shall be treated as public. The title or preamble of a statute properly forms no part of the law, but in case of doubt may be referred to for explanation. Penal statutes are construed strictly in favor of him against whom they operate. Others liberally, according to the spirit and general intent. There are many rules of interpretation, but they are of little use. Common sense is the best guide; and it is to be regretted that the letter should ever be allowed to prevail against the spirit. In case of repugnancy between two statutes, the latest prevails, for it repeals the former. (*a*) The general rule is that when a statute which repealed another is itself repealed, the other is thereby revived, without any express words. (*b*) The time when statutes shall take effect is a matter of great importance. In England, they formerly took effect from the first day of the session,—that is, before they were actually enacted, which is absurd. Here, unless some other time be provided, they take effect from their date, and consequently before they can possibly be known. (*c*) In particular cases, this evil is obviated by specifying a future day; but by omitting to do this, great hardship is often occasioned. As it is the essence of the law that it should be known before it binds, there ought to be some general regulation, as in France, fixing a day so distant that every person may know what is enacted if he will. And in the mean time the most ample provision should be made for promulgation. I do not mean that copies should be sent to every citizen. This would be a useless expense, since all will not read them. But they should be so distributed as to be conveniently accessible to all. The duty of superintending their publication usually belongs to the secretary of state, who has the custody of the originals; and the general practice is to publish them in certain newspapers, as well as in pamphlets. Copies of the latter are furnished to public officers only. Private persons are left to supply themselves as they may. This arrangement might answer the purpose if legislation were reasonably stable; and from the

(*a*) {This is called a repeal by implication, or an implied repeal, not being express. There is a very important and useful law in Ohio, R. S. § 79, in force since 1866, providing that repeals or amendments shall not affect pending actions, prosecutions, or proceedings civil or criminal, or existing causes of action, proceeding, or prosecution unless otherwise expressly provided.}

(*b*) See Commonwealth *v.* Churchill, 2 Metcalf, 118; {Kearny *v.* Buttles, 1 Ohio State, 362;} but as this result is often unintentional, it would seem wise to enact the contrary, requiring the revival to be by express words, as has been done in this State, R. S. § 78. See Milne *v.* Huber, 2 McLean, 212.

{If a statute is to take effect *from* and *after* a day named that day is excluded. Koltenbrock *v.* Cracraft, 36 Ohio State, 584.}

(*c*) {This is now changed, and by R. S. § 77 acts take effect from May 1 thereafter, unless the contrary is expressed. As to the time of day on which they are in force, see Arrowsmith *v.* Hamering, 39 Ohio State, 573.}

provision made to secure deliberation, through the forms of enactment, we might naturally suppose that statutes would be so well considered and carefully worded that when once enacted they might stand for years without alteration. Indeed this is for the most part true of the legislation of Congress; but our State legislation has been exceedingly fluctuating.

§ 18. **Unwritten Law.** (*a*) It may sound strange to unpractised ears that there should be such a thing as unwritten law; for if there be one thing which, above all others, demands all the certainty and precision which human ingenuity can attain, it is the law which governs us. Accordingly, the three divisions of written law which have just been described are required to pass the most searching scrutiny before their consummation as written law. And the question may naturally be asked, why we should have any other. Having organized a distinct department of government for the sole purpose of enacting laws, why should we recognize any other than those thus enacted? It is indeed true that our political theory seems, at the first glance, not to require, or even tolerate, unwritten law. The very terms appear to involve an absurdity. They do not, however, signify oral law, but law which has never been enacted in the shape of constitutions, treaties, or statutes. And strange as it may appear, unwritten law, as thus described, constitutes by far the greater portion of that entire body of law by which our rights are regulated. It consists of two great divisions, *common law* and *equity*, each of which I shall describe, beginning with the former.

Common Law. (*b*) This is said to be unwritten, because there is no record of its formal enactment. It is sometimes pretended that it consists of statutes worn out by time, their records having been lost. It is also called a collection of customs and traditions commencing in immemorial times, acquiesced in by successive generations, and gradually enlarged and modified in the progress of civilization. The true account, however, is, that it is the stupendous work of *judicial legislation*. Theorize as we may, it has been made from first to last by judges; and the only records it ever had are the *reports* of their decisions, and the *essays*, *commentaries*, and *digests* founded thereon. To explain its formation, we may suppose a question to have arisen in England, centuries ago, respecting which the written law contained no provision. Upon presenting this question to the judge, he must either let a wrong go unredressed, or make a law to meet the exigency. He chose the latter alternative; and in making up his decision, sought light from every available source. If a case exactly similar had before been decided, he would naturally adopt the decision then made. Or if an analogous case could be found, he would adopt

(*a*) See 1 Black. Com. 63–84; 1 Kent, Com. lec. 21, 22.

(*b*) See 1 Story, Const. § 156–158; Lindsley *v.* Coats, 1 Ohio Rep. 243, 312; Sackett *v.* Sackett, 8 Pickering, 309; Patterson *v.* Winn, 5 Peters, 233; 8 Peters, 687.

its principles so far as they would apply. (*a*) If neither of these, he would consult public policy and the abstract principles of natural justice. He would, moreover, be assisted by the arguments of the opposing counsel, who would present the case in all its bearings. With these aids, and in this manner, he would make up his decision; and if no sinister motives operated, the presumption is that it would be on the side of abstract right. Such, briefly, is the process by which the vast fabric of common law has been reared. A succession of judges, during a long lapse of years, have contributed the results of their reason and learning to elaborate and perfect it. In its *theory*, each successive adjudication has become a *precedent* for all similar cases involving the same principle; and it is obvious that just in proportion as precedents are multiplied, the number of unprecedented cases must be diminished. Legislation, moreover, has been constantly supplying deficiencies. It follows, therefore, that the field of judicial discretion, almost boundless at first, has been gradually but steadily narrowing. Still, however, admitting precedents to be absolutely binding, which is not the fact, though it is the theory, judges even at this day exercise a far wider discretion under the common law than is usually supposed by those not conversant with the subject. And to this extent there is not that complete separation between the legislative and judicial power which the theory of our government supposes.

The common law, thus slowly matured into a system in England, was introduced into this country by the first colonists, together with the statutes by which it had then been modified, so far as applicable to their condition. This was at first a matter of necessity; and when the colonies became independent, the system, which in the meantime had been much improved under their own legislation, was retained from choice. The new States, with the exception of Louisiana, which has preferred the civil code, have adopted it from the old; so that the common law now prevails generally throughout the Union. Nearly all our technical terms and forms of proceeding are borrowed from it and defined by it. Where a question arises concerning which our written law is silent, we consult the *reports*, beginning with those of our own State. We pass thence to the other American reports, and finally to the English reports, searching back to the earliest times. If none of these settle the question, we seek light from the civil law, or from

(*a*) In deciding causes, it is the custom of judges to deliver opinions, in which they give the reasons for their decisions, often at great length, and sometimes diverging from the point in issue and discussing questions not necessarily involved in it. Such opinions may be entitled to respectful consideration, according to the learning and ability of the judge, and the attention bestowed by him at the time on the subjects discussed. But they are entitled to weight as authority only so far as they were necessary to the determination of the right or title in litigation between the parties. All discussions of this character upon points whose adjudication is uncalled for, are termed *obiter dicta*. This distinction may aid the student, as he consults the reports, to separate what may be regarded as adjudged, or settled by a judicial decision, from what remains open for further argument and consideration.

any other source which can furnish it. The whole number of English reports, digests, abridgments, and other works, containing the common law, may be set down at more than one thousand volumes; and the number of corresponding works in this country at five hundred; so that the principles of common law are to be sought for through fifteen hundred volumes. (*a*) The epoch down to which the English common law is to be received in this country has been a matter of much doubt. Should it be the settlement of the country, the Declaration of Independence, or the present moment? The general sentiment has been that it should be the settlement of the country. In truth, however, there is a great reluctance in recognizing the English common law as of absolute and binding authority down to any period. The doctrine repeatedly declared by our judges is that they will be bound by it only so far as they consider it suited to our state of society and form of government. (*b*) The only certainty, therefore, is that we have something which we call common law, scattered at random over a vast surface. But precisely what it is, or how far it extends, is hidden in the breasts of our judges, and can only be ascertained by experiment.

Equity. (*c*) In its literal acceptation, equity is nearly synonymous with justice. But in its technical sense, it means *chancery law;* or that system of rules by which courts of chancery are governed in the administration of justice. It had its origin in the deficiencies of the ancient common law; which by reason of the paucity of its then settled principles, and the inflexibility of its forms, could not so shape and modify its remedies as to meet the circumstances of each particular case. When, therefore, the law furnished no remedy, or only an inadequate one, or when its rigorous enforcement would work positive injustice, the party thus aggrieved, assuming the attitude of a suppliant, peti-

(*a*) Mr. Wallace, in his book entitled "The Reporters" (1855), puts the number of reports at two thousand. {They now (1886) number about six thousand.}

(*b*) {The courts of this State will adopt the principles of the common law as the rules of decision so far only as those principles are adapted to our circumstances, state of society, and form of government. Lindsley *v.* Coats, 1 Ohio, 243, 245; Roads *v.* Symmes, ib. 281, 312; Bloom *v.* Richards, 2 Ohio State, 387; Cleveland C. & C. R. R. *v.* Keary, 3 Ohio State, 201, 205; Kerwhacker *v.* C. C. & C. R. R. ib. 172, 178.

The early English statutes did not become part of the law of Ohio. Helfenstine *v.* Garrard, 7 Ohio, 1 pt. 275; Carroll *v.* Olmstead, 16 ib. 251, 260; Crawford *v.* Chapman, 17 ib. 449, 452; Williams *v.* First Pres. Soc., 1 Ohio State, 478, 497; Drake *v.* Rogers, 13 ib. 21, 28; Thompson *v.* Thompson, 17 ib. 649, 664; Knapp *v.* Thomas, 39 ib. 377, 385; Hastings *v.* Columbus, 42 ib. 585, 590. In fact, however, an act of the Northwest Territory, passed in 1795, made the common law and general acts of Parliament prior to 4 James I. part of the law of the Territory. In 1805 the State of Ohio re-enacted this same statute, there having been doubt as to the power of the territorial legislature to pass it; but in 1806 that part was repealed and no substitute has ever been passed.}

(*c*) See 3 Black. Com. ch. 47; 1 Kent, Com. 489; 1 Story on Equity, ch. 1, 2; Pomeroy on Equity; article by Charles Sumner, 10 American Jurist, 227; the Introductions to Jeremy and Fonblanque on Equity; and the very admirable treatise of Spence on the Equitable Jurisdiction of the Court of Chancery, which traces the principles of Equity to their sources; {also Maine's Ancient Law; Campbell's Lives of the Chancellors}.

tioned to the king in person, as the fountain of justice, for relief. But it soon became inconvenient for the king to give personal attention to these petitions, and he referred them to an officer of his household called a *chancellor*. The office of chancellor, nominally derived from the Roman Empire, was at first purely ecclesiastical. The chancellor was the king's spiritual adviser or conscience-keeper, and had the custody of the great seal. Being of course distinguished for his learning and probity, it was natural that he should be thus selected by the king as the dispenser of his justice, and accordingly petitions were now addressed to him in the first instance. It therefore became necessary for the chancellor to adopt a system of rules and forms of proceeding; and as the civil law was then a part of clerical education, he borrowed from it as far as he could. Being at first without precedents, he acted according to his own ideas of natural justice, doing what he conscientiously thought right. He professed, indeed, to entertain jurisdiction of petitions only when the law furnished no adequate remedy; but being the exclusive judge of this, comparatively ignorant of the common law, and one of a class notoriously ambitious to increase their power in the State, he construed this limitation very liberally. A writ of *subpœna* was soon devised to bring parties complained of before him, which, in those superstitious times, they feared to disobey; and thus a regular court of chancery became gradually established. As early as 1394, its authority was recognized by parliament, though no record is preserved of its proceedings earlier than 1420. But in an age of bigotry, with the suffrages of the church in its favor, its influence extended so rapidly as to excite the jealousy of the courts of law; and about the year 1616, a bitter controversy grew out of this rivalry. By this time, however, the court of chancery, though founded upon usurpation, was too firmly established to be overthrown. But by way of concession to public sentiment, it gradually became separated from church influence by the selection of chancellors from the most eminent lawyers. Under their administration, its rules and forms have been improved, extended, and systematized, until they constitute, under the name of equity, one of the most regular and important branches of jurisprudence. The chancery system thus matured in England has been introduced into this country,— not, however, so universally as the common law. In some of the States, as Pennsylvania and Massachusetts, only a few special chancery powers are conferred on the courts of law; (*a*) while in others, as New York and Virginia, the entire system has been adopted. The federal and some of the State constitutions recognize chancery powers in their fullest extent, but require them to be exercised by the same tribunals which administer the law. The

(*a*) The Supreme Judicial Court of Massachusetts has now "full equity jurisdiction, according to the usage and practice of courts of equity, in all cases where there is not a plain, adequate, and complete remedy at law."

same persons, therefore officiate both as chancellors and judges; but the two jurisdictions are kept as distinct from each other as if administered by different persons.

The general nature of equity, and the points wherein it differs from law, strictly so called, cannot be fully explained until we come to consider the forms of proceeding. It resembles the common law, however, in being a mere collection of precedents, established by successive chancellors, during a long series of years, and treasured up in the reports of their decisions; and the precedents, thus established, are regarded as binding to the same extent as they are in law, but no further. Hence we perceive the fallacy of that popular notion, countenanced indeed by the early definitions, that equity consists in the application of moral principles to human transactions, without reference to positive regulations; that it addresses itself to the conscience of the chancellor, who administers relief whenever there is an honest claim; in short, that equity is something independent of law, and exercising a dispensing power over it. This may have been partially true at first; but conscience is now no more the guide of the chancellor than of the judge. Neither may decide according to his feelings. Such discretion would not be tolerated in any magistrate under a free government. In fact, the highest conception that can be formed of either a judge or chancellor, would be that of a pure intelligence, fully comprehending all legal principles, and utterly divested of passion or sympathy. If a statue could be imagined to have a mind, but no heart; an intellect, but no feeling; in a word, to be endowed with the single capacity of deciding unerringly what the law is in every case, — it would be a perfect chancellor, as well as judge; for just in proportion as this icy standard is approached, both become faultless ministers of justice, in their respective departments. But while equity agrees with law in being a system of precedents, it differs essentially in the modes of proceeding. These are so constituted as to administer remedies for which the forms of law are totally incompetent. Hence it is neither above law nor opposed to it, but merely subsidiary, serving to supply its deficiencies and help out its designs. In general, two things are necessary to bring a case within chancery jurisdiction: first, the absence of an adequate remedy at law; and secondly, the existence of some enactment or precedent to meet the case. But these things will be more fully explained hereafter. Enough has been said to show that equity forms a branch of unwritten law, not inferior in importance to the common law, and equally the work of judicial legislation.

Civil and Canon Law. I have thus far made no mention of the *civil or Roman law*, or of the *canon or ecclesiastical law*, because neither possesses any intrinsic authority in this country, except a select portion of the former in Louisiana. Yet as both are sources from which much of our unwritten law has been derived, they merit a brief description. By the *civil law* (*a*) then, is meant the body of Roman law, compiled and digested under the direction of the emperor Justinian and his successors. It consists of three principal divisions: 1. The *Institutes*, in four books which contain the elementary principles of law carefully arranged, and designed principally for students. 2. The *Pandects*, in fifty books, which contain a methodical digest of the writings and opinions of the most celebrated jurists. 3. The *Code*, in twelve books, containing the imperial edicts and decrees, to the time of its date. To these must be added the *Novels*, containing the edicts and decrees of subsequent emperors, and forming a supplement to the compilation of Justinian's. These compilations, therefore, embody the wisdom of the Romans in jurisprudence for about twelve hundred years.

By the *canon law* (*b*) is meant the body of ecclesiastical law compiled from the opinions of the early Latin fathers, the ordinances or decrees of general councils, and the bulls of the holy see. But this body of law is far less interesting to us than the civil law, because, in our total separation of church and state, its influence has been almost entirely done away. Yet in questions relating to marriage and divorce, and to the settlement of the estates of deceased persons, we still have occasion to refer to this body of law.

§ 19. **Codification.** (*c*) Before leaving this subject it may not be improper to say a few words upon the project of diminishing the importance of unwritten law, by enlarging the boundaries of written law. And first, is this practicable? In answering this question, it is sufficient to consider unwritten law merely as a collection of legal principles, no matter how established, or whence derived. Can these principles be reduced to precise language, and arranged in systematic order? For if so, they can be enacted into a code. Now operations precisely similar, and equally arduous, have been performed in every other art and science. The great difficulty has always been to find out the principles, not to arrange them; but here the principles exist in the *reports*, and the numerous *digests* and *abridgments* would greatly facilitate the construction of a code. We are not left, however, to speculation and conjecture. The thing has been done, and therefore can be done again. It is sufficient to refer to two experiments. When Justinian ascended the Roman throne, the laws had been accumulating in the same way as ours, for ten centuries, and were contained in some thousands of volumes. Yet he found commissioners

(*a*) See 1 Black. Com. 80; 1 Kent, Com. lec. 23; Gibbon's Roman Empire, ch. 44. {On the value of the Roman Law, see article in 15 Am. Law Rev. 555. Works on the Roman law have now become very numerous.}

(*b*) See 1 Black. Com. 82–85; Brown's Ecclesiastical Law; Rogers' Ecclesiastical Law. There is an American republication of the English Ecclesiastical Reports in six volumes, edited by E. D. Ingraham, of Philadelphia.

(*c*) See 1 Hoff. Leg. Out. 454; Bentham on Legislation; Grimke's Report to the Legislature of South Carolina; Story's Report to the Legislature of Massachusetts; 1 West. Law Jour. 433.

to construct from this confused mass of materials, a clear, connected, and beautiful system of law. And, in the strong language of Gibbon, "while the vain titles of the victories of Justinian are crumbled into dust, the name of the *legislator* is inscribed on a fair and everlasting monument." Almost the same remarks apply to the splendid achievement of Napoleon. When he ascended the French throne, the task of legal reform was as imperiously called for, and not less arduous. But to such a man difficulty seemed in itself a temptation. He, too, found commissioners to frame an admirable code; and, in his own vigorous language, he "will go down to posterity with that code in his hand." But we need not go abroad for examples. Codes justly renowned have already been framed for Louisiana. And, to take partial examples, our constitutional law has been codified to the admiration of the world, while that of England still remains unwritten, a heavy mass of doubtful precedents. And yet for this great work our fathers had no models, and scarcely materials. Again, the criminal law, both of the United States and of most of the States, has been likewise codified; and our citizens thereby enjoy the inestimable privilege of being able to find, on a few pages of the statute-books, every offence for which the hand of justice can punish them. (*a*) The idea of impracticability, therefore, can arise only from a misconception of what is actually proposed. Did the project contemplate the formation of a code absolutely perfect, so as to anticipate all future cases, this would indeed transcend finite capacities. For in the ever-multiplying relations of human affairs, the imagination cannot reach forward to the time when new cases will not arise. But this is not the proposition. Nothing more is sought than to incorporate into a code existing principles, and this has been shown to be practicable. A difficulty, however, has been suggested of another sort; namely, that when commissioners should have prepared a code, a legislative sanction could not be procured. The idea is that the numerous members of a legislative body could never be brought to unite upon any code, when to a single mind there would be no difficulty. It is indeed probable that many of the members would not carefully examine its provisions, and could not appreciate them if they did. But a personal inspection by every member would not be expected. This is not the way in which such bodies usually transact their business. They inquire and examine through their appropriate committees, and rely upon their reports.

(*a*) So, very recently, Codes of Procedure have been adopted in {Arkansas, California, Colorado, Connecticut, Dakota, Florida, Idaho, Indiana, Iowa, Kansas, Kentucky, Minnesota, Missouri, Montana, Nebraska, Nevada, New York, North Carolina, Ohio, Oregon, South Carolina, Utah Territory, Washington Territory, Wisconsin, and Wyoming Territory}. An act of the British Parliament passed June 30, 1852, amended by that of Aug. 12, 1854, and entitled "The Common Law Procedure Act," abolishes all forms of actions and introduces radical reforms in pleading and practice. For a summary of these changes, see 18 Boston Law Reporter (Feb. 1856), 541. The law of criminal procedure has lately been greatly simplified in England. Bishop on Law of Criminal Procedure, *passim*. The Indian codes of the English Parliament are very interesting and instructive examples of codification.

They might do so in this case. For greater security, there might be successive committees from year to year; and then, if time should disclose errors, they could be readily corrected by future legislatures.

In the next place, then, is the project expedient? There are some objections on this score, which first require to be answered. *First*, it is said that we might lose much that is really excellent in the unwritten law. The fact would seem to be otherwise. The proposition is to search thoroughly, once for all, the voluminous records of unwritten law, and abstract therefrom all the principles which are worthy of being retained. But the search need not be confined even within this range. The records of all human experience might be explored; and wheresoever in the codes of ancient or modern lawgivers, a legal principle could be found suited to our condition, it could be adopted. In this way, so far from losing, we should take the surest method of preserving all the scattered gems of jurisprudence. *Secondly*, it is said that we should effect a great, sudden, and of course disastrous change in legal rights, — a kind of civil revolution. But this does not follow. The proposition is not to reverse the law, but simply to change it from unwritten to written law. Not one legal principle need be altered, unless the public good require it. *Thirdly*, the time and expense may be deemed an objection. No doubt it would require much of both. The best exertions of the best minds, in a long and arduous labor for the public, ought to be well rewarded. But when accomplished, the work would be beyond all price. Moreover, the cost would probably be saved in a single generation by the reduced expenses of litigation. Let us then advert to some of the positive advantages of such a code: and *first*, our laws would be better adapted to our condition than they now are; since that part of the unwritten law which is suitable only for barbarians would be of course rejected, and no longer cumber our legal repositories. *Secondly*, our laws would be more generally known, for the inquirer would no longer have to search for them through thousands of volumes, and then haply not find them. *Thirdly*, they would be more simple. If statutes are not easily understood, it is the fault of those who frame them, in not using clear method and plain language. All needless technicalities which now lumber up the books would be avoided. *Fourthly*, our laws would be more certain than they now are, and it has often been said that the certainty of law is more important than the reason of it. The only uncertainty which need belong to statutes is that which arises from the imperfection of language. There would be no balancing of authorities, or arguing about fitness. The only question would be, What has the legislature enacted? Not so with unwritten law. For though in theory precedents are binding, yet in point of fact, judges do not regard precedents as absolutely imperative, like statutes, but rather as lights to aid their discretion and inform their judgment. They sometimes overrule their own prior decisions, and very often the decisions of other courts, insomuch that an immense collection (*a*) of *overruled cases* has already been published. And how is even this source of uncertainty increased, by promulgating such a doctrine as that already referred to, that the unwritten law is binding only so far as it is adapted to our condition! Ought we to depend to such an extent as this upon the discretion of any set of men? *Lastly*, our laws would be more conformable to the theory of our government, which vests legislative power in the legislature alone, and not in the judiciary. But I have not time to pursue the subject. The question of codification is by no means clear of difficulty, though abundantly deserving of serious consideration.

§ 20. **Divisions of Persons.** (*b*) Having now enumerated the various kinds of law, let us next advert to the subjects upon which law operates. These are, as we have seen, *persons* and *property*. But both persons and property are distributed by law into various divisions and subdivisions, which I shall here briefly indicate, — beginning with *persons*. 1. The law distinguishes between *natural* and *artificial* persons. By a natural person is meant simply a human being. By an artificial person is meant a *corporation*, consisting of one or more natural persons, endowed by law with certain attributes not possessed by natural persons; among which are unity and indivisibility of name and purpose, and continuity of succession and duration, unaffected by change of members. The law creating a corporation, and called its *charter*, imparts to it various other capacities according to its objects, which will be described hereafter. 2. The law distinguishes between *public* and *private* persons. Public persons include all those who occupy official stations, and will be described in connection with the departments of government. All other persons are private. 3. The law distinguishes between *citizens* and *aliens*. Citizens include all persons born within the United States, and all persons duly *naturalized*. (*c*) The process of naturalization will

(*a*) See Bigelow's Overruled Cases. One of the most remarkable instances of overruled precedents is the case of Godsall *v.* Boldero, 9 East, 72, decided in 1807, which, after being often recognized as authority by judges and text-writers, was finally overruled in 1854. Dalby *v.* India and London Life Assurance Company, 15 Com. Bench R. 365, 28 Eng. L. & Eq. 312. In the original case, an insurance had been effected on the life of the celebrated William Pitt. The policy was subsisting at the time of his death, on Jan. 23, 1806, and the debt was paid by his executors. The insurance company in a suit on the policy resisted payment, on the ground that the contract of life insurance is one of indemnity, and the creditor, having been fully paid, had been fully indemnified. The defence was sustained. The last cited case, however, decides that the contract of life insurance is not one of indemnity, but a mere contract to pay a certain sum of money on the death of a person, in consideration of the due payment of a certain annuity for his life. See Parsons on Mercantile Law, p. 550.

(*b*) See the first book of Blackstone, for these divisions and definitions.

(*c*) Also all persons born out of the jurisdiction of the United States, whose fathers were, at the time of their birth, citizens of this country, and had at one time resided therein; also, married women capable of naturalization under existing laws, whose husbands are citizens of the United States. Act of Feb. 10, 1855. 10 U. S. Stat. 604.

be described hereafter. All other persons are aliens. 4. The law distinguishes between *males* and *females*. Females have no political capacities whatsoever; that is, they have no direct voice or agency in the formation or administration of government. But while they remain unmarried, their legal capacities are the same as those of the other sex. When married, they are placed under various disabilities, which will be described when we come to speak of *husband and wife*. 5. The law distinguishes between *infants* and *adults*. Infants or minors, in many of the States, include all males under twenty-one years of age, and all females under eighteen. In others, twenty-one is the age of majority for both. All other persons are adults. Infants have no political capacities at all; and they are placed under various legal disabilities, which will be described hereafter under the heads of *parent and child*, and of *guardian and ward*. 6. The law distinguishes between persons *sane* and *insane*. Insane persons comprehend all those persons who are totally or partially deprived of reason. They are placed under various legal disabilities, which will be described under the head of *idiots and lunatics*. 7. The law distinguishes between *masters* and *slaves*, or *servants*. Slaves include those persons bound by law to involuntary and perpetual servitude, unless manumitted by their masters. They will be described hereafter. Persons voluntarily bound to service, or bound only for a limited time, will be described under the head of *master and servant*. 8. The law distinguishes *Indians* from all other persons. They are placed under various disabilities, both political and legal, which will be described hereafter. 9. The death of an individual gives rise to various legal distinctions. If he has disposed of his property by *will* or *testament*, he is called *testator;* the persons taking his property, *legatees* or *devisees;* and the person appointed by him to settle his affairs, *executor*. If he has left no will, he is called *intestate;* the persons designated by law to take his property, *heirs;* and the person appointed by court to settle up his affairs, *administrator*. All these relations will be enlarged upon hereafter.

§ 21. **Divisions of Property.** (*a.*) From the divisions of persons we pass to those of *property*. The term property includes every valuable thing which can be made the subject of exclusive ownership; and the laws which regulate the acquisition, enjoyment, and disposition of it, form a large part of the laws of every society. I shall here barely enumerate the various kinds of property, and define the terms employed to designate them. 1. The most general division of property is into *things in possession* and *things in expectation*. The former are readily understood. The latter consist of legal rights, and their corresponding obligations. If I have a legal right to any specific thing of which you are in possession, or to receive from you something valuable but not specific, and

(*a*) See the second book of Blackstone, for these divisions and definitions.

you will not voluntarily fulfil the legal obligations resulting from my right, I may enforce performance by a series of legal proceedings to be explained hereafter, constituting a *suit* or *action.* The result, therefore, of an action is to transfer into possession what was before in expectation; and the certainty of this result is what gives value to this class of things; hence they are denominated *things in action,* — or, retaining the French term, *choses in action.* Of this description are all rights resulting from *contracts*, which will occupy a wide space in our future inquiries. It is sufficient here to say that as commerce and credit increase, this kind of property increases proportionally; and it already forms an immense item in the account of individual and national wealth. 2. The next division of property is into *things real* and *things personal.* These terms, of themselves, afford no intimation of the things for which they stand, — there being just as much of *reality*, and as little of *personality*, in the one as in the other. On this account the terms *movable* and *immovable*, which are used in the civil law, would be better. For personal property includes every valuable thing of an unfixed and movable nature, so that it can follow the person of the owner; and the terms employed to designate it are *goods* and *chattels;* or, in the abstract, *personalty.* While real property includes every valuable thing of a fixed and immovable nature, so that it cannot follow the person of the owner; and the terms employed to designate it are *lands, tenements*, and *hereditaments;* or, in the abstract, *realty.* But although *immobility* is the distinguishing characteristic of realty, an *indefinite* duration of interest also enters into the idea; and therefore certain determinate interests in land, as leases for years, are called *chattels real;* because, although they have that immobility which is denoted by the term *real*, yet for want of an indefinite duration, they are treated as *chattels.* 3. Real property is divided into *things tangible* and *things not tangible.* The term *land* includes only what is tangible; that is, the soil itself, and every tangible thing permanently connected therewith, by nature or art, to an indefinite extent above and below the surface. Hence there are various articles of personalty, which become realty by being annexed thereto; and these are called *fixtures.* The term *tenement* is more comprehensive; since it includes, not only land, as above defined, but certain intangible rights or privileges connected with land, but not belonging to the same person, — as a right of way, a right of fishing, and the like. The term *hereditament* was once more comprehensive still. By the ancient law, though personalty was not descendible from ancestor to heir, yet there were certain articles of personalty, not fixtures, such as family pictures, tombstones, and the like, which by custom descended along with the family mansion. These were called *heirlooms*, and were included in the term hereditaments, which comprehend everything inheritable. Probably the law of this country does not recognize heirlooms; and, if so, the term hereditament comprehends no more than tenement. However, the division of realty now under consideration is commonly expressed by *corporeal hereditaments*, and *incorporeal hereditaments*, — the former including land only, as above defined; and the latter, all intangible rights annexed to land. These last are likewise denominated *easements*.

§ 22. **Divisions of Time.** (*a*) I shall conclude this lecture with a few remarks on the legal divisions of *time* and *place*, beginning with those of *time*. About forty-five years before Christ, Julius Cæsar undertook to reform the method of computing time; and his substitute is called the *Julian Calendar*. In this calendar the twelve months, and the number of days in each, were arranged as at present; but the year commenced on the 25th of March, and contained 365 days and 6 hours. These extra hours make one day in four years; and accordingly a day was interpolated after the 28th of February, every fourth year, which is called *bissextile* or leap year. This calendar continued in use until 1582, when Pope Gregory undertook another reformation. The Julian year was found to be too long by eleven minutes and ten seconds, which amounts to a day in about 130 years. An error therefore of ten days had now occurred; accordingly, in that year ten days

(*a*) See 2 Black. Com. 141; Herschel's Astronomy, ch. 13; 7 Com. Dig. tit. Temps; 15 Petersd. Abr. tit. Time; 4 Kent, Com. 95; Glassington *v.* Rawlins, 3 East, 407; The King *v.* Cumberland, 4 Nev. & Man. 378; Pearpoint *v.* Graham, 4 Wash. C. C. R. 232; Arnold *v.* U. S., 9 Cranch, 104. Sunday is included in the computation of time, unless excluded by statutory provision or commercial usage. Paine *v.* Mason, 7 Ohio State, 198, 206. If a note or bill payable without grace falls due on Sunday, it is not payable till Monday. But if it is entitled to grace, and the last day of grace falls on Sunday, it is payable on Saturday. 1 Parsons, Contracts, 235; Barrett *v.* Allen, 10 Ohio, 426. A contract, as the execution of a bond or promissory note, made on Sunday in contravention of the provisions of the Sunday laws, is void whether so declared by the statute or not. Pattee *v.* Greely, 13 Metcalf, 284; Towle *v.* Larrabee, 26 Maine, 464; Hilton *v.* Houghton, 35 id. 143; Allen *v.* Deming, 14 N. H. 133; Smith *v.* Bean, 15 id. 577; Lovejoy *v.* Whipple, 18 Vt. 379; Adams *v.* Gay, 19 id. 358; Watts *v.* Van Ness, 1 Hill, 76; Smith *v.* Wilcox, 19 Barb. 581; Rainey *v.* Capps, 22 Ala. 288; Johnston *v.* Commonwealth, 22 Penn. State, 102. The mere making of a contract, as for the sale of land, has been held not to be within the prohibition of the statute of Ohio forbidding "common labor" on Sunday. Bloom *v.* Richards, 2 Ohio State, 387 (overruling Sellers *v.* Dugan, 18 Ohio, 489). See Cincinnati *v.* Rice, 15 Ohio, 225. But *contra* in Indiana, where the same terms are used in the statute. Reynolds *v.* Stevenson, 4 Ind. 619; Voglesong *v.* The State, 9 id. 112; Banks *v.* Werts, 13 id. 203. See Ray *v.* Catlett, 12 B. Mon. 532; Slade *v.* Arnold, 14 id. 287; Murphy *v.* Simpson, id. 419. "Works of necessity and charity," or "works of necessity and mercy," are expressly excepted in the prohibitions of these statutes. The term *necessity*, as here used, is not a physical and absolute necessity, but denotes a moral fitness and propriety under the circumstances of the case. Such is the repair of a defect in the highway endangering the public safety. Flagg *v.* Inhabitants of Millbury, 4 Cush. 243. Or the lading of a vessel where there is danger of navigation being closed. McGatrick *v.* Wason, 4 Ohio State, 566. See also Hooper *v.* Edwards, 18 Ala. 280; Logan *v.* Matthews, 6 Penn. State, 417; Johnston *v.* Commonwealth, 22 id. 102; Phillips *v.* Innes, 4 Clark & Fin. 234. It is a question on which the authorities conflict, whether a party has any remedy for torts to property committed by one to whom he has bailed it under a contract in contravention of the Sunday laws. The point in issue is whether the owner's claim arises in such a case from a breach of the contract, or from an invasion of his right of property independently of it. In Massachusetts it has been held that he cannot recover for a conversion of his property so bailed. Gregg *v.* Wyman, 4 Cush. 322. *Contra* in New Hampshire, Woodman *v.* Hubbard, 5 Foster, 67; {and see Nagle *v.* Brown, 27 Ohio State, 7}.

were struck out from the month of October, and the day next after the 4th was reckoned the 15th. And to provide against the recurrence of a like error, it was ordained that in three centuries out of four the last year should not be a leap year. Thus the years 1700, 1800, 1900, are not leap years; but 2000 is. There is still a small error, but it will not amount to a day in 3000 years. The computation of the Gregorian calendar is called *new style*, and the year begins on the 1st of January. In England and America, the new style was not adopted until 1752. The term *month* in legal computation is somewhat ambiguous. The English rule seems to be that where a statute uses the term "month," simply, it means a *lunar month* of 28 days, while the phrase "a twelvemonth" means a *solar year*, and not forty-eight weeks; and that the same holds true in contracts and other legal instruments, except where custom has created a different understanding, as in commercial paper. But in this country the common understanding is that "month" means *calendar month*, unless the contrary is expressed. (*a*) The legal *day* begins at midnight; and fractions of a day are never noticed, except in questions of priority, as in recording deeds, and the like. (*b*) Hence it has been held that an infant becomes of age on the day before his twenty-first birthday, (*c*) but this is questionable. Where computation is to be made from an act done, the day of doing the act is included, except in case of a bill of exchange payable so many days *after sight*, when the day of sight or acceptance is excluded. But where a bill is payable so many days *after date*, the day of date is included. In a deed or lease, where the expression "from" or "after date" is used to pass an interest, the day of date is included; but where it is used as a terminus from which to compute time, it is excluded. In general, where notice of an act is required to be given a certain number of days before the act, the day of notice is included, and the day of the act excluded. (*d*)

§ 23. **Divisions of Place.** (*e*) I come, lastly, to the *divisions of place*. The division of the whole Union into States and territories has been sufficiently explained. It remains, therefore, only to describe the subdivisions of a State. The first division is into *counties*, for the purpose of municipal regulation. Our State constitution empowers the legislature to lay off new or alter old counties, with this limitation, that no new county can be laid off

(*a*) Jolly *v.* Young, 1 Esp. N. P. Cas. 186; Commonwealth *v.* Chambre, 4 Dall. 143; 4 Kent, Com. 95, note; Sheets *v.* Selden's Lessee, 2 Wallace, 178.

(*b*) {Rights will not be sacrificed to this theory. Thus the presumption that a statute takes effect from the beginning of the day of its passage will yield to an intervening claim. Arrowsmith *v.* Hamering, 39 Ohio St. 573.}

(*c*) 2 Kent, Com. 233.

(*d*) 2 Parsons on Contracts, 175–178. When an act is to be done within a given number of days from the date, or from the day of the date, the day of the date is excluded. Fuller *v.* Russell, 6 Gray, 128; 4 Cruise, Dig. (Greenl. ed.), tit. 32, c. 5, § 17, note, R. S. of Ohio, § 4951.

(*e*) See 1 Black. Com. 114. The new constitution of Ohio requires cities and villages to be incorporated by a general law applicable to all. This was done by the act of 1852.

which will be of less extent, or make that from which it is taken of less extent, than four hundred square miles. The object of this provision is not very manifest. It would seem better to have made *population* the criterion. As it is, the most populous city can never make a county by itself. Every part of the State, whether settled or not, belongs to some county. The municipal organization of counties will be described hereafter. Counties are again subdivided into *townships*. The power to lay off new or alter old townships is vested by our law in the county commissioners, with this limitation, that no township can be laid off of less extent than twenty-two square miles, unless it includes a "town corporate." (*a*) By a town corporate is here meant a *city* or *borough*, specially incorporated by the legislature with peculiar powers and privileges; whereas a township, by being properly laid off and named, becomes thereby incorporated, without a special charter. Its boundaries are recorded in a book kept for that purpose, among the county archives. Cities and boroughs always belong to some township, and fall under its municipal regulations, except when their charters otherwise provide. Townships, therefore, are the only divisions of counties which fall within the general municipal scheme.

(*a*) The validity of a law annexing one city to another was in issue in the case of Warren *v.* Mayor and Aldermen of Charlestown, 2 Gray, 84. The constitutionality of the Metropolitan Police Act of New York was affirmed in The People *v.* Draper, 15 New York, 532. As to the power of the legislature to extend the limits of a city or town, see Morford *v.* Unger, 8 Clarke (Iowa), 82; City of Covington *v.* Southgate, 15 B. Monr. 491. Under the constitution of 1851, forbidding special acts conferring corporate power, the legislature cannot by special act extend the boundaries of a city. State *ex rel.* Attorney-General *v.* Cincinnati, 20 Ohio St. 18.

PART II.

CONSTITUTIONAL LAW. (*a*)

LECTURE V.

RELATIONS OF THE STATES.

§ 24. **The Federal Government is not a League.** From the views which have been presented in the preceding lectures, it is obvious that our fundamental law is to be sought for in our constitutions. Our country claims the transcendent merit of having made the first grand experiment of limiting delegated power by written constitutions, and accordingly, constitutional law is a branch of study to which the American student should devote himself with patriotic ardor. Fortunately for him, the facilities for this study are now abundant. The text itself is found within a small compass; for, comprehensive as our constitutions are, they are as remarkable for their brevity: and the commentaries and precedents are numerous and ample. Not a word has been left unexplained; and where room has been found for difference of opinion, both sides of every question have been presented with all the force and clearness of which the subject is susceptible. With all these lights to guide the student, it must be his own fault if he do not make himself more thoroughly acquainted with constitutional law than with any other branch of legal study. Under these circumstances, perhaps I should do wisely to leave him to the guides I have named, and hasten to other branches where instruction is more wanted. But, on the whole, I have concluded to give an epitome of constitutional law, as necessarily introductory to our future inquiries. It is obvious that the most remarkable feature in our political organiza-

(*a*) On the subject of constitutional law, see the American constitutions; Story's Commentaries; 1 Kent, Com. lec. 10–19; Madison Papers; Elliot's Debates on the Federal Constitution, in five volumes (the fifth volume being the Madison Papers), 1859, Lippincott & Co., Philadelphia; Federalist; Adams's Defence; the treatises of Rawle and of Sergeant; the decisions of the U. S. Supreme Court, of which those delivered by Chief-Justice Marshall have been published in a separate volume; the Decisions of the Supreme Court of the United States, with Notes and Digest, by B. R. Curtis. See also Curtis's History of the Constitution; Sedgwick on Statutory and Constitutional Law; Cooley's Constitutional Limitations.

tion is the complex character which results from the existence of State governments under a federal government. Had we but a single representative government, framed upon the general principles before indicated, how simple would be the study of constitutional law, compared with what it now is! To adjust the relations which the States should sustain to the federal government, in such a manner as to prevent future collision and preserve general harmony, was undoubtedly the most difficult problem that ever presented itself to the framers of government. And accordingly, before we proceed to consider in detail the provisions of the federal and State constitutions, it is important that we should obtain distinct notions of the relations in which the States are actually placed by our federal organization.

And *first*, the federal government is not merely a league of the State governments, but emanates from, and expresses the sovereign will of all the people of the United States, in their original and aggregate capacity. (*a*) And herein consists the great and

(*a*) To be satisfied that this was the understanding of the convention, it is only necessary to read the debate of the first two days; during which it was resolved that a national government ought to be established, consisting of a supreme legislative, executive, and judiciary; that the legislature ought to consist of two branches, and that the members of the first branch ought to be elected by the people of the several States. These resolutions clearly point to the creation of a new system, and not to an amendment of the old; and were so regarded by the members. Mad. Pap. 746–761. The same views were again expressed in the debate upon the motion that the first branch should be elected by the State legislatures, which failed by a vote of 3 to 8 — id. 800–808. But the following facts remove all doubt upon this point. On the 13th of June, the committee of the whole reported nineteen resolutions to the house, asserting the fundamental principles of the new system — id. 858. Instead of these, Mr. Patterson, of New Jersey, proposed to substitute a series of resolutions simply amending the articles of confederation — id. 862. The two plans were debated until the 19th of June, when Mr. Patterson's plan was rejected by a vote of 7 to 3; and all the subsequent debates proceeded upon the hypothesis that an entirely new system of government was to be provided — id. 904–928. Probably the ablest exposition yet given of the nature of the federal government is to be found in the debate in the U. S. Senate on Foote's resolution, in January, 1830; and see 1 Story, Const. § 306–372. But the general nature and construction of federal powers will be best understood by reading the following quotations from opinions delivered in the Supreme Court of the United States. In Martin *v.* Hunter, 1 Wheaton, 324–27, Judge Story says: "The constitution of the United States was ordained and established, not by the States in their sovereign capacities, but emphatically, as the preamble of the constitution declares, by 'the people of the United States.' There can be no doubt that it was competent to the people to invest the general government with all the powers which they might deem proper and necessary; to extend or restrain these powers according to their own good pleasure; and to give them a paramount and supreme authority. As little doubt can there be that the people had a right to prohibit to the States the exercise of any powers which were, in their judgment, incompatible with the objects of the general compact; to make the powers of the State governments, in given cases, subordinate to those of the nation, or to reserve to themselves those sovereign authorities which they might not choose to delegate to either. The constitution was not, therefore, necessarily carved out of existing State sovereignties, nor a surrender of powers already existing in State institutions; for the powers of the States depend upon their own constitutions; and the people of every State had the right to modify and restrain them, according to their own views of policy or principle. On the other hand, it is perfectly clear that the sovereign powers vested in the State Governments, by their respective constitutions, remained unaltered and unimpaired, except so far as they were granted to the government of the United States. . . . The government of the United States can claim no powers which are not granted to it by the constitution; and the powers actually granted must be such as are radical difference between the present *government*, and that *league* or *confederacy* to which it succeeded. On this point there would be no room for doubt had the federal government been organized prior to, or simultaneously with the State governments; as, without any inherent difficulty, might have been the case. But as the

expressly given or given by necessary implication. On the other hand, this instrument, like every other grant, is to have a reasonable construction, according to the import of its terms; and where a power is expressly given in general terms, it is not to be restrained to particular cases, unless that construction grow out of the context expressly, or by necessary implication. The words are to be taken in their natural and obvious sense, and not in a sense unreasonably restricted or enlarged. . . . The constitution unavoidably deals in general language. It did not suit the purposes of the people, in framing this great charter of our liberties, to provide for minute specifications of its powers, or to declare the means by which those powers should be carried into execution. It was foreseen that this would be a perilous and difficult, if not an impracticable, task. The instrument was not intended to provide merely for the exigencies of a few years, but was to endure through a long lapse of ages, the events of which were locked up in the inscrutable purposes of Providence. It could not be foreseen what new changes and modifications of power might be indispensable to effectuate the general objects of the charter; and restrictions and specifications, which, at present, might seem salutary, might in the end prove the overthrow of the system itself. Hence, its powers are expressed in general terms, leaving to the legislature from time to time to adopt its own means to effectuate legitimate objects, and to mould and model the exercise of its powers as its own wisdom and the public interests should require."

In Houston *v.* Moore, 5 Wheat. 48, 49, Judge Story says: "The constitution, containing a grant of powers in many instances similar to those already existing in the State governments, and some of those being of vital importance also to State authority and State legislation, it is not to be admitted that a mere grant of such powers in affirmative terms to Congress does, *per se*, transfer an exclusive sovereignty to the latter. On the contrary, a reasonable interpretation of that instrument necessarily leads to the conclusion that the powers so granted are never exclusive of similar powers existing in the States, unless when the constitution has expressly, in terms, given an exclusive power to Congress, or the exercise of a like power is prohibited to the States, or there is a direct repugnancy or incompatibility in the exercise of it by the States. The example of the first class is to be found in the *exclusive* legislation delegated to Congress over places purchased by the consent of the legislature of the State in which the same shall be, for forts, arsenals, dockyards, &c.; of the second class, the prohibition of a State to coin money or emit bills of credit; of the third class, as this court have already held, the power to establish a uniform rule of naturalization, and the delegation of admiralty and maritime jurisdiction. In all other cases, not falling within the cases already mentioned, it seems unquestionable that the States retain concurrent authority with Congress, not only upon the letter and spirit of the eleventh amendment of the constitution, but upon the soundest principles of general reasoning. There is this reserve, however, that in cases of concurrent authority, where the laws of the States and of the Union are in direct and manifest collision on the same subject, those of the Union, being 'the supreme law of the land,' are of paramount authority, and the State laws, so far and so far only as such incompatibility exists, must necessarily yield."

In Cohen *v.* Virginia, 6 Wheat. 413, 414, Chief-Justice Marshall says: "That the United States form, for many and most important purposes, a single nation, has not yet been denied. In war, we are one people. In making peace, we are one people. In all commercial regulations, we are one and the same people. In many other respects, the American people are one; and the government which is alone capable of controlling and managing their interests in all these respects is the government of the Union. It is their government, and in that character they have no other. America has chosen to be in many respects and to many purposes a nation; and for all these purposes, her government is complete; to all these objects it is competent. The people have declared that in the exercise of all powers given for these objects it is supreme. It can, then, in effecting these objects, legitimately control all individuals or governments within the American territory. The constitution and laws of a State, so far as they are repugnant to the constitution and laws of the United States, are absolutely void. These States are constituent parts of the United States. They are members of one great empire, — for some purposes sovereign, for some purposes subordinate."

State governments were previously in existence, it may be well to exhibit the proofs that they were not the creators of the federal government, and that the people of the whole Union were. And *first*, the constitution itself, which is the highest authority that can be appealed to, expressly declares its origin in these words of the preamble: "We, *the people of the United States*, do ordain and establish this constitution." Had it been the work of the States, this declaration would have been a falsehood, and would not have been allowed to stand. *Secondly*, the constitution was *ratified by the people*, through their delegates in conventions, as we have already seen, and not by the State legislatures; and the ratifications all purport to be in the name of the people. *Thirdly*, the federal government operates directly upon the people as individuals, and not, like the old confederation, upon the States collectively. So far, then, as respects the mere derivation of federal powers, they are of precisely the same character as if the State governments had never existed, or had been annihilated by a complete consolidation of all powers in one general government. And every citizen of the Union is as much a constituent of the federal government as of his own State government. But although the federal government thus derives its efficiency from the whole people, as the primary source of power, it nevertheless employs the agency and influence of the State governments in several of its operations. This, however, does not conflict with the proposition before laid down, because the very power of the State governments to exert this agency and influence is conferred on them by the federal constitution, and is not an original State power. This will be evident from a bare statement of some of the particulars in which this agency is employed. And *first*, by the way of concession to the small States, the general principle of proportionate representation is departed from, so as to give all the States an equal representation in the Senate; and, for the sake of convenience, the State legislatures, and not the people, elect the senators. (*a*) *Secondly*, for similar reasons, each State, however small, is allowed at least one representative; and for the rest, instead of apportioning the representatives among the aggregate population of the whole Union, they are apportioned "among the several States," omitting any fractions below the adopted ratio. *Thirdly*, by way of concession to the slaveholding States, they are allowed a greater representation than their free population would entitle them to, by adding three-fifths of the slaves. *Fourthly*, for the sake of convenience, the States determine the qualifications of electors of representatives, and the time, place,

(*a*) The mode of electing senators was much disputed in the convention. A proposition that they should be elected by the other house was negatived by a vote of 3 to 7. A proposition that the executive should appoint them did not pass to a vote. A proposition that the people should elect them was negatived by a vote of 1 to 10. The election of them by the State legislatures was first agreed to unanimously, and afterwards by a vote of 9 to 2. Mad. Pap. 759, 814, 820, 821, 959.

and manner of elections. *Fifthly*, for the same reasons of concession and convenience, the States elect the electors of president and vice-president, the number of whom is equal to the number of senators and representatives belonging to each State. And if the election goes before the House of Representatives, the States have an equal vote. Now it is evident that in all these respects a different arrangement might have been made, so as to dispense with State influence or agency. Its actual existence, therefore, proves nothing as to the origin of federal powers.

§ 25. **It is designed for National Objects only.** The federal government is designed to unite the people of the United States into *one nation* for *national purposes* only; leaving all other matters to the control of the State governments. This is evident, not only from the history of its organization already narrated, but also from the enumeration of objects in the preamble itself. These are, *first*, "to form a more perfect union;" *secondly*, "to establish justice;" *thirdly*, "to insure domestic tranquillity;" *fourthly*, "to provide for the common defence;" *fifthly*, "to promote the general welfare;" and *sixthly*, "to secure the blessings of liberty." These are all national objects, equally affecting all the members of the Union, and in no sense local or municipal, as distinguished from national. And the truth of the proposition will be still more manifest when we come to consider the powers enumerated in the constitution as the only powers which the federal government can exercise. We shall then find the number of powers to be small, and adequate only to effect objects in the strictest sense national. In fact, there was the strongest reason for extending the federal government thus far, but no reason for extending it further. The State governments were already in existence, and fully competent to manage their internal concerns; and it would have been folly to burden the federal government with such details. Indeed, had there been no State governments before, there would have been the same reason for creating them, in aid of the federal government, as there is for dividing States into counties, or counties into townships; namely, the extreme inconvenience, if not absolute impossibility, of extending the federal arm to all the minute concerns of each particular district. Accordingly, without adverting to the strong jealousy which prevailed at the time respecting *State rights*, and which continues to this day, we find sufficient reason, on the score of expediency alone, for reserving to the States the entire control of their internal affairs.

§ 26. **It is Supreme with respect to those Objects.** (*a*) But the federal government, though limited in the *number* of its objects to those which are national, is nevertheless *supreme* in regard to those objects; and in cases of conflict the State governments must

(*a*) In the first draft of the constitution, the declaration of supremacy was confined to acts of Congress and treaties. The supremacy of the constitution was afterwards inserted by a unanimous vote. Mad. Pap. 1234, 1408; 2 Story, Const. § 1830–1836.

yield, being thus far *subordinate.* This would have resulted necessarily from the nature of the two governments; but to avoid all shadow of doubt on so momentous a subject, this supremacy is declared by the constitution itself in these explicit terms: "This *Constitution*, and the *laws* of the United States which shall be made in pursuance thereof, and all *treaties* made, or which shall be made, under the authority of the United States, *shall be the supreme law of the land;* and the judges in every State shall be bound thereby, anything in the *constitution* or *laws of any State* to the contrary notwithstanding." It would be difficult to devise language stronger than this. The latter part may almost be considered supererogation; for the subordination of the State governments would have followed as a necessary consequence from the supremacy of the federal government. And in the same spirit the next clause requires all State as well as federal officers to bind themselves, by oath, to support the federal constitution. "The senators and representatives before mentioned, and the members of the several State legislatures, and all executive and judicial officers, both of the United States and of the several States, shall be bound by oath or affirmation to support this constitution." (*a*) The relation, therefore, of supremacy and subordination is completely established by the constitution itself; and the result is the four following gradations of authority: *First*, and paramount over all, is the federal constitution; *secondly*, treaties and acts of Congress; *thirdly*, State constitutions; and *fourthly*, acts of State legislatures. With respect to these four degrees of subordination the invariable rule is that, in case of conflict, the lower must yield to the higher, — each degree being subordinate to those which go before, and superior to those which come after. Thus, in order to be valid, treaties and acts of Congress must conform to the federal constitution; State constitutions must conform to the federal constitution, treaties, and acts of Congress; and the acts of State legislatures must conform to all these, and to their particular State constitution. This idea of subordination among laws springs from the very nature of written constitutions, limiting delegated power; and our federal organization only renders it somewhat more complicated. It is, therefore, unknown where written constitutions are unknown. In England, for example, there is no such thing. Her parliament is omnipotent; and the validity of its acts cannot be called in question.

§ 27. **The Judiciary is the final Arbiter.** (*b*) In order to pre-

(*a*) Mad. Pap. 845, 1175. The debate in the convention turned upon the question whether this oath should be required of State officers, which was carried by a vote of 7 to 4.

(*b*) See 1 Story, Const. § 373–396. The Supreme Court of the United States refused leave to the State of Mississippi to file a bill in equity praying for an injunction to restrain the president from carrying into effect an act of Congress alleged to be unconstitutional, on the ground that they have no jurisdiction to control the jurisdiction of the other departments of the government. The court say: "The serve the subordination thus declared, the *judiciary* is empowered to decide, in the last resort, when either government has transcended its constitutional limits, and to declare such proceeding void. It has indeed been claimed that this power may be exercised by any one of the States, with respect to those acts of the federal government which that State deems unconstitutional. This is one of the doctrines of what is denominated *nullification;* and its existence would seem to indicate that the constitution had not been sufficiently explicit on a matter so important. But, on the contrary, its language is as clear and decisive as it could be made. "The *judicial power* shall extend to *all cases* in law and equity arising under this *constitution*, the laws of the United States, and treaties made under their authority." (*a*) This language confers the whole power of deciding constitutional questions upon the judiciary; and of course nothing is left to be exercised by any other tribunal. It is, then, the high function of the federal judiciary to arrest the arm of either branch of government, when it would overstep its prescribed limits and encroach upon the precincts of the other. And in its subordinate sphere the State judiciary exercises a similar power. Some have complained of this, as a departure from the democratic theory, in allowing a less number of men to annul the acts of a greater number. But experience has thus far shown the arrangement to be wise and salutary. It is indeed one of the noblest features in our system. One cannot easily conceive of a more sublime exercise of power than that by which a few men, through the mere force of reason, without soldiers, and without tumult, pomp, or parade, but calmly, noiselessly, and fearlessly, proceed to set aside the acts of either government, because repugnant to the constitution. (*b*)

Congress is the legislative department of the government, and the president the executive. Neither can be restrained in its action by the judicial department, though the acts of both when performed are, in proper cases, subject to its cognizance." State of Mississippi *v.* Johnson, 4 Wallace, 497.

(*a*) This clause, as originally reported to the convention, did not include the constitution or treaties. Mad. Pap. 1238. These were afterwards added by a unanimous vote; and the reason assigned was that there might be no doubt as to the power of the judiciary to expound the constitution in all cases of a judicial nature. Id. 1438.

(*b*) The courts will not declare an act unconstitutional, unless it is clearly and evidently a violation of the constitution. In all cases of doubt, the doubt must be resolved in favor of the legislative power. Hartford Bridge Co. *v.* Union Ferry Co., 29 Conn. 210; Rich *v.* Flanders, 39 N. H. 304; Baltimore *v.* The State, 15 Md. 376; Tyler *v.* The People, 8 Mich. 320; Santo *v.* The State, 2 Clarke, 165; Morrison *v.* Springer, 15 Iowa, 304; State *v.* Hitchcock, 1 Kansas, 178; Allen *v.* Silvers, 22 Ind. 491. When different parts of a statute are independent of each other, one part may be declared void for unconstitutionality, without affecting the others. Gilpin *v.* Williams, 25 Ohio State, 283; Gibbons *v.* Catholic Institute, 34 Ohio State, 289; Commonwealth *v.* Clapp, 5 Gray, 97; State *v.* Perry County, 5 Ohio State, 497; Mobile & Ohio R. R. Co. *v.* State, 29 Ala. 573; Nelson *v.* The People, 33 Ill. 390. But in determining the construction of the constitutional portion, the unconstitutional portions, though inoperative, are to be looked at. State *ex rel.* *v.* Dombaugh, 20 Ohio State, 127. But a court cannot declare a law void unless it conflicts with some provision of the constitution; opposition to a general latent spirit of the constitution is not sufficient. People *v.* Mahaney, 13 Mich. 481; Walker *v.* Cincinnati, 21 Ohio State, 14. But an act may be

§ 28. **The States are not completely Sovereign.** (*a*) It follows from what has now been said that the States are not *supreme* or *sovereign*, in the strict sense of these words, since there is a power above them. The particulars in which they have parted with their sovereignty include all the powers *exclusively* vested in the federal government, and all the powers prohibited by it to the States. These will be fully enumerated hereafter. For the present, it is sufficient to say, in general terms, that the States have ceased to be sovereign in relation to all national objects, but retain a qualified or partial sovereignty, extending to all internal objects. If there could have existed any doubt on this point, as the constitution was originally framed, such doubt was removed by the tenth amendment, which declares that "the powers not delegated to the United States by the constitution, nor prohibited by it to the States, are reserved to the States respectively, or to the people." This language, while it makes the people the source of all power, both in the federal and State governments, expressly subtracts from the sovereignty of the States all the "powers delegated to the United States," and "prohibited to the States," but leaves the States sovereign in regard to their "reserved powers." Again, the States are not altogether *foreign* with respect to each other. This is evident from the views already presented, since they are parts of the same nation. But I will here state several of the more important particulars in which they have ceased to be foreign by the express provision of the constitution. *First*, no State can refuse to give "full faith and credit to the public acts, records, and judicial proceedings" of every other State. The importance of this provision will be more fully explained in the sequel. It must be observed, however, that this provision is not intended to interfere with the great international doctrine, that no State is bound to recognize the laws of another State affecting either persons or property within the former. No laws can have, as a matter of right, an extra-territorial operation. If, therefore, we give effect to the laws of other States or nations, it is on the principle of *comity;* and this principle prevails to a very wide extent in modern times. I have only room here to say that with this general doctrine the above provision does not interfere. The States are still left to give effect or not to the laws of their sister States, on the principles of comity, established by their respective legislatures,

void as violating the intent of the constitution, though not within the letter. District Court Case, 34 Ohio State, 431, 441. An act may be constitutional in its application to certain cases, but not to others. Bowles *v.* State, 37 Ohio State. 35.

(*a*) See Bliss on Sovereignty. The relations of the States may, perhaps, be expressed in the following propositions: —

1. Each State is solely and entirely sovereign within its territorial limits, except only so far as it is made subordinate to the federal government.

2. No law of any other State can have force within its limits, except by its adoption, from comity or otherwise.

3. No rule of comity can in any case require it to allow privileges to citizens of other States which it denies to its own citizens; the demands of comity being entirely satisfied when we make others equal to ourselves.

or received as common law. *Secondly*, the "citizens of each State are entitled to all the privileges and immunities of citizens" in every other State. In other words, citizenship is made a national affair, as it should be, and the States can make no discrimination in this respect between their own people and those of other States. *Thirdly*, no State can refuse to deliver up fugitives from justice or from service escaping from other States, whereas between foreign nations this is a question of comity. *Fourthly*, the States cannot enter into any treaty, alliance, or confederation, or adopt any commercial regulations, with respect to each other. *Fifthly*, the States cannot at pleasure secede from the Union. This is nowhere expressly declared in the federal constitution, but it results necessarily from the fact that the obligations it creates are without reservation as to time. The Union was, no doubt, intended to be perpetual. The preamble declares one of the objects to be, "to secure the blessings of liberty to ourselves and our *posterity*." Provision is also made to prevent the States from ceasing to be represented in Congress, should they have such a desire. Besides, if a State could withdraw at pleasure, the Union, instead of being "a more perfect union," as the preamble declares, would be no stronger than a rope of sand. No doubt the ultimate right of revolution exists in every State, for nothing can take it away. And if one or more States were strong enough to stand out against the rest, they might thus make an effectual secession. But they could not do it in virtue of any reserved right under the constitution, unless they amounted to three-fourths of the States. Then they might amend, and of course destroy, the constitution. But in no constitutional way can a minority separate themselves from the Union. There is much looseness both of opinion and expression upon this subject. The Declaration of Independence seems to place the right of revolution upon its true foundation; namely, the failure of government to accomplish the end of its institution, that is, the welfare and happiness of the people. And whenever a majority of the people are satisfied that they can better their condition by changing their government, they have the right as well as the power to do so. Any less number would seem to want both. So long, therefore, as a majority of the people of the United States are contented with the existing government, the minority must acquiesce.

§ 29. **Classification of Constitutional Provisions.** Having thus referred to the most prominent points in our federal relations, I will now indicate the plan to be pursued in our future inquiries. Since all the States stand in the same position with respect to the federal government, and have the same internal objects to promote, it follows that there must be a strong similarity in their constitutions. Of course one will serve as a sample of the whole, and for reasons before given, I shall select the constitution of Ohio, and explain its provisions in connection with those of the federal constitution. The provisions of any constitution naturally class themselves under four general heads, namely: *first*, those which relate to the organization of the legislative department; *secondly*, those which relate to the organization of the executive department; *thirdly*, those which relate to the organization of the judicial department; and *fourthly*, those which define and limit the powers delegated and the rights reserved. Of these four classes of provisions, the first three are so nearly alike in the federal and State constitutions that they can be expressed in almost the same language. These, therefore, will be examined in immediate connection. But with respect to the fourth class of provisions, namely, those which limit delegated power, there is a very important difference, which I will here explain. The federal government being designed, as we have seen, for national objects only, and these being comparatively limited in number, it was not impracticable to enumerate specifically the substantive or primary powers requisite for their accomplishment. These are called *enumerated powers*. But it was not so easy to foresee, nor so convenient to enumerate, all the secondary or subordinate powers which might be required as means for executing those primary powers; they are conferred generally and without enumeration, and are called *incidental powers*. As these two classes include all the powers conferred on the federal government, there is of course an implied prohibition of all other powers. In other words, the theory of the federal constitution is that the grant of powers is special, and the prohibition general. But out of abundant caution, that nothing connected with so momentous a subject might be left in doubt, some special prohibitions are inserted, which form another class, entitled *powers prohibited to the federal government*. Again, in order to prevent those conflicts with the State governments which might otherwise result from the federal scheme, it was necessary to prohibit the exercise by them of various powers to which they were originally competent; and thus we have another class, entitled *powers prohibited by the federal constitution to the States*. Accordingly, in the federal constitution we have for consideration these four classes of powers, namely: enumerated powers; incidental powers; powers prohibited to the federal government; and powers prohibited to the States. But the State constitutions are much more simple. In framing them, the design was to confer powers sufficient for all the details of municipal arrangement. Of course it was impossible to enumerate, or even to provide, all the powers requisite for objects so various; and accordingly, no specific enumeration was attempted. Power is conferred, in the first place, in general terms; and then specific prohibitions are inserted, with respect to the powers intended to be withheld. In other words, the theory of the State constitutions is that the grant of power is general, and the prohibitions special; being the exact reverse of the theory of the federal constitution. In the federal constitution, all powers are to be considered as prohibited which are not expressly or incidentally conferred; and in the State constitutions, all powers are to be considered as conferred which are not expressly or incidentally prohibited. (*a*) From all which it follows that, in order to ascertain the limitations of State power, we must add to the prohibitions of the federal constitution those of the particular State constitutions; and the aggregate of these two sets of prohibitions will constitute the limitations of the power of the State in question. It must be observed, however, that there are several powers which, either from their nature or from the language of the federal constitution, may be exercised concurrently by the federal and State governments; and hence we have another class of powers, entitled *concurrent powers*. Such, then, are the classes of provisions which constitute the fourth head before mentioned; namely, those which define and limit the powers delegated and the rights reserved. In discussing these, however, it will sometimes be convenient to treat them all in connection, and sometimes to treat them separately, according to their subject-matter.

LECTURE VI.

LEGISLATIVE DEPARTMENT. (*b*)

§ 30. **Division into two Branches.** In pursuance of the plan suggested in the preceding lecture, I shall in this lecture discuss the provisions of the constitution relating to the legislative depart-

(*a*) State *v.* Gutierez, 15 La. An. 192; Commonwealth *v.* Drewry, 15 Grattan, 1; Bushnell *v.* Beloit, 10 Wis. 225; The People *v.* Smith, 17 Cal. 553; Page *v.* Allen, 58 Penn. State, 338; Lewis' Appeal, 67 Penn. State, 153; People *v.* Flagg, 46 N. Y. 401; Baker *v.* Cincinnati, 11 Ohio State, 534, 543; Cooley's Const. Lim. 164, 173. And see Sedgwick on Statutory and Constitutional Law for a summary of the cases on this subject. It will be found there that there are many weighty dicta holding the doctrine in the text, that a State legislature possesses all legislative powers, except where limited by the constitution, though Sedgwick himself seems inclined to doubt the doctrine as stated in the text.

(*b*) The history of the convention in relation to this department is as follows: The first resolution adopted was that there should be a supreme legislative, judiciary, and executive. Mad. Pap. 749. It was next resolved that the legislature should consist of two branches. At first, Pennsylvania alone objected to this, out of regard to Dr. Franklin's opinion; but the final vote stood 7 to 3 — id. 753, 925. It was next resolved that the representatives should be elected by the people. This was warmly opposed by several who were in favor of an election by the State legislatures, but was carried by a vote of 5 to 2 — id. 757. A proposition that senators should be elected by the representatives out of persons nominated by the State legislatures, was negatived, 3 to 7 — id. 759. It was then resolved, that each branch should have the power to originate laws, and that the legislative power should extend to all cases to which the State legislatures were individually incompetent, and to a negative of State laws contravening the national laws — id. 759–61. A proposition authorizing an exertion of the force of the whole against a delinquent State did not pass to a vote — id. 761. A proposition, that the State legislatures should elect the representatives was negatived after warm debate, 3 to 8 — id. 800–8. The mode of electing senators again came up; and a proposition that the executive should appoint them out of persons nominated by the State legislatures did not pass to a vote; that the people should elect them was ment. The legislative power of the United States is vested in a *Congress*, consisting of a *Senate* and *House of Representatives.* A similar arrangement exists in all the States, though until recently Vermont was an exception. We have already seen that the

negatived, 1 to 10; and that they should be elected by the State legislatures, was carried unanimously — id. 812–21. A proposition that Congress should have a negative on all State laws was negatived, 3 to 7 — id. 821–28. Thus far there had not been a great diversity of opinion. But now the rule of suffrage in Congress came up. In the continental congress, and that of the confederation, and in this convention, the States had an equal vote. Should it be so under the new constitution? The parties were nearly equally divided, and the debate was warm and protracted. The first resolution, adopted by a vote of 7 to 3, was that the rule of suffrage in the house should not be as under the confederation, but according to some equitable ratio of representation — id. 830–42. The next, adopted by a vote of 9 to 2 was, that this ratio should be according to a census, including the free inhabitants and three-fifths of the slaves, — this being the rule of contribution proposed in 1783 under the confederation, and agreed to by eleven of the States — id. 842–43. The next, adopted by a vote of 6 to 5, was that the same ratio should prevail in the senate — id. 843. The mode of choosing senators was again debated, and election by the State legislatures affirmed, 9 to 2 — id. 945–59. The term of service for a representative was first fixed at three years, by a vote of 7 to 4, and then at two years, by a unanimous vote — id. 848, 931. The term for a senator was first fixed at seven years, by a vote of 8 to 1. Afterwards, opinions ranged between four and nine years, except that some were for the term of good behavior; but six years was adopted by a vote of 7 to 4 — id. 853, 960–69. The rule of suffrage in the house again came up, and, after a long and animated debate, equality among the States was rejected, 6 to 4 — id. 974–96. But by way of compromise, equality in the senate was proposed. This was debated with great earnestness, and lost by a tie vote — id. 966–1016. The fate of the convention was now at its crisis. Happily, the whole matter of suffrage in Congress was referred to a committee of one from each State, who reported the following compromise, namely: in the house, one representative for every forty thousand, including three-fifths of the slaves, but each State to have one; an equal representation in the senate; and a prohibition to the senate either to originate or amend money bills — id. 1016–24. The various parts of this compromise were debated for several days, with sundry references to other committees — id. 1082–1108. With respect to the ratio in the house, a specific apportionment was proposed for the present, with power in Congress to regulate it in future, upon the combined principles of wealth and population — id. 1036–51. The specific apportionment was modified and agreed to — id. 1053–6. The rule of future apportionment was first agreed to, 9 to 2; but afterwards the proposition of a periodical census brought up the slave question — id. 1053–63. A proposition to consider slaves equal to freemen, was negatived, 3 to 7; and after warm debate upon the proper basis of representation, — whether wealth, or numbers, or both, and whether slaves or not, — a periodical census was unanimously negatived — id. 1069–79. It was then resolved, 6 to 2, that representation should be according to direct taxation, and that both should be determined by a census to be taken every ten years, including three-fifths of the slaves — id. 1086. The part of the compromise giving an equal vote in the senate was adopted, 6 to 3; and that relating to money bills, 5 to 3 — id. 1045–47. On the whole compromise, as thus adjusted, the vote stood 5 to 4 — id. 1107–8. The small States considered this as a triumph. The large States were dissatisfied. A breaking up was talked of. The convention adjourned for one day. Out-door meetings were had, and the next day the business of the convention was resumed — id. 1109–13. The proposition of three senators from each State was negatived, 1 to 8, and two agreed upon unanimously; and the proposition that they should vote *per capita*, and not by States, was adopted, 9 to 2 — id. 1185–6. Such was the scheme of the legislative department, as it appeared in the first draught of the constitution — id. 1226–29. The ratio for the house was modified so as not to exceed one for every forty thousand; which, on the last day of the session, was changed to thirty thousand — id. 1263, 1699. The proposition to confine the ratio to free inhabitants, was negatived, 1 to 10 — id. 1266. The restriction of the senate as to money bills was stricken out, 7 to 4 — id. 1273. But upon subsequent debate it was reinstated, with the modification that the senate might amend, but not originate them — id. 1305–16. On the general subject of this department, see the 11th lecture of Kent; the 7th–13th chapters of Story's third book; and the 2d chapter of Blackstone's first book.

motive for dividing legislative power in this manner is to obtain the utmost security for its being faithfully and beneficially exercised. The idea is not original in this country. We had a well-tried example in the structure of the British Parliament. And although, from absence of the privileged orders, we have not the same materials as exist in England for constituting two bodies with really distinct interests, yet it is obvious that if the two bodies were alike in every particular, the mere necessity of their independent concurrence in every legislative act would afford more security than if there were but a single body. To some extent they must necessarily act as a check upon each other; and the efficiency of this check will be increased in exact proportion as these two bodies can be differently constituted, either with respect to their numbers, their mode of election, or their term of service; in all which particulars it will be seen that the senate and house of representatives differ from one another. In fixing the number of each house, the aim has been to secure a medium between too large and too small in both; and at the same time to establish a difference between the two, by making the senate smaller than the other house. Accordingly, the number of federal representatives can never exceed one for every thirty thousand constituents; while every State, however small, must have at least one; whereas the federal senate can only consist of two senators from each State. This equal representation of the States in the senate is a compromise in favor of the small States, whose influence is in a measure swallowed up in the other house; and in this respect, the constitution is declared to be unalterable. Thus simply and admirably was one of the strongest objections to our present federal organization completely obviated, by departing, in the construction of the Senate, from the principle of proportionate representation. With regard to the State legislatures, a similar difference is made in the number of the two bodies. In Ohio, for example, the number of representatives is fixed at one hundred, and of senators at thirty-five.

Apportionment. (*a*) The federal method of apportionment is the result, partly of compromise, and partly of convenience. The

(*a*) The second section of the 14th article proposed as an amendment to the constitution, June 16, 1866, and ratified by the requisite number of States in the summer of 1868, provides for the apportionment of representatives as follows:—

"Section 2. Representatives shall be apportioned among the several States, according to their respective numbers, counting the whole number of persons in each State, excluding Indians not taxed. But when the right to vote at any election for the choice of electors for president or vice-president of the United States, representatives in Congress, the executive and judicial officers of a State, or the members of the legislature thereof, is denied to any of the male inhabitants of such State, being twenty-one years of age, and citizens of the United States, or in any way abridged, except for participation in rebellion or other crime, the basis of representation therein shall be reduced in the proportion which the number of such male citizens shall bear to the whole number of male citizens twenty-one years of age in such State."

It will be noticed, that, while this section may, in some cases, change the apportionment of representatives, it says nothing about a change in the apportionment of direct taxes. Therefore, cases may arise in which they will not be proportioned to the representation of the State.

provision is in these words: "Representatives and direct taxes shall be apportioned among the several States which may be included within this Union, according to their respective numbers; which shall be determined by adding to the whole number of free persons, including those bound to service for a term of years, and excluding Indians not taxed, three-fifths of all other persons." The slaveholding States demanded a greater portion of representatives than, by the rule of uniformity, their free population would entitle them to; and they were willing, in return for this advantage, to bear a like proportion of the general expense, so far as supplied from direct taxation. This compromise was assented to by the non-slaveholding States; and thus another threatening obstacle to the formation of the present government was patriotically overcome. For the purpose of apportionment, a *census* or enumeration is made every ten years; and after each census, it devolves upon Congress to determine the number of representatives for each State, according to the directions of the Constitution. The process originally adopted was, first, to fix a ratio of representation within the limit before mentioned. This ratio forms the common divisor for the representable population of each State, as ascertained by the census, pursuant to the slave compromise; and the quotient, rejecting fractions, is the number of representatives for each State. By this process, therefore, if a State happen to have such an amount of population as to leave the remainder but one less than the assumed ratio, this entire remainder must be unrepresented. But how can this evil be avoided, consistently with the words of the constitution just quoted, "among the several States, according to their respective numbers"? It has been proposed to modify the above process thus: First, agree upon the whole number of representatives. By this divide the aggregate representable population of the Union, to obtain the ratio of representation. Then proceed as before, giving to each State the nearest whole number thence resulting; that is, when the remainder is greater than one-half the ratio, adding one to the quotient. The result would be that some of the States would have one more than by the former process; but taking the aggregate, there would be no unrepresented fractions. This process was twice proposed, and strongly recommended, as more equitable than the other; but it was rejected as unconstitutional. (*a*) As to the State represent-

(*a*) By the act of May 23, 1850, the representatives are to be two hundred and thirty-three in number. They are to be apportioned in the following manner: Divide the aggregate population of the United States by this number. Then divide the population of each State by the ratio so obtained, rejecting any fraction it may contain. The quotient, disregarding fractions, is to be the number of representatives to which each State is primarily entitled. The loss resulting from the rejection of fractions is to be compensated for by assigning to so many States having the largest fractions left after the division last named one additional member each for its fraction as may be necessary to make the whole number of representatives two hundred and thirty-three. It will be noticed that this corresponds nearly to the mode suggested in the text.

By the act of March 3, 1862, the number of representatives was increased to two hundred and forty-one, and one additional member each was assigned to Pennsylvania, atives and senators, their apportionment presents no difficulty. In Ohio, for example, the ratio of representation is ascertained, for the house of representatives, by dividing the whole population of the State by one hundred, and for the Senate, by thirty-five, — with an equitable provision for fractions.

§ 31. **Elections.** (*a*) Under this head I shall speak, first, of the qualifications of electors, and secondly, of the time, place, and manner of elections.

Ohio, Kentucky, Illinois, Iowa, Minnesota, Vermont, and Rhode Island. By the act of February 22, 1872, the House of Representatives was to consist of 283 members, and if any new States were admitted, the number to which they should be entitled was to be additional. By a subsequent act in the same year, May 30, 1872, nine additional representatives were given to different States, making the whole number 292. The former act also provides that the representation of any State which shall deny the right to vote to any of the male inhabitants of the State who are twenty-one years old and citizens of the United States, shall be reduced in the proportion that the number of male citizens so deprived, bears to the whole number of male citizens twenty-one years old in the State.

(*a*) The duties of canvassers are purely ministerial, and their return is only *prima facie* evidence of election. State *ex rel.* *v.* Foster, 38 Ohio State, 599; Brower *v.* O'Brien, 2 Carter (Ind.), 423; People *v.* Van Cleve, 1 Mann. (Mich.) 362; Mayo *v.* Freeland, 10 Missouri, 629; Bacon *v.* Commissioners, 26 Maine, 491; State of Iowa *ex rel.* Rice *v.* County Judge of Marshall County, 7 Clarke (Iowa), 186; State *ex rel.* Byers *v.* Bailey Co. Judge, id. 390; Morgan *v.* Quackenbush, 22 Barb. 72; State *v.* Clerk of Passaic, 1 Dutcher, 354; Attorney-General *ex rel.* Bashford *v.* Barstow, 4 Wisconsin, 567. Omissions of the judges or clerks in making up the tally-sheets, such as a failure to sign, or to fill up the blanks in the caption, or to state the aggregate number of votes cast, may be supplied by parole on a contest. Howard *v.* Shields, 16 Ohio State, 184; Dalton *v.* State *ex rel.*, 43 Ohio State, 652, 664–67. Where an election board has once regularly dissolved after making out a tally-sheet, it is *functus officio*, and cannot subsequently reassemble and alter its return. State *ex rel.* *v.* Donnewirth, 21 Ohio State, 216. An election held on a different day from that fixed by the legislature is unauthorized and void. State *ex rel.* *v.* Dombaugh, 20 Ohio State, 167. Votes given to a person who is ineligible are not nullities, but must be counted. State *v.* Giles, 1 Chandler (Wis.), 112. Where the ballots were destroyed in one of four districts, and the returns from the other three showed an election, and it did not appear that the missing returns would have changed the result, a mandamus was granted. Heath's case, 3 Hill, 42. It is no objection that illegal votes were received, or legal votes rejected, unless the majority is thereby changed. Blandford *v.* Gibbs, 2 Cushing, 39; Sudbury *v.* Stearns, 21 Pick. 148. Where the majority would be changed, the election is void, and the ballots themselves are the highest evidence. State *v.* Judge, 13 Ala. 805; People *v.* Tisdale, 1 Doug. (Mich.) 59. But it must be made to appear affirmatively and satisfactorily that all the ballots were present in their original condition. State *ex rel.* *v.* Donnewirth, 21 Ohio State, 216. Questions of fraud and illegality can only be tried in a contest, not in a suit to enjoin the clerk from recording the result. Peck *v.* Weddell, 17 Ohio State, 271. A ballot with the whole surname, and only the initial of the Christian name, is good; it is a question of identity only. State *ex rel.* *v.* Foster, 38 Ohio State, 599; People *v.* Seaman, 5 Denio, 409; but see People *v.* Ferguson, 8 Cowen, 102; State *ex rel.* *v.* Moffitt, 5 Ohio, 358. Where votes contain a name *idem sonans* with that of a candidate, but differently spelled, they are to be counted as thrown for him. People *v.* Mayworm, 5 Mich. 146. A ballot containing the names of two persons for an office to which only one can be elected is bad so far as that office is concerned. Carpenter *v.* Ely, 4 Wis. 420. The intention of voters as to who the person voted for is, is to govern; but this intention cannot be ascertained by extrinsic evidence. People *v.* Matteson, 17 Ill. 167; People *v.* Higgins, 3 Mich. 233. Where a person was not legally elected, by reason of improperly rejecting votes, he may be ousted by *quo warranto.* People *v.* Van Slyck, 4 Cowen, 297; Commonwealth *v.* Commissioners, 5 Rawle, 75. People *v.* Mayworm, 5 Mich. 146. See the important case of Attorney-General *ex rel.* Bashford *v.* Barstow, 4 Wis. 567, where judgment of ouster from the office of governor of Wisconsin was given against the defendant. Where in one of several districts no election was held, through the fault of a deputy, and the sheriff returned an election without stating this fact, the

Qualifications of Electors. (*a*) In regard to federal representatives, this matter was left by the constitution to the determination of each State, on the principle that no more power was to be conferred on the federal government than was necessary to effect its objects. It is, moreover, a matter of convenience because the States are not uniform in this respect, — some adopting *restricted*, and others *universal suffrage*. There is, however, this limitation, that the qualifications must be the same as for electors of State representatives, in order that the States may not be tempted to pervert this power. In Ohio, the qualifications of electors are the same for all purposes of voting. 1. The voter must be a white (*b*) male adult, and not an idiot or insane person. 2. He must be a citizen of the United States. 3. He must have resided within the State for one year preceding. But no person in the military, naval, or marine service of the United States is to be considered a resident by being stationed within the State. 4. He must not have been convicted of a penitentiary offence, unless afterwards pardoned. In some of the States property qualifications are required. We seem to have chosen the wise medium. On strict democratic principles, I see not how this most precious of all our rights can be rendered much less than universal. Who would ever consent to a government which he could have no voice in framing or directing?

Time, Place, and Manner of Elections. (*c*) With regard to federal senators and representatives, these are likewise left, in the first

court refused to induct into office the person having the certificate. Marshall *v.* Kerns, 2 Swan (Tenn.), 68. And see, on the subject of elections, Gorham *v.* Campbell, 2 Hepb. (Cal.) 135; State *v.* Cadle, 2 Iowa, 400; State *v.* King, 17 Missouri, 511; Bearce *v.* Fossett, 34 Maine, 575; People *v.* Martin, 5 N. Y. 22; People *v.* Jones, 17 Wendell, 81; People *v.* Cook, 14 Barbour, 259; and on the subject of annexation of cities and towns, Warren *v.* Mayor and Aldermen of Charlestown, 2 Gray, 84.

(*a*) In the federal convention a freehold qualification for electors was debated, but it was afterwards unanimously agreed to leave the whole matter to the States. Mad. Pap. 1249–56.

(*b*) The construction given to the word "*white*" is that it only excludes negroes and mulattoes. Jeffries *v.* Ankeny, 11 Ohio, 372; Thacker *v.* Hawk, 11 Ohio, 376. Persons having "a distinct and visible admixture of African blood" are excluded by the act of April 2, 1859. This act was repealed March 13, 1865, being clearly in conflict with the Constitution as construed by the Supreme Court. In April 16, 1868, it was attempted to gain the same end by requiring from such persons such strict proofs of descent that it was practically impossible to comply, and relieving the judges of election from any penalty whatever for refusing such votes. This law was unanimously held unconstitutional in Monroe *v.* Collins, 17 Ohio State, 665, on the ground that laws to regulate suffrage must be reasonable, uniform, and impartial. This law was held to violate all these requirements. The adoption of the fifteenth amendment to the Constitution of the United States was announced by the Secretary of State, March 30, 1870. It is as follows:—

ARTICLE 15.

Sec. 1. The right of citizens of the United States to vote shall not be denied or abridged by the United States, or by any State, on account of race, color, or previous condition of servitude.

Sec. 2. The Congress shall have power to enforce this article by appropriate legislation.

{This amendment does not affirmatively give the negro a right to vote, but it may have that effect by annulling discrimination, — as, where the right to vote is given to whites only by the State Constitution. *Ex p.* Yarbrough, 110 U. S. 651.}

(*c*) See Mad. Pap. 1282, 1297. By the act of February 22, 1872, the elections in instance, to the determination of each State, for the same reasons as above stated. But in order to prevent the States from defeating the federal government, if they should be so inclined, by neglecting to make the necessary provisions, a supervisory power over these matters is reserved to Congress, except as to the place of electing senators; which, being the place of meeting of the State legislature, ought not to be under the control of Congress. As yet, however, there has been no occasion to interfere with the State regulations, except that the last law requires the States to elect by districts, instead of general ticket. In Ohio, these regulations are the same as for the State officers generally, and I shall here briefly describe them.

1. As to the *time*. Federal representatives and State senators and representatives are elected on the second Tuesday of October. This is the general election day for all but township officers, who are elected on the first Monday of April. Federal senators are elected on such day as the assembly may agree upon for each case.

2. As to the *place*. Every township is an election district; and elections are held at such places therein as the trustees may direct.

3. As to the *manner*. This may be considered under several heads. 1. All elections are *by ballot*, written or printed, and not by oral declaration. The ballot must not contain more names than the office requires, but may contain fewer, if the voter so wishes. 2. In all elections by the people, a *plurality*, and not a majority, determines the choice. But in all elections by the assembly, a majority is necessary to a choice. 3. The polls are only open for one day. They are under the management of three judges, who are the township trustees, and two clerks, of whom one is the township clerk, and the other is appointed by the judges. Each clerk keeps a *poll-book*, in order that there may be duplicates, in which the name of every voter is entered as he puts in his vote. The votes are not inspected until the final counting after the polls are closed. The name of each candidate, and the number of votes, are then entered in the poll-books; one of which, being signed by the judges and clerks, is deposited with the township clerk, and the other delivered under seal, by one of the judges, to the clerk of the court of common pleas of the county. With the assistance of two justices of the peace he makes out an abstract of the returns of the county, and forwards it to the secretary of state. Certificates of election thereupon issue to the successful candidates. Where elections are contested each house is made the exclusive judge, for its own members, and provides the mode of decision. 4. Federal senators are elected by joint ballot of both houses of

1876 and thereafter are all to be held on the Tuesday after the first Monday in November. Representatives are to be elected in districts of compact territory, as nearly equal in population as possible; and by act of May 3, 1872, all future elections of representatives are to be by ballot.

the assembly, and not by the separate ballot of each. (*a*) It has been doubted whether this is constitutional; since, as a legislature, the two houses must act separately; and in some of the States they act separately in elections. 5. Federal representatives, and State senators and representatives, are elected *by districts*, and not by *general ticket;* and for this purpose, after each apportionment, the State is divided into congressional districts, and assembly districts, as nearly according to the number of white male adults as can be done without dividing counties. The chief advantage of this system over that by general ticket is that each citizen stands a chance to know the candidate he votes for, and is not required to vote for those he cannot know. 6. To guard against abuse or fraud, each voter may be put upon oath as to his qualifications; and bribery and imposition are made penal offences.

§ 32. **Qualifications of Members.** (*b*) With respect to federal senators and representatives, these are prescribed in the federal constitution; and it is presumed that the States are precluded from adding any other. A federal representative must be twenty-five years of age, an inhabitant of the State which he represents, and for seven years a citizen of the United States. A federal senator must be thirty years of age, an inhabitant of the State which he represents, and for nine years a citizen of the United States. No person holding any office under the United States can be a representative or senator during his continuance in office. It has been decided that a person does not lose his residence by being absent on public business. It is also to be remarked that the federal constitution does not require a representative to reside in the district which he represents, — this being left to the determination of each State.

The qualifications of State senators and representatives in Ohio are, that they must have resided in their respective counties or

(*a*) In some of the States, as in Massachusetts, they are chosen by a concurrent vote.

(*b*) The qualification of age was carried by a vote of 7 to 3. Mad. Pap. 936, 937. It was proposed in the convention that there should be a qualification of landed property. "Landed" was stricken out, 10 to 1, and a property qualification carried, 8 to 3 — id. 1215, 1216. The proposition to make public debtors and those having unsettled accounts with government ineligible, was negatived, 9 to 2 — id. 1217. Seven years' citizenship for representatives was carried by a vote of 11 to 1 — id. 1257. A certain period of residence in the State, varying from one to seven years, was negatived — id. 1257–60. For senators, a citizenship of fourteen years was strongly urged, but nine years was adopted by a vote of 6 to 4 — id. 1273–79. On a subsequent day, the question of a property qualification was debated and lost, 3 to 7 — id. 1282–7. The period of citizenship was again warmly debated, but left as before — id. 1299–1305. By the third section of the 14th Article of Amendments to the Constitution of the United States, no one can sit in Congress, act as presidential elector, or hold any other office, civil or military, under the United States, or any of the States, who, having previously taken an oath as a member of Congress, or as an officer of the United States, or as a member of any State Legislature, or as an executive or judicial officer of any State, to support the Constitution of the United States, shall have engaged in insurrection or rebellion against the same, or given aid and comfort to the enemies thereof. But Congress may, by a vote of two-thirds of each house, remove such disability.

districts one year next preceding their election, unless absent on public business. And no person can be a State senator or representative who holds any office under the United States, or any "lucrative office" under the State; but this provision does not extend to township offices, justices of the peace, notaries public, or officers in the militia. Another provision very properly excludes public defaulters, so long as they continue in default. We have also a statutory provision excluding from "offices of honor, trust, or profit," persons convicted of penitentiary offences and not pardoned; but it is doubtful if this excludes from membership in the legislature, because they are not generally spoken of as "officers." Of the qualifications now described as well as of the elections and returns, each house is made the exclusive judge, because the power could be nowhere else so conveniently deposited.

§ 33. **Term of Service.** The term of service was a matter of great delicacy. A long term would not sufficiently secure responsibility. A short term would incur the danger of that fluctuation and instability to which popular governments have always been liable. At the same time it was desirable to make a difference between the two bodies, in order to secure as great a variety of influences as possible. To accommodate all these views, federal representatives are elected for two years, (*a*) and federal senators for six. (*b*) But to remove all cause for apprehension on account of the long term allotted to senators, an arrangement was made by which one third should be elected every two years. For this purpose, the first senate was divided by lot into three classes, taking care that both senators from one State should not be in the same class. The first class went out at the end of two years, the second at the end of four years; and as each class went out their places were supplied by a new election. The result is that every second year one-third of the senate, and all the house of representatives, are newly elected. Views somewhat similar have prevailed in the State constitutions. But in Ohio both senators and representatives are elected biennially, and hold office for two years, commencing on the first day of January. The term of service in all these cases is an *integral* term; so that when a vacancy occurs, by death, resignation, or otherwise, the person elected to fill it only serves out the unexpired term; and vacancies are supplied as follows: For a federal representative or a State senator or representative, the governor, by proclamation, orders a special election in the vacant district, which is conducted in the manner before described. For a federal senator, (*c*) if the vacancy occur during the recess of the assembly, the governor makes a tempo-

(*a*) The convention first fixed upon three years. Some were strenuous for one year. The term of two years was finally acquiesced in unanimously. Mad. Pap. 848, 931.

(*b*) The convention first fixed upon seven years. Afterwards, opinions ranged between four and nine years; and, after a very animated debate, the term of six years was carried by a vote of 7 to 4. Mad. Pap. 853, 960–9.

(*c*) See the debate on this subject. Mad. Pap. 1268–70.

rary appointment, to expire at its next session. Otherwise, the assembly fills the vacancy at once.

§ 34. **Duties, Powers, and Privileges of Members.** There are several provisions connected with the *duties*, *powers*, and *privileges* of members.

1. *The Time of Meeting.* (*a*) Congress is required to meet at least once a year; and this must be on the first Monday in December, unless a different day shall be appointed by law, which has not been done. On extraordinary occasions, also, the executive may by proclamation call an extra session. The regular sessions of our general assembly commence on the first Monday of January, biennially.

2. *Privilege from Arrest.* While going, attending, and returning, the members are "privileged from arrest," for any cause except "treason, felony, and breach of the peace," which terms are construed to include all criminal offences; so that the exemption from arrest extends only to civil matters; and to this extent its propriety is too obvious to need comment.

3. *Freedom of Debate.* (*b*) The words are, "for any speech or debate, they shall not be questioned in any other place." The design is to secure independence *in debate only;* and therefore the privilege extends only to what is spoken in debate. If a libellous speech be published, the member is answerable as in other cases.

4. *Security against Corruption.* (*c*) To this end, it is declared that no member "shall, during the time for which he was elected, be appointed to any civil office which shall have been created, or the emoluments whereof shall have been increased, during such time." But as the disability continues only during the time for which he was elected, this provision is not calculated to produce much effect. In Ohio this disability is extended to one year after the term.

5. *Quorum.* (*d*) By a quorum is meant the number necessary to do business. In the houses of Congress, only a majority is required to constitute a quorum; and in our assembly the same. In either, however, a less number may adjourn from day to day, and may compel the attendance of absent members. Such a provision is indispensable in order to secure the continuance of a session, which can only be effected by adjournments.

6. *Yeas and Nays.* (*e*) By yeas and nays, are meant the votes which are to be recorded on the journals of each house. In Con-

(*a*) See Mad. Pap. 1246–48.

(*b*) Rex *v.* Creevey, 1 Maule & S. 273.

(*c*) For the debate on this subject, see Mad. Pap. 937–45, 1317–26. An absolute ineligibility to any office, during the period of membership, was strongly urged. Id. 1481–5.

(*d*) See the debate, in which a smaller number than a majority was strongly urged. Mad. Pap. 1287–90.

(*e*) See the debate, Mad. Pap. 1291–94. Some thought the yeas and nays ought never to be entered, because the reasons of the vote would not appear upon the journal.

gress, they are required to be taken only at the request of one-fifth; but in our assembly they may be demanded by any two members. When the yeas and nays are not called for, members may shun responsibility, either by not voting at all or by having their voices drowned in the mass; and even if their vote be known at the time, it is not recorded for future reference. But when the yeas and nays are called and entered upon the journal, every member must vote, unless excused; and that vote may be scrutinized at any future period; so that there is no way of escaping responsibility. This shows the importance of allowing a small number to call the yeas and nays. Our State constitution requires them to be called on the passage of every bill, and there must be a majority of all members elected to each house.

7. *Protest.* (*a*) Our State constitution contains a further provision allowing any member to make his protest against any act or resolution, and have it entered upon the journal. But this does not seem calculated to answer any very salutary purpose; and the want of a similar one in the federal constitution is scarcely a matter of regret.

8. *Compensation.* (*b*) The federal constitution leaves this matter to Congress; at present, it is eight dollars per day for the members of each house, and the same for every twenty miles of travel, going and returning. The experiment was made of a fixed compensation, by way of salary; but it proved unpopular, because it did not depend upon the amount of service rendered. (*c*) In the States, the compensation is also *per diem*, but generally much less than for members of Congress. The difference, indeed, is greater than there would seem to be reason for. In both cases, the compensation is paid out of the respective treasuries, and not by the particular districts.

§ 35. **Separate Powers and Duties of each House.** There are certain separate powers and duties of each house, without the concurrence of the other, which next require notice.

1. *The Election of Officers.* With the exception of the federal

(*a*) This question was discussed in the federal convention, and negatived by a vote of 3 to 8. Mad. Pap. 1292.

(*b*) It was proposed in the convention that the compensation should be regulated by the price of wheat. Some were in favor of no compensation; some, that it should be regulated and paid by the States; some, that it should be fixed by the constitution. Mad. Pap. 849, 854, 931, 969. It was finally agreed, 9 to 2, that the compensation should be ascertained by law, and paid out of the national treasury. Id. 1326–30.

(*c*) By the act of July 8, 1866, each senator, representative, and delegate in Congress is to receive five thousand dollars per annum, and mileage for each regular session at the rate of twenty cents per mile, to be estimated by the nearest route usually travelled. The Speaker of the House is to receive eight thousand dollars. A deduction is to be made for each day's absence, unless the reason be the sickness of himself or some member of his family. By the act of March 3, 1873, which has recently caused so much discussion, the salary of senators and representatives is made $7500 in full of all pay and allowances except actual individual travelling expenses from their homes to the seat of Government by the most direct route of usual travel, once in each session. The feature which caused so much scandal was the dating of the period for which the pay was so increased back two years, to the commencement of the session then expiring. The speaker's pay is $10,000, but was not dated back.

senate, of which the vice-president of the United States is *ex officio* president, and of the State senate, of which the lieutenant-governor is *ex officio* president, each house elects its own officers; namely, a presiding officer, usually denominated speaker; a recording officer, or clerk; an executive officer, called sergeant-at-arms; and a door-keeper.

2. *The Rules of Proceeding.* These are made by each house, and are nearly the same for all deliberate bodies; but they are too numerous to be described. You will find them, with comments, in Jefferson's Manual, or Cushing's Manual. (*a*)

3. *The Journal.* (*b*) Each house is required to keep a journal of its proceedings, and publish it from time to time, in order that the constituents may know what their representatives have done; and to this end, in Ohio, all proceedings are required to be public, unless two-thirds shall otherwise determine.

4. *The Elections, Returns, and Qualifications of Members.* We have already seen that each house is made the exclusive judge of these matters, — there being no good reason for requiring the concurrence of the other.

5. *Punishment of Members.* Each house may punish its members for "disorderly behavior;" otherwise its business might be utterly prevented; and there is no restriction as to cause or manner of punishment.

6. *Punishment of Persons not Members.* (*c*) Our State constitution expressly authorizes each house "to provide for its safety, and the undisturbed transaction of its business." The federal constitution is silent on this subject; but each house of Congress has been adjudged to possess this power as necessarily inherent, and it has been exercised repeatedly. As to what amounts to a contempt, each house judges for itself.

7. *Expulsion of Members.* (*d*) With the concurrence of two-thirds, each house may expel a member. Our State constitution

(*a*) See the elaborate treatise on the Law and Practice of Legislative Assemblies in the United States, by Luther S. Cushing. Little, Brown, & Co., 1856.

(*b*) See the original debate, Mad. Pap. 1293–94; also the debate on expunging the resolution censuring President Jackson.

(*c*) See Anderson *v.* Dunn, 6 Wheat. 204; Howard *v.* Gossett, 10 Ad. & El. N. S. 359; Fenton *v.* Hampton, 11 Moore, Privy Council, R. 347; Keilly *v.* Carson, 4 id. 63; Stockdale *v.* Hansard, 9 Ad. & El. 1; 11 id. 273; 3 Perry & Dav. 349. See case of Robert Randall, 1 Benton, Abrid. 621; case of Charles Whitney, 1 id. 622; case of William Duane, 2 id. 407–26; case of John Anderson, 6 id. 90, 93; act of Jan. 24, 1857, to enforce the attendance of witnesses on the summons of either house of Congress. See proceedings and documents of the United States senate in case of Thaddeus Hyatt, first session of the 36th Congress, on a charge against him for contempt, in refusing to appear as a witness before the Harper's Ferry Committee. *In re* Falvey *v.* Massing, 7 Wis. 630. {A standing committee of either house, while engaged in carrying out the orders of the house, may send for persons and papers, and punish a refusal to obey by committal as for a contempt. *Ex p.* Dalton to appear in 44 Ohio State. But this power is not unlimited, and does not exist if the committee is not engaged in exercising powers properly belonging to the legislative department. Kilbourn *v.* Thompson, 103 U. S. 168.}

(*d*) There was no doubt in the convention as to the necessity of this power. The only question was whether it should be exercised by a bare majority, or a greater number. Mad. Pap. 1291.

provides that a member shall not be twice expelled "*for the same cause.*" In other words, if his constituents are satisfied to send him back, the house must be content to receive him. Perhaps this is right; but the houses of Congress are not thus restricted. The propriety of this power of expulsion will be felt the more strongly, if we reflect that the power of impeachment does not reach to members of the legislature. Expulsion is, therefore, the only means of removing an unworthy member.

8. *Adjournments.* (*a*) Each house can of course adjourn from day to day, without consulting the other. But as the general business of legislation requires the concurrence of both, to prevent one house from defeating or interrupting this general business, it is provided that neither house of Congress, without consent of the other, can "adjourn for more than three days, nor to any other place than that in which the two houses shall be sitting." It is the same with our assembly, except that the time is two days. Both constitutions further provide that "in case of disagreement between the two houses with respect to the time of adjournment," the executive may adjourn them "to such time as he shall think proper." This must refer to the time of final adjournment at the end of the session. And our constitution adds, what is implied in the other, that the executive shall not adjourn them to a period beyond the annual time of meeting.

§ 36. **Forms of Business.** (*b*) I come now to the *enactment of laws*, commonly called *acts* or *statutes*, which forms the chief business of legislative bodies. The course of proceeding is nearly the same in all legislatures, and I shall give a brief outline of it. Every act in its incipient stage is denominated a *bill*. In general, all bills may originate indifferently in either house. But by the federal constitution, as we have seen, *revenue bills* must originate in the house of representatives, as the branch more immediately representing the people. This exception was borrowed from England, where the house of lords, representing the landed aristocracy, are allowed neither to originate nor amend revenue bills, but simply to pass or reject them. (*c*) The object is to secure the people at large against oppressive taxation, through the influence of the peers. It is evident that we have not the same reason for placing this check upon our republican senate; and accordingly, our senate may amend but not originate revenue bills. (*d*) In Ohio there is not even this restriction; nor has expe-

(*a*) See the debate on this subject, Mad. Pap. 1294–96

(*b*) See 1 Black. Com. 181; 1 Kent, Com. 238; 1 Story, Const. § 896; Jefferson's Manual.

(*c*) The power of the Lords to reject a money bill was seriously questioned in the Commons in 1860; but the Lords insisted on their privilege, and rejected a bill abolishing a certain tax. 6 Jurist, N. S. pt. 2, 236.

(*d*) This matter of revenue bills was very much debated in the convention, the large States insisting upon it as a part of the compromise between them and the small States. Mad. Pap. 856, 1016–24, 1045, 1260, 1305–16. The clause was finally adopted by a vote of 9 to 2. Id. 1531.

rience shown the want of it. Bills may be introduced by individual members, on leave of the house, or by the report of a committee. They are required to be read three times in each house; and this must be on three different days, unless, in a case of emergency, three-fourths of the house agree to dispense with the rule. (*a*) The *first reading* is for information only; and if there be any opposition, the question is upon the rejection of the bill. If not opposed or rejected, it passes of course to a *second reading;* and the question is then upon its *commitment* or *engrossment.* If committed, it is either to a standing or select committee consisting of a few, or to a general committee of the whole house. Bills of great importance are usually discussed in committee of the whole, because greater freedom of debate is there allowed than when the same persons are sitting as a house. After discussion in committee, the bill is reported back to the house, with or without *amendment.* If with amendments, these are acted upon in the house, and others may there be offered. When the bill has in this way become sufficiently matured, the question is upon its engrossment for a *third reading;* by which is meant the copying of it in a fair large hand. After engrossment, amendments are rarely offered. A clause is, however, sometimes added by way of *ryder.* This is the stage where opposition is usually made. After the third reading, the question is upon its final passage. If it pass, it is signed by the presiding officer, and transmitted to the other house, where it goes through a similar routine. If amendments be there made, it is sent back for *concurrence;* and in case of disagreement, committees of conference are appointed. When it has thus passed both houses, it is delivered to a joint committee for *enrolment,* who see that it is correctly copied. It is then signed by the presiding officers of the two houses. And in Ohio, the process ends here; for our governor has not, as in several of the States, a *veto power.* It only remains, therefore, to deposit the enrolled law, thus authenticated, among the State archives in the custody of the secretary. Out of abundant caution, however, our constitution provides that no bill shall contain more than one subject, which shall be clearly expressed in its title, (*b*) and that no law shall be revived or amended, unless the new act contains the entire act revived, or the section amended; and the original section is thereby repealed. (*c*) The signing is

(*a*) But this provision does not require every amendment to a bill to be read three times. Miller *v.* State, 3 Ohio State, 475.

(*b*) {But this provision is directory only, and not mandatory. State *ex rel. v.* Covington, 29 Ohio State, 102.}

(*c*) Miller *v.* State, 3 Ohio State, 475; Pim *v.* Nicholson, 6 id. 176. It is held in the last-named case that this provision is directory only, and the supervision of its observance must be left to the general assembly. Under what circumstances a provision in an act that it shall take effect upon a popular vote is constitutional, see Cincinnati, &c. R. R. Co. *v.* Clinton County, 1 Ohio State, 77; Morgan *v.* Monmouth Plank R. R. Co., 2 Dutcher, 99; Morgan *v.* Unger, 8 Clarke (Iowa), 82; Pierce on American Railroad Law, 116–20. A court cannot set aside an act of the legislature duly certified and enrolled on the ground of fraud or misrepresentation or improper motives in those voting for it. Jersey City, &c. R. R. Co. *v.* Jersey City, &c. R. R. Co., 20 N. J.

also required to be done publicly, while the house is in session. And it is further provided that all laws of a general nature shall have a uniform operation throughout the State, in order to prevent the great and growing evil of special legislation.

Veto Power. (*a*) But the acts of Congress must pass another ordeal before their consummation; and that is the scrutiny of the president. In England, the king has an absolute negative upon the acts of parliament; but the negative of the president is qualified. The bill is sent to him for approval. If he approves it, he signs it. If not, he sends it back to the house where it originated, with his objections, which are entered upon its journal. The bill is then reconsidered; and if it still pass by two-thirds of both houses, it becomes a law, notwithstanding the presidential veto. The time given to the president for consideration is ten days, within which he must return the bill, unless Congress prevent him by adjournment; otherwise it becomes a law without his signature. Unfortunately, the practice is to put off important bills until within ten days of the close of the session, and thus put it in the power of the president to give them an indirect veto by mere silence. The veto power thus qualified, extends "to every order, resolution, or vote," to which the concurrence of the two houses is necessary. And although the constitution does not indicate the proper occasion for its exercise, yet as one man thereby sets his individual opinion against a majority of both houses of Congress, it was manifestly intended only for cases of emergency. The better opinion is that it can be properly exercised only on two occasions: *first*, when the bill, either from oversight in framing it or from some contingency not known at the time of its passage through Congress, has become manifestly improper to be made a law, at the time of its presentation to the president; or, *secondly*, when such an exercise of power is necessary to shield the executive department against encroachment by the legislature. Being anti-republican in its character, it ought not to be exercised upon questions of mere policy, about which fair minds may differ; for this, as has been well remarked, would be converting the extreme medicine of the constitution into its daily bread. (*b*)

Eq. 61. *Contra* in the case of an ordinance of a municipal corporation affecting private rights. State *v.* Cincinnati G. L. & C. Co., 18 Ohio State, 262.

(*a*) The first proposition in the convention was for a council of revision, to consist of the executive and judiciary, which was given up without a vote. Next, an absolute veto, which was unanimously negatived. Next, a power of suspending laws, which shared the same fate. The qualified veto, as it now stands, was then agreed upon by a vote of 8 to 2. Mad. Pap. 783–91. A subsequent motion to associate the judiciary was lost by a vote of 3 to 8 — id. 809–12. Still another motion to the same effect was debated and negatived, 3 to 4, and the present qualified veto agreed to unanimously — id. 1161–71. On a subsequent day, the association of the judiciary was negatived, 3 to 8, and three-fourths, instead of two-thirds, required to pass a law notwithstanding the executive disapprobation — id. 1332–7. By a subsequent vote of 6 to 4, two-thirds was again reinstated — id. 1562–65.

(*b*) A history of the veto power may be found in the Democratic Review for January, 1849, by E. L. Pierce. See also a history in appendix to the fourth volume of Elliot's Debates, p. 620.

§ 37. **Presentment and Trial of Impeachments.** (*a*) This is a kind of judicial proceeding, and forms an exception to the general business of legislative bodies. Impeachment is the name given to that course of proceedings by which "*civil officers*" are tried and punished for official misconduct. Civil officers include all public functionaries, except military and naval officers, and members of the legislature; the former of whom are punished by a court-martial, and the latter in the manner before described. The causes of impeachment, as stated in the federal constitution, are "treason, bribery, or other high crimes and misdemeanors;" and, as stated in our State constitution, "any misdemeanor in office." The meaning is, probably, the same in both; and comprehends any violation of official duty, whether criminal or not. The mode of proceeding, which is borrowed from the British Parliament, is also the same under both constitutions. The impeachment or charge is presented by a majority of the house of representatives, who thus discharged a function similar to that of a grand jury. It is then tried by the senate sitting under oath; of whom two-thirds must concur to produce a conviction. In England, the judgment may include banishment, and even death. But here, it can extend only to removal from office, and future disqualification. If, however, the offence be criminal, the party may be afterwards tried and punished by due course of law. In case the president should be impeached, the chief justice of the United States is to preside. The reason will be obvious, if we remember that the vice-president, who usually presides, would become president if the impeachment should be sustained; and would not therefore be in a situation to preside impartially. This liability to impeachment is, in theory, one of our strong safeguards for official integrity. In practice, however, it has not yet resulted in the conviction of either a federal officer or an officer of this State, though the experiment has been several times made. (*b*)

This terminates the view I proposed to take of the legislative department of the federal and State governments. The federal senate has indeed two other functions, but they can scarcely be called legislative. One is *to approve of treaties*, which was described in a preceding lecture. The other is *to approve of the appointment* of officers by the president, which will be described in the next lecture. I think you cannot have failed to be impressed with the striking similarity there is in the structure of the federal and State legislatures. The principal exceptions relate to the federal senate, whose organization is in many respects peculiar. But it is in consequence of these peculiarities that it has been

(*a*) The convention at first resolved that impeachments should be tried by the judiciary. Mad. Pap. 861, 1137. When the trial was given to the senate, it was proposed to except the case of the president — id. 1528.

(*b*) A judge by the name of Elliot has recently been removed by impeachment in Louisiana. 1 West. Law Jour. 380. The most remarkable instance of an impeachment trial is that of President Johnson, which also failed for want of the requisite majority.

expressly denominated the "*sheet anchor*" of the constitution. In no other part of this wonderful instrument do we find such convincing proof of the profound wisdom of its framers. They intended that the senate should be the balance of the federal system, and they have made it so. The house of representatives, being constructed to represent more directly the present feelings of the people, must necessarily represent their changing passions also. The president, whose very unity gives him strength, and who is intrusted with the vast powers to be described hereafter, without some very efficient check, would be more than a match for the other departments. But the senate, by a term of service three times as long as that of the representatives, and half as long again as that of the president, by the necessity of their concurrence in the acts of the one, and by the supervision they exercise over the most important acts of the other, are thereby enabled to constitute precisely the check which both require.

LECTURE VII.

EXECUTIVE DEPARTMENT. (*a*)

§ 38. **Unity and Duration of the Office.** — In this lecture I shall give an account of the executive department of the federal and

(*a*) The history of the proceedings of the convention, with respect to this department, is not a little remarkable. The first resolution was, that a national executive be instituted, on which all were agreed. Mad. Pap. 764. It was next resolved, 5 to 4, that the term be seven years — id. 767. A proposition to elect by electors, chosen by the people in districts, was negatived by a vote of 2 to 8, and election by Congress was carried by a vote of 8 to 2 — id. 770. A proposition by Dr. Franklin, that there should be no compensation, did not pass to a vote — id. 770–6. A proposition that the executive be removable by Congress, at the request of a majority of the States, was negatived, 1 to 10; that he should be ineligible a second time, carried 7 to 2; and that he should be removable by impeachment, carried unanimously — id. 779. A proposition that the executive should consist of a single person, was carried, 7 to 3 — id. 783. The propositions for an absolute veto, and for a power to suspend laws, were each unanimously negatived, and the present qualified veto agreed to, 8 to 2 — id. 790, 791. A proposition to associate the judiciary with the executive, in the exercise of the veto power, was negatived, 3 to 8 — id. 809–12. A proposition that the State executives should elect, was negatived unanimously — id. 830. A proposition that the people should elect, was negatived, 1 to 9; another, that the election should be by electors appointed by the State legislatures, was negatived, 2 to 8; and election by Congress unanimously affirmed — id. 1124. Ineligibility a second time was stricken out, 6 to 4 — id. 1125. Tenure during good behavior, was negatived, 4 to 6, and seven years affirmed by the same vote — id. 1129. Election by electors appointed by the State legislatures, was carried 8 to 2 — id. 1150. A term of six years was adopted, 9 to 1 — id. 1152. A specific appointment of electors, in the first instance, was carried, 3 to 7 — id. 1153. To be removable by impeachment, was carried, 8 to 2; and to receive a fixed compensation from the national treasury, 9 to 1 — id. 1160. A proposition that the judiciary should be associated in the exercise of the veto power, was again negatived, 3 to 4, and the present qualified veto affirmed unanimously — id.

State governments. The organization of this department was attended with more difficulty and contrariety of opinion, than any other part of our system. The general maxim is, that the exercise of delegated power should always require the concurrence of more minds than one. Yet a calm and thorough discussion, both of abstract principles and the lessons of history, suggested a departure from this maxim in constructing the executive department. The regular functions of this department, being chiefly ministerial, do not require the exercise of deliberation and discretion, to the same extent as those of the other departments. On the contrary, they require a promptness, decision, and energy of action, which could seldom result from the concurrence of several minds; and can only be found in perfection, when flowing from a single mind. It was accordingly resolved to vest the executive power primarily in a single person; and this is a principle of all the American constitutions. Accordingly, by the federal constitution, "the executive power is vested in a *president* of the United States of America;" and by the constitution of Ohio, "the supreme executive power of this State shall be vested in the *governor*." This word "supreme" inserted in the latter, is implied in the former; since there are many subordinate executive officers, to be described hereafter. But a single executive head is a monarchical feature, and was not assented to without much misgiving. In the federal convention, there was a considerable party in favor of a *plural executive;* and when this proposition failed,

1161–71. Election by Congress was again reinstated, 7 to 4 — id. 1188–90. Terms of eight, eleven, fifteen, and twenty years, were silently negatived, as was a proposition to elect by electors selected from Congress by lot; and a proposition that no person should serve for more than six in any twelve years, was negatived 5 to 6 — id. 1191–1207. A term of seven years, and ineligibility a second time, were reinstated, 7 to 3 — id. 1210. In this shape, the provisions, relating to the executive, appear in the first draft of a constitution, reported Aug. 6 — id. 1236, 1237. A proposition by Mr. Madison, to associate the judiciary in the exercise of the veto power, was again negatived, 3 to 8 — id. 1333. The qualified veto was again affirmed, with a substitution of three-fourths, instead of two-thirds, 6 to 4 — id. 1337. A proposition for a privy council, to consist of the president of the senate, speaker of the house, chief-justice, and the heads of departments, did not pass to a vote — id. 1398. A proposition to elect by the people, was negatived, 2 to 9 — id. 1418. A proposition that the election should be by joint ballot of Congress, was carried, 7 to 4 — id. 1419. A proposition that each State should have one vote, was negatived, 5 to 6, and that the election should be by electors, chosen by the people in each State, was negatived, 5 to 6 — id. 1420, 1421. On the 31st of August, the whole subject was referred to a committee of one from each State, who, on the 4th of September, reported substantially the scheme adopted, including for the first time the idea of a vice-president — id. 1486. This scheme was debated during five days — id. 1488–1528. A proposition to reinstate the former scheme, was negatived, 2 to 8 — id. 1498. A term of four years was adopted, 10 to 1 — id. 1508. Election by electors chosen by the people was carried 9 to 2 — id. 1508. Election by the house of representatives, in case of failure by the electors, was carried, 7 to 3 — id. 1511. The proposition that the vice-president should be president of the senate, was carried, 8 to 2 — id. 1518. The proposition for an executive council, to consist of six persons, appointed by Congress, was negatived, 3 to 8 — id. 1524. The qualified veto of two-thirds, instead of three-fourths, was reinstated, 6 to 4 — id. 1564. And thus, within five days of the close of the convention, after so many changes, the executive scheme was at last completed. For a general view of this department, see the 13th lecture of Kent, the 36th and 37th chapters of Story's third book, and 1 Black. Com. chapters from 3d to 8th inclusive.

an effort was made to procure an *executive council*, whose assent should be required to all executive measures. There is manifestly the same objection to this as to a plural executive; at least the same in kind, if not in degree. Yet such a council exists in several of the States. (*a*) But the proposition failed in the federal convention, and was not made in Ohio. Accordingly the president, with a few extraordinary exceptions, and our governor, in all cases, may discharge the duties assigned them, without the perplexity, delay, or hinderance, which would result from the necessity of consulting with other persons.

And the *unity* of the executive being thus settled, the next question was, as to the *duration of the office*. Some of the most distinguished members of the federal convention were in favor of its continuing *during good behavior*. But republican jealousy treated this proposition with little favor. It was then actually resolved that the term should be *seven years*, but it was afterwards reduced to *four*, which is intermediate between that of the representatives and senators. This term was considered long enough to give stability to the executive administration, and opportunity to complete important measures of policy, and yet not so long as to make accountability too remote. When the term of seven years was contemplated, the president was to be *ineligible a second time*. And it has become a question of grave importance, whether the public welfare does not require a similar provision now, in order to prevent the first term from being taken up with schemes to secure a re-election. This question was indeed discussed in connection with the term of four years, but experience has since imparted new light; and probably the result of such a discussion now would be different. As to the term of the State executives, there is great diversity. It varies from one to four years. Here it is two years.

§ 39. **Election of President and Vice-President.** — The next question was as to *the mode of election*. It was at first resolved in the federal convention, that the president should be chosen *by Congress*. But this resolution was reconsidered, because it was thought that the *sense of the people* could not be sufficiently expressed in such a choice, and also that there would be too much room for cabal and intrigue. Should the choice, then, be made by the State legislatures? Or by the people directly? Or by *electors* chosen for that express purpose? After much discussion, the latter method was agreed upon, and there is scarcely any part of the federal scheme more deserving of admiration. It avoids the tumult and disorder which might result from an election directly by the people, and yet gives the people, in their choice of electors, an opportunity to express their views upon this single point, without reference to other matters; which would not be

(*a*) But such a council has no control over the approving or vetoing bills by the executive.

the case if the choice were made either by the federal or State legislatures. (*a*) The number of electors for each State is the aggregate of its federal senators and representatives, and thus the compromise between the large and small States is carried out, by giving them the same representation in the *electoral colleges* as in Congress. No qualification is prescribed, except that of not being a member of Congress, nor holding any federal office, which exception was necessary to secure the electors against improper influences. For reasons already sufficiently apparent, the mode of choosing electors is left to the determination of each State, and of course there is some diversity, as by the legislature, by the people in districts, and by general ticket. Congress has power to determine the day on which the electors shall be chosen, and the day on which they shall give their votes; and the latter is required to be the same in all the States, in order to prevent intrigue and corruption. By the act of 1792, Congress fixed the day for giving the electoral votes, on the first Wednesday in December, and required the electors to be chosen within thirty-four days preceding, but did not specify the exact day. The States, therefore, have been allowed to select different days. In Ohio, it is the fifth Friday preceding the day specified. (*b*) Thus far, the provisions of the constitution remain as they were originally. But the subsequent proceedings have been considerably modified by the twelfth amendment, which was made in 1804. I shall first describe the present regulations, and then explain the points wherein they differ from the former.

On the day appointed, the electors meet in their respective States, and vote by distinct ballots, for president and vice-president, one of whom shall not be an inhabitant of the same State with themselves. A list of the votes, duly authenticated, and addressed to the president of the senate, is transmitted to the seat of government, in the manner pointed out by the act of 1792. The votes are opened and counted in the presence of both houses of Congress. A majority of all the electoral votes is necessary to a choice, both of president and vice-president. It therefore became necessary to provide for the very probable contingency of a want of a majority. In this event, the election of president devolves upon the house of representatives, voting by States, and that of vice-president, upon the senate, voting individually. In each case, two-thirds are required for a quorum, and a majority of the whole for a choice. The house must select from the three highest candidates on the list, and the senate from

(*a*) The caucus system of party nominations has rendered this part of the system inoperative, as the electors of each party are pledged to vote for the party nominee. A vote for the party electoral ticket is therefore a vote for the caucus nominee, and a vote for any other persons as electors is simply useless.

(*b*) By the act of Congress of Jan. 23, 1845, c. 1, a uniform time for holding elections for electors of presidents and vice-presidents in all the States was prescribed. The day fixed was the Tuesday next after the first Monday in the month of November of the year in which they are to be appointed.

the two highest. If the house fail to elect a president before the ensuing fourth of March, the vice-president is to act as president. Such is the substance of the twelfth amendment.

The original method differed in these particulars. *First*, the electors voted for two candidates in one ballot, without specifying the office for which each was intended. *Secondly*, the highest of all the candidates, if he had a majority, was president; and the next highest, vice-president. *Thirdly*, if two candidates had a majority and were equal, the house chose between them; but if no candidate had a majority, the house chose from the five highest. *Fourthly*, there could be no vice-president until the president was chosen; and the senate only had the choice, when the two next candidates had an equal number of votes. *Fifthly*, there was no provision made in case of failure to elect a president before the fourth of March; and of course, so far as the executive is concerned, there must have been an interregnum. This calamity had well nigh happened in 1801, when the contest was between Jefferson and Burr. The house balloted thirty-six times, and it is believed that nothing but the fear of such a crisis unprovided for, occasioned a final choice. This bitter contest is supposed to have caused the twelfth amendment. It will be observed that the present method greatly diminishes the dignity of the second office, since it is no longer placed in competition with the first. Whether this is compensated by other advantages, is a matter of opinion. There is still a case unprovided for, and that is, the failure to elect either a president or vice-president within the period prescribed. By the act of 1792, Congress has indeed provided for a new election in this event; but there is some doubt whether Congress has constitutional power to make such a provision. Another difficulty may arise in case of doubt about the authenticity of the electoral returns; and still another, in case two out of the four highest candidates for president should have an equal number of votes. These contingencies, though by no means improbable, have not as yet been provided for. (*a*)

If now we turn to the mode of electing the State executives, we find almost an entire contrast. In some few instances the governor is elected by the legislature, but generally directly by the people. In Ohio, the time, place, and manner are the same as for members of the legislature. The returns are made to the president of the senate, and counted in the presence of both houses. A plurality only is required for a choice, and in case of a tie, the

(*a*) The public attention was more forcibly called to the difficulty in case of question as to the authenticity of electoral returns at the last election than ever before. There were disputes as to some of them; but no trouble arose, as they would not have affected the result. The mode of passing on the question provided at present, each house acting separately, is highly unsatisfactory. The whole matter calls loudly for some change. It is stated that the senate committee on privileges and elections will report in favor of an amendment doing away with the electoral college, giving each congressional district one vote, and two votes to the State at large, and providing that a plurality shall elect.

choice is made by a majority of both houses on joint ballot. Contested elections are decided in like manner. If a case can be supposed, in which the assembly would fail ultimately to make the election devolving on them, that case is unprovided for.

The original scheme of the convention did not embrace such an officer as the *vice-president.* (*a*) But in the course of their deliberations, two reasons suggested themselves for creating this office. The first was, to provide a presiding officer for the senate, without depriving any State of its equal vote, by taking him from that body. The second was, to provide a suitable person to supply a vacancy in the office of president. In presiding over the senate, the vice-president only gives a casting vote in case of a tie, and never joins in their deliberations; because otherwise one of the States would have an advantage over the rest. This is the only duty annexed to the office, until by removal, death, inability, resignation, or failure to elect, the office of president becomes vacant. Then this office devolves on the vice-president, and the senate elect a *president pro tempore.* If from either of these causes, except a failure to elect, the office of vice-president also becomes vacant, Congress has power to provide what officer shall act as president; and by the act of 1792, Congress has designated first the president *pro tempore* of the senate, and next the speaker of the house of representatives. No further contingency has been provided for. The arrangement in some of the States is similar to this, in providing a *lieutenant-governor*, to fill the office of gov ernor if need be. In Ohio, the lieutenant-governor is *ex officio* president of the senate.

§ 40. **Qualifications, Compensation, Oath.** The qualifications for president and vice-president are the same. 1. The candidate must be a "natural born citizen," in order to leave no room for foreign influence or interference. An exception, however, was made in favor of "citizens of the United States, at the time of the adoption of the constitution," out of respect to those distinguished patriots from foreign lands, who had taken part in our revolution. 2. He must be at least thirty-five years of age; by which time his judgment is presumed to be matured, and his qualifications known. 3. He must have been "fourteen years a resident within the United States," so that he may be familiar with our established policy, and his countrymen acquainted with him. But "resident" is not here understood to mean that he should not have been absent on public business, or even temporarily absent on a journey. It only means that his permanent domicile must have been in the United States.

Compensation. (*b*) The compensation of the president is regu-

(*a*) This was first proposed near the close of the convention. Mad. Pap. 1486, 1516.

(*b*) When the question of compensating the president first came up in the convention, Dr. Franklin was in favor of his having nothing but his expenses, and presented an elaborate written argument to that effect. Mad. Pap. 770. It was next resolved that he should receive a fixed compensation out of the national treasury. Id. 860, 1160.

lated with a view to his independence and integrity. The constitution could not with prudence fix its amount absolutely, because circumstances might require it to be changed. But while it is left to Congress to regulate the amount, the constitution provides, that, being once fixed, it shall neither be *increased* nor *diminished* during that presidential term; and that the president shall not, during that period, receive any other emolument from the United States, or from either of the States. He is thus placed above pecuniary influence, operating either upon his hopes or fears. There is no avenue through which to address his venality. He can neither be allured nor intimidated, by pecuniary motives, to swerve from the line of his duty. By the act of 1789, Congress fixed the salary of the president at twenty-five thousand dollars, and that of the vice-president at five thousand dollars; and they have not since been altered. (*a*)

Oath. We have already seen, that all federal and State functionaries are required to take an oath "to support" the federal constitution, the form of which is prescribed by the act of 1789. This provision would include the president. But for some reason not apparent, there is a special oath prescribed for him in the constitution itself, by which he engages "to preserve, protect, and defend" the federal constitution. What difference there is between swearing to support the constitution, and swearing to preserve, protect, and defend it, cannot be readily perceived; and probably none was intended; although some executive parasites have affected to find, in this oath, something to indicate that the constitution intended to make the president its peculiar and paramount guardian. The State constitution requires all State functionaries to take an oath "to support" both constitutions, but provides no special oath for the governor. It also requires "an oath of office," to be taken before entering on duty; that is, an oath that the office shall be faithfully administered.

§ 41. **Powers and Duties of the President.** I shall consider this subject under several distinct heads.

Military Power. The president is "commander-in-chief of the army and navy of the United States, and of the militia of the several States, when called into the actual service of the United States." The governor is commander-in-chief of the army and navy of the State in time of war only, since they cannot exist in time of peace; and of the militia of the State, when not under the control of the president, by the above provision. The propriety of committing the ultimate command of the armed force of the country or State to a single hand, seems hardly to admit of dispute; and the very nature of the power demonstrates it to be peculiarly an executive power. It is not intended that the president or governor should necessarily take the field in person on all occasions; for this might

(*a*) By the act of March 3, 1873, the president's salary was made fifty thousand dollars per annum, and the vice-president's ten thousand per annum, both payable monthly.

interfere with other duties; but they are respectively made the sources whence orders are to emanate. Much apprehension was at first entertained, lest this *power of the sword* might make the executive too strong for a free government. But when we come to consider the power which the legislature exercises with respect to the army, navy, and militia, we shall find that abundant precaution has been taken to prevent the executive from abusing his share of power.

Consulting Power. (*a*) The president and governor are authorized to "require the opinion in writing of the principal officer in each of the executive departments, upon any subject relating to the duties of their respective offices." This provision seems to be a redundancy; for the power in question would result necessarily from the relation established between the chief executive officer, and those who are placed in subordination to him. Some of the State constitutions further authorize the executive to take the opinion of *the judges* on questions of law. But this seems unnecessary, because there is a special law officer appointed for this among other purposes; and improper because the judges may be afterwards called upon to try the very questions thus prejudged. (*b*)

Pardoning Power. (*c*) The president is authorized "to grant reprieves and pardons for offences, except in cases of impeachment." (*d*) There can be no doubt that the pardoning power ought to exist somewhere; because criminal justice can never be administered so perfectly, that every convict shall deserve to suffer the full and exact sentence which the law pronounces. Where then shall this benign attribute of Government be lodged? If there were no other objection to the legislature, it is not always in session; and the case has but just come from the hands of the judiciary. The executive, therefore, seems to be the only suitable depository. No doubt this power should be exercised with great circumspection, and may be exercised indiscreetly. But the executive is as likely to act judiciously as any other functionary. And should the power be sometimes abused, we have the satisfaction of knowing that the error must be on the side of mercy. In general, the pardoning power may be exercised before conviction as well as after. But the constitution of Ohio expressly confines it to cases *after conviction;* and perhaps it is well that the case

(*a*) See Mad. Pap. 1522–4. Instead of this, an executive council was warmly insisted upon, but negatived by a vote of 3 to 8.

(*b*) This provision is found only in the constitutions of Maine, New Hampshire, and Massachusetts.

(*c*) See Mad. Pap. 1433, 1587.

(*d*) By virtue of this clause, it has been held that the president may commute a sentence of death to imprisonment for life, and the condition of the pardon being accepted by the convict, his perpetual imprisonment is legal. *Ex parte* Wells, 18 Howard, 307. {Congress cannot limit this power; as by excluding the pardoned person from rights exercised by other persons, — such as prohibiting one in the late rebellion from practising in the United States courts after a pardon. *Ex parte* Garland, 4 Wall. 333, 380.}

should first be judicially investigated, in order that the exact truth may be known. In England, this power may be exercised in cases of impeachment; but these cases are properly excepted here, because the judgment in such cases is confined to removal from office and future disqualification; and cannot, as in England, involve a criminal punishment. In Ohio, the exercise of this power is guarded by requiring the governor to communicate to the assembly each case of reprieve, commutation, or pardon, with his reasons therefor.

The Treaty-making Power. (*a*) This, we have seen, is vested in the president, with the concurrence of two-thirds of the senate; and the States are prohibited from making treaties. But enough has already been said upon this topic.

Appointing Power. (*b*) The president is empowered "to nominate, and by and with the advice and consent of the senate, appoint ambassadors, other public ministers and consuls, judges of the supreme court, and all other officers of the United States, whose appointments are not herein otherwise provided for, and which may be established by law: but Congress may, by law, vest the appointment of such inferior officers as they think proper, in the president alone, in the courts of law, or in the heads of departments." Also, "to fill up all vacancies that may happen during the recess of the senate, by granting commissions which shall expire at the end of their next session." Also, "to commission all the officers of the United States." In these provisions the following points are worthy of notice:—

1. The nomination of officers is given to the president, because one person, in his situation, can select better than many. But a negative is given to the senate to protect this dangerous power against abuse. And it rests with Congress to determine whether there shall be any "inferior officers," whose appointment shall not require the consent of the senate. Congress has hitherto authorized "the courts of law" to appoint no officers but their clerk and reporter; (*c*) but has vested the appointment of a vast number of inferior officers, probably fifty thousand, "in the president alone," and "in the heads of departments;" and the enormous patronage thus placed at the disposal of the executive, without any immediate check against abuse, may be justly regarded as the most serious cause of apprehension existing in our political system. If corruption shall ever destroy the glorious fabric, it will enter through this avenue.

2. The executive can *create* no office for the purpose of filling it, because the constitution requires it to be "established by law." And as to the "filling of vacancies," the very term "vacancy"

(*a*) See *ante*, § 17.

(*b*) See Mad. Pap. 1422, 1432, 1519; Marbury *v.* Madison, 1 Cranch, 137.

(*c*) The circuit courts also appointed commissioners to take bail and affidavits in civil causes, and issue certificates for the rendition of fugitives from service. The chief-justice nominated registers in bankruptcy to be confirmed by the district judge.

implies a pre-existing office to be without an incumbent. Moreover, it must have occurred "during" the recess of the senate. And the word "happen" indicates some casualty, as death, resignation, or the like. It would seem, therefore, that the president cannot create a vacancy for the purpose of filling it, any more than an office; but on this point there is a difference of opinion.

3. When the senate have consented to an appointment, it is held to be not so far consummated, but that the president may refuse a commission; for he still has room to change his mind. But when the commission has actually been signed by him, and delivered to his secretary, the appointment is final and complete; and the secretary has no right to withhold the great seal, even by the order of the president, except where the officer is removable at his pleasure. (*a*)

4. The power of *removal* is nowhere expressly given to the president; and yet as none but judicial officers hold their offices during good behavior, this power must reside somewhere. The general opinion has been, that it is necessarily implied in the power of appointment, where the contrary is not expressed. But in 1789, it became a question, whether the consent of the senate was necessary to the removal of those officers whose appointment required their consent. After a very elaborate discussion in Congress, a small majority affirmed the power of removal to be in the president alone, and this construction, though in the opinion of many erroneous, has ever since been adopted in practice. (*b*)

5. An appointing power similar to that of the president, is conferred upon several of the governors. But the constitution of Ohio only authorizes our governor to fill vacancies during the recess of the assembly, in those offices to which the assembly have the appointment; and to commission officers generally. There is, indeed, a clause authorizing the assembly to confer on the governor the power of appointing officers not otherwise pro-

(*a*) See Marbury *v.* Madison, 1 Cranch, 137.

(*b*) {Blake *v.* United States, 103 U. S. 227.} The question whether the president has the power to remove a territorial judge has been raised, but has not been decided. United States *v.* Guthrie, 17 Howard, 284. On the 2d of March, 1867, Congress passed an act declaring that all persons who had or should be appointed to any civil office, by and with the advice and consent of the senate, should continue to hold such office until his successor was in like manner appointed, except as afterwards provided. Provided, that cabinet officers, during the term of the president by whom they were appointed, and for one month thereafter, should be subject to removal by and with the advice and consent of the senate. The act then proceeds to authorize the president during the recess of the senate, whenever he shall think there is good cause for such action, to suspend an officer until the next meeting of the senate, and appoint some one temporarily to fill the place. But the president must, within twenty days after the next meeting of the senate, report such suspension and the reasons for it to the senate, and, if the senate concur in such suspension, the president may then remove the officer and appoint some one else. If they refuse to concur, the suspended officer is thereby reinstated. The appointment of any person contrary to the provisions of this act is declared to be a high misdemeanor. This bill was vetoed by the president, and passed over the veto by Congress, and the violation of it by the president was the basis of several of the articles in the late impeachment.

vided for; but with the single exception of *notaries public*, other provision has always been made. So that, in general terms, our governor may be said to possess no appointing power, and no patronage whatsoever. (*a*)

Power as to Legislation. We have already considered the *veto power* (*b*) of the president, which constitutes his chief agency in legislation; and which our governor does not possess. But both the president and governor are connected with the legislative department by other provisions. They are required, from time to time, to communicate information respecting the general operations of government, and to recommend for consideration such measures as they shall deem expedient. This is a highly appropriate and beneficial provision. The executive is placed on an eminence whence he has opportunities of observing the errors and deficiencies in legislation, which are not possessed by the members of the legislature. The first two presidents, after the manner of the English king, met Congress in person, and delivered a speech orally, to which the two houses subsequently responded. But now the custom, both of the federal and State executives, is to send a written message, exhibiting the operations of the government during the past year, and communicating facts and suggestions to aid in legislation. The only remaining provisions under this head, are those which authorize the president and governor to convene the respective legislatures on extraordinary occasions; and, in case of disagreement between the two houses respecting the time of adjournment, to adjourn them.

Power as to Foreign Relations. In addition to the agency of the president in making treaties, and appointing and instructing our foreign ministers, it is his duty "to receive ambassadors and other public ministers" from foreign nations. No representative from a foreign power can act in that capacity here until his credentials have been examined, and he has been "*received*," or accredited by the president. And this function sometimes becomes one of exceeding delicacy and responsibility; for the refusal to receive a foreign minister is often deemed a justifiable cause of war. In cases, also, where, by civil commotion, a nation is divided into factions, each claiming the sovereign power, the reception of an ambassador from one would indirectly amount to a decision against the other. But, however important the conse-

(*a*) Under the constitution of 1851, this paragraph is not correct. The governor appoints the trustees of all the State institutions, and fills vacancies among the judges and some State officers. But his patronage is still insignificant. The legislature cannot under that constitution exercise any appointing power, and, on their undertaking to create a board to make appointments, the members of which board were designated in the act creating it, this was held to create an office and appoint to it, and therefore to be unconstitutional. State *v.* Kennon, 7 Ohio State, 546. {But the legislature can authorize a court or other body or officer to make an appointment. State *ex rel. v.* McCollister, 11 Ohio, 46; Walker *v.* Cincinnati, 21 Ohio State, 14.}

(*b*) See *ante*, § 36.

quences of a reception or refusal, the question is left solely to the discretion of the president. In fact, with the single exception of the check which the senate hold with respect to treaties, our foreign relations are under the exclusive control of the president.

Power of General Supervision. It is a duty enjoined upon the federal and State executives, "to see that the laws be faithfully executed." It would be dangerous, however, to treat this clause as conferring any specific power which they would not otherwise possess. It is rather to be regarded as a comprehensive description of the duty of the executive to watch with vigilance over all the public interests.

§ 42. **Subordinate Federal Officers.** In order to complete our view of the executive department, it remains that we take a brief notice of the subordinate executive officers, first of the federal, and then of the State government. To aid the federal executive in the discharge of his various and responsible duties, Congress has created six principal departments; namely, the *State*, *treasury*, *war*, *navy*, *interior*, and *post-office* departments. The heads of the first five are styled *secretaries;* and the last *postmaster-general.* By custom, these six officers, together with the *attorney-general*, constitute the president's *cabinet.* (*a*) They are appointed by the president, with the consent of the senate, and are removable at pleasure. With some few exceptions, each has the appointment of all the numerous subordinate officers, clerks, and other agents, employed in his department. But the scheme is too extensive and complicated to admit of a minute description. I can barely refer to the general duties intrusted to each of the departments.

State Department. This was created in 1789. The chief duties of the secretary of state are as follows: 1. To keep the custody of the originals of all treaties, laws, and other public documents; and furnish authentic copies thereof, when duly required. 2. To superintend the publication and distribution of the laws; to procure copies of all State laws; and to prepare and publish biennially a register of the names, residence, and compensation of all the civil, military, and naval officers of every degree; and of the names and condition of all public vessels. 3. To keep the great seal of the United States, and affix it, with his signature, to all commissions or other documents requiring it. 4. To superintend the *patent office;* which is attached to this department, and will be referred to hereafter. (*b*) 5. To conduct the foreign relations of the government. These relations are either political or commercial. Political relations with foreign nations are conducted through the agency of *ambassadors* or other public ministers; and commercial relations are conducted through the agency of *consuls*,

(*a*) Each of the cabinet under the act of March 3, 1873, receives $10,000 per annum.

(*b*) This duty was devolved on the department of the interior by the act of March 3, 1849.

who are stationed in all the principal ports and cities of the world. These foreign officers are all appointed by the president with the consent of the senate; but receive their instructions through the secretary of state, with whom they hold their correspondence. They are all recognized by the law of nations, and enjoy peculiar privileges and immunities wherever civilization extends. In like manner, the agents of foreign governments stationed here, conduct their intercourse through the secretary of state. So that, in a word, the whole *diplomacy* of the country is conducted by him, under the direction of the president.

Treasury Department. (*a*) This was also created in 1789. Its general duty is to manage the *fiscal operations* of the government. The secretary has cognizance of all matters connected with the *national revenue;* he has the general supervision of the *custom-houses* and their officers; and the *general land-office*, as we have already seen, is a branch of his department. (*b*) We shall see hereafter, that no money can be drawn from the treasury until Congress has made an appropriation for that purpose. But our security against the waste or improper use of the public money would be still imperfect, were it not for the admirable organization of this department; which is so framed as to establish the strictest accountability, and make the different officers act as checks upon each other. I have room barely to indicate its character. 1. There are *auditors*, whose business it is to examine all accounts with the treasury, and certify the balances; and for this purpose, certain classes of accounts are assigned to each auditor. 2. There are *comptrollers*, whose duty it is to revise the accounts certified by the different auditors, make a record of the balances, and certify them to the *register*. 3. It is the duty of the *register* to preserve these accounts thus certified to him; and also to keep an accurate account of all the receipts and expenditures of the government. 4. It is the duty of the *treasurer* to receive and keep the public money, until duly ordered to disburse it; which can only be upon warrants drawn by the secretary, countersigned by the proper comptroller and auditor, and recorded by the register. 5. By the act of 1830, the office of *solicitor* of the treasury was created, whose duty it is to superintend the litigation connected with this department. It would seem as if, under this arrangement, it would be impossible for embezzlement or peculation to extend far without detection. It is worthy of remark, that the secretary of the treasury is the only one of the heads of department who reports his proceedings directly to Congress; and to him they look for suggestions and estimates on which to base their appropriations.

(*a*) It was proposed in the convention that Congress should elect a treasurer by joint ballot, but this was negatived by a vote of 8 to 3. Mad. Pap. 1574, 1575.

(*b*) This office was transferred to the department of the interior, by the act establishing that department, of March 3, 1849.

War Department. This department was also created in 1789. The secretary has the general superintendence of *military affairs.* But as in this country the concerns of the army would not be sufficient of themselves to occupy a department, our *Indian relations* are made a branch of this department. (*a*)

Navy Department. This was not made a distinct department until 1798. It is much less extensive in its operations than either of the preceding. The secretary has the general superintendence of *naval affairs*, but no extra duties.

Interior Department. This was created in 1849. The title of the act speaks of it as the Home Department. The principal matters committed to its charge are patents, public lands, Indian affairs, pensions, the census, mineral lands, public buildings, and some matters connected with the District of Columbia.

Post-office Department. This department, though coeval with the government, derived its present organization chiefly from the act of 1810. Its patronage and influence are far more extensive than those of either of the other departments; as will be obvious from reflecting upon the immense number of postmasters and mail-contractors required in a country like ours. And there is no department of the government whose instrumentality in promoting the general happiness, is more directly felt.

§ 43. **Subordinate State Officers.** It now only remains that I describe the subordinate executive officers of this State. These may be divided into three classes; namely, *State officers*, *county officers*, and *township officers.* Of these in their order; and first, *State officers.* These are a *secretary*, *treasurer*, *auditor*, and *attorney-general.* These officers are all elected by the people for two years, except the auditor, whose term is four years. The *secretary* is keeper of the great seal of the State, and sealer of weights and measures. He has the custody of the public archives, and is the recording officer of the governor. He superintends the publication and distribution of the laws; and countersigns, seals, and registers all commissions and other documents requiring the great seal. The *auditor* and *treasurer* perform the duties suggested by their titles. The auditor examines and adjusts all accounts with the State, and issues orders for the amount upon the treasurer, who can pay out no money without such order. Each keeps a record of all orders issued and presented, and the originals, when paid, are filed as vouchers. It is further the duty of the State auditor to furnish the county auditors with all necessary forms and instructions relating to the revenue.

County Officers. These are, three *commissioners*, and *auditor*, *treasurer*, *assessor*, *recorder*, *surveyor*, *sheriff*, *coroner*, and *prosecuting attorney* (*b*) all elected by the people of each county. The

(*a*) The management of Indian affairs was transferred to the department of the interior, by the act of March 3, 1849.

(*b*) {To these must now be added in Hamilton County a county solicitor and five county *commissioners* hold their offices for three years; but one is elected each year. They may be regarded as the county legislators or managers. They have the care of the county property; of idiots and lunatics; of roads; and of paupers. They establish and alter townships and roads, and fix the amount of county taxes. But an appeal always lies from them to the court of common pleas. The *auditor* and *treasurer* are elected biennially; and their duties are so similar to those of the State auditor and treasurer, as to require no description. (*a*) The *assessor* is also elected biennially. (*b*) His duty is to assess the value of all taxable property, and report to the auditor: but an appeal lies from him to a *board of equalization*, composed of the commissioners, auditor, and assessor. The *recorder* is elected biennially; and his duty is to record all instruments for the conveyance or incumbrance of real property within the county; and make authenticated copies thereof when required. The *surveyor* is elected triennially, and his duty is to make and record surveys when required, and take testimonies in cases of disputed boundaries. The *sheriff* is elected biennially, but cannot hold the office more than four years out of six. His duties are exceedingly various. He is the executive officer of the courts; a conservator of the peace; and keeper of the jail. He also has to notify all county elections, and make returns thereof. The *coroner* is elected biennially. During a vacancy in the office of sheriff, or when the sheriff is interested, the coroner performs his duties; but his peculiar province is to hold inquests over dead bodies, when there is reason to suspect violence, and procure the verdict of a jury upon the cause of the death.

Township Officers. These are, three *trustees*, a *clerk*, *treasurer*, two *overseers of the poor*, and such number of *constables* as the trustees may direct. (*c*) These officers are all elected annually by the people of each township. *Township trustees* have nearly the same relation to the townships, that commissioners have to the counties; that is, they have the general supervision of township affairs. The general duties of the other officers are sufficiently indicated by their official designations.

It may be remarked in general, of all the officers before enumerated, that their fidelity is secured in three ways. *First*, by the official oath before described. *Secondly*, by an official bond, when there is any pecuniary responsibility. *Thirdly*, by a variety of penalties for misbehavior. There is also a general provision that they shall hold their offices until their successors are appointed. This provision saves much difficulty in case of a failure to elect

members of the Board of Control. The former attends to the law business of the county and of its offices, and the latter approve or disapprove contracts and expenditures and levying of taxes. Also a board of three infirmary directors in counties having an infirmary.}

(*a*) The duties of county auditor are prescribed in R. S. § 1013 *et seq.*

(*b*) The assessor is now elected annually, except district assessors, who only assess real estate, and are elected every ten years. R. S. § 2786.

(*c*) {Also an assessor and supervisors of roads. R. S. § 1448.}

on the proper day. I have been able barely to allude to their various duties. But enough has been said to indicate the general character of our municipal organization; and this is all I had in view.

LECTURE VIII.

JUDICIAL DEPARTMENT. (*a*)

§ 44. **Nature of this Department.** We have now reached that portion of our inquiries, which is of most immediate interest to the professional student. We are to consider the *organization* and *jurisdiction* of the judicial department of the federal and State government. To this department the people have committed the high functions of interpreting and applying the laws of the land, and of declaring them void when they contravene the provisions of the constitution. To this department, thus made to be pre-eminently the guardian of the laws, we resort in all cases of doubt

(*a*) The history of the proceedings of the convention respecting this department, is briefly as follows: It was resolved, without debate, that a national judiciary be established, to consist of one supreme tribunal, and of inferior tribunals. Mad. Pap. 791. A tenure during good behavior, and a fixed compensation, not to be increased nor diminished, were also agreed to without debate — id. 794. The subject of inferior tribunals was left to Congress, 8 to 2 — id. 800. The appointment of judges by the senate was agreed to unanimously — id. 855. A proposition that the executive should appoint, was negatived, 2 to 6 — id. 1134. A proposition that the executive should appoint with consent of the senate, was lost by a tie vote — id. 1135. The declaration that the compensation should not be increased was stricken out, 6 to 2 — id. 1136. It was at first proposed that the jurisdiction should extend to cases of revenue, impeachment, and questions involving the national peace and harmony — id. 860. Cases of impeachment were afterwards stricken out, and cases arising under the national laws added — id. 1137. On a subsequent debate, appointment by the president and senate was negatived, 3 to 6, and appointment by the senate affirmed by the same vote — id. 1171-5. Such was the condition of this department, as reported in the first plan of a constitution, except that there was a more specific enumeration of the cases of jurisdiction — id. 1238-9. A proposition to make the judges removable by the executive on the application of Congress, received but one vote — id. 1437. The last proposition was, that the judges should be appointed by the president and senate, which was adopted unanimously — id. 1520. For further information respecting the judicial department, see 2 Story, Const. chap. 38; 1 Kent, Com. lec. 14-18; Sergeant on Constitutional Law; Duponceau on Federal Jurisdiction; Conkling on the Jurisdiction and Practice of the U. S. Courts; 3 Black. Com. chap. 3-6; Kitchen on Courts; United States *v.* Ravara, 2 Dall. 297; Chisholm *v.* Georgia, 2 Dall. 419; Clarke *v.* Harwood, 3 Dall. 342; Wiscart *v.* Dauchy, 3 Dall. 321; Fowler *v.* Lindsey, 3 Dall. 411; Turner *v.* Bank of North America, 4 Dall. 8; New York *v.* Connecticut, 4 Dall. 1; Marbury *v.* Madison, 1 Cranch, 137; Clarke *v.* Bazadone, 1 Cranch, 212; United States *v.* Moore, 3 Cranch, 159; Owings *v.* Norwood, 5 Cranch, 344; Durousseau *v.* United States, 6 Cranch, 307; M'Intyre *v.* Wood, 7 Cranch, 504; Fairfax *v.* Hunter, 7 Cranch, 603; Martin *v.* Hunter, 1 Wheat. 304; Miller *v.* Nicholls, 4 Wheat. 311; Cohens *v.* Virginia, 6 Wheat. 264; United States *v.* Ortega, 11 Wheat. 467; Williams *v.* Norris, 12 Wheat. 117; Montgomery *v.* Hernandes, 12 Wheat. 129. Also, by way of comparison, the 3d, 4th, 5th, and 6th chapters of Blackstone's third book.

or controversy, as the final arbiter of our rights; and our lives, liberty, and property hang upon its decisions. It has been said that judges exercise no will of their own; but merely expound the legislative will. This is theoretically true; and if our laws were all legislative acts it might be true in point of fact. But in the present state of law, as before described, who can doubt that they exercise a high and vast discretion? Who that has ever observed the course, variety, and amount of litigation, even in the best-regulated community, will hesitate to say that judges exert a more immediate influence upon individual happiness, than any other public functionaries? Legislators, indeed, erect the temples of justice, but judges preside therein. The executive sees to the execution of the laws, when there is no doubt or difficulty; but these cases of doubt and difficulty are the very occasions when judicial interposition is required. What is the law applying to a given case? Is it constitutional? Has it been violated? What are the consequences? These are the questions which judges are ordained to answer, with reference to all the interests which men hold dear on earth, whenever these interests become the subject of controversy; and in making up their decisions, they are less limited by precise and peremptory instructions, than any other public officers, in the discharge of their prescribed duties. No wonder, therefore, that the framers of our government evinced a deep solicitude with respect to the structure of this department. They would have been unequal to their mighty undertaking, if they had not been deeply sensible how much its ultimate success must depend upon a well-constituted judiciary. And yet, while this department holds the happiness of individuals so much at its disposal, and may thus become so efficient an instrument of good, it is a gratifying reflection, that no perversion or abuse of its powers can ever make it an equally efficient instrument of evil. It holds neither the purse nor the sword of the community. It dispenses no patronage. It makes no rules but for individual cases. Its chief function is judgment, and that affects only the parties in litigation. If, therefore, it possessed the will it is utterly destitute of the power to subvert our liberties. The blow which is to destroy them, if it come at all, must come from one of the other departments. The judiciary can do little to promote such a catastrophe, but may do much to avert it.

We have seen that the want of a federal judiciary was one of the glaring defects of the confederation. The framers of the constitution, therefore, with this admonition before them, were unanimous in the opinion that such a department must be created. No one thought of leaving the interpretation of federal powers entirely to the State tribunals. There were some, however, who thought that it would be sufficient to provide one supreme federal tribunal, as a court of ultimate resort, and leave the rest to the States; but this number was small. The weight of opinion was greatly in favor of providing also for inferior federal courts, and thus forming a complete federal judiciary. Again, there were some in favor of imitating the structure of the English judiciary, as several of the States have done, by making the senate the court of final jurisdiction. But this opinion, also, yielded to the great maxim, that power, in order to be safe, must be divided among distinct departments. And the constitution accordingly declares, that "the judicial power of the United States shall be vested in one supreme court, and in such inferior courts as the Congress may from time to time ordain and establish;" and in another place, that "the Congress shall have power to constitute tribunals inferior to the supreme court." (*a*) This last provision is, of course, a pleonasm, and the most striking one in the constitution. It may now appear strange that this language of the constitution should ever have been supposed to leave it optional with Congress, to provide for a supreme and inferior courts or not. But this was once a question of much speculation; though it does not appear that Congress has ever regarded the provision otherwise than as strictly imperative. A question of more doubt has been, whether Congress is hereby required to vest the whole judicial power of the United States in the federal courts; or has an option to confer some portions of it upon the State courts. But it has been decided, that all the jurisdiction contemplated by the constitution must be vested in courts constituted by Congress. If the State courts have a concurrent jurisdiction in certain cases, it is because they possessed such jurisdiction originally, and the federal constitution did not take it away. They cannot derive it from any grant of Congress, because the constitution does not authorize Congress to confer it. (*b*) The result then is, that there must be one, and only one, supreme federal court; that the number and nature of the inferior courts are left to the discretion of Congress; and that, among these courts, all federal jurisdiction must be distributed. In this way has the constitution redeemed the pledge given in its preamble, "to establish justice."

§ 45. **Organization of the Federal Courts.** The organization of the federal courts, pursuant to the foregoing provisions, is as fol-

(*a*) The convention at first resolved that there should be one supreme, and inferior tribunals; but afterwards left the matter of inferior tribunals to Congress. Mad. Pap. 791, 800.

(*b*) Martin *v.* Hunter, 1 Wheat. 304; Prigg *v.* Commonwealth of Penn., 16 Peters, 539. See Moore *v.* People of Illinois, 14 How. 13. Nor can any State legislature confer jurisdiction upon courts of the United States. Greeley *v.* Townsend, 25 Cal. 604; Payne *v.* Hook, 7 Wall. 425. But whenever a general rule as to property, or personal rights, or injuries to either, is established by State legislation, its enforcement by a federal court in a case between proper parties is a matter of course; and the jurisdiction of the court in such case cannot be prohibited by the State legislature. So held in a case giving an action to the representatives of a man killed by negligence, and requiring the action to be brought in the State courts. Railway Co. *v.* Whitton, 13 Wall. 270. When a State law gives a right, a United States court in a proper case will give it effect. *Ex parte* McNiel, 13 Wall. 236. When a State has created a corporation, it cannot by any provision in its charter prevent its being sued in the courts of the United States, by a citizen of another State. Cowles *v.* Mercer Co., 9 Wall. 118.

lows: Besides the *supreme* court, Congress has created two inferior courts, denominated *circuit* and *district* courts. But for these three grades of courts, there are but two grades of judges; namely, *supreme* and *district* judges. (*a*) The supreme court consists of nine supreme judges; namely, one *chief justice*, and eight *associate justices*. (*b*) This court holds one session, annually, at the seat of government. For the purpose of organizing the inferior courts, the United States are parcelled off into *districts* and *circuits*. Each State forms at least one district, and sometimes more. For each of these districts, there is a district court, consisting of a single district judge, and held at least twice a year. Several of these districts constitute one circuit; for which there is a circuit court, held twice a year, in each district of the circuit, and composed of one supreme judge and the district judge. Thus, the circuit court holds an intermediate rank between the supreme and district courts. It was originally doubted, and not without reason, whether the supreme judges could constitutionally sit on the circuits at all; and perhaps it may become expedient to act upon this doubt, and create a distinct set of circuit judges.

§ 46. **Organization of the State Courts.** Here there is much diversity. In this State, the plan is similar to that of the federal courts. For three grades of courts there are but two grades of judges. The supreme court consists of five judges, who hold at least one session, annually, at the seat of government. For the purpose of organizing the other courts, the State is divided into common pleas *districts*, in each of which there are three common pleas judges. The *district court* for each district is held by one supreme judge, and the three common pleas judges. (*c*) In each county there is held a *common pleas court* by one of the common pleas judges, and each may be holding a court at the same time. There is next a *probate court* for each county, held by a single judge; and, lastly, *courts of justices of the peace for each township*.

§ 47. **Appointment, Tenure, Compensation.** The *mode of appointment* of judges is the next subject of inquiry. The federal conven-

(*a*) By the act of April 10, 1869, nine circuit judges were created with a salary of $5000 per annum, and the judges of the supreme court were required to hold court in each district in their circuit only once in two years.

(*b*) By the act of March 3, 1863, another associate justice was added, making nine associate justices. But by the act of July 3, 1866, no vacancy in the office of associate justice is to be filled until the number of associate justices is reduced to six. The supreme court is thereafter to consist of the chief justice and six associate justices, any four of whom shall be a quorum. One term is to be held annually at the seat of government, and such adjourned or special terms as may be necessary. By the act of April 10, 1869, the court was restored to its original number of one chief justice and eight associate justices, of whom six were to form a quorum.

(*c*) {By an amendment of Art. IV. secs. 1, 2, and 6 of the Constitution adopted in 1883 the legislature may increase the number of supreme judges, and lengthen the term, and may authorize the court to organize itself in divisions. The district courts are also abolished and circuit courts substituted. Pursuant to this amendment the legislature in 1884 divided the State into seven circuits, in each of which three circuit judges were elected, with terms of six years, and a salary of $4000; and every two years one circuit judge's term in each circuit expires and a successor is elected. A circuit judge can sit in circuits other than his own.}

tion at first resolved that the supreme judges should be appointed by the senate, without the nomination of the president. (*a*) But, as we have already seen, the constitution was ultimately so framed as to require them to be appointed by the president and senate. Congress has also required the inferior judges to be appointed in the same way. The excellence of this mode of appointment has been sufficiently dwelt upon. But if further illustration were wanted, it might be found in the contrast which our State constitution furnishes. Formerly, all our judges were elected by joint ballot of both houses of assembly, and our justices of the peace, by the people of each township. By the new constitution, all the judges are elected by the people. That the federal method is preferable, seems hardly to admit of doubt. One man can select better than many; and where there is a negative given to another body of men, there can be little danger of improper appointments.

Tenure of Office. (*b*) The *tenure of judicial office* comes next in order. We have seen, that a salutary republican jealousy has limited the legislative and executive functionaries to short and fixed terms of service. But various reasons seem to justify a departure from this policy, in relation to judicial officers. *First,* no danger is to be apprehended from a long term, because judicial power, from its nature, cannot enslave the people. *Secondly,* a proper discharge of judicial duty requires vast learning and experience, which a short term of service would furnish neither an adequate motive nor opportunity for acquiring. And *thirdly,* integrity, firmness, and independence, so indispensable to a well-organized judiciary, can only be secured by an independent tenure of office. Accordingly, in imitation of the best governments in Europe, and the best of our State constitutions, the federal constitution declares that "the judges both of the supreme and inferior courts, shall hold their offices during good behavior." The consequence is, that they are removable only by impeachment. They are thus placed beyond the reach of fear or favor, and have nothing to consult but the monitor within. The waves of popular commotion cannot reach them; and they have no occasion to court the good will of

(*a*) The first proposition was that Congress should appoint the judges, which was negatived by a vote of 9 to 2. Then, that the senate should appoint, which passed unanimously. Dr. Franklin mentioned the Scotch mode of a nomination by the bar, who would be sure to select the best lawyer to get him out of the way. Mad. Pap. 792, 855. Then, that the executive should appoint them, which was negatived, 2 to 6 — id. 1131–4. Then, that the executive should appoint them with the consent of the senate, which was lost by a tie vote — id. 1135. A subsequent proposition to the same effect was debated, and negatived, 3 to 6, and appointment by the senate affirmed, 6 to 3 — id. 1171–5. But ultimately, appointment by the president and senate was carried unanimously — id. 1520.

(*b*) There seems to have been no diversity of opinion in the convention upon this subject. Mad. Pap. 794. A proposition that judges should be removable by the president, on the application of Congress, received but one vote — id. 1436. By the act of April 10, 1869, any judge over seventy having held his commission at least ten years may resign, and still receive his salary for the term of his natural life. By the act of March, 1873, the salary of the chief justice was made $10,500 per annum, and of each of the associate justices $10,000 per annum.

the other departments. From the secure elevation on which they are thus placed, all disturbing influences being removed, they are left to the calm and fearless exercise of unbiassed judgments; (*a*) and there is a life before them in which to perfect themselves for duty. But here again our State constitution offers a contrast. Our judges are elected for only five years, and our justices of the peace for only three. And is it probable, with such a tenure of office, that they will be as independent, or as well qualified, as with the tenure of good behavior? There can be but one answer; and yet, when we look to some of our sister States, we have reason to be thankful that we have not annual elections. There is a provision in some of the State constitutions, making judges removable on the address of both branches of the legislature. And such a proposition was made with respect to the federal judges, but the convention wisely rejected it.

Compensation. The next topic is the *compensation* of judges. This should be so large as to secure the best abilities; and so regulated as to co-operate with the other provisions, in rendering the judges independent. Accordingly, the federal constitution provides that the judges "shall, at stated times, receive for their services a compensation, which shall not be diminished during their continuance in office." It may, however, be *increased*, since this is not prohibited. (*b*) This provision wisely proceeds upon the maxim, that the power over one's subsistence, is a power over his will; and that the power to diminish it, is much more efficient to subdue his will, than the power to increase it. Accordingly, the judicial salaries are so regulated, that while they may be prospectively altered from time to time, as circumstances may require, yet no judge can be required to receive a less salary than that with which he went into office. And by our State constitution the salary can neither be increased nor diminished during the term of service.

§ 48. **Subordinate Officers of Courts.** (*c*) To complete our view of the organization of courts, it remains that I speak briefly of the subordinate officers. These are, the *recording officer*, the *executive officer*, and the *managers of causes*. Of these, in their order.

Recording Officer. This officer is usually styled *clerk*, but sometimes *prothonotary*. His regular duties are, to keep a record of all judicial proceedings; to keep the seal of the court, and affix it to all papers requiring it; and to issue all writs proceeding from the

(*a*) A judge of a court of general jurisdiction is not liable to a judicial action for his judicial acts, even when they are in excess of his jurisdiction, and alleged to have been done maliciously or corruptly. It is only a clear absence of all jurisdiction over the subject, which would render the act a usurpation of authority, that can render him liable. For such act, no excuse is permissible. Bradley *v.* Fisher, 13 Wall. 335, 352. {See Article on Liability of Officers acting in a Judicial Capacity, 15 Am. Law Rev. 427, 491.}

(*b*) At first, the convention resolved that it should neither be increased nor diminished. Mad. Pap. 794. Afterwards, the prohibition to increase was stricken out, 6 to 2 — id. 1136, 1437.

(*c*) 1 Kent, Com. 306–9.

court. The supreme federal court and the district court have the appointment of their respective clerks; and the clerk of the district court is also clerk of the circuit court for that district. These clerks are appointed for no definite period, and are, of course, removable at pleasure. Our State courts, likewise, formerly appointed their respective clerks for each county, who held their offices for seven years, unless removed for misbehavior. But now there is a clerk elected for three years in each county, who is clerk of all the courts held in the county, except the probate court and courts of justices of the peace. His compensation is derived from fees.

Executive Officer. (*a*) The *executive officer* is variously styled *marshal*, *sheriff*, or *constable*, according to the court in which he officiates. The executive officer of the federal courts is a marshal, who is appointed for each district, by the president and senate, for the term of four years, but removable at pleasure by the president. The executive officer of the State courts is the sheriff, who is elected biennially by the people of each county, as before described. The executive officer of the courts of justices of the peace is the constable, who is elected annually by the people of each township, as before described. The various duties of these officers are minutely defined by law, and will be often referred to hereafter. It is sufficient here to say, that all writs, orders, judgments, and decrees of their respective courts, are by them carried into execution. Their compensation is derived from fees, and they are under bonds for fidelity.

Attorneys. (*b*) Although parties are permitted to manage their own causes, if they so wish, yet the successful conducting of litigation involves so much formality and technicality, as generally to require a set of men educated for that express purpose. In England, these men are variously styled *attorneys*, *solicitors*, *advocates*, *counsellors*, *barristers*, and *sergeants*, according to their rank and duties. But in this country, we have but the two classes, *attorneys* and *counsellors*. In the admiralty courts they are styled *proctors* and *advocates*. These classes are recognized in the supreme federal court, and in some of the State courts; but not in the inferior federal courts, nor in the courts of this State. Where the distinction between attorneys and counsellors prevails, it consists principally in this: that attorneys do all things necessary to prepare causes for hearing, and counsellors conduct them at the hearing. The requisites for admission at the bar are prescribed by law. In order to practise in the supreme federal court, as attorney or counsellor, one must have practised three years in the highest court of the State to which he belongs. The inferior federal courts merely require a previous admission to the State courts. The requisites for admission to the State courts vary materially in the different

(*a*) 1 Black. Com. 339; 1 Kent, Com. 309; Gwynne on Sheriffs; Murfree on Sheriffs.

(*b*) See 3 Black. Com. 25; 1 Kent, Com. 306.

States. In Ohio they are as follows: The applicant must be of age, a citizen of the United States, and of good moral character; he must regularly have studied law somewhere for two years; and must have resided one year within the State. There is an exception, however, to this last requisition, when the applicant has been in practice two years in another State. These requisites may be evinced by the certificate of some attorney in the State; and they entitle the applicant to an *examination*. This is conducted either by two judges of the supreme court, or by a committee of the bar appointed by them. If the applicant be found qualified, the oath of office is administered, and his admission recorded. He is thereby authorized to act both as attorney and counsellor at law, and solicitor in chancery, in all the State courts. (*a*) The only exception to the necessity of being thus admitted, is that of attorneys resident in other States, which permit our attorneys to practise in their courts. Attorneys are regarded as officers of court, acting under the supervision of the judges, who have authority upon good cause, to suspend them from practice. (*b*) They are not required to produce a special authority from their clients, it being always presumed until the contrary appears. (*c*) They are responsible

(*a*) By R. S. § 561, students of incorporated law colleges of Ohio, whose qualifications have been certified to by a committee of attorneys appointed by the district court, and examining such students at the commencement exercises of such college, may be admitted without further examination.

(*b*) If an attorney has applied to his own use money collected for his client, it is good cause to suspend him from practice. State *v.* Hand, 9 Ohio, 42. {So is threatening a judge out of court for his action in court. Bradley *v.* Fisher, 13 Wall. 335; People *v.* Green, 4 Colorado, 473; s. c. 7 id. 237. So is participating in a lynching or riot. *Ex parte* Wall, 107 U. S. 265.} The court will not act upon charges made against an attorney, unless they be under oath. *Ex parte* Burr, 9 Wheat. 529. That an attorney has been stricken from the rolls of one court for a contempt, is not a sufficient reason for excluding him from another court. *Ex parte* Tillinghast, 4 Peters, 108. Courts determine the qualifications of attorneys and the causes for their removal, except as limited by statute. *Ex parte* Secombe, 19 How. 9. An attorney is bound to disclose to his client if he have any adverse interest. Williams *v.* Reed, 3 Mason, 405.

(*c*) An attorney does not require a written appointment from his client as authority to appear for him. Osborn *v.* Bank U. S., 9 Wheat. 738; Pillsbury *v.* Dugan, 9 Ohio, 117; Hirshfield *v.* Landman, 3 E. D. Smith, 208. But see King of Spain *v.* Oliver, 2 Wash. C. C. R. 429. In general, the act of an attorney in court binds his client. Treasurer of Champaign *v.* Norton, 1 Ohio, 270. Otherwise, if he appeared without authority. Critchfield *v.* Porter, 3 Ohio, 518. {Secession of the client's State, and a state of war, terminates the right of the attorney in a loyal state to enter an appearance or to act for the client. Pennywit *v.* Foote, 27 Ohio State, 600.} Appearance by attorney supersedes the necessity of process; but if an attorney appear without authority, he is answerable in damages. Field *v.* Gibbs, 1 Peters C. C. R. 155, 455. If an attorney improperly sue out process, he may be ordered to pay costs. Kerr *v.* Bank of Chillicothe, Wright, 737. An attorney, as such, has no authority to make a compromise for his client. Holker *v.* Parker, 7 Cranch, 436; Mayor *v.* Foulkrod, 4 Wash. C. C. R. 511 {Whipple *v.* Whitman, 13 R. I. 512; North Whitehall *v.* Keller, 100 Penn. St. 105; Robinson *v.* Murphy, 69 Ala. 543}. His authority does not cease with recovering judgment. Langdon *v.* Castleton, 30 Vt. 285: McDonald *v.* Todd, 1 Grant (Penn.), 17. He may issue execution, though he cannot discharge it without satisfaction. Union Bank *v.* Geary, 5 Peters, 99; Erwin *v.* Blake, 8 Peters, 18. Nor can he receive the notes of third persons in discharge of it, or in payment of a debt, without special authority. Jones *v.* Ranson, 3 Ind. 327; Jeter *v.* Haviland, 27 Mo. 252. Nor sell the judgment. Campbell's Appeal, 29 Penn. State, 401. Nor release nor postpone the lien on lands acquired by it. Wilson *v.* Jennings, 3 Ohio State, 528. {An attorney employed to collect a note is not authorized to agree for the sale of chattels securfor reasonable diligence and skill, (*a*) and are generally, though not always, permitted to regulate their own charges. (*b*) To insure the utmost confidence and unreserve on the part of their clients, in giving them the necessary information, attorneys are excused from testifying in court, as to anything professionally confided to them. (*c*)

Government Attorneys. In all criminal proceedings, government is a party to the prosecution; and not unfrequently in civil proceedings. Hence the necessity of a special law officer to attend to its interests. The *attorney-general* of the United States is the regular law adviser of the president and heads of departments, and has the management of all causes in the supreme court, in which the federal government is concerned. There is, likewise, a *district-attorney* for each district, to attend to causes in the circuit and district courts. These officers are appointed by the president and senate. A similar arrangement exists in most of the States. In Ohio, there is an *attorney-general* for the State, and *prosecuting attorneys* for each county, whose duty it is to conduct all criminal proceedings, and all civil suits, in which the State is interested. These officers are elected by the people. (*d*)

ing it. Beard *v.* Westerman, 32 Ohio State, 29, 32. Nor to release a surety. Stoll *v.* Sheldon, 13 Nebraska, 207.}

(*a*) The retainer of an attorney does not imply an undertaking to recover a judgment, but only to use the diligence in the ordinary course. Gallaher *v.* Thompson, Wright, 466. He is liable for negligence and want of reasonable skill. Goodman *v.* Walker, 30 Ala. 482 ; Wilson *v.* Coffin, 2 Cush. 316 ; Parker *v.* Rolls, 28 Eng. L. & Eq. 424.

(*b*) If there be no special agreement for a fee, the attorney may recover the usual compensation. Christy *v.* Douglas, Wright, 485. An attorney's fees are not included in the term costs. McDonald *v.* Page, Wright, 121. An attorney may contract to receive part of the property recovered as a contingent compensation ; but a stipulation that no compromise shall be made without his consent, is illegal and void. Key *v.* Vattier, 1 Ohio, 132 ; {Weakly *v.* Hall, 13 id. 167. And a contract by which the client resigns all control of the claim, and is not to be liable for costs, is champertous and void. Stewart *v.* Welch, 41 Ohio State, 483. But even in such case, if the action is brought in the client's name, his right to a judgment against his debtor is not affected by the champertous agreement with his attorney. Burnes *v.* Scott, 117 U. S. 582.} An attorney has a lien on the judgment for his costs. Diehl *v.* Friester, 37 Ohio State, 473, 477 ; Mooney *v.* Lloyd, 5 Serg. & R. 412 ; Woods *v.* Verry, 4 Gray, 357 ; Currier *v.* B. & M. R. R. Co., 37 N. H. 223 ; Ward *v.* Wordsworth, 1 E. D. Smith, 598 ; Rooney *v.* Second Avenue R. R. Co., 18 N. Y. 368. *Contra*, in Indiana, Hill *v.* Brinkley, 10 Ind. 102. After he has voluntarily withdrawn from a case, he cannot withhold a paper and prevent it from being used as evidence. White *v.* Harlow, 5 Gray, 463. {On the subject of an attorney's lien for fees on his client's papers, property, or money in his hands, see article by Mr. Leonard A. Jones in 20 Am. Law Review, p. 726 (1886).}

(*c*) R. S. § 5241 ; Andrews *v.* Solomon, 1 Peters C. C. 356 ; Chirac *v.* Reinicker, 11 Wheat. 280 ; Hemenway *v.* Smith, 28 Vt. 701 ; Thompson *v.* Kilbourne, 28 id. 750 ; Coon *v.* Swan, 30 id. 6; Allen *v.* Harrison, 30 id. 219 ; Alderman *v.* The People, 4 Mich. 414 ; Martin *v.* Anderson, 21 Geo. 301 ; Parish *v.* Gates, 29 Ala. 254. The same rule extends to the clerk of an attorney. Foster *v.* Hall, 12 Pick. 93 ; Landsberger *v.* Gorham, 5 Cal. 450 ; Sibley *v.* Waffle, 16 N. Y. 183.

(*d*) In England there is no public officer answering to our prosecuting attorneys whose duty it is to attend to general criminal prosecutions. They are conducted by counsel retained by the prosecuting witness. Bills to provide such officers have been several times introduced in parliament, and the subject largely discussed, but all have yet failed to pass. Several interesting articles on the subject may be found in 2 & 3 Jurist (N. S.).

§ 49. **Jurisdiction of the Federal Courts.** (*a*) From the organization of the federal and State courts, we pass next to their *jurisdiction.* When a case is within the power of a given court, the court is said to have jurisdiction of it. This jurisdiction may either be *exclusive* or *concurrent.* A court is said to have exclusive jurisdiction of a case, when it cannot be brought before any other court; and to have concurrent jurisdiction, when the case may be brought before some other court. Again, jurisdiction may be either *original* or *appellate.* The jurisdiction is original in a given court, when the first proceedings may be commenced in that court; and it is appellate, when the proceedings must be commenced originally in some other court, and are thence transferred, for revision or correction, to the court in question. The regular methods of transferring a cause to a court of appellate jurisdiction, are by *appeal* or *by writ of error*, which will be described hereafter. It is sufficient here to say, that an appeal removes the cause entirely and in all respects, subjecting the facts, as well as the law, to a re-hearing in the court above. Whereas, a writ of error leaves the facts as determined in the court below, and only carries up questions of law for re-examination. Such being the nature of jurisdiction in general, I shall examine the jurisdiction of the federal and State courts, in each of these points of view.

In considering the jurisdiction of the federal courts, two questions arise. *First*, how much jurisdiction is conferred upon them altogether? *Secondly*, how is this jurisdiction apportioned among them? And first, as to the whole amount of federal jurisdiction. If the United States had been organized into one consolidated nation, there would have been no difficulty in determining how far the judicial power should extend. It would manifestly have embraced all subjects of judicial cognizance without exception; and of course there would have been no necessity for a specification. But the federal government being limited, as before shown, to certain specific national objects, this limitation applies as much to the judicial as to the other departments; it being an obvious maxim that the three departments should be co-extensive in their powers. The federal constitution does not, however, merely assert this general proposition and there stop; but, in conformity with its general plan, it proceeds to enumerate specifically all the objects to which the judicial powers shall extend. These are included under the nine following heads: —

1. "To all cases in law and equity, arising under this constitution, the laws of the United States, and treaties made or to be made

(*a*) The convention at first resolved, that the jurisdiction should extend to the collection of revenue, impeachments, and questions involving the national peace and harmony. — Mad. Pap. 860. The matter of impeachments was afterwards stricken out, and cases arising under national laws added — id. 1137–8. But in the first draft of the constitution, a specific enumeration of the cases of jurisdiction was contained — id. 1238, 1438–40. See Conkling on the Jurisdiction and Practice of the U. S. Courts; Duponceau on Federal Jurisdiction; 1 Kent, Com. lec. 15–17.

under their authority." (*a*) We have already seen that the federal constitution, laws, and treaties constitute the supreme law of the whole Union. And hence the clear propriety of making them cognizable by that judiciary, which alone represents the whole Union. The language, however, requires a *case* to be made; that is, a suit must be instituted, according to the regular course of judicial proceedings, to be described hereafter. The federal judges cannot be consulted upon mere abstract questions. The case may be either in law or equity, and of a civil or criminal nature. When such a case is presented, growing out of, or involving any provision of the federal constitution, laws, or treaties, it falls, for that reason, within the jurisdiction of the federal courts, without reference to the parties.

2. "To all cases affecting ambassadors, other public ministers, and consuls." The propriety of this is obvious, from the consideration, that these officers, representing foreign nations, are entitled to be treated according to the law of nations; and questions involving the law of nations ought clearly to be cognizable by the national judiciary.

3. "To all cases of admiralty and maritime jurisdiction." (*b*)

(*a*) See Osborn *v.* Bank of U. S., 9 Wheat. 738. {It seems to be now decided by the Supreme Court of the United States (1886), in *Ex parte* Royal, that a prisoner held, or convicted, under State laws, or by State authorities, if proceeded against in violation of the United States constitution, laws, or treaties, may be discharged by a circuit court of the United States, on *habeas corpus*. This doctrine has encountered criticism in legal periodicals.}

(*b*) See 3 Black. Com. 106; 1 Kent, Com. lec. 17; The Thomas Jefferson, 10 Wheat. 428; The Orleans *v.* Phœbus, 11 Peters, 175; Waring *v.* Clarke, 5 How. 441; People's Ferry Co. of Boston *v.* Beers, 20 How. 393. Judiciary Act of 1789, sec. 9, 1 Stat. at Large, 77; Act of 1845, 5 Stat. at Large, 726; The Propeller Genesee Chief *v.* Fitzhugh, 12 How. 443. This last case was decided in 1851. It overrules the preceding cases, and extends the admiralty jurisdiction to all navigable waters. And see M'Ginnis *v.* The Pontiac, 5 McLean, 359; Ward *v.* The Ogdensburg, 5 McLean, 622; Rossiter *v.* Chester, 1 Douglass (Mich.), 154. As to the jurisdiction of the United States on navigable waters within the United States, see People *v.* Tyler, 7 Mich. 161. In the cases of the Moses Taylor and the Ad. Hine *v.* Trevor, 4 Wall. 555, it was decided by the Supreme Court of the United States, in 1866, that the water-craft laws of the different States, so far as they give admiralty powers, are unconstitutional, as the grant of admiralty and maritime jurisdiction in the constitution to the courts of the United States is exclusive. This decision will undoubtedly largely increase the business of these courts, particularly upon the western waters. It does not exclude the State courts from acting by common-law remedies, or in cases not of admiralty jurisdiction. {Contracts for building, or for furnishing labor or materials in building a vessel, are not maritime contracts, and are cognizable in the State courts. Scow M. Tuttle *v.* Buck, 23 Ohio State, 565. But contracts for repairing or supplying a vessel in her home port are maritime contracts, and, as by the maritime law no lien arises therefrom, the State laws may give a lien; but the jurisdiction to enforce such lien is exclusively an admiralty one, and not cognizable by the State courts. The Lottawanna, 21 Wall. 558; Steamer Petrel *v.* Dumont, 28 Ohio State, 602.}

The lien laws have been acted on by State tribunals for many years, and have been assumed to be valid, and it seems singular that the point should never have been presented for decision before. Yet the conclusion reached seems to flow naturally and necessarily from the previous decisions of the United States courts, as is clearly shown in the opinions in the cases cited above. Some of the language in the opinions in these cases would seem to deny the power of the State legislatures to authorize their courts to maintain suits *in rem* in matters outside of admiralty jurisdiction. But in such cases it would seem that the State legislatures should have full control over the

Up to the year 1851, these cases were understood to be limited to the "*High Seas*," meaning tide-waters only, which constituted the grand highway of nations; but now the presence of *tides* is no longer the criterion; and this jurisdiction is held to embrace all the public navigable waters, whether rivers or lakes, within the United States. The subjects of admiralty jurisdiction will be considered in the lecture on Admiralty Proceedings.

4. "To controversies to which the United States shall be a party." This provision implies that the United States may sue; but does not authorize them to be sued. The presumption is held to be that government will always do right to individuals without suit; but that individuals may not be so ready to do right towards government. And hence the propriety of authorizing government to sue but not to be sued. This doctrine may be politic, but it is not magnanimous. However, the propriety that government should sue in its own courts when it does sue, is manifest.

5. "To controversies between two or more States." (*a*) This provision proceeds upon the supposition that where two States are con-

remedies of their State courts, and in Allen *v.* Newbury, 21 How. 246, and Maguire *v.* Card, 21 How. 25, it was held that admiralty had no jurisdiction over vessels plying wholly within the waters of a State. If so, it would appear that a State statute allowing suits *in rem* against such vessels for supplies furnished would not conflict with this provision of the constitution. But in the case of the Mary Washington *v.* Ayers, 5 Am. L. Reg. 692; s. c. 1 Abb. U. S. 1; Chase, C. J., says, on the authority of the Genesee Chief, 12 How. 454, and the Propeller Commerce, 1 Black, 578, that United States courts have jurisdiction in admiralty over contracts of affreightment on navigable waters wholly within a State, and that Allen *v.* Newbury turns upon the language of the act of 1845; also The Elmira Shepherd, 8 Blatch. 341. And in the case of The Belfast, 7 Wall. 624, it was held by the supreme court that a proceeding *in rem* against a vessel for goods lost in transit on navigable waters, though the contract was between citizens of the same State, and for a voyage wholly within the limits of a single State, is an admiralty proceeding, and the United States courts have exclusive jurisdiction thereof, and a State statute authorizing similar proceedings in a State court is unconstitutional. This case intimates a distinction between the jurisdiction on the lakes and waters flowing into them under the act of 1845, and tide-water and the streams flowing into it under the old judiciary act. But the question coming directly before the court in the case of The Eagle, 6 Wall. 15, it was declared that the act of 1845 does not limit the jurisdiction of the United States courts on the lakes and the navigable waters connected therewith, but has simply become entirely inoperative by virtue of subsequent decisions, and the courts possess, under the judiciary act of 1789, the same forms as to admiralty proceedings on such waters as they have on tide-water, and navigable waters connected therewith. These two cases seem finally to settle the doctrine.

But the expressions in these opinions relate solely to suits *in rem*, and must be so limited, as is shown by the case of Leon *v.* Galceran, 11 Wall. 185, 192, where the court held a suit *in personam* for mariners' wages maintainable at common law in a State court, and that the vessel might be seized or attached in such suit, when the State law gives a lien similar to the maritime lien, for the purpose of subjecting it to the judgment.

The question as to what is a navigable river has been largely discussed in the recent cases, under the registry laws which require all boats on the navigable waters of the United States to take out a license, {and will be found considered hereafter in notes under § 126}.

(*a*) It was proposed in the convention, that this, and the next class of controversies, should be decided by a singular species of arbitration, conducted under the supervision of the senate; but this proposition was negatived, 8 to 2. Mad. Pap. 1236, 1416. See Florida *v.* Georgia, 17 How. 478. Virginia *v.* West Virginia, 11 Wall. 39.

tending, the courts of neither are in a condition favorable to the administering of impartial justice to the other; whereas, the federal judiciary can be under no bias of self-interest. Besides, the general harmony is hereby better secured.

6. "To controversies between a State and citizens of another State." (*a*) Here, again, it is supposed that the State tribunals might not be impartial; and the national judiciary is therefore selected. It was early made a question, whether this provision authorized suits *by individuals against a State*, or only by a State against individuals. The federalists thought that it authorized only the latter; but the supreme court decided that it authorized both. This decision occasioned the eleventh amendment of the federal constitution, which declares that "the judicial power of the United States shall not be construed to extend to any suit in law or equity, commenced or prosecuted against one of the United States, by citizens of another State, or by citizens or subjects of any foreign State." Accordingly, no individual can now sue a State, unless it be in the courts of that State, and by its own consent. (*b*) But it has been decided, that where a State first sues an individual, and afterwards, in the progress of that suit, becomes *defendant in error*, this, not being an original suit against the State, is not prohibited by the amendment. (*c*)

(*a*) Chisholm *v.* Georgia, 2 Dall. 419; Cohens *v.* Virginia, 6 Wheat. 264.

(*b*) The sovereign power which creates a court, and from which that court therefore derives all its power, cannot be sued therein except by its own express consent. Therefore the United States courts cannot have jurisdiction in a suit against the United States, unless it be given to them by an express law. Such power is now given to the court of claims, which is created expressly to investigate the validity of claims against the United States. Nor can a State be sued in its own courts, unless there are similar statutes giving jurisdiction in such cases. Naturally, however, when the sovereign power begins a suit against one of its citizens in its own courts, the court, as is stated in the text, will have jurisdiction over a writ of error, by which the sovereign becomes, for the time being, the defendant, for the sovereign having voluntarily submitted his rights to the courts must abide by their final decision, but even in such cases the court could not grant affirmative relief against the sovereign. It could only deny the relief asked by it. So, too, when a set-off is pleaded, though it might be allowed, no judgment could be entered for the balance found due by the jury. Case *v.* Terrill, 11 Wall. 199. *A fortiori*, under our system of government, a State court cannot have jurisdiction in a suit against the United States. Thus when vessels were built for the United States, a State court could not enforce a lien to material-men for the materials used in their construction, given by the laws of the State where they were built. Briggs *v.* Life Boats, 11 Allen, 157.

Where the statute of a State has given the State courts jurisdiction in certain cases against the State, the repeal or modification of that statute will affect even cases pending at the time of such repeal or modification. The permission to sue the State was only a favor granted, not a contract. Beers *v.* Arkansas, 20 How. 527; Bank of Washington *v.* Arkansas, 20 How. 530.

(*c*) Where several persons are joined as parties, they must be such that each one of the plaintiffs could sue or be sued by each one of the defendants, and this rule extends to the members of a corporation. See Hope Insurance Company *v.* Boardman, 5 Cranch, 57; Bank of United States *v.* Deveaux, 5 Cranch, 61; Commercial Bank of Vicksburg *v.* Slocomb, 14 Peters, 60. These cases have been overruled, and it is now held that a corporation is a citizen of the State where it was created and does its business, for the purposes of suing and being sued, although some of its members are not citizens of such State. Louisville, &c. R. R. Co. *v.* Letson, 2 How. 497; Rundle *v.* Delaware & Raritan Canal Co., 14 id. 95, 96; Northern Ind. R. R. Co. *v.* Mich. Cen. R. R. Co., 15 id. 233; Covington Drawbridge Co. *v.* Shepherd, 20 id. 227, 21 id.

7. "To controversies between citizens of different States." (*a*) The word "citizens," here means *residents*, there being no such thing as State citizenship. The reason of this provision is of the same nature as of the two preceding.

8. "To controversies between citizens of the same State, claiming lands under grants from different States." Here the rights of the two States to make the grant, would be put in issue; and it is therefore supposed that the courts of neither State would be in a condition to decide without bias.

9. "To controversies between a State or the citizens thereof, and foreign States, citizens, or subjects." This provision supposes that neither foreign States nor foreign individuals could have the same assurance of impartial justice from the tribunals of a State with which, or with whose citizens, the controversy was depending, as from the federal tribunals.

It will be observed, that of these nine classes of cases, only the first and third have reference to the subject-matter of controversy. In the remaining seven, the jurisdiction depends upon the character of the parties alone, without regard to the subject-matter. Hence results the important consequence, that the jurisdiction of the federal courts embraces every possible variety of litigation. And it is this which renders the decisions of the supreme federal court so exceedingly valuable as a body of general law, having the very highest authority throughout the whole Union. These nine classes include all the cases of which the federal courts can entertain jurisdiction; so that its extent is thus definitely ascertained. (*b*) And the next inquiry is, how it has been *apportioned* among the federal courts.

Jurisdiction of the Supreme Court. This court being intended chiefly for the tribunal of last resort, exercises very little original jurisdiction. The constitution declares that, "in all cases af-

113 {Muiler *v.* Dows, 94 U. S. 444; National Steamship Co. *v.* Tugman, 106 U. S. 118}; Shelby *v.* Hoffman, 7 Ohio State, 450. {And a condition in a State statute, that a foreign corporation shall waive the right to remove cases to the federal courts before doing business in the State, is not enforceable. Home Ins. Co. *v.* Moore, 20 Wall. 445; Railway Passenger Assur. Co. *v.* Pierce, 27 Ohio State, 155.} But a corporation is not a citizen of the State creating it within the meaning of that section of the constitution, securing to citizens of one State all the privileges and immunities of citizens in another State. A State may therefore legally impose on foreign corporations coming to do business within it, taxes and requirements different from those to which their home corporations are subjected. {Cooper Mfg. Co. *v.* Ferguson, 113 U. S. 727} Paul *v.* Virginia, 8 Wall. 168; Ducal *v.* Chicago, 10 Wall. 410; Railway Co. *v.* Whitton, 13 Wall. 270. A municipal corporation, such as a county, may be sued by a citizen of another State in the courts of the United States, and the statute of the State creating it cannot prevent this. Cowles *v.* Mercer Co., 9 Wall. 118.

(*a*) In Scott *v.* Sanford, 19 How. 393, it was maintained by a portion of the court, that persons of pure African blood, whose ancestors were imported into this country and sold as slaves, cannot be citizens within the meaning of this clause, so as to sue in the federal courts. But see Tannis *v.* Doe, 21 Ala. 454; United States *v.* Ritchie, 17 How. 525; State *v.* Manuel, 4 Dev. & Bat. 24, 25; State *v.* Newsome, 5 Iredell, 253; Fisher *v.* Dabbs, 6 Yerg. 126, 127; 2 Kent, Com. 258, note (*b*). See article in Law Reporter for June, 1857, on the case of Dred Scott.

(*b*) No act of a State legislature can confer jurisdiction upon the courts of the United States. Greeley *v.* Townsend, 25 Cal. 604.

fecting ambassadors, other public ministers, and consuls, and those in which a State shall be a party, the supreme court shall have original jurisdiction." And on the principle, that the affirmation of a power in specified cases, excludes it in all cases not specified, it has been held that the original jurisdiction of the supreme court comprehends these cases only, and Congress can extend it no further. It has also been held, that even in these specified cases, original jurisdiction is not confined absolutely to the supreme court, but may be vested in the inferior courts. In a word, the supreme court can have original jurisdiction in no cases but these, and it need not necessarily have it even in these. This limitation thus interpreted, is the only limitation upon the discretion of Congress, in the *apportionment* of federal jurisdiction. For the next provision declares, that "in all the other cases before mentioned, the supreme court shall have appellate jurisdiction, both as to law and fact, with such exceptions, and under such regulations, as the *Congress shall make.*" At first there was great opposition to this proposition, on account of the phrase "*both as to law and fact.*" It was apprehended that Congress might assume to authorize the supreme court to reverse the verdict of a jury as to matters of fact, and thus greatly impair the right of trial by jury. This far-fetched objection occasioned the seventh amendment, which declares that "in suits at common law, while the value in controversy shall exceed twenty dollars, the right of trial by jury shall be preserved; and no fact tried by a jury shall be otherwise re-examined in any court of the United States, than according to the rules of the common law."(*a*) This amendment, therefore, entirely removes the objection before mentioned. And, accordingly, Congress may exercise a complete discretion in the apportionment of jurisdiction, with the above exception as to the original jurisdiction of the supreme court.

In pursuance of this discretion, Congress, by the celebrated judiciary act of 1789, (*b*) created the present judiciary system. By

(*a*) The first clause of this amendment relates solely to courts of the United States; the second, though not applicable to proceedings in the State courts, does apply to a review in the United States courts of facts so tried in a State court. Parsons *v.* Bedford, 3 Peters, 447; Justices *v.* Murray, 9 Wall. 274.

(*b*) This act of marvellous wisdom will be found in 1 Stat. at Large, 73, illustrated by elaborate notes. It should be studied in connection with the process acts of 1789, 1 Stat. at Large, 93, and of 1828, 4 Stat. at Large, 278, also illustrated by elaborate notes. Also, act of Feb. 28, 1839, 5 Stat. at Large, 321; Clearwater *v.* Meredith, 21 How. 489. A single feature requires especial mention here. It was a leading purpose of the framers of the constitution and of these laws to harmonize the action of the federal courts, as far as possible, with that of the State courts, so that no conflict should grow up between them. Accordingly, the 34th section of the judiciary act provides "that the laws of the several States, except where the constitution, treaties, or statutes of the United States shall otherwise require or provide, shall be regarded as rules of decision in trials at common law in the courts of the United States, in cases where they apply." And the process acts above referred to make similar provision in regard to the forms and modes of proceeding. So that, in a word, State law is adopted by the courts of the United States wherever it can be done without conflict with federal law. See notes to 1 Stat. at Large, 92, 93. This purpose has been carried still further by the acts of June 1, 1872, making the practice, pleadings, and modes of proceeding in other than equitable and admiralty causes, in the circuit and district courts of the United States, conform as near as may be to the practice, plead-this act the appellate jurisdiction of the supreme court is as follows: It revises, *on writ of error*, all final decisions of the *circuit court* in civil actions at law, originally commenced there, or brought there by appeal from the district court, where the value in controversy exceeds two thousand dollars. (*a*) And it revises, *on appeal*, all final decisions in cases of equity and admiralty jurisdiction involving the same amount. The reason of the distinction here made between a writ of error and appeal, is this: the supreme court has no jury to try facts in any case; but it is the peculiarity of equity and admiralty proceedings, that the court decides both law and fact without a jury; the evidence being all taken in writing. In these cases, therefore, an appeal, which brings up both law and fact, is the proper course. But in actions at law, which require a jury, the facts are settled in the court below, and the writ of error only brings up the questions of law. The value, which is thus made the predicate of appellate jurisdiction, is fixed thus high, in order to preserve the dignity of the supreme tribunal, and at the same time prevent it from being overwhelmed with a multitude of cases. It will be observed that the supreme court has no *appellate criminal jurisdiction.* Provision is made, however, that in all cases, civil and criminal, where the judges of the circuit court differ in opinion, so as to prevent a decision, the point of disagreement shall be *certified* up to the supreme court for decision. This is often done *pro forma*, when the question is new and of sufficient importance.

It has been much doubted whether the constitution intended to allow an appellate jurisdiction from the *State courts.* But inasmuch as the federal judiciary was designed to be the interpreter of federal powers, and as these powers may be brought into discussion in the State courts, it is reasonable to presume that in such cases, at least, the constitution intended that the supreme court should exercise a supervisory power over the decisions of the State courts; for otherwise, the federal government would be thus far at the mercy of the State governments. Accordingly, the judiciary act has wisely provided, that the final decisions of the highest court of law or equity in any State may be revised by the supreme court, on *writ of error*, in the two following classes of cases: 1. Where the validity or construction of the federal constitution,

ing, and forms and mode of proceeding existing at the time in like causes in the courts of record of the State within which such circuit or district courts are held. Provided, however, that this shall not alter the rules of evidence under the laws of the United States. The sixth section proceeds also to give similar remedies by attachment or other process against property as are given by State laws, and also similar remedies on judgments, by execution or otherwise. When the sum in dispute is just two (now five) thousand dollars, the supreme court has no revisory jurisdiction. Walker *v.* United States, 4 Wallace, 163 {Thompson *v.* Butler, 95 U. S. 694; First National Bank *v.* Redick, 110 U. S. 224}. When a decree of the circuit court is for a certain sum, with interest from a date named, and the interest from the date named up to the date of the decree makes the sum amount to $2,000, the supreme court has jurisdiction. The Patapsco, 12 Wall. 451.

(*a*) {This is now $5,000.}

laws, or treaties, or of any commission or authority derived therefrom, shall be drawn in question, and the decision shall be against it. 2. Where the validity of a State constitution, law, or authority, shall be drawn in question, on the ground of repugnancy to federal power, and the decision shall be in its favor. This appellate jurisdiction has been exercised in some of the most important cases that have as yet been brought before the federal judiciary; and though it even now meets with strenuous opposition from the advocates of State supremacy, yet no one can doubt that the consequences have thus far been in the highest degree salutary. (*a*)

(*a*) As to the jurisdiction of this court over the State courts, see Piqua Bank *v.* Knoup, 6 Ohio State, 342. {It can re-examine a judgment of the highest State court adverse to a land title under a United States patent. Baldwin *v.* Stark, 107 U. S. 463.} It has no jurisdiction of the question whether a law of a State and its constitution are in conflict. Withers *v.* Buckley, 20 How. 84. Nor of cases where the validity of a territorial law is drawn in question. Messenger *v.* Mason, 10 Wall. 507. The construction given to a statute of a State by the highest court thereof is held by the federal courts to be a part of the statute and as binding upon them. {Although the action involving it arose in a different State. Flash *v.* Conn, 109 U. S. 371. Except to determine the existence of a contract impaired by later legislation. L. & N. R. R. *v.* Palmer, 109 id. 244.} If such State court subsequently adopts new views of the construction, and reverses the former ruling, the federal courts follow the latest decision. Leffingwell *v.* Warren, 2 Black, 599. Even when the supreme court of the United States has followed the earlier State decision, it will, in a subsequent case, follow the later State decision and reverse its own former rule of construction. Green *v.* Neal, 6 Pet. 291. But where rights have been acquired, contracts made, or municipal bonds negotiated, upon the faith of the first State decision, the federal courts will not concede to the subsequent contradictory State decision any retroactive effect, but will hold valid all such transactions made between the dates of the two decisions. Gelpcke *v.* Dubuque, 1 Wall. 202; Havemeyer *v.* Iowa County, 3 Wall. 294; Thompson *v.* Lee County, 3 Wall. 327; Mitchell *v.* Burlington, 4 Wall. 270; Larned *v.* Burlington, 4 Wall. 275; Lee *v.* Rogers, 7 Wall. 181; Douglass *v.* County of Pike, 101 U. S. 677 {Carroll County *v.* Smith, 111 U. S. 556}. And where, in the absence of a construction given by the State court, the supreme court of the United States gives a construction, and, years after, the highest court of the State gives an opposite construction, the same rule is held as to the validity of transactions made between the dates of the two decisions. Rowan *v.* Runnels, 5 How. 134. But if, when the supreme court of the United States construes a State statute, the highest court of the State had already given a contrary construction, such State decision being not yet reported, and not cited, and such State decision is affirmed by subsequent decisions of the same State court, the supreme court of the United States will follow, in subsequent cases, the decisions of the State court, and reverse its own. Fairfield *v.* County of Gallatin, 100 U. S. 47. The federal courts are not bound by the decisions of the State courts upon questions of general commercial law. Swift *v.* Tyson, 16 Pet. 1; Oates *v.* National Bank, 100 U. S. 239.

The statutes of the United States authorize the removal of causes, in certain cases, from State courts to the circuit courts of the United States. This right is given in special cases, as in causes, civil and criminal, in any State court, against persons denied civil rights — U. S. Rev. Stats. § 641, 642; suits civil and criminal against revenue officers of the United States, and against officers and other persons acting under the registration laws — § 643; suits by aliens against civil officers of the United States under specified circumstances — § 644; and suits against corporations organized under a law of Congress, other than national banks, where the defendant has a defence arising under the constitution, or any treaty or law of the United States — § 640. Under § 639, which consolidates section 12 of the Judiciary Act, the act of July 27, 1866, and the act of March 2, 1867, in any suit commenced in any State court, wherein the amount in dispute, exclusive of costs, exceeds $500, (1) brought against an alien, or by a citizen of the State against a citizen of another State, may be removed by the defendant; (2) if the suit is against an alien and a citizen of the State, or is by a citizen of the State against another citizen thereof and a citizen of another State, it may be removed by the non-resident, if, so far as it relates to him, it is brought to

Jurisdiction of the Circuit Court. This is both original and appellate. The circuit court has *original* jurisdiction of all civil

enjoin him, or is a suit in which there can be a final determination of the controversy so far as concerns him without the presence of the other defendants as parties in the cause ; (3) if the suit is between a citizen of the State and a citizen of another State, it may be removed by the latter, whether plaintiff or defendant, if he files in the State court an affidavit stating that he has reason to believe and does believe that, from prejudice or local influence, he will not be able to obtain justice in such State court. The act of March 3, 1875, 18 Stats. at Large, 470, provides that any suit of a civil nature, at law or in equity, in any State court, where the matter in dispute exceeds, exclusive of costs, $500, and arising under the constitution, treaties or laws of the United States, or in which the United States shall be plaintiff, or in which there shall be a controversy between citizens of different States, or a controversy between citizens of the same State claiming lands under grants of different States, or a controversy between citizens of a State and foreign States, citizens or subjects, either party may remove the suit ; and when in any such suit there shall be a controversy which shall be wholly between citizens of different States, and which can be fully determined as between them, then either one or more of the plaintiffs or defendants, actually interested in such controversy, may remove the suit.

In cases arising under § 639, the party desiring to remove the suit or controversy must file his petition therefor under division 1, at the time of entering his appearance in the State court ; under divisions 2 and 3, at any time before trial or final hearing. Under the act of 1875, the petition for removal must be filed in the State court before or at the term at which said cause could be first tried, and before the trial. The petition must be accompanied by a bond as prescribed by statute.

The jurisdiction of the circuit court in such case is not appellate, but is original jurisdiction, acquired indirectly by a removal from the State court. Justices *v.* Murray, 9 Wall. 274, and Nelson, J., in Dennistoun *v.* Draper, 5 Blatch. 336 ; Fisk *v.* Railroad Co., 6 Blatch. 362, 367. Accordingly, as was said by Chief Justice Gray of Massachusetts, now associate justice of the supreme court of the United States, "it is, to say the least, a matter of grave doubt whether the circuit court of the United States, in such a case as this, could issue a writ of *mandamus* or *certiorari* to the State court ; and if it could, it would only be when no copy of the record had been filed in the circuit court, and to obtain such copy for the purpose of guiding its own proceedings, and not to restrain or control the judicial discretion of the State court." Stone *v.* Sargent, 129 Mass. 503, see 505 ; Hough *v.* Western Transportation Co., 1 Biss. 425 ; *in re* Cromie, 2 Biss. 160 ; Osgood *v.* Railroad Co., 6 Biss. 330, see 343 ; Scott *v.* Railroad Co., 6 Biss. 529, see 537.

If, upon a petition being filed within the prescribed time, the State court refuses to order a removal, but retains the case, the petitioner may still file a transcript of the record in the circuit court. If it is a proper case for removal, the circuit court has thereupon jurisdiction, and the State court cannot lawfully proceed further. The State court is governed by the averments in the petition, as it does not hear evidence to ascertain whether or not such averments are true. In the circuit court the party opposing the removal may move that the cause be remanded, if he relies upon the petition being insufficient. If he desires to controvert its allegations, he files a plea in abatement.

The jurisdiction of the State court or of the circuit court is, of course, determined, not by the assertion or denial of jurisdiction by either, but by the actual existence of cause for removal. The State court must, unless the petition be filed in vacation, examine whether or not the petition for removal presents cause. Stone *v.* Sargent, 129 Mass. 503 ; National Bank *v.* Adams, 130 Mass. 431. The decision of the *nisi prius* State court, whether in favor of or against removal, can be reviewed by the highest court of the State. If the highest court of the State decide against removal, its decision can be reviewed by the supreme court of the United States. In the following cases the supreme court of the United States affirmed the action of the State court in refusing removal. Grover & Baker Co. *v.* Florence Sewing Machine Co., 18 Wall. 553 ; Vannevan *v.* Bryant, 21 Wall. 41 ; Pechner *v.* Phœnix Ins. Co., 95 U. S. 183 ; Amory *v.* Amory, 95 U. S. 186 ; Railroad Co. *v.* McKinley, 99 U. S. 147. If the State court improperly denies the petition to remove, the petitioner may contest the action on the merits without waiving his objection to the jurisdiction, and the supreme court of the United States will, in error to the supreme court of the State, set aside all proceedings subsequent to the filing of the petition and order removal. Insurance Co. *v.* Dunn, 19 Wall. 214 ; Removal Causes, 100 U. S. 457 ; Railroad Co. *v.* Mississippi, 101 U. S. 135. In a later case that court has decided that in such case all such subsequent pro-suits at law and equity, where the value in dispute exceeds five hundred dollars, and the United States are plaintiffs; or one party is an alien; or the suit is between a citizen of the State where it is brought, and a citizen of another State; or against a citizen of the same State, claiming lands under a grant from another State. But this jurisdiction is concurrent with the State courts; and provision is made for removing such suits commenced in the State courts, at the instance of the defendant, into the circuit court. It also has original jurisdiction of all suits involving copyrights and patents; and of all crimes punishable under the federal authority. And this criminal jurisdiction is final, unless there be a disagreement between the judges, to be certified to the supreme court. The circuit court has *appellate* jurisdiction from the district court by writ of error or appeal, in the following cases; *First*, in civil actions at law, where the value in dispute exceeds fifty dollars, by writ of error; and *secondly*, in admiralty cases, where the value in dispute exceeds three hundred dollars, by appeal. But it has no appellate jurisdiction in cases of equity or in criminal cases. In these cases of appellate jurisdiction, if the judges differ in opinion, that of the supreme judge prevails, since these cannot be certified to the supreme court. (*a*)

Jurisdiction of the District Court. This court has jurisdiction of the following cases: *first*, of all admiralty cases; *secondly*, of all seizures, penalties, and forfeitures under the laws of the United States; *thirdly*, of all injuries in violation of the law of nations, or of treaties, where an alien sues; *fourthly*, of suits brought by the United States where the value in dispute amounts to one hundred dollars; *fifthly*, of suits against consuls, suits to repeal patents, and suits concerning captures; and *sixthly*, of crimes

ceedings, including the judgment on the merits rendered by the State court, are absolutely void. Kern *v.* Huidekoper, 103 U. S. 485. And where, in such a case, the petitioner filed a transcript in the circuit court, and there obtained a judgment on the merits, while the other party obtained a judgment on the merits in the State court, the circuit court can enjoin all proceedings under the judgment of the State court. Deitzsch *v.* Huidekoper, 103 U. S. 494.

Where the petition for removal of a suit is on the ground that there is, in the suit, a controversy between citizens of different States, all on one side of such controversy must be citizens of different States from all on the other side; but the position of the litigants to such controversy is not determined by the title of, or by the order of, filing, the pleadings in the State court, but by the actual interest of the parties. Meyer *v.* Construction Co., 100 U. S. 457; Ayers *v.* Chicago, 101 U. S. 184. When a suit is removed, the *res*, whether real or personal, goes with it; as do all ancillary remedies, as injunctions, attachments, receiverships. The supreme court has a revisory jurisdiction over the State courts only when it appears on the record that some one of the questions described in the act of 1789 actually did arise in the State court, and was decided there in the manner required by that act. Furman *v.* Nichol, 8 Wall. 44; Gibson *v.* Chouteau, 8 Wall. 314. And although a writ of error has been issued by one of the judges of that court, still, if the necessary facts do not appear upon the record, it will be assumed by the State court that it was improvidently issued, and will be dismissed. Nauer *v.* Thomas, 13 Allen, 572.

(*a*) {A person is not to be sued in a United States court in any district other than that of his residence or in which he may be found, unless there are two or more defendants residing in different districts, or the suit is of a local nature. R. S. §§ 739–742. A judgment of a United States court is a lien only on land in the district, but execution may issue to any district in the State, § 985.}

punishable under the federal authority, when the punishment does not exceed a fine of five hundred dollars, or imprisonment for six months, or thirty-nine lashes. In some of these cases, the jurisdiction is exclusive both of the circuit court and of the State courts; and in others, it is concurrent with both.

§ 50. **Jurisdiction of the State Courts.** (*a*) Here there is very great diversity. In Ohio, the distribution of jurisdiction very much resembles that of the federal courts. The supreme court has no jury and no original jurisdiction except that of issuing those writs which, like *mandamus* and *quo warranto*, are peculiar to the highest court. Its chief business is to hear and determine cases on *petition in error*, and such cases as may be reserved by the district court, (*b*) either from an equal division of opinion, or because of the novelty or importance of the questions involved. The district court (*b*) has appellate jurisdiction from the common pleas in all civil cases in which that court has original jurisdiction, that is, in all cases above the jurisdiction of a justice of the peace. The common pleas has exclusive original jurisdiction in criminal cases, with the exception of some minor offences assigned to the probate court, and of divorce and alimony. It has appellate jurisdiction from the probate court, from justices of the peace, and from county commissioners, in certain cases. The probate court has exclusive jurisdiction of all probate and testamentary matters, the appointment and supervision of administrators and guardians, inquests of lunacy, appropriations of private property by corporations, and sundry offences below the degree of penitentiary. *Justices of the peace* have jurisdiction of all civil cases within the value of three hundred dollars, with the exception of a few specified cases, which peculiarly require the verdict of a jury. With a few special exceptions their civil jurisdiction is confined to their respective townships. Their criminal jurisdiction, which is merely preliminary, and confined to examination and commitment for trial, comprehends all offences, and extends through the county. (*c*) They likewise have jurisdiction of some special cases, as controversies between masters and apprentices; trials of the right of property taken on execution or attachment; and actions of forcible entry and detainer. They also have the general power to administer oaths, and take acknowledgment of deeds.

(*a*) {In proceedings *in rem* where both a State court and a federal court have been applied to, and both have jurisdiction, the court first taking possession of the *res* has exclusive jurisdiction for the purposes of its suit. Heidritter *v.* Elizabeth Oil Cloth Co., 112 U. S. 294. Our supreme court, unlike that of Massachusetts, cannot decide questions not involved in the issue at the request of the legislature. State *ex rel. v.* Baughman, 38 Ohio State, 455.}

(*b*) The district courts are now superseded by the circuit courts in Ohio; see notes to § 46, *supra*.

(*c*) The defendant may demand a trial by jury, in all cases where the justice has jurisdiction to try and punish by fine or otherwise. Act of March 26, 1859. For the civil jurisdiction of justices of the peace, see act of March 14, 1853, and act of March 10, 1860.

LECTURE IX.

ENUMERATED POWERS. (*a*)

§ 51. **Power as to Revenue.** In the three preceding lectures we have examined those provisions of the constitution which relate to the organization of the three great departments of government. I have already remarked, that all the remaining provisions may be classed under the general head of *limitations of delegated power;* but that they are subdivided as follows: *first*, enumerated powers of the federal government; *secondly*, incidental powers; *thirdly*, powers prohibited to the federal government; and *fourthly*, powers prohibited to the States, by the federal constitution, and by their respective constitutions. These provisions likewise admit of a more general subdivision as follows: *first*, direct limitations, whether by enumeration or prohibition; and *secondly*, indirect limitations, by declarations of rights. But instead of following strictly either of these classifications, I shall adopt the arrangement suggested by the subject-matter, to which these provisions relate. Accordingly, while I commence with the enumerated powers of the federal government, I shall discuss in connection therewith, all the federal and State prohibitions relating to the same subject-matter.

The *revenue power* is conferred in the following words: "Congress shall have power to lay and collect taxes, duties, imposts, and excises, to pay the debts and provide for the common defence and general welfare of the United States; but all duties, imposts, and excises shall be uniform throughout the United States." (*b*) It is of course indispensable to the very existence of government, that it should have the power of raising a revenue adequate to its

(*a*) It would seem that the convention did not at first contemplate a specific enumeration of the powers of Congress. The first proposition was, that Congress should have power to legislate in all cases where the Congress of the confederation could legislate; and in all cases to which the States were incompetent, or where State legislation might interrupt the harmony of the Union; and to negative all State laws contravening the constitution or treaties. Mad. Pap. 759–61, 859. This proposition was then modified by striking out the power to negative State laws, adding the power to legislate in all cases for the general interests of the Union, and declaring the supremacy of treaties and acts of Congress — id. 1114–19, 1221. The resolution was then referred to the committee of detail, who reported a specific enumeration of the powers of Congress — id. 1221, 1232. Propositions were made to extend this enumeration much further than it actually goes; as to create corporations; to establish a national university and other seminaries of learning; to grant premiums for the promotion of useful knowledge; to encourage agriculture, commerce, and manufactures, by establishing public institutions, rewards, and immunities; to regulate stages on post-roads — id. 1354–5; to pass sumptuary laws — id. 1369, 1568; to regulate damages on protested bills — id. 1448; and to construct canals — id. 1576. See also, 1 Kent, Com. lec. 12, 18, 19.

(*b*) See Mad. Pap. 1339–43, 1485, 1549, 1611. I have put a comma, instead of a semicolon, after the word "*excises*," because it appears that the clause was so reported to the convention by the committee. See 1 Story, Const. § 907; 1 Kent, Com. 254.

necessary expenditures. But, at the same time, as the power of taxation is one of the most dangerous powers with which government is intrusted, and has been more frequently abused than any other, it requires to be guarded with peculiar care. And this is especially necessary with respect to the federal government, being professedly one of limited powers. The clause above quoted, has probably given rise to more discussion than any other in the constitution. Even its grammatical construction is a matter of controversy. Some have contended that the words, "to pay the debts and provide for the common defence and general welfare," confer distinct and substantive powers, unconnected with the taxing power. It is a sufficient objection to this construction, that it would make the federal powers unlimited, and the specific enumeration which follows this clause unmeaning, if not absurd. If Congress has the general power to do whatever it deems will promote the common defence and general welfare of the country, this single grant of power includes more than all the specifications together, and of course supersedes them all. Others, however, contend that the clause confers a general and substantive grant of power, to be explained and limited by the subsequent specifications, and in its turn to illustrate them; but having no meaning by itself alone. It is a sufficient objection to this construction, that it virtually obliterates these words from the constitution; since, if the words were taken away, the aggregate power of Congress would remain the same. What, then, is the true construction of this clause? The weight of reason as well as authority, makes these words a qualification of the taxing power. The whole provision means the same as if the words were "*in order* to pay the debts and provide for the common defence and general welfare." Thus, while Congress is not limited by this clause, as to the *subjects* upon which taxes may be levied, it is limited as to the *purposes* for which they shall be levied. Congress cannot wantonly exercise the taxing power for any purposes whatsoever; but only for the specified purposes of paying the debts and providing for the common defence and general welfare. Even this construction still leaves a vast discretion in Congress, as to the appropriation of the revenue; but it seems to be the only one which the clause will rationally bear.

Such, then, being the general import of the clause, let us examine its terms more particularly. Four words are employed to describe the taxing power; namely, "*taxes*, *duties*, *imposts*, and *excises*." Of these, the word "*taxes*" is universal, including not only the other three, but also every species of contribution levied by government; "*duties*" include impositions laid upon any kind of commodities in any situation; "*imposts*" usually signify impositions laid upon imported articles; and "*excises*" are impositions exacted upon the manufacture, retail, or consumption of commodities. Probably the only reason for employing these four terms, was an anxiety to include every species of taxation in the general grant of power. All taxes are primarily divided into *direct* and *indirect.* Direct taxes are those which are levied directly upon the person or property of individuals. Indirect taxes are those which are levied upon the privilege of doing some act; generally in relation to property, as buying, selling, importing, exporting, and the like; but sometimes in relation to certain occupations or professions, as banking, insuring, and the like; and which may consequently be avoided by foregoing the privilege taxed. The constitution elsewhere provides, as we have seen, that "direct taxes shall be apportioned among the several States according to their respective numbers;" and again, to the same effect, that "no capitation or other direct tax shall be laid, unless in proportion to the census." This was a part of the compromise between the States respecting slaves, already described. The slaveholding States bear an increased proportion of direct taxation, in return for their increased representation, both being measured by the same rule of apportionment. (*a*) In construing an act of 1794, which laid a tax upon carriages, it was decided that the constitution intended to include, under the description of direct taxes, only two species; namely, a tax upon the person, called a poll or capitation tax, and a tax upon land. (*b*) This, therefore, may be regarded as the established construction; and consequently all taxes not levied directly upon persons or land, are to be treated as indirect taxes. The constitution then declares that "all duties,

(*a*) This rule of direct taxation was adopted in the convention by a vote of 10 to 1. Mad. Pap. 1379. Since the adoption of the 14th amendment changing the proportion of representation, direct taxes will no longer be proportioned to representation.

(*b*) In Hylton *v.* United States, 3 Dallas, 171, the facts were these: In 1794, Congress passed a law laying a tax upon carriages. This tax was laid by the rule of uniformity. Hylton refused to pay, on the ground that a tax on carriages was a direct tax, and therefore could only be laid by the rule of apportionment. The court decided that it was not a direct tax, and was therefore properly laid by the rule of uniformity. This is the only point the case decides. But the court expressed their opinions fully on the nature of direct taxes. They thought there were but two kinds of direct taxes; namely, a capitation or poll tax, and a tax on land. These were the only taxes that could with any show of reason or convenience be laid by the rule of apportionment according to the census. The provision was inserted in favor of the southern States. They had a large number of slaves, and a thinly peopled territory; while the other States had but few slaves, and a thickly peopled territory. Now to make the southern States pay as much for each acre of land, or each individual person including slaves, as the other States paid — which would be the case by the rule of uniformity — was manifestly unjust. To save them, therefore, from such an imposition, was the intention of the constitution. But the same reason would not exist in regard to any other species of taxable property, as carriages for example. A carriage in the south was worth as much as a carriage in the north, and ought to pay as much tax. The inference is, that the convention had in view no other taxes, as direct, than the capitation and land taxes. These were to be apportioned to each State according to its census. As a rule of taxation, it was radically wrong on general principles; and could only be vindicated by considering that it was resorted to for the sake of compromise. The income tax is not a direct tax. Pacific Ins. Co. *v.* Soule, 7 Wall. 433. Nor is the tax on the circulation of State bank notes in the National Bank Act. Veazie Bank *v.* Fenno, 8 Wall. 533. The act of Congress requiring licenses to be taken out for particular kinds of business is constitutional. The possession of such a license does not, however, convey to the holder a vested right to carry on that business within a State contrary to the laws of that State. License Tax Cases, 5 Wall. 462; Pervear *v.* Commonwealth, 5 Wall. 475 {and see McGuire *v.* State, 42 Ohio State, 530}.

imposts, and excises shall be uniform throughout the United States." And it follows, from what has just been said, that this is equivalent to declaring that all indirect taxes shall be laid by the rule of uniformity. Again, in construing the act of 1815, which laid a direct tax upon the District of Columbia, it was decided that, although representation and direct taxation are measured by the same rule, they are not dependent upon each other; and therefore a district or territory not represented in Congress, may be constitutionally required to pay a direct tax. (*a*)

The next provision connected with revenue, is a prohibition to the United States. "No tax or duty shall be laid upon articles exported from any State. (*b*) No preference shall be given, by any regulation of commerce or revenue, to the ports of one State over those of another; nor shall vessels bound to or from one State, be obliged to enter, clear, or pay duties in another." (*c*) The object of these prohibitions is the same as of that provision which establishes uniformity as the rule of indirect taxation; namely, to secure the States against partiality or favoritism. If *exports* could be taxed, it would be in the power of Congress to injure or even destroy the staple products of a particular State, and also to cramp the general industry of the country. If inducement

(*a*) In Loughborough *v.* Blake, 5 Wheaton, 317, the single question presented to the court was, whether Congress had a right to impose a direct tax on the District of Columbia? The decision was, that Congress had this right. The general grant of power to lay and collect taxes, duties, imposts, and excises, is without limitation as to place. And the declaration that all such taxes should be uniform throughout the United States, is proof that the power was to extend through the Union. This grant of power includes direct taxes as well as others. And the provision that direct taxes shall be apportioned according to numbers, did not abridge this grant of power. The object of this provision is simply to fix a standard of apportionment, and not to exempt from taxation those who are not represented. Representation is not made the foundation of taxation. Taxes are not apportioned to representatives, but to numbers. The words are, "no capitation or other direct tax shall be laid *unless in proportion to the census.*" Now wherever a census is taken, this rule may be applied, as well in the district or territories as in the States. The district, therefore, is not only within the general grant of power, but within the restriction as to the rule. Direct taxes may be proportioned to the numbers here, as well as in the State. Congress is not obliged to extend direct taxation to the districts and territories, as it is to all the States, when it taxes any. But it has the power, if it choose to exercise it, for there is no limitation. But if Congress had not possessed this power, by the general grant, it would clearly derive it from the power of exercising "exclusive legislation in all cases whatsoever within the district." These words are as broad as words could be. But it is said they must be limited by the great principle, that representation is inseparable from taxation; what then? Is the district to be entirely exempt from taxation, because it has no representative in Congress? This is not contended for. It is admitted that indirect taxes may be laid, in the form of duties, imposts, and excises. Congress is obliged to extend such taxation to the district, if it extend it anywhere. And where is the difference, in principle, between this kind of taxation and the other? There is none. If the rule of uniformity protects the district against oppression in the one case, the rule of apportionment will equally protect it in the other. On the whole, the court could see no reason for making an exception, when the constitution makes none. The personal estate of a woman is liable to taxation, although she has no vote. The property of all inhabitants is subject to taxation, whether voters or not. Wheeler *v.* Wall, 6 Allen, 558.

(*b*) This prohibition to tax exports was strenuously resisted in the convention; but finally passed by a vote of 7 to 4. Mad. Pap. 1379–88, 1566–9.

(*c*) See Mad. Pap. 1430–2, 1440.

could be given to *import* into one State rather than another, Congress might build up the ports of one State upon the ruins of those of another. And, finally, the same result might be produced if Congress could control the *coasting trade*, so as to require vessels bound to or from one State, to enter, clear, or pay duties in another.

The only remaining provision is a prohibition to the States. "No State shall, without the consent of Congress, lay any imposts or duties upon imports or exports, except what may be absolutely necessary for executing its inspection laws; and the net produce of all duties and imposts laid by any State on imports and exports, shall be for the use of the treasury of the United States; and all such laws shall be subject to the revision and control of Congress. No State shall, without the consent of Congress, lay any duty on tonnage." (*a*) This is the only federal limitation of the taxing

(*a*) See Mad. Pap. 1447, 1584–6; Brown *v.* Maryland, 12 Wheat. 419; Raguet *v.* Wade, 4 Ohio, 107; Perry *v.* Torrence, 8 Ohio, 521; Cooley *v.* Wardens of Philadelphia, 12 How. 299. {The provision against States levying duties on imports does not apply to inter-State, but to foreign commerce. Brown *v.* Houston, 114 U. S. 622.} In Brown *v.* Maryland, 12 Wheaton, 419, the question was whether a law of Maryland, requiring *all persons selling imported articles by wholesale*, whether importers or not, to pay fifty dollars for a license in the same manner as retailers were required to do was constitutional? The court held that this law was repugnant to two provisions of the constitution: first, that which prohibits the States from laying any imposts or duties upon imports or exports; and, secondly, that which gives Congress the power of regulating commerce with foreign nations, and among the several States. I shall here abstract only what relates to the first ground of unconstitutionality. The word "imports" means "things imported." The prohibition, therefore, is not confined to duties on the *act of importation*, but includes duties on the *articles imported*. It extends to duties levied upon the articles *after* they have entered the country, as much as *while* they are entering. This is evident from the *exception* to the prohibition; namely, "except what may be absolutely necessary for executing its inspection laws." Now, inspection laws must, from their nature, act upon imported articles after they are landed. And this exception was made because the tax would otherwise have been within the prohibition. The law of Maryland, therefore, which acts upon the *selling* of imported articles, is not shielded by the fact, that it only acts upon goods after they are brought within the State. The power of requiring a license to sell, implies the power of prohibiting the sale, by making the license so great that no one will pay it. If, then, Maryland possess this power, she could, if so minded, prohibit importation entirely: for no goods would be imported, if none could be sold. It is no answer to say, that a State will have too much consideration for its own interests to do this. For, without increasing the license to the extent of prohibition, it would be very likely to be carried so far by the importing States as to impose an onerous tax upon the non-importing States. And this was the very evil against which the constitution intended to guard. It is true that there must be some period when imported goods must fall under the taxing power of the States. That period is, when they have ceased to be considered *imports*, within the meaning of the constitution. And there is great difficulty in ascertaining precisely what that period is. But it is sufficient for the present case to say generally, that when the importer has so acted upon the thing imported, that it has become incorporated and mixed up with the mass of property in the country, it has lost its distinctive character as an import, and become subject to the taxing power of the State. But while remaining the property of the importer, in his warehouse, in the original form or package in which it was imported, a tax upon it is too plainly a duty upon imports, to escape the prohibition in the constitution. No weight is due to the argument that this is not a tax upon the *article*, but upon the *person* importing it. For it is manifest that a tax on the *sale* of an article imported only for sale, is a tax on the article itself. In general, a State may tax *occupations*, because the constitution does not forbid it. But unless the persons employing the individual whose occupation is taxed, themselves pay the tax, it must still be a thing taxed through a person. A power of the States. The object manifestly is to preserve harmony, by preventing the States from exercising the taxing power to the injury of each other or of the Union. But inspection laws being designed to improve the character of State products, and prevent impositions in their sale, the States are permitted to enact them. Yet, lest this permission should be made a pretext for other objects, such laws are required to have the assent of Congress. And to remove all temptation to tax imports or exports for the purpose of revenue, the net proceeds are declared to belong to the national treasury. The same remarks apply to the prohibition of a tonnage duty. In deciding against the constitutionality of a law of Maryland, requiring all persons selling imported articles by wholesale to pay a license, it was held that this prohibition is not confined to taxes laid on the act of exportation or importation, but includes taxes laid upon the articles themselves, either before they leave the State or after they are brought into it. But it is obvious that there must be some period when imported articles fall within the taxing power of the States; and in general terms that period is, when they have become so mixed up with the mass of property in the State, as to lose their distinctive character of imports. And accordingly, a law of Ohio, laying a tax upon the capital of all merchants trading in foreign or domestic goods, was held to be constitutional; because it treated the capital of merchants like that employed in all other operations, and only indirectly and remotely affected imports or exports.

The result of the foregoing provisions is, that Congress may lay any kind of tax for the purpose of paying the debts or promoting the defence or welfare of the Union, except a tax on exports; that direct taxes, including taxes on persons and land, are to be laid by the rule of apportionment, and all other taxes by the rule of uniformity; and that the States are only prohibited from taxing imports, exports, and tonnage. It is now many years since Congress has found it necessary to lay a direct tax; and accordingly, the slaveholding States have had all the benefit without the burden of the compromise. The revenue arising from indirect taxation has been sufficient to pay off an immense national debt, besides defraying the current expenses of government; and this revenue, with the exception of the proceeds of the public lands, has been

tax on the occupation of an importer, is a tax on importations; and this a State cannot impose, because the constitution forbids it. See also Low *v.* Austin, 13 Wall. 29. But the exception is strictly limited to goods in the hands of the importer, and does not extend to cargoes sold whether before or after arrival, to be at the vendor's risk until delivered within the limits of the port, when in the hands of the vendee. Waring *v.* The Mayor, 8 Wall. 110. Nor does the prohibition extend to articles brought from one State into another, but only to foreign imports and exports. A uniform tax by a State on all sales made in it, whether made by a citizen of the State or of another State, or whether the produce of the State, or not, is valid. Woodruff *v.* Parkham, 8 Wall. 123. A State cannot tax vessels, though the property of its citizens and otherwise taxable by it, at so much per ton of the registered tonnage. State Tonnage Tax Cases, 12 Wall. 204. {But they are taxable as property the same as other property. Wiggins Ferry Co. *v.* East St. Louis, 107 U. S. 365.}

derived almost solely from duties on imports. The experiment of an excise has been tried on distilled spirits, for example; but in 1793, it produced the insurrection in Pennsylvania; a fact which strongly illustrates the unpopularity of this species of taxation. Indeed, experience has proved that a tax on imports is more cheerfully paid, because less felt by those upon whom it ultimately falls.

From the view now taken, it follows that the States must depend chiefly, if not entirely, upon direct taxation, in the literal sense of these words; since the power of indirect taxation is mostly taken away. (*a*) The constitution of Ohio contains no limitation upon the taxing power of the State, except the prohibition "to levy a poll-tax for county or State purposes." (*b*) By a *poll-tax* is here

(*a*) The doctrine is now well settled, though there is no express provision in the constitution to that effect, that the State governments cannot, without the consent of Congress at least, tax any of the instrumentalities employed by the general government in accomplishing its ends. The doctrine was first laid down in McCulloch *v.* Maryland, 4 Wheaton, 316, with reference to the Bank of the U. S. See note to § 73. Thus, certificates given by the United States to creditors for supplies in war, are not taxable by the States. The Banks *v.* the Mayor, 7 Wall. 16. Nor are United States notes intended to circulate as money, when the statute provides that they shall not be. Bank *v.* Supervisors, 7 Wall. 26. This prohibition does not apply to taxation remitted by the law of Congress as not impairing the usefulness. National Bank *v.* Commonwealth, 9 Wall. 353. It does not extend to corporations chartered by government when the charter is silent. Thompson *v.* Pacific R. R., 9 Wall. 579; R. R. Co. *v.* Peniston, 18 Wall. 5. The capital of a national bank, so far as it is invested in United States bonds, cannot be taxed, nor can the corporation be taxed in any way as the owner of them: but the stockholders may be taxed within the limitations prescribed by Congress, no matter how the capital is invested. National Bank *v.* Commonwealth, 9 Wall. 353. {The provision that the tax on such shares shall not be higher than it is on other moneyed capital, applies to prevent a more onerous mode of assessment as well as a higher percentage. People *v.* Weaver, 100 U. S. 539.} This protection of the instrumentalities of the government is reciprocal, and the United States cannot tax the salary of a judicial officer of a State. The Collector *v.* Day, 11 Wall. 113.

A State can tax property only when within its jurisdiction. So when a railroad extends into two States, and bonds are issued secured on the whole line, such bonds are not taxable in either State. Railroad Co. *v.* Jackson, 7 Wall. 262. Nor can a State tax bonds of State corporations, owned by non-residents, and compel the corporation to retain the tax. Railroad Co. *v.* Penn., 15 Wall. 300. {A vessel can only be taxed by the State where her home port is. Morgan *v.* Parham, 16 Wall. 471.} Nor can a State require non-resident traders to pay a larger license than the resident traders, as this is in contravention of the clause giving a citizen of one State all the privileges and immunities of citizens of all the States, and is a regulation of commerce. Webber *v.* Virginia, 103 U. S. 344; Ward *v.* Maryland, 12 Wall. 418; Pacific Junction Co. *v.* Dyer, 64 Iowa, 38.

(*b*) State *v.* Gazlay, 5 Ohio, 14; State *v.* Proudfit, 3 Ohio, 63; State *v.* Hibbard, 3 Ohio, 63. In State *v.* Gazlay, the taxing power of the Ohio legislature, under the first constitution, was drawn in question. This constitution contained no express grant of power to impose any tax whatever. The only provision on the subject of taxation was a prohibition, in the following words: "The levying taxes by the poll is grievous and oppressive, therefore the legislature shall never levy a poll-tax for county or State purposes." But this prohibition of one particular species of tax contains, by implication, a grant of power to lay any other, so that it be not repugnant to the State or federal constitution. And such has been the practical construction by our legislature. We levy taxes, not only upon property of every description, but upon professions and occupations. In a word, as the court observed, in Raguet *v.* Wade, 4 Ohio, 107, the power to tax, so long as it does not contravene the federal constitution, "is an unlimited sovereign power." The question in the present case was, upon the right to tax *the professions.* A law was passed, laying a tax not exceeding five dollars, upon all practising lawyers and physicians. Gazlay was regularly licensed and admitted to practice, before this meant a personal or capitation tax, the objection to which is, that it operates unequally upon the poor and the rich, by being the same for all, and not in proportion to the means of each. But the prohibition does not include taxation for township purposes; and it has also been decided not to include a tax upon professions, as those of law and medicine, sometimes called a faculty tax. We have already seen, that, by the ordinance of 1787, no tax can be laid upon the public lands within our limits until sold by Congress; and that the lands of non-residents cannot be taxed higher than those of residents. We have also seen, that, by the terms of admission into the Union, Ohio has relinquished the power of taxing lands sold by Congress until five years after the sale. (*a*)

The various *kinds* of taxes are as follows: *First*, the *State tax*, the rate of which is fixed by the legislature for each year. *Secondly*, the *county tax*, the rate of which is fixed by the county commissioners, within certain limits, varying according to the property in the county. *Thirdly*, the *township tax*, the rate of which is fixed by the township trustees. *Fourthly*, the *school tax*, the rate of which is fixed by the legislature: but the county commissioners may add one-fourth of a mill if they think proper. *Fifthly*, the *school house tax*, the rate of which is fixed by the voters of the school districts. *Sixthly*, the *poor tax*, the rate of which is fixed by the county commissioners. *Seventhly*, the *poor-house tax*, the rate of which is fixed by the county commissioners. (*b*)

law was passed, and one of his grounds for refusing to pay the tax was, that the license to practise was a contract, and subsequent taxation was a violation of that contract. But the court said that a law providing for a license was made for the public benefit, and not to confer any vested privileges. It might therefore be modified whenever the public welfare required it. Another ground of objection was, that this was a capitation or poll-tax. This the court denied. It was a faculty tax, and not a personal one. It had express reference to the ability to pay, and the amount was to be fixed by the amount of profits. In a word, it was a tax upon lucrative professions, and as proper as any other tax upon occupations or franchises. As to its being opposed to the general spirit of our institutions, this was too vague an objection to be examined.

(*a*) The rule of State taxation, as prescribed by the new constitution, has been the subject of much controversy, especially in relation to *debts* and *credits*. The intention manifestly is, to require all property of every description, whether of individuals or corporations, to be taxed by a uniform rule, according to its actual money value. The difficulty is to carry this rule into practice. The legislature, in taxing individuals, authorized *debts* to be deducted from *moneys and credits*, but not from anything else, in making up a statement for taxation; while it prohibited such deduction by banks and bankers. But the court held this provision, in favor of individuals, to be a violation of the rule of uniformity established by the constitution; and thus required credits to be taxed without any deduction of debts. See Exchange Bank *v.* Hines, and Ellis & Morton *v.* Linck, in the preface to the 2 Ohio State, 3 id. 1, 66; Latimer *v.* Morgan, 6 id. 279; Zanesville *v.* Richards, 5 id. 589; Osborn *v.* Bank U. S., 9 Wheat. 738; Portland Bank *v.* Apthorp, 12 Mass. 252. The power of the legislature to authorize municipal corporations to subscribe to the stock of railroad companies, and levy taxes for that purpose has been affirmed in this State. State *ex rel.* Smead *v.* Union Township, 8 Ohio State, 397, and cases cited; see Pierce on American Railroad Law, pp. 108–26, but not to build a link in another railway. Wyscames *v.* Atkinson, 37 Ohio State, 80. Its power to authorize assessments, as distinguished from taxes, has been affirmed. Gest *v.* Cincinnati, 26 Ohio State, 275; Bowles *v.* State, 37 Ohio State, 35, 42.

(*b*) The act of April 5, 1859, contains the present system of taxation, and repeals several previous acts. It would be impossible now to specify accurately in a short

§ 52. **Power to Borrow Money.** (*a*) Congress has the general power "to borrow money on the credit of the United States." This is intimately connected with the revenue power, and almost equally indispensable. In tranquil times, the amount required for national expenditures will not vary essentially from year to year; and by means of estimates from the treasury department, the revenue system may be easily adjusted to meet the average. But in case of war, or any other contingency, which either greatly increases the necessary expenditures, or diminishes the estimated revenue, or both, the exercise of the power to borrow money becomes absolutely necessary. When a public debt has thus been contracted, arrangements are usually made for paying it off gradually, by means of a sinking fund, and the revenue system is adjusted accordingly. In this way, the burden is so distributed as to be scarcely felt. Thus in 1816, our public debt exceeded one hundred and twenty millions. In the course of eighteen years it

space the State taxes at present. They are *generally* the State tax for State purposes, the county tax for county purposes, and local taxes, either township or municipal, as the case may be, levied for the various local purposes.

(*a*) When this clause was originally reported to the convention, it included a power "to emit bills." — Mad. Pap. 1232. This was afterwards stricken out by a vote of 9 to 2, for the avowed purpose of prohibiting paper-money — id. 1343–6.

The fourth section of the 14th amendment provides, that the validity of the public debt of the United States authorized by law, including debts incurred for payment of pensions and bounties for services in suppressing insurrection and rebellion, shall not be questioned. But neither the United States nor any State shall assume or pay any debt or obligation incurred in aid of insurrection or rebellion against the United States, nor any claim for the loss or emancipation of any slave; but all such debts, obligations, and claims shall be held illegal and void.

The power of Congress to issue bills of credit and make them a legal tender for the payment of debts, has been discussed lately in many cases. On the 25th of February, 1862, Congress authorized the issue of United States notes, not bearing interest and payable to bearer, and declared that such notes should be lawful money and a legal tender in payment of all debts public and private within the United States, except duties on imports and interest on the public debt. Subsequent issues have also been authorized. These acts have been held constitutional by the highest judicial tribunals in New Hampshire (George *v.* Concord, 45 N. H. 434), New York (Metropolitan Bank *v.* Van Dyck, 27 N. Y. 400), Pennsylvania (Schollenberger *v.* Brinton, 52 Penn. St. 1), Iowa (Hintrager *v.* Bates, 18 Iowa, 174), Nevada (Maynard *v.* Newman, 1 Nevada, 271), Michigan (Vanhousen *v.* Kanouse, 13 Mich. 303), Wisconsin (Breitenbach *v.* Turner, 18 Wis. 140), California (Lick *v.* Faulkner, 25 Cal. 404); Indiana (Thayer *v.* Hedges, 23 Ind. 141); Vermont (Carpenter *v.* Northfield Bank, 39 Vt. 46), and Massachusetts (Essex Co. *v.* Pacific Mills, 14 Allen, 389).

The supreme court of the United States held that a bond given before the passage of the acts, and made payable expressly in gold or silver, or specie, could not be discharged in legal tender notes. Butler *v.* Horwitz, 7 Wall. 258; Bronson *v.* Rods, 9 Wall. 229; Trebilcock *v.* Wilson, 12 Wall. 687. The first time the general question was decided they held the acts unconstitutional by a divided court. Hepburn *v.* Griswold, 8 Wall. 603. But afterwards by a divided court also overruled this holding, and held them constitutional as to debts contracted before as well as after their passage, without any special agreement as to the mode of payment. Legal Tender Cases, 12 Wall. 457; Bigler *v.* Waller, 14 Wall. 297 {Legal Tender Case, 110 U. S. 421, and reviews thereof in 18 Am. Law Review, 410, 618; 20 ib. 346}. A State may require its taxes to be paid in gold. Lane Co. *v.* Oregon, 7 Wall. 71. A judgment on a debt payable in gold, should be for the sum in gold, and not its equivalent in legal tenders, and the sheriff must then make the sum in gold on the execution. Phillips *v.* Dugan, 21 Ohio State, 466.

The new constitution prohibits the contracting of any debt for purposes of internal improvement. Art. xii. § 6.

was wholly paid off, and the question was, how to dispose of the surplus revenue. This power of Congress does not conflict with the exercise of a similar power by the States, for their own wants. They accordingly contract debts at their pleasure. Thus in 1825, the State of Ohio, with no surplus revenue, undertook to construct upon credit alone, her immense canals, which already extend more than four hundred miles. And it has been computed that the aggregate of debts thus contracted by the different States amounts to two hundred millions of dollars, which is about one-fifth of the public debt of France, and about one-twentieth of that of Great Britain. For these debts the creditors depend solely upon the good faith of their debtors. There seems to be a peculiar propriety in contracting debts of this kind, for lasting and valuable improvements. They are in fact contracted for the benefit of posterity, and it is but just that posterity should share the burden of paying for them. Indeed, upon no other principle would great public works be undertaken. The present generation would rather forego their share of benefit, than consent to bear the whole burden. Still it cannot be denied that this power over the public purse is the most dangerous power intrusted to government. And hence the paramount necessity of surrounding it with all possible safeguards. To this end, both the federal and State constitutions provide that "no money shall be drawn from the treasury, but in consequence of appropriations made by law." In other words, the consent of the legislature must be given beforehand, for expending money, as well as for raising it; and that the people may know what their representatives do in this behalf, it is further declared that "a regular statement and account of the receipts and expenditures of the public money shall be published," for their information.

§ 53. **Power to Regulate Commerce.** (*a*) Commerce, in its most enlarged signification, comprehends every description of intercourse between man and man. In its legal acceptation, it includes whatever relates to the exchange of commodities between individuals and nations. In civilized life, scarcely any individual consumes exactly what he produces. If the products of the earth were everywhere the same — instead of varying, as they do, with the almost infinite diversities of soil and climate — even then the division of labor, ever extending with the progress of society — until the sphere of productive effort assigned to each laborer is contracted within the smallest possible limits — would still make a countless number of individuals contribute to supply the wants of each; so that traffic between man and man would even then be immense. But when to the results of the division of labor among individuals of the same vicinity we add the results of that endless variety of soil, climate, taste, and character, by which the different

(*a*) The convention was so generally impressed with the necessity of this power, that it occasioned little debate. Mad. Pap. 1343, 1450–6. The principal question was whether two-thirds should be required to pass laws for this end.

portions of the globe and its inhabitants are distinguished from each other, we find that traffic between man and man in the same nation, almost dwindles into insignificance when compared with traffic among the nations of the earth. And it is only when we contemplate commerce on this enlarged scale — when we think of all the productions of human labor, in every region of the earth, as passing from hand to hand in an almost ceaseless process of exchange and distribution — that we can form an adequate conception of the importance of commerce, and of that part of the law, by which its vast operations are regulated. In general terms, *commercial law*, *lex mercatoria*, or the *law-merchant* comprehends all that portion of the municipal law which relates directly or indirectly to the buying, selling, or transporting of merchandise. I shall have occasion to consider its various subdivisions hereafter, and will, at present, merely indicate them. The persons engaged in commerce are called *merchants*, meaning thereby those who make a business of buying and selling. Others buy to consume; the merchant buys to sell again. He stands between the producer and consumer, buying of the former, and selling to the latter. A distinction is sometimes made between wholesale and retail dealers, according to which, those who buy and sell in large quantities, are called merchants, and those who deal in small quantities, *traders*. In this view, traders are those who buy of merchants, and sell to consumers. This, however, is a distinction in degree, rather than kind, for in the eye of the law they are all equally merchants. But seldom merchants transact business alone. Sometimes they are associated as members of a *corporation*, sometimes they form a *partnership*, and sometimes they sustain the relation of *principal and agent*. So far, then, as persons are concerned, commercial law includes that which regulates all these relations. And passing from persons to things, we come first to the law governing the contract of *sale*, the *warranty* either of title or quality connected therewith, and the *weights* or *measures* by which quantity is determined. If the sale be for cash, this brings up the law relating to *money* or other *currency*. If the sale be on credit, the law relating to *book accounts*, *bills of exchange*, *promissory notes*, and *contracts of guaranty*, comes into application; and perhaps, also, the law regulating *bankruptcy* or *insolvency*. Passing, then, from the sale to the transportation of merchandise, we have first, the law governing *carriers* in general, together with all those particular regulations which apply to *shipping;* and next, the law of *insurance*, of *stoppage in transitu*, of *lien*, *revenue laws*, and in case of war, *belligerent* and *neutral rights*. Of this extensive body of law, a large proportion is unwritten, has come down to us from distant ages, and is nearly the same in all commercial nations. But in this connection I am to discuss only those topics suggested by the provisions of the constitution.

One of the most palpable defects in the articles of confederation, as evinced by a short experience, was the absence of all provision for regulating commerce. This occasioned the meeting at Annapolis, which recommended the convention at Philadelphia, and thus led eventually to the formation of the constitution in which this defect is abundantly cured. The words of the provision are these: "Congress shall have power to regulate commerce with foreign nations, and among the several States, and with the Indian tribes." This language is construed in its most enlarged sense.

The term "*commerce*" includes navigation as well as traffic, and every description of navigation and traffic; and the power "*to regulate*" includes the power to make rules for the whole subject-matter. This may be illustrated by the case of the *United States* v. *Brig William*, (*a*) where it was held, that under this power Congress may lay an embargo or pass a law of non-intercourse, the effect of which is, for the time being, entirely to suspend foreign commerce. This power is, moreover, exclusively vested in Congress by the force of the terms employed; for how could Congress regulate commerce, if the States could pass countervailing regulations? But the clause enumerates three branches of commerce, which require a separate consideration.

Commerce with Foreign Nations. This branch of commerce is altogether a national concern; and hence the propriety of committing it to the exclusive control of the national government is obvious. This control is exercised, first, by *treaties*, and, secondly, by *acts of Congress.* (*b*)

Commercial Treaties. Free trade throughout the world, however agreeable in theory, is not a principle of the law of nations, and has not been favored by their practice. Every nation has the absolute and exclusive right, either to prohibit altogether the admission of foreign persons or products into its jurisdiction, or to prescribe and enforce the conditions upon which they shall be admitted. The terms of commercial intercourse, therefore, between the United States and every other commercial nation, are determined by treaty. What these terms are, according to existing treaties, it is not my purpose to detail. It is clear, however, that the only basis upon which a nation can treat, with due self-respect, is that of complete reciprocity. Accordingly, we extend to other nations the same commercial privileges which they extend to us. If they give us

(*a*) 2 Hall's Law Jour. 255.

(*b*) A State statute which imposes upon a shipmaster, as a prerequisite to his landing passengers, conditions which are substantially impracticable, and allows as an alternative the payment of a certain sum of money for each passenger, is a tax on the right to land passengers, and is a regulation of commerce, and void. Henderson *v.* Mayor, 92 U. S. 259. If the right of the States to pass statutes to protect themselves in regard to the criminal, pauper, or diseased foreigner landing within their borders exists at all, it is limited to such laws as are absolutely necessary for that purpose. A statute extending beyond this necessity, imposing burdensome restrictions on foreigners arriving, especially restrictions likely to bring on complications with foreign governments, is void. Chy Lung *v.* Freeman *et al.*, 92 U. S. 275; New York *v.* Compagnie Generale Transatlantique, 107 U. S. 59. A State statute which requires an inspector to make survey of sea-going vessels arriving with damaged goods, not as a sanitary precaution, but to provide for the sale of the goods, is void. Foster *v.* Master, &c., of New Orleans, 94 U. S. 245. See also Cannon *v.* New Orleans, 20 Wall. 577.

free trade, we give them the same. If they lay restrictions on our commerce, we lay corresponding restrictions on theirs. If they prohibit our commerce altogether, we prohibit theirs in like manner. So far, then, as foreign commerce is regulated by treaty, Congress, as a branch of the government, has no voice in it, but only the president and senate. At the same time the States, out of abundant caution, are expressly prohibited from entering into "any treaty, alliance, or confederation." But when the terms of commercial intercourse have thus been adjusted by treaty, it then remains to carry them into effect by legislative provisions.

Commercial Legislation. (*a*) I have already said that only a very small portion of commercial law, as before defined, has resulted from legislative enactment. The great mass of it is common to all nations, and embodies the wisdom of all times. The commercial legislation of Congress, therefore, can be briefly described. It differs very little from that of Great Britain. All our regulations have for their main object the encouragement of commercial enterprise among our own citizens, so far as this can be done without discouraging domestic production; and this encouragement is chiefly given through the exercise of the revenue power. For this purpose Congress declares from time to time what places shall be *ports of entry and clearance*, and prohibits the importing into, or exporting from, any other ports. These ports are placed under the immediate supervision of *custom-house officers*, the chief of whom is styled *collector*, and acts under the general supervision of the treasury department. No ship engaged in foreign commerce can enter or depart from any port, until the custom-house regulations have been complied with, and a permit obtained from the collector as evidence thereof. Among other things, a sworn *manifest*, containing a full statement of the entire cargo imported or exported, must be furnished to the collector; and thus complete statistics of our foreign commerce are at all times attainable. And to carry out the design before mentioned, of encouraging native enterprise, a discrimination is made between native and foreign ships, with respect to *duties*. Native ships are declared to include only those which are built here, or lawfully captured from an enemy, and which are wholly owned and officered by our own citizens. To obtain the privileges secured to such ships, they are required to be *registered* with the collector of the port to which they belong. The register contains, among other things, an accurate measurement and description of the ship, together with the names of the master and owners; and thus the whole amount of our tonnage engaged in foreign trade may be at all times known. A native ship not registered is treated as a foreign ship, and this is generally a sufficient motive to secure compliance with the registry act. Upon registering the ship, the collector makes out a *certificate* of

(*a*) See Abbott on Shipping, with notes by Judge Story; Curtis on Merchant Seamen; Flanders on Maritime Law; Flanders on Shipping; Parsons on Maritime Law.

registry for the use of such ship, and takes security from the owner that it shall be used for that ship only. Upon every change of ownership or burden, a new certificate must be obtained; and upon every change of master that fact must be reported to the collector, and be by him indorsed on the certificate. Every sale or transfer of a registered ship is required to be evidenced by a written *bill of sale*, reciting at length the certificate of registry, on peril of losing native privileges; though the transfer would be valid without such recital. Thus, by reference to the collector's office, the title of every native ship is easily traced, and the responsibility of the owners to the public and to individuals conveniently secured. If a ship not built here or obtained by capture, be wholly owned and commanded by our citizens, she is entitled to protection as American property, though not regarded as a native ship with respect to duties. The only effect, then, of the certificate of registry is to secure American privileges; for, not belonging to the law of nations, it is no voucher of national character. The document designed for this purpose is commonly called a *sea-letter*, though sometimes a *passport*, and it is essential to protect neutral ships in time of war. Another document, sometimes provided for by treaties, and here by act of Congress, is the *crew list*, which is essential for the protection of the crew in time of war. There is, also, a *certificate of property*, relating only to the cargo, which exists by the usage of the custom-house, without being specially provided for. Every seaman, for his own security, is entitled to a *certificate of citizenship*, upon satisfying the collector that he is a citizen. To secure the well-being of *passengers*, the number is not permitted to exceed two for every five tons of burden, and their names must appear in the *manifest*. There must be a *medicine chest*, amply supplied with medicines and directions; and a minimum quantity of *provisions* for each person on board. To provide a fund for the relief of sick or disabled seamen, every seaman is obliged to contribute twenty cents per month out of his wages, for which the master must account to the collector. To protect seamen from imposition, their contract for service is required to be in writing, and they have a lien on the ship to secure their wages. Finally, to protect them from ill usage abroad, it is unlawful to set them ashore in a foreign country against their consent; and if left there, it is the duty of our consuls to send them home at the public expense. There are numerous other regulations for the health, protection, and comfort of seamen, which I have not time to describe. They all proceed upon the ground that seamen are a reckless and improvident class of men, necessarily subjected to severe discipline, and requiring the most efficient safeguards against abuse and imposition. (*a*)

(*a*) Congress, by virtue of this power, passed, March 3, 1855, a law imposing numerous regulations on the carriage of passengers in steamships and other vessels sailing between our own and foreign ports, and repealing the previous laws relative thereto.

Commerce among the States. (*a*) It is obvious that if *internal commerce*, which from our varieties of soil and climate must be

(*a*) See 1 Kent, Com. 431; 2 Story, Const. chap. xv.; U. S. *v.* Brig William, 2 Hall's Law Jour. 255; Brown *v.* Maryland, 12 Wheaton, 419; Gibbons *v.* Ogden, 9 Wheaton, 1; Raguet *v.* Wade, 4 Ohio, 107; Perry *v.* Torrence, 8 Ohio, 521; Wilson *v.* Blackhead Creek Company, 2 Peters, 251; Thurlow *v.* Massachusetts, 5 How. 504; People *v.* Brooks, 4 Denio, 469. In Gibbons *v.* Ogden, 9 Wheaton, 1, the facts were these: The State of New York had passed several laws, granting to Livingston and Fulton the exclusive privilege of navigating all the waters within the jurisdiction of New York by steamboats. These laws had been decided in the State courts to be constitutional. Livingston *v.* Van Ingen, 6 Johns. 507; Ogden *v.* Gibbons, 4 Johns. Ch. R. 140, and 17 Johns. 488. But on referring the question to the supreme court of the United States, they were decided to be unconstitutional, so far as they prohibited vessels licensed according to the laws of the United States for carrying on the coasting trade, from navigating the waters of New York by means of fire or steam. Chief-Justice Marshall, who delivered the opinion, laid down the doctrine that the constitution was not to be construed narrowly, but liberally. The power to regulate *commerce* was a power to regulate *navigation*. Otherwise, Congress had no power over navigation. Again, the power to regulate commerce extends to every species of commercial intercourse between the United States and foreign nations, and among the several States. It does not stop at the external boundary of a State, although it does not extend to a commerce which is completely internal. Congress cannot regulate the commerce which is only carried on between man and man in a State, or between different parts of the same State; but it can always regulate that commerce which concerns more States than one. The power of Congress, then, comprehends navigation within the limits of every State in the Union, so far as that navigation is connected with commerce, either with foreign nations, or among the several States, or with the Indian tribes. And the power to regulate commerce is the power to prescribe the rules by which commerce is to be governed. It is a power complete in itself, and has no other limitations than those which are prescribed in the constitution. Nor is it one of the *concurrent* powers, like that of taxation. It is vested *exclusively* in Congress, and no part of it can be exercised by a State. A State may pass inspection laws, health laws, laws regulating internal traffic, and laws relating to turnpikes, ferries, and the like; but this is not an exercise of the power to regulate commerce, such being merely *police* regulations. But even admitting the States to have a concurrent power with Congress, still it is a settled doctrine that the laws of a State, which would otherwise be valid, must yield when they come into collision with the laws of Congress, the latter being supreme. And this is the case with the laws of New York now in question. They come into direct collision with the laws of Congress, regulating the coasting trade, which are the supreme laws of the land, and must prevail over those which are subordinate. These laws expressly grant to vessels a *license* to carry on the coasting trade. Now a license to do a particular thing is a *permission* or authority to do that thing. The steamboats in question, being licensed under these laws, had permission from the United States to carry on the coasting trade anywhere, between Elizabethtown and New York, as well as other places. The laws of New York interfere with this permission, by granting the *exclusive* privilege of *steam navigation* to other boats. And so far as they thus come in conflict, they are void. For the laws of Congress as much include vessels which carry passengers, as those which carry merchandise; and as much vessels propelled by steam, as those propelled by wind. In Brown *v.* Maryland, 12 Wheaton, 419, the precise point decided was, that a law of Maryland, requiring importers of foreign goods by the bale or package, and persons selling the same by wholesale, to pay for a license, was repugnant to this clause of the constitution. To arrive at this result, it was held that sale was as much a part of commerce as importation, and therefore that the power of Congress did not stop at the external boundary of a State, but entered into its interior, so far as to regulate the sale of imported articles in the first instance. But this power did not include traffic strictly internal; and when imported articles became mixed up with the general property of the State, it ceased to be subject to the control of Congress. State *v.* Shapleigh, 27 Mo. 344. A State cannot discriminate in the exercise of its taxing power in favor of its own manufactures and productions, against those of other States. State *v.* North, 27 Mo. 464. {If the rate of taxation is the same on an imported article as on that made in the State the tax is legal. Tiernan *v.* Rinker, 102 U. S. 123. And it is immaterial if the mode of collection is different. Hinson *v.* Lott, 8 Wall. 148.} A license tax upon dealers in beer and ale by the cask, not manufactured in a city, but immense between the different States, had been left to the regulation of the States themselves, a wide door would have been thrown

brought there for sale, is not unconstitutional unless it appears that the articles sold were manufactured outside of the State. Downham *v.* Alexandria, 10 Wall. 173. A law for revenue laying a distinctive tax upon the business of foreign corporations habitually doing business in this State, such business consisting in the transportation of goods and passengers *in transitu* from State to State, and the tax being graduated by the weight of the goods and the number of passengers carried, is an infringement of the clause in the constitution reserving to Congress the regulation of commerce between the States. Erie Railway Co. *v.* New Jersey, 2 Vroom, 531 ; a statute of Pennsylvania imposing a tax on railroads of so much per pound on all freight carried is unconstitutional, so far as it affects freight carried from Pennsylvania to other States, or from other States to points in Pennyslvania. State Freight Tax, 15 Wall. 232. But a tax on the gross receipts of a railroad is not, though part of the gross receipts are made up of freight on such goods. Reading R. R. Co. *v.* Penn., 15 Wall. 284 ; Pullman Palace Car Co. *v.* Commonwealth, 107 Pa. St. 148. A capitation tax of one dollar on every person leaving the State levied on the carrier transporting them is unconstitutional. Crandell *v.* Nevada, 6 Wall. 35. See also People *v.* Raymond, 34 Cal. 472. In Wilson *v.* The Blackhead Creek, 2 Peters, 245, the point decided was, that a law of Delaware, authorizing the construction of a dam across a navigable creek, was not an infringement of the constitution. This decision was expressly placed upon the ground that Congress had not, by legislating, exercised the power conferred in reference to this creek, and until this was done, the power remained in the State. Much stress was also laid upon the fact, that this dam was calculated to improve the health of those living in the vicinity. Under this clause, Congress may regulate navigation, and determine what in judgment of law shall or shall not be deemed an obstruction of it. State of Pennsylvania *v.* Wheeling & Belmont Bridge Co., 18 How. 421. A State may impose a tax on all money or exchange brokers. Nathan *v.* Louisiana, 8 How. 73 ; or on legacies, where the legatee is not a citizen of the United States, or domiciled in the State. Mager *v.* Grima, id. 490 ; or may inflict the penalty of forfeiture on enrolled vessels employed in violating its laws for the preservation of oysters. Smith *v.* State of Maryland, 18 id. 71, see Johnson *v.* Loper, 46 N. J. L. 321 ; or regulate pilotage, and the conduct of vessels in harbors. Cooley *v.* Wardens of Phil., 12 How. 299 ; Brig James Gray *v.* Ship John Fraser, 21 id. 184 ; Steamboat New York *v.* Rea, 18 id. 223 ; State *v.* Penny, 19 S. Ca. 219. See People *v.* Thurber, 13 Ill. 554 ; Hudson County *v.* State, 4 Zabris. 718. State laws imposing reasonable police regulations for the protection of markets against the sale of unfit commodities by means of an inspection of articles offered for sale, enforced by a penalty for offering uninspected articles, are not unconstitutional. State *v.* Fosdick, 22 La. An. 256. In Padelford *v.* Mayor and Aldermen of Savannah, 14 Geo. 438, the case of Brown *v.* Maryland is declared not to be binding on the State courts, and the equality of the State courts with those of the United States affirmed. A State may make regulations affecting commerce in her ports in particulars with reference to which Congress has not thought it necessary to pass laws. Port Warden *v.* Martha J. Ward, 14 La. An. 289. The State laws regulating pilotage are, in view of the various acts of Congress adopting them, to be regarded as constitutional until Congress by its own acts supersedes them. *Ex parte* McNiel, 13 Wall. 236. But though they require the vessel to take a pilot, this will not excuse the vessel from liabilities for injuries caused solely by the negligence of the pilot, at least unless the law expressly so provides ; and *quære*, as to the effects of such a proviso. The China, 7 Wall. 53. A reasonable wharfage may be charged by the owner of a wharf, whether a person or a city. Packet Co. *v.* St. Louis, 100 U. S. 423 ; Transportation Co. *v.* Parkersburg, 107 U. S. 691. The exaction of a fee for a license to carry on a certain business, by a municipal corporation, is not void as an attempt to regulate commerce. Chilvers *v.* The People, 11 Mich. 43 ; Guy *v.* Baltimore, 100 U. S. 434 ; Webber *v.* Virginia, 103 U. S. 344. In Thurlow *v.* Massachusetts, Fletcher *v.* Rhode Island, and Pierce *v.* New Hampshire, beginning 5 How. 504, and known as the *liquor cases*, these three States had passed laws prohibiting the sale of liquors, under certain conditions, and imposing penalties. In the first two cases, the liquors actually sold had been imported from abroad. In the last, the liquor had been manufactured in one State and sold in another. The decision was, that neither of these laws contravened the power of Congress. The reasons variously stated by the several judges may perhaps be reduced to these two : 1. These laws are not regulations of commerce, but of the health and morals of the people. 2. They are not in direct conflict with any act of Congress upon the subject. Beer Co. *v.* Massaopen for internal dissensions. In a word, the States would have thus far remained foreign to each other. It was wise, therefore, to give the power to Congress exclusively. And in pursuance of this power, a system of regulations has been provided for vessels engaged in the *coasting trade* and *fisheries*, similar to those provided for vessels engaged in foreign commerce. If such vessels be over twenty tons burden, they must be *enrolled* with the collector of the district, who issues a *certificate of enrolment.* The rules and requisites of enrolment are in all respects the same as of registry. If under twenty tons, no enrolment is necessary. But in either case a *license* must be taken out for the coasting trade or fishing. Otherwise, such vessels must pay foreign duties, if in ballast or laden with native products; and are liable to forfeiture, if laden with foreign products. If vessels thus enrolled and licensed, would make a foreign voyage, the enrolment and license must be surrendered, and a registry taken out, and *vice versa.* These provisions for registry and enrolment, of course include *steamboats* as well as other vessels, and the navigation of our rivers and lakes, as well as of the ocean. And it will be seen that they enable government at any time to determine the exact amount of American shipping; as well as the portions of it respectively employed in foreign and domestic commerce. At the same time, they enable all persons concerned to trace readily the title to ships, by referring to the custom-house books.(*a*) The most

chusetts, 97 U. S. 25; McGuire *v.* State, 42 Ohio State, 530. And see Pierce *v.* The State, 13 N. H. 536; Preston *v.* Drew, 33 Maine, 558; State *v.* Robinson, id. 564; Green *v.* Briggs, 1 Curtis, C. C. R. 311; Fisher *v.* McGirr, 1 Gray (Mass.), 1; Raguet *v.* Wade, 4 Ohio, 107; Perry *v.* Torrence, 8 Ohio, 521; Wynhamer *v.* The People, 20 Barb. 567; 2 Parker, Crim. Cas. 421; Smith *v.* The People, 1 Parker, Crim. Cas. 583; State *v.* Peckham, 3 R. I. 289; State *v.* Paul, 5 id. 185; State *v.* Keeran, 5 id. 497; Reynolds *v.* Geary, 26 Conn. 179. As to what State laws imposing duties and liabilities on masters of vessels for passengers brought into the State by them, are regulations of police, and therefore constitutional, or regulations of commerce, and therefore unconstitutional, see New York *v.* Miln, 11 Peters, 102; Passenger cases, 7 How. 283. People *v.* Donner, 7 Cal. 169; Mitchell *v.* Steelman, 8 id. 363; New York *v.* Compagnie Generale Transatlantique, 107 U. S. 59. A State law imposing a special tax upon a certain race of foreigners is unconstitutional, as discouraging immigration from and intercourse with that country, and thus affecting commerce. Lin Sing *v.* Washburn, 20 Cal. 534. Under this clause the question has been raised, whether Congress has the power to regulate the slave trade between the States. But as I shall have occasion to advert to this subject again, I will merely remark, that the words are broad enough to include this, provided slaves be regarded as property. Another important question is, whether Congress may not legislate upon some, if not all, of the subjects of commercial law, before mentioned, so as to produce a general uniformity throughout the Union. Why, for instance, might not the law relating to insurance, and to negotiable paper, be made the same in all the States? It is contended by very able lawyers, among them Judge Redfield, that under this clause, and also under that giving power to establish post-routes, Congress can regulate, by legislation, railroads running through different States. This may become very important, considering the immense power of the large corporations which are growing up among us, and the prominent position they hold in conducting the commerce of the country.

(*a*) The recording of a mortgage in the collector's office of the home port of a vessel puts it in force irrespective of the laws of the State regulating chattel mortgages. White's Bank *v.* Smith, 7 Wall. 646; Aldrich *v.* Ætna Co., 8 Wall. 491. "We think it may be safely said, that State legislation which seeks to impose a direct burden upon inter-state commerce, or to interfere directly with its freedom, does encroach upon the important judicial construction upon this part of the clause was occasioned by certain laws of New York, granting to individuals the exclusive privilege of navigating by steamboats all the waters within her jurisdiction. These laws, after being sustained in the State courts, were decided, by the supreme federal court, to be unconstitutional. It was held that commerce among the States does not stop at their external boundaries, but penetrates beyond. It does not include traffic between man and man, or between different portions of the same State; but it does include that which concerns more States than one. The States may pass inspection laws, health laws, and laws relating to roads, ferries, turnpikes, canals, and the like; for these, though they facilitate commerce, are not commercial regulations. But they cannot interfere with the power of Congress to regulate the coasting trade, even within their own navigable waters.

Commerce with the Indians. (a) Under this head I shall consider our Indian relations generally. We have already seen that the Europeans rested their title to this continent upon *discovery.* The Indians, however, then in possession, were admitted to have a certain *right of occupancy or use* in their lands, subject to the ultimate dominion of the discoverers. And this doctrine has ever prevailed in this country. We hold that the Indians have a kind of nondescript title, which can only be extinguished *by purchase.*

exclusive power of Congress." Waite, C. J., in Hall *v.* De Cuir, 95 U. S. 488. A city ordinance which requires of every steamer that shall moor or land in any part of the city, a sum proportioned to its tonnage, is a tonnage tax, not wharfage, and is void, as being a regulation of commerce, both inter-state and foreign. Cannon *v.* New Orleans, 20 Wall. 577. A statute of a State which requires those engaged in the transportation of passengers among the States, to give all persons travelling within that State, upon vessels employed in such business, equal rights in all parts of the vessel, without distinction of race or color, is a regulation of commerce, and, to that extent, void. Hall *v.* De Cuir, 95 U. S. 485. A statute which prohibits driving or conveying any Texas, Mexican, or Indian cattle into the State between the first day of March and the first day of December in each year, is not a legitimate exercise of the police power of the State, but is a regulation of commerce, and void. R. R. Co. *v.* Husen, 95 U. S. 465. That the power to regulate commerce among the States extends to commerce over railways was assumed in C. B. & Q. R. R. *v.* Iowa, 94 U. S. 155. And it was held to extend to telegraph lines in Pensacola Telegraph Co. *v.* W. U. Telegraph Co., 96 U. S. 1; Telegraph Co. *v.* Texas, 105 U. S. 460, but see West. Un. Tel. Co. *v.* Mayer, 28 Ohio State, 521; Mobile *v.* Leloup, 76 Ala. 401. A statute which requires a license tax for the peddling of articles not the growth, produce, or manufacture of the State, and requires no such license for peddling similar articles which are the growth, produce, or manufacture of the State, is void, though Congress has not legislated on the matter. The inaction of Congress indicates their will that such commerce shall be free from restriction. Welton *v.* Missouri, 91 U. S. 282; Webber *v.* Virginia, 103 U. S. 344. This is affirmed in Hall *v.* De Cuir, cited above. A statute giving to representatives of one deceased a right of action against the owners of a vessel engaged in inter-state commerce, on which vessel the deceased while a passenger lost his life, by the negligent collision of the vessel, is not void, so long as Congress does not regulate the liabilities of the parties in such case. Sherlock *v.* Alling, 93 U. S. 99.

(*a*) See the 50th lecture of Kent; 1 Story, Const. § 7-38, 153; 2 Story, Const. § 1097; Johnson *v.* McIntosh, 8 Wheaton, 543; Cherokee Nation *v.* Georgia, 5 Peters, 1; Worcester *v.* Georgia, 6 Peters, 515; Clark *v.* Smith, 13 id. 195. The power of regulating commerce with the Indians belongs exclusively to Congress, and a tax levied by a territorial legislature upon traders with Indians is therefore unconstitutional. Foster *v.* Commissioners, 7 Minn. 140.

The purchase is regulated by treaty, prior to which, the Indians are entitled to be protected in their possession. But the *fee-simple* in the soil, and the right of *pre-emption*, belong to the federal government.(*a*) The Indians can sell neither to the States, nor to individuals. And this principle is now extended to all their commerce, traffic, and intercourse; which are wholly under the control of the federal government. And this is without any reference to their location; since it makes no difference whether they are situated within particular States, or without the territorial limits of the Union. So that, in fact, the Indian tribes are domestic and dependent nations, sustaining towards the federal government a relation analogous to that of a ward to his guardian, and thence denominated a state of *pupilage*. They are not foreign nations, in the sense in which these words are used in the constitution; but are, nevertheless, distinct political societies capable of governing themselves, and of being parties to treaties.(*b*) In short, they are neither wholly separated from us, nor yet a part of us. They are neither citizens nor aliens; but sustain an anomalous relation, somewhere between the two.

Our relations with the various tribes have been regulated by numerous treaties and acts of Congress, but the following points are all I have room to refer to. The *Indian Bureau*, formerly attached to the war department, now belongs to the department of the interior, which has the general superintendence of Indian affairs, through the instrumentality of *agents*, stationed at convenient points. When land has been secured to the Indians by treaty, no person is permitted to reside among them, or traffic with them, without a *license*. If a crime be there committed by a white person, it is punished. Intruders among them may be apprehended by the military force. Even hunting on their grounds is prohibited. Licenses are only granted to citizens of the United States, and they are required to give security for the observance of the laws. In all trials where an Indian is a party, the burden of proof is made to rest on the white person. Foreigners are liable to be punished for being even found within their limits. The president is authorized to furnish them with domestic animals and implements of husbandry; to take measures for preventing the sale of spirituous liquors among them; and to appoint proper persons to instruct them in the arts and ways of civilization. But thus far all has been to little purpose; and philanthropy finds in the past little reason to hope for the future. The Indian seems to deteriorate by contact with the whites. His proper home is the forest. The tribes are gradually receding westward before the tide of civilization, which is sweeping them away. And everything portends that the time is not very distant, when the original possessors of the American soil will live only in history.

(*a*) See note on p. 33.
(*b*) {See article on The Legal Position of the Indian, 15 Am. Law Rev. 21, and on Indian Citizenship, 20 id. 183.}

§ 54. **Power as to Naturalization.** (*a*). The words of the constitution are, "Congress shall have power to establish an uniform rule of naturalization throughout the United States." Prior to framing the constitution, this power was exercised by the respective States, without concert or uniformity, and great inconvenience and confusion were the inevitable result. The word "uniform" now makes this power exclusive in Congress. The States have no power over the subject of *citizenship*. To remove all doubt on this point, another provision declares, that "the citizens of each State shall be entitled to all the privileges and immunities of citizens in the several States." Citizenship is thus made exclusively a national affair, without any reference to State power or limits. Who, then, are citizens of the United States? We know nothing of *denizens* in this country, and consequently all persons are divided primarily into *citizens* and *aliens*. (*b*) Citizens are either *native* or *naturalized;* and aliens are either *friends* or *enemies*.

(*a*) In 1790, Congress first exercised this power. And the only question which has been raised on the subject is, whether this power is exclusively vested in Congress. In Collett *v.* Collett, 2 Dallas, 294, the circuit court of Pennsylvania, held that the States possess a concurrent authority; that the reason for investing Congress with this power, was to guard against too narrow, and not too liberal, a mode of conferring the rights of citizenship; and, therefore, while the States cannot exclude those citizens who have been adopted by the United States, they may adopt citizens upon easier terms than Congress does. But this doctrine is now given up. For, in the United States *v.* Villato, 2 Dallas, 370, Judge Iredel said, if the case were new, he should be of opinion that the power of naturalization operated exclusively, as soon as it was exercised by Congress. In Chirac *v.* Chirac, 2 Wheaton, 269, Chief-Justice Marshall held it as a point not to be controverted, that this power belongs exclusively to Congress. And, in Houston *v.* Moore, 5 Wheaton, 1, Judge Story mentioned this power as one which was exclusive on the ground of there being a direct *incompatibility* in the exercise of it by the States. This is evidently a valid reason. For, if a State could make its own terms of citizenship, it might make terms for other States; since the moment an individual becomes a citizen of any one State, he becomes, by force of the constitutional provision, entitled to the privileges of a citizen in any other State. The power would thus operate extra-territorially, if exercised by States, and this is a sufficient reason for conferring it exclusively on Congress; as is now generally admitted to have been the intention of the constitution. The first legislation upon this subject was the act of 1790, 1 Stat. at Large, 103. This act allowed any alien, "being a free white person," who had resided within the United States two years, to become a citizen, on application to "any common-law court of record," within any State where he had resided one year, upon promising a good character, and taking an oath to support the constitution of the United States. This act was repealed by the act of 1795, 1 Stat. at Large, 414; and that again by the act of 1802, 2 Stat. at Large, 153; which, with sundry amendments, now constitutes the law of naturalization. These amendments are, the act of 1804, 2 Stat. at Large, 292; the act of 1816, 3 Stat. at Large, 258; the act of 1824, 4 Stat. at Large, 69; and the act of 1828, 4 Stat. at Large, 310; act of Feb. 10, 1855, 10 U. S. Stat. at Large, 604. See *ante*, p. 61, note. The substance of these provisions is contained in the text. The naturalization of a man makes his wife, whether married before or afterwards, a citizen of the United States. Kelly *v.* Owen, 7 Wall. 496. {But the marriage of a native-born woman to an alien does not affect her political character. Shanks *v.* Dupont, 3 Pet. 242.}

(*b*) See 1 Black. Com. 374. The first section of the 14th amendment to the constitution of the United States is as follows:—

"Sect. 1. All persons born or naturalized in the United States, and subject to the jurisdiction thereof, are citizens of the United States, and of the State wherein they reside. No State shall make or enforce any law which shall abridge the privileges or immunities of citizens of the United States; nor shall any State deprive any person of

Native citizens include, *first*, all persons born within the jurisdiction of the United States since our independence, or before that epoch, if they remained here afterwards; and, *secondly*, the children of citizens born abroad, if their parents have at some time resided here.

Naturalized citizens include, *first*, all persons who comply with the legal requisites for naturalization; *secondly*, their minor children residing here at the time; and, *thirdly*, the widow and minor children of persons complying with the preliminary requisites, but dying before their naturalization is consummated. The requisites of naturalization prescribed by Congress are briefly as follows: 1. The applicant must be a free white adult. Colored persons cannot be naturalized. (*a*) 2. The country of the applicant must be at peace with ours. 3. His intention to become naturalized must have been declared under oath, before some federal or State court, or its clerk, two years before his admission, unless he has been a resident here since 1812; or unless he be a minor, having resided here three years before his majority, with the intention of becoming a citizen. 4. He must have resided five years within the country, and one year within the State where the application is made, behaving as a good citizen; which must be proved by other testimony than his own oath. (*b*) 5. He must take an oath to support the constitution of the United States, and abjure all other allegiance. 6. If he has borne any title of nobility, he must renounce it. On these easy conditions, the high privilege of American citizenship is offered to all our white brethren of the human family. The foreigner, however unaccustomed heretofore to institutions like ours, is, by this short process of naturalization, placed on the same footing with native citizens, with a few slight exceptions before mentioned, touching eligibility to office.

All persons not citizens, are aliens, with the exception of Indians and colored persons. When their country is at peace with ours, they are called *alien friends;* and when their country is at war with ours, *alien enemies;* and their condition is very different in

life, liberty, or property, without due process of law, nor deny to any person within its jurisdiction the equal protection of the laws."

{The 14th amendment has been invoked in argument since its passage perhaps oftener than any other part of the constitution, and in a great variety of cases. Its fullest exposition is in the Civil Rights Cases, 109 U. S. 3, holding an act of Congress to be unconstitutional imposing a penalty on any person who denied to another privileges of inns, conveyances, theatres, &c., by reason of color or previous condition of servitude. The court held that the legislation which Congress was authorized to enact to carry out the amendment was not creating a code of conduct between individuals, but to correct, redress, or relieve, against State legislation subversive of the rights protected by the amendment, and that the amendment is prohibitory on the States only.}

(*a*) Not so now. R. S. of U. S. § 2169.

(*b*) By the act of July 17, 1862, any alien, of the age of twenty-one years, or upwards, who shall have enlisted, either in the regular or volunteer forces, and shall have been honorably discharged, and shall have resided within the United States one year previous to his application, may, without previous declaration of his intention, be admitted to become a citizen of the United States.

the two cases. The great and primary duty of a citizen is *allegiance*. This is the tie which binds him to his government, under a transcendent obligation of fidelity. It is that peculiar relation which is violated by treason, a crime which none but citizens can commit. We have no other oath of allegiance than that which every officer and every naturalized citizen takes, to support the constitution. But the law regards the obligation as inherent, and existing prior to any oath. It is founded on that protection which government extends over its citizens. It implies something more than obedience to the laws, for this is the duty of every alien within our jurisdiction; the citizen is further bound never to take part against his government, but always to support and defend it. And this obligation of allegiance is held to be perpetual. (*a*) No citizen can of his own will avoid it. Unless absolved from it by government, it goes with him wherever he goes, and makes him a traitor if he be found violating it. This is what is meant by the proposition, that no man can *expatriate* himself. However incompatible the obligations he may contract to other governments, this is paramount, and still continues. Such is the stern doctrine of the common law. No doubt it ought to be modified. How barbarous would it be for one of our naturalized citizens, who had spent his best days here, to be punished elsewhere as a traitor, for fighting on the side of his adopted country, in violation of a native but long-abjured allegiance to some other government! With regard to the distinctive privileges of citizenship, they are best described by stating the disabilities of aliens. Aliens, then, can neither vote, nor hold office, nor act as jurors. In many of the States they cannot hold real estate. But in Ohio, and in the new States generally, this disability is expressly removed, in order to encourage the settlement of the country. In regard to personal property, their legal capacities are the same everywhere as those of citizens, while they are friends. But in case of war their condition is at once changed. The persons and property of alien enemies are at the mercy of government, which, by the law of nations, may detain the one and confiscate the other. All trade and intercourse with them are illegal, and all contracts utterly void. The theory is, that a war between two nations is a war between all the individuals of these two nations; who are, therefore, to be regarded as personal enemies, and incapable of intercourse. This is abhorrent to all the good feelings of our nature. And, fortunately, the evils which would result from the rigorous enforcement of so barbarous a doctrine, are greatly mitigated by means of the power inherent in government, to grant *passports*, *safe conducts*, and *licenses* to alien enemies, for the protection both of their persons and property. In fact, aliens, whether friends or enemies, have

(*a*) Our government strenuously denied the doctrine that a citizen or subject cannot expatriate himself, in recent correspondence with the government of Austria relative to the release of Martin Kostza, at Smyrna, on July 2, 1853, and also in correspondence with the government of Prussia.

always been treated, in this country, with peculiar favor. Our vast public domain affords them a cheap freehold on their first arrival; and our easy terms of naturalization enable them in five years to acquire the proud title of American citizens. The fear is, that in our eagerness to open an asylum to the oppressed of other climes and to increase our population beyond all former example, we have been too liberal in the inducements held out to immigrants. It is, indeed, becoming a momentous question, whether more time should not be required to educate and prepare them for the high responsibilities of citizens of a free government. Yet, when we reflect upon the fate of the celebrated alien law of 1798, we have little reason to hope for any change in this feature of our policy. This law merely authorized the president to order out of the country such aliens as he should consider dangerous to its peace and safety, under severe penalties for disobedience. And yet it was immediately cried down, and now forms a standing topic of opprobrium.

§ 55. **Power as to Bankruptcy.** (*a*) The words are, "Congress shall have power to establish uniform laws on the subject of bankruptcies throughout the United States." This power is intimately connected with that of regulating commerce; for bankrupt laws most particularly affect merchants and traders; though they may be made to include all insolvent persons. The leading objects of a bankrupt law are four: *First*, to compel an equal distribution of the effects of the bankrupt among his creditors without preference, in proportion to their claims; for which purpose the law defines what shall be considered acts of bankruptcy; and from the moment of committing one of these acts, the power of the bankrupt over his property is at an end, and the commissioners are appointed to take possession and settle with the creditors. *Secondly*, to exempt not only the person of the bankrupt from imprisonment, but also his future acquisitions from liability for his then existing debts; for which purpose the creditors are compelled to take their respective portions of his effects, in full discharge and satisfaction of their claims. *Thirdly*, to promote honesty; for which purpose not only is the discharge made dependent upon the honesty of the bankrupt, but severe penalties are annexed to dishonesty. *Fourthly*, to encourage future efforts; for which purpose if all is found to have been fair and honest, not only is the bankrupt released from future liability for past debts, but he is allowed a small sum out of the wreck of his fortune, with which to begin the world anew. Such are the general features of a bankrupt law; and their humanity and equity would seem sufficient at once to commend

(*a*) See Mad. Pap. 1481; 2 Black. Com. ch. 31; 2 Story, Const. § 1106; 2 Kent, Com. 389; and the 5th and 6th volumes of the Law Reporter, containing numerous decisions upon the act of 1841; 1 West. Law J. 143; Chapman *v.* Forsyth, 2 How. 202; 2 Parsons on Contracts, 588. There is a full discussion of the law of bankruptcy and insolvency in the tenth chapter of the second volume (pp. 579–682) of Prof. Parsons's valuable treatise referred to. Bump on Bankruptcy.

them to every mind. The wonder is, that Congress should have so long slept over a power which might be so beneficially exerted. In 1800, a bankrupt law was enacted; but three years after, before a fair experiment could be made, it was repealed. Another bankrupt law, passed in 1841, shared a similar fate in a year after it took effect. (*a*) The States, therefore, have been compelled to take the matter into their own hands; and several of them have enacted bankrupt laws. For some time the constitutionality of these laws was doubted; but it was finally decided that the power is not vested exclusively in Congress. (*b*) If there be a bankrupt law of Con-

(*a*) In 1867, Congress again passed a bankrupt law, now no longer in force. It provides for the appointment of one or more registers in bankruptcy, in each congressional district, to assist the judge of the district court. They are nominated by the chief justice, and confirmed by the district judge. Ordinary proceedings are conducted before these registers, who certify questions of difficulty arising before them to the judge for decision. Appeal lies from such decisions to the circuit and thence to the supreme court. Any bankrupt may apply himself for the benefit of this act, in which case it is termed a voluntary bankruptcy; or any creditor of any person may, upon the commission of certain specified acts by his debtor, or upon any intention being shown of defrauding his creditors, institute proceedings against such debtor, in which case it is termed involuntary bankruptcy. As soon as the creditor is adjudged a bankrupt under either form of proceeding, he is divested of all his property, which is conveyed by the register to an assignee appointed by the creditors or the court. The assignee holds the property for the benefit of all the creditors, except certain exempted articles not to exceed a certain value, which he reconveys to the debtor. After Jan. 1, 1869, no discharge can be granted to any bankrupt who does not pay at least fifty per cent of his liabilities. This act went into operation June 1, 1867.

(*b*) In Sturges *v.* Crowninshield, 4 Wheaton, 122, a note was made in New York to a citizen of Massachusetts, *before* the passing of a bankrupt law by the legislature of New York, the effect of which was to liberate both the person and property of the debtor from all future liability for prior debts. The maker of the note was sued in Massachusetts, and there pleaded his discharge under the law of New York. The circuit court were divided in opinion, and the case was certified to the supreme court. The question submitted was, whether the law of New York *impaired the obligation of the contract*, within the meaning of the prohibition. The court decided that it did. A contract is an agreement in which a party undertakes to do or not to do a particular thing. The law binds him to perform his undertaking, and this is the obligation of his contract. Any law which releases this obligation in whole or in part, must, in the literal sense of the word, impair it. Such was the law of New York, for it gave an absolute discharge from all future liability. Parties, when they contract, have in view, not only present property, but future acquisitions. Industry, talents, and integrity constitute a fund which is as confidently trusted as property itself. Future acquisitions are, therefore, liable for contracts, and to release them for ever from this liability, impairs their obligation. But insolvent laws, which merely release the person of the debtor from imprisonment, and not his after-acquired property from liability, would not impair the obligation of contracts. The court did not seem to rest their decision upon the important fact that the note was made before the passing of the bankrupt law. They guarded their opinion by these words: "This opinion is confined to a case in which a creditor sues in a court, the proceedings of which, the legislature, whose act is pleaded, had not a right to control; and to a case where the creditor had not proceeded to execution against the body of his debtor, within the State whose law attempts to absolve a confined insolvent debtor from his obligation." In Ogden *v.* Saunders, 12 Wheaton, 213, the facts were these: The acceptor of a bill, at the time of accepting, resided in New York, and the payee in Kentucky. After accepting the bill, he removed to Louisiana, and was there sued on his acceptance. He pleaded his discharge under a bankrupt law of New York, which existed *prior* to his accepting the bill. This case, it will be seen, differs from Sturges *v.* Crowninshield in this, that the law was made before the contract; and from McMillan *v.* McNeil, 4 Wheaton, 209, in this, that the discharge was had under the law of gress in operation, the States cannot contravene its provisions. But until this be the case, they may pass bankrupt laws, provided they do not violate another constitutional provision, which prohibits them from "impairing the obligation of contracts." In relation to this provision, the decisions amount to this: that between citi-

the State where the contract was made. The court, therefore, were not bound by either of the foregoing decisions. The question was, whether a State bankrupt law impaired the obligation of *posterior contracts* entered into in that State. And it was decided, four judges against three, that it did not. The ground they took was, that where a contract was entered into, after the passage of a law relating to it, between parties subject to that law, that law is incorporated into the contract, and becomes one of its terms. It cannot, therefore, be said to impair its obligation. The meaning of the prohibition must be understood, as if the words had been, no State shall pass any law impairing the obligation of *prior* contracts. The intention was by this prohibition to guard against *retroactive* laws in relation to *contracts*, in the same manner as by another, to guard against retroactive laws in relation to *crimes*. Accordingly, *statutes of usury*, which affect the *validity* of contracts; *statutes of frauds*, which affect the *evidence* of contracts; and *statutes of limitation* and *bankruptcy*, which affect the *remedy* on contracts, — would all be constitutional as to *posterior* contracts, and unconstitutional as to *prior*. The other question raised was, whether the discharge of a debtor under a State bankrupt law would be valid against a creditor belonging to another State, who has never voluntarily submitted himself to the laws of that State, otherwise than by the origin of his contract. In the present case, the payee of the bill, as well as the drawer, were citizens of Kentucky. And the court decided that a discharge under a State law would not discharge a debt due to a citizen of another State. The report of the whole adjudication on both points, the court stated in the following words: "As between citizens of the same State, a discharge of a bankrupt by the laws of that State, is valid as it affects *posterior contracts;* but as against creditors who are citizens of other States, it is invalid as to *all* contracts." Five years before this decision was made, our supreme court came to the same conclusion, in the case of Smith *v.* Parsons, 1 Ohio, 236, where a most convincing opinion was pronounced by Judge Burnet. Still earlier, the supreme court of New York held the same doctrine in Mather *v.* Bush, 16 Johns. 233. The only opposing authority I have found, is the case of Blanchard *v.* Russell, 13 Mass. 1. This is directly contradictory on the last point above taken, as to the residence of the creditor, all the material facts being precisely the same as in Ogden *v.* Saunders. But this case arose before the question was discussed in any of the cases before mentioned. On the first point, as to impairing obligations, the decision was the same as above. To what extent State legislation on remedies existing when the contract was made is constitutional, see Bronson *v.* McKensie, 1 How. 311; McCracken *v.* Hayward, 2 id. 608; Rockwell *v.* Hubbell, 2 Doug. (Mich.) 197; Bronson *v.* Newberry, id. 38; Mundy *v.* Monroe, 1 Mann. (Mich.) 68; Quackenbush *v.* Danks, 1 Denio, 128; s. c. 3 id. 594; 1 N. Y. 129; Morse *v.* Goold, 11 N. Y. 282; Conkey *v.* Hart, 14 N. Y. 22; Falkner *v.* Dorman, 7 Wis. 388; Vedder *v.* Alkenbrack, 6 Barb. 327; Gardenhire *v.* McCombs, 1 Sneed, 83; Thorne *v.* San Francisco, 4 Cal. 127; Bacon *v.* Howard, 20 How. 22; Bank of Alabama *v.* Dalton, 9 id. 522; Bugbee *v.* Howard, 32 Ala. 713; Coosa River Steamboat Co. *v.* Barclay, 30 id. 120. A certificate of discharge under the insolvent laws of a State, is a bar to an action on a contract between two citizens of that State, though made and to be performed in another State. Marsh *v.* Putnam, 3 Gray, 551. It was held in Massachusetts, that a discharge under its insolvent laws is a bar to an action by a citizen of another State, on a contract which, by its express terms, is to be executed in Massachusetts. Scribner *v.* Fisher, 2 Gray, 43; Burrall *v.* Rice, 5 id. 539. See Whitney *v.* Whiting, 35 N. H. 457. *Contra*, Poe *v.* Duck, 5 Md. 1; Potter *v.* Kerr, id. 275; Pugh *v.* Bussell, 2 Blackf. 394; Donelly *v.* Corbett, 8 N. Y. 500. See 2 Parsons on Cont. 595. Or on a note between residents indorsed to a non-resident. Thomas *v.* Crow, 65 Cal. 470. But a debt due to a citizen of another State is not barred where there is no express stipulation that it is payable in Massachusetts. Savage *v.* Marsh, 10 Met. 594; Fiske *v.* Foster, 10 id. 597; Dinsmore *v.* Bradley, 5 Gray, 487; Houghton *v.* Maynard, 5 id. 552. State insolvent laws, in so far as they seek to discharge the debtor, are suspended by the existence of a national bankruptcy law. Boese *v.* King, 108 U. S. 379.

zens of the State where the law is made, it is valid as to posterior contracts, and invalid as to prior; but with respect to citizens of other States, it is invalid as to all contracts. It is obvious, therefore, that no consent among the States, if that were practicable, can supply the want of a general bankrupt law for the whole Union. In this State, no movement has ever been made towards a bankrupt law. There is a provision in our bill of rights, declaring that "No person shall be imprisoned for debt in any civil action on mesne or final process, unless in case of fraud." And Congress, in 1839 and 1841, adopted the legislation of the States, as to process issuing from the federal courts, in reference to imprisonment for debt. In the spirit of these provisions we have "an act for the relief of insolvent debtors," by taking the benefit of which, any insolvent person may secure himself against imprisonment for any debt then existing. The condition of this exemption is, that he make an honest assignment of all his property for the benefit of his creditors. We also have another law, which in a measure abolishes the preference of one creditor to another by an assignment of property in contemplation of insolvency, by declaring that such assignment shall enure to the general benefit of all the creditors. This is the nearest approach we have made towards a State bankrupt law.

§ 56. **Power as to the Currency.** (*a*) Congress has power "to coin money, and regulate the value thereof, and of foreign coin:" also, "to provide for the punishment of counterfeiting the securities and current coin of the United States;" and "no State shall coin money, emit bills of credit, or make any thing but gold and silver coin a tender in payment of debts." The force and importance of these provisions will be best understood by first adverting to the nature and functions of the *currency* or *circulating medium*. In civilized life no individual produces exactly what he consumes. The division of labor, ever extending as society advances, makes a countless multitude contribute to the wants of each. But this is not done gratuitously. Each gives something in exchange for what he receives. Thus all the productions of human labor are incessantly passing from hand to hand, in an endless process of distribution. But how shall these changes be effected? Barter alone will not suffice. Occasionally, I may have a commodity which you want, and you one which I want, so that we can make a direct exchange. But even in this case, we should want some known *measure of value;* and, in all other cases, we should also want a

(*a*) The provisions relating to coin occasioned no debate in the convention. Mad. Pap. 1343. But a proposition to authorize Congress to emit bills of credit was rejected by a vote of 9 to 2. The reason assigned in debate was a decided hostility to paper-money — id. 1343–6. The same sentiments were expressed upon the proposition to prohibit the States from emitting bills of credit, which was carried by a vote of 8 to 1 — id. 1442. On the whole, it seems quite clear that the convention intended to prohibit paper money in every shape. For an account of the coins current in this country, see American Almanac for 1835; for the legal-tender decisions, see *supra*, § 52.

medium of exchange. In a word, society requires, for facilitating exchanges, some convenient thing of universal notoriety, which every one will take for what he has to sell, both as measuring its value and paying for it. Such are the properties of what we call *money;* which, by universal consent, has become the measure of value and the medium of exchange in all the transactions of life. And what substance possesses the properties requisite for money in the highest degree? The voice of ages has decided in favor of the precious metals, *gold* and *silver*. *First*, because a great value can be comprised in a small bulk, which is not the case with baser metals. *Secondly*, because they waste very little with using; it having been computed that gold in circulation does not lose more than one-hundredth in twenty-five years, and silver about half that amount. *Thirdly*, because they are little liable to fluctuation in value. Value is affected chiefly by the cost of production and the regularity of supply. Since the discovery of America, neither of these elements of value has perceptibly changed. (*a*) The annual supply from all the known mines of Europe and America is nearly the same in amount, and costs nearly the same labor, one year with another. And should this quantity hereafter be found to vary considerably, still the variation would bear so small a proportion to the entire amount of these metals now in existence, which is supposed to be about five thousand millions, that the fluctuation would be scarcely felt. It is true, that of the gross amount just mentioned only about two-fifths is in the shape of money; but this does not affect the question of value, because the value is changed little, if any, by converting these metals from *bullion* into money. This is done by a process called *coining*, which consists in giving to each piece an authoritative stamp, expressing its weight and fineness; and thereby adapting it to pass currently from hand to hand, without the trouble of weighing and assaying at each transfer.

Such being the nature and functions of money, we are prepared to understand the meaning of the provisions above quoted. The power "*to coin money*" (*b*) is given to Congress, and withheld from the States, in order to insure a *uniform currency* throughout the Union. This power involves that of "*regulating its value*." But in order to insure a *sound*, as well as uniform, currency, it was further necessary either to prohibit the circulation of "*foreign coins*" altogether, or else confer the further power of regulating their value. The former alternative would produce inconvenience, and the latter was adopted. The only danger would now arise from the "*counterfeiting*" of the coins thus provided for; and accordingly power is given to prevent this by punishment. Thus, so far as *coins* are concerned, effectual means are provided for securing to the whole country that greatest of commercial blessings, a sound

(*a*) This was written before the discovery of the mines in California and Australia.

(*b*) On the subject of coins and mints, see note to 1 Stat. at Large, 246; 5 Stat. at Large, 136; act of Feb. 21, 1853; 7th section of the act of March 3, 1853.

and uniform currency. And in the exercise of this power, Congress has created *mints*, with the appropriate officers, for the purpose of coining. When bullion is brought to the mint, of the standard value, it is coined for the owner free of expense; but if below the standard value, he is required to pay the expense, which is called *seigniorage*. It will be remembered that Congress is not restricted to gold and silver; and therefore copper is used for such values as are too small to be conveniently measured by the other two. If to this we add the adoption of the *decimal scale* commonly called *federal money*, by which the dollar is made the *unit* of value, and all the other denominations are found by multiplying or dividing by ten, we have in theory a complete money system. But the practical difficulty has hitherto been to adjust accurately the relative values of gold and silver. Up to 1834, they stood in the coins as fifteen to one. But at the same time, the market value of the two metals in bullion was nearly as fifteen and eight-tenths to one. The consequence was, that gold could not be kept in circulation, being at once bought up and uncoined. By the act of 1834, the eagle was reduced from two hundred and forty-seven and a half grains of fine gold to two hundred and thirty-two grains; which makes a difference in actual value of sixty-six and a half cents. Whether the true ratio is now attained, remains to be tested by experience. If not, one will be withdrawn from circulation as before.

The remaining provisions prohibit the States from "emitting bills of credit," and from "making anything but gold and silver coin a tender in payment of debts." (*a*) In order to understand these prohibitions, we must glance at the nature and history of what is called *paper-money*. Admitting that paper can in any way be made to supply the place of metallic money, or specie, the motives for making the substitution are three; *First*, specie has an intrinsic value, equal to its current value, or nearly so; while paper has comparatively no intrinsic value at all. Hence, by substituting paper for specie, there would be a saving to the whole country of the interest on the amount of the circulating medium, which may be set down at one hundred and fifty millions of dollars. *Secondly*, paper-money is much more portable than specie; that is, more easily transferred from place to place. *Thirdly*, a paper currency is more elastic than specie; that is, more readily susceptible of contraction or expansion, to meet the occasions of a trading community, liable to sudden fluctuations; because the material can be had at any time and in any quantity. The question then is, How can paper be made to pass for money? There are but two methods. In the first place, government may *compel* the people to take it as money. Despotic governments have often resorted to such high-handed expedients. And when this course is adopted,

(*a*) By the second section of the act of Feb. 21, 1853, it would seem that silver coins are legal tenders only for sums not exceeding five dollars.

it makes but little difference whether the paper purports to be *redeemable* in specie or not; since its circulation is the result of compulsion. During our revolution, the State issued "*bills of credit*," known by the name of *continental money*, to an immense amount. These bills purported to be redeemable at some future time, by the States which issued them; but the general want of confidence soon made it necessary to bolster up their credit, by resolving, as Congress did, that whosoever should refuse to take these bills as money "should be treated as an enemy to his country." The despotic power was wanting, however, to sustain this resolve; and there was a constant depreciation in the value of these bills, until they finally ceased to be worth anything. It was to guard against the recurrence of such a state of things, that the States are now prohibited from "emitting bills of credit." And lest this prohibition might be evaded, by substituting something else equally worthless, in the place of specie, a further one was added, and designed to cover the whole ground. The States are prohibited from "making any thing but gold and silver coin" a legal tender; that is, from compelling the people to take anything but specie as money. How, then, are we to account for the fact, that so small a part of our circulating medium consists of specie? To explain this, we must advert to the other method of making paper pass for money. This does not depend upon compulsion. There is no attempt to force a value upon that which has no value. Our paper currency consists of *promises to pay specie on demand*, which we call *notes* or *bills*. Their credit depends solely upon public confidence in the ability of the promisors to redeem them whenever called on so to do. No one is compelled to receive them as money; but while all believe they will at any moment command specie, they circulate as freely as specie. How, then, is this general confidence sustained? If those who issue these bills are required to keep in reserve an equal amount of specie, in order to redeem them, dollar for dollar, at the shortest notice, there is no profit in the operation. And if not, whence the confidence in their immediate redeemability? The answer is, that the whole paper scheme is founded on the presumption that the holders of these bills will not generally ask for specie at the same time; and therefore the amount of specie kept in reserve bears but a small proportion to the notes in circulation. And this is the great evil of the system. A general and simultaneous demand for specie cannot possibly be met, and disaster must follow. To enforce a universal performance of these promises, is to insure their being broken. Every sudden panic, therefore, must produce wide-spread calamity.

But let us inquire who make these promises or issue these bills. It cannot be the States directly, for they are expressly prohibited from issuing "bills of credit." If the United States possess the power, they have not exercised it, except in the case of treasury notes. And in most of the States, as in Ohio, private individuals are prohibited, from motives of public policy. Whence, then, does this paper issue? The answer is, from incorporated companies, under the name of *banks*. A charter enables a large number of persons to unite their means, and thus do conjointly and conveniently, what neither of them could do alone. The question then arises, can the States constitutionally incorporate banks with power to emit these bills of credit? Were this a new question, I should not hesitate to say that the States cannot do indirectly what they are prohibited from doing directly. They cannot confer a power which they do not possess. No one can read the provisions before quoted, in connection with the antecedent history, without being convinced that the federal constitution intended to prevent the States from supplying, in any way, the currency of the country. For we are thus exposed to precisely the same evils, as if these bills were issued directly by the States, and against which the prohibitions were designed to secure us. But as State banks have been in existence from a period prior to the formation of the federal constitution, it is now too late to question their constitutionality. (*a*) And the same may be said of the power of Congress to incorporate a *national bank*. (*b*) It has been too long acquiesced in to be called in question now. As an original question, however, it is much less doubtful than the other, as will be shown hereafter, when we come to speak of incidental powers. Still there are many persons who hold with much plausibility, that it was the intention of the framers of the federal constitution to exclude paper-money altogether, and confine the circulating medium to the metallic money coined and regulated by Congress. The provisions we have been discussing, certainly look that way. And though it may now be too late to return to such a state of things, yet a consideration of all the evils incident to our paper system, compared with its advantages, almost inclines one to wish it had never been introduced.

The principal functions of banks are the three following: *First*, they receive money on deposit for safe-keeping, with the privilege of using it until called for; which money is drawn out as the depositor wants it, by means of *checks*, or brief orders to pay the bearer. *Secondly*, they loan money at interest, by discounting the notes and bills of their customers; for which purpose they avail themselves of the average amount of the deposits, in addition to their actual capital. *Thirdly*, in performing these operations, they issue their own notes, instead of specie, whenever their customers will take them. From the combination of these three operations, they are called banks of *deposit*, *discount*, and *circula-*

(*a*) See on this subject the cases of Craig *v.* Missouri, 4 Peters, 410, and Briscoe *v.* The Bank of Kentucky, 11 Peters, 257, where State banks, founded upon actual capital, and not upon State Credit, are held to be constitutional. The bills of a bank which has corporate property, are not bills of credit within the meaning of this clause, although the State creating the bank is the only stockholder, and pledges its faith to the ultimate redemption of the bills. Darrington *v.* The Bank of Alabama, 13 How. 12.

(*b*) See McCulloch *v.* Maryland, 4 Wheaton, 316; Osborn *v.* Bank U. S., 9 Wheaton, 738.

tion; and such are the curious and complicated engines which supply a large part of our circulating medium. Each bank is under the management of a board of directors, elected by the stockholders, and sharing a divided responsibility. Their proceedings may be conducted in profound secrecy, since the public at large have no power of inspection. They are under a constant temptation to extend their issues beyond their means of redemption, because these reserved means, consisting of specie in their vaults, constitute their only unproductive capital. They rely, as we have seen, upon the general forbearance of their creditors, whether depositors or note-holders, to demand specie, except on special occasions; which demand, if made at the same time by all creditors upon all the banks, must inevitably produce universal bankruptcy; because the effect of the system is not to keep specie enough in the country to redeem one dollar in ten of the paper. If, therefore, anything happens to disturb the general confidence upon which alone this forbearance depends, and create a panic, the consequence, even to prudent banks, is temporary embarrassment; and to imprudent banks ultimate insolvency.

§ 57. **Power as to Weights and Measures.** (*a*) The words are, "to fix the standard of weights and measures." The design of conferring this power on Congress was, that weights and measures might be uniform throughout the United States. But, although the subject has been pressed upon the attention of Congress by elaborate reports, nothing has ever yet been done. And the common understanding is, that until Congress shall fix a general standard for the States, each State is at liberty to fix one for itself. (*b*) Anything like uniformity, therefore, must be the result of accident. In Ohio, an act was passed in 1811, to regulate measures; but there was nothing on the subject of weights until 1835, when an act was passed regulating both weights and measures. This act adopts the standard of New York. The great desideratum has been to find some standard which would never vary, and, if lost, could be replaced. Such a standard would be perfect; and vast sums have been expended by the governments of Europe in experiments to attain it. Perhaps, however, ours is as nearly perfect as need be desired. The *standard of measure* is a *yard*, as used in New York on the fourth of July, 1776; the length of which bears to the length of a pendulum vibrating seconds, at Columbia College in a vacuum, at the temperature of melting ice, the proportion of one million to one million eighty-six thousand one hundred and forty-one. If, therefore, perfectly accurate experiments could be made, the constancy of this standard would be equal to the constancy of gravitation; and, if lost, such experiments could replace it. The act then declares that

(*a*) See 1 Black. Com. 226; 2 Story, Const. § 1122.

(*b*) Since the text was written, this State, by the act of 1846, adopted the standard furnished by the secretary of the United States treasury, pursuant to a resolution of Congress, adopted in 1836.

"the standard thus defined, shall be measured in a straight line between two points, engraven upon golden disks, inserted into a straight brass rod;" and this is to serve as an original standard of measure, from which all other denominations of length, surface, and solidity, are obtained by multiplication or division. The *standard of weight* is a pound, of such magnitude that the weight of a cubic foot of distilled water, at its maximum density, weighed in a vacuum with brass weights, shall be equal to sixty-two and a half such pounds. Thus the standard of weight is dependent upon that of measure. A standard pound is to be made of brass, according to this estimate, and to serve as an original standard of weight, from which all other denominations may be derived. The *standard of capacity* is a *gallon*, of which there are two kinds; one for *liquid measure*, the other for *dry measure*. The *liquid gallon* contains eight pounds of distilled water at its maximum density, at the mean pressure of the atmosphere, on the level of the sea; and the *dry gallon* ten pounds of the same. Thus the standard of capacity depends upon the standard of weight, as that does upon the standard of measure. An original standard gallon of each kind is to be made of brass, from which all other denominations are derived as before. There are divers other specifications for which I have not room. The act requires the secretary of state, who is made the State sealer of weights and measures, to procure original standards, as above defined, and keep them in a chest in his office. He is to furnish the auditor of each county, who is made the county sealer, with copies of these originals. And thus every citizen has a convenient means of procuring accurate weights and measures. To insure conformity, it is made penal to use any other weights and measures than those thus defined. (*a*)

§ 58. **Power as to Crimes and Punishment.** (*b*) As a general principle, the power of punishment is reserved to the States, as belonging properly to their internal police; and the cases in which Congress possesses this power, may be considered as exceptions created by necessity. In some of these cases, the power is expressly conferred, and in others it is incidental. I shall here confine myself to the former. Congress has the express power of punishment in the five following cases: 1. "To punish counterfeiting the securities and current coin of the United States:" which has been already considered. 2. "To define and punish piracies and felonies committed on the high seas." Without inquiring minutely into the meaning of these terms, it is suffi-

(*a*) The use of weights and measures, of what is called the metric system, which is the French system, was legalized by Congress July 28, 1866. The Chicago Chamber of Commerce, and perhaps some others, attempted to adopt the system in their reports, but it was found inconvenient on account of its newness, and, I believe, has been dropped. The act gives tables for the conversion of one system into the other.

(*b*) See 2 Story, Const. ch. xx., xxvii.; 1 Swift's Dig. 264. Mad. Pap. 1347–9, 1575. See People *v.* Tyler, 7 Mich. 61.

cient here to say, that they include all the offences on the high seas which require punishment; and their locality points out Congress as the proper power to provide for their punishment. 3. "To define and punish offences against the law of nations." Without specifying what these offences are, it is sufficient here to say that their nature makes them the proper subject of national cognizance. 4. "To declare the punishment of treason." (*a*) In the preceding cases, the power was to *define*, as well as punish. But treason being the highest of all crimes, is, for the security of the people, defined in the constitution itself. "Treason against the United States shall consist only in levying war against them, or in adhering to their enemies, giving them aid and comfort." This language would seem to indicate that there may be treason *against a State;* and the same inference may be drawn from the provision respecting fugitives from justice, to be described hereafter, which speaks of treason as a crime of which a State may have jurisdiction. Accordingly, several of the States provide for punishing treason against themselves. This was the case in Ohio, until 1824. (*b*) But the point has never been definitely settled, and is one of no small difficulty. Without some other definition, however, it is not easy to imagine a case of treason against a State, which would not also be treason against the United States. But, however this may be, it is manifestly proper that treason against the United States should be punished by the United States. There is, however, a limitation to this power. "No attainder of treason shall work corruption of blood, or forfeiture, beyond the life of the person attainted." Of this limitation it is only necessary to say that, as Congress has made death the punishment, there is no corruption of blood or forfeiture at all. There is still another provision relating to the evidence of treason. "No person shall be convicted of treason, unless on the testimony of two witnesses to the same overt act, or on confession in open court." The peculiar anxiety thus manifested, on the subject of treason, is justified by the history of England, where treason has been made a most terrific engine in the hands of arbitrary power. 5. "To punish all offences committed within the District of Columbia, and other places over which Congress exercises exclusive legislation." These places will be specified hereafter. The federal constitution contains but one other provision relating to crimes and punishments, which is, "that the trial of all crimes, except in cases of impeachment, shall be by jury; and such trial shall be held in the State where the said crimes shall have been committed; but when not committed within any State, the trial shall be at such place or places, as the Congress may by law have directed." But all these provisions will be discussed

(*a*) Mad. Pap. 1371-7; *Ex parte* Bollman, 4 Cranch, 75; Burr's case, 4 Cranch, 470; Story's Charge, 1 Story's Rep. 614.

(*b*) Another act was passed April 26, 1868, defining treason against the State, and declaring its punishment.

more at large, hereafter, when we come to the subject of criminal law. The incidental power of punishment will also be considered in its place.

§ 59. **Power as to Post-offices and Post Roads.** (*a*) The words are, "to establish post-offices and post roads." The propriety of vesting this power in Congress, results from the consideration, that the States could not have made the system what it is, because no one State could legislate beyond its own limits. At best, therefore, an arrangement of this kind, consisting of thirty-one distinct parts, must have been confused and disjointed. Whether all power relating to the subject is taken from the States, or not, is a question not decided, and of no great importance; since the grand benefits of the establishment must always be the fruits of federal legislation. If the States can do any thing, it is only in subordination thereto. But what is implied in the power to "establish post-offices and post roads?" Some have held that these words only authorize Congress to direct where post-offices shall be kept, and on what roads the mail shall be carried; and not to construct either buildings or roads for the purpose. But this construction involves the solecism of requiring Congress to effect an end, without the power of using the proper means; and, in practice, a much more liberal construction has been given to these words. Congress has derived, from this brief clause, power to create the post-office department before mentioned; to make provision for transporting the mail from every point of the Union to every other point; and to secure its safety and dispatch by adequate penalties for every obstruction or depredation. To particularize these very numerous provisions does not fall within my purpose. But no language would be too strong to describe the blessing we enjoy in this certain and rapid means of receiving and communicating intelligence. Hitherto the rates of postage have been such, that the post-office department has supported itself. But every one feels, that, were not this the case, the public money could not be better expended, than for this universal public accommodation.

§ 60. **Power as to Copyright and Patent-rights.** (*b*) The words are, "to promote the progress of science and useful arts, by securing for limited times, to authors and inventors, the exclusive right to their respective writings and discoveries." These words,

(*a*) The institution of private expresses, which now reach over nearly the whole of the civilized world, has made it a very important question how far these expresses are authorized to carry letters or other mailable matter. In the case of U. S. *v.* Adams & Co., in the district court of New York, in 1843 (see 1 West. Law Journ. 315), Judge Betts, referring to the act of 1825, held that the defendants were not liable for letters in a package, unless they knew it contained letters. And in the case of U. S. *v.* Kimball, in the district court of Massachusetts (see 1 West. Law Journ. 399), Judge Sprague, referring to the same act, held a similar doctrine.

(*b*) See 2 Black. Com. 405; 2 Kent, Com. 298, 315; 2 Story, Const. ch. xix.; 10 Amer. Jur. 63; Maugham on Literary Property; Nicklin on Copyright; Phillips on Patents; Godson on Patents; Webster on Patents; Curtis on Copyrights; Curtis on Patents; Law on Patents and Copyrights.

include "*authors*" and "*inventors*" only, and not introducers. The right intended to be secured to authors is called *copyright*, and to inventors *patent-right*. (*a*) The propriety of vesting this power in Congress, results from the consideration that the States

(*a*) Congress in 1870 passed an act for the registration, regulation, and protection of *Trademarks*, analogous to the acts protecting copyrights. The supreme court of the United States held this act was void; because a trademark, not being an invention, a discovery, or a writing, does not come within the purview of the constitution concerning copyright and patents; and the act, being applicable to all commerce, did not come within the power given to Congress over certain commerce. United States *v.* Steffens, 100 U. S. 82. In March, 1881, an act was passed for the registration and protection of trademarks used in commerce with foreign nations and with Indian tribes. These acts do not affect the right of ownership in trademarks, or the right to sue at law or in equity to maintain such rights. United States *v.* Roche, 1 McCrary, C. Ct. 385; Shaver *v.* Shaver, 54 Iowa, 208.

The right of property in trademarks was recognized at common law at an early date. Case referred to by Doderidge, J., in Southern *v.* How, Popham, 144. But as late as 1742 Lord Hardwicke refused to allow an injunction in such case, saying he knew no instance of restraining one trader from making use of the same mark with another. Blanchard *v.* Hill, 2 Atk. 484. But since Croft *v.* Day, 7 Beav. 84, the practice of protecting the exclusive right in trademarks has been firmly established.

As stated by Justice Strong in Canal Co. *v.* Clark, 13 Wall. 311, see 322, "the office of a trademark is to point out distinctively the origin or ownership of the article to which it is affixed; or, in other words, to give notice who was the producer." As stated by Lord Justice James in Singer Manufacturing Company *v.* Long, L. R. 18 Ch. Div. 395, see 412, the rule of law on which property in a trademark is founded "is, that no man is entitled to represent his goods as being the goods of another man; and no man is permitted to use any mark, sign or symbol, device, or other means, whereby, without making a direct false representation himself to a purchaser who purchases from him, he enables such purchaser to tell a lie or make a false representation to somebody else who is the ultimate purchaser." Hence the owner of a trademark will be protected in its use only so far as it serves to indicate the origin or ownership of the goods to which it is affixed. Falkinburg *v.* Lucy, 35 Cal. 52.

Any mark, sign, symbol, or device, used to identify the origin or manufacturer of an article, may be used as a trademark, as the manufacturer's own name — Burgess *v.* Burgess, 3 De Gex, M. & G. 896; England *v.* N. Y. Publishing Co., 8 Daly (N. Y.), 375; a mere number, as the figures 35 — Collins *v.* Reynolds, &c., 7 Abbott (N. Y.), New Cas. 17; the name "Charter Oak," cast on cooking-stoves — Filley *v.* Fassett, 44 Mo. 168; or the word "Pride" on cigar boxes — Hier *v.* Abrahams, 82 N. Y. 519 {"sliced" animals or objects on dissected puzzles — Selchow *v.* Baker, 93 N. Y. 59}. But letters or figures affixed to merchandise by a manufacturer for the purpose of denoting its quality only do not constitute a trademark. Amoskeag Manufacturing Co. *v.* Trainer, 101 U. S. 51. Nor do words merely denoting the ingredients of which the article is composed. Raggett *v.* Findlater, L. R. 17 Eq. 29; Ayer *v.* Rushton, 7 Daly (N. Y.), 9; Caswell *v.* Davis, 58 N. Y. 223; Van Beil *v.* Prescott, 46 N. Y. Super. Ct. 542. The name of a geographical district cannot be used as a trademark to the exclusion of other producers of the same article in the same district. The name "Lackawanna Coal" cannot be appropriated as a trademark by the owners of one coal-mine in the Lackawanna Valley, as against other coal-mines in the same valley. Canal Co. *v.* Clark, 13 Wall. 311. The word "Durham" may be used as a trademark common to all the manufacturers of tobacco in the town of Durham, to the exclusion of all other manufacturers of tobacco. The word "Durham" in connection with the figure of a Durham bull may be the exclusive trademark of a single manufacturer in that town. Blackwell *v.* Dibrell, 3 Hughes, C. Ct. 151. The name of a mineral spring, the water of which has peculiar properties, may be used as a trademark by the owner of the spring. Congress and Empire Spring Co. *v.* High Rock Congress Spring Co., 45 N. Y. 271.

If the thing on which the trademark is used is a fraud or imposition, the exclusive use will not be protected by injunction. Connell *v.* Reed, 128 Mass. 477; Palmer *v.* Harris, 60 Pa. St. 156; Seabury *v.* Grosvenor, 14 Blatchf. C. Ct. 262. If the trademark itself, or the words used on the label in connection with it, convey a deception, equity will not aid. Buckland *v.* Rice, 40 Ohio State, 526; Leather Cloth Co. *v.*

could not exercise it efficiently. A copy of patent-right confined to a single State, would afford but little encouragement to intellectual efforts; whereas, the declared object of the power is "to

American Leather Cloth Co., 11 House of Lords Cases, 523; Manhattan Medicine Co. *v.* Wood, 108 U. S. 218.

A trademark is seldom copied exactly by those who desire without right to profit by it. The question is more frequently presented by "colorable imitations," that is, by devices not a precise copy of a known trademark, but adopting so much of it, or such striking portions of it, or having such a general resemblance to it, as to beguile the ordinary purchasers of the article. A full discussion of what constitutes a colorable imitation is found in Orr-Ewing *v.* Johnson, L. R. 13 Ch. Div. 431. Instances are presented in Godillot *v.* Harris, 81 N. Y. 263; Brown *v.* Mercer, 37 N. Y. Super. Ct. 265; India Rubber Co. *v.* Rubber Comb Co., 45 N. Y. Super. Ct. 258; Enoch Morgan's Sons *v.* Swachofer, 5 Abbott (N. Y.), New Cas. 265; Same plaintiff *v.* Troxell, 23 Hun, 633; Electro Silicon Co. *v.* Trask, 59 How. (N. Y.) Pr. 189; Same plaintiff *v.* Levy, id. p. 469.

After the expiration of the patent, the words "Fairbanks' Patent," which had been used on the patented scales, could not be claimed by the former owners of the patent as a trademark, and one who made scales the same as had been patented, but did not hold them out as made by Fairbanks & Co., could not be molested for putting upon his goods, as their appropriate description, "Fairbanks' Patent." Fairbanks *v.* Jacobus, 14 Blatchf. 337. One who, during the existence of the patent for a cooking-stove, which bore the trademark "Charter Oak," manufactured and sold, with the acquiescence of the patentee, the stove with the trademark upon it, could not, after the expiration of the patent, be restrained from continuing such manufacture and sale, provided that he did not represent the stoves so made by him to be made by the former owner of the patent. Filley *v.* Child, 16 Blatchf. C. Ct. 376. In the United States it has been held that the words "Singer" and "Singer Machine" denote a particular mechanism, a particular species of machine, and can therefore be used by all who can rightfully manufacture the machine, and hence, on the expiration of the patent, the former owner of the patent has no right of action against any person who makes the machine and puts the name upon it. Singer Manufacturing Co. *v.* Stanage, 2 McCrary, C. Ct. 512. The same decision was made by Drummond, Circuit Judge. In England it was held by the House of Lords that the question whether the words "Singer" and "Singer Machine" denote a species of mechanism or denote the manufacturer is a question of fact, and the case was remanded for further evidence. Singer Machine Manufacturers *v.* Wilson, L. R. 3 App. Ca. 376. Later, in Singer Manufacturing Co. *v.* Loog, L. R. 18 Ch. Div. 395, it was held by the Court of Appeal that the defendant could not be restrained from issuing circulars stating that he was selling machines made on "the Singer system," but he could be restrained from affixing to his machines a label of the same shape, metal, and color as used by the plaintiff, placed on the same part of the machine, and bearing the word "Singer," although it did also bear other words indicating it was made by another manufacturer, which words, however, might be overlooked on casual inspection. Brill *v.* Singer Mfg. Co., 41 Ohio State, 127.

When the owner of a business and trademark sells the business and trademark to another, the purchaser has the right to the exclusive use of the trademark. Kidd *v.* Johnson, 100 U. S. 617. When a firm having a trademark dissolves, each member, after dissolution, has equal right to use it. Taylor *v.* Bothin, 5 Sawyer, C. Ct. 584. But if one partner sells his entire interest in the firm to his copartner, the right to use the trademark passes, unless specially reserved. Blackwell *v.* Dibrell, 3 Hughes, C. Ct. 151. But not when he sells to his copartner only certain real and personal estate. Hurver *v.* Dannenhoffer, 82 N. Y. 499.

Property may be acquired in a trade name, so that others than the owner may be enjoined from using it. At the suit of proprietors of the old "Irving Hotel," an injunction was allowed restraining the adoption of the same name for another hotel in the same city. Howard *v.* Henriques, 3 Sandford, 725. At the suit of the owner of a carriage repository called "The Carriage Bazaar," injunction was allowed restraining the owner of another such repository from giving his establishment the name "The New Carriage Bazaar." Boulnois *v.* Peak, L. R. 13 Ch. Div. 513. The law of trademarks, so far as applicable, is applied to trade names. Accordingly it is held that the name "Antiquarian Bookstore" cannot be appropriated by a bookseller as a trade name. Choynski *v.* Cohen, 39 Cal. 501.

promote the progress of science and useful arts." Whether there be left to the States a concurrent power, to be exercised in subordination to the legislation of Congress, has never been decided. It is clear, however, that they are not precluded from encouraging the introduction of new works and inventions. It will be observed, that Congress is no further restricted, as to the time for which these rights may be secured, than that they must be "for limited times," and not perpetual. Congress, therefore, might make them any thing short of perpetual; and why even this limitation was inserted, is not very apparent; for it would seem that on the principles of natural justice, the results of intellectual labor ought to be as much the subject of perpetual ownership, as the results of any other labor; and with respect to copyright, this was the ancient doctrine of the English law. But as the remedies for violations of this right were not deemed sufficient, Parliament passed an act in 1709, during the reign of Queen Anne, for the purpose of rendering copyrights more secure and available, during the first fourteen years; and for another equal period, if the author should be living at the end of the first. It does not seem to have occurred to the framers of this law, that it would be construed as superseding the common law, in regard to the duration of the right; but in 1774, after much controversy, it was finally decided that this act did have the effect of narrowing down a right, till then perpetual, to the short period therein designated. A subsequent act of Parliament, in 1814, extended the time to twenty-eight years, with the right of renewal. It will hereafter be seen, that, on the subject of copyrights, we have but followed the lead of England; and the same is substantially true with respect to patent-rights. These were not known at common law, but originated in England, in an exception made for fourteen years, in favor of certain manufacturers, in the general act for the prevention of monopolies. We have adopted the same period, but the right extends to other subjects than manufactures. In one respect, however, the English law is more liberal than ours. (*a*) It does not confine the privilege, either of copy or patent-rights, to citizens or residents, as is the case here with respect to copyrights. And ought we, in this solitary instance, to be outdone in liberality towards foreigners? The question is worthy of serious consideration. On the whole, it may well be doubted whether we have much to boast of, on the score of legislative encouragement of intellectual enterprise. By securing to authors and inventors, such a property in their own productions, as would descend to their posterity, if not perpetually, at least for some generations, it is very certain that the encouragement would be much greater than it now is. And would it be attended with any general evil? If not, natural justice would seem to dictate that intellectual labor should be placed on the same footing with all

(*a*) Jeffreys *v.* Boosey, 30 Eng. Law & Eq. 1-105. In this case very elaborate opinions were delivered on the subject generally, and particularly on the rights of foreigners to copyright.

other labor. In Germany, Norway, and Sweden, where the right is perpetual, no evil is experienced. In France and Russia, it extends twenty years beyond the author's lifetime. This is better than with us; and yet the public experience no evil. Indeed, the only effect to be feared, would be exorbitancy of price; but this, as in all other cases, might be safely left to the interest of those concerned. With these general remarks, I proceed to give an outline of the law of copyrights, and patent-rights, beginning with the former.

Legislation of Congress respecting Copyrights. The first act on this subject was passed in 1790. Amendatory acts were passed in 1802 and 1819. All these were consolidated and superseded by the act of 1831, which, together with an amendatory act of 1834, constitutes our present law; an abstract of which will be given under several distinct heads. (*a*)

In what Copyright consists. Copyright means something very different from property in an unpublished manuscript, which stands on the same footing with any other ownership. In fact, copyright begins where property in the manuscript ends. Without publication, the manuscript would be of little value; and without copyright, publication would be an abandonment of the manuscript for all valuable purposes; since copies accessible to all would then be as available for future publication as the original. Copyright, then, is the exclusive right of multiplying copies, and enjoying the avails thereof. Its chief value, considered as property, depends upon its being exclusive. Let competition be permitted after the first publication, and copyright would become a mere name. Copyright, therefore, is an exclusive right, so long as it continues, and, on the common principles of ownership, it would seem to be perpetual. In England, as we have seen, it was in fact so regarded, as a matter of common law, until the construction given to the statute of Anne. (*b*) In this country, it remained an open question whether there was or was not a copyright at common law, independently of the legislation of Congress, until the case of *Wheaton* v. *Peters*, (*c*) when a majority of the supreme court of the United States, upon full argument and consideration, decided, that there is no copyright at common law in this country. For the right and remedy, therefore, we are to look solely to the acts of Congress. And there, copyright is declared to be the sole right and liberty of "printing, reprinting, publishing, and vending." The right commences with the date of recording the title, and

(*a*) See act of 18th August, 1856, by which the authors and proprietors of dramatic compositions are protected. By the act of July 8, 1870, the existing laws relating to patents and copyrights were revised and consolidated. Changes made in the statements of the text are noted in their appropriate place.

(*b*) See the cases of Miller *v.* Taylor, 4 Burr. 2303; Donaldson *v.* Becket, 4 Burr. 2408; and Beckford *v.* Hood, 7 T. R. 620; in which the common law was held to be abrogated by that statute.

(*c*) 8 Peters, 591.

continues for twenty-eight years, with a qualified privilege of renewal for fourteen more. (*a*)

What may be the Subjects of Copyright. The subjects of copyright enumerated in the statutes are, "books, maps, charts, musical compositions, prints, cuts, and engravings." (*b*) These terms are broad enough to include almost every production of the press, though it would seem that newspapers, and perhaps some other periodicals, cannot become the subject of copyright.

Who may have Copyright. The first qualification for obtaining a copyright is to be a "citizen of the United States, or resident therein." In this respect, as before observed, we are less liberal than other nations; and efforts have recently been made to procure an extension of the privilege to non-resident foreigners. On this subject, as a question of policy, there prevails a wide difference of opinion. But a more interesting inquiry to us is, What kind of agency in a literary production constitutes an original or derivative title to copyright? The privilege is restricted by the statute to "those who shall be authors of any book, map, chart, or musical composition, or who shall invent, design, etch, engrave, work, or cause to be etched, engraved, or worked from their own design, any print, cut, or engraving," and the executors, administrators, or legal assigns of such persons. (*c*) Copyrights are thus made assignable either before or after being secured; and the assignment must be in writing, with two subscribing witnesses, in order to be legal; (*d*) though in *Mauman* v. *Tegg* (*e*) it was held that an equitable title will be protected in chancery. Moreover, in order to operate against a subsequent purchaser, without notice, the assignment must have all the requisites of a deed for the conveyance of land, and be recorded within sixty days with the clerk of the district court. It would seem, however, that the privilege of renewal is not assignable, being confined to the author, inventor, designer, or engraver, if living; if not, to his widow or children: but after renewal, there seems to be nothing in the way of assignment. In case of death, copyright passes to the personal representatives, under the general law for the distribution of personalty. With

(*a*) The act of July 8, 1870, declares copyright to be "the sole liberty of printing, reprinting, publishing, completing, copying, executing, finishing, and vending the same; and in the case of a dramatic composition, of publicly performing or representing it, or causing it to be performed or represented by others; and authors may reserve the right to dramatize or to translate their own works." The term continues the same, with the same right of renewal.

(*b*) The subjects in R. S. § 4952 are "Any book, map, chart, dramatic or musical composition, engraving, cut, print, or photograph, or negative thereof, or of a painting, drawing, chromo, statue, statuary, and of models or designs intended to be perfected as works of the fine arts."

(*c*) Under § 4952, the copyright may be taken out by the "author, inventor, designer, or proprietor" of the subjects specified, "and his executors, administrators, or assigns."

(*d*) The assignment may, by R. S. § 4955, be made by any instrument of writing; and the assignment must now be recorded in the office of the librarian of Congress.

(*e*) 2 Russell, 285.

respect, therefore, to derivative title, there is no difficulty, the statute being full and explicit. But great doubts must often arise with respect to original title. What shall amount to authorship is often a very difficult question. (*a*)

Preliminary Conditions. (*b*) By the act now in force, the preliminary steps for procuring a copyright are as follows: 1. To deposit a printed copy of the title before publication, with the clerk of the district court of the district in which the author or proprietor resides. 2. To give notice of having thus entered the work for copyright, by inserting the same, together with the year and the name of the proprietor, on the title-page or the page next following, of each copy of the book, or on the face or frontispiece of any other production. 3. To deposit a copy of the work with the aforesaid clerk, within three months after its publication, and also in the libraries of Congress and of the Smithsonian Institute. In case of renewal, these three conditions must be performed within six months before the expiration of the first term; and within two months of the date of the renewal, a copy of the record thereof must be published in one or more newspapers for four weeks.

(*a*) In Wheaton *v.* Peters, 8 Peters, 591, it was held that no reporter can have a copyright in the written opinions delivered by the court, though in the other matter proper for reports he may. Nash *v.* Lathrop, Supr. Ct. Mass., 1866, 6 N. E. Rep. 559; Myers *v.* Callaghan, 20 Fed. Rep. 441; Banks *v.* West Pub. Co., 27 id. 50; Little *v.* Gould, 2 Blatch. 165, 362. In Southey *v.* Sherwood, 2 Merivale, 434, it was intimated that there can be copyright in a work of a scandalous or immoral character. In Bartlett *v.* Crittenden, 5 McLean, 32, it was held that the writer of letters, and not the receiver, is the legal owner, so far as relates to copyright, and the case of Percival *v.* Phipps, 2 V. & B. 19, is to the same effect. But the receiver will not be enjoined from publication, when necessary for his own protection or vindication. In Wyatt *v.* Barnard, 3 V. & B. 77, it was held that a translation is as much a subject of copyright as an original composition. In Cary *v.* Longman, 1 East, 357, it was held that copyright may exist in part of a work, when the whole is not the subject of it; as when original notes, additions, or illustrations are affixed to an old work; and the case of Cary *v.* Kearsly, 4 Esp. 168, is to the same effect. It could not have been the intention of the statute to protect mere compilations from the works of others, when no additional labor is bestowed, for such a compiler is in no sense an author. Besides, he must either infringe the copyright of others, and thus forfeit all claim to protection, or he must avail himself of what is already common property, and incapable of appropriation. But if he makes additions and alterations in them, he has a copyright. In Gray *v.* Russell, 1 Story, 11, it was held that a work might be the subject of copyright, although the materials which compose it may be found in the works of other authors, antecedently printed, provided the plan, the arrangement, and the combination of these materials be original. See also Farmer *v.* Calvert Lith. Co., 1 Flip. 228; Banks *v.* McDivitt, 13 Blatch. 63; Lawrence *v.* Dana, 4 Cliff. 1.

(*b*) In Beckford *v.* Hood, 7 T. R. 620, it was held that the preliminary conditions in the English statute were not indispensable to vest the title. In Nichols *v.* Ruggles, 3 Day, 145, the same doctrine was held with respect to preliminary conditions in the acts of Congress; and the case of Ewen *v.* Coxe, 4 Wash. C. C. R. 487, partially countenanced the same idea. But in Wheaton *v.* Peters, 8 Peters, 591, these conditions were held to be indispensable; also in Baker *v.* Taylor, 2 Blatch. 82. The requirements under R. S., § 4956 *et seq.*, are the mailing of a printed copy of the title of the book or other article, or a description of the painting, drawing, chromo, statue, statuary, or model or design for a work of the fine arts, to the librarian of the library of congress, before publication, and within ten days after publication mailing to the same officer two copies of the book or other article, or photograph of the painting, &c. One copy must also be sent of any edition in which substantial changes are made. Such articles pass through the mails free, if distinctly marked "copyright matter." The same statement must be inserted in the book as was before required.

What constitutes an Infringement of Copyright. In general terms, when a copyright has been secured, any act which interferes with the exclusive right of multiplying copies, and enjoying the avails thereof, will be an infringement of such copyright. The spirit of the provision must have been designed, not only to secure the whole work from being published or sold, by any other person than the proprietor, but any part from being pirated. But we are not left to general inference. With respect to books, the act forbids every person but the proprietor, "to print, publish, or import; or, knowing the same to be so printed or imported, to publish, sell, or expose to sale." And with respect to the other subjects of copyright, "to engrave, etch, work, sell, or copy, either in the whole, or by varying, adding to, or diminishing the main design, with intent to evade the law; or to print or import for sale, or knowing the same to be so printed or imported, to publish, sell, or expose to sale, or in any manner dispose of." The act is silent with respect to parts of books, but expressly protects parts of the other productions named. Still the words must have a reasonable construction. (*a*) Ideas must be the common property of the whole world, and can never be exclusively appropriated. To some extent also literal quotations must be permitted.

Remedies. The remedies provided by the statute are prevention and redress. The circuit court of the United States has jurisdiction to grant injunctions to prevent the publication of manuscripts and the infringement of copyrights. Whether the State courts have this jurisdiction, has not been decided, but it is presumed that they have not. It is usual, in a bill of injunction, to pray for an account of the copies sold; and though not expressly authorized, there is little doubt, that, in a proper case, the court would decree an account, as is the English practice. (*b*) And if so, both prevention and redress may be had in equity. But when redress is the principal thing, it is generally sought for in the courts of law. And here the jurisdiction would seem to be concurrent in the federal and State courts. In England, the proper remedy is an action on the case for damages; and this is the remedy

(*a*) In Wilkins *v.* Aikin, 17 Ves. 422, fair quotation is held permissible; but at the same time, it is held that one shall not, under this pretext, appropriate the whole or any considerable portion of another's work. In like manner a fair abridgment was said, in Giles *v.* Wilcox, 2 Atk. 241, to be no infringement of copyright, but itself the subject of distinct copyright. The cases of Roworth *v.* Wilkes, 1 Camp. 94, and Mauman *v.* Tegg, 2 Russ. 285, take the same general views with respect to quotation and abridgment, applying them particularly to reviews and encyclopædias. The result is, that in such cases the intention is chiefly to be considered. But even when the intention is good, if the effect be essentially injurious to the owner of the copyright, it will be held an infringement. In Coleman *v.* Wathen, 5 T. R. 245, it was held that the acting of a dramatic work upon the stage was no infringement of copyright; and the case of Murray *v.* Elliston, 5 Barn. & Ald. 657, is to the same effect, though an injunction had previously been granted to prevent such acting. In England it would be held an infringement to take down a lecture, or any other discourse in short hand, and publish it; but probably not in this country, because not within the words of the statute; and see Story's Exrs. *v.* Holcombe, 4 McLean, 160, 306.

(*b*) {In Stevens *v.* Gladding, 17 How. 447, accounting was decreed.}

prescribed by Congress for wrongfully publishing the manuscript of another. (*a*) But for violating a copyright, no action for damages is given. The injured party can only proceed for the penalties inflicted by the statute. With respect to books, the penalty is forfeiture of every copy to the proprietor; and fifty cents for each sheet, one half to the proprietor, and the other half to the United States. With respect to the other subjects of copyright, the penalty is a forfeiture of the plates, as well as copies, and one dollar for each sheet, to be divided as before. These penalties are to be enforced by action of debt, to be commenced within two years; and it is provided that any special matter may be given in evidence under the general issue. There is a further penalty of one hundred dollars for falsely publishing on the title-page, that the copyright has been secured; but this is only to protect the public against imposition. When a part of the book is a subject of copyright, the injunction above provided for can only reach that part; and, if the rest can be published separately, it may be done without infringement. If not, the injunction will indirectly cover the whole. (*b*)

Legislation of Congress respecting Patent-rights. The first act was passed in 1790, but was repealed by the act of 1793. Additional acts were passed in 1800, 1819, and 1832, all of which were repealed by the act of 1836, which, together with the amendatory act of 1837, constitutes our present law, an abstract of which will be given under several distinct heads.

The Patent Office. There is a patent office attached to the department of state, the chief officer of which is styled commissioner of patents. (*c*) This officer and those subordinate to him are required to take an oath and give security for the faithful performance of their duty. All books, papers, models, and specimens connected with patents are kept in this office. It also has a library composed of such scientific books and publications as are adapted

(*a*) Courts of equity interfere by injunction to restrain the publication of manuscripts whereby an author's right of property is invaded. Bartlett *v.* Crittenden, 4 McLean, 300; 5 id. 32; Pulte *v.* Derby, 5 id. 328; 2 Story, Eq. § 943; 2 Kent, Com. 380. The jurisdiction of equity to restrain the publication of confidential letters of business or friendship has been asserted. 2 Story, Eq. 946; 2 Kent, Com. 381. But the weight of authority in this country is against the jurisdiction of chancery to enjoin in such cases, except to protect the author's right of property, and to confine it to restraining the publication of letters having the character of literary property. Hoyt *v.* Mackenzie, 3 Barb. Ch. R. 320; Wetmore *v.* Scovell, 3 Edw. Ch. R. 515; {Folsom *v.* Marsh, 2 Story, 100; Bartlett *v.* Crittenden, 5 McLean, 32; U. S. *v.* Tanner, 6 ib. 128; High on Injunctions, § 1012.} See an article on this subject in the American Law Register for June, 1853, by that eminent jurist, Chief-Justice Parker, formerly Professor in the Law School of Harvard University.

(*b*) This is the doctrine held in Mauman *v.* Tegg, 2 Russ. 285, a case particularly valuable for its view of the practice in questions of copyright. In England the damages to be recovered in an action on the case, are easily graduated, according to the amount of matter which is pirated, but our statute makes no provision for the apportionment of penalties, when a part only is pirated. For this and other reasons, the proceeding by injunction, with a prayer to account, is by far the most convenient and efficacious remedy; and, thus far, there is no report of an action brought for the penalty.

(*c*) The patent office was attached to the department of the interior by the act of March 3, 1849. R. S. § 475 continues it as a part of the department of the interior.

to its purposes. The office was destroyed by fire on the 15th of December, 1836, together with most of its contents; and one object of the act of 1837 was to provide, as far as possible, for replacing its records and models.

Who may obtain a Patent. The words of the statute are, "any person having discovered or invented any new and useful art, machine, manufacture, or composition of matter, or any new and useful improvement on any art, machine, manufacture, or composition of matter, not known or used by others (*a*) before his discovery and invention thereof, and not, at the time of his application for a patent, in public use or on sale, with his consent or allowance, as the inventor or discoverer." The term "*useful*" is here employed in contradistinction to mischievous; and if the invention will not be prejudicial to good morals or sound policy, the degree of utility, provided it be not absolutely frivolous, will not be drawn in question. The term "*new*" requires that the patentee should not only be the *original*, but the *first*, inventor; and accordingly, if the invention had been previously described in some printed publication, though he, in fact, never saw or heard of it, his patent will not be good. But if he honestly believed himself to be the first inventor, the fact that the invention had been previously known or used in a foreign country, but not patented or published, will not invalidate the patent. And the invention must not have been in public use or on sale, with the assent of the inventor, at the time of his application for a patent, for this will be deemed a waiver of his right. But it is no objection that a patent has been previously obtained in a foreign country and publication made there, provided the application for a patent be made here within six months thereafter. (*b*) Again, the patentee must either be the actual inventor or the *bonâ fide* proprietor of the invention; for if he surreptitiously appropriated the invention of another, who was using reasonable diligence to mature it, his patent will not avail him.

Preliminary Conditions. The application for a patent is made to the commissioner in writing. It must be accompanied by a full and clear *description* of the invention, so as to identify and distinguish it from all others; and by *drawings*, *specimens*, or *models* sufficient for a complete illustration. The description and drawings must be signed by the inventor, and attested by two witnesses. If the description be intentionally defective, either by containing too little, or too much, or being too vague, it will invalidate the patent. But if the error arise from inadvertency, it may be sub-

(*a*) R. S. § 4886 inserts here the words "in this country, and not patented or described in any printed publication in this or any foreign country." It also only requires that the same have not been in public use or on sale for more than two years prior to the application.

(*b*) By R. S. § 4887, a foreign patent is no obstacle, "provided the same shall not have been introduced into public use in the United States for more than two years prior to the application, and that the patent shall expire at the same time with the foreign patent, or if there be more than one, at the same time with the one having the shortest term; but in no case shall it be in force more than seventeen years."

sequently corrected. The applicant must also state under oath to what country he belongs, that he verily believes himself to be the original and first inventor, and that he does not know or believe that his invention was ever before known or used. The fee or duty to be paid varies as follows. If the applicant be a citizen, or an alien having resided here one year, and made oath of his intention to become a citizen, it is thirty dollars; if he be a subject of Great Britain, five hundred dollars; if he be a subject of any other country, three hundred dollars. (*a*) Provision is also made for the case where a citizen or such resident alien has not yet so matured his invention as to be ready to make his application. In this case he may, on paying twenty dollars, file his *caveat* in the patent office, describing his invention as far as can then be done, which will entitle him for one year to notice from the commissioner of any interfering application; and if within three months of receiving such notice, he shall perfect his application, he will thus retain his priority. In the mean time, until the question be decided, his *caveat* and the description by the interfering applicant are kept secret in the confidential archives of the office.

Form and Effect of the Patent. The patent is in a form of a certificate, signed by the secretary of state, and countersigned by the commissioner, under the seal of the office, setting forth that the patentee has complied with the requisitions of the law, and containing a short description or title of the invention sufficient to indicate its nature and design. For particulars, reference is made to the specifications given by the inventor, a copy of which is annexed to the patent. It then proceeds in express terms to grant to the patentee, his heirs, executors, administrators, and assigns, the full and exclusive right of making, using, and vending to others to be used, the invention for which the patent is given, for the term of fourteen years, throughout the United States. If a person entitled to a patent die before obtaining it, his personal representatives may obtain it. The whole or any part of it, either for the whole country or any particular district, may be assigned by any instrument in writing; but the assignment must be recorded, within three months, in the patent office; and if made and recorded before the patent is obtained, it may be issued to the assignee. At the expiration of fourteen years, the patentee may obtain a renewal for seven years more, on the payment of forty dollars, provided a board, consisting of the secretary of state, the commissioner of patents, and the solicitor of the treasury, shall be of opinion that he has not been sufficiently remunerated by the profits of the first period. (*b*)

(*a*) The act of 1870 changes all these fees, and makes no distinction between citizens and others.

(*b*) The act of March 22, 1848, vests the power of determining upon the question of extension in the commissioner of patents alone. The act of the commissioner, in granting an extension, is conclusive evidence of all facts which he is required to find in order to grant such extension in the absence of fraud or excess beyond his jurisdiction. Clum *v.* Brewer, 2 Curtis, C. C. 506. The extension enures only to the benefit

Issuing of the Patent. If the conditions before mentioned be complied with, and the commissioner perceive no objection, the patent is issued as a matter of course. But if the commissioner perceive objections, he notifies the applicant thereof; and he may thereupon withdraw his application and receive back one third of his fee; or he may obviate the objection if it can be done; or he may have his claim investigated before a board of three examiners to be appointed by the secretary of state, on paying twenty-five dollars towards their fees. (*a*) In case of interfering applications, the prior claim is determined in a similar manner; and in either case, the decision of the board will govern the commissioner. But if any applicant be dissatisfied with such decision, he may have his claim determined by a proceeding in chancery. At the request of the applicant, the patent may take date from the time of making the application, provided it be not more than six months before the issuing of it. If the patentee be an alien and shall neglect, for eighteen months from the date of the patent, to put and continue the same on sale to the public on reasonable terms, he thereby forfeits the right. If, after the issuing of the patent, the description be found to be erroneous through inadvertency, either by containing too little, or by claiming some material part as new, which is not, the proprietor may have the defect cured by making the correction or filing a disclaimer, as the case may be, and paying fifteen dollars. If an improvement be made after taking out a patent, it may on like terms be added to such patent. (*b*)

Remedies. Original jurisdiction, both in law and equity, of all controversies growing out of patent-rights, is given to the circuit court, with an appellate jurisdiction to the supreme court, as in other cases. The remedies provided include both prevention and redress. By a bill of injunction, the proprietor may prevent a threatened infringement of his patent, or by an action on the case he may recover damages for any injury actually done; and, in the latter case, it is in the power of the court to increase the verdict to any extent not exceeding treble the amount found by the jury. To avoid technical questions in presenting the defence in this

of the original patentee, or his legal representatives, unless the right to such extension is expressly assigned to the assignee. Wilson *v.* Rousseau, 4 How. 646; Brooks *v.* Bicknell, 4 McLean, 64; Woodworth *v.* Sherman, 3 Story, 171. But by the act of March 2, 1861, all patents granted after the passage of that act shall remain in force for seventeen years, and the extension of such patents is prohibited. And the law of 1870 continues the same provision.

(*a*) This board of examiners has been abolished, and the appeal is made to the {supreme court of the District of Columbia. R. S. §§ 4911 *et seq.*}.

(*b*) One who conceals his invention and uses it for his own profit, is not entitled to favor, if another finds out and uses the invention. But this rule does not apply to an inventor who postpones his application, in order to perfect his invention and test its value by experiments. Kendall *v.* Winsor, 21 How. 322. {Neglect to apply for a patent does not forfeit the right to one where the invention has been kept secret. Bates *v.* Coe, 98 U. S. 31, or is being perfected and tested. Agawam Co. *v.* Jordan, 7 Wall. 573. *Contra* if the circumstances show an abandonment. Planing Machine Co. *v.* Keith, 101 id. 479.}

action, it is provided that the defendant may plead the general issue, and give any special matter in evidence, by furnishing a written notice thereof thirty days before the trial.

The proprietor of a patent is required, under a penalty of one hundred dollars, to put the date of his patent upon every patented article sold. (*a*) And if any person not having a patent, shall, without the consent of the proprietor, place upon any patented article the name, stamp, mark, or device of the patentee, or any imitation thereof; or shall place upon any unpatented article any words, stamp, or device, signifying that it is patented, with the intention of deceiving the public, the penalty for every such offence is one hundred dollars. (*b*)

§ 61. **Power as to Defence.** There are several provisions relating to war, and to the organization of the army, navy, and militia, which I shall consider together under this head.

1. Congress has power "to declare war." (*c*) In England, this is the exclusive prerogative of the king. But here this power was considered too momentous to be intrusted to a single hand. We allow the president, when war has been declared, to be commander-in-chief of the forces raised to carry it on; and we allow him, with the consent of the senate, to bring war to a close by a treaty of peace. But to determine when the nation shall be involved in war, is wisely left in the hands of Congress alone. With such jealousy is this power guarded, that the constitution, in another place, declares, that "no State shall engage in war unless actually invaded, or in such imminent danger as will not admit of delay." And the propriety of this qualified prohibition to the States is obvious. If a State be actually invaded, or in imminent danger, it must necessarily have the right of self-defence; but if a State could be the aggressor by declaring war, it would be in the power of a small minority to embroil the whole Union.

2. "To grant letters of marque and reprisal." At the same time the States are expressly prohibited. Letters of marque and reprisal are one and the same thing. They are grantable by the law of nations whenever the subjects of one State have been injured by those of another, and they authorize the former to seize

(*a*) {By R. S. § 4900, the penalty now is that no damages for infringement are recovable without proof of notice to defendant.}

(*b*) The foregoing remarks apply to patent-rights as they existed prior to the act of 1842. By that act the privilege of obtaining a patent is extended to the invention of any new and original design for a manufacture, for the printing of cloth, and for stationery; and to any new and original impression, ornament, pattern, print, or picture, to be placed on any article of manufacture: and to any new and original shape or configuration of any article of manufacture. The duration of the patent in such cases is seven years, and the fees one half those paid in other cases. The applicant, if not a citizen, must have resided here one year, and declared his intention of becoming a citizen. This provision is contained in the act of 1870, but the patent in such cases may be either for three years and six months, or for seven years, or for fourteen years, as the applicant may elect.

(*c*) In the convention, some were in favor of vesting this power in the president alone, and others in the senate alone. Mad. Pap. 1351–3; Whiting's War Powers under the Constitution.

upon the persons and property of the latter, by way of satisfaction for the injury. They may, therefore, serve sometimes to prevent war, but the grant of them is usually a preliminary to the declaration of war; and it is supposed that the power to grant them would have been included in the power to declare war, without an express provision. The propriety of prohibiting the States rests on the same foundation as the other.

3. "To make rules concerning captures on land and water." There is no doubt that this power would have been included in that of declaring war, since the greater always contains the less. The States are not expressly prohibited from acting on the subject; but they are prohibited by manifest implication.

4. "To raise and support armies, but no appropriation of money to that use shall be for a longer term than two years; to provide and maintain a navy; and to make rules for the government and regulation of the land and naval forces." (*a*) This also is a part of the general power to conduct the operations of war; probably it would have been implied, had it not been expressed. The only restriction upon the power of Congress is, that no appropriation for the use of the army can be for a longer term than two years. The wise jealousy which suggested this restriction, is justified by the concurrent testimony of all history, that standing armies have been the destroyers of liberty. Instructed by this solemn admonition, it has been our settled policy to keep up during peace so small a standing army as scarcely to be prepared for a sudden war. But navies being less dangerous, and at the same time more essential, even in peace, to protect our commerce from depredations, there is no such restriction with regard to our navy. The prohibition to the States, however, includes both. "No State shall without the consent of Congress, keep troops, or ships of war, in time of peace." This implies that they may do so during war; and accordingly we have seen, that then the governor is made their commander-in-chief. The organization of the war and navy departments has already been referred to. But the regulations made by Congress for the government of each, in virtue of the provision now under consideration, are too numerous to admit of a description in this place. (*b*)

5. "To provide for organizing, arming, and disciplining the militia; reserving to the States respectively the appointment of

(*a*) These and the two preceding provisions excited very little debate. Mad. Pap. 1359–61, 1495.

(*b*) In the case of Mackenzie, commander of the United States brig Somers, who in December, 1842, had caused an officer and two men to be executed for mutiny, and who was tried by a court-martial on the charge of murder, and acquitted, the question arose, whether the case was exclusively within the jurisdiction of a court-martial. Application was twice made to the circuit court, while the court-martial was in session, to take jurisdiction of the case; but, after full argument, the application was denied. And the reasoning of the court went the length of sustaining the principle that courts-martial in the army and navy have exclusive jurisdiction of the offences committed in violation of their respective codes. The jurisdiction of a court-martial acting under a law of Congress, is affirmed in Dynes *v.* Hoover, 20 How. 65.

the officers, and the authority of training the militia, according to the discipline prescribed by Congress." (*a*) It will thus be seen that the militia falls partly under the control of Congress, and partly under that of the several States. Indeed the States were particularly solicitous on this subject. (*b*) This appears in the second amendment of the federal constitution, which is this: "a well-regulated militia being necessary to the security of a free State, the right of the people to keep and bear arms shall not be infringed." In like manner, the constitution of Ohio declares that "the people have a right to bear arms for the defence of themselves and the State." But the great difficulty was to apportion the power over the militia in a satisfactory manner, between the federal and State governments. The above provision draws a very nice distinction between the power of organizing, arming, and disciplining the militia, which is given to Congress for the sake of uniformity; and that of appointing the officers and training the militia, which is reserved to the States. By the act of 1792, Congress executed its portion of the power, by organizing a uniform militia throughout the Union; and by the acts of 1820 and 1821, the rules of discipline and field-exercise were made the same as for the regular army. We have before seen that the governor is made commander-in-chief of the militia, except when called into the actual service of the United States; in which case, that power devolves on the president. Each State makes provision for the appointment of the subordinate militia officers; but this is not a matter of sufficient general interest to justify a particular account. There is another provision, however, which is of great importance. Congress has power "to provide for calling forth the militia to execute the laws of the Union,

(*a*) See Mad. Pap. 1361, 1402; 2 Story, Const. chap. xxii.; Opinion of the Judges of Massachusetts, 8 Mass. 547; Houston *v.* Moore, 5 Wheaton, 1; Martin *v.* Mott, 12 Wheaton, 19. See Militia Act of Ohio of March 28, 1857.

(*b*) It may be doubted whether this clause of the constitution gives Congress the power to provide for *enrolling*, — that is, determining who shall constitute the militia, as the term *enrolling* may well be distinguished from that of *organizing;* the former meaning the designation of the persons who are to be included in the militia, and the latter the organization of them after they have been so designated or enrolled. Rufus King, a member of the committee who reported the provision in the federal convention, said that "by organizing, the committee meant proportioning the officers and men." 5 Elliot's Debates, 464. The act of May 8, 1792, however, provides for the enrolment of "free, able-bodied white male citizens of the respective States." It has, however, not been adhered to in practice. In Wisconsin, Indiana, Illinois, Michigan, Kentucky, Pennsylvania, New Jersey, Florida, Texas, Arkansas, unnaturalized foreigners are enrolled, the words "persons," "inhabitants," or "men" being used in those States as descriptive of the class to be enrolled. In the case of Scott *v.* Sandford, 19 How. 415, there is a *dictum* of Taney, C. J., implying that the States may determine what classes shall be enrolled in the militia. An opinion has been given by the supreme court of Massachusetts, in response to interrogatories of the governor and counsel of that State, to the effect that the States cannot enroll in the militia any persons other than those enumerated in the act of Congress. 14 Gray, 614. On March 3, 1863, Congress passed a law declaring all able-bodied male citizens of the United States, and persons of foreign birth who have declared their intention to become citizens, between twenty and forty-five, liable to military service, except those exempted. This law, I believe, was never objected to.

suppress insurrections, and repel invasions; and for governing such part of them as shall be employed in the service of the United States." By the act of 1795, Congress authorized the president to call forth the militia, when either of these three exigencies should occur. But here a question arose, Who was to determine when one of these exigencies exists? The supreme judges of Massachusetts thought it was the State governor. (*a*) But the supreme federal court has since decided that the president is the sole and exclusive judge of this matter, and that all other persons are bound by his decision. (*b*) Great as this power is, to be vested

(*a*) 8 Mass. 549.

(*b*) In Houston *v.* Moore, 5 Wheaton, 1, the facts were these: Pennsylvania passed a law providing that members of the militia of that State, refusing to serve when called out by the president, should be liable to the penalties defined by Congress; but should be tried for such delinquency by a court-martial held under the State authority. Houston was one of these delinquents. He was sentenced, under this law, by a State court-martial, to pay a fine, and his property was levied upon to collect it. This action of trespass was brought against the officer who made the levy, on the ground that the law was unconstitutional. The State court decided in favor of the law; 3 Serg. & Rawle, 109; and this decision was confirmed by a majority of the supreme court of the United States. It was held that the acts of Congress on this subject were within their constitutional power, and amounted to a full execution of that power. But until the militia are in the *actual service* of the United States, the powers of legislation over them are *concurrent* in the general and State governments. There must be some point of time when they change their character from *State* to *national* militia. Congress have not expressly fixed what this is, but from all they have said it is to be gathered, that when the militia arrive at the *place of rendezvous*, and not before, their *actual service* commences. Houston, therefore, by refusing to march to the place of rendezvous, remained within the military jurisdiction of the State. But then Congress had already legislated on the subject, and made provision for this very case; and when this is the fact, a State, though it have concurrent power, is prohibited from legislating, even though its provisions should not be repugnant. It happened, however, in this case, that the penalty inflicted on Houston was identically that provided by Congress, though inflicted by a State tribunal; and therefore the only question was whether the State court-martial had jurisdiction over the subject, so as to enforce the laws of Congress. It was held that a State court-martial had jurisdiction. Congress might unquestionably have withdrawn the whole subject from State tribunals; but not having *expressly* done so, as it had in many other cases, the presumption was, that Congress intended to leave the jurisdiction of a State court-martial *concurrent* with that of a national court-martial, in a case like the present. The fine was, therefore, properly inflicted.

In Martin *v.* Mott, 12 Wheaton, 19, the facts were these: Mott was a member of the militia of New York. During the last war a requisition was duly made by the president, for a portion of the militia of New York, of which Mott was one. He refused to obey; and, for this delinquency, was tried by a court-martial under the act of Congress, and sentenced to pay a fine, which was levied by Martin, the marshal of that district, on his property. Mott brought an action of replevin for the property so taken. The highest court of New York decided in his favor; and the case was then brought before the supreme court of the United States, and that decision was reversed. Judge Story, who delivered the unanimous opinion of the court, took the following grounds: The act of Congress of 1795, on the subject of the militia, is within their constitutional power. By this act the president is to be considered the *sole and exclusive* judge whether the exigencies have arisen, in which he is authorized to call forth the militia. This, it will be seen, is in direct opposition to the opinion of the supreme judges of Massachusetts, before mentioned. And further, it is not necessary in such a case, that it should appear in point of fact, that the particular exigency actually existed. It is sufficient that the president has so determined, and all other persons are bound by his decision. Again, though Mott, by refusing to obey the call of the president, was never actually "employed in the service of the United States," yet he was liable to be tried for such refusal, by a court-martial called under the authority of the United States. The fine was, therefore, properly inflicted. Luther *v.* Borden, 7 in a single person, it is not easy to see how a different opinion could have been reasonably entertained. Another question was, When are the militia to be deemed in "the service of the United States," so as to fall under the control of the president, as commander-in-chief? At what point of time does their character change from State to national militia? This question has also been submitted to the same tribunal; and the decision is, that the militia are not in actual service until they have reached the place of rendezvous in pursuance of the call of the president. The mere calling them forth does not subject them to martial law; but their mustering in obedience to the call does. Still another question has been raised upon this provision; namely, whether the militia, when thus placed under the command of the president, can be by him placed under the command of any officer not of the militia? This question has not been definitely settled. But if the militia, when called into service, cannot be placed under a regular officer of the army, great confusion must be the result. And the better opinion would seem to be, that the president may place them under such command as he deems best. These provisions respecting the militia, were at first assailed with more asperity than any other in the constitution. There was a general but vague apprehension, that they tended to make the federal government too strong, and the State government too weak. Time, however, has dissipated these alarms. Experience has shown, that, so far as regards the militia, the interests of the States and of the Union are one and the same. If the laws are to be executed, insurrection suppressed, or invasions repelled, the States may not only call out their own militia, but, if need be, the president will send the militia of other States to their aid. And the probability that the president will call away the militia of a State when their presence is required at home, is too remote to be feared.

There remain to be mentioned, in connection with this power of the sword, several declarations designed to guard it against abuse. 1. "No soldier shall, in time of peace, be quartered in any house without the consent of the owner; nor in time of war, but in a manner to be prescribed by law." This is the third amendment of the federal constitution; and nearly the same language is used in the Ohio bill of rights. It scarcely needs comment. By the common law, a man's house is his castle, and is privileged from all civil intrusion. This provision is designed to protect it, in like manner, against military intrusion. 2. Our State constitution declares, "that as standing armies in time of peace are dangerous to liberty, they shall not be kept up; and the military shall be kept under strict subordination to the civil power." The first part of this provision, relating to standing armies of the State, is of course superfluous. It may have been well enough to

How. 1. Signing a paper in the hands of a municipal officer, promising to serve for three years, or during the war, in the service of the United States, does not constitute a man a soldier, so as to subject him to martial law. Tyler *v.* Pomeroy, 8 Allen, 480.

declare the subordination of the military to the civil power, for without it there can be no civil liberty; but it would doubtless have resulted from the general principles of free government, without any express declaration. 3. There is another provision of the State constitution, prohibiting the infliction of corporal punishment under the military law, upon citizens in their civil capacity. But this belongs more properly to the department of criminal law.

§ 62. **Power of Exclusive Legislation.** (*a*) The words are, "to exercise exclusive legislation in all cases whatsoever over such district, not exceeding ten miles square, as may by cession of particular States, and the acceptance of Congress, become the seat of government of the United States; and to exercise like authority over all places purchased by the consent of the legislature of the State, in which the same shall be, for the erection of forts, magazines, arsenals, dockyards, and other needful buildings." This power is given in the strongest language. It is "exclusive" of the States, and embraces "all cases whatsoever," civil and criminal. The "places" must be acquired with the consent of the States in which they are situated, and must be for one of the five objects specified, or for other needful buildings. Thus limited, it would seem as if there could be no cause for apprehension. Yet the clause at first met with strong opposition as one peculiarly dangerous. It was feared that these "places" might be converted, by this "exclusive" authority, into the strongholds of tyranny. This alarm, however, has been long since quieted; and the propriety of the provision, when calmly considered, is too manifest to admit of question. Without it, how could the federal government protect itself from insult, or its property from depredation? Would it not be dependent upon the States even for a habitation and shelter? When Congress was sitting in Philadelphia, being insulted by a body of mutineers, application was made to the State authorities for protection; but it was so timidly received, and so tardily acted upon, that Congress indignantly removed to Princeton. This instance strongly illustrates the expediency of the provision. Congress can now take care of itself, its archives, and its other possessions, without being a suppliant to the States. The District of Columbia, ten miles square, selected by Washington, and ceded by Virginia and Maryland, is under the exclusive jurisdiction of the federal government. Its inhabitants do not belong to any State, and are not represented. It has been supposed that Congress might give them a local legislature, were it deemed expedient; but as yet their laws have been made directly by Congress. These laws may be extended, if there be occasion, throughout the Union; for Congress, when legislating for these places of exclusive jurisdiction, still preserves its character as a national

(*a*) See 1 Kent, Com. 429; 2 Story, Const. ch. xxiii.; Cohens *v.* Virginia, 6 Wheaton, 424; Loughborough *v.* Blake, 5 Wheaton, 322.

legislature. But it has been decided, that when this is intended, the intention must be expressed; otherwise, their operation will be confined to the particular district.

§ 63. **Power as to State Acts and Records.** (*a*) The words are, "full faith and credit shall be given in each State to the public acts, records, and judicial proceedings of every other State. And Congress may, by general laws, prescribe the manner in which such acts, records, and proceedings shall be proved, and the effect thereof." This is a very important provision. Before the adoption of the constitution, the States were in many respects foreign to each other. And it is a general rule, that the laws, acts, and records of one nation are not judicially recognized in another, without the same proof as any other facts; and even when proved,

(*a*) See Mad. Pap. 1448, 1480; 2 Story, Const. ch. xxix. In Mills *v.* Duryee, 7 Cranch, 481, an action of debt was brought in the District of Columbia, upon a judgment rendered in New York, and the plea was *nil debet.* At common law, this would have been good. The question was, whether it was good under the provisions above mentioned? The court held that it was not. The intention of the act of Congress was to give a judgment rendered in New York precisely the same *effect,* when authenticated, in the District of Columbia, as it would have in New York. Now, had this action been brought in New York, *nul tiel record,* and not *nil debet,* would have been the proper plea. *Nul tiel record* is, therefore, the proper plea here. The judgment is just as conclusive between the parties here, as it would be there; and consequently the only question is, as to the existence of the record. The mode of proof prescribed by the act, is of as high a nature as inspection, and can as well be resorted to by the court. *Nul tiel record* is, therefore, the only proper plea. Were judgments in State courts to be taken only as *primâ facie* evidence in other States, the provision in the constitution would be utterly nugatory. The common law would give them precisely the same effect. Nor can it be objected, that the courts of the States cannot issue execution; for the same objection would apply to other courts of the same State. Yet it was never doubted that *nul tiel record* was the proper plea in such cases. In Hampton *v.* McConnell, 3 Wheaton, 234, debt was brought in South Carolina upon a judgment rendered in New York, and *nil debet* was pleaded. The decision was the same as in the preceding case, the effect of which the court declared to be, "that the judgment of a State court should have the same credit, validity, and effect in every other court in the United States, which it had in the State where it was pronounced; and that whatever pleas would be good to a suit thereon in such State, and none others, could be pleaded in any other court in the United States." In Mayhew *v.* Thatcher, 6 Wheaton, 129, debt was brought in Louisiana, upon a judgment rendered in Massachusetts, where the original suit was commenced *in rem,* by a process of foreign attachment. The defendant, however, subsequently appeared, and made defence; and the court seemed to imply that without such appearance, or other evidence of personal notice, the judgment would not be conclusive. The plea in this action on the judgment was *nil debet,* and on demurrer this plea was set aside, in conformity with the preceding decision. But, as before observed, the court intimate that *nil debet* would have been a good plea, where the judgment debtor had no notice of the original suit. The reason is, that, in such case, the existence of the judgment is not conclusive evidence of indebtedness, and ought not to be the only fact put in issue. Proceedings in attachment in a State court must be allowed everywhere in the United States the same force and effect they would have had in the State where they were instituted; and if they would have been sustained there, they are binding in respect to that property in any other State in the Union in which the title to that property is drawn in question. Green *v.* Van Buskirk, 7 Wall. 139. In Shummay *v.* Stillman, 4 Cowen, 292, it was held that *nul tiel record* is not in all cases the necessary plea. The true doctrine is, that any special plea may be pleaded, which would be good to avoid a judgment in the State where it was pronounced. This is no more than following out the principle first settled, that a judgment of any State has now the same force and effect in every other State as it has in the State where it was rendered. This doctrine is adopted by our own court in Spencer *v.* Brockway, 1 Ohio, 259; and by that of New Hampshire, in Thurber *v.* Blackbourn, 1 New Hamp. 242.

the effect to be given to them is purely a matter of comity. But one of the objects of federal government was "to form a more perfect union;" and the design of this provision, among many others, was to effect that object. Two points are suggested for consideration: the *proof* and the *effect* of the public acts, records, and judicial proceedings of the States. 1. The *proof*. By the acts of 1790 and 1804, this is regulated as follows: Legislative acts are authenticated by the great seal of the State, and the certificate of the secretary. Judicial records are authenticated by the attestation of the clerk, the seal of the court, and the certificate of the presiding judge, that the attestation is in due form. (*a*) All other office records are authenticated by the attestation of the keeper thereof, with his official seal, if he have one; and the certificate of the presiding judge of the county court, or the governor or secretary of state, that the attestation is in due form; which certificate, if given by a judge, must be accompanied by the certificate of the clerk, under the seal of the court, that such judge is duly commissioned and qualified; otherwise it must be under the great seal of the State. 2. The *effect*. When State acts and records have been thus proved, the constitution declares that "full faith and credit shall be given to them;" but leaves it to Congress to declare their "effect." And by the acts before referred to, Congress has declared that they shall have in every State and territory of the Union the same faith, credit, force, and effect as they have by law or usage in the State or territory from which they are taken. The result is, that, so far as these matters are concerned, the States have ceased to be foreign with respect to each other. This provision, however, as I have heretofore remarked, is to be taken with the qualification, that the laws of one State are not binding in another, unless made so by the latter. And in this connection it may also be observed, that, by the 34th section of the judiciary act of 1789, the laws of the several States are made the rules of decision, in trials at common law in the courts of the United States, except where provision is otherwise made. The effect of this provision is, not only to supply any possible omission in the legislation of Congress, but to secure uniformity in the law as administered in each State by the State and federal courts. The construction given by the latter courts to this provision is, that it applies to State laws strictly local: that is, to the positive statutes of a State, and the construction thereof, adopted by the State tribunals, and to rights and titles to things having a permanent locality; and not to contracts or other matters of a commercial nature. (*b*) But the practical importance of the provisions

(*a*) The certificate must show that the person certifying is *the* presiding judge of the court that rendered the decision. Lothrop *v.* Blake, 3 Barr, 495; Catlin *v.* Underhill, 4 McLean, 199.

(*b*) Polk's Lessee *v.* Wendell, 2 Cranch, 87; Shipp *v.* Miller, 2 Wheaton, 316; Gardner *v.* Collins, 2 Peters, 58; Swift *v.* Tyson, 16 Peters, 1. See *ante*, p. 126, note, and cases cited.

under consideration is perhaps most strikingly illustrated with respect to judgments; for, as a general rule, a judgment rendered in any State or territory of the Union now, has the same conclusive effect throughout the Union, as it has in the jurisdiction where it is rendered. The only exception is, where the proceeding was *in rem*, as in the case of attachment, and the defendant had no personal notice of the suit. Then, and then only, is he permitted to inquire into the merits of the original judgment. (*a*) It is not, however, to be understood that execution can be issued in one State upon a judgment rendered in another; but only that such judgment is conclusive evidence of a debt, upon which a new judgment may be recovered.

§ 64. **Power as to Fugitives from Justice.** (*b*) The words are, "a person charged in any State with treason, felony, or other

(*a*) 1 Kent, Com. 260; Mayhew *v.* Thatcher, 6 Wheaton, 129; Starbuck *v.* Murray, 5 Wendell, 148 {Wood *v.* Stanberry, 21 Ohio State, 142; Pennoyer *v.* Neff, 95 U. S. 714; Pana *v.* Bowler, 107 U. S. 529. So a divorce obtained by a husband without personal service does not bar the wife from applying to establish her right as widow. Cheely *v.* Clayton, 110 U. S. 701}; Story's Confl. Laws, § 1807–12.

(*b*) Mad. Pap. 1447; 2 Story, Const. ch. xv.; The People *v.* Schenck, 2 Johns. 479; Commonwealth *v.* Deacon, 2 Wheeler's C. C. 1; Prigg *v.* Commonwealth of Pennsylvania, 16 Peters, 539; Smith's Case, 6 Law Reporter, 57. It will be seen from the text, that the power to legislate on the subject of fugitives from justice, has not been considered as residing exclusively in Congress. And in fact, were it not for long acquiescence, there would be good reason to doubt whether Congress has any power at all in the premises. The fourth article of the constitution, in which this clause occurs, is of a very peculiar character. It consists chiefly of declarations in the nature of compacts between the States, by which they are precluded from treating each other as foreign nations. The first relates to State acts and records; the second to citizenship in the different States; the third to fugitives from justice; the fourth to fugitive slaves; the fifth to the admission of new States; and the sixth to the protection of the States. With respect to two of these six subjects, namely, State acts and records, and the admission of new States, power to legislate is conferred upon Congress in express words, while, with respect to the other four, there is no express grant of power. If, then, we apply the common principles of interpretation to this article, we must conclude that it was intended to withhold from Congress the power of legislation in these four cases, and leave it to the respective States. Else, why express it in two cases, and omit it in the other four? The constitution was framed with too much care to admit the supposition that this was not designedly done; and if designedly done, then the act of Congress above referred to is a nullity. Yet, according to the case of Prigg *v.* Pennsylvania, 16 Peters, 539, precisely the reverse is true, and the States have no power to legislate on this subject. See Moore *v.* State of Illinois, 14 How. 13; *In re* Kirk, 1 Parker, Crim. Cas. 67.

Another question of great importance arises under this clause. When the demand has been made upon the executive of a State, to deliver up a fugitive, has such executive any discretion in the matter? Can the question of guilt or innocence be inquired into, in order to determine whether to deliver up or not? In other words, can such executive refuse to comply with the demand? As a matter of fact, such refusal has been given in more instances than one. But the language of the constitution is strictly imperative; the act to be done is purely a ministerial, and not a judicial act; and it would seem that the spirit as well as the letter of the clause would be violated by exercising a discretion. This is done with respect to fugitives from foreign nations; but the very object of this provision was to prevent the States from treating each other as foreign in this respect. See 1 Am. Jurist, 297; 22 id. 330; Commonwealth *v.* Deacon, 10 S. & R. 125; Johnston *v.* Riley, 13 Geo. 97. For the Virginia and Georgia controversies, see W. H. Seward's Works, vol. 2, pp. 449–546. See the Statutes of State of Ohio, §§ 95–97 and 7156–8. The supreme court of the United States has recently held that the executive of a State cannot, through the judiciary, or any other department of the general government, be compelled to deliver up a fugitive from crime, who shall flee from justice, and be found in another State, shall, on demand of the executive authority of the State from which he fled, be delivered up, to be removed to the State having jurisdiction of the crime." This is another instance in which the States have ceased to be foreign with respect to each other. When a criminal offender escapes to a foreign country, it is purely a question of comity, whether he shall be surrendered up on being demanded for punishment; there being no positive obligation so to do, which is capable of being enforced. But if the States had been left in this relation to each other, where escape from one to the other is so easy, criminal justice would have been to a considerable extent defeated; for punishment can only be administered within the jurisdiction where the offence is committed. Hence the strong motive for the provision in question, which takes from the States the power of refusing to deliver up offenders, when properly required so to do. By the act of 1793, Congress has pointed out the manner in which the demand and surrender must be made; an indictment must be found, or an affidavit made, in the State where the offence was committed, which must be certified as authentic by the executive thereof. This must be accompanied by a formal demand upon the executive of the State to which the offender has fled; who is thereupon required to cause the arrest of the offender, and his surrender to the agent of the executive making the demand, if he appear within six months. The proceeding is to be at the costs of the State demanding, and any person resisting is liable to fine and imprisonment. It will be seen at once that these provisions, strictly construed, must often be inadequate to their object. If the arrest cannot be made until these preliminaries are complied with, a fugitive may easily fly beyond the Union. This consideration has induced courts to look to the spirit rather than the letter; and to hold that a fugitive may be arrested on probable evidence, and detained for a reasonable time, to admit of the proper demand being made. And in Ohio, a statute has been enacted for this express purpose. This authorizes justices of the peace to hold examinations, and upon what they deem sufficient proof, either to commit the accused for a reasonable time, or deliver him up at once to the proper officer for removal.

§ 65. **Power as to Slaves.** (*a*) We have already seen that liberty is the natural right of every human being. It also forms one of

justice on the demand of the executive of another State, thus settling the question discussed in this note. Kentucky *v.* Dennison, 24 How. 66; Work *v.* Corrington, 34 Ohio State, 64.

{For the gradual enlargement of the scope of our extradition treaties, see article by Edwin F. Conely of Detroit, The New British-American Extradition Treaty, 18 Am. Law Review, 961.}

(*a*) One of the first acts of the first continental congress was an agreement not to participate in the slave trade. 1 Pitkin's Hist. 289. The original draft of the Declaration of Independence contained a clause severely reprobating slavery, which was stricken out at the request of South Carolina and Georgia. Mad. Pap. 18, 24. In the debate on the articles of confederation, when the proposition was to fix the quotas of the fundamental conditions of our social compact. In our various declarations of rights it is asserted to be the natural, inherent, and

taxation according to population, a motion to limit it to the *white* population was lost by a vote of 6 to 7 — id. 27–32. The articles of confederation finally made the valuation of land the measure of contribution. But this being found inconvenient, Congress, in 1783, recommended an amendment, adopting the ratio of population, with the slave compromise of three-fifths. 1 Story, Const. § 641 ; Mad. Pap. 523, 842. This amendment was never made, though agreed to by eleven States, but the same compromise was adopted by the framers of the constitution. The first vote was 9 to 2. Mad. Pap. 843. A subsequent proposition to exclude slaves from the ratio of representation was lost by a vote of 1 to 10 — id. 1261–6. On the general subject, see 2 Kent, Com. 251–8 ; 1 Black. Com. 418–25 ; Wheeler on Slavery ; Hurd on Habeas Corpus ; Hurd on the Law of Freedom and Bondage ; Cobb on Slavery.

I understand the basis of American slavery to be this : It is purely and exclusively a State institution, depending solely upon State legislation, and with which, while confined within the State where it is enacted to exist, neither the federal nor any other State government has any power to interfere in any manner whatsoever. When, therefore, a person who is enacted to be a slave in one State, is found in another which did not inflict this doom, his rights are to be determined by the law of the latter ; with the single exception of being a *fugitive*, under the clause in the federal constitution. Anderson *v.* Poindexter, 6 Ohio State, 622. And it is an established doctrine in the slaveholding States, that if a slave under their law, has once become enfranchised elsewhere, and is brought back, such person cannot again be reduced to slavery. David *v.* Porter, 4 Har. & McHen. 418 ; Spencer *v.* Dennis, 8 Gill, 321 ; Griffith *v.* Fanny, Gilmer (Va.), 143 ; Foster *v.* Foster, 10 Grattan, 485 ; Rankin *v.* Lydia, 2 A. K. Marsh. 470 ; Mercer *v.* Gilman, 11 B. Monr. 210 ; Blackmore *v.* Phill, 7 Yerg. 452 ; Commonwealth *v.* Pleasant, 10 Leigh, 697 ; Betty *v.* Horton, 5 id. 615 ; Hunter *v.* Fulcher, 1 id. 172 ; Julia *v.* McKinney, 3 Mo. 270 ; Rachel *v.* Walker, 4 id. 350 ; Charlotte *v.* Choteau, 21 id. 597 ; Marie Louise *v.* Marot, 9 Louis. 473 ; Smith *v.* Smith, 13 id. 441 ; Lunsford *v.* Coquillon, 14 Martin, 403 ; Josephine *v.* Poultney, 1 La. An. 329 ; Eugenia *v.* Preval, 2 id. 180 ; Arsene *v.* Pigneguy, 2 id. 621. But see Scott *v.* Emerson, 15 Mo. 576 ; Calvert *v.* Steamboat Timoleon, id. 597 ; Sylvia *v.* Kirby, 17 id. 434 ; Strader *v.* Graham, 10 How. 93, 94 ; Scott *v.* Sanford, 19 id. 393. The federal constitution does not regard slaves as *property*, but merely as "*persons held to service or labor ;*" and when they escape into another State, not regarding them as property, — they are there simply fugitive persons.

Congress, on the first of February, 1865, recommended the adoption of the following amendment to the constitution :

Art. 13, sect. 1 : "Neither slavery nor involuntary servitude, except as a punishment for crime, whereof the party shall have been duly convicted, shall exist within the United States, or any place subject to their jurisdiction.

Sect. 2. "Congress shall have power to enforce this article by appropriate legislation."

This amendment having been ratified by the requisite number of States, Congress passed, on the 9th of April, 1866, an act to protect all persons in the United States in their civil rights, and furnish the means of their vindication. This act declares all persons born in the United States, and not subjects of any foreign power, except Indians not taxed, citizens of the United States ; and further declares that all citizens of the United States shall have the same rights in every State and territory in the United States to make and enforce contracts, to sue, be parties, and give evidence, to inherit, purchase, lease, sell, hold, and convey real and personal property, and have the benefit of all laws for the security of persons and property equally, and that all such citizens shall be subject to like punishments, pains, and penalties, and none other, — any law, statute, ordinance, regulation, or custom, to the contrary notwithstanding.

Any person depriving any person of any of the rights secured by this act, or subjecting him to any different punishment on account of his having been held in a condition of slavery or involuntary servitude, except as a punishment for crime, or by reason of his color or race, than is prescribed for the punishment of white persons, is declared guilty of a misdemeanor, and liable to be punished by a fine not exceeding one thousand dollars, or imprisonment not exceeding one year, or both, at the discretion of the court.

Jurisdiction is given to the United States courts of all cases, civil or criminal, affecting persons who are denied, or cannot enforce, in the courts or judicial tribunals of the State or locality where they may be, any of the rights secured to them by the unalienable right of all men without exception. Hence it follows, that slavery can be justified upon no principle but that of uncontrollable necessity. If, therefore, it had not been deeply rooted in this country at the time of framing the federal constitution, there is no doubt that it would have been absolutely and for ever prohibited in the strongest language. But at this epoch, a traffic in African slaves, as lucrative as it was inhuman, was carried on by all civilized nations. Efforts had been repeatedly made by the colonies to prevent their introduction here, but they were universally frustrated by the British king. The consequence was, that before our independence, the labor of several of the colonies was chiefly performed by slaves, who constituted a considerable portion of the property of their owners; and the number continued to increase up to the moment of framing the constitution. To abolish slavery, therefore, by this instrument was out of the question. Upon such a condition, the Union could not have been formed. On the contrary, its toleration, so far as the federal government was concerned, was a matter of absolute necessity. And in this connection I shall refer to all the provisions which bear upon the subject; first remarking that the word *slaves* is not used, nor their color referred to, in the federal constitution.

Importation of Slaves. (*a*) "The migration or importation of such persons as any of the States now existing shall think proper

first section of this act; and when any such cause shall be pending in any State court against any such person, the defendant shall have the right to remove it for trial to the proper district or circuit court, in the manner provided in the habeas corpus act of 1862, and the amendments thereto. The remedies and punishments in such suits shall be in conformity to the common law, as modified by the statutes of the State wherein the court is held, so far as they are not inconsistent with the constitution and laws of the United States.

This act was vetoed by President Johnson, and passed over the veto on the 6th and 9th of April, 1866. It was held constitutional in a well-considered and able opinion, delivered by Justice Swayne, in the circuit court at Louisville, Ky. United States *v.* Rhodes, 7 American Law Register (N. S.), 233.

(*a*) Hardly a question in the convention was more obstinately contested than this. The delegates from North Carolina, South Carolina, and Georgia positively declared that these States would not consent to the constitution, if the importation of slaves was prohibited. Mad. Pap. 1388–96. The subject was referred to a special committee, who reported a compromise — id. 1415. This was afterwards modified into its present shape — id. 1427–30. And see Groves *v.* Slaughter, 15 Peters, 449; U. S. *v.* The Amistad, 15 Peters, 518. It will be observed that Congress has thus far confined its legislation to the foreign slave-trade, which is now totally abolished, so far as our citizens are concerned. But the question is beginning to be debated, whether Congress has not the power to abolish the domestic slave-trade also. Of course, I speak only of the existence of the power, not of the expediency of exercising it. The clause above quoted is not in terms confined to importation from abroad. On the contrary, the phrase, "such persons as any of the States now existing shall think proper to admit," seems rather to look to importation into the different States, than into the United States generally; and it would as well include importation into one State from another State, as from a foreign country. And since Congress has power "to regulate commerce among the several States," if we take these two provisions together, and regard slaves as property, the conclusion would seem to be, that Congress has power to regulate, and even to prohibit, the slave-trade between the different States. But if this power exists, it is confined to traffic between the States, and does not embrace that traffic between man and man, which takes place wholly within one State; because such traffic is neither "importation into any of the States," nor "commerce to admit, shall not be prohibited by the Congress prior to the year one thousand eight hundred and eight, but a tax or duty may be imposed upon such importation, not exceeding ten dollars for each person." Here was a recognition in 1787 of a power in Congress to prohibit the importation of slaves after 1808, and to discourage it by taxation before that time; and it was the first provision in any country which looked towards the abolition of the slave-trade. By the acts of 1794 and 1800, Congress did all that this provision would allow, by prohibiting citizens or residents of the United States from all concern in the slave-trade, except direct importation into this country. And no sooner was the constitutional restraint removed by lapse of time, than importation was directly prohibited, under severe penalties. The act for this purpose was passed in 1807, to take effect from the first day of the year 1808. Again, the act of 1819 authorized armed vessels to be stationed on the coast of Africa to prevent the slave-trade in any form by citizens or residents. And finally, the act of 1820 declares participation in this trade to be piracy, and punishable with death. Thus the pledge implied in the reservation of this future power, the immediate exercise of which was opposed by too many interests, has been abundantly redeemed; and the nations of Europe, in prohibiting this trade, have but followed our example.

Representation of Slaves. I have already described the compromise between the slaveholding and non-slaveholding States, by which the apportionment of representatives and direct taxes is "determined by adding to the whole number of free persons, including those bound to service for a term of years, and excluding Indians not taxed, three-fifths of all other persons."

Fugitive Slaves. (*a*) The words are, "No person held to service or labor in one State, under the laws thereof, escaping into another,

among the several States." It follows, also, that if Congress has the power in question, it is withdrawn from the States, being, as we have before seen, an exclusive and not a concurrent power. Public opinion, however, is very much divided upon this whole matter. It may be well to remark, that the constitution elsewhere declares that no amendment made prior to the year 1808 shall in any manner affect the provision relating to the importation of slaves, or that relating to their representation. But this period having long since terminated, there is no longer any express compact for the continuance of slavery. This act does not extend to the trial of a white person for the murder of a negro, in which negroes are witnesses, though the laws of the State do not allow the testimony of negroes to be taken against whites. Blyew *v.* U. S., 13 Wall. 581.

(*a*) Mad. Pap. 1456, 1589; Case of Aves, 18 Pick. 193; Commonwealth *v.* Taylor, 3 Metcalf, 72; Prigg *v.* Commonwealth of Pennsylvania, 16 Peters, 539; Jones *v.* Van Zandt, 1 West. Law Jour. 2, 56; s. c. 5 How. 225. The act of Congress mentioned in the text has been acquiesced in so long that it may now be thought too late to question its validity. But were the question new, there would be the same reason for holding that Congress has no power to legislate concerning fugitive slaves, as has before been stated with respect to fugitives from justice; there being not only no express grant of such power, but a strong implication to the contrary. And so the States are beginning to consider and treat the matter, by taking it into their own hands. In several of them, provision is already made for a trial by jury, before the slave is delivered up; and who does not feel that where liberty is the question at issue, something more than summary proceedings before a magistrate should be provided? Yet according to the case of Prigg *v.* Commonwealth of Pennsylvania, 16 shall, in consequence of any law or regulation therein, be discharged from such service or labor, but shall be delivered up on claim of the party to whom such service or labor may be due." By the act of 1793, Congress pointed out the course of proceeding. The owner of a fugitive slave or his agent is authorized to arrest him in any of the States, and take him before a federal judge or State magistrate; and, upon satisfactory proof of his title, he is to receive from the judge or magistrate a certificate thereof, which is a sufficient warrant for removing the slave back to the State from which he fled; and there is a penalty of five hundred dollars for knowingly harboring the slave or obstructing his removal. (*a*) The ordinance of 1787, framed a few months before the federal constitution, with the wisest forecast, for ever prohibited slavery in the North-western territory. "There shall be neither slavery

Peters, 539, all State legislation upon this subject is unconstitutional and void. It will be observed that the clause now under consideration includes only slaves "*escaping* from one State to another." If, therefore, a master voluntarily bring, send, or permit his slave to go into a non-slaveholding State, such case is not within the clause, there being no escape; and the slave is thereby held to be set free. The doctrine therefore now is, that none but those who are in the strictest sense fugitive slaves, can be demanded under this provision. Another serious question is, whether Congress has power to abolish slavery in the District of Columbia. The power "to exercise exclusive legislation in all cases whatsoever," clearly includes this, unless there be some prohibition of it elsewhere; and there is nowhere any express prohibition. But it is claimed that such prohibition is clearly implied from all the provisions on the subject of slaves. The course of argument may be thus stated. The existence of slavery was one of the chief obstacles to the formation of the Union. Without a liberal compromise of conflicting interests and opinions, this obstacle could not have been overcome. The result of that compromise was the recognition of slavery by the constitution. And although it is nowhere said that Congress shall not interfere with it, further than to abolish the foreign slave-trade, yet as the same conflicting interests and opinions still exist, there is the same reason for continuing the compromise that there was for making it; and therefore the spirit if not the letter, of the constitution is opposed to any interference with domestic slavery by Congress. In other words, the faith of the nation is tacitly pledged to leave the subject of slavery wholly to the States in which it exists. But, on the other hand, it is said that there can be no implication against human liberty. The result of the slave compromise is to be found in the constitution, and it goes no further than the words import. Had it been designed to prohibit Congress from abolishing slavery in the District of Columbia, or the slave-trade between the States, it would have been so expressed. But this is so far from being done, that there is an implied admission that the slave compromise itself may be changed after 1808, by declaring that it shall not be done before. There is, then, no other pledge than the constitution itself definitely expresses. It seems from a late decision that the supreme court does not regard State legislation *in aid of the claimant* as unconstitutional. Moore *v.* Illinois, 14 How. 13.

(*a*) This act of 1793 has been suspended by the act of 1850, which dispenses entirely with the agency of State officers, and adds many facilities and securities for the reclaiming of fugitives. 9 Stat. at Large, 462; Jenkin's Case, 2 Am. Law Reg. 144; Norris *v.* Newton, 5 McLean, 92; Giltner *v.* Gorham, 4 McLean, 402; Miller *v.* McQuerry, 5 id. 469; Weimer *v.* Sloane, 6 id. 259; Sims's Case, 7 Cushing, 285; 5 Opinions of United States Attorneys-General, 254; United States *v.* Morris, 1 Curtis, C. C. 23; United States *v.* Stowell, 2 id. 153; 1 Blatchford, 635; 2 id. 559; United States *v.* Reed, 2 id. 435; *In re* George Kirk, 1 Parker, Crim. Cas. 67. The act of 1850 has been declared unconstitutional in Wisconsin. *In re* Booth, 3 Wis. 1. It was pronounced constitutional in all its provisions in Ableman *v.* Booth, 21 How. 506. As to what amounts to harboring and concealing a fugitive slave under these acts, and what is sufficient notice that the person harbored is a slave, see Jones *v.* Van Zandt, 5 How. 225; Ray *v.* Donnell, 4 McLean, 504.

nor involuntary servitude in this State, otherwise than for the punishment of crimes whereof the party shall have been duly convicted." The constitution of Ohio declares: "There shall be no slavery in this State nor involuntary servitude unless for the punishment of crime." The ordinance also contained a provision similar to that before described respecting fugitive slaves. Thus even where slavery is expressly prohibited, we do not carry the prohibition so far as in England. The fetters of a slave do not in all cases fall from him, the moment he treads upon our soil; but he cannot be retained here in slavery. (*a*) When Missouri was about to be admitted into the Union, an attempt was made to prohibit slavery there, but without success. On this occasion, it was strenuously contended that Congress had not the power to prescribe such a condition of admission. In the result, however, the power seems to have been conceded; for the act expressly prohibits slavery in all the territory west of the Mississippi, and north of the latitude of 36° 30′, except Missouri. (*b*)

(*a*) With respect to the *right of transit* with slaves, the obligations of comity do not embrace it. Story, Confl. Laws, § 96. It was denied in France: 13 Causes Célèbres, 492. Also in England: Somersett's Case, Lofft's Rep. 1; 20 Howell's State Trials, 1; Forbes *v.* Cochrane, 2 Barn. & Cres. 448; 1 Black. Com. note, 424; The Amedie, 1 Acton, 240; The St. Louis, 2 Dodson, 210; The Slave Grace, 2 Haggard, 84. And in this country: People *v.* Lemmon, 5 Sandford, 681; 26 Barb. 270, affirmed 20 N. Y. 562. But in the case of Sewall's Slaves, 3 Am. Jurist, 404, there was a *dictum*, and in Willard *v.* The People, 4 Scammon, 461, a decision affirming it. And see in this connection, 2 West. Law Jour. 279; Rankin *v.* Lydia, 2 A. K. Marshall, 467; 14 B. Monr. 358; Lunsford *v.* Coquillon, 14 Martin, 401; 8 Louisiana, 475; Thomas *v.* Generis, 16 id. 483; Graham *v.* Strader, 5 B. Monr. 173; Collins *v.* America, 9 id. 565; Anderson *v.* Poindexter, 6 Ohio State, 622.

(*b*) By the act of May 30, 1854, organizing the territories of Kansas and Nebraska, this restriction, known as the Missouri compromise, was repealed. The power of Congress to frame a government for a territory has been usually referred to the clause of sect. 3, art. 4, of the constitution; namely, "The Congress shall have power to dispose of and make all needful rules and regulations respecting the territory or other property of the United States." It has also been regarded as the inevitable consequence of the right to acquire territory, and whatever its source, its possession until recently has been considered unquestionable. Sere *v.* Pitot, 6 Cranch, 336; American Insurance Co. *v.* Canter, 1 Peters, 542, 543; United States *v.* Gratiot, 14 id. 537; Cross *v.* Harrison, 16 How. 193, 194; 1 Kent, Com. 383; 2 Story, Const. § 1325. In the recent case of Scott *v.* Sanford, 19 How. 393, some members of the court, after deciding that it had no jurisdiction of the case, expressed opinions that Congress had no power to prohibit slavery in the territories; that this clause of the constitution applied only to territory owned or claimed by the United States at the time of its formation; that the prohibition of slavery in the act known as the Missouri compromise act was unconstitutional and void;—and one judge even regarded the same prohibition in the ordinance for the government of the North-western territory, as re-enacted by Congress, to be unconstitutional. But upon a familiar principle, which rejects as authority the opinions of judges, not necessary to the decision of the case, these *dicta* of a portion of the court are not likely to be considered as of binding force. There is a critical examination of this case, and of the points decided, in the Boston Law Reporter for June, 1857. This article in the Law Reporter thus states the point decided by a majority of the court. "A negro held in slavery in one State, under the laws thereof, and taken by his master, for a temporary residence, into a State where slavery is prohibited by law, and thence into a territory acquired by treaty, where slavery is prohibited by act of Congress, and afterwards returning with his master into a slave State, and acquiring a residence there, is not such a citizen of that State as may sue there in the circuit court of the United States, if he be held by the highest court of that State after his return to be a slave."

Free Colored Persons. (*a*) I will take this opportunity to say a word respecting *free negroes.* Their condition varies considerably in the different States. Some exclude them altogether. Others allow them nearly all the privileges of citizens. But in Ohio, the policy has been to discourage them as much as possible from coming here, without absolutely excluding them. In fact, the only provision in their favor is, that which punishes kidnapping them. The disabling provisions are generally confined to "blacks and mulattoes." A mulatto is a person begotten between a white and a black. Consequently, a person of any shade above half-black would not be within these disabilities. And our courts have manifested a disposition to construe these provisions strictly, in favor of liberty and equality. Some of them certainly savor of unnecessary severity.

§ 66. **Power as to the Public Domain.** (*b*) This has been already discussed under the four heads of acquisition of title; scheme of survey and sale; creation of territorial governments; and admission of new States into the Union. Nothing further, therefore, remains to be said.

§ 67. **Power to protect the States.** (*c*) The words are, "the United States shall guarantee to every State in this Union a republican form of government, and shall protect each of them against invasion; and on application of the legislature, or of the executive when the legislature cannot be convened, against domestic violence." This language makes the general protection here guaranteed, not merely a matter of power, but of duty. It binds the whole to protect the parts. Some fears were entertained at the outset that a pretext would here be found for interfering in the concerns of the States, when there was no occasion. But all agreed that there might be occasions when federal interference might be desirable, and therefore the power ought to be conferred. The only question was, whether it had been sufficiently guarded. The clause points out three occasions of interference which may be viewed separately. *First,* as to the form of the State governments. So long as they continue "republican" there is no authority to inter-

(*a*) Medway *v.* Natick, 7 Mass. 88; Gray *v.* State, 4 Ohio, 353; Jeffries *v.* Ankeny, 11 Ohio, 372; Thacker *v.* Hawk, 11 Ohio, 376; Van Camp *v.* Incorp. Village of Logan, 9 Ohio State, 406; Anderson *v.* Millikin, id. 568. The regulation of a school committee requiring colored children to attend a separate school, was held to be in conformity with the constitution of Massachusetts. Roberts *v.* Boston, 5 Cush. 198. An act in Ohio to the same effect, where equal advantages were given to the colored and white children, was held not to conflict with the 14th amendment to the constitution of the United States. State *v.* McCann, 21 Ohio State, 198.

(*b*) *Ante,* § 13, 14, 15.

(*c*) The convention at first resolved to guarantee to each State a republican constitution and its existing laws. Mad. Pap. 861. This proposition was afterwards modified by striking out existing laws, and inserting protection against foreign and domestic violence — id. 1141. A distinct power to subdue a rebellion in any State, upon the application of its legislature, was negatived by a tie vote — id. 1349–51. The clause was then agreed to in its present shape — id. 1466–8; Martin *v.* Mott, 12 Wheaton, 29. See Luther *v.* Borden, 7 How. 1, a decision relating to the Rhode Island contest in 1841 and 1842.

fere. This term comprehends such a variety of modifications as to leave the States the widest field for choice that can be desired. They are merely prevented from introducing a despotic, monarchic, aristocratic, or, in one word, anti-republican, form of government. When they shall attempt to do this, the general welfare will be threatened, and they ought to be prevented. But until they do so, there can be no interference with their form of government. *Secondly*, as to invasions. Here there can be no question. To invade a State is to invade the Union. If the State can protect itself, it is well; if not, it must need federal assistance. This power, therefore, can never do harm, but always good. *Thirdly*, as to domestic violence. Here there is more room for apprehension. The cause being domestic, interference would be a matter of extreme delicacy. And on this account it is provided, that federal interference shall not take place until the State has requested it. This will of course happen only when there is actual need; consequently, there can be no danger from this quarter. On the whole, then, it would seem that this provision is as carefully guarded as it is important to the States. It makes the stronger, as it always should be, a protector of the weaker, without the power of becoming an oppressor.

LECTURE X.

INCIDENTAL POWERS.

§ 68. **Their general Nature.** (*a*) In the preceding lecture, I have discussed all the enumerated powers of the federal constitution, together with the corresponding prohibitions. To one who has never before thought upon the subject, it may appear strange that so few specifications should be sufficient to describe the extent of federal authority. But it is to be remembered that the specifications only describe the *ends* to be effected by the federal government. The *means* to be employed in effecting these ends are not enumerated, but constitute what are termed *incidental powers*. And here the question may be asked why these means were not also enumerated? Why was not the enumeration, once begun, rendered complete? Why was anything left to implication? I will endeavor to answer these questions. In the first place there was no necessity for carrying the enumeration further. It is a general principle of common sense, running through all agencies, that where authority is given to effect a particular end, it necessarily includes the authority to use the proper means, without any specifications to that effect. In other words, where a general

(*a*) See 2 Story, Const. ch. xxiv. § 1906.

power is given to do a thing, every particular power necessary for doing it is included, without being expressed. Now the general powers deemed necessary for effecting the national purposes for which the federal government was created, having been specifically enumerated, all the particular powers necessary to carry into effect these general powers, are, on the above principle, implied, without being named; for there is nothing peculiar in the nature of this constitution, to make it an exception to this otherwise universal rule of construction. The ninth and tenth amendments were never designed to produce this effect, as has been sometimes alleged. The ninth amendment declares that "the enumeration in this constitution of certain rights, shall not be construed to deny or disparage others retained by the people." This was added out of abundant caution, to exclude a possible inference, founded on the legal maxim, that the enumeration in any instrument of certain particulars, excludes those not enumerated. It relates not to the *powers*, but to the *prohibitions* of the constitution; and merely declares, that, because some things are specially prohibited, it does not thence follow that any thing not prohibited, is therefore permitted; and that, in order to ascertain whether any particular thing is permitted, we must look further, and see whether the power to do it is conferred. And this brings me to the tenth amendment, which declares that "the powers not delegated to the United States by the constitution, nor prohibited by it to the States, are reserved to the States respectively or to the people." It is obvious that this amendment does not affect the question, What powers are in fact delegated? It merely asserts what never could have been doubted without such an assertion; namely, that Congress, being the creature of the constitution, and possessing no original and inherent powers, can only exercise such as are delegated, or, in other words, that where a grant is made, whatever is not granted, remains in the grantors. Moreover, there is one historical fact which completely rebuts the inference that this amendment was intended to confine Congress to the exercise of express powers. In the articles of confederation, the words were, "all powers not *expressly* delegated;" and when this amendment was before Congress, a motion was made to insert the word "*expressly*," and rejected; on the ground that it is impossible to confine any government to the exercise of express powers. The conclusion, therefore, is, that there was no necessity for a further enumeration.

But a still more satisfactory reason is, that such a complete enumeration as would leave nothing to implication, would have been utterly impossible. No human sagacity could have foreseen all the means which circumstances might render necessary to effect the ends which were foreseen. And even if such foresight had existed, the attempt to make such enumeration would have expanded the constitution through volumes. This alone, conceding the possibility, would have been a sufficient reason for terminating the enumeration with the ends to be effected, and leaving the means to implication. Why waste time in describing the less, when it is already contained in the greater? To what purpose is our language furnished with general terms, if they cannot supersede the necessity of enumerating the particulars they contain?

Yet, notwithstanding these very sufficient reasons for not enumerating the secondary powers, there are many who, from the fact of their not being enumerated, have denied their existence. These persons would hold the federal government to the strict letter of the constitution, and allow the exercise of no powers not specifically enumerated. I have not room to detail the arguments upon which this doctrine of *strict construction* rests. They are, however, chiefly derived from four sources; *first*, the history of the times, evincing a deep-rooted jealousy of federal power, and a strong determination to limit it in the strictest manner; *secondly*, the fact that the constitution contains several pleonasms, thereby indicating an intention to leave nothing to implication; *thirdly*, the fact that certain powers are enumerated, thereby raising the inference that those not enumerated are excluded; and *fourthly*, the amendments just referred to, which are alleged to negative the idea of implied powers. To all these arguments, however, it might be sufficient to reply, that, if any government were to be confined to the strict letter of a brief constitution, it could not fulfil the ends of its creation; and, therefore, we cannot presume an intention so to confine it. But it would seem as if the framers of the federal constitution, than whom a wiser body of men was never convened, anticipated that such arguments would be made use of, and therefore resolved to furnish, in the constitution itself, a conclusive answer to them. For, singular as the proposition may at first appear, *incidental powers are expressly conferred.* The clause conferring them immediately follows the specific enumeration, and is in these words: "Congress shall have power to make all laws which shall be necessary and proper for carrying into execution the foregoing powers, and all other powers vested by this constitution in the government of the United States, or in any department or officer thereof." (*a*) This clause, therefore, puts an end to all doubt whether Congress can exercise incidental powers. The only question that can arise is, What powers are incidental, within the meaning of the terms here employed? In other words, when is a law "*necessary and proper for carrying into execution*" the enumerated powers of the federal constitution. The answer must depend upon the meaning we annex to the words "necessary and proper." The advocates of a *strict construction* insist that the meaning is the same as if the phrase had been, *absolutely necessary*, *indispensably necessary* or *absolutely indispensable.* They hold that this provision leaves Congress no discretion whatever in the choice of means to effect the authorized

(*a*) See 2 Story, Const. § 1248; McCulloch *v.* Maryland, 4 Wheaton, 412. In the convention this clause was adopted unanimously, and without debate. Mad. Pap. 1370.

ends; and that any law passed in pursuance of this power, must be a *sine qua non;* one without which the specific end could not possibly be effected. But, on the other hand, the advocates of a *liberal construction* consider the meaning of the words "necessary and proper" to be the same as if the expression had been, *convenient*, *suitable*, *appropriate*, or some other term of like import. They hold that the provision gives Congress a discretion in the choice of means, to effect the authorized ends; and that laws passed in virtue of this power need not be the only possible means of effecting the end proposed, provided they be appropriate means. And as this is the construction upon which the government has been hitherto administered, I shall briefly state the leading arguments in favor of it.

1. The terms themselves admit of this enlarged meaning. Even had the word "necessary" been used alone, neither its grammatical nor popular sense would have required the strict construction. It generally means *needful*, *requisite*, *conducive to;* and admits of degrees of comparison. Accordingly, when we would convey the idea of extreme urgency or indispensable necessity, we prefix a qualifying word, and say *absolutely* or *indispensably necessary.* This very constitution furnishes a conclusive example, when it prohibits the States from laying any tax on imports or exports, "except what may be *absolutely necessary* for executing their inspection laws." But the word "necessary" is not used alone. It is followed by a qualifying word of another sort, which, instead of increasing, diminishes the idea of urgency. The word "proper" would have no meaning whatever, if the strict construction were adopted. But the liberal construction gives to both words their natural and appropriate signification. In the common use of language, who would ever think of using the terms "necessary and proper," to convey the idea of absolute and extreme necessity?

2. There is nothing in the character or situation of the clause to justify the strict construction; but the contrary. It is placed among the powers of Congress, and not among the limitations of power. It purports to be an additional power, and not a restriction; to enlarge, and not to diminish the powers of Congress. But even supposing it had no other effect than simply to exclude the inference against incidental powers, without enlargement or diminution, we should still arrive at the liberal construction, on the general principle of agency before mentioned; which always allows the agent a choice of means, unless the contrary be expressed.

3. The necessity of the case demands the liberal construction; since without it Congress could not beneficially promote the national interest. Probably more than half of all the legislation of Congress has no other constitutional warrant than this liberal construction of incidental powers. This will be evident from the instances to be given hereafter. Meantime, I will state the rules by which to determine whether a proposed measure comes within the sphere of incidental powers or not.

These rules are two: *first*, there must be a primary or general power, expressly conferred by the constitution; and, *secondly*, the measure in question must be a convenient and proper means of carrying into execution this primary power. These rules are deduced from the clause itself. The power declared is, in substance, to pass all laws which may be requisite for effecting any of the objects specified in the constitution. And so long as Congress adheres to these rules, there can be no danger from incidental powers. Let every measure, for which there is not a specific provision, be a manifestly proper means of effecting an end, for which there is a specific provision; and the vehement jealousy of incidental powers, which has always existed, will never be justified by experience. In order to illustrate these general views, I will now instance the most prominent of the incidental powers hitherto exercised.

§ 69. **Power to Purchase Foreign Territory.** (*a*) We have seen that since the formation of the federal government, the United States have purchased extensive territories: now. the constitution nowhere contains any express power to make these purchases. If, therefore, the power exist, it is incidental; and, by applying to it the test rules before laid down, we shall find that it requires the utmost stretch of liberal construction. To make such a purchase, involves two acts: *first*, a treaty stipulating the terms of purchase; and, *secondly*, an appropriation by Congress to pay the purchase-money. First, then, does the treaty-making power extend thus far? If so, it can only be as a general incident to national sovereignty. Secondly, has Congress power to raise and appropriate money for such purchase? If so, it can only be as incidental to the promotion of "the common defence and general welfare," upon the most enlarged construction of these terms. It is not a little singular, therefore, that this power, the most questionable perhaps of any yet exercised, should have been first exercised during the preponderance of a party including the most prominent advocates of a strict construction.

§ 70. **Power to lay an Embargo.** (*b*) The power to lay an embargo is nowhere expressly conferred. To which, then, of the enumerated powers is it incidental? It may be incidental to two of them: the war power and the commercial power; but it can only be so on the liberal construction; for it can never be absolutely indispensable to the exercise of either. But it meets the test of an incidental power, because it may be a convenient and proper means of preventing the evils of war, and of ultimately promoting the commercial welfare of the country. This power, like the preceding, was first asserted by the advocates of a strict construction.

(*a*) See 2 Story, Const. ch. xxvii.

(*b*) See 2 Story, Const. ch. xxvii.; United States *v.* Brig William, 2 Hall's Law Jour. 255.

§ 71. **Power to establish a Military Academy.** (*a*) This power is nowhere expressly conferred, but has been exercised as an incidental power. The object of such establishment being to educate young men for the army, and thus the better enable the country to prepare for, and carry on war, it is evidently a convenient and proper, though by no means an indispensable, method, of promoting the common defence and general welfare. On the liberal construction, therefore, the power to establish a military or naval academy is clearly incidental to the general power of defence; but on a strict construction it is not.

§ 72. **Power to pass Alien and Sedition Laws.** (*b*) These terms have a peculiar import. Two laws, known by this title, were enacted in 1798, and have long since expired by their own limitation. The alien law, in substance, authorized the president to order out of the country, under severe penalties for disobedience, such aliens as he should deem dangerous to its peace and safety. The sedition law, in substance, provided for punishing, by fine and imprisonment, any persons who should unlawfully combine together, with intent to obstruct any measure of the federal government; or who should write, print, utter, or publish any thing false, scandalous, and malicious, against the federal government or any department or officer thereof, with intent to bring the same into hatred and disrepute, or stir up sedition. The constitutionality of both these laws has been vehemently assailed, and no acts of the government have been more unpopular. It is admitted on all hands that there is no express authority to pass them; and it certainly is not very easy to bring them within the test rules before laid down for incidental powers. They were, however, vindicated at the time, and have since been vindicated, as exercises of powers clearly incidental to the power and duty of self-protection, which must necessarily belong to every government, whether specified or not.

§ 73. **Power to create a National Bank.** (*c*) The power to create a corporation, for any purpose, is nowhere expressly conferred; and

(*a*) See 2 Story, Const. § 1281.

(*b*) See 2 Story, Const. § 1293, 1891.

(*c*) In McCulloch *v.* Maryland, 4 Wheaton, 316, the question arose upon the validity of a law of that State imposing a tax upon the Branch Bank of Baltimore. This law was of course valid, if it did not interfere with the constitution or laws of the United States. The first inquiry, therefore, was whether the act incorporating the bank had the force of a law. Had Congress power to create such a corporation? No such power was specified among the enumerated powers. Was it included under the general grant of power to pass all laws "*necessary and proper*" for executing the specified powers? The incorporation of a bank was manifestly a *convenient and suitable* means of carrying on the fiscal operations of government. Did the words "*necessary and proper*" mean any thing more? Was no law "*necessary and proper*" within the meaning of the constitution, but one which was absolutely and altogether indispensable? This could not be the import of the words, because so narrow a construction would set aside almost half the laws of Congress. It is not absolutely necessary to punish smuggling in order to create a revenue; or to punish mail robbery, in order to have the mail transported; yet these laws can only stand upon the ground that they are "*necessary and proper*" means of effecting those ends. The import, therefore, of this provision must be, to give Congress a discretion in the choice of it is known that the proposition to confer such power was made in the federal convention, and failed. Yet this power, which was denied as an end, has been twice exercised as a means. A national bank was incorporated, first in 1791, and again in 1816; and the constitutionality of these acts has been twice affirmed, after the most ample discussion, by each of the departments of the federal government. To which, then, of the enumerated powers is this power incidental? On the strict construction it is not incidental to any one, for it is not absolutely indispensable to the execution of any one. But on the liberal construction it is incidental to the revenue power, the commercial power, the currency power, and the power of defence; for a national bank is found to be an exceedingly convenient and useful agent or instrument of the government in all its fiscal operations, which are more or less connected with each of these powers. This has been already shown in discussing the subject of currency; and on this general ground rest all the arguments in favor of its constitutionality.

§ 74. **Power to give a priority to the United States as Creditor.** (*a*)

means; and so long as the means they adopted were suitable and appropriate to effect a constitutional end, the means themselves were constitutional. It was therefore the unanimous opinion of the court, that the law incorporating the bank was constitutional. And as it was one of the provisions of this law that the directors of the bank should have power to locate branches where they should think fit; the location of the branch at Baltimore was therefore a constitutional act. This being settled, is the law of Maryland valid? There is no express prohibition in the constitution against such a law. The States are forbidden to lay duties on imports, exports, and tonnage; and this is the only *express* limitation upon their power of taxation. Is there any *implied* limitation? To answer this, we must look to the nature of the power contended for. If Maryland can lay any tax upon the bank, she can lay a high tax as well as a low one. She can thus expel the branch bank from her jurisdiction. Every other State can do the same. Thus if we admit the power of the States to tax the bank, we admit their power to destroy it. But the law incorporating the bank, being pursuant to the constitution, is declared to be "*the supreme law*" of the land. Thus a State may do indirectly, what it could not directly; it may indirectly abrogate the supreme law. The argument, then, is reduced to this: A power to create a bank, implies a power to preserve it. A power to tax a bank implies a power to destroy it. There is a direct incompatibility in the exercise of these two powers. Which must yield? That which is supreme, or that which is subordinate? Manifestly the latter. The law of Maryland is therefore unconstitutional. This is a brief sketch of the argument of the court. But it was intimated that a State might tax the real estate of a bank, and the stock owned within its jurisdiction. In Osborn *v.* The Bank of the United States, 9 Wheaton, 738, which arose under a law of Ohio imposing an enormous tax, for the express purpose of expelling the branch bank from its limits, the constitutionality of the bank was conceded; but the court was requested to review so much of its former opinion as pronounced it unconstitutional for a State to tax the bank. The argument in favor of taxation proceeded upon the ground, that the corporation was created for private and individual purposes; that its object was private trade and profit; and that the exemption from taxation was not *an incident* to any such corporation. Had the exemption been expressed in the charter the question would have been different. So also if the institution had been a public one, like the mint or post-office, taxation would not have been constitutional. But this was neither a public institution, nor expressly exempted. It was therefore liable to taxation. The court denied these premises. The bank was not created for its own sake, or for private purposes. It was never supposed that Congress could create such a corporation. The sole ground of its constitutionality was, that it was created for public purposes. Private profit was only an incident to the main purpose. The premises being false, the conclusion did not induce the court to change its former opinion. As to taxing national banks, *supra*, p. 135.

(*a*) See 2 Story, Const. § 1278; U. S. *v.* Fisher, 2 Cranch, 202; U. S. *v.* Hooe, 3

By the acts of 1797 and 1799, a priority is secured to the United States over other creditors where a debtor becomes insolvent, and though there is no express power for this purpose, yet these acts have been held constitutional upon the liberal construction of incidental powers. The ground is, that Congress being authorized to collect the revenue and defray the expenses of the government, may use all eligible means for these ends; and the law securing a priority or preference, is of this character; because, without it, many of the debts might be lost and the revenue impaired. The provisions apply to all debtors, when either of these four cases of insolvency occur: namely, *first*, when the debtor dies insolvent; *secondly*, when an insolvent debtor makes an assignment; *thirdly*, when he commits an act of legal bankruptcy; *fourthly*, when he absconds or conceals his property. The priority, however, is not in the nature of a *lien*, operating from the time of contracting the debt; for it only operates from the occurring of one of these four acts; and, accordingly, if another creditor has acquired a specific *lien* by mortgage or judgment, upon the debtor's property, the priority of government cannot supersede it.

§ 75. **Power of Punishment.** We have seen that Congress has the express power of punishment in five classes of cases: namely, offences against the currency; on the high seas; against the law of nations; in places of exclusive jurisdiction; and treason. But in point of number, these offences form but a small proportion of those actually made punishable by Congress. The rest, therefore, must have been provided for in the exercise of incidental powers. These may all be included under the six following classes: 1. Offences against the revenue laws, of which there are many; and the power to punish which is incidental to the revenue laws. 2. Offences against commerce, including the Indians, the power to punish which is incidental to the power of regulating commerce. 3. Offences against the post-office regulations, of which there are many, and the power to punish which is incidental to the power of establishing post-offices and post-roads. 4. Offences against foreign nations, other than those ascertained by the law of nations; the power to punish which is incidental to the power to manage our foreign relations. 5. Offences against the federal government, other than treason; the power to punish which is incidental to the power of self-protection. 6. Offences committed by federal officers, the power to punish which is also incidental to the power of self-protection. In all these cases, the power of punishment is clearly incidental on the liberal construction, but not on the strict construction; because, though very salutary, it is not absolutely indispensable.

§ 76. **Power to protect Domestic Industry.** (*a*) This power, so

Cranch, 73; Harrison *v.* Sterry, 5 Cranch, 289; Prince *v.* Bartlett, 8 Cranch, 431; Thelusson *v.* Smith, 2 Wheaton, 396; Conard *v.* Atlantic Insurance Company, 1 Peters, 388; Lewis *v.* United States, 92 U. S. 618.

(*a*) See 1 Story, Const. § 958–66.

important to our national prosperity, is nowhere expressly conferred. But Congress has power, as we have seen, to raise a revenue for the purpose of paying debts and providing for the common defence and general welfare; and also to regulate commerce with foreign nations. And the power to encourage our own trade and manufactures, by such *a tariff* of duties as will bring the price of imported products of foreign labor up to that for which the same commodities can be produced in this country, has been constantly exercised, since the formation of the government, as incidental to the revenue and commercial power; though not without strenuous opposition. I do not propose to examine minutely the arguments on either side. It is perfectly obvious, however, that in a new country like ours, where vacant land is so abundant and so cheap, and where the mass of the people are so independent and respectable, the price of labor must for ages be higher than in the crowded and overgrown nations of the Old World; and consequently, that if our ports were thrown open to the free and indiscriminate introduction of all foreign products, our countrymen could not sustain the competition; for it is certain that many commodities can be produced abroad and transported hither at less cost than that for which they can be produced here. Only two alternatives therefore remain: either to forego these branches of labor altogether, and depend entirely upon the supply from abroad; or to lay such duties on the importation of these commodities as will protect our own labor from a ruinous competition. And as the latter alternative is deemed, for various reasons, more conducive to the general welfare than the former, it has become a part of our general policy. And there is no doubt of the incidental power to grant this protection on the liberal construction; though not being imperatively necessary, it would not exist on the strict construction.

§ 77. **Power to make Internal Improvements.** (*a*) The phrase, internal improvements, when used with reference to the legislation of Congress, includes the construction of *roads* and *canals*, and the improvement of *watercourses*. If Congress have power to provide for any or all these things, that power is incidental; being nowhere expressly conferred. It is possible that some of these improvements may be convenient and proper means of facilitating commercial intercourse; and thus far the power to make them may, perhaps, be incidental, on the liberal construction, to the power to regulate commerce. But the power to make internal improvements is most generally derived from the revenue power. We have seen that this power may be exercised in any way which will promote the common defence or general welfare. If, therefore, a contemplated improvement be a suitable means of producing one of these results, the power *to raise and appropriate money* for making such improvement would seem, on the liberal construction, to be unquestionably incidental to the revenue power. But the terms require that the

(*a*) See 2 Story, Const. § 1267–9.

improvement be strictly national in its character, and calculated to benefit the whole Union, in one of these ways; for if it be of a merely sectional or local character, however beneficial to a particular district, it can in no sense be said to promote the *common* defence or *general* welfare. Again, while the power to raise and appropriate money, under these qualifications, is thus clear, a difficulty arises with reference to the *actual construction* of such works by the federal government, from the local jurisdiction of the States over the territory within their respective limits. The whole spirit, as well as the frequent expressions, of the constitution, indicates that without express provision for that purpose, the jurisdiction is not to be interfered with, unless by the *consent* of the States concerned; and the express provisions include only two kinds of improvements; namely, *post-roads* and *military roads*. When the construction of these becomes necessary, Congress need not consult the States; but for the construction of any other improvements within the States, it would seem that their consent should be first obtained.

I have thus briefly considered nine of the most prominent of the incidental powers hitherto exercised. I might select others of a less questionable character. I might refer to the creation of the various subordinate departments of government, and to the very numerous legislative details connected therewith; all of which are more or less the fruits of incidental power: but enough has been said to illustrate the nature of incidental powers, and the propriety of the liberal construction put upon the clause providing for them. If, instead of this, the strict construction had been adopted in practice, it must be evident that the federal government would have been comparatively inadequate to the accomplishment of the grand objects contemplated by the framers of the constitution, as we gather them from its comprehensive preamble.

LECTURE XI.

BILL OF RIGHTS. (*a*)

§ 78. **Equality of Rights.** — In the two preceding lectures, I have discussed, under the heads of *enumerated* and *incidental*, all the powers delegated to the federal government. In the same connection, I have also considered the federal and State prohibitions relating to the subject-matter of these several powers. But there still remains a number of federal and State prohibitions, relating

(*a*) See 1 Black. Com. 127; 2 Kent, Com. 1; 2 Story, Const. ch. xliv.; Mad. Pap. 1565–6.

to other matters, some direct and others indirect; and constituting, in the strictest sense of the words, our *declared* or *fundamental rights.* A brief discussion of these prohibitions will terminate our view of constitutional law. The Declaration of Independence announces the fundamental rights of man, in this strong and comprehensive language: "We hold these truths to be self-evident: that all men are created equal; that they are endowed by their Creator with certain inalienable rights; that among these are life, liberty, and the pursuit of happiness; and that to secure these rights, governments are instituted among men, deriving their just powers from the consent of the governed." The federal constitution contains no similar declaration; but in the State constitutions, the same sentiments are universally reiterated. The constitution of Ohio thus commences the declaration of rights: "All men are, by nature, free and independent, and have certain inalienable rights, among which are those of enjoying and defending life and liberty, acquiring, possessing, and protecting property, and seeking and obtaining happiness and safety." Then follows this declaration: "All political power is inherent in the people. Government is instituted for their equal protection and benefit, and they have the right to alter, reform, or abolish the same, whenever they may deem it necessary." These general and fundamental propositions furnish little matter for comment. They are rather to be regarded as prefatory to the specific declarations which follow them as corollaries. To these, therefore, let us direct our attention. I shall endeavor to group them together, as well as I may, with reference to their subject-matter, beginning with *equality.*

The nature of political equality has already been explained. (*a*) The language of our constitution is very carefully guarded, and is literally true. All men are not born absolutely equal in every respect; but there must be endless diversities of condition, capacity, means, opportunities, and the like, which no social organization can prevent. But equality of civil and political rights is the birthright of all men: and this is precisely what our constitution intends by the declaration, "that all men are, by nature, free and independent;" instead of asserting that all men shall be absolutely equal in condition. The chief provision designed to secure our political equality, is that which prohibits *hereditary distinctions.* It is in vain that Blackstone and others insist "that the distinction of rank and honors is necessary in every well-governed State;" for experience proves that men will of themselves create all the distinctions required, without the aid of government, to perpetuate them in the blood. And accordingly the federal constitution prohibits both the United States and the individual States from conferring, and our citizens from receiving, any hereditary title, emolument, privilege, or honor. The State constitutions

(*a*) 1 Black. Com. 157; 2 Story, Const. § 1351-2; Holden *v.* James, 11 Mass. 396.

also generally, though unnecessarily, contain a similar prohibition; and we have seen that before an alien can be admitted to citizenship, he must renounce every title of nobility. In one word, then, we acknowledge no nobility but that which nature gives; and no distinctions, but those which men themselves achieve. But again, equality may be counteracted by *partial legislation*, (*a*) against which we have no specific prohibition. Probably it was deemed unnecessary to express what was so manifestly implied. An arbitrary government may make partial laws without inconsistency, for it does not profess the doctrine of equality; but in a republic, such laws would be as absurd and inconsistent as they are odious. Every thing, therefore, in the shape of *monopolies*, is prohibited by the spirit, if not by the letter, of the constitution. Let us not, however, carry this doctrine too far. It is not necessary that laws should in all cases include every individual in the community; they will escape the imputation of partiality, if they include all persons similarly situated. The doctrine of equality only requires that they shall not exclude any persons coming within the principle of their operation; and hence it is that our numerous *corporations*, with special privileges and franchises, are not unconstitutional, so long as their charters exclude no class of persons from becoming members.

§ 78 *a*. **Corporal Liberty.** (*b*) As a general proposition, every individual, under our government, is at full liberty to go wheresoever, or do whatsoever he chooses, provided he does not interfere with the rights of other persons. This may be called his *corporal liberty*, or liberty of action. Again, every individual is at full liberty to adopt and practise such doctrines as he chooses on the subject of religion, provided he does not interfere with the rights of others. This is denominated his *religious liberty*. Lastly, every individual is at full liberty to speak, write, print, or publish whatsoever he chooses, provided he does not interfere

(*a*) Municipal law is a *rule*. It is not a mere direction for a particular case, or a transient order to a particular individual, but a standing regulation, operating upon all who come within the principle it establishes. This is the general limit to its extension. It must embrace an entire class, but it need not be universal. It cannot single out an individual, for this would be unjust; but neither can it be required to include all the subjects of the government, for this may be sometimes impossible. In Holden *v*. James, 11 Mass. 396, the facts were these: The defendant had been administrator of a certain estate, to which the plaintiff was creditor. The statute of Massachusetts limited actions against administrators to four years from taking out letters. In this case, the four years had expired, and the claim was barred. But the plaintiff, thinking his case a hard one, petitioned the legislature to suspend the law of limitation in his particular case. A resolve was passed to that effect; and the question now submitted to the court was, whether the legislature had this power. The court, in a very able opinion, decided, that, although the legislature has power to repeal or suspend any law as to *all* persons, it cannot exercise this power with respect to any particular individual. It was manifestly contrary to the first principles of civil liberty and natural justice, and to the spirit of our constitution and laws, that any one citizen should enjoy privileges and advantages which are denied to all others in like circumstances. The constitution of Ohio declares that "all laws of a general nature shall have a uniform operation throughout the State."

(*b*) See 1 Black. Com. 134; 2 Kent, Com. 26.

with the rights of others. This is what we understand by the *liberty of speech and of the press.* I shall consider separately the provisions relating to each of these three branches of liberty beginning with *corporal liberty.* Individuals can only be deprived of this, in three classes of cases. *First,* by arrest in civil cases; *secondly,* by arrest in criminal cases; and *thirdly,* by standing towards another in the relation of subjection. With regard to arrest and detention in civil cases, we have already considered that declaration of our State constitution, which secures every one against imprisonment for debt, if he will honestly surrender up his property for the benefit of his creditors. It only remains, therefore, to consider the detention of the person in the other two classes of cases. And, first, with regard to *arrest and detention in criminal cases,* there are numerous declarations tending to secure individuals against all injustice, from the moment of arrest down to the final conviction and punishment. I shall briefly describe these in their order.

Searches and Seizures. (*a*) It is declared by the fourth amendment of the federal constitution, that "the right of the people to be secure in their persons, houses, papers, and effects, against unreasonable searches and seizures, shall not be violated; and no warrants shall issue but upon probable cause, supported by oath or affirmation, and particularly describing the place to be searched, and the persons or things to be seized." There is a similar declaration in our State constitution. The effect is, that no person can be arrested, or his premises searched, without a warrant, from the proper authority, issued upon the oath of some individual, and particularly describing the person, place, or offence. In England, prior to 1763, a practice had grown up, of issuing general warrants for the apprehension of suspected persons, or the searching of their premises, without naming them, or describing their offence; whereby great injustice was done to innocent persons. These warrants were decided, in that year, to be against the common law, and were accordingly suppressed. (*b*) But the apprehension that they might be revived in this country, was a sufficient reason for making this declaration.

Bail. (*c*) Between the arrest and trial, the accused must either

(*a*) See 2 Story, Const. 1901; 4 Black. Com. 291; *Ex parte* Burford, 3 Cranch, 447; *Ex parte* Bollman, 4 Cranch, 75; Money *v.* Leach, 3 Burrows, 1843. As to the description to be made and other proceedings in cases of seizure, see Green *v.* Briggs, 1 Curtis, C. C. R. 311; State *v.* Robinson, 33 Maine, 564; Fisher *v.* McGurr, 1 Gray (Mass.), 1. {And the fifth amendment protecting a man from being compelled to testify against himself in a criminal case prohibits the seizure of his private papers as evidence against him, for that would be a species of testifying against himself. Boyd *v.* United States, 116 U. S. 616.}

(*b*) The legality of such general warrants, known as writs of assistance, was contested before the supreme court of the colony of Massachusetts in 1761. It was the occasion of the celebrated argument of James Otis, which was said by John Adams to have given birth to American independence. Works of John Adams, vol. 1, p. 57; vol. 2, Appendix A; vol. 10, pp. 314, 362.

(*c*) The provision of the federal constitution does not apply to the State governments. Commonwealth *v.* Hitchings, 5 Gray, 482. Privear *v.* The Commonwealth, 5 Wallace, 462.

be detained in prison, or held to bail. Our constitution declares that "all persons shall be bailable by sufficient sureties, unless for capital offences, where the proof is evident or the presumption great:" and both constitutions declare "that excessive bail shall not be required." The manner of taking bail will be described hereafter. Suffice it here to say, that these declarations sufficiently secure the liberty of the accused between the arrest and trial.

Mode of Accusation. (*a*) The fifth amendment of the federal constitution declares that "no person shall be held to answer for a capital or otherwise infamous crime, unless on a presentment or indictment of a grand jury, except in cases arising in the land or naval forces, or in the militia when in actual service, in time of war or public danger." Our constitution excepts "petit larceny and other inferior offences." The two words *presentment* and *indictment*, mean the same thing in our practice; namely, a formal accusation drawn up by the prosecuting officer, and found to be true by a grand jury, consisting of fifteen impartial persons acting under oath, of whom twelve at least must concur, before the accused can be put upon his defence; and their deliberations are conducted under an oath of secrecy, in order that, if an indictment be not found, the grounds of suspicion may not be divulged. The result is, that the common-law mode of proceeding by *information* is here abrogated, except with regard to the minor offences. This was an accusation filed by the prosecuting officer in his official capacity, upon which the accused was brought to trial, without the intervention of a grand jury. We have already seen the *impeachment* of officers for official misconduct requires an accusation to be first made and concurred in by a majority of the house of representatives. So that we are well secured against being brought to trial, in any case, without probable cause.

Trial. (*b*) Both the federal and State constitutions contain several declarations relating to the trial, in nearly the same words. 1. "In all criminal prosecutions, the accused hath a right to be heard by himself and his counsel." The ancient common law inhumanly denied the right of having counsel in capital cases, though it was permitted in trials for minor offences; but, in conformity with the above declaration, both the federal and State courts are required to assign counsel, not exceeding two, in all cases when the accused is not able to employ them; and they have access to him in prison at all reasonable hours. 2. "To demand

(*a*) See 2 Story, Const. § 1782; 4 Black. Com. 302. This provision requiring indictments does not prevent the legislature from making changes in the technical form of indictments. Lougee *v.* The State, 11 Ohio, 68; Wolf *v.* The State, 19 Ohio State, 248. Nor does it render unconstitutional the provision of the criminal code, that in case of a plea in abatement of misnomer, the true name shall be substituted and the trial proceed. Lasure *v.* The State, 19 Ohio State, 43.

(*b*) See 4 Black. Com. 355; 2 Story, Const. § 1792; People *v.* Smith, 3 Wheeler's Criminal Cases, 100. The provisions of the fifth and sixth amendments to the constitution of the United States do not apply to crimes under the State laws. Twitchell *v.* The Commonwealth, 7 Wall. 321; Prescott *v.* The State, 19 Ohio State, 184.

the nature and cause of the accusation against him, and to have a copy thereof." Accordingly, the federal and State laws provide that the accused shall be furnished with a copy of the indictment before the trial. (*a*) 3. "To meet the witnesses face to face." Accordingly, *written evidence*, by depositions, cannot be used in criminal cases, unless by consent. The accused may always claim the right of hearing the evidence against him from the lips of the witnesses, that their whole bearing and demeanor may be noticed by the jury, and any bias, evasion, or concealment detected. (*b*) 4. "To have compulsory process for obtaining witnesses in his favor." Anciently, the accused could not even have witnesses examined for him. But the federal and State constitutions not only secure this privilege, but also give him the same means of compelling their attendance that the government has. The mode of compulsion will be considered hereafter. 5. "To have a speedy public trial, by an impartial jury of the county or district in which the offence shall have been committed." (*c*) *First*, the trial shall be speedy. The accused, who is presumed innocent until proved guilty, shall not long be kept in suspense. Accordingly, it is provided, that, unless there be some strong reason for delay, he may insist upon being tried at the first term after the arrest. *Secondly*, the trial must be public. There can be no star-chamber proceedings. All must be done in the face of day. *Thirdly*, the trial must be by an impartial jury; but the various statutory provisions tending to secure their impartiality, will be considered hereafter. *Fourthly*, the jury must be taken from the county, in trials under the State law; and from the district, in trials under the federal law; unless it appear that a fair trial cannot there be had. Thus the accused is saved the expense of a distant trial, and has the advantage of the good opinion he may have established in his own neighborhood. 6. "Shall not be compelled to give evidence against himself." This does not exclude voluntary confessions, but precludes all resort to torture and the rack, or any other compulsory means, to extort confessions. 7. "Shall not be twice put in jeopardy for the same offence." (*d*) This is only the affirmance

(*a*) This right may be waived. Fouts *v.* The State, 8 Ohio State, 98.

(*b*) This clause does not exclude evidence of dying declarations, or of the testimony given by a deceased witness, on a former trial between the same parties. Summons *v.* The State, 5 Ohio State, 325.

(*c*) It has been held that the court may, at the election of the defendant, try the issue. Dailey *v.* The State, 4 Ohio State, 57; Dillingham *v.* The State, 5 id. 280. But it has since been held, that, in the higher grades of crime at least, it is not in the power of the accused to waive a trial by jury, and consent to the finding of the facts by the court. Williams *v.* The State, 12 Ohio State, 622. At common law, juries, it has been held, were the exclusive judges of evidence, but were bound both in civil and criminal cases to receive the law from the court. Commonwealth *v.* Porter, 10 Met. 263; Commonwealth *v.* Anthes, 5 Gray, 185; Williams *v.* The State, 10 Ind. 503; Pierce *v.* The State, 13 N. H. 536. Montgomery *v.* The State, 11 Ohio, 424; Robbins *v.* The State, 8 Ohio State, 131. In some of the States, there are statutes by which the jury is made the judge of the law in criminal cases. Such an act was pronounced contrary to the State constitution in Massachusetts, in Commonwealth *v.* Anthes.

(*d*) See 4 Black. Com. 335; 2 Story, Const. § 1787; People *v.* Goodwin, 18 Johns.

of a great common-law right. The meaning is, that a person shall not be tried a second time for any offence, after having been once acquitted or convicted of that same offence, by the verdict of a jury, on which judgment has been pronounced. But if the jury disagree, or a new trial be allowed, or judgment be arrested, the jeopardy here contemplated has not once existed, and another trial may be had.

Punishment. Both the federal and State constitutions declare, that "excessive fines shall not be imposed; nor cruel and unusual punishments inflicted." (*a*) We have already considered the federal power of punishment, both enumerated and incidental. For the rest, the power of punishment belongs to the States. In either case, however, if fines be imposed, they cannot be excessive; and if any other mode of punishment be provided, it must neither be cruel nor unusual. By *cruel*, is here meant barbarous. Death is a cruel punishment; yet death is inflicted in one case under the laws of Ohio, and in several cases under the laws of Congress. The declaration then only means that there shall be no unnecessary torture or barbarity. And since the punishment cannot be *unusual*, no room is left for the exercise of that horrid kind of ingenuity, which delights itself in devising new modes of punishment. And when we come to the department of criminal law, we shall find that the pledge here given has been faithfully kept. Probably the world does not furnish a more humane and simple criminal code than that of Ohio. But the proportioning of punishment to the offence has always been a matter of difficulty. No legislature can beforehand so graduate the scale of punishments, as to adapt them exactly to all the varying shades of criminality; and therefore the expedient adopted both by the federal and State legislatures is, to fix certain limits within which the discretion of the court may range, in apportioning the punishment to the facts of the case. The remaining provisions relating to punishment are found only in the State constitution, and are as follows: *First*, "no person shall be transported out of the State, for any offence committed within the same." In other words, *banishment* cannot be resorted to as a mode of punishment. *Secondly*, "no conviction shall work corruption of blood or forfeiture of estate." There is a similar provision by Congress in the act of 1790. It was a barbarous doctrine of the English law, (*b*) that a conviction of any of the high offences was followed by the two consequences here prohibited; namely, a *corruption* or *attaint* of blood, so that the convict could neither inherit nor transmit inheritance; and a *forfeiture* of his

187; Poage *v.* The State of Ohio, 3 Ohio State, 229; Dobbins *v.* The State, 14 Ohio State, 493; Stewart *v.* The State, 15 Ohio State, 155; State *v.* Behimer, 20 Ohio State, 572; Shelby *v.* Boenau, 40 Ohio State, 253; Mitchell *v.* State, 42 Ohio State, 383.

(*a*) This provision in the national constitution applies only to the legislation of the United States. Privear *v.* The Commonwealth, 5 Wallace, 462.

(*b*) See 4 Black. Com. 381.

present property. In this way, his innocent kindred suffered for his guilt.

Domestic Detention. (*a*) This may happen in consequence of the relation of a minor to his parent or guardian; an idiot or lunatic to his guardian; a wife to her husband; an apprentice to his master; and a slave to his master.

Habeas Corpus. (*b*) I have thus adverted to the constitutional declarations tending to secure corporal liberty. Any personal detention contrary to these provisions is unlawful, whether it be in the public streets, in prisons, in private houses, or elsewhere. And now the question arises, How is a person unlawfully detained to recover his liberty? Both the federal and State constitutions declare that "the privilege of the writ of *habeas corpus* shall not be suspended, unless when, in case of rebellion or invasion, the public safety may require it." By the writ of *habeas corpus* is here meant, that high and imperative writ, which issues as a matter of peremptory right, in favor of any person who is in confinement or detention, in any manner whatsoever, except it be on conviction of some offence, for which his imprisonment is the punishment, as provided in our statute. By virtue of this writ, the person so detained is carried at once before a judge to have the cause of his

(*a*) Our only constitutional provision upon this subject is, that "there shall be no slavery in this State; nor involuntary servitude, unless for the punishment of crime."

(*b*) See 2 Story, Const. § 1338; 3 Black. Com. 131; 2 Kent, Com. 26; Hurd on Habeas Corpus. This writ appears to have originated with Magna Charta, and to have taken the place of the writ *de homine replegiando*, as the great writ of liberty. It is said to be a writ *of right*, but not a writ *of course*, since cause must be shown. Lawrence's case, 5 Binney, 304; Ferguson's case, 9 Johns. 236. It issues generally to try the legality of any detention by commitment or otherwise. Among the leading cases are Gregory's case, 4 Burr. 1991; United States *v.* Greene, 3 Mason, 482; Commonwealth *v.* Briggs, 16 Pick. 203; Mercein *v.* People, 25 Wendell, 64; Commonwealth *v.* Addicks, 5 Binney, 520; Stacey's case, 10 Johns. 328; Somersett's case, 20 State Trials, 1; United States *v.* Jones, 3 Wash. C. C. R. 224. Among the debated questions are, whether the return can be contradicted; whether a writ of error will lie; and whether one tribunal will inquire into a contempt against another; as to which, see Anderson *v.* Dunn, 6 Wheaton, 204; Burdett *v.* Abbott, 14 East, 152, 201; Yeates *v.* The People, 6 Johns. 519; Holmes *v.* Jennison, 14 Peters, 540; *In re* Falvey *v.* Massing, 7 Wisconsin, 630. The power of the federal courts depends upon the 14th section of the act of 1789, 1 Stat. at Large, 73; and the 7th section of the act of 1833, 4 Stat. at Large, 634. See Bollman's case, 4 Cranch, 75; Watkins' case, 3 Peters, 201; Williams' case, 9 Peters, 704; Dorr's case, 3 How. 105; in the matter of Metzger, 5 id. 176; *In re* Thomas Kaine, 14 id. 103. The jurisdiction of the State courts, by means of the writ of *habeas corpus*, to pass upon the legality of the detention of persons who are in the custody of the United States officers, and to discharge them from such custody, has recently been passed upon in elaborate decisions. *In re* Booth, 3 Wisconsin, 1, *Ex parte* Booth, id. 145; *In re* Booth and Rycraft, id. 157; Bagnall *v.* Ableman, 4 id. 163; Ableman *v.* Booth, and United States *v.* Booth, 21 How. 506; *Ex parte* Bushnell, 8 Ohio State, 599; *Ex parte* Collier, 6 id. 55. When in an application to a State court it appears by the return that the prisoner is held under the authority, or claim and color of authority, of the United States by an officer of the government, the court can inquire no further, but must refuse the writ. Tarble's case, 13 Wall. 397. This writ cannot be used as a summary protest to review or revise errors or irregularities in the sentence of a court of competent jurisdiction. *Ex parte* Shaw, 7 Ohio State, 81; Platt *v.* Harrison, 6 Clarke (Iowa), 79 {*Ex parte* Van Hagan, 25 Ohio State, 426. The United States courts sustain a jurisdiction to release on *habeas corpus* a prisoner or convict held by State authorities in violation of the United States constitution, laws, or treaties. *Ex parte* Royall, 117 U. S. 241}.

detention investigated, and if it appear to be unlawful, he is immediately set at liberty. No comment can make the importance of this privilege more manifest than the bare statement of what it is. In fact, it is universally regarded as the grand bulwark of corporal liberty; and hence the precaution to declare that it shall never be suspended, except in cases of the most overpowering necessity. There is, moreover, in addition to the recovery of liberty, a remedy in damages for the unlawful detention, by an action for *malicious prosecution* or *false imprisonment;* but these do not belong to our present discussion.

§ 79. **Religious Liberty.** (*a*) The reason why government ought not to interfere with religion is, that religion is a matter exclusively between man and his Creator. Yet, clear as this proposition is, almost every government in the world, except ours, has made religion a matter of state; until the union of church and state had almost become a political axiom. If we take England as an example, we find that a very large portion of her laws have relation to her religious establishment. Indeed, we owe the first settlement of this country to her interference with the consciences of her subjects. The first colonists came here to enjoy that religious liberty which was denied them at home. And the doctrine for which they sacrificed so much is now incorporated into all our constitutions. The federal constitution, in the first amendment, declares that "Congress shall make no law respecting an establishment of religion, or prohibiting the free exercise thereof;" and, in another place, that "no religious test shall ever be required as a qualification to any office or public trust under the United States." Our State constitution contains a still more full and emphatic declaration, in these words: "All men have a natural and indefeasible right to worship Almighty God according to the dictates of their own conscience. No person shall be compelled to attend, erect, or support any place of worship, or maintain any form of worship against his consent; and no preference shall be given by law to any religious society; nor shall any interference with the rights of conscience be permitted. No religious test shall be required as a qualification for office, nor shall any person be incompetent to be a witness on account of his religious belief; but nothing herein shall be construed to dispense with oaths and affirmations. Religion, morality, and knowledge, however, being essential to good government, it shall be the duty of the general assembly to pass suitable laws to protect every religious denomination in the peaceable enjoyment of its own mode of public worship, and to encourage schools and the means of instruction." The result is, that we enjoy an entire freedom of conscience in religious matters; and that we have very few legislative provisions in any way connected with religion. We have seen that in the first two sales of land by the federal government, within the State, one section in

(*a*) 2 Kent, Com. 34.

each township was set apart for the support of religion: a thing which has not been done since the adoption of the federal constitution; and there are some legislative provisions relating to the management of these lands. But, with these exceptions, the only provisions we have in any way connected with religion, are those which prohibit the disturbing of religious societies when met for the purpose of worship, and which secure to such societies a perpetuity in their lands used for church purposes, without a specific act of incorporation.

§ 80. **Liberty of Speech and of the Press.** (*a*) It has been well remarked that there is little danger from error of opinion, when there is a free opportunity to expose and correct it by speech, and by the press. This, then, is one motive for securing this branch of liberty. And another is to secure the accountability of public agents. Public opinion is the tribunal before which a corrrupt or unfaithful officer most fears to be arraigned; but the efficiency of this restraint depends chiefly upon the freedom with which every one is allowed to express his opinions on public affairs. Without adverting, therefore, to the high considerations growing out of the sacredness of the right, abstractly viewed, we find in expediency alone a sufficient reason for securing to opinion the utmost freedom, both as to its formation and expression. Accordingly, the federal constitution declares that "Congress shall make no law abridging the freedom of speech or of the press." Our State constitution is more diffuse in its language. It begins by declaring that "every citizen may freely speak, write, and publish his sentiments on all subjects, being responsible for the abuse of the right, and no law shall be passed to restrain or abridge the liberty of speech or of the press." This qualification is tacitly annexed to every species of civil liberty. They who abuse it are held liable for the injury resulting from such abuse. It was well, however, to guard the above declaration against the possibility of cavil. The doctrine then is, that the liberty of speech and of the press consists in freedom from previous censorship or restraint, and not in exemption from subsequent liability for the injury which may thereby be done. And, accordingly, the law makes provision by which the person injured may have his civil action of *slander* or *libel*, to recover damages done to his reputation; and by which the libeller may be criminally prosecuted as an offender against the public peace. Again, it is declared, that "in all criminal prosecutions for libel, the truth may be given in evidence to the jury, and if it shall appear to the jury that the matter charged as libellous is true, and was published with good motives, and for justifiable ends, the party shall be acquitted." The common-law doctrine is, that in a civil action, either for verbal or written slander, the truth may always be given in evidence; but on an

(*a*) See 2 Story, Const. § 1880; 2 Kent, Com. 19; 4 Black. Com. 151; works on slander and libel by Starkie, Holt, Townsend, Odgers; R. S. of Ohio, §§ 5093, 5094.

indictment for a libel, never; because the criminality of a libel consists in its tendency to disturb the public peace, which tendency would be the same whether the libel was true or false. And this agrees with our statutory definition of a libel, which requires it to be "false *or* malicious." This provision, therefore, alters the common law only when the libel "was published with good motives, and for justifiable ends." In such cases, the truth may be given in evidence; but in other cases it is no justification. This distinction is rational and well founded. The truth ought to be published, when it concerns the public to know it; but private matters, even though true, ought not to be made public, in order to disgrace private individuals without benefiting the public.

In conclusion, it is proper to remark, that the true nature of that liberty and equality which we have now been considering, is often mistaken or misrepresented. We have seen that civil liberty is liberty protected and restrained by law; and that social equality is only an equality of rights and obligations, as determined by law. In this view, both are so mutually dependent upon each other, that neither can exist without the other. But this is true only of liberty and equality as above defined; for an absolute equality of condition is incompatible with any degree of liberty. What is it to be born free, and to live free, but to have the capability of carving out our own particular fortunes for ourselves, and thus differing indefinitely from those around us? It would require more than a Nero's despotism to reduce all men to a strict level, and keep them there. Even the most abject of slaves will differ in condition. Inequality of condition, therefore, is the natural offspring of civil liberty and equality of rights. But how often has this great truth been lost sight of! We need not go to the ostracisms, the persecutions, and the banishments of ancient Greece or Rome, for examples. We need not even go so far back as the reign of terror in France, when the guillotine was employed, in the name of liberty, to bring about an absolute equality. We may find alarming indications of the same spirit at home. Under the magic name of equality, the doctrines of agrarianism are beginning to be openly avowed; and unprincipled demagogues are industriously sowing the seeds of jealousy and disaffection between the rich and the poor, the intelligent and the ignorant, the illustrious and the obscure. These distinctions they would abolish, not by the regular results of free and generous competition, but by the combined force of numbers trampling down superiority. And liberty has been perverted in a similar manner. The people are told that their voice is the voice of God; in their self-love, they take this hackneyed saying literally; and what then is the majesty of law, if it happen to stand in the way of their capricious will! There can be but one earthly supremacy; and if this is to be found in the fitful ebullitions of popular feeling, the boasted supremacy of law becomes a mere name. This position is too clear for argument. If the people are to rise against their own laws, and suicidally trample them under foot, and if public opinion is to sustain them in so doing, there can be no such thing as security; for we shall hold our rights at the mercy of a mob of tyrants the most arbitrary and inexorable; and the signs of mob rule have of late been fearfully multiplying, both in theory and practice. Doctrines have been advanced in high places which clearly sanction popular violence against obnoxious laws; and in almost every quarter of the country, practice has followed precept, and the laws have been tumultuously set at defiance. These things may well excite alarm in every patriotic bosom. If a determined stand be not taken by the friends of order against these tendencies towards the subversion of order, the most fearful convulsions may well be apprehended. Let it never be forgotten, that the sole tenure by which we hold our rights, is the absolute and unquestioned supremacy of the law. This must be maintained, and insubordination prevented, at all hazards. The mob must be kept down, cost what it may: otherwise the days of free government are numbered. Here is our Rubicon, and it must not be crossed.

§ 81. **Right of Property.** We have seen that "the right of acquiring, possessing, and protecting property," is set down in our constitution among "the unalienable rights." Whether it be so or not, is a matter of speculation, upon which I shall not waste time. It is enough for us, that the right of property exists under the social compact, and that the protection and regulation of it form a leading object of municipal law. Property, as we have seen, is either in possession or in expectation, and the declarations now to be discussed relate to both descriptions of property, with a view to secure its inviolability by government.

Property in Possession. (*a*) The language of the ordinance of 1787 is, "Should the public exigencies make it necessary for the

(*a*) See 2 Story, Const. § 1790; 2 Kent, Com. 338; 1 West. Law Jour. 371; Bates *v.* Cooper, 5 Ohio, 115; Willyard *v.* Hamilton, 7 Ohio, 2 part, 111; Cooper *v.* Williams, 4 Ohio, 253; Cooper *v.* Warren Canal Co., 7 Ohio, 1 pt. 242; Parks *v.* Boston, 15 Pick. 207; Schuylkill Company *v.* Thobarn, 7 Serg. & R. 422; *In re* Albany Street, 11 Wendell, 153; *In re* Furman Street, 17 Wendell, 670; Gardner *v.* Newburgh, 2 Johns. Ch. Rep. 162; Beekman *v.* Saratoga Railroad Company, 3 Paige, 45; Rogers *v.* Bradshaw, 20 Johns. 735; McArthur *v.* Kelly, 5 Ohio, 139. In Gardner *v.* Trustees of Newburgh, 2 Johns. Ch. Rep. 162, the facts were these: Gardner owned a farm through which a stream flowed, which he used for various valuable purposes. The stream issued from a stream on his neighbor's farm. The legislature authorized the trustees to take water from the spring in pipes for the use of the town of Newburgh, but made no provision for making up to Gardner the loss he would sustain by diverting the water. *Held*, that he was entitled to a fair compensation before the water could be diverted; and, as the law made no provision therefor, an injunction was granted. In Rogers *v.* Bradshaw, 20 Johns. Rep. 735, the facts were these: The legislature of New York authorized the canal commissioners to take lands necessary for the canal. It became necessary to use the turnpike track for the canal, and to construct a new turnpike on Bradshaw's land. He brought trespass. *Held*, that trespass would not lie. Bradshaw was entitled to compensation; but as his land was necessary for the new road, which was rendered necessary by the canal, the commissioners were not trespassers. A turnpike is a public road. *Dictum*, that even though an act taking private property for public uses makes no provisions for compensation, it still shields the persons entering from liability as trespassers. And see 2 Kent, Com. 339, note. In Beekman *v.* Saratoga Railroad Company, 3 Paige, 45, the facts were these:

common preservation to take any person's property, or to demand his particular services, *full compensation* shall be made for the same."

The company had projected the railroad over Beekman's land, the only convenient place. He had refused his consent, and would make no agreement for compensation. Pursuant to the charter, the governor had appointed commissioners, who had appraised damages, and the amount was deposited in bank for Beekman, who had notice of the fact. He applied for an injunction, which was refused. *Held*, that a railroad was a public use, if the legislature chose so to consider it, for which private property might be taken. That the government might exercise the right of eminent domair through a private corporation. That the charter must provide a fair mode of ascertaining the compensation, but it need not be a jury, since the constitutional guaranty of a right to a trial by jury relates only to a trial of issues of fact in civil and criminal cases in courts of justice. And see Willyard *v.* Hamilton, 7 Ohio, 2 part, 111. In Cooper *v.* Williams, 4 Ohio R. 253, the facts were these: The law authorizing the construction of the Ohio canal empowers the commissioners to take any land, water, or materials necessary; and if application be made within one year for compensation, they are to appoint three or five appraisers to assess damages, deducting benefits, which award the commissioners are to pay. Cooper owned land on Mad River, commanding a large water-power, part of which he was using. The canal commissioners constructed a dam above him, and a feeder, by which they took out three thousand cubic feet per minute, which greatly diminished the water-power Cooper might use on his land. This quantity was necessary to supply the canal. On its transit, two-thirds could be used as water-power, which the commissioners proposed to sell for the use of the State. Cooper applied for an injunction, which was refused. *Held*, that Cooper was entitled to compensation for any of his land taken, or for any loss of the use of water flowing by or through his land. But he had no such right in the water of Mad River, that the State might not take so much of it as the canal required, making compensation. And having taken it, the State might use it in its transit, or sell the use of it. The same was affirmed in Cooper *v.* Williams, 5 Ohio R. 391. In Bates *v.* Cooper, 5 Ohio R. 115, the direct question of the constitutionality of the canal laws as to taking private property was presented, and their constitutionality sustained. The intimation is, that it is sufficient, if the law provides some equitable mode of ascertaining compensation, without requiring it to be assessed and paid over before proceeding with the work. In McArthur *v.* Kelly, 5 Ohio R. 139, the whole subject of jury trials is very fully considered. The particular point decided is, that, as our constitution requires the compensation to be in money, the legislature cannot authorize the canal commissioners to compensate one man for the injury he will sustain in his water-power, by constructing a mill-race on the land of another man. In Young *v.* Buckingham, 5 Ohio, 485, the legislature authorized the erection of a toll-bridge over the Muskingum, providing that damages should be estimated by three commissioners appointed by the court of common pleas. Only two of the commissioners concurred in the award. *Held*, that a toll-bridge is a public use, for which private property may be taken; and that the award of the majority of the commissioners is sufficient. A State cannot, in the exercise of the right of eminent domain, authorize the taking of property for a private use. Nesbit *v.* Trumbo, 39 Ill. 110; Tide Water Co. *v.* Coster, 3 Green (N. J.), 518. The legislature is the sole judge as to whether the exigency for the property for a public use exists, but is not sole judge of what is a public use: on this last point the court will review their decision. Tyler *v.* Beacher, 44 Vt. 649; Talbot *v.* Hudson, 16 Gray, 417; Memphis Freight Co. *v.* Memphis, 4 Cold. 419. Ground cannot be taken under this form for a private road. Osborn *v.* Hart, 24 Wis. 89; Bankhead *v.* Brown, 25 Iowa, 540; Crear *v.* Crossley, 40 Ill. 175. A city may be authorized to take the entire fee of a district of low land for the public health, fill it up, and sell it out again. Dingley *v.* Boston, 100 Mass. 554.

Since this note was written, many changes have taken place besides those made by the constitution. In this State, the exclusive jurisdiction is committed to the probate or common pleas courts, with a jury of twelve. This constitutional provision for the payment for land taken for public purposes does not execute itself. A law authorizing the appropriation of land, which does not provide a mode of assessing the value, is inoperative. Lamb *v.* Lane, 4 Ohio State, 167; Watson *v.* Pleasant Tp., 21 Ohio State, 667. Notice may be given by publication to non-resident land-owners, if the law so provide, and in such case a failure to claim within a limited time may be declared a waiver of claim. Cupp *v.* Seneca Co., 19 Ohio State, 173; Reckner *v.* Warner, 22 Ohio State, 275; Anderson *v.* McKinney, 24 Ohio State, 467. Though in case of a failure to put in a claim within a proper time, caused by inevitable accident, a court of

The language of the federal constitution is, "Nor shall private property be taken for public use without *just compensation.*" The language of our first State constitution is, "Private property ought and shall ever be held inviolate, but always subservient to the public welfare, provided a *compensation in money* be made to the owner." The language of our new constitution is, "Private property shall ever be held inviolate, but subservient to the public welfare. When taken in time of war or other public exigency, imperatively requiring its immediate seizure, or for the purpose of making or repairing roads which shall be open to the public without charge, a compensation shall be made to the owner in money; and in all other cases when private property shall be taken for public use, a compensation therefor shall first be made in money, or first secured by a deposit of money; and such compensation shall be assessed by a jury without deduction for benefits to any property of the owner." (*a*) And again, "No right of way shall be appropriated to the use of any corporation until full compensation therefor be first made in money, or first secured by a deposit of money, to the owner, irrespective of any benefit proposed by such corporation, which compensation shall be ascertained by a jury of twelve men, in a court of record, as shall be prescribed by law."(*b*)

equity might relieve, yet it will not be sufficient that a man knowing of the day, and leaving home on business, is delayed on his return by an accident to the train, as this might have been guarded against. Reckner *v.* Warner, *supra.* It may be well to observe that the clause in the federal constitution does not apply to State legislation. Barron *v.* Baltimore, 7 Peters, 243. Nor will a court of chancery interfere. Walker *v.* Mad River R. Co., 8 Ohio, 38. Where a railroad has been once located, it cannot be changed without an express authority. Moorhead *v.* Little Miami R. Co., 17 Ohio, 340. Where a canal contractor enters for materials under the written authority of the engineer, this is a justification in trespass. Bliss *v.* Hosmer, 15 Ohio, 44; Lyon *v.* Jerome, 15 Wendell, 567; Wheelock *v.* Young, 4 Wendell, 647; Fulton *v.* Monahan, 4 Ohio, 426; McClintock *v.* Inskip, 13 Ohio, 21. Whether land can now be taken in fee, for railroads and the like, or only a right of way, see Bloodgood *v.* Mohawk R. Co., 14 Wendell, 51. Raleigh & Gaston R. R. Co. *v.* Davis, 2 Dev. & Bat. 467; Heyward *v.* Mayor of New York, 3 Selden, 314; Quimby *v.* Vt. Central R. R. Co., 23 Vt. 387; De Varaigne *v.* Fox, 2 Blatchf. C. C. 95. {The legislature could authorize the fee to be taken for canal purposes. Malone *v.* Toledo, 34 Ohio State, 541; but will not be deemed to have done so without express terms. McCombs *v.* Stewart, 40 id. 647.} The owner of lots upon a public street has a private right in such street, valuable as property, and when exercising reasonable care and prudence, he makes erections on the lot in accordance with the established grade, and a subsequent alteration of the grade is made, whereby he suffers substantial injury, he is entitled to compensation. Crawford *v.* Village of Delaware, 7 Ohio State, 459. But the prevailing rule is that damages are not recoverable for such consequential injuries, unless specially provided by statute. See Pierce on American Railroad Law, pp. 173. 222, and cases cited. As to the extent of the right to appropriate beyond the track for depots, shops, and the like, see Kyle *v.* Auburn R. Co., 2 Barbour, Ch. R. 489; Kemper *v.* Cincinnati, &c. Turnpike, 11 Ohio, 392. Giesy *v.* Cincinnati, W. & Z. R. R. Co., 4 Ohio State, 308. New Orleans Second Municipality, 1 La. An. Rep. 128; Lauderbrun *v.* Duffy, 2 Barr. 398; Navigation Co. *v.* Commissioners, 11 Penn. State, 202; Hankins *v.* Lawrence, 8 Blackford, 266. For the rule of damages, see 13 Law Jour. Rep. 434; Sedgwick on Damages, ch. xxiii. The subject of taking private property for public uses, is considered in Pierce on American Railroad Law, ch. viii. and Mills on Eminent Domain.

(*a*) A jury of twelve men is intended by this clause, but the assessment may be made in the first instance by a commission, reserving an appeal to a jury. Lamb *v.* Lane, 4 Ohio State, 167.

(*b*) Giesy *v.* C. W. & Z. R. R. Co., 4 Ohio State, 308; In matter of Wells County

These declarations assert two great principles. First, the private right of an individual must yield to the *eminent domain* of government, whenever the public good requires it. And this is well; for otherwise it would be in the power of one obstinate owner to prevent the execution of any of those great public improvements which contribute so much to the general convenience and happiness. Secondly, to equalize the burden, and avoid all hardship, the owner of property so taken is to receive a compensation, which shall be full, just, and in money. Any law, therefore, which should condemn private property for any other than a public use, or which should not provide for such a compensation, would be unconstitutional. One question formerly much discussed was, whether the compensation must be paid before the property is taken. The answer was, that if a law authorizing property to be taken, provides an equitable mode of ascertaining the compensation, and directs it to be paid, the law is valid; but in any given case, if the owner of property could make it appear that his compensation would be doubtful or improbable, he might obtain an injunction against taking the property until the compensation had been secured. (*a*) Another question was, whether benefits were to be taken into view in fixing the amount of compensation. Upon this question there was much contrariety of opinion. There is an obvious distinction to be made between paying for property actually taken, and paying for consequential injury where property is not taken. To the latter case, the constitutional provisions do not apply. It is a mere question of damages; and as there can be no actual damages where the benefit exceeds the injury, there is no doubt that benefits may be properly offset against consequential injuries. (*b*) But can benefits be offset against the value of the property actually taken? In this State, where the compensation must be "*in money*," the answer must undoubtedly be in the negative; for the benefits derived from the vicinity of a public improvement, however great, are not literally money. But how is it where the compensation is only required to be "*just*," or "*full*," without specifying money? Can benefits, then, be offset against property? It would seem they cannot; for while many share in the benefits of any great public work, besides those whose property is taken for its construction, this rule would make the burden fall wholly on the latter class, which would be *unjust*. It may be said, however, that when a man is not made absolutely poorer by taking part of his property, no

Road, 7 Ohio State, 16, 21. {That the right to take private property for public use is an incident of sovereignty, and does not require constitutional recognition, see United States *v.* Jones, 109 U. S. 513.}

(*a*) Pierce on American Railroad Law, pp. 163, 509, and cases cited; Cushman *v.* Smith, 34 Maine, 247; Bloodgood *v.* Mohawk & Hudson R. R. Co., 14 Wendell, 51.

(*b*) The benefits deducted are generally confined to such as are peculiar to the land-owner, and not shared by other members of the community. Meacham *v.* Fitchburg R. R. Co., 4 Cush. 291; Nicholson *v.* N. Y. & N. H. R. R. Co., 22 Conn. 88; Robbins *v.* Mil. & Horicon R. R. Co., 6 Wis. 636. But *contra*, Alton & Sangamon R. R. Co. *v.* Carpenter, 14 Ill. 190. See Little Miami R. R. Co. *v.* Collett, 6 Ohio State, 182; Cleveland & Pittsburg R. R. Co. *v.* Ball, 5 id. 568.

injury is done him. But the answer is, that relatively he is made poorer, by so much as the property is worth, because his neighbors, whose property is not taken, share equally in the benefits. On the whole, then, the rule would seem to be, that property actually taken for public uses must be paid for, without reference to benefits, which can only be offset against consequential damages. Still another question was, whether the amount of compensation must be determined by a jury of twelve persons. It has been decided that any fair and equitable mode will be sufficient, as by disinterested appraisers or commissioners. (*a*) But in this State, these questions are all put to rest by the provisions of the new constitution, before quoted. As to what are public uses, it has been held that canals, turnpikes, railroads, toll-bridges, supplies of water for a town, and the like, are public uses; and that the legislature may exercise its right of appropriating private property for such uses through private corporations. (*b*)

Property in expectation — Contracts. (*c*) Property in expecta-

(*a*) Willyard *v.* Hamilton, 7 Ohio, 2 pt. 111; Hickox *v.* Cleveland, 8 id. 543; Beekman *v.* Saratoga & Schenectady R. R. Co., 3 Paige, 75; Lake Erie R. R. Co. *v.* Heath, 9 Ind. 558. Where a special remedy is provided for assessing damages, it is exclusive. Houston *v.* Eaton & Hamilton R. R. Co., 4 Ohio State, 685; Kramer *v.* Cleveland & Pittsburg R. Co., 5 id. 140. Pierce on American Railroad Law, pp. 168, 223.

(*b*) Giesy *v.* C., W. & Z. R. R. Co., 4 Ohio State, 308. {A right of way acquired by appropriation is held subject to the right of the State to regulate for public benefit. It is therefore held subject to a further appropriation, not subversive of the former use; hence another railway may condemn a right to cross the former. The right of the second railway is not merely acquired from the first, but is held under the State for public benefit; hence the State, in the exercise of its police powers, may require the stoppage of trains at crossings, the maintaining of watchmen, &c., for public protection. And these expenses and inconveniences do not grow out of the construction of the cross-track, but out of the future use of the franchise, and hence are not part of the damages to be assessed. Railway *v.* Railway, 30 Ohio State, 604; Mass. Centr. R. R. *v.* B., C. & T. R. R., 121 Mass. 124.}

(*c*) See Mad. Pap. 1443-4, 1581; 1 Kent, Com. 413; 2 Story, Const. ch. xxxiv.; 9 Dane, Abr. App. 77; Fletcher *v.* Peck, 6 Cranch, 87; New Jersey *v.* Wilson, 7 Cranch, 164; Terrett *v.* Taylor, 9 Cranch, 43; Dartmouth College *v.* Woodward, 4 Wheaton, 518; Sturges *v.* Crowninshield, 4 Wheaton, 122; M'Millan *v.* M'Neill, 4 Wheaton, 209; Green *v.* Biddle, 8 Wheaton, 1; Ogden *v.* Saunders, 12 Wheaton, 213; Blanchard *v.* Russell, 13 Mass. 1; Mather *v.* Bush, 16 Johns. 233; Smith *v.* Parsons, 1 Ohio, 236; Charles River Bridge *v.* Warren Bridge, 11 Peters, 421; Bronson *v.* Kinzie, 1 How. 311. In Fletcher *v.* Peck, 6 Cranch, 87, the facts were these: In 1795, Georgia passed an act authorizing the sale of a large tract of wild land; in pursuance of which, a grant was regularly made by patent, to the Georgia Company. Fletcher held a deed from Peck for a part of this land under a title derived from the patent, in which deed Peck had covenanted that the title conveyed by the patent was good and valid when the patent was made, and had not since been impaired. The fact was, that, in 1796, Georgia had passed another act, declaring the preceding act and all conveyances under it to be null and void. The pretence was, that the first act was collusively procured by bribing members of the legislature. Fletcher, therefore, brought an action of covenant against Peck, and assigned as a breach, that the patent was void by the effect of the act of 1796. This brought up the question, whether the legislature of Georgia could constitutionally repeal the act of 1795, and make void the proceedings under it. Chief-Justice Marshall pronounced the decision of the court. He said they could not go into an inquiry respecting the corruption of the sovereign power of the State; nor was it necessary. For admitting the original transaction to have been infected with fraud the parties to this suit did not participate in it, and had no notice of it. Yet if the act of 1795 be in fact repealed, their tion, as we have seen, consists chiefly of *contracts.* Without here stating the requisites of a valid contract, it is sufficient to say that

rights, innocently acquired under it, are annihilated. Had Georgia power, then, to repeal this act? She had not. The act was a grant to which Georgia was a party. A grant is a contract executed. In its own nature, it is an extinguishment of the right of the grantor, and implies a contract not to reassert that right. Such a contract Georgia had made, and rights had become vested under it. Could the legislature afterwards pass a law impairing its obligation? Certainly not; for a contract by a State is as much protected by the constitution, as a contract by an individual. The principle therefore established by this case may be thus stated: a grant is a contract, the obligation of which cannot be impaired; and it makes no difference whether the State or an individual was a party to the grant. In New Jersey *v.* Wilson, 7 Cranch, 164, the facts were these: In 1758, New Jersey passed a law declaring that certain lands to be purchased for the use of the Indians should not thereafter be subject to any tax. The Indians occupied these lands until 1803, when they were sold to individuals by authority of the legislature; but nothing was said, in the authority to sell, respecting the former exemption from taxation. In 1804, a law was passed repealing the law of 1758, which exempted the lands from taxes, and they were accordingly assessed. This brought in question the validity of the law of 1804. It had already been decided in Fletcher *v.* Peck, that the prohibition in the constitution extended to contracts to which a State was a party, as well as to contracts between individuals. In this case, therefore, the inquiry was narrowed down to the question, whether the foregoing facts amounted to a contract, which was violated by the act of 1804? The court decided that the transaction between New Jersey and the Indians had every requisite of a contract. The exemption from taxation made the lands more valuable, and they were sold by the Indians with this privilege annexed. The State, in authorizing the sale by the Indians might have stipulated for a surrender of this privilege, but did not. The purchasers therefore took the land with the privilege annexed, and the State could not afterwards take it away without impairing the obligation of their contract with the Indians. This case, then, may be considered as merely a reiteration of the doctrine of Fletcher *v.* Peck. In Terrett *v.* Taylor, 9 Cranch, 43, the facts were these: At a very early period, the *Episcopal Church,* and the common law relating thereto, were recognized in Virginia; and from 1661 to 1788, a variety of laws were passed enabling the church by its proper officers to hold lands and other property. In 1770, the Episcopal Church of Alexandria purchased, in due form of law, the land which was now the subject of dispute. Their right so to do was never doubted until 1793, when a law was passed repealing all preceding laws on the subject of the church. In 1801, another law was passed, asserting the right of the State to all the property of the Episcopal churches, and directing it to be taken for the support of the poor. The pretext was, that all the laws protective of the church were inconsistent with the principles of the constitution relating to religious liberty. On these facts, the question was referred to the supreme court, whether the laws of 1798 and 1801 were constitutional. The court decided that they were not. Be the authority of the legislature on the subject of religion what it might, they had authorized the church to purchase these lands. The revolution, though its effect was to deprive the Episcopal Church of its character as an exclusive religious establishment, could not divest them of the property which was before vested in them; for even the division of an empire creates no forfeiture of previously vested rights of property. Nor did the fact of being a corporation make any difference. The legislature may indeed change and modify *public corporations,* such as counties and towns, which exist only for public purposes; though even then the rights of property must be secured to those for whose use and at whose expense it was purchased. A legislature may, however, contract with a municipal corporation, although it is its creature; and such a contract, when made, is protected by the constitution as much as any other. Grogan *v.* San Francisco, 18 Cal. 490. And the legislature cannot take away the private property of a municipal corporation which it has legally acquired. Thus it cannot declare by act that claims for damages made against a city are valid, and order the amount to be assessed by arbitrators. Baldwin *v.* New York, 42 Barb. 549. But the legislature cannot repeal statutes creating *private corporations,* or confirming to them property acquired under the faith of previous laws; and by such repeal vest the property in the State, or dispose of it without the consent of the corporators. Against such legislation, private corporations are as much protected as individuals, by the spirit and letter of the constitution. This is a sketch of the reasoning of Judge Story, who delivered the opinion of the court. In Dartmouth College *v.* Woodward, 4 it differs from a mere promise made without consideration, chiefly in this: that there is only a *moral obligation* to perform a promise,

Wheaton, 518, the facts were these: In 1769, the British crown granted a charter to the *Trustees of Dartmouth College.* Under this charter a large amount of property was acquired, and the affairs of the College were prosperously administered until 1816, when the legislature of New Hampshire passed a law, enlarging the number of trustees, varying the mode of appointment, placing over them a board of overseers, and making other important alterations in the charter. The old trustees met and resolved not to accept the provisions of this act. The new corporation, under the name of *Trustees of Dartmouth University*, commenced operation, by taking possession of all that belonged to the college. The old trustees contested their right in an action of trover against the treasurer, to recover the books, papers, and title-deeds, which had been taken from them. The question raised upon these facts was, whether the law of 1816 came within the prohibition of the constitution against impairing the obligation of contracts. And a more important question was never brought before a court. The safety of all chartered rights was staked upon the decision. The State court decided in favor of the law. But the federal court declared the law unconstitutional. They said if this had been a public corporation, with political privileges, or if the funds had been public property, the State might have legislated as it pleased. But this corporation was a private one in its foundation, and endowed with private funds, though for public and benevolent purposes. These funds had been contributed, and trustees had taken charge of them, upon faith in the permanency of the charter. The crown, by granting the charter, had contracted with the donors and trustees that, so long as the provisions of the charter were complied with, it should not be withdrawn or impaired. At the revolution, New Hampshire had become a party to this contract in place of the crown. And though Parliament, in its omnipotence, might have violated this charter, the legislature of New Hampshire cannot, in consequence of the constitutional limitation of its powers. In fine, the charter is a contract, the obligations of which would be impaired by enforcing the law of 1816. The law, therefore, is void. In Greene *v.* Biddle, 8 Wheaton, 1, the facts were these: In the compact between Virginia and Kentucky, in 1789, prior to the admission of the latter into the Union, it was stipulated that all private rights and interests in lands, derived from the laws of Virginia before the separation, should remain valid and secure after the separation, and should be determined by the then existing laws of Virginia. This compact was made a part of the constitution of Kentucky, and thus became a compact between two sovereign States, with the assent of Congress. By the law of Virginia, as it then stood, the claimant of lands, who succeeds in his suit, was entitled to receive *mesne profits* from the occupants. But in 1797 and 1812, Kentucky had enacted laws concerning *occupying claimants*, which, however intrinsically just and equitable, materially affected the interest of the non-occupying claimants, as they would have been under the laws of Virginia; for the object of those laws was, to compel the rightful owner either to relinquish the lands to the occupant, or pay for all improvements made upon them, without his consent or default; and no possession could be obtained without complying with these requisitions. In the present case, Greene's title accrued prior to the separation, and he claimed to have his rights decided pursuant to the compact. This brought in question the validity of the laws of Kentucky, and the supreme court decided that they were unconstitutional. They said that the constitution as much embraced compacts between sovereign States, as contracts between individuals. A compact did not differ from a contract. It was an agreement to do, or not to do, some particular thing. In this compact, Kentucky had agreed that the rights of claimants to lands should be determined by the laws of Virginia; and having so agreed, could pass no laws to impair that agreement. But the laws now in question did impair the obligation of that agreement; to what extent was not material. Any deviation from the terms of a contract, by postponing or accelerating the period of performance, imposing terms not expressed in the contract, or dispensing with those which are, however minute or apparently immaterial in their effect upon the contract of the parties, impairs its obligation.

The case of Dartmouth College *v.* Woodward, affirming the inviolability of the charters of private eleemosynary corporations, has been repeatedly affirmed by the federal and State tribunals. Society, &c. *v.* New Haven, 8 Wheaton, 461; Trustees of Vincennes University *v.* Indiana, 14 How. 268; Norris *v.* Trustees of Abingdon Academy, 7 Gill & Johns. 7; Grammar School *v.* Burt, 11 Vermont, 632; Brown *v.* Hummell, 6 Barr, 86; State *v.* Heywood, 3 Rich. 389. The supreme court of Ohio, in a recent elaborate decision, which has been overruled by the supreme court of the while there is a *legal obligation* to perform a contract. And it is this legal obligation which gives such value to a contract, as to

United States, has attempted the limitation of the doctrine of this case, as it has usually been understood. Toledo Bank *v.* Bond, 1 Ohio State R. 622, 670. The charters of private civil corporations, as those of banks, turnpike and railroad companies, are equally protected by the United States constitution. Planters' Bank *v.* Sharp, 6 How. 301; People *v.* Manhattan Co., 9 Wendell, 351; Boston & Lowell R. R. Corp. *v.* Salem & Lowell R. R. Corp., 2 Gray, 1.

Grants of franchises to a corporation in which the public have an interest — as the right to open roads and lay bridges — are to be construed strictly, and nothing passes beyond what the natural force of the words used requires. Thus, in a celebrated case, it was held that where the charter, authorizing a corporation to build a bridge over a river, granted no exclusive rights above and below the bridge, no such exclusive right passed, and another corporation might be authorized to build a bridge so near as to reduce the tolls of the first bridge to a very small value. Charles River Bridge *v.* Warren Bridge, 11 Peters, 420. This case has been often affirmed. West River Bridge *v.* Dix, 6 How. 507; Richmond R. R. Co. *v.* Louisiana R. R. Co., 13 id. 81; Mohawk Bridge *v.* Utica & Schenectady R. R. Co., 6 Paige, 547; White River Turnpike Co. *v.* Vt. Central R. R. Co., 21 Vt. 591; Tuckahoe Canal Co. *v.* Tuckahoe R. R. Co., 11 Leigh, 42; Pierce on American Railroad Law, chap. iii. The franchise of a corporation, even where it is exclusive, may be taken for public uses, where compensation is made. West River Bridge Co. *v.* Dix, 6 How. 507; s. c. 16 Vt. 446; White River Turnpike Co. *v.* Vt. Central R. R. Co., 21 id. 591; Enfield Toll Bridge Co. *v.* Hartford & N. H. R. R. Co., 17 Conn. 40, 454; Boston Water Power Co. *v.* Boston & W. R. R. Co., 23 Pick. 360; Richmond, &c. R. R. Co. *v.* Louisa. R. R. Co., 13 How. 71; Boston & Lowell R. R. Corp. *v.* Salem & Lowell R. R. Co., 2 Gray, 1, 35; Crosby *v.* Hanover, 36 N. H. 404. The doctrine that the legislature of a State may, for a valuable consideration, grant to an individual or a corporation exemption from taxation of the property thereof, so that the imposition of the tax by a subsequent legislature would be in conflict with this clause of the United States constitution, has been severely contested in Ohio. Debolt *v.* Ohio Life Ins. and Trust Co., 1 Ohio State R. 563; Mechanics & Traders' Bank *v.* Debolt, id. 591; Knoup *v.* Piqua Bank, id. 603; Toledo Bank *v.* Bond, id. 622. It has also been questioned in its full extent in New Hampshire. Piscataqua Bridge *v.* N. H. Bridge, 7 N. H. 69; Brewster *v.* Hough, 10 id. 138; Backus *v.* Lebanon, 11 id. 24, and denied in Pennsylvania. Mott *v.* Penn. R. R. Co., 30 Penn. State, 9. But the repeated decisions of the supreme court of the United States have now established it beyond all controversy. New Jersey *v.* Wilson, 7 Cranch, 164; Gordon *v.* Appeal Tax Court, 3 How. 133; Piqua Bank *v.* Knoop, 16 id. 369; Dodge *v.* Woolsey, 18 id. 231; Jefferson Branch *v.* Skelly, 1 Black, 436; Franklin Branch Bank *v.* State of Ohio, id. 474. But where the payment of a certain per cent on the dividends of a corporation, prescribed in its charter, appears to be intended only as a temporary rule of taxation, this provision of the constitution does not interfere with the imposition of a higher rate. Eastern Bank *v.* Commonwealth, 10 Barr (Penn.), 442; Debolt *v.* Ohio Life Insurance and Trust Co., 1 Ohio State, 563; s. c. 16 How. 416. But unless there is a valuable consideration given for this exemption from taxation, it may be repealed, as one of the essential elements of a contract is wanting. Christ Church *v.* Philadelphia, 24 How. 300; Rouse *v.* Washington University, 7 Am. Law Reg. (N. S.) 390. See also a report to the Rhode Island Senate, by Hon. E. R. Potter, 1 Am. Law Reg. (N. S.) 718. A law allowing all persons manufacturing salt in Michigan to hold the property exempt from taxation, and receive a certain bounty per bushel on all salt manufactured, does not constitute a contract between persons erecting salt-works under it and the State, but is a mere bounty, and may be repealed at will. General encouragements held out to all persons indiscriminately to engage in a trade or manufacture in whatever shape, are always under legislative control. Salt Co. *v.* East Saginaw, 13 Wall. 373. {A State cannot contract away its right to legislate concerning the public health and morals. Butchers Union Co. *v.* Crescent City Co., 111 U. S. 746.}

Laws affecting the remedy only do not impair the obligation of a contract. Mechanics', &c. Bank Appeal, 31 Conn. 63; Cummings *v.* Maxwell, 45 Maine, 190; Rich *v.* Flanders, 39 N. H. 304; New Orleans *v.* Pontz, 14 La. An. 853; Hayward *v.* Judd, 4 Minn. 483. {But if a statute of evidence affects more than the remedy and destroys vested rights, it is void. Green *v.* Barry, 15 Wall. 622. The legislature can give a creditor or claimant a better remedy than he had before, or an additional one. Peters *v.* McWilliams, 36 Ohio State, 155. A statute may even deprive a debtor of the benefit entitle it to be considered as property. But this value would be greatly diminished, if it were left in the power of legislation to impair the obligation upon which it depends; and hence the importance of a constitutional guaranty against impairing the obligation of contracts. The ordinance of 1787 contained this declaration: "And in the just preservation of rights and property, it is understood and declared, that no law ought ever to be made, or have force in the said territory, that shall, in any manner whatever, interfere with, or affect, private contracts or engagements, *bonâ fide* and without fraud, previously formed." This was the first time that such a provision ever formed part of a declaration of rights. But so universal is the conviction of its vast importance, that it has been inserted in every American constitution since formed. In the federal constitution, the declaration is, that "no State shall pass any law impairing the obligation of contracts;" in our State constitution, that "the general assembly shall have no power to pass retroactive laws, or laws impairing the obligation of contracts; but may, by general laws, authorize courts to carry into effect, upon such terms as shall be just and equitable, the manifest intention of parties, and officers, by curing omissions, defects, and errors in instruments and proceedings, arising out of their want of conformity with the laws of this State." So far, then, as respects State legislation, we are doubly protected. Why Congress was not placed under a like prohibition, I do not understand. It will be observed, that the ordinance expressly limits the prohibition to *prior contracts;* and this is the construction put upon the language of the constitution. Indeed, if the law be made before the contract, it forms a part of its obligation, and cannot be said to impair it. The design was to protect existing contracts from *retroactive legislation;* and the effect is, that when a valid contract is once made, no future State legislation can impair its validity. The provision has been frequently the subject of judicial construction, and the following

of the statute of limitations on a debt already barred, although such a statute could not be passed as to property; for the title vests in a party after a certain time, and this would disturb vested rights. Campbell *v.* Holt, 115 U. S. 620.} A statute does not necessarily impair the obligation of a contract because it may enhance the difficulty of performance to one party, or diminishes the value of performance to the other, provided it leaves the obligation of performance in full force. So a statute passed after a sale for taxes requiring the holder of tax certificates to give notice to the occupant of the land, if there is one, before he takes his deed, is not invalid. Curtis *v.* Whitney, 12 Wall. 68. The action of forcible entry and detainer does not enter into a contract for a lease so that a repeal of it, or permission to make a new defence, impairs the obligation of the contract. Dunham *v.* Stifle, 8 Wall. 595. An increase in the amount exempted from execution does not impair the obligation of the contract. Hardeman *v.* Downer, 39 Ga. 425; Hill *v.* Kessler, 63 N. C. 437; Stephenson *v.* Osborne, 41 Miss. 119. But it does when a judgment lien has been obtained on land, securing the debt under the law existing at the time it was obtained, but which security the new law would destroy. Gunn *v.* Barry, 15 Wall. 610. Stay laws, preventing the collection of debts, are unconstitutional. Jacobs *v.* Smallwood, 63 N. C. 112; Hudspeth *v.* Davis, 41 Ala. 389.

Even though the contract expressly stipulates for a remedy, an act abolishing that remedy will deprive the party of it, without being unconstitutional on that account. Conkey *v.* Hart, 14 N. Y. 22.

See farther as to the rule in Dartmouth College *v.* Woodward, in note, p. 231.

points have been decided: 1. A grant of land, which is an executed contract, is within the prohibition, and it makes no difference whether a State or an individual made the grant. 2. A charter creating a private corporation is a contract within the prohibition; and so is a compact between two States; but a charter creating a public corporation is not. 3. The extent to which the contract is affected is of no consequence, for if any of its terms be varied, its obligation is impaired. 4. The prohibition supposes the *parties* to the contract to belong to the State which passes the law affecting it, otherwise the law cannot be said to impair it. 5. With these qualifications, it may be stated generally, that statutes of usury which affect the validity of contracts; statutes of fraud, which affect the evidence of contracts; and statutes of limitation and bankruptcy, which affect the remedy of contracts, — are all within the meaning of the prohibition. (*a*)

§ 82. **Right of Petition and Instruction.** (*b*) The right of *suffrage*, through which the people indicate their wishes in the choice of *men* to make their laws, has already been considered. But when the proper men have been selected, their constituents may desire from time to time to make known their wishes as to *measures*. Accordingly, the first amendment of the federal constitution declares that "Congress shall make no law abridging the right of the people peaceably to assemble, and to petition the government for a redress of grievances." Our State constitution goes still further. It declares that "the people have a right to assemble together in a peaceable manner, to consult for their common good; to instruct their representatives; and to petition the general assembly for the redress of grievances." The reason for thus solemnly asserting principles so self-evident probably was, that in England, where the government is less democratic, several restrictions were laid upon the exercise of these rights. The provision contains three points for consideration. 1. The right of *assembling* for consultation. The only qualification is, that the assembling be *peaceable*, and not riotous. 2. The right of *petitioning* for the redress of grievances. Correlative to this right of the people to petition, is the obligation of the legislature to receive and consider their petitions. If, however, a petition be disrespectful in its language, or demand something manifestly frivolous or wrong, a legislature

(*a*) See 2 Parsons on Contracts, ch. xi. Police regulations, incidentally affecting contracts and the rights acquired under them, are not within the constitutional inhibition which forbids the States passing laws impairing the obligation of contracts or that which gives to Congress the exclusive power to regulate commerce. Thorpe *v.* Rutland & Burlington R. R. Co., 1 Williams (Vt.), 140; B. C. & M. R. R. Co. *v.* The State, 32 N. H. 215; Galena & Chicago Union R. R. Co. *v.* Loomis, 13 Ill. 548; Hirn *v.* State, 1 Ohio State, 15; Calder *v.* Kurby, 5 Gray, 596; State *v.* Holmes, 38 N. H. 225; Cooley *v.* Board of Wardens of Philadelphia, 12 How. 299. Laws made prior to the formation of a contract do not impair its obligation. Davis *v.* Bronson, 6 Clarke (Iowa), 410; Railroad Co. *v.* McClure, 10 Wall. 511. {The right of testamentary disposition has never been deemed a vested and inalienable right, but is a product of statutory law which may be abridged; hence our statute of mortmain. See Patton *v.* Patton, 39 Ohio State, 590, 597.}

(*b*) 1 Black. Com. 143; 2 Story, Const. § 1893.

does not hesitate to reject it as soon as presented. 3. The right of *instructing* representatives. There was no occasion to assert this in the federal constitution, and it is therefore omitted. Was it necessary to assert it in the State constitution? Would the omission of it have released the representative from his corresponding obligation to obey instructions? In some of the States these are important questions. And it is argued with some plausibility, that the omission by the people to reserve the right in their constitution operates as a relinquishment of it. The people, it is said, by their constitution, have given their representatives a set of general and permanent instructions. They might unquestionably, at the same time, have stipulated for the right of giving future instructions for particular emergencies; but not having done so, they have agreed that their representatives shall be bound only by the instructions in the constitution. And this reasoning derives countenance from the fact, that several of the constitutions, like that of Ohio, take care to reserve to the people the right of instruction. On the other hand, it is contended that the right of instruction flows so directly from the relation of constituent and representative, that it requires no assertion. But as the question cannot arise here, I shall not attempt to settle it. The people of Ohio have reserved the right to instruct their representatives, and of course the representatives are bound to obey. But whether it is expedient frequently to exercise the right, and thus far convert the representative into an *automaton*, may well admit of serious doubt. If we take into view the abundant safeguards against the abuse of discretion by the representatives; the evils of party excitement; the difficulty of ascertaining the aggregate will of the constituents, in any authentic shape; and the superior advantage which the representative has to inform his judgment from being on the spot, we shall probably arrive at the conclusion, that the right of instruction should only be exercised in extreme cases. This question has lately assumed a new aspect. State legislatures have undertaken to instruct federal senators, because they elect them. Have they this right? They are not the people, and do not therefore come within the letter of the declaration. Nor is this right derived by implication from their legislative functions, for it has nothing to do with legislation. It would seem, therefore, that their instructions are not obligatory upon federal senators. The people of the States may instruct them, but not the State legislatures.

§ 83. **Security against Retroactive Laws.** (*a*) There can be but

(*a*) See Mad. Pap. 1400, 1444, 1450; Gilmore *v.* Shuter, 2 Levinz, 227; Couch *v.* Jefferies, 4 Burrow, 2460; Call *v.* Hagger, 8 Mass. Rep. 423; Dash *v.* Van Kleeck, 7 Johnson, 477; Calder *v.* Buell, 3 Dallas, 386; Fletcher *v.* Peck, 6 Cranch, 87; M'Cormick *v.* Alexander, 2 Ohio Rep. 65; Barton *v.* Morris, 15 id. 408; Butler *v.* City of Toledo, 5 Ohio State, 225; Ogden *v.* Blackledge, 2 Cranch, 272; Society, &c. *v.* Wheeler, 2 Gallison, 105; Satterlee *v.* Matthewson, 2 Peters, 380. {Judge Story's definition of a retroactive law in Society for Propagating the Gospel *v.* Wheeler, 2 Gall. 105, 139, is "Every statute which takes away or impairs vested rights acquired under existing laws, or creates a new obligation, imposes a new duty, or attaches a new disability in respect to transactions or considerations already past must be deemed one opinion as to the injustice of retroactive laws. It is a necessary maxim, that ignorance of the law forms no excuse for violat-

retroactive." This definition has been adopted by the supreme court of Ohio, Rairden *v.* Holden, 15 Ohio State, 207, and of the United States, Sturges *v.* Carter, 114 U. S. 511.} In Gilmore *v.* Shuter, 2 Lev. 227, the question was, whether the statute of frauds should be construed to act upon patrol contracts entered into before its passage. And even then, in the reign of Charles the Second, the judges held that to give the statute such a construction would make it repugnant to common justice. In Couch *v.* Jefferies, 4 Burr. 2460, Lord Mansfield held the same doctrine. He said it could never be the true construction of the act then in question to include prior cases. In Call *v.* Hagger, 8 Mass. 423, where a statute of limitations did not expressly extend to prior transactions, the court refused to give it that extent by construction. In Calder *v.* Bull, 3 Dallas, 386, the facts were briefly these: The probate court of Hartford, upon hearing, had set aside a will, the effect of which decree was to let in the heirs. By the law of Connecticut, as it then stood, no appeal could be had from this decree after eighteen months. But when this limitation had run out, the legislature passed a law setting aside the former decree, and authorizing a rehearing by the same court of probate, and an appeal therefrom; the result of which was that the will was finally established. The heirs, who by this means were deprived of their inheritance, brought the question before the supreme court, on the ground that the law in question was an *ex post facto law.* The court decided that it was not an *ex post facto law*, in the meaning of the constitution, and this is the only point actually decided, because it was the only question before the court. But occasion was taken to give a construction to this clause of the constitution which has ever since been acquiesced in. They said the prohibition related only to laws for the punishment of crimes; and its meaning was this: "That the legislatures of the several States shall not pass laws, after a fact done by a subject or citizen, which shall have relation to such fact, and shall punish him for having done it." And they considered that the following would be *ex post facto laws* within the words and intent of the prohibition: 1. Every law that makes an action done before the passing of the law, and which was *innocent* when done, criminal. 2. Every law that aggravates a crime, or the punishment thereof, after the crime is committed. 3. Every law that alters the legal rules of evidence, and receives less, or other testimony, than was required at the time of the commission of the offence, in order to conviction. These three classes may be reduced to one; namely, all laws which make an act punishable in a manner in which it was not punishable when committed. But the court did not consider any law *ex post facto* within the prohibition which *mollified the rigor* of the criminal law. They said there was a difference between making an unlawful act lawful, and making an innocent act criminal. But the character of the punishment cannot be changed even though the new punishment is of a less severe kind. The law can only stand when the new punishment is one of the same kind as that formerly imposed, but less in degree. Shepherd *v.* The People, 25 N. Y. 406. I have been thus particular in giving an account of this case, because it has often been cited as an authority on the subject of retroactive laws in general, as well as of legislation for individual cases. In M'Cormick *v.* Alexander, 2 Ohio, 65, the facts were these: Evans had obtained a judgment and taken out execution within the time required by the law as it then stood, in order to secure his *lien*, in preference to that of one M'Cormick, who had obtained a subsequent judgment. Had the law, therefore, remained unaltered, the right of Evans to the property levied upon would have been *completely* vested, as against M'Cormick. But in the mean time, a law was passed, providing, "that no judgment *heretofore* rendered, or which *hereafter* may be rendered, on which execution shall not have been taken out and levied before the expiration of one year, next after the rendition of such judgment, shall operate as a lien upon the estate of any debtor, to the prejudice of any other *bonâ fide* judgment creditor." The effect of this law was to set the right of Evans aside, and prefer that of M'Cormick, for the execution of Evans had not been levied within a year from the judgment, and that of M'Cormick had. It was no question of construction, for the statute was expressly made retroactive, including prior as well as subsequent judgments. And the court upheld the law as constitutional, although very unjust and unequal in its operation, and interfering with vested rights. They said, the right vested in Evans was not one acquired by contract or agreement; if it had been, the legislature could not have deprived him of it, because the constitution protected him. But the lien of a judgment was given him purely by legislative enactment, and the same power which gave, had taken away. In so doing, they had not exceeded the authority given them under the constitution. Arguments drawn from the ing it; because, otherwise, every transgressor would set up the plea of ignorance. When laws are prospective in their provisions, and are promulgated before they take effect, there is no hardship in this maxim; for it is at least possible to know them. But when they are made to act backwards upon that which transpired before their existence, this maxim becomes inhuman, since it holds men responsible for knowing what they could not possibly have known. Again, retroactive laws are as absurd as they are unjust. The design of a law is to *regulate* conduct; that is, to fix a rule for it; and the idea of regulating past conduct involves an absurdity in terms. You may attach a new consequence to a past transaction, but this is not regulating it; for that which is past is beyond regulation. It cannot be altered, recalled, or avoided; and, therefore, ought not to be legislated upon. Give a legislature power to pass retroactive laws, and no one can be safe; since his whole past life is liable to be animadverted upon. For such rea-

injustice of the act must be addressed to the legislature and not to the court. In Society, &c. *v.* Wheeler, 2 Gallison, 105, Judge Story is often quoted as deciding against retroactive laws in general. But the truth is, he was then construing the constitution of New Hampshire, which contains an express prohibition of *retrospective* laws generally, in these words: "Retrospective laws are highly injurious, oppressive and unjust. No such laws therefore should be made, either for the decision of civil causes, or the punishment of offences." All therefore that Judge Story decided was, "that every statute, which takes away, or impairs vested rights acquired under existing laws, or creates a new obligation, imposes a new duty, or attaches a new disability in respect to transactions or considerations already passed, must be deemed retrospective *within this prohibition.*" It has been seen that retroactive laws are now prohibited in Ohio. In Ogden *v.* Blackledge, 2 Cranch, 272, the only real difficulty occurs. There was a law of 1715, in North Carolina, limiting the time of producing claims against deceased persons to seven years. This law was repealed in 1789, and a suit was in consequence commenced by a creditor, after the former limitation had expired; he now having a legal right to sue. But a law was afterwards passed, declaring that the law of 1789 did not repeal this part of the law of 1715. The effect of this law, supposing it constitutional, was to restore the limitation, and so defeat the suit in question. But the supreme court sustained the suit, and thus virtually set aside the last law. No reasons are given in the meagre report to show the want of power to pass such a law, and we are left entirely in doubt as to how far the decision intended to go, or what were its grounds. Under these circumstances, I think very little importance is to be ascribed to the case. And so said Judge Spencer, in his opinion in the case of Dash *v.* Van Kleeck, 7 Johns. 477. He did not feel bound by a decision, not only at variance with the opinion expressed by the same court in the anterior case of Calder *v.* Bull, "but so utterly destitute of reasoning or authority to support it." On the whole, then, I leave this subject with the remark, that, however revolting to our sentiments of justice retroactive laws may be, it seems clear from the foregoing authorities, that, apart from the express prohibitions of the constitution as already explained, our only safeguard against them is to be found in the good sense and right feelings of our legislators. See 21 Law Reporter, Dec. 1858, 449, on the power of the legislature over private property. As to legislation on remedies existing when a contract was made, see cases cited *ante*, p. 152 and 217, notes. See Sedgwick on Statutory and Constitutional Law, pp. 198, 406, 479, 484, 680, 696. In McMillan *v.* County Judge, 6 Clarke (Iowa), 391, it is held that where the legislature possesses the power to authorize an act to be done, it may by a retrospective act legalize any informality in the exercise of the authority so conferred. Retrospective laws, however, will be strictly construed so as to confine their operation within as narrow limits as the language of the law will allow. Hedges *v.* Rennaker, 3 Met. (Ky.) 255; Bay *v.* Gage, 36 Barb. 447. The Ohio constitution of 1851 prohibits retroactive legislation. It has been held that a law requiring local authorities to issue bonds to pay bounties to veteran volunteers already enlisted is not retroactive, for the duty to pay is a public one, and its burdens fall equally on all. State *v.* Richland Tp., 20 Ohio State, 362.

sons as these, it is obvious that retroactive laws are fit only for tyrants to make, and slaves to submit to. Accordingly, some of the State constitutions contain a general prohibition of retroactive laws; and it is to be regretted that any should have omitted such a prohibition. But the federal constitution only prohibits three classes of retroactive laws; namely, "*ex post facto laws*," "*bills of attainder*," and "*laws impairing the obligation of contracts*." And the specific prohibition of these is so far held to sanction others, that though a court will never construe a law to be retroactive which is not made so in its terms, yet if expressly made retroactive, a court will not declare it void, on the ground of injustice, unless it comes within one of the above classes. I have already spoken of *laws impairing the obligation of contracts.* It therefore only remains that I describe the other two. 1. *Ex post facto laws.* (*a*) These have been decided to mean *retroactive criminal laws*, and no other. The prohibition extends to every law which makes an act punishable in a mode or measure in which it was not punishable when the act was committed, unless it be to diminish the punishment. With this exception, criminal laws can only operate upon future acts. Men may be benefited, but shall not be injured by laws which did not exist when the act was done. We are safe, therefore, against retroactive criminal laws. 2. *Bills of attainder.* (*b*) A bill of attainder is a special legislative act, inflicting punishment for an offence already committed, without a conviction in the ordinary course of justice. It may take life, or confiscate property, or both. It has, therefore, the double enormity of being an *ex post facto* law, and an usurpation of judicial power. The bloodiest pages of English history are those which record the inhuman exercise of this fearful power. No wonder, then, that it is universally prohibited in this country.

§ 84. **Security against the Suspension of Laws.** Our State constitution declares that "no power of suspending laws shall be exercised, except by the general assembly." Perhaps it may be asked, What other power than the legislature could suspend laws? None certainly without usurpation. The power to suspend a law is the same as the power to make it; for one law can only be suspended by making another to suspend it. Hence the exception in favor of the legislature. The provision, therefore, must have contemplated a very remote possibility of usurpation by the executive, judicial, or military departments. We have seen that there is one law, securing the privilege of the writ of *habeas cor-*

(*a*) See the case of Calder *v.* Bull, in the preceding note; Mad. Pap. 1399, 1400. Cumings *v.* Missouri, 4 Wall. 326; Gut *v.* The State, 9 Wall. 35. {Substantial amendments of criminal procedure unfavorably affecting the substantial rights of an indicted person are not valid as to him. Kring *v.* Missouri, 107 U. S. 221. But enlarging the class of persons who are competent to testify is not such a law. Hopt *v.* Utah, 110 id. 574.}

(*b*) See 2 Black. Com. 251; 4 Black. Com. 381; 2 Story, Const. § 1343; Mad. Pap. 1400. This term bill of attainder in the constitution embraces both what were known in the English law as bills of attainder, and bills of pains and penalties. Drehman *v.* Stifle, 8 Wall. 595.

pus, which cannot be suspended even by the legislature, unless in the extreme emergencies of rebellion or invasion.

§ 85. **Right of Education.** (*a*) Were it not that in times past, knowledge, more than any other of heaven's gifts, has been monopolized by the few to the exclusion of the many, it might seem superfluous to provide for it in a bill of rights. But our State constitution, copying the ordinance of 1787, declares that "religion, morality, and knowledge, being essential to good government, it shall be the duty of the general assembly to pass suitable laws to protect every religious denomination in the peaceable enjoyment of its own mode of public worship, and to encourage schools and the means of instruction." This declaration makes it not only the policy but the duty of government to promote education, and consequently the right of the people to have it. We have already seen that Congress, with a most liberal and enlightened spirit, devotes one thirty-sixth part of the public domain for ever to the diffusion of knowledge. Ohio has thus acquired, for the support of schools, more than seven hundred thousand acres. But until 1825, no efficient steps were taken to establish a regular school system. That year was signalized by the adoption of a free-school system, of which the following are the leading features: Every township is divided by the trustees thereof into districts, which are organized by the election of a clerk, treasurer, and three directors. The cost of erecting a school-house is defrayed by a special tax upon the property in the district, levied by a vote of the tax-payers. The fund for compensating teachers is made up in three ways: *First*, by the income of the school-lands before mentioned. Provision is now made for selling these lands, when those interested will consent, and investing the proceeds in a *common school fund*, the interest of which is annually paid by the State to the respective townships. When this is not done, these lands are leased, and the rents appropriated in the same way. *Secondly*, by a tax assessed upon the general tax-list; to which the county commissioners may make additions, if they think proper. *Thirdly*, by a variety of fines specially devoted to this purpose. No person can be employed as a teacher without a certificate from at least two of the *examiners* appointed in each county by the court of common pleas. While the fund lasts, the schools are open and free to all the white children residing in the district. The system is yet in its infancy, but much may be expected from it hereafter. It has this transcendent merit, that, so far as it extends, it opens the inestimable treasures of knowledge equally to the rich and the poor. So far, then, as the diffusion of knowledge far

(*a*) Since the text was written, the school system has been constantly improving by the results of experience; and its benefits have now become so universally accessible, that it is becoming a serious question, whether the right of suffrage ought not to be made dependent upon the ability to read and write. The father of a child entitled to the benefits of the public school of the sub-district of his residence may maintain an action against the teacher of the school and the local directors of the sub-district, for wrongfully expelling the child from school. Roe *v.* Deming, 21 Ohio State, 666.

and wide among the people, can give value and permanency to our free institutions, the free school system, which is the true democracy of education, is calculated to produce that glorious result.

§ 86. **Rights of the Poor.** We have seen that no property is necessary here as a qualification for office, or for the right of suffrage. We have seen that poll-taxes are prohibited for the benefit of the poor; and that they have the same access to our free schools as the rich. We have seen that in criminal cases those who cannot employ counsel have counsel assigned them by the court; and although in civil cases we have no provisions for suing *in forma pauperis,* yet the practice of not demanding costs until the end of the suit amounts to the same thing. And if to these provisions we add those abolishing imprisonment for debt, and relieving against the consequences of bankruptcy and insolvency, we shall probably conclude that the poor have no reason to complain of the law. There is no constitutional provision which directly asserts that those who cannot support themselves shall be maintained at the public expense. Yet their right of maintenance would seem to result, not only from the dictates of humanity, but from all the great principles of social organization. In a state of nature, the poor might appropriate to themselves the first property within their reach. By entering into the social compact, they have been obliged to renounce this right; and among the chances of life, it has fallen to their lot to be destitute. May they not, then, claim a bare support as a right? Life is the first and highest of all rights; but what is life without the means of living? I need not, however, pursue this reasoning; for provision is made for the support of the poor in all well-governed States. I shall briefly indicate the outlines of our system. In every county, the commissioners are authorized to lay a special tax for the erection of a poor-house, and to appoint three directors for its management. A tax may also be levied by them for the support of the poor. No pauper can be admitted into the poor-house without a warrant from the trustees of some township, setting forth the facts of his case. This warrant is submitted to the directors, and if they think such pauper is "legally a county charge," he is admitted. But in order to be a county charge, such pauper must have gained a *legal settlement* within the county, without the default of the township. The only persons who cannot gain a legal settlement are negroes and mulattoes. Indentured apprentices legally brought into the State gain a legal settlement in the township where they first served three years. Married women have the settlement which was last their husband's, if he had one; if not, that which was last theirs before marriage. All other persons gain a settlement by residing one year in any township, without being warned to leave it; or three years after being once warned, without being warned again. This warning is given by a warrant from the overseers of the poor. If neglected, without good reason, the township, and not the county, is chargeable. If there be no county poor-houses, the overseers of the poor provide for the support of those entitled to it, at the expense of the township. And if persons not so entitled are in a suffering condition, temporary provision is made for them, until they can be removed to the place of their legal settlement at the expense of the latter.

§ 87. **Right of Self-Defence.** (*a*) There are some injuries which, once committed, cannot be adequately redressed. The taking of life is an extreme case of this kind. Against the commission of such injuries, therefore, every person should not only have the protection of government, when practicable, but should also have a right to defend himself. The right of self-defence would of course exist in a state of nature, and the social compact does not take it away; but the right of avenging an injury already committed is taken away. This is a fundamental distinction. You may prevent an injury from being done, by all proper means; but when done, you may not take redress in your own hands. The social compact provides a tribunal to which you are bound to resort; and abundant provision is made for securing the redress to which you may be entitled. Thus the right of self-defence and the right of redress are two distinct things; but both are equally guaranteed by the constitution. We have already seen that "the enjoying and *defending* life and liberty" is declared to be an inalienable right. Also, "that the people have a right to *bear arms* for their defence and security." (*b*) In England, this right is qualified by the condition, that the arms must be suitable to the condition and degree of the bearer; but here, there is no qualification.

§ 88. **Right of Redress.** The words of the constitution are, "that all courts shall be open; and every person, for an injury done him in his land, goods, person, or reputation, shall have remedy by due course of law, and justice administered without denial or delay." This declaration asserts the broad doctrine, that for every injury to the *person* or *property* there shall be an appropriate legal remedy; and pledges the public faith to make the necessary provision. Thus, in return for surrendering the natural right of redressing ourselves, we have acquired the right to call the whole strength of government to our aid in procuring redress. But we must not be misled by the universality of the above language. The redress is to be administered by the "courts" and in "due course of law;" and we shall hereafter see that there are many injuries which may occasion the keenest pangs to a sensitive

(*a*) See 2 Story, Const. § 1896; 1 Black. Com. 143. A party may use reasonable force to defend the possession of his property, but he cannot use force against the person in *regaining* or *obtaining* the possession of property to which he is entitled. 3 Black. Com. 4, 179; Sampson *v.* Henry, 11 Pick. 387; 1 Bishop, Crim. Law, § 397; 1 Hilliard on Torts, ch. v. § 12, pp. 196, 197. This right is more fully considered below, under § 194.

(*b*) This provision is not infringed by a statute prohibiting the carrying of concealed weapons. State *v.* Jumel, 13 La. An. 399. {It limits the power of Congress only, and not of the States; but a State cannot forbid bearing arms so as to deprive the United States of her rightful resource for public security, or of the benefit of organization under U.S. militia laws. Presser *v.* Illinois, 116 U. S. 252.}

mind, but which, from motives of policy, the law does not undertake to redress; and this declaration cannot of course avail the sufferer, when the law does not provide for his case. But in order to furnish the best security that when the law does provide redress it shall be faithfully administered, the right of *trial by jury* is explicitly declared. The clause relating to criminal cases has been already quoted. Our State constitution contains another declaration, that "the right of trial by jury shall be inviolate." This of course includes civil as well as criminal cases. And we have already adverted to that amendment of the federal constitution, which extends the right to "all suits at common law where the value in controversy shall exceed twenty dollars." (*a*) But here, again, we must not be misled by the universality of the language. These provisions cannot be intended to prohibit a court of chancery from deciding cases without the intervention of a jury; because both constitutions, as we have seen, provide for the exercise of chancery powers. Nor can they be intended to require that justices of the peace should, in all cases, be assisted by a jury; for as their jurisdiction is never final, the parties may, by appeal, obtain the verdict of a jury, if they desire it. And lastly, it has been decided (*b*) that a jury need not necessarily consist of twelve men, though this is the usual number. The spirit of the declaration is, that the power to decide upon law and fact shall not be committed to the same individuals; but it is left to the legislature to determine how many persons shall be judges, and how many jurors. To guard against the abuse of this right of redress, it is made penal for any judicial or ministerial officer connected with

(*a*) See 2 Story, Const. § 1768. The legislature cannot make the right to a trial by jury in a criminal case dependent on giving a bond with surety for the payment of the penalty and costs. Greene *v.* Briggs, 1 Curtis, C. C. 311. It has been said that in Ohio the defendant in a criminal case cannot waive a jury trial, except by a plea of guilty. Hirn *v.* Ohio, 1 Ohio State, 15, 23. It has been held that this right can be waived in a criminal case. Daily *v.* The State, 4 id. 57; Dillingham *v.* The State, 5 id. 280. But in Williams *v.* The State, 12 Ohio State, 622, the attorney-general in open court submitted to the reversal of a judgment rendered in a prosecution for altering bank-notes, when the defendant had waived a jury and consented to be tried by the court, upon the ground "that upon the trial of an issue raised by a plea of not guilty in the higher grades of crime, it is not in the power of the accused to waive a trial by jury, and by consent submit to the facts found by the court, so as to authorize a legal judgment and sentence upon such finding;" and the court agreed in this opinion. This case, so far as it conflicts with them, overrules or qualifies those last cited. It may also be waived in a civil case. Gest *v.* Kenner, 7 Ohio State, 75. See *ante*, p. 196, note. No person can be compelled, without his assent, to submit his suit to arbitration. People *v.* Haws, 37 Barb. 440. A State law suspending the privilege of a certain class of persons to prosecute and defend actions, is a violation of the constitution of Iowa and of the United States. Wilcox *v.* Davis, 7 Minn. 23.

(*b*) {Whatever the word jury meant under the old constitution, — see Hunt *v.* McMahan, 5 Ohio, 133, — or in cases where there was no absolute right to a jury at common law, — see Work *v.* State, 2 Ohio State, 296, 302, — yet under the present constitution of Ohio it means a tribunal of twelve men, and this number cannot be diminished or its character materially varied by the legislature. Work *v.* State, 2 Ohio State, 296; Sovereign *v.* State, 4 id. 489; Lamb *v.* Lane, 4 id. 167; Norton *v.* McLeary, 8 id. 205; Jones *v.* Carr, 16 id. 420, 424; Smith *v.* A. & G. W. Ry. 25 id. 91, 102.} And outside of Ohio the general rule is, that a jury must consist of twelve men. Opinion of Justices, 41 N. H. 550; Vaughn *v.* Scade, 30 Miss. 600.

the courts, or any attorney or counsellor at law, to encourage, excite, or stir up any suit, quarrel, or controversy, with intent to injure the persons concerned. But we have no provision against *maintenance* and *champerty*, as understood at common law. (*a*) Maintenance was "an officious intermeddling in a suit that no way belongs to one, by maintaining or assisting either party with money or otherwise to prosecute or defend it." Champerty was "a bargain with a plaintiff or defendant to divide the land or other matter sued for between them, if they prevail at law; whereupon the champertor was to carry on the party's suit at his own expense." Blackstone adds, "in our sense of the word, it signifies the purchasing of a suit, or right of suing; a practice so much abhorred by our law, that it is one main reason why a *chose in action*, or thing of which one hath the right but not the possession, is not assignable at common law; because no man should purchase any pretence to sue in another's right. But although we do not punish maintenance and champerty as offences, it has been held that a contract, the making of which would constitute either of these offences at common law, is void as against public policy. (*b*) This does not prevent a lawyer from making a valid bargain or fee, and even a contingent fee; but if he should add other stipulations, such as paying all costs himself, and prohibiting a compromise without his consent, the contract would then be void. And we shall hereafter see that the doctrine of *choses in action* not being assignable, because it would encourage litigation, exists now merely in name.

§ 89. **Right of changing Government.** (*c*) If all the means before enumerated should fail to secure the happiness of the people, there remains finally, as a last resort, the right of changing their form of government. The Declaration of Independence, after enumerating the ends of government, asserts "that whenever any form of government becomes destructive of these ends, it is the right of the people to alter or abolish it." This indeed is self-evident, since all power comes from the people. They have created the government, and may destroy it, when it ceases to satisfy them. Delegated power, as above stated, is not irrevocable. The language of our State constitution does not even make the right of changing government depend upon the fact of its having failed to answer its ends; but asserts it without qualification or condition. "All political power is inherent in the people. Government is instituted for their equal protection and benefit, and they have the right to

(*a*) 4 Black. Com. 134, 135; Key *v.* Vattier, 1 Ohio Rep. 132. Cain *v.* Monroe, 23 Geo. 82; Harring *v.* Barwick, 24 id. 59. Maintenance does not extend to a fair *bonâ fide* purchase of a *chose in action* made for the purpose of securing payment of an antecedent debt. Sayles *v.* Tibbetts, 5 R. I. 270.

(*b*) Backus *v.* Byron, 4 Mich. 535; Scobey *v.* Ross, 13 Ind. 117; Weakly *v.* Hall, 13 Ohio, 167; Key *v.* Vattier, 1 id. 132; Stewart *v.* Welch, 41 Ohio State, 483. See Sedgwick *v.* Stanton, 4 Kern. 289; Roberts *v.* Cooper, 20 How. 467; Hay *v.* Cumberland, 25 Barb. 594.

(*c*) See Luther *v.* Borden, 7 How. 1.

alter, reform, or abolish the same, whenever they may deem it necessary." But it is needless to enlarge upon the general right of revolution. It must of necessity exist, whenever a majority desire it, even though the existing government should be in terms made perpetual, as some of the provisions in our constitutions are declared to be. To guard, however, against the evils of a revolution, every constitution provides for its *amendment*, (*a*) though generally by something more than a bare majority. The federal constitution may be amended as follows: Amendments may be *proposed*, either by two-thirds of both houses of Congress, or by a convention called by Congress, on the application of the legislatures of two-thirds of the States. But in either case, such amendments must be *ratified* by the legislatures or by conventions of *three-fourths* of the States, according as one or the other mode may be proposed by Congress. But no amendment can be made to deprive any State of its equal suffrage in the senate. Thus far, twelve amendments only have been made: the first ten in 1789; the eleventh in 1798, and the twelfth in 1803. (*b*) A thirteenth was proposed in 1811, and is sometimes published as an amendment, but it never was ratified by the requisite number of States. The State constitution may be amended as follows: Three-fifths of the members elected may propose amendments to be voted upon by the people. Or two thirds may propose the calling of a convention, which shall be done if a majority of the voters at the next election shall sanction the proposition. And once in twenty years, beginning with 1871, a vote is to be taken upon calling a convention, without any action of the legislature.

Here, then, terminates our view of constitutional law. I have commented, in the brief and general manner required by my plan, upon all the provisions of the federal and State constitutions. I have endeavored so to arrange the subjects as not to burden your memory, and at the same time to exhibit, in juxtaposition, the corresponding provisions of both constitutions, as well as the points of difference. If I have done any thing like justice to this great branch of law, I have exhibited the full reality of that theoretical organization described in the second lecture. In a word, I have sketched the most perfect system of civil polity the world has ever yet seen. One matter of regret, however, deserves to be mentioned.

(*a*) The first proposition in the convention was, that Congress should have no voice in amendments. Mad. Pap. 734, 844. This was afterwards stricken out. And it was simply resolved that amendments should be provided for — id. 1175. It was then proposed that Congress should call a convention, on the application of two-thirds of the State legislatures — id. 1241, 1533–41. Finally, after considerable difference of opinion, the clause was placed in its present shape — id. 1590–3. A proposition that amendments proposed by the State conventions should be referred to another general convention, was unanimously negatived — id. 1593–5.

(*b*) Since the above, a 13th, 14th, and 15th amendments have been added. The 13th amendment is given above on p. 183, note. The 14th, § 1, on p. 148, note: § 2, on p. 79, note: § 3 on p. 84, note; § 4 relates to the inviolability of the public debt, and forbids assumption of debts of insurrectionary States or claims for slaves. The 15th amendment is given on p. 81, note.

The maxim, *stare decisis*, so essential to stability in the administration of public affairs, has not been sufficiently regarded. It does not seem to be the American disposition to *adhere to established decisions.* I have remarked upon the frequency with which judicial precedents are overruled, when speaking of the common law; but I now refer more particularly to the decisions upon constitutional law. We have seen that half a century of trial has discovered many weighty questions not directly settled by the constitution itself. These have been discussed before the proper tribunals, as long as new light could be thrown upon them, and then finally decided. In most instances, all the departments of government have concurred in the determinations; and a general acquiescence in them, for a series of years, has given them, over well-constituted minds, all the authority of express constitutional declarations. And yet how few of these solemn decisions have been suffered by politicians to stand as settled principles! All have been repeatedly assailed, and many completely subverted. At this moment, hardly a single construction, once doubtful, can now be considered as established in the minds of the people. And if fifty years will not compose doubts of this kind, will as many centuries do it? The advocates of arbitrary power are, doubtless, right in pointing to this instability, this incessant fluctuation of opinion, as the most vulnerable part of our system; but I trust that this is only an accidental, and not an inevitable, result of the freedom of opinion. Surely, submission to the decisions of the constituted authorities is not incompatible with freedom of opinion. And it seems to me that one of the first lessons to be inculcated upon every American mind is to acquiesce in established constructions until they shall either be ratified or reversed by constitutional amendments. What if they do not fully meet our individual approbation? Patriotism and magnanimity require us to sacrifice our predilections for the public good. The same conciliatory and compromising spirit which produced our government can alone perpetuate it. We have an illustrious instance of this spirit in Franklin. As a member of the convention which framed the federal constitution, he had sincerely opposed many of the propositions which finally prevailed; but when the great work was finished, he addressed the convention in favor of unanimously signing the constitution; and these were a part of his words: "I consent to this constitution, because I expect no better; and because I am not sure that it is not the best. The opinions I have had of its errors, I sacrifice to the public good. I have never whispered a syllable of them abroad. Within these walls they were born, and here they shall die." Could we but adopt and practise these sentiments, with regard to the questions which have since arisen, and been constitutionally decided, there would be no shadow upon the prospect of our permanency.

PART III.

THE LAW OF PERSONS. (*a*)

LECTURE XII.

CORPORATIONS. (*b*)

§ 90. **The Nature of Corporations.** I have already observed that the chief objects of law are persons and property. I have also noticed Blackstone's division of rights, into rights of persons and rights of things, as well founded in reason, though not very accurate in point of expression. The rights of persons grow out of their relations to government or to one another; and I have mentioned the classes into which persons are divided, with respect to these relations. Before recapitulating these divisions, however, I cannot forbear to call your attention to the fundamental difference there is between personal relations in this country and in England, in consequence of our entire abolition of privileged orders. Our doctrine of equality has in this, as in everything else, been productive of simplicity. With us, in theory at least, all men start equally; they are born with equal rights; and their distinctions in after life are mainly made by themselves. This is the general rule, though, as we shall see, there are some slight exceptions founded on expediency. Whereas, in England, men set out unequally. Some are born to privileges which others never can attain. Hence, a fundamental division of persons there is into the *nobility* and *commonalty.* And this gives rise to a variety of subdivisions, rendering the classification of persons exceedingly complicated. The first book of Blackstone is almost wholly occupied with an enumeration of these distinctions; and we have only to

(*a*) On the Law of Persons in general, see the first book of Blackstone and of Swift; the Lectures of Kent, from the 24th to the 33d inclusive; and Reeves's Domestic Relations.

(*b*) On the Law of Corporations, see 1 Black. Com. ch. 18; 1 Swift, ch. 9; 2 Kent, Com. lect. 33; Angell & Ames on Corporations; Kyd on Corporations; Morawetz on Corporations; Grant on Corporations (London, 1850); Redfield on Railways; Pierce on American Railroad Law; Dillon on Municipal Corporations.

glance at the contents of that book, to see how large a portion of it is totally inapplicable to American society. Here, personal relations can be described in half the space required there. The leading divisions contemplated by law, as we have already seen, are as follows: 1. Persons are either natural or artificial. 2. They are either public or private. 3. They are either citizens or aliens. 4. They are either males or females. 5 They are either infants or adults. 6. They are either sane or insane. 7. They are either freemen or slaves, masters or servants, principals or agents. 8. Indians sustain relations different from any other persons. 9. The death of persons creates the relations of ancestors and heirs, devisors and devisees, and executors or administrators. Some of these relations have already been described in connection with the constitutional provisions relating to them. Thus we have said all that our limits will permit respecting *public functionaries*, *aliens*, *slaves*, and *Indians*. On these classes of persons, therefore, nothing further will be offered. The rest remain to be described, and will form the subject of this third part of our lectures.

I shall begin with *corporations*, to which this lecture will be devoted. The view I shall present must necessarily be brief; and for those details which do not fall within my limits, I refer to the authors above mentioned. The subject is one of growing importance; for corporations are annually multiplying to such a degree as even to excite alarm in some minds, lest individual freedom of action shall be swallowed up in the prevailing spirit of association. We have seen that corporations are called *artificial persons*, to distinguish them from persons in their natural capacity, or simply human beings. In other words, they consist of natural persons, clothed by law with an artificial character and capacity. When two or more persons desire to unite their means for the purpose of carrying on some enterprise or business which neither might be able to accomplish by himself alone, there are but two legal ways of doing it conveniently. The persons in question must either be constituted a *corporation*, by means of a legislative act or charter, or they must enter into a *partnership*, by virtue of a contract. In either case their relations will be determined, partly by the express provisions of the charter or contract, and partly by the implied conditions tacitly annexed by law to each of these relations. Thus, while corporations and partnerships both agree in being relations voluntarily assumed by the members, and also in having for their object the association of several individuals for the purpose of co-operation in business; yet they differ so materially in their mode of creation, and in many other respects, that they require a separate consideration. Accordingly, partnerships will be reserved for the next lecture.

A corporation may be defined to be a body of persons connected together by law, either contemporaneously or in succession, and endowed with the capacity of acting for various purposes as a single person. (*a*) The law knows a corporation only by its *corporate name.* (*b*) In this name all its acts are done, without a specification of its members; and this determines its continued identity, though all its members should be changed. We often hear a corporation spoken of as a body without a soul, — as an invisible, intangible, and immortal being; as existing only in the contemplation of law; and the like. But such expressions are calculated to throw darkness rather than light over the actual nature of corporations. It is sufficient to conceive of them as consisting of natural persons, united together in an artificial character by the force of law, for the purpose of concentrating or perpetuating individual ability. They are purely creatures of the law; because, though the members may voluntarily form themselves into a society or association, the law only can erect them into a corporation. We are told, indeed, that corporations may exist by *prescription.* But the theory of prescription is simply this: From considerations of general expediency, the law *presumes* that what has long been suffered to exist must have had a rightful origin. If, therefore, persons have long used the name, and exercised the franchises of a corporation, the law presumes without seeking other evidence, that they had original authority for so doing; or, in other words, that they were once duly constituted a corporation. In older countries, this theory of prescription may be very important; but, in this young country, it can be of little consequence. All our corporations, at least since the revolution, have actually derived their existence from a legislative act, which we call a *charter*, and which is to a corporation what a constitution is to a State, — its organic or fundamental law. And we may reasonably presume that no future corporation will exist but in this way. (*c*)

§ 91. **Constitutional Power to create them.** We have seen that the federal constitution confers no express power on Congress to create corporations. If this power exists, therefore, in the federal government, it is an *incidental power;* and as such it has been twice exercised by the incorporation of a *national bank.* (*d*) But

(*a*) The supreme court of the United States has intimated that the definition of a corporation could no longer be confined to its old limits, and held that a joint-stock company organized in England under an act of parliament was a corporation, though the act expressly provided that it should not be. Liverpool Ins. Co. *v.* Massachusetts, 10 Wall. 566.

(*b*) An injunction may be granted by analogy to the law of trade-marks to a corporation to restrain persons from adopting and using the same corporate name with that previously adopted regularly and in good faith by the plaintiff. Newby *v.* Oregon Central Ry., Deady, 609; Holmes *v.* Holmes Man. Co., 37 Conn. 278 {see London & Prov. Law Assur. Co. *v.* London & Prov. Joint Stock Co., 11 Jurist, 938, and as to individual's name, see DuBoulay *v.* DuBoulay, L. R. 2 P. C. 441, that no suit lies unless property rights are impaired or threatened}.

(*c*) {There may, however, be a corporation *de facto* as distinguished from one *de jure*, which, though liable to ouster by the State on *quo warranto*, cannot be otherwise questioned, and whose property interests will be protected, and rights or titles derived from it held valid. Society Perun *v.* Cleveland, 43 Ohio State, 481. See also Gaff *v.* Flesher, 33 ib. 107, 114.}

(*d*) It was proposed in the federal convention to confer on Congress the express with the States it is different. The creation of corporations by them is regarded as so essential an attribute of municipal sovereignty, that it requires no express constitutional provision. The power, not being prohibited, is therefore taken to be conferred. (*a*) In this enterprising and rapidly growing country, corporations are multiplying so rapidly that a large portion of our legislative business consists in granting and renewing charters. Many of the most important branches of trade and manufacture, nearly all banking and insurance operations, and many of our internal improvements, are undertaken and carried on by incorporated companies. Yet, although so much of good is thus effected, and without any very palpable evil, it is not uncommon to hear corporations denounced as *monopolies*, created for the benefit of the few to the prejudice of the many, and hostile to the great republican principle of equality. But corporations are not necessarily monopolies, in the odious sense of that term. A monopoly, as the name imports, is a special privilege conferred on one or more persons, to the absolute exclusion of all others. In this sense, it is deservedly odious, because it is essentially anti-republican. But our corporations are not, in this sense, monopolies. Although charters frequently and confessedly enable the members of corporations to enjoy capacities and realize advantages which they would not enjoy and realize as private individuals, and thus have something of the appearance of creating monopolies; yet so long as no *exclusive privileges* are in fact conferred upon any particular corporation, and no class of persons are prohibited from membership, they can with no propriety be said to create monopolies. Our *banks* are the nearest approach to monopolies, because individuals are expressly prohibited from banking privileges. Yet even our banks are not in fact monopolies, because no individuals are excluded from becoming stockholders, if they have the will and the means. And this objection to corporations being without foundation, there is this strong argument in their favor. Under a republican government like ours, where property is so beneficently distributed that very large fortunes are seldom accumulated, it is manifest that great enterprises, requiring large means, would seldom be undertaken by single individuals. It is only by the creation of corporations, enabling many to unite their means and act as one, that such enterprises are now achieved. It may be safely affirmed, that comparatively few of the wonderful improvements and developments in our country would have been made, if our legislatures had been divested of the power to create corporations, which they have so freely exercised. In this view, therefore, cor-

power to create corporations. Mad. Pap. 1354, 1576. That the power exists as an incidental power, see McCulloch *v.* Maryland, 4 Wheat. 316; Osborn *v.* Bank U. S. 9 Wheat. 738; Angell & Ames on Corporations, ch. ii. § 4.

(*a*) But this power is guarded by many restrictions. Thus, in Ohio, "no special privileges or immunities shall ever be granted that may not be altered, revoked, or repealed."

porations should be the favorites of republicanism; since they enable its friends to meet the only plausible argument that can be urged to sustain that unequal distribution of property which prevails in aristocratic governments. No doubt the power to create corporations may be abused. But, when exercised judiciously, it certainly produces most salutary effects. (*a*)

§ 92. **Their various Kinds.** (*b*) Corporations are divided and subdivided as follows: *First*, into *sole* and *aggregate*. A *sole corporation* consists of a single person and his successors, one after another, no two members existing contemporaneously. The member for the time being is thus endowed with a corporate capacity for the mere sake of uninterrupted succession. But such corporations being confined to the English church, require no comment here. *Aggregate corporations* are those which consist of more persons than one at the same time; and there is no necessary limit to the number who may be thus united. These are first subdivided into *ecclesiastical* and *lay*. *Ecclesiastical corporations* are likewise peculiar to the English and Romish churches. Our *religious societies*, even when incorporated by special charters, have no resemblance to them. But we have a general statute under which most of these societies are incorporated, so far as to hold their church property without any special charter. (*c*) *Lay corporations* are again subdivided into *eleemosynary* and *civil*. *Eleemosynary* or *charitable corporations* include only schools, colleges, hospitals, and the like; and have no peculiar attributes requiring comment here. *Civil corporations*, of course, include all other lay corporations. Lastly, corporations are divided into *public* and *private*. *Public corporations* are those which are founded with public means, and for public purposes. Their criterion is, that no

(*a*) Since this paragraph was written, great changes have taken place in regard to corporations, and all the recent constitutions place them under restrictions more or less severe. The new constitution of Ohio, for example, prohibits the legislature from passing "any special act conferring corporate powers." Corporations may be formed under general laws, subject, at any time, to be altered or repealed. The limit of individual liability must be at least double the amount of stock. The liability to taxation must be the same as that of private persons. Municipal corporations can only be organized under general laws, with proper restrictions as to the powers of taxation, borrowing money, contracting debts, and loaning credit. And banking powers cannot be conferred without the sanction of a subsequent popular vote. It has been held in Ohio, under these constitutional provisions, that the prohibition of any special act, conferring corporate power, extends equally to municipal and private corporations, and that any act which either creates a corporation or confers upon a corporation already existing power to do an act which it could not previously have done, confers corporate powers, and, if special, is unconstitutional. State *ex rel.* Att'y-Gen. *v.* Cincinnati, 20 Ohio State, 18. Under the general laws regulating the formation of corporations, a defect or omission in a certificate of incorporation, such as the want of a seal, may be supplied by a court under the curative statute of March 10, 1859. Warner *v.* Callender, 20 Ohio State, 190. But if the certificate of a manufacturing company is acknowledged before a notary public instead of a justice of the peace, as the statute prescribes, it will be fatal on *quo warranto*. State *ex rel.* Att'y-Gen. *v.* Lee, 21 Ohio State, 662 {but the legislature may cure this retroactively. Spinning *v.* Home B. & S. Assn., 26 Ohio State, 483}.

(*b*) 2 Kent, Com. 273; Angell & Ames, ch. i. §§ 1, 3.

(*c*) As to the powers of such corporations, see Miller *v.* Gable, 2 Denio, 492; The People *v.* Steele, 2 Barb. 397; Smith, 18 Vt. 511.

individual has any interest in their foundation, except as a member of the general body politic. To this class belong all municipal corporations, beginning with the United States, and descending down through States, counties, townships, school districts, and the like. These are, for the most part, denominated *quasi corporations;* since, with the exception of cities and boroughs, they require no special act of incorporation. They possess scarcely any other corporate properties than those of holding property and being parties to suits. But the distinguishing quality of public corporations is, that they are *alterable* at the pleasure of the public, because they involve no private interests distinct from those of the public. (*a*) *Private corporations* are those which are founded on private means. Their object may be either private or public. But their criterion is a private foundation, whereby individuals have an interest distinct from that of the community. For this reason, private corporations are not alterable at the pleasure of the public. Their charters, as we have seen, are held to be *contracts*, to which the government is one party and the corporators the other; and they are within the protection of that great constitutional guaranty, which secures contracts from being impaired by subsequent legislation. (*b*) Unless, therefore, the

(*a*) Berlin *v.* Gorham, 34 N. H. 266. And they may be altered or abolished, although by the charter they are made the trustee of a charity. Montpelier *v.* East Montpelier, 29 Vt. 12. When, however, they have acquired property under the law, this cannot be taken away (see note on p. 216), nor their duty to pay valid debts be impaired. Coddington *v.* Bispham, 36 N. J. Eq. 574.

(*b*) Dartmouth College *v.* Woodward, 4 Wheat. 518; Charles River Bridge *v.* Warren Bridge, 11 Peters, 421; Providence Bank *v.* Billings, 4 Peters, 514. See Mechanics and Traders' Bank *v.* Debolt, 1 Ohio State, 591; Toledo Bank *v.* Bond, id. 622; Knoup *v.* Piqua Bank, id. 603; 16 How. 369, 416. Jefferson Branch Bank *v.* Skelly, 1 Black, 436; Franklin Branch Bank *v.* The State of Ohio, id. 474; Wilmington R. R. Co. *v.* Reid, 13 Wall. 264. The Supreme Court did not hold in Dartmouth College *v.* Woodward that a charter is a contract. A charter may contain a contract. The ruling was that when a contract is contained in a charter, such contract is made inviolable by the constitution of the United States. But, as was said by Chief Justice Waite in Stone *v.* Mississippi, 101 U. S. 814, "it is to be kept in mind that it is not the charter which is protected, but only any contract which the charter may contain." It is held that a provision in a charter that the officers of a corporation shall be elected in a particular way is not a contract, and is repealable. State *v.* Green, 9 Mo. App. 219. A right given in a charter to dispose of lottery tickets, held not a contract but a privilege or license revocable at pleasure. State *v.* Morris, 77 N. C. 512. A provision in a charter that the corporation, when sued, shall be served in a particular way, is not a contract and may be changed by legislation. Railroad Co. *v.* Hecht, 95 U. S. 168. If the contract is one which the legislature has not power to make, such contract does not bind the State. The legislature cannot grant away the police power of the State. Hence any agreement in a charter which restricts or curtails the police power of the State is invalid; though the corporation may have paid the State a valuable consideration therefor, the legislature may annul it. Boyd *v.* Alabama, 94 U. S. 645, affirming the supreme court of Alabama; Stone *v.* Mississippi, 101 U. S. 814, affirming the supreme court of Mississippi. Butchers Union Co. *v.* Crescent City Co., 111 U. S. 746. Also, Beer Company *v.* Mass., 97 Mass. 25; Metropolitan Board *v.* Barrie, 34 N. Y. 657. The right to regulate charges in warehouses and grain elevators (Munn *v.* Illinois), and rates for freight and passengers on railways (Railroad Co. *v.* Iowa, 94 U. S. 155; Peik *v.* Railway Co., 94 U. S. 164), seems held to be a police power. The decision, however, in the first two cases was that the State, not being restricted by any agreement in the charter, had the power to regulate the charges. *Contra*, in case the charter provides against such reduction. Iron R. R.

charter of a private corporation contains an express reservation of the power to alter it, thus making the power of alteration one of the terms of the contract, the legislature can make no alteration in it, without the consent of the corporators. This doctrine, though much inveighed against by demagogues, is abundantly established by judicial decisions; and it is the foundation of that general confidence with which individuals embark their funds in corporate enterprises. Of late, however, attempts have been made to depreciate the value of this security, by broaching the doctrine, that although a State legislature cannot repeal or alter a private charter, yet the people of a State may do it, by amending the constitution for this purpose. But to this pretension, the language of the federal constitution affords a complete answer. "No State shall pass *any law* impairing the obligation of contracts." (*a*) Unless, therefore, it can be shown that a State con-

v. Lawrence Furnace Co., 29 Ohio State, 208; and in Peik *v.* Railway Co. the charter containing such a restriction was granted after the adoption of the State constitution, which provided that all charters should be repealed or amended at the pleasure of the legislature. But it is held in Illinois that, where a charter contains a clause that the company may charge such fares and rates as it may deem reasonable, the State may, in the exercise of its police power, ignore such clause and prescribe rates. Ruggles *v.* People, 91 Ill. 256; Illinois Central *v.* People, 95 Ill. 313. Chief Justice Waite, in Stone *v.* Mississippi, distinguishes between the power to tax and the police power of the State. He says that while taxation is, in general, necessary for the support of the government, it is not a part of the government itself; taxation is an incident to the exercise of the legitimate functions of government, but nothing more; and adds, "all that has been determined thus far is, that for a consideration it may, in the exercise of a reasonable discretion, and for the public good, surrender a part of its powers in this particular." Although a law of the legislature declares all charters thereafter granted subject to amendment or repeal, still if the charter of a charitable corporation, or an institution of learning, expressly suspends the statute as to it, and exempts its property from taxation, and the corporation is organized, it constitutes a contract. Home of the Friendless *v.* Rouse, 8 Wall. 431; Washington University *v.* Rouse, 8 Wall. 439. When a new power is given by an amendatory act, the exercise of the power is very strong evidence of the acceptance of the amendment by the corporation. Goodin *v.* Evans, 18 Ohio State, 150; Talladega Ins. Co. *v.* Landers, 43 Ala. 115. The concurrence of all the stockholders is not necessary to the acceptance of an amendment enlarging the powers of the corporation. Curry *v.* Scott, 54 Penn. State, 270. But if the purpose of the corporation is changed by the amendment, even though the power to amend, alter, and repeal was reserved by the legislature, every stockholder must acquiesce. Zabriskie *v.* Hackensack, &c. Co., 3 Green (N. J.), 178. See also Ireland *v.* Palestine Turnpike Co., 19 Ohio State, 369. The legislature may destroy under such a power, but cannot modify without the consent of the corporators. If, however, the corporation refuses to accept the modification, it must cease to transact business. Yeaton *v.* Bank of the Old Dominion, 21 Grattan, 593. When a general law exists, subjecting all charters to amendment or repeal, all laws passed are subject to it; and although a subsequent law exempts property from taxation during the continuance of the charter, if it does not expressly except the corporation from the general law, it will be subject to it, and therefore repealable. Tomlinson *v.* Jessup, 15 Wall. 454. When a repealable charter authorized a municipal corporation to subscribe a certain sum, and have a certain share in the directory, this proportion could be changed. Miller *v.* The State, 15 Wall. 478. And a corporation which had erected a dam, might be required to construct fishways. Com'rs of Inland Fisheries *v.* Holyoke Water Power Co., 104 Mass. 446; Holyoke Co. *v.* Lyman, 15 Wall. 500. But when the power reserved is only to repeal in case of misuser, non-user, or abuse, the legislature is not the final judge of whether a proper cause for repeal has arisen. Commonwealth *v.* Pittsburgh R. R. Co., 58 Penn. State, 26. See also note to § 81, paragraph "Property in expectation — Contracts," *ante.*

(*a*) This clause does not affect the powers of Congress. Evans *v.* Eaton, 1 Peters, C. C. 322.

stitution is not a *law*, the charter of a private corporation can no more be impaired by a State constitution than by a statute. Seldom or never has so bold and disorganizing a doctrine been reared upon so feeble a foundation. And we may congratulate ourselves that the federal constitution, which thus protects chartered rights, is "the supreme law of the land, any thing in the constitution or laws of any State to the contrary notwithstanding." In this State, however, this principle will be of no value to future corporations, because by an act of 1842 it is declared that the charter of every corporation of every description, which shall thereafter be granted, shall be subject to alteration, suspension, and repeal, in the discretion of the legislature. (*a*)

§ 93. **Their general Powers and Properties.** (*b*) As a general principle, the powers, and consequently the disabilities, of corporations are to be sought, for each corporation, in its particular charter. We have no disabling statutes like the *statutes of mortmain* in England, prohibiting corporations from receiving or holding property; nor are corporations prohibited, as in England, from being devisees, under our *statute of wills*. The charter, then, of each particular corporation is the expositor, as well as source, of its powers. And the prevailing doctrine is, that charters are to be construed strictly, (*c*) and that corporations can exercise no powers which are not expressly specified, or necessarily implied, in their charter. (*d*) In this respect, a charter is more analogous to the

(*a*) This provision is incorporated into the constitution of 1852.

(*b*) 2 Kent, Com. 277.

(*c*) {The present disposition, however, is to relax the rule of strict construction somewhat, as no longer required in view of the power of the legislature to alter charters, and to construe acts of incorporation the same as other statutes. Bank *v.* Ins. Co., 41 Ohio State, 1, 11.}

(*d*) 2 Kent, Com. 298; U. S. *v.* Arredondo, 6 Peters, 736; Beatty *v.* Knowler, 4 Peters, 162; Bartholomew *v.* Bentley, 1 Ohio State, 37; Rice *v.* Railroad Co., 1 Black, 358; *ante*, p. 210, note. Contracts made by a corporation, which are beyond its powers, are void. Straus *v.* Eagle Ins. Co., 5 Ohio State, 59. But see R. & B. R. R. Co. *v.* Odell, 29 Vt. 93. In New York, it has been held that goods bought by a corporation, although bought *ultra vires*, become its property, and it may sell them or mortgage them, and it seems they will be liable to an action for the price. Parish *v.* Wheeler, 23 N. Y. 494. See also San Francisco Gas Co. *v.* San Francisco, 9 Cal. 453; Farmers' Bank *v.* Detroit, &c. R. R. Co., 17 Wis. 372. The term *ultra vires* is used in different senses; an act is said to be *ultra vires* when it is not in the power of the corporation to do it under any circumstances; and an act is also said to be *ultra vires* with reference to the rights of certain parties when the corporation cannot perform it without their consent; and it may also be *ultra vires* with reference to some specific purpose when the corporation cannot perform it for that purpose. When the act of the corporation is *ultra vires* in the first sense it is void *in toto*, and the corporation may avail itself of the defence; but when it is *ultra vires* in the second or third senses, its right to do so will depend upon circumstances: thus, if it be an act which it might perform for some purposes, but not for others, the defence will be available if the stranger knew that it was done for the unauthorized purpose, otherwise not. Miners' Ditch Co. *v.* Zellerback, 37 Cal. 543. The modern doctrine of *ultra vires* is very recent; it dates in England from Coleman *v.* Eastern Counties Railway Co., 10 Beav. 1, decided in 1845; though it was established earlier in the United States. Yet it has already produced an excellent text-book, Brice on *Ultra Vires*, which is enlarged in the American edition by Green. The earlier American rule was clear, consistent, and rigid. A corporation existed only in conformity with its charter. An undertaking or engagement not authorized by its charter, was the undertaking or engagement of a dead federal than to a State constitution. This doctrine measures at once the powers and disabilities of corporations; for there is an implied prohibition of every power not thus conferred. Of course, the powers of different corporations must vary according to their object. Those of a college or hospital, for example, must be very different from those of a banking, insurance, manufacturing, or bridge company. So that an enumeration of the particular functions of the various existing corporations would require volumes. I can only refer to some general principles which are applicable to all.

1. The management of the affairs of a corporation, pursuant to the provisions of the charter, must depend upon the votes of the members. What shall constitute *membership* must depend upon the nature of the corporation. Generally, it is the ownership of *stock*. The charter limits the amount of *capital*, which is divided into equal *shares*, and every shareholder is a member. (*a*) But in many of the charitable corporations there is no distribution of stock; and in these, the members consist of those only who are required for managers, having no pecuniary interest. In such cases, if the endowment be private, the founder or donor may stipulate for the management or *visitation*, as it is technically called, of his charity; and the charter will constitute the persons thus indicated members of the corporation. But in whatever way the members be made such, the general rule is, that the majority shall govern, where the contrary is not provided. The will of the majority is expressed by votes, and evidenced by the records. But in business corporations, the representative principle is usually adopted; and the immediate supervision is committed to a *board of directors* elected by the stockholders, together with other appropriate officers. And in elections by the members, the general principle of voting, which requires personal attendance, is departed from, and votes are given by *proxy*, or power of attorney. For

person; was a nullity. Being a nullity, it could not be made valid by confirmation or enforced under cover of an estoppel. But this was found to be so harsh in practice that it has become barnacled over with exceptions, and muzzled by estoppels. In England the doctrine seems to have entirely shifted its ground, and the question there is held to be, not, is the act authorized, but is it prohibited; a question, not of authority, but of legality. A condensed statement of the rule and its limitations is given in Field on Corporations, §§ 257–273. But it is necessarily a tentative statement of the present condition of a portion of the law which is now in process of formation.

(*a*) {Private corporations are also recognized in Ohio as of two kinds, those formed for profit, and those not. The latter properly have no stock nor capital. State *ex rel.* *v.* Standard Life Assn., 38 Ohio State, 281. The capital and the stock are distinct species of property. The former is owned by the corporation, though in trust; while the latter is but a right to participate in the profits, and is personalty, taxable at the domicile of the owner. Bradley *v.* Bauder, 36 Ohio State, 28, 35. To perfect the legal title of transferred stock, transfer on the corporate books is necessary, if so required by the certificate. Norton *v.* Norton, 43 Ohio State, 509, 522; Henkle *v.* Salem Mfg. Co., 39 id. 547; but the claim of a pledgee of stock not transferred to him on the books is prior to that of an attaching creditor. Norton *v.* Norton, 43 Ohio State, 509. The right to issue preferred stock is a form of a power to borrow; and the terms "stock," "dividends," "profits," in effect mean respectively debts, interest, earnings. Burt *v.* Rattle, 31 Ohio State, 116.}

this, however, it is presumed there must be special provision in the charter or by-laws. Where the charter does not specify the number of members or directors who shall constitute a *quorum* for business, the rule is, that a quorum of directors shall be a majority of the whole number; but a quorum of members shall be those present, the whole having been duly notified. The power of *amotion*, by which is meant the removal of officers, is incidental to every corporation, without express provision, provided there be good cause; this being necessary to self-protection; but the power of *disfranchisement*, by which is meant the expulsion of members, requires an express provision. This is true, at least, of all joint-stock corporations. To prevent abuse, however, in the management of corporations, they are made ultimately amenable to the courts of justice. If they neglect or refuse to perform a positive duty devolved upon them by the charter, a writ of *mandamus* may be issued, to compel such performance; and if they attempt to exercise any power not conferred by the charter, a writ of *quo warranto* may be issued to compel them to desist from such usurpation. Charitable corporations, even when their visitation or supervision is provided for by the founder, as the condition of his donation, have always been held amenable to the courts of chancery for the proper discharge of their duties. And in this State, by the act of 1842, the several courts sitting in chancery have a visitorial jurisdiction over all corporations in the following cases: 1. To compel the directors or officers to account for their management of the funds of the corporation. 2. To compel them to pay the value of all property acquired to themselves, or transferred, or lost, by any violation of their duty. 3. To suspend or remove them for gross misconduct. 4. To prevent or set aside any alienation of the property of a corporation made contrary to law, or for purposes foreign to its business. Moreover, the directors or officers are made personally liable for any loss accruing to the corporation through their mismanagement. (*a*)

2. The most important property of a corporation is that of *uninterrupted succession*, so long as the charter endures, independently of the death or change of members. The common expression is, that a corporation never dies; but this is not strictly true; because it must expire with the expiration of the charter, if not before. The meaning is, that the existence and identity of a cor-

(*a*) A stockholder in a corporation can only maintain a suit in his individual capacity against a wrong-doer injuring the corporation when application has been made to the board of directors to institute the suit, and they have refused. If they have brought a suit as requested, which is pending, a stockholder has no standing in court. Memphis *v.* Dean, 8 Wall. 64. A court of equity will interfere on the application of a stockholder to restrain the governing body from doing acts within the scope of the corporate authority, if such acts, under the existing circumstances, would constitute a breach of the trust which they are charged with the execution of. Wright *v.* Oroville Mining Co., 40 Cal. 20; {Port Clinton R. R. *v.* C. & T. R. R., 13 Ohio State, 544; Hazard *v.* Durant, 11 R. I., 195; Ryan *v.* L. A. &c. Ry., 21 Kan. 365; Brewer *v.* Boston Theatre, 104 Mass. 378; Craig *v.* Gregg, 83 Penn. State, 19; Greaves *v.* Gouge, 69 N. Y. 154.}

poration are not affected by mutations of membership. One goes out, and another comes in, under the provisions of the charter, and the corporation is still the same legal entity, and experiences no interruption in its operations.

3. All the acts which a corporation can do, are done in its *corporate name*, without any specification of the members. This name is always fixed by the charter, and the shorter it is the better. The advantage of this union of many interests under a single name is at once perceived. How great would be the inconvenience, if, in suing and being sued, receiving and transferring property, making contracts, or doing any other acts to which corporations are competent, the names of all the members must be repeated.

4. Corporations are authorized to have and use a *corporate seal.* The nature and properties of a seal will be described hereafter. The ancient doctrine was, that a corporation could only speak and act under the manifestation of its seal. But this is now changed; (*a*) and corporations are not required to use a seal except in those cases where it would be necessary for individuals. They may not only contract in writing without a seal, but may even be bound by implied contracts, in the same manner as individuals. (*b*)

5. Corporations are authorized to make *by-laws* for the regulation of their business in detail. These by-laws sustain the same relation to the charter that statutes do to the constitution;

(*a*) 2 Kent, Com. 289; Bank of Columbia *v.* Patterson, 7 Cranch, 299; Fleckner *v.* U. S. Bank, 8 Wheat. 338. A deed of land by a corporation not under its corporate seal is void. Where the seal appears, it will be presumed to have been affixed by proper authority; but the contrary may be shown by parol evidence. Koehler *v.* Black, &c. Co., 2 Black, 715; C. H. & D. R. R. *v.* Harter, 26 Ohio State, 426. The private seal of one of its officers may be used, and it is not necessary to produce a resolution or order of the trustees in writing to authorize an agent to enter into a contract. Eureka Co. *v.* Bailey Co., 11 Wall. 488, 491. But it cannot contract a debt or order payment of it by the action of the individual members of the board acting separately. State *ex rel.* Steinbeck *v.* Treasurer Liberty Township, 22 Ohio State, 144.

(*b*) Smith *v.* Nashua & Lowell R. R. Co., 7 Foster, 96–98; Bank of Middlebury *v.* Rutland & Washington R. R. Co., 30 Vt. 160; Merrick *v.* Burlington, &c. Co., 11 Iowa, 74; Straus *v.* Eagle Ins. Co., 5 Ohio State, 59. But the deed of a corporation must be executed in its name, and not in that of the agent. Brinley *v.* Mann, 2 Cush. 337. But it is now generally held, that a deed running in the name of a corporation, and signed personally by its agents with their official designation, as D. E., president, is the deed of the corporation, if the agents had proper authority. Sheehan *v.* Davis, 17 Ohio State, 571; Hays *v.* Galion Gas Light & Coke Co., 29 Ohio State, 330, 334. A corporation, though it has a seal, may adopt any other. Tenney *v.* East Warren, &c. Co., 43 N. H. 343; Hutchins *v.* Byrnes, 9 Gray, 367; Haven *v.* Adams, 4 Allen, 80; Crossman *v.* Hilltown, 5 Grant's cases, 225. But see Regents, &c. *v.* Detroit, &c. Society, 12 Mich. 138. Hatch *v.* Barr, 1 Ohio, 390. And some cases go even further. Thus in Georgia, a deed made by the president of a corporation in his own name, and signed A. B., president, with his seal affixed, was held the deed of the corporation. Johnson *v.* Crawley, 25 Ga. 316. In Arkansas, however, where any seal is required, it must be the corporate seal. State *v.* Allis, 18 Ark. 269. But a deed executed on behalf of a State by a public officer, duly authorized, is the deed of the State, although the officer be named in the deed, and signs his name and affixes his private seal. Sheets *v.* Selden's Lessee, 2 Wallace, 177. As to the mode of signature of instruments not under seal by agents, see Thompson *v.* Firgu R. R. Co., 36 Barb. 79; Haverhill, &c. Ins. Co. *v.* Newhall, 1 Allen, 130.

at least the analogy sufficiently explains their nature. They must not be repugnant to the charter or other laws of the land, and they must flow expressly or impliedly from the powers conferred in the charter, as the appropriate means of executing those powers.

6. Corporations cannot commit *crimes* or *forcible injuries*, though their members may. They cannot do any strictly personal act, as giving testimony and the like; and therefore, in chancery, a corporation answers under seal; or if an oath be required, one of the officers is personally made a defendant. But corporations may be liable for the acts or omissions of their officers or agents, as much as for their own contracts and undertakings; even though such acts should in themselves be trespasses. (*a*)

7. The individual members of a corporation are not personally liable for its *debts*, beyond the amount of their shares in the capital stock, unless expressly made so by statute, which is not usual. The capital stock may consist of personalty, or realty, or both; but their shares are treated as personalty. They are usually evidenced by *certificates*, specifying the amount paid in, which is called their par value. Sometimes these certificates are made transferable by indorsement; but generally the transfer is made on the books of the company. Corporate property cannot be made liable for the individual debts of the stockholders; but their shares may be so subjected by taking the proper steps. Frequently, provision is made that in case of mismanagement, to the injury of third persons, the directors shall be personally liable for the consequences; and sometimes all the stockholders are made thus liable. The latter, however, is not accounted good policy, because few persons would become stockholders upon such a condition; though the personal liability of the directors for mismanagement furnishes an important security against corruption or abuse. But in this State, by the act of 1842, not only the directors of all cor-

(*a*) Kerwhacker *v.* C. C. & C. R. R. Co., 3 Ohio State, 172; Keary *v.* C. C. & C. R. R. Co., 3 id. 201; C. C. & C. R. R. Co. *v.* Terry, 8 id. 570; St. Louis, A. & C. R. R. Co. *v.* Dalby, 19 Ill. 353. Municipal corporations are liable for injuries arising from the negligence of subordinate officers and agents acting under their authority and direction in constructing public improvements. The City of Dayton *v.* Pease, 4 Ohio State, 80. But counties are not liable for the official delinquencies of their commissioners. Hamilton County *v.* Mighels, 7 id. 109. But a municipal corporation will not be so liable when its officers are in the discharge of a governmental duty, as for the negligence of the police. Western Med. Col. *v.* Cleveland, 12 Ohio State, 375. Or of the fire department. Wheeler *v.* Cincinnati, 19 Ohio State, 19. A corporation may publish a libel so as to be liable for damages. Phil. Wil. & Balt. R. R. Co. *v.* Quigley, 21 How. 202; Whitfield *v.* South-Eastern R. R. Co., 1 Ellis, B. & E. 115; Maynard *v.* Fireman's Fund Ins. Co., 34 Cal. 48. Or for false imprisonment. Goff *v.* Great Northern R. R. Co., 3 Ellis & E. 672. It may do a malicious act, and will be liable for it. Green *v.* London Genl. Omnibus Co., 6 Jurist (N. S.), 228. It will be liable to exemplary damages where an individual would. Baltimore & Ohio R. R. Co. *v.* Blocher, 27 Md. 277; Jeffersonville R. R. Co. *v.* Rogers, 28 Ind. 1; Atlantic & G. W. R. R. Co. *v.* Dunn, 19 Ohio State, 162, 590. It may be liable for an assault and battery committed by one of its officers under its orders, but is not so liable where the violence used exceeded what was necessary to carry out its orders. St. Louis, A. & C. R. R. Co. *v.* Dalby, 19 Ill. 353.

porations, but also the stockholders of all corporations not charitable, if they be of age, are made jointly and severally liable, in their individual capacity, for all the debts of the corporation; and any transfer of stock made by them, with intent to avoid such liability, is declared to be void. (*a*) Judgment and execution are first to be had against the corporation; and if not satisfied, they may be made parties by *scire facias;* and if one of them pays the debt, he may enforce contribution from the rest.

§ 94. **Their Termination.** A corporation may be terminated in the five following ways: —

1. *By Statute.* This applies only to future private corporations, as before explained; for we have seen that the charters of pre-existing private corporations are contracts, which the legislature cannot alter or impair, without an express reservation of the right so to do. But public corporations, being under the exclusive direction of the legislature, are alterable or dissoluble at pleasure. Yet even here, if private rights have been legally acquired under these corporations, the legislature cannot impair them.

2. *By Efflux of Time.* Almost all charters are granted for a limited period; perpetual charters not being deemed expedient. When this period terminates, the corporation is of course dissolved, unless the legislature see fit to revive it; and no more of its original functions remain than are requisite for winding up its concerns.

3. *By Surrender.* The acceptance of a charter does not involve a positive obligation to continue it until its natural expiration. Whenever, therefore, the members desire it, they may surrender their charter, and thus terminate their corporate existence. It is said, however, that there must be a formal acceptance of the sur-

(*a*) By the constitution of 1852, the private liability of all corporators must be at least equal to the amount of stock they hold, and the statutes generally fix this minimum amount as their liability. And where an amendment imposes individual liability, neither the directors nor a majority of the stockholders can accept it so as to bind dissentients. We can only do this with reference to amendments which are reasonably within the original objects of the corporation and concern the corporate property. Ireland *v.* Palestine Turnpike Co., 19 Ohio State, 369. The personal liability of stockholders under the Ohio statutes is several, but is for the common benefit of all the creditors, and is not under the control of the corporation; but as between the stockholders it is to be proportioned to the amount of stock owned by each. Wright *v.* McCormack, 17 Ohio State, 86; Umsted *v.* Buskirk, 17 Ohio State, 113. {On principle and by the preponderance of authorities, corporators or stockholders, where the corporation was never legally formed, as where there was an omission to record the certificate, or other defect in formation or organization, are not liable as partners, because there was no intention to form a partnership, and no dealings with them as such. See, for example, Ward *v.* Bingham, 127 Mass. 24; Bank *v.* Hall, 35 Ohio State, 158. Even if the court granting corporate powers had no jurisdiction. Planters' &c. Bank *v.* Padgett, 69 Ga. 159. Or though their acts are *ultra vires.* Trowbridge *v.* Scudder, 11 Cush. 83. Those actually participating in the illegal acts knowingly may be liable personally. Stafford Bank *v.* Palmer, 47 Conn. 443; Ridenover *v.* Mayo, 40 Ohio State, 9; Medill *v.* Collier, 16 id. 599. But there are a number of cases holding stockholders of an inchoate or illegal corporation liable as partners, either generally or under certain circumstances. See 79 Mo. 401, 410; 12 N. J. Eq. 31; 35 Ark. 365; 57 N. Y. 23; 25 Minn. 229; 97 Penn. State, 493; 83 Ill. 197; 78 Ind. 344; 56 Iowa, 104; 4 Neb. 416. As to the effect of ouster, see Rowland *v.* Meader Furniture Co., 38 Ohio State, 269.}

render by the legislature; but unless some interests are to be affected, other than those of the corporators, it would seem as if there can be no good reason for requiring such acceptance. (*a*)

4. *By Death.* This does not apply to joint-stock corporations; because, if all the stockholders should die, the shares would pass to their personal representatives, and the corporation still continue; but with respect to charitable corporations the case is otherwise; these may be so constituted, for want of foresight in the charter, that the death of all the members would work a dissolution, for want of the means of keeping up the succession. Such a contingency should therefore be provided for in the charter.

5. *By Forfeiture.* (*b*) A forfeiture of the charter can only be enforced by judicial proceedings. The causes of forfeiture may be included under two heads, *misuser* and *non-user;* that is, an abuse of corporate powers, or a neglect to use them. Without any express provision in the charter, either of these, when judicially ascertained, will authorize a court to adjudge the charter forfeited. But the prudent course is to specify in the charter what causes shall create a forfeiture, and how their existence shall be ascertained. In this State, however, it is provided by the act of 1842, that any corporation, other than a bank, shall be considered as having forfeited its charter, if it shall become insolvent, or wrongfully refuse to pay its debts, or suspend its ordinary business for one year, or put in circulation any paper calculated to circulate as currency, or wilfully violate any provision of its charter or other law of the State. And in such a case, any creditor or stockholder, or the prosecuting attorney of the county, may apply to either of the courts sitting in chancery for an injunction to restrain such corporation from further exercising its functions; and receivers will be appointed to wind up its concerns.

When a corporation is dissolved in either of these ways, its debts are to be first paid; and the residue of its property being converted into money, is to be refunded to the stockholders; and

(*a*) Lanman *v.* Lebanon Valley R. R. Co., 30 Penn. State, 42. A majority of the stockholders of a corporation may dissolve it, but they cannot dispose of the interest of any stockholder in its assets without his consent. McCurdy *v.* Myers, 44 Penn. State, 535; *contra*, Currien *v.* Santini, 16 La. An. 27; Polar Star Lodge *v.* Polar Star Lodge, 16 La. An. 53.

(*b*) The State *v.* Seneca Co. Bank, 5 Ohio State, 171. The power of courts of chancery to direct the appropriation of the corporate property upon a forfeiture being declared, so as to secure the rights of creditors and stockholders, is affirmed in Bacon *v.* Robertson, 18 How. 480. The power to repeal a charter may be reserved absolutely to the legislature, and can then be exercised without any judicial proceeding. If reserved conditionally, as to be exercised upon some default or abuse of corporate powers, it is not yet settled whether the decision of the legislature upon the question of such default or abuse is conclusive on the courts; but it is at least to be presumed by them to be right. McLaren *v.* Pennington, 1 Paige, 102; De Camp *v.* Eveland, 19 Barb. 81; Crease *v.* Babcock, 23 Pick. 334; Miners' Bank *v.* U. S., 1 Greene (Iowa), 561; Erie & N. E. R. R. Co. *v.* Casey, 26 Penn. State, 287; Mobile & Ohio R. R. Co. *v.* The State, 29 Ala. 573. It has been lately held that under a provision to a charter that the legislature might, in case of misuser, resume the franchise of a corporation, the misuser must be first judicially ascertained. Baltimore *v.* Connellsville & S. P. R. R. Co., Am. Law R. for October, 1865. And see article on subject, 5 Am. Law R. (N. S.) 578.

to avoid all difficulty or doubt as to the power of thus winding up affairs, it is prudent to make special provision in the charter for such winding up. But in this State, by the act of 1842, there is a general provision, that on the dissolution of any corporation, unless other special provision be made, the directors or managers acting last before the dissolution shall be trustees with full power to wind up the concerns of such corporation. (*a*)

The view now presented of corporations, meagre and imperfect as its brevity has compelled it to be, exhibits, for your more detailed examination, an admirable invention of the law, for the concentration and perpetuation of human energies and interests. The most successful projects of personal enterprise are daily and hourly liable to interruption by death; and the more persons are concerned together, the greater is this liability; for when one of the association dies, the association itself is dissolved; the agents provided by law come in to settle up the concerns of the deceased, and the survivors wind up the concerns of the association. Thus the grandest projects may be stayed or frustrated in mid career. But to prevent this inconvenience; to take away the power of death and change; to give the association a more close, and stable, and permanent union, than the natural condition of man allows, the law steps in, with its salutary power, and bids the body corporate persevere in its operations, undisturbed by such chances and changes; and the artificial persons thus formed out of many, instead of being incumbered by its numbers, conduct operations with the same energy, simplicity, and unity, as a single individual. (*b*)

(*a*) See Allen *v.* Montgomery R. R. Co., 11 Ala. 437; Nevitt *v.* Bank of Port Gibson, 6 Sm. & Mar. 513; Macon & Western R. R. Co. *v.* Parker, 9 id. 377. In a suit against a defunct corporation, service of process upon the members of its last acting board of directors is sufficient under the statute to give the court jurisdiction. Warner *v.* Callender, 20 Ohio State, 190.

(*b*) In the great growth of corporations in this country, many corporations do business in States other than those from which they derive their charter; and these powers and rights in such cases are becoming pretty well defined and settled. In the first place, courts of one State will recognize foreign corporations by what is called *comity;* and will permit them to hold property, and transact business in other States, so far at least as is not inconsistent with the policy and laws of their own State. Newburg Petroleum Co. *v.* Weare, 27 Ohio State, 343. But when the State of Pennsylvania undertook to create a corporation and to endue it with great and varied powers, but denied it the right to do any act or hold any property within the State of Pennsylvania, the court of Kansas refused to recognize it as a corporation, declaring that the rules of comity could not extend to such a case. Land Grant Railway Co. *v.* Coffee Co., 6 Kansas, 245.

So, too, it is settled that a corporation is a citizen of the State creating it, within the meaning of the act conferring jurisdiction on the courts of the United States in suits between citizens of different States. Railway Co. *v.* Whitton, 13 Wall. 270; B. & O. R. R. *v.* Cary, 28 Ohio State, 208. But it is not such a citizen within the meaning of the clause which declares that the citizens of each State shall be entitled to all the privileges and immunities of citizens of the several States; and therefore the legislature of a State may impose upon foreign corporations, doing business within its limits, conditions and taxes more burdensome than are imposed on its own corporations of a similar class, though it could not do so in the case of individuals. West. Un. Tel. Co. *v.* Mayer, 28 Ohio State, 521; Ducat *v.* Chicago, 48 Ill. 172. The court there say that the right of a corporation created in one State to do business

LECTURE XIII.

PARTNERSHIPS. (*a*)

§ 95. **The Nature of Partnerships.** It is usual to treat of partnerships under the head of Contracts, because a partnership is created by contract. But I have thought the subject properly classed among personal relations. The relation between partners, like that between corporators, is a highly important business relation; and the strong analogy between these two relations suggests the propriety of discussing them consecutively. On the subject of partnerships, we have no local provisions. (*b*) The common law of the commercial world is our law; and the subject is one of vast compass and great practical importance. I shall present only a very general outline, and refer you for details to the authors mentioned in the note. Upon the general object of partnerships, I need only remark, that it is much the same as that of corporations; that is, the association of several persons for the prosecution of any enterprise or business. The reason why a partnership is not so efficient for this purpose as a corporation, will appear in the sequel.

and make contracts in the full enjoyment of its powers in another State, is a right based upon the comity between the States, and is a voluntary act of the sovereign power, but when contrary to good policy or prejudicial to the interest of the State, the comity ceases to be obligatory. See also the same case affirmed in the supreme court of the United States, 10 Wall. 410. But its powers and the validity of its acts must be tested by its charter and the laws of its domicile. Baltimore, &c. R. R. Co. *v.* Glenn, 28 Md. 287; Talmadge *v.* N. A. C. Co., 3 Head, 327. {A corporation created by the concurrent legislation of two States, each granting it the same charter, has a domicile in each State, and may transact its business in either. Bridge Co. *v.* Mayer, 31 Ohio State, 317.}

Many questions also grow out of the consolidation of companies, or the purchase of the rights of one by another. As to these cases, it has been held that the consolidated corporation possesses all the rights and is subject to all the duties of the other corporations, each as to the property acquired from it. Thus the consolidated corporation may use a patent axle-box, the right to use which had been acquired by both the old corporations. Lightner *v.* Boston, &c. R. R., 1 Lowell, 338. But where the charter of one of the old roads exempted the property from taxation, and of the other did not, the new corporation held the property of each road just in the same way and with the same exemptions as the old road held it. Tomlinson *v.* Branch, 15 Wall. 460. When a corporation having no limit on the rate of fare it could charge, bought a road that was limited, it could not in running over the purchased road exceed the charter limit. Campbell *v.* M. & C. R. R. Co., 23 Ohio State, 168; Shields *v.* State, 26 Ohio State, 86; s. c. 95 U. S. 319. See also Black *v.* Delaware, &c. Canal Co., 22 N. J. Eq. 130.

(*a*) See the 43d lecture of Kent; the treatises on partnership by Story, Collyer, Parsons, and Lindley, and Smith on Joint Interests.

(*b*) {We now have some local provisions, viz. a limited partnership act. R. S. § 3141 *et seq.* A right to sue and be sued in the firm name in case of domestic partnerships. R. S. § 5011. Service of summons in such cases, § 5042. Execution in such cases, § 5381. Making partners parties to judgment against some of them, § 5370. Administration of the estate of a deceased non-resident partner, § 6013.}

A partnership may be said to exist when two or more persons (*a*) contribute their property or services, to be employed jointly in some enterprise or business, the profit or loss of which is to be shared among them in some fixed proportion. This definition suggests five points to be noticed: *First,* a partnership is always the result of a contract, but the contract need not necessarily be in writing. The law will always imply a contract where the persons act as partners. *Secondly*, there may be any number of persons in the partnership; but in proportion as the number is increased, the operations become more unwieldy and inconvenient; which is not the case with corporations, on account of their entire legal unity. On the other hand, we sometimes see a single person doing business under a corporate name, to give greater consequence to his concern; but this is a mere deception. *Thirdly*, each partner must contribute something valuable to the partnership means; but this contribution may consist either of money, other property, credit, labor, or skill. Anything valuable, so as to found a claim to a share of the profits, will be sufficient to satisfy the legal requisition. (*b*) *Fourthly*, a partnership may be formed either for a single project or enterprise, or for an entire and continuous branch of business, or for business in general, including all the operations of the parties. And whether a given partnership is general or special, must be ascertained from the contract, or the facts from which the contract is implied. *Fifthly*, each partner must share in the profit or loss, in some stipulated ratio. But if no ratio be agreed upon, the law implies an equal ratio, however unequal the contributions may be; (*c*) it being against the policy of the law to go into an estimate of the values contributed, in order to make for the parties a bargain, when they have omitted to make one for themselves. But in all cases there must be a sharing of profit or loss. A mere salary, though it should vary according to the profits, would not make the receiver a partner. (*d*)

(*a*) A corporation cannot form a partnership with an individual. Whittenton Mills *v.* Upton, 10 Gray, 582; Marine Bank *v.* Ogden, 29 Ill. 248; Van Kuren *v.* Trenton, &c. Co., 2 Beasley, 302. {But this is not for any reason arising from the nature of partnerships, but from the nature of corporations; corporate liability should be created only by the acts of its directors or governing body, but if the corporation were allowed to become a partner its copartners could affix unlimited liability to it without knowledge of its officers. If a corporation has received power to become a partner there is nothing in the doctrine of partnership to prevent it. Butler *v.* Am. Toy Co., 46 Conn. 136. Or perhaps if its copartner has no control in the business. See Allen *v.* Woonsocket Co., 11 R. I. 288. Pooling arrangements between railroads having connecting lines are now never considered partnerships.}

(*b*) Ward *v.* Thompson, 22 How. 330.

(*c*) Turnipseed *v.* Goodwin, 9 Ala. 372; Stein *v.* Robertson, 30 Ala. 286; Farr *v.* Johnson, 25 Ill. 522; Moore *v.* Bare, 11 Iowa, 198; Griggs *v.* Clark, 23 Cal. 427; Murray *v.* Johnson, 1 Head, 353.

(*d*) Denny *v.* Cabot, 6 Met. 82; Bradley *v.* White, 10 id. 303; Vanderburgh *v.* Hull, 20 Wend. 70; Miller *v.* Bartlett, 15 S. & R. 137; Burckle *v.* Eckhart, 1 Denio, 337; S. C. 3 N. Y. 133; Choteau *v.* Raitt, 20 Ohio, 132; Gill *v.* Geyer, 15 Ohio State, 399; Berthold *v.* Goldsmith, 24 How. 536; Wheatcraft *v.* Hickman, 9 C. B. (N. S.) 47; Conklin *v.* Barton, 43 Barb. 435; Wood *v.* Vallette, 7 Ohio State, 172. {The old leading case of Waugh *v.* Carver, Smith's Lead. Cas., holding that participating in the profits

Such, then, are the elements of a partnership with respect to the partners themselves.

But, with respect to the rest of the world, a partnership may be held to exist, without uniting all these elements. If, for example, persons having no joint interest, which would constitute them partners with respect to each other, hold themselves out to the world as partners, the law will hold them liable as partners. (*a*) And on the other hand, if persons not appearing to the world as partners, have nevertheless a secret joint interest in fact, such as would constitute them partners, the law will hold them liable to the world as partners. (*b*) Indeed, it is a general rule in the law of partnership, that no secret arrangement among partners, varying their general rights and liabilities with respect to each other, can affect their general liability with respect to third persons, unless made known beforehand. Without such a principle, partnerships might be a cloak for fraud and deception. But by holding partners responsible for the general aspect they assume before the world, and for attempting to conceal from the world the actual state of their relations, the ends of justice are effectually promoted. Thus you will perceive, that, in studying the law of partnerships, they are to be contemplated in two distinct aspects: the one embracing the mutual relations of the partners to each other; and the other, their joint relation to the rest of the world.

It is usual, in forming a partnership, to agree upon some *name* or *style*, under which all the business of the firm is to be transacted, and which each of the partners is authorized to use for that purpose. This name may or may not specify the names of all the partners; or it may not truly specify any of them; but, in either case, all the partners in fact will be bound by it; and if no name be agreed upon among the partners, a partner may act in the name of himself and company, and bind the firm. But here we see an important difference between a partnership and a corporation. The partnership name, though sufficient for many purposes, is not

as such constituted a partnership independent of the intention of the parties is now wholly overthrown in England, and} the later English cases hold the true test to be, that the business is really carried on on behalf of the party sought to be charged as principal and not as agent, and that participation in the profits, though a circumstance to show that fact, is not conclusive. Cox *v.* Hickman, 8 H. L. C. 268; Kilshaw *v.* Jukes, 3 B. & S. 847; Bullen *v.* Sharp, L. R. 1 C. P. 86; Holme *v.* Hammond, 7 Ex. 218 {Mollwo, March, & Co. *v.* Court of Wards, L. R. 4 C. P. 419. These cases are deeply influencing the law in this country, and although their doctrine is far from universal, yet it is never mentioned by our courts without praise, and has been already expressly and fully adopted in Arkansas, Michigan, Montana, New Hampshire, Ohio, Pennsylvania, Rhode Island, and West Virginia, to which might be added *dicta* in New Jersey, Illinois, Missouri, Iowa, and Tennessee. New York professes not to have adopted the doctrine, but her latest cases, for example, Cassidy *v.* Hall, 97 N. Y. 159, show a great and increasing departure from her early cases. See Bates' Limited Partnership, p. 67}.

(*a*) {This statement must be modified somewhat. A person is a partner by holding out, on the ground of estoppel; hence it is not holding out to the world strictly, but a holding out to the person deceived by the appearance of partnership that creates the liability. See Thompson *v.* First National Bank, 111 U. S. 529.}

(*b*) Fitch *v.* Harrington, 13 Gray, 468.

sufficient for all. In prosecuting and defending suits, conveying real estate, executing instruments under seal, and perhaps in some other transactions, it is necessary to use the names of all the partners; (*a*) and if they be very numerous, this may be no small inconvenience. However, these are exceptions to the general rule; which is, that the partnership name is sufficient for partnership purposes. Would it not be a salutary change, to provide by statute that the partnership name should be sufficient for all purposes? (*b*) And would it not be well, in all cases, to require partners to record the names of the members of the firm in some public place, to which all persons interested might have access? (*c*) The general interest of the community may be prejudiced, but cannot be promoted, by permitting concealment in these important matters.

§ 96. **The Capital Stock.** (*d*) This may consist of personalty, realty, or both. It includes that which is originally contributed, and the subsequent additions and accumulations. Each partner has a joint interest in the capital stock, whatever be its specific character; the extent of which interest depends upon the agreement among the partners. But what you are to observe is, that the interest is a *joint one in the whole*, and not a separate one in any particular part. It cannot be severed and made exclusive, so that one partner can claim any specific portion as his own, until all the partnership concerns have been settled, and a division made, either by mutual consent, or the intervention of a court.

(*a*) {This statement must now be modified. Statutes allowing suits in the partnership name are adopted in many States. And as to sealed instruments it is no longer necessary anywhere to use the names of all the partners, provided all have authorized or subsequently ratified the sealing of the instrument, except where the nature of the transaction requires it, as in the case of a conveyance of real estate, for the laws of conveyancing render necessary the use of the name of each partner in whom the title is.}

(*b*) By R. S. § 5011, partnerships in Ohio formed to carry on business in this State, or holding property therein, may sue or be sued in the firm name, but the partners must give security for costs, and the petition in an action brought under this statute must aver the facts necessary to show that the statute applies. Haskins *v.* Alcott, 13 Ohio State, 210; many other States have similar statutes.

(*c*) {This is required in one or two States; e. g. California. It was enacted in Ohio for a short time by the act of 1884 (81 Laws, 131), which was repealed in 1886 (83 Laws, 38).}

(*d*) The real estate of a partnership, purchased with its funds and to carry out its purposes, or taken for debts due to it, is treated as personal property. But as between the personal representative and the heirs of a deceased partner, the surplus remaining after the payment of the debts of the firm and his liabilities to it will be treated as real estate. Dyer *v.* Clark, 5 Met. 562; Hoxie *v.* Carr, 1 Sumner, 173; Buchan *v.* Sumner, 2 Barb. Ch. 165; Goodburn *v.* Stevens, 5 Gill, 1; Sumner *v.* Hampson, 8 Ohio, 328, 364; Rammelsburg *v.* Mitchell, 29 Ohio State, 22; Tillinghurst *v.* Champlin, 4 R. I. 173; Cilley *v.* Huse, 40 N. H. 358; Matlack *v.* James, 2 Beasley, 126; Buffum *v.* Buffum, 49 Maine, 108; Willis *v.* Freeman, 35 Vt. 44; Fowler *v.* Bailey, 14 Wis. 125; Ensign *v.* Briggs, 6 Gray, 329; Wilcox *v.* Wilcox, 13 Allen, 252 {*i. e.* the surplus goes to heirs and is subject to dower. This rule is almost universal in the United States. The English decisions are conflicting, but the preponderance is against this rule, holding that the surplus goes to personal representatives and not to heirs}. And real estate not purchased with partnership funds, but which, according to the agreement of the parties, is to be considered personal property, will be so considered in a court of equity. Ludlow *v.* Cooper, 4 Ohio State, 1.

For technical reasons, the law makes some distinction between realty and personalty, which will be better understood when we come to speak of *tenants in common*, in the lectures on property. But a court of chancery will treat both alike, whenever this is necessary to protect the rights of third persons; as in case of death or insolvency.

§ 97. **Authority of each Partner.** (*a*) The general rule is, that by the mere formation of a partnership, without any special agreement for that purpose, each partner becomes an *agent* for the whole firm, with authority to do in the firm name whatever the whole firm could do, *within the regular scope of partnership business.* But this authority extends only to what comes fairly within the partnership design; and beyond this the firm are not bound by the acts of one of the partners, because the world have no right to presume an authority any further. Within this general limit, the firm are bound with respect to the world, even though the act should be contrary to an express stipulation among themselves; because the world are not presumed to know of any secret limitation. If, however, a third person can be charged with actual knowledge of such limitation, then the rule ceases, because the reason ceases. The only difficulty in applying this general rule is, to determine what is within the general scope of partnership business. This is a question of fact, depending chiefly on the nature of the business. (*b*) But, in general terms, the power of a partner to bind the firm embraces the purchase and sale of property, the collection, payment, and release of debts, and the making of all contracts required in the partnership business. (*c*) The leading exceptions are these: One partner cannot, without special authority, pledge the property or credit of the firm for matters unconnected with their business; nor bind the firm by a guaranty of the credit of a third person; (*d*) nor execute a deed in the name of the firm for the conveyance of real property. (*e*) These are

(*a*) 3 Kent, Com. 40–52.

(*b*) {That is, the nature of the business as reasonably necessary or as usually conducted by similar firms in that locality. Irwin *v.* Williar, 110 U. S. 499, 505.}

(*c*) One partner has power to compromise and release a claim due to the partnership, and payment to him will be good, although notice has been given to the debtor by the other partners not to pay, unless all are present {for otherwise each partner could render it impossible for third persons to pay any debt to the firm}. But *quære*, whether it would be safe to enter into an executory contract with one partner in the name of the firm, after notice by the other partners of their dissent. Noyes *v.* N. H., N. L. & S. R. R. Co., 30 Conn. 1. This right continues, even after dissolution, unless there be some agreement to the contrary. Robbins *v.* Fuller, 24 N. Y. 570; Granger *v.* McGilvra, 24 Ill. 152.

(*d*) Sweetser *v.* French, 2 Cush. 309; Andrews *v.* Planters' Bank, 9 Sm. & Mar. 192; Langan *v.* Hewett, 13 id. 122; Gano *v.* Samuel, 14 Ohio, 592.

(*e*) Or any other sealed instrument. 3 Kent, Com. 47; McNaughten *v.* Partridge, 11 Ohio, 223. Seals are now abolished in many States. See § 171, note. But he may bind his copartner if he signs the deed in his presence and with his authority. Ball *v.* Dunsterville, 4 T. R. 313. So a previous parol authority, or a subsequent parol ratification, will make the deed good. Cady *v.* Shepherd, 11 Pick. 400; Smith *v.* Kerr, 3 N. Y. 144; Purviance *v.* Sutherland, 2 Ohio State, 478. One partner may sell the whole stock at a single trade. Arnold *v.* Brown, 24 Pick. 93; Whether one partner only the leading cases and exceptions. To give details, would carry me too far for my limits. What I have said will illustrate the general rule, and that is all I design.

§ 98. **Partnership Liabilities.** We have seen that the stockholders of a corporation, unless the contrary be provided in the charter, are not personally liable for the debts or undertakings of the corporation, beyond the amount of their shares in the capital stock; but the reverse prevails with respect to partnerships. By the common law, there is no such limited responsibility; and each partner is personally liable for all the partnership debts and undertakings. To limit this liability, a special statute is necessary. In some of the States, such provision has been made, and *limited partnerships* are permitted, whereby a partner may put into the concern a given amount of capital, and by making public record of the fact, may exempt himself from liability beyond that amount. Such provisions are deemed highly beneficial; because they take away the fear which often withholds capitalists from employing their means in this way. But as we have no such law, there can be no limited liability here; (*a*) and if the partnership means are unequal to the liabilities, the deficiency must be made up by the individual partners. The course of proceeding is this: The first claim upon the partnership fund is that of the partnership creditors. When they are satisfied, the next claim is that of the individual partners, to whom the firm may be indebted. If a surplus still remain, the creditors of an individual partner may reach his share, when ascertained; but if the partnership funds have been exhausted, without paying all the partnership debts, the unsatisfied partnership creditors have the same right to be paid out of the separate means of one of the partners, as his private creditors have; there being no preference in such cases. (*b*)

can make an assignment of all the partnership property to pay its debts is not settled. Anderson *v.* Tompkins, 1 Brock. 456; Harrison *v.* Sterry, 5 Cranch, 300; Havens *v.* Hussey, 5 Paige, 30; Kirby *v.* Ingersoll, 1 Doug. (Mich.) 477; Hayes *v.* Hayer, 4 Sandf. Ch. 485; Halstead *v.* Shepard, 23 Ala. 558; Wetter *v.* Schlieper, 4 E. D. Smith, 707; Sheldon *v.* Smith, 28 Barb. 593; Lasell *v.* Tucker, 5 Sneed, 33; Ormsbee *v.* Davis, 5 R. I. 442. Wells *v.* March, 30 N. Y. 344; Coope *v.* Bowles, 42 Barb. 87; Palmer *v.* Myers, 43 Barb. 509. One partner cannot legally confess judgment so as to bind the firm. Shedd *v.* Bank of Brattleborough, 32 Vt. 709; York Bank's Appeal, 56 Penn. State, 458; Remington *v.* Cummings, 5 Wis. 138; Edwards *v.* Pitzer, 12 Iowa, 608; North *v.* Mudge, 13 Iowa, 496. Nor can a partner submit a partnership claim to arbitration. Martin *v.* Thrasher, 40 Vt. 460.

(*a*) {*Contra* now, R. S. §§ 3141 *et seq.* Limited partnerships are now provided for in Upper Canada and in the District of Columbia, and in every State and organized territory of the United States, except Arizona, Idaho, and New Mexico.} See the recently published treatise of Bates on Limited Partnerships.

(*b*) Grosvenor *v.* Austin, 6 Ohio, 103; Allen *v.* Wells, 22 Pick. 450; Bardwell *v.* Perry, 19 Vt. 292. As to the English rule, see 3 Kent, Com. 65 and note. The act of Feb. 27, 1846, provides a mode whereby the individual property of the partners may be reached to satisfy the debts of the firm after the partnership property has been exhausted. The respective rights of the joint and separate creditors of a partnership have recently undergone elaborate discussion in Ohio. Where there are joint and separate assets for distribution in equity, the joint assets are first to be applied to the payment of the partnership debts, and the separate assets to the payment of the private debts, and in each case the surplus is to be applied to the payment of the other

§ 99. **Partnership Remedies.** Of remedies in general, I am to speak in the sixth part of these lectures; but the relations of partners, in this respect, are so peculiar, that a few words on the subject will be proper here. One partner cannot sue the firm at law for a debt due by them to him, because, in so doing, he would have to sue himself, as one of the firm. For the same reason, if one person be a member of two distinct firms, neither firm can sue the other. (*a*) Again, one partner cannot sue the rest of the firm for his share of a debt due by the firm to him; because, until the business is closed by dissolution, the joint interest cannot be thus severed. In all such cases, therefore, the only remedy is in *chancery*, which can rise above these technical difficulties. (*b*) But one partner may sue another for a breach of the partnership agreement, because this supposes the partnership at an end; and for any matter not growing out of the partnership, of course partners have the same remedies as other persons. (*c*) When the litigation

class. Rodgers *v.* Meranda, 7 Ohio State, 179; Brock *v.* Bateman, 25 id. 609. See Howe *v.* Lawrence, 9 Cush. 553; Somerset Potter Works *v.* Minot, 10 id. 592; 1 Parsons's Cont. 180. Crooker *v.* Crooker, 46 Maine, 250; Pohlman *v.* Graves, 26 Ill. 405; Hill *v.* Beach, 1 Beasley, 31; Matlack *v.* James, 2 Beasley, 126; Black's Appeal, 44 Penn. State, 503; Holton *v.* Holton, 40 N. H. 77; Treadwell *v.* Brown, 41 N. H. 12; Moline, &c. Co. *v.* Webster, 26 Ill. 233. The joint creditors of a partnership have not, as such creditors, any specific lien on the assets of the firm; and their right to enforce the application of the joint property to the payment of their claims can only be worked out through the equities of the partners, and it terminates when these equities are gone. The firm, while in the possession of such property, although unable to pay its firm debts, may sell it, or, by the consent of all the members of the firm, appropriate it to the payment of a separate debt of one of the partners. But where a firm is dissolved, and its property divided between the partners, the individual members cannot, in contemplation of insolvency, make an assignment of their property, both individual and that derived from the firm, for the benefit of the individual creditors to the exclusion of the firm creditors. Gwin *v.* Selby, 5 Ohio State, 96; Miller *v.* Estill, 5 id. 508; Sigler *v.* Knox County Bank, 8 id. 511. See Hubbard *v.* Curtis, 8 Clark (Iowa), 1; Thompson *v.* Frist, 15 Md. 24; Wintersmith *v.* Pointer, 2 Met. (Ky.) 457; Backus *v.* Murphy, 29 Penn. State, 397. As to the rights of a private creditor in levying upon or attaching a partner's interest in the property of the firm, see 1 Parsons's Cont. pp. 174, 179; Place *v.* Sweetzer, 16 Ohio, 142. The interest of a private partner in a firm can be levied upon under a judgment obtained by a private creditor. The levy must be made upon the undivided interest of the debtor partner, and the purchaser at sheriff's sale will only acquire his actual beneficial interest in the property sold. The creditor may, however, at any time before the sale, file a bill against the other partners for an account to ascertain the beneficial interest of the debtor partner, and have such interest subjected to the payment of his debt. The latter mode is, of course, preferable, as under the former it is difficult to find purchasers, on account of the uncertainty of the interest sold. Nixon *v.* Nash, 12 Ohio State, 647; Claggett *v.* Kilbourn, 1 Black, 346; Wiles *v.* Maddox, 26 Mo. 77; Haskins *v.* Everett, 4 Sneed, 531. {This subject is involved in many difficulties, owing to the hardships to the other partners necessarily attendant on any plan of subjecting a partner's interest; and each State has its own way of proceeding in such cases.}

(*a*) Englis *v.* Furniss, 21 E. D. Smith, 587.

(*b*) {These difficulties are more than technical. The technical difficulty is that the plaintiff partner appears also as a defendant, but the substantial difficulty is that the partner who is creditor of the firm to-day may be its debtor to-morrow. The fluctuations of trade and the uncertainty of uncollected debts are constantly altering the relative positions of the partners, and a multiplicity of suits would result on allowing one to sue the rest before dissolution and ascertainment of balances.}

(*c*) A suit at law may be maintained for a breach of partnership articles, where the business of the partnership has not been commenced. Vance *v.* Blair, 18 Ohio, 532. See Bailey *v.* Starke, 1 English (Ark.), 191. After the dissolution of the partnership is between a partnership and third persons, all the firm must sue or be sued jointly, and not separately; because the right or liability is always joint and not separate. And when a judgment has been obtained against the firm, a court of chancery will compel the creditor to exhaust the firm property, before proceeding against that of the individual partners. In like manner, when a judgment has been recovered against an individual partner, chancery will compel the creditor to exhaust his private property before he can proceed against his ultimate share in the property of the firm, which can only be ascertained on a final adjustment of accounts. From these remarks, it will be seen that whenever partners are concerned in litigation, the remedies in chancery are much more efficacious than those at law. (*a*)

§ 100. **Termination of Partnerships.** When a partnership embraces only a single transaction, it is of course at an end when that is completed. When it is created for an indefinite period, either of the parties may dissolve it at pleasure, unless there be an agreement that a certain notice shall be given; in which case the agreement must be complied with. In some cases, also, where a sudden dissolution would produce great injury, chancery will interfere by injunction to prevent it, even though there be no agreement as to notice; but when the partnership is for a definite period, it must continue through that period, unless all the partners agree to a dissolution, or some one of the following causes intervenes to effect a dissolution: 1. The *death* of one of the partners always works a dissolution; for his representatives cannot come in as partners, except by special consent. (*b*) All they succeed to is the share belonging to the deceased partner, to be ascertained on final settlement of accounts down to the time of his death. And the duty of winding up affairs devolves upon the surviving partners; for the representatives of the deceased have no power to act in the matter, and can neither sue nor be sued on account of partnership concerns. (*c*) 2. The *insanity* of a partner, though it does not of itself work a dissolution, will authorize a court of chancery to decree a dissolution. 3. If a single woman be a part-

and the payment of its debts, one partner may sue the other to recover a balance due. Sykes *v.* Work, 6 Gray, 433. See Robinson *v.* Green, 5 Harring. 115; McKnight *v.* McCutcheon, 27 Mo. 436.

(*a*) 1 Story, Eq. Jur. ch. xv.

(*b*) A partner may provide in his will that the partnership shall continue after his death, and in that case the liability of his estate is deemed limited to the funds embarked in it, unless otherwise expressly stated by him. Burwell *v.* Mandeville, 2 How. 560.

(*c*) Gray *v.* Palmer, 9 Cal. 616; Marlatt *v.* Scantland, 19 Ark. 443; Budow *v.* Mutual Savings Inst. 28 Mo. 181. A sole surviving partner has the entire legal title to all the partnership assets. He has a right, acting honestly and with reasonable discretion and diligence, to dispose of them as he pleases, to settle all debts against the firm, to make any compromise he may deem necessary, and to turn the assets into an available and distributable form. Barry *v.* Briggs, 22 Mich. 201; Adams *v.* Ward, 26 Ark. 135. As to his powers and duties where instructed by the will of the deceased to carry on the business, and what disbursements will be allowed him, see Tillotson *v.* Tillotson, 34 Conn. 335.

ner, her subsequent *marriage* will work a dissolution, because by marriage she loses the legal capacity of acting. 4. When the object of a partnership becomes utterly *impracticable*, a court of chancery will decree a dissolution. 5. A *war* between the different nations to which partners belong, works a dissolution, on the principle before stated, that a war between two nations disqualifies the citizens of those nations from holding intercourse with each other. 6. It has also been held that the *voluntary transfer* by one partner of all his interest to a third person amounts to a dissolution; since no partner can introduce a stranger into the concern. But this is an unreasonable rule, because it puts it in the power of a partner to dissolve at any time, against the will of the rest. The just rule would be to hold the transfer void. 7. A very strong case of *imbecility*, *fraud*, or *misconduct* in one of the partners, will induce a court of chancery to decree a dissolution. 8. Where a bankrupt law exists, the *bankruptcy* either of the whole concern or of one of the partners will effect a dissolution. And the same would be the result under our insolvent law, where an assignment is made to the commissioner. 9. Where one of the partners is an *infant*, he may dissolve the firm on becoming of age, as he may disaffirm any other contract. (*a*) The result of a dissolution is, that the authority of each partner to bind the firm ceases, unless it be continued, by special agreement, for winding up the concern, (*b*) but all the existing liabilities continue; and if those who have before dealt with the firm are not specially notified of the dissolution, a dishonest partner may still involve the firm in new liabilities to them; (*c*) for as to them, a mere advertisement of dissolution is not sufficient, unless it can be shown that they knew it. But as to all others, an advertisement is sufficient. (*d*) When

(*a*) {But the firm's assets must be devoted to paying the firm's creditors, notwithstanding such disaffirmance; that is, the infant's personal liability *in solido* only is avoided.}

(*b*) This must be limited to binding the firm in new business. After dissolution, neither partner can renew the firm notes, or incur any new responsibilities, without the consent of the others. Palmer *v.* Dodge, 4 Ohio State, 21; Bacon *v.* Hutchings, 5 Bush, 525; Montague *v.* Reakirt, 6 Bush, 323. But he may do whatever is necessary to collect debts due the partnership, and to adjust, settle, and pay its debts. Admissions by him as to the balance of account between the firm and persons dealing with it, are admissible to charge his partners. Feigley *v.* Whitaker, 22 Ohio State, 606. But see Thompson *v.* Bowman, 6 Wall. 316.

(*c*) Wardwell *v.* Haight, 2 Barb. 549; Hutchins *v.* Bank of Tennessee, 8 Humph. 418; Pitcher *v.* Barrows, 17 Pick. 361. Merrit *v.* Pollys, 16 B. Monr. 355; Clapp *v.* Rogers, 2 Kernan, 283; Brown *v.* Clark, 14 Penn. State, 469; Pope *v.* Risley, 23 Mo. 185. Little *v.* Clark, 36 Penn. State, 114; Williamson *v.* Fox, 38 Penn. State, 214; Chamberlain *v.* Dow, 10 Mich. 319. Whether the publication of such a notice in a paper, shown to be taken by the plaintiff, is evidence from which notice to them may be inferred by the jury, is a question upon which the authorities are at variance. Treadwell *v.* Wells, 4 Cal. 260; Page *v.* Brant, 18 Ill. 37; Reilly *v.* Smith, 16 La. An. 31. It is not. Zoller *v.* Janvrin, 47 N. H. 324. But a dormant partner is not liable, after retirement, to a creditor who never knew he was a partner. Grosvenor *v.* Lloyd, 1 Met. 19; Davis *v.* Allen, 3 N. Y. 168.

(*d*) {And necessary, — the theory being that those who have known of the firm by actual dealings with it are entitled to actual notice of its dissolution, to terminate the liability of each partner for the acts of another partner; but as to those who have a the dissolution is decreed by a court of chancery, a *receiver* is usually appointed to settle up the business. In all cases of a voluntary dissolution, a partner may insist upon a sale of the joint stock, for the purpose of settlement, unless a division can be agreed upon. The principles of settlement have already been stated.

The view now taken of the law of partnerships, though a mere synopsis, enables us to form an opinion upon the comparative advantages of the two kinds of associations, corporations, and partnerships; and we can hardly hesitate in giving the preference to corporations. Their ability to do all acts in the corporate name without specifying the members; their independence of the death or transfer of interest among the members; and the liability of the members only to the extent of their respective interests, are three points in which corporations have decidedly the advantage of partnerships. Yet in the common transactions of life, and more particularly in the commercial world, partnerships are deemed to answer all the purposes of association; and are much more numerous than corporations. Nor can you have failed to remark, that the law of partnership, as above explained, is pre-eminently liberal and just in its principles. Probably no branch of the law deserves a higher encomium for these qualities.

LECTURE XIV.

HUSBAND AND WIFE. (*a*)

§ 101. **Condition of Females compared with Males.** Having treated of the two principal business relations, we come now to

general knowledge of the firm, the general notice by advertisement is necessary, being the only notice possible. Actual notice is, of course, as valid as advertisement. And a publicity otherwise than by advertisement is equally valid in theory, but impossible in practice.}

(*a*) On the subject of Husband and Wife, see 2 Kent, Com. lec. 26, 27, 28; 1 Black. Com. ch. 25; 1 Swift, ch. 5; Reeves's Domestic Relations; Bishop on Marriage and Divorce; Schouler's Domestic Relations; Bishop's Law of Married Women; Wells' Separate Property of Married Women. Since the text was written, we have had some legislation in favor of the wife. By the act of 1846, with a legislative construction in 1847, the wife's realty, whether hers before marriage, or acquired after by devise, gift, inheritance, or purchase with her means, whether the legal title be in her or held in trust for her, cannot be subjected to the payment of the husband's debts; but she may unite with him in a valid conveyance. And the same is true with respect to any *chose in action*, demand, legacy, or bequest of the wife, unless so reduced to possession as to become his property; and also with respect to all furniture and household goods not provided by him. They are all exempted from liability for his debts during the life of the wife, and the heirs of her body. On the construction of this act, see Jenney *v.* Gray, 5 Ohio State, 45. Also, by the act of 1847, with respect to life insurances, the husband may insure his life for the benefit of his wife or children, and such insurance shall be exempt from liability for his debts, where the annual premium does not exceed $150; and when it does exceed that sum, a proportional part shall be so exempted. If she what are called the *domestic relations*. These are four; namely, *husband and wife*, *parent and child*, *guardian and ward*, and *master and servant*, each of which will form the subject of one lecture. To say that the law which regulates these relations is of the highest practical interest, would be to assert a mere truism. Every person, whether lawyer or not, ought to be familiar with this part of the law. We have a few statutory provisions on the subject, but, for the most part, the law of husband and wife is common law, and you will find that it savors of its origin in all its leading features. The whole theory is a slavish one, compared even with the civil law. I do not hesitate to say, by way of arousing your attention to the subject, that the law of husband and wife, as you gather it from the books, is a disgrace to any civilized nation. I do not mean to say that females are degraded in point of fact; I only say that the *theory of the law* degrades them almost to the level of slaves. With regard to *political rights*, females form a positive exception to the general doctrine of equality. They have no part or lot in the formation or administration of government. They cannot vote, nor hold office. We require them to contribute their share in the way of taxes, to the support of government, but allow them no voice in its direction. We hold them amenable to the laws when made, but allow them no share in making them. This language, applied to males, would be the exact definition of political slavery; applied to females, custom does not teach us so to regard it. Perhaps it would be difficult to deduce from any abstract reasoning, the justice of making this their political condition. But we know that it always has been what it now is, and there is no prospect of changing it; and probably the most refined and enlightened of that sex would be the last to desire a change which would involve them in the turmoil of politics. As to *legal rights*, the case is different. So long as a woman remains single in this country, her legal rights and capacities are not inferior to those of a man. I say in this country, for in England, the laws of inheritance give males altogether the advantage. With some trifling exceptions, the son or brother takes all, to the entire disinheritance of the daughter or sister. The glaring injustice of this rule of inheritance, which prefers males to females, is so palpable, that we can claim little credit for having totally abolished it. If either sex is to be preferred, it certainly ought to be females, because they are least able to make their way in poverty through the world. But our law stops at the point of perfect equality, and women inherit precisely as men. Also, in general, so far as relates to the acquisition, control, and transfer or transmission of prop-

dies before him, the benefit enures to her children. Also, by the wills act of 1852, it is questionable whether, if there be no children, the husband can, by will, place his personalty beyond the reach of his widow, any more than dower, if she elects not to take under the will. This question is removed by an amendment to this act, passed March 10, 1860, declaring that if the widow does not elect to take under the will, she shall receive her dower and such share of the personalty as she would have been entitled to, had her husband died intestate leaving children.

erty, single women stand on the same footing as men. They can make the same contracts and perform the same legal acts. In a word, the general rule is, that the legal competency of a single woman, or *feme sole*, as she is technically called, is the same as that of a man, and in some few particulars, perhaps, she may be considered as having the advantage. She attains her majority here at eighteen, (*a*) he at twenty-one. She can choose her guardian at twelve; he at fourteen. She can marry at fourteen; he at eighteen. In a word, the law considers her as arriving at maturity three or four years earlier than he does. Again, in relation to civil arrests, she has a peculiar privilege. In this State, no female can be arrested for debt; and in this exemption, she is named in company with the officers and soldiers of the revolution. This exemption does not, of course, embrace criminal matters. But when a woman marries, we call her condition *coverture*, and speak of her as a *feme covert*. The old writers call the husband *baron*, and sometimes, in plain English, *lord*. In fact, the scene is now entirely changed. The merging of her name in that of her husband is emblematic of the fate of all her legal rights. The theory is, that marriage makes the husband and wife one person, and that person is the husband. He is the substantive and she the adjective. In a word, there is scarcely a legal act of any description which she is competent to perform. The common reason assigned for this legal disfranchisement of the wife is, that there may be an indissoluble union of interests between the parties. In other words, lest the wife might be sometimes tempted to assert rights in opposition to her husband, the law humanely divests her of rights. For the arguments by which this doctrine is vindicated, I must refer you to the books. It is my province to state what the law is, and not to justify it.

§ 102. **Marriage.** Marriage, whatever may be the popular idea of it, is regarded by the law as merely a civil contract. We have not even ecclesiastical courts to take cognizance of it. I shall treat the subject in the order of events.

1. *Matters preceding Marriage.* When parties have agreed to marry, or done any acts from which such agreement can be inferred, and one of them afterwards refuses, a court of chancery cannot, as in ordinary cases, compel a specific performance; but either party may sue the other at law, for a *breach of promise;* and very heavy damages are often recovered in such suits. (*b*)

(*a*) See Stevenson *v.* Westfall, 18 Ill. 209.

(*b*) The defence of bad character or criminal conduct on the part of the plaintiff, if not sustained, may be considered in aggravation of damages. Southard *v.* Rexford, 6 Cow. 254. Whether seduction of the plaintiff may be shown in aggravation of damages, is a question on which the authorities are not agreed. Paul *v.* Frazier, 3 Mass. 73; Conn *v.* Wilson, 2 Overton (Tenn.), 233; Perkins *v.* Hersey, 1 R. I. 493; Baldy *v.* Stratton, 11 Penn. State, 316; Wells *v.* Padgett, 8 Barb. 324; King *v.* Kersey, 2 Carter (Ind.), 402; Goodall *v.* Thurman, 1 Head (Tenn.), 209. It may be so shown. Sherman *v.* Rawson, 102 Mass. 395; Kelley *v.* Riley, 106 Mass. 339; Sauer *v.* Schulenberg, 33 Md. 288. It is a good defence that the plaintiff fraudulently concealed the fact that she had had a bastard child. Bell *v.* Eaton, 28 Ind. 468. An express

But if the parties intend to consummate their agreement, there are some preliminary arrangements frequently made, to obviate the helpless condition in which the law places the wife during marriage. These are chiefly two, *jointures* and *settlements*, (*a*) both made for the benefit of the wife. A jointure is the separate provision made by the husband for the wife's support. A settlement is the separate provision made by the parents or friends of the wife for her support. These may indeed be made after marriage, but they are usually made before. (*b*) The method is to place the portion set apart for the wife under the control of trustees, who manage it, independently of the husband, for the benefit of the wife, and perhaps for the issue of the marriage. And the propriety and importance of making such arrangements will be obvious, when we come to speak of the authority which the husband exercises over the whole property, when not thus placed beyond his reach. If it be called generosity in the husband, in anticipation of some possible reverse of fortune, to provide a sure support for his wife in the day of adversity, by placing some portion of his property for her separate use beyond the control of himself or his creditors, it must be considered a sacred duty in the parent to take this precaution. And when we daily see the distress which might thus easily have been prevented, we cannot but wonder that these arrangements are not more frequently made.

2. *Who may Marry.* By our law, all male persons of eighteen and upwards, and all females of fourteen and upwards, not being nearer of kin than first cousins, (*c*) are capable of marrying. But

promise to marry need not be proved, and the promise may be implied from indirect evidence. Wightman *v.* Coates, 15 Mass. 1; Perkins *v.* Hersey, *supra*; Hoitt *v.* Moulton, 1 Foster (N. H.), 586; Waters *v.* Bristol, 26 Conn. 398. The acts and declarations of the woman are admissible in a suit brought by her to prove her acceptance of an offer of marriage. Wetmore *v.* Mell, 1 Ohio State, 26. {This case is denied, however, in Russell *v.* Cowles, 15 Gray, 582.} Moritz *v.* Methorn, 13 Penn. State, 331; Thurston *v.* Cavenor, 8 Clarke (Iowa), 155.

(*a*) See Atherly on Marriage Settlements.

(*b*) Where a post-nuptial agreement is made between husband and wife, by which property is set apart for her separate use, the agreement, although void in law, will be sustained in equity, unless the rights of creditors interfere. Wood *v.* Warden, 20 Ohio, 518. Thomas *v.* Brown, 10 Ohio State, 247. An ante-nuptial contract entered into in another country, according to its laws, by which the husband, for a valuable consideration, agreed that all the property of the wife then owned by her, and all the property which they might mutually acquire during coverture, should be her property, is not contrary to the policy of the laws of Ohio, and will be enforced in its courts against the husband's creditors. Scherferling *v.* Huffman, 4 Ohio State, 241. An ante-nuptial agreement, securing to the wife her separate property, except so far as she is specially restrained thereby, gives her full power to dispose of the same; and a gift to her husband may be presumed where she passes money to her husband, who, with her consent, invests it in lands, and takes the title in his own name. Hardy *v.* Van Harlingen, 7 Ohio State, 208. It must be shown affirmatively that all the terms of an ante-nuptial contract favorable to the wife have been fully complied with, or an ante-nuptial contract will not be enforced against her. Phillips's Ex'rs *v.* Phillips, 14 Ohio State, 308. An oral ante-nuptial contract, supported by satisfactory parol testimony, and confirmed by the continued recognition of both parties, is binding on the parties, and all claiming as volunteers under them. Southerland *v.* Southerland, 5 Bush (Ky.), 591. As to post-nuptial agreements, see Huber *v.* Huber, 10 Ohio, 371. Miller's Ex'rs *v.* Miller, 16 Ohio State, 527.

(*c*) It is now nearer of kin than second cousins. R. S. of Ohio, § 6384.

if the male be under twenty-one, or the female under eighteen, the consent of the parent or guardian must be first obtained. (*a*) Nothing is said with respect to color; and of course blacks and whites may intermarry, if their tastes harmonize. (*b*) It is required, however, that in this, as in other contracts, each party should be capable of consent or *compos mentis;* and therefore *idiots* and *lunatics* cannot marry. (*c*) Again, the parties must be single, in order to marry. If, therefore, either party has a husband or wife living at the time, not only is the second marriage void, but the crime of *bigamy* is committed, which will be described hereafter. (*d*)

(*a*) Shafher *v.* State, 20 Ohio, 1. It is held that the age of consent at common law being twelve in females and fourteen in males, a marriage between two infants, above those ages, respectively, without the consent of their parents or guardians, is, in the absence of any provision declaring it void, valid, although in violation of the specific regulations imposed by statute. Parton *v.* Hervey, 1 Gray, 119; Holtz *v.* Dick, 42 Ohio State, 23. Nor can the parent, in such case, maintain an action for enticing away his daughter, and procuring her marriage to a person of bad character. Hervey *v.* Mosely, 7 Gray, 479.

(*b*) By R. S. § 6987, marriage or carnal intercourse between persons of pure white blood, and persons having a distinct and visible admixture of African blood, was made an offence punishable by fine and imprisonment, and the minister knowingly solemnizing, and the judge knowingly issuing the license, were also punishable. It is held that State statutes prohibiting such marriages are not in contravention of the amendments of the constitution of the United States, or of the civil rights act passed in conformity thereto. Kinney *v.* Commonwealth, 30 Gratt. 858; State *v.* Hairston, 63 N. C. 451; Green *v.* State, 58 Ala. 190; Francois *v.* State, 9 Texas App. 144; State *v.* Bell, 7 Baxter (Tenn.), 9; Frasher *v.* State, 3 Texas App. 263; State *v.* Jackson, 80 Mo. 175.

(*c*) True *v.* Ranney, 21 N. H. 52; Keyes *v.* Keyes, 22 N. H. 553; Middleborough *v.* Rochester, 12 Mass. 363; Crump *v.* Morgan, 3 Ired. Eq. 91; Foster *v.* Means, Spears (S. C.) Ch. 569; Rawdon *v.* Rawdon, 28 Ala. 565; Cole *v.* Cole, 5 Sneed, 57; Waymire *v.* Jetmore, 22 Ohio State, 271; Powell *v.* Powell, 18 Kansas, 371. The court, though not expressly authorized by statute to declare the supposed marriage null, will in the exercise of its ordinary chancery power do so, in the interest of social order and public decency. Waymire *v.* Jetmore, 22 Ohio State, 271. The court will not, in the lifetime of both parties, decide the validity of such marriage, when its validity is made an issue in some collateral suit, if the statute provides for a direct proceeding between the parties for its determination, that they may be collaterally impeached. Unity *v.* Belgrade, 76 Me. 419; Stuckey *v.* Mathes, 24 Hun (N. Y.), 461; Williamson *v.* Williams, 3 Jones Eq. 446. It has been held that such marriage is not void *ipso facto ab initio*, and if not declared null during the life of both parties, it cannot afterwards be questioned. Wiser *v.* Lockwood, 42 Vt. 720; Sabalot *v.* Populus, 31 La. An. 854.

(*d*) They must not be within the prohibited degrees of kindred. 2 Kent, Com. 81. A second marriage by a woman who has a husband living is absolutely void. Appleton *v.* Warner, 51 Barb. 270. In Kentucky, under 1 Rev. St. 380, a woman whose former husband has been absent from the State of his residence more than five years, and has not been heard from within that period, is competent to contract marriage. Strode *v.* Strode, 3 Bush (Ky.), 227. When a woman lived with her first husband a few months only, and not having heard from him for four years married again, in the absence of any showing that in sixteen years thereafter the first husband had been heard from or had died, or been divorced, it was held that the presumption was that the second marriage was lawful. Kelly *v.* Drew, 12 Allen, 107.

{ After seven years' absence unheard of there is a presumption of death. Brent *v.* First, 41 Ohio State, 436. A marriage between slaves in a slave State was of imperfect obligation; and the issue of a second marriage during life of the first wife are preferred as heirs to property acquired during the second cohabitation. McDowell *v.* Sapp, 39 Ohio State, 558. A wife who after an absence claims to have obtained a divorce is estopped to claim heirship as against a second wife who relied on her statements. Edgar *v.* Richardson, 33 id. 581. }

3. *Preliminary Steps.* Before the marriage takes place, by our law, there must either be a *publication of banns*, or a *license.* Publication of banns consists in proclaiming the intention of marriage, in the presence of a religious congregation, in the county where the female resides, on two different days, the first being at least ten days before the marriage. A license is a written permission, obtained from the clerk of the court of common pleas of the county where the female resides, under the seal of the court. If either of the parties be a minor, and never married before, the clerk, before issuing the license, must be assured of the consent of the parent or guardian, either from his personal declaration, or from his written consent attested by two witnesses. And the clerk may put the applicant upon oath as to the legality of the marriage in other respects. The penalty for issuing a license, contrary to these provisions, is one thousand dollars.

4. *Who may Solemnize Marriage.* The persons who may here solemnize marriage are as follows: 1. Any regularly *ordained minister* of any religious society within the State; he having first obtained from the clerk a license for that purpose, which license is granted of course in the county where he officiates, upon exhibiting the proper credentials. Should he officiate in another county after procuring his license, he must apply to the clerk thereof, exhibiting his former license, and have his name entered as a person licensed. 2. Any *justice of the peace* within his county, who requires no special license. 3. Any *religious society*, agreeably to its forms and regulations. When parties marry, upon publication of banns, and without license, the person who is to solemnize the marriage must be satisfied that the banns have been duly published, and if either of the parties be a minor, he must have proof of the consent of the parent or guardian, in the same manner as the clerk when he issues the license. But where the parties marry upon license, a production of the license is sufficient. There is no prescribed form of solemnizing marriage; and it will be sufficient if the parties declare before the proper person that they will live together as man and wife. When the marriage has been solemnized, the person officiating must transmit a certificate thereof to the clerk of the county for record, within three months, under the penalty of fifty dollars; and this must be recorded under a similar penalty. The penalty for solemnizing a marriage contrary to these provisions is one thousand dollars; and the penalty for attempting to solemnize a marriage without authority, is five hundred dollars. But non-compliance with these requisitions does not make a marriage void. (*a*) With respect to foreign

(*a*) See Reeves's Dom. Rel. 196, 290; 2 Kent, Com. 89, 90; Milford *v.* Worcester, 7 Mass. 48; Ligonia *v.* Buxton, 2 Greenl. 102; Wycoff *v.* Boggs, 2 Halst. 138; Londonderry *v.* Chester, 2 N. H. 268; Starr *v.* Peck, 1 Hill, 270. Some of these authorities go so far as to say that a marriage according to the common law, which only requires the consent of the parties, would be valid, though none of the requisitions of the statute be complied with. But see the late cases of Queen *v.* Millis, 10 Cl. & Fin.

marriages, the rule is, that a marriage valid in the place where it was solemnized, is valid everywhere. (*a*)

534; Jewell *v.* Jewell, 1 How. 219; Clayton *v.* Wardell, 4 N. Y. 230; Clark *v.* Clark, 10 N. H. 383; Ferrie *v.* Public Administration, 4 Brad. Sur. R. 28; Caujolle *v.* Ferrie, 26 Barb. 177; s. c. 23 N. Y. 90. All that is necessary to make a valid marriage is a *present* agreement between parties competent to contract to take each other for husband and wife. Clayton *v.* Wardell, 4 N. Y. 230. Mutual promises to marry in the future, though made by parties competent to contract, and followed by cohabitation as husband and wife, do not constitute a valid marriage. Duncan *v.* Duncan, 10 Ohio State, 181; Cheney *v.* Arnold, 15 N. Y. 345. But where parties competent to contract openly and mutually consent to a contract of present marriage, and afterwards live together as husband and wife, the fact that the contract was not made before any person authorized to solemnize marriage, will not invalidate it. Carmichael *v.* The State, 12 Ohio State, 553. See also Van Tuyl *v.* Van Tuyl, 57 Barb. 235; Bissell *v.* Bissell, 55 Barb. 325; Comm. *v.* Stump, 53 Penn. State, 132; Peck *v.* Peck, 12 R. I. 485; *contra*, Commonwealth *v.* Munson, 127 Mass. 459. Mere cohabitation as man and wife is not sufficient if it is shown that no marriage ceremony whatever was performed. A contract consented to by both parties must be proved. Goldbeck *v.* Goldbeck, 3 Green (N. J.), 42. In Maryland, it is held that some religious ceremony must be superadded to the civil contract. Dennison *v.* Dennison, 35 Md. 361. In California and Oregon, it must be before a person authorized to solemnize marriage, in the presence of at least two witnesses. Holmes *v.* Holmes, 1 Abb. U. S. 525. The intention to marry must exist. A ceremony performed in jest, though before a proper officer, who was in doubt at the time whether the parties were in jest or earnest, will not create the relation. McClurg *v.* Terry, 21 N. J. Eq. 225. The lords in The Queen *v.* Millis were equally divided, and this equal division resulted in affirming that there could be no valid marriage unless contracted in the presence of a priest in holy orders; and that a dissenting minister not being episcopally ordained, a marriage solemnized by him was null. In Catteral *v.* Catteral, 1 Robertson, 580, Dr. Lushington refused to recognize the decision as going to that length, and held such a marriage in the colonies valid. But in Beamish *v.* Beamish, 9 H. L. 274, it was held that the law was established by The Queen *v.* Millis; though the Lord Chancellor declared that he would have held, prior to that decision, that the presence of a priest was not necessary; and Justice Willes, in his very learned opinion in answer to a question propounded by the lords, conclusively showed, that, down to the Council of Trent, a contract of marriage *per verba de presenti*, no clerical or official person being present, was a valid marriage throughout western Europe; and that the rule laid down in The Queen *v.* Millis was law only because it was made so by the decision in that case. The supreme court of the United States, in Meister *v.* Moore *et al.*, 96 U. S. 76, held that a marriage by declaration of the parties and cohabitation is a good common-law marriage; and that statutes merely prescribing formalities for marriage, and requiring their observance under penalty, do not invalidate the common-law marriage.

(*a*) The law was declared as stated in the text down to the case of Brook *v.* Brook, 9 House of Lords Cases, 193, decided in 1861, though Lord Brougham, in the earlier case of Warrender *v.* Warrender, 2 Clark & Fin. 529, suggested that the statement might be qualified, as was afterwards declared in Brook *v.* Brook. In Brook *v.* Brook, the House of Lords held that "the forms of entering into the contract of marriage are regulated by the *lex loci contractus;* the essentials of the contract depend upon the *lex domicilii.* If the latter are contrary to the law of the domicile, the marriage (though duly solemnized elsewhere) is there void. The marriage of a man with the sister of his deceased wife being prohibited by our law, such a marriage, contracted by British subjects, temporarily resident abroad, but really domiciled in this country, though valid in the foreign country and duly celebrated according to the forms required by the law of that country, is absolutely void here." Subsequently, the divorce court in full bench, whose decisions at that time were reviewable only by the House of Lords, held, in Simonin *v.* Mallac, 2 Sw. & Tr. 67, that foreigners who were incapable of being united in marriage in the country of their domicile could, while temporarily residing in England, contract there a marriage valid in England; so that they would be lawful husband and wife in England, while their marriage would be a nullity in their domicile. Subsequently, the court of appeal in Sottomayor *v.* De Barros, L. R. 3 Prob. Div. 1, reversing the decision of the divorce court, held, contrary to Simonin *v.* Mallac, that such marriage would be void in England as well as in the domicile of the parties; would be void everywhere. The case on being heard again in the divorce court, upon different evidence, Sottomayor *v.* De Barros,

§ 103. **Rights and Liabilities of the Husband.** The rule formerly was, that the husband has the same power over the *person* of the wife as over a child, servant, or apprentice; and, upon the same principle, the right of a master. Accordingly, if necessary in his opinion, he might administer reasonable personal chastisement. But in this country we recognize no such doctrine. A husband has no right to strike his wife, whatever may be the provocation. Against such indignity she has a twofold security. She may either have him put under bonds to keep the peace, or she may apply for a divorce. The limit of his power over her person is this: If she manifest a disposition to squander or destroy property, he may use the means necessary to prevent her; and if she leave him without cause, he may bring her back; for he has a right to her society, which he may enforce either against herself or any other person who detains her. He may also have his action for damages against any person who abducts or seduces her. (*a*) And it is said that if he should take the life of a person found in the very act of criminal connection with her, it would be excusable homicide. But his power over her *property* is much more exten-

L. R. 6 Prob. Div. 94, Sir James Hannen boldly criticised the judgment of the Court of Appeal, declaring it without precedent or warrant in English law.

In the United States the rule declared in Brook *v.* Brook was followed in Kinney *v.* Commonwealth, 30 Gratt. 858. And the same rule was held in Williams *v.* Oates, 3 Ired. 535; State *v.* Kennedy, 76 N. C. 251; Dupre *v.* Boulard's Executor, 10 La. An. 411; and State *v.* Bell, 7 Baxter (Tenn.), 9.

In Kentucky it was held that if persons who are incapacitated to intermarry by the law of their domicile go into an adjoining State or country, where no such incapacity is recognized, and are there married in accordance with the law of such State or country, the marriage, being valid by the *lex loci contractus*, though void by the law of the domicile, is valid in other States. Dannelli *v.* Dannelli, 4 Bush, 51.

In Massachusetts the rule is the reverse of that in Brook *v.* Brook. The courts there hold that where citizens of Massachusetts, who by the law of Massachusetts cannot intermarry, go, for the purpose of evading the law of the State, to another State where no such incapacity is recognized, and are there married in accordance with the law of such State, the marriage is valid not only in other States, but also in Massachusetts. Medway *v.* Needham, 16 Mass. 157; West Cambridge *v.* Lexington, 1 Pick. 506; Putnam *v.* Putnam, 8 Pick. 433; Commonwealth *v.* Lane, 113 Mass. 458. Lord Cranworth having in Brook *v.* Brook criticised the earlier Massachusetts cases, Chief Justice Gray, in Commonwealth *v.* Lane, returns the compliment with interest in an exceedingly able analysis of the opinions in Brook *v.* Brook. In New York there was no decision by the Court of Appeals till 1881. Before that there were decisions by the inferior courts, one half holding with the English rule, the other half with the Massachusetts rule. In Van Voorhis *v.* Brintnall, 86 N. Y. 18, the court of appeals, reversing the decision of the superior court of New York, adopted fully the rule established in Massachusetts.

In the United States, therefore, when two persons intermarry in a State other than their domicile, the marriage, if in accordance with the law of such State, is valid everywhere, unless the parties are by the law of their domicile incapacitated to intermarry. In such case the marriage is valid everywhere except in the State of their domicile; and some States hold it valid, others hold it void, in their domicile. The rule declared in Sottomayor *v.* De Barros, L. R. 3 Prob. Div. 1, is not law in the United States.

(*a*) He may have an action against one who harbors her, if such person has acted maliciously, and not from motives of humanity. Holtz *v.* Dick, 42 Ohio State, 23; Campbell *v.* Coster, 3 Daly (N. Y.), 165. And she may have an action against any one who entices him away from her. Westlake *v.* Westlake, 34 Ohio State, 621. So, too, against a druggist selling her opium, knowing that she used it habitually to the injury of her health. Hoard *v.* Peck, 56 Barb. 202.

sive than over her person. I have already said that property may be so secured to the wife in the form of a jointure or settlement, by means of trustees, that neither the husband nor his creditors can control it; but I shall here suppose that no such precaution has been taken. Then, by marriage, all her *personalty*, except *choses in action*, becomes at once absolutely his. And, as to *choses in action*, they become his by reducing them to possession, which he may do, by suit or otherwise, independently of her control. He may, if he choose, join her name in the suit, but he is not obliged so to do; and the only effect of so joining her will be, that if she survives him, and the judgment or decree be not collected, it will become hers by survivorship. If he was himself the debtor, the marriage cancels the debt. If she has earned money by her own labor during the marriage, he may collect it. Thus her personalty is entirely at his control. (*a*) But with respect to her *realty*, the case is somewhat more favorable. He only has control of the *income*. (*b*) Without her consent, he cannot incumber or dispose of the property itself, beyond his own life. (*c*) In this one instance, the law gives her a veto upon this power; for he cannot compel her to give consent. And, on the other hand, by marriage, the husband becomes liable for the *support* of the wife; but this liability extends only to *necessaries* suited to her condition, and not to elegancies or luxuries. Nor does it depend at all upon the amount of property he obtains by her. To the extent of necessaries which he does not supply, she may contract debts, and he will be bound for them, even though he should

(*a*) Dunseth *v.* Bank of U. S., 6 Ohio, 76; Ramsdall *v.* Craighill, 9 id. 197; Curry *v.* Fulkinson, 14 id. 100; Dixon *v.* Dixon, 18 id. 113. Where the husband has received his wife's *choses in action* in a fiduciary capacity, he may reduce them into possession by acts showing his intention to do so. Walden *v.* Walden, 7 Ohio State, 30. The husband cannot by an assignment of his wife's reversionary or contingent interests, or *choses in action*, vest the right to them in the assignee, inasmuch as they are incapable of an immediate reduction to possession. Needles *v.* Needles, 7 Ohio State, 432. *Contra*, Lynn *v.* Bradley, 1 Met. (Ky.), 232; Hill *v.* Townsend, 24 Texas, 575. These rules as to the property of the wife are all changed, in Ohio, now by R. S. § 3108 (82 Ohio Laws, 131). "All real or personal property belonging to a woman at marriage, or acquired afterwards, or due as wages, or growing out of violation of her personal rights, and all the income or profit thereof, is her separate property." See note at end of chapter.

(*b*) By statute in Ohio his interest cannot be incumbered by him or reached by his creditors {during the life of his wife or of any heir of her body. R. S. § 3108 (82 Laws, 131); Robert *v.* Sliffe, 41 Ohio State, 225}. Nor in Massachusetts will it pass to his assignees in insolvency. Lynde *v.* McGregor, 13 Allen, 182.

(*c*) But if they unite in selling land, and the proceeds be invested in other land, taking the title to the husband, it becomes his and descends to his heirs. Ramsdall *v.* Craighill, 9 Ohio, 197. A deed by a married woman, without her husband's joining with her, is a nullity, and as a contract for a conveyance is alike void. Miller *v.* Hine, 13 Ohio State, 565; Henry *v.* Henry, 27 id. 121; and Ogle *v.* Ogle, 41 id. 359, effectuating a purchase-money mortgage by her as a trust; Moore *v.* Rake, 2 Dutcher, 574; Richards *v.* McClellan, 29 Penn. State, 385; Beale *v.* Knowles, 45 Maine, 479; Eaton *v.* George, 42 N. H. 375; Gray *v.* Mathis, 7 Jones's Law, 502; Camden *v.* Vail, 23 Cal. 633. In some of the States it is held to be a sufficient joining, if the husband executes the deed. Woodward *v.* Seaver, 38 N. H. 29; Stone *v.* Montgomery, 35 Miss. 83. But, generally, he is required to join in the granting clause. It is not sufficient that an attorney in fact, having a general power from the husband to convey his lands, joins in the wife's deed. Toulmin *v.* Heidelberg, 32 Miss. 268.

give notice to the contrary, unless she had eloped, (*a*) and this is the only instance where she can bind him by her contracts, except when she acts as his agent. (*b*) If she had contracted debts before marriage he becomes liable for them, whether he obtained property by her or not; but this liability can be enforced only during the coverture; for the death of the wife discharges the husband; and the death of the husband discharges his property. (*c*) Finally, the husband is liable for any civil injuries, technically called *torts*, committed by the wife during coverture, (*d*) but not for her crimes.

§ 104. **Rights and Liabilities of the Wife.** The condition of the wife may be inferred from what has already been said. She is almost entirely at the mercy of her husband; she can exercise no control over his property or her own. As a general rule, she can make no contracts binding herself or him. (*e*) With the excep-

(*a*) Shaw *v.* Thompson, 16 Pick. 198; Sykes *v.* Halstead, 1 Sandf. 483; Read *v.* Legard, 4 Eng. Law & Eq. 523; Howard *v.* Whetstone, 10 Ohio, 365; Cummings *v.* Aldrich, 9 Foster, 63; Blowers *v.* Sturtevant, 4 Denio, 46; Cooper *v.* Lloyd, 6 C. B. (N. S.) 519; Cunningham *v.* Reardon, 98 Mass. 538; Reynolds *v.* Sweetzer, 15 Gray, 78; Hullz *v.* Gibbs, 66 Penn. State, 360. It is not necessary that the party furnishing them should make any inquiries at the time. Eames *v.* Sweetzer, 101 Mass. 78. The burden of proof is on the plaintiff to show the facts necessary to charge the husband. Keller *v.* Phillips, 39 N. Y. 351; Woodward *v.* Barnes, 43 Vt. 330. He is liable for necessaries when she lives separate from him with his consent. Corley *v.* Green, 12 Allen, 104. Even though he makes her an allowance, if that be too small for his condition in life. Baker *v.* Sampson, 14 C. B. (N. S.) 383. But he is not liable when she deserts him without good cause. Brown *v.* Mudgett, 40 Vt. 68; Munroe Co. *v.* Budlong, 51 Barb. 493; Sturdevant *v.* Starin, 19 Wis. 268. Even though she be guilty of adultery, he will be liable for necessaries if he has been guilty of the same thing. Needham *v.* Bremner, L. R. 1 C. P. 582. If the husband introduces a woman of profligate habits into his house, and permits her to remain there as an inmate, thereby rendering it unfit for a modest and chaste woman to live in it, his wife will be justified in withdrawing from his protection, and he will be bound to provide her with necessaries. Descelles *v.* Kadmus, 8 Clarke (Iowa), 51.

(*b*) Reneaux *v.* Teakle, 20 Eng. Law & Eq. 345, and *notes*. Tebbetts *v.* Hapgood, 34 N. H. 420; Gilman *v.* Andrews, 28 Vt. 241; Gill *v.* Read, 5 R. I. 343; Ruse *v.* Chilton, 26 Missouri, 598; Johnstone *v.* Sumner, 3 Hurl. & Nor. 261; Mayhew *v.* Thayer, 8 Gray, 172; Hall *v.* Weir, 1 Allen, 261; Rea *v.* Durklee, 25 Ill. 503; Keller *v.* Phillips, 40 Barb. 390; Cromwell *v.* Benjamin, 41 Barb. 558. In England, it has been held, that, although liable for necessaries furnished to the wife, the husband is not liable for money loaned to the wife, although used by her in the purchase of necessaries. Knox *v.* Bushell, 3 C. B. (N. S.) 343. In Massachusetts, however, a man was allowed to recover for money paid to a doctor for necessary medical attendance upon the wife. Mayhew *v.* Thayer, *supra*.

(*c*) 2 Kent, Com. 143, 144; Cole *v.* Shurtleff, 41 Vt. 311. This rule has been changed by statute in some of the States. In Mississippi it is done away with. Dunbar *v.* Meyer, 43 Miss. 679; Cannon *v.* Grantham, 45 Miss. 88. Done away with also in Ohio. R. S. § 3110, as amended, 81 Laws, 209. Except to the extent of property acquired from her. In Georgia it is limited to the property received by him from her by the act of 1856. The married women's act of 1861 of Ill. does not affect it. Connor *v.* Berry, 46 Ill. 370.

(*d*) 2 Kent, Com. 149; Fowler *v.* Chichester, 26 Ohio State, 9; Holtz *v.* Dick, 42 Ohio State, 23. Now altered by statute. R. S. § 3110; 81 Laws, 209. The New York act exempts the husband from liability for torts committed by her in the management of her separate property, but no further. Rowe *v.* Smith, 45 N. Y. 230; Baum *v.* Mullen, 47 N. Y. 577.

(*e*) Although it is the general rule of the common law, that a married woman cannot contract or sue alone, there are exceptions to the rule, as where there is a separation induced by his cruelty, and they are living in different countries. Wagg *v.* Gibbons, 5 Ohio State, 580. See Benadum *v.* Pratt, 1 id. 403; Smith *v.* Silence, 4 Iowa, 321. But where the ground is desertion, it must be such a desertion as amounts tion just stated her contracts are not merely voidable, but absolutely void. Nor can she make herself liable for his contracts, torts, or crimes. Her only separate liability is for her own crimes; her only joint liability is for her own *torts*, committed without his participation; and for contracts, in which the law authorizes her to unite with him. She has no power over his person, and her only claim upon his property is for bare support. In no instance can she sue or be sued alone in a civil action; and there are but few cases in which she can be joined in a suit with him. (*a*) In Ohio, but hardly anywhere else, she is allowed to make a *will*, if haply she has anything to dispose of. On the ground of an indissoluble union of interests, and in order to prevent connubial harmony and confidence from ever being disturbed, it is a general rule of law, that neither the husband nor wife can, in any case, civil or criminal, be a witness for or against the other; an exclusion which belongs to no other of the domestic relations. This rule sometimes produces hardship, but on the whole is supposed to be salutary. There are but two exceptions, which grow out of the necessity of the case. The one is where the wife has acted as the agent of her husband in business matters; the other, where she has received personal violence from him. In these cases, and these only, if there be no other witness, she is permitted to testify. Nor does the general exclusion continue only during coverture; it lasts for ever, with respect to all matters which transpired during coverture; in order that there may be every motive for the most unlimited mutual confidence. (*b*)

to a renunciation of marital rights on the part of the husband. Ayer *v.* Warren, 47 Maine, 217. See R. S. § 3111, empowering a married woman to sue in cases of desertion, neglect, or inability of the husband. Though a married woman's note is not binding upon her at law, yet she may mortgage her separate property to secure such a note, or a debt of her husband, and such mortgage will be binding. See note at end of this chapter. Bartlett *v.* Bartlett, 4 Allen, 440; Brookings *v.* White, 49 Maine, 479; State *v.* Montgomery, 35 Miss. 83; Shelby *v.* Bartis, 18 Texas, 644. But in Kentucky, she can encumber her property only by an order of court. Pell *v.* Cole, 2 Met. (Ky.) 252. Where an executory contract has been fully performed on the part of a married woman, it has been held that she can sustain an action upon it. Ham *v.* Boody, 20 N. H. 411. And in equity generally, a married woman's contracts will be sustained and made binding upon her separate estate, where made with the intention that they should bind such estate, and for its benefit, in order to prevent manifest injustice. Glass *v.* Warwick, 40 Penn. State, 140; Pentz *v.* Simonson, 2 Beasley, 232; Koontz *v.* Kalb, 16 Mo. 549; Knox *v.* Jordan, 5 Jones, Eq. 175; Parker *v.* Kane, 4 Allen, 380; Gardner *v.* Gardner, 7 Paige's Ch. 12; Ballin *v.* Dillage, 37 N. Y. 35.

(*a*) By the last amendment of R. S. of Ohio, § 4996, "a married woman shall sue and be sued as if she were unmarried, and her husband shall be joined with her only when the cause of action is in favor of or against both her and her husband."

(*b*) Cook *v.* Grange, 18 Ohio, 526. But a widow is a competent witness against her husband's administrator, where her testimony is not a violation of his confidence, or a disclosure of his conversations or admissions, or prejudicial to his interests. Stober *v.* McCarter, 4 Ohio State, 513. R. S. of Ohio, § 5241, among persons incompetent to testify classes "husband or wife concerning any communication made by one to the other or any act done by either in the presence of the other during coverture, unless the communication was made or act done in the known presence or hearing of a third person, competent to be a witness; and the rule shall be the same if the marital relation has ceased to exist." {The presence of such third person is provable by the husband or wife. McCague *v.* Miller, 36 Ohio State, 595. Such presence is a question for

§ 105. **Divorce.** (*a*) It has always been deemed the policy of the law, to hold marriage as nearly indissoluble as the nature of the case will admit; and therefore, unlike other contracts, marriage cannot be cancelled or dissolved by the consent of the parties. They may indeed agree to live separately, but the law still regards them as husband and wife. They can only cease to be such by *divorce* or by *death;* and it is generally agreed that divorces ought not to be granted but upon very urgent and pressing reasons. But on this subject there is great diversity of legislation in the different States; and, as a general remark, the English are much more strict in their requisitions than we are. In Ohio, the liberal doctrine has been carried so far, that a proposition was once discussed in the legislature, submitting all questions of divorce to the discretion of a jury; but, fortunately, we have stopped a little short of this. In Ohio, the cognizance of divorce and alimony is given to the supreme court and court of common pleas, sitting as a court of chancery. Practically, this seems not to be understood as excluding the legislature, which has often undertaken to grant divorces, though this would seem to be unconstitutional, as an assumption of judicial power. (*b*) The causes of divorce, as defined by statute, are as follows: 1. Either party having a former husband or wife living. 2. Wilful absence of either party for three years. 3. Adultery of either party. 4. Impotence. 5. Extreme cruelty. 6. Fraudulent contract. 7. Gross neglect of duty. 8. Habitual drunkenness for three years. 9. Imprisonment in the penitentiary. 10. Divorce in another State, leaving the applicant here bound by the marriage contract, when the other party has been discharged. These are the only causes expressly specified in the act relating to divorce; but there are probably two other causes; namely, being nearer of kin than first cousins, and being under the marriageable age. These causes render the parties incompetent to marry; and the only doubt is, whether void marriages can be the subject of

the court, and not for the jury. Westerman *v.* Westerman, 25 Ohio State, 500. Neither under the civil code nor the code of criminal procedure are the husband or wife competent witnesses for or against each other in criminal prosecutions. Steen *v.* The State, 20 Ohio State, 333; Schultz *v.* State, 32 Ohio State, 276. But the common-law exception arising from necessity allowing one to testify against the other where one is on trial for a personal offence committed against the other prevails in Ohio. Whipp *v.* State, 34 Ohio State, 87.} Under the last amendment, she is competent to testify for herself in an action against a third person regarding her separate property, except as to communications or acts between herself or her husband made during coverture. Robinson *v.* Chadwick, 22 Ohio State, 527. R. S., § 4997, provides that "when a husband and wife are sued together, the wife may defend for her own right; and if the husband neglect to defend, she may also defend for his right." {This section does not apply to actions in which the trial and judgment must be joint, as where both are sued for an assault and battery by her she cannot attack his confession of judgment or compromise. Coolidge *v.* Parris, 8 Ohio State, 594.}

(*a*) See the 27th lecture of Kent's Com.; Page on Divorce; Bishop on Marriage and Divorce. The English decisions, and also the English statutes on Divorce, passed in 1857, are digested in the recent work of Pritchard, entitled "A Hand-book on the Law of Marriage and Divorce."

(*b*) Bingham *v.* Miller, 17 Ohio, 445. In the constitution of 1852, the legislature is expressly forbidden to grant divorces or exercise any judicial power, not expressly conferred upon them.

divorce; but as the statute has expressly provided for one such case, where there is a former husband or wife living, I see no reason why these should not be placed on the same footing. Of the above-named causes of divorce, the only three which are vague and liable to doubt are, extreme cruelty, fraud in the contract, and neglect of duty. With respect to extreme cruelty, it is held that there must be personal violence to constitute it; mere austerity of temper, rudeness of language, or grossness of behavior, will not be sufficient. With respect to fraud, it is held that where a female, at the time of marriage, is pregnant by another man and conceals the fact, it is a case of fraud. With respect to neglect of duty, it must be so flagrant as to shock almost any conscience, or it will not be held sufficient. And generally, whatever be the cause, if it has been forgiven, and the parties have been reconciled and live together, a divorce will not be decreed. Nor will it in any case be decreed where the applicant is living in a state of adultery. (*a*) Up

(*a*) Mattox *v.* Mattox, 2 Ohio, 233; Wright's Rep. 212, 284, 563, 630, 763. It is held in Massachusetts that personal violence is necessary to constitute extreme cruelty. Ford *v.* Ford, 104 Mass. 198; and see Hoshall *v.* Hoshall, 51 Md. 72. But it is generally held otherwise. Sackrider *v.* Sackrider, 60 Iowa, 397. The ruling of Lord Stowell in Evans *v.* Evans, 1 Hagg. Const. 35: "Proof must be given of a reasonable apprehension of bodily hurt. I say an apprehension, because assuredly the court is not to wait till the hurt is actually done," is frequently cited in later English cases as the guiding rule. And "bodily hurt" is not restricted to acts of personal violence, but includes also injury to health. The matter is fully considered in Kelly *v.* Kelly, L. R. 2 Prob. and Div. Ca. 31 and 59, where the earlier cases are cited, p. 61. See also English *v.* English, 27 N. J. Eq. 579; Ruckman *v.* Ruckman, 58 How. Pr. 278; Latham *v.* Latham, 30 Gratt. 307; Friend *v.* Friend, 53 Mich. 543; Beyer *v.* Beyer, 50 Wis. 254. Recent English cases have held that it is cruelty for a husband knowingly to infect his wife with venereal disease. Divorce was granted on that ground in Brown *v.* Brown, B. L. R. 1 Prob. Div. 46; and in the United States, Cook *v.* Cook, 32 N. J. Eq. 475. Falsely and maliciously, and without probable cause, charging the wife with infidelity, is such cruelty as constitutes ground for divorce. Kennedy *v.* Kennedy, 60 How. Pr. 151; Graft *v.* Grān, 76 Ind. 136; Smith *v.* Smith, 8 Or. 100; Bahn *v.* Bahn, 62 Tex. 518; Avery *v.* Avery, 33 Kan. 1. Husband may obtain divorce on the ground of the cruelty of his wife, both in England (White *v.* White, 1 Swab. & T. 591) and in the United States (Beebe *v.* Beebe, 10 Iowa, 133; Kelly *v.* Kelly, 18 Nev. 49).

Fraudulent misrepresentations, as to wealth, social position, or character, do not constitute such fraud in the contract as to be ground for divorce. The fraud must be, not false representations anterior to the marriage, but fraud or duress in the actual contracting of the marriage, and the applicant for divorce must himself be free from guilt and laches. Leavitt *v.* Leavitt, 13 Mich. 452. The wife being pregnant by a third person at the time of the marriage, and artfully concealing the fact from her husband, constitutes such fraud. Reynolds *v.* Reynolds, 3 Allen, 605; Baker *v.* Baker, 13 Cal. 87. But if the husband had sexual intercourse with his wife before marriage, and the fact concealed was that her pregnancy was not by him but by another person, he cannot have divorce. Foss *v.* Foss, 12 Allen, 26; Crehore *v.* Crehore, 97 Mass. 330; Carris *v.* Carris, 25 N. J. Eq. 516; Hoffman *v.* Hoffman, 30 Pa. State, 417; States *v.* States, 37 N. J. Eq. 195. Even if such other person were a negro, and, in consequence, a mulatto child should be born after the marriage. Scroggins *v.* Scroggins, 3 Dev. Law, 535. But if the child were born before the marriage, and the husband were deceived without his laches into the belief that it was his child, he would be entitled to divorce. Barden *v.* Barden, 3 Dev. Law, 548. But see Farr *v.* Farr, 2 McArthur, 35. Though a marriage procured by fraud or duress may, in Kentucky, be declared null *ab initio*, it is only voidable at the instance of the injured party, not void *ipso facto ab initio.* Tomppert's Ex'rs *v.* Tomppert, 13 Bush, 326. Divorces are very rarely granted on the ground of gross neglect of duty. It seldom happens that there is a neglect of duty sufficient to warrant a divorce which does not amount on the one hand to wilful absence or desertion, or, on the other hand, to extreme cruelty. See Smith *v.* Smith, 22 Kan.

to 1833, the court had a discretion to grant a partial divorce, *a mensa et thoro*, or a total divorce, *a vinculo matrimonii;* but since that time, partial divorces have been done away; and the courts either dissolve the contract altogether, or not at all. But a wife may still file her petition for *alimony*, (*a*) without praying for a divorce. Doubts have sometimes been intimated whether divorce laws do not impair the obligation of contracts, within the meaning of the constitutional prohibition; but the better opinion is, that they do not; because they only liberate one party from a contract, when it has been broken by the other. (*b*) A much more questionable point is, whether divorces are not made too frequent in Ohio for the good of society. (*c*) It is indeed difficult to fix upon the exact medium in such cases. On the one hand, to hold the marriage contract dissoluble for slight causes, must operate as an encouragement to matrimonial strife and contention; and on the other, not to hold it dissoluble for any cause, would often occasion intolerable suffering. Perhaps the true medium would be somewhere between the severity of the English law and the liberality of our own. (*d*) With respect to *foreign divorces*, a great diversity of opinion exists in the different States; (*e*) but as our statute

699. {As to the degree of connivance of one spouse with the adultery or seduction of the other which will deprive the former of a right to divorce for such offence, see Robbins *v.* Robbins, 140 Mass. 528. A corrupt intent or wish or procurement that the offence shall be committed is necessary; a mere desire to obtain evidence of it is not sufficient.}

(*a*) A gross sum may be allowed as alimony, payable in one sum or by instalments, in the discretion of the court; and the decree may be enforced by execution for each instalment. Piatt *v.* Piatt, 9 Ohio, 37; Sheafe *v.* Sheafe, 36 N. H. 155. In determining the amount, the court will take into consideration the circumstances of the parties, their social position, the wants of the person requiring it, and the pecuniary resources of the party who is to pay it. Foote *v.* Foote, 22 Ill. 425. {And the court rendering the decree may at any time modify it in view of circumstances arising since the decree. Olney *v.* Watts, 43 Ohio State, 499. Thus it may reduce the amount on the woman's marrying again. King *v.* King, 38 Ohio State, 370, 372.} As to alimony *pendente lite* and allowance for counsel fees, see the very singular case of D'Arusmont *v.* D'Arusmont, 8 Western Law Jour. 548. A wife, who by gross abuse of her husband has been driven beyond the pale of his protection, and a separation *de facto* exists, she living and maintaining herself as a single woman, and having had specific property decreed her as alimony, may maintain an action at law in regard to such property, without the joinder of her husband, although no divorce has been decreed. Benadum *v.* Pratt, 1 Ohio State, 403. See on the subject of alimony, Bishop on Marriage and Divorce, ch. 27, and the act of April 15, 1857. After an *ex parte* divorce obtained by the husband in another State, the wife may petition for alimony here, and the court may take into consideration in awarding it property acquired since the date of the decree of divorce. Cox *v.* Cox, 20 Ohio State, 439. But see Cheever *v.* Wilson, 9 Wall. 108, 123, where the supreme court of the United States held that a decree in a divorce suit affecting real estate situated outside of the jurisdiction of the court, though it could not have extra-territorial operation, bound the parties personally, and could be enforced in the *situs rei* by proper proceedings conducted there for that purpose. In this case, however, the defendant had appeared, so that the court had jurisdiction of his person. Real estate of the husband may be decreed to the wife in fee, as alimony under the Ohio statute. Broadwell *v.* Broadwell, 21 Ohio State, 657; Gallagher *v.* Fleury, 36 Ohio State, 590.

(*b*) Cabell *v.* Cabell, 1 Met. (Ky.) 319; Adams *v.* Palmer, 51 Maine, 480.

(*c*) See 1 Western Law Jour. 170.

(*d*) The English law of divorce has been greatly liberalized by recent acts of parliament. See acts 20 and 21 Victoria, cap. 85, 28th August, 1857, and the acts amending the same passed 2d August, 1858.

(*e*) The great number of States in the Union, all foreign to each other as to their expressly authorizes divorces to be granted, when the marriage took place, or the cause of divorce occurred out of the State, we are bound to recognize the full validity of foreign divorces.

jurisdiction and judgments, and the diversity in their laws as to divorce, make the question as to the validity of foreign divorces a matter of great importance. The constitution of the United States provides that full faith and credit shall be given in each State to the judicial proceedings in every other State. But a decision pronounced by a court not having jurisdiction of the subject-matter and the parties, is not a judgment in the purview of that provision. A court to which is produced the certified record of a court of another State, is not bound by a recital, or by a finding of jurisdiction in such record, but can inquire for itself into the fact of jurisdiction. Christmas *v.* Russell, 5 Wall. 290 ; Thompson *v.* Whitman, 18 Wall. 457 ; Knowles *v.* Gas Light Co., 19 Wall. 58 ; Pennoyer *v.* Neff, 95 U. S. 714.

A decree of divorce is not the rescission of a contract, but the dissolution of a relation, the change of the *status* of the parties from married to single. The marriage is the fact which creates the relation. The offence is the fact which authorizes the court having jurisdiction, to act. But the thing acted upon and which is determined by the decree, is, the *status* of the parties. Every State has authority to determine the *status* of parties domiciled therein. Strader *v.* Graham, 10 How. 82 ; see p. 86. Sewall *v.* Sewall, 122 Mass. 156. Hence the State having jurisdiction to decree divorce, is, not the State where the marriage was solemnized, nor the State where the offence was committed, but the State where the parties are domiciled ; and, after much diversity in the earlier decisions, this is now the accepted rule. The same rule is recognized in England. Harvey *v.* Farnie, L. R. 6 Prob. Div. 35 ; Firebrace *v.* Firebrace, L. R. 4 Prob. Div. 63 ; and see Niboyet *v.* Niboyet, L. R. 4 Prob. Div. 1. Statutes prescribing the length of residence necessary to entitle a party to sue for divorce do not establish the rule that domicile is necessary, but only regulate its exercise. Hence a statute, or a provision in a constitution, authorizing a non-resident to maintain a suit for divorce against a person temporarily in such State, but not domiciled therein, is held not valid beyond the limits of the State. Hood *v.* State, 56 Ind. 263 ; Van Fossen *v.* State, 37 Ohio State, 317. A divorce granted by a court of the State wherein both parties are domiciled, the proceedings being in accordance with the law of such State, is accepted as valid everywhere. A divorce ordered by a court of a State in which neither party is domiciled, is a nullity outside the limits of that State, and a subsequent marriage by either party is bigamy ; and this is not affected by the fact that the marriage may have been solemnized, or the offence committed, or the parties or one of them should be temporarily in such State. Sewall *v.* Sewall, 122 Mass. 156 ; Hoffman *v.* Hoffman, 46 N. Y. 30 ; Strait *v.* Strait, 3 MacArthur (Dist. Col.), 415 ; Van Fossen *v.* State, 37 Ohio State, 317 ; Hood *v.* State, 56 Ind. 263 ; People *v.* Dowell, 25 Mich. 247 ; State *v.* Arrington, 25 Minn. 29 ; Litowich *v.* Litowich, 19 Kan. 451 ; and in England, Briggs *v.* Briggs, L. R. 5 Prob. Div. 163.

Since the decision by the supreme court of the United States, of Cheever *v.* Wilson, 9 Wall. 108, it has been settled law that, for the purpose of divorce, a wife may have a different domicile from that of her husband. The same appears to be held in Santo Teodoro *v.* Santo Teodoro, L. R. 5 Prob. Div. 79 ; and compare this with pp. 67, 68, in Firebrace *v.* Firebrace, L. R. 5 Prob. Div.; and p. 14 in Niboyet *v.* Niboyet, L. R. 4 Prob. Div. 1 ; also Deck *v.* Deck, 2 Sw. & Tr. 90. But no English court has gone farther than to say, an English wife may, under some circumstances, retain her English domicile ; while in the United States a wife may acquire a new domicile. When husband and wife are domiciled in different States, each State has jurisdiction of the *status* of the party domiciled in it, and can grant a divorce valid there. Can it, however, determine the *status* of the party domiciled in the other State ? Yet one party cannot be made effectively single, while the other remains married to him. The supreme court of Rhode Island in Ditson *v.* Ditson, 4 R. I. 87, cogently presented the view that a proceeding in divorce, being the determination of the *status* of the citizen, is in the nature of a proceeding *in rem ;* that a judgment rendered at the suit of a domiciled person is binding on every person, and is therefore an effective divorce as to both parties, and, as such, is valid everywhere. This view has been growing into acceptance, though it is not universally followed. States assuming to grant such divorces cannot easily deny the same power to other States. It is now agreed that where, in such suit, the non-resident defendant is personally served, or enters an appearance, the court has jurisdiction of the parties, and the cause and its judgment is valid everywhere. In Massachusetts and New York it has been held that though a married woman is a non-resident of the State where her husband is domiciled, so that in a proper

The mode of proceeding properly belongs to the sixth part of these lectures, and will be there described. In the mean time, I may here remark, that the application for divorce is, in most respects, a chancery proceeding. But to avoid the possibility of collusion between the parties to procure a divorce, their confessions can be received in evidence only when there is no reason to suspect connivance, fraud, or other improper means or motives. (*a*) And as the inclination of wise judges is against granting divorces where they can be refused, the case must be fully made out, in order to succeed. Should it appear necessary, during the pendency of proceedings, to provide for the support of the wife, the court will make an order for that purpose, and the allowance will be made large enough to enable her to carry on the suit; (*b*) and in the final decree, permanent provision is made for the wife, if she deserve it; and for the custody of the children, if there be any. (*c*)

action she can be brought in by publication as a non-resident, yet her husband's domicile remains her domicile, unless she has cause for divorce against him; that in such case, the State where the husband resides is the domicile of both, and a decree of divorce pronounced therein at his suit is valid everywhere, though the wife does not appear, and is served only by publication or other substituted mode. Hood *v.* Hood, 11 Allen, 196; Hunt *v.* Hunt, 72 N. Y. 217. In several States it has been expressly held that where the parties have different domiciles, a divorce granted in either State at the suit of the party domiciled therein, though the non-resident party does not appear, and is served only by publication, is valid everywhere. Harding *v.* Alden, 9 Greenleaf, 140; Ditson *v.* Ditson, 4 R. I. 87; Garner *v.* Garner, 56 Md. 127; Thompson *v.* State, 28 Ala. 12; Cooper *v.* Cooper, 7 Ohio R. 2 pt. 238; Cox *v.* Cox, 19 Ohio State, 502; Shafer *v.* Bushnell, 24 Wis. 372. The inclination in New Jersey seems the same way. Doughty *v.* Doughty, 28 N. J. Eq. 581; Yorston *v.* Yorston, 32 N. J. Eq. 495. A husband residing in another State may obtain a divorce for adultery committed in Massachusetts when both resided there, the wife having since remained there. Watkins *v.* Watkins, 135 Mass. 83. But it is held in New York, where divorce *a vinculo* is granted only for adultery, that at least in cases where the foreign divorce is so granted against a citizen of New York for an offence not recognized as a ground of divorce in New York, the divorce will not be recognized in New York; and the defendant in such suit, subsequently marrying in New York, is guilty of bigamy. People *v.* Baker, 76 N. Y. 78, overruling Baker *v.* People, 15 Hun, 256.

A suit for alimony, whether it is connected with a prayer for divorce or constitutes a separate action, is a personal action. The court has no jurisdiction to render a personal judgment for alimony against a non-resident husband, unless he appears to the action, or is personally served. An action may be brought for alimony after divorce has been granted. Cox *v.* Cox, 19 Ohio State, 502.

(*a*) Holland *v.* Holland, 2 Mass. 154; Billings *v.* Billings, 11 Pick. 461; Hansel *v.* Hansel, Wright, 212.

(*b*) Wright's Rep. 104, 120, 245, 308. But see Coffin *v.* Dunham, 8 Cush. 404; Baldwin *v.* Baldwin, 4 Gray, 341.

(*c*) In determining whether the father or mother shall have the custody of the child, neither party is considered to have any rights inconsistent with its welfare, and the order of the court will be made with a single reference to its best interests; and facts bearing on that question ought not to be excluded by any technical rule of evidence. Gishwiler *v.* Dodez, 4 Ohio State, 615. It is the practice to consult the wishes of the child where a parent seeks to recover it from the custody of a person to whom the parent has committed it to be brought up and instructed. Curtis *v.* Curtis, 5 Gray, 535; Gardenhire *v.* Hinds, 1 Head (Tenn.), 402; *post*, p. 279. Where the court of common pleas in a divorce case has decreed the custody of the child to one of the parties, their jurisdiction is a continuing one, and a probate court cannot afterwards interfere with the custody of the child, either by *habeas corpus* or granting letters of guardianship. If circumstances require it, application should be made to the same court to modify the existing decree, and no statute of limitations bars the court's

When husband and wife are divorced, they become single persons, to all intents and purposes; but by express provision, their children are not thereby rendered illegitimate, whatever may be the cause of divorce. Indeed, it may be questionable whether our law regards any marriage as void *ab initio;* and if not, the children would be legitimate without such provision. If the divorce be for the fault of the husband, the wife is restored to all *her realty*, and receives such part of her husband's property as the court shall think proper. This would seem to cut off his right *by curtesy*, to be described hereafter. If the divorce be for the fault of the wife, she is barred of her *dower*, to be described hereafter; and the whole provision to be made for her rests in the discretion of the court. The custody of the children, as before remarked, is also provided for by the court.

§ 106. **Rights of the Survivor in case of Death.** When the husband dies, the most important right of the widow is that of *dower*, which will be particularly described when we come to treat of property. Suffice it here to say, that it includes a life-interest in one-third part of all the *realty* owned by her husband at any time during the coverture; and of this no separate act of his can deprive her. In the worst shipwreck of his affairs, this is her plank of safety, unless she has with her own hand cast it away. If she lose her dower, it can only be by her own voluntary act. She may also remain in the *mansion-house* one year free of charge, unless her dower be sooner assigned, in the way to be described hereafter. (*a*) In England, the period was only forty days, which was called her *quarantine*. With respect to the *personalty* of her husband, she is entitled to a reasonable allowance for the support of herself and the children under fifteen years of age, for one year, to be set off by the appraisers; and if the personalty be not sufficient, it may be charged upon the realty. (*b*) She also has a right to use a variety of household articles specified in the statute so long as the minor children live with her, and if there be no minor children, they are hers absolutely. These rights take precedence of all the husband's debts, except for the last sickness and funeral. After the debts

right so to do. Hoffman *v.* Hoffman, 15 Ohio State, 427; Neil *v.* Neil, 38 Ohio State, 558.

(*a*) {She need not personally occupy the mansion-house, but may rent it. Conger *v.* Atwood, 28 Ohio State, 134.}

(*b*) Such allowance confers a vested right to property, and is not divested by death or any other contingency occurring after the amount has been fixed and allowed by the proper tribunal. Dorah *v.* Dorah, 4 Ohio State, 292. See Adams *v.* Adams, 10 Met. 170. The widow is entitled to the allowances, although she elects to take under the will. Collier *v.* Collier, 3 Ohio State, 369. Where the appraisers neglected to set off the widow's allowance, and she died after the expiration of the year without having waived or relinquished her right to such allowance, it survived to her personal representative. Bane *v.* Wick, 14 Ohio State, 505. Where the allowance has been made, it may be increased on the application of a creditor of the widow, filed after the year and after her death. Sherman's Ex'r *v.* Sherman, 21 Ohio State, 631. {But her claim to a year's support is not a debt, therefore a conveyance by the husband to defeat it is not to be set aside as a fraud upon her. Lockwood *v.* Krum, 34 Ohio State, 1.}

are paid, if there be no children, she has all the residue of the personalty. If there be children, she has one-half of the first four hundred dollars, and one-third of the residue. (*a*) With respect to the property which was originally hers, if there be no curtesy, she at once resumes her control over the realty; and if there be any of her *choses in action* not reduced to possession by the husband they again become hers. (*b*) She also has the first claim, if she be a suitable person, to administer upon the estate, and be guardian of the children. (*c*)

When the wife dies, the husband acquires an important right, somewhat analogous to dower, which is called *curtesy*, and will be described hereafter; suffice it here to say, that it includes a life-interest in all the *realty* belonging to the wife. As to her *personalty*, we have seen, that, with the exception of *choses in action*, it is already absolutely his, by the mere fact of marriage. And as to her *choses in action*, they become his by being reduced to possession. If before her death he has not reduced them to possession, he may by the common law do this as administrator, and so make them his. But under the law of this State, I doubt if this be the case. He may act as her administrator, and so collect her debts; but when collected, it would seem that they must be disposed of as assets are in all other cases of administration.

Finally, when husband or wife dies, and there is no relative of the deceased, however remote, to inherit the property, the survivor is the *heir*. (*d*) Why the most distant relative that can be hunted up should thus be preferred as heir before the nearest and dearest of all human relatives, I cannot understand: but so it is; and husband and wife can only be heirs to each other when no other heir can be found, and when the property would otherwise *escheat* to the State.

I have thus taken a general view of the relation of husband and wife; and the sum is this: Woman, married or single, has no political rights whatsoever. While single, her legal rights are the same as those of man. When married, her legal rights are chiefly suspended. When she becomes a widow, these rights revive, and

(*a*) R. S. § 6194.

(*b*) It was formerly held that a judgment recovered by the husband was not a reducing to possession, so as to cut off the wife's survivorship, without execution; but that a decree alone was sufficient. But the rule would now seem to be that if the husband sue alone, either a judgment or decree cuts off the wife; and if he join the wife in the suit, then neither cuts her off. When, however, the husband or his creditors go into equity to subject the *choses in action* of the wife, that court will go very far to protect her interest, and secure her a support. 2 Kent, Com. 137–143; Clancy on Husband and Wife, 115; Parsons *v.* Parsons, 9 N. H. 309; Wheeler *v.* Moore, 13 id. 478; Marston *v.* Carter, 12 id. 159; Poor *v.* Hazelton, 15 id. 564; Davis *v.* Newton, 6 Met. 537; Carter *v.* Buckingham, 1 Handy, 395. Needles *v.* Needles, 7 Ohio State, 432.

(*c*) An administrator can only be at the same time guardian of the person of the minor heir and not of the minor's estate. R. S. of Ohio, § 6256.

(*d*) This has been slightly modified since the text was written. See lecture on Title by Descent. The husband and wife succeed to each other, if there are no children or their legal representatives, as to personalty and as to real property that came to the deceased otherwise than by descent, devise, or gift. R. S. of Ohio, § 4159.

liberal provision is made for her support; but, from first to last, man has the advantage. Blackstone closes his chapter with an eulogium on the laws of England, for their liberality towards woman. How little this is deserved, is manifest from what has already been said. Our law is vastly more liberal towards woman than the English law; yet even here she has too much reason to regret that her lot has not fallen under the dominion of the civil law. I can see neither policy, justice, nor humanity in many of the legal doctrines with respect to married women. But there is one evil in the system which pre-eminently calls for correction. I refer to the entire helplessness of a married woman, when her husband becomes a prodigal or spendthrift. If he take care to give no cause of divorce, she has no means of providing against the utter ruin which she sees approaching. He may squander a personal estate worth a million of dollars, and leave a wife and children paupers, and the wife cannot, in this State, invoke the aid of a court to prevent it. Some of the other States have provided for such a case; others have secured to her use her own separate property, whether personal or real; (*a*) and there is evidently a strong tendency in public opinion towards securing to her some of the more important legal rights.

(*a*) We have seen that this has now been done in Ohio. As to the jurisdiction of equity in cases where the rights of married women are involved, see 2 Story, Eq. Juris. ch. xxxvii.

NOTE. — The text states the position of a married woman in relation to property as held by courts of law: her position in courts of equity was different. When a woman, having property held in trust for her, married, the trustee could pay the income to her husband, and his receipt would be a full acquittance. But if the trustee refused to pay him, and the husband went into a court of equity to have such payment enforced, the court at an early day established the rule that it would see that a suitable provision was settled upon the wife out of the property as a condition of giving any relief to the husband. When property was devised, bequeathed, or conveyed to a trustee for the separate use of a woman, whether before or after marriage, she held the property free from the control or interference of her husband. It was next held that if property was given to a woman to be held to her separate use, the instrument making such settlement separated the legal estate from the beneficial interest, and, upon her marrying, her husband took only the legal estate as a dry trust, the wife retaining the beneficial interest as her separate property. And it was established by Taylor *v.* Meads, 4 De Gex, J. & S. 597, that a married woman, where not restrained from alienation, has, as incident to her separate estate, and without any express power, a complete right of alienation of that estate by will.

As a necessary incident to her separate property, she could charge it, that is, subject it to payment for her debts. It was early held that she could so charge it by her general engagements, or bonds, bills, notes, or other written obligations, which made no reference to her separate estate. It was held by Turner, L. J., in Johnson *v.* Gallagher, 3 De Gex, F. & J. 494, that this is true of her general engagements, using the word in a wider sense as including her verbal engagements and debts contracted without any express promise to pay; but that "in order to bind the separate estate by a general engagement, it should appear that the engagement was made with reference to, and upon the faith or credit of, that estate, and whether it was so or not is a question to be judged of by the court upon all the circumstances of the case." The rule so stated has been since followed, and accordingly her separate estate is charged by her joining her husband in signing a joint and several note for money lent to him. Davies *v.* Jenkins, L. R. 6 Ch. Div. 728.

This charge upon the estate is not a lien or an appointment, but a liability of the estate to be taken in payment by decree, as a man's property may be taken on execution. Hence the charge will be defeated by a mortgage for full value, or by a conveyance of the estate, before the creditor obtains a decree subjecting it to payment. Johnson *v.* Gallagher, 3 De Gex, F. & J. 494. The charge can be enforced only against such property as was her separate estate when the engagement was made, and only so much thereof as remains when the decree is pronounced; not against what has been subsequently acquired, nor against what has been subsequently conveyed or assigned. Pike *v.* Fitzgibbon, L. R. 17 Ch. Div. 454.

The English rule as to the capacity of a married woman to charge her separate estate by her general engagements has not been uniformly followed in the United States. In Rhode Island, Pennsylvania, South Carolina, Tennessee, and Mississippi, it has been held that she cannot alienate, encumber, or charge it, unless express power is given thereto in the deed of trust or settlement. But in most of the States statutes have been enacted substantially making all her property separate estate. As a vested right cannot be taken away by statute, and a husband had vested rights in his wife's general property, these statutes do not apply to property owned, at the time of their enactment, by married women. Under these statutes the husband generally has no estate in his wife's property during her life, while he retains his curtesy in her realty after her death. While in some States she can convey or encumber her property by her sole deed; in most, she can do so only by deed or mortgage executed jointly with her husband. Generally she can, jointly with him, mortgage it for any valuable consideration, whether moving to her or not. But in Georgia, where she is not allowed to be surety for her husband, her mortgage for that purpose is void. And where, as in Alabama, and Mississippi, her statutory property can be only for the purposes stated in the statute, her mortgage for any other purpose is void.

The courts all agree that the engagements of a married woman do not charge her separate estate unless she intends them to do so at the time she enters into the engagement; but they differ as to what is competent evidence, as to what is presumptive evidence, and as to what is conclusive evidence, of such intention. The courts also differ as to the extent of her power to charge.

In some States a married woman can charge her separate estate only for the benefit of such property or of herself. Elliott *v.* Gowan, 12 R. I. 79, where it is also held that her estate is not charged unless she expressly declare at the time her intention to charge it. Perkins *v.* Elliott, 23 N. J. Eq. 526. This case was decided in 1872, and the New Jersey act of 1872, found in the Revised Statutes of 1877, allows a married woman to make any contract and to be sued thereon, except a contract of suretyship or guaranty, or to answer the debt of another. In Pennsylvania, the rule still prevails that a married woman cannot charge or encumber her separate estate created by deed or settlement, except to the extent and in the manner expressed in the instrument creating it. Maurer's Appeal, 86 Penn. State, 380. But she can charge her statutory estate by her engagements, oral or written, contracted for its or her benefit. Sawtelle's Appeal, 84 Penn. State, 306. In Maryland she can charge her separate estate only by her engagements directly affecting it. Wilson *v.* Jones, 46 Md. 349. In Georgia, § 1783 of the Code expressly provides that a married woman cannot bind her property by any contract of suretyship or by any assumption of the debts of her husband. Dunbar *v.* Mize, 53 Ga. 435. In Alabama the general property of a married woman is not made separate estate by the statute; but the statute prescribes in detail the purposes for which only it can be charged or incumbered. It cannot be charged to secure her husband's debts. Dacus *v.* Streety, 59 Ala. 254. Mississippi has an analogous statute and the same decision. Stokes *v.* Shannon, 55 Miss. 583. In Arkansas a married woman can charge her separate estate only by her engagements made for the benefit of it or of herself. Collins *v.* Underwood, 33 Ark. 265. But her mortgage executed jointly with her husband to secure his debt, is valid. Collins *v.* Wassell, 34 Ark. 17. In Indiana it has been held that she can charge her estate only by engagements made for its betterment. Insurance Co. *v.* Avery, 60 Ind. 566; Richards *v.* O'Brien, 64 Ind. 418. In Michigan a married woman cannot be surety for her husband. Kitchell *v.* Mudgett, 37 Mich. 81; Jenne *v.* Marble, id. 319. In Illinois, prior to the act of 1874, giving to a married woman the power of a *feme sole* in relation to her property, she could charge her property by her engagements only so far as was necessary to her enjoyment thereof. Thompson *v.* Weller, 85 Ill. 197.

In the following States she can charge her estate by her general engagements, including her engagement as surety for her husband or others: In Massachusetts, since 1874 — Major *v.* Holmes, 124 Mass. 108; Goodnow *v.* Hill, 125 Mass. 587. In New York — Yale *v.* Dederer, 68 N. Y. 329. In Virginia — Frank *v.* Lilienfeld, 33 Gratt. 379. In West Virginia, where, however, she can charge her estate to secure the debt of her husband or other person only by note or other engagement in writing — Radford *v.* Carwile, 13 W. Va. 572. In South Carolina, by legislation under the new constitution — Witsell *v.* Charleston, 7 S. C. 88. In Alabama, as to her separate estate created by deed or settlement — Cowles *v.* Morgan, 34 Ala. 535. Kentucky — Hart *v.* Grigsby, 14 Bush, 542. Ohio — Williams *v.* Urmston, 35 Ohio State, 296. Illinois, since 1874 — Kohn *v* Russell, 91 Ill. 138. Missouri — Siemers *v.* Kleeburg, 56 Mo. 196. Minnesota — Life Insurance Co. *v.* Allis, 23 Minn. 337. Nebraska, where there is positive actual intention to do so — Bank *v.* Scott, 10 Neb. 83. California — Woods *v.* Oxford, 52 Cal. 412.

A promissory note, signed by a married woman, has been held (1), not to be evidence of an intention to charge her separate estate — Hodgson *v.* Davis, 43 Ind. 258; Emery *v.* Lord, 26 Mich. 231; (2), not such evidence unless the intention is expressly stated in the note — Yale *v.* Dederer, 68 N. Y. 329; and the same ruling is made in New York as to her bonds and other written obligations — Gorman *v.* Cruger, 69 N. Y. 87; Woolsey *v.* Brown, 74 N. Y. 82. It is held to be presumptive evidence of such intention in Garland *v.* Pomplin, 32 Gratt. 305; Bell *v.* Kellar, 13 B. Monroe, 381; Williams *v.* Urmston, 35 Ohio State, 296. But if she gives the note in part-payment of land bought by her, she is incompetent to testify that she did not intend thereby to charge all her separate estate, Avery *v.* Vansickle, 35 Ohio State, 270 {otherwise such intention is rebuttable, Harris *v.* Wilson, 40 id. 300; but only by facts and not by her denial, Hershizer *v.* Florence, 39 id. 516. A writing is not necessary to charge her estate, Elliott *v.* Lawhead, 43 id. 171}, and has been held conclusive evidence in Kimm *v.* Wiepert, 46 Mo. 532; Bank *v.* Taylor, 62 Mo. 338; Morrison *v.* Thistle, 67 Mo. 596. {But she cannot contract with her husband, and hence cannot be his partner, even under the law of 1884 in Ohio. Payne *v.* Thompson, Supr. Ct., Ohio, 1886; nor in Mass. Kniel *v.* Egleston, Supr. Ct., Mass., 1885. Under a law enabling her to contract as if sole, a promissory note by a husband to his wife, or *vice versa*, is absolutely void. Fowle *v.* Torry, 135 Mass. 99.}

In some States a married woman is liable upon her contracts in an action at law. But in Ohio, under a statute providing that "in all cases where she may sue or be sued alone, the like proceedings shall be had and the like judgment rendered and enforced in all respects as if she were an unmarried woman," it is held that the action against her is still a proceeding to charge her separate estate, not an action upon a contract, and is therefore in substance a suit in equity, though in form an action at law; and hence the petition must aver that she has separate estate. Jenz *v.* Gugel, 26 Ohio State, 527. A court not having equity jurisdiction — for example, a justice of the peace — has no jurisdiction in such an action. Allison *v.* Porter, 29 Ohio State, 136; Elliott *v.* Lawhead, 43 id. 171. And there is no right in either party to demand trial by jury. Avery *v.* Vansickle, 35 Ohio State, 270.

In Alabama the rule was declared as it has since been declared in England, that a judgment enforcing a charge upon a married woman's separate estate attaches only to such separate estate as she owned at the time she entered into the engagement creating the charge, and only to so much thereof as remains her property at the time of the judgment. Pippin *v.* Jones, 52 Ala. 161.

The statutes of Illinois, Iowa, Kansas, and Colorado seem substantially to give a married woman equal power with a *feme sole*, as to controlling, conveying, charging and encumbering her property, putting her on the same footing as to her property that the husband has to his. There is a steady drift of legislation tending toward the complete removal of the disability of coverture of a married woman touching the ownership, control, and disposition of property, and her right to sue and liability to be sued alone. Corresponding with this is other progressive legislation tending to relieve the husband from liability for his wife's debts. It is already provided in some States, that if he is made to pay her debts contracted before marriage, he is entitled to restitution from her property; in others, if judgment is recovered against both for such debts, execution must go first against her property; in others, that he is not liable for her debts. In Iowa the laws, Rev. Stats. 1880, declare that neither husband nor wife is liable for debts contracted by the other, while both are liable for appropriate necessaries supplied to the family. In some States it is also provided that the wife shall sue alone, and in her own right, for injuries done to her, and that the husband is not liable for her torts.

LECTURE XV.

PARENT AND CHILD. (a)

§ 107. **Legitimate and Illegitimate Children.** The relation of parent and child, though in itself the most interesting that can be contemplated, is not, professionally speaking, a subject of very great importance. The law has, in fact, very little to do in regulating this relation. The sentiments of natural affection and moral obligation are so efficient for this purpose, that the sanctions of law are for the most part dispensed with; and this has become more and more the case, in proportion as mankind have become more civilized. The difference, in this respect, between ancient and modern times, is remarkable. From unlimited authority over the person, property, and even life, of the child, the parent is now curtailed to a very guarded and qualified authority over the person, during the years of minority. And even this authority finds but little aid in the law to enforce it in case of resistance. In a word, parental authority and filial obedience are left, as they should be, to the law which nature has written upon the heart. In very recent times we may discover changes in this respect, showing a regular tendency towards the doctrine of non-interference by legislators in domestic affairs. Among the earliest laws adopted in this territory, in 1788, is one providing that if a child or servant should refuse "to obey the lawful commands" of a parent or master, upon complaint to a magistrate, the offender might be sent to jail, "there to remain until he should humble himself to the satisfaction of the parent or master." And if a child or servant should "presume to assault or strike" his parent or master, upon complaint to two or more magistrates, the offender might be whipped, not exceeding ten stripes. What would be thought of such a law at the present day? The legislature would not deign to discuss a provision of this kind. But I proceed to the few legal matters that require notice under this head.

Though the law of parent and child is said to be founded in nature, yet it makes a broad distinction between *legitimate* and *illegitimate* children. By our law, legitimate children comprehend all those whose parents were married, whether lawfully or not, at the time of their being begotten or born, or who married

(a) See 2 Kent, Com. lec. 29; 1 Black. Com. ch. 16; 1 Swift, ch. 6; Reeves's Domestic Relations; Bingham on Infancy; McPherson on Infancy. See act to authorize the adoption of children, passed March 29, 1859. As to the proofs of filiation and legitimacy, see Hubback on Succession. There is a very interesting case on this subject, involving the legitimacy of John P. Ferrie, where the evidence peculiar to these questions is fully discussed. 3 Bradford, Sur. R. 151, 249; 4 id. 28; Caujolle *v.* Ferrie, 26 Barb. 177; s. c. 23 N. Y. 90.

afterwards. This is much more liberal than the English rule, which requires the marriage to precede the birth, and which bastardizes the issue of all unlawful marriages. Here, on the contrary, it is expressly provided, that if the offending parents afterwards intermarry, and acknowledge their children, they thereby become legitimate; and that the issue of marriages deemed null in law, shall nevertheless be held legitimate. In the same spirit, and nearly to the same effect, is another provision, declaring that no divorce shall render the children illegitimate. The justice and humanity of these provisions cannot fail to strike every mind. How cruel and unreasonable the law which would visit the sins of the parents upon the unoffending offspring of their unlawful intercourse! And, on the other hand, how wise and humane the law which gives to such parents the strongest of motives to repair, by subsequent marriage, the wrong they will otherwise have done! Such improvements in the law cannot be too much commended. Though apparently trifling in themselves, they indicate a spirit which, if persevered in, cannot fail to purge the law of a multitude of doctrines unsuited to the present state of civilization. It follows from the foregoing remarks, that *illegitimate* children, or *bastards*, comprehend all children whose parents never intermarried at all, or were divorced before the children were begotten. But when a doubt exists, the presumption is always in favor of legitimacy; and, therefore, if a woman have a child within a possible time after the death or absence of her husband, that child is presumed to be legitimate. Our statute respecting bastards, (*a*) corresponds in the main with the English statute, as described by Blackstone. It authorizes any unmarried woman, who is pregnant or delivered of a bastard child, to go before a justice and make oath who is the father. The putative father is then brought up by warrant, and the examination is taken in writing. If he can compound with the mother, and will give bond to the overseers of the poor, for the maintenance of the child, the matter ends there. (*b*) If not, he is bound over to appear at the next court, where the issue is tried on a plea of not guilty. The former examination is given in evidence, and the mother may testify further. If the jury find that he is guilty, the court adjudge him to be the "*reputed father*," and fix the amount of maintenance and times of payment; and unless he gives satisfactory security therefor he is committed to jail. (*c*) If the mother

(*a*) For the construction given to this statute, see Massie *v.* Donaldson, 8 Ohio, 377, and Wright's Rep. 464, 564, 690.

(*b*) Maxwell *v.* Campbell, 8 Ohio State, 265; Hootman *v.* Shriner, 15 Ohio State, 43.

(*c*) The marriage of the complainant to another man, subsequent to the institution of the suit but prior to the birth of the child, will not defeat the proceedings. The child may still be born a bastard. Roth *v.* Jacobs, 21 Ohio State, 646. {Where a man knowingly marries a woman pregnant by another man he consents to stand *in loco parentis* to the child, and is conclusively presumed to be its father except as to questions of inheritance. **Miller** *v.* **Anderson,** 43 Ohio State, 473; Haworth *v.* Gill, 30 id. 627.}

will not proceed against the father in the way here pointed out, the overseers of the poor may. From the nature of the proceeding, it will at once be seen that even an innocent man, once accused, has very little chance of establishing his innocence. The most important point of difference between legitimate and illegitimate children, is that which relates to the right of inheritance. The general rule is, that children are the first heirs to their deceased parents: but in England bastards are held to have no inheritable blood. They can neither inherit themselves, nor be the medium of transmitting inheritance to others. We have so far modified this doctrine, as to allow them to inherit and transmit inheritance on the part of the mother, who can always be known with certainty. (*a*) But with respect to the father, the law is unchanged, and they cannot inherit from or through him. The general subject of inheritance will come up hereafter. In this connection, it is sufficient to say that *posthumous* children inherit in the same manner as if born during the father's life; that no preference is given to sons over daughters, nor to the eldest son over the rest; and that the arbitrary rule, that property can never lineally ascend is done away; so that parents may be heirs to their children.

§ 108. **Rights and Duties of Parents.** (*b*) Blackstone and other writers lay down the duties of parents towards their children as consisting in their *maintenance*, *protection*, and *education*. There can be no doubt that these are duties of the highest moral obligation; and he would be an unnatural parent, who should be false to them, having the ability to perform them. But it is certainly a mistake to say that they are duties of strict legal obligation, unless there be a statute to that effect. Such they are not, because the common law furnishes no means of enforcing their performance, or punishing their non-performance. On this subject, writers seem to be beguiled by their good feelings into singular misapprehension or inexcusable vagueness of expression. How can you compel a parent to maintain, protect, or educate his child? The common law furnishes no means of doing it; and as the test of legal obligation is the means of enforcing it, this proves that the legal obligation does not exist. First, as to *maintenance* or *support*, our statute seems to presuppose that there are no means of compulsion, by authorizing the township trustees to bind children out when their parents shall not provide for them; and the principle that a parent may by will disinherit a child, or may do the same thing by giving all his property away during his life, leads to the same conclusion. It may even be doubted whether, if a parent

(*a*) Lewis *v.* Eutsler, 4 Ohio State, 354; R. S. § 4174 {Gibson *v.* McNeely, 11 Ohio State, 131, 137; Hawkins *v.* Jones, 19 id. 22}.

(*b*) 1 Black. Com. 446; 2 Kent, Com. 189; Inhabitants, &c. *v.* Mendez, 1 Raymond, 699; Cooper *v.* Martin, 4 East, 76; Mills *v.* Wyman, 3 Pick. 207; Stanton *v.* Wilson, 3 Day, 37; Van Valkinburg *v.* Watson, 13 Johns. 480; Edwards *v.* Davis, 16 id. 281.

should, without reason, turn his child out of doors, and a stranger, knowing this, should provide for the child, he could recover payment from the parent. (*a*) Next, as to *protection*, a parent may

(*a*) The law of England is well settled that the father is under no legal obligation to provide for the maintenance of a child, and cannot be made liable for necessaries furnished to him by a third person without authority express or implied. Mortimore *v.* Wright, 6 M. & W. 482 ; Shelton *v.* Springett, 11 C. B. 452 ; s. c. 20 Eng. Law and Eq. 281. Such is held to be the common law in Vermont, New York, and Illinois. Gordon *v.* Potter, 17 Vt. 348 ; Raymond *v.* Loyl, 10 Barb. 483 ; Chilcott *v.* Trimble, 13 id. 502 ; Hunt *v.* Thompson, 3 Scammon, 180. So too in New Hampshire, where it is held that the obligation cannot be implied from an omission merely of the moral obligation to furnish necessaries. Kelley *v.* Davis, 49 N. H. 187. But *contra*, in Massachusetts. Dennis *v.* Clark, 2 Cushing, 353. And see also Eitel *v.* Walter, 2 Bradford (N. Y.), 287 ; Pocock *v.* Miller, 1 Hilton (N. Y. C. P.), 108 ; Edwards *v.* Davis, 16 Johns. 281 ; Owen *v.* White, 5 Porter (Ind.), 435 ; Litchfield *v.* Londonderry, 39 N. H. 247 ; Hines *v.* Mullins, 25 Ga. 696 ; Dawson *v.* Dawson, 12 Iowa, 512 ; Tomkins *v.* Tomkins, 3 Stockton, 512 ; Gill *v.* Read, 5 R. I. 343, — holding the father liable for necessaries. In Cromwell *v.* Benjamin, 44 Barb. 558, it is said that the liability of the father to support his children where they are minors or invalids, and unable to support themselves, and remain members of his family, rests upon principles analogous to those which create a husband's liability to support his wife. But see *contra*. The father who is willing to support his child is not liable for such support to one who wrongfully withholds it from him; or to the mother who, having been divorced from him, so withholds it, or where the custody of the child was awarded to her in a decree of separation or divorce. Fitler *v.* Fitler, 33 Penn. State, 50 ; Burritt *v.* Burritt, 29 Barb. 124 ; Finch *v.* Finch, 22 Conn. 411. The obligation of the father to support his child is not removed by the circumstance that the child has property, even greater than his own. Dawes *v.* Howard, 4 Mass. 97. But a liberal doctrine now prevails, under which allowances are made to the father of a certain portion of the property of the child for its support, graduated according to the respective estates of the father and child, the ability of the former, the position and expectations of the latter, and all the circumstances of the case. Retrospective allowances are, however, not favored. Matter of Burke, 4 Sandf. Ch. 617 ; Matter of Kane, 2 Barb. Ch. 375 ; Presley *v.* Davis, 7 Rich. Eq. 105 ; Watts *v.* Steele, 19 Ala. 656 ; Osborne *v.* Van Horne, 2 Flor. 360 ; Pierce *v.* Olney, 5 R. I. 269 ; Kilburn *v.* Hosmer, 10 Cush. 150 ; 2 Kent, Com. 191 ; 1 Parsons, Cont. 256, 257 ; Tomkins *v.* Tompkins's Ex'rs, 3 Green, 303 ; Beasley *v.* Watson, 41 Ala. 234. Where a mother brings up a child who has property under circumstances which show that she did not intend it as a gratuity to the child, she may maintain an action for the expenses of maintenance and education. Whipple *v.* Dow, 2 Mass. 414. But the presumption is, that a parent's maintenance of a child is intended to be gratuitous, and the fact that the child has property while the parent has none, will not be sufficient to rebut such a presumption. Reeves's Dom. Rel. 466, note. The authority of the child to contract on behalf of the father for necessaries may be implied from circumstances. Baker *v.* Steen, 2 Stark. 501 ; Mortimore *v.* Wright, 6 M. & W. 482 ; Deane *v.* Annis, 14 Maine, 26 ; Thayer *v.* White, 12 Met. 343 ; Swain *v.* Tyler, 26 Vt. 1 ; Platts *v.* Roseburg, 4 Dutcher, 136. I think, that, upon careful examination of these apparently conflicting cases, most if not all of them will be found practically to hold the parent bound to support the child ; for where they deny this to be the doctrine, they still hold that where the parent drives the child out of the house, or refuses to furnish him with support, the authority of the child to contract for necessaries on behalf of the father will be implied. This, it is evident, practically results in holding him bound for its support, — one set of cases holding that a direct liability exists on his part, while the others, denying any such direct liability, *infer*, from the fact that he refuses to support it, an authority to contract for its own support. But a late case in New Hampshire distinctly holds that such authority to the child to contract cannot be implied from the mere failure of the father to furnish necessaries. Kelley *v.* Davis, 49 N. H. 187. Slight circumstances though will be sufficient. Fowlkes *v.* Baker, 29 Texas, 35 ; Wilkes *v.* McClung, 32 Ga. 507. The mother, according to the authorities, is not entitled to the earnings of a minor child after the death of the father, and is not liable for its support. Raymond *v.* Loyl, 10 Barb. 483 ; Pray *v.* Gorman, 31 Maine, 240 ; Bartley *v.* Richtmyer, 4 N. Y. 46 ; E. B. *v.* E. C. B. 28 Barb. 303 ; Passenger R. R. Co. Stutlen, 54 Penn. State, 375. But in New Jersey it is held that she generally is. Campbell *v.* Campbell, 3 Stockton, 268 ; Osborne *v.* Allen, 2 Dutcher, 388. See certainly go as far in defending his child from harm as in defending himself. The law permits him so to do; but it does not undertake to compel him so to do, or punish him for not so doing. And, lastly, as to *education*, the same is true. A parent of the most unbounded means may, in spite of the law, bring up his children in the most deplorable ignorance. The truth therefore is, that these are not matters of legal obligation. The law has left them to the strong impulses of natural affection. Whether wisely or not, is a question I need not discuss. The fact is all that I am now concerned with. And, on the other hand, the parent's power over the child is very little aided by law. The father is the *natural guardian* of the minor children; in which capacity he has the custody of their persons, but not of their property. He may correct them with moderation, bind them out to service, receive their earnings, and forbid their marrying. He may also by will appoint for them a *testamentary guardian*, with powers extending to their persons and property. This is a singular instance in which a person may delegate a power which he does not possess. The father, unless legally appointed guardian, cannot control the separate property of his minor child, except it be earned by the child's labor; but he may by will confer this power on another. Finally, at majority, or when a daughter marries, all power of the parent over the child ceases; and the child, to all intents and purposes, becomes emancipated from parental control. (*a*)

also Mathewson *v.* Perry, 37 Conn. 435; Hammond *v.* Corbett, 50 N. H. 501; Simpson *v.* Buck, 5 Lans. (N. Y.) 337. A step-father is not bound to support step-children. *Re* Besondy, 32 Minn. 385. Whether such support, if furnished, is a gratuity or not, must be determined from circumstances. Bond *v.* Lockwood, 33 Ill. 312. *Contra*, 54 Iowa, 591.

(*a*) In the text, I have purposely abstained from details. The right of custody of a minor child is not absolute, like that of property. The law looks mainly to the good of the child, and if a better custody exists than that of the father, the law will not disturb it. State *v.* Baird, 3 Green, N. J. 194; s. c. 21 N. J. Eq. 384; McBride *v.* McBride, 1 Bush, 15; Cole *v.* Cole, 23 Iowa, 433; Clark *v.* Bayer, 32 Ohio State, 299; Smith *v.* Bragg, 68 Ga. 650; 25 Kan. 308; 42 Mich. 509. But, as a general rule, it belongs to the father. Queen *v.* Howes, 3 El., B. & E. 322. The usual mode of testing the right of custody is by *habeas corpus*. Gishwiler *v.* Dodez, 4 Ohio State, 615; *ante*, p. 263, note (*c*); 2 Kent, Com. 194, 205. But the order can only be made on *habeas corpus*, where it appears that the child is unlawfully restrained of its liberty, as that is the office of the writ. State *v.* Baird, 3 Green (N. J.), 194. It has even been held that the father's right to the custody of his child is not lost by abandonment. Johnson *v.* Terry, 34 Conn. 259. *Contra*, Brewster *v.* Compton, 68 Ala. 299; 32 Ohio State, 299. The mother has a right to the custody of an illegitimate child. Alfred *v.* McKay, 36 Ga. 440. The father's right to the custody of the child cannot be transferred by parol. State *v.* Libbey, 44 N. H. 321; but see 26 Kan. 650. An agreement between the husband and wife that she shall have the custody of their child is not binding at law. Johnson *v.* Terry, 34 Conn. 259. The father's right to the earnings of the child is founded upon the fact of support and protection. If, therefore, the father agree with the child that he shall have his time, or send him out into the world to provide for himself, he cannot claim his earnings. 2 Kent, Com. 193, 194; 1 Black. Com. 453; Woodell *v.* Coggeshall, 2 Met. 89; Stiles *v.* Granville, 6 Cush. 458; Bray *v.* Wheeler, 29 Vt. 514; 72 Me. 509; Rush *v.* Vought, 55 Penn. State, 437. And the property so acquired by the son is not liable for the debts of the father. McCloskey *v.* Cyphert, 27 Penn. State, 220. Even though the child continue to reside with the parent and perform some services for him. 66 Ala. 362; Johnson *v.* Silsbee, 49 N. H. 543. The

§ 109. **Rights and Duties of Children.** These may be inferred from the foregoing statements. Like those of parents, they are chiefly of moral obligation, and not a subject for these lectures. We have no legal provision for compelling even an affluent child, after majority, to support an indigent parent. In some places, there is such provision, extending even to grandchildren; and it might, perhaps, be well if we had it; but as our law stands, the child or grandchild cannot be compelled to support the parent or grandparent, even to save them from the poor-house. Thus filial, like parental, duty, is left by the legislature to depend upon natural affection. (*a*) The parent may invite the love, respect, obedience, and support of the child; but the law will not help him to command them. During minority, if the child live with the parent, and there be no agreement to the contrary, the parent is entitled to his labor and earnings; but, by statute, if the child be bound out as an apprentice, any money stipulated for in the indenture must be secured to the child. If an adult child continue to reside with his parents, and live and labor in common with the family, there is no implied contract to pay him wages, and he can only claim them under an express contract. (*b*) The child can

father is not bound by the contract of the child, even for necessaries, nor liable for his torts, unless an actual authority be proved, or implied from circumstances. Baker *v.* Keen, 2 Starkie, 501; Van Valkinburg *v.* Watson, 13 Johns. 480. But in this last case, the court say, "The parent is under a natural obligation to furnish necessaries for an infant child, and if the parent neglect that duty, any other person who supplies such necessaries is deemed to have conferred upon the delinquent parent a benefit, from which the law raises an implied promise to pay, on the part of the parent." See remarks in preceding note. On the ground of a right to the services of a minor child, the father may sue for a tort committed upon such child. Hall *v.* Hollander, 4 B. & C. 660. And in case of the seduction of a daughter, the slightest proof of service will be sufficient. 2 Leigh's Nisi Prius, 1462. The father may maintain an action for the seduction of his daughter effected during her minority, after she has attained her majority. Stevenson *v.* Belknap, 6 Clarke (Iowa), 97. When a minor daughter marries, the rights of the parent are transferred to her husband; and the parent would be liable to damages for wrongfully depriving the husband of such rights. Friend *v.* Thompson, Wright's Rep. 636. In New York it has been held that an action for the seduction of a daughter may be maintained by a widowed mother. Gray *v.* Durland, 50 Barb. 100. If a law of Congress authorizes the enlistment of minors over eighteen, such enlistment will be valid and binding. In the Matter of Disinger, 12 Ohio State, 256.

(*a*) Reeves's Dom. Rel. 283; Rex *v.* Munden, 1 Strange, 190; Edwards *v.* Davis, 16 Johnson, 281. Furnishing necessary provisions to a parent is not a sufficient consideration to support a subsequent written promise by the child to pay for them. Cook *v.* Bradley, 7 Conn. 57. But a promise to pay will be implied where there is a previous request. Stone *v.* Stone, 32 Conn. 142. In New Hampshire an express request by the child to furnish the necessaries must be proved. Lebanon *v.* Griffin, 45 N. H. 558.

(*b*) Wright's Rep. 89, 133, 547, 751; 12 Ill. App. 478; Andrus *v.* Foster, 17 Vt. 556; Fitch *v.* Peckham, 16 id. 150; Ridgway *v.* English, 2 New Jersey, 409; Steel *v.* Steel, 12 Penn. State, 64; Hertzog *v.* Hertzog, 29 id. 465; Zerbe *v.* Miller, 16 id. 488; Weir *v.* Weir, 3 B. Monr. 647; Seavey *v.* Seavey, 37 N. H. 125; Munger *v.* Munger, 33 id. 581; Updike *v.* Ten Broeck, 3 Vroom, 105; Prickett *v.* Prickett, 20 N. J. Eq. 478; Haywood *v.* Brooks, 47 N. H. 231; Titman *v.* Titman, 64 Penn. State, 480; Luney *v.* Vantyne, 40 Vt. 501; Hart *v.* Hart's Adm., 41 Mo. 441; Butler *v.* Slam, 50 Penn. State, 456. But see Guild *v.* Guild, 15 Pick. 130. This rule applies to other near relatives adopted into the family. Hudson *v.* Lutz, 5 Jones (N. C.), 217. A parent who goes to live with a child is under no implied obligation to pay for board. Lynn *v.* Lynn, 29 Penn. State, 369; and where a married daughter lives or stays at her father's house, only bind the parent by his contracts, or make him liable for his torts, (*a*) when acting under his authority. The mere relation involves no such liability. Nor do the legal relations of parent and child extend to those of step-parent and step-child, unless by statute.

The course of our observations upon this relation of parent and child, naturally suggests a remark or two upon the proper scope of legislation. We have seen that the law interferes very little between parents and children; much less, in fact, than it formerly did. And why is this? Is it not because the world is learning to estimate more truly the nature and value of personal liberty? The complaint has always been, that the world was too much governed; that the law interfered too much in matters which did not concern the public, and ought therefore to be optional. This complaint has been well founded. Perchance it would not be without some foundation even now; but the tendency of legislation is certainly encouraging in this respect. Men are more and more permitted by government to manage their own affairs in their own way. This is strikingly manifested in the absence of legislation with respect to parent and child; and therefore I have remarked upon it here. But we shall have frequent occasion, in the course of our inquiries, to notice the same tendency in other matters; and it is a happy tendency. The true light in which to regard government, is that of a necessary evil. Some degree of government we must have, to preserve social order; but the less we have of it the better, provided individuals will keep themselves in order. That is the happiest condition of society in which the operations of government are the least felt in private affairs. Like the atmosphere which supports us, we are the best off with respect to it when we have the least reason to be conscious of its existence.

the husband is not under an implied contract to pay for her board. Cantine *v.* Phillips, 5 Harring. 428. When parental relations exist between or are assumed by individuals, neither an agreement to pay for services rendered, nor for the maintenance furnished, will be implied from the mere fact that the services were rendered, or the maintenance furnished. Duffey *v.* Duffey, 44 Penn. State, 399; Oxford *v.* McFarland, 3 Ind. 156; Brush *v.* Blanchard, 18 Ill. 46; Gillet *v.* Camp, 27 Mo. 511; Brown *v.* Lockwell, 26 Ga. 380; Putnam *v.* Town, 34 Vt. 429; Seidig *v.* Coover's Ex'rs, 47 Penn. State, 534; Adams *v.* Adams's Adm'rs, 23 Ind. 50.

(*a*) Paul *v.* Hummel, 43 Mo. 119. A parent is not liable for the negligent shooting of a horse by his infant child. Baker *v.* Morris, 33 Kan. 580. *Contra* if he knew the child would do so. Hoverson *v.* Noker, 60 Wis. 511, where the children were in the habit of shooting on the premises to frighten passing horses. Where the minor had contracted to clear his father's land, and in doing so negligently fired the plaintiff's property the parent was held liable. 86 Ind. 476.

LECTURE XVI.

GUARDIAN AND WARD. (*a*)

§ 110. **Appointment of Guardians.** The relation of guardian and ward is not founded in nature, like that of parent and child; but owes its origin to legal provision. When a person is not in a condition to take proper care of himself or his property, the law provides that some other person shall act for him in this behalf. The person thus designated is *guardian*, and the person placed under his care *ward*. And all the provisions of law which govern the relation thus created flow naturally from this general object of creating it. The guardian is authorized to act for his ward, only in those matters where the law requires that there should be action, and the ward is incapable of acting for himself. Beyond these limits he cannot act at all; and even within them his action is carefully controlled by law, so as to leave as little latitude as possible for the exercise of discretion. There are three classes of persons whom the law presumes to be incapable of taking care of themselves, and therefore places under guardianship; namely, *infants*, *idiots*, and *lunatics*. To these may sometimes be added a fourth class; namely, *deaf and dumb persons;* and in some of the States, but not here, there is still another class; namely, *spendthrifts*. For these classes, therefore, the law appoints guardians, or provides for their appointment. A father, (*b*) in contemplation of death, is permitted to appoint by will a guardian for his minor children; and such guardian is thence called a *testamentary* guardian. But in all other cases, under our law, guardians are appointed by the court of common pleas, and may be called *statutory* guardians. In the books of common law, we find three sorts of guardians spoken of; namely, guardians *by nature*, *for nurture*, and *in socage*. But here, these distinctions are entirely useless; for though we speak of the father as the natural guardian of his minor children, yet, until he becomes a statutory guardian, his authority reaches only to their persons, and not to their property. (*c*) The relation of guardian and ward, therefore, cannot be said to exist, until a testamentary or statutory guardian has been appointed. The other descriptions of guar-

(*a*) See 2 Kent, Com. lec. 30, 31; 1 Black. Com. ch. 17; 1 Swift, ch. 7; Reeves's Domestic Relations. Schouler's Domestic Relations. It is singular that we have no treatise expressly on this subject. Since the new constitution, jurisdiction in matters of guardianship has been vested exclusively in the probate court, instead of the common pleas.

(*b*) Or mother, if there be no father. R. S. § 6266. An executor or administrator of the estate may be appointed guardian of the person, but not of the estate of a minor. § 6256.

(*c*) Shanks *v.* Seamonds, 24 Iowa, 131.

dians belong to the feudal system, with which happily we have very little concern. I proceed, therefore, to speak of the legal condition of the persons who may be placed under guardianship; of the persons who may be appointed guardians; and of their powers and duties. (*a*)

§ 111. **Infants.** (*b*) In this State all males under twenty-one years of age, and all females under eighteen, are called *infants* or *minors*. In England, and in most of the States, the age of majority is the same for both sexes; namely, twenty-one. In other countries, it varies from this to twenty-five, and perhaps more. It is necessary to fix upon some age of legal emancipation, and perhaps twenty-one is as suitable as any. No period of minority could be selected, which would be adapted legally to all; because some arrive at maturity much sooner than others. But taking the average, at the present day, twenty-one years is at least long enough. During this period of minority, the law places infants under various disabilities, founded on their presumed want of judgment or discretion. They have no political rights; that is, they cannot vote, nor hold office, nor act as jurors. They cannot make *deeds* or *wills*. They cannot marry without the consent of their parents or guardians; and under the ages of eighteen for males, and fourteen for females, they cannot marry at all. They cannot appoint attorneys, and therefore can neither sue nor defend suits in their own names. If they have no guardian, they may sue by their next friend, technically called *prochein ami;* but they can only defend by guardian. Minority is here no ground for delaying suit; and the court at once appoint a *guardian ad litem* to defend for them. (*c*) The *contracts* of minors are not *absolutely void*, like those of married women, but only *voidable*. (*d*) During minority, a court will not uphold such contracts, unless clearly beneficial to them; and after majority, such contracts may be disaffirmed and avoided, unless they were for *necessaries* honestly furnished. (*e*) This rule is designed to protect infants against

(*a*) The marriage of a female ward determines the guardianship as to her person, but not as to her estate; and on the marriage of a female guardian, the probate court is to appoint a new guardian. R. S. of Ohio, §§ 6265, 6292.

(*b*) See Bingham on Infancy; McPherson on Infancy.

(*c*) Where a statutory guardian appears and defends a suit for his ward, it has the same effect under 1 S. & C. 673, as if he had been expressly appointed guardian *ad litem* by the court. Rankin *v.* Kemp, 21 Ohio State, 651.

(*d*) {This is the rule even when his contracts are prejudicial to him as a contract of suretyship. Harver *v.* Dipple, 31 Ohio State, 72. In some States a false representation by the infant that he is of age, renders him liable if the other party was deceived thereby. Such is not, however, the general rule. Conrad *v.* Lane, 26 Minn. 389; Sims *v.* Everhardt, 102 U. S. 300. The adult can rescind such contract, as in other cases of fraud. Bush *v.* Linthicum, 59 Md. 344; Nolan *v.* Jones, 53 Iowa, 387. In case an infant becomes a partner, the personal liability for debts of the firm is voidable, as in other contracts; but all the firm assets are available to the creditors, as in any other partnership. A ratification after the infant is of age binds him, though he did not know he was not legally bound. Anderson *v.* Soward, 40 Ohio State, 325; Morse *v.* Wheeler, 4 Allen, 570; but see 3 Penn. State, 428.}

(*e*) {The plaintiff has the burden to prove that the articles furnished were necessaries. Wood *v.* Lacey, 50 Mich. 475. And even then it seems that the infant's note imposition; and contracts for necessaries are therefore excepted, because the reason of the rule does not embrace them. But as to all other contracts, they have the option to affirm or disaffirm them on becoming of age. The only acts of minors, with respect to which they are placed on the same footing as adults, are *crimes*. From the moment they are able to discern between right and wrong, infancy ceases to form an excuse for crimes; at least this is the general rule; and the few exceptions will be stated when we come to treat of criminal law. (*a*) When testamentary guardians have been appointed, their authority continues until majority; but in all other cases, males at the age of fourteen, and females at twelve, have a right, with the approbation of court, to choose their own guardians; and it has been held in this State, that the power of guardians previously appointed ceases, of course, when the ward arrives at the age of choice. (*b*) It may be remarked, in general, that if any one of the acts which infants are disabled from doing of themselves are requisite to be done to protect their interests, they are to be done by their guardians.

§ 112. **Idiots, Lunatics, and Deaf and Dumb Persons.** (*c*) Per-

is not binding, for he is liable, not for the contract price, but for the reasonable value. See Morton *v.* Steward, 5 Ill. App. 533. }

(*a*) "The capacity of infants to commit crimes, their punishableness for criminal offences, their liability civilly for various wrongs not connected in any sense with contracts, as, for instance, for battery or slander, to say nothing of the clear right in some circumstances to maintain trover against them, are of universal recognition. But questions which have not been considered free from difficulty; whether, or how far, persons are civilly liable at law for wrongs, when such acts, if they were the acts of adults, would be wrongs, done during infancy, when connected or supposed to be connected with contracts." Per Vice-Chancellor Knight Bruce, Stikeman *v.* Dawson, 1 De G. & S. 110. The question seems to be whether the action really sounds in contract or in tort. If in contract, then the plaintiff cannot, by choosing the form of an action *ex delicto*, render the infant liable. For instance, if a horse be let to an infant, and he uses him improperly, the wrong is so connected with the contract of hire, that the hirer cannot maintain any form of action. Jennings *v.* Rundall, 8 T. R. 335.

(*b*) Perry's Lessee *v.* Brainerd, 11 Ohio, 442.

(*c*) An insane person is liable for necessaries supplied to him. He is not bound by his contracts made or deeds executed after he has been judicially declared insane, and a committee or guardian has been appointed; such contracts and deeds are void. Where the inquest finds that he not only is insane at the date of the inquest, but has been so for a specified period antecedent, such finding does not conclude persons who dealt with him during such antecedent period. Banker *v.* Banker, 63 N. Y. 409; Van Deuson *v.* Sweet, 51 N. Y. 378; Rippy *v.* Gant, 4 Ired. Eq. 443; Noel *v.* Karper, 53 Penn. State, 97. If there is a question of fraud or imposition, the fact of insanity has weight in the determination of that question. In cases where there is no question of fraud or imposition, where the honesty of the transaction is not impugned, the law has varied as to the effect of the insanity of one of the parties. In England, the law is now settled. If such party has capacity to understand the transaction, though his mind is affected or impaired, the transaction is binding. If he is in fact insane, the law in England was established by Molton *v.* Camroux, first in the Exchequer, 2 Ex. 487, afterwards in Exchequer Chamber, 4 Ex. 17; confirmed in Beavan *v.* McDonnell, 9 Ex. 309; and more definitively determined in Matthews *v.* Baxter, L. R. 8 Ex. 132. It is, that a contract made by a person who is of unsound mind, so as to be incapable of understanding its effect, is not therefore absolutely void; it is voidable at that person's option, or the option of his representatives, unless the other contracting party did not believe, and had not reasonable cause to believe, that he was of unsound mind, in which case it is binding. Accordingly, partnership, which is a continuing partnership, is not dissolved by the insanity of one of the firm, but such insanity is ground for its dissolution by the court. 1 Lindley on Partnership, 235 and cases cited. The courts sons laboring under mental incapacity are of two kinds; namely, those who have no intellect, and those who have one in a de-

of chancery intimated in Price *v.* Berrington, 3 MacN. & G. 498; Elliott *v.* Ince, 7 De Gex, M. & G. 475; Manning *v.* Gill, L. R. 13 Eq. 483; and held, in Campbell *v.* Hooper, 3 Smale & Giff. 153, that the same rule applies to deeds and mortgages. But they hold, also, that a voluntary deed, as a deed of disentailment and settlement — Elliott *v.* Ince, 7 De Gex, M. & G. 475, or a deed without consideration — Manning *v.* Gill, L. R. 13 Eq. 483, or gift — 35 Hun, 656 — is void.

In the United States, it is generally held that contracts made by one of unsound mind are voidable. Seaver *v.* Phelps, 11 Pick. 304; Arnold *v.* Richmond Iron Works, 1 Gray, 434; Jackson *v.* Gumaer, 2 Cowen, 552; Ingraham *v.* Baldwin, 9 N. Y. 45; Chew *v.* Bank of Baltimore, 14 Md. 318; Fitzgerald *v.* Reed, 17 Miss. 94; Maddox *v.* Simmons, 31 Ga. 512; George *v.* Railway Co., 34 Ark. 613; Clark *v.* Trail, 1 Metc. (Ky.) 35; Musselman *v.* Cravens, 47 Ind. 1; Allen *v.* Berryhill, 27 Iowa, 534; Crowther *v.* Rowlandson, 27 Cal. 376.

It seems to have been held that a contract is void (1) if made with one whose insanity is evident to any one of ordinary capacity and prudence, in Lincoln *v.* Buckmaster, 32 Vt. 652; Halley *v.* Troester, 72 Mo. 73; 94 Penn. State, 483; 42 Mich. 165; (2) if there is no consideration moving to him, as in a contract of suretyship — Van Patten *v.* Beales, 46 Iowa, 46; a gift to a charity, Riggs *v.* American Tract Society, 84 N. Y. 330; or as an accommodation indorser — Hicks *v.* Marshall, 15 N. Y. Supreme Ct. R. 327; Wireback *v.* Bank, 97 Penn. State, 543.

But where the contract is fair, and the other contracting party is ignorant of his condition, and the contract has been executed by him or so far executed that he cannot be put *in statu quo*, the contract will not be rescinded, but will be enforced against him, and he will be required to pay his promissory note so given. Young *v.* Stevens, 48 N. H. 133; Yanger *v.* Skinner, 14 N. J. Eq. 389; Matthieson *v.* McMahon, 38 N. J. Law, 537; Beals *v.* See, 10 Barr, 56; Lancaster Bank *v.* Moore, 78 Penn. State, 407; Carr *v.* Holliday, 5 Ired. Eq. 167; Simms *v.* McLure, 8 Rich. Eq. 286; McCormick *v.* Little, 85 Ill. 62; Copenrath *v.* Kienby, 85 Ind. 18; Abbott *v.* Creal, 56 Iowa, 175; Mut. L. Ins. Co. *v.* Hunt, 79 N. Y. 541; 51 Mich. 529.

A power of attorney, like all other volunteer deeds, executed by an insane person, is void. Dexter *v.* Hall, 15 Wall. 9.

It was decided in The Estate of Desilver, 5 Rawle, 111, that the deed of an insane person is void. The same was held in Van Deuson *v.* Sweet, 51 N. Y. 378. The case of The Estate of Desilver was decided on the ground that the law was long since settled by the case of Thompson *v.* Leach, that while the feoffment of a lunatic is only voidable, his conveyance by deed, or which takes effect only by deed, is void; and that, as in the United States there is no feoffment, but only conveyance by deed, the deed of an insane person is void. Prominence was given to this reasoning by its being adopted by Justice Strong of the Supreme Court of the United States in Dexter *v.* Hall. In that case, however, it was *obiter dictum*, as the case was upon a power of attorney, and it has never been questioned that the power of attorney of either infant or *non compos* is wholly void. Thompson *v.* Leach, which went twice to the House of Lords, is found reported in 3 Mod. 296, 301; 12 Mod. 173; 3 Lev. 284; Salk. 300, 427, 565, 576; Carthew, 435; Comberbach, 469. The rule is found in 12 Mod. 173, "The surrender is void; for whatever is done by an infant or *non compos mentis* which takes effect only by deed is void; but it is otherwise in case of a feoffment, by reason of the notoriety and solemnity thereof." It is stated in Hobart, p. 224, and other of the older books, that a lunatic's conveyance by fine, or by common recovery, when the lunatic appeared to the precipe in person and not by power of attorney, was voidable, not void. The distinction between voidable and void conveyances of a lunatic was between such public and solemn acts as a feoffment, a fine and a recovery, and secret deeds as surrender and release. The deed in Thompson *v.* Leach, though technically delivered, was retained by the surrenderer, was without consideration, and did not come to the knowledge of the surrenderee till more than five years after its execution. Lord Mansfield, in his masterly opinion in Zouch *v.* Parsons, held, announcing the decision of the court, that the ruling in Thompson *v.* Leach, so far as it referred to infants, was not law. It certainly cannot be said to be law in England now as to insane persons.

In the United States, conveyance is generally made by deed of bargain and sale. Here a deed of bargain and sale operates as a feoffment; the delivery of the deed transfers seisin. Arnold *v.* Richmond Iron Works, 1 Gray, 434; Hare *v.* Jernigan, 76 N. C. 471; and being executed in the presence of witnesses, acknowledged before a public officer, and placed on record where they are open to the inspection of all, they ranged state. As to the former, whether the want of intellect exist from birth, or be occasioned by some subsequent cause, we may call them *idiots*, though this term is usually restricted to persons born without mind. But in either case the result is the same. Here is a lack of mental power, a deficiency of intellect. As applied to crimes, the criterion is inability to distinguish right from wrong. As applied to civil matters, the criterion is inability to understand common things or manage common affairs. There need not be a total want of mind, but only such a degree of weakness or imbecility as to require guardianship.

The other class, including those who have intellect, but in a deranged state, may be called *lunatics*. There need not be frenzy or raving madness, such as to require confinement, but only a derangement, greater or less, of the reasoning faculties. And here the true criterion is *delusion*, which consists in believing without evidence, acting without motive, reasoning without premises, and treating fancies as realities. It is not enough that the delusion have an insufficient basis. It must have no basis at all; and it must so thoroughly possess the mind as to become a fixed idea, out of which the subject cannot be reasoned. This insanity may

have as great "notoriety and solemnity" as a feoffment. Accordingly, in the United States generally, the deed of an insane person is held to be voidable only. Hovey *v.* Hobson, 53 Maine, 451; Arnold *v.* Richmond Iron Works, 1 Gray, 434; Eaton *v.* Eaton, 37 N. J. Law, 108; Crawford *v.* Scovell, 94 Penn. State, 48; Evans *v.* Horan, 52 Md. 602; Riggan *v.* Green, 80 N. C. 236; Elston *v.* Jasper, 45 Texas, 409; Breckenbridge *v.* Ormsby, 1 J. J. Marshall, 239; Freed *v.* Brown, 55 Ind. 310; Scanlan *v.* Cobb, 85 Ill. 296; Mohr *v.* Tulip, 40 Wis. 66. *Contra* that it is void. Rogers *v.* Blackwell, 49 Mich. 192; Harris *v.* Harris, 64 Cal. 108. Of sale of chattels by him. 94 Ind. 535; 20 Fed. Rep. 756; s. c. 4 McCrary, C. C. 34.

A deed is wholly void, if he is under guardianship, though the guardian assents. Rannels *v.* Gerner, 80 Mo. 474.

A deed will not be avoided because the grantor is affected by monomania, unless the monomania is such that it infects the transaction. Ekin *v.* McCracken, 11 Phila. (Pa.) 534; Schuff *v.* Ransom, 79 Ind. 458; Jones *v.* Hughes, 15 Abb. N. Cas. 141. It will not be avoided because the grantor is a monomaniac on the subject of religion. Burgess *v.* Pollock, 53 Iowa, 273.

In some States it has been held that restitution of the consideration is not required before a judicial avoidance of the deed of an insane person. Gibson *v.* Soper, 6 Gray, 279; Crawford *v.* Scovell, 94 Penn. State, 48; Nichol *v.* Thomas, 53 Ind. 42; Hadley *v.* Troester, 72 Mo. 73. In the first two cases it is intimated that only such restitution would in any event be adjudged as would be equitable under the circumstances. The action in Crawford *v.* Scovell was ejectment. But in Pennsylvania ejectment can be brought upon an equitable title. By the civil code of Louisiana, a deed or contract will be avoided only on the ground of notorious insanity; and reimbursement is ordered for only so much of the consideration as accrued to the benefit of the insane person. Fecel *v.* Guinault, 32 La. An. 91; Legay *v.* Marston, 32 La. An. 170.

Where the purchase was a fair one, and made in ignorance of the insanity of the grantor, and the consideration paid, the court has, in the following cases, held the deed valid and refused to set it aside. Riggan *v.* Green, 80 N. C. 236; Rusk *v.* Fenton, 14 Bush, 490; Scanlan *v.* Cobb, 85 Ill. 296; Ashcraft *v.* De Armand, 44 Iowa, 229. Under the same circumstances, the mortgage of an insane person has been foreclosed. Insurance Company *v.* Hunt, 79 N. Y. 541; Crouse *v.* Holman, 19 Ind. 30.

An insane person is civilly liable for his torts, Morain *v.* Devlin, 132 Mass. 87; but only in compensatory, not in vindictive damages. Morse *v.* Crawford, 17 Vt. 499; Krom *v.* Schoonmaker, 3 Barb. 647; Ward *v.* Comatser, 4 Baxter (Tenn.), 64. He is not, however, liable for libel or slander. 6 Humph. 199.

be either total or partial. There may be a general kind of delusion upon all subjects, or only upon one or more subjects. The latter kind is called *monomania.* Here reason is not wholly dethroned, but delusion sits beside her. The mind is not wholly darkened, but only some of its apartments. The monomaniac may be perfectly sane on all subjects but one, and perfectly wild on that. And it is chiefly with respect to this kind of insanity that difficulties arise in jurisprudence. With respect to crimes, it is now settled that monomania is no excuse, unless the delusion be directly connected with, and the cause of, the crime. With respect to civil matters, such as contracts and wills, the better opinion is, that monomania will not set them aside, unless it be so directly connected with them as either to have wholly produced, or essentially modified them.

There is another kind of insanity called *moral* by medical writers, which exists when there is no intellectual delusion, but only a perversion of the moral sentiments and affections. But this has never been recognized in jurisprudence, and I trust never will be; because it would not only furnish an universal apology for crime, but introduce the utmost uncertainty into civil transactions. (*a*)

I may here say a word upon the subject of *drunkenness.* This is not regarded by the law as insanity, though it may lead to it. Hence mere intoxication is no excuse for crime; though where a particular state of mind must exist in order to constitute a crime, it may perhaps be taken into view in determining whether such state of mind existed. (*b*) But as to contracts, the rule now is, that if a man be so drunk at the making of a contract as not to know what he is about, the contract is void. (*c*)

As to *deaf and dumb* persons, it by no means follows that they are incapable of taking care of themselves. On the contrary, under the present provision made for educating them, they are enabled, by signs and by writing, to do almost every thing which persons blessed with speech and hearing can do. Of course the fact of being deaf and dumb does not of itself invalidate civil acts, nor excuse crime. Our statute, however, provides for such as are incapable of managing their affairs, in the same manner as for idiots and lunatics.

The substance of our statutory provision is this: (*d*) Upon application to an associate judge, by any relative, overseer of the

(*a*) State *v.* Spencer, 1 Zabriskie (N. J.), 207.

(*b*) Cline *v.* State, 43 Ohio State, 332.

(*c*) French *v.* French, 8 Ohio, 214. In England the rule as to the liability of a person upon his contracts or deeds made while drunk is the same as to his liability upon the same made while insane. Molton *v.* Camroux, 2 Ex. 487, 4 Ex. 17; Pollock on the Principles of Contract, pp. 76–82. In the United States the liability is generally the same. Morris *v.* Clay, 8 Jones, Law, 216; Jenness *v.* Howard, 6 Blackf. 240; Johns *v.* Fritchey, 39 Md. 258; Joest *v.* Williams, 42 Ind. 565; Bates *v.* Ball, 72 Ill. 108; Cavender *v.* Waddingham, 5 Mo. App. 457; R. S. of Ohio, § 6317–19 as to putting common drunkards under guardianship.

(*d*) Since 1853 this jurisdiction has been transferred to the probate court.

poor, or other inhabitant of the township, he is empowered to call a jury of five persons, not of the same township, to hold an *inquest.* If the jury find that the person complained of is an idiot or lunatic, they certify whether he is a pauper or not, and whether he ought to be confined or not. If they find that he is an idiot and pauper, he is committed to the charge of the overseers of the poor. If they find that he is a lunatic and pauper, and ought to be confined, he is committed to jail until he can be received into the lunatic asylum. If they find that he is an idiot or lunatic, but not a pauper, and not requiring confinement, the associate judges appoint a guardian (*a*) to take charge of the person and property of himself and his children. When a person indicted for homicide is acquitted on the ground of insanity, the jury are to specify this in their verdict; and if the court think it would be dangerous for him to go at large, he is committed to jail until he can be received into the asylum. In all cases, when there is reason to believe insanity has ceased, provision is made to ascertain the fact by inquest, and restore the party to his rights.

§ 113. **Powers and Duties of Guardians.** (*b*) Any person may be a testamentary guardian, whom the testator may think fit to appoint. But no executor or administrator of an estate in which a minor is interested can be his statutory guardian. Guardians are required to give bonds with security, in such sum as the court shall determine, for the faithful discharge of their duty, before the *letter of guardianship* is granted; and being amenable for all their doings to the court appointing them, they are liable to removal on good cause shown. Within three years from their appointment, and at subsequent intervals of two years thereafter, guardians of minors are required to *settle their guardianship accounts* to the approval of the court, for which purpose they must be filed one term beforehand, and public notice thereof given by the clerk, in order that any person interested may file objections. The settlements thus made are final, unless the ward, within two years after becoming of age, see fit to question them by a proceeding in chancery. In case of neglect, a settlement will be enforced by citation and attachment. The compensation of guardians for their services is a matter wholly in the discretion of the court. The general rule is, that they cannot speculate for their own advantage with the funds of their wards; that all profits must be accounted for by them; and that if they neglect to make interest on money in their hands, without good reason, they are nevertheless chargeable with interest. If the delinquency be

(*a*) And such guardian may sue in his own name. 1 West. Law Jour. 454.

(*b*) Este *v.* Strong, 2 Ohio, 401; Armstrong *v.* Miller, 6 id. 118; State *v.* Humphreys, 7 id. 1 pt. 223; Davis *v.* Ford, 7 id. 2 pt. 104; Pedan *v.* Robb, 8 id. 227; Stall *v.* Macalester, 9 id. 19; Perry *v.* Brainard, 11 id. 442; Maxsom *v.* Sawyer, 12 id. 195; Bohart *v.* Atkinson, 14 id. 228; Davies *v.* Lowrey, 15 id. 655; State *v.* Sloane, 20 id. 327; Case *v.* Ohio, 10 Western Law Journal, 163; Wright, 119, 200, 390, 562, 657.

gross, they are chargeable with compound interest. (*a*) Their power over the *persons* of their wards, is the same as that of parents over their children, with this exception, that they cannot bind them out by indenture, without the approbation of the court. Their power over the *personalty* of their wards is the same as that over their own; except that they cannot bind their wards by future contracts, without special provision of law. Their power over the *realty* is not so extensive. They have the management of it, and of the rents and profits of it, and may bring trespass and ejectment in their own names; (*b*) but they cannot sell it, as they can personalty, without express leave of court; and this leave will not be granted unless the court is satisfied that such sale will be for the advantage of their wards, or is necessary for their maintenance. (*c*) Indeed, this is going further than is generally allowed. In most places, the realty of minors can only be sold for their maintenance; but here, by special provision, it may be sold for the purpose of making a better investment. The mode of proceeding will be described hereafter. On the whole, perhaps this is well; for it often operates injuriously upon the interests of the community, as well as of the minors, that their realty, especially when unimproved, should be tied up from sale until their majority; but still it is rather a departure from the general policy of the law relating to minors, which is, to leave everything as far as possible in the condition in which it happens to be, until they become of age to change it. This power to sell real estate is extended by our statute to guardians of minors residing out of the State, upon their giving additional security, if required. (*d*)

LECTURE XVII.

MASTER AND SERVANT. (*e*)

§ 114. **Apprentices.** The title of *master and servant*, at the head of a lecture, does not sound very harmoniously to republican

(*a*) Armstrong *v.* Miller, 6 Ohio, 118; 2 Kent, Com. 231, and *note*. See *post*, § 177. Even after the ward's coming of age, the guardian is held to good faith, and a purchase of the ward's property after he or she comes of age, for an inadequate price, will be, *per se*, evidence of fraud. Eberts *v.* Eberts, 55 Penn. State, 110. And so before the termination of the guardianship, even in good faith. 61 Miss. 766.

(*b*) They may lease, but such lease is terminable on the majority of the ward or the appointment of another guardian. May lease for not over three years in Ohio without leave of court, or for not over fifteen years by leave of court. R. S. §§ 6295–6, 6301; Emerson *v.* Spicer, 55 Barb. 428; s. c. 46 N. Y. 594. See also Richardson *v.* Richardson, 49 Mo. 29.

(*c*) See R. S. of Ohio, § 6280.

(*d*) R. S. § 6290.

(*e*) See 2 Kent, Com. lec. 37, 41; 1 Black. Com. ch. 14; 1 Swift, ch. 8; Smith, Wood, on Master and Servant.

ears. And in fact *servitude*, strictly so called, does not exist in this country, except in the case of *slaves;* nor in this State at all. But the legal relation of master and servant must exist, to a greater or less extent, wherever civilization furnishes work to be done, and the difference of condition makes some persons employers, and others laborers. In fact, we understand by the relation of master and servant, nothing more or less than that of *employer* and *employed*. It is, therefore, a relation created by contract, express or implied, and might properly be treated under the head of contracts; but custom has placed it among the personal relations, and I shall so treat it. Blackstone divides servants into four classes; namely, *menial servants*, *common laborers*, *apprentices*, and *agents*. But there is no occasion here for treating separately of the first two; because we have no provisions, as in England, relating to the duration of the contract, the amount of wages, the time of laboring each day, and the like; all such matters here being settled between the employer and the employed, as matters of contract. And if there be no express contract, the law implies one, on the part of the employer, to pay a reasonable compensation, and on the part of the employed, to possess and use reasonable skill and diligence. We have, therefore, but two classes of servants to speak of; namely, *apprentices* and *agents*. With respect to apprentices, our law is chiefly statutory. Males can only be bound until twenty-one, and females only until eighteen. Beyond these ages, they may bind themselves for any length of time, if they enter freely into the indenture, and there be a *bona fide* consideration for the binding. Our statute in relation to apprentices includes "*clerks*, *apprentices*, and *servants*," and places them all on the same footing. The kind of occupation, therefore, is of no consequence; the words being broad enough to include every description of service. The mode of binding is by *indenture*, and the time is during *minority*. The minor is not, as at common law, required to be a party to the indenture. (*a*) One of the parties must, of course, be the master. The other depends upon circumstances. It is the father, if living; if not, the mother or guardian; and if the guardian, the indenture must be approved by the court of common pleas. If, however, the minor be a destitute orphan, or if his parents do not provide for him, the township trustees have authority to bind him. The term *apprentice* usually implies one bound for the learning of some particular trade; but I shall use it to signify any one bound according to the statute. The substance of the indenture is provided for in the statute. (*b*) It must in all cases

(*a*) In those States where the minor's consent must be expressed in the indenture, there must be apt words to express it in the instrument, and his simple signature is not sufficient. Harper *v.* Gilbert, 5 Cushing, 417. A contract of apprenticeship, not conformable to the statute, is voidable only by the apprentice, and cannot be avoided for that reason by any other person. Page *v.* Marsh, 36 N. H. 305. Doane *v.* Covel, 56 Maine, 527.

(*b*) The Ohio statutes now (R. S. §§ 3121-3) slightly modify the statement of the specify the age and term of service. If for a white person, it must stipulate for the education of the apprentice in reading, writing, and arithmetic; unless the binding be for less than four years. In all cases, the master must engage to give the apprentice, at the expiration of the time, a new Bible and two suits of clothes. If there be any money to be paid by the master, it must be secured to the minor, and not to his parent or guardian. Nothing is said of the covenants on the other side; except that the parent, guardian, or trustees are not to be personally bound thereby, unless they expressly stipulate so to be. The master must have the indenture recorded by the township clerk within three months. On failure so to do, the minor will be discharged: but the master will still remain liable on his covenants. Having thus provided by whom and how the binding shall be made, the statute proceeds to fix a tribunal for settling disputes. The entire jurisdiction is given to justices of the peace, without appeal. They have power, on complaint of either party, to summon the other before them, and if they can effect a reconciliation, to make such order as justice requires; if not, to summon a jury of five persons to investigate the facts. If the minor be the aggrieved party, the complaint may be made by the parent, guardian, trustees, or next friend. If the jury find that the master has broken any of his covenants, or has neglected to furnish necessary food or clothing, whether agreed for or not, or has been guilty of any kind of cruelty, they assess the damages, and the indenture is thenceforth annulled. If the complaint be by the master, for the misbehavior of the minor, the jury determine whether the master ought to be discharged or not from the indenture. If so, or if the apprentice run away, the master has his action for damages against the minor. He also has his action against any person who shall entice the apprentice away, or harbor him.

Other Incidents of Apprenticeship. (*a*) I have thus far fol-

text. The following form has been modified accordingly: *Form of indenture.* This indenture of apprenticeship, between ———, father of ———, on the one part, and ———, of the other part, witnesseth: That the said ———, aged ——— years, on the ———, is hereby bound as an apprentice under the said ———, from the date hereof until the ———, to learn the trade and occupation of a ———; and is faithfully to serve the said ———, and correctly to demean himself during the term of his apprenticeship. And the said ——— does hereby covenant that he will teach the said ——— the said trade and occupation of a ———, and will provide him, during said apprenticeship, with board, lodging, medicine, washing, clothing, and all other necessaries suitable for an apprentice; and will send the said ——— to a common school for at least twelve weeks in each school-year during the apprenticeship, after the minor is eight years of age; and at the expiration of said term of service, will furnish the said ——— with a new Bible and two good suits of clothes [all money or property stipulated to be paid by the master shall be secured to and for the sole and separate use of the minor. § 3123]. In testimony whereof, the parties have hereunto set their hands and seals this ———.

(*a*) Day *v.* Everett, 7 Mass. 145; U. S. *v.* Bainbridge, 1 Mason, 71; The King *v.* Laindon, 8 Term Rep. 379; 1 Salkeld, 66, tit. Apprentice; Thompson *v.* Tiller, 2 Strange, 1266; Hall *v.* Gardner, 1 Mass. 172; Davis *v.* Coburn, 8 id. 299; Nickerson *v.* Homard, 19 Johns. 113; James *v.* Le Roy, 6 id. 274; *Ex parte* Lansdown, 5 East, 39. A contract for servitude with no limitation but that of time, is against the policy of the law, and void. Parsons *v.* Trask, 7 Gray, 473.

lowed the statute. But statutes of a similar character have existed elsewhere for a long period, and many points have been decided respecting them. 1. This statute embraces only the case of minors bound by indenture, according to its provisions; but it does not, like the English statute, make void all other contracts for the binding of minors; such contracts, therefore, may still be good, on the common principles of law. 2. At common law the minor was not bound unless he became a party to the indenture; but as the statute does not require his assent, the binding here will be valid without it. 3. Apprentices, under the statute, are not entitled to *wages*, unless expressly stipulated for; that is, no recovery can be had upon an implied contract for work and labor, as in the case of other servants. 4. The death of the master discharges the apprentice entirely from the indenture, on the ground that the contract is strictly fiduciary. The confidence reposed in the master does not extend to his representatives; and the apprentice is under no obligation to them. But it has been held, on the other hand, that the death of the master does not discharge his representatives from the covenant to support the apprentice, although he is no longer bound. This doctrine, however, is so utterly destitute of reason, that I should presume these ancient decisions would not now be sustained. 5. The weight of authority as well as reason is in favor of the doctrine, that the master cannot assign his interest in the indenture to another, because the contract is founded on personal confidence. (*a*) It has, however, been held, that although the assignee cannot enforce the indenture against the apprentice, yet the assignment is so far valid that he may maintain an action upon it against the assignor. 6. As the rights and powers created by the indenture are derived from the statute, they can be enforced only where the statute is operative. They cease, therefore, when the master removes out of the jurisdiction, unless express provision is made for such removal, or it is required by the nature of service. 7. The master is entitled to the earnings of the apprentice under all circumstances. And it makes no difference in this respect whether the money be earned in the master's line of business or not; whether it was by his consent or not; whether the employer knew him to be an apprentice or not; or even whether he has paid the apprentice. An action will always lie by the master against the employer to recover the whole. The ground assumed is, that the master has contracted for his time, and is entitled to its avails. 8. Where a minor is wrongfully detained as an apprentice, under pretence of an indenture, he may resort to the writ of *habeas corpus* to procure his release. 9. There is nothing in this country analogous to that principle of the English law, which gives to persons who have served a regular apprenticeship at any

(*a*) Chapin *v.* Longworth, 31 Ohio State, 421.

trade the exclusive right of practising it. 10. The power of the master over the person of the apprentice is similar to that of the parent or guardian. If necessary, he may correct him with moderation, but nothing more.

§ 115. **Agents.** (*a*) The relation of principal and agent takes place wherever one person is authorized to act for and in the name of another. It is a general rule, that whatever any person has original authority to do in his own name and right, he can authorize another to do for him as his agent; and that where power is given to accomplish any object, it includes all the means proper for that object. But there is a maxim, *delegatus non potest delegare*, which prohibits delegated power from being again delegated, without special authority from the original source; therefore an agent cannot create a sub-agent, without special permission. (*b*) And, on the other hand, any person may act as agent whom the principal chooses to appoint. So comprehensive is this rule, that married women and infants, who are incapable of acting in their own behalf, may act as agents; for the appointment takes away the legal insufficiency, and enables them to bind their principals, when they could not bind themselves. (*c*) The mode of appointment depends upon the nature of the agency. By a technical rule of law, the evidence of appointment must be of as high a nature as the thing to be done. Thus, to execute a writing under seal, the appointment must be under seal. (*d*) We have a statutory provision requiring a *power of attorney* for the conveyance of realty, to be executed with all the formalities of the conveyance itself. Our *statute of frauds* requires the authority of agents to do certain acts therein named to be in writing. And we have another provision, requiring attorneys at law to have a written authority to confess judgment for their clients. (*e*) But with

(*a*) See 2 Kent, Com. lec. 41, 61; and the treatises on Agency, by Story, Wharton, Paley, and Ewell's Evans on Agency.

(*b*) Combe's Case, 9 Co. 75; Powell *v.* Tuttle, 3 N. Y. 396. Bocock *v.* Pavey, 8 Ohio State, 270. An authority to appoint a sub-agent may be implied from usage. Moon *v.* Guardians of Whitney Union, 3 Bing. N. C. 814. An agent to buy goods may employ a broker to make the purchases, if that is the usual custom of the market; and in such case, if the broker employed is competent and suitable, will not be liable for his errors or misconduct. Darling *v.* Stanwood, 14 Allen, 504.

(*c*) See *post*, § 176, *notes*. {Hence it is held in Ohio, New York, and New Jersey, that a bank receiving for collection a draft or other paper payable elsewhere, and forwarding it to its correspondent, is liable for the latter's negligence or fraud. Reeves *v.* State Bank, 8 Ohio State, 465; Exchange Bank *v.* Third National Bank, 112 U. S. 276. But most of the authorities hold that the first bank is merely bound to exercise due care in selecting suitable agents, and is not liable further. Such is the rule in Connecticut, Illinois, Iowa, Maryland, Massachusetts, Mississippi, Missouri, and Wisconsin.}

(*d*) Stetson *v.* Patten, 2 Greenl. 358.

(*e*) *Form of a power of attorney to transact ordinary business.* Be it known that I hereby constitute and appoint ———, to be my attorney in fact, with full authority to make all contracts, and do all other acts of a business nature, except the conveyance of real estate, as effectually as I could myself do, if personally present; and if need be, to substitute another attorney in his place with equal powers; and I do hereby ratify and confirm all acts lawfully done in pursuance of this power. Witness my signature and seal, &c.

Power to confess judgment. Be it known, that whereas ——— is indebted to ———.

these exceptions, the agency may be created orally, or may be implied from circumstances, or may be subsequently adopted, when there was no previous appointment by word or act. (*a*) These remarks must be understood to apply to *legal* and not *political* acts. One person cannot depute another to vote, or discharge an office for him; except in some few instances, where the law specially provides for the appointment of *deputies*. But we have seen that the members of corporations may delegate the power of voting by *proxy*. The law has a variety of special agents, such as *executors*, *administrators*, *guardians*, *trustees*, *masters in chancery*, *receivers*, *collectors*, *sheriffs*, and the like, which are elsewhere spoken of. Commerce also gives rise to a variety of agents, the most important of which are *factors*, *brokers*, and *ship-masters*. I name these various kinds of agents, for the purpose of letting you know that they exist; but in the rest of my remarks, I shall merely state the general doctrines which apply equally to all agencies. For more particular details you can consult the various titles and authors above indicated.

§ 116. **Their Powers and Duties.** The acts of an agent are done in the name and for the benefit of the principal; (*b*) and the agent can claim no other profit than his wages, or agreed compensation. (*c*) Nor does he incur any risk or liability, except for torts, so long as he keeps within his powers; but the moment he exceeds his powers he becomes personally responsible, both to the principal and to third persons. If limited by special instructions, therefore, he must adhere strictly to them; if not, he is to be governed by the established usage of his employment. (*d*) By the mere

in the sum of $——, for [state nature of indebtedness]; now, therefore, the said ——— does hereby authorize ——— or any other attorney at law, to appear in [describe the court, or say any court of record], at any regular term of said court [or specify some term], and waive the issuing and serving of process, and confess a judgment in favor of the said ———, against the said ———, for the sum of $——, with interests and costs; and thereupon to release all error, and waive the right of appeal. Witness the hand and seal of said, &c.

If the person giving this power be under arrest at the time, some attorney at law, acting for him, must attest the power as a witness.

(*a*) A power of attorney in fact is not presumed. Pillsbury *v.* Dugan, 9 Ohio, 117.

(*b*) Where an agent, A., signs for his principal, B., the most correct form is to sign "B. by A." It was for some time doubted whether the signature "A. for B." was a good execution of the contract by the principal, though it is now generally settled that it is. But the fact of the agency must clearly appear upon the face of the contract. A note running, "We, or either of us, as directors of" a corporation, "promise to pay," &c., signed by certain persons without any official designation added to their names, binds the signers individually. Titus *v.* Kyle, 10 Ohio State, 444. As to the proper mode of signing instruments for corporations, see p. 240, note (*a*).

(*c*) {And he forfeits even this by accepting inconsistent employment. Thus an agent who acts for both contracting parties, unless this is known and consented to by both, cannot recover compensation from either. Capener *v.* Hogan, 40 Ohio State, 203; Bell *v.* McConnell, 37 Ohio State, 396. An agent to sell cannot be the purchaser; and this rule of good faith is not relaxed even if the principal has named a fixed price. Peckham Iron Co. *v.* Harper, 41 Ohio State, 100, 108.}

(*d*) The necessities of maritime life give the masters of vessels peculiar powers to bind the owners under special emergencies. The master has power in a foreign port, in case of necessity, to hypothecate the vessel and to bind the owners personally for acceptance of the agency, he binds himself to the principal, for sufficient skill and diligence to execute it well; and if a loss arise for the want of either, he is therefore liable for it. (*a*) In dealing with third persons, he should disclose the fact of being an agent, or he will be held personally responsible to them; and in making written contracts, he must take care so to frame them as to bind his principal only and not himself; otherwise, though his agency appear, he will be personally liable. (*b*) Finally, an agent is

repairs and supplies, and he may bind the vessel by a loan for that purpose, but the party furnishing the supplies or repairs, or lending the money, must see to it that such a necessity apparently exists. Thomas *v.* Osborn, 19 How. 22. In cases of absolute necessity, the master may sell both vessel and cargo. Post *v.* Jones, id. 150. Contracts of affreightment entered into with the master in good faith and within the scope of his apparent authority, bind the vessel, whether the master be in the employ of the general owner or of a party to whom the entire control and management of the vessel have been committed under a contract. Freeman *v.* Buckingham, 18 How. 182.

(*a*) If his services are gratuitously rendered, he is liable for gross negligence. Grant *v.* Ludlow, 8 Ohio State, 1. But where a gratuitous agent begins to execute the work that he has undertaken, and does it negligently, he is liable in damages for ordinary negligence. Vickery *v.* Lanier, 1 Met. (Ky.) 133.

(*b*) See 2 Kent, Com. 830 (7th ed.), *notes.* Story in his work on Agency, § 268–290, lays it down as a presumption of law that where an agent contracts for a foreign principal, the credit is given to the agent. Kent differs from him. The rule in England is now settled to be, that in every case it is a question of fact to whom the credit was really given. This is said, however, not to shake Addison *v.* Gandasequi. Mahoney *v.* Kakulé, 14 C. B. 390; Green *v.* Kopke, 18 C. B. 549; Crandell *v.* James, 6 R. I. 144. But in England it is held that where an agent appears on the face of the contract to be acting as agent, he is not generally liable personally on the contract; though evidence of a custom in a special trade that he shall be so liable, is admissible. Fleet *v.* Murton, L. R. 7 Q. B. 126.

{The general rules may be summarized as follows where the contract is not under seal:

1. If the contract names the principal he and not the agent is of course the person to sue and be sued upon it unless the contrary is expressed; for the contract is with him and not with the agent. The only exception to this is the English rule that if the principal resides abroad the contract is deemed for commercial convenience to have been made on the agent's credit, and he is liable on it.

2. If the contract shows that the agent is merely agent and is not a principal, but does not disclose who the principal is, the agent is presumed to intend to bind himself personally, with the exception that an agent for the government is not supposed to intend binding himself by contracting in his own name. The reason of the rule is that credit is not supposed to be given to an unnamed person; and the agent can sue, for he is the promisee. The principal when ascertained can also be sued instead of the agent, but both cannot be sued. Yet as the fact of agency is known, a set-off against the agent of an independent demand is not allowed. If the contract is a negotiable instrument the fact that the agent signed himself "A. B., agent" will not relieve him from liability, the principal not being named in the note. Collins *v.* Buckeye State Ins. Co., 17 Ohio State, 215. Nor can the principal be sued on such note in the United States generally. See for example Cragin *v.* Lovell, 109 U. S. 194; Bank *v.* Cook, 38 Ohio State, 442.

3. If the agency was not known to the other party at all, *i. e.* if the contract is with the agent, believing him to be acting on his own behalf, he can of course sue and be sued upon it, or the principal when discovered can sue and be sued upon it; but if the principal exercises his rights as such he must take the burdens of the contract also; therefore his claim is subject to rights of set-off against the agent the same as if he had been really principal. Miller *v.* Sullivan, 39 Ohio State, 79. Both cannot be sued, but the party must elect; and merely bringing suit is not a final election (the following two cases seem to hold that even getting judgment is not a final election until the money is realized upon it. Beymer *v.* Bonset, 79 Penn. State, 298; 10 Ohio State, 313). The fact that an agent to sell has not possession of the property, is sufficient to put the other party on his guard to ascertain if he is acting for himself or not. Crosby *v.* Hill, 39 Ohio State, 100.

4. If the contract names a fictitious principal, the pretended agent being really an

personally responsible for all those injuries which the law denominates *trespasses* or *torts*, though done as agent and by order of the principal; for the law will recognize no authority to do wrong, as an excuse for doing it. (*a*)

§ 117. **Liability of Principal.** (*b*) The general liability of the principal depends upon the maxim, that the acts of his agent are his own acts — *qui facit per alium facit per se.* Hence the principal is personally responsible for whatever his agent does, in the regular course of his employment, including both contracts and

actor on his own behalf, the agent can neither sue nor be sued on the contract, for the contract was not with him. But he is liable in tort for the deception, or in contract on the implied warranty that he was authorized to act.

5. If the contractor falsely pretends to be acting as agent, but no principal is disclosed, the rule is about the same as in No 2 above; the agent is to be personally bound, and also can sue on the contract as the promisee. }

(*a*) If a horse is let to A. and delivered to B. on A.'s credit, and B. with A.'s assent and aid, who is driving another horse alongside, drives him to death, both A. and B. are jointly liable to the owner. Banfield *v.* Whipple, 10 Allen, 27.

(*b*) It is not always an easy question to determine whether the relation of master and servant exists between the employer and the employed, so as to render the former liable for the acts of the latter. According to recent English authorities, a principal contractor is not liable for damage occasioned by the negligence or wrongful act of his sub-contractor, although acting in the course of his employment. Knight *v.* Fox, 1 Eng. Law & Eq. 477; Peachey *v.* Rowland, 16 id. 442, and *notes.* In this country, there is some variety of opinion on the question. Stone *v.* Codman, 15 Pick. 297; Wiswall *v.* Bronson, 10 Iredell, 554; Blake *v.* Ferris, 5 N. Y. 48; Lloyd *v.* New York, 5 N. Y. 369; Stevens *v.* Armstrong, 2 id. 435. The English rule is now established in this country. Carman *v.* Steubenville and Indiana R. R. Co., 4 Ohio State, 399; Clark *v.* Fry, 8 id. 358; Hilliard *v.* Richardson, 3 Gray, 349; Pierce on American Railroad Law, pp. 235–42. But the principal contractor is liable if he authorized or co-operated in the injurious act. Carman *v.* Steubenville R. R. Co., 4 Ohio State, 399; Cincinnati *v.* Stone, 5 id. 38; Clark *v.* Fry, 8 id. 358. It is held that a master is not answerable to one of his servants for an injury received by him in consequence of the carelessness of another servant, while both are engaged in the same business. Priestley *v.* Fowler, 3 M. & W. 1; Farwell *v.* Boston and Worcester R. R., 4 Met. 49; Hayes *v.* Western R. R. Corp., 3 Cush. 270; Ryan *v.* Cumberland Valley R. R. Co., 23 Penn. State, 384; Coon *v.* Utica and Syracuse R. R. Co., 5 N. Y. 492; s. c. 6 Barb. 231; Whaalan *v.* Mad River and Lake Erie R. R. Co., 8 Ohio State, 249; Horner *v.* Illinois Central R. R. Co., 15 Ill. 550; King *v.* Boston and Worcester R. R. Co., 9 Cush. 112. Pierce on American Railroad Law, ch. xiii. pp. 286–310. Durgin *v.* Munson, 9 Allen, 396. It is held in Ohio, that this rule does not apply where the servant who is injured holds a subordinate position to the person through whose negligence the injury was done; for the latter stands to him in the place of the master, who is therefore liable as if personally acting. Little Miami R. R. Co. *v.* Stevens, 20 Ohio, 415; C. C. & C. R. R. Co. *v.* Keary, 3 Ohio State, 201; Timmons *v.* Central R. R. Co., 6 id. 105; Haynes *v.* East Tenn. & Ga. R. R. Co., 3 Coldwell, 222; Louisville & Nash. R. R. Co. *v.* Collins, 2 Duvall, 114. When employees are to be regarded as fellow-servants, and when as subordinates, see Manville *v.* C. & T. R. R. Co., 11 Ohio State, 417; Col. & X. R. R. Co. *v.* Webb, 12 Ohio State, 475; Pittsburg, Ft. W. & C. R. R. Co. *v.* Devinney, 17 Ohio State, 197. But the rule is undoubtedly different in England, and most of the United States. Albro *v.* Agawam Canal Co., 6 Cush. 75. But the principal will be liable if the injury resulted from his negligence or misconduct either in the act which caused the injury, or in the selection and employment of the agent by whose fault it was occasioned, or in providing improper machinery. Keegan *v.* Western R. R. Co., 8 N. Y. 175; McGatrick *v.* Wason, 4 Ohio State, 566; Carman *v.* Steubenville R. R. Co., id. 399; Mad River and Lake Erie R. R. Co. *v.* Barber, 5 id. 541. The negligence of the plaintiff, contributing to the injury, will bar recovery. Timmons *v.* Central Ohio R. R. Co., 6 Ohio State, 105. One servant is not liable to an action by another servant in the employment of the same master for damages occasioned by the negligence of the first in such employment. Albro *v.* Jaquith, 4 Gray, 99.

torts; (*a*) and this extends to all sub-agents, when the first agent has express power to appoint them; but the liability of the principal is confined to acts done within the scope of the agency; for to that extent only does he undertake with the public; and beyond that they have no right to confide in the agent. (*b*) Hence it is incumbent on those who deal with agents, knowing them to be such, to ascertain the extent of their authority; whether it be general or special, express or implied; for beyond this authority they cannot look to the principal. There is, however, this distinction between a general and special agency, in respect to binding the principal. A special agent, who exceeds his authority, in no case binds his principal; but a general agent, though he act contrary to private instructions, will bind his principal, if the act done were within the general scope of the agency, and the person dealt with did not know of the private instructions. (*c*) What is the general scope of the agency, must be determined by the custom of the

(*a*) The principal is liable on a contract made by the agent within the scope of his authority, though the other party dealt solely with the agent, and did not know at the time that he was acting as agent. But where in such a case the principal in good faith settles with the agent, the third party still trusting to the agent alone, this liability ceases. Armstrong *v.* Stokes, L. R. 7 Q. B. 610. Where an agent acting within the scope of his authority perpetrates a fraud for the benefit of his principal, and the latter knowingly receives the fruits of it, he is liable as if for his own wrong. Smith *v.* Tracy, 36 N. Y. 79; Maple *v.* R. R. Co., 40 Ohio State, 313; Tucker *v.* Jerris, 75 Me., 184. A principal is not criminally responsible for the acts of his agent, done without his authority, knowledge, or consent. State *v.* Bacon, 40 Vt. 456. The master is liable, though the act be contrary to instructions, if it is done by the employee to accomplish something that he thinks best for the interest of his master. But if the act be done to effect a purpose of the servant, without reference to the master's interest, the master is not liable. Limpers *v.* London, &c. Co., 1 Hurl. & Colt. 526. But a railroad company is not liable for injuries inflicted upon a passenger by a baggage master with a hatchet furnished him for use in the performance of his duties, such injuries being inflicted to gratify his own personal resentment in the course of a quarrel provoked by the importunate behavior and abusive language of the passenger, though the quarrel arose during the performance by the servant of the duties he was employed to perform. Little Miami R. R. Co. *v.* Wetmore, 19 Ohio State, 110. But where the act done is in the course of his employment, and a person is injured thereby, the motive or intention of the servant in doing the act will not discharge the master. So a conductor, being clothed with the implied authority to determine who shall be admitted, and who excluded, the company will be responsible for the wrongful exercise of the power, whatever the motive. The intent can only be looked at, where the nature of the act is such as to render it doubtful whether it is within the scope of the servant's employment or not. Passenger R. R. Co. *v.* Young, 21 Ohio State, 518. Where a travelling agent of a firm, employed to solicit orders for goods, without particular orders as to route and travel, hires a buggy at a livery stable, for use in the prosecution of his agency, without disclosing his employers, and through his negligence some damage is caused, he is the servant of the firm in the transaction, and it will be liable for such damage. Pickens and Blummer *v.* Diecker and Bro., 21 Ohio State, 212. A principal, whether a corporation or an individual, may be subjected to exemplary or punitive damages for the tortious acts of agents or servants, when done within the scope of their employment, in all cases where natural persons, acting for themselves, if guilty of like tortious acts, would be liable to such damages. Atlantic & G. W. R. Co. *v.* Dunn, 19 Ohio State, 162; Baltimore and Ohio R. R. Co. *v.* Blocher, 27 Md. 277; Jeffersonville R. R. Co. *v.* Rogers, 28 Ind. 1.

(*b*) Simons *v.* Monier, 29 Barb. 420; Henshaw *v.* Noble, 7 Ohio State, 226, 231. As to the liability of a railroad corporation for injuries to third parties by their agents, see C. C. & C. R. R. Co. *v.* Terry, 8 Ohio State, 570.

(*c*) Williams *v.* Getty, 31 Penn. State, 461; Smith *v.* Maguire, 3 Hurl. & Nor. 554; Baltimore *v.* Esclebuck, 18 Md. 276.

business. (*a*) And it is well settled that no general agency to sell will authorize the agent to pledge or barter. (*b*) The chief difficulty in determining the liability of the principal arises in those cases where the agency is inferred from mere employment; as where a common servant, for example, obtains money or goods in the name of his master. In all such cases, the rule is, that if the principal receives the benefit of the agency, he is responsible for the consequences; and if he does not receive the benefit of it, in this particular case, yet if he has before recognized the authority of the agent, and has not countermanded it, or if he has done anything amounting to a subsequent ratification, he is held responsible. (*c*)

§ 118. **Termination of the Agency.** The appointment of an agent is revocable at any moment by the principal, unless, for a valuable consideration, the agent has acquired a vested and permanent interest in the continuation of the agency. Such powers are called *powers coupled with an interest;* and they are not revocable at pleasure. A familiar instance is that of a power of attorney in a mortgage, to sell the land on default of payment, which will be described hereafter. Such a power would be of no value, if revocable at pleasure; and therefore it is not so held; but all powers not coupled with an interest are revocable at pleasure; (*d*) and with respect to the manner of revocation, the rule is, that if the

(*a*) Layet *v.* Gano, 17 Ohio, 466, 473; Lobdell *v.* Baker, 1 Met. 201–3; Story on Agency, § 17–22. And private instructions to a special agent which are not made known, or designed to be made known, to persons dealing with him, do not limit the liability of the principal. Hatch *v.* Taylor, 10 N. H. 538. Parties dealing with a special agent are generally chargeable with notice of the extent of his authority. White *v.* Langdon, 30 Vt. 599; Black *v.* Shreeve, 2 Beasley, 455.

(*b*) Guerreiro *v.* Peile, 3 B. & Ald. 616; Stevens *v.* Wilson, 6 Hill, 513. {An agent to sell goods is presumed to have authority to warrant their quality and condition unless perhaps the property is of a kind not usually sold with a warranty. Dayton *v.* Hooglund, 39 Ohio State, 671; Randall *v.* Kehlor, 60 Me. 37. Nelson *v.* Cowing, 6 Hill, 337; Peters *v.* Farnsworth, 15 Vt. 155; Skinner *v.* Gunn, 9 Port. (Ala.) 305; Smith *v.* Tracy, 36 N. Y. 79; Howard *v.* Sheward L. R., 2 C. P. 148.}

(*c*) Paley on Agency, 161–71. A ratification of an unauthorized contract, in order to be obligatory, must be shown to have been made with a full knowledge of all essential facts connected with the transaction. Hovey *v.* Brown, 59 N. H. 114; Dickinson *v.* Conway, 12 Allen, 487; Humphrey *v.* Havens, 12 Minn. 298. It makes no difference that the ignorance arose solely from the neglect of the principal to make inquiries. Coombs *v.* Scott, 12 Allen, 493. {Ratification is equivalent to antecedent authority, and relates back to the time of the agent's act as between principal and agent, but not so as to interfere with intervening third persons' rights. Holland *v.* Drake, 29 Ohio State, 441; Pollock *v.* Cohen, 32 id. 514; Cook *v.* Tullis, 18 Wall. 332.}

(*d*) If the power is given for a valuable consideration, it is irrevocable by the principal during his life. Walsh *v.* Whitcomb, 2 Esp. 565; Gaussen *v.* Morton, 10 B. & C. 731; Wheeler *v.* Knaggs, 8 Ohio, 169. But the *interest*, which will enable the power to survive the death of the principal, must be an interest in the subject on which the power is to be exercised, and not merely an interest in that which is produced by the exercise of the power. The interest must pass with the power, and vest in the person by whom the power is to be exercised, so that he can act in his own name. Hunt *v.* Rousmanier, 8 Wheaton, 201; Bergen *v.* Bennett, 1 Caines' Cas. 1; Knapp *v.* Alvord, 10 Paige, 295. Hartley's Appeal, 53 Penn. State, 212; Barr *v.* Schroeder, 32 Cal. 609. {For example, a power to sell and receive a certain proportion of the proceeds as compensation is not a power coupled with an interest, and is therefore revocable. Simpson *v.* Carson, 11 Oregon, 361; Chambers *v.* Seay, 73 Ala. 372.}

appointment was made under seal, the revocation must be under seal; otherwise it may be either in writing or oral. But until notice of such revocation, the acts of the agent will bind the principal. The death of the principal, however, works a revocation from the moment it takes place; although notice of the fact be not received until some time after: and this severe rule makes it hazardous to deal with an agent whose principal lives at a distance. (*a*) It would perhaps be well to alter this rule, by express provision, so as to make the law uniform, that no power should be considered as revoked, by death or otherwise, with respect to any third person, who had previously dealt with the agent, until notice of such revocation. So the death of the agent terminates the agency, because the law does not transfer such a trust to his personal representatives. So lunacy of the principal, when ascertained by inquest, revokes the agency, (*b*) and, in most cases, his bankruptcy would have the same effect. (*c*) So the marriage of a woman revokes an agency created by her when single. (*d*)

I have heretofore spoken of the relation of master and servant, as one of the domestic relations; but the view now presented shows that it belongs more properly to the business relations. It has, in fact, very little to do with domestics, or domestic life; and here again we have a strong illustration of the growing policy of non-interference. Our law wisely abstains from attempting to regulate the relation of master and servant, strictly so called, except where the servant is a minor, and incapable of contracting for himself. What a contrast is here presented to the laws of England, which leave hardly any thing to the discretion of the employer and the employed! There is manifestly no more reason for providing by law what wages shall be paid, and how many hours servants shall work, and how long the contract shall continue, than there would be in prescribing what dress each person shall wear, by what title he shall be called, and how much money he shall expend. Such laws have, in fact, been tolerated in former times; and perhaps some relics of them may even now be found in England, under the name of *sumptuary laws*. But who does not feel that personal liberty must be a mere name, where all the most common

(*a*) 2 Kent, Com. 646. Michigan Ins. Co. *v.* Leavenworth, 30 Vt. 11; Saltmarsh *v.* Smith, 32 Ala. 404; Travers *v.* Crane, 15 Cal. 12; Lewis *v.* Kerr, 17 Iowa, 73; Bank of New York *v.* Vanderhorst, 32 N. Y. 553. Easton *v.* Ellis, 1 Handy (Cincinnati), 70. The rule, that the death of the principal operates as a revocation of the agency, is fully discussed in Ish *v.* Crane, 8 Ohio State, 520; reaffirmed 13 Ohio State, 574, and it is held not to apply to acts of an agent not necessary to be done in the name of the principal, as matters *in pais* and done in good faith without the knowledge of the principal's decease. See also Cassiday *v.* McKinzie, 4 Watts & Serg. 282; Dick *v.* Page, 17 Mo. 234.

(*b*) But see Davis *v.* Lane, 10 N. H. 156, where it is held not to revoke the authority to the damage of innocent partics dealing with the agent. In Bunce *v.* Gallagher, 7 Am. L. Reg. (N. S.) 32; S. C. 5 Blatchf. 481, the court held that the insanity of tho principal revoked the agency as soon as it became known to the agent, whether it was ascertained by inquest or not.

(*c*) Parker *v.* Smith, 16 East, 382; Minet *v.* Forrester, 4 Taunt. 541.

(*d*) Charnly *v.* Winstanley, 5 East, 266; Wambole *v.* Foote, 2 Dak. 1.

affairs and relations of life are thus imperatively prescribed by law? I must be pardoned for recurring so often to this topic; for we cannot fully appreciate the value of our freedom, until we contemplate it in the absence of those vexatious details of municipal regulation, which have been elsewhere endured.

LECTURE XVIII.

EXECUTORS AND ADMINISTRATORS. (a)

§ 119. **Who may Appoint and be Appointed.** The relations we have been considering are those which exist among the living. We are now to consider one which results from death. When a person dies, there must be some one authorized to settle up his affairs. The law permits the living to designate who shall perform this office for them. This is done by making a *will* or *testament*, to take effect after death; the nature of which instrument will be explained hereafter. The deceased is then called *testator*, and the person so nominated to settle his affairs, *executor*. But if the living neglect to make such provision before death, the law undertakes to make it for them. When a person dies without a will, he is said to die *intestate*, and the person designated by law to settle his affairs is called *administrator*. In most places, there is a distinct court for the cognizance of all probate and testamentary matters, under the name of an orphan's court, or court of probate. But here the court of common pleas discharges all these functions. The powers and duties of executors and administrators are here chiefly regulated by statute; and I shall give a synopsis of its provisions.

The only persons incapable of appointing executors are infants, idiots, and lunatics, who are prohibited from making wills. And any person, except a married woman, may be appointed executor, to whom the testator is willing to commit the trust; though a minor cannot act during his minority. As to administrators, the directions of the statute are, that the widow of the intestate shall be first entitled to letters of administration; next, the nearest of kin who are competent; next, any creditor who will accept the trust; and lastly, any other suitable person. The fidelity both of executors and administrators is secured by an official oath, and by bond and sureties, in such amount as the court shall determine; usually double the value of the personalty coming into their hands. If from any cause the executorship becomes vacant, the court

(c) See Kent, Com. lec. 37; 2 Black. Com. ch. 32; Treatises on Executors by Wentworth, Williams, and Toller; Robertson on Personal Succession; Roper on Legacies; and the treatises of Jarman, Roberts, Ram, and Redfield, on Wills.

appoints an *administrator with the will annexed.* If the administratorship becomes vacant, the court appoints an *administrator de bonis non;* that is, *of the estate yet unsettled.* (*a*) If there be a contest concerning a will or other good cause, *a special administrator* is appointed. If a will be discovered after an administrator has been appointed, he is compelled to surrender in favor of the executor therein named. The executor of an executor has no authority, as such, to settle the estate of the first testator. The time within which administration may be originally granted is limited to twenty years from the death of the testator or intestate. Both executors and administrators are removable for good cause. If a single woman be appointed executrix or administratrix, and afterwards marry, her authority ceases; and her husband does not acquire the power in her right, as is generally the case elsewhere. If a minor be appointed executor, he cannot act as such until majority, and provision must be made by court for the intermediate period. The proper county to make the appointment, is that in which the deceased resided; but if he were a non-resident, then any county in which he left property.

§ 120. **Their Course of Proceeding.** The first duty of an executor is to have the will *proved.* (*b*) Until this is done, he has no authority to act. The mode of making probate will be described when we come to speak particularly of wills. After probate of the will, the executor is to follow its directions as far as they go; and for the rest, he is to be governed by the law regulating administrators. The next duty of an executor or administrator, is to have the *personalty* of the intestate *appraised* by three persons under oath, who are appointed by the court; and a sworn *inventory* thereof must be returned to court within three months from the day of appointment. Five days' notice of taking this inventory and appraisement must be given to those interested in the estate. If the court so order, this inventory must also include an appraisement of the realty; but generally, it will only include the movables, debts due the estate, and money on hand, all which must be specifically set forth; and the annual crops and emblements, whether severed from the land or not, are to be treated as movables and included in the inventory. The only case where an inventory is not required, is when an executor is residuary legatee, and has given bond to pay all the debts and legacies. If there be property in another county requiring appraisement, a justice of the

(*a*) Without legislative provision an administrator *de bonis non* cannot maintain an action either against the representatives of the deceased administrator or against the sureties in his official bond. Blizzard *v.* Filler, 20 Ohio, 479; Tracy *v.* Card, 2 Ohio State, 431. Under the act of April 7, 1864, such an action may be maintained against the sureties on the official bond, but not against the personal representatives. Curtis *v.* Lynch, 19 Ohio State, 392; Douglas *v.* Day, 28 Ohio State, 175.

(*b*) An executor is not bound to assume the burden of defending a will against the heirs-at-law, but may throw the same on the legatees or devisees; and where the will is adjudged invalid, he is not entitled to charge the estate in his account with the expense of maintaining the defence. Executors of Andrews *v.* His Administrators, 7 Ohio State, 143.

peace may appoint the appraisers. If there be a widow or minor child, certain specified articles, including clothing, pictures, books, utensils, and furniture, are given to them, and not made assets. These, therefore, are inventoried, but not appraised. If, after making the first inventory, new assets be discovered, a further inventory must be made. It is also the duty of the appraisers to make an *allowance* for the widow and children under fifteen years of age, sufficient for their support one year. The items of this allowance are returned in a separate schedule; and if the personalty be not sufficient for this purpose, they certify what further sum should be allowed, and this must be made up out of the realty. The next duty of the executor or administrator, is to take measures for paying the debts. For this purpose, he must notify the public of his appointment by advertisement within three months. He then proceeds to collect the debts due to the estate, which, if need be, he may compound by leave of court; (*a*) and to convert the chattels into money by a sale at public auction, upon fifteen days' notice; unless the widow will take them at the appraisement, and secure the payment. Our statute requires that all such sales, to an amount exceeding three dollars, shall be on a credit of from three to nine months, to be secured by note or bond with two or more approved sureties. When the sale is by an executor, the chattels specifically bequeathed are only to be sold when the other personalty is insufficient to pay the debts. The sale bill must be made out in the same order as the inventory, and specify the disposition made of each article. A return of the sale must be made within three months; and if the proceeds thus realized from the debts and chattels prove insufficient to pay the debts due from the estate, application is made to the court for leave to sell enough of the realty to make up the deficiency. The mode of doing this will be explained hereafter. If all the property of the deceased, which for this purpose is called *assets*, be insufficient to pay the debts, the estate is declared *insolvent*, and the entire proceeds, being converted into money, are applied in the following order: *First*, to pay the expenses of the last sickness, funeral, and administration. *Secondly*, to make up the year's allowance for the widow and children under fifteen. *Thirdly*, to pay debts entitled to a preference under the laws of the United States. *Fourthly*, to pay public rates, duties, and taxes. *Fifthly*, (*b*) to pay debts due to individuals, which are liens upon the estate either by judgment, decree, or mortgage. *Sixthly*, to pay all other debts *pro rata*. When a claim is presented against the estate, the executor or administrator may require, in addition to the usual vouchers, an affidavit that the claim is justly due. If such claim be allowed, the allowance is

(*a*) He has, at common law, authority to submit a claim to arbitration. The statute of Ohio giving special power to submit to reference does not take away this common-law right. Childs *v.* Updyke, 9 Ohio State, 333.

(*b*) {By act of 1883 (80 Laws, 78) claims for wages for manual labor performed within twelve months and not exceeding $150 each are preferred to the fifth class above.}

indorsed thereon. If rejected, it may by agreement be referred to arbitrators; and if not so referred, and the estate has not been declared insolvent, it must be sued within six months, or it will be barred. Debts due to an executor or administrator must be allowed by court, and are not entitled to a preference. Debts not yet due may be paid, deducting interest for the unexpired time. If due notice of appointment has been given, and claims have not been presented within one year sufficient to show the estate insolvent, debts may be paid without liability to any creditor who has not given notice of his claim, except for his *pro rata* share of what may remain. But if the estate prove *solvent*, then, after paying the debts which have the first claim, the residue is to be distributed as follows: *First*, the surplus proceeds of the personalty are given to the widow, if there be no children; and to the children, if there be no widow. But if there be both, the widow has one-half of the first four hundred dollars, and one-third of the residue, and the children have the rest. If there be neither widow nor children, the distribution is made according to the law of *descent* and *distribution*, to be described hereafter. *Secondly*, the realty over which the administrator has no control, except it be given him by the court, for the purpose of paying debts, is divided among the widow and heirs, according to the law of *dower* and *descent*, which will be described hereafter.

The time allowed to executors and administrators, for settling estates, is eighteen months, within which time the first account must be rendered; but if there be good cause, the court may extend this time from year to year, not exceeding five in all; and even after this period the office does not expire until the estate has been entirely settled. (*a*) Within the time thus allowed, they are required to present to the court from time to time their accounts, with proper vouchers for all money disbursed where the sum exceeds ten dollars; and in case of delay, they may be compelled so to do by citation and attachment. Their final account is continued open for one term, subject to examination by all persons interested, who are notified thereof by advertisement of the clerk, and may file written exceptions to any of the items. The account is then *audited* by the court, and such order made thereon as the case requires. Upon *final distribution* made pursuant to such order, a return is made thereof, with *proper vouchers*, and the same proceedings are had as before. If the court allow the final settlement, an order is made to that effect; and the executor or administrator, and his sureties, are thenceforth discharged, unless within five years good cause be shown for setting such allowance aside. (*b*) If the compensation of an executor has been fixed by the will, and he acquiesce therein, he can receive no other; but he

(*a*) {In Taylor *v.* Thorn, 29 Ohio State, 569, assets were discovered and administered twenty-three years after settlement of the estate}.

(*b*) For proceedings against executors, administrators, and guardians, on the part of creditors, legatees, and distributees, see act of April 17, 1857.

may renounce that, and take the compensation fixed by law for an executor or administrator; which is, on the personalty and the proceeds of realty sold by them, six per centum on the first thousand dollars; four per centum on the excess up to five thousand dollars; and two per centum on the excess above five thousand; together with such special allowance as the court may see proper to make for extraordinary services. But in no case can they speculate upon the funds of the estate; (*a*) and they are chargeable with interest when they have or ought to have made interest.

§ 121. **Their Powers and Liabilities.** Executors and administrators may sue and be sued in their official capacity; but the general rules relating to actions for and against them will be considered hereafter. I will only remark, that our law presents no motive for suing them, until after the time fixed by the statute or the court for the settlement of the estate, unless the claim be one which would not be affected by the insolvency of the estate, or have been presented and disallowed; for in no other case would the person suing recover costs. All suits are barred after four years from the date of appointment, if notice thereof has been duly given, unless assets have since come to hand, or the claim accrued since, or a new administrator has been appointed; in which latter case, one year is added to the four. In no case can execution issue against an executor or administrator, without special permission of the court, and then it runs against the assets in his hands, unless he has been guilty of waste. If executors or administrators *waste* the estate of the deceased, — that is, wilfully or carelessly diminish the amount of assets, — they and their sureties become liable for such deficiency: but in no other case do they become personally liable, unless they voluntarily undertake so to be; and by the statute of frauds, this undertaking must be in writing. Express provision is made, that judgments against them shall specify that they are to be satisfied *out of assets* in their hands; and that if they have occasion to appeal, they need not give bonds as in other cases. Executors and administrators from other States are expressly authorized to act here, upon making application with proper exhibits; but this is an exception to the general rule, which is, that they must derive their authority from the law of the place where the property is, without regard to the domicile of the deceased.

Here terminates our view of the law of persons. There is, indeed, one other relation, and a very important one too, which might have been embraced in this division of lectures: I mean the relation of *debtor and creditor;* but the title is so comprehensive, that, had I undertaken to discuss it, I should hardly have

(*a*) It is against the policy of the law for administrators to purchase the property of the deceased at a public sale held for the purpose of raising money to pay debts; and such a sale may be set aside in equity by the *cestui que trust,* without proof of fraud or actual injury. Barrington *v.* Alexander, 6 Ohio State, 189; Sheldon *v.* Newton, 3 id. 494; Piatt *v.* Longworth, 27 Ohio State, 159.

known where to stop. It includes, in fact, the greater part of what remains to be said, except that relating to crimes. Nor is it usual to class this among the personal relations, since it belongs quite as properly to the law of property, and the law of procedure, as to the law of persons.

PART IV.

THE LAW OF PROPERTY. (*a*)

LECTURE XIX.

PRELIMINARY CONSIDERATIONS.

§ 122. **General Explanations.** In the third lecture, I described the origin of title to the American continent, and traced the history of title to that portion of it which constitutes the United States. I also gave a general account of the acquisition and disposition of that vast extent of territory which constitutes our *public domain.* In the fourth lecture, I described the general divisions and subdivisions of property, for municipal purposes, and defined the terms connected therewith. These it will now be useful briefly to recapitulate. 1. The term *property* includes every valuable thing which can be made the subject of exclusive ownership. 2. The most general division of property is into *things in possession* and *things in expectation.* Things in possession include all things which are under the present and immediate control of the owner. Things in expectation consist of *rights* which may require the intervention of law to render them available. To this class belong all *contracts* and *legal obligations*, which pass under the general description of *choses in action.* 3. Property is again divided into *things real* and *things personal.* Things real include every valuable thing of a fixed and immovable nature, and pass under the general description of *lands, tenements*, and *hereditaments*, or simply *realty*. Things personal include every valuable thing of an unfixed and movable nature, and pass under the general description of *goods* and *chattels*, or simply personalty; and there are certain things occupying a sort of intermediate position

(*a*) On property, in general, see the 2d book of Blackstone, 2d and 3d books of Swift; and 3d and 4th volumes of Kent. On real property, see Flintoff on Real Property; Lomax's Digest; Hilliard's Digest; Coke upon Littleton; Cruise's Digest, by Greenleaf; and treatises by Washburn, Digby, and Tiedeman. Those curious as to the growth of rules of property among the most ancient nations, will find a learned and curious discussion of this subject in Maine's Ancient Law.

between the two, some of which are called *chattels real*, others *heirlooms*, and others *fixtures*. 4. Real property is again subdivided into *things tangible* and *things not tangible*. Things tangible, include *land* and every corporeal thing permanently connected therewith to an indefinite extent above and below the surface; and pass under the general description of *corporeal hereditaments*, or simply *land*. Things not tangible, include certain rights, privileges, or easements, annexed to land in the ownership of another, and pass under the general description of *incorporeal hereditaments*.

By the right of property, I understand, in the language of Blackstone, "that sole and despotic dominion which one man claims and exercises over the external things of the world, in total exclusion of every other individual." (*a*) This is the definition of *exclusive ownership*, and it has been a question of much speculation, whence this right originated; whether from nature or society. We know, as a matter of history, that in the beginning God gave to man a general dominion over the earth, and all things appertaining thereto; but this would only make the first inhabitants *owners in common* of the whole, and not exclusive owners of any specific part. The historical inference, therefore, is, that exclusive ownership did not commence until some subsequent period, when a division of the common property was made, either by compulsion or voluntary agreement. In other words, the right of exclusive ownership is conventional, and not divine or natural; and the same inference results from our theory of the social compact. An island or continent, for example, which no man had ever seen, would be the property of no one; but if a number of persons should be cast upon it, and take possession, they would own it in common, until some agreement should be made concerning it; after which, the nature of their ownership, whether exclusive or common, would depend upon their agreement. In either view, therefore, it would seem that the exclusive ownership of property is a social and not a natural right, though our State constitution declares the contrary. But the question is only of speculative interest; for whatever be the origin of the right of property, its efficiency and value depend upon the provisions of municipal law. Our security for the enjoyment of the right of property may be considered in two aspects, with reference to government and to each other. As before explained, we are protected against encroachments on the part of government, by the constitutional assurance, that, except in the way of regular and just taxation, private property shall not be taken for public use, without compensation to the owner; and that existing contracts shall not be impaired by legislation. And with respect to one another we are protected against encroachment by the whole remedial force of the law, which defines our rights and redresses our

(*a*) 2 Black. Com. ch. 1; 3 Kent, Com. lec. 50.

wrongs. The right of property is, therefore, abundantly protected; and we shall find as we proceed, that the rules which govern the acquisition, enjoyment, transfer, and transmission of it, form the larger portion of the entire body of municipal law.

§ 123. **The Feudal System.** (*a*) There was a time when real property comprehended almost every thing of sufficient importance to be the object of municipal regulation; but that time has long since passed away. In the progress of civilization, personal property has been constantly augmenting in quantity and value, until it has probably turned the scale. At the present moment, it forms a large, if not the largest, part of the wealth of nations. And this difference is destined to be constantly growing greater; for while the basis of real property, that is, the surface of the globe, is limited by nature, so that it cannot be increased, the quantity of personal property, consisting of all the various commodities of life, and depending on the creative genius of man, can be increased to an indefinite extent. This fact in the history of the two divisions of property, has had an important influence upon the character of the law by which they are respectively regulated. The law of personalty, being almost entirely of modern origin, is characterized by the spirit of modern improvement; and as a body, it is comparatively simple, rational, and liberal. Whereas the law of realty, having acquired its form and shape in the days of darkness and barbarism, is characterized by a spirit almost directly the opposite; being, in a remarkable degree, abstruse, technical, and artificial. He who begins with the establishment of the *feudal system*, and traces down the history of the law of real property, will do it with mingled feelings of disgust and gratification. He cannot fail to be thoroughly disgusted with the narrow, arbitrary, and mystifying spirit which dictated all the early doctrines; nor to be equally gratified with the bold, liberal, and determined spirit which has since been manifested, to substitute new ones in their place. But it is remarkable with what a tenacious grasp the laws of real property adhere to the soil in which they have once taken root. Notwithstanding all the improvements which have hitherto been effected, with so much effort, this branch of law is still obnoxious to the charge of being complicated and cumbrous, to a degree totally at variance with the spirit of the age in other respects.

For the origin of the law of realty, we go back to the *feudal system*, and although, for reasons which will be hereafter mentioned, we feel the influence of this system but slightly in this State; yet even here this branch of law cannot be fully understood without some knowledge of the law of feuds. I shall merely mention some of the leading features. The feudal system in its

(*a*) On the feudal system and the doctrine of tenure, see 2 Black. Com. ch. 4, 5, 6; 3 Kent, Com. lec. 53; Sullivan's Lectures; Dalrymple on Feudal Property; Wright on Tenures; Gilbert on Tenures; the Histories of English Law by Reeve, Hale, and Crabbe; Hallam's Middle Ages, ch. ii.

origin was purely a *military establishment*, founded by conquerors. The title to the whole conquered territory vested at once in the *commander in chief* as the ultimate owner, who was called the *lord paramount*. By him it was apportioned, in the first place, among his *principal officers*, who *held* it of him on certain terms of *tenure*, but did not absolutely *own* it. By such *holding*, they became his *vassals;* their interest in the land thus held was called a *feud*, *fief*, or *fee;* and the ultimate right still remaining in the lord, was called his *seigniory*. These principal officers again apportioned their respective feuds in a similar manner among their *inferior officers*, and they among theirs, until, by repeated *subinfeudations*, the feuds became small enough for the purpose of cultivation. Even the lowest *feudatories*, however, did not labor upon the soil. This was the lot of the vanquished inhabitants, who were held in the most abject servitude, and called *serfs* or *villeins*. Thus the feudal system may be properly compared to a stupendous pyramid, of which the lord paramount was the vertex, and whose base rested on slaves. The most important feature in the law of feuds, was that of *tenure*, as distinguished from *absolute ownership*. The terms by which vassals held their feuds, whatever link they formed in the chain of subinfeudation, were chiefly two, *fealty* and *service*. *Fealty* consisted in the obligation of fidelity to the lord; and from certain words used in the ceremony, the assumption of this obligation was called *doing homage*. This is supposed to be the origin of the oath of allegiance. *Service* was the recompense made to the lord for the use of the land, and consisted in attending him in his court during peace, and in his army during war. The mode, manner, and quantity of service were settled at the time of creating the feud; and when scribes could be found, were reduced to writing. This was the origin of the *deed of feoffment*. But the creation of the feud was not complete, until there had been what was called a *corporeal investiture;* which consisted in a *symbolical delivery of possession*, by the lord to the vassal, in sight of the land, and in presence of the neighboring vassals. This gave rise to the modern ceremony, called *livery of seisin*, which will be described hereafter. Originally, feuds were only granted for the life of the feudatory; but, in process of time, they began to be granted to the feudatory *and his heirs*, and thus became *hereditary*. As they were granted upon personal considerations, and created a very intimate and confidential relation between the lord and the vassal, it was a fundamental doctrine that they were *unalienable*, without mutual consent. That is, the lord could not transfer his seigniory without the consent of his vassal; nor could the vassal transfer the feud without the consent of the lord. Such were some of the leading features of the feudal system, while it retained its purely military character; and nowhere was that system more firmly established than in England. The progress of civilization, however, for eight centuries, has effected many important changes. The original *military tenures* gradually gave place to *civil tenures*, such as *grand sergeanty*, *petit sergeanty*, *free socage*, *villein socage*, and divers other tenures, designated by equally euphonious names. But it would be a waste of time to dwell on these tenures, because they are now obsolete. It is sufficient in this connection to observe, that the mighty revolution which has gradually been effected in the law of realty, may be traced to two fundamental innovations upon the original law of feuds. The first relates to hereditary estates, and consists in substituting *absolute ownership* in the place of *holding upon terms of tenure*. The second relates to estates not hereditary, and consists in substituting a *pecuniary compensation* or *rent* in the place of *personal service*.

§ 124. **Slight traces of it here.** It was necessary to present this brief sketch of the feudal system, in order to account for the exceedingly technical character of the law of realty, and to explain the several existing doctrines to which reference must hereafter be made. At the same time it is unnecessary to give a detailed account of that system, because very few traces of it are perceptible in our law. In this respect, the citizens of the new States are much more fortunate than those of the original States, to which the principles of the English law were directly transplanted. For although no feudal conquerors parcelled out the American territory among their victorious followers, yet, as we have before seen, the first settlers brought with them, as their birthright, the general doctrines of the English common law, and among them those feudal principles which time had not been able there to eradicate. But our historical summary has shown that this region was settled under happier auspices. The ordinance of 1787, by a few sweeping provisions, respecting the title, descent, and transfer of land, effectually prevented many of those feudal doctrines, which still cumber the land laws of the older States, from attaching themselves here. The author of the ordinance has himself said that "the titles which were planted by this ordinance, in 400,000 square miles of territory, are more purely republican, and more completely divested of feudality, than any titles in the Union were at that time." (*a*) In fact, the ancient notions of *tenure* do not exist here even in theory, as they do in some of the older States. (*b*) Our citizens hold of no superior. What they own, they own absolutely and independently. All estates are in the broadest sense of the word *allodial*. The only provision in our law which bears the most remote analogy to the doctrine of holding of a superior is, that the people of the State, in their collective and sovereign capacity, have an ultimate right to all land within their jurisdiction, when it so happens that there is no other legal owner; in which case, the law makes it *escheat* to them; and this *right of*

(*a*) Dane's Abr. App. 77.

(*b*) The right of eminent domain is by some jurists based on the principle of the feudal tenure, and by others on sovereignty or public necessity. West River Bridge Co. *v.* Dix, 6 How. 532, 533, 539; 2 Parsons on Contracts, 519.

escheat bears some resemblance to that of the lord paramount. But it has its origin in the most obvious considerations of public policy, and can in no sense be regarded as a relic of the feudal system. We do, indeed, still retain some of the legal terms to which that system gave rise. Thus we speak of the manner of holding as a *tenure*, of the thing holden as a *tenement*, and of the person holding as a *tenant;* but we use all these terms in a modified sense. So we recognize a relation of *landlord and tenant*, respecting which, some of the rules have taken their complexion from the feudal relation of lord and vassal. But this is all; and we may therefore dismiss the subject of *tenure* as having no other than a speculative interest for us.

I have stated that the law of realty improves more slowly than any other branch of law, owing to the nature of the subject; and that much yet remains for reform, even here. At the same time, it is a matter of congratulation that so much has been effected. I have no doubt that the law of realty in Ohio could be written in one third of the space which would be required for the law of realty in England. The truth of this will be felt as we proceed; though it cannot now be demonstrated without anticipation. I will, however, here indicate some of the leading points in which the most marked improvement has been made. 1. We have much fewer incorporeal hereditaments than the English. 2. We have none of the distinctions growing out of their manorial establishments. 3. We have none of the particular customs which prevail there. 4. The statutes of uses, of mortmain, and of entails, are not in force here. 5. All our tenancies, which are not in severalty, are in common. We have no joint tenancies or tenancies in coparcenary, distinct therefrom. 6. Our conveyances are greatly simplified. 7. We have but one real action, and that is ejectment, which answers for all purposes. (*a*) In these, and other similar respects, which will be enlarged upon hereafter, we have reason to boast of our improvement in the law of realty; and because we have innovated so much and so well, I shall treat this branch of law with more fulness than has been my custom hitherto.

The law which regulates the acquisition, use, and transfer of personalty, differs so much from the corresponding provisions with respect to realty, that I at first doubted whether it would not be advisable to treat the subjects separately; but, upon reflection, I have concluded to treat the two in connection. The distinguishing character of personalty is, its *movable nature;* and upon this is founded a great variety of distinctions relative to the mode of acquiring it, the evidence of ownership, the injuries which may be done to it, and the mode of disposing of it. In general, it may be remarked, that in all these respects the law of personalty is much less formal and technical, and in most of them much more simple and reasonable, than the law of realty. All this will be

(*a*) This form of action is superseded by the Code. For actions concerning real property, see R. S. § 5779 *et seq.*

illustrated as we proceed. But in the mean time, I would call your attention to the wide compass embraced by the law of personalty. Whatever relates to the money or currency of the country; to contracts in general, and more particularly to the various commercial contracts, such as bills of exchange, promissory notes, bailments, sales, insurance, and other marine contracts; to corporations; to partnerships; and generally to the relation of debtor and creditor; all this comes more or less directly within the comprehensive scope of the law of personalty. You will not, therefore, expect from me anything more than an abstract or synopsis of these various matters, with a reference to the sources whence more particular information may be had. The subjects of *commercial law* alone, occupy many volumes; while I can devote to them only a few pages; but I shall take some notice of all these subjects; enough at least to indicate how much is to be learned, and what are the landmarks to direct your progress.

LECTURE XX.

INCORPOREAL HEREDITAMENTS, EASEMENTS, AND FIXTURES. (a)

§ 125. **In what they Consist.** We have seen that realty includes not only those *tangible things*, which, in legal contemplation, constitute *lands*, but also certain *intangible rights* annexed to land, and included among *tenements* or *hereditaments.* For this reason, it has been customary to make two divisions of the subject. Hereditament, being formerly the most comprehensive term, has been selected for this purpose, and the division is into *corporeal hereditaments* and *incorporeal hereditaments:* the first, including land only; and the second, every thing real which is not land. I shall first consider incorporeal hereditaments, under the name of *easements;* and then close the lecture with a brief account of fixtures. Incorporeal hereditaments comprise certain rights and privileges connected with land, but belonging to different persons from the proprietors of the land. They are not things of substance, cognizable by the senses, but exist merely in idea. In England, they make a very important portion of real property. No less than eleven different kinds are enumerated by Blackstone; namely, *advowsons*, *tithes*, *offices*, *dignities*, *franchises*, *corodies*, *pensions*, *annuities*,

(a) See 2 Black. Com. Ch. 3; 3 Kent, Com. lec. 52; Woolrych on Ways; Gilbert on Rents; Angell on Watercourses; Angell and Gould on Tide Waters; Cox, Latham, and Woolrych on Window Lights; Amos on Fixtures; Ewell on Fixtures: Angell on Highways; Gale, Goddard, and Washburn on Easements.

commons, *ways*, and *rents*. But this list is very much reduced in this country. For in regard to the first two, namely, *advowsons* and *tithes*, it is sufficient to say that they grow exclusively out of the *English church establishment*, which happily has no existence in this country; and we are thus relieved from a great variety of perplexing questions. In regard to the next six, namely, *offices*, *dignities*, *franchises*, *corodies*, *pensions*, and *annuities*, they have, in the first place, no necessary connection with realty; and in this country, they are not, and cannot be hereditary. On the contrary, they are strictly personal in their character; and with the exception perhaps of *annuities*, in some cases, are neither transferable nor descendible. Not only some express provisions of the federal and State constitutions, but the whole spirit and tendency of our institutions, are opposed to the English doctrines and practice in regard to these hereditaments, if such they can be called in this country. For these reasons, I shall not stop to describe them. Again, as to the English right of *common*, which is the right that one man has to feed his cattle, dig turf, cut wood, or take fish, on the lands of another; it originated under the *manorial establishments* of England, where the lord of the manor was in the habit of setting apart certain portions, to be used in common by tenants or copyholders. It there forms quite a diffusive and intricate branch of law. It has also prevailed in some of the older States of this Union. But in the sense of the English law, this right of common is not known here, and will not therefore be discussed. Again, *rent* is defined to be, "a certain profit issuing yearly out of lands and tenements corporeal." According to this definition, rent may properly be classed with incorporeal hereditaments. But we commonly understand by rent, nothing more than a *periodical compensation*, in money or other property, for the use of land; and, in this sense, it can in no respect be considered as an incorporeal hereditament. I shall accordingly reserve the consideration of rent to its proper place, in connection with estates for years.

§ 126. **Public Easements.** (*a*) But there are certain other rights

(*a*) On the general subject of dedications to public uses, see Lade *v.* Shepherd, 2 Strange, 1004; McConnell *v.* Lexington, 12 Wheaton, 582; Cincinnati *v.* White, 6 Peters, 431; Gowen *v.* Philadelphia Exchange Co., 5 W. & S. 141; U. S. *v.* Chicago, 7 How. 185; Rowan *v.* Portland, 8 B. Monroe, 232; Glover *v.* Powell, 3 Am. Law Reg. 367; 2 Stockton, Ch. 211. A dedication of ground for public uses may be made in Ohio under the statute or according to the common law, the latter requiring and the former dispensing with the assent or acceptance of the public. Fulton *v.* Mehrenfield, 8 Ohio State, 440. {Dedication refers to public and not private uses, and its doctrines do not apply to purposes not public. For example, a proprietor who subdivided a tract, marking streets, alleys, public squares, and marked a lot "Depot of the O. & P. R. R. Co," does not dedicate the depot lot. Todd *v.* P., Ft. W., & C. R. R., 19 Ohio State, 514. Dedicated land reverts to the grantor or his heirs, if the use is abandoned or becomes impossible. Bd. of Education *v.* Edson, 18 Ohio State, 221. But not by mere misuser. Williams *v.* Presbyterian Soc., 1 Ohio State, 478.}

Public Common. Where land was dedicated for the use of public buildings for the county, and it was proposed to lease part of it for private purposes, chancery would of considerable importance connected with land, which I shall now discuss under the head of *easements;* a convenient term, sanctioned by the best usage, and sufficiently broad to include all incorporeal hereditaments known in this State. By *easements*, are meant rights or privileges relating to the land of other persons. They are divided into two classes, *public* and *private. Public easements* comprehend all such as are open and free to the enjoyment of every citizen. They apply chiefly to *commons, roads*, and *rivers*.

Public Commons. By our statute, whenever the proprietor of

not interfere by injunction. Smith *v.* Hueston, 6 Ohio, 101. Where the proprietors by their agent recorded a plat, designating one lot as a "public square," and lots were sold described as adjoining it, the proprietors were enjoined from converting it to any uses inconsistent with the dedication. Brown *v.* Manning, 6 Ohio, 298. Where land in Cincinnati was designated on the plat as for "public uses," it was proper to use it for a court-house and jail, but not to lease it for private purposes. Here the city sued the county, and failed because the statute vested the fee in the county. Cincinnati *v.* Hamilton County, 7 Ohio, 1 pt. 88. Where land had been designated and used as a public square, the legislature could not authorize it to be sold and the proceeds applied to other purposes. Le Clercq *v.* Gallipolis, 7 Ohio, 1 pt. 217. And see Lebanon *v.* Warren County, 9 Ohio, 80. Land dedicated for a public square may be improved and ornamented for recreation and health, or used for public buildings and the transaction of public business. Langley *v.* Gallipolis, 2 Ohio State, 107.

Public Roads, Streets. An order opening a county road forty feet wide, when the law requires sixty, will be set aside. Burrows *v.* Vandevier, 3 Ohio, 383. Chancery cannot decree compensation for property taken for a street, nor correct irregularities in the proceedings. Armstrong *v.* Cincinnati, 5 Ohio, 223. Nor prevent the destruction of a road on the application of a supervisor. Putnam *v.* Valentine, 5 Ohio, 187. Where damage has been done by grading a street and the owner has neglected to prefer his claim pursuant to law, he cannot afterwards recover of the corporation. Hickox *v.* Cleveland, 8 Ohio, 543. The liability of a lessee for rent continues after appropriation for a street, and he is therefore entitled to compensation. Foote *v.* Cincinnati, 11 Ohio, 408. Before the new constitution, "*benefits*" might be considered, in assessing damages. Symonds *v.* Cincinnati, 14 Ohio, 147; Browne *v.* Cincinnati, id. 541; Kramer *v.* Cleveland & Pittsburg R. R. Co., 5 Ohio State, 140; Columbus, Piqua, & Indiana R. R. Co. *v.* Simpson, id. 251. The damages must now be assessed by a jury of 12 men. Lamb *v.* Lane, 4 Ohio State, 167. And they must be assessed without deduction for benefits. County commissioners may lay out a road through an incorporated town or city, unless expressly prohibited by the charter. Wells *v.* McLaughlin, 17 Ohio, 99. And see on the general subject, Cincinnati *v.* Coombs, 16 Ohio, 181; Culbertson *v.* Cincinnati, id. 574; Bingham *v.* Doane, 9 id. 165; Fox *v.* Hart, 11 id. 414; McMicken *v.* Cincinnati, 4 Ohio State, 394; Ferris *v.* Bramble, 5 id. 109; Shaver *v.* Starrett, 4 id. 494. As to the power to authorize assessments for such purposes, see Reeves *v.* Treasurer of Wood County, 8 Ohio State, 333; Butler *v.* City of Toledo, 5 id. 225; Hill *v.* Higdon, id. 243; Ernst *v.* Kunkle, id. 520; Strader *v.* Cincinnati, 1 Handy, 446, 464. A State road and a county road may coexist together. Bisher *v.* Richards, 9 Ohio State, 495.

Public Rivers. On the general subject see Angell on Watercourses, and on Tide Waters; 3 Kent, Com. 497, 516; 3 Western Law Journal, 310, 337; 4 id. 145, 190. With regard to the Ohio River, it has been held that the cession of Virginia reserved the bed of the river to low-water mark on the Ohio side. Handly *v.* Anthony, 5 Wheaton, 374; Booth *v.* Shepherd, 8 Ohio State, 243. And see State *v.* Hoppess, 2 Western Law Journal, 279. But with respect to jurisdiction, see 11th section of the Virginia Compact of 1789, 1 Revised Statutes of Kentucky, 45, which makes the jurisdiction of Virginia and Kentucky "concurrent with the States which may possess the opposite shores of the said river." With regard to the provision in the ordinance of 1787, see Hutchinson *v.* Thompson, 9 Ohio, 52; La Plaisance *v.* Monroe, 1 Walker's Ch. Rep. (Mich.) 155; Gavit *v.* Chambers, 3 Ohio, 495; Hogg *v.* Zanesville, 5 id. 410; As to navigable waters generally, see Walker *v.* Board of Public Works, 16 Ohio, 540; Hopkins *v.* Kent, 9 id. 13; Blanchard *v.* Porter, 11 id. 138; Carson *v.* Blazer, 2 Binney, 475; Shrunk *v.* Schuylkill, 14 Serg. & R. 71; Smith *v.* State of Maryland, 18 How. 71.

land wishes to lay out a *town*, or an *addition* thereto, he is required to have a *plat* thereof surveyed, acknowledged, and recorded, specifying the *streets*, *alleys*, and *commons*. And the effect of complying with these requisitions, is to vest in the *town*, for the use of the public, the fee-simple of all such portions as are designated to be for public use. Here, then, while the land on which the streets, alleys, and commons are laid out, belongs to the town, the easement belongs to the public at large. But apart from this statutory provision, it is not necessary that the fee in the land should pass, in order to secure the easement to the public; or that the dedication should be made in any particular form; all that is required is the assent of the owner of the land, and the fact of its being used for the public purposes intended by this appropriation. Thus where an individual lays out a public street over his land, or where the proprietor of a town reserves a spring or common for the public use, the easement vests at once in the public, without regard to length of possession; and the owner cannot revoke the dedication.

Public Roads. (*a*) By these, I mean roads laid out by the public authorities. The mode of proceeding to lay out State, county, and township roads, is detailed at length in the statutes, with the particular provisions of which I shall not tax your memory. The government has authority under the constitution, as we have seen, to appropriate the land of individuals for these purposes, on making them a compensation. But the public acquire thereby only an easement in the land so appropriated. The fee-simple, subject to the easement, still remains in the former proprietor. (*b*) And where land is granted bounded upon a road, the grant extends to the middle of the road, unless the contrary be expressed. (*c*) The difference, then, between streets laid out by individuals, and roads laid out by government, is, that in the former the fee is in the town, and in the latter the fee is in individuals; while in both the easement belongs to the public. In either case, if the road becomes impassable, the public have a right to pass over the adjoining land without becoming trespassers, provided they do no unnecessary injury.

Public Rivers. The general doctrine of the common law is, that the owners of land bounded by the sea, or by navigable rivers, where the tide ebbs and flows, own only to ordinary high-water mark; while the shore below belongs to the public. But

(*a*) The right of passing on a highway is subject to such incidental, temporary, and partial obstructions as manifest necessity requires, such as those occasioned by delivering freight at stores or houses, repairing the street, constructing sewers, or building or repairing houses on adjoining lots. Clark *v.* Fry, 8 Ohio State, 358.

(*b*) The owner still retains the trees, shrubs, &c., growing in the road, for all purposes not incompatible with the easement. Where a growing hedge stood within the limits of a public highway, leaving ample room for public travel, which was not thereby incommoded or annoyed, and it was cut down by a person not acting under official authority, he will be liable therefor to the owner of the adjoining land. Phifer *v.* Cox, 21 Ohio State, 248.

(*c*) Phillips *v.* Bowers, 7 Gray, 21.

on navigable rivers, *above tide water*, the adjacent owners own to the middle of the stream, subject to the public easement of navigation. Of this latter class are all the navigable rivers within this State; there being no tide within its limits. By the fourth article of compact in the ordinance of 1787, "the navigable waters leading into the Mississippi and St. Lawrence, and the carrying places between them," were declared to be "public highways, and forever free to all citizens;" and by the ninth section of the act of Congress of 1796, "all navigable rivers within the North-western Territory," were declared to be and remain "*public highways;*" and where the opposite banks of any stream, *not navigable*, belonged to different persons, "the stream and the bed thereof" were declared to be *common to both*. In regard to this provision, our court has decided that in the case of navigable rivers, the easement only is reserved to the public, while the fee of the bed of the river belongs to the adjacent owners; and that this act only affirms the common law, in relation both to navigable and unnavigable streams; namely, that opposite owners should own to the middle of the stream, as in case of roads they own to the middle of the road. (*a*) It will be observed that the words of the provision are "the stream and the bed thereof shall be common to both." A literal interpretation of these words would make the opposite owners *tenants in common* of the bed of the stream, instead of each being a tenant in severalty to the middle, as the court intended above. Perhaps this distinction may be of importance hereafter. Our court has also decided that the legislature has no authority to obstruct a public easement in navigable rivers; and that where a dam was permitted to be laid across, by reason of which navigators sustained damage, the owners of the dam were liable, although they were authorized by law to build the dam, and used all diligence to prevent it from being an obstruction. But the State may legislate respecting these rivers, and even affect their navigation, provided all persons are equally subjected to the inconvenience resulting from such navigation, and provided the navigation, though affected, be not actually destroyed. It may become a difficult question hereafter to determine what are navigable rivers within this act. The second section of the act of Congress of 1796 provides that navigable rivers shall not be included in *public surveys;* but does not indicate what shall be considered such; and it is left to the discretion of the *surveyor* to include a given river or not. But of course his decision cannot be conclusive. In the deed of cession by Virginia, the description specified "all the territory to the northwest of the river Ohio." And from these words it has been decided, that the owners on this side have no right of soil, further

(*a*) {Gavit *v.* Chambers, 3 Ohio, 596; Lamb *v.* Rickets, 11 id. 311; Walker *v.* Bd. Pub. Works, 16 id. 544; and this is the doctrine in Connecticut, Illinois, Indiana, Massachusetts, Maine, Michigan, Mississippi, New Jersey, New York, and Wisconsin.}

than to the edge of the river at low-water mark. But as a matter of expediency, amounting almost to necessity, the States bordering on this river have habitually exercised a common jurisdiction. The question whether the right of fishing in these navigable rivers is a public right open to all, or a private right belonging to the adjacent owners, has not been judicially decided in this State. (*a*) In practice, it has been treated as a public and common right. And in Pennsylvania, such has been the decision with respect to the rivers of that State. (*b*).

§ 127. **Private Easements.** (*c*) Private easements comprehend all those which belong to particular individuals. They relate chiefly to the use of *land, water, air*, and *light.*

As to Land. (*d*) The most important easement under this head is the right of *private way* over another man's ground. This right may arise in three ways: from *contract*, as where I expressly grant this right to you; from *prescription*, as where you have enjoyed the right unmolested for a certain period, which, under our statute of limitations, would probably be twenty-one years; (*e*) or from *necessity*, as where I sell you land so hemmed in by mine, that you

(*a*) {It is well settled, however, that the right of fishery in our fresh-water lakes and their bays is not limited to the riparian owners, but is common to the public. Sloan *v.* Biemiller, 34 Ohio State, 492 ; Hogg *v.* Beerman, 41 Ohio State, 81 ; s. c. 52 Am. Rep. 71.}

(*b*) It has been frequently held that the ebbing and flowing of the tide in a river is not in this country the test of its navigability. Whether a river is navigable or not, is a question of fact to be determined in each case upon the facts. This is clearly the doctrine of the United States courts. Russell *v.* The Empire State, Newberry's Adm. R. 541 ; Spooner *v.* McConnell, 1 McLean, 337 ; Propeller Genesee Chief *v.* Fitzhugh, 12 How. 443 ; The Ad Hine *v.* Trevor, 4 Wallace, 555 {Lawson *v.* Blaver, 2 Bin. 475 ; Cates *v.* Wadling, 1 McCord, 580 ; Wilson *v.* Forbes, 2 Dev. 30 ; Collins *v.* Benbury, 3 Ired. 277 ; Elder *v.* Burrus, 6 Humph. 358 ; Bullock *v.* Wilson, 2 Porter, 436 ; Castner *v.* Steamboat Dr. Franklin, 1 Minn. 73 ; McManus *v.* Carmichael, 3 Iowa, 1 ; The Daniel Ball, 10 Wall. 557 ; The Montello, 11 Wall. 411}. Those rivers must be regarded as public navigable rivers in law, which are navigable in fact ; and they are navigable in fact when they are used, or are susceptible of being used, in their ordinary condition, as highways for commerce, over which trade and travel are, or may be, conducted in the customary modes of trade and travel on water. The Daniel Ball, 10 Wall. 557 {The Montello, 20 Wall. 430. At some seasons of the year with tolerable regularity. Little Rock & C. R. R. *v.* Brooks, 39 Ark. 403 ; Walker *v.* Allen, 72 Ala. 456 ; Shaw *v.* Oswego Iron Co., 10 Oregon, 371}. For other cases, see note on admiralty jurisdiction in chapter on Judicial Department. An act of Congress declaring a bridge built over a navigable river dividing two States to be a lawful structure, and a post route, legalizes the bridge as built, and abates a suit brought to declare the bridge a nuisance, though ready for hearing. The Clinton Bridge, 10 Wall. 454. See also the Wheeling Bridge case, 18 How. 429. But in a late case in Kentucky, these decisions are said not to apply to questions as to the ownership of land under the water, and subject to the easement of the public, and the court held that a grant of land bounded on the Ohio extends to the centre of the stream. Barry *v.* Snyder, 3 Bush (Ky.), 266. But see Martin *v.* Nance, 3 Head (Tenn.), 649 ; Tomlin *v.* Dubuque, &c., R. R. Co., 32 Iowa, 106 ; Pollard's Lessee *v.* Hagan, 3 How. 212 ; Martin *v.* Waddell, 16 Peters, 410 ; Mumford *v.* Wardwell, 6 Wall. 436. The courts of Pennsylvania, New York, Iowa, and several other States, have decided the question in the same way. Mississippi and Illinois, however, hold differently. For a full discussion of the cases on this subject, see an article in the Am. Law Rev. for July, 1868.

(*c*) Morgan *v.* Mason, 20 Ohio, 401.

(*d*) See 2 Black. Com. 35 ; 3 Kent, Com. 434 ; Lasala *v.* Holbrook, 4 Paige, 169 ; Rust *v.* Low, 6 Mass. 90 ; Stackpole *v.* Healy, 16 id. 33.

(*e*) 3 Kent, Com. 441.

cannot come at it without crossing mine. (*a*) This right of way is always confined to one particular track, which the owner of the right is bound to keep in repair; and if he suffers it to become impassable, he cannot, as in case of public highways, pass over the adjoining land. There are several other easements under this head, which are denominated *urban*, from being confined chiefly to cities and populous towns. Such are the right of *support*, as where I have a right to rest my timbers on the wall of your house; (*b*) the right of *drip*, as where I have a right to let the water fall from my roof upon your premises; and the right of *drain*, as where I have a right to convey water through your premises. These rights may arise either from *contract* or *prescription*, but I presume not from *necessity*. When a *party wall* stands equally on the land of each adjacent owner, and has been erected at joint expense, each owner thereby acquires a right to the use of such wall, and is bound to contribute towards all necessary repairs; and the same is true, where the wall stands wholly on the land of one, provided the other has acquired, either by contract or prescription, a right to use it as a party wall. (*c*) But without special provision, which is made in many cities, neither party can be compelled to contribute to the original erection of a party wall, or to furnish a portion of his land for that purpose. At common law, the same rules govern *partition fences*, but in most of the States these are the subject of statute regulation. In Ohio, for example, a partition fence between two enclosures, without any agreement, is at the joint expense of both proprietors. But if one owner

(*a*) Pinnington *v.* Galland, 20 Eng. Law & Eq. 561; N. Y. Life Ins. & Trust Company *v.* Milnor, 1 Barb. Ch. 353. Carbrey *v.* Willis, 7 Allen, 364; Taylor *v.* Warnaky, 55 Cal. 350. A way of necessity ceases as soon as the necessity to use it ceases. Abbott *v.* Stewardstown, 47 N. H. 228; Carey *v.* Rae, 58 Cal. 189; 132 Mass. 582; 59 N. H. 7; 136 Mass. 575; 77 Me. 193; 51 Conn. 70.

(*b*) Richards *v.* Rose, 24 Eng. Law & Eq. 406. As to the right of the owner of the surface to the support of mineral strata when the mines are owned by another, see Humphries *v.* Brogden, 1 Eng. Law & Eq. 241.

(*c*) As to the liability of the owners of a party wall to contribution, see Sherred *v.* Cisco, 4 Sandford, 480, which decides that where a party wall, which has been jointly built by two adjoining owners, one half on land which each owns in severalty, is destroyed by fire, there is no obligation resting upon either to rebuild it, or to unite in building another party wall. The parties are not tenants in common of the wall; but each owns in severalty the portion of the wall situated on his own land, with no qualification except that neither has a right to pull it down without the other's consent. See Campbell *v.* Meisier, 4 Johns. Ch. 334; Wolf *v.* Frost, 4 Sandf. Ch. 72. Where the agreement to build a party wall contains no express stipulations for its perpetual continuance, such a stipulation will not be implied, although it has been used by both parties for a period of more than twenty-one years. If it becomes reasonably proper, through the increased value of the property, to erect a building for which the old wall is not suitable, the owner of one lot may, in such a case, pull down his portion of the party wall, using only reasonable care to avoid injury to his neighbor. Hieatt *v.* Morris, 10 Ohio State, 523. A covenant in an agreement for the erection of a party wall, by which the other party is to pay half the cost when he uses it, runs with the land, and binds assignees. Platt *v.* Eggleston, 20 Ohio State, 414 {Roche *v.* Ullman, 104 Ill. 11. But the right to receive the compensation is personal to the promisee, and does not follow his land. Hart *v.* Lyon, 90 N. Y. 663; Holden *v.* Gibson, 16 Ill. App. 411. If the wall is built by an owner of both houses, and he sells one, including the whole wall, to A., and the rest to B., A. cannot remove it against B.'s will, if it supports B.'s house. 80 Ky. 391}.

does not choose to enclose his land, he is not bound to contribute. As to the *foundations* of buildings in compact towns, in the absence of special provision, the rule is, that each man may pull down his, or lay new ones, on giving notice and using ordinary care, without liability for injury to those next to him.

As to Water. (*a*) Of the use of water in general, it must be observed, that water, like light and air, was undoubtedly intended to be the property of all mankind; and therefore, while the *use* of *running water* may belong to a particular individual, the thing itself can never be exclusively appropriated. An easement is all the property that can be had in it. If, either from owning the soil covered by water, or from contract, or prescription, I am entitled to use a certain body of water, either for turning a mill, or for fishing, or for any other purpose, the law protects me in the enjoyment of that right, but at the same time forbids the appropriation of that water to myself, any further than is necessary for that particular use. (*b*) We have seen that the navigable waters of this State are common highways; but that the adjacent owner owns to the middle of the stream. It follows that he may have a private easement in the water not inconsistent with the public easement. For example, he has the exclusive right of drawing nets upon his own bank. So he may take the water to turn a mill or perform any other service which does not interfere with navigation. As to waters not navigable, we have seen the only difference to be, that the public has no easement therein. Accordingly, no individual can have a right even to fish in the stream, except the adjacent owner, unless by contract or prescription. The exclusive use of the water belongs to the adjacent owner, subject to the great leading principle of not interfering with the rights of

(*a*) See 2 Black. Com. 14; 3 Kent, Com. 439; Angell on Watercourses. An act relative to the location and construction of ditches, drains, and watercourses, was passed March 24, 1859.

(*b*) Newhall *v.* Ireson, 8 Cush. 595; Luther *v.* Winnisimmet Co., 9 id. 171; Eliott *v.* Fitchburg R. R. Co., 10 id. 191; Ashley *v.* Wolcott, 11 id. 192; Thurber *v.* Martin, 2 Gray, 394; Chandler *v.* Howland, 7 id. 348. An action for a nuisance, caused by diverting or obstructing the water, will not lie unless the damage is real, material, and substantial. Cooper *v.* Hall, 5 Ohio, 320; McElroy *v.* Goble, 6 Ohio State, 187. As to the right of a mill-owner, in order to improve the easement, to build a bridge over a public highway, see Bisher *v.* Richards, 9 Ohio State, 495. An action is not maintainable against a person who by digging a well intercepts from a stream water which would otherwise have flowed into it by percolation through the soil, though such loss of water was a natural effect reasonably to be expected from digging the well. Chasemore *v.* Richards, 26 L. J. (N. S.) Ex. 393; same case in House of Lords 29 L. J. (N. S.) Ex. 81.

{Two different doctrines prevail as to the duty of a lower proprietor to receive the surface water flowing from higher land upon him. The common law permits the lower proprietor to obstruct such flow; and this prevails in Arkansas, Indiana, Kansas, Massachusetts, Maine, Minnesota, Missouri, New Jersey, New York, Rhode Island, Vermont, and Wisconsin. But the civil-law doctrine is that the lower estate is subject to the servitude; and a dam or change of grade cannot be made to prevent it. This is adopted in Alabama, California, Illinois, Iowa, Louisiana, North Carolina, Ohio, Pennsylvania, and Tennessee. Under either doctrine the upper proprietor cannot gather the surface water and discharge it upon the lower proprietor in a different course or larger body than nature has provided. Tootle *v.* Clifton, 22 Ohio State, 247.}

owners above and below. (*a*) As to grants of lands adjoining rivers, the principle is as in case of roads, that they extend to the middle, unless the words of a grant exclude such an inference. The implication is always in favor of the extension. But when the words of the grant expressly limit it to the edge of the stream, low-water mark is the boundary line; and the adjacent owner would have no right to use the water beyond that line. (*b*)

As to Light and Air. (*c*) In these elements, as in water, there can be no absolute property; but the owner of land may acquire a right to use them in a certain way, so that his neighbor can do nothing to obstruct him in that use. For example, if, for the period of prescription, I have had the light admitted into my house in a certain direction, and have enjoyed a pure atmosphere, I have acquired such a right, that my neighbor can do nothing on his land, either to obstruct the light or taint the atmosphere, without being guilty of a *nuisance ;* at least the rule is so laid down in the books. But it must be taken with so many qualifications, particularly in cities, and the application of it is of so rare occurrence, that a bare allusion to it is as much as I have room for.

§ 128. **Fixtures.** (*d*). From the view heretofore given of what

(*a*) Embrey *v.* Owen, 4 Eng. L. & Eq. 466 ; Wood *v.* Sutcliffe, 8 id. 217 ; Tyler *v.* Wilkinson, 4 Mason, 397 ; Cooper *v.* Williams, 4 Ohio, 253, 286 ; Buckingham *v.* Smith, 10 id. 288, 297. As to the rights of adjoining owners to water flowing in subterranean courses, see Acton *v.* Blundell, 12 M. & W. 324, limited by Dickinson *v.* Grand Junction Canal Co., 9 Eng. L. & Eq. 513.

(*b*) M'Cullock *v.* Aten, 2 Ohio, 307 ; Hopkins *v.* Kent, 9 Ohio, 13 ; Benner *v.* Platter, 6 Ohio, 504 ; Lamb *v.* Rickets, 11 Ohio, 311.

(*c*) See 2 Black. Com. 14 ; 3 Kent, Com. 358. The English law on this subject is not favorably received in this country. Myers *v.* Gemmell, 10 Barb. 537 ; Palmer *v.* Wetmore, 2 Sandf. 316 ; Ray *v.* Lynes, 10 Ala. 63 ; Fifty Associates *v.* Tudor, 6 Gray, 255 ; Hubbard *v.* Town, 33 Vt. 295 ; Ward *v.* Neal, 35 Ala. 602. It has since been settled in Ohio that an easement in light and air cannot be gained by prescription in this State. Hieatt *v.* Morris, 10 Ohio State, 523 ; Mullen *v.* Stricker, 19 Ohio State, 135 ; Richardson *v.* Pond, 15 Gray, 387. Nor will the law of implied grants, or implied reservations in the case of the sale by the owner of two adjacent lots or one of them, growing out of the nature or use of the structures existing upon the lots at or prior to the time of the conveyance, be applied to such easements. Mullen *v.* Stricker, *supra* {*contra,* Sutphen *v.* Thirkelson, 38 N. J. Eq. 318. The English law is received in Delaware. Clawson *v.* Primrose, 4 Del. Ch. 643}.

(*d*) See Brown on Fixtures; Ewell on Fixtures, Chitty's Blackstone, 282, note ; 2 Kent, Com. 341 ; 1 Swift's Dig. 74 ; 10 American Jurist, 53 ; Elwes *v.* Maw, 3 East, 38 ; Whiting *v.* Drastow, 4 Pick. 310 ; Wall *v.* Hinds, 4 Gray, 270 ; King *v.* Johnson, 7 id. 239 ; Hill *v.* Wentworth, 28 Vt. 429 ; Fullam *v.* Stearns, 30 id. 443 ; Martin *v.* Roe, 7 El. & B. 237 ; s. c. 40 Eng. L. & E. 68 ; Van Ness *v.* Pacard, 2 Peters, 137. An article annexed by a tenant may not be fixed which would have been a fixture, if annexed by a vendor. Many annexations are removable by a tenant, as being trade fixtures, which a vendor could not deprive his vendee of. In Teaff *v.* Hewitt, 1 Ohio State, 511, where this subject is discussed at length, the united application of the following requisites was regarded as the safest criterion of a fixture : 1. Actual annexation to the realty, or something appurtenant thereto. 2. Appropriation to the use or purpose of that part of the realty with which it is connected. 3. The intention of the party making the annexation to make the article a permanent accession to the freehold ; this intention being inferred from the nature of the article affixed, the relation and situation of the party making the annexation, the structure and mode of annexation, and the purpose or use for which the annexation has been made. See also Voorhees *v.* McGinnis, 48 N. Y. 278 ; Fortman *v.* Goepper, 14 Ohio State, 558 ; Hill *v.* Sewald, 53 Penn. State, 271 ; Meig's Appeal, 62 Penn. State, 28. "The general principle to be kept in view, which underlies all questions of this kind, is the distinction between constitutes realty, it is obvious that there may be certain articles of property which occupy so nearly a middle place between realty and personalty, that it is difficult to say at once to which class they belong. This is the case with what are called *fixtures*, including those chattels, which, by being *annexed* as appendages to the realty, become parcel thereof. The annexation may be either *actual* or *constructive.* Thus locks, doors, windows, blinds, wainscots, and the like, are actually annexed, while title-deeds, keys, and the like, are constructively annexed. It is of little consequence what are fixtures and what are not, until there is a change of possession, but then it will be a question of great importance: and this will happen in the three following cases: 1. When the owner dies. In this case it is not important to his *creditors*, because if the personalty will not satisfy their claims, they can resort to the realty. But between the *widow* and *heirs*, it is important; because, if there be no children, the widow has the whole of the personalty: otherwise, half of the first four hundred dollars, and a third of the residue; and this she has absolutely; whereas, she can in no case have more than a life-estate, in one-third of the realty. (*a*) 2. When the owner sells. In this case, the privileges and appurtenances, in which fixtures are included, pass with the land; and it is of course material, as between the vendor and vendee, what are to be considered fixtures. 3. When the owner leases. In this case, the question is more important than in either of the preceding; for the lessee often finds it necessary for his business or comfort to make various additions and improvements, during the continuance of the lease; and it is therefore of the utmost consequence for him to understand, whether, at the expiration of his lease, these are to belong to his landlord or himself. Now in all these cases the ancient rule was, that all chattels, when once fixed to the realty, became parcel thereof, and pass or remain therewith; but in modern times, this rule has been very much relaxed, for the benefit of trade and agriculture, in favor of lessees; while in regard to the other persons above named, it remains very nearly as at first. Thus a lessee has been allowed to take away kettles fixed in mortar, steam-engines, mills, and even buildings, which he had constructed during his lease. On the whole, the rule, as it now stands, seems

the business which is carried on in or upon the premises, and the premises or *locus in quo.* The former is personal in its nature, and articles that are merely accessory to the business, and have been put in the premises for that purpose, and not as accessories to the real estate, retain the personal character of the principal to which they appropriately belong, and are subservient. But articles that have been annexed to the premises as accessory to whatever business may be carried on upon it, and not peculiarly for the benefit of a present business, which may be of a temporary character, become subservient to the realty, and acquire and retain its legal character." Applying these principles, the stone piers of a railroad bridge were held not fixtures as between the railroad company and the owner of the land. Wagner *v.* Cleveland & T. R. R. Co., 22 Ohio State, 563, 577–8.

(*a*) The widow now in many cases takes a larger estate than this, and often the fee. See chapter on Title by Descent, notes.

to be, that if the articles in question are annexed for the special purpose of immediate profit, and make no necessary or customary appendage to the realty, and if they can be severed without injury to the value of that which remains, they belong to the lessee; otherwise to the owner. It is hardly necessary to add that these remarks apply only to cases where the parties have made no special provision concerning the fixtures. They can make what contract they please, and the law will enforce it; but when they are silent the law gives the construction I have mentioned.

I have before named the American law of incorporeal hereditaments, as one of the instances of improvement in the law of realty. If the student will now take the trouble to read Blackstone or Cruise on the same subject, he will feel the truth of the remark; and he will see that the chief difference is to be traced to two causes: our entire disunion of church and state permitting nothing like a religious establishment; and our total abolition of hereditary personal distinctions. In a word, he will find in this very comparison, one of the best illustrations of the proposition, that the essential genius of republicanism is simplicity.

LECTURE XXI.

ESTATES WITH RESPECT TO DURATION. (a)

§ 129. **Nature of Estates.** The inquiry next in order, relates to the various kinds of *estates*. The term *estate* when applied to realty, signifies the *interest* which the owner has therein: so that if I grant *all my estate* in a certain parcel of land, all my interest thereby passes, without any other words. In common language, the term is used in a broader sense. Thus when we speak of the estate of a certain person, we mean by it all he is worth, whether of personalty or realty. But at present we are concerned with estates in their technical acceptation: and here they divide themselves into various classes, depending, *first*, upon their duration; *secondly*, upon their commencement; *thirdly*, upon the number of owners; and *fourthly*, upon the conditions which may be annexed to them. In this lecture, I shall consider estates only with reference to their duration; and in this view they divide themselves into five classes; namely, estates in fee, for life, for years, at will, and at sufferance. It has been customary to make a more general division of estates into two classes; namely, *freehold estates* and *estates less than freehold;* and then estates in fee and for life are included in the first class, being the only estates of freehold dignity. For by the common law an estate for the longest fixed

(a) See 4 Kent, Com. lec. 54-56; 2 Bl. Com. ch. 7-9; 1 Swift, b. 2, ch. 2-7.

term of years, though it might exceed a hundred lives, is accounted no more than a *chattel interest;* while an estate for life, however short that life may be, is a *freehold interest.* This doctrine originated in feudal reasons, which have long since ceased to exist. As a feud, when once created, could not be terminated by the mere will of the lord, whatever could be held as a feud was called a *frank tenement* or *freehold.* Now feuds could not be conferred for a term of years, but were either for life or hereditary; and hence freeholds included only estates in fee, and for life. Again, feuds were always conferred by *corporeal investiture;* and hence by the common law, freeholds could not be created without *livery of seisin.* (*a*) This term *seisin, seisina,* originally signified actual possession of land under a feudal grant. But when feuds became hereditary, and the heir succeeded by law to the rights of the ancestor, a distinction was made between *seisin in fact,* which was the actual possession before mentioned, and *seisin in law,* which was the right of possession acquired by the heir before *entry,* but not perfected into actual possession until entry. A similar distinction is said to prevail now, where the ceremony of *livery of seisin* is still in use, which signifies that formal delivery of possession required to perfect the conveyance of a freehold. The parties, grantor and grantee, with their witnesses, go to or upon the land, and the grantor actually delivers to the grantee a key, twig, or some other thing, as a symbol of the delivery of the land. But the case was entirely different with estates for years; not being created with feudal solemnities, they were held by the most precarious tenure; it depended upon the will of the feudal owner to terminate the tenancy when he pleased; and though he should violate an express agreement, the tenant had no remedy for the recovery of possession. An estate for years, therefore, when held by so frail and slavish a tenure, could with no propriety be called a *freehold.* And such continued to be the law until the year 1530, when it was altered by act of Parliament; and the tenant for years was made as secure in his possession as a tenant for life. From that time, the real difference between freehold and other estates ceased; but the technical difference in the mode of creating them continues to this day in England, and perhaps in many of the States; and from this difference resulted another;

(*a*) As to *livery of seisin,* the court, in Holt *v.* Hemphill, 3 Ohio, 232, say: "We have always held that a complete title may be created, without an actual entry, and where the grantee may never have been within hundreds of miles of the property granted. The delivery of the deed has been considered as giving possession, in contemplation of law, and the grantee is presumed to have entered, unless that presumption is rebutted by facts. . . . And that I may not be misunderstood on this important point, I repeat that I do not consider a formal *livery of seisin,* as practised in former times, or an actual corporeal entry, as being at all necessary to consummate a title, or to vest a seisin in deed, in any case where the premises are vacant, or occupied by a person holding under the grantor, or otherwise, without claim of title. In all such cases, the execution and delivery of the deed vests the seisin, completes the title, and puts the grantee in the same situation as if he had made a formal entry, and received the twig and turf from the hand of the grantor." And see Borland *v.* Marshall, 2 Ohio State, 308, 313.

namely, that freeholds could not be made to commence *at a future time*, while other estates could. (*a*) The reason was, that *livery of seisin*, being in its nature a present act, could not have a future operation; whereas, estates for years, requiring no *livery of seisin*, might commence at any time the parties should agree. In this State, however, these technical differences have also ceased; for here, *livery of seisin*, as will appear in the sequel, is never necessary in the creation of any estate. The distinction, then, between freehold and other estates, is of no further use to us, than as it serves to determine who are entitled to exercise certain civil functions, which by our law are confined to *freeholders*. And I shall accordingly consider estates, with reference to their duration, as divided into the five classes before named.

§ 130. **Estates in Fee.** (*b*) An estate in fee, is one, which, at the death of its owner, if not otherwise disposed of by him, *descends* to his heirs. In feudal times, as we have seen, the term *fee* had a different signification; but now it means nothing more than a *descendible estate;* so that an estate in fee is the same thing as an estate of inheritance. Of the various ways in which this estate may be created, I shall speak hereafter. It is sufficient now to say, that where it is created *by deed*, the word *heirs*, is indispensable, unless otherwise provided by statute; which is not the case here. This is an inflexible rule of the common law, and no words of *perpetuity* will supply the place of the word *heirs*, except in the grant to corporations, where the word *successors*, though not essential, is usually substituted. (*c*) Accordingly, if in creating this estate by deed the word *heirs* happen to be omitted, however clear may be the intention to create a fee, the grantee will take only a life-estate. But in regard to *wills*, this severity is relaxed, on account of the hurry and want of advice with which they are often made; and there, any words of perpetuity signifying an intention to create a fee will have that effect. Several of the States have, by express provision, put deeds upon the same footing as wills, in this respect; and I cannot help looking upon the common-law rule as arbitrary and unjust. It is certainly in direct opposition to one of the prevailing rules of interpreting contracts; which is, to construe them most strongly

(*a*) {But a freehold *in futuro* could always be created to begin *in futuro* by deed of bargain and sale, for no *livery of seisin* was required thereunder. The early Massachusetts ruling to the contrary is regarded as anomalous.}

(*b*) 2 Black. Com. chap. 7; 4 Kent, Com. lec. 54; 1 Cruise's Dig. 1.

(*c*) Congregational Society *v.* Stark, 34 Vt. 243. A fee may be conveyed to a corporation without the word "successors." Ross *v.* Adams, 4 Dutcher, 160. This case intimates that by the use of language indicating a clear intention, a fee-simple might be conveyed to an individual without the word "heirs." {It is so held in Ohio, in Brown *v.* First National Bank, 44 Ohio State, decided May 11, 1886. But not unless such intention is plain. Ford *v.* Johnson, 41 id. 366.} But this is entirely contrary to the common law. The necessity of the word "heirs" to the creation of an estate in fee simple is removed by statute in the following States: Alabama, Arkansas, Georgia, Illinois, Indiana, Iowa, Kentucky, Mississippi, Missouri, New York, Tennessee, Texas, and Virginia, — the presumption in those States being declared to be, that the deed passes all the grantor's estate, unless some limitation appears.

against the maker or grantor; and most beneficially for the other party. But its origin is to be traced to the feudal system. At first, as we have seen, feuds were not hereditary. At length they began to be conferred on feudatories and their heirs. At this stage of the law, if the word *heirs* was omitted, the presumption was that the lord only intended to create an original feud, not hereditary; and this presumption, which was then reasonable, has ever since prevailed in courts of law. In courts of equity, however, when a contract for conveyance is to be construed, this rigid rule is departed from; and the omission of the word *heirs* is supplied, whenever this appears to have been the intention of the parties.

What has now been said applies to all estates in fee. But it is usual to divide these estates into two classes, *fees simple* and *fees conditional*. Since, however, conditions may be annexed to every other species of estate as well as an estate in fee, I have thought it better to consider conditional fees, in connection with other conditional estates, in a separate division. At present, therefore, I am only concerned with *estates in fee-simple*. This is the highest possible interest which a man can have in real property, whether corporeal or incorporeal. It includes all interests, present and future. It forms a unit or whole, of which all other estates are but fractions or parts. It comes to the owner with the unlimited power of alienation during life; and unless he does something to encumber it, passes in the same absolute character to his heirs. Such estates are obviously more in harmony with the free spirit of our institutions than those which are clogged with conditions and limitations. It does not suit the genius of our citizens to be put under restrictions with regard to the disposition of property. Hence, those "fettered inheritances," which are so common in England, are rare in this country. The prevailing estate is a fee-simple. And this is one leading cause of the exceeding simplicity of our land system.

§ 131. **Estates for life.** (*a*) Estates for life rank next in importance to estates in fee. We have seen, that for feudal reasons, they are esteemed of higher dignity than the longest estate for years. An estate for life is so much taken off from a complete estate in fee. The future estate in fee expectant on the termination of the life-estate, is called either a *reversion* or *remainder*, as will be explained hereafter; and the two together constitute one complete estate in fee. An estate for life may either be for the life of him who has it, or for the life of a third person. In the first case, the owner is called *tenant for life*, simply; in the second, *tenant for another's life*, or in law French, *tenant pur autre vie;* while he for whose life the estate is held, is called *cestui que vie.* Both these estates are of freehold dignity, though the former is justly regarded as the preferable estate, because it certainly must

(*a*) 2 Black. Com. ch. 8; 4 Kent, Com. lec. 55; 1 Cruise's Dig. 59.

last as long as the owner lives, while the latter may not. But connected with an estate for another's life, is one curious question. Suppose the owner dies before the man for whose life it is held; to whom does the residue of this estate belong? It does not revert to the grantor, for the time has not expired; and it does not descend to the heirs of the grantee, unless they are expressly mentioned. This was the reasoning of the ancient common law; and to solve the difficulty, any person was permitted to take possession by way of *special occupancy*, as of a vacant estate, and hold it till the death of him by whose life the estate was measured. In England, and in many of the States, this doctrine has been altered by statute. In this State, we have no provision on the subject; but yet I would venture to say that our courts would never recognize so absurd a doctrine, as to allow a stranger to take possession. Undoubtedly, the residue of the estate would go to the representatives of the deceased owner, according to our rules of distribution. And whether we call this residue a *freehold*, or a *chattel interest*, is of little consequence; for in either case the heirs will have it, if there be no debts to pay. But from the phraseology of our statute of descent, which confines its operation to real estates of inheritance, of which the above is certainly not one, I presume that this remaining interest would be distributed as personal property. Estates for life may be created either by the *act of the parties*, or by the *operation of law*. Thus, if I grant land to you for the term of your life, I create in you an estate for life, by express words. If I grant land to you without any specification of time, I create in you an estate for life, by legal construction. For it cannot be a fee, because it has not the word *heirs;* and it cannot be an estate for years, because the years are not specified. It is therefore construed as a life-estate. There are but two estates for life by the operation of law: namely, *dower* and *curtesy;* both resulting from marriage, and both having the same general incidents as other life-estates. Of these general incidents only I shall now speak; reserving what is peculiar to these two estates for a more appropriate place, in connection with the mode of acquiring title.

Termination. (*a*) An estate for life, in this country, terminates only with the *natural death* of the person. We know no such thing as *civil death* under the English law. Monastic seclusion does not exist among us; bills of attainder are prohibited by the federal constitution; and no crime creates a forfeiture of estate; for our constitution declares "that no conviction shall work corruption of blood, or forfeiture of estate." And I presume the same principle exists in all the States.

Estovers. (*b*) A tenant for life has a right to take reasonable

(*a*) See 2 Black. Com. 121.

(*b*) See 2 Black. Com. 122; 4 Kent, Com. 73 {A dowress may sell timber on woodlands to raise means to pay taxes upon it and other lots, and to pay for care in overseeing the land. Crockett *v.* Crockett, 2 Ohio State, 180}.

estovers; that is, *wood* and *timber* necessary for the purpose of *building*, *burning*, *ploughing*, and *fencing;* but he has no right to cut down timber for any other purpose, as to sell it. The general principle is, that he is entitled to nothing more than what is necessary for the temporary enjoyment of the estate. The law prevents him from impairing the value of the inheritance, as we shall see more particularly under the head of *waste*. On the subject of estovers, we have no statutory provision.

Emblements. (*a*) On the death of a tenant for life, his representatives are entitled to the *emblements* not yet severed from the land; that is, to those *annual crops* which were the immediate fruits of his labor; such as *grain*, *garden-roots*, and the like. Grass and fruits are not emblements, because they do not owe their existence to the annual cultivation of man. The doctrine of emblements is, that the tenant who could not foresee his death, planted in expectation of reaping; and it would be hard if those things which he planted that year, should go to the next owner of the estate. But where the tenant knows when the estate is to expire, the emblements go to the next in estate. (*b*) In this State, (*c*) emblements, though not yet severed from the land, are regarded in all respects as personalty. As such, they must be included in the inventory made by an executor or administrator, and as such they are levied upon and sold on execution. As a general rule, no person, having a right to emblements, becomes a trespasser by entering upon the land to take them away.

Alienation. (*d*) A tenant for life, unless the contrary be stipulated, has the power of disposing of his entire estate, or any less portion. And if he undertakes to create an estate in fee, this does not work a forfeiture. The common-law doctrine of forfeiture, by attempting to grant a greater estate than one has, never existed in this State, (*e*) and probably not in this country. For-

(*a*) 4 Kent, Com. 73; R. S. § 6026; Cassilly *v.* Rhodes, 12 Ohio, 88; Jenney *v.* Gray, 5 Ohio State, 45. Growing crops pass by a deed or lease as appurtenant to land, unless excepted; but parol evidence is admissible to show that the parties intended to consider them personalty and accept them. Baker *v.* Jordan, 3 Ohio State, 438; Youmans *v.* Caldwell, 4 id. 71; Backenstoss *v.* Stabler, 33 Penn. State, 251. Budd *v.* Hiler, 3 Dutch, 43; Shofner *v.* Shofner, 5 Sneed, 94. Such parol evidence is not admissible in Indiana. Chapman *v.* Long, 10 Ind. 465. Nor in Maine. Brown *v.* Thurston, 56 Maine, 126. A sheriff's sale under partition proceedings does not pass growing crops to the purchaser. Houts *v.* Showalter, 10 Ohio State, 124. But the judgment debtor, or mortgagor, sowing crops after a judicial sale of the premises, loses them, if the sale be confirmed. Parker *v.* Storts, 15 Ohio State, 351. In England, a mortgagor is not entitled to growing crops. Walmsley *v.* Milne, 7 C. B. (N. S.) 115.

(*b*) But in such a case, the tenant may avail himself of a general custom, giving to a tenant from year to year the away-going crops. Foster *v.* Robinson, 6 Ohio State, 90.

(*c*) Where mortgaged lands are sold under a decree of foreclosure, the emblements of a lessee are protected, and do not pass to the purchaser. Cassilly *v.* Rhodes, 12 Ohio, 88. A purchaser of land at judicial sale acquires no right to the landlord's share of the tenant's growing crops, in Ohio. Albin *v.* Riegel, 40 Ohio State, 339.

(*d*) See 4 Kent, Com. 82; 2 Black. Com. 265.

(*e*) {Carpenter *v.* Denoon, 29 Ohio State, 379; Koltenbrock *v.* Cracraft, 36 id. 584.}

feiture took place only under the common-law conveyances, which, as we shall see under the proper head, were never adopted here. If therefore a tenant for life undertakes to convey a greater estate than he has, the conveyance will be good for so much as he has.

Incumbrances. (*a*) If a tenant for life takes an estate charged with an incumbrance, he is not required to pay off the incumbrance; but only to keep down the interest, leaving the principal to be paid by the owner of the fee. If this were not the rule, the life-estate might be of no value, but even run the tenant in debt. Equity, therefore, has established this rule.

Waste. (*b*) A tenant for life is liable for *waste.* In general terms, waste may be defined to be, a spoiling or destroying of the estate with respect to *houses*, *wood*, or *soil*, to the lasting injury of the inheritance. But no damage resulting from the act of God, as lightning or tempest; or from public enemies, as an invading army; or from the reversioner himself, is waste. There are two kinds of waste, *voluntary* and *permissive.* Voluntary waste is that which results from *actual commission*, as felling timber, defacing buildings, opening mines, and changing the course of husbandry. Permissive waste is that which results from *omission*, as suffering buildings or other improvements to go to decay. But in every provision against waste, *estovers* are of course excepted. And it has been held that where timber has been cut down and sold, to purchase boards for making repairs, this is not waste. The circumstances of this country have also made one change in the law respecting waste; which is, that in case of *wild lands*, the tenant may clear a reasonable portion, for the purpose of cultivation, without being guilty of waste. With respect to *repairs*, in the absence of any special agreement between the tenant and the next in estate, the rule is, that the tenant shall keep the premises in as good condition as he found them, inevitable accidents only excepted. And where there is a special agreement to repair, the tenant is not excused even by inevitable accident, unless he so stipulates. The obligation of the tenant to preserve the premises from waste, extends also to the acts of strangers, for which he is liable, having his remedy against them. In some of the States, waste is guarded against by the statutory penalty of forfeiture of the place wasted and treble damages. In Ohio, the only case of forfeiture for waste is that of a dower estate. (*c*) But, as will be seen hereafter, in all cases of waste, a court of equity will prevent it by injunction, or if it be already committed, the party injured may recover damages in an action at law.

(*a*) See 4 Kent, Com. 74; Decker *v.* Decker, 3 Ohio, 157, 165; Cumberland *v.* Codrington, 3 Johns. Ch. R. 227; and as to taxes, R. S. § 2852; M'Millan *v.* Robbins, 5 Ohio, 28.

(*b*) See 2 Black. Com. 281; 4 Kent, Com. 75; Loomis *v.* Wilbur, 5 Mason, 13; Jackson *v.* Brownson, 7 Johns. 227; Pynchon *v.* Stearns, 11 Met. 304; Clark *v.* Holden, 7 Gray, 8; Crockett *v.* Crockett, 2 Ohio State, 180.

(*c*) But now a tenant by the curtesy or in dower who commits or suffers waste forfeits the estate. R. S. §§ 4177, 4194.

§ 132. **Estates for Years.** (*a*) An estate for years has been defined to be, a contract for the possession and profits of land, for a *certain* period. Its distinguishing characteristic is, that it must expire at a fixed period or *terminus*, which is always ascertained at the creation of the estate; hence, the estate itself is called a *term*, and the tenant a *termor*. (*b*) This estate is never

(*a*) On the general subject, see 2 Black. Com. ch. 9; 4 Kent, Com. lec. 56; 1 Cruise's Dig. 243; treatises on Landlord and Tenant, by Archibald, Taylor, and Woodfall.

As to Permanent Leaseholds. By the act of 1821, they were declared to be real estate as to judgment and execution. By an act of 1837, they were declared to descend as estates of inheritance. By an act of 1839, both these were consolidated. Previously, they had been treated as chattels. Bisbee *v.* Hall, 3 Ohio, 449; Reynolds *v.* Stark county, 5 Ohio, 204; Murdock *v.* Ratcliff, 7 Ohio, 1 pt. 119. Since, they were once adjudged to be real estate for all purposes. Loring *v.* Melendy, 11 Ohio, 355. This is doubted in Boyd *v.* Talbert, 12 Ohio, 212; and the better opinion is that they are so only as to judgments, executions, liens, sales, and descents. See Abbott *v.* Bosworth, 36 Ohio State, 605; Northern Bank *v.* Roosa, 13 Ohio, 334; M'Lean *v.* Rockey, 3 McLean, 235.

Miscellaneous. Although a tenant cannot deny the title of his landlord, as it was when he became tenant, he may show that it has terminated. Devacht *v.* Newsam, 3 Ohio, 57. A landlord leasing to a cropper for one year, reserving as rent a part of the crop, has a lien upon the growing crop for his part, and may maintain trover therefor. Case *v.* Hart, 11 Ohio, 364. A wife cannot make a valid lease of her husband's land. His ratification will not help it. Tullis *v.* Young, 6 Ohio, 294. Where a parol lease is made for one year, with talk about longer time, and the tenant occupies for several years, without further stipulation, it is a tenancy from year to year, at the rent of the first year. Moore *v.* Beasley, 3 Ohio, 294. Where the lessee assigns part of the premises, though for the whole term of his lease, it is still only a sub-letting, and the original lessor cannot sue the sub-lessee. Fulton *v.* Stuart, 2 Ohio, 215. So where the lessor of a house and furniture assigns his reversion, the assignee cannot sue for rent in his own name, unless the entire interest was assigned to him. Jones *v.* Smith, 14 Ohio, 606; Crawford *v.* Chapman, 17 Ohio, 449. Under the Code, an assignee of the reversion may sue in his own name for breach of covenant, when he is the party beneficially interested. Masury *v.* Southworth, 9 Ohio State, 340. Where a lease is only signed by the lessor, he cannot maintain covenant for rent, although the lease had words for such a covenant, and the lessee took possession. Trustees *v.* Spencer, 7 Ohio, 2 pt. 149. Where husband and wife leased for her life, without covenant for quiet enjoyment, and after his death she sold to another, who ejected the lessee, and thereupon he sued the husband's administrator upon an implied covenant, it was held that the words "have rented" did not imply a covenant in relation to a life-estate, though they might for years. Worthington *v.* Young, 6 Ohio, 313; Young *v.* Hargrave, 7 Ohio, 2 pt. 63. A., owning a four-story building, leased to B. for three years "the store-room and cellar thereunder." The other portions of the building were leased to other persons. The entire building was destroyed by fire. B., against the will of A., built a kind of shed over the cellar, not higher than the ceiling of the storeroom, and claimed to hold for the term; but it was held that he had no such right, and he was ejected. The opinion is worth reading as a curiosity. Winton *v.* Cornish, 5 Ohio, 477. The express contract of the lessee fixes his liability for rent for the whole term. Even an assignment of the lease, with the assent of the lessor, and his acceptance of rent subsequently from the assignee, will not discharge the first lessee from his liability. Sutliff *v.* Atwood, 15 Ohio State, 186; Harmony Lodge *v.* White, 30 id. 569, and the same in a perpetual lease. Taylor *v.* De Bus, 31 id. 468; Smith *v.* Harrison, 42 id. 180; Frank *v.* Maguire, 42 Penn. State, 77. {The lessor is not liable to third persons who came into the tenant's store, for injury by the falling of insecurely fastened shelves erected by such lessor. Burdick *v.* Cheudle, 26 Ohio State, 393. Nor for defects arising during the term. Shindelbeck *v.* Moon, 32 id. 264. Where the landlord had agreed to keep the elevator in repair, this means to repair on notice of its being out of order, and he is not liable for an accident in the absence of notice of its being out of order. Sinton *v.* Butler, 40 Ohio State, 158.}

(*b*) {A lease to a person not mentioning heirs or assigns so long as he uses the leased property as a factory is a lease for life. Warner *v.* Tanner, 38 Ohio State, 118. Where there is a privilege of renewal of the term, the tenant's merely holding over is not necessarily an election to renew. Elevator Co. *v.* Brown, 36 Ohio State, 660.}

created by the operation of law, but always by the act of the parties. The instrument creating it is called a *lease*, and the parties *lessor* and *lessee*, or *landlord* and *tenant*. These latter terms are derived from the feudal system, though the relation itself did not exist under that system, all feuds being freehold. An estate for years originally differed from a freehold in the five following particulars: 1. Livery of seisin, as we have seen, was not necessary in creating it. Hence, the tenant could not be said to be *seised*, but merely *possessed*, of the land. He had no interest in the *soil itself*, but merely in the profits of the soil. His estate was therefore treated as a *chattel;* and this technical distinction still continues, though the reason has ceased, livery of seisin not being now necessary in the creation of any estate. 2. An estate for years might be made to commence at a future time, while a freehold could not. But this distinction, as we have seen, no longer exists. 3. An estate for years was originally held, as we have seen, by precarious tenure; but now the law makes this tenant as secure in his possession as the tenant of a freehold. 4. An actual *entry* by the tenant was necessary to perfect this estate. But now an actual entry is not required in any case. The execution and delivery of the lease, perfects the title of the lessee, to all intents and purposes. 5. It made no difference as to the nature of this estate, whether it were for only a part of a year, or for any number of years. It might be for a month, or for a thousand years; but it was still no more or less than an estate for years, with precisely the same legal incidents. In fact, by a very common practice, this estate could be so created as to last for ever, without altering its character. This is the case with what are called *perpetual leases*, in which a certain term is created, *renewable for ever*. Yet at common law, these estates, although they may continue for ever, are nothing more than estates for years. The fee still remains in the lessor, and the lessee has only a chattel interest. But by our statute, these permanent leasehold estates are made subject to the same law of descent and distribution, and of sale on execution or by decree, as estates in fee. Though as to dower and curtesy, and in all other respects but those above mentioned, they still continue to be chattel interests. The *incidents* of estates for years are nearly the same as those of estates for life, except in regard to *emblements*. Thus tenants for years, in the absence of a special agreement to the contrary, have the same right to *estovers*, (*a*) the same power of *underletting*, are in the same manner exempt from *forfeiture*, for creating a greater estate, and are equally liable for *waste*. The reason why they are not entitled to *emblements* is, that the termination of their estate is fixed and certain; and it is their own folly to sow what they know cannot come to maturity during their term.

(*a*) A tenant for years has a right to cut wood on the farm for fires and repairs, the quantity cut being reasonable. Hubbard *v.* Shaw, 12 Allen, 120.

Rent. (*a*) But here is one additional incident, belonging sometimes to estates for life, and generally to estates for years, which remains to be described. I mean *rent.* According to Blackstone, rent is "a certain profit issuing yearly out of lands and tenements corporeal;" and there are three kinds of rent: namely, *rent-service*, where the fee remains in the landlord, and the tenant is bound to render some corporeal service in partial or full return for the use of land, which service may be enforced by *distress; rent-charge*, where the fee is granted with a reservation of rent, and with a special clause of distress, charging the rent upon the land; and *rent-seck*, where the fee is granted with a reservation of rent, and without a clause of distress. (*b*) The term *distress* here signifies a summary mode allowed to the landlord, of seizing and selling the tenant's property to satisfy the rent which he owes. But in Ohio and several other States, the power of enforcing payment by distress is confined to the collection of public dues; and the landlord stands on the same footing as any other creditor. Accordingly, the foregoing distinctions are of little importance; and we may consider rent simply as a periodical compensation, in money or otherwise, agreed to be given by the tenant to the landlord for the use of realty, the payment of which may be enforced like any other demand. I say agreed to be given, because where one occupies another's land without a lease containing a special agreement to pay a fixed rent, the compensation which may be recovered is not in the shape of rent, but of damages in an action for *use and occupation*, or for *mesne profits*, as will be explained hereafter. (*c*) When the relation of landlord and tenant has been created, the estate of the landlord is denominated a *reversion*, to which rent is said to be incident. If, therefore, he conveys the reversion, the future rent passes with it, and when he dies, it goes to his heirs; but it is otherwise if the rent be already due. (*d*) If the tenant be evicted by a paramount title in a stranger, or actually expelled by the landlord, his obligation to pay rent ceases; (*e*) but no destruction of

(*a*) Van Rensselaer *v.* Hays, 19 N. Y. 68; Van Rensselaer *v.* Ball, id. 100. {Where, after termination of the tenancy, the landlord regains possession by removing all the doors and windows so that the tenant is driven out by the exposure, this is not tortious and no action lies, there having been no breach of the peace. Say *v.* Stoddard, 27 Ohio State, 478.}

(*b*) Van Rensselaer *v.* Chadwick, 22 N. Y. 32; Wallace *v.* Harmstad, 44 Penn. State, 492. Where a right of re-entry is reserved, in a conveyance in fee reserving rent, upon default in payment of rent, the grantor has a lien for rents superior to the lien of the mortgagee of the grantee. Stephenson *v.* Haines, 16 Ohio State, 478. Where fixtures are leased with the realty, with liberty to the tenant to replace them, and a lien reserved upon the whole for rent, this is not such a chattel mortgage as requires filing to make it valid. Metcalfe *v.* Fosdick, 23 Ohio State, 114.

(*c*) When land is occupied by a person, not the owner, in such a manner and under such circumstances that a contract to pay rent cannot in law be implied, rent for such occupancy cannot be recovered in the absence of an express contract to pay it. Mitchell *v.* Pendleton, 21 Ohio State, 664.

(*d*) Kimball *v.* Pike, 18 N. H. 419; Gibbs *v.* Ross, 2 Head, 437; Gale *v.* Edwards, 52 Maine, 363.

(*e*) Shumway *v.* Collins, 6 Gray, 227; Leishman *v.* White, 1 Allen, 489. But see Fuller *v.* Raby, 10 Gray, 285.

the premises by fire, flood, or other inevitable accident, will discharge the obligation, unless the lease contains a provision to that effect. (*a*) Where the lease provides for a forfeiture in case of non-payment of the rent when due, a tender or readiness to pay on the premises at any time, before sunset on the day stipulated, will be sufficient. The tenant is not obliged to seek the landlord away from the premises unless he agrees so to do, but he may make such tender, and it will be good. (*b*) When leased property becomes divided, either by the act of the landlord or by operation of law, if the parties cannot agree upon an apportionment of rent, it must be made by a jury.

§ 133. **Estates at Will.** (*c*) An estate at will was originally where the tenant occupied at the mere pleasure of him who had the next estate; and who could terminate the tenancy at any moment without previous notice. Such a connection between landlord and tenant harmonized perfectly with the arbitrary notions of a landed aristocracy. It had but one redeeming quality, and that was with regard to *emblements.* The tenant at will, having no knowledge when he might be obliged to quit the premises, was entitled to emblements on the same ground as the representatives of a tenant for life. But as notions of liberty began to gain ground, the slavish character of this tenancy became gradually changed. It was first settled that an estate at will *was equally at the will of both parties;* and that neither could terminate the tenancy without fair notice to the other. (*d*) The next improvement was to determine, that, unless there was an express agreement to hold at will,

(*a*) *As to Forfeiture and Notice.* In order to forfeit a lease for the non-payment of rent, the exact sum due must be demanded before sunset on the day when due, on the land, at the most notorious place. Boyd *v.* Talbert, 12 Ohio, 212 ; Connor *v.* Bradley, 1 Howard, 211 ; Smith *v.* Whitbeck, 13 Ohio State, 471 ; Chapman *v.* Wright, 20 Ill. 120 ; Jewett *v.* Berry, 20 N. H. 36. An entry to forfeit a lease of school lands must be for the entire tract in the original lease, without reference to sub-leases of any part. Hart *v.* Johnson, 6 Ohio, 87. The only notice to quit required in Ohio is that provided for bringing ejectment, or forcible entry and detainer. Spencer *v.* Marckel, 2 Ohio, 263 ; Baker *v.* Gittings, 16 Ohio, 485. The statutory notice to leave the premises necessary to be given in an action of forcible entry and detainer, before beginning an action against a tenant holding over his term, may be served either before or after the termination of his term. Leutzey *v.* Herchelrode, 20 Ohio State, 334.

(*b*) Peterson *v.* Edmondson, 5 Harrington, 378 ; Graham *v.* Perry, 29 Mo. 245. But where premises are destroyed by fire before the commencement of the term, though after the execution of the lease, the lessee will be discharged. Wood *v.* Hubbell, 10 N. Y. 479. {But in Ohio, by R. S. § 4113, the lessee of a building destroyed or rendered unfit for occupancy by the elements or other cause, without his fault, is not liable for rent afterwards, unless the lease expressly stipulates otherwise, if he surrender the premises. That a third party by cutting off light and air by building on an adjacent lot has rendered the premises uninhabitable is no defence to an action for rent. Hilliard *v.* Gas Coal Co., 41 Ohio State, 662.}

(*c*) See 2 Black. Com. ch. ix. ; 4 Kent, Com. lec. 56 ; 1 Cruise's Dig. 269 ; Moore *v.* Beasley, 3 Ohio, 294; Coffin *v.* Lunt, 2 Pick. 70, and note to that case ; Spencer *v.* Marckel, 2 Ohio, 263.

(*d*) The death of the lessor terminates a tenancy at will, and the lessee becomes a tenant at sufferance only. Reed *v.* Reed, 48 Maine, 388 ; Esty *v.* Baker, 50 Maine, 325. {A tenancy to continue as long as mutually agreeable, and terminable by either party on four days' notice, is a tenancy at will, and the lessee has no interest which is assignable ; and an assignment by him terminates it, and death of either party terminates it. Say *v.* Stoddard, 27 Ohio State, 478.}

all tenancies for no stipulated term, should be construed as *periodical tenancies from year to year*, or some shorter period, according to the facts of the case. The establishment of this wholesome doctrine, is a virtual abolition of estates at will; and it has been fully recognized in this State. But since the creation of this periodical tenancy, there has been much diversity of opinion in different places, in regard to the *notice to quit*. In England, it is half a year; in some of the States, the same; (*a*) in others, a reasonable time; but here, nothing is settled. We have two ways of dispossessing a refractory tenant; namely, by the action of *ejectment*, and of *forcible detainer*. In ejectment, our statute requires ten days' notice before the commencement of the term at which the appearance is to be made; and in forcible detainer, three days' notice before the commencement of the suit; but this is a different thing from notice to quit. Whatever this be, it must be so given as to expire before or at the time the period expires; for if the tenant has been allowed to enter upon a new period without notice, he cannot be dispossessed until the end of this period. And the chief criterion to determine whether a tenancy is from year to year, from quarter to quarter, or from month to month, is the pay-day of rent. On account of the uncertainty whether his term will be renewed, a tenant from term to term is entitled to *emblements* as much as if he was strictly a tenant at will. In this respect, and in the right to notice to quit, he differs from a tenant for years. In other respects, his powers, privileges, and liabilities are nearly the same.

§ 134. **Estates at Sufferance.** (*b*) An estate at *sufferance* is where one comes rightfully into possession of land, but holds over after his interest is determined. A tenant at sufferance differs from a mere *intruder* in this, that he is not a trespasser. But he has no interest capable of being transferred or defended; and it is said that, independently of statutory provision, he is not liable to pay rent. We have no statute on the subject; but the doctrine is so absurd on the face of it, that I presume our courts would not recognize it. The tenant could not indeed be sued for *rent* technically speaking, under the lease, because it has expired; but I have no doubt he might be liable in an action *for use and occupation*. At common law, this tenant is not entitled to notice to quit. But here, this point is of very little importance; because, as we have seen, there must be ten or three days' notice, as the case may be, before he can be dispossessed *by action*. The landlord may indeed *enter* at any time, without notice, and will not thereby become a trespasser; and if he can turn the tenant out *peaceably*, he will thus acquire possession immediately. But if the tenant refuses to go out, he cannot use force upon his person; for though we have no statute making *forcible entry* an indictable offence, yet

(*a*) Baker *v.* Adams, 5 Cush. 99. In Massachusetts, it is three months in ordinary cases by statute. The notice must terminate at one of the regular intervals of payment. Prescott *v.* Elm, 7 Cush. 346.

(*b*) 2 Black. Com. ch. ix.; 4 Kent, Com. lec. 56; 1 Cruise's Dig. 269.

in the case supposed, the landlord could not justify an assault and battery. Unless, therefore, he can expel the tenant at sufferance peaceably, he must give the required notice, and then bring his action. This tenant therefore has an undue advantage over his landlord. In England, and in many of the States, a penalty of *double rent* is imposed by statute for holding over; while here, there is not only no penalty, but in our course of proceeding, an obstinate tenant cannot be expelled under perhaps several months. This is an evil which calls loudly for remedy.

It will be seen that the foregoing observations have related to realty only. In fact no such distinctions prevail with respect to personalty, on account of its transitory nature. There may indeed be a qualified ownership; that is, a man may have possession of an article of personalty, and a right to use it for an indefinite or definite period, without being the absolute owner of it. But there can be no such distinction as a fee-simple, or freehold, with respect to it. Technically speaking, personalty is not hereditary. On the death of the owner, it passes according to the law of *distribution*, to the personal representatives, but does not *descend* to the heirs like the fee of land. But all this will be explained hereafter. It is sufficient here to remember that the distinction of estates with respect to duration belongs exclusively to realty.

LECTURE XXII.

ESTATES IN REVERSION AND REMAINDER. (*a*)

§ 135. **Estates in Reversion.** (*b*) Estates are divided, with respect to their commencement, into estates in *possession*, in *reversion*, and in *remainder*. Of estates in possession, there is nothing to be said. All the remarks hitherto made, apply to estates in the actual possession of the owner. This is their most natural and obvious situation. But the first three of the foregoing estates, namely, estates in fee, for life, and for years, while they are in the present occupation of one person, may belong in expectancy, either in *reversion* or *remainder*, to another. To these accordingly we turn our attention. An *estate in reversion* may be defined to be, the residue of an estate remaining in the grantor or his heirs, to come to his or their possession, after the determination of some particular estate granted away. It grows out of this legal maxim with regard to property, that whatever interest a man has, and does not dispose of, remains in him and his representatives. A

(*a*) See 2 Black. Com. ch. 11; 4 Kent, Com. lec. 59, 60; 1 Swift's Dig. b. 2, ch. 9; 2 Cruise's Dig. title Remainder and Reversion; Fearne, on Remainders.

(*b*) 2 Black. Com. 175; 4 Kent, Com. 353; 2 Cruise's Dig. 154; 1 Hilliard's Dig. 418.

reversion may be in fee, for life, or for years. Thus, if I have an estate in fee, and grant you any smaller estate, the reversion in fee still remains in me. If I have an estate for life, and grant you any smaller estate, the reversion for life still continues in me; and if I have an estate for years, and grant you an estate for a less number of years, the reversion for years still continues in me. In this way, there may be any number of reversions existing in the same estate, in the same manner as a unit may be divided into any number of parts; and all these estates in reversion, added to the estate in possession, make together only one fee-simple estate in possession. An estate in reversion is considered as a *present interest*, though it can only take effect *in future;* and as such, is transferable and descendible in the same manner as an estate in possession. Formerly, the usual incidents to a reversion were *fealty* and *rent.* But fealty does not exist here; and rent is not inseparable. I may have a reversion with or without rent. If I lease you an estate for years, I have a reversion with rent. If I sell you a life-estate outright, I have a reversion without rent. In like manner I may separate rent from the reversion, when originally connected; for I may grant the rent without the reversion, or the reversion without the rent. The latter, however, can only be done by express words. If I grant the reversion simply, the rent passes as an incident. But if I grant the rent simply, the reversion does not pass. Estates in reversion, however, being always created by operation of law, and never by positive grant, are so simple and so easily comprehended, that no further remarks are necessary.

§ 136. **Estates in Remainder.** (*a*) An estate *in remainder* may be defined to be, an estate limited by the grantor to take effect and be enjoyed by the grantee, after another previous estate shall be terminated. For example, if I grant land to you for life, and then to your brother and his heirs, the latter estate is a remainder. The estate which precedes the remainder is called a *particular* estate. Remainders differ from reversions in this, that they are always created by the express act of the parties, while reversions result from the operation of law; and also in this that remainders are never limited to the grantor, while reversions are always reserved to him or his heirs. In other words, a remainder is something granted; a reversion is something reserved. Estates in remainder form by far the most abstruse and intricate subject connected with the law of realty. They had their origin in the English fondness for family settlements. It is not uncommon to find in such settlements eight or ten remainders limited one

(*a*) 2 Black. Com. 163; 2 Cruise's Dig. 258; 4 Kent, Com. lec. 59, 60; 1 Hilliard's Dig. ch. 41–51, pp. 362–418; Campbell *v.* Watson, 8 Ohio, 498. Cross-remainders are not favored. As between more than two, they are never implied, but must arise from the most explicit expressions in the deed or will. Therefore, a devise "to my four sons or the survivors of them, and their heirs and assigns, to be equally divided among them when the youngest becomes of age," was so construed that each took a fee. Lawrence *v.* McArter, 10 Ohio, 37. See Collins *v.* Collins, 40 Ohio State, 353.

after the other, in order to prevent the possibility of the estate passing out of the family of the grantor. Fortunately, the spirit of our institutions is utterly opposed to these entangled and cumbrous arrangements; and accordingly our books contain few discussions on the subject. In this State, so far as I know, there has not been a single case; not from any legal prohibition, but from the general disposition of our citizens to keep property as little trammelled as possible. On this account, I shall attempt no more than to give a very general statement of the leading properties belonging to remainders.

To whom Remainders may be Limited. (*a*) 1. In this State, we have a statutory restriction, that "no estate shall be given or granted by deed or will to any persons but such as are in being, or the immediate issue or descendants of such as are in being, at the time of making such deed or will." (*b*) There is some ambiguity in these words. Had the statute said only "*immediate issue*," we should not hesitate to say that estates could only be limited to *persons in being* or *their children*. But the addition of the word "descendants," raises a doubt. It must either mean nothing at all, or it must be intended to include lineal descendants more remote than children. We have had no construction of this statute; but from the strong aversion the law manifests to *perpetuities*, and from the existence of the common-law doctrine, when this act was passed, that the contingencies upon which estates were limited, must happen within a life or lives in being, and twenty-one years afterwards, I should presume that our legislature intended to restrict the limitation of estates to persons in being and their children. (*c*) 2. Another restriction grows out of *the rule in Shelley's case*, (*d*) which may be thus stated: Whenever a person, either by deed or will, takes an estate for life, and in the same instrument, there is a remainder limited, either immediately or otherwise, to his heirs in fee, that person takes the whole estate in fee.

(*a*) 4 Kent, Com. 264; R. S. § 4200.

(*b*) {N. B. Our statute forbids perpetuities in lands and tenements in this State, and does not cover personal property. That the rule against perpetuities does not apply to charitable trusts, see Jones *v.* Habersham, 107 U. S. 174.}

(*c*) {The words "immediate issue or descendants" mean those descendants who would take as heirs under the statute of descents, and are not confined to children, but may mean grandchildren. Turley *v.* Turley, 11 Ohio State, 173; or great-grandchildren, McArthur *v.* Scott, 113 U. S. 340, 383.}

(*d*) 1 Coke's Rep. 104; 4 Kent, Com. 214; Preston, on Estates, 263; 4 Cruise's Dig. 369; M'Feely *v.* Moore, 5 Ohio, 464; 2 Black. Com. 242; 2 Hilliard's Dig. 22; King *v.* King, 12 Ohio, 390; Williamson *v.* Williamson, 18 B. Monr. 329; Hampton *v.* Rather, 30 Miss. (Cush.) 193; Allen *v.* Markle, 35 Penn. State, 117; Kennedy *v.* Kennedy, 5 Dutcher, 185; Thurston *v.* Thurston, 6 R. I. 296; Simpers *v.* Simpers, 15 Md. 160; Williams *v.* Houston, 4 Jones Eq. 277; Lloyd *v.* Rambo, 35 Ala. 709; Dennett *v.* Dennett, 43 N. H. 499; English *v.* Beekle, 32 Mo. 186; Norris *v.* Hensley, 27 Cal. 439. In M'Feely *v.* Moore, 5 Ohio, 464, a devise to a husband and wife "to have the use during their respective lives, then to descend to their heirs, to whom I bequeath the same, and to their heirs and assigns forever," was held to be within the rule in Shelley's case as part of our common law. But by R. S. § 5968, this rule is abolished with respect to wills. And see Armstrong *v.* Zane, 12 Ohio, 287; King *v.* Beck, 15 Ohio, 559, but not when it does not defeat the intent. Carter *v.* Reddish, 32 Ohio State, 1.

This rule is said to have been established as early as 1325. But the case from which the rule took its name is one reported by Coke. The existence of this rule is fully recognized in this State, with respect to conveyances by deed; and it was applied to conveyances by will until 1840, when the legislature abrogated it, with respect to wills, by providing that when lands are devised to any person for life, and after his death to his heirs in fee, the devise shall be construed to create an estate for life in the devisee, with a remainder in fee-simple to his heirs. In other words, the intention of the testator shall be literally carried into effect. And it is to be hoped that the legislature will abrogate it with respect to deeds; for though professedly a rule of construction, adopted to effectuate the intention of the parties, its obvious tendency is to frustrate such intention by converting what was meant for a life estate into a fee-simple. Besides, there is scarcely a principle of our law, which has been the subject of so much controversy. But I am at present concerned with this rule only so far as it is connected with remainders. The result of its existence is, that remainders in fee cannot be limited by deed to the heirs of the same person to whom the life-estate is granted; for this would be construed to be an estate in fee-simple. 3. The only other restriction grows out of the distinction between remainders and reversions. An ultimate remainder cannot be limited to the grantor himself, or to his heirs general, because this would already be in them as a reversion. This follows from the definition of a reversion before given.

How Remainders are Created. It is a fundamental property of remainders, that they must always be created by *the same instrument or act* which creates the particular estate; for if by one instrument I should grant a present estate to you, and by another the future estate to some one else, this last would not be the creation of a remainder, but the grant of a reversion growing out of the first grant. There have been three ways in which remainders could be created: *first*, by the ancient common-law conveyances; *secondly*, by conveyances under the statute of uses; *thirdly*, by wills; and the law varied considerably according to the manner in which they were created. But in this State, as will be explained hereafter, the common-law conveyances have never been in use; and although we have adopted the conveyances which grew out of the *statute of uses*, yet the statute itself is not in force here, as will also be explained hereafter. The proper division, therefore, is into remainders *created by deed*, and remainders *created by will* or *executory devises.*

The leading properties of remainders created by deed, are as follows: 1. There must be a present particular estate to precede the remainder. This is implied in the very term; something must be taken out, to leave a remainder. Such is the reason usually given; and in mathematics it would be perfectly satisfactory. But the student of law, who perceives no inherent difficulty in creating a future estate, after a present estate reserved to the grantor, will require some further explanation. The necessity, then, for a particular estate, only exists where the freehold is to pass in remainder; and then it results from the doctrine before referred to, that a freehold cannot be made to commence *in future.* Accordingly, when a man wishes to convey a freehold, to commence at a future time, he must first create a particular estate, to continue until he wishes the next estate to commence, and then limit the freehold thereon. In so doing, livery of seisin is made to the particular tenant, and enures to the benefit of the remainder-man. Such is the artificial reasoning upon which the whole system of remainders is founded. But under our law, this reason for creating a particular estate, for the mere purpose of limiting remainders thereon, does not exist, because we do not make livery of seisin. I may grant an estate of freehold, to commence at any time I please; and although this would not be a remainder, it would answer precisely the same purpose. This fact certainly renders the law of remainders unnecessary here, but whether it alters the law in any respect, remains to be decided. 2. This particular estate must be at least an estate for years; for an estate at will or sufferance, having no certain measure of duration, is of too slender a nature to support a remainder; since it would depend upon the pleasure of the grantor, whether the remainder should ever take effect at all. 3. This particular estate must be less than fee-simple; for after a fee-simple nothing can remain; hence, it follows that the greatest estate upon which a remainder can be limited is a conditional fee. 4. This particular estate must not fail or be defeated before its natural termination; for when the particular estate fails, the remainder also fails. The one is said to *support* the other, and the maturity of the particular estate may be likened to a condition precedent, which must be fulfilled before the remainder can take effect. This rule seems to be entirely arbitrary, and founded in no substantial reason. The idea that one estate supports the other, is purely metaphorical; it does not have this effect from any inherent necessity, but merely because the law so ordains. The consequence is to place all the remainder-men more or less at the mercy of him who has the first estate; and to destroy the whole chain because one link happens to fail. This can only be obviated by the cumbrous arrangement of appointing *trustees*, to preserve the remainders; an expedient now universally adopted in creating these estates, but which I have not room particularly to describe. 5. The remainder must vest in the grantee, either during the continuance of the particular estate, or at the instant of its termination. The reason is, that the particular estate and the remainder, being created by the same act, are considered but one entire estate, divided into parts; and if there could be an interval or hiatus between the expiration of the particular estate and the commencement of the remainder, there would be an immediate reversion in the grantor, which would destroy the unity of his grant. This rule, like the foregoing, seems to be purely arbitrary. The reason here given would be good in mathematics, but need not be adopted in law. What harm could possibly arise from allowing the grantor to enjoy the intervening estate, until by the terms of the grant the remainder-man could take it, and then giving it to him? There is surely no necessity for breaking up the whole grant, when the deficiency could be so easily supplied; yet such is the law; and its effect can only be obviated, as before, by the appointment of trustees to preserve the remainders. These several rules, and particularly the last, give rise to the distinction between *vested* and *contingent* remainders, which I shall now proceed to explain.

§ 137. **Vested and Contingent Remainders.** (*a*) *A vested remainder* is where a present interest passes to a determinate person, to be enjoyed in future. Thus, if I grant an estate to you for life, with remainder to your brother and his heirs in fee, your brother acquires a present interest which he may dispose of at pleasure, though it can only be enjoyed by him and his heirs or assigns after your death. In this case, you perceive there is no doubt that the remainder will take effect at the moment your particular estate expires. In other words, the moment you die your brother or his representatives will be ready to take, since the law will not presume an entire failure of heirs. On account of this certainty, the remainder is considered as vesting at once; and becomes as much a present interest as a reversion is. A *contingent remainder* is where no present interest passes, on account of the uncertainty whether there will be any one to take it when the particular estate expires. Thus, if I grant an estate to you for life, with remain-

(*a*) A future contingent interest in real estate, in the nature of a contingent remainder or executory devise, may be devised or conveyed. Thompson *v.* Hoop, 6 Ohio State, 480. Otherwise, of a naked or remote possibility. Needles *v.* Needles, 7 id. 432; Jeffers *v.* Lampson, 10 Ohio State, 101; Gilpin *v.* Williams, 25 id. 283, 300; Hart *v.* Gregg, 32 Ohio State, 502; Miller *v.* Emaus, 19 N. Y. 384; but if conveyed by warranty, the subsequently acquired title might feed the estoppel, and thus pass. Rosenthal *v.* Mayhugh, 33 Ohio State, 155, 158. In New Hampshire, a conveyance of a contingent interest is only good by way of estoppel. Hayes *v.* Tabor, 41 N. H. 521; Ackerman *v.* Vreedland, 1 McCarter (N. J.), 123. But a vested remainder may be conveyed like any real property. Glidden *v.* Blodgett, 38 N. H. 74. Courts always incline to construe remainders as vested, if the words creating them admit of such a construction. Linton *v.* Laycock, 33 Ohio State, 128; Chew's Appeal, 37 Penn. State, 23; Burd *v.* Burd, 40 Penn. State, 182; Gourley *v.* Woodbury, 42 Vt. 395. For cases where remainders have been construed to be vested, see Blanchard *v.* Blanchard, 1 Allen, 223; Brown *v.* Brown, 44 N. H. 281; Pike *v.* Stephenson, 99 Mass. 188. remainder is not contingent, unless there is a collateral contingency after the determination of the primary estate. Weehawken Ferry Co. *v.* Sisson, 2 Green (N. J.), 475. But a devise in remainder to the children of C., now in existence or hereafter to be born, who should be living at the happening of a contingency specified, creates a contingent, not a vested, remainder. Stephens *v.* Evans, 30 Ind. 39; Smith *v.* Block, 29 Ohio State, 488. And prior to birth of the children who are to take the remainder, seisin is not *in nubibus*, but remains in the testator's heirs. Gilpin *v.* Williams, 25 Ohio State, 253.

der to the heirs of your brother in fee; here, as it is doubtful whether your brother will die before you, and as he can have no heirs while he lives, the remainder to his heirs is contingent. If he dies before you, the remainder at once vests in his heirs, and becomes in them a disposable interest; but if he survives you, the remainder never vests at all, because the particular estate has previously terminated. In this case, the remainder is contingent, because limited to an uncertain person. It may likewise be contingent, by being limited upon an uncertain event. Thus, if I give you an estate for life, with a remainder to your brother if he survives you, here the uncertainty whether your brother will survive you makes his remainder contingent. Whenever the contingency upon which the remainder depends is changed into certainty, the remainder vests of itself in the person to whom it is limited, without any act by him; but until then, his interest, being a mere possibility, is not the subject of bargain and sale. The leading rules which govern contingent remainders are as follows: 1. The event upon which a contingent remainder is limited must not be *unlawful.* Thus, a remainder limited to a bastard expected to be begotten, or to a man upon his murdering another, would be void for unlawfulness. 2. The event must be a common and not a remote possibility. Thus, it is said that a remainder to a corporation not yet in existence, or upon the termination of a war not yet commenced, would be void from the beginning, on account of the remoteness of the contingency. 3. The event must not be such as to defeat the particular estate. Thus, if I grant an estate to you for life, with remainder to another immediately, on his paying to me a given sum, this remainder would be void in its very creation, because it would defeat the life-estate. 4. If the contingent remainder be a freehold, some vested estate of freehold must precede it. The reason is, that the freehold must pass out of the grantor at the time of creating the remainder; and, when it passes out of the grantor, it must vest somewhere else, since it cannot remain in *abeyance.* (*a*) Now, it cannot pass in the contingent remainder, because that vests nowhere; it follows that it must pass in some preceding estate, which may either be the particular estate, or a preceding vested remainder. This rule is founded upon the technical doctrine that *livery of seisin* is necessary to create a freehold. Whether the rule will be recognized in this State, where the reason has ceased, must be left to conjecture.

§ 138. **Executory Devises.** (*b*) Remainders created by will differ so much from remainders created by deed, that they have taken the distinct name of *executory devises.* These differences are to be ascribed to that indulgence which the law on all occasions shows to testators, by giving effect to their intentions, however untechnically expressed. A statement of them will

(*a*) 2 Black. Com. 107; 1 Hilliard's Dig. 408.
(*b*) 2 Black. Com. 173; 6 Cruise's Dig. 461; 4 Kent, Com. lec. 60.

justify what has been said respecting the arbitrary character of the law of remainders, strictly so called. 1. No particular estate is necessary to precede an executory devise, since by will a freehold might always be made to commence at a future time. Thus, if I devise to you an estate in fee, to commence six months after my death, this is a good executory devise. 2. The limitation of an estate, by will, after an estate in fee-simple, is said to be a good *executory devise.* For example, if I devise land to you and your heirs forever, but if you die within age, then to your brother and his heirs, the limitation to your brother and his heirs is good by way of executory devise, although the first estate was a fee-simple. (*a*) 3. We have seen that remainders created by deed are defeated by the failure of the particular estate. But this is not the case with executory devises, which cannot be affected by any subsequent alteration of the estates upon which they are limited. (*b*) Such is the liberal spirit of the law of executory devises in these three important particulars. For the purpose of effectuating the will of the testator, the law rises above the technical doctrines of remainders, and follows the dictates of reason. Yet it seems to do so with great reluctance; for the rule is, that no limitation by will shall be construed as an executory devise when it can be treated as a contingent remainder. And, accordingly, whenever there is a preceding estate, capable of supporting a contingent remainder, the next estate limited by devise is construed to be a remainder, and as such is liable to all the incidents of contingent remainders. (*c*) Executory devises are expressly within the statutory provision before mentioned, restricting the limitation of estates to persons in being and their issue; and they are within the policy of the law which requires the event upon which they are limited to be a common and not a remote possibility. (*d*) Accordingly, if I should devise an estate to your sons to be born of a second wife, while a first is living, this would be void for remoteness. So if I should devise an estate to some person, to take effect after a general failure of your heirs, without first devising the estate to you and your heirs, such devise would be void for remoteness.

The foregoing observations on reversions and remainders have applied exclusively to realty. In the law of personalty, no such

(*a*) I take this rule and illustration as I find them in the books. But it seems to me that, after a fee-simple, nothing remains; and that the example here given is one of a fee conditional. See Taylor *v.* Foster, 17 Ohio State, 166; Niles *v.* Gray, 12 Ohio State, 320; Lapham *v.* Martin, 33 Ohio State, 99; Ratliff *v.* Warner, 32 id. 334.

(*b*) Thompson *v.* Hoop, 6 Ohio State, 480; Holt *v.* Lamb, 17 id. 374.

(*c*) Thompson *v.* Hoop, 6 Ohio State, 480.

(*d*) See the case of the Church in Brattle Square *v.* Grant, 3 Gray, 142, wnere it was declared to be the settled rule in England that all limitations by way of executory devise, which may not take effect within the term of a life or lives in being at the death of the testator, and twenty-one years afterwards, as a term in gross, or in case of a child *en ventre sa mere* twenty-one years and nine months, are void as too remote, and tending to create perpetuities.

distinctions are known, because there are no reasons for them. On account of the movable and transitory nature of personalty, there are few occasions when it is desirable to make a future disposition of any specific article; and therefore the law makes no provision for such disposition. (*a*) But a future amount of value, either in money or goods, may be stipulated for, in the ordinary course of contracts; and by recourse to trustees, as will be explained hereafter, future settlements of personalty can be made, as well as of realty. What, therefore, you are here to remember is, that there is no technical reversion or remainder in any specific article of personalty.

The view I have taken of estates in remainder, is too brief and general to do any thing more than excite your curiosity to examine further; unless, perhaps, it should lead you to discuss the policy of adhering to rules, when the reasons of them no longer exist. There is clearly no absolute necessity for perpetuating a branch of law so purely arbitrary and technical. A few brief statutory provisions would enable persons to make future dispositions of realty as easily as of personalty, and to any extent which might be deemed expedient. Let it be expressly provided that any estate might be made, by deed or will, to commence at a future period; and that, where several successive estates should thus be created, the failure of any one should not affect the rest, but the lapsed estate should revert to the grantor or his heirs, until the next estate could take effect; and the whole fabric of remainders would fall to the ground. I hope the day is not far distant when such a reform will be undertaken.

LECTURE XXIII.

ESTATES IN COMMON. (*b*)

§ 139. **Different kinds of Joint Ownerships.** I have hitherto spoken of estates as if they belonged to a single person. But in

(*a*) But it has been held, that an estate in remainder may be created by will in personal property, even where an absolute power of disposition in favor of particular objects, or for the accomplishment of particular purposes, is given to the first taker, and the devise will be valid as to whatever is not so appropriated. Pruden *v.* Pruden, 14 Ohio State, 251 {Ratliff *v.* Warner, 32 id. 334; Flickinger *v.* Saum, 40 id. 591; and an executory devise may be created in personalty. Lapham *v.* Martin, 33 id. 99; and a not uncommon American ruling is that a future estate may be created in chattels by deed as well as by will. See Gray on Perpetuities, p. 57}.

(*b*) See 2 Black. Com. ch. xii.; 2 Kent, Com. lec. 64; 1 Swift's Dig. b. 2, ch. 10; 2 Cruise's Dig. 497; 1 Hilliard's Dig. ch. 53–55; pp. 429–62. In Sergeant *v.* Steinberger, 2 Ohio, 305, the court say: "It has more than once been decided on the circuit, that estates in joint-tenancy do not exist in Ohio. The reasons which gave rise to this description of estate in England never existed with us. The *jus accrescendi* is not founded in principles of natural justice, nor in any reasons of policy applicable to our society or institutions. But, on the contrary, it is adverse to the understanding, habits, and feelings of the people. We have no statute recognizing the existence of any such principle as the right of survivorship. But we have various statutory pro-the estates before described, several persons may have a common interest. I speak not now of corporations which may happen to own realty; because the interest of corporations, whether in personalty or realty, is of the same nature, being measured by the shares they hold; which shares only give them an interest in the *proceeds* of the corporate property; and not an interest in the specific property itself. But I refer to natural persons having an undivided interest in the same parcel of realty, no matter how acquired; and in this lecture I am to explain the light in which the law regards such common interest. At common law, estates were divided, with respect to the number of owners, into four classes; namely, estates, *in severalty*, *in joint-tenancy*, *in coparcenary* and *in common.* But an estate in severalty means nothing more than that the land belongs to a single owner, and therefore requires no comment. With respect to the other three estates, the distinctions at common law were numerous and important. In this State, however, the prevailing sentiment in favor of simplicity, has reduced these three estates to one; namely, an estate in common. As this is an important proposition, I will briefly state the grounds on which it rests. In the *first* place, our legislature has generally treated them as one. In the *second* place, our court has expressly decided, that *joint-tenancies* do not exist in Ohio. The case was one where land had been devised to husband and wife, by such words as at common law would have created a joint-tenancy in any other persons; and in husband and wife would have given each the entirety, with the indestructible *right of survivorship;* for as neither could sever the jointure, the whole would belong to the survivor. But the court said, that inasmuch as our legislature had uniformly treated a joint-tenancy as a tenancy in common, and inasmuch as the right of survivorship, which cut off the heirs of the deceased joint-tenant, is not conformable to the spirit of our institutions, or the feelings of our people, they would not recognize a joint-tenancy. And as the same reasons applied to the peculiar tenancy of husband and wife, it should be treated as a tenancy in common. (*a*) And in another case,

visions inconsistent with it. . . . It is from this evident that the legislature have treated a joint-tenancy as a tenancy in common. It is well settled that the joint-tenancy of husband and wife varies in many principles from other joint-tenancies. . . . But the right of survivorship was the same as in other cases of joint-tenancies; and in the case of husband and wife, is as much at variance with our laws and usages as in the common case." This was the case of a devise to husband and wife and their heirs. In Wilson *v.* Fleming, 13 Ohio, 68, it was held that they could not be joint-tenants even of an equitable estate. And in Miles *v.* Fisher, 10 Ohio, 1, it was held that a joint-tenancy could not be created by using the very words, "to hold as joint-tenants, and not as tenants in common."

(*a*) Wilson *v.* Fleming, 13 Ohio, 68. But in most of the States, the rule of the common law still prevails, and a deed or devise to a husband and wife and their heirs makes them joint-tenants with a right of survivorship. Bates *v.* Seely, 46 Penn. State, 248; Woodford *v.* Higbee, 1 Winston (N. C.), No. 1, 237; Babbitt *v.* Scroggin, 1 Duvall, 272; Ketchum *v.* Wadsworth, 5 Wis. 95; Wright *v.* Sadler, 20 N. Y. 330; Thornton *v.* Thornton, 3 Randolph, 183; Elliott *v.* Nichols, 8 Am. Law Reg. (N. S.) 398. In New Jersey, by the Act of 1812, it was declared that no estate should be conwhere the devise expressly specified that the devisees should hold as joint-tenants, and not as tenants in common, it was held that they were tenants in common. In the *third* place, although it has never been decided that coparceners differ in no respect from tenants in common, yet this follows from the reason above given, that our legislature has uniformly treated them as the same. The single exception with respect to *waste*, only strengthens this conclusion; for at common law, one joint-tenant or tenant in common might maintain an action for waste against another, but a coparcener could not. So that our statute, by extending this privilege to a coparcener, only operates to do away the sole remaining difference between tenants in common and coparceners.

§ 140. **Tenants in Common.** (*a*) The leading incidents of estates in common are as follows: 1. The only *unity* required between tenants in common, is the unity of possession. They may differ in regard to interest, title, and time. They own undivided parts, and occupy promiscuously, because neither knows his own severalty. In legal language, they take by distinct moieties, and have no entirety of interest; and therefore, there is no right of survivorship, as there would be in a joint-tenancy; but on the death of either, his undivided interest descends to his heirs. 2. Tenants in common may have *partition* made at any time, by pursuing the course pointed out in the statute, and thus become tenants in severalty. Or they may make partition by mutual agreement. The proceedings in partition will be described hereafter. (*b*) 3. Tenants in common may maintain waste against each other, the nature of which has been already described. (*c*) 4. The possession of one tenant in common is the possession of the other. Therefore neither

sidered an estate in joint-tenancy unless it is expressly set forth in the deed creating it that such is the intention of the parties. This act, it has been held, applies also to conveyances to trustees. Boston, &c. Co. *v.* Condit, 4 Green (N. J.), 394.

(*a*) See 2 Black. Com. 191; 4 Kent, Com. 367; 2 Cruise's Dig. 549; 1 Hilliard's Dig. chap. 54, page 438. A tenant in dower, being also tenant in common of the remainder, may have partition. Morgan *v.* Staley, 11 Ohio, 389. Where land is purchased with partnership funds, the partners are tenants in common. Greene *v.* Graham, 5 Ohio, 264. A levy and sale of the interest of a tenant in common, setting off his share by metes and bounds, instead of taking his undivided share in the whole tract, is only good for his share in the portion so set off. Treon *v.* Emerick, 6 Ohio, 391. One tenant in common cannot make partition by conveying a portion of the common property by metes and bounds. His deed will only convey his undivided share in the portion conveyed. Dennison *v.* Foster, 9 Ohio, 126. But see White *v.* Sayre, 2 Ohio, 110. Where husband and wife conveyed in trust to reconvey to them "jointly, their heirs and assigns, and to the survivor of them," &c., which was done, the husband took the entire fee on the death of the wife. Lewis *v.* Baldwin, 11 Ohio, 352. Where land is devised to a brother and his wife, they take as tenants in common, and if the wife die without issue, her brothers will inherit her share, though not of the blood of the ancestor. Penn *v.* Cox, 16 Ohio, 30. Where the owner and occupier of a farm are, according to a contract between them, to share the crops, they are tenants in common of the crops until a division. Walker *v.* Fitts, 24 Pick. 191; Caswell *v.* Districh, 15 Wend. 379; Putnam *v.* Wise, 1 Hill, 234; Case *v.* Hart, 11 Ohio, 364; Frost *v.* Kellogg, 23 Vt. 308; Smyth *v.* Tankersley, 20 Ala. 212; Carr *v.* Dodge, 40 N. H. 403; Knox *v.* Marshall, 19 Cal. 617.

(*b*) It is held in New York that partition may be made by parol, if followed by actual enjoyment in accordance with the agreement. Wood *v.* Fleet, 36 N. Y. 499.

(*c*) R. S. § 5774. But see Darden *v.* Cooper, 7 Jones, Law, 210.

becomes a trespasser by entering upon any part of the common premises; but if one *actually ousts* the other, and claims the whole to himself, ejectment may be brought against him. Nor does an actual ouster imply force. Whenever one tenant in common, either by words or actions, denies the common tenancy, and claims to hold the whole, as exclusive owner, this will be equivalent to an actual ouster. (*a*) But the mere taking of all the rents by one, will not amount to such ouster. The other can only compel him to account in equity. (*b*) 5. Estates in common are liable to curtesy and dower, and are alienable, descendible, and devisable, like any other estates. These various matters will be explained hereafter. 6. Tenants in common may be compelled to contribute for *necessary repairs*, but not for new improvements; the law presuming that the former must be beneficial to all concerned. (*c*) 7. Tenants in common may convey their *undivided shares* in the same manner as property held in severalty; but it is generally held that one tenant in common cannot convey a *distinct portion* of the common estate by metes and bounds. Our court, (*d*) however, has decided differently. The facts were, that partition was made among eight heirs, and the portions set off to each. The plaintiff purchased three of these shares, and took separate deeds from each of the owners. After this, the partition was set aside for error. The plaintiff then brought ejectment. The court held that he could recover one undivided eighth part of the land conveyed by each of the deeds. The correctness of this decision is very questionable; and in the dissenting opinion of Judge Burnet, the objections to it are placed in a very strong light. The decision, in fact, amounts to this, that one tenant in common may

(*a*) Defending an ejectment suit brought by his cotenant, and setting up the statute of limitations is an ouster. Noble *v.* McFarland, 51 Ill. 226.

(*b*) A tenant in common, it has been held, who has received in money more than his share of the profits of the estate, is liable to his cotenant, in an action at law for the surplus. But mere occupancy and taking the profits, without receiving money for the same, will not give such right of action. Shepard *v.* Richards, 2 Gray, 424; Peck *v.* Carpenter, 7 id. 283. And mere occupation of the entire premises, without attorning to his cotenant or excluding him from his rights, does not render him liable for use and occupation, to his cotenant. Badger *v.* Holmes, 6 Gray, 118. See Huff *v.* McDonald, 22 Geo. 131; Davis *v.* Lottich, 46 N. Y. 393; Crow *v.* Mack, 52 Ill. 332; Israel *v.* Israel, 30 Md. 120; Crane *v.* Waggoner, 27 Ind. 52; Ballou *v.* Hale, 47 N. H. 347; Webster *v.* Calef, 47 N. H. 289. There must be either an actual conversion or destruction of the property. Strong *v.* Colter, 13 Minn. 82. But the destruction need not be total. An action of tort for misuse of the property, as for wasting water in an aqueduct, may be maintained. McLellan *v.* Jenness, 43 Vt. 183. By our statute R. S. § 5774, one tenant in common may recover his share of the rents and profits from another; and the same right may arise from contract, as where all agree to rent to one of their number. Cahoon *v.* Kinen, 42 Ohio State, 190.

(*c*) The repairs must be absolutely necessary to the enjoyment of the property. Dech's Appeal, 57 Penn. State, 467. In Massachusetts it seems to be held that he cannot claim for repairs made without the consent of his cotenant. Calvert *v.* Aldrich, 99 Mass. 74.

(*d*) See White *v.* Sayre, 2 Ohio Rep. 110. Such a deed, though void as to the cotenants, is good as against the grantor by estoppel. McKey *v.* Welch, 22 Texas, 390; Holcomb *v.* Coryell, 3 Stockton, 548. A levy upon the undivided interest of a tenant in common in a part only of the land held in common is void as against his cotenants. Whitton *v.* Whitton, 38 N. H. 127.

of himself make a partition which shall bind the rest. 8. Where partners hold real estate, they are treated in all respects as tenants in common. 9. Tenants in common must join in an action of trespass (a) and in debt for rent; but in ejectment they have an option, either to join or sever. It has been said that they cannot declare on a *joint demise*, because tenants in common cannot in fact make a join demise; but such is not the law here. By our statute, they may either declare on a joint demise or on several demises. These matters will be better understood hereafter, when we come to consider the technicalities of practice.

§ 141. **Joint Interest in Personalty.** (b) In general, the joint owners of personalty are partners, whose relation to each other has already been described. Their interest is rather that of joint-tenants, than of tenants in common; because there is a qualified right of survivorship. And this is true generally of all joint interests in personalty, though the owners be not strictly partners. Either of the joint owners may control the possession, and even transfer the title, during the lives of all; and when either of them dies, this power remains in the survivors. The representatives of the deceased can only call the survivors to account for their doings, and for a proper share of the ultimate proceeds of their management. Nor can any one of the joint owners convey his undivided share of any specific article to a third person. To avoid the effect of any of these rules of law, recourse must be had to chancery. But the maritime law makes an exception with respect to ownership of vessels, which extends also to steamboats and other kinds of water craft used on our interior waters. Joint owners of vessels are called *part owners*, (c) to distinguish them from partners. They are strictly tenants in common; for each part owner may dispose of his undivided share during life, and at death it goes to his representatives. Nor can one of the part owners control or dispose of the vessel without authority from the rest. A court of admiralty will even restrain a majority from employing a vessel against the will of the minority, without giving them security.

I have heretofore mentioned the consolidation of all tenancies of realty, into that of a tenancy in common, as one of the instances in which our land law has been simplified. The brevity of this lecture proves this proposition. It would have required four times the space to discuss this title of the English law, even in the same general manner. Here, then, we have a decided gain on the score of simplicity, and without any countervailing disadvantage.

(a) This rule is not changed by the code. Depuy *v.* Strong, 37 N. Y. 372.

(b) 2 Kent, Com. 350.

(c) Abbott, on Shipping, 68–84; 3 Kent, Com. 151. Nor can he insure the interest of all without their authority. Knight *v.* Eureka F. & M. Ins. Co., 26 Ohio State, 644.

LECTURE XXIV.

ESTATES UPON CONDITION.

§ 142. **Conditions in general.** (*a*) Hitherto, I have considered estates only in their simple and absolute character, unaffected by any conditions or qualifications; but in the creation of estates, it often happens that certain conditions are annexed, according to which they either become vested, enlarged, or defeated; and these conditions may be as various as the dispositions of men. They are not, however, of frequent occurrence here, our conveyances being generally of the most simple character. With the exception of leases and mortgages, which form classes by themselves, we rarely meet with conditions in a deed; whereas in the English law they are very frequent. Indeed, under the feudal system, as we have seen, all estates were held upon conditions, on failure of which, they might be resumed by the lord of whom they were held. I shall give a very general description of the conditions which may be met with here, and of the rules which govern them. Conditions may be annexed to estates in fee, for life, and for years. Thus, if I grant an estate to you and your heirs, so long as you continue to reside in this State, this would be a conditional fee. It is a fee, because it may continue for ever; but since its continuance depends upon your residing in this State, it is called a *qualified*, *base*, or *determinable fee*. Again, if I grant an estate to you as long as you continue in a certain occupation, this is in like manner a conditional estate for life. Lastly, if I lease you an estate for a term of years, on condition that you occupy it in a certain way, this is a conditional estate for years. Conditions are either *express* or *implied*. Express conditions are those which are inserted in the deed, and are called *conditions in deed*. Implied conditions are those which are created by the common or statute law, without express words in the deed. But as none of the examples of implied conditions which are given in the books, will apply to the law of this State, we should probably be safe in saying that none but express conditions would be here recognized. (*b*) Again, conditions are either *precedent* or *subse-*

(*a*) 2 Black. Com. ch. 10; 4 Kent, Com. lec. 57; 1 Hilliard's Dig. ch. 27, 28, pp. 247–255. {There has been said to be a peculiarity in the American law as to conditions, viz. that the rule against perpetuities does not apply to them. For example, a conveyance on condition that liquor shall not be sold on the premises, or that the grantee shall keep a mill thereon, or shall not build on part, is said to be good between the life in being and the immediate issue thereof, or whatever be the limit of remoteness allowed in each State. Gray, in Restraints on Alienation, p. 23, note, gives a full list of cases and *dicta* on this proposition, while he deplores its effect.}

(*b*) A condition is not created by a clause in a deed in fee, stating that "it is expressly understood between the parties that the said tract or parcel of land is not *quent.* (*a*) Conditions precedent are those that must be performed before the estate can commence. Thus, if I grant you an estate upon your marrying a particular person, this is a condition precedent; you must marry before taking the estate. Conditions subsequent are those upon the failure of which, an estate already vested is defeated. Thus, if I grant you an estate so long as you reside upon it, this is a condition subsequent. Besides these, there are conditions which operate to enlarge a vested estate. Thus I may grant you an estate for life, with the condition that, if you have children, it shall be an estate in fee. This condition, although subsequent to the commencement of your estate, is precedent to its enlargement, and therefore strictly belongs to neither of the above classes. The most important rules relating to conditions are the following: —

1. Conditions must be annexed at the time of creating the estate, and not afterwards; because, when an estate is once created, the grantor's power is at an end. Accordingly, if the conditions are contained in a separate deed, both must be executed at the same time.

2. Conditions must operate upon the whole estate. If I should grant you an estate in fee, with a provision that upon the happening of a certain event your estate should cease for a certain number of years, this would not be good, it is said, because it would destroy the unity of the estate. But a condition may operate upon part of the land and not upon the rest. Thus one-half might be made to revert, upon a certain event. There may be good reason for this distinction under the technical rules of

to be put" to any other than a specified use. Thornton's lessee *v.* Trammell, 39 Ga. 202. Nor by words in the *habendum* clause requiring the grantees to hold for a particular purpose, there being no clause of re-entry or forfeiture. Packard *v.* Ames, 16 Gray, 327. But a covenant against a certain use will be enforced by injunction. Stines *v.* Dorman, 25 Ohio State, 580.

(*a*) The intention of the parties, as it appears in the deed, determines whether the condition is precedent or subsequent. Parmelee *v.* Oswego and Syracuse R. R. Co., 6 N. Y. 74; S. C. 7 Barb. 599; Underhill *v.* Saratoga and Washington R. R. Co., 20 Barb. 455; Robbins *v.* Gleason, 47 Maine, 259. A condition precedent, which is possible and lawful, must be strictly performed to give the right of action which depends on it. Balt. & O. R. R. Co. *v.* Polly, 14 Grattan, 447. Conditions subsequent are strictly construed against the grantor. Thus, if a grant be made upon condition that the *grantee* shall forever keep up a fence on the line between the land of the grantor and the land conveyed, the grant will not be forfeited by neglect to keep up the fence by the heirs of the grantee after his death. Emerson *v.* Simpson, 43 N. H. 475; Labaree *v.* Carleton, 53 Maine, 211; Voris *v.* Renshaw, 49 Ill. 425. And their non-performance will not reinvest the title in the grantor. Black *v.* Hoyt, 33 Ohio State, 203, 212. The heirs will not be bound, unless expressly named. Page *v.* Palmer, 48 N. H. 385. If it be doubtful whether a clause in a deed is a condition or a covenant, the latter construction must be adopted. Hoyt *v.* Kimball, 49 N. H. 322. Cf. State *ex rel. v.* Board of Public Works, 42 Ohio State, 607, 615, and Hornback *v.* C. & Z. R. R., 20 id. 81. Where a condition required a certain institution should be permanently located on the land within a year, it is satisfied by the location of the institution there *bonâ fide*, and the erection of buildings, though they are subsequently burned down, and rebuilt on another spot. Mead *v.* Ballard, 7 Wall. 290. Where land is deeded to a school board for school purposes only, a mere sale of the land is not a breach of the condition. Taylor *v.* Binford, 37 Ohio State, 262.

the common law, but I can perceive none in the nature of the subject. (*a*)

3. Conditions can only be reserved to the grantor and his heirs. Except by statutory provision, which we have not, they cannot be reserved to strangers. (*b*) The reason assigned is, that estates upon condition, do not, *ipso facto*, cease upon the happening of the condition, but only when there has been an *entry* for condition broken, or some act equivalent thereto, as the commencement of an action. In order to discourage *champerty* and *maintenance*, (*c*) or the fomenting of litigation, it was a maxim of the English law, as we have seen, that no right of action could be assigned by one person to another. Consequently, the right of entry for condition broken could not be reserved to a stranger. But here the reason of this rule does not exist, because we have no law against champerty or maintenance. The doctrine, however, that there must be an *entry*, to defeat an estate upon condition, has been recognized by our court, (*d*) and it was held that the bringing an ejectment was equivalent thereto. In this respect, an estate upon condition differs from a *conditional limitation*. For example, if I simply grant you an estate upon condition of your remaining in Ohio, and you break the condition by removing, either I or my heirs must enter and assert our claim, in order to defeat your estate; and until we do so, the estate continues in you. But if I make a conditional limitation, by granting an estate to you so long as you remain in Ohio, and then to another person, the very act of removing defeats your estate; and it vests instantly in the next person, without any act done by him (*e*).

4. Conditions which are impossible at the time of making them, or which afterwards become impossible by the act of God, or by the act of the grantor himself, are void; and an estate already vested thus becomes absolute. The reason is, that the moment that a condition becomes impossible, it ceases to be a condition in the sense intended by the grant; and when this is not the fault of the grantee, he is not to be prejudiced thereby. Accordingly, the estate being vested, he holds it discharged of the condition. Thus, if I should grant you an estate, upon condition that within

(*a*) And a condition cannot be severed. A grant of a part of the reversion will defeat the whole condition. Tinkham *v.* Erie R. R. Co., 53 Barb. 393.

(*b*) Underhill *v.* Saratoga and Washington R. R. Co., 20 Barb. 455. Forfeiture, by breach of condition, can only be taken advantage of by the grantor or his heirs. Dewey *v.* Williams, 40 N. H. 222; Hooper *v.* Cummings, 45 Maine, 359. A right of entry on condition broken passes only to heirs, and is not devisable or assignable. Southard *v.* Cent. R. R. Co., 2 Dutcher, 13; Norris *v.* Milner, 20 Ga. 563.

(*c*) See 4 Black. Com. 134; Key *v.* Vattier, 1 Ohio Rep. 132, 141.

(*d*) Sperry *v.* Pond, 5 Ohio Rep. 387; Osgood *v.* Abbott, 58 Maine, 73; Guild *v.* Richards, 16 Gray, 309.

(*e*) An executory devise is the substitution of another estate on the happening of an event cutting off the prior estate. The term has been used also to denote a proviso determining an estate, without itself substituting another; the best treatises apply the term to the former case only. See Gray on Restraints on Alienation, p. 12, note. A condition ends the estate without limitation over, — that is, only the heir can enforce it.

five years you should marry a certain woman, and she should be dead at the time, or should die within the five years, or I should marry her; in either case you would hold the estate discharged of the condition.

5. Conditions, the performance of which is unlawful, are void. Thus, if I grant you an estate, the continuance of which depends upon your doing something which is illegal or immoral; or omitting something which is your duty, the condition is void, and the estate which is vested becomes absolute. (*a*)

6. Conditions which are repugnant to the nature of the estate, are void. Thus, if I grant you an estate in fee, upon condition that you shall not part with it, or shall not receive the profits of it, these conditions would be void for repugnancy, since the rights of alienation, and of taking the profits, are the essential incidents of an estate in fee. But the grantor may prohibit alienation to a particular person; (*b*) for this is not within the reason of the rule. So if the estate be for life or years, a condition against alienation will be good, for here is no repugnancy to the nature of the estate. And in this case, a sale on execution will not be considered as an alienation so as to defeat the estate. (*c*)

7. Conditions in absolute prevention of marriage are void on grounds of public policy, except in the case of widows taking lands from their deceased husbands. (*d*) But the grantor may

(*a*) A condition in a will forfeiting the devise of any one who goes to law to break the will is valid here, both as to realty and personalty, though such is not the English law. Bradford *v.* Bradford, 19 Ohio State, 546, 548.

(*b*) Langdon *v.* Ingram, 28 Ind. 360.

(*c*) But the condition may interfere with or control the mode of enjoyment of the estate. Thus, a condition against partition has been held valid. Hunt *v.* Wright, 47 N. H. 396. So, also, one against the sale of intoxicating liquors on the premises sold. Plum *v.* Tubbs, 41 N. Y. 442. And a condition in a grant of a fee-simple, that a perpetual rent shall be paid, is valid. Van Rensselaer *v.* Barringer, 39 N. Y. 9.

{Two rules may be framed as being generally accepted: 1. A forfeiture or limitation over on alienation of a fee-simple is void, unless alienation merely to specific persons is forbidden, or unless the condition takes effect to prevent the estate vesting, — *i. e.* is a condition precedent to its vesting. But as to all other estates, whether in tail, for life, or for years, such a limitation is valid. 2. A clause prohibiting alienation, but without forfeiture or limitation over — *i. e.* leaving the estate in the owner's hands without power to alienate — is wholly void as to every estate, whether legal or in trust, excepting only married women's separate property trusts. See Gray on Restraints on Alienation, for a full statement of rules and all the cases. In Ohio it has been specifically ruled that a condition in a devise in fee restraining alienation is void. Anderson *v.* Cary, 36 Ohio State, 506. So is a condition that land be exempt from the devisee's creditors. Hobbs *v.* Smith, 15 id. 419. So is a condition forbidding alienation, except to a certain person, even for a few years. Anderson *v.* Cary, 36 Ohio State, 506. An exception to the second rule above given occurs in Pennsylvania, and lately in Massachusetts. Broadway Bank *v.* Adams, 133 Mass. 170. And see also Miller, J., in Nichols *v.* Eaton, 91 U. S. 716, permitting a testator to devise a life interest or lesser interest in trust for the support of the beneficiary, but free from claims of his creditors. Some States by statute also allow a certain amount of income to be thus limited. The name of "spendthrift trusts" has attached to these. See Gray on Restraints on Alienation, *passim.*}

(*d*) Lingart *v.* Ripley, 19 Ohio State, 24; Commonwealth *v.* Stouffer, 10 Barr, 350; McCullough's Appeal, 12 Penn. State, 197. But see Parsons *v.* Winslow, 6 Mass. 169; Otis *v.* Prince, 10 Gray, 581. But in Pennsylvania, by the use of proper words, the enjoyment of a bequest can be limited to the period during which the legatee shall remain unmarried, although the general rule is recognized. Where a bequest was provide that the grantee shall not marry without his consent; because this does not absolutely prevent marriage.

8. Conditions may be performed by any person having an interest in the subject-matter. And if a particular time be appointed, the performance must be at or before the time. The law is strict on this subject, though equity will relieve against mere failure in point of time.

9. Equity will relieve against all forfeitures for breach of conditions, where a compensation can be made in damages; and this renders the legal doctrines respecting conditions of little practical consequence. (*a*)

10. When the condition has been broken, the grantor may, by his own act, debar himself from taking advantage of it. (*b*) Thus, where a lease contains a clause of re-entry, for non-payment of rent at a certain time, and the lessor accepts rent afterwards, he cannot enter for condition broken.

§ 143. **Estates Tail.** (*c*) My limits will not allow a further consideration of the general subject of estates upon condition. But there are certain particular estates upon condition, known by specific names, which, though not in existence here, require a brief notice, on account of the frequent reference made to them by way of illustration and analogy. These are *estates tail*, *estates by statute merchant*, *by statute staple*, and *by elegit*. And first, *estates tail*. An estate tail is an estate given to a man and some particular description of his heirs, to the exclusion of all other heirs. It was originally treated as a fee-simple, upon condition that the grantee had the required heirs; and accordingly, as soon as the condition was performed, by the birth of the specified heirs, the estate became absolute. But as this construction tended to defeat the design of creating the estate, — which was to tie up the property from alienation, and create a perpetuity in particular families, — the aristocracy of England had influence enough to procure the enactment of the famous statute, *de donis conditionalibus*, the effect of which was to fetter an estate tail, with the ancient restraints upon alienation. The estate was to go to the stipulated heirs at all events, if there were such; and if not, to revert to the donor. With the long struggles in England, to avoid the effect of this statute, I shall not occupy your time. Happily, estates tail have been rare in this country. They were introduced here

made to A., "during the term she shall remain the wife or widow of my son," it was held that A. could only enjoy it while she complied with the conditions. Holtz Estate, 38 Penn. State, 422. But an absolute prohibition of marriage, until the devisee shall be twenty-one years old, is reasonable, and marriage before reaching that age will defeat the estate. Shackleford *v.* Hall, 19 Ill. 212.

(*a*) A court of equity will not allow its powers to be used in any way to assist to divest an estate for a breach of a condition subsequent. Smith *v.* Jewett, 40 N. H. 530; Livingston *v.* Tomkins, 4 Johns. Ch. 431; Warner *v.* Bennett, 31 Conn. 468.

(*b*) Ludlow *v.* N. Y. & Harlem R. R. Co., 12 Barb. 440.

(*c*) See 2 Black. Com. 110; 4 Kent, Com. 12–15. See act of April 4, 1859, providing for the sale or lease of estates tail in certain cases.

before the revolution, but were so manifestly opposed to the spirit of our republican institutions, which favor a free distribution of property, that most, if not all of the States, have altogether prohibited them. This is partially the case in Ohio. By the act of 1811, (*a*) no estate can be in any way limited to any persons, but such as are in being at the time, and their immediate issue or descendants; and all estates attempted to be entailed, become absolute fees in the issue of the first grantee in tail. Thus by a statute of ten lines, while the dead are prevented from domineering over their posterity, by means of restraints upon their property, the students of law are relieved from investigating this extensive and intricate branch of English jurisprudence.

§ 144. **Estates by Statute Merchant, Staple, and Elegit.** (*b*) The object of these three estates was the same; namely, to make land available to pay debts. Under the feudal system, real estate could not be made available to a creditor, because there was no process by which it could be reached. The first act making land chargeable with debts, was the *statute de mercatoribus*, or *statute merchant*, passed in 1284; and the second was the *statute staple*, passed in 1354. Both these were designed for the benefit of commerce, and originally confined to traders. They enabled creditors of this description to secure debts acknowledged to be due, by taking possession of the debtor's land, and appropriating the profits until their debts were satisfied; and while so in possession, they were called tenants by *statute merchant*, or *statute staple*, as the case might be. It follows that they held possession upon condition subsequent. We have had nothing similar to these provisions in this country. The estate *by elegit* was created the same year as that by statute merchant, for the common benefit of all judgment creditors, whether merchants or not. The judgment creditor, who until then had recourse only upon the body, goods, and annual profits of the lands of his debtor, was allowed his *election*, in case there was not sufficient personalty, to take possession of one-half of his lands, until the debt was paid out of the rents and profits; and while so in possession, he was called *tenant by elegit:* this estate, therefore, like the other two, was an estate upon condition subsequent. We once had something like it, as will be seen by referring to our early laws on the subject of judgment and execution; but the modern policy has been to sell

(*a*) Under this statute, the first tenant takes a fee-tail, the heirs of his body take a fee-simple. King *v.* King, 12 Ohio, 390. The same construction is given to similar statutes. Clark *v.* Smith, 49 Md. 106; Lippitt *v.* Huston, 8 R. I. 415. The heirs of the body of the first tenant, while taking by descent, yet take *per formam doni* from the person who created the estate, and are therefore not estopped by the deed of the first tenant, though he conveyed the land in fee-simple with covenant of general warranty. Pollock *v.* Speidel, 17 Ohio State, 439; s. c. 27 id. 86. And the surviving husband of the first tenant is tenant by curtesy. Harkness *v.* Corning, 24 Ohio State, 416. Estates tail are not favored, and the presumption is against the intention to create them, and the presumption must be overcome by language free from ambiguity. Collins *v.* Collins, 40 Ohio State, 353, 363.

(*b*) See 2 Black. Com. 160.

the land at once on execution, as will be explained hereafter. I have barely alluded to these estates, because frequently referred to for analogies.

The remarks hitherto made have related exclusively to realty. Conditions may, however, be annexed to personalty, in the common course of business transactions. (*a*) But as their nature and effect will always depend upon the terms of the contract by which they are created, they involve no technical questions of law which require notice here. The most common cases of personalty held upon condition, are those coming under the head of *bailments*, which will be considered hereafter in connection with contracts. I therefore leave the subject of estates upon condition, with the remark that this title furnishes still another instance of the simplicity of our law of real property, compared with the ancient English law.

LECTURE XXV.

MORTGAGES. (*b*)

§ 145. **Object of a Mortgage.** I have already observed that mortgages are usually treated under the head of estates upon condition.

(*a*) A sale and delivery of personal property on condition that the title shall not vest in the vendee until the price is paid, passes no title until the condition is performed. Sanders *v.* Keber, 28 Ohio State, 630 ; Coggill *v.* H. & N. H. R. R. Co., 3 Gray, 544 ; Sargent *v.* Metcalf, 5 id. 306 ; Buson *v.* Dougherty, 11 Humph. 50 ; 1 Parsons, Cont. 449.

(*b*) See 2 Black. Com. 157 ; 4 Kent, Com. lec. 58 ; 2 Cruise's Dig. 82 ; and the treatises of Powell, Coote, Patch, Hilliard, and Jones. The last two are American works.

What is a mortgage, and what estate it creates. Where a deed is absolute upon its face, yet was intended merely as security for a debt, it will be treated as such ; and this may be proved by parol. Stratton *v.* Sabin, 9 Ohio, 28 ; Morris *v.* Way, 16 id. 469 ; Marshall *v.* Stewart, 17 id. 356 ; Irwin *v.* Longworth, 20 id. 581 ; Slutz *v.* Desenberg, 28 Ohio State, 371 ; Wilson *v.* Giddings, id. 554 ; Emerson *v.* Atwater, 7 Mich. 12 ; Hartnett *v.* Ball, 22 Ill. 43 ; Lokerson *v.* Stillwell, 2 Beasley, 357 ; Shaw *v.* Woodward, 28 Ill. 277 ; Belote *v.* Morrison, 8 Minn. 87 ; Tillson *v.* Moulton, 23 Ill. 648 ; Crews *v.* Threadgills, 35 Ala. 354. As in case of a sale and lease back as security only. Patrick *v.* Littell, 36 Ohio State, 79. When shown to have been intended for a mortgage, it continues such until the equity of redemption is released or foreclosed. Decamp *v.* Crane, 4 Green (N. J.), 166 ; Holliday *v.* Arthur, 21 Iowa, 19 ; Phœnix *v.* Gardner, 13 Minn. 430 ; Bingham *v.* Thompson, 4 Nev. 244. Such release may be by parol. Shaw *v.* Walbridge, 33 Ohio State, 1. Yet the grantor's equity in the case of such deed is not subject to be sold on execution. Baird *v.* Kirtland, 8 Ohio, 21 ; Morris *v.* Way, 16 id. 469. But in case of a mortgage the legal title remains in the mortgagor, and may be sold on execution. In case of sale, the appraisement must be of the entire value, without deducting encumbrances. Ely *v.* M'Guire, 2 Ohio, 223 ; Phelps *v.* Butler, id. 224 ; Farmers' Bank *v.* Commercial Bank, 10 id. 71 ; Moore *v.* Rittenhouse, 15 Ohio State, 310, 314. An instrument intended for a mortgage, but not under seal, is not valid against an assignee under a subsequent assignment for the benefit of creditors. Erwin *v.* Shuey, 8 Ohio State, 509. Such an instrument is not entitled to

But their practical importance makes it proper to devote to them a distinct lecture. They are pledges to secure the payment of

record, and if recorded it will not affect subsequent purchasers or encumbrancers with notice. So too in California. Racouillat *v.* Sanserain, 32 Cal. 376 ; Racouillat *v.* Rene, 32 Cal. 450. Where the certificate leaves a blank for the name of the mortgagor, it is only an equitable mortgage. Smith *v.* Hunt, 13 Ohio, 260. So where there is only one witness. White *v.* Denman, 16 Ohio, 59 ; s. c. 1 Ohio State, 110. So where the name of the second witness is added after recording. Bank of Musk. *v.* Carpenter, 7 Ohio, 1 pt. 21. Where the consideration is illegal, the mortgage is void ; but this cannot be inquired into in ejectment. Raguet *v.* Roll, 7 Ohio, 1 pt. 76, and 2 pt. 70 ; Williams *v.* Englebrecht, 37 Ohio State, 383. See also Cowles *v.* Raguet, 14 Ohio, 38. Where the mortgage was to secure a note in one bank, and it was discounted in another, this does not invalidate, unless a subsequent encumbrancer was actually misled. Patterson *v.* Johnson, 7 Ohio, 1 pt. 225. Mere changes in the evidences of the debt do not affect the lien of the mortgage. Choteau *v.* Thompson, 3 Ohio State, 424; Seymour *v.* Darrow, 31 Vt. 122 ; Spring *v.* Hill, 6 Cal. 17 ; Williams *v.* Starr, 5 Wis. 534. A renewal of a note is not a payment of the debt, so as to discharge the mortgage debt, unless the parties so intended. Choteau *v.* Thompson, 3 Ohio State, 424 ; Kuhns *v.* McGeah, 38 id. 468, 492 ; Brown *v.* Kuhn, 40 id. 468, 490 ; Parkhurst *v.* Cummings, 56 Maine, 155. Such is the rule as to all collateral. Dayton National Bank *v.* Merchants' National Bank, 37 Ohio State, 208. When mortgage notes have been paid before maturity, and delivered to the mortgagor without cancelling the mortgage, and he reissues them to innocent third parties, he and all subsequent mortgagees will be estopped from denying their validity. Jordan *v.* Forlong, 19 Ohio State, 89. As to the description of the debt, see Tousley *v.* Tousley, 5 Ohio State, 78. A mortgage, duly executed and recorded, is not invalid as to third parties from a want of certainty in the description of the debt secured, if upon the well-known principle; extrinsic evidence may be introduced to apply it to its subject-matter. Hurd *v.* Robinson, 11 Ohio State, 232 ; Gill *v.* Pinney, 12 Ohio State, 38. A release by a prior to a subsequent mortgagee, creates no new estate, but only extinguishes the prior mortgage. Hill *v.* West, 8 Ohio, 222. The effect of mortgages of franchises by railroad companies is treated of in Redfield on Railways, § 235 ; Pierce on American Railroad Law, ch. xx. Bonds of a corporation, which pledge the real and personal property of a corporation for the payment of a debt, will be treated and enforced by a court of equity as a mortgage. White Water Canal Co. *v.* Vallette, 21 How. 414.

Priorities, &c. Since the act of 1838, all mortgages, whether executed before or since, take effect as to third persons only from the time of their delivery to the recorder. Magee *v.* Beatty, 8 Ohio, 396 ; Fosdick *v.* Barr, 3 Ohio State, 471 ; Paine *v.* Mason, 7 id. 198. A mortgage handed in for record on the first day of the term, but before the opening of court, has priority over a judgment recovered at that term. Follett *v.* Hall, 16 Ohio, 111 ; Holliday *v.* Franklin Bank, id. 533 ; Hemminway *v.* Davis, 24 Ohio State, 150. An unrecorded mortgage or equitable assignment is valid as between the parties, but as to third persons only from the time it is recorded. White *v.* Denman, 16 Ohio, 59 ; s. c. 1 Ohio State, 110 ; Fosdick *v.* Barr, 3 id. 471; Bloom *v.* Noggle, 4 id. 45 ; Erwin *v.* Shuey, 8 id. 509 ; Tousley *v.* Tousley, 5 id. 78; Sidle *v.* Maxwell, 4 id. 236 ; Stewart *v.* Hopkins, 30 Ohio State, 502. A defectively executed mortgage, as having no seal or only one witness, though recorded, stands on the same footing as an unrecorded mortgage as to third persons, for it is not entitled to record. Erwin *v.* Shuey, 8 Ohio State, 509 ; Van Thorniley *v.* Peters, 26 id. 471. But the omission of a notarial seal is doubtless not part of the execution in this sense. Ashley *v.* Wright, 19 id. 291.

An elder mortgage to secure a specific debt and future advances will be postponed as to advances made after the recording of the junior mortgage. Spader *v.* Lawler, 17 Ohio, 371 ; Choteau *v.* Thompson, 2 Ohio State, 114. But see Kramer *v.* F. & M. Bank, 15 Ohio, 253 ; Griffith *v.* N. J., &c. Co., 3 Stockton, 39. In Connecticut, it is held good also as to advances agreed to be made on the faith of it before the recording of the junior mortgage. Boswell *v.* Goodwin, 31 Conn. 74. It is good against a judgment for all advances made before the judgment, although the debt on which the judgment was founded was incurred before the mortgage was made. Robinson *v.* Williams, 22 N. Y. 380. In New Jersey it is good as to all advances made on the faith of it before actual notice of the subsequent incumbrance. Ward *v.* Cooke, 2 Green (N. J.), 93. A mortgage to secure future advances to a specified amount is good to that amount. Lawrence *v.* Tucker, 23 How. 14. See also Soule *v.* Albee, 31 Vt. 142 ; Gookins *v.* Gilmore, 47 Maine, 9. In New Hampshire, by statute, it is money; and in the present wide extension of credit, they form one of the most frequent subjects of judicial cognizance. The

void as to future advances. Johnson *v.* Richardson, 38 N. H. 353. In England now a second mortgage will be preferred to advances under a first mortgage made with notice of the second, and subsequent to it. Rolt *v.* Hopkinson, 4 Jurist (N. S.), 919. Overruling Gordon *v.* Graham, 2 Eq. Abr. 598. A junior mortgage recorded has priority over a senior mortgage unrecorded, though given for purchase-money, and the junior had notice of it. Stansell *v.* Roberts, 13 Ohio, 148; Mayham *v.* Coombs, 14 id. 428; Bloom *v.* Noggle, 4 Ohio State, 45. Though mentioned in the second mortgage, unless its priority is expressly reserved. Bercaw *v.* Cockerill, 20 Ohio State, 163. But if so reserved, the defective execution of the prior mortgage will not impair its priority. Coe *v.* Columbus, &c. R. R. Co., 10 id. 372. A judgment confessed during the term, has priority over a mortgage executed before the first day of the term, but not recorded until after. Jackson *v.* Luce, 14 Ohio, 514. Where mortgaged premises have been sold in parcels to different persons, either by judicial or voluntary sale, the mortgagee, in foreclosing, must proceed first against that which was last sold. Cary *v.* Folsom, 14 Ohio, 365; Sternberger *v.* Hanna, 42 Ohio State, 305; Root *v.* Collins, 34 Vt. 173; Gaskill *v.* Line, 2 Beasley, 400; Day *v.* Patterson, 18 Ind. 114; Ogden *v.* Gliddon, 9 Wis. 46; Mobile, &c. Co. *v.* Huder, 35 Ala. 713; McCullum *v.* Turpie, 29 Ind. 146; Lock *v.* Fulford, 52 Ill. 166; Payne *v.* Avery, 21 Mich. 524. *Contra*, Barney *v.* Myers, 28 Iowa, 472. And see Green *v.* Ramage, 18 Ohio, 428. As to the effect of a special agreement to release the parcels on payment of definite amounts, see Iglehart *v.* Crane, 42 Ill. 261. Where the different conveyancers of parcels are all expressly made subject to the mortgage, the rule does not apply; they must then share *pro rata*. Briscoe *v.* Power, 47 Ill. 447. When the portion primarily liable is released by the mortgagor in a proceeding against the rest, he must be charged with the whole value of the parcel released. Hoy *v.* Bramhall, 4 Green (N. J.), 74, 563; Iglehart *v.* Crane, 42 Ill. 261. And see Stillman *v.* Stillman, 21 N. J. Eq. 126.

Where the recorded chain of title would not lead a searcher for encumbrances to the finding of a mortgage, such mortgage will be postponed to subsequent liens. Leiby *v.* Wolf, 10 Ohio, 83. Though a mortgage deed is recorded in the record of deeds (instead of the record of mortgages), if it be indexed in both the volume index and the general index with the letters "mtg" annexed, it will be operative against a subsequent purchaser for value without actual knowledge of it. Smith *v.* Smith, 13 Ohio State, 532. An index to the record of a conveyance is not necessary to make the record constructive notice. If the purchaser is misled, his remedy is against the recorder. Green *v.* Garrington, 16 Ohio State, 548. A mortgage, recorded after a contract for the sale of the land is made, but before the execution of the deed, will bind the land. Kyle *v.* Thompson, 11 Ohio State, 616. An elder equitable mortgage has priority over a younger judgment lien. Bank *v.* Carpenter, 7 Ohio, 1 pt. 21. Where the indorser of a note executes a mortgage to secure his indorsement, it will not be discharged by the failure of the mortgagee to make the demand, and give the notice necessary to charge the indorser personally. Hilton *v.* Catherwood, 10 Ohio State, 109. The failure of the husband to disclose to the wife the contents of a mortgage she executes at his request, the grantee being ignorant of the fact, is not such a fraud that she can impeach the acknowledgment by parol. Baldwin *v.* Snowdon, 11 Ohio State, 203. Although the debt secured is barred by the statute of limitations, the mortgagee may have his remedy in equity upon the mortgage. Fisher *v.* Mossman, 11 Ohio State, 42; Pratt *v.* Huggins, 29 Barb. 277; Wilkinson *v.* Flowers, 37 Miss. 579. *Contra*, Ross's Heirs *v.* Mitchell, 28 Texas, 150.

Assignment. A mortgage is very rarely assigned by deed. It is ordinarily assigned by an unsealed indorsement on the mortgage, or by a mere transfer of the debt secured by it. A mortgage may be itself the only evidence of the debt; the assignment of such a mortgage is a transfer also of the debt. A mortgage may be given to secure a bond or a negotiable note. The assignment of such a mortgage without a transfer of the debt is nugatory. If such assignment is by deed, the assignee takes a naked legal title, and holds it for the benefit of the owner of the debt secured by it. But if it is by unsealed writing, it can operate only to transfer an equity; but as the only equity is the debt, and that is not transferred, nothing passes. A transfer of the debt is a transfer of the beneficial interest in the mortgage, and such transferee though the mortgage be not actually assigned, is the beneficial assignee and owner of the mortgage. If the debt is evidenced by a bond, not negotiable, the assignee takes subject to equities. The assignment of mortgages securing negotiable instruments has given rise to a conflict of decision. One line of decisions treats the mortgage as a mere in-law which governs them is the common law modified by a very few statutory provisions. Of the derivation of the word *mortgage*, Blackstone gives, in substance, this account: *Vivum vadium*, or living pledge, is when a debtor pledges land to his creditor, to hold until the debt is paid out of the rents and profits; this is likewise called a Welsh mortgage. *Mortuum vadium*, dead pledge, or *mortgage*, is where a debtor actually conveys land to his creditor, upon condition that the conveyance shall be void, if the debt be paid at a given time; but otherwise shall be absolute. In the former case, which now rarely if ever occurs, the debtor still retains a subsisting title to the land, though encumbered by the debt to be paid from the rents and profits. In the latter case, which is that of the common mortgage, the debtor, by the terms of the conveyance, retains no subsisting title; and therefore the pledge is said to be *dead;* though in fact, as we shall see, the law still gives him a subsisting interest, not warranted by the terms of the conveyance. The object of a mortgage, as already stated, is to secure the payment of money by a pledge of real estate; but the law of mortgages has in the course of time undergone so many changes, that scarcely one of the original doctrines on the subject now remains. I shall describe the *form* of a mortgage, in its proper connection with other deeds. But for the purpose of being understood in my present remarks, I will here observe, that, in form, a mortgage differs in no respect from a common deed of conveyance in fee-simple, except in the *condition of defeasance.*

cident to the note, and, held like it, discharged of equities when the transfer is made without notice before maturity of the note. Carpenter *v.* Longan, 16 Wall. 271; Pierce *v.* Faunce, 47 Maine, 507; Bloomer *v.* Henderson, 8 Mich. 395; Cicotte *v.* Gagnier, 2 Mich. 381; Cornell *v.* Hilchens, 11 Wis. 353; Croft *v.* Bunster, 9 Wis. 503. In the case of Taylor *v.* Page, 6 Allen, 86, the transferee of the mortgage held the legal title, and holding both legal title and equity, the case rests upon a different principle. The other line of decisions treats the mortgage as a separate security, additional to the note; not negotiable, and therefore subject to equities, though the note secured by it and transferred with it is held discharged of equities. Baily *v.* Smith, 14 Ohio State, 396; Olds *v.* Cummings, 31 Ill. 188; Johnson *v.* Carpenter, 7 Minn. 176; Bouligny *v.* Fortier, 17 La. Ann. 121. The opinions pronounced in these cases are irreconcilable; but the actual decisions upon the facts, in all except the cases in Illinois and Minnesota, are consistent with the proposition that in case of the assignment of a mortgage securing a negotiable interest, where the assignment is not by deed, the assignee holds free from all equities which affect the debt, but subject to all defects and equities which affect the validity of the mortgage. The deed of the mortgage or an assignment of the mortgage without an assignment of the debt conveys no interest to the grantee or assignee unless the mortgagee is in possession of the premises; and such is the rule as to all securities, an assignment of the security apart from the debt conveys nothing. Hill *v.* West, 8 Ohio, 222, 224; Smith *v.* Smith, 15 N. H. 55; Hobson *v.* Roles, 20 id. 41; Johnson *v.* Cornett, 29 Ind. 59; Peters *v.* Jamestown Bridge Co., 5 Cal. 334. When the debt is also assigned it is of course good. An assignment of the debt carries the mortgage as an incident. Paine *v.* French, 4 Ohio, 419; Swartz *v.* Leist, 13 Ohio State, 419; Allen *v.* First Natl. Bk. 23 id. 97; Mapps *v.* Sharp, 32 Ill. 13; Gower *v.* Howe, 20 Ind. 396; Jones *v.* Quinnipiack Bank, 29 Conn. 25; Blake *v.* Williams, 36 N. H. 39; Croft *v.* Bunster, 9 Wis. 503; Ord *v.* M'Kee, 5 Cal. 515; Crow *v.* Vance, 4 Iowa, 434; Martin *v.* McReynolds, 6 Mich. 70. And such is the rule as to all collaterals, — they follow the debt. The purchaser of the property at foreclosure of the mortgage, if the foreclosure proceedings are defective, is considered as being the assignee of the mortgage. Childs *v.* Childs, 10 Ohio State, 339.

And if its legal import were now to be gathered from its words, it would be the conveyance by the mortgagor to the mortgagee of an estate in fee-simple, upon condition that if the stipulated sum of money for which the mortgage is given, were paid upon a fixed day, the estate should revert to the mortgagor; but otherwise, should become absolute in the mortgagee. Accordingly the mortgagee would take immediate possession, and exercise all acts of ownership, until the pay-day arrived, and then would give it up or hold it absolutely, according to the fact of payment or non-payment. Such, I say, would be the inference drawn from the form and language of a mortgage; and such was in fact the early construction given to it by law; but such is not now the construction; and it is matter of regret that the form of the instrument has not been changed with the law, so that the words might now express the present legal nature of the transaction. (*a*)

§ 146. **Right of Redemption.** (*b*) The original construction of a mortgage as just explained, was found to be productive of extreme hardship. Land is often mortgaged to secure a debt much less than its value; and if a failure to pay this debt punctually at the day, were to involve the forfeiture of the land absolutely, the mortgagee would obtain an unconscionable advantage. On this ground, the court of equity early took up the subject, and allowed

(*a*) {A mortgage of an equity is not wholly null. Thus where the vendee under a title bond mortgages his interest, the mortgage will be deemed to be an assignment *pro tanto* by him to the mortgagee. Churchill *v.* Little, 23 Ohio State, 301. And when the mortgagor obtains the legal title it will enure to the mortgagee as against subsequent claimants. Philly *v.* Sanders, 11 id. 490. In Ives *v.* Comm. of Insolvents, Wright, 626, it was said to be a mortgageable interest. See also Jarvis *v.* Hannan, 40 Ohio State, 334; Tarbell *v.* West, 86 N. Y. 280, 287.}

(*b*) The right of redemption may be barred by an adverse possession for twenty-one years, by the mortgagee claiming to hold as owner. Clark *v.* Potter, 32 Ohio State, 49; Fox *v.* Reeder, 28 id. 181. But it will be saved, notwithstanding such possession, by any deliberate act of the mortgagee by which he recognized the mortgage as subsisting. Robinson *v.* Fife, 3 Ohio State, 551. As a general rule, a party seeking to redeem must redeem the whole, and not a part; otherwise, however, where the mortgagee has become the absolute owner of a part. Id. A widow, who, in the lifetime of her husband, united with him in a mortgage of his lands, has in equity a right to redeem, and a foreclosure to which she was not a party, during her husband's life, does not divest her of this right. McArthur *v.* Franklin, 16 Ohio State, 193. Parmenter *v.* Binkley, 28 id. 32. But she need not be made party to foreclosure of a purchase-money mortgage. Folsom *v.* Rhodes, 22 Ohio State, 435; nor if the mortgage was made before marriage. Wilson *v.* Scott, 29 id. 636. *Semble*, that she must pay the whole debt, unless by the consent of the mortgagee. McArthur *v.* Franklin, *supra;* McCabe *v.* Bellows, 7 Gray, 148. A widow who joined in a mortgage of her husband's property, where the mortgaged land on sale pays the debt and leaves a surplus, is entitled to dower in the surplus, but in that only, not in the entire proceeds, to be satisfied out of the surplus. State Bank *v.* Hinton, 21 Ohio State, 509; but see Kling *v.* Ballentine, 40 Ohio State, 391. A release of dower in a mortgage releases it as to the holder of the mortgage and his privies only, and not as to third persons; hence if the sale is under a lien in which she has not released dower, she is dowable in the property in the hands of the purchaser. Ketchum *v.* Morris, 28 Ohio State, 503. Hence, also, if a mortgage is given without release of dower, and a second mortgage is given to another party with release of dower, and on foreclosure to which she is a party the proceeds are insufficient to pay off the first mortgage, the amount of the dower claim must be given to the second mortgagee before the first mortgage is paid. Black *v.* Kuhlman, 30 Ohio State, 196. Not even an express agreement in the mortgage itself, can abridge the time allowed for redemption. Chase *v.* McClellan, 49 Maine, 375.

the mortgagor to redeem the land, after the time stipulated, by paying the debt and interest, provided this were done within the period allowed for bringing an action of ejectment, which is here twenty-one years. This right is thence called an *equity of redemption;* and it extends to the heirs and assigns of the mortgagor, and to every other person interested in the lands; the grand principle being, that the only right of the mortgagee is, to be secured for his debt. (*a*)

§ 147. **Right of Foreclosure.** (*b*) Had the interference of equity

(*a*) A mortgagee in possession must account for rents and profits, less taxes and the cost of reasonable repairs to keep up the premises. Anderson *v.* Lanterman, 27 Ohio State, 104; Moore *v.* Titman, 44 Ill. 367; Strang *v.* Allen, 44 Ill. 428. So must a buyer at foreclosure when one having a right to redeem is enforcing that right. McArthur *v.* Franklin, 16 Ohio State, 193; Childs *v.* Childs, 10 id. 339. But where he has used reasonable diligence to rent, he will not be charged with more than he obtained, because of an offer of more by the mortgagor's agent after the arrangement was made, especially if it appears he had not authority to bind his client. Hubbard *v.* Shaw, 12 Allen, 120. He cannot charge for permanent improvements, however, though necessary for the protection of crops, or to enhance the rental value. Hidden *v.* Jordan, 32 Cal. 397.

(*b*) *Remedies.* If the debt secured by the mortgage is not paid at maturity, the mortgagee has three remedies: an action at law for the debt, an action of ejectment to recover possession of the land, and a suit in equity to foreclose the mortgage. Any or all of these remedies may be prosecuted at the same time. The code of civil procedure does not affect this right of the mortgagee, but only the name given to the three proceedings. Williams *v.* Englebrecht, 37 Ohio State, 383, and cases cited. A power of attorney, in a mortgage, to sell on default, is valid; and will extinguish the equity of redemption, if exercised fairly, and upon notice, though a bill of foreclosure was pending at the time. Brisbane *v.* Stoughton, 17 Ohio, 482; Mitchell *v.* Bogan, 11 Rich. 686. In Texas, it cannot be executed after the death of the mortgagor, it being inconsistent with the laws for the settlement of estates. Robertson *v.* Paul, 16 Texas, 472. But in other States, it is held to be a power coupled with an interest, and therefore irrevocable by death or in any other way. Bancroft *v.* Ashurst, 2 Grant's Cases, 513; Bradley *v.* Chester, &c. R. R. Co., 36 Penn. State, 141; Brewer *v.* Winchester, 2 Allen, 389. The conditions of the power must be complied with, in order to make the title good. Roarty *v.* Mitchell, 7 Gray, 243. Smith *v.* Provin, 4 Allen, 516; Bancroft *v.* Ashurst, *supra;* Bradley *v.* Chester, &c. R. R. Co., *supra.* Where a misapprehension prevented competition, and the mortgagee purchased at a great bargain, if he be secured in any event, a resale will be ordered. Hey *v.* Schooley, 7 Ohio, 2 pt. 48. But it is held in Illinois, that where the mortgagee purchases at a sale under a power, the sale will be set aside at the application of any party, without proof that the price was too small, or that any injury has resulted. Unless the right to purchase is expressly given him by the mortgage. Hall *v.* Towne, 45 Ill. 493. See also Elliott *v.* Wood, 53 Barb. 285; Montague *v.* Dawes, 14 Allen, 369. A mortgagee may maintain an action on the case against one who unjustly lessens his security. Allison *v.* M'Cune, 15 Ohio, 726. Carpenter *v.* Canal Co., 35 Ohio State, 307. Where the mortgagee makes the mortgagor his executor, the mortgage is not extinguished. Collard *v.* Donaldson, 17 Ohio, 264. Different debts secured by the same mortgage are in case of deficiency of proceeds to be paid in the order they fall due, whether assigned or not. Winters *v.* Bank, 33 Ohio State, 250, and cases cited; Anderson *v.* Sharp, 44 Ohio State, —; Wood *v.* Trask, 7 Wis. 566; Murdock *v.* Ford, 17 Ind. 52; Sangster *v.* Love, 11 Iowa, 580. But where several mortgages are all executed and recorded at the same time, it is for the jury to find which was delivered first, and the dates fixed for the performance of their conditions are not even competent evidence to go to the jury for this purpose. Gilman *v.* Moody, 43 N. H. 259. Where one of the mortgages is for the purchase-money, that has priority. Clark *v.* Brown, 3 Allen, 509. Where a mortgagor sells before foreclosure, and his grantee is not made a party to the bill, he cannot maintain ejectment against the purchaser, but may redeem. Frische *v.* Kramer, 16 Ohio, 125. A junior mortgagee may foreclose without first redeeming from the prior mortgage, Stewart *v.* Johnson, 30 Ohio State, 24, although the prior mortgagee has already foreclosed and bought in the property, if the junior stopped here, the mortgagor would have had the advantage; for though the mortgagee should obtain possession of the land, yet for the period of twenty-one years, he would not dare to make any valuable improvements, because he would be liable to lose them by a redemption of the land; and if the land happened to rise in value in the mean time, faster than the interest increased, this would be wholly for the benefit of the mortgagor when he chose to redeem; whereas, if it should greatly depreciate, the loss might fall entirely on the mortgagee. For these reasons, the court of equity interfered again, in favor of the mortgagee, and allowed him at any time within twenty-one years from the day the money fell due, to *foreclose the mortgage;* or, in other words, to cut off the equity of redemption, and thus quiet his title. But this was required to be done upon such terms as were just and equitable for both parties. The rule here adopted is this: the land is appraised as for sale on execution; and if two-thirds of the valuation exceed the debt and interest, the land is sold at public auction, and the surplus proceeds paid over to the mortgagor; if not, the title is passed in fee-simple to the mortgagee, and the right to redeem for ever taken away; but in this latter case, if the real value of the land is less than the debt and interest, the mortgagee still has his right of action against the mortgagor, for the deficiency. (*a*) This equitable proceeding by foreclosure, in which all the parties interested in the mortgaged premises are brought before the court, and their claims adjusted, is the only one by which the equity of redemption can be cut off. (*b*)

§ 148. **Other Incidents.** (*c*) These leading determinations of

encumbrancer was not made a party to such suit. In the latter suit the proceeds must be first applied to paying off the prior claimant free of costs. Id., and Holliger *v.* Bates, 43 id. 437. Where the mortgage debt is payable by instalments, there may be a foreclosure when the first falls due. But the decree can only be for what is due; and if the property cannot be divided, and the whole must be sold, the surplus must be brought into court for equitable disposition. King *v.* Longworth, 7 Ohio, 2 pt. 231. Where the mortgagee recovers a judgment for any part of the debt, and the land is sold on execution, the purchaser takes it discharged from the mortgage. Freeby *v.* Tupper, 15 Ohio, 467. And see Fosdick *v.* Risk, id. 84; Ireland *v.* Hull, 10 Johnson, 481. R. S. § 5316 provides that in the foreclosure of a mortgage, a sale of the mortgaged property shall in all cases be ordered. The mortgagee may have a personal judgment for his debt, and levy execution on the premises instead of foreclosing, or he may (R. S. § 5021) seek a personal judgment and also a foreclosure. But in such case he must pray for a personal judgment in the petition, or it cannot be granted for a deficiency arising on sale of the property; the court may, however, find the balance due and order execution for it. Giddings *v.* Barney, 31 Ohio State, 80. Formerly, a conveyance might be decreed without sale under certain circumstances. Anonymous, 1 Ohio, 235; Higgins *v.* West, 5 Ohio, 554. As to the old proceeding by *scire facias,* see Reedy *v.* Burgert, 1 Ohio, 157; Allen *v.* Parish, 3 Ohio, 187; Dennison *v.* Allen, 4 Ohio, 495; Biggerstaff *v.* Loveland, 8 Ohio, 44; Hubbell *v.* Broadwell, id. 120.

(*a*) By § 5316, the land is to be sold in all cases.

(*b*) Proceedings to foreclose are not void because of the non-joinder of interested persons, but are simply of no effect as to the rights of persons not parties, while perfectly valid as to parties. Childs *v.* Childs, 10 Ohio State, 339.

(*c*) Ely *v.* M'Guire, 2 Ohio Rep. 223; Phelps *v.* Butler, id. 224; Miami Exp. Co. *v.* Bank U. S., Wright's Rep. 249. A mortgagee may make advances necessary to protect his security and charge them to the property as a lien prior to other claims also benefited; thus he may pay taxes, although such taxes are not legal. Bates *v.* People's, equity have led to very essential modifications in the legal character of a mortgage. The execution and delivery of the instrument no longer create an estate upon condition in the mortgagee, but simply give him a lien; while the legal title to the land continues in the mortgagor, to all intents and purposes, until default of payment; so that he can exercise all acts of ownership over it, precisely as if no mortgage had been made. And even after default the title does not pass *ipso facto* to the mortgagee. The default only lays the foundation for an action of ejectment, by which the mortgagee may obtain possession of the premises. This, however, does not affect the equity of redemption, which still continues in the mortgagor until cut off by lapse of time or foreclosure; and is, in the mean time, descendible and transferable like any other legal estate. The only restriction upon the power of the mortgagor, while he continues in possession, is, that he cannot commit *waste;* that is to say, a court of equity will interfere by injunction to prevent any act which will impair the mortgagee's security; though if waste were actually committed, a court of law could give no remedy, because the mortgagee is not now considered the legal owner of the estate. His rights before ejectment or foreclosure, are all determined by the leading principle, that the mortgage is now a mere security for a debt. The mortgagee, therefore, has nothing but a *specific lien* upon the land; that is, a power of subjecting it to the payment of his debt, by taking the proper steps, in preference to any other creditor or subsequent incumbrancer. He has not an estate in the land, but a mere inchoate right which may be strengthened into an estate. His interest is not liable to be sold on execution, but may be made available to his creditor by proceedings in equity. It is likewise capable of being assigned or transmitted, in the same manner as a chattel, being considered of no higher nature. Our statute expressly provides that if a mortgagee die before foreclosure, the debt and mortgage shall be personal assets in the hands of the executor or administrator; and if possession be obtained by them, they shall hold in trust for the persons who would have been entitled to the money if the debt had been paid. This general view of the present nature of a mortgage, shows that the interest of the mortgagee is no longer an *estate upon condition*, in the strict sense of that phrase; since even after the condition is broken, he cannot obtain possession without the intervention of a court; and that in fact the execution of a mortgage cannot now be said to create a legal estate of any description in the mortgagee. (*a*) It is only therefore in compliance with custom, that I have treated the subject under the head of legal estates; for it would fall more

&c. Assn., 42 Ohio State, 655. May pay for gathering a mortgaged crop. McKennon *v.* May, 39 Ark. 442.

(*a*) Phelps *v.* Butler, 2 Ohio, 224; Ely *v.* McGuire, id. 223; Moore *v.* Rittenhouse, 15 Ohio State, 310, 314; McArthur *v.* Franklin, 16 Ohio State, 193, 206. *Contra*, Allen *v.* Everly, 24 Ohio State, 97; 15 Ohio, 735; 18 Ohio, 273, 277; Fletcher *v.* Holmes, 32 Ind. 497; Mack *v.* Wetzlar, 39 Cal. 247; Williams *v.* Beard, 1 S. C. 309; Jorham *v.* Arnold, 22 Mich. 247. *Contra*, Stewart *v.* Barrow, 7 Bush (Ky.), 368.

properly under that of *equitable estates.* But I will now state a few other matters, serving still further to illustrate the rights of the parties.

The mortgagee has three modes of collecting his debt, which he may pursue either successively or simultaneously, as he chooses. These are an action of contract for the money, an action of ejectment for the land, and a bill of foreclosure in chancery. If all are pursued at the same time, a satisfaction in either way will of course bar proceedings in the other. In this State, from 1795 to 1831, there was an additional remedy by *scire facias*, created by statute; and it was held that a resort to this remedy precluded other proceedings. But this superfluous remedy is now taken away; and it would be well if the others could be in some way consolidated, or the option restricted. When the mortgaged property is sufficient to satisfy the debt, the most common and effectual mode of proceeding is by foreclosure; and it has been decided, that, if there be several instalments, this course may be adopted when the first becomes due, though it be only of the interest. Whether ejectment can be brought until all the payments are due, I do not find decided. But from the general maxim, that a condition cannot be apportioned in law, it would seem that all the payments must be due, before the mortgage, considered as a legal conveyance, is forfeited, so as to lay the foundation of this action. The only objections to the remedy by foreclosure are the expense and delay attending it. But an expedient has been adopted to obviate these; which is to give the mortgagee a *power of attorney* in the mortgage itself to sell the mortgaged premises, on default of payment, without recourse to a court of chancery; and account for the surplus to the mortgagor. Owing to the maxim, "Once a mortgage, always a mortgage," it has been doubted whether a sale under such a power, unless the mortgagor joined in the conveyance, would cut off his equity of redemption; but it is now settled that such a sale, fairly conducted, will be conclusive against him; and to insure fairness, the power is sometimes conferred on a third person; but this is not absolutely necessary. (*a*) This power to sell is in its nature irrevocable, and passes to any assignee of the mortgage; being coupled with an interest, as has been explained before. The only doubt therefore is, whether such sale will be conclusive against subsequent mortgagees, or whether they may still redeem by indemnifying the purchaser; but as they have notice of the power to sell, and may bid at the sale, I see not how they can have any claim to redeem. It is usual to accompany the mortgage with a bond or note for the money; but

(*a*) Brisbane *v.* Stoughton, 17 Ohio, 482. The power of sale is cumulative, and does not deprive the mortgagee of the remedies, whether by strict foreclosure, or a sale by order of court, to which he would be otherwise entitled. Shaw *v.* Norfolk County R. R. Co., 5 Gray, 162; Hall *v.* Sullivan R. R.; Pierce on American Railroad Law, p. 524, note; Carradine *v.* O'Connor, 21 Ala. 573; Byron *v.* May, 2 Chandler (Wis.), 103; 2 Story, Eq. §§ 1024, 1026, 1027; Morrison *v.* Bean, 15 Texas, 267.

this is not essential. A mortgage may be taken to secure future advances and responsibilities, if this intention be clearly expressed in the mortgage. But when the debt is evidenced by a bond or note, the holder can assign the mortgage by a simple indorsement of the bond or note; for the security follows the debt as an incident.

If there be several mortgages, their respective priorities are determined by the record. Formerly, our law allowed a mortgage recorded within six months, to take effect from date. But now the provision is, that mortgages shall take effect from the time of presentation to the recorder; and thus a wide door to fraud is effectually closed. If, however, a subsequent mortgagee have actual notice of a prior unrecorded mortgage at the time of taking his mortgage, the fact of placing his mortgage first on record, will not give him the priority; for this would be to convert the statutory provision into an instrument of fraud, by placing constructive above actual notice. The American doctrine is, that if a deed be properly executed, the record is constructive notice to all the world; and precludes the averment by another of a want of actual notice; but it is not the only notice which the law will recognize. (*a*) Again, the English doctrine of *tacking* a subsequent debt upon a prior mortgage, so as to cut out an intermediate debt due to another, has never been adopted here, on account of its manifest incompatibility with our doctrine of notice. (*b*) Each comes in according to his priority; and whoever may commence proceedings, the oldest lien is first satisfied. It is provided by our statute, that when the mortgagee shall have entered satisfaction of the mortgage, either upon the mortgage itself or upon the record, such entry shall operate as a release of the mortgage; and it has been decided that the mere fact of payment discharges the mortgage, and that this may be proved by parol. (*c*)

§ 149. **Mortgage of Personalty.** (*d*) The foregoing remarks have

(*a*) But in Ohio, it is now settled that, contrary to the doctrine in the text, a mortgage properly recorded will have priority over a prior unrecorded mortgage, though with notice. See note on p. 354.

(*b*) {The doctrine of tacking never existed in this State. Towner *v.* Wells, 8 Ohio, 136; Fitch *v.* Mendenhall, 17 id. 578. Nor in Vermont. Chandler *v.* Dyer, 37 Vt. 345. And it has now disappeared generally in the States, if it ever existed.}

(*c*) Hill *v.* West, 8 Ohio, 222. The cancellation of a mortgage on record by the person appearing upon the record to be the owner of it, will discharge the mortgage as to subsequent *bonâ fide* purchasers without knowledge of the facts, although the cancellation was made through fraud or mistake. Swartz *v.* Leist, 13 Ohio State, 419; Ely *v.* Schofield, 35 Barb. 330. The mortgagee's purchase of the mortgaged premises extinguishes the mortgage by merger. Jennings *v.* Wood, 20 Ohio, 261. Unless otherwise intended by the parties. Factors, &c. Ins. Co. *v.* Murphy, 111 U. S. 738.

(*d*) See 4 Kent, Com. 138; Story on Bailments, 196; Miller *v.* Cassilly, Wright's Rep. 208; Hilliard on Mortgages. {The interest of the mortgagee is that of general owner; and he is entitled to possession even before the debt is due, unless the contrary is stipulated. Robinson *v.* Fitch, 26 Ohio State, 659. But he is not the owner at any time, and therefore cannot sell the property after the debt is due, in order to realize, but must resort to legal proceedings. Beard *v.* Westerman, 32 Ohio State, 29, 32. And must account for the surplus after satisfying his debt. Hanes *v.* Tiffany, 25 id. 549, 554. A chattel mortgage cannot be made upon related to *realty;* but personalty may also be mortgaged. A mortgage of personalty differs from one of realty, chiefly in one par-

mere choses in action. Tingle *v.* Fisher, 20 W. Va. 497. Thus it cannot be made upon the mortgagor's interest as distributee of an estate in an administrator's hands; the instrument, however, will be effectuated as an assignment. Horst *v.* Dague, 34 Ohio State, 371.} A mortgage of personal property, where the mortgagor retains possession of the property, with power of sale, is void as against subsequent purchasers and execution creditors. Collins *v.* Myers, 16 Ohio, 547; Freeman *v.* Rawson, 5 Ohio State, 1; Harman *v.* Abbey, 7 id. 218; Gardner *v.* McEwen, 19 N. Y. 123. But it seems not if his sales are not to be for his own benefit, but for that of the mortgagor. Kleine *v.* Katzenberger, 20 Ohio State, 110. See Gay *v.* Bidwell, 7 Mich. 519. Ever since the statute of 1866, unrecorded chattel mortgages are good as between the mortgagee and the mortgagor, or subsequent mortgagees or purchasers from him with notice. They are also good, therefore, as against an assignee in bankruptcy, who simply stands in the shoes of the bankrupt. Gibson *v.* Warden, 14 Wall. 244. {*Contra*, Blandy *v.* Benedict, 42 Ohio State, 295; s. c. with note, 24 Am. Law Reg. 256, holding that being void as to creditors, it is void as to an assignee for creditors; and such is the rule as to an administrator of the insolvent estate of a mortgagor of an unrecorded chattel mortgage. Kilbourne *v.* Fay, 29 Ohio State, 264.} Since 1846, we have had a law providing for the registration of personal mortgages, which declares void all mortgages of personalty, where there is not an actual and continued change of possession, as against subsequent creditors, purchasers, or mortgagees, unless the original, or a copy, shall be deposited with the township clerk; and this must be renewed every year. For the construction of this act, see Paine *v.* Mason, 7 Ohio State, 198. Refiling it out of time does not make it a new mortgage. Biteler *v.* Baldwin, 42 Ohio State, 125. The lapse of a full year without renewal renders the instrument invalid as against creditors. The year begins to run from the exact hour of the prior filing. Seaman *v.* Eager, 16 Ohio State, 209. It is a sufficient filing to hand the mortgage to the proper officer, and have him indorse it, though he subsequently misplaces it, and another mortgagee inquiring at the office is incorrectly informed that there is no mortgage there. Jordan *v.* Farnsworth, 15 Gray, 517. If the mortgage be executed by joint owners it must be filed or refiled in all the townships in which they reside. Aultman *v.* Guy, 41 Ohio State, 598. A description of the property, which will enable third persons to identify it, aided by inquiries which the mortgage itself indicates, is sufficient. Lawrence *v.* Evarts, 7 Ohio State, 194. A chattel mortgage cannot, of itself, give a lien on, and title to, subsequently acquired property, but the mortgagee may acquire a valid lien on such property where it is actually delivered to him, pursuant to the provisions of the mortgage. Chapman *v.* Weimer, 4 id. 481; 74 Me. 332; 18 S. Ca. 157; 49 Mich. 425; 30 Minn. 132. *Contra*, 58 Iowa, 499. The mortgagor's interest is subject to execution or attachment; and if the mortgagee's security is placed in jeopardy by proceedings of other creditors of the mortgagor, his remedy is in equity. Curd *v.* Wunder, 5 id. 92; Carty *v.* Fenstemacher, 14 Ohio State, 457; Morgan *v.* Spangler, 20 Ohio State, 38, 55. And if the mortgagor has the right of possession, the mortgagee's remedy is in equity in such case. Curd *v.* Wunder, *supra*. Otherwise he may replevy, but the lien of the other creditors is not divested by the replevying. Carty *v.* Fenstemacher, *supra*. When a mortgage, which gives the mortgagor the right to retain the goods, contained an express provision that if the mortgagor should commit waste, or attempt to secrete or remove the goods, the mortgagee might take possession, and the goods were levied on by other creditors and removed from the possession of the mortgagor, and the township of his residence, the mortgagee might replevy them before condition broken. Ashley *v.* Wright, 19 Ohio State, 291. And see Gooding *v.* Shea, 103 Mass. 360; Fuller *v.* Day, 103 Mass. 481; Tuesley *v.* Robinson, 103 Mass. 558; Brown *v.* Phillips, 3 Bush, 656. A clause giving the mortgagee a right to take possession when he deems himself in danger gives him the right to judge of the necessity, provided he acts in good faith. Barrett *v.* Hart, 42 Ohio State, 41. A mortgage of personal property, situated in another State, if executed and recorded in such State, according to its laws, is valid in this State, without any new record or filing, where the mortgagor has, after the execution of such mortgage, removed into the State, and brought the property with him without the consent of the mortgagee. Kanaga *v.* Taylor, 7 Ohio State, 134. Cobb *v.* Buswell, 37 Vt. 337. A person taking a chattel mortgage with actual notice of an unsatisfied prior mortgage upon the same property, is not a *bonâ fide* mortgagee under this act; but constructive notice, not in accordance with the statute, will not alone be sufficient to constitute *mala fides*. Day *v.* Munson, 14 Ohio State, 488. But this rule does not ticular; namely, as to the party who shall have *possession* during the mortgage. As possession of personalty is usually taken by the world to be evidence of ownership, and credit given accordingly; and as there are no records of personalty where titles can be traced and incumbrances ascertained; it would seem to be the policy of the law, in order to prevent fraud upon third persons, that the mortgagee should have possession of the thing mortgaged. But the decisions only go to this extent, that where the retaining of possession by the mortgagor produces actual fraud upon third persons, the rights of the mortgagee are postponed to theirs; but where third persons are not actually defrauded, the mortgage is good to the mortgagee, though the mortgagor retains possession. (*a*) In other respects, the rights and remedies of the parties are nearly the same as with respect to realty. If the mortgagee be not in possession, he may, on default, either obtain possession by action at law, or foreclose by suit in chancery. If he be in possession, there is no occasion for a bill of foreclosure. In this case, the mortgage does not differ from a pledge or pawn to which possession is essential, except in the mere form of the writing. When the mortgagee is in possession, and there is a default, he may sell, on reasonable notice to the mortgagor; but until sale, the right of redemption continues. If no pay-day be fixed, there may be a redemption at any time before sale on notice. But there are some cases where the mortgagee of chattels never has possession; as maritime pledges, on *bottomry* and *respondentia*, (*b*) which the master of a ship is authorized to make in a foreign port, in cases of necessity. To secure a loan on *bottomry*, the ship and freight are hypothecated to the lender. To secure a loan on *respondentia*, the cargo only is hypothecated. In neither case, of course, does possession accompany the pledge; and the hypothecation is evidenced by bond. The lender stands in the place of an insurer, for

apply to a general creditor; his levy of execution with notice of an unrecorded mortgage gives him a prior lien. Houk *v.* Condon, 40 Ohio State, 569. A chattel mortgage, where the mortgagee is in possession, is good even as against judgment creditors, though the mortgage is so imperfect as to amount only to an executory contract. Coe *v.* Columbus, P. & I. R. R. Co., 10 Ohio State, 372. As to what is sufficient possession by the mortgagee in such case, see Carpenter *v.* Snelling, 97 Mass. 452; Parshal *v.* Eggart, 52 Barb. 367. The want of a notary's seal to his certificate to the affidavit, will not invalidate a mortgage. Ashley *v.* Wright, 19 Ohio State, 291; Gibson *v.* Warden, 14 Wall. 244. A lease reserving a lien on personalty on the premises, to be valid as against subsequent mortgages, must be filed as a chattel mortgage. Smith *v.* Worman, 19 Ohio State, 145. Where a mortgagee takes the property to his store, and sells it as the chance comes with other lots of similar goods, but keeps the accounts separately, there is no such confusion of goods as to charge him with the value at the time he took them there. Armstrong *v.* McAlpin, 18 Ohio State, 184. A power of sale in such a mortgage is valid. Cobb *v.* Farr, 16 Gray, 597; Hawkins *v.* Hastings Bank, 1 Dill. 462. It is not necessary in foreclosing that the property be within the jurisdiction of the court if the parties are. Hence a court can order sale of a vessel under a chattel mortgage though she be out of the jurisdiction. Means *v.* Worthington, 22 Ohio State, 622.

(*a*) McGarran *v.* Haupt, 9 Iowa, 83; Forest *v.* Tinkham, 29 Ill. 141; Marrow *v.* Forney, 35 Ala. 131; Hackett *v.* Manlove, 14 Cal. 85.

(*b*) 3 Kent, Com. lec. 49. What is sufficient necessity to justify a bottomry bond, is fully discussed in The Grapeshot, 9 Wall. 139.

he takes the risk of the voyage. If the ship or cargo be lost, he receives nothing; if not, he receives the principal loaned, and the extraordinary interest agreed upon; and he has a lien upon the thing hypothecated, for payment.

LECTURE XXVI.

EQUITABLE ESTATES. (*a*)

§ 150. **In what they Consist.** The estates before described, with the exception of mortgages, are strictly *legal estates;* that is, such

(*a*) See 2 Black. Com. 327 ; 4 Kent, Com. lec. 61, 62 ; the title Uses and Trusts in the Digests of Hilliard and Cruise ; Bacon on Uses ; Saunders on Uses and Trusts.

In General. With respect to equitable estates, it is a general maxim, that as between equities otherwise equal, the elder is preferred. Woods *v.* Dille, 11 Ohio, 455. Unless the former has so acted as to raise an estoppel in favor of the younger. Brown *v.* Kuhn, 40 Ohio State, 468. Thus a bill of peace by a patentee under a junior entry will not be sustained against an equitable title under a senior entry. Wallace *v.* Porter, 14 Ohio, 272. And see Nisewanger *v.* Wallace, 16 Ohio, 557. An equitable estate is descendible, and liable to be sold for payment of debts. Avery *v.* Dufrees, 9 Ohio, 145. Prior to the statute of 1810, a decree for a conveyance did not operate as a conveyance, but had to be enforced by attachment or sequestration. And this is still the case with decrees of the federal courts. Randall *v.* Pryor, 4 Ohio, 424 ; Shepherd *v.* Ross County, 7 Ohio, pt. 1, 271. An equitable title, even with possession, is no bar to an action of ejectment. Spencer *v.* Marckel, 2 Ohio, 263. It can only be enforced in equity. Barr *v.* Hatch, 3 Ohio, 527. This, of course, is not so now under the code. Powers *v.* Armstrong, 36 Ohio State, 357. But an equitable title with possession for more than twenty-one years is good, even in ejectment, against the naked legal title. Barton *v.* Morris, 15 Ohio, 408. So after an undisputed possession for forty years, an equitable title will be presumed against a naked legal title. Bierce *v.* Pierce, 15 Ohio, 529. Though a decree for a conveyance here operates as a conveyance, it is as between the parties subject to the contingency of reversal ; but not as to a purchaser before notice of proceedings to reverse. Taylor *v.* Boyd, 3 Ohio, 337.

Innocent Purchaser without Notice. This question cannot arise where neither party has the legal title. Woods *v.* Dille, 11 Ohio, 455 ; Anketel *v.* Converse, 17 Ohio State, 11 ; Elslner *v.* Fife, 32 Ohio State, 358. A mere volunteer or claimant on a past consideration cannot have the rights of a *bonâ fide* buyer as an assignee for the benefit of creditors. Morgan *v.* Kenney, 38 Ohio State, 610, 613 ; or judgment or execution lienholder. Sessions *v.* Trevitt, 39 id. 259 ; Page *v.* Thomas, 43 id. 38 ; but if the prior claim is a mere equity, as a defectively executed mortgage, a grantee for a past consideration holds free of it. Clements *v.* Doerner, 40 Ohio State, 632, 634. Recitals in a deed or patent are notice. Bell *v.* Duncan, 11 Ohio, 192 ; Mack *v.* Brammer, 28 Ohio State, 508 ; Seegar *v.* Harrison, 25 id. 14. Parties dealing with heirs in regard to descended lands, are chargeable with notice of the extent of their rights. Piatt *v.* St. Clair, 6 Ohio, 227. Notorious actual adverse possession is an answer to the plea of innocent purchaser, that being notice which would put a prudent man upon inquiry. House *v.* Beatty, 7 Ohio, 2 pt. 84 ; Reeder *v.* Barr, 4 Ohio, 446 ; Woodworth *v.* Paige, 5 Ohio State, 70 ; Williams *v.* Sprigg, 6 id. 585 ; Sternberger *v.* Hanna, 42 Ohio State, 305 ; Day *v.* R. R. Co., 41 id. 392 ; Morrison *v.* Kelly, 22 Ill. 610 ; 90 N. Y. 298 ; 18 Fla. 688 ; Warren *v.* Richmond, 53 Ill. 52 ; Hoppin *v.* Doty, 25 Wis. 573 ; Russell *v.* Streezy, 22 Mich. 235 ; Phillips *v.* Costley, 40 Ala. 486 ; Pell *v.* McElroy, 36 Cal. 268. Where real estate belonging to a partnership, but held in the name of one, is used for partnership purposes, this would doubtless be notice to a buyer from such partner of the rights of the firm. Notice of facts sufficient to put a reasonable man on inquiry is good. Baker *v.* Bliss, 39 N. Y. 70. The knowledge need not come from as courts of law can recognize and enforce. And in the earliest period of the English law, no other estates were known. But the

the claimant: it is sufficient if it come from any source worthy of credit. Butcher *v.* Yocum, 61 Penn. State, 168. The doctrine of notice does not apply to mortgages in Ohio, as they take effect against third parties only when recorded. Bloom *v.* Noggle, 4 Ohio State, 45; Sidle *v.* Maxwell, id. 236; Tousley *v.* Tousley, 5 id. 78; Erwin *v.* Shuey, 8 id. 509; Building Ass'n *v.* Clark, 43 id. 427. Nor can this plea protect a title originally defective against a better adverse title. McArthur *v.* Phœbus, 2 Ohio, 415. This doctrine of innocent purchaser applies to permanent leaseholds. Ludlow *v.* Kidd, 3 Ohio, 541; and to mortgagees not for past considerations. Farmer's Bk. *v.* Teeters, 31 Ohio State, 36. Where the legal title has been fraudulently obtained against a superior equity, and conveyed to an innocent purchaser without notice, redress can only be had against the party committing the fraud. Ludlow *v.* Kidd, 4 Ohio, 244; Booraem *v.* Wells, 4 Green, 87. To sustain the plea of innocent purchaser without notice, the purchase-money must have been paid in money or its equivalent: giving notes secured by mortgage is not sufficient. Haughwout *v.* Murphy, 21 N. J. Eq. 118; Bowen *v.* Prout, 52 Ill. 354. A purchaser with notice from a vendee without notice, will be protected. Ramsey *v.* Jones, 41 Ohio State, 685; Harrison *v.* Forth, 2 Prec. Ch. 51. A decree in chancery, curing a defective deed, is not notice to a purchaser under an attachment, not being party to the decree. Paine *v.* Mooreland, 15 Ohio, 435. And see Warner *v.* Webster, 13 Ohio, 505. A decree curing a defective mortgage is only effectual from its rendition as against third persons. Clements *v.* Doerner, 40 Ohio State, 632. A purchaser at a sheriff's sale, without notice of a secret equity, is protected, though he had notice before confirmation. Oviatt *v.* Brown, 14 Ohio, 285.

Title Bonds and Defective Deeds. It is not unusual to sell land, with an obligation to convey upon payment of the purchase-money, instead of executing a deed, and taking back a mortgage. This obligation must be in writing, to comply with the statute of frauds, and is usually in the shape of a title bond. Now this only conveys to the purchaser an equitable estate, even when the purchase-money has all been paid. And the same is true of an intended legal conveyance, which happens to lack any of the legal requisites of a deed. Accordingly, the equitable owner can only perfect his legal title by a decree in chancery for a deed, in the nature of a decree for specific performance of a contract to convey. And this may be had against the heirs of the vendor, if the title descends to them. But where the declaration is in covenant upon a title bond, and only the condition is relied upon, without the penal part, it is not a covenant. Huddle *v.* Worthington, 1 Ohio, 423. A vendor's lien arises only in case of an actual sale and does not exist where one holding land as security reconveys it to the debtor without payment. O'Connor *v.* Smith, 40 Ohio State, 214. Where land is sold by title bond and the vendee in possession, a judgment against the vendor will bind the land to the extent that the purchase-money remains unpaid. Lefferson *v.* Dallas, 20 Ohio State, 68. Such a vendee in possession has a superior equity to a subsequent purchaser from the vendor. Goings *v.* Allen, 4 Bush (Ky.), 608. Where the vendor under a title bond, after delivering possession to the vendee mortgages the land, subsequent payments of the purchase-money by the vendee to the vendor prior to a claim by the mortgagee's assertion of a right to receive them from the vendee will be protected. Ranney *v.* Hardy, 43 Ohio State, 157. A defective deed to a *bonâ fide* buyer creates an equity superior in merit to a vendor's lien. Hume *v.* Dixon, 37 Ohio State, 66.

Equitable Liens. The most common case of equitable lien is that of a vendor for the purchase-money. Although the vendee has obtained the legal title, yet if he has not paid for it, he is not in good conscience entitled to the absolute ownership. Accordingly the vendor retains a lien against the vendee, and all claiming under him *with notice.* But this is only when the vendor has done no act to indicate that he does not intend to rely upon the land, as by taking a mortgage upon only a part of the land, or by taking any collateral security. Williams *v.* Roberts, 5 Ohio, 35; Dietrich *v.* Folk, 40 Ohio State, 635; Shall *v.* Biscoe, 18 Ark. 142; McCarty *v.* Penet, 4 Ind. 226; Pierson *v.* David, 1 Clarke, 23; McAlpine *v.* Burnet, 19 Texas, 497; Gnash *v.* George, 58 Iowa, 492; Hett *v.* Collins, 103 Ill. 74; Boyer *v.* Austin, 75 Mo. 81. But see Stevens's Appeal, 38 Penn. State, 9; Follett *v.* Reese, 20 id. 551. But a lien dates from the date of the contract of sale, and subsequently taking a mortgage at the time of conveyance upon the property for the balance of the purchase-money will not defeat it. Neil *v.* Kinney, 11 Ohio State, 58; Anketel *v.* Converse, 17 Ohio State, 11; Wasson *v.* Davis, 34 Texas, 159. *Contra,* Pease *v.* Kelly, 3 Oregon, 417. But it has been institution of a court of chancery has given rise to another kind of estates, which may be denominated *equitable*, and which now

held in some States that even taking collateral security, though *primâ facie* a waiver, may be prevented from operating as such by an express agreement. Schwartz *v.* Stein, 29 Md. 112; McGonigal *v.* Plummer, 30 Md. 422; Adams *v.* Buchanan, 49 Mo. 64. In Illinois a distinction is taken where a lien is reserved in the deed of conveyance, and in such case the taking of other security will not waive the lien. Carpenter *v.* Mitchell, 54 Ill. 126. But the mere taking of notes or bonds of the vendee without endorsement does not rebut the lien. Gnash *v.* George, 58 Iowa, 492; Bradley *v.* Curtis, 79 Ky. 327; Whetsel *v.* Roberts, 31 Ohio State, 503; Chilton *v.* Braidlee, 2 Black, 458; Burger *v.* Potter, 32 Ill. 66; Walker *v.* Sedgwick, 8 Cal. 398; Griffin *v.* Blanchard, 17 Cal. 70; Buntin *v.* French, 16 N. H. 592. And there are cases where collateral security does not rebut the lien; namely, where the sale is by title bond, or contract to convey, the vendor retaining the legal title. Rogers *v.* Blum, 56 Tex. 1. This equitable lien of the vendor is superior to the right of dower in the widow of the vendee. Elliott *v.* Plattor, 43 Ohio State, 198. There is also what is called an equitable mortgage, which is where a debtor deposits his title deeds with a creditor as security for a debt. This was very common in England, but is rarely done here, if at all. It has been held that no lien is created in Ohio by such a deposit, though such is the declared intention. . Probasco *v.* Johnson, 2 Disney, 96. But it seems to be recognized in New Jersey. Griffin *v.* Griffin, 3 Green, 104. The vendor's lien is founded upon an implied trust between him and the vendee, and therefore does not pass to the assignee of a note given for the purchase-money. Jackman *v.* Hallock, 1 Ohio, 318; Brush *v.* Kinsley, 14 Ohio, 20. Keith *v.* Horner, 32 Ill. 524; Walker *v.* Williams, 30 Mo. 165; Shall *v.* Biscoe, 18 Ark. 142; Ross *v.* Heintzer, 31 Cal. 313. But see, *contra*, Kern *v.* Hazelrigg, 11 Ind. 443; Moore *v.* Raymond, 15 Texas, 554; Rakestraw *v.* Hamilton, 14 Iowa, 147; Griffin *v.* Camack, 36 Ala. 695; Lewis *v.* Pusey, 8 Bush, 615; Watt *v.* White, 33 Texas, 421; Wakefield *v.* Johnson, 26 Ark. 506. It may be preserved when assigned in terms, though not otherwise. Smith *v.* Smith, 9 Abb. Pr. (N. S.) 420; Hooper *v.* Logan, 23 Md. 201; Walsh *v.* Bagle, 30 Md. 262. When the lien is expressly reserved in the deed of conveyance, it will pass by the assignment of the right to receive the purchase-money. Carpenter *v.* Mitchell, 54 Ill. 126. Nor will this lien pass by a sheriff's sale, so that the purchaser can set it up against the widow's dower. McArthur *v.* Porter, 1 Ohio, 99. The vendor does not extinguish his lien simply by taking a mortgage; and therefore it will have priority over a judgment between the date and recording of the mortgage. Boos *v.* Ewing, 17 Ohio, 500; Anketel *v.* Converse, 17 Ohio State, 11. Even though the mortgage be on other property. Elliott *v.* Plattor, 43 Ohio State, 198. *Contra*, Harris *v.* Harlan, 14 Ind. 439; Mattix *v.* Weand, 19 Ind. 151; Selby *v.* Stanley, 4 Minn. 65. Where a guardian has given a lien upon rents to improve his ward's land, this will hold good against a paramount title purchased by the ward when of age. Este *v.* Strong, 2 Ohio, 401. The advancement of money to pay an intestate's debts creates no equitable lien on the property descended to his heirs. Lieby *v.* Parks, 4 Ohio, 469. But a vendor's lien will pass by devise along with the legal title. Tiernan *v.* Beam, 2 Ohio, 383. Where several tracts have descended to heirs, subject to the debts of the ancestor, some of which have been aliened by the heirs, equity will compel the creditors to exhaust first those which have not been aliened; and as to those which have been aliened, to begin with the last and proceed back in regular order. Piatt *v.* St. Clair, 6 Ohio, 227. The vendor's lien is preferred to that of a judgment without notice, and to that of a mortgage with notice. Patterson *v.* Johnson, 7 Ohio, 1 pt. 225. Where one creditor has a lien upon only one fund, and another has a lien upon two, the former may compel the latter to exhaust the fund upon which he has no lien. Bank of Musk. *v.* Carpenter, 7 Ohio, 1 pt. 21; Fassett *v.* Traber, 20 Ohio, 540; Sternberger *v.* Hanna, 42 Ohio State, 305. In Kentucky, by statute, the vendor's lien does not exist unless reserved in the deed. 2 Stanton's Rev. St. 230; Maupin *v.* McCormack, 2 Bush, 206. It has there become a common method of securing unpaid balances of purchase-money instead of taking back a mortgage. It is not lost by renewing notes. Lush *v.* Hopper, 3 Bush, 179. What is a sufficient reservation in the deed, see Keith *v.* Wolf, 5 Bush, 646; Ledford *v.* Smith, 6 Bush, 127. If the reservation was omitted by mistake, it may be corrected. Phillip *v.* Skinner, 6 Bush, 662. In Kansas the lien is not recognized at all. Simpson *v.* Munder, 3 Kans. 172; Brown *v.* Simpson, 4 Kans. 76.

Uses and Trusts. If the English statute of uses was ever in force here, it became so by the territorial law of 1795, or by the State law of 1805, which were repealed by the law of 1806. 1 Chase, Stat. 190, 512, 528. Since then, it certainly has not been occupy a very important place in the law of realty. It is not common in the books, to find such a title as *equitable estates;* but I have selected it for the purposes of discussing a variety of rules relating to property, which could not well be embraced under any other head; and which are essential to a proper understanding of this branch of law. By an equitable estate is meant any right or interest in land, which not having the properties of a legal estate, requires the aid of a court of chancery to make it available. What are the requisites of a legal estate will be explained hereafter. It may be laid down in the mean time as a general proposition, that whenever one man has a legal title to land, to which another, on the established principles of equity, has a right, the latter may, by recourse to a court of chancery, render his equitable title available against the legal title. In all such cases, the owner of the legal estate is held to be a *trustee* for the owner of the equitable estate; and chancery will compel him to execute the *trust*, for the *use* of the latter. Hence equitable estates have acquired the name of *uses* or *trusts;* under which name their properties will now be considered.

§ 151. **Origin of Uses and Trusts.** (*a*) In the civil law, a distinction existed between a right to enjoy the rents and profits of land, and a right of property in the land itself; and thus one person might have the naked legal ownership, while the whole beneficial interest belonged to another. In the early part of the fourteenth century, this distinction was introduced into the English law through ecclesiastical influence. The efforts of the church to enrich itself by the acquisition of lands had been opposed by a series of statutes, known as the *statutes of mortmain*, (*b*) the object

in force. Helfenstine *v.* Garrard, 7 Ohio, 1 pt. 275; Thompson *v.* Gibson, 2 Ohio, 339. This statute is commonly referred to as 27 Henry the 8th, chap. 10. The doctrine of charitable uses has been recognized in the case of Bryant *v.* McCandless, 7 Ohio, 2 pt. 135, where certain persons calling themselves the Licking Land Company, in making partition, appropriated sundry tracts "to be a perpetual fund for the support of the ministration of the gospel on the premises of the company," but created no trustee or donee. After thirty years, the legislature appointed a trustee, and the dedication was sustained. And see McIntire *v.* Zanesville, 9 Ohio, 203; McIntyre's Adm'rs *v.* Zanesville, 17 Ohio State, 352; Girard *v.* Philadelphia, 7 Wall. 1. Where a trust was created in Virginia, of lands in Ohio, and, on the death of the trustee, his place was supplied by appointment of the Virginia court of chancery, it was held that the conveyances of the second trustee could not be recognized here. Henry *v.* Doctor, 9 Ohio, 49. Where a conveyance in trust is fraudulent, it may be set aside in chancery, without making the beneficiaries parties. Campbell *v.* Watson, 8 Ohio, 498. The obligations of a trustee of lands descend to his heirs, and if infants, they must have a guardian *ad litem* duly appointed and notified. St. Clair *v.* Smith, 3 Ohio, 355. As to trusts for religious societies, see Price *v.* Methodist Church, 4 Ohio, 515; Keyser *v.* Stansifer, 6 Ohio, 363; Smith *v.* Swormstedt, 16 How. 288; The Dublin Case, 38 N. H., 459; Att'y-Gen. *v.* Proprietors of Meeting-house, &c., 3 Gray, 1.

(*a*) 2 Black. Com. 327, 332. Religious societies are authorized under order of court to convey their real estate by act of March 24, 1860.

(*b*) Id. 268. In Ohio R. S., § 5915, is the only statute of mortmain, and provides that a gift or devise to charitable, &c., purposes by a person leaving issue or an adopted child shall be void unless the instrument was made at least a year prior to the donor's decease. Such bequest is not valid by being made contingent on the extinction of lineal descendants. Patton *v.* Patton, 39 Ohio State, 590.

of which was, to disable religious corporations from receiving conveyances of real estate. But these various restrictions related to legal estates only; and to avoid their effect, recourse was had by the clergy to the above distinction made in the civil law. Conveyances, therefore, instead of being made directly to the church, were made to individuals, with the understanding that the church was to have the beneficial enjoyment. This usufructuary or beneficial interest, thus separated from the legal ownership, was denominated *use;* and the court of chancery, then directed by the clergy, assumed the entire jurisdiction of *uses*, on the ground that they were exclusively matters of *conscience*, and not of law. By degrees, therefore, under the decision of shrewd and interested chancellors, the doctrine of uses grew up into a regular and established system. For various reasons, the *use* of land thus severed from the *legal ownership*, was deemed a more beneficial estate than where both the use and the legal title were united. It was discharged from all the feudal burdens; was not liable to forfeiture for treason; and could be transferred from hand to hand, without the tedious formalities of the common law. For these and other reasons, individuals who were not within the statutes of mortmain, entertained a decided preference to uses over legal estates. The consequence was that by the end of the fifteenth century, a large proportion of the real property of the kingdom was incumbered in this complicated and double manner; one person having the legal estate and another the use. This state of things gave rise to a series of legislative acts, which ended with the enactment, in 1536, of the celebrated *statute of uses*, of which some account must now be given. The intention of this statute was to destroy the double property in land, which had resulted from the introduction of uses; not by destroying the use, but by changing it from an equitable into a legal estate. Accordingly, it was enacted in substance, that whenever one person was *seised* of land for the use of another, he who had the use, should *ipso facto* have a legal estate of the same measure and quality. Wherever this statute could operate, therefore, its effect was to abolish the intervening legal estate, by annexing it to the use and making that a legal estate; and had the language of the statute been as comprehensive and explicit as its object required, the court of chancery would have been completely deprived of its jurisdiction over real property, which was the main motive of the provision. But this effect was not produced; and after a long and severe contest between the courts of law and chancery, the doctrines of *uses* were revived under the name of *trusts*. The great preliminary question under the statute was, whether the statute *executed the use;* that is, converted it into a legal estate. If it did, the jurisdiction belonged to the courts of law, if not, to the courts of chancery. Of the manner in which the object of the statute was thus defeated, I can speak but briefly. In the first place, it did not in its letter, include *estates for years*, but only *freeholds;* and of course *trust terms* to any length could be created to evade it. But a more effectual mode of evasion was this: A conveyance was made to A. for the use of B., in trust for C. The statute was construed as only transferring the legal estate from A. to B. Here its operation terminated. B. then took the legal estate in trust for C.; which trust the court of chancery stood ready to enforce. And thus, after a series of protracted and bitter discussions, a statute from which so much had been expected, resulted only in changing the name of an equitable interest from *use to trust.* But, happily for us, the mass of learning connected with this statute has here no other than a speculative interest; for if it was ever in force in this State, it certainly has not been in force since 1806. The question arose in one case, (*a*) and the court was divided in opinion; two of the judges holding that the statute was in force here from 1795 to 1806, and two holding that it never was in force. But whatever opinion may be formed on this point, it is admitted on all hands, that the statute has not been in force here since 1806; and this is enough for our purpose; for the important consequence follows, that we retain the original doctrines of uses as settled in chancery, without any of the subsequent doctrines derived from the statute. In other words, uses and trusts are here synonymous terms, and belong exclusively to chancery jurisdiction. We shall see hereafter, that our only conveyances are those which originated under the statute of uses; but in all other respects, our law of real property is the same as if that statute had never been enacted. I shall consider equitable estates under two heads, *express trusts* and *implied trusts;* confining myself to a very general outline of their nature and properties.

§ 152. **Express Trusts.** (*b*) Our *statute of frauds,* which will be considered hereafter, requires all transactions relating to land, to be expressed in writing. The English statute of frauds contained a special exception in regard to trusts. Our statute does not make this exception, but it is held to be implied. The doctrine is so universal, that *implied trusts* will be enforced in equity, that without citing authorities to prove it, I shall take it for granted; and shall therefore speak of *express trusts as a distinct class.* In the creation of every express trust, three parties are concerned: *first,* the person who creates the trust, and who is called the *grantor; secondly,* the person who is to execute the trust, and

(*a*) Thompson *v.* Gibson, 2 Ohio, Rep. 339; Helfenstine *v.* Garrard, 7 Ohio, 1 pt. 275.

(*b*) To establish an express trust in the case of a conveyance by deed absolute on its face, the evidence of such trust, and of its terms and conditions, must be clear and conclusive, and when made in consideration of love and affection, it is repugnant to the existence of the trust. Miller *v.* Stokely, 5 Ohio State, 194. A sale by a trustee will be held a breach of the conditions of the trust-deed only where the purposes of the trust are clearly shown to be inconsistent with the exercise of such a power. Stall *v.* Cincinnati, 16 Ohio State, 169. The general doctrine is, that an express trust cannot be created by parol. Cook *v.* Barr, 44 N. Y. 156; Smith *v.* Hollenback, 51 Ill. 223. But Ryan *v.* O'Connor, 41 Ohio State, 368, and Harvey *v.* Gardner, 41 Ohio State, 642, seem to settle for Ohio that an express trust can be established by parol evidence. In Kentucky, it seems that it may be. Barkley *v.* Lane, 6 Bush, 587.

who is called the *trustee; thirdly*, the person for whose benefit the trust is made, and who has been designated by the awkward phrase of *cestui que trust;* in the place of which I shall substitute the term *beneficiary*. The parties will then be grantor, trustee, and beneficiary. With these explanations, I proceed to a summary description of the leading properties of express trusts.

1. Express trusts are usually declared in the same instrument which creates the legal estate: but this is not always the case. Land may be conveyed to a trustee upon such trusts as the grantor, or some other person named in the conveyance, shall afterwards declare; and in either case the trustee will hold the land subject to these future declarations.

2. All persons may convey land in trust, who are capable of making a deed or will. Who these are will be pointed out hereafter.

3. All persons may be made trustees, not excepting infants or married women; because the mere capacity of being a trustee involves nothing more than the capacity of receiving a legal conveyance. It is obvious, indeed, that there may be certain acts required in the execution of a trust, to which persons under disability would not be legally competent in their own right. But in such cases, the power conferred by the grantor gives the trustee a capacity which the law does not give; for example, in the execution of a trust, an infant, or a married woman without her husband, may make a valid conveyance.

4. All persons without exception may be beneficiaries; since no disability whatever can disqualify one for enjoying the benefit of a trust properly created.

5. Every description of property, real or personal, is capable of being settled in trust; there being no valuable thing which one man may not hold for the benefit of another.

6. Express trusts of realty, when properly created, attach to the land itself, and not merely to the person of the trustee. Therefore, if a proper trustee should be afterwards wanted, chancery will see that the trust is executed by any person having a legal title to the land.

7. Trust estates are in all valuable respects as beneficial as legal estates. Where the contrary is not expressly provided, they are in like manner alienable, devisable, and descendible. They cannot indeed be sold on execution; but they may be made liable for debts by analogous proceedings in chancery, which will be explained hereafter. They are also equally liable to curtesy and dower. Formerly, by force of some early and arbitrary decisions, they were not liable in any case to dower, but this distinction does not exist here.

8. Trust estates may not only be limited in remainder to the same extent as legal estates, but owing to what may be called their flexibility or elasticity, they are susceptible of a much greater variety of future provisions. For while the legal estate

continues in the same trustees, the beneficial interests may be made to shift from hand to hand, almost at the pleasure of the grantor. Thus, he may omit to declare the trust at first, and reserve to himself or others the right of future appointment in such manner as he chooses; or he may declare a trust at first, subject to future revocation, and may afterwards revoke the trust, and declare a new one; or he may declare trusts to arise of themselves, upon future contingencies, reserving the enjoyment of them to himself in the mean time; or, lastly, he may declare trusts to take effect immediately, and yet be capable of changing of themselves, from hand to hand, according to future events.

9. The abuse of this power to create trusts, is provided against by our *statute of frauds*, which declares void all trust conveyances made to defraud creditors and purchasers; and by our statute against *perpetuities*, which prohibits the limitation of any estate further than to persons in being and their immediate issue.

10. Though *trustees* (*a*) have the legal title to the trust property, it is not subject to their debts, nor to dower and curtesy in their hands. They cannot convey or incumber it for their own use, except in the single case where the purchaser has no notice of the trust either actual or constructive; and this cannot happen where the trust is expressed, because then the record is constructive notice to everybody. The general principle is, that the trustee can do nothing that can prejudice the interest of the beneficiary; and the reason of the above exception is, that he who appoints a trustee holds him out to the world as a trustworthy person; and if, in violation of the confidence and credit thus given him, he sell or incumber the land, for a valuable consideration, to a person having no notice of the trust, the innocent purchaser will hold it discharged of the trust; and the beneficiary must seek his redress from the trustee in whom his benefactor reposed the first confidence. But if the purchaser either paid no consideration, or had notice of the trust, either actual or constructive, he puts himself in the place of the trustee, and still holds the land subject to the trust. For the protection of beneficiaries, it is an established rule that where the declared trust is to sell the land for the payment of specified debts or legacies, the purchaser is bound to see the money applied to the specified purposes; though it is otherwise if the trust be to pay debts generally, without any specification, because then the purchaser cannot know

(*a*) See Thompson on Trustees; Willis on Trustees; Fletcher on Estates of Trustees; Hill on Trustees; Lewin on Trusts; Perry on Trusts. A sale of the trust property to the trustee may be set aside by the *cestui que trust*, without showing fraud or actual injury. Barrington *v.* Alexander, 6 Ohio State, 189; Piatt *v.* Longworth, 27 id. 159; Cox *v.* John, 32 id. 532; Rammelsburg *v.* Mitchell, 29 id. 22. So where a trustee holding a mortgage for the estate bought in the property at foreclosure, his vendee with notice holds subject to the *cestui's* rights. Holgate *v.* Eaton, 116 U. S. 33. It is voidable at the election of the *cestui que trust.* Huff *v.* Earl, 3 Ind. 306. This rule has been held not to apply where a sale is made by a public officer under a proceeding adverse to the *cestui que trust*, and the trustee has no means to prevent the sale. Chorpenning's Appeal, 32 Penn. State, 315.

what they are. So far as the powers and duties of the trustees are pointed out in the deed, they are bound to follow them to the letter. A power to sell land, for example, does not include a power to barter or exchange it for other land; though it may include a power to mortgage or lease it, when the intention is merely to raise money for certain purposes. But where a trust is simply created for the benefit of another, without any specific directions, the duties which chancery will enforce upon the trustee are chiefly three: *first*, to permit the beneficiary to receive the rents and profits; *secondly*, to execute such conveyances as the beneficiary shall direct; *thirdly*, to defend the title when this is necessary. And, as a general principle, the trustee can make no profit from his management of trust property. His necessary expenses are of course allowed, but he can charge nothing for his care and trouble, unless by express provision in the instrument. This severe rule is deemed necessary for the protection of the beneficiary. (*a*) Trustees are accountable in chancery for their conduct; and when the circumstances require it, they may be removed and others appointed. (*b*) If there be several, they must all act together, unless there be express provision to the contrary; and if one improperly refuse to unite with the others, he will be compelled to resign. (*c*)

11. The republican habits of our citizens being opposed to complicated family settlements, we have very few express trusts created by deed, though they occasionally occur. But trusts created by will are more frequent. The leading motive for creating a trust is to prevent property from being improvidently squandered. If a father wishes to provide with certainty for a child about to marry, and for the issue of such marriage, instead of conveying property to the child directly, he conveys it to trustees, with a declaration of his wishes; and thus while he gives the annual income to the married couple, he secures the principal to their children. In like manner, if a man wishes to guard with certainty against the prodigality of his heirs, he devises his property to trustees, with specific instructions; and thus limits the power of his heirs, as far as he considers expedient. (*d*) These examples will serve for illustra-

(*a*) Richardson *v.* Spencer, 18 B. Monroe, 450; Warbass *v.* Armstrong, 2 Stockton, 263.

(*b*) Gilbert *v.* Sutliff, 3 Ohio State, 129; Montpelier *v.* East Montpelier, 29 Vt. 12; Bliss *v.* Am. Bible Society, 2 Allen, 334. A trustee, in doubt as to his powers, may apply to a court of equity to define them. Wiswell *v.* First Congregational Church, 14 Ohio State, 31; 29 Ohio State, 147; 25 Ohio State, 128; 35 Ohio State, 503. Trustees acting in good faith, and with reasonable care, are not responsible for losses. They may be excused even for ignorance of law, where they acted under the advice of counsel. Miller *v.* Proctor, 20 Ohio State, 442.

(*c*) Sloo *v.* Law, 3 Blatch. C. C. 459. But in the case of a public trust the rule is, that a majority of the trustees can act, unless some other rule be pointed out in the instrument. Ibid.

(*d*) But a trust estate cannot be made incapable of alienation by the beneficiary, nor prevented from becoming liable for the payment of his debts. "It is a settled rule of law that the beneficial interest of the *cestui que trust*, whatever it may be, is liable for the payment of his debts. It cannot be so fenced about by inhibitions or tion; and a little reflection will convince any one of the very great utility of this description of estates.

§ 153. **Implied Trusts.** (*a*) Implied trusts, as their name imports, are those which result from the established doctrines of equity, without any declaration by the parties. They are sometimes called *resulting trusts*, and are chiefly upheld to prevent fraud. In most cases, the question whether there be an implied trust or not, depends upon circumstances connected with the consideration of real contracts. The following are the cases in which implied trusts have been most generally sustained: —

1. If I purchase land, and take the title in my own name, but you pay the consideration, I become thereby a trustee for you. (*b*)

restrictions as to secure to it the inconsistent characteristics of right to enjoyment by the beneficiary and immunity from his creditors. A condition precedent that the provision shall not vest until his debts are paid, and a condition subsequent that it shall be divested and forfeited by his insolvency, with a limitation over to another person, are valid, and the law will give them full effect. Beyond this, protection from the claims of creditors is not allowed to go." Swayne, J., in Nichols *v.* Levy, 5 Wall. 441. This is altered by statute in Tennessee. Nichols *v.* Levy, *supra;* Turney *v.* Massingill, 7 Lea, 353. In Pennsylvania, Massachusetts, and Kentucky, where the doctrine of spendthrift trusts obtains, such a provision is allowed if the beneficiary is entirely excluded from control of the fund. Broadway Bank *v.* Adams, 133 Mass. 170; Vaux *v.* Parke, 7 W. & S. 19; Pope *v.* Elliott, 8 B. Monr. 56. In New York, the court will leave him a reasonable sum for support, and so in several States by statute. Genet *v.* Beckman, 45 Barb. 382; Campbell *v.* Foster, 35 N. Y. 361; Adams, Eq. *43; Perry on Trusts, § 386. This doctrine is examined and all the cases given in Gray on Restraints on Alienation. The only exceptions to this rule are the separate use and pin-money trusts for married women. Adams, Eq. *43; Perry on Trusts, § 387.

(*a*) Barr *v.* Hatch, 3 Ohio R. 527; Bond *v.* Swearingen, 1 Ohio R. 395, 411; M'Arthur *v.* Porter, 1 Ohio R. 99; Williams *v.* Roberts, 5 Ohio R. 35; 2 Story on Equity, ch. 32; Capen *v.* Richardson, 7 Gray, 364. A *bonâ fide* purchaser of a land warrant, without notice that a previous assignment was forged, who had located it and received a patent for the land, will not be declared a trustee for the true owner of the warrant. The addition of the legal title to his equity will prevail; but had the true owner brought suit before the patent was obtained, his older equity would have been superior. Dixon *v.* Caldwell, 15 Ohio State, 412. Parol evidence is competent to establish a resulting trust. Byers *v.* Wackman, 16 Ohio State, 441; Swinburne *v.* Swinburne, 28 N. Y. 568; Collins *v.* Smith, 18 Ill. 160; McGinity *v.* McGinity, 63 Penn. State, 38; Farris *v.* Dunn, 7 Bush, 276; Caldwell *v.* Caldwell, 7 Bush, 515. But it must be very clear. Witts *v.* Harney, 59 Md. 584; Noel *v.* Noel, 1 Clarke, 423; Kendall *v.* Mann, 11 Allen, 15.

Resulting trusts are only raised in cases of frauds, or by the payment of the purchase-money at the time the title is acquired. Subsequent payment is not sufficient. Barnet *v.* Dougherty, 32 Penn. State, 371; Kelly *v.* Johnson, 28 Miss. 249; Francistown *v.* Deering, 41 N. H. 438; Kellum *v.* Smith, 33 Penn. State, 158; Rothwell *v.* Dewees, 2 Black, 613; Barnard *v.* Jewett, 97 Mass. 87. Though the implication of a resulting trust may be rebutted by proof of a contrary intent, it will not be controlled by proof of an intent which is fraudulent. Hutchins *v.* Heywood, 50 N. H. 491.

The mere contribution of a part of the purchase-money is not sufficient; it must be some definitely ascertainable aliquot part of the purchase-money. Reynolds *v.* Morris, 17 Ohio State, 510; McGowan *v.* McGowan, 14 Gray, 119; Cutter *v.* Tuttle, 4 Green, 549.

(*b*) But the mere fact that the consideration paid for land was borrowed by the grantee for that purpose, does not make him a trustee for the lender. Whaley *v.* Whaley, 71 Ala. 159. When the husband takes the title of land purchased with the wife's separate money in his own name in whole or in part without her consent, a trust results to her *pro tanto*. McGovern *v.* Knox, 21 Ohio State, 547; Sessions *v.* Trevitt, 39 id. 259; Newton *v.* Taylor, 32 id. 399. In Kentucky, by statute, when one person accepts a deed of land at the request of another who has paid the consideration, no trust results in favor of the latter. Martin *v.* Martin, 5 Bush, 47.

2. If, being already your general trustee, I purchase land in my own name with money belonging to you, I hold this land as trustee for you.

3. If I convey land to you without any consideration, you become a trustee for me. (*a*)

4. If I contract with you for the purchase of real estate, by title bond, or otherwise, you thereby become a trustee for me, until the legal conveyance is made. And the same is true, if through a mistake you make me a defective conveyance. You hold the legal title in trust to me, until a good conveyance is made.

5. If I convey land to you when I have not the legal title, and afterwards acquire the legal title, I hold it in trust for you, and the same doctrine extends to my heirs taking by descent from me.

6. If I convey land to you, and take no collateral security for the payment of the purchase-money, you become a trustee for me, until the purchase-money is paid. But it is otherwise, if I do any thing to manifest an intention not to rely upon the land for security. This is called an *equitable lien.*

7. If I, being your debtor, deposit my title-deeds with you, I thereby become a trustee for you until the debt is paid. This is called an *equitable mortgage*, but it is of little consequence in this country, owing to the difficulty of affecting another claimant with notice of such deposit.

8. If I convey land to a trustee, and declare the trust as to a part, there is a resulting trust to me for the residue. If the conveyance be upon such trusts as I shall afterwards declare, and I fail to declare them, there is a resulting trust to me for the whole. And, generally, if I create a trust for any particular purpose, there is a resulting trust to me as soon as that purpose is accomplished.

9. The only apparent exception to the above doctrines is in transactions between parents and children. If I purchase land in the name of my infant child, though I take the profits during his minority, there is no resulting trust to me, but the purchase will be treated as an *advancement* to the child, because blood is a sufficient consideration in such cases, and my taking the rents and profits during his minority only implies that I act as a guardian. (*b*) And the same is true, where a husband purchases

(*a*) But see concurring opinion of Welch, J., in Thompson *v.* Thompson, 17 Ohio State, 649, 662, in which he maintains that no consideration is necessary in fact, nor need any be stated to constitute an absolute conveyance. In New Jersey, when the deed expresses a consideration, though merely nominal, and never paid, no trust results, nor can it be shown by parol that such was the intention of the parties. Hogan *v.* Jaques, 4 Green, 123.

(*b*) Creed *v.* Lancaster Bank, 1 Ohio State, 1; Vanzant *v.* Davies, 6 id. 52; Wheeler *v.* Kidder, 105 Penn. State, 270; James *v.* James, 41 Ark. 301; Tremper *v.* Barton, 18 Ohio, 418; Dickenson *v.* Davis, 43 N. H. 647; Mutual Ins. Co. *v.* Deal, 18 Md. 26; Russ *v.* Mevius, 16 Cal. 350. So, too, if the deed is taken in the name of a son-in-law. Baker *v.* Leathers, 3 Ind. 558. Nor will a trust result on a conveyance to a son-in-law. When such a conveyance is made in consideration of the "natural love and in the name of his wife. (*a*) But an adult child under similar circumstances might be treated as a trustee for his father.

affection" of the grantor for her daughter and the grantee, and for the purpose of "advancing" the grantee "in life," no trust is created in favor of the daughter. Thompson *v.* Thompson, 18 Ohio State, 73; Mosely *v.* Mosely, 87 N. Ca. 89. But cf. Creswell *v.* Jones, 68 Ala. 420. But the presumption that it is intended as an advancement, may be rebutted by evidence. Browne *v.* Burke, 22 Geo. 574; Hodgson *v.* Macy, 8 Ind. 121. Woolery *v.* Woolery, 29 Ind. 249; McCaw *v.* Busk, 31 Ind. 56. A mere preponderance of testimony is sufficient. Middleton *v.* Middleton, 81 Iowa, 151. The partial disposition of an estate by will, does not exclude the operation of the Ohio statute as to advancements in the distribution of the intestate residuum. Dittoe *v.* Cluney, 22 Ohio State, 436; Peer *v.* Peer, 3 Stockton, 243. An implied or resulting trust cannot be shown against an absolute deed in consideration of love and affection. Miller *v.* Stokely, 5 Ohio State, 194; Farringdon *v.* Barr, 36 N. H. 86.

An executed trust is one the terms of which are fully and completely declared. An executory trust is one which is indicated or sketched, but the terms of which are to be finally and completely declared by another instrument. An executed trust may be created, passing a vested irrevocable interest to the *cestui que trust*, without the knowledge of either the trustee or the *cestui que trust*. Fletcher *v.* Fletcher, 4 Hare, 67; *In re* Way's Trust, 2 De Gex, J. & S. 365; Brown *v.* Winthrop, 1 John. Chy. 330; Mann *v.* Coates, 109 Mass. 581.

An assignee for the benefit of creditors is in England merely an agent appointed by the debtor for the management of the debtor's business. Such an assignment is therefore revocable by the debtor at any time before the creditors express their assent to it. In the United States such an assignment is a conveyance of property in trust, and, if accepted by the assignee, is irrevocable without the consent of the *cestuis que trust*, i. e., the creditors.

An ordinary trust must be certain and definite in the designation of the beneficiaries, so that they may be able to assert their rights in court. If the declaration of trust is uncertain in this particular, the trust is invalid and fails. A charitable trust, on the other hand, designates only the class of persons, not the individuals, who are to receive the bounty. "A charity is a gift to be applied, consistently with existing laws, for the benefit of an indefinite number of persons, either by bringing their minds and hearts under the influence of education or religion, by relieving their bodies from disease, suffering, or constraint, by assisting them to establish themselves in life, by erecting or maintaining public buildings or works, or otherwise lessening the burdens of government." Jackson *v.* Phillips, 14 Allen, 539.

The rules of English chancery are extremely liberal in sustaining charitable bequests. Where property is left directly to indefinite persons without the intervention of a trustee (Attorney-General *v.* Powell, 3 Merivale, 48), or to such charity as is designated in another paper, and no such paper is found or is proved ever to have been written (Attorney-General *v.* Syderfin, 1 Vern. 224), or to such charity as my executor shall designate, and the executor dies before the testator (Moggridge *v.* Thackwell, 7 Ves. 36), a scheme for a charitable trust to utilize the bequest will be determined. If the charity cannot be established or contrived in the mode prescribed by the testator, because such mode is illegal or impracticable, the property will be given to a charity *cy près*, i. e., as near as may be, the one proposed by the testator. Where property was bequeathed for the maintenance of religion, but a form of religion prohibited by law, it was given by sign-manual to the Established Church. Baxter's Case, 1 Vern. 248; Da Costa *v.* De Pas, 1 Ambler, 228, 2 Swans. 489, note; Isaac *v.* Gompertz, Ambler (Blunt's ed.), 228, note. A bequest of funds being made to supply beer to the inmates of a poor-house where the use of beer was illegal, the chancellor decreed it to be held by the rector of the parish to supply the inmates of the poor-house with tea, sugar, &c. Attorney-General *v.* Vint, 3 DeG. & Sm. 704. Where a fund was left to provide for the ransom of Christian captives from the Barbary States, and, in the course of time, piracy being swept from the Mediterranean, the object of the charity became extinct, the chancellor directed the fund to be appropriated to other charities for which provision had been made by the testator. Attorney-General *v.* Ironmongers' Co., 2 M. & Keene, 576.

In the United States it was for a time supposed that chancery derived its authority from the statute of 43 Elizabeth, which created boards of commissioners, with super-

(*a*) Seibold *v.* Christmas, 75 Mo. 308.

10. As the evidence upon which an implied trust is set up must be parol evidence, so parol evidence is admissible to rebut the equitable presumption of a trust, by showing either from words or actions what was the actual intention of the parties.

11. Implied trusts are much less safe than express trusts, because there is no such thing as constructive notice with respect to them. Perchasers can only be affected by proof of actual notice of the facts which create the implied trusts. This circumstance renders the interest of him to whom the implied trust results a very precarious one.

It only remains to be observed on the general subject of equitable estates, that the dividing line between them and legal estates is as distinctly observed in Ohio as in any other place. (*a*) They cannot be sold on execution; nor taken advantage of in an action of ejectment. In a word, courts of law will not take notice of them; and they are left exclusively to the cognizance of chancery. The policy of keeping up this distinction of jurisdictions has been

visory powers over such trusts. And as in some States this statute was held to be in force as part of the common law, in others it was held not to be in force in this country, and in others it was expressly repealed by statute, so in some States the courts were held to possess all the judicial authority over charitable bequests that was exercised by the chancellor in England, while in other States it was held the same rules must be applied to charities that apply to other trusts. This diversity of ruling still exists, though the supposition on which it was based has been ascertained to be unfounded.

Where a charity is general and the testator neither prescribes a plan or scheme, nor authorizes any one to do so, no case arises for the exercise of judicial authority. In England, a plan or scheme will be devised by exercise of prerogative, either by the king, under his sign-manual, or by the chancellor representing the king. American courts, having only judicial power, cannot establish a trust in such cases, but the bequest fails. In Kentucky, however, where the court inferred that the will gave the executors power to devise a scheme, it was held that the court would do so if the executors failed to act. Attorney-General *v.* Wallace, 7 B. Monroe, 611. In Virginia and Maryland a charity cannot be established unless it comes within the rules of private trusts. Rizer *v.* Perry, 58 Md. 112. The later decisions in Indiana and Wisconsin hold substantially the same. Erskine *v.* Whitehead, 84 Ind. 357; Ruth *v.* Overbrunner, 40 Wis. 228; Heiss Ex'r *v.* Murphy, 40 Wis. 276. In New York the matter is strictly regulated by statute. But in most of the States a charitable trust, as defined in Jackson *v.* Phillips, will be upheld; and where property is left to such charitable trusts as a designated person or body shall declare, the trust becomes effective upon such declaration being made; and an executory devise of land for such purpose to a corporation to be created *in futuro* will be sustained if the corporation be formed within a reasonable time. This view has been fully adopted by the Supreme Court of the United States in Ould *v.* The Washington Hospital for Foundlings, 95 U. S. 303; Jones *v.* Habersham, 107 U. S. 174; Russell *v.* Allen, 107 U. S. 163; Simpson *v.* Welcome, 72 Me. 496.

The doctrine of *cy près*, as held in the United States, is defined by the Court of Appeals of Kentucky, in Moore's Heirs *v.* Moore's Devisees, 4 Dana, 366; "Where there is an available charity to an identified or ascertainable object, and a particular mode, inadequate, illegal, or inappropriate, or which happens to fail, has been prescribed, a court of equity may prescribe or sanction any other mode that may be lawful and suitable, and will effectuate the declared intention of the donor." Examples of the application of this rule are: Jackson *v.* Phillips, 14 Allen, 359; and McIntire's Adm'rs *v.* Zanesville, 17 Ohio State, 352. But the authorities are variant as to what degree of vagueness in the objects will defeat a charity.

For the topic of Charitable Trusts, see Tudor on Charitable Uses, Perry on Trusts, vol. ii., and the masterly opinion of Justice Gray in Jackson *v.* Phillips.

(*a*) Roads *v.* Symmes, 1 Ohio R. 281, 314; Spencer *v.* Marckel, 2 Ohio R. 263; Moore *v.* Burnet, 11 Ohio, 234.

sometimes questioned. It is agreed on all hands that the *legal doctrines* alone would form a very imperfect system of land law, and the same is true of the *equitable doctrines* taken by themselves. But it is an important question, whether by a combination of the two into one entire and regular system, to be administered by the same tribunal, the body of land law would not be greatly improved. I merely state this for your consideration, having no time to discuss the subject. My hope is that this is among the great reforms towards which public sentiment is now tending.

For the sake of simplicity, the foregoing remarks have related exclusively to realty. But trusts may be created of personalty, to the same extent, and nearly on the same principles, as of realty. In fact, courts of chancery, for the purpose of giving complete effect to settlements in trust for any of the purposes aforementioned, will sometimes virtually reverse the distinctions between the two kinds of property, by treating realty as personalty, and personalty as realty. From the nature of personalty, moreover, it must be obvious, that where infants or married women are concerned, the best way to secure personalty for them, so that they may be certain of enjoying the proceeds, is to place it in the hands of trustees. We have seen that the guardian or husband has only a limited power over realty; but with regard to personalty it is nearly absolute; and therefore the motives for creating trusts of the latter are often stronger than with respect to the former.

LECTURE XXVII.

TITLE BY OCCUPANCY.

§ 154. **What constitutes Title.** (*a*) Having finished our view of the various kinds of estates, I am now to consider the different methods of acquiring *title* to property. According to Blackstone, there are three gradations of title: namely, first, mere possession without right; secondly, the right of possession, which may be enforced by action; thirdly, the absolute right of property without possession or the present right of possession; and a perfect title consists in the union of these three gradations. But such refinements serve rather to perplex, than inform, the mind. The truth is, that title means the same thing as *ownership*. A man may be in possession of a thing which he does not own; and he may own a thing of which he is not in possession. Possession, therefore, though it creates a presumption of ownership, and though it may ripen in time into actual ownership, is not of itself ownership.

(*a*) 2 Black. Com. chap. 13, 16, 17; 2 Kent, Com. 318.

He who is in possession without right, is liable to be dispossessed by him who has the right; and he who has the right without possession, may acquire possession by recourse to the law. One of the elementary principles in the action of ejectment, is, that the plaintiff must rely solely upon the strength of his own title, and not upon the weakness of the defendant's title. The reason is, that actual possession is *primâ facie* evidence of title, and gives the occupant a right against every person who cannot show, not simply a better, but a good, title. If, however, the person in possession be a mere intruder, he is not permitted to question the validity of the plaintiff's title, unless the latter were also a mere intruder; for any shadow of right in the plaintiff will be sufficient against mere possession without right. The first step, then, is for the plaintiff to exhibit a sufficient title; and until he do this the defendant may rely simply on his possession without further proof. But when this is done, the defendant must meet it by showing a better title either in himself or some third person. It would seem, therefore, that the perfection of title consists in the union of possession with the right of possession; for where these meet in the same person, he cannot be rightfully dispossessed. In other words, he is the lawful present owner of the property; and this is the whole of the matter. The question, then, is, what constitutes legal ownership of property? and this is answered by describing the ways in which ownership may be acquired, and what is evidence of such acquisition. In the acquisition of ownership there is a marked difference between personalty and realty. I shall, however, continue to treat them in connection, noticing the distinctions as they occur. By the English law, all the different modes of acquiring title are reduced to two; namely, by *descent* and by *purchase.* (*a*) In other words, he who acquires title in any other way than by descent or inheritance, is technically called a *purchaser.* Property acquired by purchase, differs from that acquired by descent, and thence denominated *ancestral*, in two important particulars, which will be more fully explained hereafter. *First*, *ancestral property* descends in the blood of the ancestor from whom it came; whereas, *purchased property* descends to the heirs of the last owner, without regard to the blood of any preceding ancestor. And, *secondly*, *ancestral property* becomes assets in the hands of the heir, and liable to the debts of the ancestor; whereas, *purchased property* is independent of any such liability. I am here speaking of the doctrines of the English law. In this country, or at least in this State, they have been so far altered, that ancestral property, as will be seen hereafter, includes all realty acquired from an ancestor, either by descent, devise, or deed of gift, where blood is the only consideration; and purchased property includes realty ac-

(*a*) See 2 Black. Com. 241; 4 Kent, Com. 373.

quired in any other way, and personalty. For this reason, I shall not notice the distinction between descent and purchase, except when discussing the law of descent; and I shall generally use the term *purchase* in its popular, and not in its technical, acceptation. There are, then, five ways of acquiring title to property; namely, by *occupancy*, by *marriage*, by *descent*, by *devise*, and by *purchase*. Each of these will form the subject of a distinct lecture. I shall discuss them in the above order, beginning with *occupancy;* which, as far as relates to realty, is often treated of under the head of *prescription.*

§ 155. **Realty acquired by Occupancy.** Where property of any description is without an owner, it fairly belongs to the first person who takes possession. This is a dictate of the law of nature; and if ever there was a time when there was no such thing as exclusive individual property, occupancy may have given the first title. This, too, is the foundation of title by discovery. And accordingly we have seen that the whole American continent was parcelled out among the various European nations according to the priority of discovery; the occupancy of the aborigines not being regarded as sufficient to prevent the acquisition of title by discovery. At present, however, there is so small an amount of property which has not a legal owner, that the right of acquiring property by occupancy is of very little consequence. But there are some cases in which this right is even now called into exercise. It is settled, that if soil be formed from the sea or a river, by gradual alluvion, it is the property of the adjacent owner. If an island be formed in a river, it belongs to the owner of the nearest bank; or if the middle line of the river passes through it, the portions on each side of this line belong to the respective owners of the adjacent banks. Again, with regard to the use of air, water, and light, as connected with the ownership of land, great weight is always given, as we have seen, to prior occupancy. The doctrine is, that he who has made the first appropriation of either of these elements to a particular use, is entitled to protection in the enjoyment of that use; but this doctrine is modified by so many considerations growing out of the increase of population and public policy, that it is difficult to lay down any precise rules on the subject. The above cases suppose the ownership to be vacant, and the right originates in the law of nature. But we have two important statutes, the effect of which is to enable persons to acquire title by occupancy, where the ownership was not vacant when the possession was taken. These are the *statute of limitations*, and the *statute of occupying claimants.*

Effect of the Statute of Limitations. (*a*) This statute, which

(*a*) In Ludlow *v.* McBride, 3 Ohio, 240, the court say, "The doctrine is now too well settled to be disturbed, that a prior possession is presumptive evidence of title, and, unexplained or uncontradicted, is a sufficient title to recover upon in ejectment against a mere intruder. The authorities upon this point are numerous and decisive, will be considered more particularly hereafter, provides, in substance, that no action of ejectment, or any other action for the recovery of the title or possession of real estate, shall be maintained after twenty-one years from the time the cause of such action accrued, unless the person entitled to such action was at that time under one of the four disabilities of infancy, coverture, insanity, or imprisonment; in which case, the action may be maintained, after the twenty-one years have elapsed, so that it be within ten years after the removal of such disability. The object of this statute is to discourage negligence in the assertion of claims, and prevent the raking up of dormant titles; and the consequence of its enactment is, that if any person has been in exclusive adverse possession of land for the space of twenty-one years, or the additional ten years allowed in case of disability, although he has no shadow of title at first, yet by the mere effect of occupancy for this length of time, his title has become impregnable. But this occupancy must be what is termed *adverse;* that is, one which disclaims the title of the negligent owner; for if it be in subordination thereto, the limitation of the statute does not apply. The question of *adverse possession* (*a*) is a question of fact for the jury under the instruction of the court. It must be exclusive of any other right; but it need not be under claim of a rightful title. And there are four classes of cases, where the possession of another is not adverse to that of the owner. 1. Where both parties claim under the same title, as by the same descent, devise, or conveyance, the possession of the one is not, of itself, adverse to the

both in the English and American courts. It is not necessary that there should be a continued possession for twenty years to furnish this presumption of right. Such possession, when both adverse to all others, and continued, rises at length to a right even against the legal owner of the fee, if once within the protection of the statute of limitations. And when continued less than twenty years, may prevail as a presumptive right until rebutted by proof of prior possession, right of succession, legal title, or other evidence sufficient to defeat such presumption. In cases where no other evidence of title than possession, is given by either party, the prior possession must prevail, especially, when connected with an assertion of ownership, unless such prior possession has been abandoned, or the subsequent possession has been continued until protected by the lapse of time and the statute of limitations." And this is true where the possession commenced without color of title. Paine *v.* Skinner, 8 Ohio, 159. In some of the States, persons are protected in the possession of real estate, who have been in possession in good faith and under color of title, and paid the taxes for seven years, or who have been in open and notorious possession under a conveyance purporting to convey a fee-simple, or under judicial sales, or sales for taxes. Wright *v.* Mattison, 18 How. 50; Lea *v.* Polk County Copper Co., 21 id. 493; Scott *v.* Hickox, 7 Ohio State, 88. The original possession must have been taken under the judicial sale, or the statute will not apply. Coarser *v.* Mefford, 11 Ohio State, 575. Title by prescription may be acquired by twenty-one years' adverse enjoyment of an easement, and the period begins to run from the time the right of action accrues. Tootle *v.* Clifton, 22 Ohio State, 247. The possession need not be all by one person; and if successive transfers were in fact made, it matters not whether they were by instruments sufficient to convey a title or not. McNeely *v.* Langan, 22 Ohio State, 32. Actual notorious possession for twenty-one years makes a perfect title, though it was by mutual mistake of the parties. Yetzer *v.* Thoman, 17 Ohio State, 130; Bobo *v.* Richmond, 25 id. 115.

(*a*) Adams on Ejectment, 50–7; Abram *v.* Will, 6 Ohio, 164; Paine *v.* Skinner, 8 id. 298; Wallace *v.* Miner, 6 id. 366; s. c. 7 id. 1 pt. 249; Ludlow *v.* M'Bride, 3 id. 240; Ludlow *v.* Barr, 3 id. 388; Starke *v.* Smith, 5 id. 455.

other, but requires some positive act or declaration to make it so. 2. Where the possession of one party is consistent with the title of the other, it is not, of itself, adverse, but requires other circumstances to make it so; as where a grantor remains in possession after conveyance, or where the beneficiary is in possession instead of the trustee, or the mortgagor after executing the mortgage, in all these cases the presumption is against adverse possession. 3. Where the other party has never, in contemplation of law, been out of possession, the actual possession is not of itself adverse. Thus a tenant for years, at will, or at sufferance, does not, unless by some positive demonstration, hold adversely to his landlord; and the possession of one tenant in common, unless there be an actual ouster, is the possession of all. (*a*) 4. Where the possessor has once acknowledged the title of the other party, as by offering to purchase, paying rent, requesting a lease, and the like, the possession is not adverse; nor can it be rendered so by a subsequent denial; and this doctrine of acknowledgment extends even to the predecessors of him in possession. With these explanations, it may be laid down as a general rule, that where neither party can show any other than a possessory title, the prior possession, however short, is the better one, unless the defendant has been in possession so long as to be protected by the statute of limitations; but against a regular paper title no possession short of the statute will avail, this being the term fixed for the presumption of title; and then the presumption is so conclusive that a person out of possession may recover upon a prior possession, for the period of the statute, against a regular paper title with possession for a less period. But it is held that possession of government land before a patent has been issued, even for twenty-five years, is not protected by the statute, because the statute does not run against the government.

Effect of the Statute of Occupying Claimants. (*b*) This statute

(*a*) Youngs *v.* Heffner, 36 Ohio State, 232.

(*b*) The subject of an occupying claimant law, in all its bearings, is very fully discussed in Greene *v.* Biddle, 8 Wheat. 1. See 2 Parsons on Contracts, 495, 496; Rawle on Covenants for Title, 263–72. The costs of the proceeding are recovered by the party who prevails in the application. Martin's Case, 1 Ohio, 156. The claim may embrace improvements made before the occupant's title commenced. Shaler *v.* Magin, 2 Ohio, 235; Davis *v.* Powell, 13 id. 308. No personal judgment for the value of the improvements can be rendered against the true owner; and if the owner obtains possession without resorting to an action at law, he is not liable for the improvements. Webster *v.* Stewart, 6 Clarke (Iowa), 401; Dungan *v.* Von Puhl, 8 id. 263. A purchaser at a void administrator's sale, cannot obtain compensation in equity for taxes and improvements paid for before eviction by the heir. Winthrop *v.* Huntington, 3 Ohio, 327. But see Nowler *v.* Coit, 1 Ohio, 519. A purchaser at sheriff's or administrator's sale is within the act. Sellers *v.* Corwin, 5 Ohio, 398, and Longworth *v.* Wolfington, 6 id. 9. That the valuers are three, instead of twelve, is no objection to the constitutionality of the law. Hunt *v.* M'Mahan, 5 Ohio, 132; also, Bank of Hamilton *v.* Dudley, 2 Peters, 492. In relation to school lands, the office of the township trustees is a public office within the meaning of the law. Hart *v.* Johnson, 6 Ohio, 87, 538. A purchaser from a judgment debtor after execution levied, when evicted by the creditor, cannot have the benefit of the act. Vincent *v.* Goddard, 7 Ohio, 2 pt. 188. The valuation is invalid, without reasonable notice to the adverse party. Patterson *v.* Prather, 11 Ohio, 35. Where the defendant fails in ejectment because of error in boundary, he is intended to benefit those persons only, who have taken possession of land supposing they had an undoubted title; and in this confidence have made valuable improvements, which, by the common law, they would utterly lose, on being evicted by a superior title; accordingly, those persons called *squatters*, that is, mere intruders, occupying without claim of title, are not within its provisions. The act enumerates five classes of occupants, whom it protects: namely, *first*, those who can show a plain and connected title either in law or equity, derived from the records of some public office; *secondly*, those who claim by descent, devise, deed, or title bond, under the foregoing; *thirdly*, those who claim under a sale on execution against either of the foregoing; *fourthly*, those who claim under a regular tax sale; *fifthly*, those who claim under a regular sale by executors, administrators, guardians, or other persons, by order of court. (*a*) If a person of either of these descriptions has occupied land without fraud or collusion, he cannot be evicted by any claimant having a superior title, until he has been fully paid for all lasting and valuable improvements, made previous to the commencement of the suit, unless he refuse to pay the claimant the value of the land without the improvements. The act proceeds upon the plain equitable ground that the improvements honestly made ought in fairness to belong to the occupant, and the land itself to the claimant. But as they cannot be separated, and one must take both, the party taking both must pay the other the fair value of his share. The mode of ascertaining the respective claims is as follows: The title is first tried by the regular action of ejectment, and judgment goes against the occupant, who thereupon claims the benefit of this act. A jury is then impanelled to ascertain, *first*, the naked value of the land at the time of the judgment; *secondly*, the value of improvements made before suit; *thirdly*, the rents and profits; and *fourthly*, the damages done to the land by any species of waste. These rents and profits, together

cannot claim under the act. Waldron *v.* Woodcock, 15 Ohio, 13. Where possession was taken in good faith of the wrong land, the statute does not apply. King *v.* Potter, 18 Mich. 134. Nor where the improvements were made under a mistake as to the quality and duration of the estate taken under a certain instrument, through which title is traced. Taylor *v.* Foster, 22 Ohio State, 255. Where plaintiff elects to convey, after valuation, and tenders the warranty deed of the person to whom he had sold pending suit, this is sufficient; but he cannot claim interest since the judgment. Wilkins *v.* Huse, 15 Ohio, 285. The holder of a tax title is entitled to the benefit of this law. Neiswanger *v.* Gwynne, 13 Ohio, 74. And see Stuart *v.* Parish, 6 Ohio, 476. Robinson *v.* Fife, 3 Ohio State, 551. A mere notice of the claim which is afterwards successfully asserted, is not conclusive evidence of fraud and collusion on the part of the purchaser. Harrison *v.* Castner, 11 Ohio State, 339. The Kansas statute is copied from the Ohio one, and construed in the same manner. Stebbins *v.* Guthrie, 4 Kan. 353.

(*a*) ⟨ But one holding by contract of purchase from a *cestui que trust* is not on eviction by the trustee entitled to the value of his improvements, for he was not holding under an adverse title. Preston *v.* Brown, 35 Ohio State, 18. An occupier will be protected as far as just, independently of the statute. Thus if one tenant in common makes improvements on the property, the improved part will if possible be awarded him on partition. Youngs *v.* Heffner, 36 Ohio State, 232. So an occupier who has permanently improved the property but is not entitled under the occupying claimant law, will, if sued by the owner for rents and profits, be allowed for the improvements. Preston *v.* Brown, 35 Ohio State, 18, 28. ⟩

with damages, are of course to be subtracted from the value of the improvements, or *vice versa*. If the balance be in favor of the claimant, then, as nothing is due the occupant, the claimant has judgment for the land and for such balance. But if the balance be in favor of the occupant, then the claimant has his option, either to take the assessed value of the land and release to the occupant, or pay the assessed balance for the improvements and take the land. (*a*) It would be difficult to conceive of a set of provisions more perfectly equitable and just. The principle of the common law, which gave all improvements in the nature of fixtures to the successful claimant, was always productive of hardship, but peculiarly so, in a new country, where the settlers are proverbially improvident respecting the security of their title. The present statute was enacted in 1831, and differs considerably from that of 1820. Under the latter, the valuation, instead of being made by a jury of twelve, as at present, was made by three commissioners; and it was objected that on this account the act was unconstitutional, being in contravention of the provision that the right of trial by jury should be inviolate; but the court held that even in this form the law was constitutional, no particular number being necessary to constitute a jury. At all events, the present statute silences this objection. It has also been decided that under this act, it makes no difference whether the improvements were made before or after the occupant's supposed title commenced. Neither the words nor the reason of the act restrict its operation to subsequent improvements. It is sufficient, if at the time of action he can show such a supposed good title as the act requires. The words of the act are, that the occupant "shall be paid the value of all lasting and valuable improvements, made on said land by such occupying claimant," or those under whom he claims, prior to the commencement of the suit.

§ 156. **Personalty acquired by Occupancy.** (*b*) It is more easy to acquire personalty by occupancy, than realty, on account of possession being stronger evidence of ownership. It is a general rule, as will be shown hereafter, that the ownership of realty must be evidenced not only by writing, but by record; whereas personalty does not usually require even written evidence of ownership. The consequence is, that personalty is more frequently acquired by occupancy than realty. The most common instances are as follows: 1. The finder of *things lost* is entitled to them, unless the original owner appears to claim them; and still more, if there be no such owner. (*c*) We have a statute respecting *stray animals* and *boats*

(*a*) The Act of March 22, 1849, which gives to the occupying claimant, after judgment rendered against him, the option to require of the true owner the full value of his permanent improvements, or to take the land by paying the owner the value thereof, without the improvements, has been declared unconstitutional, for the owner cannot be deprived of his property, and it is he that should have this option. McCoy *v.* Grandy, 3 Ohio State, 463.

(*b*) 2 Kent, Com. lec. 36; 2 Black. Com. ch. 26.

(*c*) 2 Kent, Com. 356; Bridges *v.* Hawkesworth, 7 Eng. Law & Eq. 424; McGoon *v.* Ankeny, 11 Ill. 558. See Forster *v.* Juniata Bridge Co., 16 Penn. State, 393.

adrift, requiring the finders to have the things found appraised, and to advertise the fact of finding; and if the owner does not appear within one year and pay charges, the property vests in the finder. 2. The captor of *wild animals*, including all, on land or water, which have not been tamed or domesticated, is entitled to them, provided that in taking them, he does not trespass on the rights of others. 3. *Emblements*, which have been already described, are acquired by occupancy. 4. The increase of value by *accession*, is referred to this head. The general rule is, that if a thing in the possession of another receive an accession of quantity or value by natural or artificial means, as by the growth of vegetables, the pregnancy of animals, or the application of mechanical labor and skill, such increase belongs to the possessor. (*a*) 5. The acquisition of value by invention, discovery, or authorship, in art, science, or literature, comes likewise under this head. But enough has been said on this topic, when speaking of *copyrights* and *patent-rights*. (*b*) 6. In case of the *confusion* of goods, the rule is, that if goods belonging to different persons be mixed or confounded together by mutual consent, the owners have a proportionable interest therein; but if done by one without consent of the other, the latter has the whole. (*c*) 7. The *capture* of an enemy's goods in time of war, is referred to the head of occupancy; but a discussion of this topic would occupy too much space. 8. To this head may also be referred the subject of *good-will*, (*d*) by which is meant the advantage accruing to any trade or business from an established custom. It is partly dependent upon mere locality, and partly upon personal reputation. The presumption is, that customers will continue to deal where they have been in the habit of dealing, all other things being equal; and this renders an old stand more valuable than a new one, independently of the reputation of those who conduct the business. Thus far, good-will is merely local; all beyond is personal. Both law and equity regard good-will as a valuable interest, capable of being bought and sold; but it is obviously difficult to measure its value, as we measure that of actual property; and therefore the parties interested must expressly fix a value by agreement, if they would have it recognized by courts. Questions of

(*a*) Pulcifer *v.* Page, 32 Maine, 404. See note (*c*).

(*b*) See generally on this subject, and particularly the rights of foreigners to copyright, the recent learned and elaborate opinions in the House of Lords, in the case of Jeffreys *v.* Boosey, 30 Eng. Law & Eq. 1–105. To these may be added trademarks and trade names, — for which see note, p. 162.

(*c*) Commissioners *v.* Springfield, 36 Ohio State, 643. But a party does not lose his property by an intermixture, unless it is caused by his wilful or unlawful act, and the property of each cannot be distinguished. Smith *v.* Sanborn, 6 Gray, 134; Willard *v.* Rice, 11 Met. 473; Pratt *v.* Bryant, 20 Vt. 333; Beach *v.* Schmultz, 20 Ill. 185; Low *v.* Martin, 18 id. 286; see Inglebright *v.* Hammond, 19 Ohio, 337. {If A. cut timber from B.'s land and convert it into railroad ties, which are then purchased by one without notice, the latter, in Ohio, is not liable to B. for the increased value, but only for the value of the timber. R. R. Co. *v.* Hutchins, 37 Ohio State, 282; *contra*, Wooden Ware Co. *v.* United States, 106 U. S. 432.}

(*d*) See Collyer on Partnership, 88; Smith on Commercial Law, 109. 1 Parsons on Contracts, 130.

this sort generally arise upon a relinquishment of business. If the owner of a shop sells it, the local good-will passes of course to the purchaser without specific mention; but the personal good-will remains with the person, unless the contrary be stipulated; and even then he is not precluded from prosecuting the same kind of business at another stand, because contracts in restraint of trade are against public policy. Attempts have been made to draw a distinction between an agreement not to pursue the same business, and not to pursue the same kind of business; but it is too shadowy to be available. When a partner leaves or enters a firm, good-will is never taken into account, unless by express provision in the contract. So when a partner dies, the survivor succeeds to the entire good-will, without liability to account, unless the contrary was expressly stipulated. (*a*) When, however, a court of equity decrees a sale of an entire stock in business, care is taken so to regulate the sale as to bring an increased price on account of the good-will, if this be practicable.

LECTURE XXVIII.

TITLE BY MARRIAGE.

§ 157. **Dower.** (*b*) The nature of marriage has already been described. One of the consequences of marriage, after the death of one of the parties, is to give the other a life-estate in a part or the whole of the realty owned by the deceased. If the husband dies, the title thus acquired by the wife is called her *dower*. If the wife dies, the title thus acquired by the husband is called his *curtesy*. These have been already mentioned under the head of estates for life, their general incidents being the same as belong to all life-estates; but in this connection they require a more particular consideration. By *dower* is meant the interest which the wife has in the realty of her husband after his death. At common law, there were several kinds of dower, and a full discussion of the subject involved a variety of nice distinctions; but in this country, or at least in this State, there is but one kind of dower which is provided for by statute; and thus we have another instance of simpli-

(*a*) {See Rammelsberg *v.* Mitchell, 29 Ohio State, 22.}

(*b*) See 2 Black. Com. 128, 4 Kent, Com. 35; Park on Dower; Clancy on Husband and Wife; Bishop on Marriage and Divorce; Bright on Husband and Wife; Scribner on Dower. The history of dower is given at much length in Allen *v.* M'Coy, 8 Ohio, 418. Under the ordinance, it embraced all lands of which the husband was seised during coverture, whether descendible or not. Betts *v.* Wise, 11 Ohio, 219. During the husband's life, it is too remote a contingency to be the subject of sale as a distinct estate. Douglass *v.* M'Coy, 5 Ohio, 522. A suit for dower abates by the death of the wife, and cannot be revived for any other purpose. Miller *v.* Woodman, 14 Ohio, 518. A widow in possession of dower, being evicted by title paramount, cannot sue on the covenant of warranty made to her husband. St. Clair *v.* Williams, 7 Ohio, 2 pt. 110.

fication in the law of realty. Referring for details to the books, I shall consider who may be endowed; of what; how barred; and how assigned.

Who may be endowed. The words of the statute are, "the widow of any person dying." She must have been the *actual wife* of the party at the time of his death, unless divorced for his aggression. (*a*) Nor may she at the time have been living with an adulterer, though the mere fact of former adultery, if her husband has afterwards been reconciled, is not an objection to dower. Nor is the fact of her being an *alien;* since in this State aliens have the same capacities in regard to real estate as citizens. There is nothing in our statute of dower, or in that which prescribes the formalities of marriage, to determine whether a *legal* marriage according to the statute is necessary; but I presume the general rule applies in this case; which is, that in the absence of positive testimony of a legal marriage, proof of reputation and cohabitation as husband and wife will be received as *primâ facie* evidence of a legal marriage. (*b*)

Of what. (*c*) The words of our statute, R. S. § 4188, are, "one full and equal third part of all the lands, tenements, and real estate of which her husband was seised, as an estate of inheritance, at any time during the coverture, and all lands, tenements, and real estate of which her husband at his decease held the fee simple in remainder or reversion. (*d*) She shall in like manner be endowed of one-third part of all the right, title, or interest which her husband, at the time of his decease, had in any lands and tenements held by bond, article, lease, or other evidence of claim." The common law did not give dower in *equitable* estates; but the above words are understood to include all equitable estates; and thus a very unreasonable doctrine of the common law, which denied dower, while it allowed curtesy, in equitable estates, is here abolished. (*e*) The term "*lease*" used in the statute, probably has no meaning. For the interest of a lessee for a life terminates at his death; and that of a lessee for years, though renewable for

(*a*) As to effect of divorce, see note on p. 391. A widow's creditors may subject her unassigned right of dower. Boltz *v.* Stolz, 41 Ohio State, 540.

(*b*) Case of Ferrie, 3 Bradford, Sur. R. 151, 249; 4 id. 28; Caujolle *v.* Ferrie, 26 Barb. 177; s. c. 23 N. Y. 90.

(*c*) The widow must elect between her dower and the provision made for her by her husband in his will, unless it plainly appears by the will that it was intended she should have both. R. S. § 5963.

(*d*) She is, therefore, not entitled to dower in estates in reversion or remainder. Brooks *v.* Everett, 13 Allen, 457; Butler *v.* Cheatham, 8 Bush, 594. In New York it is extended to cases where the husband at the time of his death held land under a contract to convey. Hicks *v.* Stebbins, 3 Lans. 39.

(*e*) In Maryland, the law is the same as it is in Ohio. Lyon *v.* Gephart, 29 Md. 547. In Illinois, the wife has dower in all equitable estates of which the husband was equitably seised during coverture. Atkins *v.* Merrill, 39 Ill. 72. In Oregon she has no dower in equitable estates. Farnum *v.* Loomis, 2 Oregon, 29. {Whether there is dower in a perpetual leasehold estate in Ohio which the husband had sold before his death is not settled. The statute makes such estate follow estates in fee as to descent. R. S. § 4181. And it had been held below that dower was not by descent, and therefore there was no dower in such estate; but the point in the case was not decided by the Supreme Court. Abbott *v.* Bosworth, 36 Ohio State, 605.}

ever, is a mere chattel interest, except in certain cases pointed out by another statute, of which dower is not one. The effect of this statute, therefore, is simply to extend the right of dower to equitable estates in fee. You will, however, note this distinction, that a dower in *legal* estates extends to all land owned at any time during the coverture; but in *equitable* estates, only to land owned at the time of the decease. The statute does not say that the right thus acquired by the widow shall be for her life only; but this is implied in the very term dower. The widow is likewise entitled to remain one year in the mansion-house free from expense, unless her dower is sooner assigned. As to the *seisin* of the husband, we have already seen that there is no livery of seisin in Ohio, and that actual entry is never necessary to constitute a seisin. (*a*) The word here means nothing more than ownership; and there is no distinction between seisin *in law* and seisin *in deed.* But there are several cases in which the mere legal seisin or ownership will not give a right of dower. Thus a trustee, without beneficial interest, has not such an ownership as will create the right of dower; (*b*) nor a mortgagee, who does not obtain possession either by ejectment or foreclosure; nor a purchaser who, at the same time that he obtains title, mortgages the land back for the purchase-money; (*c*) nor a purchaser against whom the vendor has an equitable lien for the purchase-money; (*d*) nor a partner, where the lands have been purchased with partnership funds, under articles stipulating that the whole property should be sold to pay the debts, and the firm is insolvent; (*e*) nor the heir upon whom

(*a*) At common law, the widow could have dower only in lands of which her husband was seised during coverture. Apple *v.* Apple, 1 Head (Tenn.), 348. By the Act of March 27, 1858, the widow has dower in real estate of which, at his decease, her husband held the fee-simple in remainder or reversion, after the termination of the prior estate. Upon her petition for dower, the grantee of her husband is not estopped from denying the seisin of her husband. Coakley *v.* Perry, 3 Ohio State, 344.

(*b*) White *v.* Drew, 42 Mo. 561; Derush *v.* Brown, 8 Ohio, 412; Firestone *v.* Firestone, 2 Ohio State, 415.

(*c*) Welch *v.* Buckins, 9 Ohio State, 331; Culver *v.* Harper, 27 id. 464. Mills *v.* Van Voorhies, 20 N. Y. 412; Boynton *v.* Sawyer, 35 Ala. 497; Wing *v.* Ayer, 53 Maine, 138; Fletcher *v.* Holmes, 32 Ind. 499; Folsom *v.* Rhodes, 22 Ohio State, 435. But when the mortgage was not acknowledged or delivered until sixteen days after the deed, held that the grantee acquired a sufficient seisin for the dower right of his wife to attach. Rawlins *v.* Lowndes, 34 Md. 639. Nor where a mortgage was given before marriage, and the equity of redemption released after, without her joining. Rands *v.* Kendall, 15 Ohio, 671. Nor where she joined in a mortgage of one lot, and this, with all others, was sold for less than the mortgage debt, by the administrator. St. Clair *v.* Morris, 9 Ohio, 15. She has dower in property of her husband mortgaged, of which he was seised during coverture, against all persons but the mortgagee. As to the effect of assigning dower on the rights of a mortgagee where he was a party to the proceeding, see Affleck *v.* Snodgrass, 8 Ohio State, 234. Carter *v.* Goodwin, 3 Ohio State, 75. A sale under the act "to provide for the partition of real estate," of an estate held in common, divests the wife of a cotenant in fee of the estate of her inchoate right of dower therein. Weaver *v.* Gregg, 6 Ohio State, 547.

(*d*) Walton *v.* Hargraves, 42 Miss. 18; Cocke *v.* Bailey, 42 Miss. 81. So where lands subject to a vendor's lien are reconveyed by the vendee to the vendor in satisfaction of such lien, they pass free from dower, though the vendee's wife does not join in the conveyance. Rawlins *v.* Lowndes, 34 Md. 639.

(*e*) {She cannot have dower in partnership lands, except in such balance as may lands descend, charged with the debts of the ancestor; for in all these cases, there is a claim superior to dower existing in some other person. Nor can there be dower in lands owned for public or private burial-grounds; nor in lands dedicated by the husband to public uses, as for a street, common, or market-place; because in these cases the use is incompatible with dower. (*a*) But there may be dower in wild lands, though while they remain such it is of no value. (*b*) With these qualifications, this right of dower is of so transcendent a character, that the husband cannot by any separate act, as by alienating the land, or incumbering it with debts, deprive the widow of her right. Moreover, the statute expressly provides that if he should give up the lands by collusion or fraud, or lose them by default, the widow may still claim her dower; so that in this respect, he has no more power than he has over the separate lands of his wife.

How Dower is Barred. There are several ways in which a widow may be deprived of dower, when the ownership of the husband would have been sufficient. 1. *By Jointure.* (*c*) The statute provides that if any estate be conveyed to a woman as a jointure, in lieu of dower, to take effect immediately after the death of the husband, and to continue during her life, this will bar her dower; but here her free consent is presupposed; and therefore if the jointure was made before she was of age, or after the marriage, she has her option, on becoming a widow, to take the jointure or her dower; and if she be legally evicted from any part of her jointure, she may recover an equal amount as dower; but on the other hand, should a conveyance intended to be in lieu of dower, from any legal defect, fail to be a bar, and the widow in consequence demand her dower, such conveyance to her shall be void. 2. *By Devise in lieu of Dower.* (*d*) By our statute of wills, if a husband by his will make any provision for his widow, it will be taken in lieu of dower, unless it plainly appears to have been his intention that such provision should be in addition to dower; and she has six months within which to make known her election to the court, whether she will take the legacy or dower; which

be found to be her husband's share after paying all the debts and winding up the partnership.} Greene *v.* Greene, 1 Ohio, 535; Sumner *v.* Hampson, 8 id. 328. See *supra*, p. 248.

(*a*) {Gwynne *v.* Cincinnati, 3 Ohio, 24; 85 Ind. 104.}

(*b*) Allen *v.* M'Coy, 8 Ohio, 418; Schnebly *v.* Schnebly, 26 Ill. 526; Brown *v.* Richards, 2 Green (N. J.), 32. *Contra*, in some other States. Connor *v.* Shepherd, 15 Mass. 164; Johnson *v.* Perlee, 2 N. H. 56; Phillips *v.* Williams, 14 Maine, 411; Stevens *v.* Owen, 25 id. 94.

(*c*) R. S. § 4189. A reasonable antenuptial agreement will bar dower, though not amounting strictly to a jointure. Stilley *v.* Folger, 14 Ohio, 610; Grogan *v.* Garrison, 27 Ohio State, 50; Mintier *v.* Mintier, 28 Ohio State, 307. It must, however, have been fully executed. Murphy *v.* Murphy, 12 Ohio State, 407; Johnson *v.* Johnson, 30 Mo. 72.

(*d*) R. S. § 5963. Devise suitable for dower, but not saying in lieu of dower. Wife does not elect within the time, but agrees with heirs, reciting that it was in lieu of dower, and accepts other things as such. She is thereby barred. Shotwell *v.* Sedam, 3 Ohio, 5.

election must be entered on the minutes of the court; and the election of either bars the other. (*a*) If she makes no election, the law considers her as relinquishing her legacy, and gives her dower; and in one case, where the legacy was not specified to be in lieu of dower, but the widow made an agreement with the heir, reciting that it was in lieu of dower, and stipulating to accept certain things in satisfaction of the devise, the court held this agreement to be a bar. (*b*) 3. *By joining her husband in a deed.* (*c*)

(*a*) The time within which she is to make her election is now one year. When the election has once been made and entered upon the minutes of the court, the probate judge has no power to cancel it, on her application, on the ground of an alleged mistake. This can only be effected by a petition filed in a court having general equity powers. Davis *v.* Davis, 11 Ohio State, 386. Where the will gave the widow a life-interest in the whole property so long as she remained a widow, and she elected to take under it, she forfeited the whole by marrying again. Lingart *v.* Ripley, 19 Ohio State, 24. When the provision in the will includes the dower, as where the widow is given a life-estate in all the realty, it is equivalent to a provision in addition to dower, and she will still have her dower right, free from the claims of creditors. In such a case, if she actually accepts the provisions of the will, but dies without having made her formal election, or having been cited to do so, she will be held to have taken under the will. Baxter *v.* Bowyer, 19 Ohio State, 490.

(*b*) See note (*d*) on page 389.

(*c*) See Brown *v.* Farran, 3 Ohio, 140; Connell *v.* Connell, 6 Ohio, 353; Hubbell *v.* Broadwell, 8 Ohio, 120; Hughes *v.* Lane, 11 Ill. 123; Garrett *v.* Moss, 22 id. 363. The result of these cases is, that it is sufficient if the certificate state the substance without the exact language of the statute. With respect to joining in a mortgage, the wife thereby only bars herself with respect to the mortgagee and his representatives or assigns. If the debt be paid without a sale of the land, dower is restored; if by sale of part only, dower is restored in the residue; but if the land be sold to pay the debt, it makes no difference whether it be by the administrator of the husband, or under a decree; for dower is equally barred. St. Clair *v.* Morris, 9 Ohio, 15; Ketchum *v.* Shaw, 28 Ohio State, 503. Curative statutes enacted for the purpose of healing defective acknowledgments, are unconstitutional and void as respects married women. Good *v.* Zercher, 12 Ohio, 364. The same doctrine was held in Meddock *v.* Williams, 12 Ohio, 377, and in Silliman *v.* Cummins, 13 Ohio, 116. But in Chestnut *v.* Shane, 16 Ohio, 599, the three preceding decisions were overruled, the curative statute of 1835 held valid, and the omission to certify that the contents were explained, held not to be fatal. Card *v.* Patterson, 5 Ohio State, 319; Browder *v.* Browder, 14 Ohio State, 589; Dengenhart *v.* Cracraft, 36 id. 549; Koltenbrock *v.* Tracroft, id. 584. The acknowledgment by the husband and wife may be at different times and before different magistrates. Ludlow *v.* O'Neil, 29 Ohio State, 181. Where the wife joins in the granting clause, this is sufficient without anywhere stating that she relinquishes dower. Smith *v.* Handy, 16 Ohio, 191. Edwards *v.* Sullivan, 20 Iowa, 502. But where she is only mentioned in the testatum clause, as signing and sealing, without granting words, she is not barred. Lufkin *v.* Curtis, 13 Mass. 223; Stevens *v.* Owen, 25 Maine, 94. When she is the owner in fee, her title does not pass by a deed executed by herself and husband, unless she joins in the granting clause. Purcell *v.* Goshorn, 17 Ohio, 105; Cincinnati *v.* Newell, 7 Ohio State, 37. Where A., in possession of land, sold to B., and put him in possession, which possession had continued ever since, B. cannot defeat A.'s wife claiming dower by showing title in some third person, without connecting himself with such title. Ward *v.* Mackintosh, 12 Ohio State, 231. The wife's separate deed will not bar her dower. Dodge *v.* Ayerigg, 1 Beasley, 82. Dower can be released to the owner of the land, but cannot be conveyed to a third person, until after assignment. Hoots *v.* Graham, 23 Ill. 81; Cornwall *v.* Wilson, 21 Ark. 62; Harrison *v.* Gray, 49 Maine, 537; Miller *v.* Woodman, 14 Ohio, 518; Bailey *v.* West, 41 Ill. 298; Chicago Dock Co. *v.* Kinzie, 49 Ill. 289. Before assignment, however, it is an interest in lands within the statute of frauds. Finch *v.* Finch, 10 Ohio State, 501. Where a wife has joined in a mortgage, and the land is worth more than the debt, she has dower in the surplus. Bank of Commerce *v.* Owens, 31 Md. 324. But she is not entitled to be endowed of the whole estate, to be paid out of the surplus. State Bank *v.* Hinton, 21 Ohio State, 509; Culver *v.* Harper, 27 id. 464; Fox *v.* Pratt, 27 id. 512. But see Kling *v.* Ballentine,

Our statute provides that a woman may bar herself of dower, by joining with her husband in a deed or mortgage, she being eighteen, in the same manner as if she were conveying her separate estate. But in this case, to avoid the possibility of deception or coercion, the wife must be examined separately by the person taking the acknowledgment, who must explain the contents of the deed; and she must declare that she executed the deed of her own free will, and without fear, and that she is still satisfied therewith. All these things must be stated in the certificate. 4. *By fraud in the wife.* (*a*) Our court has decided that, where a widow agreed with the administrator, that the land should be sold free from dower, and was present when the land was so put up for sale, and did not contradict it, and the land in consequence brought a higher price, she is thereby barred. 5. *By her misbehavior.* (*b*) Our statute provides that if a woman be divorced for her own aggression, or if she voluntarily leave her husband and live with an adulterer without a subsequent return and reconciliation, she thereby forfeits her right of dower; and if she wantonly commit or suffer any *waste*, she thereby forfeits that part of the dower estate in which such waste was committed. (*c*)

How Dower is assigned. (*d*) Dower may be assigned in two

40 id. 391. Where a wife has joined in a mortgage releasing her dower, she stands only in the position of a surety, and is entitled to have the debt paid out of the personalty. Peckham *v.* Hadwen, 8 R. I. 160. She may maintain a bill to redeem her inchoate right of dower. Davis *v.* Wetherell, 13 Allen, 60.

(*a*) See Smiley *v.* Wright, 2 Ohio, 506; Taggart's Appeal, 99 Penn. State, 627. But in M'Farland *v.* Febiger, 7 Ohio, 1 pt. 194, it was held, that where a wife signed and acknowledged a deed with her husband, knowing that it was defective in the granting clause, and that the purchaser was thereby deceived, this will not bar her dower; because the fraud was committed while she was under coverture. Carter *v.* Goodin, 3 Ohio State, 75. She has dower in real estate in the conveyance of which, without consideration to defraud her husband's creditors, she joined with him in executing during coverture. Woodworth *v.* Paige, 5 id. 70.

(*b*) Divorce barring dower. Barrett *v.* Failing, 111 U. S. 523. Marriage in Kentucky in 1816; separation in 1818; wife ever since residing in Ohio. Husband sells land in Ohio, and then procures divorce in Kentucky for her wilful absence. After his death she claims dower, and succeeds on the ground that the statute barring dower for her aggression only applies to divorces granted in this State. Mansfield *v.* M'Intyre, 10 Ohio, 27. A woman having a husband living at the time of her second marriage, is not entitled to dower in the estate of her second husband, — the second marriage being void. Smith *v.* Smith, 5 Ohio State, 32. A woman divorced *a vinculo matrimonii*, although for the husband's aggression, who marries again, cannot have dower in the lands of her first husband dying after such marriage. She is not then the widow of the first husband within the meaning of the statute. Rice *v.* Lumley, 10 Ohio State, 596; Charlton *v.* Miller, 27 Ohio State, 298, 305. Under the statute of 1840, where a woman obtained a divorce for the aggression of her husband, she retained her dower, even though at the time of his death she was married to another man. Lamkin *v.* Knapp, 20 Ohio State, 454.

(*c*) R. S. § 4194; or by not paying taxes, § 2852. Crockett *v.* Crockett, 2 Ohio State, 180; Woodward *v.* Dowse, 10 C. B. (N. S.) 722. *Contra*, Lakin *v.* Lakin, 2 Allen, 45; Bryan *v.* Batchelder, 6 R. I. 543.

(*d*) By the statute of 1843, the widow, in addition to the lands set off to her, is entitled to one-third of the net profits of the lands subject to dower, accruing between the time of filing her petition and the time of assigning dower, to be ascertained by the commissioners; but if the lands had been aliened by her husband, the commissioners are to exclude from their estimate all permanent improvements subsequently made. It had previously been decided that dower is to be estimated according to the ways, *voluntarily* or *by petition.* When the land is not encumbered, the heir or other person interested may assign the widow her dower, "by writing under his hand and seal," and if she accepts the assignment it is conclusive. It would seem from the above words, that a deed of assignment of dower need not be attested and acknowledged like other deeds. But we have no judicial construction of those words. If dower be not assigned voluntarily as above, the widow must file her petition against the heirs or other persons interested, setting forth all the facts necessary to sustain her right and enable the court to act; and if the court decree in her favor, the sheriff is ordered to have the dower set off by three judicious men, and possession given to the widow. (*a*) We have no action at law to recover dower, unless ejectment would lie in the first instance, which, under the above provision, is improbable. After assignment thus made, there is no doubt ejectment would lie to recover possession. In case the heirs should file a bill for partition before the assignment of dower, the persons directed to make partition must first set off the dower; and in like manner, when land is directed to be sold by administrators, it is the first duty of the appraisers to set off the dower. Where the property is of such a nature that it cannot well be divided, dower is assigned in a special manner, as one-third of the rents and profits, to be ascertained by the above persons.

From this view it will be seen that our law of dower differs from the common law, in there being but one kind of dower, instead of four or five; in comprehending equitable as well as legal estates; and in being cognizable in chancery, and not at law, in the first instance. And on the whole, it is believed to be inferior to no system in the great points of simplicity and liberality. The subject of personalty acquired by the wife has already been considered in the lecture on husband and wife. (*b*) We there saw

value of the land at the time of assignment, excluding all increase resulting from improvements made after alienation, but including all other increase. Dunseth *v.* Bank U. S., 6 Ohio, 76, and 10 id. 18; Allen *v.* M'Coy, 8 id. 418. And so by statute now. R. S. § 5716. This mode of estimating dower is adopted in Gore *v.* Brazier, 3 Mass. 544; Thompson *v.* Morrow, 5 Serg. & Rawle, 289; Powell *v.* M. & B. Man. Co., 3 Mason, 375; Fritz *v.* Tudor, 1 Bush (Ky.), 28. But not in New York. Dorchester *v.* Coventry, 11 Johns. 510; Shaw *v.* White, 13 Johns. 179. Where the husband dies seised, dower is to be assigned according to the law in force at the death of the husband. The wife's right does not vest until that time, so as to be beyond the power of the legislature. Lucas *v.* Sawyer, 17 Iowa, 517; Boyd *v.* Harrison, 36 Ala. 533. But in cases where the husband aliened before death, the legislature cannot, as against the purchaser, afterwards, but during the husband's life, enlarge the dower rights of the wife. Young *v.* Walcott, 1 Clarke, 174; Thomas *v.* Hesse, 34 Mo. 18. But the right to dower accrues at the death of the husband, and is barred in twenty-one years from that time. Tuttle *v.* Wilson, 10 Ohio, 24. Dower cannot be assigned in a gross sum. Johnson *v.* Nyce, 17 Ohio, 66. In assigning dower out of rents and profits, deductions are to be made for reasonable repairs and taxes, but not for water-rents or taxes. Hillgartner *v.* Gebhart, 25 Ohio State, 557. By R. S. § 5719, in executor's and administrator's sales of real estate, and in guardian's sales, partitions, and all other judicial sales upon the request of the widow, made by answer filed, the premises may be sold free from dower, and a gross sum assigned to the widow from the proceeds.

(*a*) The court now appoints the appraisers.

(*b*) In Ramsdall *v.* Craighill, 9 Ohio, 197, it is held that if they unite in selling her that with respect to personalty, the advantage is altogether on the side of the husband. The wife not only acquires no interest in his personalty, but loses the control of her own personalty. Except the right to a mere support, narrowed down to the measure of necessaries, she acquires no interest in personalty by marriage, until her husband's death; (*a*) in which event, if there be no debts and no children, she has all; if there be children, after payment of the debts, she has half the first four hundred dollars, and one-third of the residue.

§ 158. **Curtesy.** (*b*) This estate is recognized both by our legislature and our courts; and I shall consider its general nature; but of the origin of the term *curtesy*, I shall not take up your time with giving an account. At common law, an estate by curtesy is where a man marries a woman seised of real estate in fee, and has by her issue born alive. In this case, on the death of his wife, he is entitled to hold such real estate for life as tenant by curtesy. This curtesy differs from dower in two important respects: first, it extends to all the real estate of the wife, instead of a third part; and secondly, it depends upon having issue born alive, which was not the case in dower. As to the *marriage*, it must be the same as in case of dower; that is, a marriage consummated pursuant to the statute, and actually existing at the death of the wife; for if there has been a divorce for the husband's aggression, our statute provides that the wife shall be restored to all her real estate; which expressly takes away his curtesy; but if the divorce be for the aggression of the wife, the statute provides that she may be restored to the whole or a part of her real estate, as may seem just. What is meant by this last vague provision, is somewhat doubtful; but I presume it only means to allow the husband to retain possession, after the divorce, during the life of the wife, as a kind of punishment to her; and not to give him an estate by curtesy; for at her death the right of her heirs attaches, which would not be affected by this order of court. We have seen that by express provision, the adultery of the wife, without subsequent reconciliation, cuts off her dower. As to the *seisin* required in the wife, nearly the same remarks apply as in case of dower. (*c*) She must have a beneficial ownership in fee;

land, the proceeds become his; and if these proceeds be invested in other land, and he takes the title, this also is his. But there has been subsequent legislation, protecting the property of the wife. See Lecture on Husband and Wife.

(*a*) But see act of April 17, 1857, *ante*, note at the end of chap. 14; Slanker *v.* Beardsley, 9 Ohio State, 589.

(*b*) 2 Black. Com. 126; 4 Kent, Com. 27-35; 1 Cruise's Dig. 105; Lowry *v.* Steele, 4 Ohio, 170; Fleming *v.* Donahoe, 5 Ohio, 255; Canby *v.* Porter, 12 Ohio, 79.

(*c*) In Ohio, it is held that a husband may have tenancy by the curtesy, though the wife may never have been seised, either actually or constructively, of the lands, and though the same be held adversely during coverture by another person. Borland *v.* Marshall, 2 Ohio State, 308; Merritt *v.* Horne, 5 id. 307; Mitchell *v.* Ryan, 3 id. 377; Stephens *v.* Hume, 25 Mo. 349; Buchanan *v.* Duncan, 40 Penn. State, 82. Curtesy initiate is abolished in Ohio. Curtesy is not a vested estate until the wife's death and in property of which she died seised. Hershizer *v.* Florence, 39 Ohio State, 516. The husband cannot be tenant by the curtesy of a remainder expectant upon but she need not have entered upon the land, because here entry is never necessary to perfect title. Nor need she be in actual possession; for where a woman before marriage created a term of years in trust for herself during the coverture, she was still considered by our court as having such a seisin as entitled her husband to curtesy; and it makes no difference at what time of the coverture the seisin commenced, so that it continues till her death. Nor is curtesy confined to the *legal* estate of the wife; as I have before mentioned, it has long been held to extend to her *equitable* interest. The only exception is, where the trust is expressly declared to be for her sole and separate use, in such a manner as to negative the idea of curtesy in the husband. As to the necessity of *issue* born alive and capable of inheriting, which is not the case in respect to dower, whatever may have been the origin of the doctrine, it seems now to be a purely arbitrary and technical requisition; for if the infant should live but for one instant after birth, so as to prove that it was born alive, this is sufficient; the right to curtesy from that moment attaches, and becomes perfect on the death of the wife. Were we to look to the reason of the thing alone, we should say that there is more reason why a husband should have curtesy when there had been no issue, than if there were issue surviving; and just as much reason as when there were issue born which did not survive. However, such is the law. (*a*) We have seen that dower may be barred or forfeited in a variety of ways. Not so with curtesy. No conduct of the husband, however wrong, which does not result in divorce, deprives him of his right. Nor does he incur a forfeiture for *waste*, as in case of dower, because there is no express provision to this effect. (*b*) He only renders himself liable in damages. There is of course no occasion for an assignment of curtesy, as there is of dower, because the husband takes the whole.

We have already seen, that the husband takes control of all

a life-estate, unless the life-estate is determined during coverture. To entitle him, the wife must have had, during coverture, a right to the present possession of the land. Watkins *v.* Thornton, 11 Ohio State, 367; Shores *v.* Carley, 8 Allen, 425; Orford *v.* Burton, 36 N. H. 395; Stewart *v.* Barclay, 2 Bush, 550; Moore *v.* Culvert, 6 Bush (Ky.), 356; Reed *v.* Reed, 3 Head (Tenn.), 491. The married women's statutes in Ohio are expressly declared not to affect tenancy by the curtesy. Nor does the Illinois Act of 1861. Cole *v.* Van Riper, 44 Ill. 58. Nor the New York acts of 1848 and 1849. Burke *v.* Valentine, 52 Barb. 412. But see Matter of Winne, 1 Lans. 508. Nor the New Jersey act. Porch *v.* Fries, 3 Green, 204. It is entirely abolished in Iowa. Shields *v.* Keys, 24 Iowa, 298. A husband is not tenant by the curtesy of land settled to the sole and separate use of the wife. Pool *v.* Blakie, 53 Ill. 495.

(*a*) By a statute passed in 1853, R. S. § 4176, the birth of issue is not necessary in Ohio {and there is no curtesy in the interest of the issue of the wife, by a prior marriage, unless she obtained the property by gift from the surviving husband or his ancestors. And this provision is not affected by the wife's having devised the land to others than her children. Tilden *v.* Barker, 40 Ohio State, 411.

A husband's estate by curtesy cannot be subjected to his debts nor can a mortgage of it by him be enforced, as long as issue of the marriage survives. Robert *v.* Sliffe, 41 Ohio State, 225. This rule was altered by statute in 1884, 81 Ohio Laws, 209, and then restored in 1885. 82 Ohio Laws, 131}.

(*b*) {Except for non-payment of taxes. R. S. § 2852}.

his wife's personalty. If *choses in action* be not already reduced to possession, he may collect and dispose of them. In a word, therefore, by marriage, the husband acquires a right to all the wife's personalty, unless previously settled in trust for her separate use; and the law gives her no power to prevent his wasting it.

LECTURE XXIX.

TITLE BY DESCENT. (a)

§ 159. **Preliminary Explanations.** When the owner of land dies without making a disposition thereof, the law makes it for him. Leaving no will, *testamentum*, he is said to die *intestate*, and in legal phrase is called *the intestate*. The persons to whom the law gives his property are called his *heirs*, and he their *ancestor;* and the title by which the heirs take the property is called *title by inheritance or descent.* But before the property of the ancestor can avail his heirs, there are certain prior claims to be satisfied. In

(a) See 2 Black. Com. chap. 14–29; 4 Kent, Com. lec. 65; 2 Hilliard, chap. 22; 3 Cruise's Dig. 369; Reeve on Descents; Chitty on Descents. By an act of 1854, R. S. § 4182, any person capable of making a will may appear before the probate judge, with two witnesses, and by a written declaration designate who shall be his heir-at-law, and the person so designated shall occupy the same position, in respect to inheritance, as a child born in lawful wedlock. This singular statute has received no construction, but is mentioned in Lathrop *v.* Young, 25 Ohio State, 451, 463. On the death of the ancestor, lands descend at once to the heir, and become liable to sale on execution against him, but subject always to the ancestor's debts, if due steps be taken to charge them. Douglass *v.* Massie, 16 Ohio, 271. Hence the heir and not the administrator is entitled to the rents prior to a sale to pay debts, although the estate be insolvent. Overturf *v.* Dugan, 29 Ohio State, 230. In the mean time, the heir is bound to pay the taxes; and if he permits a sale for delinquency, and becomes the purchaser, he cannot set up a title against the creditor. Piatt *v.* St. Clair, 6 Ohio, 227. The lien for debts can only be discharged by payment or lapse of time. Ramsdall *v.* Craighill, 9 Ohio, 197. Prior to 1831, there was a proceeding by *scire facias* to charge descended lands. McVickar *v.* Ludlow, 2 Ohio, 246; Gray *v.* Askew, 3 Ohio, 466; Union Bank *v.* Meigs, 5 Ohio, 312; Piatt *v.* St. Clair, 6 Ohio, 227. But neither the personal representatives nor creditors of a decedent acquire by his death such an interest in his land, as to preclude the legislature from repealing a law authorizing a sale for the payment of debts. Ludlow *v.* Johnston, 3 Ohio, 553. The title of the widow and heirs to their distributive shares of the personalty vests immediately at the death of the intestate, subject only to administration to pay the debts and funeral expenses, which are to be first paid by the administrator. Conger *v.* Barker, 11 Ohio State, 1; Armstrong *v.* Grandin, 39 Ohio State, 368. The common-law doctrine of shifting inheritance does not apply at all to our law of descents. The property of the intestate vests at once in the heirs in being, and this title is not divested by the subsequent birth of others. This rule does not exclude children *en ventre sa mere*, as they are in being in the eye of the law. Drake *v.* Rogers, 13 Ohio State, 21; Cox *v.* Matthews, 17 Ind. 367. In Cutlar *v.* Cutlar, 2 Hawk. 324, the contrary was held, but the legislature soon afterwards amended the law so as to exclude the doctrine. The course of inheritance is subject to legislative control before death. Pollock *v.* Speidel, 27 Ohio State, 86, 94; Gilpin *v.* Williams, 25 Ohio State, 283, 300; Nimmons *v.* Westfall, 33 Ohio State, 213; Oyler *v.* Scanlan, 33 Ohio State, 308; Denny *v.* McCabe, 35 Ohio State, 576.

the first place, the rights of *dower* and *curtesy*, if either exist, take precedence of heirship, and cannot be affected by the law of descent. And in the next place, the claims of creditors must all be satisfied. When these prior claims are satisfied, the heirs succeed by descent to the residue; or, rather, at the instant of the ancestor's death, his property vests in his heirs incumbered by these prior claims. It was formerly held that an *actual entry* by the heir was necessary to perfect his title; but for the same reason that actual entry is not necessary under a deed in this State, I presume it is not necessary for the heir. It is the general spirit of our laws to dispense with these empty ceremonies; though I am not aware that this particular point has been decided. The rules of descent vary considerably in the different States, but all the States agree in departing from the English law so far as to promote equality among the heirs. For example, the two great characteristics of the English *canons of descent*, namely, *primogeniture*, or a preference of the eldest son over all the other children, and a *preference of males over females*, are probably found nowhere in the United States. But before describing our rules of descent, some preliminary explanations will be necessary.

1. I have already had occasion to observe that realty alone is strictly *inheritable*. Technically speaking, personalty does not descend in any case to the heirs. On the death of the owner, it vests in the executor or administrator; and is by him distributed in the manner heretofore pointed out. Those who take the residue, after payment of debts, are said to take, not as heirs, but as *distributees*. They are called *personal representatives*, to distinguish them from heirs who are called *real representatives*. Nevertheless, I shall, in this lecture, include succession to both realty and personalty; for, with the exception of the widow's claims, personalty passes in this State to the same persons, as non-ancestral realty. The statute of descent and distribution, not in force here, was enacted in 1853. It prescribes some of the fundamental rules of inheritance; but yet leaves many questions to be settled by authority and analogy, respecting which I would refer you for particulars to the books before indicated. The same statute provides both for the descent and distribution of estates; that is, for the disposition both of realty and personalty. With regard to the property of non-residents, the general rule is, that realty descends according to the law of the place where it is situated; that is, realty in this State descends according to the law of this State; whereas personalty is distributed according to the law of the place where the deceased resided. (*a*)

(*a*) Where lands of an intestate are sold to pay debts, the surplus is to be regarded as real estate; but if the heir dies before distribution of the proceeds intestate, the surplus, as regards the distribution of his estate, must be treated as personalty. Pence *v.* Pence, 11 Ohio State, 290; Griswold *v.* Frink, 22 Ohio State, 79. A devise of the proceeds of land is personalty, and goes to the devisee's administrator. Richey *v.* Johnson, 30 Ohio State, 288; Horst *v.* Dague, 34 id. 371; Collier *v.* Grimesey, 36 id. 17; Hanes *v.* Munger, 40 id. 493. A requirement that an executor sell to pay a void

2. Our statute says that real estate shall descend "*in parcenary;*" but we have already seen that in this State there is no distinction between estates in parcenary and estates in common. Of course the phrase means nothing more than that the heirs, until partition is made, are tenants in common.

3. Where heirs of a certain description are all in the same degree, they take "*per capita;*" otherwise, "*per stirpes.*" The meaning is this: heirs take *per capita*, or *by the head*, when each individual has the same share: as, for example, if there be five children, or five grandchildren, or five brothers and sisters all living, and none of any other degree, each takes one-fifth. But heirs take *per stirpes*, or *by representation*, when the children of a deceased heir take only their deceased parent's share: as, for example, if there had been five heirs in the same degree, but one was dead, the children of the deceased would together take only one-fifth. (*a*)

4. Our statute makes a distinction between the cases where realty came to the intestate "*by descent, devise, or deed of gift, from any ancestor,*" and where it came to him in any other way. This distinction has been already noticed. For the sake of convenience, I express it by calling the first property *ancestral*, and the second *non-ancestral*. By *ancestral property*, then, is meant that realty which came to the intestate from his ancestor, *in consideration of blood*, and without a pecuniary equivalent, and which must have come either by descent or devise from a now dead ancestor, or by deed of actual gift from a living one. (*b*)

bequest falls with the bequest and the heir takes as realty. Patton *v.* Patton, 39 id. 590.

(*a*) Dutoit *v.* Doyle, 16 Ohio State, 400.

(*b*) Under the act of 1805, where one inherited land from his father, and died without issue, or brothers and sisters, the estate went to his mother, in preference to his father's sister. McCollough *v.* Lee, 7 Ohio, 1 pt. 15. Where land descended from the father to an infant son, was sold by the guardian, and the proceeds held in money, when the ward died without issue, the sale was held to change the property to non-ancestral, so that it went to the half-brothers, issue of the mother's second marriage. Armstrong *v.* Miller, 6 Ohio, 118. Under the statute of 1824, where land descended to a posthumous child, who died without issue, or brother or sister, but leaving a mother, who afterwards married, and had a child, that child was held to be the heir of the first child. Dunn *v.* Evans, 7 Ohio, 1 pt. 169. Where land was devised in trust to a married sister if living, if not, to her children, and she died before the testator, and the children shortly after, the land was held to be ancestral property in the children, which could not pass to her half-brother not of the testator's blood, nor to their father, but to the next of kin of the blood of the testator. Brewster *v.* Benedict, 14 Ohio, 368. The term "ancestor," in the act of 1831, means any one from whom the estate is inheritable, and the term "the ancestor from whom the estate came," designates the person from whom it was immediately inherited. Prickett *v.* Parker, 3 Ohio State, 394; Clayton *v.* Drake, 17 Ohio State, 367. Where land was devised to a brother and his wife, they take as tenants in common, and if the wife dies without issue, her brothers will inherit, though not of the blood of the ancestor. Penn *v.* Cox, 16 Ohio, 30. Where one tenant in common, in proceedings in partition, elects to take the land at its appraisement, and after obtaining the deed for it dies intestate, that portion of the land which he inherited descends as ancestral property, and the remaining title which he acquired under proceedings in partition as non-ancestral. Freeman *v.* Allen, 17 Ohio State, 527. But if two heirs after partition or devisees exchange their shares by deeds the property becomes non-ancestral. Brower *v.* Hunt, 18 Ohio State, 311. An estate which came to the intestate by descent from a

And by *non-ancestral property* is meant all personalty, and that realty which came to the intestate in any other way, whether by purchase from his ancestor or from a stranger, for an equivalent paid, or by actual gift from a stranger, so that the consideration of blood is out of the question; for this makes the sole distinction. (*a*)

5. We have already seen that *aliens* have here the same rights and privileges in regard to real estate as citizens. The statute of descent expressly provides that it shall be no objection to heirship that it is derived through an alien ancestor; from which it follows that aliens may not only inherit, but transmit, inheritance as well as citizens. And the statute further provides, in the same spirit of liberality, that alien heirs, residing out of the State, may have ten years within which to appear and assert their claims. (*b*) Our statute is equally liberal on the subject of *legitimacy*. *Bastards* are made capable of inheriting or transmitting inheritance *on the part of their mother*, (*c*) who can always be certainly known, but not on the part of their father, for want of such certainty. And if a man have children by a woman, and afterwards marry her and recognize such children, they thereby become legitimate, and capable of inheriting. Again, where a marriage is deemed null in law, the issue of such marriage are still held legitimate, and capable of inheriting. (*d*) By these humane provisions, children are

deceased husband is not ancestral property, but passes under the second section as non-ancestral. This second section governs the descent of all lands not included in the first. To constitute ancestral property, the title under which the intestate immediately holds must have come by descent, &c., from an ancestor. Brower *v.* Hunt, 18 Ohio State, 311; Lathrop *v.* Young, 25 id. 451.

(*a*) Where land was purchased by the husband, and devised by him to the wife, is this in her hands ancestral or non-ancestral property? This question is raised in Birney *v.* Wilson, 11 Ohio State, 427; and a strong opinion is intimated that it is non-ancestral, as though, under our law, his heir, she is not of his blood. It was not necessary to decide this point, as the land came to the wife under the old statute, when she was not the husband's heir. It has been held to be non-ancestral property in her hands in Pennsylvania. Opdyke's Appeal, 49 Penn. State, 373.

(*b*) Even in those States where the disability of aliens to take lands still exists, if there are no other heirs, they may take lot by deed or devise, and hold it against any one but the sovereign, until office found. Cross *v.* De Valle, 1 Wallace, 5. But naturalization will not retroact, so as to confirm a title, where at the death of the ancestor the disability of alienage existed. Henry *v.* Brooklyn Benevolent Society, 39 N. Y. 333. Under the law of 1807, aliens can hold land in the territories, and inherit and transmit inheritance in the absence of special legislation to the contrary. People *v.* Folsom, 5 Cal. 373.

(*c*) Where a bastard inherited from his mother, survived her, and died intestate, leaving no issue, but leaving a widow; held, that the land should go to the widow, and not to the heirs of the mother. Little's Lessee *v.* Lake, 8 Ohio, 289. But see act of March 14, 1853, regulating descents. Lewis *v.* Eutsler, 4 Ohio State, 354. Under this act, it was held that a bastard, though he might inherit from his mother, could not inherit from her relatives. Gibson *v.* McNeely, 11 Ohio State, 131; Hawkins *v.* Jones, 19 Ohio State, 22. But this was changed April 3, 1867, so that bastards may inherit and transmit inheritance from and to the mother, and from and to those from whom she may inherit, or to whom she may transmit inheritance in like manner as if born in lawful wedlock. The word issue in a will does not include illegitimate children. Gibson *v.* McNeely, *supra*. And see Stevenson *v.* Sullivant, 5 Wheaton, 207. The issue of a slave marriage are in Ohio lawful heirs of their father. Morris *v.* Williams, 39 Ohio State, 554.

(*d*) This is not only true in cases where the marriage is voidable only, and re-exempted as far as possible from punishment for the faults of their parents, and parents have a motive to atone for their faults by rendering their children legitimate. It hardly need be added that *posthumous* children may inherit as well as those born before the death of the father. This is a principle of general law. It is only necessary that the birth occur within a possible time after the father's death. (*a*) There was an important maxim of the English law, which we have abolished, namely, that no one could be an ancestor, so as to transmit inheritance, unless he had been *actually seised* of the land; for the heir must be heir to the person last actually seised; or, as it was expressed in Latin, *non jus sed seisina facit stipitem;* not the right to the land, but the seisin, makes the stock. It is unnecessary to point out the consequences of this technical doctrine, because we do not recognize it. For, besides that we have no such thing as technical seisin, as has been repeatedly observed, the very words of the statute extend the rules of descent to the heirs "of any person who shall die intestate having *title or right* to any real estate of inheritance." (*b*) These words include whatever amounts to an ownership in fee, whether legal or equitable, without any reference to the question of actual seisin. Besides, the statute expressly provides that "permanent leasehold estates, renewable for ever, shall be subject to the same law of descent and distribution as estates in fee."

6. There are two modes of computing the degrees of kindred; namely, by the *canon law*, and by the *civil law*. In England, the former is adopted; in this country, the latter. (*c*) The difference is this: the canon law begins at the common ancestor and reckons downward, and in whatever degree the two persons whose relationship is sought, or the most remote of them, is distant from the common ancestor, that is the degree of relationship; whereas the civil law, which we follow, begins with the intestate, ascends to the common ancestor, and then descends to the person in question, reckoning a degree for each person, in both the ascending and descending lines. With these explana-

quires a judicial decree to dissolve it; but even where a man, during the life-time of his first wife, married another woman, who was ignorant of the first marriage, and lived with her, and had children by her, these children are legitimate, although the second marriage was, in the eye of the law, an entire nullity. Wright *v.* Lore, 12 Ohio State, 619.

(*a*) § 19 of the act of 1853, makes this rule general, whereon representation is allowed. The amended section of 1862 (59 Ohio Laws, 50), adds the qualification: "but in no case shall any person inherit unless living at the time of the death of the intestate." In 1 Beck's Med. Jour. 449, the ordinary term of gestation is said to be ten lunar months, or forty weeks, equal to nine calendar months and a week. In Chitty's Med. Jour. 409, it is said to be thirty-nine weeks and one day, or nine calendar months. This alone is sufficient to show that there is no exact and uniform period. In fact, although the ordinary period is about nine calendar months, it may fall short two months, and it may overrun nearly one month, as agreed by both these authors.

(*b*) Bond's Lessee *v.* Swearingen, 1 Ohio, 395; Rice *v.* White, 8 Ohio, 216; Avery's Lessee *v.* Dufrees, 9 Ohio, 145.

(*c*) 2 Black. Com. 206; 4 Kent, Com. 412; Clayton *v.* Drake, 17 Ohio State, 367.

tions, I proceed to state and illustrate the rules of descent, as prescribed in our statute.

§ 160. **Rule for Lineal Descendants.** First of all, property descends to children and their issue, *per capita*, where all are in the same degree, and *per stirpes*, where they are not. This rule operates wherever there are children or children's issue, whether the property be ancestral or non-ancestral, to the exclusion of all collateral relations. (*a*) If all the living heirs are children, all grandchildren, and so on, they take equal shares; but if any one of the heirs be dead, leaving children, these children together take their parent's share by representation. The only exception to the first rule is when any of the children of the intestate or their issue have received from him, in his lifetime, any property by way of *advancement.* (*b*) Property is said to be given by way of advancement, when it is given with an express view to a portion or settlement for life; and not when it is given for maintenance or education. In case of advancement, our statute provides that if it be equal to or greater than the other shares, it shall pass for a full share; and if less, it shall be taken as part of a share, the value being estimated at the time it was made.

§ 161. **Rule for Brothers and Sisters.** (*c*) If there be no lineal descendants, property descends collaterally to the brothers and sisters, and their issue, *per capita*, where all are in the same degree; and *per stirpes* where they are not. The effect of this rule is to prefer brothers and sisters, and their lineal descendants, to all other collateral kindred. But, under this rule there is a difference when the property is ancestral, and when not. If the property is ancestral, it passes to the husband or wife relict for life, (*d*) and then to brothers and sisters of the whole and

(*a*) {An adopted child has all the rights of a child born to the parents, but he does not become of the blood of the adopting parents' ancestors so as to inherit from them property that the adopting parents had they lived would have inherited. Quigley *v.* Mitchell, 41 Ohio State, 375. And his natural mother inherits his personal estate to the exclusion of the adopting parents and their children. Upson *v.* Noble, 35 Ohio State, 655.}

(*b*) As to *advancements*, see 4 Kent, Com. 418; Grattan *v.* Grattan, 18 Ill. 167. By the statute of wills of 1852, where an absent or after-born child is not provided for, such child is to inherit as if there were no will, subject to any deduction by way of advancement. By the statute of descents of 1853, an advancement may include realty or personalty, or both, and is to be treated as part of the heritable or distributive share; but if it exceeds such share, there is to be no refunding. If an advancement of realty exceeds the heritable share of realty, or if that of personalty exceeds the distributive share of the personalty, the excess of either may be applied towards the supplying of any deficiency in the other. As to valuation, the rule is, that if the deed, or the book charge of the intestate, or the receipt of the heir specifies the value, that is to govern; otherwise, the value is to be estimated at the date of the advancement. Prior to this statute, there was no provision as to advancements of personalty. Putnam *v.* Putnam, 18 Ohio, 347; Tremper *v.* Barton, 18 Ohio, 418; Myers *v.* Warner, 18 Ohio, 519. An agreement made by the son with the father, on receiving an advancement, not to set up any claim as heir against his father's estates, imposes no legal obligation on the son. Needles *v.* Needles, 7 Ohio State, 432.

(*c*) Ewers *v.* Follin, 9 Ohio State, 327.

(*d*) {The word "relict" designates relationship, and subsequent marriage does not half blood indiscriminately, provided they are of the blood of the intestate's ancestor. But if non-ancestral, it passes first to the husband or wife, if there be such; if not, (*a*) to the brothers and sisters, and their issue of the *whole blood*, if there be such; if not, to those of the *half blood*. Suppose, for example, the intestate's father had two or more wives, and children by each; in which case the intestate would have brothers and sisters both of the whole and half blood. Now if the property were ancestral, and came from the intestate's father, it would pass, after the life estate of the wife relict, to his brothers and sisters, both of the whole and half blood, because both would equally be of the blood of the ancestor from whom the estate came; that is, of the intestate's father; but if the property were ancestral, and came from the intestate's mother, then the children of his father by his other wife or wives, being of half blood with the intestate, and not of the blood of the ancestor from whom the estate came, could not take at all, except in a case to be mentioned under the third rule. If, however, the property in this case were non-ancestral, it would pass first to the husband or wife relict; and if there is none, then to the brothers and sisters of the whole blood, and next to those of the half blood. The reason of the above distinction is this: The law endeavors, as far as is possible, by fixed rules, to effectuate what would probably have been the wishes of the intestate. For this purpose, it recurs to the universal feeling of attachment to those of the same blood, and endeavors to keep property within that limit. Under the first rule, no distinction was necessary. The lineal descendants of the intestate necessarily partake through him of the blood of all his ancestors. But, under the second rule, brothers and sisters of the half blood share the blood of only half the intestate's ancestors. One parent is common to both, the other not. If the property came to the intestate through the common parent, then it cannot pass out of the blood of the ancestor by passing to both alike, and accordingly, the law ordains that it shall so pass. But if the property came from or through the ancestor not common to both, by passing to the half blood, it would pass out of the blood of the ancestor; this, accordingly, the law will not allow, unless in a contingency provided for under the third rule.

§ 162. **Rule for other Specified Relatives.** (*b*) If there be no heirs who can take under the preceding rules, ancestral property

prevent such survivor being "relict." Spitler *v.* Heeter, 42 Ohio State, 100. The provision in favor of a surviving husband or wife only applies where the decedent was seised. A surviving husband can take no interest in the estate of a parent of his wife who died after the wife did. Lane *v.* McKinshey, 31 Ohio State, 640. }

(*a*) {The text has been modified to express the present law of Ohio. }

(*b*) For the legal meaning of the word "*relatives*," see Mahon *v.* Savage, 1 Sch. & Lef. 111; Bennet *v.* Honywood, Ambler, 708; Harding *v.* Glyn, 1 Atkyns, 469; Spring *v.* Biles, 1 T. R. 435, *note* (*f*); Storer *v.* Wheatley, 1 Barr, 506; Williams *v.* Veach, 17 Ohio, 171.

passes to the ancestor from whom it came, if he be living; if not, to the children of such ancestor, or their issue, if any; (*a*) if not, to his brothers and sisters and their issue, if there be such; (*b*) if not, to the brothers and sisters of the half blood of the intestate not of the blood of the ancestor, if there be such; if not, to the "*next of kin*" of the intestate, being of the blood of the ancestor. And non-ancestral property, including personalty, ascends to the father, if living; if not, to the mother, if living; if not, it passes to the "*next of kin*." This rule, it will be seen, provides for the contingency before mentioned, where ancestral property, when neither the ancestor himself, nor any of his children, or brothers or sisters, or their issue, are living, passes out of the blood of the ancestor, by passing to the half blood of the intestate. The last part of this rule, which allows non-ancestral property to ascend to the parents, is an innovation upon the English law, under which property could never lineally ascend. Under this rule, the doctrine of representation terminates. It extends only to the lineal descendants, and the brothers and sisters of the intestate or the ancestor, as the case may be, and their descendants. Beyond these, therefore, the next of kin, who are living, take the whole, without regard to the representatives of any in the same degree who are dead.

§ 163. **Rule for the next of Kin.** The question now arises, *who are the next of kin?* The statute says, that if the specified persons cannot take, the next of kin shall. But who these are, it leaves to the common law to determine; and, as I have already mentioned, the common law of this country has adopted the rule of the civil law. By this rule, the first degree of kindred embraces parents and children; the second, brothers and sisters, and grandparents and grandchildren; the third, great-grandparents, great-grandchildren, uncles and aunts, and nephews and nieces, and so on, to the more remote degrees. But among these, the lineal descendants, the brothers and sisters and their descendants, the parents, and the brothers and sisters of the ancestor from whom the estate came, and their descendants, have been specifically provided for in the statute. Accordingly we have to seek for the next of kin among grandparents, great-grandparents, uncles and aunts, cousins, and so on, without regard to the doctrine of representation, but having regard to the distinction between property ancestral and non-ancestral; for if the property be ancestral, the next of kin must be of the blood of the ancestor; if not, of the blood of the intestate.

(*a*) See note at end of chapter.

(*b*) The term brothers and sisters in the fifth clause of the first section includes the half blood. Cliver *v.* Sanders, 8 Ohio State, 501. This fifth clause is not limited, like the fourth, to estates coming by gift from a living ancestor. So when an infant died seised of property which had descended from her grandfather to her father, and from him to her, it passed to the half brothers and sisters of her father, though not of the blood of the grandfather, rather than to the brothers and sisters of the grandfather. White *v.* White, 19 Ohio State, 531.

I shall point out some of those whom the law would probably select. I say *probably*, because we have had no decisions on the subject. 1. Parents were the last persons expressly provided for. Next come the grandparents, who, being in the second degree, would be preferred to the uncles and aunts of the third degree. But though both grandparents are equally near of kin, and though in general there is no distinction of sex, yet, as the father has been expressly pointed out to take before the mother, by analogy, the grandfather will take before the grandmother, unless the estate came from or through her; in other words, they do not take together, as tenants in common. (*a*) 2. Next come the uncles and aunts of the intestate. If the property was ancestral, it will pass to the brothers and sisters of that parent from whom the estate came, under the third rule; so that our present inquiry is confined to the case where the property is non-ancestral. In this case, it will probably pass to the brothers and sisters of the father, in preference to those of the mother, from the analogy before mentioned, of fathers being preferred to mothers in the statute. 3. Great-grandparents would come next. Indeed, they are in the same degree as uncles and aunts, that is, the third. But they would probably be postponed to the latter, because the law dislikes lineal ascent when it can be avoided, — a prejudice which the statute exemplifies, by preferring more remote heirs to parents. However, this question, from the nature of things, can seldom arise. 4. Cousins would probably come next; for though grand-uncles and aunts are likewise in the fourth degree, yet from the preference to *descent* before *ascent*, the estate will sooner descend to the children of uncles and aunts, than ascend to the brothers and sisters of grandparents, unless the estate came from them; but as property rarely passes to degrees so remote, it would be unprofitable to pursue this inquiry further. 5. If there be no one of kin, real estate passes to the husband or wife of the intestate, if such there be; if not, it escheats to the State. It may seem singular, considering the closeness of the connection, that the husband or wife should be the most remote of all the heirs; and that they are only permitted to inherit to each other, when otherwise the property would escheat to the State; and in fact, I cannot conceive of a single argument in favor of such a doctrine; but such is the law, and it is not my province to vindicate it. (*b*) The propriety of the State taking property by escheat, when it has no other owner, is too obvious to need comment.

A brief recapitulation will serve to impress these rules the better on your memory. When heirs take by descent, they take as tenants in common. Posthumous children may inherit. Bastards can inherit and transmit inheritance from the mother. Children born before marriage and acknowledged after, and children born

(*a*) See Knapp *v.* Windsor, 6 Cushing, 156.
(*b*) But see note at end of chapter.

during a marriage void in law, are legitimate, and may inherit. Aliens can inherit and transmit inheritance. Actual seisin of the ancestor is not necessary. Males are not preferred to females, except in case of husband and wife. Descent *per capita* is where all the heirs in the same degree take alike. Descent *per stirpes* is where the heirs are of different degrees; and the children of those dead take together the shares of their deceased parents. It extends no further than to children and their issue, brothers and sisters and their issue, and the brothers and sisters of the ancestor from whom the estate came, and their issue. Ancestral property is realty which came to the intestate by descent or devise from a now dead ancestor, or by deed of actual gift from a living one; there being no other consideration than that of blood. Non-ancestral property is realty which came to the intestate in any other way, and personalty. *Ancestral property* passes as follows: 1. To the children and their issue, however remote. 2. To the husband or wife relict for life. 3. To the brothers and sisters and their issue, however remote, whether of the half blood or the whole blood, provided they be of the blood of the ancestor. 4. To the ancestor from whom it came, if living. 5. To the ancestor's children, and their issue; then to the ancestor's husband or wife relict if a parent of the decedent, for life; then to the ancestor's brothers and sisters, and their issue; then to the half brothers and sisters of the intestate and their issue though not of the blood of the ancestor. 6. To the next of kin to the intestate, being of the blood of the ancestor, determined by the rule of the civil law. 7. To the State. *Non-ancestral property*, including personalty, descends as follows: 1. To the children and their issue, however remote. 2. To the intestate's husband or wife relict. 3. To the brothers and sisters of the whole blood, and their issue, however remote. (*a*) 4. To the brothers and sisters of the half blood and their issue, however remote. 5. To the father, then to the mother. 6. To the next of kin of the blood of the intestate. 7. To the State. (*b*)

LECTURE XXX.

TITLE BY DEVISE. (*c*)

§ 164. **Preliminary Explanations.** The modes of acquiring title hitherto described, derive their effect from the operation of the law.

(*a*) Jenks *v.* Langdon, 21 Ohio State, 362.

(*b*) I have taken the liberty to modify the text in accordance with the present law.

(*c*) See 2 Black. Com. ch. 23; 4 Kent, Com. lec. 67; 2 Hilliard's Dig. ch. 36; 6 Cruise's Dig. 1; Powell on Devises; Roper on Legacies; Toller on Executors; Jarman on Wills; Redfield on Wills; Hawkins on Wills. The English statute of wills devising lands dates back to the 32d of Henry 8th, explained by the 34th and

That is to say, in the cases of *occupancy*, *marriage*, and *descent*, there is no express transfer or conveyance from the party who had title to the party who thereby acquires title. But in the remaining modes of acquiring title, there is an express transfer of title from one person to another. *Title by devise* is where a person, in anticipation of death, makes a disposition of his property by *will testamentum*. It was not until the year 1543, that real estate could be disposed of by will; for, as we have already seen, the holder of land, under the feudal system, was very far from being considered as the absolute owner; at present, however, subject to the claims of creditors, and of dower and curtesy, every person capable of acting for himself is free to dispose of his property by will to whomsoever he pleases. There is an idea prevailing among the more ignorant classes, that a father, in making a will, must give something, no matter how little, to each of his children, or the will will not be good; but this opinion is without foundation. A man may give his property to whomsoever he pleases, to the complete disherison of his children; and however unnatural and inhuman this may appear, it will not affect the validity of the will. Indeed, it may be laid down, as a general proposition, that all restraints upon alienation of property are in opposition to the prevailing spirit and policy of our institutions. When a person dies leaving a will or testament, he is called a *testator*. The property disposed of by will is called a *bequest*, *legacy*, or *devise*, and the persons who take it, *legatees* or *devisees*. The person appointed in the will to settle the estate is called *executor*. Wills are here chiefly regulated by statute, and I shall give a synopsis of its provisions.

Who may make a Will. In this State, any person of full age, and of sound mind and memory, (*a*) and not under any re-

35th of that reign. This statute excepts married women, infants, and persons of unsound mind, from making a will, and corporations from taking by will. But in this State, a married woman could always make a will without the consent of her husband. Allen *v.* Little, 5 Ohio, 65. Nor is it necessary that the testator be actually seised of land at the time of making the will; for if he had possession under a parol contract of purchase, which was afterwards perfected, the land would pass by will. Smith *v.* Jones, 4 Ohio, 115. For an excellent synopsis of Ohio legislation with respect to wills, see Bailey *v.* Bailey, 8 Ohio, 239. See also Smith *v.* Berry, 8 Ohio, 365. By the wills act of 1852, it is provided, that, if the widow shall fail to make her election to take under the will, she shall retain her dower, and such share of the personalty as she would be entitled to in case her husband had died intestate. And this provision raises a serious question, whether, if there be no children, the widow may not take all the personalty, in spite of the will. But, by the amendatory act of March 10, 1860, if she fail to make her election to take under the will, she retains her dower, and such share of the personal estate of her husband as she would be entitled to by law, in case her husband had died intestate, *leaving children*. When the widow has once made her election, the judge of probate cannot set it aside on her application. She must apply to a court of equity. Davis *v.* Davis, 11 Ohio State, 386. Where a widow has actually taken under a will, and all parties have acquiesced, they may be estopped to deny her election to take under it. Thompson *v.* Hoop, 6 Ohio State, 480; Stockton *v.* Wooley, 20 Ohio State, 184.

(*a*) Mere defects of the senses, or of memory, or of extreme old age, do not, of themselves, render a person incapable of making a will. If a person can understand what he is doing, and how he is disposing of his property, he has sufficient capacity to make a will. Blecker *v.* Lynch, 1 Bradf. 458; Weir *v.* Fitzgerald, 2 Bradf. 42; Clarke *v.* Davis, 1 Redf. 249; Julke *v.* Adams, id. 454; Gaither *v.* Gaither, 20 Ga.

straint, (*a*) may make a valid will. Married women are not excluded. Corporations are excluded, because in judgment of law they never die. (*b*)

Who may take by Will. In this State, all natural persons, without exception, are capable of taking by will, provided they be in being at the time of making the will, or be the immediate issue of persons then in being. We never have had anything in the nature of the *statutes of mortmain* to limit the capacity of corporations; and whether they can take by will or not, will depend upon the express provisions of their charters. As to aliens, we have seen that in this respect they enjoy all the privileges of citizens. There is, however, a contingent exception to the above universality, in the case of a *subscribing witness* to a will, whom the rules of evidence require to be disinterested; and accordingly the statute provides, that if a legacy be left to him, and the will cannot be proved without him, such bequest is void, unless he would be entitled to a portion as heir, in case there had been no will; in which case so much of that portion shall be saved to him as is equal to the legacy.

What may pass by Will. In this State, every description of property, real and personal, whether held by legal or equitable title, will pass by will. This is settled not only by the various words employed in the statute, but also by the decisions of our court. But it is expressly provided that no will shall affect the claims of creditors; thus legalizing the principle of justice, that all a man can dispose of, in anticipation of death, is the surplus which remains after all his debts are paid. And it is further provided, that the widow's dower cannot be affected by will, unless a legacy be given her in lieu of dower; and even then she has an option, which she may exercise at any time within six months; but she

709; Sutton *v.* Sutton, 5 Harrington, 450; Stubbs *v.* Houston, 33 Ala. 555; Delafield *v.* Parish, 25 N. Y. 9. This last case is also published separately in full as "The Parish Will Case." St. Ledger's Appeal, 34 Conn. 434. Capacity is presumed until the contrary is shown. Perkins *v.* Perkins, 39 N. H. 163; Stubbs *v.* Houston, 33 Ala. 555; Landis *v.* Landis, 1 Grant's Cases, 248. But see Sutton *v.* Sadler, 3 C. B. (N. S.) 87. That a person is under guardianship as an habitual drunkard, is *primâ facie* evidence of incompetency to make a will, but no more. Leckey *v.* Cunningham, 56 Penn. State, 370; Lewis *v.* Jones, 50 Barb. 645.

(*a*) Undue influence, to avoid a will, must be such as to impose a restraint upon the testator, in the disposition of his property in accordance with his own independent judgment and wishes. Monroe *v.* Barclay, 17 Ohio State, 302; Eckert *v.* Flowry, 43 Penn. State, 46; Clarke *v.* Davis, 1 Redf. 249; Julke *v.* Adams, id. 454; Norris *v.* Stokes, 21 Ga. 552; Dunlap *v.* Robinson, 28 Ala. 100; Turley's Ex'rs *v.* Johnson, 1 Bush (Ky.), 106. Gross inequality in the disposition of property is not ground for setting aside will, though it may be considered as bearing on the question of capacity, fraud, or undue influence. Kevil *v.* Kevil, 2 Bush (Ky.), 614. That the principal devisee was one with whom the deceased had illicit intercourse, does not raise a presumption of undue influence. Monroe *v.* Barclay, 17 Ohio State, 302; Roe *v.* Taylor, 45 Ill. 485.

(*b*) Two persons may make a joint will where the bequests are severable and the instrument is not in the nature of a compact, but is the will of each, and revocable by him, and capable of probate as the will of each. Betts *v.* Harper, 39 Ohio State, 639, limiting the earlier case of Walker *v.* Walker, 14 id. 157. And see *Ex parte* Day, 1 Bradf. 476; Lewis *v.* Schofield, 26 Conn. 452.

cannot take both. This option must be made known to the court of common pleas, and entered on the minutes thereof. If the widow neglect so to make it known, she is held to have waived her legacy, and will have her dower, together with such portion of the personalty as she would have had if no will had been made. It is also provided, that any devise of property shall be held to convey all the testator's interest therein, unless it shall clearly appear by the will that the testator intended to convey a less estate. (*a*) And if the testator has acquired property after making his will, such property will pass by the will, if it appear that he intended to dispose of all the property he might have at the time of his death. But where property descends, in consequence of not being disposed of by the will, it is, by our statute, the first to be chargeable with the testator's debts, unless the contrary be directed; and where property specifically devised has been taken to pay the testator's debts, the other devisees are to contribute *pro rata* to make up the loss, unless the contrary be directed. If either of the devisees be insolvent, his share is to be made up by the rest; and if he be dead, his estate must contribute. All questions of contribution arising under wills may be adjusted in chancery. We have before seen that land taken by devise from an ancestor is here made ancestral property, in the same manner as if taken by descent.

§ 165. **Execution of a Will.** (*b*) The form of a will is of no manner of consequence, provided the intention of the testator is manifest. Not a technical word is absolutely necessary. It is common enough to preface a will with an appeal to the Almighty, an allusion to the uncertainty of life, and an averment of the testator's soundness of mind, but all this is unnecessary. In general, the more direct and concise a will is, the better. But there are certain formalities required by the statute which cannot be dispensed with.

1. A will must be in *writing.* (*c*) This is required, not only by the statute of frauds, which requires all conveyances of realty to

(*a*) A will disposing of lands in Ohio must be construed according to Ohio rules; and in such case a widow will not be entitled to dower, in addition to the provision made for her, unless such clearly appears to have been the testator's intention. Jennings *v.* Jennings, 21 Ohio State, 56. It is governed by the law in force at the testator's death. Hartshorne *v.* Ross, 2 Disney, 15, 444.

(*b*) To pass real estate, a will must be executed with the formalities required by the law of the country where the real estate is situated. To pass personalty, it must have the formalities required by the law of the place of his domicile, or of the place where he actually is at the time of his death. If a person temporarily absent from his domicile makes a will according to the law of the place where he then is, but which does not comply with the law of the place of his domicile, and afterwards returns to his domicile and dies there, the will is not valid even as to personalty. Manuel *v.* Manuel, 13 Ohio State, 458.

(*c*) A mistake in a will cannot, therefore, be shown by parol and corrected, as in such a case a will would be made by parol, or if the mistake were shown by writing, still it would be without the formalities required by the statute. Bacon *v.* Wetmore, 2 Green, 250; Wallige *v.* Wallige, 55 Penn. State, 209; McAlister *v.* Butterfield, 31 Ind. 25; Skipwith *v.* Cabell, 19 Grattan, 758.

be in writing, but also by the statute of wills, which expressly requires all wills to be in writing except *nuncupative wills.* These last cannot pass *realty;* (*a*) but they are good for *personalty*, if they were made in the *last sickness*, reduced to writing within ten days after the uttering of the testamentary words, and subscribed by two witnesses, who can testify that the testator was of sound mind and not under restraint, and that he called upon some person present to witness that such was his will; and they must be proved within six months.

2. A will must be *signed* at the end thereof by the testator, (*b*) or by some other person in his presence, and by his *express* direction; but since 1825, a will need not be under seal.

3. It must be *attested* and *subscribed*, in the *presence* of the testator, by two or more competent witnesses, who either saw the testator sign the will, or heard him acknowledge the signing. Prior to 1795, three subscribing witnesses were required. The witnesses need not subscribe in the presence of each other, nor know the contents, nor attest every page. As to being in the *presence of the testator*, it has been held sufficient to be in the same room, so that the testator *might* see them, though in fact he did not. (*c*)

§ 166. **Revocation of a Will.** (*d*) The statute points out several ways of revoking a will, or a particular part of it, by the testator.

(*a*) R. S. § 5991. But under the statute of 1824, a nuncupative will was sufficient to pass realty. Gillis *v.* Weller, 10 Ohio, 462; Ashworth *v.* Carleton, 12 Ohio State, 381.

(*b*) Where the testator wrote his name at the end of a will, without any witnesses, then asked for the will to "finish it," and wrote a bequest below his name, and the witnesses then signed, but the testator did not sign again, held invalid. Glancy *v.* Glancy, 17 Ohio State, 134. The validity of the execution of a will must be determined by the law in force at the death of the testator. Jones *v.* Robinson, 17 Ohio State, 171.

(*c*) 4 Kent, Com. 515. The witnesses need not attest the instrument at the same time, or in the presence of each other. The acknowledgment of the signature by the testator, when the witness did not see him sign, may be by signs and motions, or conduct, as well as by express words. Raudebaugh *v.* Shelley, 6 Ohio State, 307; Haynes *v.* Haynes, 33 Ohio State, 598; Logue *v.* Stanton, 5 Sneed, 97; Haysradt *v.* Kingman, 22 N. Y. 372; Matter of McElwain, 3 Green, 490; Reed *v.* Watson, 27 Ind. 443; Willis *v.* Mott, 36 N. Y. 486. But the signature of the testator must be affixed before that of the witnesses. Jackson *v.* Jackson, 39 N. Y. 153. But, although a testator may adopt a signature previously made by acknowledgment before the witnesses, it is held in England that a witness cannot do this. Cooper *v.* Bockett, 7 Eng. Ec. Rep. 537. This appears to be an unreasonable distinction, and has been repudiated in Pennsylvania, in Sturdevant *v.* Birchett, 10 Grattan, 67; Kentucky, in Smith *v.* Wylie, 1 B. Monroe, 114; and some other States; and is disapproved of in Redfield on Wills, pp. 230, 247. But it has lately been so held in Massachusetts. Chase *v.* Kittredge, 11 Allen, 49. In Illinois it is not necessary that the witness should know that it is a will; he is only a witness to the signature; no publication is required. Dickie *v.* Carter, 42 Ill. 376.

(*d*) A conveyance subsequent to the date of a will does not revoke the will, except so far as relates to the property conveyed. Brush *v.* Brush, 11 Ohio, 287. A duly executed written will can neither be wholly nor partially revoked by a subsequent nuncupative will. M'Cune *v.* House, 8 Ohio, 144. Where a will was made, containing a residuary devise of all his freehold estate, and afterwards other land was acquired in fee, and the testator declared, in the presence of two witnesses, that he now republished his former will, but without signing any new instrument, it was held that all his realty passed. Reynolds *v.* Shirley, 7 Ohio, 2 pt. 39; Pruden *v.* Pruden, 14 Ohio State, 251.

1. By intentionally destroying, tearing, cancelling or obliterating such will, or causing the same to be done in his presence, or by his direction. (*a*)

2. By making and publishing a subsequent will; for when there are two wills, it is only the last which takes effect. But the revocation of a subsequent will does not revive a prior one, without express words to that effect, or a republication of such prior will. Nor will a nuncupative will revoke a prior written one.

3. By making a *codicil* for the express purpose of revocation; for a codicil being in general only a sequel to a will, of which it forms a part, does not *ipso facto* work a revocation, like a subsequent will; but only when it expressly provides for such revocation, or contains provisions repugnant to those of the will; and the codicil must be executed with the same formalities as the will itself. (*b*)

4. By having a child subsequently born, there being none alive before, and no provision for such child in the will or otherwise. (*c*) For if the testator had a child when the will was made, the subsequent birth of another does not revoke the will; but provision is made that the after-born child shall take, *as heir*, the same portion of the estate as if there had been no will; to which portion, all the legatees contribute proportionably; and the case is the same where a child was supposed to be dead at the time of making the will, and the contrary turns out to be the fact; but in either case, a deduction is made from the amount to be contributed, of so much as such child may have received by way of *advancement*. But a testator may expressly provide so that the subsequent birth or discovery of a child shall not alter the dispositions made by the will. It is only in the absence of such express provision, that the law steps in to supply the omission. A subsequent marriage, without the

(*a*) Where a testator, being blind, told J. to bring him his will, and he handed it to him in an envelope with three seals, and the testator felt the seals and handed it back, directing it to be thrown into the fire and burned, but J. put it into his pocket, and threw something else into the fire, and called to the deceased to listen and hear it burn, and the deceased smelt the burning paper, and died in the belief that the will was destroyed, it was held not to be a revocation, and the court refused to declare the devisee a trustee for the heirs. Kent *v.* Mahaffey, 10 Ohio State, 204. *Contra*, Smiley *v.* Gambill, 2 Head, 164; Blanchard *v.* Blanchard, 32 Vt. 62. As to what is sufficient evidence of a revocation, see Price *v.* Powell, 3 Hurl. & Nor. 341; Smock *v.* Smock, 3 Stockton, 156; Andrew *v.* Motley, 12 C. B. (N. S.) 514; Brown *v.* Brown, 8 Ellis & B. 876.

(*b*) Where the disposition made by the codicil is inconsistent with that made by the will, it will operate as a *pro tanto* revocation. Larabee *v.* Larabee, 28 Vt. 274. But it will not revoke the will further than is required by express terms, or necessary implication. Collier *v.* Collier, 3 Ohio State, 369.

(*c*) This is the rule in the absence of any statutory provision on the subject. McCullum *v.* McKenzie, 26 Iowa, 510. When deceased had no child at the time the will was made, the subsequent birth of a child revokes the will, and it is not revived by the fact that the parent survives the child. Ash *v.* Ash, 9 Ohio State, 383. Where a will was made June 12, 1830, and the testator died July 7, 1830, and a child was born on the 4th of December following, held that the testator had no child *in esse* at the time of the execution of the will, within the meaning of the statute of wills, and that the will was therefore avoided by the birth of such child. Evans *v.* Anderson, 15 Ohio State, 324.

birth of a child, does not in any case revoke the prior will, either of the husband or wife. (*a*)

5. As to the effect of a subsequent conveyance, we adopt the common law, which holds the will to be revoked as to the particular portion of the estate conveyed. This is reasonable, because the conveyance, though made after the will, takes effect first. But our statute provides that no subsequent contract, incumbrance, or other act, which does not wholly divest property from the testator, shall revoke the prior will in reference to such property, unless such contract, incumbrance, or other act, be wholly inconsistent with the previous devise or bequest. With this exception, the property passes by the will, subject to all the rights created by the subsequent acts of the testator. (*b*)

§ 167. **Probate.** (*c*) A will is of no effect until *probate* has been made. For this purpose, the executor, or any person interested, may bring the will before the probate court. The probate must be made in the county where the property lies; or if it lie in several, then in either. (*d*) The subscribing witnesses, and such others as any person interested may desire, if within the jurisdiction, must be examined in open court; if absent, their depositions must be produced, if possible; but if dead or gone to parts unknown, any other legal testimony may be taken. The testimony so taken is reduced to writing by the clerk and filed; and if it appear to the court that the testator was competent at the time to make a will, and not under restraint, and that the will was duly executed and attested, such will and proof are recorded in the clerk's office; and a certified copy thereof is as valid and effectual as the original. This probate, however, is not absolutely conclusive as to the validity of the will; which is liable to be contested by bill in chancery, at any time within two years from the probate; or in case of disability, two years from the removal thereof. (*e*) And here I would remark, that besides the four disabilities usually provided

(*a*) In New York, by statute the subsequent marriage of a woman does revoke prior wills, and the married women's acts have not altered this rule. Loomis *v.* Loomis, 51 Barb. 119.

(*b*) A devise to an intended wife whom the testator subsequently marries, is not revoked by her desertion and divorce. Charlton *v.* Miller, 27 Ohio State, 298.

(*c*) By the act of 1852, when a will is propounded for probate, the court only examine witnesses in favor of the probate. In other words, the contest cannot be made until after the probate. This was decided in the case of Hathaway's will, 4 Ohio State, 383. By the same act, in case probate be refused, an appeal lies to the common pleas, but not from the granting of probate. And see Chapman's will, 6 Ohio, 148; Hunter's will, 6 id. 499; Swazey *v.* Blackman, 8 id. 5. As to the practice in contesting will, see Green *v.* Green, 5 Ohio, 278; Raudebaugh *v.* Shelley, 6 Ohio State, 307. The verdict of a jury, as to the validity of a will, may be reviewed on petition in error. Glancy *v.* Glancy, 17 Ohio State, 134. Spoliated or destroyed wills cannot be established under the statutes of Ohio, unless existing subsequently to the testator's decease. In matter of Sinclair's will, 5 Ohio State, 290.

(*d*) If the testator were a resident of this State at the time of his death, letters testamentary can only issue from the probate court of the county in which the testator resided. Limes *v.* Irwin, 16 Ohio State, 488.

(*e*) Where a proceeding is commenced within the two years as to some of the parties, the right of action is saved as to all, who are ultimately made parties to the proceeding. Bradford *v.* Andrews, 20 Ohio State, 208.

for in our statutes, namely, *infancy*, *coverture*, *insanity*, and *imprisonment*, we have in this one case a fifth, namely, *absence from the State*, which corresponds to being " beyond seas," in the English law. When a will is contested in chancery, our statute requires an issue to be made up, whether the writing produced be the last will of the testator or not, which issue is tried by a jury, the defendant having the affirmative. If any devisee in a will know of its existence, and do not, within three years, produce it for probate, he thereby forfeits his devise. (*a*) And any person having control of a will, and failing to produce it for probate after being duly cited, may be attached for a contempt, and is liable in damages to the party injured. Provision is made for depositing a will for safe-keeping with the clerk of the court of common pleas; in which case the will must be sealed up in a wrapper, and the name of the testator indorsed on the outside; and if, after the death of the testator, there be no person indorsed on the wrapper, as authorized to produce the will for probate, it will be publicly opened in court, and the proper proceedings had. When a will has been admitted to probate, and is not contested, as above provided, it binds everybody interested. If lands affected by a will lie in several counties, one probate is sufficient; for an authenticated copy of the will and probate will be admitted to record in any other county. I have said that a will is of no effect until probate has been made; but after probate it relates back, and takes effect from the death of the testator.

§ 168. **Other Incidents.** (*b*) It is universally agreed that wills are to be construed *liberally*. The great object is to ascertain the *intention* of the testator, and this always governs the construction; although for want of time, advice, or learning, he may have omitted the proper legal words. (*c*) On this principle, the law dis-

(*a*) This does not apply to the failure to record a copy of the probate of a foreign will for over three years. Carpenter *v.* Denoon, 29 Ohio State, 379.

(*b*) Where the will says, "I give one third of all my land to A.," he takes in fee-simple. Smith *v.* Berry, 8 Ohio, 365. But though the first words might be sufficient to pass a fee, any subsequent provision, showing a contrary intention, will limit the operation of the general words. Stableton *v.* Ellison, 21 Ohio State, 527. Where the will directs land to be converted into money, and the interest of one-third to be secured to the wife, and the rest to heirs, and there are no heirs, the wife takes the whole. Ferguson *v.* Stuart, 14 Ohio, 140. Where the will gives all to the wife, but directs the executor to lease, &c., and pay proceeds to the wife, the legal title is in the executor. Boyd *v.* Talbert, 12 Ohio, 212. Where a devise is to three children, "providing they live to legal age," they take a present vested interest, subject only to be divested by dying before majority. Foster *v.* Wick, 17 Ohio, 250. Where property is devised for specific purposes, it reverts when those purposes have been entirely accomplished. Bigelow *v.* Barr, 4 Ohio, 358; Williams *v.* Veach, 17 id. 171. And see Decker *v.* Decker, 3 Ohio, 157; Davison *v.* Wolf, 9 id. 73. As to the construction of a devise to the heirs of a person in existence, see Williamson *v.* Williamson, 18 B. Monr. 329.

(*c*) Worman *v.* Teagarden, 2 Ohio State, 380; Collier *v.* Collier, 3 id. 369; Thompson *v.* Thompson, 4 id. 333. The testator may charge his personal estate with the payment of incumbrances on his real estate, either by express words or by provisions inconsistent with any other intention. Id. The intention of the testator to charge pecuniary legacies on real estate, so as to make the charge a lien upon it, may be declared in express words or derived by implication from the provisions of the will.

penses with words in wills, which would be absolutely necessary in any other instruments. We have seen an instance of this when speaking of the necessity of the word "*heirs*" in a deed, in order to create a fee, which word is not necessary in a will. We have also seen that the *rule in Shelley's case* is abrogated with respect to wills, and the intention of the testator carried literally into effect, by limiting the estate as he limited it. Again, as to what are called *lapsed legacies*, our statute provides that if a devise be made to a person without naming issue, and such person die before the testator, his issue shall take, unless the contrary be expressed in the will. Another maxim of construction is that where there are repugnant clauses in a will, that which is last in order shall prevail, though the contrary holds in a deed. Our court has repeatedly sanctioned the doctrine that the intention of the testator, whenever it can be ascertained, is the rule of construction. For example, although *manufacturing stock* is personal property, and would pass under a general bequest thereof, yet where it appeared that the testator intended to discriminate between that and other personalty, the will was so construed. Also, where property was devised to educate a child, and the child soon after died, yet as it appeared that the testator intended that the devisee should have a life-estate, the will was so construed; although the general principle is, that a grant is void when its purpose is fulfilled. There are very few powers, in relation to the management of property, which the testator cannot confer either on the executors or trustees. If a vacancy occur in the office of executor or trustee, by reason of any contingency not provided for in the will, the court has power to fill such vacancy; and where an administrator has been appointed on the supposition that there was no will, and the will has been afterwards discovered and proved, the power of the administrator is thereby superseded, and the executor takes his place. We have seen that the testator cannot in any way limit his property further than to such persons as are in being at the time, and their immediate issue. But with this restriction, the testator may settle his property in almost any use or trust he pleases, in defiance of all the ancient technicalities. In relation

Clyde *v.* Simpson, 4 id. 445. The word "heirs" may be construed to mean "legatees," when that is the manifest intention of the testator. Collier *v.* Collier, 3 Ohio State, 369. Where there is a devise in fee to A., but if he "die without heirs," or "without children," or "without issue," then to B. in fee, the words "if he die without issue," or words of similar import, are to be interpreted according to their popular and natural meaning, and as referring to the time of the death of A., unless the contrary intention is plainly expressed in the will, or is necessary to carry out its undoubted purposes; and if A. have no children or issue living at the time he dies, B. takes under such devise. Parish *v.* Ferris, 6 Ohio State, 563; Stevenson *v.* Evans, 10 Ohio State, 307; Niles *v.* Gray, 12 Ohio State, 320. But see Creswell's Appeal, 41 Penn. State, 288; Condict *v.* King, 2 Beasley, 375. Words of survivorship are to be referred to the period of payment or distribution of the subject-matter of the gift, unless a contrary intention is evidenced by the language of the will. Sinton *v.* Boyd, 19 Ohio State, 30. A condition that any legatee trying to break a will shall forfeit his legacy is valid, and a legacy thus forfeited will pass to general residuary legatees. Bradford *v.* Bradford, 19 Ohio State, 546.

to his children, the testator has power by his will to appoint guardians, until they arrive at majority; and guardians so appointed have the same power over the persons and property of such children, unless modified by the will, as other guardians. With respect to creditors, we have already seen that no disposition of property by will can defeat their claims. Even the express discharge of a debt due to the testator will not be valid as against creditors. Nor does the appointment of a debtor to be executor operate as a discharge of the debt, as was formerly held.

Foreign Wills. (*a*) The general doctrine is, that wills relating to land must be executed according to the prescribed formalities of the State where the land lies; but our statute has made an exception in favor of wills made in any of the States or territories of the Union; which, if made and proved according to the law of the place where made, have the same validity as if made here; and authenticated copies, when placed on record in the county where the property lies, are as effectual as domestic wills. And the same is provided with respect to wills executed and proved in a foreign country; except that notice of the application to have such foreign wills admitted to record, must be given through the newspapers, in order that all persons interested may have an opportunity to make resistance.

LECTURE XXXI.

TITLE BY PURCHASE.

§ 169. **Forms of Conveyance.** (*b*) We come now to the last method of acquiring title; namely, by *purchase*. Under this head, I shall discuss the subject of *conveyancing* at some length, on account of its great practical importance. In the course of our inquiries, you will have abundant reason to observe how much this branch of law has been already simplified; and how much yet

(*a*) A will made in another State must be recorded here, before title to land situated here vests in the devisee. Wilson *v.* Tappan, 6 Ohio, 172; Bailey *v.* Bailey, 8 id. 239. But the title dates back to the death of the testator, and not merely to the date of registration here. Hall *v.* Ashby, 9 Ohio, 96.

(*b*) See 2 Black. Com. ch. 20; 4 Kent, Com. lec. 67; the various works upon Conveyancing, by Curtis, Oliver, Barton, Watkins, and Wood; Roberts on Fraudulent Conveyances; Sugden on Vendors. In Lindsley *v.* Coats, 1 Ohio, 243, the court say, "In no instance have the ancient common-law modes of conveyance, as such, been adopted in this State; and long anterior to the settlement of this country, they had given way to the comparatively modern mode of assurance by deeds of lease and release, bargain and sale, &c. From the first organization of the government to the present time, it has been the policy of our laws that the title to real estate should be matter of record, subject to the inspection of every individual interested." And accordingly, in this case, a parol exchange of lands with possession under it, was held void here, though good at common law. And see Starr *v.* Starr, 1 Ohio, 321; Bentley *v.* Deforest, 2 id. 221; Hall *v.* Ashby, 9 id. 96.

remains to be done. In England the law of conveyancing is so technical and abstruse, and the forms are so voluminous, and complicated, that this is made a distinct and important branch of the legal profession; and a long apprenticeship is required to make an expert conveyancer. In all enlightened nations a fundamental distinction has been made between realty and personalty in regard to the modes of transfer. Personal property, on account of its movable and transitory nature, has generally been transferable by *mere delivery*, without any form or ceremony whatever. This was expressly declared to be the law of this territory by the ordinance of 1787, and has ever since continued so to be. But from the earliest periods of the English law, something more than mere delivery has been necessary to transfer real estate. From its fixed and permanent character, no transfer can be evidenced by change of place; and as it is in every point of view important that the owner should be known, a variety of forms and ceremonies have been resorted to in order to insure *notoriety*. For the purpose of placing this matter in a clear light, I shall briefly refer to the three principal common-law conveyances, namely, *by feoffment*, *by fine*, and *by common recovery*, though neither has ever been in use here; after which I shall describe the forms in actual use.

Feoffment. (*a*) Feoffment was the ancient mode of conveying any corporeal hereditament. It was commenced by an instrument in writing, signed, sealed, and delivered; in other words a deed. Then followed the ceremony, so often referred to before, called *livery of seisin*, without which the deed was of no effect. This ceremony consisted in a corporeal transfer or delivery of the land to the purchaser. The parties went to the land, or in sight of it, and there, in the presence of as many witnesses as could be had, the feoffer declared the contents of the deed, and then made a symbolical delivery of the land therein described to the feoffee, by actually delivering a twig or turf, or something else thereto belonging. This ceremony completed the conveyance. Blackstone says of this conveyance, that it was "the most ancient, the most solemn and public, and, therefore, the most easily remembered and proved." The notoriety depended upon the number of persons who witnessed the livery of seisin. The corresponding conveyance of an incorporeal hereditament was termed a *grant*, which differed in nothing from a feoffment, but that there was no livery of seisin, it being impossible from the intangible nature of the subject.

Fine. (*b*) This is the name given to a conveyance by record of court. It proceeds from beginning to end upon *fictions*. The person who is to be the grantee sues the grantor on a pretended contract to convey the land to him. The grantor thereupon comes into court, acknowledges the right of the grantee, and asks leave to compromise the suit. This leave is granted upon payment of

(*a*) See 2 Black. Com. 310.

(*b*) Id. 348.

a *fine* to the king; whence comes the name of the conveyance. A record is then made of all the proceedings, of which the parties take indented copies; and a proclamation thereof completes the conveyance. This conveyance is absolutely conclusive upon *parties* and *privies*, from the moment, and upon all other persons after five years, without claim. Here, then, the publicity of proceedings in court is substituted for livery of seisin.

Common Recovery. (*a*) This, like a fine, is a conveyance by record of court. It consists, like that, of a series of *fictions*, but is much more complicated. Here the person who is to be the grantee sues for the land, alleging that the grantor is in possession without any title. The grantor thereupon prays that some person, who, as he alleges, warranted the title to him, may be called in to defend in his place, disclaiming all title in himself. This alleged warrantor makes default; whereupon a twofold judgment is rendered: first, that the plaintiff or intended grantee recover the premises; and, secondly, that the alleged warrantor indemnify the defendant, or intended grantor, for the loss of his land. This conveyance was devised for the express purpose of cutting off estates tail, and all remainders and reversions expectant thereon: and it was permitted to have this searching effect, on account of the two fictions involved in the judgment; namely, a pretended recompense to the defendant by the fictitious warrantor.

Bargain and Sale. (*b*) The ancient forms of conveyance, just described, may have prevailed in some parts of the Union; but they never were adopted in this State. The ordinance of 1787, which was the first act of legislation over the territory, prescribed two other modes of conveyance; namely, *by bargain and sale*, and *by lease and release;* and no other has ever been used. Both these forms originated under the *statute of uses*, which we have seen, if ever in force here, has not been since 1806. The original object of both these conveyances was to avoid the necessity of livery of seisin, without resorting to the records of court. I shall begin with the conveyance by *bargain and sale.* It will be remembered that the effect of the statute of uses was, to annex the legal title to the use, by providing that when any person was *seised* of land to the use of another, the legal estate should *ipso facto* pass to the latter. Prior to this statute, a bargain and sale of land was held to be nothing more than a *contract to convey*, which, if made upon a valuable consideration, equity would enforce by decreeing a legal conveyance. This very fact, of a valuable consideration, was held to raise a *trust* or *use* in favor of the bargainee, and give jurisdiction to the court of chancery to carry it into effect. This being the existing doctrine, the effect of the statute was to change a

(*a*) Id. 387. R. S. of Ohio, §§ 5803 *et seq.* provides for a proceeding in certain cases to sell property held by other than a fee-simple title for the benefit of the holder of the present estate and not injurious to the succeeding proprietors.

(*b*) See 2 Black. Com. 238; 4 Petersdorf's Abr. 5; 4 Kent. Com. 495; Lindsley *v.* Coats, 1 Ohio, 243; Thompson *v.* Gibson, 2 id. 339; Holt *v.* Hemphill, 3 id. 232.

bargain and sale into a legal conveyance. The execution of the deed for a valuable consideration raised a use in the bargainee, to which the statute, superseding the action of a court of chancery, at once transferred the legal estate. Here, then, was no troublesome ceremony of making livery of seisin, or going through the forms of a suit in court; and it is not strange that this simple mode of conveyance was at once adopted into general use. To secure, however, the notoriety which this form would otherwise want, it was enacted in the same year, that a bargain and sale should not be held to convey a *freehold*, unless it were made by indenture, and *enrolled* within six months in one of the courts, where all persons might take cognizance of it. This *enrolment* was undoubtedly an improvement upon the preceding modes of securing notoriety, and is the origin of our present law for recording deeds. Such is the theory of a bargain and sale, under the statute of uses; and such is its theory with us, though we have not adopted that statute. We hold that the mere execution and delivery of the deed, without any other ceremony, completes the conveyance. We also hold, as a matter of form, that some consideration must be stated in the deed, which was not necessary in a feoffment, because without such consideration, a *use* could not be raised in the bargainee. Under the English law, a corporation could not convey by bargain and sale, because it could not be seised to a use; which is not the case here, because we require no seisin to a use; the conveyance taking effect here without the intervention of the statute.

Lease and Release. (*a*) This mode of conveyance was invented to evade one of the provisions above referred to. We have seen that the necessity of *enrolment* was confined to the conveyance of *freeholds*. Consequently, a bargain and sale of an *estate for years* would be good without enrolment. Accordingly, a person wishing to make a secret conveyance, executed a lease for one year or more, which, without enrolment, vested in the lessee the *use* of the term for that time; to which use the statute at once annexed the possession. Now, by the common law, a person in possession as lessee could receive a *release* of the freehold and reversion without livery of seisin. Accordingly, a release was executed immediately after the lease, and thus the conveyance was completed without either livery or enrolment. This is said to be the most common conveyance in England; but so far as I know, it is not practised at all in Ohio, though, as we have seen, it is provided for in the ordinance of 1787. At any rate, the main reason for preferring it in England, does not exist here; for such a conveyance would require to be recorded as much as a deed of bargain and sale; and the latter is the more simple and economical, because it requires but one instrument, while the former requires two. This is probably the reason why a bargain and sale is here generally preferred.

(*a*) See 2 Black. Com. 339; 4 Kent, Com. 494.

It will thus be seen that our law of conveyancing has been greatly simplified. By a slight attention to the form of a deed of bargain and sale, every man might, for all common purposes, become his own conveyancer. It will also be seen, that while personalty may be transferred by mere delivery, without even a bill of sale, realty can only be transferred by means of a deed, which must be recorded in a public office, for notice to all the world. The form and requisites of a deed will be fully described in the course of this lecture. But in the mean time, there are several preliminary considerations which require a brief notice. With respect to personalty, I shall have very little to say here, on account of the simplicity of the mode of transfer; but when I come to speak of the *contract of sale*, my remarks will relate chiefly to the sale of personalty. It must not, however, be inferred that no right whatever to realty can be transferred without a regular and formal deed. This is the only method of conveying a complete legal title from one person to another among the living; but an equitable title, as before explained, may be transferred by any instrument of writing which complies with the statute of frauds; and this equitable title may be perfected into a legal title, by the decree of a court of chancery. Indeed, where the purchase-money is not to be paid down, instead of making a deed and taking back a mortgage, it is very common for the vendor to make only a *title bond*, which is a contract to convey when the stipulated payments shall have been made. Such a contract makes the vendor a trustee for the vendee; and when the latter has complied with his part of the contract, if the vendor should refuse to make a deed, he may be compelled to do so by a decree in chancery.

§ 170. **Preliminary Conditions of a Valid Conveyance.** Under this head, I shall consider several matters affecting the validity of a conveyance, though it may have all the formalities required by law.

Fraudulent Conveyances. (*a*) I shall reserve what I have to say on the general subject of fraud, until I come to treat of contracts, when the statute of frauds will be examined at some length. It will be sufficient here to say, that this statute not only requires every conveyance of realty to be in writing, as before remarked, but also makes void every conveyance made with intent to defraud creditors or purchasers. Under the head of crimes, moreover, we shall see that severe penalties are annexed to the fraudulent transfer of property, whether real or personal. In fact, it is a general rule, that fraud vitiates every thing into which it enters. A fraudulent conveyance, therefore, will not be permitted to take effect; and in our subsequent remarks we shall presuppose that the parties to a conveyance are acting in good faith. If not, a court of law, when it is possible, and a court of equity always, will set aside the fraudulent conveyance.

(*a*) See Hovenden on Frauds; Roberts on Frauds, and Roberts on Fraudulent Conveyances; Crumbaugh *v.* Kugler, 2 Ohio State, 373; 3 id. 544.

Conveyance without Title. In this State, it is made a penitentiary offence, *knowingly* to convey land without having a title thereto, either legal or equitable, properly evidenced, *with intent* to defraud the purchaser. (*a*) It will be observed that three things are necessary to constitute the criminality: *First*, the entire want of title; *secondly*, a knowledge of that fact; and *thirdly*, the intent to defraud the purchaser. But if the first two exist, the third almost necessarily follows. If a man who knows that he has no shadow of title, undertakes to make a conveyance, he can have no other motive than to defraud the purchaser; but where the guilty knowledge does not exist, the criminality is taken away; and the only effect of a conveyance without title would be to lay the foundation of an action by the purchaser, either on the covenants in the deed, or to recover back the purchase-money.

Conveyance without Possession. (*b*) At common law, the conveyance of land, which at the time was in the adverse possession of another, was void; and this is the law in several of the States. Also by a statute of the 32d of Henry 8th, it was made unlawful for any person to make a conveyance of land, unless he, or those under whom he claimed, had been in actual or constructive possession within one year. In this State, we have no statutory provision on the subject; we have no law against *champerty* or *maintenance*, which prohibited a right of action from being assigned or purchased; and we have no express decision on the question. But the reason of the ancient common-law doctrine does not exist here. When livery of seisin was necessary, as it could only be made by a person in possession, a conveyance by a person not in possession must of course be void. But where the execution and delivery of a deed consummates a conveyance, without livery of seisin on the one hand, or entry on the other, there is no good reason why a conveyance of land to which the grantor has a good legal claim, should not be valid. On the whole, then, I think we are safe in concluding that a conveyance by a person who has a legal claim to land, held adversely by another, is valid. The ancient idea that litigation is thereby encouraged, is utterly without foundation. An action by the vendee would do no more harm than an action by the vendor.

Conveyance Pending Suit — Lis Pendens. (*c*) Wherever there

(*a*) {R. S. § 7079. The crime of conveying land without title applies to deeds purporting to convey lands situated out of the State as well as within; the word "convey" here does not render the statute void for repugnancy, but means to execute an instrument in the form of a conveyance. Kerr *v.* State, 36 Ohio State, 614.}

(*b*) 2 Black. Com. 290; 4 Kent, Com. 446; Key *v.* Vattier, 1 Ohio, 132; Backus *v.* McCoy, 3 id. 211; Cresinger *v.* Welch, 15 id. 156; Hall *v.* Ashby, 9 id. 96; Rawle on Covenants for Title, pp. 31–51; Cain *v.* Monroe, 23 Geo. 82; Harring *v.* Barwick, 24 id. 59.

(*c*) *Pending Suit — Lis Pendens.* R. S. § 5055, — "when the summons has been served or publication made, the action is pending so as to charge third persons with notice," &c., but by § 4987 at the date of the summons served on defendant or at the date of the first publication, § 4988, an attempt to commence an action is equivalent to commencement, if there is diligence and a service within sixty days. Upon the general subject of *lis pendens*, see 4 Kent, Com. 449; 6 Dane's Abr. 741; Jackson *v.* Ketchum, is a statute existing against champerty, or where champerty is an offence at common law, a conveyance of land during the pendency of a suit concerning it, is an act of champerty. As we recognize no such misdemeanor, the only effect of the pendency of a suit is to make the conveyance void; and this effect always follows, though the purchaser knew nothing of the existence of the suit, and paid a full price for the land. The pendency of a suit, for reasons of public policy, is held to be constructive notice to all the world, not to purchase the subject in litigation; and as against the plaintiff, such purchase, however honestly made, is totally void; though as against the defendant, if he should finally prevail in the suit, the conveyance would be good, because he would not be allowed to disaffirm his own deed. This may be often a very hard doctrine, but without it there would be no end to litigation; for before the plaintiff had got through his suit, the defendant would convey to some one else, and thus make another suit necessary, and so on without end.

Conveyance of more than one has. (a) At common law, as we have seen, the attempt to convey a *greater estate* than the grantor had, was not only void as to the grantee, but worked a forfeiture

8 Johns. 479. The doctrine of *lis pendens* does not apply to the party in interest who is not a party to the suit. Irvin *v.* Smith, 17 Ohio, 226. Where a trustee before suit by him who has the equity, contracts to sell to one ignorant of the equity, and conveys to him after suit is brought, the doctrine does not apply. Trimble *v.* Boothby, 14 Ohio, 109; Gibler *v.* Trimble, id. 323. After a final decree there is no *lis pendens.* Turner *v.* Crebill, 1 Ohio, 372; Taylor *v.* Boyd, 3 id. 337. Nor does the doctrine apply where the plaintiff in ejectment conveys during suit. Dawson *v.* Porter, 2 Ohio, 304. Nor where the conveyance was made between final decree and reversal on bill of review. Ludlow *v.* Kidd, 3 Ohio, 541. A chancery suit is considered as pending from the time of publication of notice. Bennett *v.* Williams, 5 Ohio, 461. A bill of divorce praying for alimony, but not referring to any particular property, is not a *lis pendens* as to that property. Hamlin *v.* Bevans, 7 Ohio, 1 pt. 161; *contra* if it describes property and claims equities in it. Tolerton *v.* Williard, 30 Ohio State, 579. Where a bill was filed to subject land to a judgment, which was afterwards reversed, and remanded, and another judgment obtained, a conveyance between the two judgments was held to be *pendente lite.* Stoddard *v.* Myers, 8 Ohio, 203. A grant of letters of administration is not a *lis pendens.* Davis *v.* Livingston, 6 Ohio, 225. Where a creditor's bill does not allege that there are no leviable means, a conveyance by the judgment debtor is good. Clark *v.* Strong, 16 Ohio, 317. After final judgment against A., and proceedings to subject a debt due from W. to A. to the judgment, and notice to W. of such proceedings, the fact that such judgment is set aside, and a new judgment entered, will not authorize W. to pay A. Such a payment is made *lite pendente.* Gibbon *v.* Dougherty, 10 Ohio State, 365. {Laches in prosecuting a suit may prevent its being a *lis pendens* as to third persons. Fox *v.* Reeder, 28 Ohio State, 181; Trimble *v.* Boothby, 14 Ohio, 109. But a delay of eight months in making service by publication where property was attached is no ground for dismissal. Bacher *v.* Shawhan, 41 Ohio State, 271; *contra* by statute in a justice's court. The doctrine of *lis pendens* does not apply to negotiable paper before due; and a *bonâ fide* purchaser takes it free of a decree against the maker and payee subjecting the debt. Stone *v.* Elliott, 11 Ohio State, 252; Howe *v.* Hartness, id. 449; Secor *v.* Witter, 39 id. 218. A failure to indorse on a summons served by a private person his authority to serve it does not constitute the action a *lis pendens,* except from the date of such indorsement. Barry *v.* Hovey, 30 Ohio State, 344. An assignment for benefit of creditors after the date of the summons, but before service and taking of the property, will not defeat a replevin. Collier *v.* Bickley, 33 Ohio State, 523.}

(a) See 4 Kent, Com. 106; White *v.* Sayre, 2 Ohio, 113. Deed in fee by tenant for life not a forfeiture. Carpenter *v.* Denoon, 29 Ohio State, 379.

as to the grantor. For example, if a lessee for years undertook to convey a freehold, his term was thereby forfeited to the next owner in reversion or remainder. This depended upon technical reasons arising from the feudal relation of lord and vassal. And accordingly, after the statute of uses, when the courts adopted many of the equitable doctrines already established in chancery, this doctrine of forfeiture was given up, and it was held that when a person attempted to convey a greater estate than he possessed, the conveyance should be good for his whole interest. This is the doctrine here, and it seems to be the only rational doctrine that could be adopted. In like manner the conveyance of *more land* than one has, is good for whatever he has. Thus, if I undertake to convey, as sole owner of a tract of land, when in fact I only own an undivided share, this will be good for such undivided share. Indeed, our court has gone so far as to hold, that if I own an undivided fourth, for example, of a given tract, and I undertake to convey a specific portion thereof, by metes and bounds, the conveyance will be good for an undivided fourth of the portion attempted to be conveyed. (*a*) This is a novel doctrine, but it must stand as law till overruled.

§ 171. **Formalities of a Deed.** (*b*) I now come to the particular consideration of deeds. According to Blackstone, "a deed is a writing sealed and delivered by the parties." It is said to be called a *deed*, by way of eminence, "because it is the most solemn and authentic act that a man can possibly perform in relation to the disposal of his property." The above definition does not describe a deed of the present day, because by our law *signing* is essential. With us, any instrument is a deed, which is *written, signed, sealed*, and *delivered*. But, in common language, we confine the term deed to an instrument for the conveyance of real estate. I proceed, therefore, to describe the properties of such a deed. The formalities of a deed are provided for by statute. But from the ordinance of 1787 to the present time, there has been a great deal of fluctuating legislation on the subject.

A deed must be in writing: or it may be *printed*, all but the signature. The common custom is to have blank forms printed, to be filled up with writing; but the deed must be filled up before the execution. A writing not under seal may be made over a sig-

(*a*) White *v.* Sayre, 2 Ohio, 103.

(*b*) See 4 Kent, Com. 450; 2 Black. Com. 295. A deed must conform to the law in force at the time of its execution, to be valid. Though the law be altered to require less formality before it is recorded, still it will be void. Boyle *v.* Chambers, 32 Missouri, 46; Switzer *v.* Knapps, 10 Iowa, 72. Since the internal revenue law, it must be stamped fifty cents for every five hundred dollars, or fractional part thereof, in the value of the property conveyed. The act of June 6, 1872, taking effect Oct. 1, 1872, statutes at large, session of 1871, 1872, p. 230, 256, § 36, repealed stamp duties on all instruments except bank checks, to take effect Oct. 1, 1872. {But this act never was held to exclude the instrument as evidence in the State courts where the omission to stamp was not with intent to evade the law. Stewart *v.* Hopkins, 30 Ohio State, 502, and cases cited. Or when offered by one not a party to it. Reis *v.* Hellman, 25 id. 180.}

nature in blank; but for technical reasons, no sealed instrument can be thus made. (*a*)

It must be signed: or if the grantor cannot write, some one else must write his name, and he must ratify it. In early times, when seals had a distinctive character, signing was not necessary, but it became so under the English statute of frauds. Even without the statute, however, signing has always been necessary in this State. But I presume it would be sufficient for the grantor's name to appear in any part of the deed.

It must be sealed. (*b*) And it is provided by statute, that whenever a specific seal is not expressly required, "a seal either of wax, wafer, or of ink, commonly called a scrawl seal, shall be alike valid, and deemed sufficient." In consequence of this provision, it is very rare to see any other seal to a deed than a mere flourish of a pen opposite to the signature, with the word "seal," or the initials "L. S.," to show that it is meant for a seal; and this flourish is hardly ever made by the grantor himself, but usually by the scrivener, so that it becomes his only by adoption. More need not be said to demonstrate the utter insignificance of the formality of sealing; yet the conveyance would be good for nothing without it. The use of seals originated in the inability of men to write their names; and then they had a distinctive character, which identified the grantor as well as his signature. But ever since men have been able to write, and their signature has been required, and especially since a mere scrawl has been made sufficient, the requisition of a seal has been purely arbitrary. The theory is, that the affixing of a seal evinces solemnity and deliberation; but as seals are usually affixed, this is mere theory; and even were it fact, still the formalities which remain to be men-

(*a*) Ayres *v.* Harness, 1 Ohio, 368; Day *v.* Brown, 2 id. 345. Blanks cannot be filled in a deed after execution. Drury *v.* Foster, 2 Wallace, 24; Burns *v.* Lynde, 6 Allen, 305. {That a power may be given to alter or file a blank in a deed, see Drury *v.* Foster, 2 Wall. 24, 33; but if a grantee's name is not inserted before delivery by the party authorized to fill the blank, the deed is void. Allen *v.* Withrow, 110 U. S. 119. But an intentional omission of the grantee's name was said not to prevent the instrument being valid in equity as a contract in favor of the vendee; and perhaps the grantor would be estopped to claim that the name was inserted after execution. Holden *v.* Belmont, 32 Ohio State, 585, 589. But the omission of the name of a mortgagee when it is specified that he is to hold in trust for a named person will not invalidate it between the parties or as a lien. Hitesman *v.* Donnel, 40 Ohio State, 287.} But in Iowa it has been held that an agent may be authorized to fill blanks as to third persons. Owen *v.* Perry, 25 Iowa, 412; Durie *v.* Himer, 29 Iowa, 297. As to the question of presumption as to the time of alterations appearing on the face of a deed, the decisions are conflicting. On the one hand, it is said that in the absence of any proof on the subject the alteration must be presumed to have been made before delivery. Little *v.* Herndon, 10 Wall. 26. On the other, that when the alteration is beneficial to the grantee he must explain and justify it. Robinson *v.* Myers, 67 Penn. State, 9. Where a deed has once been executed and delivered, parol evidence is not admissible to show that at the time the grantor reserved a right to cut timber on the property. Jones *v.* Timmons, 21 Ohio State, 596.

(*b*) 2 Black. Com. 295; Erwin *v.* Shuey, 8 Ohio State, 509; Richardson *v.* Bates, 8 id. 257. {Private seals and all distinctions between sealed and unsealed instruments are now abolished in Arkansas, California, Dakota, Indiana, Iowa, Kansas, Kentucky, Mississippi, Montana, Nebraska, Ohio, Oregon, Tennessee, and Texas.}

tioned, are amply sufficient for every useful purpose. But such is the law, and I shall consider the policy of seals in another place.

It must be attested. (*a*) The words of the statute are: "Such deed shall be signed and sealed by the grantor, or such signing or sealing shall be acknowledged by the grantor in the presence of two witnesses, who shall attest such signing and sealing, and subscribe their names to such attestation." The witnesses, then, must either see the grantor sign and seal, or hear him acknowledge the same, before they subscribe their names. But this need not be done in the presence of each other. It has been decided by our court, that a deed without subscribing witnesses, though not operative as a conveyance, is nevertheless a good *license* to enter and occupy for the purposes specified. Because if a license to enter be in writing, so as to comply with the statute of frauds, it is sufficient; and if possession be taken under it, it will be a good defence to an action of trespass or ejectment by the grantor. But in general, where a deed is thus defective, it is not constructive notice when recorded, and cannot operate as any thing more than a contract to convey, which a court of equity will enforce, unless there has intervened an innocent purchaser without notice; though when there are two subscribing witnesses, the fact that one is incompetent on the ground of interest, will not invalidate the deed.

It must be acknowledged. (*b*) The words are, "such signing and

(*a*) *Attestation.* The ordinance required two witnesses. This was changed by the law of 1795, and until 1805 no witnesses were required. Since then there must be two witnesses, or no legal title passes, but only an equitable title. Moore *v.* Vance, 1 Ohio, 1; Courcier *v.* Graham, 1 id. 330. Nor is there even an estoppel, though there be a covenant of warranty. Patterson *v.* Pease, 5 Ohio, 190. But such a deed is a good license to enter. Sullivant *v.* Franklin County, 3 Ohio, 89. When there are two witnesses the deed will be valid, though one was incompetent on the score of interest. Johnson *v.* Turner, 7 Ohio, 2 pt. 216. The want of an attestation and acknowledgment of a lease is not cured by the fourth section of the statute of frauds. Richardson *v.* Bates, 8 Ohio State, 257.

(*b*) *Acknowledgment.* No acknowledgment will be presumed from lapse of time. Roads *v.* Symmes, 1 Ohio, 281. The officer must state his official character. Johnston *v.* Haines, 2 Ohio, 55; Beckel *v.* Petticrew, 6 Ohio State, 247. But he need not state that the law authorizes him. Livingston *v.* McDonald, 9 Ohio, 168. Prior to 1818, the officer's seal was not required, except in the case of a married woman. Paine *v.* French, 4 Ohio, 318. From that time until 1831, it was necessary in all cases. Since then it is not required in any case. Fund Commissioners *v.* Glass, 17 Ohio, 542. See Ashley *v.* Wright, 19 Ohio State, 291; Gibson *v.* Warden, 14 Wall. 244. Where a deed of land in Ohio is acknowledged in another State before an Ohio officer, who happens to be there, it is sufficient. Kinsman *v.* Loomis, 11 Ohio, 475. So where it is acknowledged before a justice out of his county. Crumbaugh *v.* Kugler, 2 Ohio State, 373, 379. Learned *v.* Riley, 14 Allen, 109. Or by a mayor without the limits of his city. Moore *v.* Moore, 3 id. 154; Ordiorne *v.* Mason, 9 N. H. 24; *contra*, Share *v.* Anderson, 7 Serg. & R. 43. In some of the States, deeds are held valid as between parties without acknowledgment. Pierce *v.* Sampson, 5 Allen, 60; Merrill *v.* Gould, 16 N. H. 347; Haynes *v.* Sechrest, 13 Iowa, 455. As to what is a sufficient acknowledgment of the deed of a corporation in Ohio, see Sheehan *v.* Davis, 17 Ohio State, 571. As to the presumptions governing the certificate, see Carpenter *v.* Dexter, 8 Wall. 513. Where the officer does not sign the certificate, the deed is invalid. Hout *v.* Hout, 20 Ohio State, 119. As to the effect of an unacknowledged deed between the parties, see Hout *v.* Hout, 20 Ohio State, 119; McMahon *v.* McGraw, 26 Wis. 614.

sealing shall be acknowledged;" but it is sufficient if the grantor says, "I acknowledge this to be my deed," for it could not be his deed without signing and sealing. The officers before whom the acknowledgment may now be taken are, a judge of either court, a justice of the peace, a notary public, and a mayor, or other presiding officer of an incorporated town or city. The officer is required "to certify such acknowledgment on the *same sheet*, and subscribe his name to such certificate." (*a*) It has been held that the acknowledgment cannot be presumed from lapse of time. In fact, this follows necessarily from the provision, requiring the certificate to be on the same sheet. The presence of the certificate is the only evidence, unless when the existence of the deed is presumed; and then all the required formalities are presumed. It has also been held that the official character of the officer must appear on the face of the certificate, either in the body of it, or at the end with the subscription. The case before the court was a certified copy of a deed, in which the official character of the justice was not stated, though it could have been proved by parol. And the court said, however it might be with an original deed having this omission, it was fatal to the copy. And I can see no good reason why a difference should be made in this respect between a certified copy and the original. As to the expression "*on the same sheet*," I presume it is not intended thereby to require a deed to be upon one sheet only: the meaning is, that the certificate of acknowledgment shall not be on a separate piece of paper. The foregoing remarks embrace all acknowledgments by all descriptions of persons, with the single exception of the case where husband and wife join in a deed, either to convey the wife's land or to relinquish her right of dower. (*b*) In this case the officer is required to examine the wife apart from her husband, and make known to her the contents of the deed; and if she then declares that she did voluntarily sign, seal, and acknowledge the deed, and that she is still satisfied therewith, her conveyance will be good. And all these facts must appear in the certificate; namely, the

(*a*) A certificate of a commissioner for Ohio in another State upon a separate strip of paper attached to the deed by a wafer, with the officer's seal upon the same, does not comply with the requirements of the act of Jan. 26, 1844. Winkler *v.* Higgins, 9 Ohio State, 599. A mortgage on two sheets of paper, the latter of which contains the testatum clause, signatures, and acknowledgment, is not void. Norman *v.* Shepherd, 38 Ohio State, 320. Where a conveyance, defective because the instrument is written on different sheets, or the instrument and acknowledgment are on different sheets, is corrected, the act of Feb. 10, 1860, makes the correction relate back to the time of filing the original conveyance in the recorder's office.

(*b*) As to acknowledgments where the wife joins her husband, see Brown *v.* Farran, 3 Ohio, 140; Connell *v.* Connell, 6 id. 353; Good *v.* Zercher, 12 id. 364; Ruffner *v.* McLenan, 16 id. 639; Chesnut *v.* Shane, 16 id. 599; Bocock *v.* Pavey, 8 Ohio State, 270; Williams *v.* Robson, 6 id. 510; Newell *v.* Anderson, 7 id. 12; Card *v.* Patterson, 5 id. 319; Ward *v.* Mackintosh, 12 id. 231; Browder *v.* Browder, 14 id. 589. But it is not indispensable that she acknowledge at the same time and place and before the same officer as her husband; but her deed does not bind her until signed and acknowledged by her husband. Ludlow *v.* O'Neil, 29 Ohio State, 181.

separate examination, the explanation, the voluntariness of the act, and the present satisfaction therewith. But our court has decided that it is sufficient if the certificate contains the substance of these facts, without following the express words of the act. The reason of this formality is, that in law, unless the contrary appear, the wife is presumed to act under the restraint and fear of her husband. In fact this presumption is carried so far that in every other case her deed is void. In other words, but for this provision of the statute, she could not make a deed at all. In 1835, a healing act was passed, making good all prior deeds by husband and wife, though it should not appear in the certificate that the contents of the deed were explained to the wife; but this was only retrospective.

It must be delivered. (*a*) If all the preceding formalities have

(*a*) *Delivery.* Where a deed has been once delivered, no return or redelivery of it will reconvey the title. Starr *v.* Starr, 1 Ohio, 321; Baldwin *v.* Bank of Massillon, 1 Ohio State, 141; Jones *v.* Neale, 2 P. & H. (Va.) 339; Strawn *v.* Norris, 21 Ark. 80; Gimon *v.* Davis, 36 Ala. 589. Nor will a destruction of the deed by mutual act of the parties with intent to revest the title in the grantor have that effect, nor estop the grantee. Dukes *v.* Spangler, 35 Ohio State, 119. The cancellation of a deed does not revest the title in the grantor, though it is done with that intention. Steel *v.* Steel, 4 Allen, 417; Wilson *v.* Hill, 2 Beasley, 143; Schaeffer *v.* Fithian, 17 Ind. 463; Parshall *v.* Shirts, 54 Barb. 99; Killey *v.* Wilson, 33 Cal. 690; Lawton *v.* Gordon, 34 Cal. 36. But see Sawyer *v.* Peters, 50 N. H. 143. Nor will any parol agreement retransfer the title. Washington *v.* Ogden, 1 Black, 450. Where the grantor first records and then delivers, the deed need not be again recorded. Kemp *v.* Walker, 16 Ohio, 118. Where the grantor orders the deed to be recorded and then delivered, this is equivalent to a delivery. Steele *v.* Lowry, 4 Ohio, 72. Boody *v.* Davis, 20 N. H. 140; Thompson *v.* Jones, 1 Head (Tenn.), 574. The delivery of the deed to the recorder to be recorded, is *primâ facie* evidence of delivery, which may be rebutted by clear evidence to the contrary. Mitchell *v.* Ryan, 3 Ohio State, 377; Hoffman *v.* Mackall, 5 id. 125; Boardman *v.* Dean, 34 Penn. State, 252. Masterson *v.* Cheek, 23 Ill. 72. While the grantee's acceptance is necessary, yet this will be presumed if the conveyance is beneficial to him, until the contrary is shown. Mitchell *v.* Ryan, 3 Ohio State, 377. But where it was delivered to the recorder without the knowledge of the grantee, and taken from the recorder by the grantor, and kept until his death, this will not be presumed to be a delivery, without proof that the grantor intended it to be. Hayes *v.* Davis, 18 N. H. 600; Baker *v.* Haskell, 47 N. H. 479. Where the grantor, after handing the deed to the recorder, returns it to him, and instructs him not to let the grantees have it without his orders, and one of them obtains possession of it by misrepresentations, a court of equity will set it aside. Armstrong *v.* Armstrong, 4 Green, 357. In the absence of proof, delivery at the date of the deed will be presumed. Elsworth *v.* Central R. R. Co., 34 N. J. L. 93; Lyon *v.* McIlvaine, 24 Iowa, 9; Jayne *v.* Gregg, 42 Ill. 413; Blake *v.* Fash, 44 Ill. 302. A deed delivered as an escrow, and so remaining, cannot be used to show an outstanding title. Lloyd *v.* Giddings, 7 Ohio, 2 pt. 50. But where the escrow has been performed, the delivery takes effect, whether it come to the grantee or not. Shirley *v.* Ayres, 14 Ohio, 307. And see on the general subject, 4 Kent, Com. 454; Souverbye *v.* Arden, 1 Johns. Ch. 240; Greenleaf's Cruise, tit. xxxii. § 68–77; 4 Kent, Com. 454. A deed placed in the hands of a third person, to be by him delivered to the grantee on the happening of some future event, without such delivery being dependent on any conditions, is a valid deed, binding the grantor — but otherwise, if the grantor retains the right to recall the deed. Cook *v.* Brown, 34 N. H. 460. Where the deed is deposited with a third person, to be delivered upon the performance of a condition, no title passes by the grantee's obtaining possession of it improperly without the performance of such condition. Ogden *v.* Ogden, 4 Ohio State, 182. Smith *v.* South Royalton Bank, 32 Vt. 341; Cincinnati, &c. R. R. Co. *v.* Iliff, 13 Ohio State, 235; Black *v.* Shreeve, 2 Beasley, 425; Abbott *v.* Alsdorf, 19 Mich. 157. The agent of the grantee may hold an escrow, where it does not involve a violation of duty. Cincinnati, &c. R. R. Co. *v.* Iliff, *supra.* One who been complied with, the deed is executed and ready for delivery. The attesting words commonly used, namely, "signed, sealed, and delivered in the presence of," imply that the delivery is made in the presence of the subscribing witnesses; but this is hardly ever the fact, and it is not required by the statute. The delivery, however, is an essential part of the conveyance; for, as a general principle, so long as the deed remains in the hands of the grantor it is inoperative; and it would be in like manner inoperative if taken from the possession of the grantor without his consent. In a word, until he performs some act equivalent to a delivery, he retains the power to change his mind. It has been decided, however, that if a deed has been once delivered, it will be effectual, though it afterwards remain in the custody of the grantor. And our court has said what comes to nearly the same thing: namely, that the redelivery of a deed once delivered, does not operate as a reconveyance of the title; also, that where a man makes a deed of trust, and directs it to be delivered and recorded, the acceptance of the trust by the grantee, and the recording of the deed, amount to a delivery, though there was no delivery in fact; also, that where a father conveys to an infant son, and puts the deed on record, this is a delivery to the son, though the father, as natural guardian, retains the custody of the deed. The delivery need not be an actual handing of the deed by the grantor to the grantee; any words or actions signifying the intention to deliver are sufficient. In fact, whenever the deed is not found in the possession of the grantor, a proper delivery will be presumed, and it will fall upon the party impeaching the deed to prove a *non-delivery*. A deed is often delivered to third persons to hold for the parties until the happening of a given event. During this interval it is called an *escrow*, and until the event happens no estate passes. Its effect as a deed commences from the second delivery, except in certain cases, when, to prevent injustice, it is allowed to relate back and take effect from the first delivery. Where a deed has no date, its operation commences from the date of delivery; and even where it has a date, if it were not delivered until after that date, it can only operate from the day of delivery, so as to affect the rights of third persons. Our court has said that the doctrine of relation back to the date, applies only to the immediate parties. The

delivers a deed to the grantee as an escrow, is estopped from denying its valid delivery as against a *bonâ fide* purchaser. Resor *v.* Ohio & M. R. R. Co., 17 Ohio State, 139. Delivery to a third person for the benefit of the grantee, to be delivered at once or at the grantor's death, is a good delivery, when assented to by the grantee, and in the latter case the title passes as of the date of the first delivery; and after the grantee's death, parol declarations of his are competent evidence to show such acceptance. Black *v.* Hoyt, 33 Ohio State, 203; Crooks *v.* Crooks, 34 id. 610; Ball *v.* Foreman, 37 id. 132; but if revocable this is no delivery. Williams *v.* Schatz, 42 id. 47. A delivery by one of several without authority by the others does not bind them. Williamson *v.* Carskadden, 36 Ohio State, 664. Alteration of a deed by a grantor, at the request of the grantee, and redelivery of the deed, is, in legal effect, a re-execution of the deed. Malarin *v.* United States, 1 Wallace, 282.

delivery of the deed completes the conveyance, without livery of seisin or entry, and is effectual to pass the title of the grantor, although the land be in the adverse possession of another.

It must be recorded. (*a*) When a deed has been duly executed and delivered, the grantor has nothing more to do concerning it. The putting it upon record, which must be done within six months, is the business of the grantee. The reason of the law requiring it to be recorded, is to protect the grantee and the public against secret conveyances. The notoriety thereby given to the transfer is superior to that resulting from livery of seisin, and equal to that of enrolment in England. Any person who has an interest in knowing in whom the legal title to land rests, can always ascertain it by going to the records. If he find no incumbrance there, and no lien for taxes, or by judgment or decree, and have no notice of any equitable claim, he is safe in purchasing. For as an equitable title is not required to be on record, it is postponed to a legal title acquired without

(*a*) *Record.* The act of 1795, establishing a recorder's office, required all deeds to be recorded within one year. The act of 1802 reduced the time to six months, but now no time is allowed, R. S. § 4134, as amended, 82 Ohio Laws, 230. In these provisions, the intention was to make the penalty of not recording a loss of the title as against a subsequent *bonâ fide* purchaser; but as to the grantor and his heirs, the deed is valid without recording. Allen *v.* Parish, 3 Ohio, 107. Where neither of two deeds is recorded within six months, and the second is recorded first, it will prevail in the absence of notice. Northrup *v.* Brehmer, 8 Ohio, 392. Recording after six months is constructive notice from the time of recording. Irvin *v.* Smith, 17 Ohio, 226. The record or registry of a deed is constructive notice only to those who claim through or under the grantor by whom it was executed. Blake *v.* Graham, 6 Ohio State, 580. The law of notice does not apply to mortgages under the statute of Ohio, — mortgages having no effect against third parties until recorded. Bloom *v.* Noggle, 4 Ohio State, 45; *ante*, § 145, note. A deed absolute, but intended as security, is subject to the recording laws as to deeds, and not as to mortgages, and a record within six months was held good as against an intervening assignment for creditors. Kemper *v.* Campbell, S. C. of Ohio, 1886. The Ohio act applies only to legal titles. As between equitable titles it makes no difference whether they be recorded or not. Churchill *v.* Little, 23 Ohio State, 301. Though the statute does not mention deed of corporations, they are within its policy, and must be recorded. Sheehan *v.* Davis, 17 Ohio State, 571. Error of the recorder in recording will not invalidate. Conklin *v.* Hinds, 16 Minn. 457. *Contra*, Terrell *v.* Andrew Co., 44 Mo. 309. But if the deed as recorded would not give actual notice, it will not give constructive notice; therefore a mistake of the recorder in entering the grantor's name as "Samuel" for "Lemuel," invalidates the record. Jennings *v.* Wood, 20 Ohio, 261. But it is also held that if the instrument be properly recorded, an error in indexing will not affect it. Bishop *v.* Schmidt, 46 Mo. 472. Or a total failure to index. Green *v.* Garrington, 16 Ohio State, 548. Actual or presumptive notice will avoid the effect of omission to record. Cunningham *v.* Buckingham, 1 Ohio, 264. Open and visible occupation of land is notice to put a party on inquiry. Morrison *v.* Kelly, 22 Ill. 610; Williams *v.* Sprigg, 6 Ohio State, 585; Woodworth *v.* Paige, 5 id. 70; McKinzie *v.* Perrill, 15 id. 162. It must be open, notorious, and exclusive possession. Holmes *v.* Stout, 2 Stockton, 419; Vaughn *v.* Tracy, 28 Mo. 318. A purchaser at a sheriff's sale may avail himself of the registry act to protect his title. Scribner *v.* Lockwood, 9 Ohio, 184. A marginal note by the recorder that a deed was erroneously placed on record, cannot affect the validity of the deed. Foster *v.* Dugan, 8 Ohio, 87. Recording an instrument not authorized or required to be recorded, is not notice. Erwin *v.* Shuey, 8 Ohio State, 509; Graves *v.* Graves, 6 Gray, 391; Burnham *v.* Chandler, 15 Texas, 441; Bossard *v.* White, 9 Rich. Eq. 483; Galpin *v.* Abbott, 6 Mich. 17. For directions as to searching records, particularly in Ohio, see Curwen on Abstracts of Title. Under the recording acts a lease for years is treated as real estate, and a mortgage of it is to be recorded as a real estate and not chattel mortgage. Paine *v.* Mason, 7 Ohio State, 198.

actual notice of the equity; whereas the existence of a deed on record is *constructive notice* to all the world, and no one can plead the want of actual notice. By express provision of the statute, mortgages are now required to be recorded forthwith. In other words, they *take effect* from the time of recording, or rather from the time of presentation; for from the moment they are left in the office, their operation commences. But until 1831, mortgages were placed on the same footing as other deeds still are; that is, they might be recorded at any time within six months from date, and then related back and took effect from date; this opened a wide avenue to fraud: a dishonest man might raise five times the value of his land by successive mortgages to different persons, when each supposed he was the first mortgagee; and the present law in regard to other deeds seems to be almost equally objectionable. Why should not a purchaser be required to put his deed on record immediately, so that no subsequent incumbrancer could be defrauded by a dishonest grantor? It is true we have the threat of imprisonment in the penitentiary, to protect us against such acts; but this punishment is no compensation to the man who has paid his money for a title already passed to another. The statute provides that if a deed be not recorded within six months, it shall be deemed fraudulent as against any subsequent *bonâ fide* purchaser, having no knowledge of its existence; but that it may be put on record after the six months, and from the date of recording, shall be notice to any subsequent purchaser. It must be borne in mind, then, that, as between the parties to the deed, the fact of recording is of no consequence; since the deed is not void by omitting to record it. The sole object of recording it is to give notice to subsequent purchasers and incumbrancers; and even as to them, our court has decided that if they can be affected with positive or even strong presumptive notice, in any other way, they cannot impeach the unrecorded deed; and the fact of such notice may be established by parol evidence. This doctrine can never produce hardship; for the burden of proving the actual notice will fall upon him who has neglected to record his deed; and if the subsequent purchaser knew of the former deed, it was folly to purchase, and he deserves to suffer. But if there be two deeds, and neither recorded within six months, the second deed, if executed before the first is recorded, will prevail in the absence of notice; and this doctrine has been extended to the case of a sale on execution, where the sale was confirmed before the prior deed was recorded, the six months having elapsed. The constructive notice resulting from recording, applies only to deeds, mortgages, and leases, duly executed; and if there be any defect in the execution, or if the instrument be not a deed, mortgage, or lease, the recording will have no effect, because the statute does not apply to such. But when the recorded instrument is within the statute, it is declared that a certified copy thereof shall be *primâ facie* evidence of the existence of the instrument, and conclusive evidence of the existence of the record; and it has been held that even the immediate grantee may give such certified copy in evidence, without accounting for the original.

Exceptions. (*a*) The seven requisites of a deed now enumerated, namely, that it must be in *writing*, *signed*, *sealed*, *attested*, *acknowledged*, *delivered*, and *recorded*, are expressly extended by the statute to every "instrument of writing, by which any land, tenement, or hereditament, shall be conveyed, or otherwise affected or incumbered in law," *with the exception of* "leases of school or ministerial lands, for any term not exceeding ten years; and of any other lands for any term not exceeding three years." But there is some ambiguity in the phraseology of the statute, which it may be well to notice. The words are, "nothing in this act contained shall be construed to affect the validity of any excepted lease, or to require such lease to be attested, acknowledged, or recorded." Now the question is, whether it was intended to except such leases altogether from the operation of the act, as the first of the clause implies; or only as to the requisites of attestation, acknowledgment, and recording, as enumerated in the last part of the clause. If the former be the intention, then these leases are left to the operation of the statute of frauds, which simply requires them to be in writing, without a seal; if the latter, then such leases are still required to be under seal. I should have little hesitation in saying that the former was the intention, and that these excepted leases would be good if made in writing without a seal; but I do not know that the question has been raised. It will be observed that these requisites are expressly limited to estates "*in law*," and hence it is that any written agreement to convey will be good in equity. Moreover, where a legal conveyance was intended, but has been frustrated by the want of any one of these formalities, a court of equity will still consider it a valid contract to convey, as between the parties, and will enforce a specific performance; but a legal title cannot be conveyed, if any one of these formalities be wanting. There is a case, where the grantee in a deed by an indorsement on the back assigned "all his right and title in the deed" to another; and the court held that there never was a time in this State when such an assignment would be of any avail in law; but that equity might hold it to be a valid contract to convey. The words "*conveyed, or otherwise affected or incumbered*," are as comprehensive as could have been selected; and, but for the exception in regard to leases, would include the transfer of the smallest degree of interest. It has been held, however, that a certificate of entry or a mortgage may be assigned by mere delivery;

(*a*) R. S. § 4112. See Bentley *v.* Deforest, 2 Ohio, 221; Barr *v.* Hatch, 3 id. 527; Paine *v.* French, 4 id. 318; Reed *v.* McGrew, 5 id. 375; Atkinson *v.* Dailey, 2 id. 212.

thus taking the case both out of the statute of frauds and of deeds: and the reason is, I presume, because, by the assignment, the land is not *affected* by any new incumbrance; but the ownership remains precisely as it was before the assignment.

The Consideration. (*a*) Of the consideration of contracts I shall speak more at large hereafter. The general principle of law is, that a consideration is essential to a contract, and where the contract is in writing, must be stated therein; but instruments under seal form an exception to the necessity of stating the consideration; because, in the eye of the law, the solemnity of affixing a seal is itself evidence of a consideration. As, therefore, a sealed instrument generally *imports* a consideration, none need be stated; and this was the doctrine in regard to the common-law conveyances; but conveyances under the statute of uses form an exception to this exception; that is, they fall under the general principle, which requires a consideration to be stated in the contract; and the reason is this: before the statute of uses, some consideration was held necessary, as we have seen, in order to raise a use; and as the statute merely annexed the legal estate to the use, without varying the evidence necessary to create the use, the courts of law still retained the doctrine established in equity; indeed, it may be added, that the very idea of a bargain and sale, which in theory is something different from a gift, supposes a valuable consideration; accordingly, it is a settled doctrine that a valuable consideration must be stated in the deed; but the amount is of no consequence; it being only necessary to comply with the technical

(*a*) See, in general, 4 Kent, Com. 461; Sheppard *v.* Little, 14 Johns. 210. Where a deed purports to be executed for a valuable consideration, and none such existed, it cannot be supported by natural affection. Burrage *v.* Beardsley, 16 Ohio, 438. But a different consideration from that expressed may be set up, if not inconsistent. Steele *v.* Worthington, 2 Ohio, 182; Vail *v.* McMillan, 17 Ohio State, 617; Hannan *v.* Oxley, 23 Wis. 519; Bryant *v.* Hunter, 6 Bush, 75. See on the proof of another or different consideration. Hitz *v.* Natl. Metropolitan Bank, 111 U. S. 722; McCrea *v.* Purmount, 16 Wendell, 460; Frink *v.* Green, 5 Barb. 455; 1 Parsons on Cont. 355. Where a husband has received property with his wife, this is a good consideration for a conveyance of a property to her use. Hill *v.* West, 8 Ohio, 222. Where the consideration was the compromising of a suit, or forbearance to prosecute, a court of equity will not set the conveyance aside, on showing that there was no real foundation for such suit or prosecution. Moore *v.* Adams, 8 Ohio, 372. A court of chancery will not set aside a deed executed upon the consideration of a bet on an election, but will leave the parties as it finds them. Thomas *v.* Cronise, 16 Ohio, 54. And see as to gaming consideration, Bond *v.* Swearingen, 1 Ohio, 395. Mere inadequacy of price, though it may prevent a decree for specific performance, will not be sufficient to set aside a conveyance, unless it be so gross as to suggest actual fraud. Smith *v.* Loring, 2 Ohio, 440; Newton *v.* Mahoning County, 26 Ohio State, 618; Steele *v.* Worthington, 2 id. 182; Knobb *v.* Lindslay, 5 id. 468; Watkins *v.* Collins, 11 id. 31; Galloway *v.* Barr, 12 id. 354; Osgood *v.* Franklin, 2 Johns. Ch. 1; Hyer *v.* Little, 20 N. J. Eq. 443; Holmes *v.* Holmes, 1 Abb. U. S. 525. The doctrine in the text, that the recital of a *valuable* consideration in a deed is essential to its validity in Ohio, is overruled in Thompson *v.* Thompson, 17 Ohio State, 649. The judges were unanimous that it is sufficient if the deed recites a good consideration, as natural affection for a child. Two out of the five judges declared their opinion that a deed was valid, although no consideration whatever was named in it. Where a deed purports to be made for a valuable consideration, it cannot, when impeached, be sustained by proof of a good consideration. Burrage *v.* Beardsley, 16 Ohio, 438; Miller *v.* Stokely, 5 Ohio State, 194.

requisition; and where one consideration is stated, so as to make the deed *primâ facie* sufficient, a different one may be proved, so that it be not repugnant to the first. How, then, it may be asked, is a father to convey to his child, in consideration of natural affection, where no money passes? I answer, that he must resort to a fiction. There was a conveyance under the statute of uses, adapted to this very case; namely, by a *covenant to stand seised to the use of the child;* for which the consideration of blood was sufficient: but as this conveyance, not being mentioned in the ordinance of 1787, has never been adopted here; a conveyance to a child, in consideration of blood, being in the form of a bargain and sale to the child, must purport to be upon some valuable consideration for the sake of form; as one dollar, for example. This doctrine, respecting the consideration of a conveyance is sufficiently absurd, at best; but perhaps its absurdity will not be quite so striking if the reason be stated thus. There is a manifest difference between a bargain for the sale of land and a legal conveyance of that land; the former being a contract to be executed, and the latter the execution of that contract; now, at common law, a contract for the sale of lands would not have been binding without a consideration; but when a subsequent legal conveyance was made in execution of the prior contract of sale, this consideration was presumed, and was not, therefore, required to be stated. Under the statute of uses, however, the contract of sale and the conveyance became one act, and were effected by one instrument; and accordingly before this instrument could operate as a good conveyance, it must contain enough to make a good *primâ facie* contract of sale; that is, a valuable consideration. The result, then, of the doctrine of a consideration is, that the deed must *appear on its face* to have been made upon a sufficient one: and then, as between parties, a court of law will not inquire into the fact. A deed without any consideration in fact, or with only a very inadequate one, would be perfectly binding in a court of law, except as to creditors and purchasers, under the statute of frauds; and even in equity, mere inadequacy of consideration would not vitiate a deed, unless there had been gross deception and misrepresentation.

Foreign Deeds. (*a*) Our statute provides that all deeds out of this State, executed, and acknowledged or proved, pursuant to the law of the place, or pursuant to the law of this State, shall be as valid as if executed here. But the time for recording is the same as for deeds executed within the State. The words of the statute are, "in any other State, territory, or country," thus including all deeds wherever made.

§ 172. **Parties to a Deed.** (*b*) With respect to the grantees in a

(*a*) Allen *v.* Parish, 3 Ohio, 107; Foster *v.* Dennison, 9 id. 121; M'Cullough *v.* Rodrick, 2 id. 234; Rogers *v.* Allen, 3 id. 488; Sortwell *v.* Jewett, 9 id. 180; Nowler *v.* Coit, 1 id. 519; Wills *v.* Cowper, 2 id. 124; Henry *v.* Doctor, 9 id. 49.

(*b*) 4 Kent, Com. 462; Sloane *v.* McConahy, 4 Ohio, 157; Bryant *v.* McCandless, deed, there is little to be said. Every natural person is capable of receiving a conveyance, and there is no general law disabling corporations. As before observed, their ability to take and hold real estate depends entirely upon their charters. The only question as to grantees arises when there is no person in existence competent to take; and in such case, the grant is necessarily held to be void, except it be to charitable uses; in which case, the legislature may appoint a trustee of the legal title, and until such appointment the fee remains in the donor, subject to the trust. But with respect to the grantors, there are various restrictions and qualifications, both as to the ability to convey and the mode of conveying. I shall consider these in connection with the different classes of persons to whom they apply: namely, *infants, idiots, and lunatics, married women, partners, corporations, attorneys in fact, sheriffs, commissioners of insolvents, auditors,* and *executors* or *administrators.*

Infants and Guardians. (*a*) As a general principle, we have seen that an infant can make no binding obligation. The deed of an infant, however, is not absolutely *void,* but only *voidable.* When he becomes of age, he may either confirm or annul it. If he confirm the deed, it becomes good *ab initio;* if not, it is void *ab initio.* It follows, then, that an infant can only make a valid conveyance, through his guardian, who is expressly empowered "on good cause shown, to sell all or any part of the property, whether real or personal, of his ward." This *cause* must be shown to the court of common pleas, without whose sanction a conveyance by guardian would be utterly void. And it will not be a *good cause,* unless, in pursuance of another provision of the statute, "the court shall be satisfied that the sale will be for the advantage of the ward, or is necessary for his maintenance." The statute makes no difference between *testamentary* and other guardians; but it is manifest, that if a will, appointing a guardian, expressly authorize him to sell the property of his ward, he may do it without leave of court; otherwise, not. In case the court authorizes a sale by the guardian, he is to be governed by the same *regulations* in every respect as an executor or administrator. What these regulations are, I shall state under that head.

Idiots and Lunatics. (*b*) Idiots, as we have seen, are utterly incapable of making a valid conveyance; and lunatics can only

7 id. 2 pt. 135; Helfenstine *v.* Garrard, 7 id. 2 pt. 275; Sergeant *v.* Steinberger, 2 id. 305; Greene *v.* Graham, 5 id. 264; Fleming *v.* Donohoe, 5 id. 255; Trustees of McIntire School *v.* Zanesville Co., 9 id. 203. A mere misnomer apparent on the face of a deed will not affect its validity. As where Charles A. Clark and Sarah Clark gave a mortgage, but in the *testatum* clause and acknowledgment they were called Charles *B.* Clark and *Mary* Clark, it is valid against every one. Dodd *v.* Bartholomew, S. C. of Ohio, 1886.

(*a*) Drake's Lessee *v.* Ramsay, 5 Ohio, 251; Massie's Lessee *v.* Long, 2 id. 287, 293; Tucker *v.* Moreland, 10 Peters, 58; Cresinger *v.* Welch, 15 Ohio, 156.

(*b*) Lacy *v.* Garrard, 2 Ohio, 7; French *v.* French, 8 id. 214. As to the duty of the insane person or his guardian to restore the consideration when the deed is avoided, see Arnold *v.* Richmond Iron Works, 1 Gray, 434; Gibson *v.* Soper, 6 id. 279.

convey during their lucid intervals. But their guardians have the same power to sell the real estate of their wards, as guardians of minors; and are under the same regulations. The statute, however, mentions the payment of the debts of an idiot or lunatic, as a sufficient cause for selling real estate, which is not the case with regard to minors; also, where an idiot or lunatic, when sane, had contracted to convey, the guardian is specially empowered to execute the conveyance; and all these provisions apply to *deaf and dumb persons*, if they are incapable of managing their estates. As to persons intoxicated, it has been held that if the grantor was so much intoxicated as not to know what he was doing, his deed will be set aside in chancery, although the grantee had no agency in procuring the intoxication.

Married Women. (*a*) On account of the legal presumption that a married woman is under the power and control of her husband, to such a degree that she cannot act freely, it is a general principle, as we have seen, that her deed is absolutely void. But as it

(*a*) There has been so much controversy as to how far contracts to convey may be enforced, or mistakes in conveyances corrected, as against married women, that we have recently had legislation tending, at least as to mistakes, to place them on the same footing as single persons. I shall in this note refer to a number of cases. Where a married woman agreed to surrender or levy a fine, and the husband died, she was compelled to perform. Baker *v.* Child, 2 Vernon, 61. Where a married woman with others had been ordered to execute a conveyance, the order was enforced. Jordan *v.* Jones, 16 Law Jour. R. Ch. 93. An imperfect conveyance, which, if valid, would have barred dower, was validated in equity, and had that effect. McCall *v.* McCall, 3 Day, 402. A mere signing and sealing with the husband will not be sufficient. There must be words in the body of the deed showing the intent to be bound. Constantine *v.* Van Winkle, 6 Hill, 177; Catlin *v.* Ware, 9 Mass. 218; Lufkin *v.* Curtis, 13 id. 223; Powell *v.* Monson M. Co., 3 Mason, 347; Cox *v.* Wells, 7 Blackford, 410. A wife may act as the attorney of her husband, but only to convey his interest. Fowler *v.* Shearer, 7 Mass. 14. Where the wife joined in all but the acknowledgment, which she refused, her interest was not affected. Martin *v.* Dwelly, 6 Wendell, 9. Where a wife only united in a deed because she was advised it was so defectively drawn as not to bar her dower, she knowing that the purchaser was not aware of this, it was held that fraud could not be imputed to her, being a married woman. McFarland *v.* Febiger, 7 Ohio, 1 pt. 194. This was going to the extreme verge, and there appeared to be a disposition to recede somewhat. Chestnut *v.* Shane, 16 Ohio, 599; Smith *v.* Handy, id. 191. But in Purcell *v.* Goshon, 17 Ohio, 105, where the fee was in the wife, and she joined, with the intention of conveying it for a cemetery, but by a blunder of the scrivener, only relinquished dower, it was held the mistake could not be corrected. By statute in Ohio, courts are now authorized to correct and relieve against any errors, mistakes, and defects occurring in a conveyance of land, by a husband and wife. 54 Ohio Laws, 199. Under this statute, the case of Purcell *v.* Goshorn came up again, and the deed was corrected. 11 Ohio State, 641. But this is limited by the courts strictly to cases of omissions, defects, or errors. Hence it does not apply to a deed which she acknowledged, but had neither signed nor sealed, for that is not her deed or instrument in writing. Koltenbrock *v.* Cracraft, 36 Ohio State, 584. But an omission to certify that she acknowledged separately, can be cured under these acts if she actually did so. Kilbourn *v.* Fury, 26 Ohio State, 153. And if her acknowledgment was before an officer not authorized to take it, this also is curable. Dengenhart *v.* Cracraft, 36 Ohio State, 549; Miller *v.* Hine, 13 Ohio State, 565; Carney *v.* Hopple, 17 Ohio State, 39. This statute is only permissive, not mandatory. It still remains for the courts to determine under what circumstances, and on what principles, they will grant relief. Hout *v.* Hout, 20 Ohio State, 119. Where a deed was intended by husband and wife to convey the entire interest in land of which they were tenants in common, but by mistake his interest only was conveyed, and she released dower, the court corrected the mistake. Parol evidence was admitted. Smith *v.* Turpin, 20 Ohio State, 478, 492.

is often desirable that she should be able to part with her own real estate, or relinquish her dower in that of her husband, it is provided by statute that if she be eighteen years of age she may *join with her husband* in the deed, and thus make a valid conveyance. The precautions taken to ascertain that the whole has been done by her free assent, have been already stated. Unless, however, she thus join with her husband, her conveyance is utterly void; and his power to incumber her estate, without her joining, is expressly limited by another statute to the duration of the marriage. Accordingly, any separate contract made by the husband touching the wife's land would instantly cease on the termination of the marriage, either by the death of one of the parties or by divorce. But to this inability of the wife to make a separate conveyance of her estate, there is one exception; and that is, where she acts in pursuance of a *power* legally conferred. If in the deed or will conveying to her the estate, she be expressly authorized to dispose of it in a certain manner, she can execute that power without the co-operation of her husband. With respect to conveyances to each other, the legal doctrine, that the husband and wife cannot contract with one another, makes it necessary to resort to a circuity, when either wishes to convey to the other. The conveyance is first made, with specific directions, to a trustee, who by another conveyance, in execution of the trust, vests the title in the party intended. But since the law allows this to be thus done indirectly, what evil could result from allowing it to be done directly? Surely the trouble thereby saved would be a sufficient reason for making this case an exception to the general rule; and in equity this is done.

Partners. If partners own real estate, as partnership property, although in equity such property, as we have seen, is bound for the joint debts, yet in law, partners stand on the same footing as any other tenants in common; and, accordingly, if a conveyance is to be made even for partnership purposes, all the partners must join in the deed, with their separate signatures and seals. A conveyance in the name of the firm, with one seal for all, would not be sufficient, for two reasons. In the first place, partners are not like corporations, authorized to use a common seal; and, in the next place, one partner is not, as such, authorized to sign and seal for another. He must have a regular power of attorney for that purpose, as much as if acting for a stranger. It has indeed been held, that if all the partners be present and consent, a signing and sealing by one will make the instrument the deed of the whole. But I presume this decision would not embrace conveyances under our statute. (*a*) At all events, the safer course would be for all the partners to execute the deed, either personally or by attorney.

Corporations. Whether corporations can hold real estate or not, depends, as we have seen, upon their charter. But, having

(*a*) Undoubtedly true: though not ruled on in Ohio, decisions in other States are numerous.

this power, their conveyances are made under the corporate seal, which is affixed by the proper officer. The corporation itself is named as grantor, its corporate name is subscribed, and the acknowledgment is made by the same officer. There is a case in our reports, where the president of a bank executed a deed in his own name, and under his own private seal; and, although the corporation was properly named as grantor, yet this defect in the execution was held fatal to the deed as a legal conveyance. A court of equity, however, afterwards held the deed to be good as a contract to convey, and enforced a specific performance. (*a*)

Attorneys in Fact. (*b*) The parties hitherto spoken of have been owners of the land to be conveyed. Those hereafter to be mentioned are the agents of the owners, authorized to make the conveyance either by the act of the owner or by the operation of law. As to attorneys in fact, we have seen the general principle of law to be, that they must derive their authority to act from an instrument of as high a nature as that which they are required to execute; for example, to execute an instrument under seal, they must be authorized by a writing under seal. But the statute of deeds goes much further. It provides that all powers of attorney,

(*a*) Hatch *v.* Barr, 1 Ohio, 390; Barr *v.* Hatch, 3 id. 527; Webb *v.* Moler, 8 id. 548. Where the deed of a corporation is signed by the cashier with his own name, describing himself as such officer, and the corporate seal is affixed, this is sufficient. Sheehan *v.* Davis, 17 Ohio State, 571. *Contra*, Zoller *v.* Ide, 1 Neb. 439. The corporate seal affixed to a deed is presumptively affixed by proper authority. Sheehan *v.* Davis, 17 Ohio State, 571, 79 Ill. 450.

(*b*) Where the power was defective, but the principal recognized the act, it was held to cure the defect. Buchanan *v.* Upshaw, 1 How. 56. A power given by an infant is absolutely void. Lawrence *v.* McArter, 10 Ohio, 37. A power given by a married woman must be acknowledged by her in order to bind her. Bocock *v.* Pavey, 8 Ohio State, 270. Where the terms of the power are departed from by the parol assent of the principal, equity will sustain the act. Webster *v.* Harris, 16 Ohio, 490. Where the wife does not join in the power, but joins with the attorney in the conveyance, her title passes. Glenn *v.* Bank U. S., 8 Ohio, 72. A recorder's copy of a defective power is not evidence to prove execution of the lost original, but only its contents. Webster *v.* Harris, 16 Ohio, 490. Where the power to sell land has become coupled with an interest before revocation, the revocation is null. Wheeler *v.* Knaggs, 8 Ohio, 169. A power to a son-in-law to conduct a farm for his own benefit, and to do with it as if it were his own, gives no power to lease the farm in payment of a debt. Ward *v.* Thrustin, 40 Ohio State, 347.

Form of a Power of Attorney to Convey Land. Be it known that ———, and ———, his wife, do, by these presents, constitute and appoint ——— their attorney in fact, with full authority to sell and convey, without reservation of dower, or any other right whatsoever, the following real estate in fee-simple, viz. [describe the property], and to execute a warranty deed therefor to the purchaser; and generally, to do all acts necessary for conveying as complete a title thereto as the said constituents could themselves convey; hereby covenanting with all whom it may concern to ratify and confirm all lawful acts done in pursuance of this power. Witness the hands and seals of the said constituents, this ———. [Signatures and seals of the constituents, and attestation by two subscribing witnesses.]

The State of ———, county of ———. Before me, ———, a ———, personally appeared ——— and ——— his wife, the above named constituents, and acknowledged the signing and sealing of the above power of attorney to be their voluntary act and deed for the uses and purposes therein expressed. And the said ———, wife of the said ———, being examined by me separate and apart from her said husband, and the contents of the above power of attorney being explained to her, declared that she did voluntarily sign and seal, and does now acknowledge the same, and that she is still satisfied therewith. Witness my signature, this ———. [Signature without seal.]

authorizing the conveyance or incumbrance of real estate, shall be signed, sealed, attested, acknowledged, and certified in the same manner as deeds; and also that such powers shall be recorded in the proper county, before the conveyance or incumbrance is made. If husband and wife join in a power of attorney, to convey her estate or relinquish her dower, the statute provides that the wife may revoke such power at any time before the sale or conveyance, provided her revocation be recorded in the county; but if not so revoked, and her name be inserted in the deed made by the attorney, her rights will be thereby concluded. A conveyance by attorney is made in the name of the principal. The attorney does not affix his own signature and seal, but those of his principal. It is always well to recite the substance of the power, and refer to the book and page of the record; though a conveyance would be good without. An executor, authorized by the will, or a trustee by deed or will, is to all intents and purposes an attorney in fact. But where the power is conferred by will, there is an exception to the general principle above stated, that the power to sign and seal must be given under seal; since, as we have already seen, a will is not required to be under seal.

Sheriffs. (*a*) The parties which remain to be described are

(*a*) On the general subject of sales on execution, see 2 Black. Com. 436; 4 Kent, Com. 428; Wheaton *v.* Sexton, 4 Wheaton, 503; Voorhees *v.* Bank, U. S., 10 Peters, 449. In this note I shall refer to local decisions, under the head of judgment liens, and proceedings on execution, levy, sale, &c.

Judgment Liens. The first requisite for a good title under a judgment is, that such judgment should have been a lien on the land in question. In Roads *v.* Symmes, 1 Ohio, 281, which referred back to 1800, there was no statute making it a lien, but it was held to be such at common law. And see M'Cormick *v.* Alexander, 2 Ohio, 65, where the history of judgment liens is fully considered; also Waymire *v.* Staley, 3 Ohio, 366. It was early decided that the validity of the original judgment cannot be questioned collaterally. Starr *v.* Starr, 1 Ohio, 321. But, on this subject, in Paine *v.* Mooreland, 15 Ohio, 435, the court say, "The distinction is between the lack of power, or want of jurisdiction in the court, and a wrongful or defective execution of power. In the first instance, all acts of the court not having jurisdiction or power are void; in the latter voidable only. A court then may act, first, without power or jurisdiction; second, having power of jurisdiction, may exercise it wrongfully; or third, irregularly. In the first instance, the act or judgment of the court is wholly void, and is as though it had not been done. The second is wrong, and must be reversed upon error. The third is irregular, and must be corrected by motion." And see, to the same effect, Cochran *v.* Loring, 17 Ohio, 409; but where it is held that a title acquired while a judgment is in force, is not affected by a subsequent reversal. Also, Hunt *v.* Yeatman, 3 Ohio, 15, and R. S. § 5409. A judgment is not a lien upon after-acquired land aliened before levy. Miller *v.* Murphy, 4 Ohio, 92; Phelps *v.* Butler, 2 id. 224. A levy on part releases the rest, as to younger judgments. Walpole *v.* Ink, 9 Ohio, 142. A justice's judgment is not a lien until made so by proceedings in a court of record. Jackman *v.* Hallock, 1 Ohio, 318; Hill *v.* Kling, 4 id. 135; Edmiston *v.* Edmiston, 2 id. 251. Land *bonâ fide* sold but not conveyed, is not subject to a subsequent judgment lien. Manley *v.* Hunt, 1 Ohio, 257. But a mortgagor's equity of redemption is. Phelps *v.* Butler, 2 Ohio, 224. So are permanent leaseholds. Northern Bank *v.* Roosa, 13 Ohio, 334. The equitable estate of a vendee under a contract for the sale of lands, who is not in possession thereof, cannot be levied upon and sold to satisfy a judgment against him. Haynes *v.* Baker, 5 Ohio State, 253. A decree for money is a general lien, but a decree of foreclosure is not a lien upon other lands. Myers *v.* Hewitt, 16 Ohio, 449. Chancery will not aid in enforcing a judgment lien because there is a remedy at law. Miami *v.* Turpin, 3 Ohio, 514; Douglass *v.* Huston, 6 id. 156. A judgment in the United States circuit court is agents appointed by the law to make conveyances for the payment of debts. They do not, like attorneys, act in the name of

a lien from the first day of the term on all lands in the District. Lawrence *v.* Belger, 31 Ohio State, 175. When a judgment becomes dormant the lien ceases, and a revival does not relate back. Lytle *v.* Cincinnati, 4 Ohio, 459 ; Norton *v.* Beaver, 5 id. 178; Hutchinson *v.* Hutchinson, 15 id. 301. A recognizance notwithstanding its terms, is not a lien until judgment. Dewitt *v.* Osburn, 5 Ohio, 480. A *supersedeas* in error only suspends the lien. Conn *v.* Doyle, 2 Ohio, 318. Where defendant on *ca. sa.* turns out land, the residue is not discharged. Douglas *v.* Wallace, 11 Ohio, 42. By R. S. § 5375, a confessed judgment only binds land from its date. And see Urbana *v.* Baldwin, 3 Ohio, 65 ; Riddle *v.* Bryan, 5 id. 48. Since 1824, to save priority, execution must be levied within the year. Norton *v.* Beaver, 5 Ohio, 178. If there be several judgments, and none levied within the year, they are all equal, and the first levy will be preferred. But a junior judgment levied within the year prevails over a senior judgment not so levied, though levied first. Patton *v.* Sheriff, 2 Ohio, 395 ; Shuee *v.* Ferguson, 3 id. 136 ; Earnfit *v.* Winans, id. 135 ; Sellers *v.* Corwin, 5 id. 398 ; Scoggins *v.* Atherton, 6 id. 30. As to priorities between mortgages and judgment liens, see Brazee *v.* Lancaster, 14 Ohio, 318 ; Holliday *v.* Franklin Bank, 16 id. 533 ; Myers *v.* Hewitt, 16 id. 449 ; Fitch *v.* Mendenhall, 17 id. 578 ; Tousley *v.* Tousley, 5 Ohio State, 78. The lien of a levy under an execution is not vacated by a subsequent appeal of the case to the supreme court by the judgment debtor. When a court of equity is called upon in the enforcement of legal liens, the legal priorities of such liens will control their rights in equity. Moore *v.* Rittenhouse, 15 Ohio State, 310. The balance found by the court to be due after sale in foreclosure, where the proceeds did not satisfy the whole debt, is not a judgment where no personal judgment was asked, and therefore not a lien until levy of execution. See Conn *v.* Rhodes, 26 Ohio State, 644.

Execution, Levy, Sale, &c. Execution may issue upon an order of maintenance under the bastardy act. Darby *v.* Carson, 9 Ohio, 149. Where the plaintiff purchases on his own execution and the title fails, he cannot have a new execution. Vattier *v.* Lytle, 6 Ohio, 477. There must be good cause to justify the relinquishment of a levy to the prejudice of subsequent lien-holders. Com. Bank *v.* Western, 11 Ohio, 444 ; Ford *v.* Skinner, 4 id. 378. The return of a levy cannot be amended so as to affect liens acquired between the levy and amendment. Ohio Trust Co. *v.* Urbana Ins. Co., 13 Ohio, 220. A second levy before the first is disposed of is void ; but a levy is not vacated by *supersedeas* in error, nor by quashing a *vendi*. Arnold *v.* Fuller, 1 Ohio, 458. Taking out a *fi. fa.* instead of a *vend. ex.* does not avoid a previous levy. Bouton *v.* Lord, 10 Ohio State, 453. The levy operates as a satisfaction while undisposed of. Cass *v.* Adams, 3 Ohio, 223 ; but see Reynolds *v.* Rogers, 5 id. 169 ; Walsh *v.* Ringer, 2 id. 327. When set aside, the parties stand, with respect to liens, as if no levy had been made. Patton *v.* Sheriff, 2 Ohio, 395. Where the execution is issued and levied after the death of the defendant, it is null. Massie *v.* Long, 2 Ohio, 287 ; Cartney *v.* Reed, 5 id. 221. But if levied before death a sale after death is valid, without making the heirs or representatives parties to the judgment. Bigelow *v.* Renker, 25 Ohio State, 542. A levy upon sufficient goods, afterwards discharged, discharges lien upon land, as against a purchaser. Ford *v.* Skinner, 7 Ohio, 2 pt. 148. Where the writ has no seal, the levy is void. Boal *v.* King, 6 Ohio, 11. Where there are several levies only one sale is necessary. Douglas *v.* M'Coy, 5 Ohio, 522. An ambiguous description in a levy may be explained by parol. Matthews *v.* Thompson, 3 Ohio, 272. Morgan *v.* Spangler, 14 Ohio State, 102. Prior to 1824, a sheriff after office expired, might complete proceedings commenced by him. Fowble *v.* Rayberg, 4 Ohio, 45. As to *appraisement* and *advertisement*, see Allen *v.* Parish, 3 Ohio, 187 ; Fitch *v.* Dunlap, 2 id. 78 ; Patrick *v.* Oosterout, 1 id. 27 ; 1 id. 235 ; Roads *v.* Symmes, 1 id. 281 ; Wiles *v.* Baylor, 1 id. 509. Where lands subject to lien have been sold by the debtor, the sheriff must sell in the inverse order. Commercial Bank *v.* Western, 11 Ohio, 444. If the plaintiff purchases, he is affected by error in the judgment, though a stranger would not be. Walpole *v.* Ink, 9 Ohio, 142. A purchase by one of the appraisers is not strictly void, and will be set aside only on a direct proceeding by a party in interest. Terrill *v.* Auchauer, 14 Ohio State, 80. The purchaser is subrogated to all the rights of the plaintiff, as against the defendant. Barr *v.* Hatch, 3 Ohio, 527 ; Riddle *v.* Bryan, 5 id. 48. But queried in Endel *v.* Leibrock, 33 Ohio State, 254, 270. Where the return is not sold because the purchaser refused to pay, and there was a sale upon a *vendi*, without objection at the time, it cannot be questioned afterwards. Bisbee *v.* Hall, 3 Ohio, 449. And see further as to title of purchaser, Beggs *v.* Thompson, 2 Ohio, 95 ; Phelps *v.* Butler, 2 id. 224.

the owners; but simply describe themselves as officers of the law. They are *sheriffs*, *insolvent commissioners*, *auditors*, and *executors or administrators*. I shall begin with the *sheriff*, who acts in all cases where property is sold to satisfy a judgment or decree, except where the court of chancery appoints a master for this purpose; and the proceedings are the same on a judgment as on a decree. There was a time when realty could not be sold for debt; and even now, in some places, the rents and profits only can be appropriated to this object. But here the only distinction between realty and personalty is, that the latter must be sold first. The execution commands the officer to make the money out of the personalty; and for want thereof, out of the realty.

1. *Levy*. The first step in executing the writ is to *levy* it upon the property. If it be personalty, the sheriff takes actual possession, and returns an inventory. (*a*) If it be realty, the levy is made, without taking possession, by returning a description of the property.

2. *Appraisement*. The next step with respect to realty, is the *appraisement*. This is made upon actual view of the premises, by three freeholders of the county, selected and sworn by the sheriff; and a copy is deposited in the clerk's office. The object of the appraisement is to prevent the land from being sacrificed; for it cannot be sold for less than two-thirds of its appraised value; unless it be for a debt or tax due the State, or to make up the default of a public officer. But, though a contrary opinion was once held, it is now settled upon the fullest argument, that this provision requiring an appraisement, is merely directory to the sheriff; if he omits to have it made, he is liable to a penalty, and either of the parties to the judgment may have the proceedings stayed or set aside, at any time before the execution of the deed; but afterwards, the fact that there was no appraisement, will not affect the title of the purchaser. With respect to per-

A deed is valid if executed by the deputy sheriff. Haines *v.* Lindsey, 4 Ohio, 88; Anderson *v.* Brown, 9 id. 151; and evidence may be received to show that a sheriff's deed does not cover all the land included in the description. Longworth *v.* Bank U. S., 6 Ohio, 536. The order of confirmation is indispensable to support the sheriff's deed. Curtis *v.* Norton, 1 Ohio, 278; Buckingham *v.* Granville, 2 id. 360. A sheriff's deed takes effect from the day of sale. Boyd *v.* Longworth, 11 Ohio, 235. Thomas *v.* Crofut, 14 N. Y. 474. And see further, Armstrong *v.* McCoy, 8 Ohio, 128; Scribner *v.* Lockwood, 9 id. 184; Goudy *v.* Shank, 8 id. 415; Foster *v.* Dugan, 8 id. 87; Rhonemus *v.* Corwin, 9 Ohio State, 366. Where the order of confirmation of a sale is set aside on error, after the execution of the sheriff's deed, but before any legal conveyance by the purchaser, the title acquired by the deed is divested by the order setting aside the order of confirmation. McBain *v.* McBain, 15 Ohio State, 337.

(*a*) A levy must be public, open, and unequivocal. When personal property is so cumbrous that the sheriff cannot take it into his manual possession, he must use proper diligence to notify the owners or their agents, or the levy will be postponed to junior liens without notice. Minor *v.* Smith, 13 Ohio State, 79. { An actual seizure is necessary; merely indorsing a paper levy on the execution is void; but leaving the property in the debtor's custody is not necessarily an abandonment or insufficient, unless the debtor is left in absolute control with power of sale. Murphy *v.* Swadener, 33 Ohio State, 85. But after an actual levy, a constructive levy of subsequent executions by the same officer by indorsement is sufficient. Id. An entry on real estate by the sheriff is not essential to the levy. Morgan *v.* Kenney, 38 Ohio State, 610. }

sonalty, there was no appraisement until the act of 1843 put it in the power of the judgment debtor to claim an appraisement if he saw proper. (*a*)

3. *Advertisement.* The next step is to *advertise* the property. The notice for realty must be given *thirty days*, and for personalty, *ten days* before the sale; either by advertisement in some newspaper printed in the county, or, if there be none, then in some newspaper circulating therein; and by posting up a notice at the court-house door, and in five other public places. The statute expressly provides, that if a sale be made without such advertisement, it may be set aside on motion. But this provision like that requiring an appraisement, is merely directory to the sheriff, and if a sale be completed without it, the title of the purchaser is not thereby affected. (*b*)

4. *Sale.* The next step is the *sale.* Realty is sold at auction, at the court-house door; and personalty is sold where it happens to be. Neither the sheriff nor appraisers can purchase directly or indirectly. A private sale is never permitted; the property is sold at public auction because the law presumes that in this way it will be most likely to bring its fair value. (*c*)

(*a*) {An appraisement is necessary, and the court cannot dispense with it. Wiles *v.* Baylor, 1 Ohio, 500. But is not jurisdictional, and a sheriff's deed therefore conveys title, though in fact there was no appraisement. Allen *v.* Parish, 3 Ohio, 187. The appraisement must be of the entire estate without deduction for incumbrances. Baird *v.* Kirtland, 8 Ohio, 21. If there is more than one levy on the same property separate appraisements are not necessary; yet if they are had and are not the same, a sale under one levy cannot be had under an appraisement in another. Daniels *v.* McBain, 2 Ohio State, 406, 408. If a lot is but 27 feet front, and the appraisers value it as if 30 feet, at so much per front foot, there can be no deduction from the price in consequence. Ohio Life Ins. & Tr. Co. *v.* Goodin, 10 Ohio State, 557. The purchaser's title is not open to collateral impeachment, because the appraisers were disqualified by not being residents of the county. Mauarr *v.* Parrish, 36 Ohio State, 636.}

(*b*) {The day of the first notice may be included, but that of the sale must be excluded. Hagerman *v.* Ohio Build. & Sav. Assn., 25 Ohio State, 186. If the weekly paper is not always published on the same day of the week, it is no objection if there is a full thirty days. Wilson *v.* Scott, 29 Ohio State, 636. If the advertisement was in a paper which the court is satisfied was not of general circulation, it may refuse confirmation, though the proceedings are regular. Craig *v.* Fox, 16 Ohio, 563. The advertisement must be in papers in the English language, unless the statute expresses the contrary. See Cincinnati *v.* Bickett, 26 Ohio State, 49.}

(*c*) {There is no authority to incur the expense of an auctioneer. Ingham *v.* Lindemann, 37 Ohio State, 218. A purchase by an appraiser is voidable and not void, and though a ground for refusing confirmation, will be held void only on a proceeding by a party in interest. Terrill *v.* Auchauer, 14 Ohio State, 80; Bohart *v.* Atkinson, 14 Ohio, 228; Armstrong *v.* Huston, 8 Ohio, 552. So if an executor or administrator or guardian buys at his own sale, no matter what the degree of good faith, the sale will at any time be held fraudulent and void; and so if a third person buy and convey to the wife of the administrator. Riddle *v.* Roll, 24 Ohio State, 572; Piatt *v.* Longworth, 27 id. 159; Glass *v.* Greathouse, 20 Ohio, 503. The plaintiff's attorney may buy, but if his client's debt is not paid in full by the sale, the client may within a reasonable time claim the benefit of the purchase. Wade *v.* Pettibone, 14 Ohio, 557. If the proceedings and sale do not embrace all the land intended to be sold and supposed to be bought, the court cannot as against minors correct the proceedings and give the purchaser the additional land. Dickey *v.* Beatty, 14 Ohio State, 389. Error in the number of acres sold is no defence to an action for the deferred payments; and so although the sale was a private one by order of court; it is still a judicial sale. Dresbach *v.* Stein, 41 Ohio State, 70. Defective description not affecting the price is no reason for not confirming. Wilson *v.* Scott, 29 Ohio State, 636.}

5. *Return.* The next step is to *return* the writ with the proceedings thereon to the court at its next term, pursuant to the command thereof. But provision is made, that when land has been twice offered, and remains unsold for want of bidders, the court, on motion of the plaintiff, may, if they see proper, order a new appraisement, or a new levy and appraisement, as the case may require.

6. *Confirmation.* Upon the return of a sale of realty, the court examine the proceedings of the sheriff, and hear objections, if any are offered. If the proceedings are found to be correct, an *order* is entered on the journal, that the sheriff make a deed to the purchaser. Until this order is made, he may retain the purchase-money in his hands. And it has been decided that this order of court is absolutely necessary to the validity of the deed; and if not made and entered on the journal, the deed is good for nothing. On a motion for this order, it has been held, that the court will only look to the execution, and the proceedings of the sheriff, and not to any defects prior to the execution; though on a motion to set aside the execution and proceedings, every thing after the judgment is examinable. (*a*)

7. *Deed.* All is now ready for the *execution of the deed.* This is done by the sheriff, who signs, seals, and acknowledges the deed in his official capacity. The statute expressly provides what the deed shall recite; namely, the parties to the judgment, the kind of action, the amount of the judgment, the term when it was rendered, and the substance of the several executions. The intention is, that the deed shall show upon its face whatever is material to the title of the purchaser; and accordingly, the appraisement and advertisement are not required to be recited, because they are not essential to the validity of the deed. But at the same time the statute omits to mention the order of court, which, as we have seen, is material, though it need not be recited. The deed thus made, is declared to be *primâ facie* evidence of the legality of the sale and the proceedings therein, until the contrary be proved; that is, the burden of impeaching the deed, for want of correctness in the proceedings, falls upon the other party; while the purchaser is required in the first instance merely to produce his deed, without proving any of the preliminaries. And the statute further declares that such deed shall vest in the purchaser as good a title as was vested in the party, at, or after, the time when his land became liable to the satisfaction of the judgment.

Commissioners of Insolvents. (*b*) We have seen that by the act

(*a*) {The purchaser has only an equity before possession or sheriff's deed, but after sale; hence an execution against him levied then on the premises is invalid. Gorrell *v.* Kelsey, 40 Ohio State, 117. Rents falling due after the title is vested in the buyer belong wholly to him. Albon *v.* Riegel, 40 Ohio State, 339, 340. If the debtor pays the judgment after sale and before confirmation, the court should not confirm if he objects. Reed *v.* Radigan, 42 Ohio State, 92.}

(*b*) See 2 Black. Com. 285; 2 Kent, Com. 389. The two cases alluded to in the text, M'Cullough *v.* Roderick, 2 Ohio, 234, and Rogers *v.* Allen, 3 id. 488, appear to for the relief of insolvent debtors, a commissioner of insolvents is appointed in each county, to receive and dispose of their property for the benefit of their creditors. Every person applying for the benefit of this act, is required to deliver to the commissioner a written inventory of all his property, both real and personal, together with a written assignment thereof. And this assignment operates as a *conveyance* to the commissioner of all the interest of the applicant, though it is expressly provided that no particular form of assignment shall be required. Here, then, is a case where real estate may be conveyed by the act of the owner, without the formalities of a deed. It is sufficient if it be in writing, and the property will pass, though not particularly specified, either in the inventory or schedule; such being the express provision. But as this is in derogation of the general law, our court has decided that an assignment by an insolvent debtor in Pennsylvania, does not pass his real estate in Ohio, for this can only be transferred in pursuance of our own laws. As this point has been twice decided, we must consider it the law; but I cannot perceive its propriety, for in the statute of deeds it is expressly provided, that conveyances made pursuant to the laws of other States shall be good here. The commissioner, being thus made the trustee of the legal title, is directed to have the property appraised, and sell the same at public auction, after giving at least thirty days' notice. This is all that the statute says on the subject. It is entirely silent with respect to the deed to be made by the commissioner. But it is manifest that such deed will convey all the title which the insolvent had at the time of application, and must be executed with all the formalities of any other deed. As to the recitals, it would be proper after the analogy of a sheriff's deed, to recite the *application*, *assignment*, and *sale;* though, as these are not expressly made necessary, the deed would be valid without them.

Auditors — Tax Titles. (*a*) By the present law, the auditor is

be overruled by Sortwell *v.* Jewett, 9 Ohio, 180, where it was held that an assignment elsewhere of land in Ohio, which would be good if made in Ohio, will prevail over a subsequent attachment made in Ohio. Cf. Johnson *v.* Sharp, 31 Ohio State, 611, 617. To convey real estate to an assignee for the benefit of creditors, the deed of assignment should be acknowledged before an officer. Kingman *v.* Loyer, 40 Ohio State, 109.

(*a*) See Blackwell on Tax Titles. With regard to tax titles, our court has said, in Holt *v.* Hemphill, 3 Ohio, 232: "In deciding upon tax titles, great strictness has always been observed, and less latitude given than in proceedings on judgment and execution. A collector who sells land for taxes must act in conformity with the law from which he derives his power; and the purchaser is bound to inquire whether he has done so or not. He acts at his peril, and cannot sustain his title without showing the authority of the collector, and the regularity of the proceeding. In these cases, the maxim *caveat emptor* applies." Taxes are both a personal debt of him in whose name the lands are listed, as also a lien upon them, — and where the lands have been sold on execution after the taxes had been assessed, proceedings for the collection of the taxes may be had either against the land or against the party in whose name they were listed, — and in either case such party or the purchaser of the land, when compelled to pay the taxes, has no right of action against the other to recover the amount. Creps *v.* Baird, 3 Ohio State, 277. Where town lots were separately listed, advertised, and sold, but assessed in gross, the sale is invalid. Willey *v.* Scoville, 9 Ohio, 43. Where the listing was so many acres, in a named subdivision, which contained more, the sale was invalid. Burchard *v.* Hubbard, 11 Ohio, 316; Turney *v.* Yeoman, the person appointed to make conveyance of land sold for taxes. In discussing this topic, therefore, the whole subject of *tax titles* comes under consideration; and our court has laid down, and reiterated, the doctrine, that much greater strictness is to be observed with respect to these titles, than with respect to titles acquired under execution. The purchaser is bound to inquire whether all the preliminary requisitions of the law have been complied with; and it therefore becomes important to know what these are.

1. The land must have been regularly *listed* by the assessor for taxation.

2. The land must be *assessed* and returned by the *assessor*.

3. There must be a *duplicate of assessments*, made by the auditor, and a copy handed to the treasurer for collection.

4. There must be a *notice* of the aggregate amount of taxes for each hundred dollars in value. This must be given by the treasurer, immediately after receiving the duplicate, by advertising six weeks in the newspaper, and posting in three places in each township.

16 id. 24; Lafferty *v.* Byers, 5 id. 458. A description upon a duplicate and a sale for taxes of a tract of land, as one hundred and fifty acres, part of section 36, N. W. corner, is defective, unless the 150 acres were situate on the N. W. corner of the section and in a square form. Stewart *v.* Aten, 5 Ohio State, 257. See Winkler *v.* Higgins, 9 id. 599, as to an undivided share. Humphries *v.* Huffman, 33 id. 395. Unless the auditor's book show a legal advertisement, the sale is void. Kellogg *v.* McLaughlin, 8 Ohio, 114. The assessment upon part of a lot, without specifying what part, is too vague. Massie *v.* Long, 2 Ohio, 287. After the survey of an entry has been recorded, the withdrawal of the entry will not avoid the tax lien of the State. Holt *v.* Hemphill, 3 Ohio, 232. When land is regularly sold for taxes, it is not merely the interest of him in whose name it is listed, but the land itself which passes in fee-simple. M'Millan *v.* Robbins, 5 Ohio, 28. Even where the tax sale is invalid, a lien-holder cannot have it set aside without tendering the tax, penalty, and interest. Gillett *v.* Webster, 15 Ohio, 623. Every thing required to be done in the auditor's office must be proved by transcripts therefrom. Carlisle *v.* Longworth, 5 Ohio, 368. And see as to the strictness required, Lafferty *v.* Byers, 5 Ohio, 458; Treon *v.* Emerick, 6 id. 391; Winder *v.* Sterling, 7 id. 2 pt. 190; Buckley *v.* Osburn, 8 id. 180; Wilkins *v.* Huse, 9 id. 154; Barger *v.* Jackson, 9 id. 163; Hollister *v.* Bennett, 9 id. 83; Harmon *v.* Stockwell, 9 id. 93; Jones *v.* Devore, 8 Ohio State, 430; Skinner *v.* Brown, 17 Ohio State, 33. As to injunctions to restrain the collection of an illegal tax, see Burnet *v.* Cincinnati, 3 Ohio, 73; M'Coy *v.* Chillicothe, 3 id. 370; Osborn *v.* Bank U. S., 9 Wheaton, 751; Cin. Gas Co. *v.* Bowman, 1 Handy, 289; Christopher *v.* Mayor, 13 Barbour, 567; De Baum *v.* Mayor, 16 id. 392. The certificate of purchase at tax sale passes to the heirs of the purchaser. Rice *v.* White, 8 Ohio, 216. For proceedings in redemption of land sold for taxes, see Street *v.* Francis, 3 Ohio, 277; Masterson *v.* Beasley, 3 id. 301; Rawson *v.* Boughton, 5 id. 328; Reynolds *v.* Leiper, 7 id. 1 pt. 17. The provision for forfeiture of a life-estate for non-payment of taxes is constitutional. M'Millan *v.* Robbins, 5 Ohio, 28. The forfeiture only operates against those claiming under the State. Thevenin *v.* Slocum, 16 Ohio, 519. Where a forfeiture is claimed, the law must be strictly complied with. Hannel *v.* Smith, 15 Ohio, 134; Vanzant *v.* Davies, 6 Ohio State, 52. The statute of limitations does not run against the tax lien of the State. Monroe *v.* Morris, 7 Ohio, 1 pt. 262. As to the title acquired by the purchaser, see Stuart *v.* Parish, 6 Ohio, 476; Wallace *v.* Seymour, 7 id. 1 pt. 156; Rennick *v.* Wallace, 8 id. 539; Douglas *v.* Dangerfield, 14 id. 522; Turney *v.* Yeoman, 14 id. 207; Gwynne *v.* Niswanger, 15 id. 367; Milliken *v.* Starling, 16 id. 61. A valid sale for non-payment of taxes bars all rights of dower. Jones *v.* Devore, 8 Ohio State, 430. A county auditor's deed, duly executed, is *primâ facie* evidence of title in the purchaser. Stanbery *v.* Sillon, 13 Ohio State, 571; Woodward *v.* Sloan, 27 Ohio State, 592; but cf. Rhodes *v.* Gunn, 35 id. 387; and see Thompson *v.* Gotham, 9 Ohio, 170.

5. A *delinquency* does not exist until the twentieth day of December. After which the treasurer may *distrain* personal property. But payment may be made at any time before distress, by paying *five per cent* penalty.

6. On the first Monday of January, the treasurer must settle with the auditor, and make return of the *delinquent taxes* under oath.

7. By the first day of October, in each year, the auditor must make out a *list* of all land returned delinquent for the preceding year, charging the delinquent tax with a penalty of twenty-five per cent and interest, and the current tax. This list, certified and signed, must be published for four weeks, together with a notice that such land will be sold to pay the taxes and charges, on the second Monday in January, unless payment be previously made. This list and notice, with the name of the paper in which it was published, must be recorded by the auditor, in a book to be kept for the purpose.

8. On the second Monday of January, the treasurer must sell the land at the court-house, for cash only; that is, the person offering to pay the taxes and charges due on a given tract for the *least quantity* thereof, upon immediate payment, becomes the purchaser of such quantity, of all which the auditor, who is required to be in attendance, must make a record. The auditor must also give the purchaser a *certificate* of purchase, specifying the price and quantity, which certificate is assignable.

9. At any time within two years from the sale, or in case of disability, two years from the removal thereof, the owner may *redeem* the land sold, by application to the court of common pleas. But he must give six weeks' notice of his intention, in some newspaper; and must deposit in court the amount for which the land was sold, all taxes subsequently paid and interest, together with *fifty per cent* on that amount, as redemption money. If, on hearing, the court allow him to redeem, he must also pay the costs of the application, and compensate the purchaser for all valuable improvements made on the land since the sale. And he must, within thirty days, cause a certified copy of the *order of redemption* to be recorded in the recorder's office. This order vests in the applicant all the title which passed by the sale.

10. After the lapse of two years, the holder of the certificate of purchase, if the land has not been redeemed, may produce the same to the auditor and require a *deed;* and the auditor is then bound to make the deed. Nothing is said about *recitals*, but it would seem from analogy to a sheriff's deed that the auditor's deed should recite all the essential preliminaries before enumerated; though probably a deed would not be void for want of these recitals.

11. The statute then provides as follows: "that the deed *so made* by the auditor shall vest in the grantee a good and valid title both in law and equity, and shall be received in all courts

as *primâ facie* evidence of a good and valid title." And upon this provision, our court has decided, that before an auditor's deed can be offered in evidence to prove the title of the purchaser, proof must be given of the legality of the sale, by transcripts from the various records of the proceedings on which the sale is founded; and then the deed will be *primâ facie* evidence of title; that is, it will not be necessary to go back beyond these proceedings, unless it be to answer objections raised on the other side. As the right owner may not always be known, it is provided that the fact of the land being listed in any other name, shall not invalidate the sale, provided the land were in other respects sufficiently *described.* And to prevent any transfer from affecting the claim of the State, it is provided that the *lien of the State* for taxes shall attach on all real estate, on the first day of March annually, (*a*) and shall be perpetual for all taxes due or to become due. Also, that when sold for delinquency, this lien shall be transferred to the purchaser; so that if his title should fail, he should still have a valid claim upon him for the amount by him paid.

12. If land offered for sale be not sold for want of bidders, the land is thenceforth *forfeited* to the State; but may be redeemed at any time before being sold by the State, by payment of all taxes and charges, and those which would have accrued, in case the land had continued on the tax duplicate. Sales of forfeited lands are made biennially, on the second Monday in December, from 1831 onward, pursuant to advertisement, continued four weeks from the 15th of October. (*b*)

13. On the subject of tax titles, the following additional points have been decided: Upon a sale of land for taxes, an agreement among several that they will advance funds and one shall buy, so as to prevent competition, and afterwards to divide the land among them, is illegal, and equity will set aside the sale, on payment of the purchase-money and interest, with fifty per cent penalty and costs. (*c*) On an application to redeem land sold for taxes, the *validity of the title* of the applicant cannot be called in question. All he has to show is a *right to redeem;* and for this purpose it is sufficient that he, or those whom he represents, are in some way connected with the title, as by deed, descent, contract, or possession under claim of title. When lands are advertised to be sold for taxes, they must be described with such certainty that the real owner, though his name were not given, may know the land; and that persons intending to purchase may also know it.

(*a*) The lien attaches now on the day preceding the second Monday of April annually.

(*b*) A forfeiture sale is void if the land was not previously on the delinquent list: Woodward *v.* Sloan, 27 Ohio State, 592; and must have been offered at the delinquent sale: Magruder *v.* Esmay, 35 Ohio State, 221.

(*c*) The purchaser at a void tax sale cannot recover any penalty, but merely interest: Johnson *v.* Stewart, 29 Ohio State, 498; Chapman *v.* Sollers, 38 id. 378; but if only part of the tax was illegal, he may recover the penalty on the balance: Younglove *v.* Hackman, 43 Ohio State, 69.

On the whole, then, it will be perceived from this outline, that tax titles must always be liable to great uncertainty. Indeed, as our court has observed, the general impression is, that they are good for nothing; and for this reason, land sold for taxes is almost always sacrificed for a small part of its value.

Executors, Administrators, and Guardians. (a) In this connection, I am only to consider the proceedings of executors and administrators, so far as connected with the sale of property; their general powers and duties have been before described. Where an executor is expressly empowered by the will to sell the land for any purpose, he may act without any order of court. The will is his letter of instructions, and this he must obey, unless it be contrary to law. But where no such power is given by the will, the executor, like the administrator, acts

(a) For the construction of a power to sell contained in a will, see Taylor *v.* Galloway, 1 Ohio, 232; Wills *v.* Cowper, 2 id. 124; Steele *v.* Worthington, 2 id. 182; Dabney *v.* Manning, 3 id. 321. Prior to 1795, our courts had no power to order a sale of decedent's property, nor between the years 1805 and 1808. At all other times there has been such a power. Ludlow *v.* Johnston, 3 Ohio, 553; Ludlow *v.* M'Bride, 3 id. 240; Paine *v.* Skinner, 8 id. 159. An order of sale is indispensable, and the record must show it. Goforth *v.* Longworth, 4 Ohio, 129; Ludlow *v.* Wade, 5 id. 494; Ludlow *v.* Park, 4 id. 5; Newcomb *v.* Smith, 5 id. 447. The power is statutory, and must be strictly pursued. Lieby *v.* Parks, 4 Ohio, 469; Ludlow *v.* Wade, 5 id. 494; Avery *v.* Pugh, 9 id. 67. Since 1824, the heirs must be parties. Ewing *v.* Hollister, 7 Ohio, 2 pt. 138; Adams *v.* Jeffries, 12 id. 253. As to the jurisdiction of the court appearing upon the records, see Sheldon *v.* Newton, 3 Ohio State, 494. If infants, they may answer by general guardian, or guardian *ad litem*, but the general guardian cannot purchase. Massie *v.* Matthews, 12 Ohio, 351; Robb *v.* Irwin, 15 id. 689. Sheldon *v.* Newton, 3 Ohio State, 494; Merritt *v.* Horne, 5 id. 307. Nor can an executor, or perhaps appraiser. See p. 438, note (c). Actual notice to the infant heirs is not essential to the jurisdiction of the court. Benson *v.* Cilley, 8 Ohio State, 604. The guardian is not to unite in the petition of the administrator, since he only sells for the benefit of the wards. Newcomb *v.* Smith, 5 Ohio, 447; Maxsom *v.* Sawyer, 12 id. 195. On motion to confirm, the court may exercise some discretion, even where the letter of the law has been complied with. Craig *v.* Fox, 16 Ohio, 563. The reversal of an order of a sale after its confirmation, does not divest the title of the purchaser. Irwin *v.* Jeffers, 3 Ohio State, 389. A guardian appointed for a female before twelve, cannot, by petition after, sell land without a re-appointment. Perry *v.* Brainard, 11 Ohio, 442. But in favor of a purchaser, many irregularities will be overlooked. Stall *v.* Macalester, 9 Ohio, 19. When the law is repealed under which an order of sale was made, and the sale was made afterwards, it was void. Perry *v.* Clarkson, 16 Ohio, 571. A purchaser takes the title free from incumbrance of debts. Stiver *v.* Stiver, 8 Ohio, 217; Bank *v.* Carpenter, 7 Ohio, 1 pt. 21. But if his title fail, he has no equity against the decedent's estate. Salmond *v.* Price, 13 Ohio, 368. The sale may be of a part, although the petition and order name the whole of a tract. Ewing *v.* Higby, 7 Ohio, 1 pt. 198. So an equitable title may be sold. Ibid. Where the sale proves void, the heir who seeks to annul it must pay past taxes, but not the purchase-money. Nowler *v.* Coit, 1 Ohio, 519. There is no power, under an order of sale, to create a trust. Piatt *v.* St. Clair, 6 Ohio, 227; but see 7 Ohio, 2 pt. 165. The conveyance may be made to the assignee of the purchaser. Ewing *v.* Higby, 7 Ohio, 1 pt. 198. A petition may be granted to sell for payment of taxes. Welsh *v.* Perkins, 8 Ohio, 52. {The statute requires the petition to describe all the ward's lands; it will be presumed that those described constituted all; and the sale of a lot as No. 174, when the petition described lot 74, will be presumed to be of the same. Mauarr *v.* Parrish, 26 Ohio State, 636. Only the court in the county where the guardian was appointed has jurisdiction to sell the real estate. Foresman *v.* Hoag, 36 Ohio State, 102. The probate court cannot authorize an administrator to sell subject to a mortgage or other lien; it must order the sale free therefrom: Stone *v.* Strong, 42 Ohio State, 53; nor subject to a homestead assigned therein by metes and bounds: Wehrle *v.* Wehrle, 39 id. 365.}

simply as an officer of the law and must resort to the court for instructions. In speaking, therefore, of their proceedings in the sale of real estate, it will be unnecessary to name both. If there be any provision which does not apply to both, it will be pointed out. By our law, all the property, real and personal, of a deceased person, is liable for the payment of his debts; the personalty first, and then the realty. But though the personalty has been exhausted in the manner pointed out by the act, without paying all the debts, the realty cannot be touched without an order of court; to obtain which, application must be made by petition to the court of common pleas, to which all persons interested must be made defendants, and notified thereof by subpœna or otherwise. And if the court are satisfied that a sale is necessary, three appraisers are appointed to assign dower, if there be a widow, and then to return an appraisement of the value of the estate. Upon this return, the court order a sale of the whole or part, as the case may require. If there be no dower to assign, the order of appraisement and sale may be made at the same time; and if an appraisement of the realty was returned by the executor or administrator originally, a new appraisement is not required. The notice of sale must be given by advertisement for four weeks, after which the sale is made at auction at the door of the court-house; and if the land be improved, it must sell for *two-thirds* of the appraised value; if not, for *one-half*. But after being twice offered and not sold, the court may either direct the amount for which it shall be sold, or order a new appraisement. Our statute declares that the sale shall be upon deferred payments, not exceeding two years with interest. But persons interested in the land may prevent a sale by giving security for the payment of the debts mentioned in the petition. If a sale of so much as would pay the debts would injure the value of the residue the whole may be sold, and the surplus distributed under the order of the court; but in all cases of surplus from the sale of realty, such surplus goes to those who would have had the realty. After the sale, a return must be made of the proceedings to the next term of court; and if the court are satisfied that the sale has in all respects been legally made, they order the sale to be confirmed, and that a deed be made to the purchaser. The statute then declares that such deed shall be received in all courts as *primâ facie* evidence that the executor or administrator has in all respects observed the directions and complied with the requisitions of the law, and shall vest the title in the purchaser, in like manner as if conveyed by the deceased in his lifetime. Nothing is said concerning the *recitals* in the deed; but from the strong analogy between this and a sheriff's deed, it would certainly be proper to recite all the essential preliminaries, though perhaps not absolutely necessary. The power to sell is expressly extended to equitable as well as legal estates. It has been decided that an order of court is absolutely necessary to sustain the sale; and where the records do not show such order, it cannot be presumed, or proved by parol. Where the court making the order has jurisdiction of the case, the question whether it was made on a proper state of facts cannot be collaterally examined. So far as the rights of purchasers are concerned, such orders are as available as judgments. This power to sell land under an order of court is strictly a legal power, and cannot be aided in equity. The order must precede the sale. A subsequent order cannot be given in evidence to sustain the sale.

§ 173. **Form of a Deed.** (*a*) No particular form of words is re-

(*a*) *Form of a Quitclaim Deed.* Be it known that ——, and ——, his wife, in consideration of $—— to them paid by ——, do hereby bargain, sell, and quitclaim to the said ——, his heirs and assigns for ever, the following real estate, viz. [describe the property], together with all the privileges and appurtenances to the same belonging; to have and to hold the same, to the said ——, his heirs and assigns for ever; hereby covenanting that the title so conveyed, is clear, free, and unincumbered by any act of the grantors herein. In witness whereof, the said ——, together with ——, his wife, who hereby releases all claim of dower, hereunto set their hands and seals, this ——. [Signatures and seals of the grantors, and attestation by two subscribing witnesses.]

State of ——, county of ——. Before me ——, a ——, personally appeared ——, and ——, his wife, the grantors in the above conveyance, and acknowledged the same to be their voluntary act and deed. And the said ——, wife of the said ——, being examined by me separate and apart from her said husband, and the contents of the above deed being made known and explained to her, declared that she did voluntarily sign and seal, and does now acknowledge the same, and that she is still satisfied therewith. Witness my signature, this ——. [Signature of the officer.]

Form of a Warranty Deed. Be it known that ——, and ——, his wife, in consideration of $—— to them paid by ——, do hereby bargain, sell, and convey to the said ——, his heirs and assigns for ever, the following real estate, viz. [describe the property], together with all the privileges and appurtenances to the same belonging; to have and to hold the same to the said ——, his heirs and assigns for ever; hereby covenanting that they own the property so conveyed in fee-simple and without incumbrance, and that they will warrant and defend the same against all claims whatsoever. In witness whereof the said ——, together with ——, his wife, who hereby releases all claim of dower, hereunto set their hands and seals, this ——. [Signatures and seals of the grantors, attestation by two subscribing witnesses, and certificate of acknowledgment, as before.]

Form of a Mortgage with Power to Sell. Be it known that ——, and ——, his wife, in consideration of $—— to them paid by ——, do hereby bargain, sell, and convey to the said ——, his heirs and assigns for ever, the following real estate, viz. [describe the property], together with all the privileges and appurtenances to the same belonging; to have and to hold the same to the said ——, his heirs and assigns for ever; hereby covenanting that they own the property so conveyed in fee-simple and without incumbrance, and that they will warrant and defend the same against all claims whatsoever.

Provided, however, that if the said ——, or any other person for him, shall pay to the said ——, or those claiming under him, the sum of $——, in —— months after this date, according to the tenor and effect of a promissory note of this date, then this conveyance shall be void.

And for the better securing the aforesaid payment, as well as to save the expense and delay of legal proceedings, the said ——, and ——, his wife, hereby appoint ——, his heirs, executors, administrators, and assigns, his attorneys in fact, with power to keep the buildings on the said premises fully insured and in repair, at the expense of the said ——, until payment; and in case of default of payment at maturity, to lease the said premises and receive the rents, and apply them towards such payment, or to sell the said premises at public auction, giving such notice thereof as quired by law to make a deed valid. The following words would be amply sufficient to convey a fee-simple with warranty: "I, A. B., in consideration of ——— dollars to me paid by C. D., do hereby bargain and sell to C. D. and his heirs the following tract of land, viz., ——— and do hereby warrant the title. Witness my hand and seal this ———." But the universal practice is, to extend a deed, by means of repetition, tautology, and circumlocution, over many times the above space. The origin of this abuse is to be traced to the cupidity of conveyancers. In England, as before observed, conveyancing forms a profession by itself, to a much greater degree than it does here, on account of the admirable simplicity of our land laws; and the charges being in proportion to the labor, it becomes the interest of this branch of the profession to make the forms as prolix as possible. Accordingly, wherever a word could be inserted to increase the length of a deed, it has been done; and this abuse, though considerably diminished, is by no means entirely corrected in this country. In proof of which, as well as for the purpose

is required in sales on execution, and execute a warranty deed to the purchaser; and out of the proceeds of sale, to pay the said debt, together with interest, costs, charges, and assessments, and the balance, if any, to pay over to the said ———; hereby covenanting with all concerned to ratify and confirm all acts lawfully done in pursuance of this power. In witness whereof, the said ———, together with ———, his wife, who hereby relinquishes all claim of dower, hereunto set their hands and seals this ———. [Signatures and seals of the mortgagors, attestation by two subscribing witnesses, and certificate of acknowledgment, as before.]

Form of a Lease. This indenture of lease, made this ———, between ———, of the first part, and ———, of the second part, witnesses; that the party of the first part, in consideration of the rents and covenants hereafter mentioned, does demise and lease to the party of the second part, his representatives and assigns, the following real estate, viz. [describe the premises], together with all the privileges and appurtenances to the same belonging; to have and to hold the same for the term of —— years from the date hereof, at the annual rent of $——, payable [state the terms of payment]; and it is hereby covenanted between the said parties, that the said party of the second part, his representatives and assigns, shall pay the rents above reserved, at the times above specified, unless the premises shall be destroyed by inevitable accident; but shall not be liable for ordinary wear and tear, nor for any injury which can be insured against, nor for any taxes, charges, or assessments, nor for repairs, except voluntary waste; and that in case of default of payment at any time, for the space of —— days after rent becomes due, the party of the first part, his heirs and assigns, may re-enter upon the leased premises, and have and hold the same, as if this lease had not been made; but, otherwise, shall keep the premises in good repair, and not molest the party of the second part; who, performing his covenants, shall quietly hold and enjoy the leased premises during the term aforesaid, and peaceably surrender possession thereof at the expiration of said term. In witness whereof, the said parties hereunto, and to a duplicate hereof, set their hands and seals, the day and year aforesaid. [Signatures and seals of lessor and lessee, attestation by two subscribing witnesses, and certificate of acknowledgment, as before.]

Form of a Bill of Sale of a Ship or Steamboat. Be it known that ———, in consideration of $—— to him paid by ———, does hereby bargain and sell to said ———, his representatives and assigns, the body of the steamboat called the ———, with her apparel, tackle, and furniture, now lying at the port of ———, the certificate of whose enrolment [or registry] is as follows, viz. [copy it in full]; and the said ——— does avow himself to be the lawful owner of the same, and does hereby warrant the title thereto. Witness the signature [and seal, though not essential] of the said ———, this ———. [Signature and attestation by one or more witnesses, the latter not essential.]

To make this a mortgage, add a proviso as in a mortgage of realty.

of explaining the nature of a deed, I shall carefully analyze one of our common forms, consisting of the following parts, namely, the *introduction*, *granting clause*, *description*, *habendum clause*, *covenants*, *conclusion*, and *certificate of acknowledgment*.

Introduction. "This indenture made this ——— day of ——— in the year of our Lord ———, between the *grantor* [naming him], of the city of ———, county of ———, and State of ———, of the first part, and the *grantee* [naming him], of the same city, county, and State, of the second part, witnesseth." Here the deed is described as an "*indenture*." The meaning of an indenture originally was, that the deed was executed by two or more parties, each of whom took *copies or counterparts;* and these copies or counterparts were so *indented* as exactly to fit each other. This formality of indenting is of no use whatever, and is now seldom practised; but the instrument is still called an indenture, because made or purporting to be made between two or more *parties*. But no person is strictly a *party* who does not execute the deed; and in a simple conveyance in fee, it is only the grantor who executes; though in a lease, where there are mutual covenants, both lessor and lessee execute; in strict accuracy, therefore, an indenture is not the proper form of conveying in fee. It is in common use, however, and has this advantage, that if there be several grantors or several grantees, having been once named at length in the *introduction*, they may, through the rest of the deed, be indicated as "parties to the first part" or "parties to the second part," and thus shorten the deed. In the above introduction, the *date* is contained; and it is usually expressed in words and not figures, because figures are so easily altered; but the deed would undoubtedly be good, if all the *numerals* were in figures, or even if there were no date. The *residence* also of the parties is expressed by city, county, and State; but this is not essential; for if the question becomes necessary, it can be proved by parol. Formerly, the *office* or *occupation* of the parties was also stated, or in law phrase, their "*addition*," but this is useless. When a deed is not an indenture, it is called a *deed poll*, or single deed; and then the introduction is as follows: "Know all men by these presents, that I," &c. In this form, the date does not appear until the end of the deed, and the grantor speaks in the first person. The phrase "these presents" has this apology, that it is a literal translation of the Latin words, *hæc presentia*. I hardly need add that the appeal "to all men" is without use or meaning.

Granting Clause. (*a*) After the introduction, the only difference between the *indenture* and *deed poll* is that above indicated; and therefore I shall confine myself to the indenture. After the word "witnesseth," the granting clause is as follows: "That the said *grantor*, for and in consideration of the sum of —— dollars,

(*a*) Ewing *v.* Higby, 7 Ohio, 1 pt. 198; Hart *v.* Johnson, 6 id. 87; Hall *v.* Ashby, 9 Ohio, 96; Foster *v.* Dennison, 9 Ohio, 121; Piatt *v.* St. Clair, 7 Ohio, 2 pt. 165; M'Farland *v.* Febiger, 7 Ohio, 1 pt. 194.

in lawful money of the United States, to him in hand paid by the said grantee, the receipt whereof is hereby acknowledged, has given, granted, bargained, sold, aliened, released, conveyed, and confirmed, and does by these presents give, grant, bargain, sell, aliene, release, convey, and confirm, unto the said grantee, his heirs and assigns for ever, all," &c. Here you have an insight into the art of amplification. I shall first indicate the words which may be left out, and then comment upon what is essential. The expressions "for" and "in consideration of," need not both be used. The money need not be stated to be "in lawful money of the United States." The expressions "to him in hand paid" and "the receipt whereof is hereby acknowledged," need not both be used. The statement of the conveyance in the past and present tenses, "has given," &c., and "does give," &c., is an insult to common sense; either tense is sufficient; and the use of eight different words, "give, grant, bargain, sell, aliene, release, convey, and confirm," to express the act of conveying, is without apology. The proper words in this State are "bargain and sell." But any other words which indicate the intention, as "grant," or "convey," would do equally well. The word "sell," would alone be sufficient. The word "heirs," we have seen, is necessary; but the "assigns" is not; for the right of alienation is inseparable from a fee, without being expressed. In fact, any words inserted in restraint thereof, would be rejected as repugnant to the estate granted. The word "forever" is not necessary, for perpetuity is implied in the word "heirs." When the granting clause has been thus pruned of about three-fourths of its verbiage, it will contain simply a statement of the *receipt* (*a*) of the consideration, and the *conveyance* of the estate. The nature of the consideration has been already described. As to the *receipt* expressed in the deed, it is not conclusive, and parol evidence will be admitted to show that the money was not in fact paid. But it is *primâ facie* evidence of payment, and throws the burden of proving a non-payment on the grantor. In a lease, the granting clause varies considerably from the above. The consideration usually stated is, "the rents and covenants hereinafter mentioned." The operative words are "lease," or "demise." The word "heirs," is not used; and the word "assigns," is not necessary, because the power of assigning or underletting is implied, where the contrary is not stated. It has been decided (*b*) that where a wife signs and acknowledges the deed, but is not named in the granting clause nor elsewhere, as conveying any interest, her dower is not barred. Also, that if she only be named in the conclusion as relinquishing dower, the deed will not convey a fee held in her own right. If there be any *recitals* (*c*) in a deed, their proper place is between

(*a*) See Shepard *v.* Little, 14 Johns. 210.

(*b*) M'Farland *v.* Febiger, 7 Ohio, 194; Foster *v.* Dennison, 9 id. 121; Purcell *v.* Goshorn, 17 id. 105; Cincinnati *v.* Newell, 7 Ohio State, 37; *ante*, p. 369, note.

(*c*) Douglas *v.* Scott, 5 Ohio, 194; Wallace *v.* Miner, 6 Ohio, 366; Reeder *v.* Barr, their introduction and the granting clause, but they may occur elsewhere. Their effect is to preclude those who trace title through deeds containing them, from denying their truth or notice of what they contain. But if such recitals contain errors in fact, they may be corrected by parol, when they are not the essential part of the conveyance.

Description and Boundary. (*a*) The description of the premises is an essential part of the deed; and the general principle is, that it should contain particulars enough to enable a man to ascertain with certainty the land conveyed from the deed itself. This results from a rule of evidence, that *parol* testimony cannot be introduced to modify a written contract. In regard to deeds, the rule is thus stated: Parol evidence is not admissible to contradict, vary, or add to, the terms of a deed. Of the various exceptions and modifications of this rule, I cannot here speak. As applied to the description of the premises in a deed, the result is this: If there be a *patent ambiguity*, that is, an ambiguity apparent on the face of the deed, such that the mere reading of the description will show that it does not identify the land, the deed is void for uncertainty. But if the ambiguity be *latent*, that is, discoverable, not from the words employed, but only from a reference to extrinsic facts and circumstances, then the description may be aided by parol evidence. (*b*) But what is necessary to make a good description will be best understood from a statement of particulars. The means made use of to describe land are chiefly three: first, *specific boundaries*, commonly called *fixed monuments*, or *metes* and *bounds;* secondly, *courses* and *distances*, as determined

4 Ohio, 446; Matoon *v.* Clapp, 8 Ohio, 248; M'Chesney *v.* Wainwright, 5 Ohio, 452; Scott *v.* Douglas, 7 Ohio, 227; Glover *v.* Ruffin, 6 Ohio, 255; Ludlow *v.* Park, 4 Ohio, 5.

(*a*) See 4 Kent, Com. 455; 1 Phillips on Evidence, 473–480; 4 Comyn's Dig. 287; Worthington *v.* Hylyer, 4 Mass. 196; Blake *v.* Doherty, 5 Wheaton, 359; Reisch *v.* Dickson, 1 Mason, 10; Jackson *v.* Clark, 7 Johns. 217; Revere *v.* Leonard, 1 Mass. 91; Powell *v.* Clark, 5 id. 355; Howes *v.* Barker, 3 Johns. 506; Stebbins *v.* Eddy, 4 Mason, 414; M'Chesney *v.* Wainwright, 5 Ohio, 452; McCulloch *v.* Aten, 2 Ohio, 307; Douglass *v.* M'Coy, 5 Ohio, 522; Walsh *v.* Ringer, 2 Ohio, 327; Alshire *v.* Hulse, 5 Ohio, 534; M'Coy *v.* Galloway, 3 Ohio, 282; Benner *v.* Platter, 6 Ohio, 504; Gavit *v.* Chambers, 3 Ohio, 495; Hopkins *v.* Kent, 9 Ohio, 13; Throckmorton *v.* Moon, 10 Ohio, 42; Hollister *v.* Hunt, 9 Ohio, 8; Galloway *v.* Brown, 16 Ohio, 428; Reed *v.* Marsh, 8 Ohio, 147; Marsh *v.* Stephenson, 7 Ohio State, 264; Richardson *v.* Chickering, 41 N. H. 380; Opdyke *v.* Stephens, 4 Dutcher, 83; Robinson *v.* White, 42 Maine, 209. In M'Coy *v.* Galloway, 3 Ohio, 282, the court say, "It is admitted that course and distance must give way to natural objects; but this rule has its limits, and must be used with sound discretion. Where a natural object is distinctly called for and satisfactorily proved, it becomes a landmark, not to be rejected, because the certainty which it affords excludes the probability of mistake; while course and distance, depending for their correctness on a great variety of circumstances, are liable to be incorrect. Difference in the instruments used, and in the case of surveyors and their assistants, must lead to different results. Hence it is that this rule has been established." And see Hare *v.* Harris, 14 Ohio, 529. But parol evidence may show that a reference to a monument, in a sheriff's deed, which would greatly enlarge the quantity, was a mere mistake. Spiller *v.* Nye, 16 Ohio, 16. Where the monument referred to is notorious, a mistake in stating its distance is not material. Buckley *v.* Gilmore, 12 Ohio, 63.

(*b*) Dougherty *v.* Purdy, 18 Ill. 206; McAfferty *v.* Conover, 7 Ohio State, 99.

by the *compass* and *chain;* and thirdly, *quantity*, as determined by computation of the number of *acres*. With regard to these, the established principle is this: specific boundaries control courses, distances, and quantity; that is, if a description contain specific boundaries alone, without course and distance or quantity, it will be sufficient; if it contain all three, and the course and distance or quantity be incompatible with the specific boundaries, the latter prevail; if it contain only course and distance and quantity, and the quantity disagree with the course and distance, the latter prevail; and if it contain course and distance only, it will be sufficient; but quantity only is never sufficient. When all the particulars mentioned are necessary to ascertain the property conveyed, they must all agree; but when there are particulars sufficiently certain to designate the property, the addition of circumstances, false or mistaken, will not frustrate the conveyance. Where land is described as "*between*" certain limits, the limits themselves are excluded. If the description name a monument not existing at the execution of the deed, and the parties afterwards agree to fix one, such agreed monument prevails, though not exactly coincident with the line described in the deed. The mention of the quantity of acres, after a specific description, does not amount to a covenant as to that of quantity; but if the land has been paid for according to the quantity stated, and the quantity turns out to be less, the grantee may resort to chancery. When the quantity is qualified by the words "more or less," or similar words, the buyer takes the risk, and cannot be relieved even in equity, unless there be actual fraud. (*a*) When land is sold at so much for the entire parcel, as for a field enclosed, or an island in a river, any surplus over the stated quantity belongs to the grantee. Where the description is "part of a lot," or "one acre of a lot," it is too vague to sustain a sale. Where a deed refers to another deed for the description, and the land can be ascertained by such reference, the description is good. Neither the town nor county need be stated in the description, if the land can be otherwise identified. Where the description is "so many acres in the south-west corner of a given section," it is good, and the land must be laid out in a square. (*b*) But if it be "so many acres on the south side," the whole south line must be the base of a rectangle. Where the description specifies "a tree on the bank of a creek, thence down the creek with the meanders thereof," low-water mark is the boundary, even though the tree be at some distance from the bank; for neither corner trees nor

(*a*) Ketchum *v.* Stout, 20 Ohio, 453. Words expressing quantity yield to monuments, courses, and distances; and where these are sufficient to determine the boundaries of the land conveyed, there is no covenant that the land described contains that quantity. Mann *v.* Pearson, 2 Johns. 37; Perkins *v.* Webster, 2 N. H. 287; Powell *v.* Clark, 5 Mass. 355; Davis *v.* Rainsford, 17 id. 207; Flagg *v.* Thurston, 13 Pick. 145; Newhall *v.* Ireson, 8 Cush. 595; Pierce *v.* Faunce, 37 Maine, 63; Emery *v.* Fowler, 38 id. 99; Chandler *v.* McCard, 38 id. 564.

(*b*) See Stewart *v.* Aten, 5 Ohio State, 257; Winkler *v.* Higgins, 9 id. 599.

line trees are required to be in the actual line; the nearest and most permanent objects may be selected. (*a*) We have seen that where land is advertised to be sold for taxes, the description must be as certain as in a deed; but our court has decided that a defective description in a levy upon land, may be supplied by parol. When the description has been given according to the foregoing principles, it is usual to find the following addition: "and all the estate, right, title, interest, claim, and demand of the said grantor, of, in, and to the said premises and every part thereof; together with all and singular the privileges and appurtenances to the same belonging; and the rents, issues, and profits thereof." But this can have no other effect than to lengthen the deed; for it is a general principle, that when land passes, all that is appurtenant thereto passes with it, whether mentioned or not. (*b*) We have seen that when a man grants "all his estate" in a certain piece of land, all his interest thereby passes; and even if it were not so, the brief expression, "*with the appurtenances*," would express as much as all the above verbiage.

Habendum Clause. (*c*) Immediately after the description, it is usual to insert the following words: "To have and to hold the premises hereby bargained and sold, or meant, or intended so to be, with the appurtenances, to the only proper use and behoof of the said grantee, his heirs and assigns for ever." The original purpose of this clause, which is a literal translation from the Latin form, was, to explain the nature of the grant, and specify the *tenure* by which the land was to be held; but as we have no peculiarity of tenure, and as the nature of the estate conveyed has been already specified in the granting clause, this clause is utterly useless in common deeds. In deeds of trust, however, it is convenient to insert the *habendum* clause, for the purpose of specifying therein the trust created; though it is not necessary even there. In leases, also, it is usual to state the duration of the lease and the terms of rent in this clause, in the following language: "To have and to hold the said demised premises with the appurtenances to the said *lessee* and his assigns, from the said ——— day of ——— for and during, and to the full end and term of ——— years from thence next ensuing, and fully to be complete and ended:" but of this it is sufficient to say, that the whole might be expressed with equal force, by inserting immediately after the description the following words: "for the term of ——— years from the said ——— day of ———:" and in com-

(*a*) {Where a description calls for the meanders of a stream, giving course and distance, in subsequent conveyances by the same description, after changes by accretion and attrition, the meander line will control course and distance even if the stream in very dry weather occasionally ceases to flow over the ripples. Niehaus *v.* Shepherd, 26 Ohio State, 40.}

(*b*) For example, Meek *v.* Breckenridge, 29 Ohio State, 642, a sale by metes and bounds carries such right as the grantor had to have the eaves of the house projecting beyond his bounds.

(*c*) 4 Kent, Com. 468.

mon deeds, where there is no trust to be expressed, the clause had better be omitted altogether. I will only add, that where it is inserted, it becomes void, if it be repugnant to the estate created by the granting clause.

Covenants. (*a*) We have before observed that, by our criminal

(*a*) 4 Kent, Com. 457 ; Patterson's Lessee *v.* Pease, 5 Ohio, 190 ; Kingdom *v.* Nottle, 1 Maule & Selwyn, 355, and 2 id. 53 ; Greenby *v.* Wilcox, 2 Johns. 1 ; Hamitton *v.* Wilson, 4 id. 72 ; Bickford *v.* Page, 2 Mass. 455 ; Wyman *v.* Ballad, 12 id. 304 ; Backus *v.* McCoy, 3 Ohio, 211 ; Sprague *v.* Baker, 17 Mass. 586 ; King *v.* Kerr, 5 Ohio, 154 ; Foote *v.* Burnet, 10 id. 317, where the whole law of covenants real is fully detailed in the note. This subject is well treated in Rawle on Covenants for Title. See also 2 Parsons on Contracts, 494–508 ; Sedgwick on Damages, ch. vi.

The Covenant of Warranty. The rule of damages is the purchase-money and interest. Clark *v.* Parr, 14 Ohio, 118 ; King *v.* Kerr, 5 id. 154 ; Lloyd *v.* Quimby, 5 Ohio State, 262. Or expenses and counsel fees if the paramount title was gotten rid of by litigation. Lane *v.* Fury, 31 Ohio State, 574. In the case of King *v.* Kerr it is also held, that notice to the warrantor of being sued in ejectment is not required to hold him ; and where there are several successive warrantors, though each may be sued separately, there can be but one satisfaction. Also that where the benefit of the occupying claimant law is demanded, and results in the defendant's retaining the land by paying its value, this is an eviction. Wilson *v.* Taylor, 9 Ohio State, 595. In the New England States generally, the measure of damages for the breach of this covenant is the value of the land at the time of eviction. 2 Parsons on Contracts, 500. A mortgagee, even after a decree of foreclosure, may maintain an action against the mortgagor for breach of the covenant of warranty in the mortgage ; and the measure of damages is the debt due to him, with interest, notwithstanding the encumbrance which constitutes the breach is a less amount. Lloyd *v.* Quimby, 5 Ohio State, 262 ; Elder *v.* True, 32 Maine, 104. A widow evicted from her dower, after assignment, by title paramount to that of her husband, cannot sue on the warranty to him. St. Clair *v.* Williams, 7 Ohio, 2 pt. 110. But dower assigned by metes and bounds, is an eviction under this covenant. Johnson *v.* Nyce, 17 Ohio, 66 ; Nyce *v.* Obertz, 17 id. 71. And so is dower assigned in rents and profits. McAlpine *v.* Woodruff, 11 Ohio State, 120. Though a married woman, uniting with her husband, cannot be sued upon this covenant, she is estopped by it. Hill *v.* West, 8 Ohio, 222. And so though she convey without her husband. Rosenthal *v.* Mayhugh, 33 Ohio State, 155. Where land in a deed is declared to be conveyed subject to a certain encumbrance, this is an exception of such encumbrance from the subsequent covenant of warranty, although the warranty is general in its terms. Bricker *v.* Bricker, 11 Ohio State, 240. *Contra,* Estabrook *v.* Smith, 6 Gray, 572.

The Covenant of Seisin. This covenant is broken as soon as made if the grantor has no title, without waiting for eviction, and the rule of damages is, the purchase-money and interest, the same as in warranty. Innes *v.* Agnew, 1 Ohio, 386 ; Backus *v.* M'Coy, 3 id. 211 ; Spurk *v.* Vangundy, 3 id. 307 ; Robinson *v.* Neil, 3 id. 525 ; Kincaid *v.* Brittain, 5 Sneed, 119. But these cases also decide that where the grantor, at the time of making this covenant, was in actual possession, claiming title, the covenant is then a real one, and runs with the land. The covenants of seisin and of power to convey are not identical. The former is more comprehensive. But they agree in this, that if the grantor was in possession, they run with the land. Devore *v.* Sunderland, 17 Ohio, 52 ; Raymond *v.* Raymond, 10 Cush. 134. But in several of the States the covenant of seisin is not satisfied by an actual seisin, and it is regarded as a covenant for *title.* See Lockwood *v.* Sturdevant, 6 Conn. 385 ; Comstock *v.* Comstock, 23 id. 349 ; Parker *v.* Brown, 15 N. H. 186 ; Rawle on Covenants for Title, p. 48.

Covenants in General. A covenant to warrant and defend, "as executors are bound by law to do," is not binding. Day *v.* Brown, 2 Ohio, 345. The same case decides that where the name of the covenantor is left blank, it cannot be filled by implication. But fiduciary vendors may, by apt words, bind themselves by personal covenants. Rawle on Covenants for Title, pp. 571–3 ; Lockwood *v.* Gibson, 12 Ohio State, 526. It is erroneous to decree that infants shall convey with covenants, since they cannot so bind themselves. St. Clair *v.* Smith, 3 Ohio, 355. A covenant with county commissioners thereafter to be elected is void. Sloane *v.* M'Conahy, 4 Ohio, 157. A covenant for conveyance may be discharged by a parol contract upon a sufficient consideration. Reed *v.* M'Grew, 5 Ohio, 375. A contract to convey so soon as the purchase-money law, if a man conveys land to which he knows he has no title, with intent to defraud, it is a penitentiary offence; but where there is no intention to defraud, the mere fact of conveying does not amount to a warranty of title. The liability of the grantor for the goodness of the title, in conveyances in fee, depends upon the *express* covenants inserted in the deed. I think it may be safely laid down, that, unless otherwise provided by statute, there is no such thing as an *implied warranty* (*a*) of a title in fee to real property, unless, perhaps, by using the word *give*. Hence the grantee always requires an express covenant, when he means to hold the grantor; and the grantor always gives a *quitclaim* deed, when he intends to exempt himself from liability. But in leases for years, the words "*grant and demise*" are held to imply a covenant of title and for quiet enjoyment; and perhaps any other words creating the contract of lease would have the same effect. It follows, then, that the man who purchases land must observe the maxim, *caveat emptor;* and if he means to hold the grantor liable, he must require express covenants. It has been specially provided in several of the States, that the words "grant, bargain, and sell," shall amount to a covenant against the acts and encumbrances of the grantor: but we have no such provision; and therefore, however excellent the principle, I presume that even this covenant would not be implied. The *ancient warranty* was a covenant real, whereby the grantor warranted the title, and bound himself, in case of eviction, to furnish other land of equal value. But in this country, the ancient warranty has been entirely superseded by specific covenants, of which there are five. 1. That the grantor is lawfully seised: "And the said ——— [grantor], for himself, his executors, and administrators, does hereby covenant, promise, and agree to and with the said ——— [grantee], his heirs, executors, administrators, and assigns, that he is lawfully seised as owner of the premises hereby bargained and sold, or meant and intended so to be." 2. That the grantor has good right to convey: "And that he has good right, full power, and lawful authority to sell and convey the same in manner and form

shall be paid, requires simultaneous performance or tender of performance. Webb *v.* Stevenson, 6 Ohio, 282. Where the covenant is "to convey land in fee-simple, clear of all encumbrance, the title to be indisputable," there must be a clear, connected paper-title. Courcier *v.* Graham, 1 Ohio, 330. Where the covenant is to convey without naming the day, and on the other side, to pay part on demand, and the rest on a day named, the covenants are mutual as to time, and the purchaser cannot sue without payment or tender of the whole purchase-money. M'Coy *v.* Bixbee, 6 Ohio, 310. The covenant against encumbrances covers taxes which are a lien upon the land when the deed is made, though not yet due, and also all other encumbrances, though known to the parties, unless excepted in the deed; and parol evidence is not admissible to show that the parties intended them to be excepted. Long *v.* Moler, 5 Ohio State, 271. Also an assessment for street or road improvement payable in annual instalments running through several years is covered by this warranty through the entire series of years. Craig *v.* Heis, 30 Ohio State, 550.

(*a*) Grannis *v.* Clark, 8 Cowen, 36; Barney *v.* Keith, 4 Wend. 502; Young *v.* Hargrage, 7 Ohio, 2 pt. 63. Statutes exist in several of the western States, by which the words "grant," &c., imply a warranty. King *v.* Gilson, 32 Ill. 348; Blossom *v.* Van Court, 34 Missouri, 390.

aforesaid." 3. That the land is free from encumbrances: "And that the said premises are now free, clear, discharged, and unencumbered of and from all former and other grants, titles, leases, encumbrances, charges, estates, judgments, liens, mortgages, taxes, and assessments, of what kind or nature soever." 4. That the grantee shall quietly enjoy: "And that the said ——— [grantee], his heirs and assigns, shall and may, at all times hereafter, peaceably and quietly have, hold, use, occupy, possess, and enjoy the above-granted premises, and every part and parcel thereof, with the appurtenances, without any let, suit, trouble, molestation, eviction, or disturbance of any person or persons lawfully claiming or to claim the same." 5. That the grantor will warrant and defend: "And further, that the said ——— [grantor], his heirs, executors, and administrators will warrant and for ever defend the aforesaid premises, with their appurtenances, and every part and parcel thereof, unto the said ——— [grantee], his heirs and assigns, against all persons claiming, or to claim, by, from, or under him, them, or any of them, or by, from, or under any other person or persons whomsoever." The first three of these covenants have usually been considered as personal covenants, operating presently; and the last two, as real covenants, operating prospectively. In fact, a strict analysis would reduce these five covenants to two; one importing a clear title now, and giving an immediate right of action if this be not true; the other looking to the ultimate security of title, and giving a future right of action whenever such title should be actually defeated. Accordingly, the covenant of *seisin*, which is a present covenant, and the covenant of *warranty*, which is a future covenant, are the two most commonly used in our deeds. Very rarely is any other covenant inserted, unless it be in the covenant *against encumbrance*, which is also a present covenant. But the tendency of recent decisions is to remove all distinction between present and future covenants, by making them all run with the land, and operate prospectively. The only exception is where the covenantor, at the time of the conveyance, was not in possession claiming title; in which case, the covenant of seisin is held to be a present personal covenant, not running with the land, but broken, if at all, as soon as made, and giving an immediate right of action before eviction. With this exception, the three covenants, of seisin, of warranty, and against encumbrances, are real covenants, running with the land. Those of seisin and warranty give no right of action until eviction. (*a*) That against encumbrance gives no right of action until the encumbrance has

(*a*) Gilman *v.* Haven, 11 Cush. 330; Lothrop *v.* Snell, 11 id. 453; Picket *v.* Picket, 6 Ohio State, 525; Hannah *v.* Henderson, 4 Ind. 174; Norton *v.* Jackson, 5 Cal. 262; Stipe *v.* Stipe, 2 Head, 169; Brady *v.* Spurck, 27 Ill. 478. The purchaser cannot plead defect of title in bar to an action on the note for the purchase-money, unless he has been evicted by title paramount. Id. But this is now altered by statute. R. S. § 5780; and in such action the purchaser by counter-claim can set up outstanding titles or encumbrances covered by the covenants. Purcell *v.* Heeny, 28 Ohio State, 39; Cincinnati *v.* Brachman, 35 id. 289; Craig *v.* Heis, 30 id. 550.

been paid off. In all three the measure of damages is the same; namely, the purchase-money, with interest and charges of litigation. And this is the case even when the removing of the encumbrance has cost more than the above amount. But the covenants of seisin and warranty being of such universal importance, I will be a little more explicit respecting them.

The *covenant of seisin*, stripped of its surplusage, amounts to this: that the grantor is the lawful owner in fee-simple. As this covenant is in the present tense, if the grantor has not the title at the date of the deed, there is a breach of the covenant instantly; whence it has been sometimes held, that the covenant of seisin is merely a *personal* covenant, and not a *real* covenant running with the land; and accordingly that the "assigns" of the grantee, though expressly named, cannot avail themselves of it, because a personal contract cannot be assigned. This is the doctrine of several of the States. But in this State, the established doctrine with regard to the covenant of seisin is this: if, at the time of executing the deed, the grantor was not *seised either in fact or in law;* that is, if the grantor, or some person claiming under him, was not in actual possession claiming title, the covenant of seisin is broken instantly, and does not pass with the land to the *heirs or assigns* of the grantee: but on the other hand, if the grantor was in possession with claim of title, then this covenant runs with the land, and is not broken until actual *eviction* by a paramount title; in a word, it has in the latter case the same operation as a covenant of warranty; and this is now the English doctrine. (*a*) The *covenant of warranty* (*b*) is an undertaking to indemnify against all existing claims which may in future be presented. It is in express terms made prospective; it runs with the land into whosesoever hands it passes, and is not broken until there has been an actual eviction by a paramount title. Where the land has passed through several hands, with covenants of warranty, the last holder may, upon eviction, maintain a separate action against every prior warrantor, or may single out either at his pleasure; but he can obtain only *one* satisfaction, and the person who makes that can immediately sue either or all of those who precede him. (*c*)

Such being the legal effect of these covenants, we can now ascertain how much of surplusage there is in the forms above given. The grantor expressly names "his heirs, executors, and

(*a*) Backus *v.* McCoy, 3 Ohio, 211; Devore *v.* Sunderland, 17 Ohio, 52; Lane *v.* Fury, 31 Ohio State, 574, 577; Betz *v.* Bryan, 39 id. 320.

(*b*) Innes *v.* Agnew, 1 Ohio, 386; King *v.* Kerr, 5 id. 154; St. Clair *v.* Williams, 7 id. 2 pt. 110; Day *v.* Brown, 2 id. 345; Bond *v.* Swearingen, 1 id. 395; Douglass *v.* McCoy, 5 id. 522; Allen *v.* Parish, 3 id. 107. But even a covenant of warranty does not run with the land, if the grantor was not in possession when he conveyed. Moore *v.* Merrill, 17 N. H. 75. Nor does it run with the land after it has once been substantially broken. Hall *v.* Plaine, 14 Ohio State, 417. A covenant to keep up fences runs with the land to a certain extent at least. Easter *v.* Little Miami R. R. Co., 14 Ohio State, 48.

(*c*) Wilson *v.* Taylor, 9 Ohio State, 595.

administrators." Is this necessary in order to bind them? One would suppose so, from the care taken to insert them; but the fact is, that as a general rule heirs, devisees, executors, and administrators are liable for the debts and undertakings of the deceased, so far as they have *assets*, whether mentioned or not at the contracting of the debt; and there is nothing in the nature of these covenants to distinguish them from other pecuniary obligations; it cannot therefore be necessary in any case to specify them, in order to bind them. Whenever the cause of action by law survives, they are liable without being mentioned, if they have assets; and when it does not by law survive, no words of the deceased could bind them. Again, the grantor covenants "with the grantee, his heirs, executors, administrators, and assigns:" is this necessary in order to extend the benefit of the covenant to them? If the covenant runs with the land, the "heirs and assigns" may take advantage of it without being named, as our court has declared; and if it does not run with the land, they cannot, although named, avail themselves of it; as has been also declared: therefore it can be in no case necessary to mention them: and as to "executors and administrators," if the covenant runs with the land, they cannot sue although mentioned, and if it does not run with the land, they can sue, though not mentioned, as in case of any other debt or liability due to the deceased. The conclusion then is, that in any of the covenants in a deed, it is sufficient to name the grantor and grantee, without their representatives or assigns. As to the tautology of the words, "promise, covenant, and agree to and with," it is hardly necessary to say that the words, "covenant with," have the same force. So of the expressions, "good right, full power, and lawful authority" — either is as good as all. So the phrase, "every part and parcel thereof," after "appurtenances," is superfluous, because the whole includes every part. And the whole expression, "against all persons claiming or to claim by, from, or under him, them, or any of them, or any other person or persons whomsoever," means no more than "against all claims whatsoever." Accordingly, if all surplusage be left out, these two covenants will run as follows: "and the said grantor does hereby covenant with the said grantee, that he is the lawful owner of the said premises, in fee-simple; and that he will warrant and defend the title against all future claims."

A deed containing the above covenants is usually called a "*warranty deed*," to distinguish it from a "*quitclaim deed*," which either contains no covenant at all, or only a covenant against the acts of the grantor. This covenant is usually in the following form: "That the said grantor has not done or suffered any thing whereby the title of the said premises to the said grantee can be frustrated or annulled." To which is sometimes added another, which when abbreviated is as follows:

"And further, that he will warrant and for ever defend the said premises against all persons claiming under him, his heirs, or assigns." The only other difference of form between a quitclaim and a warranty deed, is in the granting clause, where in the former, the word "quitclaim," or "release," is usually inserted.

In a *lease* there are usually covenants by the lessor and lessee. (*a*) Those by the lessor are: 1. A covenant to *renew* the lease at the expiration of the term. Without this covenant, the lessor is not bound to renew; and when inserted, it runs with the land, and binds any one who obtains the reversion. 2. A covenant to *repair.* Without this, the lessor is not bound to repair or allow for repairs. But the lessee would be compelled to repair at his own expense, or incur a liability for permissive waste. 3. A covenant for *quiet enjoyment.* Without this, the lessee who should be disturbed during his term, could have no remedy. Those by the lessee are: 1. A covenant *to pay the rent.* Unless there be such a covenant, the lessor can only recover his rent by an action for use and occupation. But where there is an express covenant to pay, the lessee will be liable, although the premises should be destroyed by fire, or other inevitable accident. (*b*) 2. A covenant *not to assign or underlet.* Without such a covenant the lessee may do either, this power being implied where it is not denied, as we have already seen. 3. A covenant to yield possession to the lessor at the expiration of the lease. The only effect of this covenant is to make the lessee answerable in damages for any detention. For the lessor can recover *possession* as speedily without this covenant as with it; but he cannot recover damages. There is also a clause of *re-entry or forfeiture for non-payment* of rent, which is peculiarly necessary in this State, because there is no remedy *by distress;* but there is this nice distinction to be observed: If the proviso be that upon non-payment by a given day, the *lease shall be void,* no after-acceptance of rent will operate as a confirmation. But where the proviso is only for *re-entry,* and the lessor afterwards accepts rent, the breach is cured. And the tenant is not bound to seek the landlord off of the land. The rent must be demanded on the premises; though a personal tender off of the

(*a*) A covenant in a lease to insure, when the money realized in case of loss is to be expended in rebuilding or repair, is such a covenant as may run with the land. Masury *v.* Southworth, 9 Ohio State, 340; but in the absence of an agreement to employ it in rebuilding, see as to the lessee's interest in insurance gotten by him for the lessor's benefit. Gilbert *v.* Port, 28 Ohio State, 276. The covenant of the lessee to pay rent, fixes his liability for the rent for the whole term of the lease; and he will continue to be liable for it, although he has assigned the lease with the consent of the lessor, and the lessor has accepted rent from the assignee. Sutliff *v.* Atwood, 15 Ohio State, 194; Harmony Lodge *v.* White, 30 Ohio State, 569. And though the lease be a perpetual one. Taylor *v.* De Bus, 31 id. 468. And he is, in Ohio, liable to the assignee of the reversion, though there is neither privity of estate nor of contract between them. Smith *v.* Harrison, 42 id. 180.

(*b*) Linn *v.* Ross, 10 Ohio, 412; Fowler *v.* Bott, 6 Mass. 63, now altered by statute, R. S. § 4113; but under this statute the conduct of third parties cutting off light and air by building and thus rendering the rented property uninhabitable, does not absolve the lessee.

land will be good. I have mentioned that an actual eviction is necessary before proceeding on the covenant. But our court has decided that where the defendant in ejectment, after judgment against him, claims the benefit of the occupying claimant law, and so is not *actually* evicted, he may nevertheless, in this case, proceed upon his covenants.

All that has been said on the subject of covenants, applies chiefly to those cases where the owner of the land conveys *in propriâ personâ*. An attorney in fact may bind his principal by covenants, if expressly authorized so to do by the power. But those agents who derive their authority from the law, as guardians, executors, administrators, insolvent commissioners, sheriffs, and auditors, have no authority to bind those whom they represent, and therefore their covenants, if binding at all, would only bind themselves. In such deeds, therefore, covenants are seldom inserted. There is, however, a case in which executors covenanted "to warrant and defend, as executors are bound by law to do;" and the court held this to be no covenant by them, because they are not bound by law to warrant at all. (*a*) In the same case, the covenant of seisin contained a *blank*, instead of the name of the party seised, and the court held this covenant void on that account.

Estoppel. (*b*) In this connection, it is proper to say a word on

(*a*) Day *v.* Brown, 2 Ohio, 345.

(*b*) On the general subject of estoppel, see 2 Black. Com. 295; 4 Kent, Com. 97, 254, 440; 2 Parsons, Cont. 340; Merritt *v.* Horne, 5 Ohio State, 307; Buckingham *v.* Hanna, 2 id. 551; Coakley *v.* Perry, 3 id. 344; Hamilton *v.* Zimmerman, 5 Sneed, 39. Estoppels are not favored by courts of law, and still less by courts of chancery. Lieby *v.* Parks, 4 Ohio, 469. A deed not legally attested does not work an estoppel. Wallace *v.* Miner, 6 Ohio, 366; Patterson *v.* Pease, 5 id. 190. But see Douglas *v.* Scott, 5 Ohio, 194. Where a patent issues to the heir, on the entry and survey of his ancestor, he is estopped from denying his ancestor's title. Bond *v.* Swearingen, 1 Ohio, 395; Douglass *v.* McCoy, 5 id. 522; Jackson *v.* Williams, 10 id. 69. Where the grantor had only an equitable title, and afterwards obtains the legal title, if there was a warranty, his heirs are estopped. Allen *v.* Parish, 3 Ohio, 107; Broadwell *v.* Phillips, 30 Ohio State, 255; Moore *v.* Rake, 2 Dutcher, 574; Lindsey *v.* Ramsey, 22 Ga. 627; Robertson *v.* Wilson, 38 N. H. 48; Hayes *v.* Tabor, 41 N. H. 521; Philly *v.* Sanders, 11 Ohio State, 490; Carbrey *v.* Willis, 7 Allen, 364; Ross *v.* Adams, 4 Dutcher, 160; Goodman *v.* Beacham, 24 Ga. 150. He is estopped also, if there was a covenant, for further assurance. Bennett *v.* Waller, 23 Ill. 97. Where a deed is in the ordinary form of a release, purporting only to convey all the right, title, and interest of the grantors, it conveys only the vested interest of the grantors in the premises at the time, and the covenant of warranty is only coextensive with the grant, and does not therefore estop from the assertion of an after-acquired title. White *v.* Brocaw, 14 Ohio State, 339; Ballard *v.* Child, 46 Maine, 152; Lownsdale *v.* Portland, 1 Oregon, 381. In ejectment, where both parties claim under the same chain of title, the defendant is estopped from denying its validity. Hart *v.* Johnson, 6 Ohio, 87. Recitals work an estoppel, even in the deed of a remote grantor. Kinsman *v.* Loomis, 11 Ohio, 475. A recital in a deed, that the grantor has a certain interest in the land, which interest the deed purports to convey, estops the grantor, and all persons in privity with him, to deny that fact, and therefore prevents them from asserting any subsequently acquired title inconsistent therewith. French *v.* Spencer, 21 How. 228. But recitals can only affect parties and privies. Miller *v.* Holman, 1 Grant's Cases, 243; Moore *v.* Littel, 40 Barb. 488. Those covenants only work an estoppel which run with the land and contain an express warranty. Boyd *v.* Longworth, 11 Ohio, 235. Such covenants will estop a wife who unites with her husband: Hill *v.* West, 8 Ohio, 222; or a wife who supposed her husband dead after seven years' absence, and made a deed without him:

the subject of *estoppel.* By estoppel is meant that a party is not allowed to contradict what he has agreed to under seal. The doctrine of estoppel is confined to instruments under seal, on account of the *theoretical* solemnity attending their execution. By the effect of estoppel, if a man who has no interest at the time, or only an equitable interest, makes a conveyance, and afterwards obtains the legal title, this relates back to supply the prior conveyance, and enures to the benefit of the grantor or his assigns. For though the original deed conveyed nothing at the time, the grantor is estopped from averring that fact; and so are his heirs and all persons claiming under him. The case would be the same, if the legal title had been acquired after the death of the grantor. But the estoppel of the heirs, and other representatives of the grantor, depends upon the fact whether the deed contains covenants of title. If the heirs should recover against their ancestor's grantee, on the ground that the ancestor had no title at the time of conveying, and that the deed contained a warranty, the grantee might immediately turn round and sue the heirs on the covenant; and it is to avoid this circuity of action, that the heirs of the ancestor are estopped whenever the deed contains a covenant of warranty. But no deed will operate by estoppel, unless it be executed with all the legal formalities; and accordingly where an instrument, intended for a deed, and containing a covenant of title, had but one subscribing witness, it was held not to estop the heirs of the grantor under the laws of this State.

Conclusion and Attestation. (*a*) The conclusion of the deed is in these words: "In witness whereof the said grantor has hereunto set his hand and seal, this ——— day of ——— in the year ———." But I presume the signature and seal would be sufficient without any *concluding words* averring the fact. Their presence would speak for themselves. Whether the signatures of the two witnesses alone would be sufficient without any *attesting words*, is doubtful, for the statute requires the signing and sealing to be done or acknowledged "in the presence of two witnesses who shall attest such signing and sealing, and subscribe their names *to such attestation.*" But the fact of delivery need not appear

Rosenthal *v.* Mayhugh, 33 Ohio State, 155. For something like an equitable estoppel, see Reily *v.* Miami Exp. Co., 5 Ohio, 333. If a man stands by and suffers another to purchase land to which he has a title, without making it known to the purchaser, he will be estopped in equity from exercising his legal right. Cochran *v.* Harrow, 22 Ill. 345; Smiley *v.* Wright, 2 Ohio, 506; McAfferty *v.* Conover, 7 Ohio State, 99. And see Wilson *v.* Hicks, 40 id. 418. But a mortgagee, under a duly recorded mortgage, is not estopped from asserting his claim under the mortgage by the fact that he was present at a sheriff's sale of the land under a judgment against the mortgagor, and did not mention his mortgage, in the absence of evidence of actual fraud on his part. Fisher *v.* Mossman, 11 Ohio State, 42. To create an estoppel, *in pais*, the acts relied upon must have been done with a design to induce the party setting up the estoppel to act upon them. Andrews *v.* Lyons, 11 Allen, 349; Morgan *v.* Spangler, 14 Ohio State, 102; Beardsley *v.* Foot, 14 Ohio State, 414.

(*a*) Smith *v.* Crooker, 5 Mass. 538; Hurst *v.* Adams, 6 id. 519; Hatch *v.* Hatch, 9 id. 307; Courcier *v.* Graham, 1 Ohio, 330; Patterson *v.* Pease, 5 Ohio, 190.

in the attestation, because the statute does not require it. If there be any erasures, alterations, or interlineations, a memorandum should be made of them in the attesting clause, to show that they were done with the consent of parties; for any material alteration of a deed by one party, after the execution, and without the consent of the other, destroys it. And the most convenient proof of the time and manner of making the alterations, is by this memorandum, though undoubtedly other proof would be admitted.

A *mortgage* follows in every respect the common form of a deed, with the addition of a *clause of defeasance*, immediately before the *conclusion*. This clause, when abbreviated according to the foregoing principles, may be in the following words: "Provided, nevertheless, that if the said *mortgagor* shall pay to the said *mortgagee*, the sum of ——— dollars, on the ——— day of ———, in the year ———, according to a promissory note of this date, then, this mortgage is to be void." If there be a power of attorney to sell, it is inserted immediately after this clause of defeasance. We have already seen that the construction put upon a mortgage is far different from what its language imports; and for this reason, its form ought to be so altered as to contain the precise stipulations which the law implies; but a still greater improvement would be to provide by law, that an instrument of the following form, duly executed and recorded, should have the force and effect of a mortgage: "I, A. B., do hereby mortgage to C. D. the following real estate, to which I warrant the title; viz., ———, to secure the payment of ——— dollars, due on the ———, according to my note of the same tenor and date. Witness my hand and seal," &c. Why would this not answer every purpose?

Certificate of Acknowledgment. The nature of an acknowledgment having been before considered, it only remains to consider the form of the certificate; which is usually as follows: "The State of ———, county of ———. Before me ———, a ——— of said ———, personally appeared ———, the above-named grantor, and acknowledged the signing and sealing of the above deed, as his voluntary act. Witness my hand," &c. But where the wife joins her husband, the following addition must be made: "And the said ———, wife of the said ———, being examined by me separate and apart from her husband, and the contents of the above deed being explained to her, declared that she did voluntarily sign, seal, and acknowledge the same, and is still satisfied therewith. Witness my hand," &c.

In concluding my remarks on the form of deeds, I will merely observe that there are three arguments in favor of observing set forms. *First*, the legal effect of *words* is thereby settled; *secondly*, the instrument is more readily drawn, and with less liability to mistake; and *thirdly*, we can more readily refer to any particular part. For these reasons, I am in favor of established forms; but every consideration shows that these forms ought to be as concise as possible; and I hope that the somewhat minute examination I have given establishes the fact that the customary prolixity which I have exposed, in the common form of deeds, is an abuse worth reforming. And when we consider the whole number of deeds made annually in the United States, and all required to be recorded, it will be conceded that this single reform would produce in the aggregate an immense saving of time, material, and expense. What, then, would be the result, if a similar reform were effected in regard to all legal forms and instruments? But it is time to leave the subject of title by purchase. I have made the lecture a very long one, on account of its great practical importance. I trust I have sufficiently proved the truth of the remark made in the beginning, that much improvement has been made in this branch of law, and that there is room for much more. In a matter of such universal interest as the transfer of property, whether real or personal, there is peculiar reason for endeavoring to attain the utmost degree of simplicity and brevity. We have improved our law in both these respects; but wise legislation might go much further. With regard to transfers of realty, the two great points to be regarded are certainty and notoriety. Whatever forms and ceremonies conduce to these ends are salutary, and ought to be retained; all beyond are worse than useless, and ought to be abolished. On the subject of personalty there is less fault to find. This part of the law is simple enough. If it be defective in any respect, it is in the want of certainty, with the single exception of a ship or steamboat; but I reserve remarks on this subject till we come to the contract of sale.

LECTURE XXXII.

CONTRACTS IN GENERAL. (*a*)

§ 174. **What constitutes a Contract.** To complete our view of the law of property, it only remains that we examine the law of contracts. I have already spoken of the constitutional guaranty which secures existing contracts against being impaired by legislation; and on this important provision, I have nothing now to add to the views then presented, though hardly any language would be too strong in commendation of its utility. In this lecture, I am to consider the general law of contracts; and in the next, the law regulating particular classes of contracts; and I

(*a*) See 2 Black. Com. ch. 30; 2 Kent, Com. lec. 38, 39, 40; 1 Dane's Abr. ch. 1; the treatises of Smith, Parsons, Metcalf, Bishop, Langdell, Anson, Wharton, Leake, Pollock by G. H. Wald, Chitty, Pothier, and Newland, the latter on Contracts as regarded in equity.

desire, at the outset, to impress you strongly with a feeling of the practical importance of this division of law, not merely to the professional man, but to every citizen. Nearly all the business transactions of life have some connection with contracts. Even our currency is chiefly made up of contracts in the shape of bank-notes. A large proportion of the wealth of every man consists of contracts. In short, few of us pass a single day without having something to do with contracts. The outline, therefore, of the law of contracts should be in the mind of every person pretending to business qualifications; and this is all I shall undertake to exhibit. Writers have given various definitions of a contract, of which I shall quote but three. Blackstone says it is "an agreement, upon sufficient consideration, to do or not to do a particular thing." (*a*) Powell says it is "a transaction in which each party comes under an obligation to the other, and each reciprocally acquires a right to what is promised by the other." (*b*) The French definition, taken from the civil law is, "a convention by which one or more persons obligate themselves to one or more other persons, to give, or to do, or not to do something." (*c*) It makes little difference which of these definitions we adopt. The effect of every valid contract is to create reciprocal rights and obligations. A distinction is, however, made between *executed* and *executory* contracts. Thus if I agree to deliver property to you, and forthwith deliver it, this is an executed contract on my part; and the effect is to convey to you *something in possession.* But if you do not, at the time, pay the price agreed, the contract so to do is *executory* on your part; and as I may be compelled to resort to an action against you to enforce payment, the effect is to give me a *right of action.* Hence the interest of a party in an executory contract is technically called *a thing or chose in action.* (*d*) The remedy which a party has, in case of non-performance by the other party, is two-fold. By a suit at law, he may in all cases recover damages; and by a suit in chancery, he may in many cases compel specific performance. But these points are explained elsewhere. In thus describing the effect of a contract, I have presupposed its legal sufficiency or validity; but according to the foregoing definitions, this must depend upon three things; namely, the *consideration*, the *parties*, and the *subject-matter.* I shall speak of these in their order.

§ 175. **Consideration.** We have seen that Blackstone makes a

(*a*) 2 Black. Com. 442.

(*b*) 1 Powell on Contracts, p. 6.

(*c*) "A contract is an agreement in which a party undertakes to do, or not to do, a particular thing." Marshall, C. J., Sturges *v.* Crowninshield, 4 Wheat. 197. This definition, omitting the element of consideration, is preferred by Metcalf, J., the learned contributor to the American Jurist on the subject of Contracts, vol. 20, p. 1. Whether the term "agreement," as used in the statute of frauds, includes the consideration, has been a disputed point. Wain *v.* Walters, 5 East, 16; Saunders *v.* Wakefield, 4 B. & Ald. 595; Packard *v.* Richardson, 17 Mass. 122.

(*d*) 2 Black. Com. 443. A grant is an executed contract. Fletcher *v.* Peck, 6 Cranch, 136.

"*sufficient consideration*" part of the definition of a contract. (*a*) In fact, this is what distinguishes a *contract* in legal contemplation from a mere *promise*. An agreement without any consideration is called, in law language, a *nudum pactum*, or naked promise, which the law will not recognize. (*b*) But what is meant by a consideration, in this technical sense, will be best understood by an illustration. Thus, if I promise to do something for you, without your having done or promising to do anything for me in return, there is no motive or consideration for my promise. The benefit is all on your side, and the burden all on mine, without any mutuality or reciprocity. If I fail to perform, you suffer no *damage*, but remain in the same condition as before the promise was made. Hence, though I may be *morally bound* to perform, yet the law will neither enforce performance, nor give damages for non-performance. But if, on the other hand, my promise to you is based upon something done or to be done by you for me, which will either benefit me or incommode you, there is then a consideration for my promise, which converts it into a contract, and makes it binding in law. There is now a mutuality, and each party may call upon the other to perform his part, or pay damages for non-performance. But we must take care not to confound a consideration with an *equivalent*, as we are at first apt to do. The law does not require that what you do or agree to do for me shall be the same in kind or equal in value, with what I agree to do for you. (*c*) It merely requires that something be done or suffered

(*a*) 2 Kent, Com. 463; 2 Black. Com. 443. For an admirable essay on this subject, see Am. Law Reg. for March, May, and June, 1854, by Mr. E. L. Pierce.

(*b*) 2 Black. Com. 445. The *nudum pactum* of the civil law and the gratuitous promise of the common law are now distinguished from each other. 1 Fonb. Eq. bk. 1, ch. 5, § 1, Art. *Nudum pactum*, English Law Review, May, 1849. The policy of the rule, requiring a consideration to uphold a contract, has been maintained by some jurists, and assailed by others. Eastwood *v.* Kenyon, 11 Ad. & El. 438; s. c. 2 P. & D. 276; Story on Bailm. § 169; 1 Fonb. Eq. 337, *note;* Fitch *v.* Redding, 4 Sandf. 130, per Duer, J. {Motive and consideration are not the same. Gratitude or expectation of results may be motives, but are not considerations. Philpot *v.* Gruninger, 14 Wall. 570.}

(*c*) This rule is sometimes expressed in strong language, as "The law does not weigh the quantum of the consideration." "The least spark of a consideration will be sufficient." Pillans *v.* Mierop, 3 Burr. 1663, 1666; Whitney *v.* Stearns, 16 Maine, 397; Sanborn *v.* French, 2 Foster (N. H.), 246; Train *v.* Gold, 5 Pick. 384; Hubbard *v.* Coolidge, 1 Met. 93; Austyn *v.* M'Lure, 4 Dall. 226; Wolford *v.* Powers, 85 Ind. 294; Worth *v.* Case, 42 N. Y. 362; Williams *v.* Jensen, 75 Mo. 681; Giddings *v.* Giddings, 51 Vt. 227. In the absence of fraud or warranty, the sale of a chattel which proves to be utterly worthless is a sufficient consideration: Johnson *v.* Titus, 2 Hill, 606; Brown *v.* Budd, 2 Carter (Ind.), 442; Eagan *v.* Call, 34 Penn. State, 236; or the release of a supposed dower right which clouded a title: Sykes *v.* Chadwick, 18 Wall. 141. But it is to be observed that these are not cases of a money consideration; for the benefit derived from money is capable of measurement in regard to adequacy, and was so held in Shepard *v.* Rhodes, 7 R. I. 470; Wolford *v.* Powers, 85 Ind. 294, 301. The general rule is that if the promisor got all he bargained for, he must perform his promise. But gross inadequacy of consideration is often an important fact in connection with circumstances of distress, improvidence, or mental incompetency, or where peculiar confidential relations exist between the parties from which the presumption of fraud may be raised, so as to avoid the contract or to prevent a decree of specific performance. Griffith *v.* Spratley, 1 Cox, 383; Preble *v.* Boghurst, 1 Swanst. 329; Moth *v.* Atwood, 5 Ves. Jr. (Sumner's ed.) 845, and *notes;* Crowe *v.* Ballard, 1 id. 215; Morton your part, as an inducement to my undertaking, and a foundation for damages in case of my failure, which something we call a consideration; and it makes no difference whether it be beneficial to me or some other person not a party, or merely prejudicial to you; for in either case it will be a sufficient consideration. (*a*) The general idea is, that a consideration must be something by which one party is to gain, or the other to lose, in a *pecuniary sense;* as the payment of money, performance of work, delivery of property, forbearance to sue, and the like. But this is not always the case; for a *moral obligation* alone is held sufficient to support an express promise, though not to raise an implied promise. Thus, if an adult person promise to pay a debt contracted during infancy; (*b*) or if any person promise to pay a debt barred by the statute of limitations, (*c*) or bankruptcy; such promise will bind him, though there was no existing legal obligation. The rule then is, that a moral obligation, founded on a once existing legal obligation, will support an express promise. (*d*) *Marriage*

lock *v.* Buller, 10 id. 291; Osgood *v.* Franklin, 2 Johns. Ch. 1, 23; Knobb *v.* Lindslay, 5 Ohio, 468; Watkins *v.* Collins, 11 id. 31; Tracy *v.* Sacket, 1 Ohio State, 54; Follett *v.* Rose, 3 McLean, 332; Davidson *v.* Little, 22 Penn. State, 245; Robinson *v.* Schly, 6 Geo. 515; 1 Story, Eq. Juris. § 246. A promise to pay one cent is not a consideration for a promise to pay six hundred dollars. Schnell *v.* Nell, 17 Ind. 29.

(*a*) Com. Dig. art. B. 1; Pillans *v.* Mierop, 3 Burr. 1673; Bunn *v.* Guy, 4 East, 194; Morley *v.* Boothby, 3 Bing. 113; Violet *v.* Patton, 5 Cranch, 150. Benefit to a third person is the ordinary consideration of guaranties. Stadt *v.* Lill, 9 East, 348; Leonard *v.* Vredenberg, 8 Johns. 29; Bailey *v.* Freeman, 11 id. 221. A mutual concurrent promise may be a consideration if capable of performance. Nott *v.* Johnson, 7 Ohio State, 270; Forney *v.* Ship, 4 Jones, Law, 527; Funk *v.* Hough, 29 Ill. 145; Philpot *v.* Gruninger, 14 Wall. 570. {A mutual concurrent promise, as distinguished from its performance, may always be a consideration for a promise, subject to the following qualifications: 1st, It must be capable of performance and of enforcement; 2d, it must not be a promise of something valueless on its face, for example, a promise to relinquish a mere possibility, as a child's expectancy in his living parent's estate; 3d, it must not be the performance of a legal obligation, as the payment in whole or in part of a debt overdue, or to perform a duty or contract in consideration of extra pay or reward.}

(*b*) 2 Kent, Com. 234-239.

(*c*) Lonsdale *v.* Brown, 3 Wash. C. C. 90.

(*d*) That a *moral obligation* is a sufficient consideration to sustain an express promise is supported by numerous *dicta.* Atkins *v.* Hill, Cowper, 284; Hawkes *v.* Saunders, 1 id. 290; Trueman *v.* Fenton, id. 544; Lee *v.* Muggeridge, 5 Taunt. 36; Seago *v.* Deane, 4 Bing. 459; Wells *v.* Horton, 2 C. & P. 383; Gleason *v.* Dyke, 22 Pick. 390; Doty *v.* Wilson, 14 Johns. 381; Com'rs Canal Fund *v.* Perry, 5 Ohio, 56; Montgomery *v.* Lampton, 3 Met. (Ky.) 519; Musser *v.* Ferguson, 55 Penn. State, 475. Stated in this general form, it has been of late discountenanced by the courts. Wennall *v.* Abney, 3 B. & P. 249, *note;* Littlefield *v.* Shee, 2 B. & Ad. 811, per Lord Tenterden; Jennings *v.* Brown, 9 M. & W. 501, per Parke, B.; Kaye *v.* Dutton, 7 Man. & Grang. 807, per Tindal, C. J.; Hamor *v.* Moore, 8 Ohio State, 239; Shepard *v.* Rhodes, 7 R. I. 470. On the other hand, however, the promise of a widow to perform a contract made by her when married, which was not then binding on her separate estate, but was void, is not enforceable without a new consideration. Musich *v.* Dodson, 76 Mo. 624; Hayward *v.* Barker, 52 Vt. 429. See, more fully, Pollock on Contracts, by G. H. Wald, 169 (*g*). The cases, to explain which it has been employed, are now based on a less sweeping rule, which allows a party to waive some special privilege or exception in his favor, but for which there would have been a valid contract enforceable against him. {It follows that the rule should be stated thus: A past consideration or the mere moral obligation of a benefit conferred without request will not support a promise; but the past consideration must have been performed or rendered on a promise of payment, or on the known expectation of payment, from which a promise would be implied; and also is a sufficient consideration to support a promise predicated upon it, though not necessarily a valuable one. (*a*) But *natural affection* among kindred is not. (*b*) A consideration which is *impossible*, will not support a contract, (*c*) nor will the law uphold one which is *illegal* or *immoral*, (*d*) as will be seen hereafter. Considerations are of three kinds; namely, *executed*, *executory*, and *concurrent*. An *executed* consideration is something done before making the promise; and the rule is, that such consideration will not be sufficient, unless induced by the previous request of the other party, or there be a subsequent new consideration. (*e*) Thus, if I promise you to pay a debt *already due* by another, this promise is not binding, because the consideration is past; but if I first request you to trust him, promising to see the debt paid, the promise is binding; and so it is, if, upon the strength of it, you agree not to sue him; for this forbearance is a new consideration. (*f*) An *executory* consideration is something to be performed before the other party can be required to perform. This is called a *condition precedent*, and performance must be done or tendered to make the contract binding on the other party. Thus, if I agree to do so much work for so much money, I must perform the work, or offer to perform it, before I can claim the compensation. A *concurrent* consideration is where there are mutual engagements to be performed *at the same time*, as in the case of

right to resist performance of the original promise must be a personal privilege which is waived by the new promise, as infancy, bankruptcy, limitations; whereas the contract of a married woman, being void and not voidable, is not in the category of personal privileges. The statute of limitations is a deprivation of remedy rather than an annulling of the contract. As to services rendered on request without fixing a compensation, the subsequent promise may be regarded merely as an agreement of their value. } For statement of the rule, see American Law Register, June, 1854, art. Consideration of a Contract; Parsons on Contracts, vol. 1, p. 360; Selwyn, N. P. 55 (11th ed.); Gee *v.* Archer, 2 Barb. 420; Nash *v.* Russell, 5 id. 566; Valentine *v.* Foster, 1 Met. 520; Beaumont *v.* Reeve, 8 Q. B. 483; and an elaborate opinion of the late Lord Denman in Eastwood *v.* Kenyon, 11 Ad. & El. 438; s. c. 2 P. & D. 276.

(*a*) 2 Black. Com. 297, 444; Story *v.* Arden, 1 Johns. Ch. 261; Bradish *v.* Gibbs, 3 id. 523; Newburyport Bank *v.* Stone, 13 Pick. 420.

(*b*) Pennington *v.* Gittings, 2 Gill & Johns. 208; Duvoll *v.* Wilson, 9 Barb. 487; Mills *v.* Wyman, 3 Pick. 307; Cook *v.* Bradley, 7 Conn. 57.

(*c*) Co. Lit. 206 *a*; Nerot *v.* Wallace, 3 T. R. 17; Powell on Contracts, 161, 164. But this impossibility must be natural or physical, not merely personal to the promisor; and difficulty or improbability is no excuse. Huling *v.* Craig, Addison, 343; Gilpin *v.* Consequa, 1 Peters, C. C. 86; Yonqua *v.* Nixon, id. 224; Tufnel *v.* Constable, 7 A. & E. 798.

(*d*) Collins *v.* Blantern, 2 Wils. 347; Toler *v.* Armstrong, 11 Wheaton, 258.

(*e*) Lampleigh *v.* Braithwaite, Hob. 106; s. c. Smith's Lead. Cas.; 22 American Jurist, 2–16; Dodge *v.* Adams, 19 Pick. 429; Dearborne *v.* Bowman, 3 Met. 158; Chilcott *v.* Trimble, 13 Barb. 502; Webb *v.* Cole, 20 N. H. 490; Kelley *v.* Lindsey, 7 Gray, 287. But an entire promise, founded partly on an executed and partly on an executory consideration, will be sustained. Bret *v.* J. S. *et ux.*, Cro. Eliz. 756; Loomis *v.* Newhall, 15 Pick. 159; Roberts *v.* Griswold, 36 Vt. 496; Wiggins *v.* Keizer, 6 Ind. 252. A previous request may be implied from tacit acquiescence in the service or an acceptance of the benefit conferred. Livingston *v.* Rogers, 1 Caines, 583; Oatfield *v.* Waring, 14 Johns. 188; Law *v.* Wilkin, 6 Ad. & El. 718; Wilson *v.* Edmonds, 4 Foster (N. H.), 517. It is held that if after the payment of my debt by a third person I make an express promise to pay him the amount, this last promise is binding. Gleason *v.* Dyke, 22 Pick. 390; Paynter *v.* Williams, 1 Cr. & Meeson, 819.

(*f*) Leonard *v.* Vredenberg, 8 Johns. 29; 2 Kent, Com. 122, 123.

marriage; and here, as neither party can perform without the other, a tender of performance is sufficient. The principal exceptions to the necessity of a consideration were formerly two; namely, contracts under seal, and negotiable contracts after being negotiated. I shall speak of these hereafter. For the present it is sufficient to say, that we have a statutory provision authorizing a total or partial failure of consideration to be set up in defence to all written contracts, whether under seal or not, except negotiable contracts after being negotiated. (*a*)

(*a*) Where a part of the consideration is merely void, the note will be good in part and bad in part. Wilson *v.* Forder, 20 Ohio State, 89. But where a portion is illegal, then the whole is void. Widoe *v.* Webb, 20 Ohio State, 431. Forbearance of legal proceedings either against the promisor or a third party, is a frequent consideration, and it is not necessary that the promisor should be at all interested in the suit. Smith *v.* Algar, 1 B. & Ad. 603; King *v.* Upton, 4 Greenl. 387; Silvis *v.* Ely, 3 W. & S. 420; Jennison *v.* Stafford, 1 Cush. 168; Call *v.* Calef, 4 id. 388; Rood *v.* Jones, 1 Doug. (Mich.) 188; Holzworth *v.* Koch, 26 Ohio State, 33; Ford *v.* Rehman, Wright (Ohio), 434; Boyd *v.* Freize, 5 Gray, 553; Vinal *v.* Richardson, 13 Allen, 521. But the forbearance is not a valid consideration, if the proceedings are entirely unfounded. Jones *v.* Ashburnham, 4 East, 455; Newell *v.* Fisher, 11 Sm. & Marsh. 431; Wade *v.* Simeon, 2 M. G. & S. 548. But if the result is a matter of reasonable doubt, it is sufficient. Gould *v.* Armstrong, 2 Hall (N. Y.), 266; Longridge *v.* Dorville, 5 B. & Ald. 117. A promise in consideration of forbearance is not binding unless accepted by the other party. Shupe *v.* Galbraith, 32 Penn. State, 10. An agreement to give time is a sufficient consideration for a note of a third party. Mechanics' Bank *v.* Wixson, 42 N. Y. 438; Brownell *v.* Harsh, 29 Ohio State, 631.

Compromise of a right of action or waiver of legal rights, is a valid consideration, whatever might have been the result of a suit. Penn *v.* Lord Baltimore, 1 Ves. Sen. 450; Union Bank *v.* Geary, 5 Peters, 114; Barlow *v.* Ocean Insurance Co., 4 Met. 270; McKinley *v.* Watkins, 13 Ill. 140; Pierce *v.* Pierce, 25 Barb. 243; Burnham *v.* Dunn, 35 N. H. 556; Mayo *v.* Gardner, 4 Jones (N. C.), 359; Gates *v.* Shutts, 7 Mich. 127. Burnham *v.* Dunn, 35 N. H. 556; Mayo *v.* Gardner, 4 Jones, Law, 359; Cook *v.* Wright, 1 Ellis, B. & S. 559; Scott *v.* Warner, 2 Lans. 49. The claim compromised must not be unfounded, or else it will not support a compromise; but an honest difference of opinion is sufficient. Edwards *v.* Baugh, 11 M. & W. 641; Longridge *v.* Dorville, 5 B. & Ald. 117; Jarvis *v.* Sutton, 3 Ind. 289. Palfrey *v.* Portland, &c. R. R. Co., 4 Allen, 55. But the compromise will not be sustained if the public have an interest in the prosecution of the legal proceedings. Coppock *v.* Bower, 4 M. & W. 360; Gardner *v.* Maxey, 9 B. Monr. 90; Clark *v.* Ricker, 14 N. H. 44; Walbridge *v.* Arnold, 21 Conn. 424.

The acceptance of part payment of a debt by a creditor has been held from an early period of the common law, to be no bar to an action for the sum unpaid, there being no consideration for the discharge of the residue which the law would recognize. The conduct of a creditor in prosecuting a claim for the part thus discharged, in violation of his promise, has been thought so unfair and unconscionable by the courts, that they have materially impaired the original force of the rule, excluding from its operation cases where any other property but money was received in satisfaction, or any collateral benefit could be fixed upon as a consideration, or where third parties would be defrauded if the creditor was allowed to recover the residue. Howe *v.* M'Kay, 5 Pick. 44; Brooks *v.* White, 2 Met. 283; Smith *v.* Bartholomew, 1 id. 276; Kellogg *v.* Richards, 14 Wendell, 116; Goodwin *v.* Follett, 25 Vt. 386; Harper *v.* Graham, 20 Ohio, 105; Lee *v.* Oppenheimer, 32 Maine, 253; Silvers *v.* Reynolds, 2 Harrison, 275; Browne *v.* Stackpole, 9 N. H. 478; Warren *v.* Skinner, 20 Conn. 559; Sibree *v.* Tripp, 15 M. & W. 23; Rose *v.* Hall, 26 Conn. 392; Bowker *v.* Harris, 30 Vt. 424; Liening *v.* Gould, 13 Cal. 598; State *v.* Davenport, 12 Iowa, 335; Pemberton *v.* Hoozier, 1 Kansas, 108; Trumbull *v.* Brock, 31 Ohio State, 649; Smith *v.* Phillips, 77 Va. 548; Thompson *v.* Robinson, 34 Ark. 44; Warren *v.* Hodge, 121 Mass. 106. Payment of a portion of the money before it is due is a good consideration. Newsam *v.* Finch, 25 Barb. 175; Wright *v.* Bartlett, 43 N. H. 548; Warner *v.* Campbell, 26 Ill. 282. *Contra*, after it is due. Turnbull *v.* Brock, 31 Ohio State, 649. A composition agreement between a debtor and his creditors, by which they agree to receive a certain sum in hand, and a note

Gifts. In this connection, I will say a word respecting gifts. Every competent person has an undoubted right to give his prop-

for a portion of the remainder, as a satisfaction of their claims, is valid and binding at law. Way *v.* Langley, 15 Ohio State, 392; Pierson *v.* McCahill, 21 Cal. 122. In this latter case, the consideration for the promise of one creditor is found in the promise of the other creditors, and it is said that such an agreement with a single creditor would not be binding. In Massachusetts, it is still held that payment of a portion of a debt is no consideration for a satisfaction of the whole. 12 Gray, 341; Watts *v.* Frenche, 4 Green, 407. But see 20 Ohio, 105. The mere performance of that which one is legally bound to do is no consideration. Withers *v.* Ewing, 40 Ohio State, 400, 407; Gilmore *v.* Lewis, 12 Ohio, 281; Dodge *v.* Stiles, 26 Conn. 463; Tilden *v.* New York, 56 Barb. 340; Parmalee *v.* Thompson, 45 N. Y. 58.

It is an interesting question now constantly calling for the adjudication of the courts, in what cases voluntary subscriptions to public institutions, or private enterprises of benevolence, are supported by a valid consideration. The law on this point is as yet unsettled. There are opinions and *dicta* which seem to make all such subscriptions binding, on the ground that the promise of each is a good consideration for the promise of all. George *v.* Harris, 4 N. H. 533; Cong. Soc. in Troy *v.* Perry, 6 id. 164; Trustees Baptist Society *v.* Robinson, 21 N. Y. 234. On the other hand, some actual benefit to the subscriber, or some actual expenditure on faith of his subscription, or some agreement on the part of the party to whom the promise of the subscription runs, has been required to sustain it; and such is the prevailing current of authorities. Johnson *v.* Otterbein University, 41 Ohio State, 527; Boutell *v.* Cowden, 9 Mass. 254; Phillips Academy *v.* Davis, 11 id. 113; Bridgewater Academy *v.* Gilbert, 2 Pick. 579; Thompson *v.* Paige, 1 Met. 565; Ives *v.* Sterling, 6 id. 310; Comm'rs Canal Fund *v.* Perry, 5 Ohio, 56; Stewart *v.* Trustees of Hamilton College, 1 N. Y. 581; s. c. 2 Denio, 403; Barnes *v.* Perine, 9 Barb. 202; 15 id. 249; 12 N. Y. 18; Wilson *v.* Baptist Education Society, 10 Barb. 308; Phipps *v.* Jones, 20 Penn. State, 260; Ryerss *v.* Congregation of Blossburg, 33 Penn. State, 114; Norton *v.* Janvier, 5 Harring. 346. Reformed, &c. Church *v.* Brown, 29 Barb. 335; Doyle *v.* Glasscock, 24 Tex. 200; Pryor *v.* Cain, 25 Ill. 292; Eyclesheimer *v.* Van Antwerp, 13 Wis. 546; McDonald *v.* Gray, 11 Iowa, 508; Richmondville Seminary *v.* Brownell, 37 Barb. 535; Ohio W. F. College *v.* Love, 16 Ohio State, 20. But the expenditures need not be by the parties to whom the subscriptions are payable, if others have acted on the faith of them. Miller *v.* Bollard, 46 Ill. 377. There is an elaborate discussion of the rules governing such subscriptions in Lathrop *v.* Knapp, 27 Wis. 214. The obligation assumed by the party to whom the subscription runs, to see and to make the application of the money, was held sufficient in Troy Academy *v.* Nelson, 24 Vt. 189. But see Dayton, &c. Turnpike Co. *v.* Coy, 13 Ohio State, 84. A subscription to secure the rebuilding of a woollen mill belonging to private persons will be valid; the public interest in such an enterprise is sufficient. Pitt *v.* Gentle, 49 Mo. 74.

Where A. promises B., from whom the consideration moves, to confer a benefit on C., it is a controverted question whether C. has a right of action in his own name to enforce the promise. The American authorities generally allow C. this right of action. Bliss, Code, Pl. § 242; Pomeroy's Rem. § 139, note 2; Thompson *v.* Thompson, 4 Ohio State, 333; Crumbaugh *v.* Kugler, 3 Ohio State, 544; Bagaley *v.* Waters, 7 Ohio State, 366. Though it be under seal, and the third party be not named in it. Emmitt *v.* Brophy, 42 Ohio State, 82. The original parties may rescind at any time before acceptance by such third person. Trimble *v.* Strather, 25 Ohio State, 378. A recent opinion of a learned jurist, Metcalf, J., essentially limits the rule, as stated in the earlier decisions in Massachusetts, and requires some privity on the part of the third party to entitle him to sue. Mellen *v.* Whipple, 1 Gray (Mass.), 317; Dow *v.* Clark, 7 id. 198. Page *v.* Becker, 31 Mo. 466. The consideration of a written contract may be proved by extrinsic evidence. M'Crea *v.* Purmort, 16 Wendell, 460; Frink *v.* Green, 5 Barb. 455; Willson *v.* Betts, 4 Denio, 201; Arms *v.* Ashley, 4 Pick. 71; Livermore *v.* Aldrich, 5 Cush. 431. If it belongs to the class required by the statute of frauds to be in writing, the consideration must appear in writing in England. Wain *v.* Walters, 5 East, 10. The English rule has been followed in New York and some other States. Sears *v.* Brink, 3 Johns. 210; Rogers *v.* Kneeland, 10 Wendell, 218; Edelen *v.* Gough, 5 Gill, 103; Henderson *v.* Johnson, 6 Geo. 390; but the current of judicial opinion in this country is in favor of dispensing with its expression. Packard *v.* Richardson, 17 Mass. 122; Cummings *v.* Dermitt, 26 Maine, 397; Gillighan *v.* Boardman, 29 id. 79; Reed *v.* Evans, 17 Ohio, 128; How *v.* Kimball, 2 M'Lean, 103; Sage *v.* Wilcox, 6 Conn. 81. Steadman *v.* Guthrie, 4 Met. (Ky.) 147; Shirley *v.* Black, 45 Penn. State, 345.

erty to whom he pleases, provided he do not thereby injure his creditors. And although a promise to give is not binding, for want of a consideration, yet a gift perfected is irrevocable by the giver; and to perfect a gift, there must in all cases be an actual delivery of the thing given, if it be such as to admit of actual delivery. (*a*) This is equally true of gifts *inter vivos*, between the living, and gifts *causâ mortis*, in anticipation of death. But the latter differ from the former in this, that being made in anticipation of death, if the giver recover, the condition of the gift fails, and he may reclaim the thing given. This species of gift differs from a nuncupative will in two respects: The forms are dispensed with, and there is an actual delivery. But courts are inclined to watch such gifts with great caution, and require very clear evidence to support them. (*b*)

§ 176. **Parties.** The general rule is, that all persons are capable of contracting. But there are several exceptions, all but one of which are founded on the actual or presumed want of mental capacity. The very idea of a contract supposes the *assent of mind* on each side. The term *agreement*, which is nearly synonymous with "contract," has been supposed to be formed by two

(*a*) Noble *v.* Smith, 2 Johns. 52; Pearson *v.* Pearson, 7 id. 26; Phipps *v.* Hope, 16 Ohio State, 586; Woodruff *v.* Cook, 25 Barb. 505; Mechling's Appeal, 2 Grant's Cases, 157; Reid *v.* Spalding, 42 N. H. 114; Marsh *v.* Fuller, 18 N. H. 360. Delivery need not be simultaneous with the words of donation. Gillespie *v.* Burleson, 28 Ala. 551. Nor will a written instrument, purporting to be a gift of personalty, be sufficient without delivery. Payne *v.* Powell, 5 Bush, 248. The delivery must be proven; it cannot be inferred from the mere possession of the article by the donee where that might have been otherwise accounted for. Grey *v.* Grey, 47 N. Y. 552. A mere parol declaration cannot cancel a debt, or transform it into a gift; but where the intent of the original transaction is doubtful, subsequent declarations of the donor as to the intention are admissible. Doty *v.* Wilson, 47 N. Y. 580. *Choses in action* not negotiable, and negotiable paper not indorsed, may be the subjects of a gift; and delivery sufficient to vest an equitable title in the donee, though not the legal one, is sufficient. The delivery of a savings bank book was held to pass the deposits. Camp's Appeal, 36 Conn. 88.

(*b*) Parish *v.* Stone, 14 Pick. 198; Carpenter *v.* Dodge, 20 Vt. 595; Withers *v.* Weaver, 10 Barr, 391; 2 Kent, Com. 437–48, ch. 38; Hamor *v.* Moore, 8 Ohio State, 239; Starr *v.* Starr, 9 id. 74; Singleton *v.* Cotton, 23 Geo. 260; Jones *v.* Brown, 34 N. H. 439; Kenney *v.* Public Administrator, 2 Bradf. Sur. R. 319; Merchant *v.* Merchant, 3 id. 432; Bates *v.* Kempton, 7 Gray, 382. *Choses in action*, such as bonds, mortgages, and promissory notes not indorsed, may be transferred by delivery only as a valid *donatio causâ mortis*. Westerlo *v.* De Witt, 38 N. Y. 340; House *v.* Grant, 4 Lans. 296; Southerland *v.* Southerland, 5 Bush (Ky.), 591. So the delivery of a savings bank book *in extremis*, will pass the deposits. If the delivery in terms give the donee power to control the fund only after the donor's death, and not presently, it is testamentary, and therefore not valid as a gift, — as here, an indorsement on a certificate of deposit of "Pay to B. not till my death," — for no property passes until death. Basket *v.* Hassell, 107 U. S. 602; Gano *v.* Fisk, 43 Ohio State, 462; Tillinghast *v.* Wheaton, 8 R. I. 536. *Contra*, Ashbrook *v.* Ryan, 2 Bush (Ky.), 228. The donee's own note cannot be the subject of such a gift. Brown *v.* Moore, 3 Head, 671. Nor his check until it is paid or accepted by the bank. Simmons *v.* Savings Soc., 31 Ohio State, 457. But a receipt for money may be so given to the debtor. Champney *v.* Blanchard, 39 N. Y. 111. Where a soldier deposited money, taking a written agreement to return it if he came back alive, if not to pay it to an infant sister, it was held valid. Baker *v.* Williams, 34 Ind. 547. Delivery cannot be proved by subsequent declaration of the donor to persons not connected with the gift. Rockwood *v.* Wiggins, 16 Gray, 402.

words, *aggregatio mentium*, which expresses this idea. (*a*) The parties, then, must be capable of giving an intelligent consent. But a want of capacity may arise either from *actual destitution* of reason, or from such *constraint* as prevents its free action; and hence, *insane persons*, *drunkards*, *infants*, *married women*, and *persons under duress*, are placed under a total or partial disability. *Alien enemies* are likewise disabled, on the ground of public policy. I shall speak of these six classes in their order.

(*a*) The mutual assent of the parties to the terms of a contract is essential to its validity. But the assent must be evinced by some speech or act; a mere mental determination to accept is not sufficient. Nor does an act not in itself an acceptance, become such in consequence of such a determination. White *v.* Corliss, 46 N. Y. 467. If the acceptance by the one party varies from the proposition made by the other, no contract subsists between them. Bruce *v.* Pearson, 3 Johns. 534; Hazard *v.* Marine Ins. Co., 1 Sumner, 218; Hutchinson *v.* Bowker, 5 M. & W. 535; Peltier *v.* Collins, 3 Wendell, 459; Suydam *v.* Clark, 2 Sandf. 133; Esmay *v.* Groton, 18 Ill. 483. Jenners *v.* Mt. Hope Co., 53 Maine, 20; Myers *v.* Smith, 48 Barb. 614; Cornwell *v.* Kreugel, 41 Ill. 394; Northwestern Iron Co. *v.* Mead, 21 Wis. 474; Van Valkenburg *v.* Rogers, 18 Mich. 180. An offer not yet accepted by the party to whom it is made, may be withdrawn by the party making it, as in the case of a bid at auction, which is not binding until the hammer falls. Page *v.* Cave, 3 T. R. 148. Sometimes the party making an offer promises to give the other a certain period of time within which he may accept it, or, in common parlance, gives him the refusal of it. Such an offer, unless a consideration for its being kept open has been agreed upon, may be withdrawn at any time previous to its acceptance, during the period it was promised to be kept standing. Boston & Maine R. R. *v.* Bartlett, 3 Cush. 224; Erskridge *v.* Glover, 5 Stew. & Port. 264; Chevey *v.* Cook, 7 Wis. 412. An acceptance may be implied. Sanford *v.* Howard, 29 Ala. 684. See Cooke *v.* Oxley, 3 T. R. 653. Contracts are now constantly being made by correspondence through the mails. It has become well settled that if A. receives a letter through the mail from B., containing an offer, and with due despatch deposits a letter in the mails, accepting it before receiving any notice of revocation, a bargain is concluded, notwithstanding B. had, before the acceptance, deposited another letter revoking the offer, which had not reached A. at the time of the acceptance. But no contract would subsist if A. had received the second letter before he had deposited his own letter of acceptance in the mails. Adams *v.* Lindsell, 1 B. & Ald. 681; Potter *v.* Saunders, 6 Hare, 1; Gibbins *v.* The Northeastern, &c., 11 Beavan, 1; Dunlop *v.* Higgins, 1 House of Lords Cases, 381; Duncan *v.* Topham, 8 M. G. & S. 225; Eliason *v.* Henshaw, 4 Wheaton, 328; Tayloe *v.* Merchants' Fire Ins. Co., 9 How. 390; Mactier *v.* Frith, 6 Wendell, 103; Brisban *v.* Boyd, 4 Paine, 17; Averill *v.* Hedge, 12 Conn. 436; Levy *v.* Cohen, 4 Geo. 1; Chiles *v.* Nelson, 7 Dana, 281; Halls *v.* Gaither, 9 Porter, 605; Hamilton *v.* Lycoming Mutual Ins. Co., 5 Barr. 339; Palo Alto, Daveis, 344, 357; Vassar *v.* Camp, 14 Barb. 341; Martin *v.* Black, 12 Ala. 721; Moore *v.* Pierson, 6 Clarke (Iowa), 279; Hallock *v.* Insurance Co., 2 Dutcher, 268; Hong *v.* Brown, 19 N. Y. 111; Abbott *v.* Shepard, 48 N. H. 14; Stockham *v.* Stockham, 32 Md. 196; Brown *v.* N. Y. &c. R. R. Co., 44 N. Y. 79. In British and Am. Telegraph Co. *v.* Colson, L. R. 6 Ex. 108, the Court of Exchequer expressed an opinion that this rule of the completion of a contract by letter on the mailing of the acceptance was subject to the condition that if the letter of acceptance does not arrive in due course of post, the parties may act on the assumption that the offer has not been accepted. This was doubted by the Lords Justices in *Harris' Case, L. R. 7 Ch.* 587, *In re Imperial Land Co. of Marseilles*, who both expressed the opinion that the contract was actually and finally made when the letter was posted. But the question did not actually come up in that case. Id.; Townsend's case, 13 Eq. 148. I have not found this distinction noticed in any American case, though the language and reasoning used would seem to exclude it. The same principles apply to contracts by telegraph. Trevor *v.* Wood, 36 N. Y. 307. Where an agreement not within the statute of frauds is complete, and there is no understanding that it is not to be binding on the parties until reduced to writing, it will bind them at once, although there was an understanding that it should subsequently be reduced to writing, and executed. Blaney *v.* Hoke, 14 Ohio State, 292.

Insane persons, (*a*) whether *idiots* or *lunatics*, as we have seen, are incapable of contracting during the disability. On this ground, guardians are appointed to manage their concerns. But sanity is always presumed until insanity has once been established; after which, the continuance of insanity is presumed until the contrary has been proved. (*b*) And the decision of an inquest, under our statute, is not conclusive when a contract is in question. The fact still remains open to contest. (*c*) The old doctrine, that a man cannot be permitted to stultify himself, that is, to set up the defence of insanity, is now exploded. As to idiots, the test is incapacity of understanding and acting in the ordinary affairs of life. Mere mental imbecility, not reaching this point, will not invalidate a contract fairly made. (*d*)

Drunkards, though formerly held liable, both in law and equity, to perform their contracts, unless the intoxication were procured by the other party, are now regarded with more favor. Courts have lately inclined to consider a contract, made by a person so drunk as not to have the use of his reason, as void, though the intoxication was voluntary, and there was no actual fraud on the other side. (*e*)

Infants, (*f*) as we have seen, are only partially disqualified from contracting. They are held bound by contracts made for *necessaries*, suited to their age and condition; and their other contracts are *voidable* only, and not absolutely *void*. They may be ratified by assent after becoming of age. But infancy is a personal privilege of the infant, and the other party cannot take advantage of it. (*g*) If beneficial to the infant, the contract will be enforced against the adult; and this is perhaps the only case in which the obligation is not mutual. Prudence, therefore, dictates that dealings where infants are concerned, should be conducted with their guardians. As to real property,

(*a*) *Ante*, § 112.

(*b*) White *v.* Wilson, 13 Ves. 88; Jackson *v.* Vandusen, 5 Johns. 144; Hix *v.* Whittemore, 4 Met. 545. But the contracts of an insane person are only voidable, and may be ratified after the insanity has ceased. His deed, made while insane, may be avoided by his guardian or himself, without first restoring the consideration to the grantee. See note on p. 277–8.

(*c*) Sergeson *v.* Sealey, 2 Atk. 412; Faulder *v.* Silk, 3 Camp. 126. But see Leonard *v.* Leonard, 14 Pick. 280.

(*d*) 2 Kent, Com. 452; Dennett *v.* Dennett, 44 N. H. 531; Bond *v.* Bond, 7 Allen, 1.

(*e*) Barrett *v.* Buxton, 2 Aiken (Vt.), 167; Gore *v.* Gibson, 13 M. & W. 623; 1 Parsons on Contracts, 310, 311; 2 Kent, Com. 451, 452; French *v.* French, 8 Ohio, 214; Menkins *v.* Lightner, 18 Ill. 282. Where the intoxication is only partial, and not induced by the other party, it does not avoid the contract. Caulkins *v.* Fry, 35 Conn. 170; Henry *v.* Ritenour, 31 Ind. 136. But where the contract might be rescinded, it will be affirmed by the subsequent receipt of benefits under it. Willoughby *v.* Moulton, 47 N. H. 205.

(*f*) *Ante*, § 111.

(*g*) Beardsley *v.* Hotchkiss, 96 N. Y. 201. Thus an infant is not liable to an action for breach of promise of marriage, but may bring an action against an adult. Hunt *v.* Peake, 5 Cowen, 475; Willard *v.* Stone, 7 id. 22; Rush *v.* Wick, 31 Ohio State, 521.

this is indispensable; for infants cannot convey at all; and guardians, as we have seen, can only convey with leave of court. (*a*)

Married women, (*b*) as a general rule, are utterly disqualified for making any contract whatsoever. Their contracts, as we have seen, are held to be absolutely void, to all intents and purposes. Even when living separately from their husbands, they cannot bind themselves for necessaries; and for this reason their husbands are made liable. The only exception is, where the statute allows married women to join with their husbands in conveyances of land. (*c*)

Persons under duress, whether from actual violence, or the threat thereof, are not bound by contracts made during such duress. (*d*) There have been many nice distinctions as to what constitutes duress; but they result in this general principle, that if the contract be made from a reasonable apprehension of violence or constraint, it will not be binding, because the mind does not act freely. (*e*)

Aliens, while their country is at war with ours, are prohibited,

(*a*) But an infant is liable for his torts, and even it has been held for a fraudulent representation that he was of age, whereby he obtained goods. Fitts *v.* Hall, 9 N. H. 441; Wallace *v.* Morss, 5 Hill, 391. For a full classification of the cases on the rights and liabilities of infants, see 1 Am. Leading Cases, 230–67. Also, 1 Parsons on Contracts, 242–82; 2 Kent, Com. 233–45.

(*b*) *Ante*, pp. 263 to 274.

(*c*) *Ante*, pp. 423, 432; 1 Parsons on Contracts, 283–307. Unlike the infant, the married woman's promise to pay for money expended during coverture after the disability is removed, is not binding. Watkins *v.* Halstead, 2 Sandf. 311; Goulding *v.* Davidson, 28 Barb. 438; Story, Prom. Notes, § 185; Meyer *v.* Haworth, 8 Ad. & L. 467. But *contra*, Lee *v.* Muggeridge, 5 Taunt. 147. Perhaps she would be bound by the ratification where the original promise was made on faith of her separate estate. Vance *v.* Wells, 8 Ala. 399; Kennerly *v.* Martin, 8 Mo. 698. The wife, as agent of the husband, may have an implied authority to order goods necessary for family use, and otherwise manage household affairs. Renaux *v.* Teakle, 20 Eng. Law & Eq. 345; Shelton *v.* Pendleton, 18 Conn. 417. Infants may be agents. Story on Agency, § 7. Slaves may be agents. Chastain *v.* Bowman, 1 Hill (So. Car.), 270; Gore *v.* Buzzard, 4 Leigh, 231. But slaves cannot enter into contracts for themselves under the legislation of the Slave States, and a marriage between them produces no civil effect. Girod *v.* Lewis, 6 Mart. 559; State *v.* Samuel, 2 Dev. & Bat. 177. Seamen receive the peculiar protection of courts of admiralty, so that stipulations in the shipping articles in derogation of their general rights and privileges are void. Brown *v.* Lull, 2 Sumner, 444.

(*d*) Doolittle *v.* McCullough, 7 Ohio State, 299; Mays *v.* Cincinnati, 1 id. 268; Knox County Bank *v.* Doty, 9 id. 505; Baker *v.* Cincinnati, 11 Ohio State, 534.

(*e*) Duress, such as will avoid a contract, may arise in the case of an arrest for improper purposes without just cause, or an arrest for just cause but without lawful authority, or an arrest for a just cause and under lawful authority for an improper purpose. Richardson *v.* Duncan, 3 N. H. 508; Watkins *v.* Baird, 6 Mass. 506; Severance *v.* Kimball, 8 N. H. 386. In England, duress of goods does not avoid a contract, although money paid under such duress may be recovered back. Atlee *v.* Backhouse, 3 Meeson & Welsby, 642; Skeate *v.* Beale, 1 Ad. & El. 983; Oates *v.* Hudson, 5 Eng. Law & Eq. 469. But in this country duress of goods as well as of person avoids a contract. Collins *v.* Westbury, 2 Bay, 211; Foshay *v.* Ferguson, 5 Hill, 154. Where a son forged the father's name, and the bankers, though without threatening a prosecution, insisted on the father's assuming the indebtedness, which he agreed to do, and gave them an agreement to make a mortgage, it was held that a father under such circumstances was not a free agent, and the agreement was set aside. Williams *v.* Bayley, L. R. 1 H. L. 200.

as we have seen, from contracting with our citizens, on grounds of public policy, unless by special license from government. The theory is, that when two nations are at war, all the individuals are at war with each other. The fact we know to be different; but the rule still continues. (*a*)

§ 177. **Subject-matter.** The general rule is, that parties may contract about whatsoever they choose; but there are several exceptions founded on reasons of public policy. The law will not uphold a contract, when the subject-matter is prejudicial to the general welfare. On this ground four classes of contracts are held to be invalid; namely, contracts which are *immoral*, *impolitic*, *fraudulent*, and *illegal*. I shall consider these in their order.

Immoral Contracts. Where the undertaking on either side is to do or permit something decidedly immoral, as prostitution, making indecent books or pictures, and the like, the law will not aid either party in enforcing performance. The immorality, however, must be of a marked character; for the law does not observe a fastidious delicacy. On nice points parties are left to their own moral sense. This is merely an application of the principle of non-interference, and does not militate against the doctrine before advanced, that questions of abstract morality are beyond the scope of human laws. The law simply refuses its aid in the enforcement of immoral contracts. But the question of morality is not always open to discussion. In general, only those contracts are held void for immorality which the precedents have settled to be immoral. (*b*)

Contracts against Public Policy. Where the subject-matter of a contract is in opposition to public policy, this is a sufficient reason for refusing to enforce it. On this ground, a contract in restraint of trade or marriage, or tending to stifle or prevent a criminal prosecution, or to induce an officer to swerve from his duty, will not be enforced. These examples sufficiently illustrate the idea. But you are not to suppose that the question, what is public policy, is always open for discussion whenever a contract is sought to be enforced. This would be to convert the court into an arena for party politics. It is only in those cases which the consent of ages has settled to be against public policy, that the defence is now admitted. What is public policy, has thus become a question of precedent, not depending upon the varying opinions of different judges. (*c*)

(*a*) But an alien enemy resident in this country, and not ordered away by the proper authority, may sue and be sued as in times of peace. Clark *v.* Morey, 10 Johns. 69; Russell *v.* Skipwith, 6 Binney, 241. During war, a person cannot appoint an agent in an enemy's country, though if appointed before he may still act. So if a creditor direct a debtor if he cannot remit to purchase cotton and hold it, this is illegal, for it is the creation of an agency, and the creditor gets no title. United States *v.* Grossmeyer, 9 Wall. 72.

(*b*) Chitty on Contracts, 577–9.

(*c*) See 2 Parsons on Contracts, 253–9, where the numerous recent cases in which contracts have been held to be in restraint of trade are collected. Alger *v.* Thacher, 19 Pick. 51, is a leading American authority. Lange *v.* Werk, 2 Ohio State, 519;

Fraudulent Contracts. (*a*) It is a general rule, both in law and equity, that fraud vitiates every contract into which it enters. Fraud signifies any kind of artifice, surprise, trick, dissembling, misrepresentation, concealment, or deceit, by which the parties or third persons are cheated or deceived. The varieties of fraud are so great that it is difficult to lay down any specific rules concerning it, without occupying too much space. I shall briefly consider the subject in two points of view: first, with reference to the *parties;* and secondly, with reference to *third persons*, particularly as provided against in the statute of frauds.

Fraud between the Parties. The law requires that when parties are about to enter into a contract, neither shall misrepresent or conceal any material fact upon which it is predicated. It is as clearly fraudulent to suppress truth, as to assert falsehood, because deception is equally the result. But here a distinction is to be noted. Intentional misrepresentation is always fraudulent. But there may be intentional concealment which is not fraudulent. The point is to determine what kind of knowledge a contracting party may lawfully keep to himself. And the best rule I can lay down is this: If you have any peculiar or extraordinary informa-

Thomas *v.* Miles, 3 id. 274; Grasselli *v.* Lowden, 11 Ohio State, 349; Crawford *v.* Wick, 18 id. 190; Oregon Steam Nav. Co. *v.* Winsor, 20 Wall. 64. An agreement to procure a person a contract to furnish supplies to the government is void as against public policy. Tool Co. *v.* Norris, 2 Wallace, 45; Frost *v.* Inhabitants of Belmont, 6 Allen, 152; Sedgwick *v.* Stanton, 4 N. Y. 289; Powers *v.* Skinner, 34 Vt. 274. But the employment of an agent regularly to put in a bid and make a contract, is not. Winpenny *v.* French, 18 Ohio State, 469. A contract to advocate a claim before a legislature in session, or its committees, is legal, but not a contract to advocate a claim with individual members of such legislature. Sedgwick *v.* Stanton, *supra;* Bryan *v.* Reynolds, 5 Wis. 200; Trist *v.* Child, 21 Wall. 441. An agreement for a consideration to withdraw opposition to a divorce is void as against public policy. Stontenburg *v.* Lybrand, 13 Ohio State, 228. So is an agreement by a public officer to share fees. Martin *v.* Wade, 37 Cal. 168. So are all agreements entered into to aid a rebellion. Hanauer *v.* Doane, 12 Wall. 324. In Ohio only the principals can make the defence of illegality. An agent holding the proceeds of the illegal transaction cannot avoid accountability to his principal. Norton *v.* Blinn, 39 Ohio State, 145.

(*a*) See Roberts on Frauds; Roberts on Fraudulent Conveyance; Hovenden on Frauds; Broom's Legal Maxims, 571–3, 605–38; 1 Story, Eq. Juris. ch. vi.; 2 Kent, Com. 482–92; 2 Parsons on Contracts, 264–84; Tracy *v.* Sackett, 1 Ohio State, 54. Where a grantor was so drunk as not to have the exercise of his judgment, his deed will be held null, though the grantee had no agency in making him drunk. French *v.* French, 8 Ohio, 214. Where one has dealt with parties to a conveyance treating it as valid, he cannot afterwards impeach it as fraud. Rennick *v.* Bank, 8 Ohio, 529. The merely making a good bargain, by purchase at a small price, or otherwise, will not be ground for setting aside a contract, unless there has been actual imposition. Steele *v.* Worthington, 2 Ohio, 182; Knobb *v.* Lindsay, 5 id. 468; Hough *v.* Hunt, 2 id. 495; Douglas *v.* Houston, 6 id. 156; Hunter *v.* Goudy, 1 id. 449. Where a widow stands by and allows the auctioneer to sell the land as free from dower, and so increase the bid, she cannot afterwards claim dower. Smiley *v.* Wright, 2 Ohio, 506. It is not fraud in an attorney who holds a recorded mortgage, to prepare a subsequent one for his client without mentioning his own. Paine *v.* French, 4 Ohio, 318. A fraudulent grantee may convey a good title to an honest purchaser for a fair price, though the latter knew of the fraud. Piatt *v.* St. Clair, 7 Ohio, 2 pt. 165. It is fraud in a mortgagee to stand by and see an ignorant purchaser making valuable improvements, without disclosing his lien. Carter *v.* Longworth, 4 Ohio, 384. As to false statements of quantity in the sale of real estate, see Ketchum *v.* Stout, 20 Ohio, 453; *ante*, p. 451.

tion, which the other party, exercising ordinary knowledge and diligence, cannot be presumed to have, you are bound to disclose it; and the concealment of it will be a fraud. Thus, while the law requires a full and fair disclosure of all the facts necessary to enable each party to make up his mind, the rule has a reasonable construction. The law will not relieve against the common inequalities of knowledge, judgment, skill, and experience. It does not discountenance speculation and enterprise, by requiring bargains to be perfectly equal. It allows one party to obtain the advantage, when there is no positive unfairness. Accordingly, slight inadequacy of consideration, or ignorance of the subject-matter, or mental imbecility not amounting to idiocy or insanity, will not of themselves avoid a contract. So in regard to the quality and value of articles contracted for, the rule is, that if a defect be open and obvious to common inspection, there can be no ground to complain of fraud. But when the defect is latent and not readily perceived, the party knowing it is bound to make disclosure. When a contract has been absolutely concluded, neither party can alter it, without the consent of the other, in any essential part, without avoiding it altogether. As a general rule, if any part of one entire contract is fraudulent, it is void throughout. Courts of law will not undertake to apportion fraud. This can only be done by courts of equity, whose jurisdiction of fraud will be considered hereafter.

The Statute of Frauds. (*a*) Fraud with respect to third persons,

(*a*) Browne on the Statute of Frauds. *First Section.* By a statute of 1846, provision is made for depositing a mortgage of chattels, or a copy, with the township clerk or recorder, and renewing the same thirty days before the end of each year. And unless this be done, the retaining of possession by the mortgagor is declared to render the mortgage absolutely void, as against creditors and subsequent purchasers in good faith. Prior to this act the rule was, that the retaining of possession, after bill of sale or mortgage, was *primâ facie* fraudulent, but might be explained. Hombeck *v.* Vanmetre, 9 Ohio, 153; Collins *v.* Myers, 16 id. 547; Stanley *v.* Brannon, 6 Blackf. 196; Read *v.* Wilson, 22 Ill. 377; Constant *v.* Matteson, 22 id. 546. See Gay *v.* Bidwell, 7 Mich. 519.

Second Section. The expression "*utterly void*" applies only to creditors and purchasers, not to the parties. Burgett *v.* Burgett, 1 Ohio, 469; Douglas *v.* Dunlap, 10 id. 162; Barton *v.* Morris, 15 id. 408; Brown *v.* Webb, 20 id. 389; 3 Ohio State, 246; Crumbaugh *v.* Kugler, 2 Ohio State, 373; 3 id. 544; Webb *v.* Roff, 9 id. 430; Scott *v.* Purcell, 7 Blackf. 66; Randall *v.* Phillips, 3 Mason, 378. There must be a fraudulent intent in both parties in order to render the conveyance or sale void. Ewing *v.* Runkle, 20 Ill. 448; Brown *v.* Riley, 22 id. 45. And the retaining of possession by the mortgagor does not necessarily make it fraudulent. Id.; Oliver *v.* Eaton, 7 Mich. 108; Gay *v.* Bidwell, 7 id. 519. See Hudgins *v.* Kemp, 20 How. 45. Where a debtor, while a suit is pending, conveys his whole estate, with a stipulation for repurchase, and retains possession under an agreement to pay rent, this is *primâ facie* fraudulent, but may be explained. Barr *v.* Hatch, 3 Ohio, 527; Hood *v.* Brown, 2 id. 266; Starr *v.* Starr, 1 id. 321; Minns *v.* Morse, 15 id. 568. Where a father who is embarrassed conveys property to his wife or children, the question of fact is, whether his circumstances were such that a prudent man should have apprehended insolvency. If so, the honesty of his intention will not support the conveyance. Brice *v.* Myers, 5 Ohio, 121; Miller *v.* Wilson, 15 id. 108; Reade *v.* Livingston, 3 Johns. Ch. 481; Robinson *v.* Bates, 3 Met. 40; Crumbaugh *v.* Kugler, 2 Ohio State, 373. A conveyance made without consideration by one indebted at the time, cannot be avoided by subsequent creditors without showing actual fraud, or a secret trust for the benefit of the grantor. Webb *v.* Roff, 9 Ohio State, 430. Before our statute abolishing preferences, is chiefly provided against by the "*act for the prevention of frauds and perjuries*," commonly called the statute of frauds. Our pres-

made by assignments in contemplation of insolvency, such preferences were not of themselves held to be fraudulent. Atkinson *v.* Jordan, 5 Ohio, 293; Hull *v.* Jeffrey, 8 id. 390; Harshman *v.* Lowe, 9 id. 92; Mitchell *v.* Gazzam, 12 id. 315; Hatch *v.* Smith, 5 Mass. 42; Bradshaw *v.* West, 7 Peters, 615; Cumber *v.* Wayne, 1 Smith, L. C. 258, *note;* Bancroft *v.* Blizzard, 13 Ohio, 30; Doremus *v.* O'Harra, 1 id. 45; Arnold *v.* Maynard, 2 Story, 349; Freeman *v.* Deming, 2 Sandf. Ch. 332. As to the consideration of a purchase being an antecedent debt, see Lupin *v.* Marie, 2 Paige, 215; Riley *v.* Johnson, 8 Ohio, 526; Swift *v.* Tyson, 16 Peters, 1; Bank of Sandusky *v.* Scoville, 24 Wendell, 115. Riley *v.* Johnson, 8 Ohio, 526, holding that the payment of an antecedent debt was not a consideration, was overruled by Carlisle *v.* Wishart, 11 Ohio, 172, holding that it was, and following Swift *v.* Tyson. In Roxborough *v.* Messick, 6 Ohio State, 448, the doctrine was established to be, that taking the note merely as collateral for an antecedent debt, without any change in the relation of the parties, was not a valuable consideration; but if there were such change, or if at the time of the creation of the debt there were an agreement for further security, it would be valid.

Third Section. This has been proved to be of no practical importance.

Fourth Section. Prior to our first statute of frauds, which was passed in 1810, though a legal title could not be conveyed by parol, yet an express trust might be both created and proved by parol. Fleming *v.* Donahoe, 5 Ohio, 255. When a parol contract for the sale of lands is admitted by the defendant in his answer without relying upon the statute of frauds, the contract will be enforced. Woods *v.* Dille, 11 Ohio, 455; 2 Story, Eq. Jur. § 755. Where a purchaser by parol is put in possession, the vendor cannot set up the statute, nor even a parol agreement to rescind. Kelley *v.* Stanbery, 13 Ohio, 408. A parol contract for a new lease, when the tenant is in possession under a former lease, is within the statute of frauds. Armstrong *v.* Kattenhorn, 11 Ohio, 265; Crawford *v.* Wick, 18 Ohio State, 190. But where possession is given under it, it is withdrawn from the operation of the statute. Grant *v.* Ramsey, 7 Ohio State, 157. The owner gave a parol license to erect abutments of a mill-dam, and afterwards entered and destroyed them; *held,* that the license, being executed, was not within the statute, and the owner was a trespasser. Wilson *v.* Chalfant, 15 Ohio, 248. A parol contract for the purchase of a land-office certificate, with part performance, will take the case out of the statute. Kay *v.* Watson, 17 Ohio, 27. A parol contract to clear and fence, and raise a crop of corn as a compensation, if part performed by clearing and fencing, entitles the party to the crop of corn. Wilber *v.* Paine, 1 Ohio, 251. Mere payment of the purchase-money, under a parol contract, without possession, does not take the case out of the statute. Crabill *v.* Marsh, 38 Ohio State, 331; Sites *v.* Keller, 6 Ohio, 483; Pollard *v.* Kinner, 6 id. 528; Sanborn *v.* Sanborn, 7 Gray, 142; Campbell *v.* Campbell, 3 Stockton, 268. But in Indiana, it is held that it may do so. Single *v.* Clemens, 17 Ind. 124. But it is otherwise where possession is delivered. Waggoner *v.* Speck, 3 Ohio, 292; Moore *v.* Beasley, 3 id. 294; Randall *v.* Turner, 17 Ohio State, 262. For other constructions of this section, see Town *v.* Needham, 3 Paige, 546; Woods *v.* Farmare, 10 Watts, 195; Sage *v.* M'Guire, 4 Watts & Serg. 228; Wood *v.* Leadbetter, 13 Mees. & W. 840; Stevens *v.* Stevens, 11 Met. 251; Mumford *v.* Whitney, 15 Wendell, 381; Wible *v.* Wible, 1 Grant's Cases, 406; Chadwick *v.* Felt, 35 Penn. State, 305; McGregor *v.* Brown, 10 N. Y. 114; Harrell *v.* Miller, 35 Miss. 700. An agreement relating to land entered of record in a proceeding to appropriate land by a railroad company is a contract of record, and binding under the statute. Huston *v.* Cincinnati, &c. R. R. Co., 21 Ohio State, 235. The memorandum need not be made at the time of the contract. It is sufficient if it be made any time before trial. Webster *v.* Zully, 52 Barb. 482. None but the parties can take advantage of the statute. Creditors cannot insist upon their debtors setting it up. Lefferson *v.* Dallas, 20 Ohio State, 68; Crawford *v.* Woods, 6 Bush (Ky.), 200; Chicago Dock Co. *v.* Kinzie, 49 Ill. 287; Patterson *v.* Underwood, 22 Ind. 607. The memorandum must contain a sufficient description of the property sold to enable it to be located. White *v.* Herman, 51 Ill. 243; Whelan *v.* Sullivan, 102 Mass. 204. A contract to make a will of all the testator's property real and personal, in favor of a third person, in consideration of that person's making a similar will in favor of him, is a contract for the sale of lands. Gould *v.* Mansfield, 103 Mass. 408. A contract for standing timber to be taken off at the vendee's discretion is for an interest in land. Pattison's Appeal, 61 Penn. State, 294. But a contract by the contractor to cut wood on his own land and deliver it at so much a cord, is not. Kilmore *v.* Howlett, 48 N. Y. 569.

ent act was passed in 1810, prior to which we had no provision on the subject. It is copied with some variations from the English

Fifth Section. This is the fourth section in the English statute, 29 Charles II. Upon the general subject of this section, see Chitty on Cont. 211; Story on Cont. § 561, 590 ; 2 Parsons on Cont. 284–341 ; Wain *v.* Walters, 5 East, 10 ; Saunders *v.* Wakefield, 4 Barn. & Ald. 595 ; Violet *v.* Patten, 5 Cranch, 142; Packard *v.* Richardson, 17 Mass. 122 ; Gage *v.* Wilcox, 6 Conn. 81 ; Hoover *v.* Morris, 3 Ohio, 56 ; Anderson *v.* Harold, 10 id. 399 ; Sears *v.* Brink, 3 Johns. 210 ; Griffith *v.* Young, 12 East, 513 ; Philbrook *v.* Belknap, 6 Vermont, 383. The statute may be complied with by letters passing between the parties where the terms of the contract can be collected with certainty from them. Jackson *v.* Lowe, 1 Bing. 9 ; Macrory *v.* Scott, 5 Wels. Hurls. & Gordon, 907 ; Archer *v.* Baynes, id. 625 ; Dobell *v.* Hutchinson, 3 Ad. & El. 355. The contract may be on different pieces of paper. Esmay *v.* Groton, 18 Ill. 483 ; Lee *v.* Mahoney, 9 Iowa, 344. But if some only of the pieces of paper are signed, reference must be specifically made in those which are signed to those which are not. If all are signed, then such reference is not necessary, if by inspection and comparison, it appear that they severally relate to, or form part of, the same transaction. Thayer *v.* Luce, 22 Ohio State, 62. An entire contract must comply with the statute throughout or it will be entirely void, but a severable contract may be sustained so far as it complies with the statute. Thayer *v.* Rock, 13 Wendell, 53 ; Loomis *v.* Newhall, 15 Pick. 159 ; Irvine *v.* Stone, 6 Cush. 508 ; Rand *v.* Marther, 11 id. 1 ; Paige *v.* Monks, 5 Gray, 492 ; McMullen *v.* Riley, 6 id. 500 ; Noyes *v.* Humphreys, 11 Grattan, 636 ; Collins *v.* Merrill, 2 Met. (Ky.) 163 ; Mayfield *v.* Wadsley, 3 B. & Cr. 356 ; Wood *v.* Benson, 2 Cr. & Jerv. 94.

As to the words, "*debt, default*, or *miscarriage*," see Birkmyr *v.* Darnell, 1 Smith, L. C. 134 ; Green *v.* Creswell, 1 Perry & Dav. 430 ; Doyle *v.* White, 26 Maine, 341 ; Benman *v.* Russell, 20 Vt. 205 ; Wilson *v.* Coupland, 5 B. & Ald. 228; Johnson *v.* Gilbert, 4 Hill, 178 ; Murphy *v.* Merry, 8 Blackf. 295 ; Barker *v.* Bucklin, 2 Denio, 45 ; Sanford *v.* Howard, 29 Ala. 684. A promise to answer for another's *tort* is within the statute. Kirkham *v.* Marter, 2 B. & Ald. 613. Although the effect of the promise is to pay the debt of another, yet if the leading object of the undertaker is to subserve some interest of his own, it is not within the statute. Nelson *v.* Boynton, 3 Met. 396 ; Allen *v.* Thompson, 10 N. H. 32 ; Fish *v.* Thomas, 5 Gray, 45 ; Emerson *v.* Slater, 22 How. 43 ; Cross *v.* Richardson, 30 Vt. 641 ; Kutzmeyer *v.* Ennis, 3 Dutcher, 371 ; Mason *v.* Hall, 50 Ala. 599. A verbal promise by A. to B. to indemnify him against loss and damage, in becoming surety for C., is within this section. Easter *v.* White, 12 Ohio State, 219 ; Kelsey *v.* Hibbs, 13 Ohio State, 340 ; *contra*, Mills *v.* Brown, 11 Iowa, 314. The guaranty of a *del credere* factor is not within the statute. Swan *v.* Nesmith, 7 Pick. 220 ; Wolff *v.* Koppell, 5 Hill, 458 ; s. c. 2 Denio, 368 ; Bradley *v.* Richardson, 23 Vt. 731, 732 ; Couturier *v.* Hastie, 16 Eng. Law & Eq. 562 ; s. c. 8 Exch. 40 ; Sherwood *v.* Stone, 14 N. Y. 267. So the promise of a party, which has the effect of discharging the original debtor, as where he is accepted by the creditor in place of the original debtor, is not within the statute. Bird *v.* Gammon, 3 Bing. N. C. 883 ; Curtis *v.* Brown, 5 Cush. 488 ; Stanly *v.* Hendricks, 13 Iredell, 86; Watson *v.* Jacobs, 3 Wms. (29 Vt.) 169 ; Woods *v.* Corcoran, 1 Allen, 405 ; Warren *v.* Smith, 24 Texas, 484 ; Andre *v.* Bodman, 13 Md. 231 ; Meriden Brit. Co. *v.* Zingsen, 48 N. Y. 247 ; Yale *v.* Egerton, 14 Minn. 194. The promise must be made to the party to whom the party undertaken for is under a liability. Thus where A. is indebted to B., and C. promises A. to pay his debt to B., this last promise of C. is not within the statute. Eastwood *v.* Kenyon, 11 Ad. & El. 538 ; Hargreaves *v.* Parsons, 13 M. & W. 561 ; Barker *v.* Bucklin, 2 Denio, 45 ; Westfall *v.* Parsons, 16 Barb. 645 ; Pratt *v.* Humphrey, 22 Conn. 317 ; Preble *v.* Baldwin, 8 Cush. 549 ; Tibbetts *v.* Flanders, 18 N. H. 284 ; Day *v.* Cloe, 4 Bush, 563. If there is no consideration whatever moving between the creditor and the new promisor, the only one being a conveyance of property to the new promisor by the original debtor, it is within the statute. Furbish *v.* Goodenow, 98 Mass. 296.

As to the words "*in consideration of marriage*," they do not refer to the marriage contract itself, which is seldom in writing. Smith on Cont. by Rawle, 58 ; 1 Parsons on Contracts, 546. But it has been held that a promise to marry after a period longer than a year is within the statute. Derby *v.* Phelps, 2 N. H. 515. A verbal antenuptial contract is an agreement made in consideration of marriage, and unless there has been a part performance, is within the statute. Finch *v.* Finch, 10 Ohio State, 501. {But such part performance must not be attributable to any other motive. Henry *v.* Henry, 27 Ohio State, 121.} As to the words, "*contract or sale of lands*," see 1 Greenl.

statutes of the 13th and 27th of Elizabeth, and the 29th of Charles the Second. It consists of five sections, and in this connection

Ev. § 271; Sug. Vend. 99; Reed *v.* M'Grew, 5 Ohio, 375; M'Clintock *v.* Inskip, 13 id. 21; Wisely *v.* Barclew, 4 West. L. I. 281; Bridgman *v.* Wells, 13 Ohio, 43; Vaughan *v.* Hancock, 3 Man. Gr. & Scott, 766; Green *v.* Armstrong, 1 Denio, 550; Warren *v.* Leland, 2 Barb. 613; Whitmarsh *v.* Walker, 1 Met. 313; Nettleton *v.* Sikes, 8 id. 34.

It will be seen, by reference to the latter decisions, that the sale of growing trees or crops is not within this clause, where no interest in the realty is contemplated {or even a dwelling house to be severed from the land. Long *v.* White, 42 Ohio State, 59}.

As to the words, "*one year from the making,*" they do not mean contracts which may or may not, but which must, outrun the year. Peter *v.* Compton, 1 Smith's L. C. 143; Jones *v.* Pouch, 41 Ohio State, 146; Lanch *v.* Strawbridge, 2 Man. Gr. & Scott, 814; Morse *v.* Fox, 10 Johns. 244; Kent *v.* Kent, 18 Pick. 569; Roberts *v.* Rockbottom, 7 Met. 47; Lyon *v.* King, 11 id. 411; Hill *v.* Hooper, 1 Gray, 131; Randall *v.* Turner, 17 Ohio State, 262; Hutchinson *v.* Hutchinson, 46 Maine, 154; Dresser *v.* Dresser, 35 Barb. 573; Houghton *v.* Houghton, 14 Ind. 505; Rogers *v.* Brightman, 10 Wis. 55; Blanchard *v.* Weeks, 34 Vt. 589; Sherman *v.* Champlain Trans. Co., 31 Vt. 162; Jilson *v.* Gilbert, 26 Wis. 637. If the contract is not wholly to be performed within a year, it is void. Broadwell *v.* Getman, 2 Denio, 87; Herrin *v.* Butters, 20 Maine, 119. If the understanding of the parties is that the contract is not to be performed within a year, it is void. Peters *v.* Westborough, 19 Pick. 364. An agreement to renew a fire policy from year to year, terminable at the will of either party, is not within the statute. Trustees First Baptist Church *v.* Brooklyn Fire Ins. Co., 19 N. Y. 305; Sheehy *v.* Adarene, 41 Vt. 541; Updike *v.* Ten Broeck, 3 Vroom, 105; McClellan *v.* Sanford, 26 Wis. 595. If the contract has been entirely executed on one side, and nothing remains to be done but the payment of the consideration, it may be recovered. Donellan *v.* Read, 3 B. & Ad. 899; Cherry *v.* Heming, 4 Wels. Hurls. & Gordon, 631; Brackett *v.* Evans, 1 Cush. 79; Thomas *v.* Dickinson, 14 Barb. 90. Where all the plaintiff's part of the contract should be completed within a year, and it was not intended by the parties that any part of his portion should not be completed within that time, the contract is not within the statute, although the performance on the part of the defendant may be extended beyond that period. Smith *v.* Neale, 2 C. B. (N. S.) 67. An agreement within the clause to work for a specified time, cannot be set up in defence to an action on a *quantum meruit* for services performed under it. King *v.* Welcome, 5 Gray, 41. But see Swanzey *v.* Moore, 22 Ill. 63.

The Memorandum. As to the *consideration being expressed,* see Wain *v.* Walters, 5 East, 10; Sears *v.* Brink, 3 Johns. 210; Packard *v.* Richardson, 17 Mass. 122; Reed *v.* Evans, 17 Ohio, 128; 1 Greenleaf, Ev. § 268; Boydell *v.* Drummond, 11 East, 142; Sivewright *v.* Archibald, 6 Eng. L. & Eq. Rep. 286; *ante,* "Consideration," note (*a*).

As to the words, "*signed by the party to be charged,*" they mean that the name, initials or mark must appear somewhere on the paper, written with pen or pencil, for the purpose of authentication. Penniman *v.* Hartshorn, 13 Mass. 87; Clason *v.* Bailey, 14 Johns. 484; Anderson *v.* Harold, 10 Ohio, 399; 2 Kent, Com. 511; Phillimore *v.* Barry, 1 Comp. Cases, 513; Lobb *v.* Stanley, 5 Ad. & Ellis (N. S.) 574; Sweet *v.* Lee, 3 Man. & Gr. 452. But both names are not required. Smith *v.* Smith, 8 Blackford, 208; Lathrop *v.* Bryant, 2 Bing. N. C. 735. The party signing the instrument will be bound, although the other party has not signed it, provided he has manifested his assent in some other way. Old Colony R. R. Co. *v.* Evans, 6 Gray, 25. Smith *v.* Neale, 2 C. B. (N. S.) 67; Justice *v.* Lang, 42 N. Y. 493; Thayer *v.* Luce, 22 Ohio State, 62. It is immaterial in what part of the instrument the name is put, provided it appears to have been written there to give effect to the instrument and complete the contract. Anderson *v.* Harold, 10 Ohio, 399; Messitt *v.* Clason, 12 Johns. 102; Clason *v.* Bailey, 14 id. 484; Johnson *v.* Dodgson, 2 M. & W. 653; Profert *v.* Parker, 1 Rus. & My. 625; Stokes *v.* Moore, 1 Cox, 219; M'Crea *v.* Purmort, 16 Wendell, 469; Fenly *v.* Stewart, 5 Sandf. 101; Penniman *v.* Hartshorn, 13 Mass. 87; Barstow *v.* Gray, 3 Greenl. 409; Shirley *v.* Shirley, 7 Blackf. 452. The contract may be signed by an agent so as to satisfy the statute. Hawkins *v.* Chace, 19 Pick. 502; Bickett *v.* White, 27 Ohio State, 405. Where the written authority of an agent fully sets out the contract he is authorized to make with a third person, and he delivers this as the proposition of his principal, this is a sufficient memorandum. Himrod Furnace Co. *v.* Cleveland & M. R. R. Co., 22 Ohio State, 451. And his authority may be proved by parol evidence. Truman *v.* Loder, 11 Ad. & El. 589. An auctioneer may sign for both parties. Cleaves *v.* Foss, 4 Greenl. 1; Morton *v.* Deane, 13 Met. 385; M'Comb

I shall remark upon them all, though the last three might be reserved until I come to speak of written contracts.

First Section. "That all deeds of gifts, and conveyances of goods and chattels, made in trust, for the use of the person making the same, shall be void and of no effect." This section, it will be observed, is confined to personal property only. As a general rule, the possession of personal property is regarded as evidence of ownership. Among business men, credit is ordinarily given upon the mere fact of such possession, without further inquiry; and hence this provision of the statute. It prohibits persons from putting such property out of their hands, while they still retain the beneficial interest, by having it held for their own use. It is obvious that there can seldom be any other motive than fraud upon third persons, for such a nominal transfer. Why should I suffer you to hold my property for my use, if it be not either to defraud my creditors, or to enable you to defraud yours? But as this section is probably included in the next, I will not make further comment upon it.

Second Section. "That every gift, grant, or conveyance of lands, tenements, hereditaments, rents, goods, or chattels, and every bond, judgment, or execution made or obtained with intent to defraud creditors of their just and lawful debts or damages, or to defraud or deceive the person or persons who shall purchase such lands, tenements, hereditaments, rents, goods, or chattels, shall be deemed utterly void, and of no effect." The substance of this provision is, that every conveyance or encumbrance of real or personal property made with intent to defraud *creditors* or *purchasers* is void. Its design is twofold: first, to give legal efficacy to the grand principle, that all the property which a debtor has shall be responsible for his debts; and secondly, to promote honesty and fair dealing between vendors and purchasers. I shall make some general remarks upon both of these heads.

As to Creditors. (*a*) The words are, "with intent to defraud."

v. Wright, 4 Johns. Ch. 659. And a broker may sign for both parties, if he acts as agent for both. Hinckley *v.* Arey, 27 Maine, 362; Shaw *v.* Phinney, 13 Met. 453. In Massachusetts a full entry by a broker on his books in the regular course of business, containing the names of the parties, though not subscribed, is held sufficient. Coddington *v.* Goddard, 82 Mass. 436. The manipulations of a telegraph operator in sending the name of the party amount to a signature within the statute. Dunning *v.* Roberts, 35 Barb. 463; Trevor *v.* Wood, 36 N. Y. 307. As to a *parol discharge* of a contract required to be in writing, the better opinion is in favor of its validity. Greenleaf Ev. § 302; Goss *v.* Nugent, 5 Barn. & Ad. 58; Stead *v.* Dawber, 2 Perry & Dav. 457. {If possession has not been delivered. Jones *v.* Booth, 38 Ohio State, 405; *contra*, after delivery of possession.} Kelley *v.* Stanbery, 13 Ohio, 408. A verbal agreement, to be effectual and binding as an alteration of the express terms of a prior written contract between the parties, must be supported by a new and valid consideration, and a mere executory contract of the kind to constitute an exception to this rule, must have been so far acted upon, that a refusal to carry it out would work a fraud on one of the parties. Thurston *v.* Ludwig, 6 Ohio State, 1; Willey *v.* Hall, 8 Clarke (Iowa), 62; Emerson *v.* Slater, 22 How. 41. See Low *v.* Forbes, 18 Ill. 568; McGrann *v.* North Lebanon R. R. Co., 39 Penn. State, 83. McDonald *v.* Mountain Lake Water Co., 4 Cal. 335; Cox *v.* Carroll, 6 Clarke, 350; Jones *v.* Alley, 4 Greene, 181.

(*a*) The act of April 6, 1859, regulates the mode of administering assignments in

It is seldom possible to prove such intent by positive testimony, because no man can look into the heart of another; and hence the law resorts to presumption. If, for example, a fraud has been actually committed, the intent will always be presumed. And in relation to creditors, one of the strongest grounds for presuming fraud, is the want of *consideration.* It is fair to conclude that when a man who is in debt disposes of his property for much less than it is worth, there is a secret understanding between him and the purchaser, by which creditors are to be defrauded. Indeed, this collusion may take place when the full value is paid; for if the object be to convert property into money for the purpose of secreting it, and this be known to the purchaser, he becomes a party to the fraud, and must suffer the consequences. But in the absence of collusion, if a debtor receives the fair value of his property, the conveyance will be good; for it does not render him the less able to pay his debts. The corresponding section of the English statute expressly excepts conveyances made in good faith, and for a valuable consideration; and though there is no such exception in ours, yet there is no doubt that our courts would make it, for the plain reason that the presumption of a fraudulent intent is thereby rebutted. But questions of this kind most frequently arise upon conveyances made in consideration of natural *affection*, which is never deemed a valuable consideration, though good as between the parties. On this subject, our courts lay down the reasonable doctrine, that a conveyance to a child, by a parent who was indebted at the time, is presumptive evidence of fraud; but this presumption may be rebutted, by showing that the parent was in prosperous circumstances, and not embarrassed; that his debts were small, and sufficient property was retained to pay them; and that the gift was no more than a reasonable provision for the child. Other circumstances which create presumptions of fraud as to creditors, are, that the conveyance was made when a judgment was expected against the debtor; that he remained in possession after the conveyance; that there was an agreement to reconvey at a future time, if the grantee should so wish; and the like. But all these presumptions may be rebutted by proving the actual honesty of the transaction. There has been much controversy upon the question, how far an *insolvent debtor* can give one creditor a *preference* over another. (*a*) Our court has held that an *actual conveyance* or *transfer*, for a fair value, in payment of a preferred debt, is not within the statute, being no fraud upon other creditors; but that a *general assignment* to trustees for the purpose of preferring creditors is to be watched with great jealousy. In

trust for the benefit of creditors. See also act of March 16, 1860, and March 26, 1860. See Burrill on Assignments; Meeker *v.* Sanders, 6 Clarke (Iowa), 61; Hoffman *v.* Mackall, 5 Ohio State, 124; Conklin *v.* Coonrod, 6 id. 611.

(*a*) Livermore *v.* Jenckes, 21 How. 126.

fact, the opinion has been rapidly gaining ground that an equal distribution ought to be made among all the creditors of a living, as much as of a deceased, insolvent debtor. Preferences are certainly inequitable, if not actually fraudulent. But in this State, all doubt is now removed by our statute, which declares "that all assignments of property in trust, which shall be made by debtors to trustees in contemplation of insolvency, with the design to prefer one or more creditors, to the exclusion of others, shall be held to inure to the benefit of all the creditors, in proportion to their respective demands; and such trusts shall be subject to the control of the courts." (*a*) Henceforward, therefore, if an insolvent debtor desires to prefer a creditor, he must do it by an actual payment to him in money or other property.

As to Purchasers. The purchasers who are protected by the statute are those who have purchased in good faith. Thus, if I have purchased property of you, and before delivery of possession you convey it to some one else who knew of my purchase, this conveyance will be fraudulent as to me: but if he knew nothing of my right, and purchased in good faith, and for an actual consideration, he will be protected as an innocent purchaser without notice. But in such case, there are conflicting opinions as to whether the payment of an antecedent debt is such a consideration as will protect the subsequent purchaser, because he parts with nothing new. Again, if you convey land by deed to me, and I omit to record the deed for the purpose of enabling you to make a sale to some one else, my collusion with you makes the conveyance to me void; but if I merely retain the deed for the six months allowed before recording, without any knowledge of your subsequent sale, my title will be good: from which it follows that, in order to invalidate a conveyance on the ground of fraud as to another purchaser, there must be collusion between the grantor and that purchaser whose conveyance is to be set aside. The fraudulent conveyance described in the statute is said to be "utterly void and of no effect." In the corresponding section of the English statute, such conveyance is declared void only as to the persons intended to be defrauded; namely, creditors and purchasers. As to the fraudulent grantor himself, and all strangers to the transaction, the conveyance is binding; and our court has decided that this is the true construction of our statute, and that none but creditors and purchasers can impeach the conveyance. To allow the grantor to take advantage of his own wrong would promote fraud instead of preventing it; and to allow strangers not affected by the transaction to take advantage of it, would encourage an officious intermeddling with what does not concern them.

Third Section. "That where any loan of goods and chattels shall be pretended to have been made to any person with whom,

(*a*) Bloom *v.* Noggle, 4 Ohio State, 56; Harkrader *v.* Leiby, 4 id. 602; Dickson *v.* Rawson, 5 id. 218; Bagaley *v.* Waters, 7 id. 359; Floyd *v.* Smith, 9 id. 546.

or those claiming under him, possession shall have remained for the space of five years, such goods and chattels shall be deemed the property of the person having had such possession, unless a reservation of the right to such goods and chattels shall have been made to the lender in writing, and such writing shall have been recorded within six months from the time of making such loan, in the recorder's office of the county where one or both of the parties shall then have resided." The substance of this provision is, that where personal property under color of loan has been suffered to remain in the possession of another for five years, the lender shall lose his title thereto, unless a written reservation of his right was made and recorded within six months after the lending. There is no such provision in the English statute, and we have no decision upon it. The intention, probably, is not to interfere between the lender and borrower, but to protect the interests of creditors against the concealment of property by the real owner, under pretence of loan. To prevent such deception, the owner who is not in possession is required to place the evidence of ownership on record as notice to the world; but the time is made so long as to defeat the object in a great measure; the tendency is rather to promote than prevent fraud. We are accustomed to regard the person whom we find in the possession of personalty as the owner, and to credit him as such. But this provision would seem by implication to allow a man at any time within five years after parting with possession, without any record, to assert his ownership, to the injury of those who had been induced to treat the borrower as owner. Perhaps the best provision on this subject would be to require that he who would claim, as against third persons, the ownership of personalty, which he had suffered to remain for six months in the possession of another, should produce recorded evidence of his ownership, made within that length of time, after the possession and ownership were severed.

Fourth Section. "That no leases, estates, or interests, either of freeholds or terms for years, or any uncertain interests, of, in, or out of lands, tenements, or hereditaments, shall at any time hereafter be assigned or granted, unless it be by deed or note, in writing, signed by the party so assigning or granting the same, or their agents thereunto lawfully authorized, by writing or by act and operation of law." The substance of this provision is, that no interest whatsoever in real property shall be conveyed by one person to another without a written instrument of conveyance; and where the conveyance is made by the agent of the owner, the authority to convey must also be in writing. The design is to prevent perjury and fraud in proving title to realty. As to personalty, it can be transferred from hand to hand by mere delivery. This was expressly declared in the ordinance of 1787, and is a part of the common law of the world. But realty cannot change its place like personalty; and something else is required to mark a change of ownership. The statute declares that this shall be written evidence. In speaking of deeds and wills, we have already seen that these instruments of conveyance must not only be in writing, but must also be executed with many formalities. This provision, however, is silent as to the form of the instrument; it only requires that it be in writing; and even to this requisition there are some apparent exceptions. *Implied* or *resulting trusts* in real estate, as we have seen, are not within it; their very nature requires them to be excepted; since to require them to be in writing would be to annihilate them. It has also been held that a *certificate of entry* under the land laws of the United States may be transferred by parol; because this is not an assignment of the interest in the land, but merely of a prior right to acquire an interest. Again, it has been held that a mortgage may be transferred by mere delivery, if the debt secured by it is at the same time duly assigned; because the interest of a mortgagee is but a chattel interest.

Fifth Section. "That no action shall be brought whereby to charge the defendant, upon any special promise, to answer for the debt, default, or miscarriage of another person; or to charge any executor or administrator upon any special promise to answer damages out of his own estate; or to charge any person upon any agreement made in consideration of marriage; or upon any contract or sale of lands, tenements, or hereditaments, or any interest in or concerning them; or upon any agreement that is not to be performed within the space of one year from the making thereof; unless the agreement upon which such action shall be brought, or some memorandum or note thereof shall be in writing, and signed by the party to be charged therewith, or some other person thereunto by him or her lawfully authorized." The substance of this provision is, that upon the five classes of contracts enumerated, no action shall be brought unless they have been reduced to writing and signed by the party or his authorized agent. It will be observed that, under this section, the authority of the agent is not, as under the preceding, required to be in writing; but only the contract itself. The agent must be *lawfully* authorized; and what will constitute a lawful authority is to be gathered from the law of principal and agent. It is settled, however, that one party to the contract cannot sign as agent for the other; but that an auctioneer is an agent for both parties. As to the *signature*, it is sufficient if the name be written with ink or pencil by the party himself in any part of the contract; and if he be in the habit of printing it, this will be sufficient. But the question of greatest difficulty has been, whether the *consideration* of the contract must be stated in writing. It is admitted that the statute does not require a formal agreement drawn up with technical precision; but in England and in New York, it has been held that the consideration must be expressed. In Massachusetts and Ohio, the contrary has been held. (*a*) The phrase "some memorandum or note thereof" would seem to indicate that the consideration may be omitted; and the reason of the law would lead to the same conclusion; for perjury would be as effectually prevented in one way as in the other. With these general explanations, I shall take up each of the five classes of contracts above enumerated, and make such remarks as may seem necessary; first observing that the phraseology is the same, word for word, as in the English statute.

1. "Any special promise to answer for the debt, default, or miscarriage of another person." This language describes what is technically called a *guaranty;* which is, where one person becomes responsible for the debt of another, without making it his own. The criterion is, that the undertaking is for the debt of another; it is collateral, and not original. (*b*) Hence, if you come with your friend to buy goods of me, saying you will be responsible, and I deliver the goods to him, giving the credit to you, your verbal promise will be sufficient, because you make the debt your own in the first instance. But if you had told me to charge the goods to him, and if he did not pay, you would; this promise would not bind you unless in writing. (*c*)

2. "Any special promise by an executor or administrator to answer damages out of his own estate." An executor or administrator, as such, is, of course, not personally liable for the debts of the deceased beyond the amount of assets. If, therefore, he become so liable, it must be by his own special undertaking. And this provision requires such undertaking to be in writing, and so expressed as to create a personal liability.

3. "Any agreement made upon consideration of marriage." It has been decided that this does not include mutual promises to marry, but only agreements to pay money or perform some other collateral act in consideration of marriage; therefore an action may be brought for the breach of a verbal promise to marry.

4. "Any contract or sale of lands, tenements, or hereditaments, or any interest in or concerning them." At first view, this provision might seem to be included in the fourth section; but there are the following differences: *first*, that relates to conveyances only; this includes all contracts concerning realty, as, for example, a contract to convey; *secondly*, there, an agent must be authorized by writing: here, he is merely required to be lawfully authorized; *thirdly*, there, the instrument of conveyance must be

(*a*) So, too, in Indiana. Hiatt *v.* Hiatt, 28 Ind. 53.

(*b*) {The use of the word "guarantee" is not decisive that the contract is collateral. Moorehouse *v.* Crangle, 36 Ohio State, 130.}

(*c*) {Thus also a promise to indemnify one if he will go surety for a third person is a promise to answer for the debt of another. But if the promisor is already a surety for such third person, his promise of indemnity is not a promise to answer for another's debt, for it is to secure his own default. Ferrell *v.* Maxwell, 28 Ohio State, 383.}

in writing: here, a note or memorandum is sufficient; *fourthly*, there, the conveyance is declared to be absolutely void; here, it is merely declared that no action shall be brought against the party. Since, however, every conveyance is a contract executed, it follows that this section would include all those cases under the fourth, where an action should be brought on the instrument of conveyance against a party thereto; so that covenants in deeds or leases are equally within both sections. The provision now in question has been held to embrace a contract for the produce of land, *while growing*, but not *when severed.* (*a*) Also an agreement to take lodgings at a future day. (*b*) A sale of land at auction is also within it, but the auctioneer is held to be the agent of both parties, and his memorandum complies with the statute. In fact, it may be laid down as a general rule, that any executory contract in relation to realty, must be in writing, and signed. (*c*)

5. "Any agreement that is not to be performed within one year from the making thereof." The word "performed" here means *completed.* An inchoate performance, or partial execution to take place within the year, leaving something to be done after the year, will not take the case out of the statute. Thus, a contract for a year's service, to commence at a future day, must be in writing. (*d*) But a contract to deliver goods within a year, to be paid for after a year, may be verbal, because on one side the performance is all to be within the time; and the statute does not include contracts which *may* be performed within the time, or may reach beyond, depending on a contingency. Thus, a contract to pay money on the arrival of a ship, or the acquisition of a legacy may be verbal.

I have thus examined each of the five classes of contracts enumerated in the fifth section. But in construing them, courts have always observed that the object of the statute is to prevent fraud as well as perjury; and have accordingly held that *part performance*, or performance on one side, takes a case out of the statute. The doctrine is, that if one of the parties to a verbal contract within the statute, has honestly performed his part, the other shall not set up the statute to avoid performance on his part, because this would make the statute an instrument of fraud. Thus, if I put you into the possession of land, upon a verbal agreement that if you make certain improvements you shall occupy rent free for a certain period, and you make the improvements, I cannot turn

(*a*) {An oral contract for the sale of a dwelling-house, to be severed from land, and delivered on rollers when severed, is not within the statute. Long *v.* White, 42 Ohio State, 59.}

(*b*) {A contract to pay in land *or* money is within the statute; for as there cannot be a breach shown of the first alternative, the contract cannot be shown to have been broken. Howard *v.* Brower, 37 Ohio State, 402.}

(*c*) {A contract for the purchase of real estate may be orally rescinded if possession has not been taken. Jones *v.* Booth, 38 Ohio State, 405.}

(*d*) {Not a good illustration, for it has been disputed whether deferring the beginning of the services for a few days brings the contract within the statute. 9 Bush, 460; 37 Ohio State, 431, 434.}

you out within the period; and on the other hand, if you have occupied my land under a verbal agreement to pay rent, you cannot refuse to pay rent, because the contract was not in writing. But the mere payment of money is not such part performance as takes the case out of the statute. (*a*) Accordingly, if I verbally agree to sell and convey land to you, and you pay the purchase-money, you cannot compel me to make the conveyance. You can only abandon the contract, and recover back the money. The English statute contains one provision relative to the sale of goods exceeding ten pounds in value (the seventeenth section), which is not in ours: namely, that a contract for such sale shall not be valid, unless, *first*, the buyer actually receive some part of the goods; or, *secondly*, pay something by way of earnest to bind the bargain; or, *thirdly*, unless the contract be in writing. If we had some such provision, it would tend to prevent much doubt and litigation. (*b*)

Illegal Contracts. (*c*) By illegal contracts is here meant, not those which lack some of the legal requisites of a valid contract; but those, the subject-matter of which is in contravention of some positive law. The general principle is, that if a statute forbids an act to be done, or provides a penalty for doing it, any contract to do such act is invalid, whether the statute declares so or not. (*d*)

(*a*) Crabill *v.* Marsh, 38 Ohio State, 331; 2 Story, Eq. Juris. § 759, 760. {The doctrine of part performance only applies to contracts specific performance of which would be decreed, as interests in real estate. Entire performance of other contracts, as for services not to be completed within a year, will entitle the party to recover their value, which may or may not be the contract price. Towsley *v.* Moore, 30 Ohio State, 184. But part performance will not. Reinheimer *v.* Carter, 31 id. 579. Part performance, to take a contract out of the statute, is in general terms such a part performance by one that he cannot be put *in statu quo.*}

(*b*) A contract to manufacture goods and sell them is not within this section. Parsons *v.* Loucks, 48 N. Y. 17. Nor one to sell corn to be gathered and shucked before delivery. Reutch *v.* Long, 27 Md. 181; *contra*, Pitkin *v.* Noyes, 48 N. H. 294. It is not necessary that the payment on account be made at the time of the agreement. If it be afterwards made and received, the agreement becomes complete. Bissell *v.* Balcom, 39 N. Y. 275.

(*c*) See Spurgeon *v.* McElvaine, 6 Ohio, 442; State *v.* Buttles, 3 Ohio State, 309; Roys *v.* Johnson, 7 Gray, 162; Lee *v.* Walbridge, 19 N. Y. 134; Clark *v.* Protection Insurance Company, 1 Story's Rep. 109; De Begnis *v.* Armistead, 10 Bing. 107; General Insurance Company *v.* Belt, 1 West. Law Jour. 261; Chitty on Contracts, 577–626.

(*d*) Whether contracts made contrary to the provisions of a penal statute are void or not, depends upon the intention of the legislature, as determined from an examination of the whole statute. Union Ins. Co. *v.* McMillen, 24 Ohio State, 67; Vining *v.* Bricker, 14 Ohio State, 331; Bemis *v.* Becker, 1 Kansas, 226. Both parties to a transaction forbidden by statute are not necessarily *in pari delicto.* He only is criminal on whom the penalty is imposed. The court will relieve the other party where justice requires it. Musser *v.* Chase, 29 Ohio State, 577; Smith *v.* Bromley, 2 Douglas, 696; Atlas Bank *v.* Nahant Bank, 3 Met. (Mass.) 581; Tracy *v.* Talmadge, 4 Kernan, 162. See also Ins. Co. *v.* Ellis, 32 Ohio State, 388. A defaulting treasurer cannot set up as a defence that the securities he converted were obtained in unauthorized banking contrary to the statute. German Congregation *v.* Stegner, 21 Ohio State, 488. Nor are an embezzling treasurer and the county officials who take securities from him to secure the defalcation *in pari delicto.* Shanklin *v.* Madison Co., 21 Ohio State, 575. Where part of the consideration is illegal, the whole contract is void. Widoe *v.* Webb, 20 Ohio State, 431. {But if the consideration is legal, but supports two promises one of which is illegal, the legal promise is enforceable. See State *ex rel. v.* Bd. of Educ.

Courts of law will not aid parties who contract to infringe the law. A contract, therefore, to commit any of the crimes, offences, or immoral practices specified in our criminal code, could not be enforced; although there is no such express declaration. Our statute for the prevention of gaming declares all contracts to be absolutely void, when any part of the consideration is money, or other property, won, lost, staked, or betted, upon any game or wager whatsoever: or lent to another for that purpose. The language is so broad as to cover every species of gaming contract, under whatsoever name it may be designated. (*a*) Even negotiable contracts are, in this one instance, void after being negotiated.

Usury. (*b*) In England, and in most of the States, *usurious contracts* have also been prohibited. *Usury* signifies the taking of greater interest than the law allows. It has been the policy of most nations to limit the rate of interest, and prohibit the taking of more, by declaring the entire contract void, and sometimes by severe penalties; but public sentiment has been gradually inclining in favor of a more liberal policy. It is undoubtedly convenient to fix the rate of interest for those cases where the parties make no contract on the subject. But if it were now proposed for the

35 Ohio State, 519, 527.} Bonds issued in aid of rebellion cannot be a good consideration, as they are not imposed upon the people by irresistible force. Hanauer *v.* Woodruff, 15 Wall. 439. Where a contract is void, when made because in contravention of a statute, a subsequent repeal of the statute will not render it valid. Banchor *v.* Mansel, 47 Maine, 858.

(*a*) R. S. § 4269. Hoss *v.* Layton, 3 Ohio State, 352. In Massachusetts it is held, that although a contract be in violation of a statute, yet if the plaintiff can make out a case for relief without showing the contract, he can recover, and the defendant will not be allowed to defeat him by showing the contract; but if he is obliged to show the contract to make out a case he must fail. Welch *v.* Wesson, 6 Gray, 505; Commonwealth *v.* Harrison, 11 Gray, 309. Thus in Ladd *v.* Rogers, 11 Allen, 209, the court held, that where a horse had been sold on the Lord's Day, contrary to the statute, an action could not be maintained for the contract price, although the defendant retained the horse afterwards, for to maintain such an action the plaintiff must show the illegal contract; but that an action of tort in the nature of trover would lie. For various views upon this subject, some of them differing from the above, see Woodman *v.* Hubbard, 5 Foster, 67; Morton *v.* Gloster, 46 Maine, 520; Adams *v.* Gay, 19 Vt. 358; Parsons on Cont. (4th ed.) 262, note (*f*).

(*b*) 2 Black. Com. 454; an English Treatise on Usury by Comyn; La Fayette Society *v.* Lewis, 7 Ohio, 80; Reddish *v.* Watson, 6 id. 510; Brockway *v.* Clark, Wright, 727; State of Ohio *v.* Taylor, 10 Ohio, 378; Shelton *v.* Gill, 11 id. 417; Creed *v.* Commercial Bank, id. 489; Bank of Chillicothe *v.* Swayne, 8 id. 257; Baggs *v.* Louderback, 12 id. 153; Graham *v.* Cooper, 17 id. 605; Mattocks *v.* Humphrey, id. 336; Bank of Wooster *v.* Stevens, 1 Ohio State, 235; Palmer *v.* Yarrington, id. 253; Selser *v.* Brock, 3 Ohio State, 302; Bank of Wooster *v.* Stevens, 6 id. 262; Dunkle *v.* Renick, 6 id. 527; Lockwood *v.* Mitchell, 7 id. 387. It is immaterial what devices are resorted to for the concealment of the usury, and if detected the contract is affected with its incidents. Whether illegal interest has been intended to be stipulated by the parties, is a question for the jury. Andrews *v.* Pond, 13 Peters, 65; Stevens *v.* Davis, 3 Met. 211; Thomas *v.* Catheral, 5 G. & J. 23; Corcoran *v.* Powers, 6 Ohio State, 19. A contract untainted with usury when made will not become void by the subsequent receipt of usurious interest. Busby *v.* Finn, 1 Ohio State, 409. On the topic of usury, see 2 Parsons on Cont. 383–431. But it is not a usurious contract for a man to agree to sell a piece of land for a certain sum in cash, or a much larger sum, even if it be double, on a long credit. Hogg *v.* Ruffner, 1 Black, 115. An agreement between partners allowing a partner who is to bear his share of losses interest above the legal rate on moneys advanced, is not usurious. Cunningham *v.* Green, 23 Ohio State, 296.

first time to prohibit men from contracting for what rate they please, we should probably with one voice oppose such a measure, as an arbitrary interference with our personal liberty. We cannot easily perceive why the *price* to be paid for the use of money should be regulated by law, when the price of every other commodity is allowed to regulate itself, upon the principle of fair and free competition; and as to *value*, all agree that it cannot be regulated by law. A thing is worth what men will give for it, let the law declare what it will. Besides, the actual value of money to a given person, at a given time and place, depends upon circumstances, which the individual himself only can appreciate. Nothing is more variable and fluctuating. It is said, however, that the necessitous and the improvident must be protected against extortion. Then why not appoint guardians at once to manage their affairs? It is futile to guard them against one class of contracts only. You close up one avenue to ruin, and leave open all others. This argument therefore fails, and this is the only one of any plausibility; whereas the objections to usury laws are numerous. They cannot be made effectual; for men who want money, and cannot obtain it at the legal rate, will give more; and the rate will be increased proportionally to the hazard. A tempting bribe is held out to knavery. The law offers a premium for violating the contract. The business of lending against law naturally passes into the hands of Shylocks; and they must charge enough to insure against the risk of refusal to pay on the ground of usury. The rate of interest is thus actually increased by the very means intended to limit it; but I will not pursue the argument. In this State, in the year 1824, a law was passed, entitled, "an act fixing the rate of interest," in these words: "That all creditors shall be entitled to receive interest on all money, after the same shall become due, either on bond, bill, promissory note, or other instrument of writing, or contract for money or property; on all balances due on settlement between parties thereto; on money withheld by unreasonable and vexatious delay of payment; and on all judgments obtained, from the date thereof; and on all decrees obtained in any court of chancery, for the payment of money, from the day specified in such decree for the payment thereof; or if no day be specified, then from the day of entering thereof, until such debt, money, or property is paid; at the rate of six per centum per annum, and no more." (*a*) Taking this

(*a*) Since the text was written, a law was passed, in 1848, authorizing the excess of all payments of interest above the lawful rate, whether made in advance or not, to be treated as payments on account of the principal. See Baggs *v.* Louderback, 12 Ohio, 153. In 1850, a law was passed authorizing parties to stipulate in writing for a rate of interest not exceeding ten per centum per annum, until payment. Curwen's Laws of Ohio in Force, 921. This law was repealed Feb. 25, 1859, and more than six per cent could not then be secured by a special contract. But by the act of May 4th, 1869 (66 Ohio Laws, 91), it became lawful to stipulate for eight per cent per annum; and on such contracts interest is to be reckoned at the stipulated rate until paid, and judgments on them to bear the stipulated rate also. This act has been held not to apply to banks. Shunk *v.* First National Bank of Galion, 22 Ohio State, 508.

act by itself, though nothing is said of usury or forfeiture, yet the concluding words, "six per centum per annum, and no more," would seem at least to render a contract void for any *excess* above that rate, if they do not create an entire forfeiture; but taking it in connection with the act of 1804, which it repeals, and which was expressly designed to prevent usury by providing for an entire forfeiture, it has sometimes been thought that the intention of the act was merely to fix the rate of interest where the parties had not fixed it; and that they are left free to stipulate for any other rate. Our court, however, after much vacillation, and some apparently contradictory decisions, have finally concluded that no more than six per cent interest can be secured by express stipulation. For any excess above this rate the contract is void. But illegal interest once paid cannot be recovered back; and a court of equity will not enjoin a judgment at law on the ground of illegal interest, unless there has been a tender of what is lawfully due. Nor can the interest law be evaded by a stipulation for a certain percentage by way of collection fee; for all such stipulations are held to be void. And where a corporation is limited by its charter to a certain rate of interest, any contract for more is wholly void, not as against the interest law, but as an excess of power. (*a*)

Lawful Interest. In this connection, as interest is an incident to almost all contracts, I will state some of the leading rules by which it is governed. We have seen that the statute provides for interest in four classes of cases; viz.: 1. (*b*) On contracts for money or other property, after the same shall be due. This includes all contracts payable on a day certain, which is called the day of *maturity;* but where the contract is to pay on demand,

Under the National Bank Act, taking usurious interest avoids the debt only to the extent of the interest. The act of 1850 of this State does not apply to those banks. First National Bank of Columbus *v.* Garlinghouse, 22 Ohio State, 492; Ewing *v.* Bank, 43 id. 31. In the absence of provision in the law to the contrary, a debt bearing by stipulation a rate of interest higher than the usual rate, but permitted by law, will, after maturity, only bear the regular rate. Gray *v.* Briscoe, 6 Bush (Ky.), 687; Holden *v.* Trust Co., 100 U. S. 72. But such is not the Ohio law. Monnett *v.* Sturges, 25 Ohio State, 384; Marietta Iron Works *v.* Lottimer, 25 id. 621; Hydraulic Co. *v.* Chatfield, 38 Ohio State, 575. It has been held in Indiana, that where a contract is made for a rate of interest higher than is allowed at the time the contract is made, but prior to suit the law is changed, and such rate is authorized, the higher rate may be collected. Klingensmith *v.* Reed, 31 Ind. 389. *Sed quære.*

(*a*) {The leading Ohio case on this proposition is Bank of Chillicothe *v.* Swayne, 8 Ohio, 257, holding the entire contract void for want of power; but the court has lately shown a disposition, where possible to distinguish the case, to adopt another rule. See National Bank *v.* Ins. Co., 41 Ohio State, 1; Larwell *v.* Hanover Sav. Soc., 40 id. 274; Ewing *v.* Bank, 43 id. 31.}

(*b*) Blaney *v.* Hendricks, 2 Black, Rep. 761; Kennerly *v.* Nash, 1 Stark. Rep. 452; M'Clure *v.* Longworth, Wright, 582; City of Ohio *v.* Cleveland & Toledo R. R. Co., 6 Ohio State, 489; Darling *v.* Wooster, 9 id. 517. In the subjoined authorities, the principles applicable to this subject are thoroughly discussed, and illustrated by the numerous cases. Selleck *v.* French, 1 Conn. 31; Reid *v.* Rensselaer Glass Factory, 3 Cowen, 387–93; s. c. 5 id. 587; Pierce *v.* Rowe, 1 N. H. 179; Vaine *v.* Wilkins, 12 id. 474; 1 Am. Leading Cases, 493–523; 2 Parsons on Contracts, 380–3. As to the liability of a garnishee to pay interest during the pendency of attachment proceedings, see Candee *v.* Webster, 9 Ohio State, 453.

interest is not chargeable until demand; though the contrary has been held where the contract was expressed to be for money lent. By our statute, interest is recoverable on bank-notes from the time of demand and refusal; but the bank may give six weeks' public notice of intention to redeem, and then interest will cease after so commencing to redeem. Lastly, where the contract is to pay at a future day *with interest*, it is recoverable from date. 2. On balances due upon settlement of *accounts* between the parties. This only includes interest on the balance found due, from the date of the settlement, and not on the separate items from their date; and yet there is no doubt that each party may charge interest on the separate items, whenever from the custom of business, or the course of dealing between the parties, it can be inferred that such was their intention. 3. (*a*) On money withheld by unreasonable and vexatious delay of payment. This class is very indefinite. Perhaps it includes all cases of indebtedness after demand of payment. It undoubtedly includes money obtained by fraud, whether the party has used it or not. The theory of interest, when there is no express contract to pay it, is that it takes the shape of *damages for detention*. This implies something wrongful in withholding the principal; accordingly, if a tender be made even after suit brought, it stops the running of interest after that time. So if an administrator pay a debt in full, and the estate afterwards turn out insolvent, he can only recover interest on the excess so paid, from the time the insolvency is decreed. 4. On judgments and decrees from the date thereof; that is, the first day of term. (*b*) On this class no comment is necessary. But the authorities establish another class of cases, viz.: 5. (*c*) When it can be proved that the money has been used, and interest actually made. On this ground executors, administrators, guardians, trustees, receivers, and the like, are chargeable with interest on money in their hands; but interest is not chargeable, in favor of the other heirs, upon money given to a child by way of

(*a*) Mason *v.* Waite, 17 Mass. 560; Wood *v.* Robbins, 11 id. 504; Walker *v.* Bradley, 3 Pick. 261; Hogg *v.* Zanesville, 5 Ohio, 410.

(*b*) {Under the statute allowing a judgment to bear the same rate of interest as the contract on which it was rendered, no rests are allowed; thus if the interest on the contract is seven per cent payable quarterly, the interest on the judgment is seven per cent without annual rests. Marietta Iron Works *v.* Lottimer, 25 Ohio State, 621.}

(*c*) Wyman *v.* Hubbard, 13 Mass. 232; Fay *v.* Howe, 1 Pick. 527; Osgood *v.* Breed, 17 Mass. 356. See *ante*, p. 288. But an administrator is not chargeable with interest unless he uses the funds of the estate in his business, or derives from them some benefit, or is guilty of negligence. Gooch *v.* Irwin, 7 Ohio State, 22. Trustees and other parties standing in such fiduciary relations are chargeable, it has been held, with compound interest, if they have been grossly delinquent in the investment of the funds intrusted to them, or, having used them for their own advantage, refuse to account for the profits. Fay *v.* Howe, *supra*; Boynton *v.* Dyer, 18 Pick. 1; Swindall *v.* Swindall, 8 Iredell, Eq. 285; Schieffelin *v.* Stewart, 1 Johns. Ch. 620; Clarkson *v.* De Peyster, 2 Wend. 177; s. c. 1 Hopkins, Ch. 424; Ackerman *v.* Emott, 4 Barb. 626; 2 Kent, Com. 230, 231; Knott *v.* Cottee, 13 Eng. Law & Eq. 304; Pearson *v.* Darrington, 32 Ala. 227. But see as to the rule in Pennsylvania, Dieterrich *v.* Heft, 5 Barr, 87.

advancement. These five classes of cases probably include all those in which interest can be recovered, without any express contract for that purpose. But there are some other points which require to be noticed. 6. (*a*) Where by special agreement interest is due before the principal, a separate action can be brought to recover it; and in Ohio, if no suit be brought and it remain due and unpaid, interest upon interest, or compound interest, will be allowed. (*b*) But the law varies in other places; and the weight of authority, though not of reason is against it. 7. (*c*) Where partial payments have been made on a debt, the common rule is to compute interest down to the first payment, then deduct that payment, and so on for each of the successive payments. But in Massachusetts, the rule is thus modified: compute the interest down to the time when a payment or payments have been made exceeding the interest then due; add the interest and subtract the payment or payments; and thus proceed to the time of computation. This modification is made to avoid compound interest, by preventing the interest in any case from forming part of the principal. 8. (*d*) Where the contract is made in one place and payable in another, the rate of interest is governed by the law of the latter place; otherwise, by the law of the place of making the contract.

§ 178. **Express Contracts.** The remarks hitherto made apply generally to all contracts; but it now becomes necessary to distinguish between the various kinds of contracts. The distinction between executed and executory contracts has been already explained. The next general division is into *express* and *implied.* Express contracts are those the terms of which are actually stipulated in uttered language; if the words are reduced to writing, they are termed *written contracts;* if not, *oral* or *verbal* contracts. Implied contracts are those which the law infers from the acts of the parties. (*e*) *Parol* or *simple* contracts signify all contracts which are not under seal, whether express or implied. (*f*)

What Contracts must be in Writing. The general rule is, that oral contracts are as valid as written; but there are certain classes of contracts, which, for special reasons, the law requires should be in writing. These are provided for in the third, fourth, and fifth sections of the statute of frauds, which have been already described. This statute, it will be remembered, was designed to prevent *perjury* as well as fraud; and it will be readily seen, that to require a contract to be reduced to writing, is the best possible

(*a*) Cooley *v.* Rose, 3 Mass. 221; Fobes *v.* Canfield, 3 Ohio, 17; Watkinson *v.* Root, 4 id. 373; Hastings *v.* Wiswalt, 8 Mass. 373; Fake *v.* Eddy, 15 Wend. 76.

(*b*) {But though the interest be at a higher rate, interest on unpaid interest will be only at six per cent. Cramer *v.* Lepper, 26 Ohio State, 59; Cook *v.* Courtright, 40 Ohio State, 218.}

(*c*) Miami Exp. Co. *v.* Bank U. S., 5 Ohio, 261; Dean *v.* Williams, 17 Mass. 417; Hammer *v.* Neville, Wright, 169.

(*d*) Story's Conflict of Laws, § 291–301.

(*e*) Herzog *v.* Herzog, 29 Penn. State, 465.

(*f*) Rann *v.* Hughes, 7 T. R. 351, note; Beckham *v.* Drake, 9 M. & W. 79.

safeguard against perjury, and consequent fraud, in relation to such contract. But I need not repeat a description of the contracts which must be in writing, by the last three sections of this statute.

Contracts under seal. (*a*) There is another division of contracts into *specialties* and *parol* or *simple contracts.* Specialties include *contracts under seal* and *obligations of record.* Simple contracts, otherwise denominated *parol contracts*, include all other contracts, whether oral or written. It is then the *seal* or the *record* which constitutes the specialty. Seals are of two kinds, *public* and *private.* Public or official seals are those used by public officers, for the authentication of public documents. With these we have at present no concern. Private seals are those used by private individuals, in the execution of private contracts. A sealed contract is technically called a *specialty*, *deed*, *bond*, *covenant*, or *writing obligatory.* Every contract may be under seal, if the parties so elect; and there are some contracts which are invalid without a seal; as deeds for the conveyance of real estate, and various kinds of bonds prescribed by statute. The law relating to these contracts abounds with technical and arbitrary distinctions, which serve no other purpose than to confuse the mind. There is, perhaps, no branch of law in which reform would be more salutary. It may be safely asserted that the total abolition of private seals would be an immense improvement, without any admixture of evil; for they are not only of no conceivable use, but positively injurious, from the complexity which they occasion. This will be evident from a brief examination. According to Blackstone, seals were first introduced because men could not write. (*b*) Not being able to ratify contracts by *signature*, each person had his own particular *seal*, with some distinctive *device*, which he used in the place of a signature. The moment, therefore, that writing became general, the reason of using seals ceased; but the custom nevertheless continued. From the origin of seals, then, we gather this: that instead of being a "relic of ancient wisdom," as the books declare, they are in reality a monument of ancient ignorance. We further learn that the original purpose of a seal has been entirely lost sight of in modern times; for we not only never affix a seal without a signature, but where a person cannot write his own name, we write it for him, and he ratifies it. In fact, seals are so far from being used to identify contracts, that they very seldom have any distinctive character to indicate to whom they belong. They are generally affixed by the scrivener, as a part of his business. For what purpose, then, are seals continued in use? The

(*a*) 2 Black. Com. 305; 4 Kent, Com. 452; Platt on Covenants; Hurlstone on Bonds.

(*b*) 2 Black. Com. 295; 4 Kent, Com. 452; Jackson *v.* Wood, 12 Johns. 73; Jackson *v.* Stevens, 13 Johns. 316; Bond's Lessee *v.* Swearingen, 1 Ohio, 402; Ayres *v.* Harness, 1 id. 368; Violett *v.* Patten, 5 Cranch, 142; Hall *v.* Phelps, 2 Johns. 451; Fox *v.* Reil, 3 Johns. 477; 1 West. Law Jour. 385; Farmers' Bank *v.* Haight, 3 Hill, 463; Addison on Contracts, p. 5.

pretext is, that they add *solemnity* to the instrument to which they are affixed. To judge from the language of the books, one might suppose that a seal was some mystic symbol or amulet; and that the ceremony of affixing it was attended with something like religious pomp. But according to Lord Coke, "a seal is wax impressed, because wax without an impression is not a seal." (*a*) The solemnity, then, which is attached to a seal, must consist in melting the wax, and making the impression; a rite which certainly cannot be very august or awful. But how is even this solemnity diminished, when we come to the definition of a seal in our statute; which may be "either of wax, of wafer, or of ink, commonly called a scrawl seal." Chancellor Kent considers this substitution of a "flourish with a pen at the end of the name," in place of the ancient seal, as a virtual abolition of seals. (*b*) It does indeed show how utterly insignificant seals are; but it does not take away one of their legal consequences. The "scrawl," which we have substituted, possesses the same mysterious virtue as the wax described by Coke; yet it is upon this theoretical solemnity of a seal that the principal distinctions between sealed and unsealed writings are founded. Some of these distinctions I will now enumerate. 1. The presence of the seal is said to *estop* the party, that is, to preclude him, from proving any thing to the contrary: when by the same words without a seal, he would not be *estopped*. (*c*) Now common sense would indicate that if the doctrine of *estoppel* be ever proper, it should be founded upon the nature of the averment, and not upon the mere presence of a seal. 2. The presence of a seal is said to *import a consideration*, without its being expressly stated, and to preclude a denial of that fact; (*d*) when the same words without a seal would have no such effect; and such is the doctrine of the common law; but it is so unreasonable, that a statute has lately been passed in this State, allowing the consideration of all contracts, whether sealed or not, to be called in question; with the exception of negotiable contracts, after being negotiated. (*e*) 3. At common law, a debt due upon a sealed contract was entitled to a priority of payment out of the assets of a deceased person, before any debt due upon a contract not under seal; but this doctrine is also deemed so unreasonable that our statute of distribution allows no such preference. 4. A contract cannot be filled up over a seal and signature in blank, though left for that express purpose; whereas the same words may be written over a mere signature in blank, and the contract will be valid. This distinction, though palpably unreasonable,

(*a*) Inst. 169.

(*b*) 4 Kent, Com. 453. Brackets with the word "seal" between them printed on a paper by a third person, opposite the blank space for signature, is a sufficient scrawl seal; it is adopted by signing. Osborn *v.* Kistler, 35 Ohio State, 99.

(*c*) Co. Litt. 352, *a*; 4 Kent, Com. 260.

(*d*) Sharington *v.* Stratton, Plowden, 308; 2 Kent, Com. 464.

(*e*) A similar change of the common law has been introduced in New York and Indiana.

has been recognized by our own court. 5. If there be a subscribing witness to a sealed instrument, the confession of the party who executed it will not be admitted to prove the execution, if the witness can be had; whereas, if there be no seal, the confession will be sufficient. This distinction is so utterly absurd, that it is matter of astonishment it should ever have been adopted; it has, however, been recognized by the courts of this country. 6. No agent can affix the seal of his principal, unless his authority so to do be under seal; whereas, a mere verbal authority will be sufficient for affixing the signature of the principal. And the same doctrine applies to the revocation of an agent's authority by the principal. 7. A surety upon a contract under seal, is not released by giving time to the principal, unless the agreement for extension be under seal; whereas, a mere verbal agreement for extension will release a surety upon a contract not under seal. 8. A contract under seal being of a higher nature, supersedes a simple contract upon the same subject-matter. The latter is said to be *merged* in the former. 9. The remedy upon contracts under seal is, from beginning to end, entirely different from that upon contracts not under seal. This will be demonstrated when we come to speak of the modes of proceeding. Such are a few of the distinctions, founded upon the presence or absence of a seal, which render the law of contracts, otherwise so simple and reasonable, in this one respect a collection of arbitrary principles. What an immense superstructure to be built on so slight a foundation! Yet such is the common law; and such it must remain, until legislation shall do away with private seals. (*a*) It is not denied that some contracts should be executed with more formality, and proved with more care, than others. On this principle, we have seen that the statute of frauds properly requires certain contracts to be in writing; that the statute of *wills* as properly requires them to be *attested*, and that the *statute of deeds* requires them to be both *attested* and *acknowledged*. But the reason of these requisitions has not the most remote application to the use of seals; for it cannot be pretended that seals add any thing to that vigilance and precaution in executing and proving contracts, which these provisions are intended to secure.

Deeds. The foregoing remarks apply generally to all sealed instruments. I shall now refer to the particular classes, beginning with *deeds*. The term *deed*, as we have already seen, is applicable to all contracts under seal, by way of eminence, because, in the language of Blackstone, it is the most solemn and authentic act that a man can possibly perform, with relation to the disposal of his property; but it is now most frequently used in a restricted sense to denote an instrument for the conveyance or encumbrance of real estate. Its form and requisites for this

(*a*) {Private seals and all distinctions between sealed and unsealed instruments are now abolished in Arkansas, California, Dakota, Indiana, Iowa, Kansas, Kentucky, Mississippi, Montana, Nebraska, Ohio, Oregon, Tennessee, and Texas.}

purpose have been fully considered. Deeds are divided into two kinds, *deeds poll* and *indentures*. A *deed poll*, or *single deed*, is a deed executed by only one party; and was so called, because, when forms were more regarded than substance, the edge of such deed was not *indented*, but *polled* or shaved quite even. Whereas, an *indenture*, which is a deed executed by more parties than one, was so called, because as many *copies* or *counterparts* were required to be executed as there were parties; and the edges of each were so notched or indented as to correspond one with another. This useless formality is now obsolete, but the name remains; and whenever parties enter into mutual covenants or engagements under seal, the instrument is an indenture. The most frequent instances are *indentures of lease*, and *indentures of apprenticeship*, which have been already described.

Bonds. (*a*) The term bond is used to denote the *acknowledgment* of an existing debt under seal. It differs from a *covenant* in this, that the latter is always an executory contract for something future: though each is technically called, by way of eminence, a *writing obligatory*. Bonds are of two kinds, *single bonds* and *penal bonds*. A *single bond*, more frequently called a *single bill*, is a simple acknowledgment of indebtedness without any condition of qualification; as if I, under hand and seal, acknowledge myself indebted to you in a given sum. A *penal bond* is an acknowledgment of indebtedness, accompanied by a *condition*, upon compliance with which such acknowledgment is void. The sum here named as a debt is called a *penalty*, because it is inserted merely to secure the performance of the condition, which is the principal thing; as if I, under hand and seal, acknowledge myself indebted to you in a given sum, upon condition that it is to be void upon my doing a certain thing, as to pay money or to convey land. And it has been decided that an action will not lie to recover a penalty, unless it be under seal. Besides the penal bond given by individuals in their private transactions, our statute requires that all bonds given in the course of judicial proceedings, and all official bonds given for the performance of duty, shall be in this form. Penal bonds, therefore, occupy a wide space in the law. But the very idea of a penalty supposes that the amount is greater than the value of the condition, the performance of which it is designed to secure; yet, as the law formerly stood, if the condition was not strictly performed, the entire penalty could be recovered. The hardship thus frequently occasioned induced chancery to interfere and prohibit the recovery of any thing more than reasonable damages, for the non-performance of the condition. But now the application to chancery is unnecessary, because our statute enables the courts of law to do the same thing. As a matter of form, the judgment is given for the entire penalty; but the actual damages are assessed by a jury, and execution issues for no more than the

(*a*) Huddle *v.* Worthington, 1 Ohio, 423; Nelson *v.* Ford, 5 id. 473.

amount of their verdict. The result, therefore, is that a penal bond now amounts to no more than a covenant to perform the condition, and may be treated as such. (*a*)

Specialties of Record. These include obligations of indebtedness evidenced by judicial records. Such records form the highest possible kind of evidence; insomuch that the only question which can be controverted is, whether the record exists. If it does, it imports absolute verity. So that specialties of record are the highest kind of specialties. And as a simple contract is merged in a sealed contract upon the subject-matter, so a sealed contract is merged in a specialty of record. These specialties are of two kinds: *recognizances*, and *judgments* or *decrees*. A recognizance is an acknowledgment of indebtedness made before the court or some authorized officer thereof, with a condition to be void on doing certain things therein named; which acknowledgment is made part of the record of the cause to which it relates. The object of a recognizance is to secure the appearance of a defendant or witness. The statute provides when it may be taken, and what shall be its form. As to *judgments* and *decrees*, they are barely mentioned under this head, because they are the highest kind of specialties; but as they have little or nothing in common with contracts, a discussion of them is reserved for another occasion.

§ 179. **Implied Contracts.** There is, perhaps, no branch of law, which the mind of an unprejudiced person will contemplate with more satisfaction, than that which regulates implied contracts. The broad principle which governs them may be thus stated: Every member of society has impliedly contracted to do whatever the law requires of him; if, therefore, without any special contract, he acts in such a manner as to create a legal liability, he is as much bound to fulfil that liability as if he had expressly contracted so to do. On this theory, every kind of indebtedness, which is not by express contract, may be referred to an implied contract. The most common instances of implied contracts are these: If you, with my consent, or at my request, have done work of any kind for me, without any express agreement as to compensation, I have impliedly contracted to pay you a *quantum meruit*, what it is reasonably worth. If you have sold me goods of any description, and I have consented to receive them, without any agreement as to price, I have impliedly contracted to pay you a *quantum valebant*, what they are reasonably worth. If you and I have settled

(*a*) If the sum stated in an obligation is to be regarded in the nature of a penalty, it is not recoverable on default of the obligor, and only actual damages will be allowed. But if it may be regarded as damages liquidated and assessed by the parties, then it may be recovered on a breach of the condition. For late leading cases which illustrate this distinction, see Beale *v.* Hayes, 5 Sandf. 640; Bagley *v.* Peddie, id. 192; Mead *v.* Wheeler, 13 N. H. 351; Brewster *v.* Edgerly, id. 275; Atkins *v.* Kinnier, 4 Exch. 776; Berry *v.* Wisdom, 3 Ohio State, 241; Cairnes *v.* Knight, 17 Ohio State, 68; Fisk *v.* Gray, 10 Allen, 132; Lampman *v.* Cochran, 16 N. Y. 275; Clement *v.* Cash, 21 N. Y. 257; Bagley *v.* Reddie, 16 N. Y. 469.

accounts, and agreed upon a balance due from me to you, I have impliedly contracted to pay that balance. If you have lent me money, I have impliedly contracted to pay you. If, at my request or with my consent, you have paid money to another for my use, I have impliedly contracted to pay you. If you have received money from me or any other person, which on the principles of justice ought to be paid to me, you have impliedly contracted to pay it to me. If you have undertaken the custody of property belonging to me, you have impliedly contracted to use due diligence in keeping it safely. If I have permitted you to use property belonging to me, you have impliedly contracted that you will not abuse it. And if I have employed you to do some service requiring a certain amount of skill, you have impliedly contracted to apply such skill. These examples sufficiently explain the nature of implied contracts; and when we come to the law of procedure, we shall find that the common counts in debts and assumpsit have been framed with a special view to furnish a remedy upon such contracts. In fact, there are many cases where, though an express contract was made, it may be waived and a remedy sought upon the implied contract. Thus, where an express contract for service has been fully performed on one side, or where it has been put an end to by the act of the parties, compensation for the service rendered may be sought on the implied contract for a *quantum meruit*. But for technical reasons, where the express contract is a specialty, the remedy must be sought upon the specialty itself, with the single exception of an action of debt for rent. (*a*)

(*a*) 1 Chit. Plead. 339, 346, 348; Kelley *v.* Foster, 2 Binney, 4; Bank of Columbia *v.* Patterson, 7 Cranch, 299; Fitch *v.* Sargeant, 1 Ohio, 355; Hollister *v.* Reznor, 9 Ohio State, 1. A party who has abandoned a contract after part performance, without a just cause or the assent of the other party or his acceptance of the unfinished work, cannot recover *pro tanto* for the labor and materials. Allen *v.* Curles, 6 Ohio State, 505. But where there is a substantial performance of a contract of building with unintentional deviations or deficiencies, a party may recover, it has been held, the contract price, deducting therefrom the amount necessary to complete the work according to the contract. {Goldsmith *v.* Hand, 26 Ohio State, 101; Cullen *v.* Bimm, 37 id. 236; Mehurin *v.* Stone, 37 id. 49} Hayward *v.* Leonard, 7 Pick. 182; Snow *v.* Ware, 13 Met. 42; Bassett *v.* Sanborn, 9 Cush. 58; Gleason *v.* Smith, id. 484; Smith *v.* Gugerty, 4 Barb. 614. See Smith *v.* Brady, 17 N. Y. 173; White *v.* Hewitt, 1 E. D. Smith, 395. The authorities on this subject are conflicting. 2 Parsons on Contracts, p. 35. According to the current of authorities, there can be no recovery, even *pro tanto*, upon a contract for personal service for a time certain, where it is abandoned without the consent of both parties, or some legal excuse, before its expiration. 1 Parsons on Contracts, 522; Angle *v.* Hanna, 22 Ill. 429. A contract to work for six months certain, at eleven dollars per month, is an entire contract. Larkin *v.* Buck, 11 Ohio State, 561; Hansel *v.* Erickson, 28 Ill. 257; and if the laborer is dismissed without cause, he may recover for the whole period covered by the contract. Davis *v.* Marshall, 6 Hurl. & Nor. 916. "I have this day hired the barge Mary Jane of Albert Stein, for the sum of ten dollars per day until delivered back at Cincinnati in like good order as received," is an entire contract, and a recovery in a suit thereon is a bar to any further action. Stein *v.* Prairie Rose, 17 Ohio State, 471. But in New Hampshire and Iowa, this doctrine does not prevail, and the laborer is entitled, notwithstanding the breach of the contract, to recover the value of his services, deducting therefrom the damages to his employer resulting from the breach. Britton *v.* Turner, 6 N. H. 481; Pixler *v.* Nichols, 8 Clarke (Iowa), 106. See Ashbrook *v.* Hite, 9 Ohio State, 365; Loomis *v.* Eagle Bank, 10 Ohio State, 327; Ryan *v.* Dayton, 25 Conn. 188; Coe *v.* Smith, 4 Ind. 79; Wolfe *v.* Howes, 20 N. Y. 197; Stein *v.* Prairie Rose, 17 Ohio State, 471.

32

LECTURE XXXIII.

PARTICULAR CONTRACTS.

§ 180. **Negotiable Contracts.** (*a*) In the preceding lecture I have considered the nature and general divisions of contracts; but there are certain classes of contracts which, on account of their peculiar practical importance, seem to require a distinct consideration. These are, *negotiable contracts; the contract of sale; the contract of bailment; the contract of principal and surety; the contract of insurance;* and *liens.* I propose in this lecture to describe, of course very briefly, each of these contracts, beginning with *negotiable contracts.* It was an ancient doctrine of the common law, *that contracts could not be assigned.* The reason of this doctrine is said to be, that the right of a party to a contract is a right to sue in case of non-performance; and to permit a party to assign or transfer this right to another would encourage litigation.(*b*) This reason is not true in point of fact; since the assignee of a contract could have no motive to sue, which would not equally operate upon the original party. Still it was an ancient rule that *choses in action* could not be assigned. But like most rules not founded in reason, this rule has now become merely technical in law, and does not exist in equity. (*c*) It prohibits me from so

It is sometimes required in contracts that the work shall be accepted or approved by a third party, as an architect, or even by the employer; and such acceptance or approval has been considered a condition precedent to a recovery by the other party. Smith *v.* Brady, 17 N. Y. 173; McCarren *v.* McNulty, 7 Gray, 139; Vanderwerker *v.* Vt. Central R. R. Co., 27 Vt. 130; Herrick *v.* Belknap, 27 id. 673; Barker *v.* Troy & Rutland R. R. Co., 27 id. 766; Mansfield & Sandusky R. R. Co. *v.* Veeder, 17 Ohio, 385 {Kane *v.* Stone Co., 39 Ohio State, 1. In the absence of fraud or of mistake so gross as to imply fraud. Martinsburg, &c. R. R. *v.* Marsh, 114 U. S. 549}. A written agreement may be discharged by a subsequent oral agreement upon a new and valid consideration, or by an agreement without such new consideration, which has been so far acted upon by the parties, that a refusal to carry it out would be a fraud on one of the parties. Thurston *v.* Ludwig, 6 Ohio State, 1; Willey *v.* Hall, 8 Clarke (Iowa), 62; Emerson *v.* Slater, 22 How. 28.

(*a*) See 3 Kent, Com. lec. 44; 2 Black. Com. 466; Story on Bills; Bayley on Bills; Chitty on Bills; Kyd on Bills; Cunningham on Exchange; Byles on Bills; Parsons on Bills and Notes.

(*b*) Lampet's case, 10 Co. R. 48.

(*c*) When the assignee of a chose in action became by practice authorized to bring an action in the name of the assignor, entitling the action "A. who sues for the use of B.," choses in action became substantially assignable at law. Choses in action were assignable in equity, and are, under the codes, assignable. The assignee is held in equity, under the codes, the owner, and sues in his own name. But such assignee takes the chose in action "subject to equities;" that is, subject to such defences as were valid against it between the original parties.

A negotiable instrument is something more than an assignable instrument. When a negotiable instrument is duly transferred, the transferee is called a *bonâ fide* holder, and holds it as an absolute obligation, discharged of all defences to which it may have been liable in the hands of prior parties. Bills of exchange, promissory notes, bank checks, corporate and municipal bonds, certificates of stock and certificates of deposit, transferring to you my interest in a contract as to enable you to sue at law in your own name; but I can so transfer my interest

are negotiable {and by a confusion with the doctrines of symbolic delivery in sales, bills of lading have been called quasi-negotiable}.

When a negotiable instrument is transferred in the manner stated in the text before maturity, the transferee takes absolute title, though it may have been obtained by the transferor by fraud, or though it had been lost and he found it, or though it was stolen. And this is true, although it never became a complete instrument by being delivered by the maker, but was obtained by fraud, or in case it is made payable to bearer, or was indorsed in blank and was lost or stolen before it was made complete by delivery. If it was originally subject to set-off or counter-claim, or was delivered only for a particular purpose and disposed of for other purposes, or delivered as an escrow, or upon condition, and disposed of in disregard of the condition, such transferee holds by absolute title. A *bonâ fide* holder has, as incident to his ownership, the right to confer an absolute title. Hence, one knowing of infirmities in the note, purchasing from a *bonâ fide* holder, takes an absolute title. After maturity the instrument loses its proper negotiability; a purchaser does not get a better title than his assignor had. But one who purchases after maturity from a *bonâ fide* holder takes an indefeasible title. A purchaser after maturity takes the title of his assignor. This prevailing rule has also been held in Ohio — McKesson *v.* Stanberry, 3 Ohio State, 156, although the Ohio statute provides that if any such instrument "be indorsed or delivered after the day on which it is made payable, and the indorsee institute an action thereon against the maker, drawer, or acceptor, the defendant shall be allowed to set up any defence he might have made had the action been instituted in the name and for the use of the person to whom the bond, note, bill, or check was originally made payable." A note due on demand is due at its date; the statute of limitations begins to run at its date. But it is strictly negotiable for a reasonable time after its date.

A sealed instrument, though negotiable in form, is not negotiable at common law or under the statute of Anne: it is made negotiable by statute in Massachusetts, North Carolina, Georgia, Florida, Tennessee, Ohio, Illinois, Kansas, Nebraska, Dakota, and Colorado. The following instruments are not negotiable, but are invalid even in the hands of a *bonâ fide* holder: a forged instrument; one made by a married woman who has no separate estate, or which is not a charge upon her separate estate; accommodation paper made by one of unsound mind, and any paper made by such after inquest of lunacy found, — the law as to other paper made by a lunatic is unsettled; where such paper is held void, it is not negotiable, where it is held only voidable, it is negotiable; paper made void by statute, such as notes or drafts given for gambling debts, — Bayley *v.* Taber, 5 Mass. 286; Vallett *v.* Parker, 6 Wend. 615; Aurora *v.* West, 22 Ind. 88; instruments signed by an infant, or signed by one purporting to be an agent, the signer having in fact no authority; or made by one who, without any negligence on his part, is fraudulently induced to sign in the belief that he is executing an instrument of a wholly different character, as, for example, a power of attorney or contract for service, — De Camp *v.* Hamma, 29 Ohio State, 467; Hubbard *v.* Rankin, 71 Ill. 129; Auten *v.* Gruner, 90 Ill. 300; Anderson *v.* Walker, 34 Mich. 113; Griffith *v.* Kellogg, 39 Wis. 290; Bank *v.* Lierman, 5 Neb. 247; but such maker, though unable to read, must not be chargeable with any negligence in failing to ascertain the character of the paper which he signs — Ross *v.* Doland, 29 Ohio State, 473; Swannell *v.* Watson, 71 Ill. 456; Anderson *v.* Warne, 71 Ill. 20. This rule is not admitted in Indiana. Kimble *v.* Christie, 55 Ind. 140; Bank *v.* Weckerly, 67 Ind. 345. But see Fisher *v.* Van Behren, 70 Ind. 19; Ruddell *v.* Dillman, 73 Ind. 518.

The rule that instruments negotiable in form, purporting to be issued by an agent, are not valid in the hands of a *bonâ fide* holder, if such assumed agent has no authority, applies to municipal bonds. The governing or representative body, the board or officers issuing the bonds is an agent; the people or taxpayers are the principal. A board or officer issuing municipal bonds without authority cannot validate them by subsequent ratification. Marsh *v.* Fulton County, 10 Wall. 676; Gould *v.* Sterling, 23 N. Y. 463; Treadwell *v.* Commissioners, 11 Ohio State, 183; Clark *v.* Des Moines, 19 Ind. 201; Veeder *v.* Lima, 19 Wis. 298. {So of reissued bonds. Bd. of Educ. *v.* Sinton, 40 Ohio State, 504.} But the taxpayers can validate them by laches or conduct which estops them from denying their validity in the hands of a *bonâ fide* holder, as by failing to enjoin their issue — Supervisors *v.* Schenck, 5 Wall. 581; by voting for and submitting to payment of principal or interest — Supervisors *v.* Schenck, 5 Wall. 581; Mercer County *v.* Hubbard, 45 Ill. 142; Shoemaker *v.* Goshen Township, 14 Ohio State, 585; Railroad *v.* Marion County, 36 Mo. 295; or by receiving and keeping the pro-as to enable you to use my name in a suit for your benefit; and the law will protect such a transfer; so that for all substantial

ceeds and benefits of them — Pendleton County *v.* Amy, 13 Wall. 305; State *v.* Van Horne, 7 Ohio State, 331; State *v.* Union Township, 8 Ohio State, 403; Barrett *v.* County Court, 44 Mo. 199.

As to the power of municipal corporations to issue negotiable bonds, it has been held that a municipal corporation has implied power to contract a debt whenever necessary to carry out any power conferred upon it. Lynde *v.* County, 16 Wall. 6. Whenever it may contract a debt it may borrow money to pay it. Lynde *v.* County, 16 Wall. 6; Bank *v.* Chillicothe, 7 Ohio, 2 pt. 31; Galena *v.* Corwith, 48 Ill. 424; Mills *v.* Gleason, 11 Wis. 470. And when it may contract a debt or borrow money, it may issue negotiable bonds for its payment. Commonwealth *v.* Pittsburg, 34 Penn. State, 496; Commonwealth *v.* Pittsburg, 88 Penn. State, 66; Reinbath *v.* Pittsburg, 41 Penn. State, 278; De Voss *v.* Richmond, 18 Gratt. 338; Railroad *v.* Evansville, 15 Ind. 395; Galena *v.* Corwith, 48 Ill. 423; Lynde *v.* County, 16 Wall. 6. In New York it has been held that the implied authority is only to issue bonds directly to the creditor in payment of the debt, not to sell the bonds in order to raise money to pay the debt. Ketchum *v.* Buffalo, 14 N. Y. 256.

A municipal body issuing bonds has ordinarily from the legislature specific authority to issue bonds for a specified purpose, and after compliance with specified conditions; the condition frequently is that the bonds should be voted for by a majority of the qualified voters of the city or county, or should be petitioned for by a specified proportion of the taxpayers. If issued for a purpose other than that authorized, they are invalid in the hands of a *bonâ fide* holder. Marsh *v.* Fulton County, 10 Wall. 676; Lewis *v.* Shreveport, 3 Woods, C. Ct. 205. Where the conditions precedent to the existence of authority are not performed, the bonds are not valid in the hands of a *bona fide* holder. Starin *v.* Genoa, 23 N. Y. 440; Gould *v.* Sterling, 23 N. Y. 456; Treadwell *v.* Commissioners, 11 Ohio State, 183; Middleport *v.* Insurance Co., 82 Ill. 502; Eagle *v.* Cohn, 84 Ill. 292; Wallace *v.* Mayor of San Jose, 29 Cal. 188. But the non-performance must be in matter of substance, not of mere formalities. Supervisors *v.* Galbreath, 99 U. S. 214; Roberts *v.* Bolles, 101 U. S. 119; Smead *v.* Union Township, 8 Ohio State, 394; Mercer County *v.* Hubbard, 45 Ill. 142; Steines *v.* Franklin County, 48 Mo. 179.

The rule as to non-performance of conditions precedent, avoiding municipal bonds in the hands of *bonâ fide* holders, is subject to the following limitations: A *bonâ fide* holder holds the bond free from all infirmities of origin, except want of power in the makers, and prohibited consideration. Cromwell *v.* Sac County, 96 U. S. 51. When the question of performance is by law to be determined by any particular person or body, such determination, though erroneous, binds, and bonds issued in pursuance thereof cannot be questioned in the hands of a *bonâ fide* holder. Commissioners *v.* Aspinwall, 21 How. 539; Kennicott *v.* Supervisors, 16 Wall. 464; St. Joseph Township *v.* Rogers, 16 Wall. 659; Block *v.* Bourbon County, 99 U. S. 686; Bank *v.* Rome, 19 N. Y. 23; Belo *v.* Commissioners, 70 N. Ca. 489; Knox County *v.* Nichols, 14 Ohio State, 271; State *ex rel. v.* Comm'rs, 37 id. 526. Accordingly bonds negotiated after being held valid by the supreme court of the State in which they are issued are not affected by such decision being disapproved and held erroneous by a subsequent decision of the same court, rendered after such negotiation. Douglass *v.* Pike County, 101 U. S. 677. And while a mere recital, in the bond, of the act of the legislature conferring authority is notice to every purchaser to see at his own peril that the requirements of the statute have been complied with — McClure *v.* Oxford, 94 U. S. 429; Silliman *v.* Railroad, 27 Gratt. 119; Aurora *v.* West, 22 Ind. 89; Fisk *v.* Kenocka, 26 Wis. 29; a recital in the bond that all conditions have been performed estops the maker from questioning the validity of the bond in the hands of a *bonâ fide* holder. Town of Coloma *v.* Eaves, 92 U. S. 484; Venice *v.* Murdock, 92 U. S. 494; County of Moultrie *v.* Bank, 92 U. S. 631; Marcy *v.* Oswego, 92 U. S. 637; Wilson *v.* Salamanca, 99 U. S. 499; Pompton *v.* Cooper Union, 101 U. S. 196 {State *ex rel. v.* Bd. of Education, 27 Ohio State, 95; State *ex rel. v.* Comm'rs, 37 id. 526}. A recital, however, that the bond is issued in pursuance of an act of the legislature, does not estop the municipality from contending against a *bonâ fide* holder that the act was not constitutionally passed. South Ottawa *v.* Perkins, 94 U. S. 260. In Illinois, on the contrary, it has been held that recitals in a bond which is issued without authority in fact are no protection to a *bonâ fide* holder. Lippincott *v.* Pana, 92 Ill. 24; Gaddis *v.* Richland County, 92 Ill. 119; People *v.* Jackson County, 92 Ill. 441.

The instrument, to be negotiable, must be payable in money. Gold and silver are purposes, contracts in general are now as much assignable as any other property; and even to this technical prohibition, there is a

the money of the world. U. S. treasury notes are, by law, money in the United States. Bank notes commonly pass current as money. It has been held that the words "current funds" mean money, or funds or notes circulating as money, at par, without any discount; and that evidence will not be admitted to show any other meaning. Marc *v.* Kipper, 34 Ill. 286. "Current money" or "good current money" means money, *i. e.*, legal tender. Wilburn *v.* Greer, 6 Ark. 255; Black *v.* Ward, 27 Mich. 193. Hence it is held in some States that bills and notes payable in "currency," or "current funds," or "current bank notes," being payable in current par paper, the equivalent of money, are negotiable. Pardee *v.* Fish, 60 N. Y. 265; Deberry *v.* Darnell, 5 Yerg. 451; Howe *v.* Hartness, 11 Ohio State, 449 {Swetland *v.* Creigh, 15 Ohio, 118; White *v.* Richmond, 16 id. 5}; Marc *v.* Kipper, 34 Ill. 286; Butler *v.* Paine, 8 Minn. 324; Drake *v.* Markle, 21 Ind. 433; Fry *v.* Dudley, 20 La. An. 368; Mitchell *v.* Hewitt, 5 Smedes & M. 361; Cockrell *v.* Kirkpatrick, 9 Mo. 688. In other States they are not negotiable unless payable in actual money or legal tender. Collins *v.* Lincoln, 11 Vt. 268; Jones *v.* Fales, 4 Mass. 245; McCormick *v.* Trotter, 10 Serg. & R. 94; State *v.* Corpening, 10 Ire. 58; Lange *v.* Kohne, 1 McCord, 115; Warren *v.* Brown, 64 N. C. 381; Simpson *v.* Moulden, 3 Cold. 429; Lampton *v.* Haggard, 3 Munroe, 149; Black *v.* Ward, 27 Mich. 193; Huse *v.* Hamblin, 29 Iowa, 244. If made payable in the bills of a particular bank. Irvine *v.* Lowry, 14 Pet. 293; Hawkins *v.* Watkins, 5 Ark. 481; Shamokin Bank *v.* Street, 16 Ohio State, 1. In England, bills and notes payable in notes of the Bank of England are not negotiable. *Ex parte* Iveson, 2 Rose, 225; *Ex parte* Davison, Buck, 31.

The addition of the words "with current exchange" does not affect the negotiability of the instrument. Hill *v.* Tod, 29 Ill. 101; Bullock *v.* Taylor, 39 Mich. 137; Leggett *v.* Jones, 10 Wis. 34.

A promissory note must contain a promise to pay. A mere acknowledgment of indebtedness is not a negotiable instrument, though the law implies therefrom a promise. The instrument must contain either an express promise or words which amount in legal effect to a promise. A form in common use in England, "I. O. U. £110," is not a promissory note. A mere due-bill, "Due A. B. $100," has been held to be negotiable. Jacquin *v.* Warren, 40 Ill. 459; Brady *v.* Chandler, 31 Mo. 28; Kimball *v.* Huntington, 10 Wend. 675; Lowe *v.* Murphy, 9 Ga. 338. The contrary has been held. Currier *v.* Lockwood, 40 Conn. 348; Read *v.* Wheeler, 2 Yerg. 50. If in the form "Due A. B. or bearer," "Due A. B. or order," "Due A. B. on demand," it is without contest, negotiable. {A certificate of deposit is negotiable. Miller *v.* Austen, 13 How. 218.}

The engagement to pay must be absolute. Hence, if the instrument is payable only out of a particular fund, it is not negotiable. Read *v.* Buffalo, 67 N. Y. 526. But if the engagement is absolute, the appropriation of a particular fund to the payment, or the recital that the maker has deposited securities upon certain conditions as collateral, does not affect the negotiability. Littlefield *v.* Hodge, 6 Mich. 326; Towne *v.* Rice, 122 Mass. 67. If payable "when A. shall come of age," it is not negotiable, for A. may die a minor. Kelley *v.* Hemingway, 13 Ill. 604. But if payable "on demand after my decease" — Bristol *v.* Warner, 19 Conn. 7; or "one day after date or at my decease" — Conn *v.* Thornton, 46 Ala. 588, it is negotiable, for death is certain. So, if it is to be paid "in the course of the coming season." Cota *v.* Buck, 7 Metc. (Mass.) 588. {But not if it is to be paid "on settlement of canal operations." Weidler *v.* Kauffman, 14 Ohio, 455.} A note to be paid "by 20th May, or when he completes the building according to contract," is held to be payable on or before the 20th May, and therefore negotiable. {Stevens *v.* Blunt, 7 Mass. 240; Goodloe *v.* Taylor, 3 Hawks, 458. A note payable "on or before" a date is negotiable. Jordan *v.* Tate, 19 Ohio State, 586; Ackley School Distr. *v.* Hall, 113 U. S. 135; Charlton *v.* Reed, 61 Iowa, 166.}

Various stipulations or recitals are sometimes incorporated with bills and notes. The question is then presented, are such stipulations or recitals independent, leaving the separate engagement to pay money absolute, and therefore negotiable; or are they inseparable, making the engagement to pay conditional or uncertain, and therefore not negotiable? A stipulation that if the bill or note be not paid at maturity, or be sued, the obligor will pay to the holder a collection fee or attorney's fee, has been held to be an independent agreement, not affecting the negotiability of the instrument. Dietrich *v.* Bayhi, 23 La. An. 767; Gaar *v.* Louisville B. Co., 11 Bush, 180; Stoneman *v.* Pyle, 35 Ind. 103; Nickerson *v.* Sheldon, 33 Ill. 373; Bullock *v.* Taylor, 39 Mich.

class of contracts denominated *negotiable*, which have always formed an exception; it being the very essence of these contracts

137; Sperry *v.* Horr, 32 Iowa, 184; Seaton *v.* Scoville, 18 Kansas, 433; Heard *v.* Bank, 8 Neb. 10; Trader *v.* Chidester, 41 Ark. 242. In other States it is held that such a stipulation makes the instrument non-negotiable. Woods *v.* North, 84 Penn. State, 407; Bank *v.* Gay, 63 Mo. 33. {Some States allow a reasonable attorney's fee to be stipulated for in a note in case of litigation, as Illinois, Indiana, Oregon, Pennsylvania, Tennessee, Texas. Clawson *v.* Munson, 55 Ill. 394; Smith *v.* Silver, 32 Ind. 321. *Contra*, by statute in 1875. Nelson *v.* White, 61 Ind. 139; Peyser *v.* Cole, 11 Or. 39; McIntire *v.* Cayley, 37 Iowa, 676; Imler *v.* Imler, 94 Penn. State, 372; Minor *v.* Paris Exchange Bank, 53 Texas, 559; Parham *v.* Pulliam, 5 Coldw. 407. While other States regard it as usurious and void, as Arkansas, Ohio, Kentucky, Michigan, Nebraska. State *v.* Taylor, 10 Ohio, 378; Shelton *v.* Gill, 11 id. 417; Martin *v.* Bank, 13 id. 250; Witherspoon *v.* Musselman, 14 Bush, 214; Myer *v.* Hart, 40 Mich. 517; Dow *v.* Updike, 11 Nebr. 95; Boozer *v.* Anderson, 42 Ark. 167.}

A note with a power of attorney to confess judgment is held in Pennsylvania not to be negotiable. Sweeney *v.* Thickstun, 77 Penn. State, 131. In Ohio it is negotiable. Osborn *v.* Hawley, 19 Ohio, 130. A power of attorney is not a negotiable instrument; hence, if the power is simply to confess judgment in favor of the payee, it does not enure to the benefit of an indorsee. Osborn *v.* Hawley. But if made "in favor of the holder of the note," it is valid in accordance with its terms, for the benefit of every holder. Clements *v.* Hull, 35 Ohio State, 141.

The negotiability of a note is not affected by a recital therein that it is given in payment of specified property — Collins *v.* Bradbury, 64 Maine, 37; nor by the additional recital that a lien is reserved on the property — Duncan *v.* Louisville, 13 Bush, 378; or that the maker has deposited certificates upon certain conditions as collateral; or that the thing sold is also warranted — Mitchell *v.* McCabe, 10 Ohio, 405.

A note payable on its return to the maker is negotiable. Frank *v.* Wessel, 64 N. Y. 155. But if payable on the return of it and also of other independent writings, it is not. Smilie *v.* Stevens, 39 Vt. 316.

A negotiable instrument altered in any material particular becomes a different contract from the one which the obligor made, and is nullified and destroyed as a legal obligation. In England, the consequence is the same whether the change is made by a party to the instrument or by a stranger. Davidson *v.* Cooper, 13 M. & W. 778. In the United States, when the change is made by a stranger to the instrument, it is called a spoliation, has no more effect than an accidental obliteration, and does not affect the validity of the instrument in the hands of a *bonâ fide* holder, if the instrument in its original form can be discerned and identified. Fullerton *v.* Sturges, 4 Ohio State, 529; Bigelow *v.* Stephen, 35 Vt. 521; Ford *v.* Ford, 17 Pick. 418; Davis *v.* Carlisle, 5 Ala. 707; Crocket *v.* Thomason, 5 Sneed, 342; Lee *v.* Alexander, 9 B. Monroe, 25; Cochran *v.* Nebeker, 48 Ind. 459; Vogle *v.* Ripper, 34 Ill. 106; Lubbering *v.* Kohlbrecker, 22 Mo. 596; Bank *v.* Roberts, 45 Wis. 373. {An alteration by one of two joint payees avoids it as to both. Thompson *v.* Massie, 41 Ohio State, 307. An alteration to conform to a previous agreement is harmless. Wardlow *v.* List, 41 Ohio State, 414. In some States any intentional alteration is fatal; for it destroys the identity of the paper. In others the alteration must be material to avoid it; thus adding a guaranty to a note is not material to the maker's obligation. Deming *v.* Trustees, 31 Ohio State, 41. *Contra*, of change in the rate of interest. Harsh *v.* Klepper, 28 id. 200. Or adding a place of payment. Sturges *v.* Williams, 9 id. 443.} If the alteration, by a party, is fraudulent, not only is the instrument destroyed, but the debt for which it was given is extinguished. Wheelock *v.* Freeman, 13 Pick. 165. {The ignorance of the payee that the maker has altered the note will not save it as against the surety. Jones *v.* Bangs, 40 Ohio State, 139; Wood *v.* Steele, 6 Wall. 80.} If the alteration is innocent, the instrument only is destroyed; the indebtedness for which it was given can still be recovered. Clute *v.* Small, 17 Wend. 242; Merrick *v.* Boury, 4 Ohio State, 60; Clough *v.* Seay, 49 Iowa, 111; Matteson *v.* Ellsworth, 33 Wis. 488. A note which has been altered and then restored to its original form, in which condition it passes into the hands of a *bonâ fide* holder, is valid in the hands of such holder. Shepherd *v.* Whetstone, 51 Iowa, 457. When the drawer or maker is guilty of contributory negligence, as where he leaves a blank which is subsequently filled so skilfully as not to excite suspicion, or writes a stipulation in pencil, which is rubbed out, or on the margin, which is cut off, so that the suspicions of a prudent man would not be aroused, the instrument in its altered form is valid in the hands of a *bonâ fide* holder. Zimmerthat they can be transferred absolutely from hand to hand, so as to authorize the holder to sue at law in his own name.

man *v.* Rote, 75 Penn. State, 188 ; Seibel *v.* Vaughan, 69 Ill. 257 ; Bank *v.* Armstrong, 62 Mo. 59 ; Vischer *v.* Webster, 8 Cal. 109 ; Holland *v.* Hatch, 15 Ohio State, 464. But the contrary has been held in Kitchen *v.* Place, 41 Barb. 465 ; Bank *v.* Clark, 51 Iowa, 264.

A stranger to the instrument, who indorses in blank before the payee, is, in most of the States, *primâ facie* a joint maker ; in Ohio and Illinois if he is not in the chain of title he is *primâ facie* a guarantor {but on proof that he signed before the delivery to the payee, he is chargeable as joint maker. Seymour *v.* Mickey, 15 Ohio State, 515, and cases cited ; and Church *v.* Swope, 38 id. 493} ; Parkhurst *v.* Vail, 73 Ill. 343 ; Boynton *v.* Price, 79 Ill. 145 ; in Indiana he is *primâ facie* indorser — Browning *v.* Merritt, 61 Ind. 425. If the evidence simply shows that such indorsement was made at the time of the execution of the note, or before delivery to the payee, he is held to be a joint maker. As between such person and the payee, it is competent to show by parol evidence just what the understanding of the parties was, and fix the consequent liability as maker, or guarantor, or indorser. In New York and Pennsylvania such person is an indorser. Phelps *v.* Vischer, 50 N. Y. 69 ; Shafer *v.* Bank, 59 Penn. State, 144. This whole topic of blank indorsement before the payee is fully discussed in Good *v.* Martin, 95 U. S. 90.

A guarantor differs from a surety. A surety is, along with his principal, an original and primary debtor ; his liability is not affected by notice being given or not given of his principal's default, or by demand being made or not made upon the principal. The liability of a guarantor is collateral, and he may be discharged by the creditor's failure to make demand on the principal or give notice of his default to the guarantor. The guarantor differs from an indorser. The indorser's liability is conditional ; he is entirely discharged unless demand and notice be promptly and strictly given ; or, rather, he does not become liable except upon such prompt and strict demand and notice. The guarantor is entitled only to reasonable demand and notice, and is discharged only so far as he is damaged by the creditor's delay.

Negotiable paper payable to order could be assigned at common law and under the statute of Anne only by indorsement. But an assignee without indorsement was recognized as owner in equity ; and, all titles that were valid in equity being valid under the code, such assignee is owner, and can sue in his own name in States that have adopted the code of civil procedure. But such assignee, having not the legal title, but only an equitable title, he holds the paper subject to the equities between the original parties which grow out of the transaction in which the instrument was given. And this rule is the same whether the note is negotiable or non-negotiable. Eversole *v.* Maule, 50 Md. 95 ; Reddish *v.* Ritchie, 17 Fla. 867 ; Garratt *v.* Jaffray, 10 Bush, 413 ; Combes *v.* Chandler, 33 Ohio State, 178 ; Thompson *v.* Shoemaker, 68 Ill. 256 ; Patterson *v.* Cave, 61 Mo. 439 ; Hayward *v.* Stearns, 39 Cal. 58. {But there are only such equities as inhere in the paper, and not independent claims such as set-off and the like. See Knisely *v.* Evans, 34 Ohio State, 158.} If the instrument is negotiable, and has come into the hands of a *bonâ fide* indorsee so as to be discharged of equities, the assignee, without indorsement of such indorsee, would also undoubtedly hold it discharged of equities.

A *bonâ fide* indorsee must be a purchaser in good faith, in the ordinary course of business, and for value. This was the rule from the first. In 1824 Lord Tenterden pronounced the judgment of the Court of Common Pleas, that in the case of a lost or stolen bill or note, although the holder had given value for it, yet, if he took it under circumstances which ought to have excited the suspicions of a prudent man, he could not recover. Gill *v.* Cubitt, 3 Barn. & Cress. 466. The effect of this ruling was to discredit English paper on the Continent. Twelve years later the Court of King's Bench restored the old rule, holding that gross negligence alone would not defeat the title of the holder ; gross negligence sometimes being proof of, or tending to prove, *mala fides*, but not being the same thing. Goodman *v.* Harvey, 4 Ad. & El. 870. The rule as restored in Goodman *v.* Harvey remains, without question, the rule in England. For a time, Gill *v.* Cubitt was accepted as authority in the United States, and was followed in a number of the States, but the rule as restored in Goodman *v.* Harvey now prevails. Farrell *v.* Lovett, 68 Me. 326 ; Bank *v.* Savery, 127 Mass. 75 ; Insurance Co. *v.* Hachfield, 73 N. Y. 226 ; Hamilton *v.* Vought, 34 N. J. Law, 187 ; Battles *v.* Laudenslager, 84 Penn. State, 446 ; Bank *v.* Hooper, 47 Md. 88 ; Matthews *v.* Poythress, 4 Ga. 287 ; Johnson *v.* Way, 27 Ohio State, 374 ; Shreeves *v.* Allen, 79 Ill. 553 ; Hamilton *v.* Marks, 63 Mo. 167 ; Helbrun *v.* Krolick, 36 Mich. 371 ; Pond *v.*

Requisites of Negotiability. Negotiable contracts were introduced in modern times for the benefit of commercial intercourse.

Agricultural Works, 50 Iowa, 596; Murray *v.* Lardner, 2 Wall. 710; Collins *v.* Gilbert, 94 U. S. 753.

In order to be a purchaser for value, it is of course not necessary to pay the face of the note or bill. A purchase of a note secured by mortgage for half its face — Baily *v.* Smith, 14 Ohio State, 402, and the purchase of the unsecured note of a maker known to be solvent for less than half — Phelan *v.* Moss, 67 Penn. State, 59, have been held to constitute the purchaser a *bonâ fide* holder. Any amount, indeed, seems to be sufficient, unless it is so inconsiderable as to be evidence of bad faith, evidence that the purchaser must have known of the existing infirmities in the instrument. {Tod *v.* Wick, 36 Ohio State, 370; Rooker *v.* Rooker, 29 id. 1.} Whether or not it is such evidence is a question for the jury.

Chancellor Kent, in Bay *v.* Coddington, 5 Johns. Ch. 54, held that an indorsee who took the indorsed paper only as security for a precedent debt was not a *bonâ fide* holder. This decision was affirmed by the Court of Errors in Coddington *v.* Bay, 20 Johns. 637. The Supreme Court of the United States, in Swift *v.* Tyson, 16 Pet. 1, declared that taking negotiable paper in payment of, or as collateral security for, a precedent debt, is taking it for value and in due course of trade, and such indorsee, acting in good faith, is a *bona fide* holder. The Court of Errors of New York subsequently, in Stalker *v.* McDonald, 6 Hill, 93, criticised the reasoning in Swift *v.* Tyson, and reaffirmed Coddington *v.* Bay. It would be a vain labor to assort the countless decisions in the United States bearing upon this vexed question. To a certain extent, there is now a general accord. The fact seems to be, as stated by Justice Harlan in Railroad Co. *v.* Bank, 102 U. S. 14, see p. 25, that, in the absence of statute to the contrary, "where negotiable paper is received in payment of an antecedent debt, or where it is transferred by indorsement as collateral security for a debt created, or a purchase made, at the time of the transfer; or the transfer is to secure a debt not due, under an agreement, express or to be clearly implied from the circumstances, that the collection of the principal debt is to be postponed or delayed until the collateral matures; or where time is agreed to be given, and is actually given, upon a debt overdue, in consideration of the transfer of negotiable paper as collateral security therefor; or where the transferred debt takes the place of other paper previously pledged as collateral security for a debt, either at the time such debt was contracted or before it became due, — in each of these cases the holder who takes the transferred paper, before its maturity, and without notice, actual or otherwise, of any defence thereto, is held to have received it in due course of business, and, in the sense of the commercial law, becomes a holder for value." "Upon these propositions there seems at this day to be no substantial conflict of authority." The courts of New York, however, still dissent as to one of the above clauses. "A mere receipt of a bill or note *in payment of*, or as security for, an antecedent debt, has never, in this State, been held sufficient to protect the title of the holder as against the equities of third persons; and some new credit must be given, new advance made, or some prior security parted with, or a debt absolutely satisfied and extinguished, in order to complete the title of the holder." Weaver *v.* Barden, 49 N. Y. 286, see p. 294; Turner, Adm'x *v.* Treadway, 53 N. Y. 650; Moore *v.* Rider, 65 N. Y. 438. A note taken in payment of a simple-contract debt, no securities being surrendered, is subject to equities. Turner *v.* Treadway, 56 How. Pr. R. 56.

The rule in Ohio is, "When a debt is created without any stipulation for further security, and the debtor afterward, without any obligation to do so, voluntarily transfers a negotiable instrument to secure the pre-existent debt, and both parties are left in respect to the pre-existent debt *in statu quo*, no new consideration, stipulation for delay, or credit being given, or right parted with, by the creditor, he is not a holder of the collateral for value in the usual course of trade, and receives it subject to all the equities existing against it at the time of the transfer." Roxborough *v.* Messick, 6 Ohio State, 448. This rule prevails in New York, as seen by the cases above cited, and in some other States. Nutter *v.* Stover, 48 Me. 163; Rice *v.* Riatt, 17 N. H. 116; Royer *v.* Bank, 83 Penn. State, 248; Fenouille *v.* Hamilton, 35 Ala. 319; Bowman *v.* Van Kuren, 29 Wis. 220; Craighead *v.* Wells, 8 Baxter, 38; and see Tyrrell *v.* Railroad Co., 7 Mo. App. 294. The Supreme Court of the United States holds that even in the case described in Roxborough *v.* Messick, the transfer is in the due course of trade, and the assumption of responsibility by the indorsee by the mere fact of the indorsement is sufficient consideration, and such indorsee holds the instrument discharged of equities. Railroad Company *v.* National Bank, 102 U. S. 14. The rule as

They are designed to circulate readily from hand to hand, and thus multiply the facilities of traffic and credit; and in order to answer this purpose, they must evidently carry upon their face all the means of determining their worth. Accordingly, the following properties are requisite to render a contract negotiable; *first*, it must be in writing; *secondly*, it must be for the payment of money only, and not for other property; *thirdly*, it must be for the payment of a sum certain, and not for unliquidated damages: *fourthly*, the sum promised must be payable absolutely, and without conditions; *fifthly*, the contract must contain words of negotiability, as "*to order*," "*to assigns*," or "*to bearer;*" and *sixthly*, it must import a *consideration*, so as to preclude the necessity of inquiry and proof. A contract possessing these properties is fitted for negotiation, since it is liable to no other question than what relates to the responsibility of the parties.

Mode of Transfer. The transfer is effected in two ways: *first*, where the contract is payable "to order," or "to assigns," it is negotiable by *indorsement:* that is, by writing upon the back; and *secondly*, where it is payable "to bearer," it is negotiable by mere *delivery*, without writing. (*a*) Indorsements are of two kinds: *first*, a *blank indorsement*, where the holder simply writes his name, without any other words, which is equivalent to an order to pay to bearer, for it thenceforth passes by mere delivery; and any subsequent holder may fill up the indorsement so as to make the contract payable to himself; and *secondly*, a *special indorsement*, which specifies the person to whom the contract is transferred. If it be indorsed to him or his order, he can only transfer it by another indorsement. But the indorsement does not require negotiable words. The first indorser may stop the negotiability by expressing that intention; as by indorsing to one person *only*, to one person and *no other*, and the like; but in the absence of such restrictive words, the negotiability remains; and it is said that none but the indorser can, even by express words, restrict the negotiability. (*b*)

laid down by the Supreme Court of the United States is also the rule in England — Poirier *v.* Morris, 2 El. & Bl. 89; Currie *v.* Misa, L. R. 10 Ex. 153; and in many of the States, Fisher *v.* Fisher, 98 Mass. 303; Osgood *v.* Bank, 30 Conn. 27; Cobb *v.* Doyle, 7 R. I. 550; Straughan *v.* Fairchild, S. C. Ind. Apl. 1882; Morris *v.* Preston, 93 Ill. 215. The Supreme Court of Ohio declines to follow Railroad Co. *v.* National Bank, 102 U. S. 14; Pitts *v.* Foglesong, 37 Ohio State, 676.

An indorsee who, taking negotiable paper as collateral security, is held to take subject to equities between the original parties, still has legal title to the paper, and can recover against an accommodation indorser who indorsed without restriction as to the use to be made of the paper. Grocers' Bank *v.* Penfield, 69 N. Y. 502; Lord *v.* Ocean Bank, 20 Penn. State, 384; Pitts *v.* Foglesong, 37 Ohio State, 676.

(*a*) Under the Ohio statute, it is held that a promissory note, payable to a person or bearer, is negotiable by delivery, and a sealed bill or note in the same form is only negotiable by indorsement. Avery *v.* Sawyer, 14 Ohio, 542; Osborn *v.* Kistler, 35 Ohio State, 99.

(*b*) {That a blank indorsement by a party to the paper is a written contract, the terms of which are supplied by the law, and cannot be varied by parol, was held in Martin *v.* Cole, 104 U. S. 30; Daniel on Neg. Instr. 707, but such is not the rule in Ohio. Bailey *v.* Stoneman, 41 Ohio State, 145; Hudson *v.* Wolcott, 39 id. 618; and

What Contracts are Negotiable. At common law, *bills of exchange* were the only negotiable contracts; by the statute of Anne, *promissory notes* were placed upon the same footing; and by our statute, *bills, notes,* and *bonds* are made equally negotiable; (*a*) but this statute does not vary the requisites of negotiability before enumerated; indeed it is sufficient, so far as negotiability is concerned, to consider all negotiable instruments as divided into two classes, *orders* and *promises:* for a bill of exchange is a *written order* for the payment of money; which definition equally embraces *checks, drafts,* and *orders* commonly so called: and a promissory note is a *written promise* for the payment of money, which definition equally embraces promises under seal, whether denominated *bonds* or *single bills.* The parties are thus designated. In a bill, the person who makes the order is called a *drawer:* the person in whose favor it is made, the *payee:* and the person to whom the order is addressed, the *drawee,* and after acceptance, the *acceptor.* In a note, the person who makes the promise is called the *maker;* and the person to whom it is made, the *payee.* When the payee, either of a bill or note, has indorsed it to a third person, it is then said to be *negotiated.* He becomes the indorser, and the person to whom it is transferred, the *indorsee.* He may in his turn become the indorser, and so on indefinitely. The person having a right to the bill or note at any particular time is called the *holder.*

Common form of Notes and Bills. No set form of words is necessary, either for a note or bill. (*b*) It is usual and expedient to begin with naming the *place* and *date,* but not indispensable; since these may be proved by parol. The bill then proceeds substantially in a form like this: "*Three months after date, pay to the order of C. one thousand dollars for value received.*" This is signed by B., the drawer, and addressed to A., the drawee; who accepts, by writing the word "*accepted*" on the face, and signing his name. A note usually proceeds thus: "*Three months after date I promise to pay to the order of B. one thousand dollars for value received.*" This is signed by A., the maker; and thus far we perceive little resemblance between the two; but when B., the payee of the note, has indorsed it to a third person, thus: "*Pay to the order of C.,*" the resemblance is complete; for the note is

see Robinson *v.* Abell, 17 Ohio, 36. But contemporaneous writings may be used to qualify an indorsement as between parties having notice of them. Davis *v.* Brown, 94 U. S. 127.}

(*a*) {Overdue coupons detached from a municipal bond not matured, are negotiable. Thompson *v.* Perrine, 106 U. S. 589. The orders of a municipal officer or the municipal treasurer are not negotiable instruments. McCortle *v.* Bates, 29 Ohio State, 419, 421; State *ex rel. v.* Liberty Township, 22 id. 144.}

(*b*) As to the words which will constitute a bill or note, see cases cited in 1 Am. Leading Cases, 312–27; Weidler *v.* Kauffman, 14 Ohio, 455; Mitchell *v.* McCabe, 10 id. 405; Moore *v.* Gano, 12 id. 300; Osborne *v.* Hawley, 19 id. 130; Jury *v.* Barker, 1 Ellis, B. & E. 459; Watson *v.* Evans, 1 Hurl. & Colt. 662; Ives *v.* Farmers' Bank, 2 Allen, 236; Arnold *v.* Sprague, 34 Vt. 402; Carver *v.* Hayes, 47 Maine, 257; Yates *v.* Nash, 8 C. B. (N. S.) 581.

then converted into a bill. B., the indorser of the note, corresponds to B., the drawer of the bill; A., the maker of the note, to A., the acceptor of the bill; and C., the holder of the note, to C., the holder of the bill. Their liabilities, too, are identical. In both cases, A. is the party first liable to the holder, and B. undertakes to pay if A. does not, upon due notice of the *dishonor.* The words "*for value received*" are above inserted, because they are customary: but they are never indispensable. (*a*) If present, they do not prevent the denial of a consideration, as between the original parties; and if wanting, the consideration cannot be denied after negotiation, except it be for gaming. The *time of payment*, which is called the *maturity*, is, in the above examples, a given time *after date.* It may, however, be *on demand*, or a given time *after sight.* In the former case, the demand may be made at any time; and this determines the maturity: (*b*) in the latter, which applies to bills only, *sight* means *presentation for acceptance.* In this case, the acceptor dates his acceptance, and this determines the maturity. As bills are usually drawn upon some distant place to which they are transmitted for acceptance, to guard against accident or miscarriage, it is common to draw two or three on the same account, which constitute a *set.* In this case, the first is specified to be payable, "*the second and third of the same tenor and date being unpaid;*" and in like manner the rest, so that the payment of the one which first arrives makes the rest void. It is not necessary to specify the particular *place of payment;* but when this is done, it becomes a part of the description of the bill or note; and although no demand need be made there, in order to charge the acceptor or maker, yet if he had the money there, he is not in default, and cannot be subjected to costs. (*c*)

(*a*) In the making and indorsement of negotiable bills and notes, the consideration is implied by law, even when not expressed. Swift *v.* Tyson, 16 Peters, 1; Benjamin *v.* Tillman, 2 M'Lean, 213; Jennison *v.* Stafford, 1 Cush. 168 {Dean *v.* Caruth, 108 Mass. 244. Though non-negotiable. Dugan *v.* Campbell, 1 Ohio, 115.} *Aliter*, in Connecticut, if the note is not negotiable. Bristol *v.* Warner, 19 Conn. 7. And in Ohio, where the note contracts for the delivery of specific articles. Niswanger *v.* Staley, 8 West. Law Jour. 493.

(*b*) As to the time within which notes and bills, payable on demand, must be indorsed, so as to shut out equities between the maker and indorser, 1 Parsons on Contracts, 217; as to the time of their presentment so as to charge the indorser, id. 221; Chitty on Bills, 377; Harker *v.* Anderson, 21 Wendell, 372; Seaver *v.* Lincoln, 21 Pick. 267. A promise to pay when the maker can make it convenient, with interest from date, is a valid promise to pay in a reasonable time. Lewis *v.* Tipton, 10 Ohio State, 88. A note specifying no time for payment is, in legal effect, payable immediately, although it stipulates that interest is to be paid annually. Jones *v.* Brown, 11 Ohio State, 601. {In a series of notes maturing successively, with an independent stipulation that all shall fall due on failure to pay any one, those not due except for the stipulation are for purposes of demand and notice deemed due irrespective of the stipulation. McClelland *v.* Bishop, 42 Ohio State, 113.}

(*c*) In this country, contrary to the decision of the House of Lords in England, in Rowe *v.* Young, 2 Brod. & Bing. 180, a demand at the place named is not a condition precedent to a suit against the maker or acceptor. It is, however, necessary in order to hold the indorser, and if the maker or acceptor was there at the time with his money, he will be exonerated from costs and damages. United States Bank *v.* Smith, 11 Wheaton, 171; Wallace *v.* M'Connell, 13 Peters, 137; Hartwell *v.* Candler, 5 Blackf. 215; Conn *v.* Gano, 1 Ohio, 483; Armistead *v.* Armistead, 10 Leigh, 512; Cook *v.*

A bill or note may be filled up over a signature *in blank* left for that purpose; and if a blank be left for the payee's name, any rightful holder may insert his own name, (*a*) but a bill or note payable to one or two persons or order, would be void for uncertainty. It is sufficient, however, to make it payable *to bearer*, without specifying any name, and if the payee be a fictitious person, and his name purport to be indorsed, it may be treated as payable to bearer. A subscribing witness is never indispensable, unless by special provision, and sometimes creates inconvenience; because, in proving the execution, such witness must be produced, or his absence accounted for. Where several persons unite in a note, it may be *joint* only, or *joint and several.* If they simply say, "*we promise*," or "*we jointly promise*," it is a joint liability only, and all must be sued; but if they say, "*we or either of us promise*," or "*we jointly and severally promise*," the liability is both joint and several, and either or all may be sued. It has also been held that when a note says, "*I promise*," but is signed by two or more, they are severally liable. (*b*)

Acceptance. (*c*) This is to be considered with reference to bills only; for notes, as we have seen, are accepted in the act of making, and before the indorsement which converts them into bills. The holder of a bill is required to present it to the drawee for acceptance. If payable at a given time after date, it need not be presented until maturity; if payable at sight, or a given time after, it must be presented within a *reasonable time;* for the

Martin, 5 S. & M. 379; Fitler *v.* Beckley, 2 W. & S. 458; Green *v.* Goings, 7 Barb. 653; Otis *v.* Barton, 10 N. H. 438; Payson *v.* Whitcomb, 15 Pick. 212; Hills *v.* Place, 48 N. Y. 520.

(*a*) One who intrusts his name in blank to another to procure a discount is liable to the full extent to which that other may see fit to bind him where the paper is taken in good faith without notice that the authority has been exceeded. Fullerton *v.* Sturges, 4 Ohio State, 529; Schryver *v.* Hawkes, 22 Ohio State, 308; Van Duzer *v.* Howe, 21 N. Y. 531; Mich. Ins. Co. *v.* Leavenworth, 30 Vt. 11; Michigan Bank *v.* Eldridge, 9 Wall. 544; McDonald *v.* Muscatine National Bank, 27 Iowa, 319; Smith *v.* Lockridge, 8 Bush (Ky.), 423.

(*b*) {Hance *v.* Hair, 25 Ohio State, 349; First Natl. Bank *v.* Fowler, 36 Ohio State, 524.} A material alteration in the note by the party holding it, which changes its meaning or legal operation, vitiates it. Huntington *v.* McIntyre, 3 Ohio State, 445; Sturges *v.* Williams, 9 id. 443. As to what is a material alteration, see Boalt *v.* Brown, 13 Ohio State, 364; Holland *v.* Hatch, 15 Ohio State, 464. Patterson *v.* McNeely, 16 Ohio State, 348; Derby *v.* Thrall, 44 Vt. 413. Adding a third person as joint maker is a material alteration. But if he signs in such a place as would, unexplained, make him a joint maker by mistake, not intending to become so, this fact may be shown. Wallace *v.* Jewell, 21 Ohio State, 163. {Adding a surety does not discharge the maker. Mersman *v.* Werges, 112 U. S. 139.} When it was not received in payment of a precedent debt, and was materially altered by the holder, but without any fraudulent intent, he may recover upon the original cause of action. Merrick *v.* Boury, 4 Ohio State, 60. An alteration, though material, made without a fraudulent intent, but under a mistake of facts, though it avoids the note, will leave the original liability of the parties untouched. Louis *v.* Schenck, 3 Green (N. J.), 459. An alteration by a third person without the privity of the party claiming rights under it will not prejudice him. Fullerton *v.* Sturges, 4 Ohio State, 529.

(*c*) 3 Kent, Com. 82–8. When a promise to accept amounts to an acceptance, see Lonsdale *v.* Lafayette Bank, 18 Ohio, 126; Sherwin *v.* Brigham, 39 Ohio State, 137. As to parol acceptances, see Spaulding *v.* Andrews, 48 Penn. State, 411; Arnold *v.* Sprague, 24 Vt. 402.

drawer does not undertake to be liable for ever; and what is a reasonable time will depend upon circumstances, among which the distance, the custom of trade, and the fact of being kept in circulation, are the most important. If the drawee have a place of business, the presentment must be made there; if not, at his residence; and if that cannot be found, diligent inquiry must be made. If the drawee be dead, the presentment is made to his representatives. The acceptance may be oral, but is usually in writing. A promise to accept will be equivalent to an acceptance, if it has given credit to the bill; and an acceptance has been implied from the conduct of the drawee. The holder is not bound to take a qualified acceptance, as for part only, or for a different time, or for some contingency, and if he consents so to do, he discharges the drawer. (*a*)

Protest and Notice. If the bill be not accepted, the next step is to have it protested for *non-acceptance;* at least this is the law in England and in most of the States. In some States, however, it has been held not to be necessary to protest for *non-acceptance*, but only for *non-payment.* In this State, nothing has been decided; but our statute regulating damages on protested bills, recognizes a protest for non-acceptance, and it would not be safe to dispense with it. The protest is made by a *notary public*, (*b*) an officer recognized in all commercial nations. In this State, he is appointed by the governor for three years, and is under official bond and oath. His notarial acts are verified by his *official seal.* The statute declares that due faith and credit shall be given to his protestations, attestations, and other instruments of publication. At present, however, we are concerned only with his agency in protesting bills. His protest is an official declaration under seal, of the fact of presentation and refusal; and is everywhere received as *primâ facie* evidence thereof, to save the trouble of

(*a*) But when a bill is addressed to a drawee at a place generally, he may accept it, payable at a particular place, and presentment for payment may be made at that place without notice to, or the assent of, the drawer, and will be sufficient to bind him. Myers *v.* Standart, 11 Ohio State, 29.

(*b*) See Brooke's Treatise on the Office and Practice of a Notary; also Roelker's Manual for Notaries Public, recently issued. See act concerning Notaries Public and Commissioners, of March 13, 1858. A protest is evidence only of the facts it recites. Bradshaw *v.* Hedge, 10 Iowa, 402; Dunn *v.* Devlin, 2 Daly, 122. But it is not evidence of facts recited in it unnecessarily, such as a statement of the drawee that he had no funds. Dakin *v.* Greaves, 48 N. H. 45. A waiver of protest before maturity dispenses with demand and notice. A promise to pay, after maturity, with knowledge that demand had not been made or notice given, is also a waiver. Ligerson *v.* Matthews, 20 Howard, 476; Edwards *v.* Tandy, 30 N. H. 540; Blodgell *v.* Davis, 32 Vt. 361; Loose *v.* Loose, 36 Penn. State, 528; see Hudson *v.* Wolcott, 39 Ohio State, 618. But a promise to pay made under the belief that a demand was made, is not binding. Arnold *v.* Dresser, 8 Allen, 435. But where an indorser, not knowing whether demand has been made or not, writes to the holder promising to pay, this is a waiver, though without reference to the latter, and before its receipt the holder had failed to make demand and give notice. Yeager *v.* Farwell, 13 Wall. 6. And see Cordery *v.* Colvin, 14 C. B. (N. S.) 574. Where a waiver of protest is contained in the face of a bill, it is part of the contract, and binds the indorsers. Bryant *v.* The Merchants' Bank, 8 Bush, 59; Lowry *v.* Steele, 27 Ind. 168; Carran *v.* Little, 40 Ohio State, 397.

taking other testimony. The next step is to *notify* the drawer and indorsers in order to fix their liability; since they impliedly engage to pay only in case of failure by the drawee, and due notice thereof. The notice must be given in a reasonable time, which is a mixed question of law and fact. The rule is, that notice must be sent by the first regular conveyance, by mail or otherwise. If it be put in the post-office properly directed, this is sufficient. The same remarks apply to the presentation for payment, protest for non-payment, and notice thereof; and need not therefore be repeated. (*a*) But a protest is only required in case

(*a*) As a general rule the bill or note must be presented on the last day of grace during customary business hours. If the last day of grace falls on Sunday, or some public holiday, it must be presented the day before. If there are no days of grace, and the day of payment falls on Sunday, or some public holiday, the presentment must be on the day following. Piatt *v.* Eades, 1 Blackf. 81; Farmers' Bank of Maryland *v.* Duvall, 7 G. & J. 79; Salter *v.* Burt, 20 Wendell, 205; Sheldon *v.* Benham, 4 Hill, 129; Montgomery Co. Bank *v.* Albany City Bank, 8 Barb. 397; Bank of Vergennes *v.* Cameron, 7 id. 143; Dana *v.* Sawyer, 22 Maine, 244; Lunt *v.* Adams, 17 id. 230.

The notice of dishonor to the indorser must so describe the note that he cannot mistake which one is intended. A misdescription, which would not mislead him, will not vitiate the notice. Mills *v.* Bank of United States, 11 Wheaton, 431; Bank of Alexandria *v.* Swann, 9 Peters, 34; Gilbert *v.* Dennis, 3 Met. 498; Townsend *v.* Lorain Bank, 22 Ohio, 345; Bank *v.* Woods, 28 N. Y. 561; Thompson *v.* Williams, 14 Cal. 160. If the parties reside in the same place, notice must be delivered to the indorser himself, or left at his residence or place of business, and notice by mail is not sufficient. Pierce *v.* Pendar, 5 Met. 352; Phipps *v.* Chase, 6 id. 491; Cayuga Co. Bank *v.* Bennett, 5 Hill, 236; Curtis *v.* State Bank, 6 Blackf. 312; Bowling *v.* Harrison, 6 Howard, 248. The mode of serving notice depends not upon the question, whether the indorser resides in the place where presentment must be made or not, but upon his residence being in the same place with the party seeking to charge him with notice or not. West River Bank *v.* Taylor, 7 Bosworth, 466.

Where the parties reside in different places, as to what post-office the notice should be sent, see Bank of United States *v.* Carneal, 2 Peters, 543; Bank of Columbia *v.* Lawrence, 1 id. 79; Choteau *v.* Webster, 6 Met. 1; Walker *v.* Stetson, 14 Ohio State, 89. Where the parties reside in different places, notice may be personal or sent by mail. If sent by mail, it must be sent by the earliest practicable mail after the day of presentment. If the mail closes at an unseasonable hour on the day following the day of presentment, it may be sent in the next mail, and Sundays and other public holidays are not counted. Each indorser has the same privilege of time in notifying preceding indorsers. Lenox *v.* Roberts, 2 Wheaton, 373; Bank of Alexandria *v.* Lawrence, 1 Peters, 79; Eagle Bank *v.* Chapin, 3 Pick. 180; Eagle Bank *v.* Hathaway, 5 Met. 213; Palen *v.* Shurtleff, 9 id. 581; Prescott Bank *v.* Coverly, 7 Gray, 217; Sanderson *v.* Reinstadler, 31 Wis. 483; Nevins *v.* Bank, 10 Mich. 547; Grinman *v.* Walker, 9 Iowa, 426; Chick *v.* Pillsbury, 24 Maine, 458; Carter *v.* Burley, 9 N. H. 559; Howard *v.* Ives, 1 Hill, 263; Sheldon *v.* Benham, 4 Hill, 129; Brown *v.* Turner, 11 Ala. 752; Sussex Bank *v.* Baldwin, 2 Harrison, 488; Denny *v.* Palmer, 5 Iredell, 611; Remington *v.* Harrington, 8 Ohio, 507; Lawson *v.* Salem Bank, 1 Ohio State, 206; West *v.* Brown, 6 id. 542; as to place of demand, id.; Davis *v.* Hanly, 7 English (Ark.), 645; Linn *v.* Horton, 17 Wis. 151. An agent of the party in the allowance of time has the same privilege. Story on Bills, § 292; Ohio L. Ins. & Trust Co. *v.* M'Cague, 18 Ohio, 54; Lawson *v.* Farmers' Bank, 1 Ohio State, 206. What constitutes due diligence when the facts are ascertained is a question of law for the court. Walker *v.* Stetson, 14 Ohio State, 89. It is not necessary to show that the notice was received, but only that it was mailed in due time, and properly directed. Loud *v.* Merrill, 45 Maine, 516; Woods *v.* Neeld, 45 Penn. State, 86. Notices addressed to all the indorsers, and enclosed altogether to the last indorser, will charge all the indorsers, though the last indorser was only an agent to collect, and never received the enclosed notices. Wamesit Bank *v.* Buttrick, 11 Gray, 387.

The notice must inform the indorser either in express terms, or by reasonable implication, of the dishonor of the note, and it is not sufficient according to the current of of bills drawn upon a place out of the State. (*a*) Notes and domestic bills need not be protested in order to charge the indorser. Notice of non-payment is all the law requires. (*b*)

authorities to state merely that it is unpaid. Mills *v.* Bank of United States, 11 Wheaton, 431; Gilbert *v.* Dennis, 3 Met. 498; Pinkham *v.* Macy, 9 id. 174; Dole *v.* Gold, 5 Barb. 490; Sinclair *v.* Lynah, 1 Spears, 244. And dishonor is implied in the statement of a protest. Cayuga Co. Bank *v.* Warden, 1 Comst. 414; Spies *v.* Newbery, 2 Doug. (Mich.) 425; Smith *v.* Little, 10 N. H. 526; Crocker *v.* Getchell, 23 Maine, 392; Saltmarsh *v.* Tuthill, 13 Ala. 390; Townsend *v.* Lorain Bank, 2 Ohio State, 345; Wood *v.* Watson, 53 Maine, 300. It is sufficient if it would naturally and fairly convey to a person of ordinary intelligence, that the bill was presented at maturity and dishonored, and that he is looked to for payment. Burkham *v.* Trowbridge, 9 Mich. 209. It is held in Ohio, that a demand upon one of three joint and several promisors not partners, is sufficient to charge the indorser. Harris *v.* Clark, 10 Ohio, 5. But *contra*, State Bank *v.* Slaughter, 7 Blackf. 133; Union Bank *v.* Willis, 8 Met. 504. And see Greenough *v.* Smead, 3 Ohio State, 423. Notice of non-payment to one joint drawer is not notice to the other drawers, unless all the drawers are partners. Miser *v.* Trovinger, 7 Ohio State, 281. A drawer who has no assets in the hands of the drawee, and has no reason to expect that the drawee will pay the bill, is not entitled to notice. Miser *v.* Trovinger, 7 Ohio State, 281; Walker *v.* Rogers, 40 Ill. 278; Case *v.* Morris, 31 Penn. State, 100. Every person who has a right to draw, or reason to believe that his bill will be honored, is entitled to notice. Dickens *v.* Beal, 10 Peters, 572; French's Executors *v.* Bank of Columbia, 4 Cranch, 153. Where the maker is insolvent, no demand is necessary. Hawkins *v.* Olson, 48 Ill. 277 {*contra*, Bank *v.* McGuire, 33 Ohio State, 295. Notice to an insolvent indorser is sufficient without notice to his assignee; but notice to the latter does not bind either. House *v.* Vinton Natl. Bank, 43 Ohio State, 346, 353.}

(*a*) Farmers' Bank of Canton *v.* Brainard, 8 Ohio, 292; Case *v.* Heffner, 10 id. 180; Estep *v.* Cecil, 6 Ohio State, 536: West *v.* Valley Bank, 6 id. 168.

(*b*) A bank-bill, though payable at a future day, is not such a bill as requires either protest or notice to charge the drawer. In the matter of Brown, 2 Story, 502. A certificate of deposit, negotiated by indorsement, has been held not to bind the indorser; the certificate being a mere special agreement, and not a promissory note. Patterson *v.* Poindexter, 6 W. & S. 227; Charnley *v.* Dulles, 8 id. 353; Sibree *v.* Tripp, 15 M. & W. 23. But *contra*, Kilgore *v.* Bulkley, 14 Conn. 363; Bank of Orleans *v.* Merrill, 2 Hill, 295; Laughlin *v.* Marshall, 19 Ill. 390. Bank checks are payable on presentation and demand, and are not entitled to days of grace. The holder must present them within a reasonable time, but delay in presenting them does not discharge the maker, unless he has been injured thereby. Morrison *v.* Bailey, 5 Ohio State, 13; Werk *v.* Mad River Valley Bank, 8 id. 301; Stewart *v.* Smith, 17 Ohio State, 82; Laws *v.* Rand, 3 C. B. (N. S.) 442; Morrison *v.* McCartney, 30 Missouri, 183. The mere loss of secret equities between the drawee and payee is not such an injury. Stewart *v.* Smith, 17 Ohio State, 82. But a check payable on a future specified day is *primâ facie* a bill of exchange, and entitled to grace, but the intention of the parties may be shown to be otherwise. Andrew *v.* Blatchley, 11 Ohio State, 89. As to what is a reasonable time to present a check in, see O'Brien *v.* Smith, 1 Black, 99. As to the payments upon forged checks, see Ellis *v.* Ohio Life Ins. & Trust Co., 4 Ohio State, 628.

A bank check is not an assignment of the fund, if for a sum greater or less than the whole sum in bank, until it is presented to the bank, and certified by it. And *quære* whether it is until then, even if for the exact sum standing to the drawer's credit. Bullard *v.* Randall, 1 Gray, 605; Dana *v.* Third National Bank, 13 Allen, 445; Lloyd *v.* McCaffrey, 46 Penn. State, 410; Butterworth *v.* Peck, 5 Bosworth, 341. {A draft for the exact amount of the fund drawn on is an assignment of it, as against the drawer or his assignee for benefit of creditors if no third party's rights intervene. Gardner *v.* National City Bank, 39 Ohio State, 600. But not merely on account of a fund, but for part of it only. Whitney *v.* Eliot Bank, 137 Mass. 351; Mandeville *v.* Welch, 5 Wheat. 277.} The fact that a check is taken in good faith and for value, several days after it is drawn, will not expose the taker to defences existing between the parties. Ames *v.* Merriam, 98 Mass. 294. The banker must ascertain that the person presenting a check drawn to order is the proper person, at his peril. Dodge *v.* National Exchange Bank, 20 Ohio State, 234 {and must ascertain whether a check dated before the drawer's assignment for the benefit of creditors known to the bank was not drawn after

Rights and Liabilities of the Parties. The holder of a note or bill is positively the owner thereof, until the contrary be shown, unless there be something on the paper itself to raise a doubt. (*a*) The acceptor of a bill, or the maker of a note, is the party primarily liable for its payment. He is liable to every other party on the paper, as well as to the holder; and with respect to the drawer and indorsers, the rule is that each is liable to all that come after him on the paper, unless the indorsement be *without recourse;* and, on the other hand, has a claim upon all who come before him on the paper. In other words, each successive indorser contracts with all who come after him that he will pay, if the maker or acceptor do not, the proper steps having been taken to charge them. The holder, therefore, on non-payment by the maker or acceptor, and notice, may elect to proceed against any one of the other parties; or may begin with the last and proceed against each successively up to the first; or may proceed against each of them contemporaneously; and the party who pays him, may do the same with respect to every party prior to himself; and so on up to the first party. We have a statute requiring holders of a note or bill to join the drawer and indorsers in the same suit, under the penalty of not recovering costs in separate suits. We also have a statute affirming the doctrine of commercial law, that where paper is negotiated after maturity, the maker, drawer, or obligor may set up any defence against the holder, which he might have done against the original payee; because such holder ought to suspect such paper; and even when negotiated before maturity, if the holder has actual notice that a portion has been previously paid, though not minuted on the paper, he can only recover the residue. The common rule is, that *accommodation paper* is placed on the same footing as business paper. But our court has decided, from the peculiar wording of our statute, that where persons indorse for the accommodation of another, they are to be considered, with respect to each other, as *co-sureties;* and each must make good his contributive share to the one who is compelled to take up such paper. But the decision would not embrace an accommodation acceptor. (*b*) By our statute, where the consideration even of negotiable paper is a gambling consideration, the paper is utterly void even in the hands of an innocent holder, without knowledge of the fact. This seems unreasonable and un-

the assignment and antedated. Chaffee *v.* Bank, 40 Ohio State, 1. The doctrine of *lis pendens* does not apply to mercantile paper. See p. 418–9}.

(*a*) Chauffee *v.* Taylor, 3 Allen, 598. Such possession, with proof of payment of a consideration, will sustain an action on a note payable to bearer, although the note bears the indorsement of a third party directing payment to be made to the order of a fourth, who has not indorsed the note nor consented to the bringing of the action. Rider *v.* Taintor, 4 Allen, 356. The doctrine of *lis pendens* does not apply to negotiable paper before maturity. Stone *v.* Elliott, 11 Ohio State, 252.

(*b*) Douglas *v.* Waddle, 1 Ohio, 413. {The decision of Douglas *v.* Waddle was criticised, regretted, and not followed as to bills of exchange in Barnet *v.* Young, 29 Ohio State, 7}. *Contra,* Fentum *v.* Pocock, 5 Taunt. 72; McDonald *v.* Magruder, 3 Peters, 470; Murray *v.* Judah, 6 Cowen, 484; Montgomery *v.* Walker, 9 Serg. & R. 229.

necessary. The paper ought to be void only with respect to those who have knowledge of the fact. *Damages* can only be recovered on protested bills, not on notes. (*a*) The amount varies according to the statutes of the different States. Here, the amount is twelve per centum, if the bill be drawn upon a person without the United States, and six per centum if drawn upon a person without the State, but within the United States. This amount is exclusive of interest and charges of protest; and may be recovered, either upon protest for non-acceptance or non-payment, against any party but the acceptor. These damages are designed to indemnify the holder for the disappointment and expense of making good the bill in the distant place on which it is drawn; and to save the drawer and indorsers from this increased liability, it is a principle peculiar to this branch of law, that any person may, after protest for non-acceptance or non-payment, volunteer to accept or pay *supra protest*, as it is called, for the honor of any or all the parties to the bill; and by so doing, and giving due notice thereof, he becomes entitled to all the rights of a regular holder of the bill, as to those parties for whose honor he intervenes. (*b*) This is almost the only instance where one can become the creditor of another without his knowledge or consent. But it is not the only instance in which the law shows a particular favor to negotiable paper. We have a statute providing that the plaintiff, suing on a note, bill, or bond, need not prove the signature of the defendant, unless he first denies it under oath. This provision often saves much trouble and expense to the holder, without any unfairness to the other party. We also have a provision on the subject of *days of grace*, adopting the usual custom of allowing three days after maturity before default, with respect to all negotiable paper. It is very common in this part of the country (*c*) to find contracts in the form of notes or orders, "payable in currency," or "payable in goods." Such contracts, however, are not negotiable, because not payable in money; but it has been decided that if not paid at maturity, in currency or goods, the full amount may be recovered in money. (*d*)

(*a*) 3 Kent, Com. 115–21; West *v.* Valley Bank, 6 Ohio State, 168. Where the rule of damages in such cases has been established by usage, the court cannot alter it on account of the depreciation of the currency in a monetary crisis. Wood *v.* Watson, 53 Maine, 300.

(*b*) 3 Kent, Com. 87.

(*c*) Dugan *v.* Campbell, 1 Ohio, 115; Byington *v.* Geddings, 2 id. 227; Rhodes *v.* Lindley, 3 id. 51; Niswanger *v.* Staley, 8 West. Law Jour. 493.

(*d*) Pinney *v.* Gleason, 5 Wendell, 397; Brooks *v.* Hubbard, 3 Conn. 58; Perry *v.* Smith, 22 Vt. 301; Stewart *v.* Morrow, 1 Grant (Penn.), 204; Brown *v.* Richardson, 20 N. Y. 472; Peddicard *v.* Whittam, 9 Iowa, 471; Horton *v.* Arnold, 17 Wis. 139; Gaulden *v.* Sheehee, 24 Ga. 438. But see *contra*, Cole *v.* Ross, 9 B. Monr. 393; Clark *v.* Pinney, 7 Cowen, 681; Mason *v.* Phillips, Addison, 346. Where the agreement is to pay a certain sum in goods at a fixed price, by weight or measure, the debtor may discharge his obligation by paying the amount in money. Trowbridge *v.* Holcomb, 4 Ohio State, 38. But there are authorities which hold that the measure of damages for breach of the contract is the value of the goods and interest. 2 Parsons, Cont. 490; and this is the rule of damages wherever it appears, from the subject-matter of the contract or the circumstances of the case, that the parties did not intend that the

With respect to *bank-notes*, our statute prohibits them from being made payable at a future day. Being on demand, they do not carry interest until demand is made. Then they carry interest until the bank redeems or offers to redeem them; and banks cannot refuse to receive their own notes in payment of debts. In Massachusetts, it is held that the giving of a promissory note or bill of exchange, in payment for goods, unless there be a stipulation to the contrary, is so far payment, as to extinguish the right of action against persons originally liable for the goods, but not parties to the note or bill. But the contrary is held in New York, and, it would seem, on better reasoning. (*a*) A similar question has arisen with respect to bank-notes of broken banks, and there is a like contrariety of decision. In New York, it is held that although neither party knew that the bank was broken, yet if in point of fact the bank was at the time insolvent, the loss falls upon the payer, and the receiver may recover of him the original consideration, as if nothing had been paid. But in Pennsylvania and elsewhere, the loss is held to fall on the receiver, when there is no fraud; and this would seem to conform to the common understanding of mankind, which is to treat bank-notes as money. (*b*)

§ 181. **Contract of Sale.** (*c*) When discussing the subject of *title by purchase*, my remarks were chiefly confined to realty. I then observed that personalty is generally transferred by mere delivery. In fact, but two exceptions to this rule now occur to me. One is the transfer of contracts not payable to bearer, which, as we have just seen, must be *by indorsement*. The other is the transfer of vessels, which, as we have seen when speaking of the regulations of commerce, must be evidenced by a written *bill of sale*. On these exceptions I have nothing further to remark; and shall confine my observations to the incidents belonging to the general contract of sale.

What constitutes a Sale. (*d*) We have seen that by the English

debtor should have his election to deliver the articles or pay the specified amount of money. Cleveland & Pittsburgh R. R. Co. *v.* Kelley, 5 Ohio State, 180.

(*a*) Chapman *v.* Durmit, 10 Mass. 47; Schermerhorn *v.* Loines, 7 Johns. 311; Muldan *v.* Whitlock, 1 Cowen, 290; Wilkins *v.* Reed, 6 Greenl. 220; Waydell *v.* Luer, 3 Denio, 412; Van Epps *v.* Dillaye, 6 Barb. 252; 2 Greenl. Ev. § 520; Merrick *v.* Bowry, 4 Ohio State, 60; 2 Parsons, Cont. 136.

(*b*) Lightbody *v.* Ontario Bank, 1 Wendell, 1; same case in Error, 13 id. 101; Miller *v.* Race, 1 Bur. 452; Young *v.* Adams, 6 Mass. 182; Scruggs *v.* Gass, 8 Yerger, 175; Bayard *v.* Shunk, 1 W. & S. 592; Imbush *v.* Mechanics' Bank, 1 West. Law Jour. 49; 3 Kent, Com. 86, note; Parsons on Contracts, 220; Fogg *v.* Sawyer, 9 N. H. 365.

(*c*) 2 Black. Com. 446; 2 Kent, Com. lec. 39; Long on Sales; Pothier on the Contract of Sale, by Cushing; Benjamin on Sales. Where the identical property delivered is to be returned, the transaction is a bailment, and the property does not pass. But where the obligation is only to return a like quantity of a similar article, there is a sale of the article delivered, and the title passes. Lonergan *v.* Stewart, 55 Ill. 45; Ives *v.* Hartley, 51 Ill. 520.

(*d*) The subject-matter of a sale must have an actual or potential existence, and a mere possibility or contingency not coupled with an interest is not the subject of a sale. 2 Kent, Com. 468. It was ruled by Lord Tenterden, that a contract by which the seller agrees to sell goods to be delivered at a future day, which he has not now, statute of frauds, no contract for the sale of goods exceeding ten pounds in value will be valid, unless the buyer actually receives some part of the goods; or pay some part of the price by way of earnest; or there be a written memorandum of the contract signed by the party to be charged. It is to be regretted that we have not such a provision in our statute; because now, to determine what constitutes a sale, we have to refer to the general elements of a contract before described. There must, then, be something more than mere *words*, or there will not be a consideration. For example, if you say you ask so much for an article, and I say I will give it, and nothing more pass between us, this is not a binding contract, because there is not yet a consideration. Something else must be *done* by one of the parties to bind the contract; the buyer either must pay or offer to pay some part of the price, or the seller must deliver or offer to deliver some part of the goods, or the contract will not be complete. But almost any thing demonstrating an understanding that the contract is completed, will be held sufficient. Thus, if the goods have been marked, or laid aside, or sent to any place by the direction of the buyer, he will be held responsible. We say, then, in general terms, that the contract of sale is completed, when the buyer has acquired the right to demand the goods; or the seller, to demand the price of the goods; and that this happens whenever, in addition to the mere words of a bargain, either party has done any act, no matter how trifling, which can be construed into a consideration. In sales conducted *by letter*, the true rule would seem to be, that the sale is complete when a letter containing the proposal has been received, and an answer containing the acceptance has been despatched, provided it be in a reasonable time. But where a specified time has been given for an answer, the proposal may be withdrawn at any time before acceptance. (*a*) In sales *by number*, *weight*, *or measure*, the sale is not complete, until the specific property sold is separated and identified. (*b*) In sales *at auction*, the auctioneer acts

and has made no contract for purchasing, and has no reasonable expectation of receiving by consignment, but intends to go into market and buy, is not valid. Bryan *v.* Lewis, 1 Ry. & M. 386. But this doctrine cannot now be considered law. Hibblewhite *v.* M'Morine, 5 M. & W. 462; Mortimer *v.* M'Callan, 6 id. 58; Stanton *v.* Small, 3 Sandf. 230. A bare expectancy, as the anticipated interest of an heir in his ancestor's estate, has been held to be the subject of a valid contract of sale. Fitzgerald *v.* Vestal, 4 Sneed, 258. But see Needles *v.* Needles, 7 Ohio State, 432.

(*a*) See *ante*, p. 470, note (*a*).

(*b*) Aldridge *v.* Johnson, 7 Ellis & B. 885; Cartwright *v.* Leonard, 11 Iowa, 32. As to articles called in the later civil law "fungible," articles sold not by selection, but by weight, measure, or count, out of a mass, of which mass all portions are equivalent, it has sometimes been held that a sale is complete where intended to be so or such is the usage, though there be no separation of the particular portion sold from the mass. As five hundred bushels of oats out of a larger quantity in an elevator, Cushing *v.* Breed, 14 Allen, 376; Kimberly *v.* Patchin, 19 N. Y. 330; Warren *v.* Milliken, 57 Maine, 97; Newhall *v.* Langdon, 39 Ohio State, 87. Where grain is deposited in an elevator, the owner of which is a dealer as well as a warehouseman, and by the terms of the receipt, or by the usages of the business, the owner of the elevator, on presentation of the receipt, can deliver either the grain, or its market value, such deposit is a sale, not a bailment. For a considered collection of cases as the agent of both parties. The bidder may retract his bid before the hammer is down, but not after. Here, then, the bid on one side, and the acceptance on the other, by knocking down the hammer, complete the sale. (*a*)

The Warranty. (*b*) When the article sold is in the possession

upon the questions growing out of the business of grain elevators, see Rahilly *v.* Wilson, 3 Dillon, 420 and note; Mr. Holmes' note to 2 Kent, Com. 12th ed. p. 590, and an article in 6 Am. Law Review, 450. And see Hurff *v.* Hires, 40 N. J. Law, 581; Whitlock *v.* Hay, 58 N. Y. 484; Broadwell *v.* Howard, 77 Ill. 305.

(*a*) Payne *v.* Cave, 3 T. R. 148; Boston and Maine R. R. *v.* Bartlett, 3 Cushing, 224.

(*b*) Mere words of commendation do not constitute a warranty. McGrew *v.* Forsythe, 31 Iowa, 179. In Gallagher *v.* Waring, 9 Wendell, 28, it was held, that a warranty that an article is merchantable, will be implied, though no sample was exhibited at the sale. In Lain *v.* Fidgeon, 6 Taunt. 108, the same doctrine was held. In Jones *v.* Bright, 5 Bing. 533, it was held that if a man sells generally, he warrants the goods fit for some purpose; if he sells for a particular purpose, he undertakes they shall be fit for that purpose. In Bridge *v.* Wain, 1 Stark. 504, it was held that goods sold as goods of a certain kind are warranted to be such. In this case, the goods were scarlet cuttings; there was proof what scarlet cuttings were; the goods furnished were scarlet cloth, but of an inferior quality to that known by the above name: judgment was for the plaintiff, on the ground above mentioned. In Gardiner *v.* Gray, 4 Camp. 144, Lord Ellenborough says, "the purchaser has a right to expect a salable article answering to the description in the contract. Without a particular warranty, this is an implied term in every such contract." In 13 Mass. 145, Chief-Justice Parker cites a case where it was held that an advertisement in the newspaper amounts to a warranty. In Jones *v.* Bowden, 4 Taunt. 847, Justice Heath cites the following case decided by himself. Some sheep were sold for stock; it was in evidence that stock sheep meant sheep that were sound, and he held that there was an implied warranty that the sheep were sound. In Shepard *v.* Kain, 5 B. & Ald. 240, the following was the case: A ship was advertised as a copper-fastened vessel, with these words, "to be taken with all faults, and without allowance for any defects whatsoever." The plaintiff had had opportunities to examine. The vessel was but partially copper-fastened. *Held*, that the meaning of the advertisement must be, with all the faults that a copper-fastened vessel may have. Here the vessel was not copper-fastened. There was a warranty that she was a copper-fastened vessel. In Seixas *v.* Wood, 2 Caines, Rep. 48, it was held, that to entitle the plaintiff to recover where one article was sold for another, there must be a warranty or fraud. If the defendant knew that the article was not what he sold it for, that would be fraud. In Springwall *v.* Allen, 2 East, 448 (*in note*), it was adjudged that the *scienter* was the gist of the action where there was no warranty. Seixas *v.* Wood has been overruled in 4 Cowen, 444, and 12 Wend. 566. In Chandelor *v.* Loper, 4 Cro. Jac., a jewel was sold as a bezoar stone, which was not such; and it was held, if the defendant did not know that it was not a bezoar stone, no action lies. This case is denied in 13 Mass. 143; and see Greenleaf's Overruled Cases, 75. In the case of a sale in good faith without warranty to a refiner of "Manilla sugar," the vendor was held entitled to recover, though the article contained four per cent of sand. Gossler *v.* Eagle Sugar Refinery, 103 Mass. 331. In Sweet *v.* Colgate, 20 Johns. 196, plaintiff sold defendant an article by both supposed to be barrilla; it proved to be a different article. Held, that as there was no warranty or fraud, the plaintiffs must recover. The plaintiff in this case was but an agent, selling the goods on commission. It was also decided that an advertisement, or invoice entry, did not amount to a warranty. But, say the court, if a vendor agrees to sell Madeira wine, and sends Teneriffe, the vendee would not be bound to pay for it. In this case the sale was by sample; the bulk of the article corresponded with the sample, and that absolved the plaintiff from further responsibility. In Hart *v.* Wright, 17 Wend. 267, the doctrine which raises, on a fair sale of an article of goods or merchandise, the implied warranty that it is merchantable or fit for the purpose intended is repudiated; but a contract to deliver goods generally of a certain description is another matter. There the vendee may insist that they shall be merchantable, and if they prove not to be so, they may be returned. In Salisbury *v.* Stainer, 19 Wendell, 159, hemp was sold in bales. Salisbury was told to examine them, and did examine some, but this was held to be no sale by sample, and no warranty that the bulk should correspond of the seller, there is an implied warranty of *title;* but if not in possession of the seller, there is no implied warranty, and the maxim is *caveat emptor*, let the buyer take the risk, for he is put upon inquiry. (*a*) As to *quality*, there is no implied warranty in any case where there has been an opportunity for inspection. In sales by *sample*, the only implied warranty is, that the bulk shall correspond to the sample; (*b*) and in sales by *description*, that the articles shall be of the *kind* described, and not a different article. With regard to the *deception* which will render the seller liable, it may be either an intentional concealment of the truth, or an intentional statement of falsehood. It is difficult to lay down any precise rule upon this subject. The law does not expect minds to be equal, or knowledge to be equal; but it expects men to be honest; and this requires, first, that nothing shall be misrepresented; and secondly, that any peculiar or extraordinary information, which one of the parties has, and knows that the other has not, should be made known. As to the ordinary skill or information belonging to the subject-matter, the law expects each man to possess it, and will not relieve him against the want of it, (*c*) unless it amount to a

with the part examined. Where the purchaser has had such an opportunity to examine, the seller is not liable in the absence of fraud. It is held in Illinois that there is an implied warranty that wheat sold in the stack is merchantable. Fish *v.* Roseberry, 22 Ill. 288. A contract to deliver "corn" requires it to be in good order and merchantable. Peck *v.* Armstrong, 38 Barb. 215.

(*a*) Coolidge *v.* Brigham, 1 Met. 551; Darst *v.* Brockway, 11 Ohio, 462; Shattuck *v.* Green, 104 Mass. 42. Where the vendor was not in possession at the time of the sale, and had no title then, a good title to the goods subsequently acquired by him would not inure to the benefit of the grantee. Scranton *v.* Clark, 39 N. Y. 222. The rule of *caveat emptor* applies to purchasers at judicial sales. Creps *v.* Baird, 3 Ohio State, 277.

(*b*) Where the article is in packages in a sale by sample, the general rule is, that each package shall correspond to the sample; but where the goods consist of different varieties of the same articles, and the sample is usually formed by mixing proportionate parts of each package together, there is no breach, though some of the packages are inferior to the sample, if it fairly represents the whole. Leonard *v.* Fowler, 44 N. Y. 289. {And the Ohio rule is that a substantial compliance with the terms is sufficient, subject to proper deductions. Cullen *v.* Bimm, 37 Ohio State, 236.} And though the offer is made by sample, if opportunity for inspection is given, and the vendee inspects some, and is offered an opportunity to inspect the others, but declines, there is no warranty, though the goods were deceitfully packed, if the vendor was ignorant of it, and acted in good faith. Barnard *v.* Kellogg, 10 Wall. 384.

(*c*) 2 Kent, Com. 478–92; 1 Parsons on Contracts, 456–76. No warranty is implied from the payment of a fair price. Mixer *v.* Coburn, 11 Met. 559; Moses *v.* Mead, 1 Denio, 378. In executed contracts of sale of personal property, where there is an opportunity of inspection, and the defects are not latent, the rule of the common law is *caveat emptor*, and there is no implied warranty as to the quality of the article sold. The rule of *caveat emptor* does not apply, however, in cases where the vendor has acted fraudulently. Hadley *v.* Clinton Co. Imp. Co., 13 Ohio State, 502; Hoe *v.* Sanborn, 21 N. Y. 552; Weimer *v.* Clement, 37 Penn. State, 147; Deming *v.* Foster, 24 N. H. 165; Mason *v.* Chappel, 15 Grattan, 572; Emmerton *v.* Matthews, 7 Hurl. & Nor. 586. *Contra*, in Arkansas. Boyd *v.* Whitfield, 19 Ark. 447. But where articles are ordered to be made for a particular purpose, there is an implied stipulation that they shall be free from all such defects of material and workmanship as will render them unfit for that purpose. Rodgers *v.* Niles, 11 Ohio State, 48; Kellogg Bridge Co. *v.* Hamilton, 110 U. S. 108; Cunningham *v.* Hall, Sprague, 404; Overton *v.* Phelan, 2 Head, 445; Hamilton *v.* Gangyard, 34 Barb. 204; Brown *v.* Murphee, 31 Miss. 91; Lespard *v.* Van Kirk, 27 Wis. 142; Field *v.* Kinnear, 4 Kans. 476.

case of idiocy, lunacy, or drunkenness. *Markets overt*, as they exist in England, are not known in this country; (*a*) and we have adopted the broad, though sometimes unjust, principle, that no person can transfer a greater right or better title to any chattel than he himself possesses. If therefore a thief, or even the bailee of a chattel, sell it to a person who does not know that he is not the owner, and it pass through ever so many hands of innocent purchasers without notice, still the original owner may reclaim it wheresoever he can find it. (*b*)

Other Matters. (*c*) When the bargain has been struck, and the sale is complete, the goods are entirely at the risk of the buyer. And the sale is complete, when the seller has done all he has to do with respect to the goods. (*d*) A delivery to the carrier, or to the agent of the buyer, is a delivery to the buyer

Nor will taking from the manufacturer an express warranty in certain respects be a waiver of the implied warranty as to other qualities. Boothby *v.* Scales, 27 Wis. 626. Where manufactured articles are sold by the maker, there is an implied warranty against latent defects. Hoe *v.* Sanborn, *supra.* But not where they are sold by a person not the maker, who is ignorant of such defects. Dickenson *v.* Gay, 7 Allen, 29. In the case of the sale of articles to be used for food, there is an implied warranty that they are not unwholesome. Hoover *v.* Peters, 18 Mich. 51; Divine *v.* McCormick, 50 Barb. 116. In Kentucky, it is held that where an article is sold for a particular purpose, there is an implied warranty that it is fit for that purpose. Miller *v.* Gaither, 3 Bush (Ky.), 152.

(*a*) Roland *v.* Gundy, 5 Ohio, 202; Hoffman *v.* Carow, 22 Wendell, 285; Fawcett *v.* Osborn, 32 Ill. 411.

(*b*) A sale of goods conditional upon the payment of the price, passes no title to the vendee until the price is paid, even in favor of a *bonâ fide* purchaser from the vendee to whom they had been delivered. Coggill *v.* H. & N. H. R. R. Co., 3 Gray, 545; Sargent *v.* Metcalf, 5 id. 306; Blanchard *v.* Child, 7 id. 155; Burbank *v.* Crooker, 7 id. 158; Sanders *v.* Keber, 28 Ohio State, 630; Hodgson *v.* Barrett, 33 id. 63. See Sawyer *v.* Fisher, 32 Maine, 28; Dudley *v.* Osborn, 41 N. H. 326; Ballard *v.* Burgett, 40 N. Y. 314; Putnam *v.* Lamphear, 36 Cal. 151. But see Wait *v.* Green, 36 N. Y. 556; Murch *v.* Wright, 46 Ill. 48. Where one agrees to buy, and the other to sell, an article for a certain price, without any other stipulations, it is a sale for cash; the delivery of the goods in the expectation of immediate payment is not an absolute delivery, and vests no title in the purchaser until the payment of the price. Wabash Elevator Co. *v.* First National Bank of Toledo, 23 Ohio State, 311. But where the possession is delivered under fraudulent representations, though the sale may be rescinded, the title passes to the vendee so far that he may give a good title to a *bonâ fide* purchaser. Padden *v.* Taylor, 44 N. Y. 371. But an attaching creditor of the fraudulent vendee stands in no better position than his debtor. Field *v.* Stearns, 42 Vt. 106.

(*c*) Macomber *v.* Parker, 13 Pick. 183; Tarling *v.* Baxter, 6 B. & C. 360; Farnum *v.* Perry, 4 Law Reporter, 276; Riddle *v.* Varnum, 20 Pick. 280.

(*d*) {Actual delivery is not necessary to pass title to specific personal property. Hooban *v.* Bidwell, 16 Ohio, 509.} Where a quantity of corn is sold to be delivered in lots at a future time and place, and to be paid for as delivered, at a specified rate per bushel, the contract is executory, and no title passes until delivery. Ormsby *v.* Machis, 20 Ohio State, 295. Where the article is to be manufactured, the title does not pass until it is complete, and in some way delivered to or accepted by the vendor. West Jersey R. R. Co. *v.* Trenton R. R. Co., 3 Vroom (N. J.), 517. Where the goods are in bulk, a separation is necessary. Randolph *v.* Elliott, 34 N. J. L. 184. Though the contract is entire, when the vendor has performed every thing that he is to do as to a portion the title to that portion passes, though the vendor has still something more to do as to the rest. Thompson *v.* Conover, 3 Vroom (N. J.), 466. Where the contract is that the title shall not pass until the whole purchase-money is paid, the payment of a part does not give the vendee any interest which can be levied on. Sage *v.* Sleutz, 23 Ohio State, 1. {For symbolic delivery by transfer of bill of lading, see Emery *v.* Irving Natl. Bank, 25 Ohio State, 360.}

himself. As to the time of delivery and payment, the rule is, that when no time is agreed upon, they are concurrent acts to be performed forthwith. Either may tender performance, and then demand performance of the other; and on the other hand, either may refuse to perform, unless the other will. But if goods have been actually delivered and received in good faith, before payment, the buyer has acquired a title to the goods, and the seller can only recover the price agreed upon; or if no price was agreed upon, then a reasonable price. To this rule, however, the right of *stoppage in transitu*, forms a partial exception. This is an equitable right, which the law gives to the vendor, when the vendee becomes insolvent, and the goods were sold on credit, to resume possession of the goods anywhere on their *transit* to the vendee, and before they come into his actual possession. There is much nice learning connected with this right, for which I have not room. The right is confined strictly to vendor and vendee, and the chief question is, when the transit begins and terminates. This being settled, the rule is clear, that while the goods are *in transit*, the vendor may stop them for his own security, as against the insolvent vendee. But if the vendee is actually in possession of the goods; or if before reaching him, he has honestly sold them to a third person, the vendor cannot *seize* them. He must then take his chance with the rest of the creditors. (*a*) When the sale has been perfected, and the buyer refuses to accept the article, the vendor may sell it at auction, and recover the difference. (*b*) When no place of delivery is specified in the contract, the law implies that it is the place where the article is at the time of sale. (*c*)

(*a*) 1 Parsons on Contracts, 476–91; 2 Kent, Com. 540–52; O'Neil *v.* Garrett, 6 Clarke (Iowa), 480; Rogers *v.* Thomas, 20 Conn. 54; Newhall *v.* Vargas, 15 Maine, 314; 13 id. 93; Sawyer *v.* Joslin, 20 Vt. 172; Mottram *v.* Heyer, 5 Denio, 628; s. c. 1 id. 483; Chandler *v.* Fulton, 10 Texas, 2; Benedict *v.* Schaettle, 12 Ohio State, 515; Lee *v.* Kimball, 45 Maine, 172; Pottinger *v.* Hecksher, 2 Grant's Cases, 309; Blackman *v.* Pierce, 23 Cal. 508; Reynolds *v.* Boston, &c. R. R. Co., 43 N. H. 580; Caheen *v.* Campbell, 30 Penn. State, 254; Gilford *v.* Smith, 30 Vt. 49; Markwald *v.* Creditors, 7 Cal. 213. Seizure by the creditors of the vendee before delivery to him does not terminate the right; nor is the commencement of a suit for the price, by the vendor's agent, without his knowledge, necessarily a waiver of it. Callahan *v.* Babcock, 21 Ohio State, 281. Though a portion of the goods has been delivered, the right still exists as to those not delivered. Mohr *v.* Boston, &c. R. R. Co., 106 Mass. 67.

(*b*) Girard *v.* Taggart, 5 S. & R. 19; Sands *v.* Taylor, 5 Johns. 395. And in New York, it is held that the sale need not be at auction, but may be in the ordinary manner upon notice to the purchaser. Crooks *v.* Moore, 1 Sandf. 397; Conway *v.* Bush, 4 Barb. 564. The vendee cannot recover back the consideration which he has paid, where, through his own default, the contract has not been completed, although, after such default, the vendor sells the goods to another party. Ashbrook *v.* Hite, 9 Ohio State, 357. Where the vendee fails to comply with his contract, the vendor has the choice of three courses. 1. He may hold the property for the purchaser, and recover the entire price from him. 2. He may sell the goods as agent of the purchaser, and recover the difference between the contract price and that realized on the sale. 3. He may rescind the contract and recover the difference between the contract price and the market price at the time and place of delivery. If he elects to resell the goods, he must use reasonable care and diligence like any other agent. {Shawhan *v.* Van Nest, 25 Ohio State, 490; s. c. with note, 15 Am. Law Reg. 153} Dustan *v.* McAndrew, 44 N. Y. 72.

(*c*) Goodwin *v.* Holbrook, 4 Wendell, 380; Bronson *v.* Gleason, 7 Barb. 472. In

§ 182. **Contract of Bailment.** (*a*) The most approved definition of this contract is, a delivery of goods in trust, upon a contract, express or implied, that the trust shall be duly executed and the goods restored to the owner, as soon as the purpose of the delivery shall be answered. The person making the delivery is called *bailor*, and the person receiving it *bailee*. The transaction itself, and sometimes the thing bailed, is called *bailment*. The term is derived from a French word, signifying *to deliver*. It will be obvious from the above definition, that bailments bear a strong analogy to *trusts*, which have been before described. In fact, courts of law have, in an eminent degree, applied to them the equitable doctrines which govern trusts. You will, however, observe that parties may make such express stipulations in regard to liability, as they please. The only question arises, when there are no express stipulations. Then the law deduces a contract from the nature of the transaction. The law of bailments, therefore, is chiefly the law of implied contracts. Bailments are divided into five sorts, namely, *deposits*, *mandates*, *loans*, *pledges*, and *lettings*. I shall speak briefly of each.

1. *Deposit*, or *depositum*. This is a delivery of goods to another to be safely kept until called for, without recompense. Here, if there be no special undertaking to the contrary, the trouble of safe-keeping being without reward, the depositary impliedly undertakes for no more than slight diligence in keeping the *deposit;* and in case of loss or injury, is only liable for gross negligence. The terms *diligence* and *negligence*, being the opposites of each other, both admit of the same degrees, of which the law makes three. Thus, *ordinary diligence* is that which men of common prudence use with respect to their own affairs; and the absence of it is ordinary negligence. *Slight diligence* is that which even careless men use with respect to their own concerns; and the absence of it is extraordinary or gross negligence. *Extraordinary diligence* is that which very prudent men use with respect to their own concerns; and the absence of it is slight negligence. These specifications are, perhaps, as accurate as the nature of the subject admits of. A jury, looking at the circumstances

the absence of express stipulation, the law implies that the payment is to be made in money at the time and place of delivery. Coil *v.* Willis, 18 Ohio, 28.

(*a*) The outline of the law of bailments, originally derived from the civil law, was indicated by Lord Holt, in the celebrated case of Coggs *v.* Bernard, 2 Lord Raymond, 909; s. c. Smith's Lead. Cases. Afterwards Sir William Jones wrote a small treatise on the subject, which every student ought to read for the sake of its admirable style and analysis. The fortieth lecture of Kent is also an excellent summary of this branch of law. But the recent treatise by Judge Story will supersede the necessity of referring to any other source. On the subject of Carriers, see the treatise of J. K. Angell, Esq.; also, Edwards on Bailments; 1 Parsons on Contracts, ch. xi. The bailee cannot set up title in himself to justify his refusal to return the thing bailed. Simpson *v.* Wrenn, 50 Ill. 222. But this rule, that the bailee cannot dispute the title of the bailor, does not apply where the bailee has been compelled to pay for the property to one having actual title, in a suit of which the bailor had notice. Cook *v.* Holt, 48 N. Y. 275. In case of adverse claims, the bailee may delay a reasonable time to examine into the facts. Ball *v.* Liney, 48 N. Y. 6.

of a case, will readily determine between these three degrees; and then the law will apply the rule. And the general rule is, that a depositary for safe-keeping merely, without recompense, only undertakes for slight diligence, as above defined; but the degree of diligence varies somewhat with circumstances. (*a*) Thus, if I deliver to you a box of jewels or precious metals, for safe-keeping, and you know them to be such, you will be held to greater care than if the articles had been less valuable. In other words, slight diligence in keeping gold, is more than slight diligence in keeping iron. (*b*) So if you become the depositary in consequence of your own voluntary or officious proposal, you are held to greater diligence than if the request had first come from the depositor; (*c*) but still the general rule for this kind of bailments is the equitable one above stated; that slight diligence only is required, and nothing but gross negligence makes the depositary liable.

2. *Mandate*, or *mandatum*. This is a delivery of goods to another, to have some act done with respect to them, in addition to safe-keeping, without recompense. Here, then, are two things to be considered, *custody* and *feasance*. As to custody, the mandate does not differ from a deposit, and the rule of liability is the same. But feasance is the principal thing, and here if there be no special undertaking to the contrary, the trouble of doing the thing required being without reward, the mandatary impliedly undertakes only for slight diligence, and is liable only for gross negligence. There is no liability for mere *nonfeasance*, or an omission to do the thing undertaken; but only for *misfeasance*, which is doing it improperly; or *malfeasance*, which is doing some other wrong. (*d*) But the amount of diligence varies according to the nature of the thing to be done. Thus, an undertaking to carry glass requires greater care than to carry cloth; and an undertaking to repair a watch requires greater care than to grind an axe. (*e*) So where the very nature of the thing to be done presupposes a certain kind of professional skill, the mandatary is responsible for possessing

(*a*) Foster *v.* Essex Bank, 17 Mass. 479. The distinction between "negligence" and "gross negligence," has of late been discountenanced as unintelligible. Steamboat New World *v.* King, 16 How. 471; Griffith *v.* Zipperwick, 28 Ohio State, 388, 402. The term is well defined by Alderson, B., in Blyth *v.* Birmingham Water Works Co., 36 Eng. L. & Eq. 506, 508; Maury *v.* Coyle, 34 Md. 235.

(*b*) Tracy *v.* Wood, 3 Mason, 132; Dorman *v.* Jenkins, 2 Ad. & El. 256; Griffith *v.* Zipperwick, 28 Ohio State, 388.

(*c*) Jones on Bailments, 48. In a regular deposit the specific thing deposited must be returned and if the depositary has the option of returning another of like kind and value, the property in the thing passes to him. Chase *v.* Washburn, 1 Ohio State, 244. {In case it becomes impossible to return a like article, but without the depositary's fault, see Fosdick *v.* Greene, 27 Ohio State, 484.} As to the liability in the case of a gratuitous deposit of money, see Spooner *v.* Mattoon, 40 Vt. 300; Darling *v.* Younker, 37 Ohio State, 487.

(*d*) Elsee *v.* Gatward, 5 T. R. 143; Thorne *v.* Deas, 4 Johns. 84; Balfe *v.* West, 22 Eng. Law & Eq. 506; Lyons *v.* Tams, 6 Eng. (Ark.) 189; Fellowes *v.* Gordon, 8 B. Monr. 415; Dart *v.* Lowe, 5 Ind. (Porter) 131.

(*e*) Tracy *v.* Wood, 3 Mason, 182; Whitney *v.* Lee, 8 Met. 93; Grant *v.* Ludlow, 8 Ohio State, 10.

that skill. (*a*) Still the general rule is the equitable one before stated; that slight diligence only is required, and nothing but gross negligence makes the mandatary liable. (*b*)

3. *Loan*, or *commodatum*. This is a delivery of goods to another, to be used by him, without recompense to the lender. Here, if there be no special undertaking to the contrary, as the benefit is all on the side of the borrower, he impliedly undertakes for extraordinary diligence, and is liable for slight negligence. He cannot apply the thing borrowed to any other purpose than that for which it was lent; he must take the utmost care not to let the article be lost or injured; and must return it when the lender calls for it. But he is not responsible for a loss resulting from inevitable accident. (*c*) The three kinds of bailments now described, are called gratuitous bailments, because the benefit is all on one side, and the burden on the other. In those which remain, there is a mutual benefit and interest.

4. *Pledge*, or *pignus*. (*d*) This is a delivery of goods by a debtor to his creditor, to be kept as a security till the debt be discharged. Here the bailment is mutually beneficial to both parties. The pledgor thereby procures credit, and the pledgee security. Therefore, there being no express agreement to the contrary, the pledgee undertakes for ordinary diligence in keeping the goods, and becomes responsible for corresponding negligence. If the article can be used without injury, he may use it; otherwise not. If the keeping of it be expensive, he may use it in a reasonable manner to defray such expense. But in either case if a profit be made, it must go in liquidation of the debt. As to the redemption of the pledge, we have remarked on this, when speaking of mortgages of personalty.

5. *Letting*, or *locatio*. This is a delivery of goods to another to be used by him for a compensation to be paid, or to have something done about them by him for a compensation to be received. This class of bailments is much more comprehensive and important than either of the preceding; and the above designation of

(*a*) Shiells *v.* Blackburne, 1 H. Bl. 158; Wilson *v.* Brett, 11 M. & W. 113; Leighton *v.* Sargent, 7 Foster (N. H.), 460.

(*b*) A distinction has been taken in some cases between the diligence required where the bailment was solicited by the bailee and where it was not, he being held to greater diligence in the former case than in the latter. Jourdan *v.* Reed, 1 Clarke, 135; Newhall *v.* Paige, 10 Gray, 366; Hills *v.* Daniels, 15 La. An. 280; Dougherty *v.* Posegate, 3 Clarke, 88. And in Mississippi, it has been held, that a bailee without compensation, if he accepts the bailment, will be bound to use ordinary diligence. Moore *v.* Gholson, 34 Miss. 372.

(*c*) Coggs *v.* Bernard, 2 Ld. Raym. 909; Wilcox *v.* Hogan, 5 Ind. (Porter) 546. The bailor, in such a case, is responsible for any injury that may happen to the bailee in the use of the article lent from defects in it, if he lends it knowing it to be in a dangerous condition, but not otherwise. McCarty *v.* Young, 6 Hurl. & Nor. 329.

(*d*) See 2 Kent, Com. 577; 1 Parsons on Cont. 591–602; Tyler on Pledges; Wilson *v.* Little, 2 N. Y. 443; s. c. 1 Sandf. 351. Where a party receives a note as collateral security for an existing debt without any special agreement, he is bound to use ordinary care and diligence in collecting it. Roberts *v.* Thompson, 14 Ohio State, 1.

letting does not very accurately indicate the nature of the contract. There are, in fact, three distinct subdivisions.

1. *Letting for Use*, or *locatio rei*. This is where the letter for a compensation gives the temporary use of a thing to the hirer. Here the letter and hirer are mutually benefited; the one gaining a right to the price, the other, to the use of the thing hired. Accordingly, the hirer impliedly undertakes for ordinary diligence, and becomes liable only for corresponding negligence. (*a*) He must use the thing hired for that purpose only for which it was hired; and must take ordinary care so to use, as not to abuse it. Then if loss occurs, he is clear; but if he departs from the use contemplated by the contract, he then becomes answerable for all casualties. (*b*)

2. *Letting for Work*, or *locatio operis faciendi*. This is where the receiver, who cannot properly be called hirer, is to do some work about the goods, for a compensation, either stipulated or reasonable. Here, both skill and care enter into the contract; and being mutually for the benefit of the employer and employed, the latter impliedly undertakes for ordinary care in keeping the article, and ordinary skill and diligence in doing the work; and he becomes liable only for corresponding negligence or deficiency. It often happens, however, that *custody* is the sole object of this bailment; and then it differs from the deposit, only in the fact of compensation; whence the difference in the degree of diligence. But when there is work to be done about the article, in addition to safe-keeping, or *feasance*, in addition to *custody*, then this bailment differs from the *mandate*, only in the fact of compensation; whence the difference in the degree of diligence. (*c*) The most

(*a*) Millon *v.* Salisbury, 13 Johns. 211; Harrington *v.* Snyder, 3 Barb. 380; Columbus *v.* Howard, 6 Geo. 219. As to the responsibility of hirers of slaves, see Mullen *v.* Ensley, 8 Humph. 428; Swigert *v.* Graham, 7 B. Monr. 661; Hawkins *v.* Phythian, 8 id. 515; Heathcock *v.* Pennington, 11 Iredell, 640. But if the chattel was taken from him without fault or negligence by the military forces of the United States, the bailee will not be liable to the bailor for a failure to return it. Watkins *v.* Roberts, 28 Ind. 167. As to the burden of proof in England, it is held, that it is on the plaintiff to show some negligence on the part of the defendant. There is a conflict in the American cases. In Connecticut, in a late case, it was held that in the absence of any proof by the bailee that the goods had been lost, or of the exercise of reasonable care, the plaintiff was not required to show affirmatively how they had been lost, or that the bailee had been negligent. Boies *v.* Hartford, &c. R. R. Co., 37 Conn. 272.

(*b*) Harrington *v.* Snyder, 3 Barb. 383; Columbus *v.* Howard, 6 Geo. 219. *Semble* that a bailor for hire is liable for damages caused by the thing hired not being reasonably fit for the purpose, without proof of personal negligence or misconduct. Fowler *v.* Lock, L. R. 7 C. P. 272. Where there is a hiring of goods not agreed to as specific chattels, and where the person hiring has no reasonable means of ascertaining their quality, the hirer is bound to supply such as are reasonably fit for the purpose, and liable for damages caused by their unfitness. Id. p. 281.

(*c*) As to liability of warehousemen, and forwarding merchants, and when common carriers are liable as such. Railroad Co. *v.* Barrett, 36 Ohio State, 448. Roberts *v.* Turner, 12 Johns. 232; Teale *v.* Sears, 9 Barb. 317; Garside *v.* Trent and Mersey Navigation Co., 4 T. R. 581; Ackley *v.* Kellogg, 8 Cowen, 223; Thomas *v.* Boston and Providence R. R. Co., 10 Met. 472; Norway Plains Co. *v.* Boston and Maine R. R. Co., 1 Gray (Mass.), 263; Holtzdaw *v.* Duff, 27 Mo. 392. Dufour *v.* Mepham, 31 Mo. 577; Jackson *v.* Sacramento R. R. Co., 23 Cal. 268; Myers *v.* Walker, 31 Ill. 353; McCullum *v.* Porter, 17 La. An. 89; Ala. R. R. Co. *v.* Kidd, 35 Ala. 209; Titeworth important bailees under this head are *innkeepers.* Who are inn keepers, and what are their duties, must be determined by the common law. (*a*) Our statute merely requires them to take out a license from year to year, without specifying their duties. The following may be taken as a sufficient definition of an inn or tavern; namely, a house, the owner of which holds out that he will receive all travellers or sojourners who are willing to pay an adequate price, and are in a situation fit to be received. (*b*) As a peculiar confidence is reposed in innkeepers by their guests, to whom they are often entire strangers, they are placed by law under very high obligations. They are held responsible for the safe-keeping of the property of their guests, from the moment of being brought to the inn, unless the loss or injury arise from the acts of God or of public enemies, comprising whatever comes under the head of inevitable casualties. (*c*) In other words, they

v. Winnegar, 51 Barb. 148; Baltimore R. R. Co. *v.* Schumaker, 22 Md. 168; Chicago, &c. R. R. Co. *v.* Scott, 42 Ill. 132; Aldrich *v.* Boston, &c., R. R. Co., 180 Mass. 31. But a warehouseman who delivers the articles intrusted to him to an unauthorized person is liable. Jeffersonville R. R. Co. *v.* White, 6 Bush (Ky.), 251. Where a warehouseman has failed to deliver up goods intrusted to him, the burden of proof rests on him to show that they were lost without fault. Cass *v.* Boston & Lowell R. R. Co., 14 Allen, 448. A warehouse receipt in the absence of statute is not negotiable. Second National Bank *v.* Walbridge, 19 Ohio State, 419. As to liability of a warehouseman when he mixes the depositor's goods with his own, see Chase *v.* Washburne, 1 Ohio State, 244.

(*a*) As to lodging-houses, see Dansey *v.* Richardson, 24 L. J. Rep. 217; S. C. 25 Eng. Law & Eq. 76; 52 London Law Mag. 153; Holder *v.* Soulby, 8 C. B. (N. S.) 254; Pinkerton *v.* Woodward, 33 Cal. 557.

(*b*) Thompson *v.* Lacy, 3 B. & Ald. 283. See also Com. *v.* Wetherbee, 101 Mass. 214; Krohn *v.* Sweeny, 2 Daly, 200.

(*c*) Mason *v.* Thompson, 9 Pick. 280; Grinnell *v.* Cook, 3 Hill, 488; Thickstun *v.* Howard, 8 Blackf. 536; Shaw *v.* Berry, 31 Maine, 478; Washburn *v.* Jones, 14 Barb. 193; Mateer *v.* Brown, 1 Cal. 221; Willard *v.* Reinhardt, 2 E. D. Smith, 148; Gill *v.* Libby, 36 Barb. 70; Morgan *v.* Ravey, 6 Hurl. & Nor. 265; Hulett *v.* Swift, 42 Barb. 230. There are recent cases which hold that the innkeeper is not liable for losses occasioned without any negligence of himself or his servants. Merritt *v.* Claghorn, 23 Vt. 177; Dawson *v.* Chamney, 5 Ad. & El. (N. S.) 164; Hill *v.* Owen, 5 Blackf. 323; Metcalf *v.* Hess, 14 Ill. 129; Laird *v.* Eichold, 10 Ind. 212; Hoorth *v.* Franklin, 20 Texas, 798. But the peculiar liability of innkeepers is for the protection of guests or wayfarers. It does not extend to boarders. Manning *v.* Wells, 9 Humph. 746. But payment of fare by the week does not necessarily make one "a boarder." Berkshire Woollen Co. *v.* Proctor, 7 Cush. 423-4. But see Willard *v.* Reinhardt, *supra.* It has been held that if a person commits his horse to an innkeeper to be fed, he is a guest, although he do not himself lodge or receive any refreshment at the inn. Mason *v.* Thompson, 9 Pick. 280; Towson *v.* Havre de Grace Bank, 6 H. & J. 52. But see Grinnell *v.* Cook, 3 Hill, 485; Thickstun *v.* Howard, 8 Blackf. 535; Smith *v.* Dearlove, 6 M. G. & S. 132; Ingalsbee *v.* Wood, 33 N. Y. 577. Purchasing liquor at an inn is sufficient to constitute the purchaser a guest. McDonald *v.* Egerton, 5 Barb. 560. {Simply depositing money with the clerk without requiring present accommodations does not constitute its owner a guest. Arcade Hotel Co. *v.* Wiatt, 44 Ohio State.} A townsman or neighbor may be a traveller, and therefore a guest at an inn, as well as a stranger. Walling *v.* Potter, 35 Conn. 183. The innkeeper is not liable if the loss is occasioned by the fault of the guest. Burgess *v.* Clements, 4 M. & S. 306; Armistead *v.* White, 6 Eng. Law & Eq. 349; Fuller *v.* Coats, 18 Ohio State, 343; or if the guest retains the exclusive possession of the goods. Farnworth *v.* Packwood, 1 Stark. 249; Richmond *v.* Smith, 8 B. & C. 9; Packard *v.* Northcraft, 2 Met. (Ky.) 439; Weisinger *v.* Taylor, 1 Bush (Ky.), 275; Vance *v.* Throckmorton, 5 Bush (Ky.), 41. The goods, to render the innkeeper chargeable, must be within his custody. Albin *v.* Presby, 8 N. H. 408; Hawley *v.* Smith, 25 Wendell, 642. See are bound for the highest possible degree of care and diligence. A theft by their servants does not exculpate them, because they are bound to keep honest servants. There are many details connected with their responsibility, but I have only room for the general principles. (*a*)

3. *Letting for Transportation*, or *locatio operis mercium vehendarum*. This is where goods are intrusted to a *carrier*, to be transported from place to place, for a compensation, either stipulated or reasonable. Here the transaction is mutually beneficial; and on the common principle, the carrier would impliedly undertake only for ordinary diligence, and be liable only for corresponding negligence. In fact, this is the rule with respect to a *special carrier*, or one who only undertakes to carry goods in a particular case. (*b*)

Clute *v.* Wiggins, 14 Johns. 175; Piper *v.* Manny, 21 Wendell, 282. The innkeeper's liability extends to all the money and goods of the guest placed in the inn, and is not confined to such as are necessary and designed for ordinary travelling purposes. Berkshire Woollen Co. *v.* Proctor, 7 Cush. 417; Wilkins *v.* Earle, 44 N. Y. 172. His liability as an insurer is co-extensive with his right to a lien. Ingalsbee *v.* Wood, 36 Barb. 452. But see Giles *v.* Fauntleroy, 13 Md. 126. He is bound to receive all proper persons who resort to his house as travellers, at suitable times, and in a proper manner, and are able to pay their fare, so long as he has the means of accommodation for them, and it has been held that he is bound under proper limitations to admit drivers of stage coaches and those persons who have business with his guests. Markham *v.* Brown, 8 N. H. 523; Rex *v.* Ivens, 7 C. & P. 213.

(*a*) R. S. § 4427 declares that innkeepers providing a good safe, and posting certain notices of that fact, shall not be liable for articles of value not given to them to be placed in the safe. Similar laws exist in many of the other States. Under these statutes, it has been held, that although the statutory notice has not been given, still if the guest had actual notice, it will be sufficient. Purvis *v.* Coleman, 1 Bosw. 321; s. c. 21 N. Y. 111; Stanton *v.* Leland, 4 E. D. Smith, 88. The New York statute relieves the innkeeper from liability for all "money, jewels, or ornaments," which the traveller neglects to deposit in the safe, though they be such as are reasonably required for travelling expenses and personal convenience. Hyatt *v.* Taylor, 42 N. Y. 259. But the words will be taken strictly, and will not include a gold watch and chain worn as a part of the ordinary apparel. Remaly *v.* Leland, 43 N. Y. 539. *Contra*, in Wisconsin, Stewart *v.* Piersons, 24 Wis. 241. Where articles are properly deposited the act has no effect; the liability of the innkeeper is then the same as at common law. Wilkins *v.* Earle, 44 N. Y. 172. Where there is no neglect on the part of the guest in failing to deposit the goods, as after he has packed his trunk to depart, and given the key to the clerk to have it brought down, the statute does not relieve the innkeeper. Bendetson *v.* French, 46 N. Y. 266; Kellogg *v.* Sweeny, 46 N. Y. 291. The Maryland statute does not apply to sums of money reasonably necessary for travelling expenses. Maltby *v.* Chapman, 25 Md. 307.

(*b*) Whether a carrier is a private or common carrier is often an important question to be determined. Generally, a common carrier is one who undertakes to carry the goods of all persons indifferently, or of such as choose to employ him. U. S. Express Co. *v.* Backman, 28 Ohio State, 144; Gisbourn *v.* Hurst, 1 Salk. 249; Robertson *v.* Kennedy, 2 Dana, 430; Dwight *v.* Brewster, 1 Pick. 53; Pennewill *v.* Cullen, 5 Harring. 238; Verner *v.* Sweitzer, 32 Penn. State, 208; Haynie *v.* Baylor, 18 Texas, 498. A common carrier cannot discriminate between different classes of persons. He must take all persons who offer themselves under such reasonable regulations as he may establish. Keeny *v.* Grand Trunk R. R. Co., 59 Barb. 104; Fish *v.* Clark, 2 Lans. 176. Thus the following classes of persons, when their employment answers this definition, are common carriers, and subject to their peculiar liabilities: Proprietors of *Stage Coaches:* Beckman *v.* Shouse, 5 Rawle, 179; Dwight *v.* Brewster, 1 Pick. 50; Jones *v.* Voorhees, 10 Ohio, 145; Clark *v.* Faxton, 21 Wendell, 153; Merund *v.* Butler, 17 Conn. 138; Frink *v.* Coe, 4 Greene, 555. *Railroad Companies:* Thomas *v.* Boston & Providence R. R. Co., 10 Met. 472; Norway Plains Co. *v.* Boston & Maine R. R., 1 Gray (Mass.), 263. Masters and Owners of *Vessels:* Elliott *v.* Rossel, 10 Johns. 1; M'Arthur *v.* Sears, 21 Wendell, 190; King *v.* Shepherd, 3

But *common carriers*, or those who make a business of carrying goods, whether by land or water, have been placed, by the policy of the law, under the highest degree of responsibility. Their reputation for care and prudence cannot be known by the multitude, whose goods they carry; and therefore they are held responsible for all losses or injuries not resulting from the acts of God or public enemies. (*a*) In other words, the degree of their

Story, 360. *Canal Boatmen:* Parsons *v.* Hardy, 14 Wendell, 215; Teall *v.* Sears, 9 Barb. 317; De Mott *v.* Laraway, 14 Wendell, 225; Commander-in-Chief, 1 Wallace, 43. *Ferrymen:* Harrington *v.* Lyles, 3 Barr, 342; Cohen *v.* Hume, 1 M'Cord, 439; White *v.* Winnisimmet Co., 7 Cush. 155; Willoughby *v.* Horridge, 16 Eng. Law & Eq. 437; Wilson *v.* Hamilton, 4 Ohio State, 722; Fisher *v.* Clisbee, 12 Ill. 349; Richards *v.* Fuqua, 28 Miss. 792; Hall *v.* Renfro, 3 Met. (Ky.) 51; Griffith *v.* Care, 22 Cal. 534. *Expressmen:* U. S. Express Co. *v.* Backman, 28 Ohio State, 144; Sherman *v.* Wells, 28 Barb. 403; Haslam *v.* Adams Ex. Co., 6 Bosw. 235; Place *v.* Union Express Co., 2 Hilton (N. Y. C. P.), 19; American Ex. Co. *v.* Baldwin, 21 Ill. 504; Hooper *v.* Wells, 27 Cal. 11; Christenson *v.* Am. Ex. Co., 15 Minn. 270; Southern Ex. Co. *v.* Crook, 44 Ala. 468. For an excellent epitome of the law and cases on this subject, see an article in 5 Am. L. Register (N. S.), 1, by Judge Redfield; and for the argument against holding them to be common carriers, see id. 449 and 513. The weight of authority is decidedly that they are. {Whether a *sleeping-car company* is a common carrier or an innkeeper, see article by Morris Gray, Esq., 20 Am. Law Rev. 159 (1886).} Owners of *Omnibus Lines:* Parmelee *v.* McNulty, 19 Ill. 556. *Steamboats:* Citizens' Bank *v.* Nantucket Steamboat Co., 2 Story, 16; Jencks *v.* Coleman, 2 Sum. 221; Propeller Niagara *v.* Cordes, 21 How. 7; Cincinnati, &c. Co. *v.* Boal, 15 Ind. 345. But *steam tow-boats* are not common carriers: Leonard *v.* Hendrickson, 18 Penn. State, 40; Wells *v.* Steam Navigation Co., 2 N. Y. 204; Ashmore *v.* Penn. &c. Co., 4 Dutcher, 180; Merrick *v.* Brainard, 38 Barb. 574; Arctic Ins. Co. *v.* Austin, 54 Barb. 559. A *barge-owner*, who lets barges for the conveyance of goods to any customers who apply to him, is a common carrier, though each voyage was made under a special contract, and each barge only let to one person for the same voyage, and though the owner did not ply between fixed termini, but the customer fixed in each particular case the points of arrival and departure. Liver Alkali Co. *v.* Johnson, L. R. 7 Ex. 267. And see the Northern Belle, 9 Wall. 526. Where persons are engaged in other trades, and make the business of carrier subordinate or incidental to some other, it is sometimes a controverted question whether they are to be affected with the liabilities of a common carrier. The case of a *wagoner*, whose general occupation is that of a farmer, has involved some contrariety of opinion. For cases where he has been held as a common carrier, see Gordon *v.* Hutchinson, 1 W. & S. 285; Powers *v.* Davenport, 7 Blackf. 497; Chevalier *v.* Strahan, 2 Texas, 115. *Contra*, Samms *v.* Stewart, 20 Ohio, 69; Fish *v.* Chapman, 2 Kelly (Geo.), 349; Satterlee *v.* Groat, 1 Wendell, 272. For cases in which persons within the above classes have been held not to have so held themselves out as to render themselves common carriers, see Shoemaker *v.* Kingsbury, 12 Wall. 369; Allen *v.* Sackreder, 37 N. Y. 341.

(*a*) An "act of God" is defined by Lord Mansfield to mean "something in opposition to the act of man." Forward *v.* Pittard, 1 T. R. 33. It must be something in which human agency does not concur, whether of a carrier or a third person. Thus accidental fire, except when caused by lightning or collisions at sea, without the fault of either party, is not "an act of God." M'Arthur *v.* Sears, 21 Wendell, 190; Fish *v.* Chapman, 2 Kelly (Geo.), 357; Plaisted *v.* Boston & Kennebec Steam Navigation Co., 27 Maine, 132; Fergusson *v.* Brent, 12 Md. 9; Porter *v.* Chicago, &c. R. R. Co., 20 Ill. 375; Propeller Niagara *v.* Cordes, 21 How. 7; Miller *v.* Steam Nav. Co., 10 N. Y. 431; Goold *v.* Chapin, 20 N. Y. 259. But a violent and unusual storm will excuse from liability for goods thrown overboard to relieve the ship, notwithstanding the throwing overboard is done by man. Price *v.* Hartshorn, 44 N. Y. 94. And where the loss arises from natural decay, the carrier is not responsible. Express Co. *v.* Smith, 33 Ohio State, 511; Farrar *v.* Adams, Bull. N. P. 69; Warden *v.* Greer, 6 Watts, 426; Clark *v.* Barnwell, 12 How. 282. Nor where the loss is caused by defective packing of the goods. Klauber *v.* Am. Ex. Co., 21 Wis. 21. But *delay* by the carrier in delivering goods is excused by the freezing of water, which he navigates, or by boisterous weather, low tides, adverse winds, or failure of wind, and the like. Express Co. *v.* Smith, 33 Ohio State, 511; Clark *v.* Barnwell, 12 How. 283; Boyle *v.* M'Laughlin, 4 Harr. &

responsibility, and the reason of it, are the same as in the case of

J. 291; Parsons *v.* Hardy, 14 Wendell, 215; Bowman *v.* Teall, 23 id. 306. Or an unusual influx of freight exceeding the ability of the carrier to transport. Galena and Chicago Union R. R. Co. *v.* Rae, 18 Ill. 488. *Contra*, Deming *v.* Grand Trunk R. R. Co., 48 N. H. 455. A carrier is only bound to carry in a reasonable time under ordinary circumstances. Briddon *v.* Great Northern R. R. Co., 4 Hurl. & Nor. 847. The burden of proof is always on the carrier to show circumstances exempting him from liability. Gaines *v.* Union Transp. & Ins. Co., 28 Ohio State, 418; Emma Johnson, Sprague, 527; Hall *v.* Cheney, 36 N. H. 26; Ferm *v.* Thompson, 4 E. D. Smith, 276 {Michaels *v.* N. Y. &c. R. R. Co., 30 N. Y. 564; Read *v.* Spaulding, 30 N. Y. 630; but in the United States courts the rule is different, and} where the common carrier shows that the loss was by some *vis major*, as by a flood, he need not show affirmatively that he was guilty of no negligence. The burden of showing that the loss was really caused by the carrier's negligence, if relied on, rests on the plaintiff; negligence, which was merely a remote cause, will not in such a case render the carrier liable. Railroad Co. *v.* Reeves, 10 Wall. 176. The plaintiff may, however, recover in such a case, on showing that the loss under the circumstances might have been avoided by the exercise of proper care and skill on the part of the defendant. Transportation Co. *v.* Downer, 11 Wall. 129, 132. *Contra*, Graham *v.* Davis, 4 Ohio State, 362. See p. 530.

The liability of a common carrier begins as soon as he or some duly authorized agent of his has received the goods. Fitchburg & Worcester R. R. Co. *v.* Hanna, 6 Gray, 539; Merriam *v.* H. & N. H. R. R. Co., 20 Conn. 354. But it does not begin as long as any thing remains to be done by the consignor before the goods are ready for transportation. Judson *v.* Western R. R. Corp., 3 Allen, 18. Or if they are received to await orders of the consignor. Railroad Co. *v.* Barrett, 36 Ohio State, 448; Barron *v.* Eldridge, 100 Mass. 455. Or detained at his request. St. Louis R. R. Co. *v.* Montgomery, 39 Ill. 335. But if a passenger retains his baggage in his personal possession, the carrier is not liable in case of loss. Tower *v.* Utica, &c. R. R. Co., 7 Hill, 47; Wilson *v.* Hamilton, 4 Ohio State, 722; Steamer Crystal Palace *v.* Vanderpool, 16 B. Monr. 302. Nor is the carrier liable for money kept in the sole custody of a passenger, and carried without notice to the defendant for a purpose unconnected with the object of his journey, though such loss was caused by the negligence of the carrier's servants. First National Bank of Greenfield *v.* Marietta & Cincinnati R. R. Co., 20 Ohio State, 260. The liability of the carrier terminates with delivery to the owner or consignee, or his authorized agent, the place of which may be determined by an express contract or one implied from usage, or the course of business between the parties. Gibson *v.* Culver, 17 Wendell, 305; Farmers' & Mechanics' Bank *v.* Champlain Transportation Co., 16 Vt. 52; s. c. 18 id. 131; 23 id. 186. Where goods are carried in a ship, delivery on the usual wharf is sufficient to discharge the carrier. Hyde *v.* Trent & Mersey Navigation, 5 T. R. 397; Cope *v.* Cordova, 1 Rawle, 203. But delivery to a drayman or cartman on the landing not authorized by the consignee to receive the goods, is at the risk of the carrier, and he cannot justify such delivery by proof of a custom. Dean *v.* Vaccars, 2 Head, 488. There must be a landing of the goods, notice to the consignee, and a reasonable time to take them away. The Mary Washington, 1 Abb. U. S. 1; Shenk *v.* Phil. Steam Prop. Co., 60 Penn. State, 109. Personal delivery is also dispensed with in the case of railroads, the proprietors of which, after the goods have been transported and placed in a warehouse, are only liable as warehousemen for want of ordinary care. Ill. Central R. R. Co. *v.* Alexander, 20 Ill. 23; Smith *v.* N. & L. R. R. Co., 7 Foster (N. H.), 86; Mich. South & North R. R. Co. *v.* Schurtz, 7 Mich. 515; Thomas *v.* Boston & Providence Railroad Corp., 10 Met. 472; see Pennsylvania Co. *v.* Miller, 36 Ohio State, 541; Norway Plains Co. *v.* Boston & Maine Railroad, 1 Gray (Mass.), 263; and it seems from this last case that notice to the consignees of the arrival of the goods is not necessary to exonerate them from the liability of common carriers. See Rome R. R. Co. *v.* Sullivan, 14 Geo. 277; Michigan Central R. R. Co. *v.* Hall, 6 Mich. 243; Michigan, &c. R. R. Co. *v.* Bivens, 13 Ind. 263; Morris, &c. R. R. Co. *v.* Ayers, 4 Dutcher, 393; Francis *v.* Dubuque, &c. R. R. Co., 25 Iowa, 60. In New Hampshire, the liability of the company as a common carrier is not changed into that of warehouseman until the consignee has had a reasonable time after the arrival of the goods to take them away. Moses *v.* Boston & Maine R. R., 32 N. H. 523. Jeffersonville R. R. Co. *v.* Cleveland, 2 Bush (Ky.), 468; Winslow *v.* Vermont, &c. R. R. Co., 42 Vt. 700. See Pierce on American Railroad Law, pp. 425–54. In Illinois, such notice is not necessary. Richards *v.* Mich. Southern & Northern Indiana R. R. Co., 20 Ill. 404; Porter *v.* Chicago & Rock Island R. R. Co., 20 id. 407; Davis *v.* Mich. South. & North. Ind. R. R. Co., 20 id. 412. Nor in North Carolina.

innkeepers. It is usual for them to sign a *bill of lading*, (*a*) acknowledging the receipt of the goods, specifying the price of carriage, and agreeing to deliver them in good condition, at the end of their transit; but this does not vary the liability from that of the implied contract. If the articles are not in good condition at the end of the transit, the carrier is responsible, unless he can prove that the injury was done before he received them; for the whole burden of proof falls on him. Nor can he vary his liability by any notice that he will only be responsible in a certain way. The policy of the law will not give effect to such a notice. (*b*)

Neal *v.* Wilmington R. R. Co., 8 Jones Law, 482. As to notice in case of common carriers by water, see Price *v.* Powell, 3 Const. 322; Barclay *v.* Clyde, 2 E. D. Smith, 95. In the case of an express company, actual delivery is necessary. Witbeck *v.* Holland, 45 N. Y. 13. If the delivery be made to the wrong person, the carrier is liable. Jeffersonville, &c. R. R. Co. *v.* White, 6 Bush (Ky.), 251.

It has been held in England, that when a railway company take into their care a parcel directed to a particular place, and do not by positive agreement limit their responsibility to a part only of the distance, that is *primâ facie* evidence of an undertaking to carry the parcel to the place to which it is directed, although that place be beyond the limits of its line. Muschamp *v.* Lancaster, &c. Railway, 8 M. & W. 421; Watson *v.* Ambergate, &c. Railway, 3 Eng. L. & Eq. 497; Fowles *v.* Great Western Railway Co., 16 id. 531; s. c. 7 Exch. 696; Railroad Co. *v.* Campbell, 36 Ohio State, 647. This doctrine was affirmed in New York, St. John *v.* Van Santvoord, 25 Wendell, 660; and Iowa, Angel *v.* Miss. &c. R. R. Co., 9 Iowa, 487. But *contra*, the decision of the court of errors, 6 Hill, 157; and decisions in Vermont, Massachusetts, and Connecticut. Farmers' & Mechanics' Bank *v.* Champlain Transportation Co., 18 Vt. 140; s. c. 23 id. 209; Hood *v.* N. Y. & N. H. R. R. Co., 22 Conn. 1; Nutting *v.* Conn. River R. R. Co., 1 Gray (Mass.), 502; Barclay *v.* Clyde, 2 E. D. Smith, 95; Noyes *v.* Rut. & Bur. R. R. Co., 27 Vt. 110; Elmore *v.* Naugatuck R. R. Co., 23 Conn. 457; Naugatuck R. R. Co. *v.* Waterbury Button Co., 24 id. 408; Hart *v.* R. & S. R. R. Co., 8 N. Y. 37; Kyle *v.* L. R. R. Co., 10 Rich. 382; Darling *v.* Worcester R. R. Co., 11 Allen, 295; Perkins *v.* Portland, &c. R. R. Co., 47 Maine, 573. But see Russell *v.* Livingston, 16 N. Y. 515. And see Brown & Co. *v.* Mott & Bros., 22 Ohio State, 149. Where a company is liable as forwarder only beyond its own route, its liability ceases when the goods have arrived safely at the end of its route, and have been delivered safely with proper instructions to the next carrier. Reed *v.* United States Ex. Co., 48 N. Y. 462; Ill. Central R. R. Co. *v.* Frankenburg, 54 Ill. 88; Wahl *v.* Holt, 26 Wis. 713. But a failure to transmit special instructions will make the first company liable. Little Miami R. R. Co. *v.* Washburn, 22 Ohio State, 324.

(*a*) A bill of lading, so far as it is a contract, is conclusive; so far as it is a receipt, it may be explained. So it may be shown that the freight mentioned in the bill was never actually delivered. The Lady Franklin, 8 Wall. 325; Dean *v.* King, Pennock, & King, 22 Ohio State, 118; B. & O. R. R. Co. *v.* Wilkins, 44 Md. 11.

(*b*) It is now well settled that a common carrier may limit his common-law liability by special contract with the owner. N. J. Steam Navigation Co. *v.* Merchants' Bank, 6 How. 381–5; Reno *v.* Hogan, 12 B. Monr. 63; Farmers' & Mechanics' Bank *v.* Champlain Transportation Co., 23 Vt. 186; Parsons *v.* Monteath, 13 Barb. 353; Moore *v.* Evans, 14 id. 524; Dorr *v.* N. J. Steam Navigation Co., 4 Sandf. 136; Stoddard *v.* Long Island R. R. Co., 5 id. 180; Davison *v.* Graham, 2 Ohio State, 131; Austin *v.* Manchester, &c. R. R. Co., 11 Eng. Law & Eq. 506, and notes; Carr *v.* Lancashire & Yorkshire R. R. Co., 14 id. 340, and notes; Pierce on American Railroad Law, pp. 415–25; Mich. Central R. R. Co. *v.* Hale, 6 Mich. 243; Thayer *v.* St. Louis R. R. Co., 22 Ind. 26. But the carrier is not exempted by such special contract from liability in cases of misfeasance or gross negligence. See cases cited, *supra.* Sager *v.* Portsmouth, &c. R. R. Co., 31 Maine, 228; Ill. Central R. R. Co. *v.* Morrison, 19 Ill. 136; Ashmore *v.* Penn. &c. R. R. Co., 4 Dutcher, 180; Farmers' & Mechanics' Bank *v.* Champlain Trans. Co., 23 Vt. 186; Berry *v.* Cooper, 28 Ga. 543. But in New York, it has recently been held that he may lawfully contract with a passenger, in consideration of an abatement of fare for exoneration from liability from negligence. Bissell *v.* N. Y. &c. R. R. Co., 25 N. Y. 442; Lee *v.* March, 43 Barb. 102; Kinney *v.* Cent. R. R. Co., 3 Vroom (N. J.), 407. *Contra,* Cleveland P. & A. R. R. Co. *v.* Curran,

The owners of stage-coaches, steamboats, and railroad cars, are common carriers with respect to baggage, and subject to the general rules. (*a*) As to the persons of passengers, they are not

19 Ohio State, 1; C. H. & D. R. R. *v.* Pontius, 19 Ohio State, 221; Knowlton *v.* Erie R. R. Co., 19 Ohio State, 260. And according to the weight of authorities, he is liable, notwithstanding such contract, for the want of ordinary care. Goldey *v.* Penn. R. R. Co., 30 Penn. State, 242; Pierce on American Railroad Law, pp. 420, 421; Farnham *v.* Camden & Amboy Co., 55 Penn. State, 43; American Ex. Co. *v.* Sands, 55 Penn. State, 140; School District *v.* Boston, &c. R. R. Co., 102 Mass. 552; Christenson *v.* Am. Ex. Co., 15 Minn. 270; Southern Ex. Co. *v.* Crook, 44 Ala. 468. In Ohio, he is still liable for losses arising from a neglect of that high degree of diligence enjoined upon him by his public employment, which still remains greater than that required of an ordinary bailee for hire. Davidson *v.* Graham, 2 Ohio State, 131; Graham *v.* Davis, 4 id. 362; 28 Ohio State, 418; 26 Ohio State, 595; Evansville, &c. R. R. Co. *v.* Young, 28 Ind. 516; Indianapolis, &c. R. R. Co. *v.* Allen, 31 Ind. 394; Michigan, &c. R. R. Co. *v.* Heaton, 31 Ind. 397. An exception of "losses by fire" will not excuse the carrier for fire caused by his own negligence; but the burden of proof is on the plaintiff to show that it was so caused. Lamb *v.* Camden, &c. R. R. Co., 46 N. Y. 271; Caldwell *v.* N. J. St. Co., 47 N. Y. 282; Erie R. R. Co. *v.* Lockwood, 28 Ohio State, 358; Bankard *v.* Baltimore, &c. R. R. Co., 34 Md. 197. He cannot, even by express contract, exempt himself from liability for accidents arising from the improper and unsafe condition of his conveyance. Welch *v.* Pittsburgh, &c. R. R. Co., 10 Ohio State, 64. A general notice, as, "all baggage at the risk of the owners," is generally held not to exempt the common carrier from his liability as insurer, on the ground that he is bound to accept goods such as he usually carries, and transport them under the responsibility which the law imposes on him, and the owner is not to be presumed to assent to a notice which relieves him of it. Hollister *v.* Nowlen, 19 Wendell, 234; Cole *v.* Goodwin, id. 251; Clark *v.* Faxton, 21 id. 153; Dorr *v.* N. J. Steam Navigation Co., 4 Sandf. 142; Fish *v.* Chapman, 2 Kelly (Geo.), 349; Jones *v.* Voorhees, 10 Ohio, 145 {Railroad Co. *v.* Campbell, 36 Ohio State, 647; Gaines *v.* Union Transp. & Ins. Co., 28 id. 418}; Judson *v.* West R. R. Corp., 6 Allen, 486; Steele *v.* Townsend, 1 Ala. (S. C.) 201. Such general notice is, however, held in Pennsylvania to exempt the common carrier from his stringent liability. Laing *v.* Colder, 8 Barr, 484; Camden & Amboy R. R. Co. *v.* Baldauf, 16 Penn. State, 67. But it is held that the carrier may, by notice brought home to the owner, limit his responsibility for carrying goods beyond the line of his general business, or make it dependent on certain conditions, as having notice of the kind and quantity of the goods, and an increased rate paid. Orange Co. Bank *v.* Brown, 9 Wendell, 85; Farmers' & Mechanics' Bank *v.* Champlain Transportation Co., 23 Vt. 206. In Jones *v.* Voorhees, 10 Ohio, 145, and Davidson *v.* Graham, 2 Ohio State, 131, the distinction between a general and qualified notice does not seem to have been noted. See Graham *v.* Davis, 4 id. 376. But such a notice must be brought home to the owner's knowledge. Brown *v.* Eastern R. R. Co., 11 Cush. 97; Camden & Amboy R. R. Co. *v.* Baldauf, 16 Penn. State, 67; Verner *v.* Sweitzer, 32 Penn. State, 208. In Illinois, a general notice, though brought home to the owner, is not sufficient. Western, &c. R. R. Co. *v.* Newhall, 24 Ill. 466; Mann *v.* Birchard, 40 Vt. 326. Such notices and contracts are strictly construed; thus a limitation of liability to one hundred dollars for any article, means for any article in the trunk. Earle *v.* Cadmus, 2 Daly, 237; Hopkins *v.* Westcott, 6 Blatch. 64.

(*a*) Notwithstanding no distinct price be paid for the transportation of the baggage. Orange Co. Bank *v.* Brown, 9 Wendell, 85. But this liability does not extend to merchandise or any articles not properly included in baggage, or necessary for the personal convenience of the traveller. Pardee *v.* Drew, 25 Wendell, 459; Hawkins *v.* Hoffman, 6 Hill, 586; Pennsylvania Co. *v.* Miller, 35 Ohio State, 541; Bomar *v.* Maxwell, 9 Humph. 621; Dibble *v.* Brown, 12 Geo. 217; Bell *v.* Drew, 4 E. D. Smith, 59; McCormick *v.* Hudson River R. R., id. 181; Collins *v.* Boston & Maine R. R. Co., 10 Cush. 506; Smith *v.* Boston, &c. R. R. Co., 44 N. H. 325; Richards *v.* Westcott, 2 Bosw. 589. In Porter *v.* Hildebrand, 14 Penn. State, 129, a carpenter recovered for a reasonable number of tools as a part of his baggage. The wife's jewelry was held properly included, in M'Gill *v.* Rowand, 3 Barr, 451. But not jewelry for presents to friends. Nevins *v.* Bay State, &c. Co., 4 Bosw. 225. A watch, in Jones *v.* Voorhees, 10 Ohio, 145. *Contra*, Bomar *v.* Maxwell, *supra*. Pocket pistols: Woods *v.* Devin, 13 Ill. 746; Davis *v.* Mich. &c. R. R. Co., 22 Ill. 278. Manuscripts insurers of safety, but are liable for the slightest negligence of themselves or their servants. But when an injury happens from upsetting, explosion, or the like, the presumption is negligence, and the carrier has the burden of proving due care. (*a*)

carried by a student, author, or professional man, for study, or use, or business. Hopkins *v.* Westcott, 6 Blatch. 64. An opera glass: Toledo, &c. R. R. Co. *v.* Hammond, 33 Ind. 379. So money necessary to defray travelling expenses, but not money intended for trade or investment or transportation. Johnson *v.* Stone, 11 Humph. 419; Weed *v.* S. & S. R. R. Co., 19 Wendell, 534; Jordan *v.* Fall River R. R. Co., 5 Cush. 69; Orange Co. Bank *v.* Brown, 9 Wendell, 85; Illinois, &c. R. R. *v.* Copeland, 24 Ill. 332; Hickock *v.* Naugatuck R. R. Co., 31 Conn. 281; Merrill *v.* Grinnell, 30 N. Y. 594. But see Hawkins *v.* Hoffman, 6 Hill, 586. In Ohio, as well as in several other States, the owner of a trunk as well as his wife are competent witnesses to prove its contents in a suit against a common carrier; but this evidence is not admitted to prove articles which are not properly baggage. Mad River & Lake Erie R. R. Co. *v.* Fulton, 20 Ohio, 318.

(*a*) Talmadge *v.* Zanesville & Maysville Road Co., 11 Ohio, 218; Stokes *v.* Saltonstall, 13 Peters, 181; Ingalls *v.* Bills, 9 Met. 1; Maury *v.* Talmadge, 2 M'Lean, 157; Laing *v.* Colder, 8 Barr, 482, 483; Caldwell *v.* Murphy, 1 Duer, 233; Derwort *v.* Loomer, 21 Conn. 245; Fuller *v.* Naugatuck R. R. Co., id. 557; Farish *v.* Reigle, 11 Grattan (Va.), 697; Hegeman *v.* Western R. R. Co., 16 Barb. 353; Fuller *v.* Talbot, 23 Ill. 357; Willis *v.* Long Is. R. R. Co., 32 Barb. 398; Bowan *v.* N. Y. Cent. R. R. Co., 18 N. Y. 408; Edwards *v.* Lord, 49 Maine, 274. {So of a collision. R. R. *v.* Mowery, 36 Ohio State, 418. Or the upper berth of a sleeping-car falling on a passenger. Railway *v.* Walrath, 38 Ohio State, 461.} A carrier is liable for a defect in the axle of a car, though it could not have been detected without taking the car to pieces. Alden *v.* New York, &c. R. R. Co., 26 N. Y. 102; Boyce *v.* Cal. Stage Co., 25 Cal. 460. The carrier is not liable where the passenger, by the want of ordinary care, has contributed to the injury. Pierce on American Railroad Law, 476. {But a passenger obeying the conductor is not deemed a free agent. R. R. *v.* Manson, 30 Ohio State, 451; but see Ry. *v.* Krouse, 30 id. 222.} The plaintiff need not prove that he was not guilty of contributory negligence. That is a defence that is to be proved by the other side. R. R. Co. *v.* Gladmore, 15 Wall. 401. He is bound to furnish reasonably safe and convenient means of travel, and to exercise the utmost skill in the use of the means he employs, but he is not bound to adopt every new improvement that may be better than the means he is using, regardless of cost. He may consider the nature and amount of his business, and the cost of such improvement may be of itself a sufficient reason for not adopting it. Le Barron *v.* East Boston Ferry Co., 11 Allen, 313. See also Hegeman *v.* Western R. R. Co., 13 N. Y. 9. The responsibility of the carrier for the carriage of slaves is to be measured by the law applicable to passengers. Boyce *v.* Anderson, 2 Peters, 150; McClenaghan *v.* Brock, 5 Rich. 17. As to the burden of proof, see Holbrook *v.* Utica & Schenectady R. R. Co., 12 N. Y. 236; Lucas *v.* Taunton & New Bedford R. R. Co., 6 Gray, 70. Pierce on American Railroad Law, p. 490; Curtis *v.* Rochester & Syracuse R. R. Co., 18 N. Y. 534. The fact that a train was several hours behind time is proof of gross negligence. Chicago B. & C. R. R. Co. *v.* George, 19 Ill. 510. Carriers of passengers are liable to a passenger carried gratuitously for injury done to him by the gross negligence of themselves or their servants; and it was said that when carriers undertake to convey persons by the powerful but dangerous agency of steam, any negligence may well deserve the epithet of "gross." Philadelphia & Reading R. R. Co. *v.* Derby, 14 How. 486; see Carroll *v.* N. Y. & N. H. R. R. Co., 1 Duer, 571; Steamboat New World *v.* King, 16 id. 471; Pierce on American Railroad Law, pp. 476–83; Todd *v.* Old Colony, &c. R. R. Co., 3 Allen, 18; Ind. &c. R. R. Co. *v.* Munday, 21 Ind. 48. *Contra*, when the pass is on that condition. Wells *v.* N. Y. &c. R. R. Co., 24 N. Y. 181. Common carriers of passengers are bound to take all passengers who apply, so long as they have convenient accommodation for their safe carriage, and there is no sufficient excuse for their refusal. Jenckes *v.* Coleman, 2 Sumner, 221; Bennett *v.* Dutton, 10 N. H. 481; Crouch *v.* L. & N. W. R. Co., 25 Eng. Law & Eq. 287. Common carriers must carry all who apply, without distinction of color, religious belief, or political relations or prejudices, but they may separate their passengers by other distinctions than those of sex, if doing so is a sound regulation to preserve peace, promote comfort, secure order, or maintain the rights of both carriers and passengers. Westchester & Phila. R. R. Co. *v.* Miles, 55 Penn. State, 210. {Nor can they discriminate in their charges in favor of large

§ 183. **Contract of Principal and Surety or Guaranty.** (*a*) The contract of principal and surety or guaranty takes place whenever one person to procure credit for another, undertakes to be answerable for him. The original debtor is called *principal*, and the collateral debtor, *surety* or *guarantor*. The criterion of the contract is, that there is an original debt or duty, for the payment or performance of which a third person intervenes, by way of additional security. The surety does not take the place of the

shippers. Scofield *v.* Railway Co., 43 Ohio State, 571. } Neither entry into the cars, nor payment of fare is necessary to constitute one a passenger. Being in the waiting-room of a company, waiting for a train, is sufficient. Gordon *v.* Grand S. &c. R. R. Co., 40 Barb. 546 ; Ohio, &c. R. R. Co. *v.* Muhling, 30 Ill. 9. They are not liable for injury to a passenger caused by a mob along the line of the road, unless negligent in regard to it. Pittsburg, &c. R. R. Co. *v.* Hinds, 53 Penn. State, 512. *Telegraph Companies* were held in the earlier cases in the United States to be common carriers of messages, and were held to the responsibility of common carriers. They are now held responsible only for diligence. A good discussion of the ground and measure of responsibility is found in Ellis *v.* Am. Tel. Co., 13 Allen, 226 ; and in Grinnell *v.* West. Un. Tel. Co., 113 Mass. 299. The company is liable to the sender of a message for failure to forward, and for mistakes in the transmission. The company is not liable to the person to whom a message is directed for failure to forward it, unless such person had contracted with the company for its transmission. In the United States, the company is liable to the receiver of a message for mistake in transmission. N. Y. & Wash. Print. Tel. Co. *v.* Dryburg, 35 Penn. State, 157 ; Ellis *v.* Am. Tel. Co., 13 Allen, 226 ; Elwood *v.* West. Un. Tel. Co., 45 N. Y. 459; Lowry *v.* West. Un. Tel. Co., 60 N. Y. 198 ; Aiken *v.* West. Un. Tel. Co., 5 S. Ca. 358 ; and is liable to the receiver for a message forged and sent by one of its employees. Bank of Cal. *v.* West. Un. Tel. Co., Supreme Court of Cal., July, 1877. In the United States the sender of the message also has been held liable to the receiver for mistake in transmission made by the company. Durkee *v.* Vermont Cent. R. R. Co., 29 Vt. 127 ; Saveland *v.* Green, 40 Wis. 431. In England it is held that the company is not the agent of the sender, and hence the sender is not liable to the receiver for mistake in transmission. Henkel *v.* Pape, L. R. 6 Ex. 7. And also that a tort, which consists in the imperfect performance of a contract, does not give a right of action to one who is not a party to the contract, and hence the receiver has no action against the company for mistake in transmission. Playford *v.* Un. King. El. Tel. Co., L. R. 4 Q. B. 706 ; Dickson *v.* Reuter's Tel. Co., L. R. 2 C. P. Div. 62, affirmed on appeal, L. R. 3 C. P. Div. C. A. 1. Where a cipher despatch, which the company's agents had no means of understanding, was by negligence sent incorrectly, the company was held liable only in nominal damages. Saunders *v.* Stewart, L. R. 1 C. P. Div. 326. For failing to send such message, the company is held liable only in nominal damages. Candee *v.* West. Un. Tel. Co., 34 Wis. 471. { But a message, "Will give you 50 for 25," is not obscure or in cipher. Telegraph Co. *v.* Griswold, 37 Ohio State, 301. And a company cannot stipulate against its own negligence ; and negligence is presumed from inaccurate transmission. Id. } A condition that the company will not be liable for damages unless claim therefor be presented in writing within sixty days after sending the message, held valid and binding. Young *v.* West. Un. Tel. Co., 65 N. Y. 163. { It is only liable for damages that naturally would follow and might be in contemplation. Bank *v.* Tel. Co., 30 Ohio State, 555. } The condition on the printed blanks that the company will not be liable beyond the cost of the message, unless the message is repeated and an additional charge paid therefor, held in Indiana unreasonable, and invalid. West. Un. Tel. Co. *v.* Fenton, 52 Ind. 1. Held valid in Passmore *v.* West. Un. Tel. Co., 78 Penn. State, 238 ; Grinnell *v.* West. Un. Tel. Co., 113 Mass. 299, in which last case, the cases previous to it are collated. But such condition is valid only against the sender ; it is not valid against the receiver, whose right of action is based not on contract, but on tort. La Grange *v.* Kelly, 25 La. Ann. 383.

(*a*) See 3 Kent, Com. 121 ; Brandt on Principal and Surety ; Baylies on Principal and Surety ; Fell on Guaranty ; Reed *v.* Evans, 17 Ohio, 128 ; Selser *v.* Brock, 3 Ohio State, 302 ; Hall *v.* Williams, 9 id. 17. A surety against whom judgment has been rendered may, without making payment himself, proceed in equity against his principal, to subject the estate of the latter to the payment of the debt. Hale *v.* Wetmore, 4 Ohio State, 600.

principal, and make the debt absolutely his own; but merely undertakes to pay in case the principal does not. We have seen that the fifth section of the statute of frauds requires the contract of the surety to be in writing, because it is for the debt of another, and not his own debt. Like other contracts, too, there must be a consideration; but whether this must be expressed in writing, we have seen is doubtful. It is not necessary that the fact of being surety should appear on the face of the writing; for it may be proved by parol. From what has been said of indorsers of negotiable paper, you will perceive that they become sureties for the parties before them on the paper, and differ in no respect from common guarantors, except that by becoming parties to the paper successively, each becomes a distinct and not a joint surety, and is entitled to notice. The most common cases of sureties, strictly so called, are those of bail in civil and criminal proceedings, to be described hereafter, and of sureties in bonds for the performance of official duty. It follows from the nature of the obligation, that it cannot exceed that of the principal, though it may be less; that it must be for the same identical thing as that of the principal; and that it must be extinguished by the extinction of the principal obligation. Any compromise, therefore, with the principal by which he is discharged, discharges the surety; and any alteration in the terms of the original liability, without the consent of the surety, discharges him; for it is no longer the same thing for which he undertook. The most common instance under this head, is that of *giving time* to the principal. (*a*) If the creditor, without the consent of the surety, enters into an agreement, or does any act by which he precludes himself from proceeding against the principal the moment the debt becomes due, he thereby discharges the surety; but mere delay to enforce payment does not have this effect. (*b*) If the surety is compelled to pay the debt, he has his

(*a*) Smith's Mercantile Law (Holcombe & Gholson), 465, 466. If a surety voluntarily pays money on a void obligation, his co-surety is not liable to contribution. Russell *v.* Failor, 1 Ohio State, 327. An alteration to discharge a surety must be made by a binding contract, and therefore upon a new consideration. Woodworth *v.* Brinker, 11 Ohio State, 593; Jones *v.* Brown, 11 Ohio State, 601; Ide *v.* Church, 14 Ohio State, 372; People's Bank *v.* Parsons, 30 Vt. 711. In Ohio, it has been held that the payment of usurious interest, or even a promise to pay it, is a sufficient consideration for a promise to extend the time of payment, to discharge the surety. Blazer *v.* Bundy, 15 Ohio State, 57; Wood *v.* Newkirk, 15 Ohio State, 295. {Or a promise to pay the same interest. Fawcett *v.* Freshwater, 31 Ohio State, 637. Part payment of an overdue debt is not. Turnbull *v.* Brock, 31 id. 649. Payment of more interest than is due is not an extension unless so intended. Vose *v.* Woodford, 29 id. 245. If the surety holds ample indemnity he is not discharged. Kleinhaus *v.* Generous, 25 id. 667. A wife mortgaging her property to secure her husband's note is a surety within this rule, and is discharged by a contract extending the note. Ins. Co. *v.* McDonnell, 42 Ohio State, 650. Not so of a retiring partner. Rawson *v.* Taylor, 30 id. 389.}

(*b*) 3 Kent, Com. 111, 112. Nor will failure to present the claim to the assignee where the principal made an assignment for the benefit of his creditors. Dye *v.* Dye, 21 Ohio State, 86. {Nor failure to sue until the debtor becomes insolvent. Newton *v.* Hammond, 38 id. 430. Nor allowing the claim to be barred by limitations against the principal's administrator. Moore *v.* Gray, 26 Ohio State, 525.} The strict rules of demand and notice necessary to charge the indorsers of negotiable paper, do not apply to guaranties. But in the case of a guaranty that a note is action against the principal. If there be several co-sureties, and one pays the debt, the rest are liable to contribute their share; and for this purpose we have seen that accommodation indorsers are held to be co-sureties in this State. (*a*) At common law, the surety could not proceed against the principal, until he had first actually paid the debt; and he had no means of compelling the creditor to take any steps to hasten payment by the principal; but we have a statute for the relief of sureties and bail, by which a surety, by bond, bill, or note, being under apprehension that the principal may remove, or become insolvent, may notify the creditor in writing to sue the principal, and if he fail to do so, the surety will be discharged. (*b*) But this statute does not include sureties for guardians, executors, administrators, or public officers. Also, when a judgment is rendered against principal and surety, by our statute the latter may require it to specify that he is surety; and may have an execution first issued against the principal, until his property is exhausted, before proceeding against himself; and should he ultimately be obliged to pay the debt, he may at once sue out process against the principal, and have judgment rendered immediately upon the return of such process, instead of waiting until the next term, as in other cases.

§ 184. **Contract of Insurance.** (*c*) The subject of insurance is

collectible, the holder is bound to use reasonable diligence in collecting the note and to give reasonable notice to the guarantor of the failure of the maker to pay it, — and the guarantor is discharged where he suffers damage by reason of the neglect of the holder. Bashford *v.* Shaw, 4 Ohio State, 263; Wolfe *v.* Brown, 5 id. 304. And if the creditor, in his agreement to delay the prosecution of a suit against the principal debtor, reserves all rights and remedies against the surety or indorser, the surety or indorser is not discharged. Story on Prom. Notes, § 416; Rees *v.* Berrington, 2 Ves. Jr. (Sumner's ed.) 544, *notes;* Sohier *v.* Loring, 6 Cush. 537. {But abandoning a levy on the property of the debtor releases the surety *pro tanto* if the plaintiff knew he was surety. Day *v.* Ramey, 40 Ohio State, 446.}

(*a*) *Supra*, p. 512, n. (*b*); 1 Story, Eq. Juris. §§ 492–504. As to the rights of subrogation, see Constant *v.* Matteson, 22 Ill. 546.

(*b*) {R. S. § 5833; Baker *v.* Kellogg, 29 Ohio State, 663; Iiffe *v.* Weymouth, 40 id. 101; Clark *v.* Osborn, 41 id. 28; Meriden Silver Plate Co. *v.* Flory, 44 id. (1886); and R. S. § 5845 authorizes the surety to maintain suit against the principal to compel him to pay the debt. Wilkins *v.* Bank, 31 Ohio State, 565. That he would have such right of suit in equity independent of the statute, see Horst *v.* Dague, 34 id. 371, 375.}

(*c*) On the subject of Insurance, see the English treatises of Park, Marshall, Miller, Hughes, Ellis, and Arnold; 3 Kent, Com. lec. 48, 49, 50; and the American treatises of Phillips, Duer, Angell, Flanders, and Wood.

Much of the litigation respecting insurance has relation to *concealment, misrepresentation*, or *warranty*, as to which, see 1 Phillips, § 524; 2 Duer, 381; Angell, § 174. A fact is *material* to the *risk*, when it tends to show its nature and extent, and might reasonably influence the taking or refusing it, or the amount of premium. *Concealment* is the suppression of such a fact, when the other party has not the means of knowing, or is not presumed to know it. *Misrepresentation* is a false statement with regard to such a fact. Both are supposed to precede the making of the policy, and to have an influence thereupon; and the rule as to both is, that if either party, whether by design or oversight, conceals or misrepresents a material fact, the contract will be void. Materiality is a question of fact for the jury. A *warranty* is either *expressed*, in words contained in the policy, or *implied* from such words. Its consequences flow from the policy, and not from any thing preceding. It is not an inducement to making the contract, but a part of the contract when made, and operates as a condition of its validity. Hence the materiality of the fact warranted is not in quesone of vast compass and importance. It comprehends three principal subdivisions or branches: namely, *marine*, *fire*, and *life insurance;* on each of which volumes have been written. The utility of insurance is beyond all question. It serves to equalize misfortunes, by distributing the effects of an individual calamity among many; or to shift inevitable losses from those who can ill afford to bear them, to those who, in the aggregate, derive profit therefrom. It is, therefore, a contract highly favored by the law. We have no law prohibiting individuals from insuring, but the business is chiefly conducted by incorporated companies. The contract of insurance may be defined to be, a contract in which one party, for a stipulated sum, agrees to indemnify another against certain risks or perils therein specified. The contract itself is called policy, from the Italian word *polizza;* the price paid for insurance, *premium;* the party insuring, *insurer* or *underwriter;* and the other party *insured* or *assured.* I shall make some general remarks on each of the three branches of insurance above named.

1. *Marine Insurance.* Here the object is indemnity against the *perils of navigation.* These perils are usually specified in the policy; and they may include all casualties to which the ship or cargo may be exposed, except those which good morals or public policy require should not be insured against. The most common perils are lightning, tempest, fire, shipwreck, capture, robbery, blockade, embargo, and barratry. *Barratry* here means fraudulent misconduct of the master or his mariners, without the consent or connivance of the owner; for no man can insure against his own misconduct. (*a*) Yet on the score of morality, the law of insurance is not over scrupulous; for it permits a party to insure against the perils incident to an *illicit* or *contraband* trade, as it respects foreign nations. The ordinary *subjects* of insurance are the ship, including tackle and furniture, the cargo and freight, and sometimes profit and commissions. Seamen are not permitted to insure their wages, because this would take away a strong stimulus to exertion. The propriety of allowing *wager policies*, where persons insure upon the mere hope or expectation of profit without having any actual interest at risk, may well be doubted. Such policies are expressly prohibited in many places, and would probably come

tion. There must be a strict and literal, not merely a substantial, compliance. This is a hard rule, and there is a tendency to relax it. For leading cases on these topics, see Carter *v.* Boehm, 3 Burrows, 1905; Lynch *v.* Dunsford, 14 East, 494; Curry *v.* Com. Ins. Co., 10 Pick. 535; Fowler *v.* Ætna Ins. Co., 6 Cowen, 673; Bufe *v.* Turner, 6 Taunt. 338; N. Y. Bowery *v.* N. Y. Fire Ins. Co., 17 Wendell, 359; Jennings *v.* Chenango, 2 Denio, 75; Duncan *v.* Sun, 6 Wendell, 488; Shaw *v.* Robberds, 1 Neville & Perry, 279; S. C. 6 Ad. & El. 75; Smith *v.* Columbia, 17 Penn. State, 253; Gates *v.* Madison, 5 N. Y. 469; Protection *v.* Harman, 2 Ohio State, 452; Clark *v.* Man. Ins. Co., 8 How. 235; Wall *v.* East River, 3 Selden, 370; Meade *v.* North Ins. Co., 3 id. 530; Miller *v.* W. F. M. Ins. Co., 1 Handy, 208. As to the party in whose name the suit is to be brought. Protection Ins. Co. *v.* Wilson, 6 Ohio State, 553.

(*a*) {If the conduct is free from fraud, gross negligence, or wilful violation, it is not barratry, though it causes loss. Germania Ins. Co. *v.* Sherlock, 25 Ohio State, 33. Negligence of officers or employees, is one of the perils insured against. Perrin *v.* Protection Ins. Co., 11 Ohio 147. Phœnix Ins. Co. *v.* Erie Transp. Co., 117 U. S. 312.}

within our statute against gaming. Indeed, such policies are contrary to the fundamental idea of insurance, which is indemnity against loss; for there can be no apprehension of loss, when there is nothing at risk. Yet wager policies of this description have sometimes been sustained, when the underwriter knew that the insured had nothing at risk. There is a distinction between *open* and *valued* policies. An *open policy* is where the amount of interest is not specified, but left to be proved in the event of loss. A *valued policy* is where the parties have fixed a value to the subject insured, which shall be binding in case of loss. It is obvious that all wager policies must be valued policies; but the fact of valuation will not of itself sustain them, because the valuation in the policy is held not to be so entirely conclusive but that the insurer may prove that the whole subject of insurance was never at risk. Still more, he may show that there was no interest whatever at risk. When a loss occurs within the perils insured against, it is either *partial* or *total.* It is usual to insert a memorandum in the policy, that the insurer shall not be answerable for any *partial loss* within a certain *per centum*, commonly five. The object is to exclude trifling injuries, and sometimes, on certain articles liable to gradual deterioration, all partial loss is excluded, for the same reason. Where the policy is open, the value is estimated at the place of departure, adding expenses. The policy contains a special authority to the master to incur expense in preventing loss or saving property; and from the moment of disaster, he becomes the agent as well for the insurer as the insured. In adjusting a partial injury to the ship, where the insurer pays for the repairs, the rule is, to allow one-third of the value of the new materials, for their increased value above the old. A *total loss*, strictly so called, seldom occurs; and when it does, the custom is to stipulate that the insurer shall deduct a small *per centum*, say two or three, from the whole amount of insurance, in order to take from the insured all motive to desire a total loss, from the certainty of a full indemnity. But a technical total loss occurs whenever the damage exceeds one-half the amount at risk; because then the insured has a right *to abandon* to the insurer, and proceed for a total loss. From the moment of such abandonment, the thing insured becomes the property of the insurer, and everything is done at his risk and expense. (*a*) The contract of insurance is pre-eminently one of good faith. The insured is bound to make a full disclosure, at the time of taking out the policy, of all matters affecting the risk, within his particular knowledge. And during the continuance of the risk, he must do nothing, by deviation, negligence, or otherwise, to increase the risk. The loss may have

(*a*) {Globe Ins. Co. *v.* Sherlock, 25 Ohio State, 50, as to the difference between actual total loss and constructive total loss.} Cincinnati Ins. Co. *v.* Duffield, 6 Ohio State, 200. {There can be no claim for a total loss without abandonment where the boat remains *in specie.* Globe Ins. Co. *v.* Sherlock, 25 id. 50. The right of abandonment only obtains in marine insurance.}

occurred before the insurance is effected, but the insured must not know this. The expression "*lost or not lost*," in the policy, does not save the insured, if he knew of the loss. There is also an implied warranty on the part of the insured that the ship is in all respects *sea-worthy* at the commencement of the risk; which includes not only a sufficient ship, tackle and furniture, but also a sufficient master and crew. In case of *double insurance*, where policies do not stipulate the contrary, the rule of contribution applies, and each insurer contributes in proportion to his amount.

2. *Fire Insurance.* (*a*) Fire is one of the perils in marine insurance; but I speak now of insurance against fire on land. In this, however, there is little that is peculiar. The character and situation of the building must be fully described by the applicant, and the purpose for which it is occupied; and no change in either can be made by which the risk is increased. (*b*) If the fire happen

(*a*) When the agreement to insure is complete, and the applicant has complied with all the conditions imposed, the risk commences, although the policy may not have been issued. Hamilton *v.* Lycoming Ins. Co., 5 Barr (Penn.), 339; Palm *v.* Medina Fire Ins. Co., 20 Ohio, 529; Kentucky Mutual Insurance Co. *v.* Jenks, 5 Ind. (Porter) 96; Lightbody *v.* North American Ins. Co., 23 Wendell, 18; Carpenter *v.* Mutual Safety Ins. Co., 4 Sandf. Ch. 408; Suydam *v.* Columbus Ins. Co., 18 Ohio, 459; Neville *v.* Cincinnati Ins. Co., 19 id. 452; Hallock *v.* Commercial Ins. Co., 2 Dutcher, 268. The contract of insurance may be made by letter. Tayloe *v.* Merchants' Fire Ins. Co., 9 How. 390; Mactier *v.* Frith, 6 Wendell, 103. In the absence of any statute, a verbal contract of insurance is binding. Trustees First Baptist Church *v.* Brooklyn Fire Ins. Co., 19 N. Y. 305; Mobile Marine Dock & Mut. Ins. Co. *v.* McMillan, 31 Ala. 711; Post *v.* Ætna Ins. Co., 43 Barb. 351; Kelly *v.* Commonwealth Ins. Co., 10 Bosworth, 82; Audubon *v.* Excelsior Fire Ins. Co., 27 N. Y. 216; Commercial Mut. Marine Ins. Co. *v.* Union Mut. Ins. Co., 19 How. 318; Ins. Co. *v.* Wall. 31 Ohio State, 628. Though the charter of an insurance company provides that the policies are to be signed by the president, this does not prevent the corporation from making an oral contract for insurance. Sanborn *v.* Fireman's Ins. Co., 16 Gray, 448; Walker *v.* Metropolitan Ins. Co., 56 Maine, 371. But see Henning *v.* United States Ins. Co., 47 Mo. 425. The question has been raised whether the stamp laws affect this, but I do not see why they should prevent this contract being verbal any more than any other. All contracts are required to be stamped, if on paper, but it has never been thought that this required all contracts to be written. West Mass. Ins. Co. *v.* Duffey, 2 Kansas, 347. Statements in the application when referred to "as forming a part of the policy," will have the effect of a warranty. Byers *v.* Ins. Co., 35 Ohio State, 606; Burrett *v.* Saratoga County Mutual Fire Ins. Co., 5 Hill, 188; Murdock *v.* Chenango County Mutual Ins. Co., 2 N. Y. 210; Sexton *v.* Montgomery County Mutual Ins. Co., 9 Barb. 200; Kennedy *v.* St. Lawrence County Mutual Ins. Co., 10 id. 285; Williams *v.* N. E. Mutual Fire Ins. Co., 31 Maine, 224. *Contra*, if not thus referred to. Jefferson Ins. Co. *v.* Cotheal, 7 Wend. 72; Snyder *v.* Farmers' Ins. Co., 13 id. 92; s. c. 16 id. 481. See Sheldon *v.* Hartford Fire Ins. Co., 22 Conn. 235; Jennings *v.* Chenango Mutual Ins. Co., 2 Denio, 75; Protection Ins. Co. *v.* Harmer, 2 Ohio State, 452.

(*b*) Sillem *v.* Thornton, 26 Eng. Law & Eq. 238; Glen *v.* Lewis, 20 id. 364; Stetson *v.* Mass. Mutual Fire Ins. Co., 4 Mass. 330; Jefferson County Ins. Co. *v.* Cotheal, 7 Wendell, 72; Grant *v.* Howard Ins. Co., 5 Hill, 10; Richards *v.* Protection Ins. Co. 30 Maine, 273; Moore *v.* Protection Ins. Co., 29 id. 97; Billings *v.* Tolland, 20 Conn. 130; Harris *v.* Columbiana Ins. Co., 4 Ohio State, 285; Washington Mutual Ins. Co. *v.* Mer. & Man. Mutual Ins. Co., 5 id. 450; Sarsfield *v.* Metropolitan Ins. Co., 61 Barb. 479. Want of explicitness to the answers to interrogatories is waived by the issuing of the policy. Nichols *v.* Fayette, &c. Ins. Co., 1 Allen, 63; Liberty Hall Ass. *v.* Housatonic Mut. Fire Ins. Co., 7 Gray, 261. Where the "*storing*" of hazardous articles is prohibited, the policy is held not to be vitiated where the storing is not the principal object of the deposit, but is merely incidental to it, as only for consumption or other temporary purposes. N. Y. Equitable Ins. Co. *v.* Langdon, 6 Wendell, 623;

through the gross misconduct or the intentional act of the insured, the insurer is clear. (*a*) The policy may be either open or valued, but is usually valued; and an insurance upon a building does not cover the movables in the building, unless by express stipulation. Whatever is saved from the fire goes to the benefit of the insured; that is, the insurer, to the extent of his undertaking, must make good the amount actually lost, and not merely the proportion which the amount lost bears to the whole amount. (*b*) There is no such thing as abandonment for a total loss. The insurer may always repair, if he chooses; but the rule of one-third new for old does not here apply. (*c*) It is usual to enumerate certain articles, and certain occupations, which, by reason of the very great hazard of fire, are excluded from the policy. (*d*)

s. c. 1 Hall, 226; O'Neil *v.* Buffalo Fire Ins. Co., 3 Comst. 122; Hynds *v.* Schenectady County Mutual Ins. Co., 16 Barb. 119; Rafferty *v.* New Brunswick Fire Ins. Co., 3 Harrison, 480; Harris *v.* Columbiana Ins. Co., 4 Ohio State, 285. But see Glen *v.* Lewis, 20 Eng. Law & Eq. 364. See Mead *v.* Northwestern Ins. Co., 7 N. Y. 530; Westfall *v.* Hudson River Fire Ins. Co., 2 Kernan, 289; Lee *v.* Howard Fire Ins. Co., 3 Gray, 583; Macomber *v.* Howard Fire Ins. Co., 7 id. 257. As to misstatements of the distance of other buildings, see Burritt *v.* Saratoga County Mutual Ins. Co., 5 Hill, 188; Jennings *v.* Chenango County Mutual Ins. Co., 2 Denio, 75; Wilson *v.* Herkimer Co., &c., 6 N. Y. 53; Wall *v.* East River Mutual Ins. Co., 3 id. 370; Gates *v.* Madison County Mutual Ins. Co., 2 N. Y. 43; s. c. 5 N. Y. 469; Hall *v.* People's Mutual Fire Ins. Co., 6 Gray, 185; Allen *v.* Charlestown Mutual Fire Ins. Co., 5 id. 384. As to misstatements of title, see Smith *v.* Bowditch Mutual Fire Ins. Co., 6 Cush. 448; Allen *v.* Charlestown Mutual Fire Ins. Co., 5 Gray, 384; Jenkins *v.* Quincy Mutual Fire Ins. Co., 7 id. 370; Byers *v.* Ins. Co., 35 Ohio State, 606.

(*a*) But the mere negligence of the assured or his servants, where there is no fraud, is not sufficient to defeat the policy. Shaw *v.* Robberds, 6 Ad. & El. 75, 83; s. c. 1 N. & P. 279; Columbia Ins. Co. *v.* Lawrence, 10 Peters, 517, 518; Waters *v.* Merchants' Louisville Ins. Co., 11 id. 225; Perrin *v.* Protection Ins. Co., 11 Ohio, 147, overruling Lodwick *v.* Kennedy, 5 id. 433; St. Louis Ins. Co. *v.* Glasgow, 8 Missouri, 713; Mathews *v.* Howard Ins. Co., 13 Barb. 234, overruling Grim *v.* Phœnix Ins. Co., 13 Johns. 451; Hynds *v.* Schenectady County Ins. Co., 16 id. 119; St. John *v.* Am. Mut. F. & M. Ins. Co., 1 Duer, 371; Copeland *v.* N. E. Ins. Co., 2 Me. 432; Chandler *v.* Worcester Fire Ins. Co., 3 Cush. 328; Butman *v.* Monmouth Fire Ins. Co., 35 Maine, 227; Catlin *v.* Springfield Fire Ins. Co., 1 Sumner, 434; Henderson *v.* Western Marine and Fire Ins. Co., 10 Rob. (La.) 164; Cumberland, &c. Co. *v.* Douglas, 58 Penn. State, 419. But if the negligence of the insured himself amounts to real recklessness or misconduct, it will, it seems, be a defence to an action on the policy. Johnson *v.* Berkshire Ins. Co., 4 Allen, 388. As to the distinction between recklessness or misconduct and mere negligence, see Citizens' Ins. Co. *v.* Marsh, 41 Penn. State, 386. Where the policy is payable to a third party in case of loss, he is affected by the acts of the assured, in the absence of any special provision relieving him from responsibility for such acts of the assured. Fogg *v.* Middlesex Mutual Fire Ins. Co., 10 Cush. 346; Hale *v.* Mechanics' Mutual Fire Ins. Co., 6 Gray, 169; Grosvenor *v.* Atlantic Fire Ins. Co., 17 N. Y. 391.

(*b*) Trull *v.* Roxbury Mutual Fire Ins. Co., 3 Cushing, 267.

(*c*) Brinley *v.* National Ins. Co., 11 Met. 195.

(*d*) The insurance being against fire, there must generally be actual ignition to bring the loss within the policy. Therefore, a loss by intense heat, the explosion of steam, lightning, or the removal of goods through apprehension of a neighboring fire, is not within the policy. Austin *v.* Drewe, 6 Taunt. 436; s. c. 4 Camp. 360; Millaudon *v.* N. O. Ins. Co., 4 La. An. 15; Babcock *v.* Montgomery County Mutual Ins. Co., 6 Barb. 537; s. c. 4 N. Y. 326; Kenniston *v.* Mer. Co. Mutual Ins. Co., 14 N. H. 341; Hillier *v.* Alleghany County Mut. Ins. Co., 3 Barr (Penn.), 470. But losses through *bonâ fide* efforts to extinguish the fire, as by wetting and soiling goods, or losses by theft, consequent upon their forced removal, are fairly within the policy. Witherel *v.* Maine Ins. Co., 49 Maine, 200; Newmark *v.* Liverpool, &c. Ins. Co., 30 Missouri, 160; Talamon *v.* Home, &c. Ins. Co., 16 La. An. 426; Whitehurst *v.*

3. *Life Insurance.* (*a*) This is a contract by which the insurer,

Fayetteville, &c. Ins. Co., 6 Jones Law, 352 ; Tilton *v.* Hamilton Ins. Co., 1 Bosworth, 367. And where the loss is incurred in the *bonâ fide* removal of goods in consequence of the dangerous proximity of a fire, it is within the policy, though the building in which they were contained never actually catches. Leiber *v.* Liverpool, &c. Ins. Co., 6 Bush (Ky.), 639 ; White *v.* Republic, &c. Ins. Co., 57 Maine, 91. Where the policy contains an exception of "explosion," what language will include as loss by fire consequent upon the explosion, and what will not, see United L. F. & M. Ins. Co. *v.* Foote, 22 Ohio State, 340 ; Boatmen's F. & M. Ins. Co. *v.* Parker, 23 Ohio State, 85. The insurer must have an interest in the property insured, both when the insurance is effected and when the loss occurs, and this interest may be legal or equitable. M'Givney *v.* Phœnix Ins. Co., 1 Wendell, 85 ; Tyler *v.* Fire Ins. Co., 12 Wendell, 507 ; s. c. 16 id. 385 ; Swift *v.* Vt. Mutual Ins. Co., 18 Vt. 305 ; Perry County Ins. Co. *v.* Stewart, 19 Penn. State, 45 ; Insurance Co. *v.* Updegraff, 21 id. 513 ; Fowler *v.* New York, &c. Ins. Co., 26 N. Y. 422.

Thus the mortgagor and mortgagee may each insure the premises. The mortgagor, in case of loss, can recover the full value of the premises, not exceeding the sum insured. But the mortgagee can only recover the value of his debt, and if it is paid, he can recover nothing. Carpenter *v.* Providence Ins. Co., 16 Peters, 495 ; Motley *v.* Manuf. Ins. Co., 29 Maine, 337 ; French *v.* Rogers, 16 N. H. 177. It has recently been held, that the mortgagee may recover of the insurers the sum insured, and that the insurers are not entitled to be subrogated to his rights against the mortgagor. King *v.* State Mutual Fire Ins. Co., 7 Cushing, 1. But see the authorities there cited, and Smith *v.* Columbia Ins. Co., 17 Penn. State, 253 ; Insurance Co. *v.* Updegraff, 21 id. 513 ; Pentz *v.* Ætna Fire Ins. Co., 3 Edw. Ch. 341 ; s. c. 9 Paige, 568 ; Morrison *v.* Tennessee M. & F. Ins. Co., 18 Missouri, 262 ; Cushing *v.* Thompson, 34 Maine, 496 ; Quebec Fire Ins. Co. *v.* St. Louis, 22 Eng. Law & Eq. 73 ; Loomis *v.* Eagle Life & Health Ins. Co., 6 Gray, 396 ; Concord Ins. Co. *v.* Woodbury, 45 Maine, 447.

The alienation of the interest of the insured avoids the policy, unless made with the consent of the insurer. Ins. Co. *v.* Archer, 36 Ohio State, 608 ; Carpenter *v.* Providence Washington Ins. Co., 16 Peters, 502 ; Wilson *v.* Hill, 3 Met. 66. But a mortgage is held not to be such an alienation. { Byers *v.* Ins. Co., 35 Ohio State, 606. The retirement of a partner is not an alienation. West *v.* Citizens Ins. Co., 27 Ohio State, 1. } Jackson *v.* Mass. Mutual Fire Ins. Co., 23 Pick. 418 ; Conover *v.* Mutual Ins. Co., 3 Denio, 254 ; Shepherd *v.* Union Mutual Fire Ins. Co., 38 N. H. 232 ; Smith *v.* Monmouth, &c. Ins. Co., 50 Maine, 96. *Contra*, M'Culloch *v.* Indiana Mutual Fire Ins. Co., 8 Blackf. 50. Where notice is required to be given of all alterations in the ownership, or encumbrances, a mortgage is included. Edmonds *v.* Mutual Ins. Co., 1 Allen, 311 ; Hutchins *v.* Cleveland Mutual Ins. Co., 11 Ohio State, 477. Where the charter of a Mutual Insurance Company requires encumbrances to be noticed in the written application, or the policy is to be void, a verbal notice of an incumbrance is not sufficient. Smith *v.* Farmers' Ins. Co., 19 Ohio State, 287. The seizure and sale of the property on execution, even when the assured has only an equity of redemption, are not an alienation so long as the right to redeem the property seized remains. Strong *v.* Ins. Co., 10 Pick. 40 ; Clark *v.* N. E. M. F. Ins. Co., 6 Cush. 342 ; Rice *v.* Tower, 1 Gray, 426 ; see Buffum *v.* Bowditch, 10 Cush. 540. Whether the divesting of all interest of the assured by operation of law, as by the foreclosure of a mortgage, is an alienation, may be considered an open question ; but the better opinion is that it is an alienation. McLaren *v.* Hartford Fire Ins. Co., 5 N. Y. 151; Bragg *v.* N. E. Mutual Fire Ins. Co., 5 Foster (N. H.), 289. Such a sale has been held an alienation, although subsequently to the loss the sale is set aside by consent. Mt. Vernon Man. Co. *v.* Summit Co. Mutual Ins. Co., 10 Ohio State, 347. {But not if set aside before loss. Ins. Co. *v.* Sampson, 38 id. 672. } A conveyance in trust for creditors, though in fraud of the insolvent laws, is an alienation. Dadmun Man. Co. *v.* Worcester Mutual Fire Ins. Co., 11 Met. 429. An assignment in insolvency is an alienation. Little *v.* Ins. Co., 38 Ohio State, 110 ; Young *v.* Eagle Ins. Co., 14 Gray, 150. A contract to convey is not an alienation. Trumbull *v.* Portage County Mutual Ins. Co., 12 Ohio, 305 ; Masters *v.* Madison County Mutual Ins. Co., 11 Barb. 624 ; Perry County Ins. Co. *v.* Stewart, 19 Penn. State, 45 ; Morrison *v.* Tennessee Marine and Fire Ins. Co., 18 Missouri, 262. As to the time when the insurance begins, see Kentucky

(*a*) {Life insurance, unlike fire and marine, is not a contract of indemnity. } See, in addition to the treatises on Insurance already cited, the recent works of Reynolds, Bunyon, and Bliss on Life Insurance.

for a fixed premium, undertakes to pay a stipulated sum, if the person whose life is insured die within the time for which insurance is effected. The sum paid, by way of premium, may be either a sum in gross, or a sum annually. The term of insurance may be either a given number of years, or for life; and the life insured may be either that of the person who procures the insurance, or that of any other person in whose life he is actually interested. (*a*) The rules by which life insurance is governed are founded upon a calculation of the average chances of human life in certain regions, and they are as fixed and certain as any other rules. The applicant is required to furnish a written answer to a set of queries relating to his age, habits, occupation, constitution, and the like; and similar queries are usually addressed to his medical adviser, and to some intimate friend. These answers become part of the contract; and any misrepresentation or concealment vitiates the policy. (*b*) Restrictions are usually inserted, as to the places to

Mutual Ins. Co. *v.* Jenks, 5 Ind. (Porter) 96. A condition in an insurance policy that a suit upon the same shall be brought only in the county where the company is established, is not binding on the assured. Nute *v.* Hamilton Mutual Ins. Co., 6 Gray, 174; Hall *v.* People's Mutual Fire Ins. Co., 6 id. 185. But a provision limiting the time within which the suit is to be brought, is valid. Burton *v.* Buckeye Ins. Co., 26 Ohio State, 467; Portage Co. Mutual Fire Ins. Co. *v.* West, 6 Ohio State, 599; Cray *v.* Hartford Fire Ins. Co., 1 Blatchford, C. C. 280; Wilson *v.* Ætna Ins. Co., 20 Vt. 99; Amesbury *v.* Bowditch Mutual Fire Ins. Co., 6 Gray, 596; Fullam *v.* N. Y. Union Ins. Co., 7 id. 61.

(*a*) A contract by which an association for a consideration engages to pay money at the death of a member to one who has an interest in his life, is a contract of insurance, notwithstanding the amount to be paid is not a gross sum, but is graduated by the number of members holding similar contracts; notwithstanding the premium to be paid depends upon the contingency of the death of members; and notwithstanding it provides no means of enforcing the payment of the consideration. Com. *v.* Wetherbee, 105 Mass. 162.

(*b*) Vose *v.* Eagle Life and Health Ins. Co., 6 Cush. 42; Miles *v.* Conn. Mutual Life Ins. Co., 3 Gray, 580; Geach *v.* Ingall, 14 Meeson & Wels. 95; Anderson *v.* Fitzgerald, 24 Eng. Law & Eq. 1; Duckett *v.* Williams, 2 Cr. & Mees. 348; S. C. 4 Tyrwh. 240; Hartman *v.* Keystone Ins. Co., 21 Penn. State, 466. As to the effect of the husband's declarations in relation to his health, where the policy is taken out in the wife's name and for her sole use, see Fraternal Mut. Life Ins. Co. *v.* Applegate, 7 Ohio State, 292; Ins. Co. *v.* Cheever, 36 id. 201.

Estoppel of the Company by act of agent. The change introduced into the business of insurance by the use of soliciting agents has induced a modification of the old rules as to representations, and, in some cases, as to warranties. The supreme court of the United States has held, and affirmed and re-affirmed the holding, that the agent acts as agent of the company, not of the applicant, in taking the application; that the powers of the agent will not be narrowed by limitations not communicated to the person with whom he deals, and the company must be held responsible to parties with whom it transacts business by the acts and declarations of the agent within the scope of his employment. Hence, if the applicant makes a fair statement of what he knows, and the agent fills out the application incorrectly by using his own judgment in omitting or describing, or interpreting what the applicant said, the company cannot defeat a suit on the policy by proof of the untruth of such statements. The assured is allowed to give oral proof of his statements made to the agent, not to contradict the written application or to show a contract different from that contained in the policy, but to estop and disable the company from showing the untruth of the written statements. Un. M. L. Ins. Co. *v.* Wilkinson, 13 Wall. 222; Ins. Co. *v.* Mahone, 21 Wall. 152; N. J. M. Life Ins. Co. *v.* Baker, 94 U. S. 610; also McBride *v.* Republic L. Ins. Co., 30 Wis. 562; Boos *v.* World Ins. Co., 4 Hun, 133. Where the applicant signed the application in blank and the agent of the company filled it without authority or direction from the applicant, the company is liable on a policy issued which the insured may go; and should he go without permission, to any of the prohibited places, the policy is forfeited. (*a*) Death by suicide, duelling, or at the hands of justice, is likewise excepted from the policy. (*b*) The warranty, that the person is in good health at the date of the policy, and has no disease tending to shorten life, is construed liberally for the insured: and only requires that he should have been in reasonably good health, and without any manifest and palpable disease. (*c*) When one person insures the life of another, he is required to have a pecuniary interest in that life, to avoid the objection to a wager policy; as, for example, the interest of a creditor in the life of his debtor, or a wife in the life of her husband, and the like. (*d*) It is a settled

thereon, notwithstanding misstatements made in the application. Hingston *v.* Ætna Ins. Co., 42 Iowa, 46; Ins. Co. *v.* McGookey, 33 Ohio State, 555. Where the agent took a genuine application, but imposed a spurious one on the company, the company is liable on a policy issued thereon. Ins. Co. *v.* Eshelman, 30 Ohio State, 603. Where the agent fraudulently inserted answers not given by the applicant, but the applicant signed the application without reading it or hearing it read, and such incorrect answers were warranties, the applicant was held inexcusably negligent, and the company was not bound. Ryan *v.* World Mut. L. Ins. Co., 41 Conn. 168; N. Y. Life Ins. Co. *v.* Fletcher, 117 U. S. 519. The company is not estopped from proving their falsity. Galbraith *v.* Arlington Mut. L. Ins. Co., 12 Bush, 29. The same ruling as to warranties has been made in Fire Insurance. State M. F. Ins. Co. *v.* Arthur, 30 Penn. State, 315. In Massachusetts it is held that the agent of the company is, in filling out applications, the agent of the applicant, and hence no estoppel arises against the company, and hence parol testimony is not admissible for any such purpose as in the cases cited above. Vose *v.* Eagle L. Ins. Co., 6 Cush. 42. *Contra*, Ins. Co. *v.* Williams, 39 Ohio State, 584.

Special limitation. A condition that suit must be brought within twelve months after loss, is valid. But if the assured waits longer than twelve months at the instance of the company, either pending negotiations for settlement or to enable the company to investigate the loss, he is not barred. Andes Ins. Co. *v.* Fish, 71 Ill. 620; Merchants' M. Ins. Co. *v.* Lacroix, 45 Texas, 158; and see Curtis *v.* Home Ins. Co., 1 Biss. 485, and McFarland *v.* Peabody Ins. Co., 6 W. Va. 425.

(*a*) Hathaway *v.* Trenton Mutual Life & Fire Ins. Co., 11 Cush. 448. This restriction may be waived by the acceptance of premiums after notice of the departure. Wing *v.* Harvey, 27 Eng. Law & Eq. 140.

(*b*) The Amicable Society *v.* Bolland, 4 Bligh (N. S.), 194; S. C. Bolland *v.* Disney, 3 Russel, Ch. 351; Harper *v.* The Phœnix Ins. Co., 18 Missouri, 109; Spruill *v.* N. C. Mut. Life Ins. Co., 1 Jones (N. C.), 126; Hartman *v.* Keystone Ins. Co., 21 Penn. State, 466.

Suicide of insured while insane. When the policy provides that, in case the insured should die by his own hand or act, the policy shall be void, this clause does not prevent a recovery if the insured kills himself in a fit of insanity, which overcomes his reason and will. Schultz *v.* Ins. Co., 40 Ohio State, 217; Life Ins. Co. *v.* Terry, 15 Wall. 580; Hathaway *v.* Nat. L. Ins. Co., 48 Vt. 335; Weed *v.* Mut. Benefit L. Ins. Co., 41 N. Y. Superior Ct. 476; Knickerbocker L. Ins. Co. *v.* Peters, 42 Md. 414; John Hancock M. L. Ins. Co. *v.* Moore, 34 Mich. 41. But if the policy provides that it shall be void in case of the death of the insured by his own act whether sane or insane, no recovery can be had though the insured be insane at the time he commits suicide. Bigelow *v.* Berkshire L. Ins. Co., 93 U. S. 284; De Gogorza *v.* Knickerbocker L. Ins. Co., 65 N. Y. 232; Pierce *v.* Travellers' L. Ins. Co., 34 Wis. 389; Chapman *v.* Republic L. Ins. Co., 6 Biss. 238. In this country, it is held that the exception of "suicide" designates *felonious* self-destruction, and not self-destruction when the life assured is insane. Manhattan L. Ins. Co. *v.* Broughton, 109 U. S. 121; Breasted *v.* Farmers' Loan & Trust Co., 4 Hill, 73; S. C. 8 N. Y. 299. *Contra* in England. Borradaile *v.* Hunter, 5 Man. & Gr. 639; Clift *v.* Schwabe, 3 Man. G. & S. 437.

(*c*) Ross *v.* Bradshaw, 1 Wm. Black, 312.

(*d*) Lord *v.* Dale, 12 Mass. 155, 118; Reed *v.* Royal Exchange Assurance Co., Peake, Ad. Cas. 70; St. Johns *v.* American Mutual Life Ins. Co., 2 Duer, R. 429. A rule that the death must occur within the period of the policy; and it will not be sufficient that the cause of death occurred within that period, if life continued beyond. (*a*)

§ 185. **Liens.** (*b*) Lien is of French derivation, and signifies an obligation, tie, or claim attached to property, as security for a debt, and to that extent controlling the rights of the owner. I have included liens under the head of contracts, because though they may exist by the operation of law, they are usually created by contract, either express or implied. Liens may attach either to realty or personalty; and I shall consider both kinds, with reference to the various methods in which they may be acquired.

Liens by Mortgage. We have already considered mortgages both of personalty and realty. I therefore merely name them under this head.

Liens by Judgment or Decree. The nature of liens by judgment and decree, and the proceedings which lead to them, will be considered hereafter.

Builder's Lien. (*c*) At common law, ship-builders are the only

father has an insurable interest in the life of his minor son. Loomis *v.* Eagle Life & Health Ins. Co., 6 Gray, 396. Mitchell *v.* Union, &c. Ins. Co., 45 Maine, 104. A creditor of a firm has an insurable interest in the life of one of its members. Morrill *v.* Trenton Mutual Life & Fire Ins. Co., 10 Cush. 282. Rawls *v.* Am. Life Ins. Co., 36 Barb. 357. It is now held in England (overruling Godsall *v.* Boldero, 9 East, 72, which has been repeatedly approved), that the contract of life insurance is not one of indemnity; that the creditor need only have an interest in the debtor's life when the policy is affected, and that although the debt be afterwards fully discharged, he may recover the sum insured in the policy in case of a death within its terms. This doctrine has very recently been held on both sides of Westminster Hall. Dalby *v.* India & London Life Assurance Co., 28 Eng. Law & Eq. 312; s. c. 18 Jurist, No. 935; 15 C. B. 365. See *ante*, p. 61, *note;* Law *v.* London Indisputable Life Policy Co., 19 Jurist, 178; Loomis *v.* Eagle Life and Health Ins. Co., 6 Gray, 396. The rule in Dalby *v.* I. & L. L. Ins. Co. is now the established rule in the United States. Hence, if a wife insures the life of her husband, and is afterwards divorced, her right to recover on the policy is not thereby affected. Conn. Mut. L. Ins. Co. *v.* Schaeffer, 94 U. S. 457; McKee *v.* Phenix Ins. Co., 28 Mo. 383. In Conn. Mut. L. Ins. Co. *v.* Schaeffer, the court say, "where the insurance is effected merely by way of indemnity, as where a creditor insures the life of his debtor for the purpose of securing his debt, the amount of insurable interest is the amount of the debt," p. 462. It was so held by the court of Queen's Bench in Herndon *v.* West, 3 B. & S. 579; but the decision rests upon the English statute. It was decided in Warnock *v.* Davis, 104 U. S. 775, that an assignment of a life policy to a person who has no insurable interest in the life insured, is not valid; but if such assignee has agreed to pay and has paid any premiums on the policy, or is in any way a creditor of the assured, to that extent he has an interest in the insurance money, and may recover that amount. {But the Supreme Court of Ohio refuse to follow this, and permitted a person to assign his policy to the infant child of a friend. Eckel *v.* Renner, 41 Ohio State, 232.}

(*a*) Lockyer *v.* Offley, 1 T. R. 260.

(*b*) See Whitaker on Liens.

(*c*) The term "owner," in the first section of the mechanics' lien law, includes ownership of an estate, less than an estate in fee. Choteau *v.* Thompson, 2 Ohio State, 123; Dutro *v.* Wilson, 4 id. 101. {But the lien law does not apply to public buildings or to county commissioners. Lumber Co. *v.* Purdum, 41 Ohio State, 373.} For provisions enforcing liens against steamboats and other watercrafts, see R. S. §§ 3184 and 5880–94. The lien covers all materials furnished in good faith for the purposes of building, though not used. Beckel *v.* Pettigrew, 6 Ohio State, 247. As to the degree of explicitness required in the account to be filed, see Davis *v.* Hines, 6 Ohio State, 473; Thomas *v.* Huesman, 10 Ohio State, 152. The lien cannot be created on the lands of a married woman by work done under a contract with the husband, nor class of builders who have a lien for their compensation, and this only continues while the ship is in their possession. Nor does it extend to those who furnish materials or make repairs, except when the ship is in a foreign port, where the owners are either not known, or not accessible. But by our statute of 1843, all persons who perform labor or furnish materials for constructing, altering, or repairing any building or vessel, may have a lien thereon, without retaining possession, by taking the required steps. To this end they must, within four months after their claim accrues, make out a specific account, swear to it, and have it recorded in the recorder's office; and thus they secure a lien for two years from the commencement of their work or furnishing. During this time they may commence suit for their claims, and then the lien continues until final judgment and satisfaction. If the property upon which the lien attaches cannot be sold on execution, provision is made for leasing it until the lien is satisfied. Provision is also made for securing sub-contractors, in case the principal contractor does not pay them. (*a*)

Vendor's Lien. We have seen that the vendor of realty has an equitable lien thereon for the purchase-money, unless, by taking collateral security, or some other act, he evinces an intention to waive such equitable lien; and the rule is nearly the same with respect to the vendor of personalty before delivery. Unless it appear manifest, from the circumstances of the sale, that he intended to rely solely upon the personal credit of the vendee, he may retain possession of the chattel until the purchase-money be either paid or tendered (*b*)

Bailee's Lien. (*c*). It may perhaps be stated as a general rule, that *a bailee for reward* has a lien upon the thing bailed, until payment of his compensation. If this be not universally true, there are very few exceptions. Of tradesmen it may be said

can it affect her dower. Spinning *v.* Blackburn, 13 Ohio State, 131; Gray *v.* Pope, 35 Miss. 116; Iaege *v.* Bossieux, 15 Grattan, 83. But it may be created by work done under a contract with the wife, on her property, at least to the extent of reasonable repairs. Machir *v.* Burroughs, 14 Ohio State, 519; Edwards *v.* Edwards, 24 id. 402. Still more is this true since the acts of 1861 and 1866. See note, p. 272. Any owner of land knowingly standing by and seeing work done on his land for another person, thereby subjects his land to a lien for such work. Donaldson *v.* Holmes, 23 Ill. 85. The lien only extends to articles furnished with reference to the erection of a particular specified building. Hill *v.* Bishop, 25 Ill. 349. An architect is within the provisions of the law. Bank of Penn. *v.* Gries, 35 Penn. State, 423. Such a lien is postponed to a prior mortgage duly executed. Reid *v.* Bank of Tenn., 1 Sneed, 262. {But an apportionment was suggested in Choteau *v.* Thompson, 2 Ohio State, 114.}

(*a*) Under this law all mechanics' liens for the same building shared equally, but in the case of sub-contractors the one first giving notice acquired a priority. Copeland *v.* Manton, 22 Ohio State, 398. Under R. S. § 3198 sub-contractors share *pro rata*. But if the sub-contracts are on independent jobs separately let, the liens are respectively confined to the amount unpaid on the particular contract. Dunn *v.* Rankin, 27 Ohio State, 132. As against a sub-contractor the owner cannot set off claims against the contractor not growing out of the contract though previously acquired. Bullock *v.* Horn, 44 Ohio State (1886).

(*b*) *Supra*, p. 518, note (*b*); Wentworth *v.* Day, 3 Met. 352.

(*c*) R. S. §§ 3212 *et seq.*, provides for enforcing the liens of certain bailees {and their enforcement, including livery-stable keepers, warehousemen, and carriers}.

generally, that whenever an article is delivered to them to exercise their trade upon it, they may retain it until payment of their charges. (*a*) Thus, if you incur charges at an inn, the innkeeper has a right to retain your baggage until you pay your bill. (*b*) If you commit goods to a carrier for transportation, either by stage, wagon, boat, or ship, he may retain them until his freight be paid. (*c*) If you send a horse to a farrier to be shod, he may retain the horse until you pay him for his work. If you land goods on a wharf, or send them to a warehouse for storage, the wharfinger or warehouseman may retain them until payment of his dues. (*d*) If you send cloth to a tailor to be made into a garment, he may retain the garment until you pay him his charges. (*e*) These examples sufficiently illustrate the general principle.

Miscellaneous Liens. Under this head, I shall enumerate a few liens which do not come within either of the foregoing classes. In the case of *salvage* at sea, the salvors have a lien upon the goods saved for their compensation, which is always liberal, in order to encourage the utmost exertions; but this right is limited to goods lost or exposed in the course of navigation, usually called *wrecks*. (*f*) The finder of things on land has no lien unless the statute give him one. (*g*) We have a statute by which persons who take up *stray animals, or boats adrift*, have a lien thereon for their compensation, provided they take the proper steps, by advertisement and other proceedings. The master of a ship has no lien thereon for his wages, because he engages upon the credit of the owners; but all the rest of the crew have such lien, and in a court of admiralty may prevent the ship from sailing, and even cause her to be sold, if their wages be not paid. (*h*)

(*a*) Morgan *v.* Congdon, 4 N. Y. 551; M'Intyre *v.* Carver, 2 W. & S. 392; Nevan *v.* Roup, 8 Clarke (Iowa), 207.

(*b*) Grinnell *v.* Cook, 3 Hill, 485. A landlord not an innkeeper has no such lien, nor has a boarding-house keeper. Preston *v.* Neale, 12 Gray, 222; Willard *v.* Reinhardt, 2 E. D. Smith, 148. And an innkeeper taking boarders under a special contract, has no such lien as to them. Hursh *v.* Ryers, 29 Missouri, 469.

(*c*) Ellis *v.* James, 5 Ohio, 88; Bowman *v.* Hilton, 11 id. 303; Hunt *v.* Haskell, 24 Maine, 339; Galena & Chicago Union R. R. Co. *v.* Rae, 18 Ill. 488. But where the goods are delivered to the carrier by a party whose possession is wrongful, the carrier, although innocent of the wrongful possession, has no lien. Robinson *v.* Baker, 5 Cush. 137; Fitch *v.* Newbury, 1 Doug. (Mich.) 1; Stevens *v.* Boston, &c. R. R. Co., 8 Gray, 262; Clark *v.* Lowell, &c. R. R. Co., 9 Gray, 231. But an innkeeper in such a case has a lien. York *v.* Greenaugh, 2 Ld. Raym. 866; Black *v.* Brennan, 5 Dana, 312; Broadwood *v.* Granara, 28 Eng. Law & Eq. 443; 10 Exch. 417; Snead *v.* Watkins, 1 Com. Bench (N. S.), 267.

(*d*) But only persons regularly carrying on the business of warehousemen are entitled to this lien. Alt *v.* Weidenberg, 6 Bosworth, 176.

(*e*) R. S. §§ 3212 *et seq.*; Steinman *v.* Wilkins, 7 W. & S. 466. An agister of cattle, in the absence of a special agreement to that effect, has no lien on them for the keeping. Goodrich *v.* Willard, 7 Gray, 183.

(*f*) Abbott on Shipping, 399; Post *v.* Jones, 19 How. 150.

(*g*) Nicholson *v.* Chapman, 2 H. Bl. 254; Forster *v.* Juniata Bridge Co., 16 Penn. State, 393. But the finder of goods, for which a reward has been offered, has a lien. Wentworth *v.* Day, 3 Met. 352; Wilson *v.* Guyton, 8 Gill, 213.

(*h*) 3 Kent, Com. 165, 197; Abbott on Shipping, 475.

General and Particular Liens. I have thus far spoken of what are called *particular liens*, as distinguished from *general*. The distinction is this: a particular lien extends only to the charge made upon the identical property then in hand; but a general lien is that which covers any general balance of account. (*a*) Thus, when you put your horse to a livery stable, the keeper only has a particular lien for the expense incurred at that particular time; but if you leave your papers with an attorney, he may retain them not only for his fees for that particular service, but for his general balance of account against you. General liens are not favored in law: they exist only by the long-established usage of particular trades, or by express contract. Thus factors, wharfingers, bankers, insurance brokers, and attorneys are said to have a general lien by the force of usage alone; and in any other case, if you notify those who employ you that you will not receive property for the purposes of your trade, without a general lien, those who employ you with that notice are bound by it. (*b*)

When a Lien does not Exist. You cannot acquire a lien by a voluntary or wrongful act: for instance, if you pay charges upon goods for the mere sake of getting possession, you do not thus acquire a lien. Again, you cannot acquire a lien by misrepresentation. If by a false statement you obtain possession of goods, you cannot retain them, though money be actually due you on account of them. (*c*) Again, you cannot acquire a lien where the person who gave you possession had no authority so to do. (*d*) Again, you cannot insist on a lien, when there has been any agreement or other circumstance, from which it may be inferred that you intend to waive the right of lien. (*e*) Finally, you cannot acquire a lien by assignment from another; for, as a general rule, a lien is a personal privilege which cannot be assigned. (*f*)

How a Lien may be Lost. With the exception of liens by mortgage or judgment, where possession does not usually accompany the lien, the general rule is that possession is essential to the existence of a lien. It would be highly prejudicial to the general

(*a*) Oppenheim *v.* Russell, 3 B. & P. 494; M'Farland *v.* Wheeler, 26 Wend. 467. {An undertaker has no lien on a corpse; if he ships it in a casket C. O. D. he has no claim against the carrier for taking out the corpse and sending back the casket unpaid for; for it is against public policy to hold the carrier for not returning the body (Ohio District Ct. 1876) Express Co. *v.* Epply, 1 Cincinnati Weekly Law Bull. 79; s. c. 4 Am. Law Record, 672.}

(*b*) Knap *v.* Alvord, 1 Paige, 205; Bryce *v.* Brooks, 26 Wendell, 367; Dennet *v.* Cutts, 11 N. H. 163; 2 Kent, Com. 634; Smith's Merc. Law (Holcombe & Gholson), 559. A carrier has no general lien for back freights. Leonard *v.* Winslow, 2 Grant's Cases, 139.

(*c*) Lempriere *v.* Pasley, 2 T. R. 485; Taylor *v.* Robinson, 2 Moore, 730.

(*d*) Robinson *v.* Baker, 5 Cush. 137; Fitch *v.* Newbury, 1 Doug. (Mich.) 15; Daubigny *v.* Duval, 5 T. R. 606. But see Arendale *v.* Morgan, 5 Sneed, 703, and as to innkeepers' liens, see Sneed *v.* Watkins, 1 C. B. (N. S.) 267.

(*e*) Hewison *v.* Guthrie, 2 Bing. N. C. 755; Cowper *v.* Green, 7 M. & W. 633; Jackson *v.* Cummins, 5 id. 351; Chase *v.* Westmore, 5 M. & S. 180; Burdick *v.* Murray, 3 Vt. 302.

(*f*) Daubigny *v.* Duval, 5 T. R. 606; Holly *v.* Huggeford, 8 Pick. 76.

interest of trade and traffic, if a lien could attach to goods in the market; because no one could know when he might safely buy them. It follows, therefore, that you lose your lien by parting with possession. (*a*)

There are some other particular contracts to which I have not adverted in this lecture. Maritime loans on *bottomry* and *respondentia* were referred to in the lecture on mortgages. The *charter party* and the general contract of *affreightment*, are peculiar to the law of shipping, and I have not room for a description of them here; and the same is true of the implied contract of *general average*, by which all the parties interested in a ship and cargo, tacitly agree to contribute their proportions, if it becomes necessary to sacrifice a part of the cargo for the safety of the rest. (*b*) Here, then, we close the consideration of property and contracts, which constitutes the fourth division of these lectures.

(*a*) Hutton *v.* Bragg, 7 Taunt. 14; M'Farland *v.* Wheeler, 26 Wend. 473; Bailey *v.* Quint, 22 Vt. 474; Nevan *v.* Roup, 8 Clarke (Iowa), 207. But delivery for a special and temporary purpose, Roberts *v.* Wyatt, 2 Taunt. 268; Reeves *v.* Capper, 5 Bing. (N. C.) 136; Hays *v.* Riddle, 1 Sandf. 248; or when obtained by fraud, does not dissolve the lien. Bigelow *v.* Heaton, 6 Hill, 43; s. c. 4 Denio, 496. {But as between the original parties a lien may exist apart from possession if so agreed. Thus where a lien-holder by attachment surrenders the property to the debtor's assignee in insolvency under an agreement to apply the proceeds to the debt, the latter and the debtor are estopped to claim that the lien was thereby lost. Holland *v.* Drake, 29 Ohio State, 441. An agreement to pay for goods out of the proceeds of the sale of the stock of goods including them creates no lien, but simply the relation of debtor and creditor. Stewart *v.* Hopkins, 30 Ohio State, 502.} The bailee loses his lien as against an innocent purchaser, where he redelivers the article to the bailor, even for a special and temporary purpose. Bodenhammer *v.* Newsom, 5 Jones (N. C.), 107. Continued possession is not necessary, however, in the case of equitable liens, such as the vendor's lien for purchase-money.

(*b*) For all these maritime contracts, see the 42d, 45th, 46th, 47th, and 49th lectures of Kent; and Abbott on Shipping, with American notes by Judge Story; and the two valuable treatises of Flanders on Shipping and on Maritime Law; also, Parsons on Maritime Law.

PART V.

THE LAW OF CRIMES.

LECTURE XXXIV.

CRIMES AND PUNISHMENTS IN GENERAL.

§ 186. **Preliminary Considerations.** We have now reached that division of our inquiries, which is usually denominated *criminal law*, and to which, under the head of *public wrongs*, Blackstone devotes the fourth book of his commentaries. The distinction between *civil* and *penal* sanctions has already been adverted to. Society does not invite obedience to its regulations by the offer of *rewards*, but deters from disobedience by the threat of *punishments*. It is therefore to the *terrors of the law* that our thoughts are now to be chiefly directed. We are to contemplate the dark side of the human condition, and make ourselves familiar with the consequences of transgression. To the philanthropic inquirer, this is perhaps the most interesting branch of legal study. I cannot indulge myself in tracing the history of criminal legislation in ancient and modern times; but I can assure you that there is no aspect in which the different ages present a greater diversity. An impartial survey cannot fail to conduct you to the gratifying conclusion, that mankind have been steadily improving in this department of legislation. It is hardly a metaphor to say that the ancient codes were written in blood; whereas the characteristics of modern criminal jurisprudence are mildness, compassion, and benevolence. In a word, humanity has kept even pace with the progress of civilization. In their anxiety to protect the life, liberty, and property of the whole community from aggression, legislatures have ceased to be altogether unmindful of the life, liberty, and happiness of the offenders themselves. The divine attribute of mercy has been brought to temper justice, and sanguinary laws are found to be as unnecessary as they are hateful. In this country, at the present moment, we can hardly perceive a trace of that fierce and savage spirit which dictated the ancient penal codes. The grand problem in criminal legislation is to preserve the peace and order of society, with the least possible exercise of severity. All punishment is in itself an evil; but as disobedience of the laws is a still greater evil, there is a point beyond which humanity cannot safely go; and many affect to fear that in this country that point has been passed; but I trust that such persons have not made due allowance for the natural tendency of good laws to protect themselves. As a general principle, it is only bad laws which require very severe sanctions. Let all the regulations of society be wise and equitable, and they will go far towards sustaining themselves by their own intrinsic excellence; whereas obedience to laws which are palpably unjust, can only be enforced by the most terrific denunciations. I do not, of course, mean to intimate that, in any possible condition of society, penal enactments can ever be entirely dispensed with; but merely to assert the proposition, that the better the government becomes, the fewer will be the occasions of punishing transgression; and the view we are about to take of criminal law in this country will prove that I am correct.

§ 187. **The Nature of Crimes.** A *crime*, in its legal acceptation, signifies any act to which the law attaches a penalty or punishment, without any reference to its moral turpitude. The terms *offence* and *misdemeanor* are nearly synonymous, though commonly used to indicate a less degree of enormity. To constitute a crime, there must first of all be an *act;* since a mere opinion or intention, however wrong in a moral or religious point of view, if not carried into an act, cannot be treated as a crime; although the criminality of the act when done, may be partially or entirely dependent upon the intention of the actor. This results from that entire freedom of the mind, which is a fundamental condition of human nature. And although it will be found that most of those acts which the law declares to be *criminal*, are likewise *wicked* or *sinful* in a moral or religious view, yet it is because of their tendency to do temporal injury to society, and not because of their abstract wickedness or sinfulness, that human law interposes to punish them. This idea has been sufficiently developed before. Every crime indeed involves a private injury as its immediate consequence; for society can only be reached through individuals. And the right to a civil remedy is only suspended, not annihilated, by making it punishable. (*a*) In some instances, as we shall see, special provision is made for private compensation as well as punishment. But the true and only reason for making any given act a crime, is the public injury that would result from its frequent perpetration. Each single instance is an individual injury; frequent repetition would make it a social injury. Accordingly, society

(*a*) {This doctrine is not in force here, and the civil action for the tort may be at once pursued without awaiting the conviction of the accused. Howk *v.* Minnick, 19 Ohio State, 462.}

takes the most efficient measures for its prevention, by appealing to the fears of mankind. The crime is first accurately defined, and the requisite punishment meted out to it; and then government itself becomes a party to the prosecution of the offender, in order to insure its being carried into effect; for the certainty of punishment is even more effectual in preventing crimes, than any degree of severity with a probability of escape. But while the only legitimate object of punishment is to protect society against the repetition of crimes, humanity dictates that the reformation of the offender should also be effected, if possible. Yet as government has no concern with men, except as members of society, it is obvious that their moral improvement can never properly be made the primary object of punishment. Nor, on the other hand, can vengeance ever properly be an object of punishment, even in the slightest degree. To suppose this would be to clothe government with the attributes of a fiend. Self-protection, then, is at once the foundation and the end of the power which society exercises, of punishing its members. So true is this, that if a case could be supposed, in which it would be perfectly certain that an act, however atrocious, would never be repeated by the same or any other person, there would be no motive for punishing it. In preventing the repetition of crimes, punishment is designed to operate both upon the individual offender, and upon the community at large. Upon the offender himself it operates in one of these ways: namely, by physically disabling him from repeating the offence; or by dissuading him from it through the recollection of past suffering; or by both of these together. Upon the community at large, it operates only by the terror of example. Hence it follows, that the mode and measure of punishment are to be determined, not so much by the abstract nature of the offence, as by its liability to frequent repetition; and also that no act should be punished at all, the repetition of which does not injuriously affect the temporal welfare of society. In England and in several of the States, the common law prevails in the punishment of crimes; and many acts are punishable from precedent, which have never been made so by legislative provision. But the manifest evil of this doctrine is, that the majority of men, unskilled in the law, cannot be supposed to know beforehand, whether a given act will be criminal or not. In fact, the accumulation of precedents through the lapse of centuries, must render it difficult for the most consummate lawyer to be able to pronounce at once with certainty on the subject. And yet it is absolutely necessary to act upon the well-known maxim, that ignorance of the law is no excuse for its violation; because, otherwise, ignorance would always be pretended. (*a*) This consideration alone is sufficient to demonstrate the importance of requiring every offence to be defined by the legislature, together

(*a*) {Ignorance of facts, however, may always be shown to rebut guilty intention Farrell *v.* State, 32 Ohio State, 456; Crabtree *v.* State, 30 id. 382.}

with its punishment; and accordingly it has become a fundamental doctrine in the federal courts and in the courts of this State, that they have no common-law jurisdiction of crimes; and cannot treat any act as an offence, until the proper legislature has declared it to be such, and meted out the punishment. (*a*) With regard to the federal courts, this doctrine rests upon the absence of any power in the federal constitution to punish crimes except in certain specified cases before enumerated, for which Congress is to provide. A different opinion has been sometimes entertained; but this is now the universal sentiment: and the happy consequence is, that on a few pages of the statute book may be found enumerated all the offences which can be punished by the federal or State government, and the measure of punishment annexed to each. So that the only use now made of the criminal part of the common law, is to furnish the outlines of criminal procedure, and define the terms employed in the statutes. If there be any evil to be apprehended from this doctrine, it is that cases may arise in which men cannot be punished, however they deserve it, because the legislature has not anticipated their offences; but this objection weighs hardly a feather against the inestimable privilege of having every offence, for which punishment can be inflicted, distinctly and accurately defined; (*b*) instead of being left to be collected from doubtful precedents, established in a very different state of society, and scattered at remote intervals, through the reported decisions of seven or eight centuries.

(*a*) U. S. *v.* Hudson, 7 Cranch, 32; U. S. *v.* Coolidge, 1 Wheat. 415; Key *v.* Vattier, 1 Ohio R. 132; Smith *v.* State, 12 Ohio State, 466; Anderson *v.* Soward, 40 id. 325. The same rule prevails in Indiana and Iowa, though in those States it is specifically prescribed by statute. Beals *v.* State, 15 Ind. 378; State *v.* O. & M. R. R. Co., 23 Ind. 362; Estes *v.* Carter, 10 Iowa, 400. {For otherwise a long list of acts would be punishable which were crimes by the common law, but which the more civilized and enlightened people of modern times do not regard as such. Per Johnson, J., in Davis *v.* Brown, 27 Ohio State, 326, 331.} In the other States formed out of territory formerly under the British crown, the courts have a common-law criminal jurisdiction. Punishments, indeed, in such States are provided for by statute; there being, generally, a provision that all crimes and offences the punishment whereof is not specifically provided for by statute, shall be punishable by fine or imprisonment, or both. In such States common-law process and procedure are used, so far as not otherwise provided by statute; crimes are mostly defined, but in many cases are only named; the common-law supplying the definition. But common-law crimes, even if not named, are indictable. As it is held in Minnesota that conspiracy is an indictable offence, though not in any way named in the statute. State *v.* Pulle, 12 Minn. 164.

(*b*) The State constitutions generally contain a provision that the indictment must exhibit the nature and the cause of the accusation against the defendant. Under this it has been held that the legislature has not power to dispense with such allegations in an indictment as are essential to reasonable particularity and certainty in the description of the offence. McLaughlin *v.* State, 45 Ind. 338. But this constitutional provision does not require time, place, circumstances, or mode of commission to be stated. Hence a statutory provision that in an indictment for murder in the second degree or manslaughter, it shall not be necessary to set forth the manner in which, or the means by which, the death was caused, but it shall be sufficient to charge that the defendant did purposely and maliciously, or did unlawfully, kill the deceased, is not unconstitutional. Wolf *v.* State, 19 Ohio State, 248. A city ordinance providing for the punishment of "any known thief" found within the limits of the city is valid. Morgan *v.* Nolte, 37 Ohio State, 23.

The present condition of our penal legislation is this: First, we have an act for the punishment of *crimes*, including murder and all crimes punishable by imprisonment in the penitentiary, except two or three which are elsewhere provided for. This act contains a general provision for punishing those who aid, abet, or procure; and another provision disfranchising the convict from the privilege of voting, holding office, or being a juror or witness, unless he obtain a general pardon, in all cases except manslaughter and duelling. Secondly, we have an act for the punishment of *offences*, including a great variety of offences punishable by fine, or imprisonment in jail, or both; but there is no general provision against aiding, abetting, or procuring, nor for disfranchisement. Thirdly, we have an act for the prevention of *immoral practices*, and another for the prevention of *gaming*, including a variety of offences against good order and good morals, chiefly punishable by small fines. Fourthly, we have a great number of distinct penalties scattered through the statutes, relating mostly to the neglect of official duties, but including several other miscellaneous matters. It will thus be seen that, however excellent in other respects, our criminal law is greatly deficient in method and concentration. We have the disjointed fragments, but not a complete system. And the same is, in a great measure, true of the criminal legislation of Congress. What we want, therefore, is a revised criminal code, in which all penalties should be brought together and arranged in systematic order. And in framing this code, occasion might be taken to correct an evil in our mode of defining crimes, which I will here point out. Instead of giving such general definitions as will include all cases coming within the reason of the law, our legislature has undertaken to enumerate, in each case, the particular subjects, with respect to which the offence may be committed. For example, in defining forgery, instead of using some general term which would include all matters that may be forged, and not exclude any, the statute attempts to specify every writing which can be the subject of forgery. The same is true of the definitions of perjury, larceny, arson, burglary, and many other offences. Now, to say nothing of the want of brevity in this mode of definition, the obvious objection is, that no legislative foresight can be expected to particularize so fully as not to omit any thing coming within the principle. And yet on the maxim that where enumeration is attempted, all particulars not mentioned are excluded, it follows that if a single particular be omitted, there can be no punishment for that case. Finally, the framing of such a code as is here suggested, would furnish the best possible opportunity for making any other improvements suggested by experience. In a system so arranged, the slightest want of harmony or symmetry would at once be seen; and although absolute perfection could not be attained, this would be the surest method of approximating towards it.

Again, not only must all offences be expressly provided for by the legislature, but the law must be made before the act is committed. In other words, there can be no *retroactive criminal legislation;* and this doctrine prevails throughout the United States. Both the federal and State constitutions, as we have seen, prohibit the enactment of *ex post facto* laws; and by these are meant retroactive criminal laws. (*a*) Any law, therefore, which makes criminal an act which was innocent at the time of its commission; or which aggravates the punishment of a crime after its commission; or which renders conviction more easy than it was when the crime was committed, would be unconstitutional and void. But it is presumed that laws which favor the offender, by diminishing the punishment, or rendering conviction more difficult, would be valid, although retroactive; because they are to operate for the benefit of the accused. The result is, that we enjoy the glorious privilege of knowing that the past is secure, so far as punishment is concerned. Under no state of excitement can a vindictive legislature animadvert upon past transactions. If we take care to escape existing penalties, we need be under no apprehension as to retrospective ones. But with regard to the acts which may be declared criminal, there is no express constitutional restriction, either upon Congress or the State legislatures. This is properly left to be determined by the exigency of time. Whatever act, therefore, tends to injure society, in a degree sufficient to attract public animadversion, may be declared criminal; but with regard to the mode and measure of punishment, as well as the forms of proceeding from the commencement to the conclusion of a criminal prosecution, there are, as we have seen, a variety of constitutional provisions, all tending to secure the offender against unnecessary suffering. All these provisions have been commented upon in connection, and will be referred to again. I shall here merely recapitulate those which relate to the mode and measure of punishment. 1. Excessive *fines* cannot be imposed. 2. Neither *cruel* nor *unusual* punishments can be inflicted; that is, there can be no unnecessary torture or barbarity in administering punishment; and no exercise of invention in devising new modes of punishment. 3. Banishment cannot be resorted to as a mode of punishment. 4. There can be no corruption of blood or forfeiture of estate; or, in other words, the consequences of punishment must terminate with the person of the offender. The result is, that our criminal code cannot fail to be humane, so long as the constitution endures. As the power of punishment is the most dangerous to the safety and liberty of the citizen, with which any government can be intrusted, so no power has been guarded with more scrupulous jealousy by all the American constitutions. In this respect, we have immeasurably the advantage of all other nations, ancient

(*a*) See Calder *v.* Bull, 3 Dallas, 386; *ante*, p. 219. When a criminal statute is repealed, and there is no provision in the repealing act saving offences committed or prosecutions pending, no conviction can legally be had after such repeal under such statute. Calkins *v.* The State, 14 Ohio State, 222.

or modern, as will be abundantly evinced in the course of our observations. In the two great points of simplicity and humanity, the criminal code of this State, for example, might safely challenge a comparison with any code in the civilized world. It often wants method and congruity in its structure, but the principles upon which it is framed are such as philanthropy must ever contemplate with satisfaction.

§ 188. **Modes of Punishment.** The punishments now in use may be divided into four classes; namely, corporal punishments, fine, imprisonment, and death. Of these in their order.

Corporal Punishment. Perhaps confinement in the *stocks* and *pillory* would hardly rank among corporal punishments; their object being disgrace, rather than pain. These punishments, however, once so prevalent, have nearly, if not entirely, gone out of fashion, in this country; whether wisely or not may admit of much doubt. There are some offences for which disgraceful punishments would seem to be peculiarly appropriate; and there are many persons upon whom they would operate with peculiar efficiency. But by corporal punishment we commonly understand *whipping*, *branding*, *cropping*, and the like. These, however, like the other, have nearly ceased to be inflicted. Whipping is indeed authorized in two or three cases, under the acts of Congress; (*a*) and is practised to some extent in several of the States; but in this State there has been none of it since 1815. The fact is, the spirit of the age is opposed to corporal punishment in every shape. There is too much of the appearance of savage ferocity in causing the human body to smart and bleed under the lash or the iron. Such things are bad enough for brutes; they are too bad for men. This at least seems to be the growing opinion of the age; and it speaks well for the march of humanity.

Fine. Punishment by fine is very generally practised throughout the United States. The constitution sanctions moderate fines, by declaring that they shall not be excessive. These considerations should induce one about to question their expediency to doubt the correctness of his own judgment; nevertheless, I cannot help regarding mere pecuniary punishments as impolitic at least, if not unjust. If we can forget the imposing authority of usage, and view the matter as a new proposition, we shall see that punishment by fine practically amounts to a sale of criminal licenses. Government virtually says that for so much money so much crime may be expiated. The question for the citizen, not otherwise restrained, is, can he afford to pay the price? The answer will depend upon an examination of his purse. If he be rich, the penalty is nothing; if poor, it may amount to a prohibition; so that a fine operates as a great punishment, a small punishment, or no punishment at all, according to the state of the offender's coffers. This inequality is

(*a*) It is now abolished as a punishment both on land and in the navy and merchant service. 5 U. S. Stat. at Large, 322; 9 id. 515. { Imprisonment for non-payment of a fine is constitutional. *In re* Beall, 26 Ohio State, 195. }

one strong objection; and another is that government is strongly tempted to push punishment to extremes, when paid for it in the receipt of fines. This danger may be small in this country at this time; but under a corrupt government, what an alacrity to punish would this motive produce! We know that there have been times when all crimes, however atrocious, could be expiated by money; and that corrupt governments have thus managed to draw an immense revenue from the depravity of their subjects. Even false accusations have been invited, in the most effectual manner, by giving the informer one-half the fine; but to the honor of our laws be it said, they hold out scarcely any encouragement to that most despicable class of men, mercenary informers. With some trifling exceptions, they hold out no other motive to citizens to inform against transgressors than that which they find in their regard for the public good. They even discourage informations without manifest cause, by a provision which exposes the wanton or malevolent informer to the payment of costs; and our experience has thus far proved that the office of informing may be safely left to the public spirit of a high-minded people, without the temptation of a bribe; but I shall not pursue this topic. Since fines are so much in favor, we have reason to rejoice that they cannot be excessive; and must content ourselves with this assurance.

Imprisonment. This punishment is effected either in *penitentiaries*, which are state prisons; or in *jails*, which are county prisons. The United States have no prisons, but make use of the prisons of the different States with their consent. As a mode of punishment, imprisonment has many strong recommendations. *First*, there is a peculiar fitness and propriety in withholding the benefits of the social compact from those who have violated its obligations. Society guarantees our civil liberty, on the condition that we obey and uphold the laws made to protect it. If, therefore, we break this condition by transgressing these laws, the deprivation of liberty is a just and natural forfeiture. Society enters, as it were, for condition broken, and resumes its grant; while the offender is left to learn from the loss of liberty how great is its value. *Secondly*, imprisonment operates more equally than any other punishment upon all descriptions of persons; since liberty is of very nearly the same priceless value to every one. *Thirdly*, imprisonment is more efficient than the punishments before described; since it physically disables the offender, for the time being, from continuing his depredations upon society. The man who has been whipped or fined, is forthwith let loose upon society, with the power, and probably a disposition sharpened by exasperation, to repeat his transgression. But the man who is immured between prison walls cannot do harm. *Fourthly*, imprisonment admits of all degrees of severity, and can therefore be graduated better than any other punishment to meet all offences. It may take place in the gloomy dungeon or the cheerful light; it may be at hard labor or at listless ease; it may be solitary or in the company of other offenders; and it may be for any period, from a single hour to the whole of life. For these, and perhaps other reasons, imprisonment is unquestionably the best of all the methods of punishment. Moreover, convicts are not unfrequently compelled to support themselves by their own labor, and thus relieve the public of the burden. In our penitentiary, "hard labor" is always a part of the sentence; in our jails it is not; but the expense of aliment is there trifling, being confined by the sentence to "bread and water." Of late, public sentiment has been strongly inclining in favor of solitary imprisonment, and there are three strong arguments in favor of it. *First*, the convict cannot corrupt or be corrupted by others having less or greater experience in crime than himself; whereas promiscuous imprisonment must necessarily operate to some extent as a school for crime, even where prison discipline is the most perfect. *Secondly*, in solitary confinement there is always some prospect of reformation; and this should always be kept in view as a secondary object of punishment. Of this at least we may be sure, that if, in the long and lonesome hours, during which the solitary prisoner's mind must be thrown back upon itself, for want of other objects to fix it upon, reflection does not make him better, he is beyond reformation by any human means, and may be given up as a hopeless reprobate. *Thirdly*, solitary imprisonment is more effectual, as an example, than promiscuous imprisonment. It is sad for a man to be alone under any circumstances; but in a prison it must be terrible. To be convinced of this, we need not resort to the high-wrought picture of Sterne's captive; we need only to think of a man's social nature. The imagination cannot conceive of a fate more utterly appalling than that of solitary imprisonment for life. What are the momentary pangs of the most painful death, in comparison with the unutterable despair of entering a dungeon, never to come out? This is, indeed, a living and enduring death. It has all the awfulness of actual death, without its speedy oblivion.

Death. This is the last resort of the law. In this country, except under the military law, the punishment of death is always inflicted by hanging; the sheriff or marshal, as the case may be, is the executioner; and in order that even this punishment may not come within the prohibition of "cruel," it is attended by none of those aggravations of barbarity and torture which strike us with such horror in the codes of other countries. Formerly, executions were always *public*, under the belief that the example must have a salutary effect upon the thousands who throng to witness such spectacles; but this opinion is gradually changing in favor of *secret executions;* and I think the change a wise one. For the victim himself, there is no doubt that a secret death is best; because his thoughts are not drawn off from the contemplation of his awful situation, by a desire to make a last exhibition of hardihood, which the vulgar will applaud as heroism; and as to the rest of the community, it would seem that the tolling of a bell or the mere announcement in a newspaper, without any of the pomp and parade which make us forget the crime in our sympathy with the criminal, is calculated to produce at least as salutary an effect as a view of his struggles in the presence of a noisy crowd. But another question of much more importance is beginning to attract public attention; namely, ought death to be in any case inflicted as a punishment? Without attempting an elaborate discussion of this question, I shall briefly indicate the leading views entertained on each side. The question is twofold; first, as to the *right;* and secondly, as to the *expediency*, of capital punishment.

Those who maintain that society has the *right*, place it on the ground of self-defence. They admit that a strong necessity must exist, before society can be justified in taking the life of its members; but when such a case does arise, the right of self-defence takes precedence of every other, and the life that would be dangerous to society may be rightfully terminated. They also find authority for the exercise of this right, in the Old Testament, and in the general practice of mankind. On the other hand, those who deny the right, reason in this way: Society, they say, has no power but that which it derives from the consent of its members. But life is one of the *inalienable* rights of man. He cannot part with it if he would, until his Creator calls for it. No man can give a valid consent to his own death. As between individuals, the most unequivocal consent would not shield the slayer from the guilt of murder; and if one individual cannot authorize another to take his life, he cannot have authorized society to do it. Society, therefore, cannot have derived this power from consent; and consequently has not got it. Nor can the doctrine of self-defence be the foundation of such a right; since no individual can endanger the existence of society. Self defence authorizes one person to take another's life, in order to preserve his own; it is purely preventive, and has nothing to do with punishment. But society can never be placed in this predicament towards an individual, and therefore can never have occasion to kill in self-defence. Again, the language of Scripture brings no aid to the argument, because none is more solemn and explicit than that which says, "thou shalt not kill." Besides, the doctrine of governing men by divine right is now exploded; and the fact that Jehovah, the author of life, in his immediate government of a peculiar people, did authorize the punishment of death, by no means justifies the inference that he has delegated this power to human governments. Such arguments, drawn from the ancient theocracy, would prove vastly too much; and therefore cannot be used; and the same may be said of the argument from custom. What wrong can be named, that custom has not, at some period, sanctioned? Such, briefly, are the arguments for and against the right of capital punishment.

And the question of *expediency* is equally debatable, when the right is conceded. The great argument in favor of death as a punishment, is the terrific example it holds out to others. Not only does death render it certain that the same offender will never repeat the offence, but it has the strongest possible tendency to deter others from committing it. On the other hand, however, it is urged that the same result may be attained without inflicting death. Solitary imprisonment for life renders it almost equally certain that the offender will not repeat the offence; and as a terror to others, it is scarcely less effectual than death itself. At the same time, our sentiments of humanity are much less shocked at seeing the prison doors closed for ever upon a fellow-creature, than at seeing him suspended from the gallows. We feel that he has a space for repentance and reformation; instead of being sent suddenly away, reeking with guilt, to the presence of his final Judge. We also feel that he may, after all, be innocent: so uncertain is human testimony. We know that innocent men have often been condemned and executed; and in such cases an infinite wrong has been done, without the possibility of undoing it. The vital spark has been rashly put out, and all earth cannot rekindle it: whereas the prisoner, when his innocence is discovered, can be set free, and thus be indemnified, in some degree, for the wrong he has sustained. These considerations, and others of a similar nature, are strongly turning public sentiment towards the abolition of capital punishment. The experiment was made by Catharine of Russia, and is said to have been entirely successful.

Apportionment of Punishment. Having thus described the actual modes of punishment now in use, the question arises, how these punishments are to be apportioned, so as to be just sufficient for each offence, and no more; for that punishments ought to be thus apportioned, is self-evident. But to effect the desired apportionment, not only as to different offences, but also as to different degrees of the same offence, has proved the most difficult problem in criminal legislation. In fact, while reason teaches that the degrees of criminality must be almost infinitely various, experience at the same time proves that no human legislation can specifically provide beforehand for those minute and shadowy differences. To remedy this defect, therefore, recourse is had to judicial discretion. Whenever the nature of the punishment admits of degrees, which is the case with all but death, a limited discretion is given to the judges, as to the amount of punishment. The law fixes the extremes; that is, it prescribes for each offence the largest and smallest fine, and the longest and shortest time of imprisonment; and between these extremes judicial discretion is permitted to range, for the purpose of adapting the punishment to the aggravating or palliating circumstances of each case. Perhaps a safer depositary of this delicate power could not be suggested, whether we consider the rights of the public or the offender. Humanity being a prevailing sentiment, the presumption is, that if the judges are biassed at all, it will be in favor of the criminal; he, therefore, will have nothing to complain of;

and, on the other hand, the public are protected against the consequences of too much lenity, by having the limits of judicial discretion in all cases ascertained by the statute. But in this connection, there is one important defect, both in the State and federal divisions, which ought to be mentioned. It is, that with one or two exceptions, no provision is made for punishing the second offence more severely than the first; though the propriety of so doing is self-evident; for the very fact of repetition by the same offender, proves that the first punishment was not sufficient.

§ 189. **Who are Exempted.** (*a*) The general rule is, that no

(*a*) It is not strictly true, and has not been since McNaughten's case, 10 Clark & Fin. 200, that no insane man is criminally responsible, or that proof of the fact of insanity is proof of incapacity to commit crime. The law undertakes to determine what degree or form of insanity amounts to such incapacity. In that case the judges reported to the House of Lords: "To establish a defence on the ground of insanity, it must be clearly proved that, at the time of the committing of the act, the party accused was laboring under such a defect of reason, from disease of the mind, as not to know the nature and quality of the act he was doing, or, if he did know it, that he did not know he was doing what was wrong." They also reported that in case of partial insanity, or insane delusion, "he must be considered in the same situation as to responsibility as if the facts with respect to which the delusion exists were real."

In the United States, inability to distinguish between right and wrong as to the act charged as a crime is the generally accepted, and in some States the exclusive, test of such insanity as exempts from criminal responsibility. Commonwealth *v.* Rogers, 7 Metc. (Mass.) 500; State *v.* Johnson, 40 Conn. 136; Moett *v.* People, 85 N. Y. 374; State *v.* Spencer, 1 Zabriskie, 196; Commonwealth *v.* Mosler, 4 Barr, 267; Brinkley *v.* State, 58 Ga. 296; McAllister *v.* State, 17 Ala. 434; Bovard *v.* State, 30 Miss. 600; Dove *v.* State, 3 Heisk. (Tenn.) 348; Loeffner *v.* State, 10 Ohio State, 598; Hopps *v.* People, 31 Ill. 385; State *v.* Huting, 21 Mo. 476; State *v.* Mewherter, 46 Iowa, 88; People *v.* McDonnell, 47 Cal. 134.

The insanity of delusion is recognized as a defence in Commonwealth *v.* Rogers, 7 Met. 500.

The insanity of uncontrollable impulse produced by mental disease is recognized as a defence in Commonwealth *v.* Rogers, 7 Met. 500; Anderson *v.* State, 43 Conn. 514; Commonwealth *v.* Mosler, 4 Barr, 267; People *v.* Sprague, 2 Parker's Crim. Cases, 43; Scott *v.* Commonwealth, 4 Met. (Ky.), 227; Kriel *v.* Commonwealth, 5 Bush, 365; Shannahan *v.* Commonwealth, 8 Bush, 464; Stevens *v.* State, 31 Ind. 485; State *v.* Felter, 25 Iowa, 67.

The Supreme Court of New Hampshire in State *v.* Pike, 49 N. H. 399, and State *v.* Jones, 50 N. H. 369, discarded all tests of insanity adopted by other courts as rules of law, and held that insanity is a mental disease; that whether the defendant had a mental disease, and whether the act charged as crime was the product of such disease, are the decisive questions, and they are questions of fact for the jury. Accordingly the same court holds that it is not competent for a witness who is not an expert to give his opinion as to the sanity of the defendant. Boardman *v.* Woodman, 47 N. H. 120; State *v.* Pike, 49 N. H. 399.

The question how far drunkenness is admitted as a defence to a prosecution for crime, is fully discussed in the note to United States *v.* Drew, 1 Leading Crim. Cases (2d ed.), 131, where there is a full citation of cases. The note closes with the following conclusions: "*First.* That fixed insanity, or *delirium tremens*, though the result of voluntary dissipation, is as much an excuse for crime as any other form of insanity. *Second.* That voluntary intoxication, not depriving the party of all knowledge of what he was doing, is not of itself an excuse for any crime. *Third.* That when some specific intent *must be proved*, in order to constitute a particular crime, the jury may consider the fact and degree of intoxication in determining whether the party had capacity to form such intent. {Cline *v.* State, 43 Ohio State, 332.} *Fourth.* That intoxication will not reduce an *unprovoked* homicide from murder to manslaughter; but if *legal* provocation has been given, it may be considered in determining whether, in fact, the party acted upon such provocation, or from malicious motives, in giving the fatal blow." See Davis *v.* Nichols, 25 Ohio State, 369, 373. The *Second* includes such person who commits an act made punishable by the law, is exempted from liability to the punishment prescribed. But to this rule there are several exceptions, founded on the absence of *criminal intention.* The principle is, that in the perpetration of a crime the mind must concur with the body, the will with the muscular organs, or the actor is not to be held responsible. If, therefore, either from imbecility, insanity, mischance, or necessity, one does an act which would be criminal if done intentionally, he stands excused on the ground of having no criminal volition. Thus *idiots* always, *lunatics* during the intervals of insanity, and *infants* while too young to know the distinction between right and wrong, are held excusable for those acts which would otherwise be punishable, because they cannot harbor a criminal design; but *drunkenness*, which is a voluntary insanity, is no excuse. Again, if the act which would otherwise be criminal, is the result of an *accident* or *mistake*, which the law calls *mischance*, the actor is not responsible, because he did not do it wilfully; but mere ignorance of the criminality of the act, when the act itself is done intentionally, is no excuse; because every person of sound mind is held bound to know what acts are declared by the law to be criminal. Lastly, if the act which would otherwise be criminal, be the result of *inevitable necessity*, the actor is excused, because he could exercise no volition. Thus, if the compulsion be physical, or if it result from an injunction of law, the exemption is absolute. But the command of no superior, except the law, can excuse the commission of a crime; for there is no necessity for obeying such a command. It was indeed formerly held, as we have seen, that a wife was excusable for concurring with her husband, on the ground of constraint, but this absurd idea is now nearly exploded. There is, however, a species of moral compulsion, which the law always allows to palliate, and often to excuse,

cases as Pigman *v.* State, 14 Ohio R. 555, where it was held that on a charge of passing counterfeit money, if the accused was so drunk that he did not know that he passed a bill that was counterfeit, he is not guilty.

At the common law an infant under the age of seven years was conclusively presumed to be *doli incapax;* between the ages of seven and fourteen, he was presumed to be *doli incapax*, but the presumption could be controverted and overcome by evidence. There was one exception; a boy under fourteen was conclusively presumed to be incapable of rape. In the United States the same presumptions prevail. State *v.* Learned, 41 Ver. 585; Godfrey *v.* State, 31 Ala. 323; State *v.* Doherty, 2 Overt. (Tenn.) 80. And see Commonwealth *v.* Mead, 10 Allen, 398; People *v.* Kendall, 25 Wend. 399; State *v.* Handy, 4 Harr. (Del.) 566; Stephenson *v.* State, 28 Ind. 272. In Ohio, however, it is held that the presumption of incapacity to commit rape between the ages of seven and fourteen is in all cases open to be controverted by evidence of the fact being to the contrary. Williams *v.* State, 14 Ohio R. 222. This decision has been followed in New York. People *v.* Randolph, 2 Parker, Crim. Cases, 174. Hiltabiddle *v.* State, 35 Ohio State, 52.

There is a general presumption that a wife who commits a crime in the presence of her husband does it under his coercion, and therefore cannot be held guilty. But this presumption does not arise in treason, homicide, or robbery; nor does it arise in offences of a character in which women are supposed especially to participate, such as keeping brothels and other disorderly houses. This presumption may always be rebutted by evidence, and the wife be shown to have acted from her own will. See Tabler *v.* State, 34 Ohio State, 127.

the commission of a crime. Thus, where the act is done strictly in *self-defence*, it is excused on the ground that the actor in violating a human law, did but obey a still higher law. So where the act is done in a moment of strong and overpowering excitement, before the passions, suddenly provoked, have had time to cool, the guilt, if not wholly excused, is greatly palliated, out of regard to the infirmity of our nature. It has often been made a question, whether extreme want of food, clothing, or shelter, ought not to be a justification of the acts done to relieve immediate necessities. Humanity would incline us to answer in the affirmative, but the plea of want, if once allowed, would open so wide a door to depredation, that the policy of the law is against admitting it. I have thus briefly indicated the general principles upon which crimes are palliated or excused, for want of criminal intention in the perpetrator. The application of these principles will be made, when we come to the description of crimes.

§ 190. **Principals and Accessories.** (*a*) We have already seen that, to constitute a crime, there must be an act. In perpetrating this act more persons than one may be concerned; and they may be concerned more or less directly. This has led to some important distinctions. He who directly and absolutely perpetrates the act, is denominated *principal in the first degree*. He who is present aiding and abetting, is denominated *principal in the second degree;* and this presence may either be *actual*, as where one stands immediately by and assists; or it may be *constructive*, as where one keeps watch at a convenient distance. Again, he who is neither chief actor, nor actually or constructively present, may still be guilty of participating in the perpetration or in its results; in which case he is denominated an *accessory*. If he procure, advise, or command the act to be done, he is an *accessory before the fact*. If, knowing the act to have been done, he receives, comforts, or assists the criminal, or shares in the avails of the crime, he is an *accessory after the fact*. And the general rule has been that though an accessory cannot be punished until the principal has been convicted, yet then he is liable to the same punishment as the principal. But the distinction between principals and accessories applies only to crimes standing in the middle rank of guilt; for in treason, on account of its magnitude, and in petty offences, on account of their littleness, all participators have been treated as principals. Such are the doctrines and distinctions of the common law; and it would not be difficult to show that some of them are arbitrary, and all of them unnecessary. For why make these distinctions in name, when the criminality and punishment are the same? If the distinction be well founded in middling crimes, why not extend it to all? And why allow the accessory to escape merely because the principal cannot be found? But these distinctions are greatly

(*a*) See 2 Swift's Dig. b. 5, chap. 14; 4 Black. Com. chap. 3.

modified in this State. We have a general provision, that if any person "*aid, abet, or procure*" another to commit any offence punishable with death or imprisonment in the penitentiary, he shall be liable to the same punishment as the chief actor would be liable to, if convicted. This provision embodies the essence of the common-law distinctions without their complexity or arbitrariness; and there are similar provisions in the federal code. But they are all defective in one respect; they do not extend to all offences; though there can be no good reason for excluding any. In fact, there are several special provisions designed particularly to remedy this imperfection. But why might there not be, in place of all these, one universal provision, punishing all who aid, abet, procure, or participate, with the same punishment as those who actually perpetrate the offence; and inflicting this punishment whether the chief actor be found or not? Such a provision would be at once simple and comprehensive; and I can perceive no objection to it. (*a*)

§ 191. **Improvement Suggested.** From the general views now presented, it will be seen that though criminal law has undergone important changes in this country, all of which are very decided improvements, yet many deficiencies still remain to be supplied. In addition to those already indicated, the want of a general provision for *compensation* to the injured party, when the case admits of it, is worthy of notice. There are some special provisions to this effect; but the principle thus recognized should be made universal. In all cases but homicide, compensation of some sort can be made to the individual himself; and in the case of homicide, it might be made to his family. Where the offender is able, this compensation should be made by him as a part of his sentence; and where he is unable, the principle of equality would seem to require that it be made at the public expense. Another very important desideratum, is a more general uniformity in the criminal laws of the different States. So great is the present diversity, that in contemplating it, one might almost be tempted to suppose that criminal legislation is an affair altogether arbitrary and capricious; not governed by fixed and immutable principles, but varying like climate, with geographical limits. Yet surely this is not the fact. The diversity does not spring from the nature of the subject. What is criminal in Maine should be so in Louisiana. There is nowhere a sufficient difference in the social condition, to make any important difference in criminal legislation. But whatever be the cause of the diversity, it does exist to a remarkable extent; and among many evil consequences, one not the least to be regretted, is that it becomes a matter of calculation among the vagabond portion of our community, who live by preying upon society, in

(*a*) {And such is now the law of Ohio. See R. S. § 6804; Hanoff *v.* State, 37 Ohio State, 178; Stephens *v.* State, 42 id. 150; Hartshorn *v.* State, 29 id. 635. Except that the statute makes the procurement of a felony an offence distinct from its commission. Chidester *v.* State, 25 Ohio State, 433.}

which of the States they may commit the greatest number of outrages, with the fairest prospect of mild punishment or entire impunity. Accordingly, that State which ventures to be most humane, will be most likely to be thronged with rogues and knaves; since, in addition to the usual proportion of its own population, it must bear the burden of immigration from those States where the laws are more sanguinary. But we are not without hope that time will bring about a greater degree of uniformity. Throughout the civilized world, the spirit of inquiry and reform is now more generally directed to the subject of crimes and punishments, than to any other matter affecting our social condition. Commissioners are appointed to visit distant regions, and compare criminal codes; and a general improvement must be the ultimate result.

LECTURE XXXV.

CRIMES UNDER THE STATE LAW.

§ 192. **General Division of Crimes.** In this lecture, I propose to consider the principal offences punished by State legislation, but without attempting a complete enumeration. And at the very outset I find difficulty in selecting any suitable classification. The most general division of crimes is into the three following classes: 1. *Crimes affecting the public welfare.* The theory of criminal law is, that all crimes affect the public welfare; otherwise, society would not interfere with them. But there are some which have this tendency much more directly and immediately than others. Such are all those offences against the justice, health, morals, peace, and property of the public, which do not directly affect either the persons or property of individuals. 2. *Crimes affecting private persons.* The personal rights of individuals, expressed in general terms, include life, liberty, health, reputation, and happiness, which, as we have seen, are declared in our constitution to be inalienable rights. All offences, therefore, which tend directly to injure or destroy either of these rights, would fall within this class. 3. *Crimes affecting private property.* This class would of course include all offences having a direct reference to the property of individuals. In the present lecture, my object is to present a mere sketch of the crimes punishable in this State, in the order indicated by the above classification. The minor offences will be barely referred to, for the purpose of grouping them together. Of the higher offences, I shall speak somewhat more at length. And although the subject of indictments belongs properly to a future lecture on criminal procedure, I shall so far anticipate that subject here, as to give, in connection with some of the higher offences, that part of the indictment which describes the offence. If the student will particularly note the technical description of the offence, he will be enabled the more accurately to remember in what the offence consists. I have before said that an indictment is a formal accusation of an offence, drawn up by the prosecuting officer, and found to be true by a grand jury; and that no man can be put upon his trial upon any criminal charge, except those of the lowest grade, until such an indictment has been found against him. The caption and conclusion of the indictment, which are merely formal and the same in all indictments, will be omitted, and only that part given which describes the offence.

§ 193. **Crimes Affecting the Public Welfare.** Under this head I shall consider a variety of offences, which scarcely admit of a more particular classification. In defining them, especially those of a minor sort, I shall use all possible brevity. (*a*)

Perjury and Subornation. (*b*) To understand the nature of perjury, we must first consider the purpose of an oath. The dictionary definition of an oath is, "an affirmation, negation, or promise corroborated by the attestation of the Divine Being." But in terms an oath differs from an affirmation in this: an oath is a direct appeal to God for the truth of what one says, or the performance of what one promises; while an affirmation appeals only to the pains and penalties of perjury. The one presupposes a belief in a future retribution; the other does not. The law requires an oath or affirmation from three classes of persons: namely, witnesses, jurors, and public officers; and as many persons have conscientious scruples against taking an oath, it is in all cases optional to affirm. Which is the more binding upon

(*a*) An act was passed April 26, 1861, declaring it treason against the State to levy war against, or knowingly adhere to the enemies of, the State, or the United States. The penalty is imprisonment for life. Betraying military posts, &c., supplying arms and ammunition to enemies, and not giving information of treason to the proper officials, are punishable by imprisonment for not less than ten nor more than twenty years. Setting on foot any military enterprise against the territory or people of any one of the United States, is punishable by imprisonment for not less than one nor more than ten years.

(*b*) *Indictment.* That heretofore, to wit, at the court of ——, begun and holden at ——, in the county aforesaid, before the [presiding judge] on the —— a certain action of trespass for assault and battery was pending, in which —— was plaintiff, and —— was defendant; in which action issue had before that time been joined; which issue then and there came on to be tried by a jury of said county in due form of law; and then and there, upon the trial of said issue, one —— being produced as a witness on behalf of said plaintiff, did make oath before the said [presiding judge], who was then and there duly authorized to administer such oath, that the evidence which he should give to the said court and jury, touching the matters in question on the said issue, should be the truth, the whole truth, and nothing but the truth; and it then and there became a material question, upon the trial of said issue, whether the said defendant had struck the said plaintiff, and how many blows; and thereupon the said —— did then and there, under the oath aforesaid, falsely, wilfully, and corruptly declare that the said —— did see the said defendant on —— at ——, strike the said plaintiff blows with his fist; whereas in truth and in fact the said —— did not see said defendant on ——, at, or at any other time or place, strike the said plaintiff at all, with his fist or otherwise; but the said declaration of the said ——, under oath as aforesaid, was then and there wholly false and untrue, as he the said —— then and there well knew; and so the said —— did then and there, in manner and form aforesaid, commit wilful and corrupt perjury.

the conscience, is a question which the conscience alone can answer; but it would seem that every human being is at all times under so strong a moral obligation to tell the truth and perform his promises, that no act of his can increase it. At any rate, the legal sanction of both is the same; namely, the pains and penalties of perjury. We say, then, that the purpose of the law, in punishing perjury, is to secure the telling of truth and performance of promises, in all things pertaining to the administration of justice, by an appeal to purely temporal sanctions, operating equally upon believers and unbelievers in a future retribution. According to Blackstone, (*a*) perjury is "when a lawful oath is administered, in some judicial proceedings, to a person who swears wilfully, absolutely, and falsely, in a manner material to the issue or point in question." This definition involves four distinct matters: 1. The oath must be administered by some person authorized by law. (*b*) 2. It must be in some judicial proceeding. (*c*) 3. The person must knowingly swear falsely. 4. The false swearing must be in relation to some material matter. (*d*) In this State, perjury is made to consist in wilfully and corruptly declaring, under oath or affirmation, any matter to be fact, knowing the same to be false; or denying any matter to be fact, knowing the same to be true; such oath or affirmation being administered by a person and upon an occasion authorized by law. The punishment is imprisonment in the penitentiary from three to ten years. The statute undertakes to specify all the cases in which perjury can be committed, instead of saying generally all cases in which the law authorizes an oath or affirmation; but in other respects the definition does not differ essentially from that of Blackstone. It suggests, however, the following queries: 1. If a person not having certain knowledge, swear against his belief, or without having any belief, would this be within the definition? 2. Since the oaths and affirmations of jurors and public officers are not statements of facts, but promises, are they within the definition? If either of these questions be answered in the negative, the definition is defective, and ought to be amended. *Subornation* of perjury consists in procuring another to commit perjury, and would consequently be included in any general provision against aiding, abetting, or procuring. The punishment is properly made the same as for committing perjury.(*e*) Formerly, an indictment for

(*a*) 4 Black. Com. 137.

(*b*) {Where the oath is not administered by the proper officer in a proper proceeding, there can be no perjury; therefore, false testimony of persons other than the complainant on the preliminary examination in bastardy, is not perjury. Hamm *v.* Wickline, 26 Ohio State, 81. Nor where the oath is administered in arbitration proceeding by a notary, when the statute says justice of the peace. State *v.* Jackson, 36 Ohio State, 281. Or before a mere *de facto* officer. Staight *v.* State, 39 id. 496.}

(*c*) Perjury may be committed in swearing falsely to an application for a marriage license. Call *v.* The State, 20 Ohio State, 330. {Though before a deputy clerk. Warwick *v.* State, 25 id. 21.}

(*d*) Dicher *v.* State, 30 Ohio State, 130.

(*e*) As to subornation of perjury, see Commonwealth *v.* Smith, 11 Allen, 243. It is perjury was exceedingly voluminous; it being held necessary to set forth the authority under which the oath was administered, together with a complete record of the proceedings in which the oath was taken; but these are dispensed with by our statute, and it is made sufficient to set forth the substance of the offence.

Bribery. In the ordinary acceptation of the term, bribery consists in hiring or being hired to swerve from public duty, and it would be easy to make one general and comprehensive provision against bribery under all circumstances, punishing equally him who offers and him who receives a bribe. Such a provision should embrace electors, jurors, witnesses, and all public officers. But our statute falls far short of the generality here proposed. It punishes bribery in the following cases: 1. Bribery of a juror, referee, arbitrator, umpire, commissioner, or appraiser, before or after appointment, and the acceptance or solicitation by such person of a bribe — imprisonment within sixty days, and fine within five hundred dollars, or both. 2. Similar conduct towards or by any member or officer of the general assembly, or any State judicial, or other officer — imprisonment within five years, and fine within five hundred dollars, or both, and disqualification. 3. Bribery to obtain escape of prisoner — fine within two hundred dollars, and imprisonment within thirty days. 4. A county commissioner taking a bribe in the execution of his office — fine between three hundred and one thousand dollars. 5. Delegate to a political convention, seeking or taking a bribe — fine within five hundred dollars, and imprisonment two to five years. 6. A candidate bribing a delegate for nomination — fine one hundred to five hundred dollars, and ineligibility. 7. Bribery of an elector — fine within five hundred dollars, and imprisonment within six months. 8. Bribery by a candidate to obtain a vote — fine five hundred to one thousand dollars, and imprisonment within three years, and perpetual disqualification. 9. Bribery by one not a candidate, including treating or threats, or refusal to allow an employee to vote — fine one hundred to two thousand dollars, and imprisonment within three years. 10. Taking or seeking a bribe at primary elections — fine within one hundred dollars, and imprisonment one to two years.

False Personation. If any person with fraudulent intent falsely personate another, that is, take the name of and pretend to be another, in any judicial proceeding, or in the acknowledgment of a deed or power-of-attorney, or in procuring a marriage license, the punishment is imprisonment in the penitentiary from one to six years. The object of this provision is to guard the public against impostors, in those weighty matters in which successful imposition would be most deleterious.

Refusing to Testify. Being legally called upon to testify and

essential that the accused should know not only that the witness will swear to what is untrue, but also that he will do so corruptly and knowingly. Stewart *v.* The State, 22 Ohio State, 477.

refusing to take the oath or affirmation — imprisonment not over ninety days, and fine from ten to five hundred dollars.

Refusing to Assist Officers. Being legally called upon by the sheriff or other officer to aid him in arresting or securing an offender, and refusing so to do — fine within fifty dollars.

Resisting Officers. Resisting or abusing any judge, justice, sheriff, constable, or other officer, in the execution of his office — fine within five hundred dollars, or imprisonment within thirty days, or both. (*a*)

Taking Unlawful Fees. Any officer, judicial or ministerial, knowingly receiving any other fee or reward for doing his duty than that which the law prescribes — fine within two hundred dollars, or imprisonment within twenty days, or both; and forfeiture of office and disqualification from holding any office.

Stirring up Suits. Any judicial or ministerial officer of court, or attorney, stirring up or encouraging any suit, quarrel, or controversy, with intent to injure the persons litigating — fine within five hundred dollars, and civil liability in treble damages.

Aiding in the Escape of Prisoners. 1. Any officer in the penitentiary procuring, aiding, or abetting any convict to escape — same punishment as the escaped convict. 2. Any other officer voluntarily suffering an offender in his custody to escape — fine fifty to five hundred dollars, or imprisonment within three months, or both. 3. Any person rescuing or attempting to rescue an offender from custody — same punishment.

Usurpation of Office. Assuming to be an officer without authority — fine within three hundred dollars, and imprisonment within twenty days, or both.

Oppression in Office. Wilfully and corruptly oppressing another, under color of office — fine within three hundred dollars, and imprisonment within twenty days, or both.

Offences connected with Elections. 1. A resident of any county voting in any township in such county, in which he does not actually reside — fine within five hundred dollars, or imprisonment from three to six months. 2. A resident of the State voting in any county in which he does not actually reside — penitentiary from one to three years. 3. Voting more than once at the same election — penitentiary from one to five years. 4. A resident of another State voting in this State — penitentiary from one to five years. 5. Voting without having the qualifications of an elector — jail from one to six months. 6. Procuring, aiding, or advising another to vote contrary to law — fine from one hundred to five hundred dollars, and jail from one to six months. 7. Procuring, aiding, or advising another to go, for the purpose of voting, to a place where he has no right to vote — penitentiary from one to five years. 8. Influencing or attempting to influence a voter, by bribery or threats, to vote contrary to his inclination

(*a*) Faris *v.* State of Ohio, 3 Ohio State, 159. {It is not necessary that the officer be assaulted to constitute the offence. Woodworth *v.* State, 26 id. 196.}

— fine within five hundred dollars, and jail within six months, and if a candidate and elected, removal from office. 9. Deceiving a voter who cannot read, as to the contents of his ballot, or fraudulently changing a ballot — penitentiary from one to three years. 10. Fraudulently putting a ballot into the box after the polls are opened — penitentiary from one to three years, and if a judge of the election, and knowingly permitting the counting of such ballot, same penalty. 11. Any judge or clerk of an election knowingly violating his duty as prescribed by law — penitentiary from one to five years. 12. A judge of election postponing the count or removing the ballot-box — fine one hundred to one thousand dollars, and imprisonment within ten days. 13. Obtaining possession of the ballot-box, or attempting to do so — imprisonment from one to three years. 14. Destroying or attempting to destroy any ballot-box, ballot, or poll-book — imprisonment one to five years. 15. Adding fictitious names on poll-book or list — imprisonment one to three years. 16. Having possession of an altered or counterfeit poll-book, list, or return — imprisonment one to three years. 17. Marking the ballot of another to ascertain how he voted — fine within fifty dollars, and imprisonment within ten days. 18. Bribery by a candidate — fine five hundred to one thousand dollars, or imprisonment within three years, and perpetual ineligibility. 19. Bribery, treating, or threatening, by one not a candidate, or sale of influence — fine one hundred to one thousand dollars, and imprisonment within three years. 20. Demanding or receiving from a candidate a bribe, or offering to sell him tickets with a view of being influenced — fine fifty to three hundred dollars, or imprisonment within sixty days, or both. 21. Betting on elections — fine between five and five hundred dollars, or imprisonment between ten days and six months, the fine to equal the amount hazarded if between those sums.

Offences connected with Banking. 1. Any officer of an incorporated bank refusing to indorse, on notes presented for redemption and not redeemed, the date and fact of presentation — fine from five to fifty dollars for each note. 2. Any officer of an incorporated bank knowingly making a false statement to bank commissioners — penitentiary from one to ten years. 3. Acting as an officer of a bank not incorporated by law — fine of one thousand dollars. To constitute a bank, there must be a company or association which lends money or some evidence of debt, and issues paper designed to circulate as money, or causes the same to be done; and any person is declared to be an officer who in any way intermeddles with the concerns of such bank for its benefit. 4. Acting as an officer or agent of an incorporated bank, which issues notes less than five dollars, or notes payable elsewhere, or at a future day, or in anything else than gold and silver, or dealing in such paper as a broker — fine of one hundred dollars for each offence. 5. Acting as an officer or agent of a municipal corporation which issues paper intended to circulate as money

— fine of fifty dollars. 6. Passing or paying out paper designed to circulate as money and not authorized by law — fine and imprisonment as for misdemeanor. 7. Acting as an agent of any bank incorporated out of this State, or of any individual or association out of this State, engaged in banking with a view to give circulation to their paper — fine of a sum equal to one fourth of the amount of the notes brought here. 8. Any receiving or disbursing officer of the State receiving or paying out unauthorized paper — fine of one hundred dollars.

Neglect of Official Duty. Under this head might be enumerated a great number of fines, imposed upon officers for the neglect of the duties assigned them by law. But suffice it to say, there is scarcely a duty imposed upon a citizen, connected with the municipal concerns of the State, the neglect or refusal to perform which does not involve a penalty or forfeiture.

Offences against the Public Health. (*a*) These are commonly called *nuisances*, and are as follows: 1. Putting the carcass of any dead animal into any river, creek, pond, road, alley, lot, field, meadow, or common, or permitting the same to remain there — fine from one to fifty dollars. 2. Putting the same into a well, stream, or brook of running water, used for domestic purposes — fine from five to fifty dollars, or imprisonment within sixty days, or both. 3. Knowingly selling unwholesome provisions — fine within fifty dollars, or imprisonment within twenty days, or both. 4. Creating or keeping up ponds of stagnant water — fine within five hundred dollars. It is perhaps a matter of regret that our provisions against nuisances do not extend further. A variety of other nuisances will suggest themselves, equally offensive with those above specified, which are punishable at common law, but cannot be punished here, for want of express provision.

Offences against Public Morals. (*b*) Under this head are included the following: —

Lotteries. 1. Being concerned in getting up any lottery or scheme of chance — fine fifty to five hundred dollars, and imprisonment ten to ninety days. 2. Selling lottery tickets or having any agency therein — fine within five hundred dollars, or imprisonment within six months, or both. 3. Advertising a lottery — fine within five hundred dollars, or imprisonment within six months, or both.

Gaming. (*c*) 1. Playing at any game, except for athletic exercise, or betting on either side, in any ordinary, tavern, race-field, or place connected therewith; or playing at any game whatever in any place for gain; or betting upon any matter whatsoever — fine within one hundred dollars, or imprisonment ten days to six months. 2. Keeping any gaming table, device, or machine, or suffering one to be kept, for the sake of gain — fine

(*a*) See 3 Black. Com. 216; 4 id. 167.
(*b*) See 2 Swift's Dig. b. 5, ch. 8; 4 Black. Com. chap. 4.
(*c*) The act for prevention of gaming is amended by the act of Feb. 21, 1859.

between fifty and five hundred dollars, and imprisonment from ten to ninety days, and security to desist. 3. The keeper of any tavern, ordinary, or house of public resort, permitting gaming of any kind in or about the premises — fine between fifty and two hundred dollars, and forfeiture of license. 4. All gaming contracts are declared void; money lost may be recovered at any time within six months, by the loser, or any other person on his behalf; and a bill of discovery may be filed, or any person present or concerned may be made a witness to prove the fact. (*a*)

Offences against Religion. 1. Sporting, rioting, quarrelling, hunting, fishing, or laboring on Sunday — fine within twenty dollars, or imprisonment within twenty days, or both. But this is declared not to include persons under fourteen; nor persons who conscientiously observe the seventh day; nor families moving or emigrating; nor ferry-men, water-men, or toll-receivers; nor works of necessity or charity. (*b*) 2. Selling spirituous liquors on Sunday, except to travellers — fine within five dollars. 3. Disturbing any religious or other lawful meeting at any time — fine within fifty dollars, or imprisonment within ten days, or both. 4. Profanely cursing or damning; or swearing by the name of God, Jesus Christ, or the Holy Ghost — fine within one dollar. (*c*) But this is declared not to include persons under fourteen. 5. Selling liquor within four miles of a religious meeting — fine ten to one hundred dollars. But this does not include those whose usual places of selling liquor are there.

Miscellaneous. 1. Playing bullets, or running horses, or shooting at a target, along or across the street of any town or village, or running a horse-race on any public road in common use — fine five to fifty dollars. 2. A tavern-keeper or retailer of liquors, keeping or permitting a ball or ninepin alley — fine from ten to one hundred dollars. 3. Exhibiting any public show without license — fine one hundred dollars. 4. Exhibiting for gain any

(*a*) Hoss *v.* Layton, 3 Ohio State, 352; Craig *v.* Andrews, 7 Clarke (Iowa), 18.

(*b*) Bloom *v.* Richards, 2 Ohio State, 387. For construction of the phrase "necessity and charity," see Omit *v.* Commonwealth, 21 Penn. State, 426; Commonwealth *v.* Nesbit, 34 id. 398; Johnston *v.* Commonwealth, 22 id. 102; Commonwealth *v.* Knox, 6 Mass. 76; Pearce *v.* Atwood, 13 id. 350–2; Bosworth *v.* Swansey, 10 Met. 363; Robeson *v.* French, 12 id. 24; Pattee *v.* Greeley, 13 id. 284; Gregg *v.* Wyman, 4 Cush. 322; Flagg *v.* Millbury, 4 id. 143; Phillips *v.* Innes, 4 Clark & Finnelly, 234. In this last case, it was held by the House of Lords that the shaving by barbers of their customers was not a work of necessity. McGatrick *v.* Wason, 4 Ohio State, 566. See *ante*, p. 64, note (*a*) and cases cited. The Sunday act has been held unconstitutional in California, as being contrary to the constitutional provision for the free exercise and enjoyment of religious profession and worship. *Ex parte* Newman, 9 Cal. 502. The opinion of Terry, C. J., is indeed a singular one. Field, J., dissented. A municipal ordinance prohibiting the opening of shops and other places of business on Sunday, without excepting cases of necessity and charity, or exempting from its operation persons who conscientiously observe the seventh day of the week as the Sabbath, is inconsistent with the laws of the State, and void. City of Canton *v.* Nist, 9 Ohio State, 439 {but an ordinance prohibiting keeping open liquor shops without such exceptions, is valid under the power to regulate. Piqua *v.* Zimmerlin, 35 Ohio State, 507}.

(*c*) As to the crime of blasphemy, see People *v.* Ruggles, 8 Johns. 290; Commonwealth *v.* Kneeland, 20 Pick. 210; Updegraph *v.* Commonwealth, 11 S. & R. 394.

puppet show, wire dancing, tumbling, juggling, or sleight of hand — fine within ten dollars. 5. Being concerned in bull or bear baiting or cock-fighting, or fighting of other animals — fine five to one hundred and fifty dollars, or imprisonment ten to thirty days. (*a*)

Offences against the Public Peace. (*b*) These are as follows: —

Riots. (*c*) 1. Three or more persons assembling together, with intent to do an unlawful act, with force and violence, against the person or property of another, or against the peace; or, when lawfully assembled, agreeing to do such unlawful act, and making motion or preparation thereto, or continuing together after proclamation to disperse — fine within five hundred dollars, or imprisonment within thirty days, or both, and giving security. 2. Abusing judicial officer, or resisting or obstructing other officers — fine within five hundred dollars, or imprisonment within thirty days. 3. It is also declared that if rioters be killed, wounded, or maimed, in the exercise of necessary and proper means to disperse them, it shall be no crime.

Affrays. Two persons by agreement wilfully fighting or boxing at fisticuffs — fine within fifty dollars, or imprisonment within ten days, or both.

Digging up Dead Bodies. Being concerned in digging up or carrying away any dead human body from any cemetery or burial-ground, or attempting so to do — fine within one thousand dollars, or imprisonment within six months, or both.

Offences against Public Property. (*d*) These are as follows: —

Infractions of the Canal Regulations. The highest offence of this kind is that of wilfully and maliciously breaking or destroying any lock, bank, dam, aqueduct, or culvert of any canal belonging to the State; the punishment of which is imprisonment in the penitentiary from three to seven years, and liability for damages; and there are numerous minor offences under this head; but not being of general interest, I shall not enumerate them.

Destruction of Public Buildings, Bridges, and other Property. These offences will be described in connection with similar injuries to private property.

Obstruction of Navigable Rivers. (*e*) We have seen that all the navigable rivers within the State are declared to be public highways. Interference with any buoy, beacon, channel, stake, or other aid to navigation, is punished by fine within five hundred dollars, or imprisonment within six months, or both. Obstructing the passage of navigable water, or public ground or highway — fine within five hundred dollars.

(*a*) Carrying concealed weapons, — fine not exceeding two hundred dollars, or imprisonment not more than thirty days. Act of March 18, 1859. See act of May 1, 1854, in relation to the sale of intoxicating liquors. Miller *v.* The State, 3 Ohio State, 475; Aultfather *v.* The State, 4 id. 467.

(*b*) 2 Swift's Dig. b. 5, ch. 6; 4 Black. Com. ch. 11.

(*c*) As to the powers to suppress riots, see 1 West. Law Jour. 418; 2 id. 49.

(*d*) See 2 Swift's Dig. b. 5, ch. 5.

(*e*) See 4 Black. Com. 167.

§ 194. **Crimes affecting Private Persons.** The personal rights or immunities of individuals, expressed in general terms, include life, liberty, health, reputation, and happiness. These rights, as we have seen, are declared to be inalienable. Accordingly, the acts which tend directly to endanger or destroy them, are generally prohibited under severe penalties.

Homicide. (*a*) According to Blackstone, "homicide, or the killing of any human creature, is of three kinds, *justifiable*, *excusable*, and *felonious*. The first has no share of guilt at all; the second very little; but the third is the highest crime against the law of nature that man is capable of committing." But I shall confine my remarks to felonious or criminal homicide, that alone being punishable; and I shall say nothing of suicides, because, however wrong in the sight of Heaven, our law does not attempt to punish it even by disgrace. By the law of England, felonious or criminal homicide is of two kinds, *murder* and *manslaughter*, which are thus defined by Blackstone: "Murder is when a person of sound memory and discretion unlawfully killeth any reasonable creature in being and under the king's peace, with malice aforethought, either expressed or implied." — "Manslaughter is the unlawful killing of another without malice either express or implied; which may be either voluntarily, upon a sudden heat; or involuntarily, but in the commission of some unlawful act." (*b*)

(*a*) *Indictment for Murder in the First Degree.* That heretofore, to wit, on ———, at ———, to wit, at the county aforesaid, one ———, with force and arms, in and upon one ———, purposely and of deliberate and premeditated malice, did make an assault; and the said ——— did then and there, with a certain knife, held in his right hand, purposely, and of deliberate and premeditated malice, strike and thrust the said ———, in and upon the left side of the body, and between the ribs of him, the said ———; thereby giving to the said ——— then and there, with the knife aforesaid, upon his body aforesaid, one mortal wound, of the breadth of three inches, and of the depth of six inches; of which said mortal wound the said ———, from the said date [date of wound], until [date of the death], at the county aforesaid, did suffer and languish, and languishing, did live; on which said [date of the death], in the county aforesaid, the said ———, of the said mortal wound did die; and so the said ———, in manner and form aforesaid, did purposely, and of deliberate and premeditated malice, kill and murder the said ———.

Indictment for Murder in the Second Degree. This form is the same as the preceding, except that the words "purposely and maliciously, but without deliberation and premeditation," are to be used throughout in place of the words "purposely, and of deliberate and premeditated malice."

The form under the criminal code of Ohio is, that A. B. on the ——— day of ———, in the year of our Lord one thousand eight hundred and ———, in the county of ——— aforesaid, did unlawfully, purposely, and maliciously kill C. D. then and there being.

Indictment for Manslaughter. This form is the same as the first, except that the words "unlawfully and feloniously" are to be used instead of the words "purposely, and of deliberate and premeditated malice;" and the word "murder" is to be omitted, leaving only the word "kill."

The form under the criminal code of Ohio is the same as the form above given for manslaughter, except that the words "purposely and maliciously" are omitted.

In all the forms above given, the caption and conclusion are omitted. These can be found in the form given under § 240.

See the very recent work of Wharton on Homicide.

(*b*) 4 Black. Com. 177, 191, 195. The degree of the crime must be found by the jury and specified in their verdict. Dick *v.* The State, 3 Ohio State, 89; Parks *v.* The State, 3 id. 101.

But in this State there are four kinds of criminal homicide; namely, *murder in the first degree*, *murder in the second degree*, *manslaughter*, and the *destruction of a child before birth*, which are defined by our statute as follows: —

Murder in the first degree is where one kills another purposely, and of deliberate and premeditated malice, or in the perpetration of, or attempt to perpetrate any rape, arson, robbery, or burglary, or by administering poison, or causing the same to be done, or kills by placing an obstruction on a railroad. (*a*) The punishment is death, which is here reserved for this crime only. (*b*)

Murder in the second degree is where one kills another purposely and maliciously, except as provided in murder in the first degree. The punishment is imprisonment in the penitentiary for life.

Manslaughter is where one unlawfully kills another, except as provided in murder in the first and second degrees. The punishment is imprisonment in the penitentiary from one to twenty years.

(*a*) Neither fraud nor violence are necessary ingredients in the crime of administering poison. It includes furnishing poison to another, for the purpose or with the intent that the person to whom it is delivered shall commit suicide with it; and also being present at the taking of poison by a suicide, participating in it by assistance, persuasion or otherwise, though the person thus participating at the time intends and agrees also to commit suicide. Blackburn *v.* The State, 23 Ohio State, 146.

(*b*) It has been held in Ohio by three judges against two, that the purpose or intent to kill is in all cases an essential ingredient in the crime of murder, the statute of the State in that respect changing the common law; and that killing another in committing rape, burglary, arson, abortion, and the like, without intending to kill, is not murder as at common law. Robbins *v.* The State, 8 Ohio State, 131; Fouts *v.* The State, 8 id. 98; Kain *v.* The State, 8 id. 306. See State *v.* Gillick, 7 Clarke (Iowa), 287. Homicide is the killing of a human being by a human being. A child not completely born and separated from the person of the mother, is not, in criminal law, a human being. Its destruction is a crime, but is not homicide. Murder is, at common law, homicide with malice aforethought. Malice is the intent to do an unlawful injury. Malice may be expressed or implied. It need not be directed against the person injured, and, in some cases, it need not be directed against any particular person. But the malice must be of grave character to constitute murder. The intent to commit a misdemeanor or to inflict slight personal injury is not sufficient; while the intent to commit a felony or to do grievous bodily harm, is sufficient, as is also a wanton and reckless disregard of human life. Hence, at common law, death caused though unintentionally in perpetrating a felony, or in doing grievous bodily harm, or by such reckless conduct as throwing building material from a house down into a frequented street of a city, or riding a vicious horse into a crowd to frighten the people, is murder. Fouts *v.* The State, 8 Ohio State, 98, though followed in subsequent cases in the same court, was never satisfactory. The Supreme Court of Indiana, under a statute in the same words with the Ohio statute, held that an intent to kill was not necessary to constitute murder in the first degree where the killing happened in perpetrating or attempting to perpetrate rape, arson, robbery or burglary. Stocking *v.* The State, 7 Ind. 326. The Ohio criminal code of 1877, removes doubt by inserting the word "either," "Whoever purposely, and either of deliberate and premeditated malice, or," &c. The Ohio code also provides that whoever maliciously obstructs a railroad with intent to endanger any locomotive or car, and thereby occasions the death of another, is guilty of murder in the first degree; that killing purposely and maliciously which does not amount to murder in the first degree, is murder in the second degree; and that any unlawful killing which is not murder, is manslaughter. Though in Ohio, there must be an intent to kill some person, except in the case of obstructing a railway, in order to constitute murder, it need not be an intent to kill the person who is actually slain. Wareham *v.* The State, 25 Ohio State, 601.

Destroying a child before birth, is where a physician or other person intentionally causes the death of an unborn but living child, by administering any drug or substance, or employing any instrument or other means whatsoever, unless the same be necessary to preserve the life of the mother, or be advised by two other physicians. The punishment is imprisonment in the penitentiary from one to seven years. (*a*)

The grand distinction between murder and manslaughter is, that in murder the killing is always with *malice*, while in manslaughter it is without malice. The precise legal idea of malice, as an ingredient in crime, can hardly be expressed by a brief definition. It does not mean simply the intention to kill, for I may intentionally kill another in self-defence. Nor does it mean anger in the common acceptation of that term; for anger is precisely that "*sudden heat*" which determines the killing not to be murder. But it means that dark, sullen, malevolent disposition of the mind which, in the prosecution of its mischievous purposes, is equally reckless of divine and human law. The description of malice given by Blackstone is as follows: (*b*) "Malice prepense, *malitia prœcognitata*, is not so properly spite or malevolence to the deceased in particular, as any evil design in general: the dictate of a wicked, depraved, and malignant heart." — "Express malice is when one with a sedate, deliberate mind and formed design doth kill another: which formed design is evidenced by external circumstances discovering that inward intention; as lying in wait, antecedent menaces, former grudges, and concerted schemes to do him some bodily harm." — "Also, in many cases where no malice is expressed, the law will imply it; as where a man wilfully poisons another, in such a deliberate act, the law presumes malice, though no particular enmity can be proved. And if a man kills another suddenly, without any, or without a considerable, provocation, the law implies malice."

The distinction between the two degrees of murder, though apparently well founded in reason, and certainly commendable for its humanity, does not exist under the laws of England, nor of the United States, nor of many of the States. It consists in this: (*c*) In both, the killing is done purposely and maliciously; but in one there is *deliberation* and *premeditation*, while in the other there is not. As to the length of time necessary to constitute deliberation or premeditation, no definite rule can be laid down. It varies with persons and circumstances. In some minds a minute would be as effectual as a month. The questions for the jury are: Had the slayer space and opportunity for reflection? Did he think over what he was about to do?

(*a*) Robbins *v.* The State, 8 Ohio State, 131.

(*b*) 4 Black. Com. 198–200.

(*c*) Respublica *v.* Mulatto Bob, 4 Dall. 149; Pennsylvania *v.* Lewis, Addison, 279; Shoemaker *v.* The State, 12 Ohio, 43; State *v.* Turner, Wright's Rep. 20; State *v.* Town, id. 75; State *v.* Williams, id. 199; State *v.* Gardiner, id. 392; State *v.* Thompson, id. 617; Sutcliffe *v.* The State, 18 Ohio, 469.

Did he coolly form a settled purpose? Was his mind sedately and considerately made up to take life? If these questions be answered in the affirmative, the verdict must be murder in the first degree. If not, and yet the killing was done purposely and maliciously, it must be murder in the second degree. But there are five cases in which our statute precludes the question of deliberation; namely, where the killing takes place in the perpetration of rape, arson, robbery, burglary, or poisoning. In these cases, from their peculiar enormity, the law presumes both malice and premeditation. (*a*)

If the killing be not malicious, and yet be unlawful, it is manslaughter; of which there are two kinds: the one *voluntary*, resulting from a sudden quarrel; the other *involuntary*, resulting from some unlawful act. In Pennsylvania and Virginia, (*b*) a distinction is made in the punishment of these two offences, and involuntary manslaughter is regarded as a misdemeanor only, and not a felony. Our statute makes no such distinction, although it would seem to be as well founded as in the two degrees of murder. To constitute voluntary manslaughter, there must be intention to kill at the moment of killing; but this intention must be the result of sudden heat, and without the least malice or premeditation. It is often very difficult to distinguish between voluntary manslaughter and murder in the second degree, since the question turns upon the presence or absence of malice at the moment of killing; and this must be determined by circumstances developing themselves on the instant. The most important of these are the kind and degree of provocation. If the provocation be such as greatly to excite the passions, the offence will be manslaughter; if not, malice will be inferred, and the case will be murder in the second degree. If the killing be involuntary, that is, if there be no intention to kill at the moment of killing, but yet the slayer is in the commission of some unlawful act, the case is one of involuntary manslaughter. And it is not every unlawful act which makes an unintentional killing manslaughter. The mere withholding from another any legal right is an unlawful act, but this cannot be what the law intends. Nor would an ordinary trespass be such an act. If, for example, in getting over another's wall, to cross his field, I should accidentally cause a stone to fall and kill some one, this would not be manslaughter. But while the books leave the question as to the exact nature of the unlawful act in doubt, reason would seem to require that it should either be a misdemeanor or an aggravated trespass, because it is the unlawfulness of this precedent act, and not the killing of itself, which constitutes the crime. And it may happen that a sudden quarrel is the unlawful act in question. In this case, the inquiry would seem to be, who was first in fault for bringing on the quarrel?

(*a*) See *ante*, p. 571, note (*b*).
(*b*) 7 Serg. & Rawle, 423; 5 Black. Com. (Tucker), 192.

If the person slain commenced the quarrel, and the killing were unintentional, the slayer would be innocent; for as to him the quarrel was not an unlawful act.

It is a familiar maxim of criminal law, that every man is presumed to be innocent, until proved to be guilty. Yet in cases of homicide, when the fact of killing is once proved, the legal presumption is that of murder; and it lies upon the accused to prove any circumstances of justification or palliation. The doctrine is thus stated by Blackstone: (*a*) "We may take it for a general rule that all homicide is malicious, and of course amounts to murder; unless when *justified* by the command or permission of the law; *excused* on the account of accident or self-preservation; or *alleviated* into manslaughter, by being either the involuntary consequence of some act not strictly lawful, or, if voluntary, occasioned by some sudden and sufficiently violent provocation. And all these circumstances of justification, excuse, or alleviation, it is incumbent on the prisoner to make out to the satisfaction of the court and jury." But where a distinction exists between the two degrees of murder, this rule is so far modified, that the presumption is only that of murder in the second degree. (*b*) To make out murder in the first degree, the burden of proof falls upon the State. To make out manslaughter or entire innocence, the burden of proof falls on the accused.

Upon the maxim, that the greater always includes the less, it has become a rule in cases of homicide, that under an indictment for murder in the first degree, the prisoner may be convicted either of murder in the second degree or manslaughter. (*c*) This rule has been so long acquiesced in, that it may now be too late to call it in question. But it seems to be in direct opposition to that constitutional guaranty which secures to the accused the privilege "of demanding the nature and cause of the accusation against him, and having a copy thereof." The meaning of these words appears to be, that the accused shall not be tried for any offence not charged in the indictment, be it greater or less; the object of an indictment being to notify him precisely what charge he is called upon to meet.

The most common defence set up in cases of homicide is that of *self-defence*, of which I have before spoken. On this subject the

(*a*) 4 Black. Com. 201. See for a full examination of the presumptions in cases of homicide, York's case, 9 Met. 103; Commonwealth *v.* Webster, 5 Cush. 304; and an able article in the North American Review for January, 1851, p. 178–204, by Hon. Joel Parker, Royall Professor of Law in Harvard University.

(*b*) State *v.* Turner, Wright's Rep. 20, 28. In some States it has been held that where there has been a conviction for murder in the second degree, and a new trial granted, the prisoner at the second trial can only be convicted of murder in the second degree. But in Ohio it is settled that the whole previous trial is set aside, and the prisoner may be convicted of any offence of which he might have been convicted at the first trial; and such seems to be the most reasonable rule. State *v.* Behimer, 20 Ohio State, 572.

(*c*) 2 Chitty, C. L. 739; 2 Hale, P. C. 402; 7 Serg. & Rawle, 423.

authorities do not seem to be entirely in harmony. Blackstone, (*a*) quoting from Hale, says that "the party assaulted must flee as far as he conveniently can, either by reason of some wall, ditch, or other impediment; or as far as the fierceness of the assault will permit." But Foster, in his Crown Law, (*b*) states the doctrine thus: "In the case of justifiable self-defence, the injured party may repel force by force in defence of his person, habitation, or property, against one who manifestly intendeth or endeavoreth, by violence or surprise, to commit a known felony upon either. In these cases, he is not obliged to retreat, but may pursue his adversary till he findeth himself out of danger: and if in a conflict between them he happeneth to kill, such killing is justifiable." I understand by this, that if I am attacked, it is not necessary that my life be endangered before I can resort to self-defence. It is enough if there be danger of great harm. Nor is it necessary that the danger should actually exist. It is enough if there be reasonable ground for apprehension. Chief Justice Parker, on the trial of Selfridge, stated the doctrine thus: (*c*) "When, from the nature of the attack, there is reasonable ground to believe that there is a design to destroy life, or commit a felony upon the person, the killing of the assailant will be excusable homicide, although it should afterwards appear that no felony was intended." And this is the good sense of the matter. The party assailed must judge from the circumstances of the moment, and act upon the hasty conclusion thus formed. The cowardly doctrine, therefore, of retreating as far as possible before resisting would seem to have no more foundation in law than it has in the common feelings or practice of mankind. (*d*) And although it is clear that no words, however provoking, will justify the taking of life, it may well be questioned whether, in this country, any man is bound to submit quietly to a blow, though intended only to disgrace him. Such I understand to be the doctrine held in the celebrated cases of Selfridge and Goodwin. It was thus stated by the late Mr. Dexter, in his defence of the first of these cases: "I respect the laws of my country and revere the precepts of our holy religion; I should shudder at shedding human blood; I would practise moderation and forbearance to avoid so terrible a calamity; yet should I ever be driven to that impassable point where degradation and disgrace begin, may this arm shrink palsied from its socket, if I fail to defend my own honor." (*e*)

(*a*) 4 Black. Com. 185.

(*b*) Foster, C. L. 273.

(*c*) Selfridge's Trial, 160; 1 Western Law Jour. 23; Stewart *v.* State, 1 Ohio State, 66.

(*d*) {One who is assaulted without fault on his part need not retreat, although able to do so safely, but may kill to save his own life or prevent grievous bodily harm. Erwin *v.* State, 29 Ohio State, 186. The danger of death or great bodily harm need not be actual, but the belief of the slayer that it exists must be upon reasonable grounds. Marts *v.* State, 26 Ohio State 162; Darling *v.* Williams, 35 id. 58; State *v.* Peacock, 40 id. 333.}

(*e*) One who first makes a malicious assault upon another, cannot, during the con-

Rape upon Daughter or Sister. (*a*) Having carnal knowledge of a child under twelve years of age, or one's daughter or sister, forcibly and against her will — penitentiary for life. This offence has all the turpitude of rape and incest combined.

Rape upon any other Woman. (*b*) Having carnal knowledge of any other female than one's daughter or sister, forcibly and against her will; or a male of seventeen or more having carnal knowledge of a female under ten, with her consent — penitentiary from three to twenty years. This definition does not exclude the wife, but the law implies such exclusion. For a man cannot be punished for a rape upon his own wife, though he may for aiding and abetting another to ravish his wife. But a strumpet or paramour may be the subject of rape as much as a virtuous female.

Carnal Knowledge of an Insane Woman. A male over seventeen having carnal knowledge of any insane woman, not his wife, knowing her to be insane — penitentiary from three to ten years. This offence might properly be called a rape, since an insane person is incapable of consenting.

Bigamy. Marrying a second time, while a former husband or wife is living, unless such husband or wife shall have been continually and wilfully absent and unheard from, for five years next preceding — penitentiary from one to seven years.

Incest. (*c*) Sexual intercourse between persons nearer of kin by consanguinity, or affinity, than cousins, the parties knowing their relationship — penitentiary from one to ten years. Our statute includes step-parent and step-child; (*d*) and it limits the criminality as between brother and sister, to above sixteen years

tinuance of the conflict thus provoked, justify taking the life of the assailed as an act of self-defence, however imminent his peril. But that conflict over, and he being once more in good faith in a position of apparent security, his right of self-defence returns. Stoffer *v.* The State, 15 Ohio State, 47. The burden of proof where the homicide is excused on the ground of self-defence rests on the accused; but it must be established by a preponderance of evidence only. Silous *v.* The State, 22 Ohio State, 90.

(*a*) *Indictment.* That heretofore, to wit, on ———, at ———, to wit, at the county aforesaid, one ———, with force and arms, in and upon ———, a female, did make an assault; and her the said ——— did then and there feloniously ravish and carnally know, by force and against her will: she the said ——— then and there being the daughter of him the said ——— as he the said ——— then and there well knew.

If the rape be upon any other woman not insane, the form is the same, except that the allegation of being daughter or sister is omitted; and if the female be under ten, and the male seventeen or more, these facts are alleged, and the words "by force and against her will," may be omitted. If the female be insane, this and the *scienter* must be alleged, and also, probably that she was not the wife of the accused; and the force may be admitted as before.

(*b*) As to the capacity of infants to commit or attempt rape, see Williams *v.* The State, 14 Ohio, 222. As to evidence admissible, see McCombs *v.* The State, 8 Ohio State, 643. McDermott *v.* The State, 13 Ohio State, 332. Emission is still a necessary part of the offence. Blackburn *v.* The State, 22 Ohio State, 102.

(*c*) Emission is a necessary ingredient of the crime. Noble *v.* The State, 22 Ohio State, 541.

(*d*) The relation of step-father and step-daughter, to constitute this crime, does not exist after the termination of the marriage relations between the step-father and the step-daughter's mother. Noble *v.* The State, 22 Ohio State, 541.

of age. But there are two singular omissions, probably accidental. The intercourse between mother and son is not provided for, while that of a step-mother and step-son is; and the language is not such as to make the daughter or step-daughter punishable. Nothing is said as to half-brother and sister.

Adultery and Fornication. (*a*) Adultery usually signifies criminal conversation between two married persons, or a married and an unmarried person, which introduces, or tends to introduce, a spurious offspring into the family. To constitute adultery, there must be carnal connection. In England, the punishment of adultery is left to the spiritual courts. In this country it is generally punished by fine and imprisonment. In this State, a single act is a good cause for divorce; and if a wife leave her husband and dwell with her adulterer, it bars her dower unless forgiven by the husband. In addition to which, we have the following penal provisions: For fornication — fine within two hundred dollars, and imprisonment within three months. It will be observed that an unmarried woman is not punishable for intercourse with a married man, though an unmarried man is punishable for intercourse with a married woman. I can see no reason for this discrimination, and presume it to be accidental. It will also be observed that a *single act* is not punishable. There must be a *living and cohabiting in a state of adultery*, to constitute the offence. This cannot be oversight; though I see no good reason for such an indirect toleration of single acts. (*b*)

Assault with Criminal Intent. (*c*) Assaulting another with intent to kill or commit rape, or robbery — penitentiary from one to fifteen years. (*d*) Here two things are to be considered, the *assault* and *intent*. An assault is any attempt, with force or violence, to

(*a*) *Indictment.* That heretofore, to wit, on ———, at ———, to wit, at the county aforesaid, one ———, being then and there a married man, did then and there desert ———, his lawful wife, and from the day aforesaid until the ——— did there live and cohabit with another woman, to wit, one ———, in a state of adultery, by having carnal knowledge of the body of her the said ———, at divers times between the days aforementioned.

(*b*) In Massachusetts, a man who marries and cohabits with a woman who has not heard from her husband for more than seven years, supposing him to be dead, is guilty of adultery. Commonwealth *v.* Thompson, 11 Allen, 23.

(*c*) *Indictment.* That heretofore, to wit, on ———, at ———, to wit, at the county aforesaid, one ——— with force and arms did make an assault upon one ——— with a dangerous weapon, to wit, with a drawn sword, which he the said ——— in his right hand then and there held, with intent purposely and of deliberate and premeditated malice to kill and murder him the said ——— with the drawn sword aforesaid.

Under an indictment for this offence there may be a conviction of assault and battery merely. Stewart *v.* State, 5 Ohio, 241. And where the intent was to commit a rape, it is sufficient so to allege, without specifying the age of the female, or whether or not she was a daughter or a sister of the accused. Bowles *v.* State, 7 Ohio, 2 pt. 343. An attempt to carnally know a female child under ten years of age with her consent is not an indictable offence under the laws of Ohio. The presumption is that such a child is incapable of giving such consent, but such presumption may be rebutted by proof that she understood the nature of the act. Smith *v.* The State, 12 Ohio State, 466; O'Meara *v.* The State, 17 Ohio State, 515. As to assault with intent to kill, see Sharp *v.* The State, 19 Ohio, 379.

(*d*) Now penitentiary from ten to fifteen years. Act of March 31, 1865.

do a corporal injury to another, coupled with a present ability to carry such intent into effect. Hence mere words never amount to an assault, though they serve to explain the intent of the act constituting the assault. And it follows, that an assault is complete without effecting the corporal injury attempted. As to the intent, it must be to kill or commit a *rape*, or *robbery;* and it must be ascertained from the declarations of the party, or the circumstances of the assault. The rule is, that persons are presumed to intend the natural and probable consequence of their acts. Hence if the weapon be such, and so used, as probably to produce death, the inference is that death was intended. With respect to the intent to commit murder, the test is, that the circumstances must be such, as if death had taken place, would have made it a case of murder in the first or second degree. If it would have been manslaughter, the offence cannot be greater than assault and battery. As to rape and robbery, the intent is much more easily deducible from the circumstances of the assault.

Mayhem. According to Blackstone, mayhem is "the violently depriving another of the use of such of his members as may render him the less able in fighting, either to defend himself or to annoy his adversary." (*a*) But our statute makes it a very different thing; namely: Unlawfully and purposely cutting, slitting, or biting the nose, ear, lip, tongue, or other member, or putting out the eye of another, or cutting off or disabling a member, or throwing any scalding water or acid, or assaulting with a dangerous instrument, with intent to maim, or disfigure—penitentiary from one to twenty years. The word "kill" is here used in connection with murder; but if I am right in the preceding conjecture, it has no meaning. If you can infer an intent to take life in this way, it must be from such circumstances as would have made the killing murder in the first or second degree, had the purpose been effected. As to the intent to maim or disfigure, it cannot admit of doubt.

Shooting or Stabbing. (*b*) Maliciously shooting, stabbing, cutting, or shooting at another, with intent to kill, wound, or maim—penitentiary from one to twenty years. With respect to *shooting*, it is immaterial whether the shot takes effect or not, if the party was shot at. (*c*) But it is essential that the gun or pistol should have been loaded with something calculated to kill, wound, or maim. With respect to *stabbing*, it must be done with some pointed weapon which actually penetrates the body. The intent to wound or maim would seem to be a necessary inference from the single fact of shooting or stabbing. The intent to kill may require the addition of other circumstances; and they must be such, that had death ensued, the killing would have been murder

(*a*) 4 Black. Com. 205.
(*b*) Nichols *v.* The State, 8 Ohio State, 435.
(*c*) Nor need the intent be to hit the person that is wounded. If one maliciously intending to kill B. by mistake shoots at and hits A., supposing him to be B., he is properly convicted on an indictment for maliciously shooting A. with intent to kill. Callahan *v.* The State, 21 Ohio State, 306.

and not manslaughter; for though the word murder is not used, yet as the act must be *malicious*, it amounts to the same thing; since a malicious killing is murder. It will be observed that whenever the intent is to kill, the shooting or stabbing would be included in the offence before described, of an assault with intent to commit murder.

Duelling. Fighting a duel; being second; giving, accepting, or knowingly bearing a challenge; or advising, prompting, or encouraging a duel, though none be fought — penitentiary from one to ten years, and perpetual disqualification for office. (*a*) If death ensue, the offence is murder; and though the statute seems to suppose that it may sometimes be in the second degree, it would seem as if the manifest deliberation of a duel must always make death murder in the first degree. It will be observed that the language is so comprehensive as to include all persons in any way concerned in a duel.

Poisoning with Intent to Kill. Administering poison to another, with intent to kill or injure, or mingling poison with that intent, so that it be taken, or poisoning a well, spring, cistern, &c. — penitentiary from two to fifteen years. Here the intent to kill can hardly admit of doubt, when the facts are proved. (*b*)

Kidnapping. Carrying or decoying out of this State, by force or fraud, without lawful authority, any white or colored person, or attempting so to do, or enticing a female under eighteen from her custodian to a house of prostitution, or harboring her there — penitentiary from one to seven years. (*c*)

Assault and Battery. Unlawfully assaulting or threatening another in a menacing manner, or unlawfully striking or wounding another — fine within two hundred dollars, or imprisonment within six months, or both; besides a civil liability to the party injured. (*d*) As to what constitutes an assault, we have already seen that it must be something more than mere words; there must be some menacing motion, which, if carried into effect, would complete the battery or beating.

Sending Threatening Letters. Knowingly sending or delivering any letter or writing to another, with or without any name, or with a fictitious name, containing wilful and malicious threats of injury, with intent to extort money or other value from such person —

(*a*) {See Constitution, Art. XV. § 5.}

(*b*) Robbins *v.* The State, 8 Ohio State, 131. The amendment of April 8, 1861, makes the crime administering poison to another with intent to destroy life, or mixing poison in water, food, drink, or medicine with that intent.

(*c*) But according to the case of Prigg *v.* Commonwealth of Pennsylvania, 16 Peters, 539, this provision is unconstitutional with respect to fugitive slaves, who may therefore be kidnapped with impunity so far as this provision is concerned. An act to prevent and punish child-stealing was passed March 24, 1860.

(*d*) A person procuring another to commit an assault, though not present, may be punished as a principal. Baker *v.* The State, 12 Ohio State, 214. An indictment for an assault and battery is not sustained by proof that A. struck B. in a prize fight. That is an affray, and differently punished. Champer *v.* The State, 14 Ohio State, 437.

fine within five hundred dollars, or imprisonment within thirty days, or both. Blackmailing — penitentiary one to five years, and fine within one thousand dollars.

Malpractice of Physicians. 1. Any physician or other person, wilfully administering to a pregnant woman any medicine, drug, or other thing, or using any instrument, with intent to procure a miscarriage, unless the same shall be necessary to preserve her life, or be advised by two physicians — imprisonment one to seven years. We have already seen that if a living child be thus destroyed before birth, it is a penitentiary offence. 2. Prescribing, while in a state of intoxication, any poison, drug, or medicine to another, which shall endanger life — fine within one hundred dollars, and imprisonment within twenty days. 3. Prescribing any drug or medicine to another, endangering life, without first declaring its true nature and composition, if inquired — fine within one hundred dollars, and imprisonment within twenty days. This last is aimed against quackery; but it is so framed as to make conviction very difficult.

Libel. (*a*) Writing, printing, or publishing any false or malicious libel of or concerning another, or causing or procuring the same to be done — fine within five hundred dollars, or imprisonment within six months, or both; but publication is necessary. (*b*) We have already considered the constitutional provisions relating to liberty of speech and of the press. The mere uttering of slanderous words, though it may render the party liable to a civil action for damages, does not constitute a libel, and cannot be prosecuted criminally. There must be a writing, printing, or publishing of the slander; and it must be done maliciously, that is, with intent to injure the party libelled: if false, the malicious intent will be inferred, of course; if true, it may or may not be malicious, according to the circumstances. If it concern public men or measures, the constitution makes the truth a justification. As to publication, it is held that the communicating of the libel to a single individual is a publication; and that pictures as well as writings may be libellous, if made public.

§ 195. **Crimes Affecting Private Property.** This division includes a variety of offences having direct reference to the property of individuals or companies; though for convenience I have in-

(*a*) *Indictment.* That heretofore, to wit, on ———, at ———, to wit, at the county aforesaid, one ———, maliciously intending to injure, vilify, and defame the character of one ———, and to bring him into disgrace, contempt, and infamy, did write, print, and publish, and cause to be written, printed, and published in a certain newspaper called the ———, a certain false, scandalous, and malicious libel of and concerning the said ———, which said false, scandalous, and malicious libel is of the purport and effect following, to wit [here set forth the libel with the proper innuendoes]; to the great damage, infamy, and scandal of him the said ———.

(*b*) On the general subject of libel, see 4 Black. Com. 150; 2 Swift's Dig. 340; Holt on Libel; Starkie on Slander; 1 Am. Leading Cases, 103–208; see *post*, § 209. By the new constitution: "In all criminal prosecutions for libel, the truth may be given in evidence to the jury, and if it shall appear to the jury that the matter charged as libellous is true, and was published with good motives, and justifiable ends, the party shall be acquitted."

cluded some injuries to public property. In those which relate to buildings and habitations, the ultimate purpose may be to commit a personal injury; but I have not thought it worth while to divide these into a distinct class.

Larceny and other Stealing. (*a*) The usual definition of larceny is, "the felonious taking and carrying away of the personal goods of another." (*b*) *First*, there must be a *felonious taking*, that is, a taking with intent to steal, which intent must exist at the very moment of the taking. *Secondly*, there must be a *felonious carrying away;* but a mere removal of the articles from their place, for the purpose of carrying them away, is held sufficient. *Thirdly*, the thing stolen must be *personalty* belonging to another; for realty, being immovable, cannot be stolen. (*c*) Our statute enumerates the following offences under this head: —

Grand Larceny. 1. Stealing any money (*d*) or other personal goods or chattels belonging to another, of the value of thirty-five dollars and upwards (*e*) — penitentiary from one to seven years. 2. Horse-stealing is especially provided for, without reference to the value of the animal, and the time of imprisonment is from one to fifteen years. 3. The same punishments are prescribed for

(*a*) *Indictment.* That heretofore, to wit, on ———, at ———, to wit, at the county aforesaid, one ——— did feloniously steal, take, and carry away one gold watch of the value of ——— dollars, of the goods and chattels of one ———, and in his possession then and there being found.

If the indictment be for stealing written documents, they need not be set forth literally, but may be described generally; as, "one promissory note given by ——— to ——— for the payment of ——— dollars, and of the value of ——— dollars," and the *scienter* must be alleged. Gatewood *v.* State, 4 Ohio, 386; Rich *v.* State, 8 Ohio, 111. If the indictment be for horse-stealing, it would seem that no value need be stated, but this is doubtful. The kind of horse must be specifically stated as in the statute; and it has been held that a charge of stealing a "gray horse" cannot be sustained by proof of stealing a "gray gelding." Hooker *v.* State, 4 Ohio, 348. If the indictment be for knowingly receiving or buying stolen goods, the old practice was to set forth the larceny as above, and then say, "that one ——— did then and there receive and buy the said goods and chattels so as aforesaid stolen, to wit, &c., he the said ——— then and there well knowing the same to have been stolen." And a similar practice prevailed, when the indictment was for harboring or concealing the thief. But now the practice is to omit the specification of the larceny, and say, "did buy and receive one [describe the property] of the value of ——— dollars, of the goods and chattels of one ——— then lately before stolen; he the said ——— then and there well knowing the same to have been stolen." And it has been held that the confessions of the thief made in presence of the accused cannot be received as proof of the theft. Morrison *v.* State, 5 Ohio, 438.

(*b*) 2 Swift's Dig. 309; 4 Black. Com. 229.

(*c*) Severing and carrying away trees and vegetables, where if severed the taking would be larceny, is now punished as a crime. Act of March 11, 1857. Personal chattels, though constructively annexed to the freehold, are subjects of larceny. Jackson *v.* The State, 11 Ohio State, 104.

(*d*) It was held under the act of 1831, that bank-bills were not money under this provision. Johnson *v.* The State, 11 Ohio State, 324. On March 21, 1863, the legislature amended this section, defining money to include "all bank bills or notes, United States treasury notes, or other bills, bonds, or notes issued by lawful authority and intended to pass and circulate as money." See Hummel *v.* The State, 17 Ohio State, 628.

(*e*) When several articles are taken at the same time, the transaction being the same, they may be embraced in one count, and the taking constitute one offence, though they belong to different persons. State *v.* Hennessey, 23 Ohio State, 339.

knowingly receiving, buying, or concealing, any of the above stolen articles, or harboring the thief. (*a*) This is in accordance with the common saying, that the partaker is as bad as the thief. But no provision is made for remunerating the owner, and making this a part of the sentence. This, therefore, must be the subject of a separate proceeding. The reason why horse-stealing, or participating therein, is punished more severely than other theft, and without regard to value, perhaps, is, that in a grazing country like ours, horses are more exposed than other property. The statute is very minute in enumerating the various kinds of money securities and of horses, which may be the subject of larceny. I have already doubted the expediency of such minute specifications. In the present case, for example, if there be one written security, or one description of horse not specified, it may be stolen with impunity; and the danger is, that no legislative foresight can enumerate all.

(*a*) Coin is embraced in the term "goods and chattels," in the provision punishing the receiving of stolen "goods and chattels." Hall *v.* The State, 3 Ohio State, 575. Foreign bank-bills, the circulation of which is prohibited in this State, may be the subject of larceny. Starkey *v.* The State, 6 Ohio State, 266. Under § 26 of the Crimes Act, the person may be convicted of receiving stolen goods, though the goods were taken by robbery. Shriedley *v.* The State, 23 Ohio State, 130.

Larceny at common law is the wilful wrongful taking possession of the goods of another with the intent to deprive the owner of his property therein. To constitute larceny, there must be a taking possession of the goods of another; this taking must be wrongful, and must be accompanied at the time with an intent to deprive the owner of his property in them. Taking into the hand an article lying in a drawer, and lifting it merely from the bottom of the drawer, is a complete taking possession. Taking an article from a man's pocket, but not severing it from his person by reason of its being fastened by a guard or chain, is not taking possession. Goods delivered by a master to his servant are still in the possession of the master, only in the custody of the servant. If the servant should afterwards convert such goods to his own use, that would be taking possession from his master. Goods delivered by the owner to a bailee are in the possession of the bailee. If the bailee should subsequently convert them to his own use, there would be no taking possession, and hence no larceny; except that if he should open a package and take separate articles therefrom, that would be a taking, and would be larceny. Goods delivered by a stranger to a servant, to be taken to his master, not yet having been in the possession of the master, are in the possession of the servant; and if he convert them to his own use, such conversion is not a taking, and is not larceny. To meet this defect in the definition of larceny, such breaches of trust were made criminal by statute, and this crime is called embezzlement. If one finds goods lost without any apparent means of ascertaining the owner, such taking is not wrongful, though the finder means to keep them for himself. If one finds goods not really lost, but in such place, or with such marks, that he has reason to believe the owner can be ascertained, his intention at the time determines the question of criminality. If his intention at the time of taking possession is to keep them from the owner, he commits larceny; if his intention at the time is to restore them to the owner, and he subsequently makes up his mind to keep them, he does not commit larceny. It is not necessary that in taking possession the intent should be to convert the goods to his own use. If one wrongfully takes a horse from the possession of the owner merely to destroy it, that is larceny. Bonds, bills, notes, and other *choses in action* are not held goods and chattels in criminal law, hence taking them was not larceny at common law. Various statutes have been passed to make the stealing of such larceny. The criminal code of Ohio of 1878, in place of a multitudinous enumeration, makes the stealing of "a thing of any value" larceny. In larceny, as in burglary, fraud is equivalent to force. Hence, obtaining goods from another by fraudulent pretence, is taking them. If a person intending to appropriate goods fraudulently induces the owner to part with possession merely, he commits larceny; but if he so induces the owner to part with his ownership as well as possession, the act is obtaining goods under false pretences.

Hence, a general and comprehensive description, such as I have chosen, for convenience and brevity, would be preferable in principle.

Petit Larceny. Stealing any of the above-mentioned articles, except horses, when the value is less than thirty-five dollars, or knowingly concealing the same — fine within two hundred dollars, or imprisonment within thirty days, or both.

Knowingly harboring or concealing a thief or robber, one to seven years. Knowingly concealing a horse-thief, one to fifteen years. Buying, receiving, or concealing anything stolen, embezzled, or obtained by false pretences is larceny. Stealing or fraudulently destroying or secreting a will — imprisonment one to ten years. Fraudulently tapping a gas-pipe and stealing the gas — fine within two hundred and fifty dollars, or imprisonment within thirty days, or both. You will observe that the distinction between grand and petit larceny is made to depend upon the value stolen, and thirty-five dollars is made the turning-point. Some have doubted the expediency of this. That there should be a distinction between stealing a large amount and a small one, though there may be the same inward depravity in both cases, is undoubtedly expedient; for the severity of punishment should be proportioned to the necessity of prevention, which is itself proportioned to the temptation to steal; and the temptation increases with the value of the article. But admitting this, ought not the punishment to vary regularly with the amount, instead of making a single dividing line? Undoubtedly a law might be framed, apportioning the punishment uniformly according to the value, which the present law does not. A cent above the dividing line sends the convict to the penitentiary, and the largest amount does no more. A cent below saves him from the penitentiary, but punishes him no more than the smallest value. But this is matter of speculation. There is no doubt, however, that our law of larceny will admit of improvement in the several points before indicated; and would it not be well so to generalize the definition of the subject-matter, as to include in one comprehensive expression every species of movable value which can be feloniously taken? This question is at least worthy of consideration.

Embezzlement. (*a*) An officer, attorney at law, agent, clerk, guardian, executor, administrator, trustee, assignee in insolvency, servant, or employee of any person, except apprentices and persons under eighteen, who embezzles, or converts to his own use, or fraudulently makes away with, or secretes; or any public officer, or the agent, clerk, servant, or employee of such officer, or of a board of such officers — same punishment as for larceny of the thing embezzled. In fact, the only difference between larceny and embezzlement, as thus defined, is, that there is no felonious taking. Why apprentices and persons under eighteen should be

(*a*) The act of April 12, 1858, defines and punishes an embezzlement of public money. It applies to township treasurers. State *v.* Morton, 21 Ohio State, 667.

exempted, if they be old enough to distinguish between right and wrong, is not very apparent.

Robbery. (*a*) Taking forcibly from the person of another, by violence or putting in fear, any money or personal property of any value whatever, with intent to rob or steal — penitentiary from three to fifteen years. This, it will be seen, is only a more aggravated species of larceny. In addition to the felonious taking of property, there is violence, or putting in fear. On account of this aggravation, the amount taken is held immaterial, and the smallest value thus taken completes the offence. According to the definition, the taking must be from the person; but it is held sufficient if the taking be in the presence of the owner. The definition here includes money and *personal property.* That of larceny includes money and *personal goods and chattels.* Hence it was there necessary to make a special provision for money securities, which is not necessary here, because they are personal property, though not strictly goods or chattels. This shows the policy of using general and comprehensive terms.

Forgery and Counterfeiting. (*b*) By the English definition for-

(*a*) *Indictment.* That heretofore, to wit, on ———, at ———, to wit, at the county aforesaid, one ——— with force and arms did feloniously make an assault upon one ———, and did then and there put the said ——— in fear and danger of his life; and did then and there feloniously, by violence and putting in fear, steal, rob, take, and carry away from the person, and against the will of the said ———, one gold watch of the value of one hundred dollars, of the goods and chattels of the said ———.

As our statute makes the value immaterial, in case of robbery, it may be doubted whether value need be alleged; but as the thing taken must be of some value, it would not be safe to omit the allegation.

(*b*) *Indictment.* That heretofore, to wit, on ———, at ———, to wit, at the county aforesaid, one ——— did falsely make, alter, forge, and counterfeit a certain promissory note for the payment of money, purporting to be made and signed by one ———, for the sum of ——— dollars, which said false, forged, and counterfeit promissory note is of the purport and effect following, to wit [here set forth a true copy of the note {but see R. S. §§ 7218–19}]; with intent then and there to injure and defraud the said ———.

If the indictment be for uttering, &c., say, "did utter, &c., as true and genuine, a certain, &c., with intent, &c., he the said ——— then and there well knowing the said, &c., to be false, forged, and counterfeit." The person whose name is forged is a competent witness to prove the forgery, without calling the subscribing witness. Simmons *v.* State, 7 Ohio, 1 pt. 116. The degree of resemblance between the forged and genuine instruments is not material, if it be such as might deceive persons of ordinary observation. Hess *v.* State, 5 Ohio, 1. An indictment for forgery must specifically set forth the forged instrument, and the proof must correspond to the description. McMillen *v.* State, 5 Ohio, 268; Pickens *v.* State, 6 id. 274. But the indorsement on a note need not be set forth. Hess *v.* State, 5 Ohio, 1. An indictment for selling counterfeit notes need not set forth the consideration, nor that the sale was to the injury of any one. Hess *v.* State, 5 Ohio, 1. If an unincorporated association in actual existence issue bills, the passing of them is not an offence within the provisions now under consideration. Sutton *v.* State, 9 Ohio, 133. The provisions respecting coins include foreign as well as domestic coins, if they be current in the State; but the indictment for putting off counterfeit coins need not allege the fact of being current; though it is otherwise for counterfeiting. Sutton *v.* State, 9 Ohio, 133; Smith *v.* State, 8 id. 294; Fight *v.* State, 7 id. 1 pt. 180. Where the indictment states that the prisoner secretly kept instruments of counterfeiting, this is a sufficient *scienter.* Sutton *v.* State, 9 Ohio, 133. On the general subject, see 4 Black. Com. 83, 247; 2 Swift's Dig. 305. The instrument must be such that it does or may prejudice another's rights. Barnum *v.* The State, 15 Ohio, 717. The indorsement of a promissory note is the subject of forgery. Poage *v.* The State, 3 Ohio State, gery consists "in fraudulently making or altering any writing, to the prejudice of another's right." This is clear and comprehensive. Counterfeiting, in England, is confined to the current coin of the realm, and is treated as a species of treason. But our statutory provisions are very minute in specifying the subjects and the manner both of forgery and counterfeiting. In describing them, however, I shall generalize as much as possible. 1. Falsely making, altering, forging, counterfeiting, printing, or photographing any writing of whatever kind, upon which any claim or evidence of claim to any species of property, money, or value is founded; or knowingly uttering or publishing the same, as true and genuine; or causing the same to be done; with intent in either case to injure or defraud another — penitentiary from one to twenty years. And if it be of any currency or security issued under an act of Congress, fine within five thousand dollars, and imprisonment within fifteen years. The statute enumerates a long list of writings which may be thus forged or counterfeited, but the above description probably includes them all. You will observe that four words are employed to designate the manner of committing the offence; but the first two probably include all; for it is difficult to conceive of any other species of forgery or counterfeiting, than that of *falsely making* the instrument in question, or *falsely altering* it, when already made; but the mere making or altering the writing does not complete the offence. It must be done *with intent to defraud;* otherwise, taking the strict letter, a merely sportive use of the pen might be converted into a crime. 2. Counterfeiting any of the coins of gold, silver, or copper, current in the State; or knowingly passing or putting them off; or knowingly making or keeping any instrument for counterfeiting them — penitentiary from one to fifteen years. 3. Knowingly selling, exchanging, or passing any counterfeited bank-note or bill, or having the same in possession with that intent, whether such note have signatures or not, or have fictitious signatures; or knowingly making, altering, or passing any note or bill purporting to be of a bank which never existed — penitentiary from one to fifteen years. 4. Gilding any silver coin or other metal, so as to give it the appearance of a gold coin, with intent to defraud; or knowingly passing such gilded coin — penitentiary from one to five years. 5. Knowingly engraving any plate or other instrument for counterfeiting or altering bank-notes or bills; or causing the same to be done; or having the same in possession for that purpose — penitentiary from three to fifteen years. 6. Knowingly attempting to pass any counterfeit coin, bank-note, or bill — penitentiary from one to five years. It would thus appear that the purity of the currency is well protected; and

229. As to what constitutes "an order for the payment of money" under the statute, see Evans *v.* The State, 8 Ohio State, 196; Bynam *v.* The State, 17 Ohio State, 142. It is forgery to counterfeit foreign bank-bills under ten dollars, the circulation of which is prohibited in this State. Thompson *v.* The State, 9 Ohio State, 354.

yet so great is the temptation to counterfeit money, and especially bank-notes, that scarcely any crime is more prevalent. Such are the provisions against forgery and counterfeiting. The two terms are very nearly, if not altogether, synonymous; and here, again, the question may be asked, why so many distinct provisions are necessary to describe these offences. Might not a single comprehensive expression be found, which would include every description of forgery and counterfeiting, both in reference to the agent, the instrument, the manner, and the matter? This would seem to be both possible and expedient.

Burglary and other Housebreaking. (*a*) The substance of the English definition of burglary is "breaking and entering into a mansion-house by night, with intent to commit a felony." (*b*) 1. There must be a breaking as well as entering, though they need not be at the same time; but the raising of a window or the opening of a door, without breaking the fastenings, will be sufficient. And it will be an entering, if any part of the body be within, or even an instrument or a weapon held in the hand. 2. It must be a house where some person dwells. 3. It must be in the night; and this means not the whole interval between sunset and sunrise, but the interval between the termination of evening twilight and the commencement of morning twilight, when a man's features cannot be clearly seen. But whether it be moonlight or not, makes no difference. 4. The intent must be to commit a felony in the house; though nothing need be done towards effecting such intent. By our statute there are five offences of this kind, which differ from the foregoing, and from each other, in several respects. 1. Forcibly breaking or entering, or attempting it, any building or railroad-car at night, with intent to commit a felony or to steal, — one to ten years; possession of burglar's tools, with intent to use them burglariously — one to five years. 2. The same in the daytime with intent to steal — fine within three hundred dollars, and imprisonment within sixty days. This is the substance of the definition, though much abridged. The difference between this and the English definition is, that here the offence is not confined to dwelling-houses, but may be committed in almost any species of building, the enumeration being very full. (*c*) 3. Maliciously

(*a*) *Indictment.* That heretofore, to wit, on ———, at ———, to wit, at the county aforesaid, one ———, did in the night season, to wit, about the hour of ——— in the night of said day, wilfully, maliciously, and forcibly break and enter into the dwelling house of one ———, there situate, with intent then and there feloniously and burglariously to steal, take, and carry away the goods and chattels of the said ———, in the said dwelling-house then and there being.

If the intent were to commit any other offence than stealing, describe it in the language of the statute. The burglary is complete without carrying the intent into effect. But if the intended offence was actually consummated, add another count for the offence itself.

(*b*) See 4 Black. Com. 223–30; 2 Swift's Dig. 300; Ducher *v.* The State, 18 Ohio, 308.

(*c*) But it is still not exhaustive. The building must be properly described. It is not sufficient to describe it as a "still-house," though built and used originally for that purpose, and generally known by that name, if the distillery has been abandoned, and entering, by day or night, any of the aforementioned buildings, and attempting to commit a felony — penitentiary from one to ten years. The points of difference between this and the preceding offence are, that this may be committed indifferently by day or night; there is no forcible breaking, but only a malicious entry; and there must be an actual attempt, and not a mere intent, to commit the crimes specified, which do not, like the other, include all penitentiary offences. I have said any of the aforementioned buildings; but in fact, there are one or two exceptions, which, there being no reason for them, I conclude are accidental. 4. Unlawfully breaking and entering by night, into any mansion-house, shop, store, ship, boat, or other water-craft, in which any person shall reside or dwell, and committing or attempting any personal violence or abuse, or being so armed with a dangerous weapon as to indicate a violent intention — fine within three hundred dollars, and imprisonment within thirty days. This offence differs from any of the preceding, *first*, with respect to the buildings, which must be those where persons reside; and *secondly*, with respect to the intent or attempt, which is personal violence only. (*a*) Hence the difference in the punishment; and though the kind or degree of violence is left to inference, it must, doubtless, be less aggravated than the preceding. 5. Committing the same offence last mentioned, in the daytime — fine within one hundred dollars, and imprisonment within twenty days. But here nothing is said about being armed with a dangerous weapon; the reason of the omission is not apparent. In general, it will be observed that these five offences of house-breaking all differ from a mere trespass upon the premises of another, which is the subject of civil redress only, in the intent with which the offence is committed; which is, in each of the cases, to do some criminal act. Whereas, in a mere trespass, there is no criminal intent. Unlawfully entering premises to disturb or take any receptacle for bees or honey, or to injure or take poultry, or take grain — fine within five hundred dollars, or imprisonment within sixty days, or both.

Arson and other Burning. (*b*) The substance of the English definition of arson is, "the malicious and wilful burning of a dwelling-house, or out-house belonging thereto; and it is punished

the structure is used for a mill for chopping corn. Thalls *v.* The State, 21 Ohio State, 233.

(*a*) It has been held necessary to allege in the indictment for this offence that the house broken is the residence or dwelling-place of some one; and that where one enters such a house by night with the intention of committing adultery with the owner's wife, by her consent, it is an offence within this provision. Forsythe *v.* State, 6 Ohio, 19.

(*b*) *Indictment.* That heretofore, to wit, on ——, at ——, to wit, at the county aforesaid, one ——, with force and arms, did wilfully and maliciously set fire to, burn, and consume the dwelling-house of one —— there situate.

If the building be not one of the specified ones, the value must be alleged. If the building were not burned, say, "did wilfully, &c., set fire to, with intent to burn." On the general subject of arson, see 4 Black. Com. 220-3; 2 Swift's Dig. 304. It is an indictable act for the lessee of a warehouse in possession to procure another to burn such warehouse. It is "not his own." Allen *v.* The State, 10 Ohio State, 287.

with death. But here, as in the case of burglary, we not only do not confine the offence to dwelling-houses, but we make various other alterations in the subject and manner of the crime. 1. Wilfully and maliciously burning or attempting to burn any dwelling-house, kitchen, smoke-house, shop, barn, stable, store-house, warehouse, malt-house, stilling-house, mill, or pottery, not his own, or any other building not his own, of the value of fifty dollars, or containing property of that value; or any ship, boat, water-craft, or bridge of that value; or any public building whatever — penitentiary within twenty years, and if of a less value, fine within two hundred dollars, or imprisonment within thirty days, or both. Thus it will be seen that we have extended the crime of arson, with regard to the buildings which may be the subject of it, in the same manner as burglary. Considering the nature of the offence, the punishment is remarkably lenient. There is no offence short of murder which indicates greater depravity of heart than this. It has not even the poor excuse of a desire of gain. The mischief is altogether gratuitous and malicious, and in a city may be immense. Therefore, even when life is not endangered, the punishment ought to be exemplary. 2. Firing one's own property of the value of fifty dollars in order to prejudice the insurer — imprisonment within twenty years. 3. Wilfully and maliciously setting fire to, burning, or causing to be burned, any hay, fodder, or grain, in stacks, or any corn-crib, fence, boards, timber, rails, or tan-bark, etc., belonging to another, if the value of the property is over thirty-five dollars, — imprisonment from one to three years, and if of a less value, fine from five dollars to one hundred dollars, or imprisonment within thirty days, or both. The enumeration is much more particular than I have stated; but though designed to include every thing, it omits wood, and many other things of a similar character, which equally require this kind of protection. 4. Wilfully and maliciously setting fire to any woods, prairies, or other grounds belonging to another; or causing the same to be done; or intentionally suffering fire to pass from one's own ground to another's — fine within one hundred dollars, or imprisonment within twenty days, or both. Such are the provisions against the malicious destruction of life or property by burning. But why might there not be one general provision, punishing the malicious burning of every kind of property whatever, instead of these numerous and yet very imperfect specifications? I can see no objection. The highest punishment might be for the burning of buildings where life is endangered; and the rest might depend upon the amount of property endangered or destroyed. As the provisions stand, there is great want of discrimination in this respect.

Fraudulent Conveyance and Swindling. To guard the business transactions of men against fraud, deception, and imposition, in addition to the civil liability which they involve, the following penalties are provided: 1. Knowingly selling or conveying any tract of land, without having a title thereto, either in law or equity, by descent, devise, or other written evidence, with intent to defraud the purchaser — penitentiary from one to seven years. This has been mentioned before (p. 418). 2. Obtaining from another, by any false pretence, any money or other value, with intent to cheat and defraud him, or procuring his signature, or disposing of, or offering to dispose of, securities, knowing the signatures have been so obtained, of the value of thirty-five dollars or more — imprisonment from one to three years; and if of less value — imprisonment from ten to sixty days, or fine ten to one hundred dollars, or both. 3. Fraudulently making and transferring any instrument of writing, with intent to defraud creditors — fine from twenty to five hundred dollars, or imprisonment within ten days, or both. (*a*) These are the only provisions we have against what is commonly called *swindling*. It will be at once perceived that they are very far from including all the cases in which knaves may cheat honest men. (*b*)

Malicious Destruction of Property. (*c*) We have already considered one way of maliciously destroying property; namely, by burning. The other provisions on the subject are as follows: 1. Knowingly or maliciously destroying any landmark or boundary properly established — fine within five hundred dollars, or imprisonment within thirty days, or both. 2. Knowingly and maliciously destroying or defacing any monument or tombstone or fence, etc., around a cemetery, or tree or plant therein — fine within five hundred dollars, or imprisonment within thirty days, or both. 3. Knowingly and maliciously altering or defacing any ear-mark or brand upon any horse, sheep, swine, cattle, etc., of another — fine within fifty dollars, or imprisonment within twenty days, or both. 4. Knowingly and maliciously destroying any horse, sheep, swine, or cattle of another, if the value is thirty-five dollars or more — imprisonment from one to five years; and if the value is below that amount — fine from twenty to two hundred dollars, or imprisonment within three months, or both; administering poison to any such animal — fine from fifty to two hundred dollars, or imprisonment within thirty days, or both. 5. Knowingly and maliciously destroying or injuring any tree, bush, vine, etc., or other product, or thing attached to land, not his own, if the value is thirty-five dollars, or more — imprisonment from one to three

(*a*) State *v.* Green, 7 Wis. 676; Commonwealth *v.* Drew, 19 Pick. 179. The false pretence must relate to a past event or an existing fact, and not be merely an assurance as to the future. Dillingham *v.* The State, 5 Ohio State, 280. Counterfeiting trademarks. Act of March 29, 1859. Executing and delivering false and fictitious bills of lading. Act of March 22, 1860. One who obtains money upon a mortgage of personalty which he falsely represents as his, is guilty of obtaining money under false pretences. Commonwealth *v.* Lincoln, 11 Allen, 233. So is one who obtains money by falsely stating that in a former transaction proper change was not given to him. Commonwealth *v.* Norton, 11 Allen, 266.

(*b*) {The provisions against fraud and deception, adulterations, &c., are now very numerous. See §§ 7067 to 7090.}

(*c*) 4 Black. Com. ch. 17. {The enumeration of property under this head is now greatly changed and enlarged. See R. S. §§ 6861–6885.}

years, and if value is less, fine five to one hundred and fifty dollars, or imprisonment from one to thirty days. (*a*) 6. Knowingly and maliciously destroying or defacing any mile-stone or guide-board, on any public road—fine within fifty dollars, or imprisonment within ten days, or both. 7. Intentionally obliterating or destroying any public notification set up by authority of law, or defacing any sign affixed to any bridge—fine within twenty dollars, or imprisonment within twenty-four hours, or both. 8. For riding or driving over a public bridge faster than a walk, or refusing to pay toll, or driving more than twenty head of cattle over—a fine of one to ten dollars. (*b*) The above specifications furnish a remarkable instance of the particularity which I have so often referred to in the definition of offences. There certainly could be no difficulty in providing a general penalty for the malicious destruction of every kind of property without specification, but varying according to the value destroyed.

We have thus reviewed, as briefly as possible, the principal offences made punishable in this State, and the measure of punishment assigned to each. This examination has shown, that although our criminal code is yet crude and imperfect, its spirit is deserving of all commendation. The Dracos among mankind have had no part in it. Humanity has presided over every enactment. How remarkable the contrast between this country and England, where, in the time of Blackstone, there were no less than one hundred and sixty capital offences. (*c*) Our whole number of penal enactments scarcely amounts to this. We have but one capital offence; but two penitentiary offences for life; and the rest never exceed twenty years, and do not average more than ten. Then as to the minor punishments, imprisonment in jail is very rarely over thirty days, and does not average ten; and fines rarely exceed five hundred dollars, and do not average one hundred. On the score of humanity, then, we may reasonably congratulate ourselves. Nor has experience thus far shown that we have erred in this benevolent way. Our criminal records will probably show as few prosecutions and as few depredations, in proportion to our population, as those of any other state or nation; although our local exposure to travelling depredators is very great. It will be observed that there is no provision against *compounding* or compromising a crime, between the party injuring and the party injured, as there is in England. (*d*) This will probably be considered as a defect. Again, there is no provision against *misprisions*, (*e*) or the concealment of crimes having knowledge of their commission, as there is under the acts of Congress. Whether this be a defect, may be more

(*a*) {Compare R. S. §§ 6864 and 6880. They cover the same ground, except that the latter is independent of value.}

(*b*) {These are the principal offences against property. There are numerous other minor provisions also.}

(*c*) See 4 Black. Com. 18.

(*d*) {There is now such a provision. R. S. § 6901.}

(*e*) {For misprision of treason. R. S. § 6807.}

questionable. Perhaps the duty of information may be safely left to the public spirit and private interest of individuals, without punishment, as we have seen it is without reward. On the whole, then, with little to censure, we have a great deal to admire, in our criminal law. The defects exist only in the details, and can be easily remedied; while the merits are fundamental, and characterize the entire system. You can hardly appreciate them as they deserve, unless by a comparison with some other system; and if you take that of England, it will be a contrast rather than a comparison.

LECTURE XXXVI.

CRIMES UNDER THE LAW OF THE UNITED STATES. (a)

§ 196. **Crimes Relating to the Currency.** The federal government, being framed and designed for national purposes only, as distinguished from local or municipal, we have seen that its power to define and punish crimes is limited, by this consideration, to a comparatively small number of cases, rendered absolutely necessary for its well-being; while the general power of punishment is reserved to each State, as belonging to its internal police. We have already enumerated the cases to which the federal power of punishment extends, whether by express provision or incidentally; but it will be proper here briefly to recapitulate them. Congress, then, has the *express power* of punishment in five classes of cases; namely: 1. Offences relating to the public securities and currency. 2. Offences committed on the high seas. 3. Offences against the law of nations. 4. Treason. 5. Offences committed in places of exclusive legislation. And Congress has exercised the *incidental power* of punishment in six classes of cases, making in all eleven; namely: 6. Offences against the revenue laws. 7. Offences against commerce. 8. Offences against the post-office regulations. 9. Offences against foreign nations. 10. Offences against the federal government below treason. 11. Offences committed by federal officers. Instead, therefore, of classifying these offences according to the subject-matter, as in the preceding lecture, I shall adopt the arrangement just indicated; except that the fourth and tenth classes will be united, in order to present at one view all the offences against the federal government. The description will contain all offences of any considerable importance, though some trivial ones may be omitted; at the same time, in aiming at brevity, I shall generalize, where the acts of Congress particularize.

(a) See a good analysis of the criminal law of the United States in the preface to 2 Wheeler's Crim. Cases; Wharton's Criminal Law, 124-47.

By the federal constitution, Congress has power "to provide for the punishment of counterfeiting the securities and current coin of the United States." (*a*) Under this provision, the following offences are made punishable; the description being abbreviated as much as possible. 1. Falsely making, altering, forging, or counterfeiting with intent to defraud, any treasury note, or any writing, to obtain money from the United States, or their officers; or any certificate of public debt, or any letters-patent, or any writing to transfer public stock, or to receive any dividend thereon, or any pension from the United States, or any abstract or official copy of the registry, license, or enrolment of any vessel; or any certificate of ownership, passport, sea-letter, or clearance granted to any vessel; or any permit, debenture, or other document, granted by the officers of the customs; or procuring the same to be done; or assisting therein; or knowingly using any such writing or document; or attempting so to do — fine within five thousand dollars, and imprisonment within ten years, varying according to the nature of the instrument. The act of 1790 punished some of these forgeries with death, but this is virtually repealed by milder provisions since enacted. 2. Falsely making, forging, altering, or counterfeiting any coins resembling the gold or silver coins of the United States, or foreign coins current therein; or procuring the same to be done, or assisting therein; or knowingly using or passing such coins or attempting so to do; or bringing such coins into the country for the purpose of using or passing them — fine within five thousand dollars, and imprisonment within ten years. For similar offences upon the copper coin — fine within one thousand dollars, and imprisonment within three years; and there is a penalty of ten dollars for using any copper coins except cents and half-cents. 3. Any person employed at the mint debasing or making too light any of the coins there struck, with intent to defraud; or embezzling any of the metals left there to be coined, — fine within ten thousand dollars, and imprisonment within ten years. 4. Impairing, clipping; diminishing, or falsifying, any of the gold or silver coins current in the country with intent to defraud — fine within two thousand dollars, and imprisonment within two years. It only remains to be observed, that, as to most of the offences now described, the jurisdiction of the State courts is expressly reserved; and we have already seen that State legislation has undertaken to provide for them. As to the coins, however, doubt exists on two points; namely, *first*, whether the State legislatures have any authority to legislate on the subject; and *secondly*, whether in the absence of State legislation, the State courts can entertain jurisdiction of the offences provided for by Congress with an express reservation of State jurisdiction. I merely state these questions, without intending to discuss them; having already considered the subject of jurisdiction as fully as my limits will permit.

(*a*) 2 Wheeler's Crim. Cases, Pref. 57.

§ 197. **Crimes on the High Seas.** (*a*) Congress has express power "to define and punish piracies and felonies committed on the high seas;" because *the high seas* are not within the jurisdiction of any particular State. They are the common highway of all nations, and crimes there committed are the proper subjects of national cognizance. The high seas include not only the ocean proper, but also every river, haven, harbor, basin, bay, or roadstead, without the jurisdiction of particular States, or where the tide ebbs and flows. The offences provided for are the following, very much abridged: 1. *Piracy.* This is an offence against the law of nations, a pirate being considered as the enemy of all mankind; and by the law of nations piracy is robbery on the high seas, and is punishable with death. By the acts of Congress, piracy is also punishable with death, and the following offences, committed on the high seas, are declared to be piracy; namely: *First*, any person committing robbery or murder, or any other capital offence by the laws of the United States. *Secondly*, any master or mariner piratically running away with any vessel, or with goods or merchandise of the value of fifty dollars; or voluntarily giving up a vessel to pirates. *Thirdly*, any seaman laying violent hands upon his commander, to prevent his fighting in defence of his vessel or goods, or making a revolt in the vessel. But in these cases, if the vessel be foreign, and the offence be not committed by or upon any American citizen, our courts will not entertain jurisdiction. *Fourthly*, any American citizen committing any piracy aforesaid, or any act of hostility against the United States or citizens thereof, under color of any foreign commission or authority. *Fifthly*, any person, on land or water, knowingly procuring, assisting, or commanding a piracy to be committed, and thus becoming an accessory before the fact. *Sixthly*, any person committing piracy, as defined by the law of nations. But this being merely robbery, is provided for before. *Seventhly*, any person committing the crime of robbery upon any vessel, cargo, or crew. But this is also provided for before. *Eighthly*, any person belonging to any piratical vessel, or engaged in any piratical enterprise, landing from such vessel and committing robbery on shore. But this does not affect the local jurisdiction. *Ninthly*, (*b*) any American citizen belonging to a foreign vessel, or any person belonging to an American vessel, landing upon a foreign shore, and by force or otherwise, bringing away any negro or mulatto, not a slave by the laws of the United States, or receiving him on board; or forcibly detaining him on board; or assisting therein; or attempting to sell him; or transferring

(*a*) See acts of 1790, 1804, 1819, 1820, 1825; 4 Black. Com. 71; U. S. *v.* Ross, 1 Gallison, 624; U. S. *v.* Smith, 1 Mason, 147; U. S. *v.* Bevans, 3 Wheaton, 336; U. S. *v.* Palmer, 3 id. 610; U. S. *v.* Wiltberger, 5 id. 76; U. S. *v.* Smith, 5 id. 153; U. S. *v.* Pirates, 5 id. 184; U. S. *v.* Holmes, 5 id. 412; 2 Wheeler's Crim. Cases, Pref. 27; People *v.* Tyler, 7 Mich. 61.

(*b*) 2 Wheeler's Crim. Cases, Pref. 45.

him to another vessel; or landing him on shore, with intent to make him a slave. This language is designed to be sufficiently comprehensive to include any agency or concern whatever in the slave-trade. 2. *Being accessory to piracy after the fact*, by knowingly harboring or concealing a pirate; or receiving or taking charge of any vessel or cargo taken by a pirate — fine within five hundred dollars, and imprisonment within three years. 3. *Manslaughter*. But this, not being defined by Congress, the common-law definition is adopted, which has before been given, — fine within one thousand dollars, and imprisonment within three years. 4. Endeavoring to induce any officer or mariner of a vessel to turn pirate; or yield up the vessel to pirates; or run away with the vessel or cargo — same punishment as above. 5. Knowingly confederating with pirates; or trading with them; or furnishing them supplies — same punishment as above. 6. Confining the master of a vessel, or endeavoring to make a revolt therein — same punishment as above. 7. *Murder or rape;* or inflicting a mortal blow or wound, or poisoning so that death afterwards ensues on shore; or aiding or advising therein — death. Here, again, the common-law definition of murder is adopted: which is the unlawful killing of another with malice aforethought, either express or implied; and there are no degrees. So of rape, which is the having carnal knowledge of a woman forcibly and against her will; and there are no distinctions as under the State law. 8. Attacking any vessel with intent to plunder, rob, or despoil the same — fine within five thousand dollars and imprisonment within ten years. 9. Breaking or entering any vessel, boat, or raft, with intent to kill, rob, or steal, or to commit a rape or other felony — fine within one thousand dollars, and imprisonment within five years. 10. Maliciously cutting or destroying any cordage, cable, buoy, buoy-rope, headfast, or other fastening of any vessel, boat, or raft — same punishment as above. 11. Plundering from any vessel, boat, or raft which has been wrecked, or is in distress — fine within five thousand dollars, and imprisonment within ten years. 12. Wilfully obstructing the escape of any person from any vessel, boat, or raft which has been wrecked, or is in distress — same punishment as above. 13. Wilfully decoying a vessel, boat, or raft into danger, by showing false lights, or extinguishing true lights — same punishment as above. 14. Any commander of an American vessel putting any officer or mariner thereof belonging to this country on shore in a foreign country, and leaving him there; or refusing to bring him home, he being able and willing to return — fine within five hundred dollars, and imprisonment within six months. 15. Assaulting another on board an American vessel, with a dangerous weapon; or with intent to kill, rob, or steal, or to commit a rape, mayhem, or other felony — fine within three thousand dollars, and imprisonment within three years. 16. Committing mayhem on board an American ship, by cutting, disabling, putting out, or destroying the eye, nose, lip, tongue, ear, or other limb or member, with intent to maim or disfigure — fine within one thousand dollars, and imprisonment within seven years. 17. Committing larceny to any amount on board an American ship, or aiding therein — fine of fourfold the value stolen, and stripes not exceeding thirty-nine. Thus there is no distinction between grand and petit larceny, as under the State law; but the criterion of the offence is the same as there; namely, the felonious taking and carrying away. 18. Being accessory to larceny after the fact, by receiving or concealing the goods or thief — same punishment as above; but by a subsequent act — fine within one thousand dollars, and imprisonment within three years. 19. Being guilty of misprision; that is, having knowledge of the commission of a felony, and concealing the same, or not disclosing it to the civil or military authorities of the United States — fine within five hundred dollars, and imprisonment within three years. We have seen that there is no such provision under the State law. 20. Wilfully casting away, burning or otherwise destroying any public or private American vessel, or procuring the same to be done, or aiding therein — death. 21. Conspiring to destroy any vessel as aforesaid, or to procure the same to be done; or fitting out any vessel with intent that the same may be thus destroyed — fine within ten thousand dollars, and imprisonment within ten years. 22. Any American citizen, without our jurisdiction, being concerned in fitting out or arming any vessel to cruise against our citizens — fine within ten thousand dollars, and imprisonment within ten years. Such are the offences committed upon, or having reference to, the high seas, for which Congress has made specific provision. To avoid nice questions of jurisdiction, it is further declared that if any of the foregoing offences be committed on board of an American vessel lying at a foreign port, they shall be punished in the same manner as if such vessel had been at sea. The only ground for fear is, that the above enumeration is not sufficiently extensive. Are there not offences deserving of punishment which cannot be punished under these provisions? To provide for such cases, if there be any, there might be a general provision, punishing every other act committed on the high seas, which would be punishable if committed on land, in those places which are within the exclusive jurisdiction of the United States. It is to be regretted that the constitution did not employ a word more definite than *felony;* or that Congress, in repeating it, did not give it a definition. As the provision now stands, it seems to imply every offence for which Congress sees fit to provide. There is not the same objection to the use of the terms murder, manslaughter, rape, robbery, and larceny, without defining them; because they are sufficiently defined by recourse to the common law. You will observe that murder and manslaughter in these provisions, taken together, include the same offences as murder and manslaughter under the State law. But the addition of murder in the second degree, by the State law, makes the transition from murder to manslaughter less abrupt than it is here; and is therefore an improvement.

§ 198. **Crimes against the Law of Nations.** (*a*) What constitutes the law of nations has already been briefly explained; and the reason why the power to punish infractions of this law has been expressly conferred on Congress has also been considered. Blackstone has described these offences with great clearness and brevity, under three heads. 1. Violation of safe-conducts. 2. Infringement of the rights of ambassadors. (*b*) 3. Piracy. Congress has adopted this division, except that piracy is provided for under the preceding head. 1. Violating any safe-conduct, or passport duly issued under the authority of the United States — fine at the discretion of the court, and imprisonment within three years. 2. Doing any species of violence to any foreign ambassador, or other public minister — same punishment. Nor is this all; for if any person sue out or prosecute any writ or process, from any federal or State court, against any foreign ambassador or other minister, or against his domestic or servant, not only is such process absolutely void, but the person ordering it, and his attorney, and the officer executing it, are each liable to the punishment before indicated. (*c*) This provision, however, does not protect such domestic or servant, as to debts contracted before entering into such service; nor in any case, unless his name is registered with the secretary of state, and by him transmitted to the marshal of the district. Congress has made provision for punishing several other offences against foreign nations, in violation of our peace or neutrality; but these, not being defined by the law of nations, are arranged under another head. The importance of the foregoing provisions is at once perceived. Safe-conducts and passports are granted, as we have before seen, for the protection of aliens within our jurisdiction, and the national honor is pledged for their being respected; while the complete immunity of foreign ministers and their families is a fundamental condition of diplomatic intercourse. If they misbehave themselves, their recall may be demanded; but while they remain here, their persons must be inviolate.

§ 199. **Treason, and other Crimes against the General Welfare.** Under this head, besides treason, which is expressly provided for, I shall include a variety of offences injurious to the general good, which Congress has provided for, in virtue of its incidental power, and which do not properly fall within either of the other provisions.

1. *Treason.* (*d*) This offence stands highest on the list of

(*a*) See 4 Black. Com. ch. 5.

(*b*) 2 Wheeler's Crim. Cases, Pref. 56.

(*c*) An ambassador from one sovereign State to another, while travelling through the territories of a State to which he is not accredited, in the execution of the duties of his mission, is privileged from arrest on civil process. Holbrook *v.* Henderson, 4 Sandf. 619.

(*d*) See act of 1790; 3 Story, Com. 169; 4 Black. Com. ch. 6; Swift's Dig. 254;

crimes, because it strikes directly at the welfare of society. Being a violation of that allegiance which every citizen owes to his government, it can only be committed by a citizen. Under arbitrary governments it has always been made a ready pretext for cutting off obnoxious individuals. Even in England, some of the best and purest blood has been shed in its name. By reference to Blackstone, it will be seen that a variety of acts, and even of imaginations, are there declared to be treason; and the punishment is the most horrible that language can express. But the framers of our constitution, as we have seen, took special care to guard our citizens against the unwarrantable exercise of so tremendous a power, by declaring what should constitute treason, by what testimony it should be proved, and what should be the extent of its punishment. "Treason against the United States shall consist only in levying war against them, or in adhering to their enemies, giving them aid and comfort." Here, then, we have two acts, and only two, which can amount to treason. This language is copied literally from one of the English statutes, and the English decisions may therefore be consulted for its interpretation; with regard to the meaning of the phrase, "*levying war*," we have interpretations of our own. War can only be levied by employing actual force. Troops must be openly raised and embodied. A secret meeting of conspirators, though with a treasonable intent, would not amount to a levying of war; nor would the mere enlistment of men to serve against government. There must be an actual and visible demonstration of war, by gathering together in hostile array. With regard to the other branch of the definition, we have happily had no occasion to give it a construction; but its meaning obviously is, taking part with our enemies in time of war; and rendering them actual assistance against our own government; either by joining their ranks and fighting for them, or by furnishing them with information or materials, provisions, or ammunition. "No person shall be convicted of treason, unless on the testimony of two witnesses to the same overt act, or on confession in open court." This declaration excludes circumstantial evidence, and the evidence of private confessions, except by way of corroboration, after two witnesses have sworn to the same overt act. In all other cases, a single witness, uncontradicted, may procure a conviction; but in treason, there must not only be two witnesses, but they must testify to the same act, and that must be an overt act. The importance of this provision can be fully appreciated by those only who have read the English trials for treason, and seen upon what slender and pitiful testimony convictions have there been procured. "Congress shall have power to declare the punishment of treason; but no attainder of treason shall work cor-

2 Wheeler's Crim. Cases, Pref. 23; Burr's Trial, reported in two volumes; U. S. *v.* Vigol, 2 Dall. 346; U. S. *v.* Mitchell, 2 Dall. 348; *Ex parte* Bollman, 4 Cranch, 75; Opinion in the case of Burr, 4 Cranch, 470; Story's Charge, 1 Story's Rep. 614; U. S. *v.* Hanway, 2 Wallace, Jr. 139; 3 Greenl. Ev. § 237.

ruption of blood, or forfeiture, except during the life of the person attainted." Congress has declared that the punishment shall be death by hanging; and without any of those barbarous and disgusting aggravations mentioned by Blackstone. We have before seen that it is questionable whether treason may not also be a State crime. Many of the States so regard it, and make provision for its punishment. Such was the fact in this State until 1824. But it is evident that to make treason a State crime, there must be some different definition; because each State being a part of the United States, the acts embraced in the foregoing definition, though committed against a single State, would still be treason against the United States.

2. *Misprision.* (*a*) The literal meaning of misprision is neglect or contempt. At common law, all high offences below the degree of capital were punishable as misprisions. They were divided into two classes; negative misprisions, which consisted in the concealment of something which ought to be revealed; and positive misprisions, which consisted in doing something which ought not to be done. To the first class belonged the concealment of any treason, or felony, in which the person so concealing his knowledge had no participation. To the second class belonged misconduct of public officers, and contempt of the constituted authorities. But we have no such general provisions against misprisions. In the statutes of this State the term is not mentioned; nor is there any provision resembling it, unless it be that which punishes the concealing of stolen goods or harboring the thief. But Congress have provided for punishing misprision of treason and felony. Misprision of treason is where any person, knowing of the commission of treason, does not forthwith disclose the same to the executive or judicial authorities of the United States, or of one of the States. The punishment is imprisonment not exceeding seven years, and a fine not exceeding one thousand dollars. Misprision of felony consists in the concealing of any felony made punishable by the United States, or not revealing the same to the civil or military authorities. The punishment is imprisonment not exceeding three years, and a fine not exceeding five hundred dollars. It is unfortunate that this term *felony*, so often used in criminal legislation, has not been defined by statute. At common law, (*b*) it was the general name for every crime which occasioned a forfeiture of lands or goods. But such cannot be the criterion in this country, because forfeiture is here abolished as a part of punishment. When Congress use the term felony, they seem to include in it every capital offence except treason, and this is the sense in which Blackstone, after much discussion, concludes to use the term. Under the law of Congress, then, the concealment of any capital offence other than treason, is punishable as a misprision of felony.

(*a*) 4 Black. Com. chap. 9. (*b*) 4 Black. Com. chap. 7.

3. *Criminal Correspondence with Foreign Powers.* Any resident alien, or any citizen, resident or not, being concerned in any correspondence with a foreign government, with intent to influence its measures in relation to any controversy with this government, or to defeat the measures of this government — fine within five hundred dollars, and imprisonment between six months and three years. This offence, it will be seen, partakes somewhat of the nature of treason. But it is declared not to include the case where an individual merely seeks from a foreign government redress for a private injury.

4. *Bribery.* 1. Directly or indirectly bribing any judge of the federal courts, with respect to any order, judgment, or decree — fine and imprisonment of both parties, at the discretion of the court, and future disqualification of the judge to hold any office. 2. Bribing a custom-house officer to swerve from his duty — fine for both parties between two hundred and two thousand dollars.

5. *Resistance of Officers.* Knowingly obstructing or resisting any officer in the execution of any judicial order or process of the federal courts; or assaulting, beating, or wounding such officer — fine within three hundred dollars, and imprisonment within one year.

6. *Rescuing Prisoner.* 1. Rescuing or liberating, by force, any person convicted of a capital offence — death. 2. Rescuing a prisoner under any other circumstances — fine within five hundred dollars, and imprisonment within one year.

7. *Vacating Records.* Feloniously stealing, altering, falsifying, or otherwise avoiding any record, process, or other proceeding in the federal courts, so as to defeat any judgment therein — fine within five hundred dollars, or imprisonment within seven years, or stripes not exceeding thirty-nine.

8. *False Personation.* Acknowledging any recognizance, bail, or judgment in the federal courts, in the name of any person not privy or consenting thereto — same punishment as above.

9. *Perjury.* Wilfully and corruptly committing perjury, or procuring perjury to be committed, in any matter pending in the federal courts, or in any deposition required by law — fine within eight hundred dollars, imprisonment within three years, pillory one hour, and future incompetency as a witness. But by a subsequent act of 1825, perjury, or subornation of perjury, in any case where the laws of the United States require an oath or affirmation to be taken, is punished by a fine within two thousand dollars, and imprisonment within five years. This last provision, in addition to the above, includes perjury in relation to public money, provided for in the act of 1823; perjury before committees of Congress, provided for by the act of 1798; perjury in relation to the customs, provided for by the act of 1799; and perjury under the insolvent act, provided for by the act of 1800. It therefore virtually repeals the former acts. You will observe that the act of Congress does not specify in what perjury shall consist; and

therefore recourse is had to the common-law definition before adverted to.

§ 200. **Crimes Committed in Places of Exclusive Federal Jurisdiction.** (*a*) We have seen that Congress has power "to exercise exclusive legislation, in all cases whatsoever, over such district, not exceeding ten miles square, as may, by cession of particular States, become the seat of government of the United States; and to exercise like authority over all places, purchased by the consent of the legislature of the State in which the same shall be, for the erection of forts, magazines, arsenals, dock-yards, and other needful buildings." In these places, therefore, Congress provides for the punishment of crimes. And as the power to do a thing implies the power to do it effectually, Congress may provide for apprehending an offender escaping from these places, and for transporting such offender to or from these places, for trial or execution. And unless State jurisdiction over such places has been expressly reserved, in the cession thereof, it entirely ceases. The offences, in these places, provided for by Congress, are as follows: 1. *Murder*, the punishment of which is death, and there is no distinction of degrees. 2. *Manslaughter*, as defined by the common law — fine within one thousand dollars, and imprisonment within three years. 3. *Arson.* Maliciously burning any dwelling-house, or any barn, stable, or other building connected therewith; or advising or aiding therein — death. 4. *Other Burning.* Maliciously setting fire to or burning any other building, vessel, timber, stores, provisions, or other property, specified in the act; or advising or aiding therein — fine within five thousand dollars, and imprisonment within ten years. 5. *Misprision*, *mayhem*, *larceny*, and *being accessory to larceny after the fact* — the same as on the high seas, before described. There is also a general provision, that if any offence be committed in these places of exclusive federal jurisdiction, for which Congress has not made specific provision, the punishment shall be the same as the State in which the same is situated provides for such offence. This is a convenient method of supplying the manifest deficiencies in the foregoing specifications.

§ 201. **Crimes against the Revenue Laws.** The power to punish these offences is incidental, as we have seen, to the power to raise and disburse the revenue. There are nearly fifty in number; and they are so framed as to meet every anticipated attempt, either by revenue officers or other persons, to defeat or defraud the revenue. The punishments consist entirely of fines and forfeitures; and the prosecutions may be commenced at any time within five years. I shall omit a description of these offences, for two reasons: first, on account of their peculiar character, they affect only that class of persons immediately connected with the revenue, and have no general application to the public at large; and, secondly,

(*a*) See Cohens *v.* Virginia, 6 Wheaton, 264; Commonwealth *v.* Cleary, 8 Mass. 72.

they could not be described so as to be understood, without a full account of our revenue system, for which I have not room.

§ 202. **Crimes against Commerce, including the Indians.** The power to punish these offences is incidental to the power to regulate commerce. And the following is a summary of the offences provided for as to the Indians. 1. Any citizen or resident of the United States entering any territory secured by treaty to the Indians, for the purpose of hunting or grazing therein — fine within one hundred dollars, and imprisonment within six months. 2. Entering the territory secured to the Indians, south of the Ohio River, for any purpose whatever, without a passport from the proper authority — half the above penalty. 3. Entering the Indian territory with a hostile intention, and committing any offence against the person or property of any friendly Indian, which would be punishable if committed upon a citizen within our jurisdiction — fine within one hundred dollars, and imprisonment within one year; if property be taken or destroyed — remuneration in double value; and if murder be committed — death. 4. Surveying or settling upon any land belonging to Indians, or attempting so to do — fine within one thousand dollars, and imprisonment within one year. 5. Attempting to reside among the Indians as a trader, without license from government — fine within one hundred dollars, imprisonment within thirty days, and forfeiture of merchandise. 6. Purchasing from Indians any utensil for hunting or cooking, or any article of clothing except skins or furs — fine within fifty dollars, and imprisonment within thirty days. 7. Purchasing a horse from an Indian, without license — fine within one hundred dollars, imprisonment within thirty days, and forfeiture of the horse. 8. An Indian agent being concerned in any trade with Indians on his own account — fine within one thousand dollars, and imprisonment within one year. 9. Treating with Indians for the purchase of land, without authority from government — same punishment. 10. A foreigner going into the Indian territory without a passport — same punishment. 11. Any Indian or other person committing, within the Indian territory, any offence which would be punishable, if committed within places of exclusive federal jurisdiction — the same punishment as is there provided for. (*a*) All these provisions are intended for the benefit of the Indians, and their spirit cannot be too much applauded. But experience has proved them to be altogether insufficient to protect these helpless children of nature against circumvention and imposition by white adventurers among them.

Among the offences not relative to Indians, the most important offence affecting internal commerce, is that of a *conspiracy to destroy a ship*. (*b*) According to the definition, a conspiracy formed,

(*a*) {Congress cannot punish crimes by white men upon white men, or Indians upon Indians in Indian country, if within State limits; for this is not a regulation of commerce with Indians. 15 Am. Law Rev. 30.}

(*b*) See 23d section of the act of 1825, 4 Stat. at Large, 122; U. S. *v.* Cole, 5 either on the high seas, or within the United States, to cast away, burn, or otherwise destroy any ship or vessel, or to procure the same to be done, with intent to injure underwriters upon the vessel or cargo, or lenders upon bottomry or *respondentia*, is punishable by fine not exceeding ten thousand dollars, and imprisonment not exceeding ten years. This provision does not, in terms, confine the place of intended destruction to the high seas. And it has been held to include all the navigable waters within the United States.

§ 203. **Crimes against the Post-Office Regulations.** (*a*) The power to punish these offences is incidental, as we have seen, to the power to establish post-offices and post-roads; and the offences provided for are as follows: 1. Any person connected with the post-office department, unlawfully detaining or opening any letter, or packet, or mail of letters not containing money or other evidence of value — fine within three hundred dollars, or imprisonment within six months, or both. If such letter, packet, or mail contain money or other evidence of value — imprisonment from ten to twenty-one years. For the same offence with respect to newspapers — fine within fifty dollars. 2. Any person not connected with the department, stealing, opening, or destroying the mail, or any letter or packet therein, not containing money or other evidence of value — fine within five hundred dollars, and imprisonment within one year. If the same contain money or other evidence of value, imprisonment from two to ten years. For the same offence with respect to newspapers — fine within twenty dollars. 3. Buying, receiving, or concealing any thing, knowing the same to have been robbed, stolen, or embezzled from the mail; or otherwise becoming accessory after the fact — fine within two thousand dollars, and imprisonment within ten years; with special provision that the principal need not be first convicted. 4. Any person having charge of the mail, quitting or deserting the same before delivering it to the proper person at the end of the route — fine of five hundred dollars; and if such person receive or carry any letter or packet, otherwise than in the mail, or procure the same to be done — fine within fifty dollars. 5. Robbing any carrier of the mail, or person intrusted therewith, of such mail or any part thereof — imprisonment from five to ten years for the first offence, and death for the second. But if, in committing the first offence, the carrier be wounded or his life threatened by dangerous weapons, the punishment is death. 6. Attempting to rob the mail, by assaulting or threatening the carrier — imprisonment from two to ten years. 7. Doing any injury to the bag, valise, or portmanteau, in which the mail is carried, with intent to rob or steal therefrom — fine from

M'Lean, 513. See also, as bearing upon the question, act of 1804, 2 Stat. at Large, 290; U. S. *v.* Johns 1 Walsh. C. C. Rep. 363; U. S. *v.* Amedy, 11 Wheaton, 392; act of 1790, 1 Stat. at Large, 116; U. S. *v.* Hamilton, 1 Mason, 152; act of 1825, 4 Stat. at Large, 115; U. S. *v.* Coombs, 12 Peters, 72; U. S. *v.* Bailey, 1 M'Lean, 234.

(*a*) 2 Wheeler's Crim. Cases, Pref. 39.

one hundred to five hundred dollars, and imprisonment from one to three years. 8. Concealing a letter or other writing in a newspaper, pamphlet, or magazine, or writing any thing thereon, for the purpose of avoiding letter postage — fine of five dollars, and full charge as for letter postage. 9. Advising, procuring, aiding, or assisting in the commission of any of these offences — same punishment as the principal. Where the punishment is a fine, in all these cases, one-half goes to the informer. This is one of the very few cases in which pecuniary inducement is held out to informers.

§ 204. **Crimes against Foreign Nations.** (*a*) Under this head I shall include several offences, made punishable by virtue of the incidental power which the federal government has to keep peace with foreign nations, and preserve a strict neutrality with respect to their controversies. 1. Any American citizen, within our jurisdiction, accepting and exercising a commission to serve one foreign government, by land or sea, against another foreign government at peace with us — fine within two thousand dollars, and imprisonment within three years. The design of this provision being to prevent our citizens from involving this nation in the quarrels of other nations, to the injury of our neutral policy, it prohibits foreign service only in those cases where it would have that tendency. 2. Any resident, whether citizen or alien, within our jurisdiction, enlisting or procuring another to enlist, in the service of any foreign government, on board of any vessel of war, letter of marque, or privateer — fine within one thousand dollars, and imprisonment within three years. The design of this provision being the same as of the preceding, it does not include an enlistment made by a foreigner, on board of a foreign ship which happens to be temporarily within our jurisdiction. 3. Any person within our jurisdiction, whether citizen or not, being concerned in fitting out or arming any vessel for the service of one foreign government against another, with whom we are at peace — fine within ten thousand dollars, imprisonment within three years, and forfeiture of the vessel and furniture. 4. Any person, within our jurisdiction, whether citizen or not, being concerned in augmenting the force of any vessel in the service of one foreign government in war with another, with whom we are at peace — fine within one thousand dollars, and imprisonment within one year. 5. Any person within our jurisdiction, whether citizen or not, being concerned in setting on foot any military expedition against any foreign government with whom we are at peace — fine within three thousand dollars, and imprisonment within three years.

§ 205. **Crimes committed by Federal Officers.** These offences are provided for by virtue of the incidental and inherent power which every government has to protect itself from injury by its own functionaries. Some of them have already been described; others are

(*a*) 2 Wheeler's Crim. Cases, Pref. 48.

peculiar to certain particular officers, and are not of sufficient general interest to call for any description; but the following apply to all coming within their principle: 1. Any officer connected with the judicial department, knowingly receiving or demanding unlawful fees — fine within five hundred dollars, and imprisonment within six months. 2. Any officer of the federal government being guilty of extortion under color of his office — fine within five hundred dollars, and imprisonment within one year. 3. Any person having charge of the public arms, stores, munitions of war, or other property, wilfully embezzling or purloining the same — fine of fourfold the value, and stripes not over thirty-nine.

The view now presented of the criminal code of the United States, is necessarily imperfect, from its brevity; but it answers the purpose I had in view, which was to make you acquainted with the extent of federal power, on the subject of crimes and punishments. Should you have occasion to prosecute or defend for any of these crimes, you will of course consult the statutes for their exact definition. On the score of lenity, you will remark a considerable difference between the State and federal provisions. Here we have nine capital offences; namely, forgery, piracy, murder, rape, destroying a vessel, treason, rescuing a prisoner convicted of a capital offence, arson, and mail-robbery. The average of fines, too, is very much higher; but on the other hand there is only one case of imprisonment for more than ten years. Again, whipping may be inflicted in two instances, and the pillory in one. (*a*) You will also remark that the provisions are more general for the punishment of accessories before and after the fact; but even here, they are not universal, as they should be. Nor is there any general provision, that the accessory may be punished without the conviction of the principal, though this is provided for in some cases. The provision against misprisions is general, but there is none against compounding offences. Taking all the provisions together, however, they probably meet sufficiently the chief exigencies of the federal government. In their details, as we have seen, they are obnoxious to criticism, in not clearly defining the terms employed. They are also deficient in method and arrangement, from having been made by piecemeal. For these reasons, a general and systematic revision of the whole subject would be an improvement.

(*a*) These modes of punishment have been abolished.

PART VI.

THE LAW OF PROCEDURE. (*a*)

LECTURE XXXVII.

CIVIL PROCEEDINGS IN COURTS OF LAW. (*b*)

§ 206. **Redress without Suit.** I now enter upon the sixth part of these lectures, in which I am to consider *the law of procedure*, or, as it is more commonly called, *practice.* I have reserved this branch of our inquiries until now, in compliance with the general

(*a*) Since the text was published, great changes have taken place in the law of procedure, not only in England but in this country, all having for their object greater brevity and simplicity. In several of the States, codes of procedure have been framed, which, by abolishing all distinctions between proceedings in law and chancery, and between forms of action, have created an entirely new system. Such is the case in Ohio. But as the old forms are still retained in the federal courts, as well as in many of the State courts, I have deemed it proper to leave the text as originally written, making notes occasionally to show the operation of the Code, taking that of Ohio as a specimen. In its general outlines, it does not greatly differ from the codes of New York, Kentucky, and Missouri. It took effect July 4, 1853. For the States adopting codes, see *ante*, p. 59, note.

I take this occasion to say, that for more than twenty years I have been a persevering advocate for a reform of this nature. My views were earnestly urged in the first edition of this book. They were afterwards repeatedly pressed in the Western Law Journal, of which I had the editorial charge. See vol. 5, p. 338 ; vol. 6, p. 557 ; vol. 7, p. 216. Standing almost alone, at the first, and not daring to hope for so radical a change to begin with, as these codes have made, I prepared a bill to abolish common-law forms, in all cases, and substitute chancery forms in their place. This bill twice passed the lower house, once by a vote of 38 to 27, and at the next session, by a vote of 40 to 15 ; but on each occasion failed in the Senate on the pretext of want of time. This was in the years 1848 and 1849, and before the completion of any of the codes. They are now in the course of experiment, and promise the realization of all I ever anticipated. The only point in which they can be assailed is their novelty, which give rise to so many questions requiring adjudication. This objection could not have been made to my project, at least not to the same extent. For chancery forms have stood the test of many centuries ; are not difficult to understand ; and have been thoroughly expounded and settled.

(*b*) On the general subject of practice, see the third book of Blackstone ; the third book of Swift ; Howe's Practice ; Duer's Practice ; Tidd's Practice ; Chitty's Practice ; Archbold's Practice ; Selwyn's Nisi Prius, with notes by Wheaton ; Buller's Nisi Prius ; Espinasse's Nisi Prius ; Chitty, Stephen, Gould, and Lawes on Pleading ; Wilcox's Forms ; Leigh's Nisi Prius ; Stephen's Nisi Prius.

custom, which is to treat of rights first, and then remedies; or, in other words, to discuss law in the abstract, before attending to its practical application. But for this general custom, I should have been inclined to prefer the synthetic to the analytic method; for I believe that the simplest way of teaching the elements of law, would be to begin with a single case of injury or wrong, and trace the proceedings with respect to it historically, from the first violation of the law up to the last step in the attainment of the remedy, in every form in which it can be administered. The student would thus be the better prepared for understanding legal rights in all their bearings and relations, by having first acquired a general idea of the mode in which legal remedies are applied. This may be mere conjecture; but the experiment would be worth making. I have, however, complied with the general custom, and reserve remedies until the last. Having, therefore, considered what our rights are, I am now to indicate the course of proceeding when those rights are violated. This is regulated almost entirely by the common law, and is, of course, very nearly the same in all the American as well as English courts. The organization of our federal and State courts, and the general apportionment of jurisdiction among them, have been sufficiently considered in the eighth lecture, on the judicial department. And our remaining inquiries naturally fall into four divisions: namely, *first*, civil proceedings in courts of law; *secondly*, civil proceedings in courts of chancery; *thirdly*, admiralty proceedings; *fourthly*, criminal proceedings; to each of which I shall devote one lecture. But before proceeding to the main subject of this lecture, I shall notice the principal modes of redress without suit.

1. *Defence of Persons and Property.* This falls more properly under the head of prevention than of redress, and has been before referred to. As a general rule, every one is allowed to prevent a threatened injury to the person or property, either of himself, or of those who stand in the relation of husband or wife, parent or child, master or servant, guardian or ward, by using just so much force as is necessary to prevent the injury and no more. To exceed this limit would be to convert defence into aggression. The law designs to furnish a shield only, not a sword.

2. *Reprisal.* (*a*) If, without personal violence amounting to a breach of the peace, one can, by seizure or entry, as the case may be, recover the possession of any property, or the custody of a wife, child, servant, or ward, wrongfully withheld from him, the law justifies him in so doing. But no personal violence is permitted, in making such re-caption or reprisal; because, as a general rule, this would be to redress one wrong by doing another and greater. (*b*)

3. *Abatement of Nuisances.* (*c*) The causing of certain speci-

(*a*) 3 Black. Com. 4.

(*b*) See *ante*, p. 225, note.

(*c*) 3 Black. Com. 5. An individual citizen may abate a private nuisance injurious to him when he could also bring an action, but he can abate a common nuisance only fied nuisances is usually punished as an offence. But the term "nuisance" comprehends whatsoever unlawfully annoys or does damage to another, in contravention of that great rule of right, "so use your own as not to injure others." When therefore one suffers from a nuisance, as thus defined, the law permits him to abate it; that is, remove it in a summary manner, if this can be done without riot or personal violence. Moreover, damages may be recovered at law for the injury thus sustained, in an action on the case, to be described hereafter.

4. *Distraining Property.* (a) Under the English law, the right of distraining property is deemed of great importance. When rent is in arrear, landlords are permitted to seize the chattels of their tenants on the leased premises, in satisfaction thereof; and trespassing animals may likewise be seized by the owners of the land on which they trespass, to indemnify themselves for the injury thus committed. To try the legality of such seizures, the action of *replevin* is resorted to, as will be seen hereafter. But in this State no such summary proceeding is allowed, except for the collection of debts due to the State. Landlords cannot distrain for rent, and trespassing animals are the subject of special statutory regulations.

5. *Accord and Satisfaction.* (b) This takes place when the parties themselves agree upon the satisfaction to be rendered for any injury, which they are permitted to do in all cases not criminal; and if such agreement be performed, the accord and satisfaction form a complete bar to any action by the injured party. The law, which always endeavors to discourage litigation, will not disturb a compromise thus made.

6. *Arbitration.* (c) This takes place when parties refer any matter in controversy to the decision of third persons. The act of reference is technically called *submission;* the persons to whom the reference is made, *arbitrators;* and the decision made by them, *award.* At common law, any thing may be the subject of arbitration, which is not criminal. The usual mode of submission is by a penal bond, specifying the particulars submitted, and conditioned for the performance of the award when made; but any other form of agreement will be valid, if sufficiently specific. A court of equity will not compel the specific performance of an agreement for submission; but when an award has once been made, it is held conclusive between the parties, unless it be set aside for fraud, accident, or mistake; and if either party refuse to perform it, the other may resort to chancery for a specific performance, or seek

when it obstructs his individual right. State *v.* Paul, 5 R. I. 185; State *v.* Keeran, 5 id. 497; Brown *v.* Perkins, 12 Gray, 89; s. c. 1 Allen, 89.

(a) 3 Black. Com. 6.

(b) 3 Black. Com. 16. An accord and satisfaction moving from a stranger or person having no pecuniary interest in the subject-matter, if accepted in discharge of the debt, is a good defence to an action against the debtor. Leavitt *v.* Morrow, 6 Ohio State, 71. See *post,* § 211.

(c) 3 Black. Com. 16; 2 Story on Equity Juris. chap. 40.

damages at law for non-performance; or if either party should sue upon the original subject of controversy, the award may be pleaded in bar of such suit. These general principles of arbitration have been long settled by the common law, but in almost every State statutory provisions have been superadded. Thus our statute provides for submitting all controversies to arbitration, except those which involve the title to realty, and for making such submission a rule of court; the advantage of which is, that judicial process may then be had for the procurement of testimony, and when the award has been properly made, the court will enforce its performance, as if it were a verdict, without a separate suit. To attain this advantage, the directions of the statute must be strictly pursued; but the common law of arbitration is not thereby abrogated; and therefore proceedings in arbitration may be effectual at common law, when they cannot be made a rule of court.

§ 207. **Redress by Suit.** The result of violating any legal right is an *injury* or *wrong*. If it be of a highly dangerous or atrocious character, the *public* take it up, and punish it as a *crime*. If not, it is regarded merely as a *private* affair between man and man, for which the injured party has his *civil remedy* against the other. This remedy is secured, as we have seen, by a solemn assurance in the constitution, "that all courts shall be open; and every person, for an injury done him in his lands, goods, person, or reputation, shall have remedy, by due course of law, and right and justice administered, without denial or delay." Indeed, this is only the expression of one of the fundamental articles of the social compact, by which, in return for the relinquishment of private redress, society undertakes to settle controversies between its members, according to the principles of justice, as defined by law. We must observe, however, that it is not every injury in the estimation of individuals, for which a remedy is promised; but only those injuries for which a remedy can be had "*by due course of law;*" and these injuries must relate either to the "*lands, goods, person,* or *reputation*" of individuals. The terms "*lands and goods,*" as before explained, are technical words, used to designate property; the former embracing *real property*, and the latter *personal;* while the terms "*person* or *reputation,*" are in like manner used to designate our *personal rights* or *immunities.* The meaning therefore is, that all injuries which the law can redress must relate either to the *person* or *property* of individuals; and this agrees with the remark heretofore made, that all laws have such relation. Hence, it will be inferred that some of the keenest injuries to the feelings or affections which persons of refined sensibilities can suffer, must be left unprovided for; and this agrees with another remark, that the law does not undertake to regulate *moral right and wrong.* The terms above employed, "*for an injury done him,*" might seem to imply, that the law only undertakes to redress *injuries of commission* or *positive injuries.* But, in fact, provision is equally made for *injuries of omission,* or *negative injuries.* Every denial to another of that which is his legal right, is as really a wrong as that which results from a direct act; otherwise there would be no remedy for the non-performance of contracts, or the refusal to comply with any other legal obligations. Such, then, is the general character of *civil injuries or wrongs;* but it should be observed that the law commonly uses the Latin word *delictum* or the French word *tort* instead of our equally significant English words. The remedies thus provided are called *civil*, to distinguish them from *criminal proceedings.* They are of two kinds; namely, those which are administered by *courts of law*, and those which are administered by *courts of equity;* and they will be found to differ essentially from each other, both in point of form and efficiency.

§ 208. **Actions.** (*a*) We are now to consider in what manner the law proceeds to administer civil remedies. These remedies are administered by courts, through the instrumentality of what are called *actions.* The term *action* includes the whole course of legal proceedings to obtain redress for a civil injury. The *parties* to an action are denominated *plaintiff* and *defendant;* and the former is said to *sue* or *prosecute* the latter. Hence, the term *suit* is sometimes used instead of action. In some few instances the redress sought by a civil action consists in the recovery of *some specific article of property*, wrongfully withheld from the plaintiff by the defendant; but most frequently the object of an action is to obtain *compensation in money* for an injury complained of, which compensation is technically called *damages.* (*b*) It is obvious that for *injuries to property*, this is generally the most easy and natural kind of redress, since money is the universal measure of value; and besides, it is often impracticable to obtain *satisfaction in kind.* But it may at first view appear strange, that pecuniary damages should be the redress sought for *personal injuries*, since we are accustomed to hold personal immunities to be beyond all price. If my property has been injured, or my dues withheld, I can readily tell the exact sum which will make me whole; but if my body has been bruised, my health impaired, or my reputation slandered, how can I tell what amount of money will compensate me for the injury? It is evident that, strictly speaking, there can be no *equivalent* in such cases; but it is also evident, that unless we resort to the principle of *retaliation*, which vindictively doubles the amount of injury, pecuniary damages, though often inadequate, constitute the only satisfaction which the law can furnish. Were we now at liberty to classify actions, upon any principle of analysis, it would follow, from what has been said, that only two classes would be necessary; and these might be, *first*, for injuries to the person, and for injuries to

(*a*) See 3 Black. Com. 116; 1 Chit. Plead. 83.

(*b*) On the subject of damages, see Sedgwick on Damages; Sutherland on Damages; 2 Parsons on Contracts, pp. 432–508; and the leading case of Suydam *v.* Jenkins, 3 Sandf. 614.

property; or, *secondly*, for injuries of commission, and for injuries of omission; or, *thirdly*, for the recovery of the specific thing, and for the recovery of pecuniary damages. But instead of a simple and natural division of actions, such as either of these would be, we are compelled, by peculiar circumstances in the history of the common law, to recognize a perplexing variety of actions abounding with arbitrary and technical distinctions. The customary division of actions is into *real*, *personal*, and *mixed*. *Real actions* are those used for the recovery of real property only, without damages. *Personal actions* are those used for the recovery of personal property or damages. And *mixed actions* are those used for the recovery of real property and damages. But in this, and several other States, real actions are not in use; their place being supplied by the mixed action called *ejectment*, which answers every useful purpose, and is the only mixed action now in use. Personal actions are again subdivided into *actions ex contractu*, or *actions of contract*, and *actions ex delicto*, or *actions of tort*.

To account for this diversity of civil remedies, we must look back to the history of actions; and let me apprise you beforehand, that you will find very little of that adaptation of means to ends, which is calculated to gratify a philosophic mind. On the contrary, you will find that the remedial part of the law resembles a mass of patchwork, made up at intervals and by piecemeal, without any preconceived plan or system, for the purpose of meeting the exigencies of the times by temporary expedients. It will be well to bear this in mind, while considering the forms of action; for it will help you to account for combinations and classifications, which would otherwise be unaccountable. At the earliest period of the English law of which we have any definite account, *specific forms* of action were in use, for such cases as had then most frequently occurred. These had been collected into a book called *registrum brevium* or *the register of writs;* and were denominated *brevia formata*, or *fixed writs*, being held to be immutable by any authority except that of Parliament; that is, the courts could not change them. Such was the state of things until 1284, when an act was passed, known as the *statute of Westminster 2d*, to provide for the formation of *new writs* in *cases* for which the register contained no appropriate form, but for which the progress of society made it necessary to provide; and from certain words used in this statute, the new actions formed under it are called *actions on the case*. (*a*) Our present actions, then,

(*a*) The words of the statute, as early translated, are as follows: "That if it shall fortune in the chancery, that in one case a writ is found, and in *like case* falling under like law, and requiring like remedy, is found none, the clerks of the chancery shall agree in making the writ, or adjourn the plaintiffs until the next Parliament; and that the cases be written in which they cannot agree, and that they shall refer such cases until the next Parliament: and by consent of men learned in the law, a writ shall be made, lest it might happen after that the court should long time fail to minister justice unto complainants." 1 Chitty on Pleading, 84; 3 Black. Com. 123, 183; 3 Reeve's Hist. E. L. 89; Crabb's Hist. E. L. 290.

are traced either to the register of writs, or to the statute of Westminster; and though, judging from their form, they would seem to be adapted only to the redress of a few specific injuries, yet they have been gradually extended in their scope, by means of fictions and innovations, of which the common law has been peculiarly fond, so as to cover all the cases which usually occur. If, however, a case should now arise, for which the precedents thus framed furnish no established form, the question whether there be a remedy or not, is to be determined by the application of this rule: If the case be *new in principle*, the courts must wait until the legislature provides for it; but if it be only new in the *particular instance*, and comes clearly *within* a settled principle, the courts will entertain a *special action on the case*, founded on the authority of the statute before mentioned. The names of the actions now in use are, *debt*, *covenant*, *assumpsit*, *trespass*, *trover*, *detinue*, *replevin*, *case*, and *ejectment*. Of these, the first eight are *personal actions*, and the last *mixed*. The first three are *actions of contract;* and the other six, *actions of tort*. Assumpsit and trover are in fact *actions on the case*, for they originated under the statute of Westminster; but from their very general use they have become specific designations; while the word *case* has become a generic term, including a large class of actions for which there is no specific designation. I shall now give a very brief description of each of these actions, with reference to the injuries they are designed to remedy, taking them in the above order. The first point which a practising lawyer has to decide, is the proper action for the case presented. To decide this, he must be familiar with the scope and purpose of all the actions; and this is a matter of no small labor and difficulty, on account of the frequent want of correspondence between the original form of a particular action, and the actual purpose for which it is now employed. In describing these actions, I shall have frequent occasion to speak of the *declaration*, which forms a part of the pleadings to be described hereafter. For the present it is sufficient to say, that the declaration contains the plaintiff's statement of his case in court. Its form varies in each of the actions, as will appear from the specimens given in the notes. A careful examination of one declaration in each of the actions will best impress upon the memory the distinctive features of such action. In these specimens, I shall omit the caption and conclusion; which are merely formal, and the same in all declarations. I shall also omit the allegations of time and place, which cannot now be conveniently explained.

Debt. (*a*) The action of debt is one of those which we trace up to the register of writs. It is the remedy *for recovering a debt*, strictly so called; that is, a certain and liquidated sum of money due from the defendant to the plaintiff. It makes no difference

(*a*) See 1 Swift's Dig. 572; 1 Chit. Plead. 100; Steph. Plead. 14.

whether the debt be evidenced by a sealed contract, a written contract not sealed, an implied contract, or a mere legal obligation without any contract, provided the sum be capable of being reduced to certainty beforehand, and does not depend upon a mere arbitrary estimate of damages by a jury. *Interest* can be recovered in this action, because the amount is rendered certain by the law regulating the rate of interest; but it is in no case adapted to the recovery of uncertain damages. It has, however, been so far extended in modern times, without any alteration of its form, that there are now very few, if any, merely pecuniary claims, which may not be recovered by the action of debt. Thus it may now be brought to recover the *price* of any property sold, or the *compensation* for any service performed, although such price and compensation were not stipulated between the parties; for the amount in such cases is liquidated by proving the market-price or customary compensation. But this action has never been extended beyond strictly pecuniary claims, as distinguished from consequential and unliquidated damages. When such, therefore, become the subject of a suit, even though founded on contract, some other action must be resorted to. Originally, the defendant in this action was allowed to *wage his law;* that is, to swear that he did not owe the debt, and procure twelve of his neighbors to swear that they believed him; and this may partially account for its circumscribed scope; but the anomaly of wager of law has never been admitted in this country, and is now obsolete in England. (*a*)

Covenant. (*b*) The action of covenant is likewise one of those found in the register of writs. It is the remedy provided for *the recovery of damages for the breach of a contract under seal.* These contracts, on account of the theoretical solemnity of their execution, which has before been remarked upon, are called *covenants*, by way of eminence; and this action is confined to them only. It makes no difference what the covenant be for; whether to pay money, or to perform or abstain from any other act; if damages can be recovered at all for the breach of a contract under seal, they may always be recovered by this action. But it is evident that there are many cases in which covenant is a *concurrent remedy* with debt; and the plaintiff may have his option between them. Thus, whenever there is a sealed contract to pay a specific sum of money, this sum with interest may be recovered as a debt, by the action of debt; or in the shape of damages, by the action of covenant. When, however, the sealed

(*a*) *Declaration in Debt.* For that the defendant made his certain writing obligatory of the date aforesaid, sealed with his seal, and now to the court here shown, and then and there delivered the same to the plaintiff, and thereby bound himself to pay to the plaintiff, or his order, the sum of ——— dollars, in ——— days after the date thereof, which period has now elapsed. Yet the defendant has not paid the said sum of money or any part thereof to the plaintiff; but still owes the same to, and unjustly detains the same from, him.

It will thus be seen that the elements of a declaration in debt are, the fact of indebtedness in a liquidated sum, and the manner of such indebtedness.

(*b*) See 1 Swift's Dig. 570; 1 Chitty's Plead. 109; Steph. Plead. 76.

contract is for any thing else than to pay money, the action of covenant is the sole remedy. It is obviously unnecessary that there should be more than one form of action for the same identical injury; and a perfect system of remedial law would probably avoid concurrent remedies, for the sake of simplicity; but we shall find that under the existing system, most of the injuries for which redress is sought, admit of concurrent remedies by different actions. (*a*)

Assumpsit. (*b*) The action of assumpsit has no precedent in the register of writs, but originated under the statute of Westminster. It is, therefore, one of the actions *on the case;* but from its general use, as before observed, it has acquired a generic character. It is the remedy provided for the recovery of damages *for the breach of contract not under seal.* It makes no difference whether the contract be written or verbal, express or implied; or what it be for; whether to pay money, or to perform or abstain from any other act. If the facts be such as to make out a contract, promise, or undertaking, by expression or inference, and there be no seal, assumpsit will lie. It takes its name from the Latin word *assumpsit,* originally used when the proceedings were in that language, to describe the undertaking or promise. It will be observed that assumpsit can never be a concurrent remedy with covenant, on account of the seal; but it is concurrent with debt, whenever there is an unsealed contract to pay a liquidated sum of money, or a sum capable of being liquidated. It will also be observed, that by taking the seal away from any contract whatever, assumpsit will lie upon such contract, instead of covenant. By abolishing seals, therefore, the two actions would be consolidated; and by going one step further and abolishing the action of debt, which might be readily dispensed with, we should have a simple remedy for all cases of contract. (*c*)

(*a*) *Declaration in Covenant.* For that by a certain indenture then and there made between the parties, sealed with their seals and having the date aforesaid, one part of which indenture is now to the court here shown, the plaintiff did lease to the defendant the following property, to wit [describe it], for the term of —— years, at the annual rent of $——, payable on the —— day of —— in each year; and the defendant, among other things, did thereby covenant with the plaintiff to pay him the said rent, as it should become due; by virtue of which lease the defendant then and there took possession of said premises for the term aforesaid. And the plaintiff avers that afterwards, to wit, on ——, a large sum of money, to wit, $—— of the said rent, for —— years of the said term then elapsed, was and still is in arrears and unpaid; and so the said defendant has broken his said covenant.

It will thus be seen that the elements of a declaration in covenant are, the fact of making a contract under seal, the substance of that contract, and the breach of it.

(*b*) See 1 Swift's Dig. 574; 1 Chitty's Plead. 88; Steph. Plead. 18.

(*c*) *Declaration in Assumpsit.* For that the defendant was indebted to the plaintiff in the sum of —— dollars, for divers goods, wares, and merchandise before that time sold and delivered by the plaintiff to the defendant at his request; and in consideration thereof the defendant then and there undertook and promised the plaintiff to pay him the said sum of money on request. Yet although often requested, he has not paid the same, or any part thereof, to the plaintiff, but refuses so to do.

From this specimen it will be seen that the elements of a declaration in assumpsit are, the fact of making a contract not under seal, the substance of that contract, and the breach of it.

Trespass. (*a*) We now come to the *actions of tort.* The action of trespass is found in the register of writs, and was probably the first one reduced to form. The word *trespass* literally includes every kind of transgression or wrong; and hence the action on the case is often described as "*trespass on the case.*" But when the word is used by itself, it designates this particular action. It is the remedy made use of to recover damages for *every violent or forcible injury either to the person or property.* Force, therefore, is the *gist* or criterion of the action; and hence the injury is always described in these proceedings as committed *vi et armis et contra pacem, with force and arms, and against the peace.* To judge from this technical language, the action must have originated in those turbulent times, when armed force and violence were so common, that injuries not thus accompanied were scarcely noticed; but at present the *degree of force* made use of is of no consequence. If one *assault*, that is, make a motion to beat another, it is as much a forcible trespass as if there had been an actual *battery.* So if one merely walk upon another's unenclosed grounds, it is as much a forcible trespass, as if he had first broken down a fence to get in. Perhaps the legal idea of trespass will be best understood, if thus stated: Every injury to the person or property, which is the direct, immediate, and necessary effect of some act done by the defendant, however great or small the violence used, is viewed by the law as *a forcible injury*, and the proper remedy is *trespass;* from which it follows that no injury which is the result of negligence or omission, or which is merely the indirect consequence of any act not directly and necessarily injurious, or which is not done by the defendant himself, but by some one for whose acts he is responsible, can be redressed by this action. In fact, it will be found that forcible injuries to the person, and to real property, are almost the only ones for which trespass is the exclusive remedy: since for forcible injuries to personal property, some one or more of the other actions will nearly always lie concurrent with this. The following are specimens of the nice distinctions observed in relation to this action: If a log be put down in the gentlest manner upon my foot, the action is trespass; but if you dam up a watercourse so as to flood my land, trespass will not lie. If you row your boat directly against mine, the action is trespass; but if the wind or stream urge it against mine, trespass will not lie; and the remedy must be an action on the case. From this description it follows that the injuries redressed by trespass may be divided into three classes: *First*, direct injuries to the body, where the action is called trespass for an *assault and*

(*a*) See 1 Swift's Dig. 5, 27; 1 Chitty's Plead. 162; Case *v.* Mark, 2 Ohio, 169; Steph. Plead. 16; Cooley, Bigelow, on Torts; Henshaw *v.* Noble, 7 Ohio State, 226. The wrongful act, in order to be actionable, must be the proximate cause of the injury. The rule *in jure causa proxima, non remota, spectatur,* is well discussed in Marble *v.* City of Worcester, 4 Gray, 395.

battery; secondly, direct injuries to realty, where the action is called trespass *quare clausum fregit*, or trespass for breaking the close, because in legal contemplation every man's land is considered as enclosed; and *thirdly*, direct injuries to personalty, which may consist either in wrongfully taking and carrying it away, or directly injuring, without taking it, where the action is called trespass *de bonis*. (*a*)

Trover. (*b*) The action of trover, as we have seen, originated under the statute of Westminster. It takes its name from the French word *trouver*, signifying *to find*. It was originally designed as the remedy for recovering damages *whenever personal property had been literally lost by the plaintiff and found and made use of by the defendant*. It was one of the actions on the case; but it has passed into such extensive use, as to acquire, like assumpsit, a generic character. By a resort to fiction, its sphere has so much enlarged in the process of time, that it now extends to all cases where the personal property of one person has been wrongfully *converted* by another to his own use. The word *conversion*, in this action, has a technical signification. It implies either a *wrongful taking* of the goods of another; or a *wrongful detention* of what may be rightfully taken; or a *wrongful using* of what may have been neither wrongfully taken nor detained. Whenever one commits either of these three acts, with respect to personal property belonging to another, he is guilty of what the law calls a *conversion* of such property to his own use, and trover lies to recover damages. Conversion, as thus explained, is the gist or criterion of the action; although, for the sake of adhering to the original form, the property is still alleged, by way of fiction, to have been *lost* by the plaintiff, and *found* and *converted* by the defendant. It follows, therefore, that trover is concurrent with trespass in all cases of *wrongful taking*. We shall also find that trover is concurrent with detinue and replevin, in all cases of *wrongful detention*. The following are specimens of the nice distinctions which prevail in regard to this action: If my trees have been cut down, but not carried away, trespass is the only

(*a*) *Declaration in Trespass for Assault and Battery*. For that the defendant, with force and arms, did assault, beat, bruise, and wound the plaintiff, and other wrongs to him then and there did, against the peace.

Declaration in Trespass quare clausum fregit. For that the defendant, with force and arms, broke and entered the close of the plaintiff, situate [describe the premises], and then and there cut down and destroyed a large number, to wit, one hundred oak trees, of great value, to wit, of the value of five hundred dollars; and other wrongs to the plaintiff the defendant then and there did against the peace.

Declaration in Trespass de bonis. For that the defendant, with force and arms, took and carried away the following goods and chattels of the plaintiff, to wit, ten bales of cotton, of great value, to wit, of the value of ——— dollars, and other wrongs to the plaintiff the defendant then and there did, against the peace.

From these examples it will be seen that the elements of a declaration in trespass are, the fact of committing a trespass, the fiction that it was done with force and arms and against the peace, and the particulars of the trespass.

(*b*) See 1 Swift's Dig. 533; 1 Chitty's Plead. 147; Steph. Plead. 18.

remedy, because growing trees form part of the realty; but if they have been carried away, trover or trespass will lie concurrently, because, after being severed, they are personalty. If coals have been dug from my pit, but not thrown out upon the surface, trespass is the only remedy; but if thrown out, trover or trespass will lie, for the same reason as before. (*a*)

Detinue. (*b*) The action of detinue is one of the original actions found in the register of writs. It is recognized in this State, but seldom resorted to, on account of the extension we have given to the action of replevin. It is the remedy originally provided *for recovering specific personal property wrongfully detained from the rightful owner, together with damages for the detention.* It is the only action, except replevin, adapted to this purpose; all the others being to recover damages alone. Besides the thing itself, damages may be recovered for the detention, and may include the value of the thing itself, when it cannot be had. No matter how the defendant came by the article, provided the plaintiff has a right to it; for the wrongful detention is the gist or criterion of the action. It follows from the very nature of the recovery, that the action can only be used where the detained article can be specifically identified. It also follows that detinue may be concurrent with trespass, trover, and replevin; for a wrongful detention is the sole gist of replevin, and is one of the gists of trover; and where goods have been wrongfully taken, the plaintiff may waive the taking, which would be the gist of trespass, and proceed for the detention only. (*c*)

Replevin. (*d*) The action of replevin, at common law, was the remedy for *the recovery of specific personal property, wrongfully distrained, together with damages for the wrongful act.* To distrain, is to seize upon property for payment of rent, taxes, and the like. The act of distraining as well as the thing taken, is called a

(*a*) *Declaration in Trover.* For that the plaintiff was lawfully possessed, as of his own property, of certain goods and chattels, to wit [describe the goods generally, as ten chairs, ten horses], of great value, to wit, of the value of $——; and afterwards, on the same day, the plaintiff lost the same; and afterwards on the same day, the same came into the possession of the defendant by finding; yet the defendant, well knowing the same to belong to the plaintiff, but intending to injure and defraud him thereof, refused to deliver the same to the plaintiff, though often requested so to do, and then and there converted the same to his own use.

It will thus be seen that the elements of a declaration in trover are, the fact that the plaintiff owned the goods, the fiction that he lost, and the defendant found them, and the fact that the defendant converted them to his own use.

(*b*) See 1 Chitty's Plead. 117; Steph. Plead. 18.

(*c*) *Declaration in Detinue.* For that the defendant was possessed of certain goods and chattels of the plaintiff, to wit [describe them], of great value, to wit, of the value of —— dollars, to be delivered to the plaintiff when the defendant should be thereto requested; yet though often requested, the defendant has not delivered the same or any part thereof to the plaintiff, but still wrongfully detains the same.

It will thus be seen that the elements of a declaration in detinue are, the fact that the plaintiff has a right to the possession of the goods, and that the defendant wrongfully detains them. The fiction of a bailment is commonly made use of, as in the above form, but is believed not to be essential.

(*d*) See 1 Swift's Dig. 522; 1 Chitty's Plead. 157; Steph. Plead. 19; Curd *v.* Wunder, 5 Ohio State, 92; Bigelow *v.* Comegys, 5 id. 256.

distress: and the object of the action was to try the legality of the distress. But the summary method of compelling payment by distress, is not practised here, except in collecting taxes and canal tolls; and therefore, if the scope of the action had not been greatly enlarged, it would have been of little use. But by our statute, it is made a much more general remedy. It now lies *whenever personal property is wrongfully detained from the owner;* or in other words, a wrongful detention is now made the gist of replevin. The object of the action is twofold: to recover the specific property detained, and damages for the detention. In these respects, it coincides entirely with detinue; but in the mode of proceeding, it is entirely different from any other action, and forms an anomaly in our practice. The plaintiff makes affidavit that the property belongs to him; that it is wrongfully detained by the defendant; and that it was not taken on any process against the plaintiff, nor for any debt or tax due the State; and thereupon the sheriff *replevies* the property: that is, he takes it out of the hands of the defendant, and delivers it to the plaintiff, upon his giving *security* to try his title, and abide the event of the suit; which security must be in double the value of the property, ascertained by *appraisement,* for which the statute provides. The suit then goes on to trial; and if the plaintiff fails in proving his title, he is answerable to the defendant for the value of the property replevied, and damages for taking it away, but the defendant cannot recover back the specific goods. If the plaintiff succeeds, he already has the property, and of course only recovers damages for the previous detention, while in the hands of the defendant. From this view of replevin, as it exists here, you will observe that it may be concurrent with trespass, trover, and detinue, as before explained in speaking of detinue. But in general, the choice will lie between trover and replevin. If you wish to recover the specific chattels, and can find and identify them, you will bring replevin; but if you cannot identify them, or cannot come at them, or do not want them, you will bring trover for the damages you have sustained. (*a*)

Case. (*b*) The action on the case originated, as we have seen under the statute of Westminster 2d, and took its name from words used in the statute. It stands for a *genus,* of which assumpsit and trover were *species.* We sometimes say, "*trespass on the case,*" but the single word "*case*" is sufficiently definite. Case is, then, the remedy provided for the recovery of damages *for any injury to the person, property, health, reputation, or domestic comfort of individuals, not accompanied by force, either actual or*

(*a*) *Declaration in Replevin.* For that the defendant was possessed of certain goods and chattels of the plaintiff, to wit [describe them], to be delivered to the plaintiff when the defendant should be thereto requested; yet the defendant, though often requested, would not deliver the same or any part thereof to the plaintiff, but wrongfully detained the same until replevied.

Thus the declaration in replevin is nearly identical with that in detinue.

(*b*) See 1 Swift's Dig. 539; 1 Chitty's Plead. 133; Steph. Plead. 17.

constructive. Whenever the matter affected is not tangible, as reputation, so that force cannot be applied to it; or whenever the injury complained of is not immediate but consequential; or is the result of negligence or omission, this action will lie. Of course, it embraces a much greater variety of injuries than any other action. It is in fact what the statute of Westminster intended it to be, a general remedy for all civil injuries, not before provided for by the established forms in the register. Case is often rendered concurrent with covenant and assumpsit, by waiving the contract, and proceeding for the negligence or *tort.* It may also in some cases be rendered concurrent with trespass or trover, by waiving the force or conversion, and proceeding for *negligence* in not returning or taking care of chattels. In fact, all these actions are in their nature separated by such minute shades of difference, and their original boundaries have been so often enlarged for the furtherance of justice, which was too much hampered by the ancient forms, that the most accomplished practitioner is often at a loss which one of two or more actions he ought to adopt. (*a*)

Ejectment. (*b*) The action of ejectment is the remedy now used

(*a*) *Declaration in Case.* For that whereas the plaintiff has always sustained a fair reputation for honesty, and has never been guilty or suspected of the crime of larceny; yet the defendant, well knowing this, but maliciously intending to injure the reputation of the plaintiff, and expose him to the penalties of the law for larceny, did utter and publish, in the hearing of sundry persons, of and concerning the plaintiff, the following false and scandalous words, to wit: You [meaning the plaintiff] are a thief, and I [meaning the defendant] can prove it; by means whereof the plaintiff is greatly injured in his reputation, and has been rendered liable to a prosecution for larceny.

The above is but a single example of a declaration in case for slanderous words. No general form can be given; for, from the very nature of the action, the declaration must vary with each particular case.

(*b*) See 1 Swift's Dig. 504; 1 Chitty's Plead. 188; Steph. Plead. 11; 3 Black. Com. 199; Adams on Ejectment, with notes by Tillinghast; Runnington on Ejectment. Although the action of ejectment is superseded by the Code, I have deemed it advisable to add some particulars to the very general view presented in the text. In Holt *v.* Hemphill, 3 Ohio, 232, the court say, "From the practice which has prevailed since the passing of the limitation act of 1804, it would seem that the action of ejectment has been considered the proper remedy for the recovery of real property under all circumstances; although neither that act, nor those which have since been passed, can be considered as prohibiting real actions, yet there is reason to conclude, and such appears to have been the prevailing opinion, that by a fair interpretation of those acts, the writ of ejectment may be used in all cases in which the writ of right can be sustained at common law."

Parties. If one having the exclusive title, unite with himself in a joint demise persons having no title, it will be erroneous. Adams *v.* Turner, 7 Ohio, 2 pt. 136. Tenants in common are authorized by statute to declare upon a joint demise; but if they be infants, they cannot demise by *prochein ami.* Massie *v.* Long, 2 Ohio, 287; Wilkinson *v.* Fleming, 2 id. 301. Where the owners were non-residents, and their tenants did not ask to be admitted to defend, the owners were allowed to remove the case to the federal court. Gwynne *v.* Roe, 4 Ohio, 435.

Title. The plaintiff must rely wholly upon the strength of his own title, and cannot be aided by the weakness of his adversary's, because bare possession is good against all who cannot show something better. Hence the defendant may prove a superior title in a third person. But this privilege is confined to him. If the plaintiff should endeavor to rebut the defendant's title, by showing one still better than either, he would defeat his own first set up. Ludlow *v.* Barr, 3 Ohio, 388; Devacht *v.* Newsam, 3 id. 57; Treon *v.* Emerick, 6 id. 391; Abram *v.* Will, 6 id. 164; Dresback *v.* M'Arthur, *for recovering the possession of real property.* In Ohio, and several other States, it is the only action employed for this purpose, having

7 id. 1 pt. 146 ; Fenno *v.* Holme, 21 How. 481, and evidence of an equitable title is not sufficient, id. {But *contra,* now under the Code, if pleaded. Powers *v.* Armstrong, 36 Ohio State, 357.}

Evidence. The points to be established are, a legal title in the plaintiff, with a present right of possession ; and the fact of possession by the defendant, which is usually admitted by the consent rule. But if the defendant is in as tenant, he cannot dispute his landlord's title.

If the claim rest upon *occupancy* only, it may be shown by proving such facts as enclosing, cultivating, taking the profits, and the like. If this has continued for twenty-one years, a deed will be presumed. If for a less time, it will still be good against a subsequent occupancy for a less term. Courcier *v.* Graham, 1 Ohio, 330 ; Ludlow *v.* Barr, 3 id. 388 ; Stark *v.* Smith, 5 id. 455 ; Wallace *v.* Minor, 7 id. 1 pt. 249 ; Armstrong *v.* M'Coy, 8 id. 128.

If the claim rest upon *marriage,* it must be *dower* or *curtesy.* And dower is not here recovered by ejectment, but curtesy is. In either case, the facts to be proved are, a legal marriage, seisin during coverture, and death. In curtesy there was a fourth fact, the birth of a living heir, but the statute dispenses with this. With regard to marriage, if an actual one be proved, it will be presumed to be legal. The best evidence is that of an eye-witness of the ceremony, or a certified copy from the legal register. In the absence of these, proof of cohabitation and general reputation is sufficient.

If the claim rest upon *descent,* the points to be established are, title in the ancestor and heirship. Where births are required to be registered, a certified copy is the most convenient proof of pedigree. But in the absence of this, or of direct testimony, we resort to general reputation, declarations of deceased members of the family, entries in family books, monumental inscriptions and the like.

If the claim rest upon devise, the production of a certified copy of the will and probate is sufficient.

If the claim rest upon a deed, or a succession of deeds, our practice is to require only the last deed to be produced, and to receive recorder's copies of all prior conveyances. Burnet *v.* Brush, 6 Ohio, 32. Ancient deeds are said to prove themselves, and thirty years will make a deed ancient ; but in these cases it is important that possession has corresponded. So if a deed not recorded has been lost, its contents may be proved in the best way possible. Allen *v.* Parish, 3 Ohio, 107 ; Blackburn *v.* Blackburn, 8 id. 81.

Judgment and Execution. A judgment in execution is conclusive as to the right of possession for the time laid in the declaration, until reversed on error or made void by a subsequent adverse recovery in another action. Hinton *v.* M'Neil, 5 Ohio, 509. If judgment by default has been rendered against the casual ejector, a writ of error may be prosecuted in his name. Roe *v.* Bank U. S., 3 Ohio, 26. When the plaintiff has been put in possession under the writ of *habere facias,* if he be disturbed he cannot have a second writ, but must bring a new action. Hinton *v.* M'Neil, 5 Ohio, 509 ; Hough *v.* Norton, 9 id. 45.

Injunction to prevent repeated Actions. The question with a court of equity is, whether the litigation, from any cause, either in the number of trials or the loss of evidence, has become vexatious. 2 Story, Eq. Juris. § 859 ; Bath *v.* Sherwin, Finch, Prec. 262 ; 1 Brown, P. C. 266 ; Leighton *v.* Leighton, 1 Peere Wms. 672 ; 2 Brown, P. C. 217 ; Tenham *v.* Herbert, 2 Atkyns, 483 ; Weller *v.* Smeaton, 1 Brown, Ch. Rep. 573 ; Huntington *v.* Nicoll, 3 Johns. 586 ; Harmar *v.* Gwynne, 5 M'Lean, 313.

Declaration in Ejectment. For that one ——— [the lessor and real plaintiff] had demised to John Doe the following real estate situated in said county, to wit [describe the land], together with the appurtenances, for the term of ——— years from the date aforesaid, which is not yet expired ; by virtue of which demise the said John Doe entered into possession thereof for the said term ; and Richard Roe afterwards, to wit, on ———, at the county aforesaid, with force and arms entered into the said demised premises, and ejected the said John Doe therefrom, and other wrongs to him then and there did, against the peace.

Notice. To ——— [the person in possession and real defendant]. Sir, — I am informed that you are in possession of, or claim title to, the premises in the above declaration mentioned, or some part thereof ; and I, being sued in this action as casual ejector only, and having no claim to the said premises, do advise you to appear at the next term of the [describe the court], to be holden in said county, on the ———, by silently taken the place of all *real actions*, strictly so called. Ejectment was not originally designed for *trying the title* to land; but has been adapted to this object by means of a series of fictions. In arriving at its present state, it has passed through three distinct stages. At first, it was only used by the lessee of land, who had been ejected or ousted therefrom *by a stranger*, to recover damages for the ouster. We have seen that in early times a lessee for years had no security for the permanence of his title. As against the lessor, if there was no covenant for quiet enjoyment, the lessee was without remedy; for the lessor could not be treated as a trespasser. But if the ejector was a stranger, the lessee might sue him for the ejectment in an action of trespass, and recover damages, but not possession of the land. In process of time, however, the courts of chancery undertook to compel the ejector, unless he could justify the ejectment under a superior title, to make restitution of the land to the lessee. In this the courts of law soon followed them, though without altering the form of the action. The next stage, therefore, was to enlarge its scope, so as to enable the lessee to recover possession of the land for the unexpired term, as well as damages for the ouster. But for this purpose it was necessary to show a better title than the *ejector*, which incidentally brought up for examination the *title of the lessor*, since the lessee could have no other title than that derived from him. In this state of things it was perceived by the lawyers that, by recourse to several fictions, the trial of the lessor's title might be made the direct and main object of the action, instead of being an incidental circumstance. For this purpose there were only wanting a fictitious lessee, a fictitious ejector, and a fictitious ouster: and for the sake of getting rid of the almost endless technicalities and subtleties of real actions, the courts readily sanctioned the introduction of these fictions, which have now been acquiesced in for more than three centuries; and the result is, that if I claim title to a piece of land of which you are in possession, I begin by serving upon you a *declaration* and *notice*, which in this action takes the place of a writ. The declaration states that I made a lease or demise to a fictitious person, say John Doe; that he entered into possession; and that another fictitious person, say Richard Roe, forcibly ejected or ousted him from the premises. Thus John Doe becomes the nominal plaintiff, and Richard Roe the nominal defendant. But appended to this declaration is a notice purporting to be written by Richard Roe to you, informing you that he has been sued, but that being a *casual ejector* only he shall not defend, and advising you to appear and defend. This the court will permit you to do, by entering into a *consent rule*,

some attorney of said court, and by a rule of said court, to cause yourself to be made defendant in my stead; otherwise I shall suffer judgment by default, and you will be turned out of possession.

Consent Rule and Plea. The defendant comes and confesses the lease, entry, and ouster in the declaration mentioned, and admits himself to be in possession of the premises therein described, and says that he is not guilty of the trespass and ejectment complained of.

by which you confess the fictions of a *lease*, *entry*, and *ouster*, as alleged in the declaration, and agree to try the question of title only. Such is the circuitous manner in which one of the most important actions is made to effect its purpose. The form still remains that of trespass to recover damages for the ouster; but these damages are now merely nominal. You cannot even recover, in this action, the intermediate profits of the land, while the defendant has been in the unlawful possession of it; but must bring a separate action of *trespass for mesne profits*. Nor is a final judgment in ejectment conclusive of the controversy, as it is in other cases. Ordinarily, a final judgment is conclusive between the same parties, in relation to the same matter. But in ejectment, the parties, being fictitious, may be changed at will, and the same matter litigated again, until a court of chancery should interfere by injunction. While, therefore, much has been gained by thus superseding real actions, a still further improvement would be to abolish these fictions, and so shape the action as to recover not only possession, but mesne profits.

§ 209. **Analysis of Wrongs and Remedies.** I have thus glanced at the various actions by which civil remedies are administered. Perhaps you will now be tempted to inquire, what necessity there is for such a variety? Why one action of contract would not answer all the purposes of three? Why the five actions of *tort* might not be reduced to two; namely, one for the recovery of the specific thing, and the other for the recovery of damages for injury or detention? And why the action of ejectment would not be equally efficient and still more conclusive when divested of its circuitous and fictitious character? It might be difficult to satisfy a philosophic mind that all these changes would not be improvements. If the forms of civil redress were now for the first time to be prescribed, and the task were committed to capable men, it is not probable they would much resemble those in present use; because no analysis, either of contracts or torts, would produce such a result. If each minute difference were to require a peculiar form, the number would be infinitely greater. If not, there would be no reason for making it so great. But these forms have come down to us through the lapse of centuries; and by the various contrivances before alluded to, they have been gradually moulded and extended so as to meet the increasing wants of civilization; and the true question now is, whether a reform be on the whole expedient? No doubt this part of the law is susceptible of great simplification; and it is equally clear that a consolidation of the forms of action would render litigation much less expensive. It would likewise go far to exculpate the remedial part of the law from the charge of unnecessary intricacy and technicality. The number of cases decided upon mere questions of form would be vastly diminished. Fictions would no longer occupy the place they now so unworthily hold in the administration of justice, and the common law would approximate more nearly to the common sense of mankind. But would these advantages compensate for the evil always attendant upon any radical reform in jurisprudence? Upon this grave question the inexperienced may well hesitate; for it now divides the best opinions of the age. But one can hardly help wishing that the experiment might be made; for as the system now exists, it probably takes more time to become familiar with the forms of law, than to comprehend its abstract principles. Should these suggestions have no other effect, I trust they will stimulate your curiosity to examine the more carefully whether the evils alluded to really exist. In the mean time, before describing the proceedings in these actions, I shall give a brief analysis of the wrongs they are designed to redress, with a view to impress the scope and purpose of each more deeply on the memory. We have before seen that all wrongs have relation either to the person or property, and that those of a more atrocious character than ordinary are punished as crimes; but the present inquiry will be confined to civil injuries.

Wrongs relating to the Person. These are either to the body, liberty, health, reputation, or domestic comfort of individuals. 1. If one unlawfully *threaten* me with bodily harm, so as to interrupt my business, I may sue him in *trespass*, and recover damages for such interruption, although mere threats, which do not interrupt business, furnish no cause of action. Here, then, the interruption is the injury, and must be specially counted upon under what is called a *per quod*, or special allegation. Again, if one unlawfully *assault* me, that is, attempt or offer to beat me, though my business be not interrupted, I may sue him in *trespass*, and recover damages for assault merely; for here is something more than mere threats. Again, if one unlawfully *beat* me, I may sue him in trespass and recover damages for such battery. Every battery, of course, includes an assault, and hence this injury is commonly called an *assault and battery*. The degree of violence is of no further consequence than to enhance or reduce the damages; for if one barely touch me unlawfully, it is a battery; and it is no more than a battery, if he wound, maim, or otherwise hurt me, to the very verge of taking life. But the damages to be recovered will be in proportion to the injury; and very exemplary or vindictive damages are often recovered, under the name of *smart money*. I am, of course, supposing that there is no justification for the wrong thus done. For the law permits a parent, master, guardian, or teacher, in reason and moderation, to correct his child, apprentice, ward, or pupil, without becoming a trespasser. So one may defend himself, his property, wife, child, ward, servant, or pupil, against an unlawful attack, if he use no unnecessary violence, without becoming a trespasser. Here the defence is termed *son assault demesne*, meaning that the plaintiff made the first assault. 2. The only wrong to one's *liberty*, is the unlawfully depriving him of it; and it makes no difference whether this be done by confining him in prison or in a private house, or by forcibly detaining him anywhere else. The injury thus done is termed a *false imprisonment*, and the remedy is by an action of trespass, because in any unlawful detention of another, the law presumes force. Nor is the time or manner of the detention material, except to increase or diminish the amount of damages, which are often very great. In addition to this, we have before seen that a speedy restoration to liberty may be had through the writ of *habeas corpus;* so that the remedy for this great wrong is theoretically complete. 3. The *health* of individuals may be injured, without any direct personal violence, by the malpractice of physicians, or by nuisances; and the remedy for such injury is by an action on the *case*. Here, too, on account of the exceeding value of the subject injured, the damages are often very great. 4. (*a*) The *character* of a man strictly signifies what he is in himself, independently of the opinion others may entertain of him. When, therefore, we speak of defamation of character, we use terms inaccurately. But the *reputation* of a man depends wholly upon the estimation in which others hold him, and may therefore be injured by defamation. The remedy for such injury is by an action on the case, because the thing affected being intangible, cannot be the subject of direct violence. *Slander* may be either spoken or written. In the latter case it is called a *libel*. In either case, the words must be both false and malicious, in order to constitute a civil injury. The law makes an important distinction between words which are actionable in themselves, and those which only become actionable by alleging and proving some special damage. Words actionable in themselves, and requiring no proof

(*a*) As we have before seen, the truth is a complete defence to an indictment; if the libel was "published with good motives, and for justifiable ends." And the Code provides that in a civil action, "the defendant may allege the truth of the matter charged as defamatory, and may prove the same, and any mitigating circumstances to reduce the amount of damages, or he may prove either." The Code also dispenses with the very awkward and clumsy allegations termed *innuendoes*, § 124, 125. As to *privileged communications*, meaning those which, from the occasion, do not carry the presumption of malice, which would otherwise arise from the publication, see {Liles *v.* Gaster, 42 Ohio State, 631; Lanning *v.* Christy, 30 id. 115}; Wright *v.* Woodgate, 2 Cromp. M. & R. 573; Child *v.* Affleck, 9 B. & C. 403; Lake *v.* King, 1 Saund. 131; Astley *v.* Younge, 2 Burr. 807; The King *v.* Creevey, 1 Maule & S. 273; Oliver *v.* Bentwick, 3 Taunton, 456; Woodward *v.* Lander, 25 E. C. L. Rep. 537; Warr *v.* Jolly, 25 id. 508; Cockayne *v.* Hodgkisson, 24 id. 448; Howard *v.* Thompson, 21 Wendell, 319; Cook *v.* Hill, 2 Sandf. S. C. Rep. 341; Forbes *v.* Johnson, 11 B. Monr. 48; Somerville *v.* Hawkins, 3 Eng. L. & E. Rep. 503; Taylor *v.* Hawkins, 5 id. 253; Harrison *v.* Bush, 32 id. 173; Curtis *v.* Mussey, 6 Gray, 261. The better opinion is, that this defence cannot be set up on demurrer, because malice is a question for the jury. White *v.* Nichols, 3 How. 266; Fry *v.* Bennett, 5 Sandford, 72; Cooper *v.* Stone, 24 Wendell, 442; Budington *v.* Davis, 6 How. Prac. Rep. 401. The making, hearing, and deciding upon accusations against their members, by churches and religious societies, and pronouncing the decision, when done in good faith and according to the discipline and usages of the church and society, is a privileged communication; but it loses this character on proof of actual malice. Farnsworth *v.* Storrs, 5 Cush. 412; Fairchild *v.* Adams, 11 id. 59; Dial *v.* Holter, 6 Ohio State, 228. The same rule applies to the proceedings of other associations. Barrows *v.* Bell, 7 Gray, 301. The publication of a correct account of the proceedings in a court of justice is generally a privileged communication. But the privilege does not extend to the publication of preliminary proceedings of an *ex parte* character. Such publication can only be justified by showing its truth. Cincinnati Gazette Co. *v.* Timberlake, 10 Ohio State, 548.

of special damage, are those which charge another with any thing criminal, or which would exclude him from society, or which would injure him in his business. (*a*) Any other words require proof of actual damage under a *per quod*, because the law does not presume it. A libel may consist of words only, or of signs, pictures, caricatures, and the like; and on account of the more permanent nature of the injury, many words would be actionable in themselves when published, which would not be so when merely spoken. To make libellous matter actionable, it seems only necessary that it should bring one into public hatred, contempt, or ridicule. The only remaining injury to the reputation is that which results from a *malicious prosecution*, which may be either a civil or a criminal prosecution. To support the action for this injury, there must be *malice*, either express or implied, *want of probable cause* for the prosecution, and an injury to the defendant, either in his liberty by the imprisonment, in his reputation by the disgrace, or in his property by the expense. (*b*) The remedy is by an action on the case. 5. The *domestic comfort* of individuals may be affected by the following injuries, for which the law affords a remedy: ***First***, a husband may maintain trespass for the abduction of his wife, whether forcibly or by persuasion. (*c*) So he may maintain trespass for the battery of his wife, whereby he loses her society for a time. So he may maintain trespass for adultery with his wife. In the cases of abduction and adultery, the action is trespass, because the wife cannot in the eye of the law give her consent. In the case of battery, the husband and wife must join in the action, unless where he proceeds under a *per quod* for the special injury he sustains by loss of her society. The old expression was *per quod consortium amisit*. ***Secondly***, a parent may maintain trespass, and perhaps

(*a*) The general rule of the common law is, that where the charge, if true, would subject the plaintiff to an indictment for a crime involving moral turpitude, or to an infamous punishment, the words are actionable in themselves; otherwise, not. Alfele *v.* Wright, 17 Ohio State, 238. Words spoken of another, charging him with maliciously removing the corner-stone of lands, are, *per se*, actionable. Dial *v.* Holter, 6 Ohio State, 228. Evidence of particular facts and circumstances calculated to have misled the party publishing the slander, also of a common report of the truth of the alleged charge, is admissible to rebut the presumption of malice. Evidence of other actionable words, or libels, is admissible to show the *quo animo*. Vanderveer *v.* Sutphin, 5 Ohio State, 293; Reynolds *v.* Tucker, 6 id. 516. When the truth of the words spoken is pleaded in defence in good faith, the plaintiff is not entitled to exemplary damages on account of a failure to sustain it, nor should it be regarded as an aggravation of the injury sustained by the defendant. Rayner *v.* Kinney, 14 Ohio State, 283. { *Contra*, if recklessly uttered, though under belief of truth. Hayner *v.* Cowden, 27 id. 292. }

(*b*) {The prosecution must also have terminated, and favorably to the plaintiff. } To rebut malice, the defendant may show that at the time he commenced the prosecution, he believed the defendant guilty; that he stated the facts he knew to a magistrate, and upon his assurance that such facts constituted the crime charged, he instituted the prosecution. White *v.* Tucker, 16 Ohio State, 468. A conviction of a party by a jury, even upon false testimony, and though the verdict is subsequently set aside, is conclusive evidence of a probable cause for the prosecution. Parker *v.* Huntington, 7 Gray, 36.

(*c*) { But not against her parents seeking to protect their daughter. Holtz *v.* Dick, 42 Ohio State, 23. By a wife for enticing away her husband. Westlake *v.* Westlake, 34 Ohio State, 621. }

case, for seducing and debauching his daughter. But so little does the law profess to regard wounded feelings as a cause of action, that in this case the damage must be laid under a *per quod* for the loss of service, *per quod servitium amisit.* The slightest proof of service, however, will be sufficient to maintain the action, and then the jury may give damages to any extent they see proper for wounded feelings. The same doctrine has been held in regard to an adopted daughter, and even a niece. And it would seem that on the ground of loss of service, a parent might maintain trespass for the battery of his child, or case, for enticing the child away. (*a*) *Thirdly*, a master has a similar remedy for seducing, beating, or enticing away his apprentice or servant; except that he can have no damages for wounded feelings. But it would seem that a guardian could have no such remedy with respect to his ward, unless the relation of master and servant existed.

Wrongs to Real Property. (*b*) All wrongs to *real property*

(*a*) {As to grandparent's right when he has the custody. Clark *v.* Bayer, 32 Ohio State, 299.}

(*b*) The action of *ejectment* is superseded by the Code. Its nature has been before described. In this note, therefore, I shall give some account of other actions having relation to land.

1. *Forcible Entry and Detainer.* This action, under the name of *Forcible Entry* and *Detention*, is regulated by the act of 1853, which may be regarded as a supplement to the Code; § 125–38. It may be brought whenever there is an unlawful and forcible entry and detention, or, the entry being lawful, an unlawful and forcible detention. This will include all judicial sales where the defendant holds over; all sales by executors, administrators, guardians, and on partition, where any of the parties holds over; and all other cases where one without color of title holds over against one who has the right of possession. It is tried on three days' notice before a justice of the peace, with a jury, if either party claims it. The proceeding may be reviewed by petition in error, but no judgment is a bar to another action {but the judgment of the common pleas is not reviewable on error. Rothwell *v.* Unterstein, 42 Ohio State, 249}. The writ of possession must be executed within ten days after judgment. For decisions upon prior statutes, see Murphy *v.* Lucas, 2 Ohio, 255; Yager *v.* Wilber, 8 id. 398; Kelly *v.* Hunter, 12 id. 216; Aubrey *v.* Almy, 4 Ohio State, 524.

Trespass Quare Clausum. There must be actual possession to maintain this action. A right of possession is not sufficient. Beggs *v.* Thompson, 2 Ohio, 95; Miller *v.* Fulton, 4 id. 433. The actual owner, not in possession, is liable to be sued. Wilber *v.* Paine, 1 Ohio, 251; and see Dabney *v.* Manning, 3 id. 321; Rowland *v.* Rowland, 8 id. 40. Prior to the statute abolishing the distinction between trespass and case, a corporation could not be sued in trespass, either alone or with others. Foote *v.* Cincinnati, 9 Ohio, 31. Where several are concerned in the trespass, they may be sued jointly or separately, but there can be only one satisfaction. Wright *v.* Lathrop, 2 Ohio, 33; Ellis *v.* Bitzer, 2 id. 89.

Trespass for Mesne Profits. This action is consequent upon ejectment. Adams on Ejec. 327–34; 2 Chitty, Pl. 435. The judgment is conclusive of the right, back to the date of the demise, and beyond that assumpsit will lie. Sinnard *v.* M'Bride, 3 Ohio, 264. But a purchaser at sheriff's sale, who has been kept out of possession, cannot maintain the action. Beggs *v.* Thompson, 2 Ohio, 95. Nor can an ejected tenant, under a lease allowing him to remove buildings, set off their value in defence to this action. Worthington *v.* Younge, 8 Ohio, 401. As to the provision in the Code, see M'Kinney *v.* M'Kinney, 8 Ohio State, 423.

Action for Waste. The statute of Marlbridge, 1268, gave an action to recover full damages for waste against tenants occupying under lease. 1 Cruise, Dig. 69. The statute of Gloucester, 1277, gave an action to recover the place wasted, and treble damages against all tenants. The statute of Anne, 1708, exempted tenants from accidental damages. And there was an ancient writ of *estrepement* which authorized the sheriff to prevent waste. 3 Black. Com. 225; 4 Kent, Com. 77, 80. The more modern *writ of waste* also authorized the recovery of the place wasted, and treble damages.

must consist in detaining the possession from him who is entitled thereto, or doing some injury to the property without detaining the possession. 1. Real actions not being in use here, the general remedy, where possession of land is unlawfully withheld, is *ejectment*, which may be maintained against the person wrongfully in possession, by any one who has a legal right to such possession. But for certain cases requiring a more speedy remedy, as where one unlawfully and forcibly enters and detains the premises of another, or having lawfully entered, unlawfully and forcibly detains the same, a more summary remedy has been provided in this State, by an action for *forcible entry and detainer*, to be tried before a justice of the peace. At common law, this forcible entry and detainer was an indictable offence, but is not so here. In addition to these general remedies, there are proceedings in dower and partition, as will be seen hereafter, adapted to those particular claims; and a court of chancery will often enable one to recover possession of land when there is no remedy at law. 2. For injuries done to real property without detaining the possession, the general rule is, that if the injuries be forcible, the remedy is *trespass*, if not *case;* these being the only actions which can be maintained for such injuries. The theory of the law is, that the land of every person is enclosed and set apart from that of his neighbor, either by a visible and tangible fence, or by an ideal and invisible boundary; and therefore every unwarrantable entry upon the land of another is deemed a forcible breaking of his close, and the remedy is by an action of *trespass quare clausum fregit.*

Id. But those have never been in force here. The remedy has been an action on the case, to recover simple damages for the waste committed, unless in case of dower, when by statute the place itself is forfeited.

Action for a Nuisance. Where the alleged nuisance is a dam erected across a water-course, some actual damage must be proved. Cooper *v.* Hall, 5 Ohio, 320. Injury to health will be sufficient. Story *v.* Hammond, 4 Ohio, 376. Damages may be recovered in Ohio, though occasioned by the diversion of a watercourse in Pennsylvania. Thayer *v.* Brooks, 17 Ohio, 489. And one digging away the bank of a stream on his own land is liable for flooding land below him. Byrd *v.* Blessing, 11 Ohio State, 362. The vendee of land in possession, under an existing contract of sale, is not liable to an action by the vendor for an injury to the land. Stauffer *v.* Eaton, 13 Ohio, 322. Where the owner below grants land above, with the privilege of draining the creek as low as he pleases at all times, he cannot sue, though the creek be wholly diverted. Potter *v.* Burton, 15 Ohio, 196. When a city has established a grade, and improvements are made with reference to it, and the grade is afterwards changed, the city is liable for damages thereby occasioned. Goodloe *v.* Cincinnati, 4 Ohio, 500; McCombs *v.* Akron, 15 Ohio, 474; Akron *v.* McCombs, 18 Ohio, 229; Crawford *v.* Delaware, 7 Ohio State, 459. But this doctrine is not held, I believe, in any other State. Radcliff *v.* Mayor, &c. of Brooklyn, 4 Comst. 195, and cases there cited.

Actions for the Use or Price of Land. The action for use and occupation presupposes a tenantry. Butler *v.* Cowles, 4 Ohio, 205; Richey *v.* Hinde, 6 id. 371; Moore *v.* Beasley, 3 id. 294. It may have been under a parol lease or a void lease. Wilson *v.* Trustees, 8 Ohio, 174. The action will not lie where the tenant holds adversely; nor by a purchaser, on foreclosure, against a tenant of the mortgagor. Peters *v.* Elkins, 14 Ohio, 344. The action may be in debt or assumpsit, and the common count is sufficient; Armstrong *v.* Clark, 17 Ohio, 495; unless there be something peculiar in the contract. Tullis *v.* Wiley, 6 Ohio, 294; Potts *v.* Rider, 3 id. 70. Where the title to land fails in part or in the whole, the purchase-money may be recovered to the extent of the failure. Taft *v.* Wildman, 15 Ohio, 123; Michael *v.* Mills, 17 id. 601.

In order to maintain this action, the plaintiff must at the time have the actual possession of the land, which alone will be sufficient against a mere intruder. But if the defendant entered under color of title, then the plaintiff must show a legal right of possession. This is regarded as merely a possessory action; and therefore a person entitled to the emblements or vesture of land, may maintain trespass even against the owner of the land, who forcibly prevents him from taking them away. We have seen that in ejectment the damages are merely nominal, the main object of the action being to recover possession. If, therefore, the plaintiff would recover damages for the wrongful detention of the land, or in other words, the intermediate profits during the period of wrongful possession, he must bring a separate action, which is termed *trespass for mesne profits.* Of the injuries to land not accompanied by force, one of the most frequent is that of *waste*, which we have seen to be, where the tenant for life or years does some permanent injury to the inheritance, with respect to the buildings, timber, or soil; and the remedy is by action on the *case*, because the wrong-doer is rightfully in possession. Another injury is *slander of title*, which is redressed by an action on the *case*. But there is rarely occasion for such remedy now, because the goodness or badness of title is readily ascertained by searching the records, and, therefore, the most false and malicious assertions respecting it can do very little harm. The remaining injuries to land may be classed under the general head of *nuisances*, the remedy for which, besides abatement of the nuisance, is an action on the *case*. The most important of these nuisances are, overhanging another's dwelling so as to throw the water upon his roof; obstructing another's ancient lights, that is, lights enjoyed for twenty years or more; corrupting the atmosphere with noisome smells, so as to render another's residence unhealthful or uncomfortable, and overflowing another's land by diverting or interrupting established watercourses. This part of our law relating to realty furnishes a strong contrast to the corresponding portion of the English law in respect to its simplicity. Blackstone devotes to it seven chapters, replete with technical learning about *abatement*, *intrusion*, *disseisin*, *discontinuance*, *deforcement*, *subtraction*, and *disturbance*, with all of which we may dispense entirely, unless we choose to study it as a matter of curiosity.

Wrongs to personal property may be considered, *first*, with reference to things in possession, and *secondly*, with reference to things in action. First, *things in possession* are liable to two kinds of injuries: namely, wrongful deprivation of possession, and abuse without deprivation of possession; with respect to which the following general rules may be laid down. 1. If goods be wrongfully taken from my possession, whether I be the absolute owner or only entitled to the temporary possession thereof, I may bring *trespass de bonis asportatis*, for such wrongful taking; or waiving the wrongful taking, I may bring *trover* for the wrongful detention; or, if I would recover the specific goods, rather than their value, together with damages for the detention, I may bring *detinue* or *replevin*. If the original taking were rightful, and the detention only is wrongful, I cannot bring *trespass*, but must choose between *trover*, *detinue*, and *replevin*. 3. If goods be forcibly injured while in my rightful possession, I may bring *trespass*, and, perhaps, waiving the force, I may bring *case*, but this is doubtful. 4. If goods in my rightful possession be injured through the neglect or misconduct of another, without force, my only remedy is *case;* for trover, detinue, and replevin presuppose a wrongful possession in the defendant. 5. If my goods, rightfully in the temporary possession of another, be injured in any way not amounting to a *conversion*, whether by force, neglect, or misconduct, my only remedy is an action on the *case*.

Secondly, *things in action*, consisting of contracts and legal obligations, are liable only to one kind of injury, namely, non-performance; but the nature of the remedy varies according to the nature of the obligation; respecting which the following rules may be laid down: 1. If a debt, technically so called, be due me, that is, a sum of money already liquidated, or capable of being liquidated with certainty, whether it be a statutory penalty, or a voluntary indebtedness by contract under seal, or writing without seal, or simply implied by law, I may bring the action of *debt*. 2. If this liquidated sum be evidenced by a contract under seal, I have an option between *debt* and *covenant;* and if by a contract not under seal, whether express or implied, I have an option between *debt* and *assumpsit*. 3. If there be a contract for any thing else than a liquidated sum of money, and it be under seal, the only remedy is *covenant;* and if not under seal, the only remedy is *assumpsit*.

§ 210. **Process.** (*a*) The preceding remarks have prepared the student to answer the first question of practice; namely, what is the proper action to be brought? The next inquiry is, how is such action to be commenced and prosecuted? Judicial proceedings naturally divide themselves into five parts. 1. The *process*, including the means whereby the parties are brought before the court. 2. The *pleadings*, including the means of making up an issue between the parties. 3. The *trial*, including what relates to jurors and witnesses. 4. The *judgment*, including what relates to appeals and writs of error. 5. The *execution*, including the means of carrying the judgment into effect. I am to speak first, then, of *process*, a term which embraces all writs and orders issued by courts to their executive officers in the course of judicial proceedings. In England, where the king is in theory the fountain

(*a*) With respect to the federal courts, the act of Congress of 1798 adopted the State laws in regard to process as they existed in 1789. The act of 1828 adopts the State laws, in regard to final process both in law and equity, as they then existed; but provides that the federal courts may by rules conform such process to the alterations since made by State laws. See Bronson *v.* Kinzie, 1 Howard, 311; Duncan *v.* Darst, id. 301.

of justice, the first step in any civil action is to obtain an *original writ*, (*a*) which is a mandatory letter in the king's name and under the great seal, issuing out of the court of chancery, and commanding the defendant to satisfy the plaintiff, or else appear in the proper court and answer for his default. This writ is there deemed necessary to give the courts of law jurisdiction. In modern practice, however, it is usually dispensed with by recourse to a fiction, and a proceeding by bill substituted. But in this country there is no occasion for an original writ, and nothing in the nature of a proceeding by bill. Our courts derive their jurisdiction from the constitution, and require no writ to confer it in particular cases. Accordingly, all process is here divided into *mesne* and *final;* the former signifying all process before judgment, and the latter all process after judgment. The constitution requires all process to issue in the name of the State; but it issues under the seal of the proper court, and is attested by the clerk. As a general rule, all courts are invested with power to enforce obedience to any process they are authorized to issue. We have express provision to this effect, though the power would exist incidentally. Disobedience is technically denominated a *contempt*, (*b*) and may be punished by attachment, fine, imprisonment, and sometimes sequestration of property. Moreover, the officer who is charged with executing any process may call to his aid the *posse comitatus*, or power of the county; and it is made the duty of every person to render assistance when called upon, under penalties for refusal. Even the military force of the county may be called out, if necessary. The theory is, that every writ, properly issued, must be obeyed at all hazards.

Precipe. (*c*) The first step, then, is to procure the proper writ

(*a*) Steph. on Plead. 5.

(*b*) Until a recent date, the power of courts to punish contempts has been left to their discretion, controlled only by precedents. By our statute of 1834, it is confined to three classes of cases. 1. To the misbehavior of any person in their presence, or so near as to obstruct the administration of justice. 2. To the misbehavior of their officers in their official transactions. 3. To disobedience or resistance, by any person, to any lawful writ, process, order, rule, decree, or command of said courts. And see State *v.* Goff, Wright, 78; State *v.* Coulter, id. 421; State *v.* Nixon, id. 763; Morris *v.* Marcy, 4 Ohio, 83; Lowe *v.* The State, 9 Ohio State, 337; Baldwin *v.* The State, 11 Ohio State, 681; Coe *v.* Columbus, P. & I. R. R. Co., 10 Ohio State, 372; in the matter of Hackley, 24 N. Y. 74; Shaw *v.* Shaw, 2 Swab. & T. 519; *Ex parte* Chetwynd, *Re* Mulock, 4 Am. Law Register (N. S.), 298; *Ex parte* Langdon, 25 Vt. 680; 32 Vt. 253; id. 258; Clarke's case, 12 Cush. 320. The power to punish contempt is inherent in legislative and judicial tribunals; and see as to the practice in such cases, State *v.* Mathews, 37 N. H. 450. A party committed until he purge the contempt by appearing before the grand jury, is entitled to his discharge when the grand jury has been discharged. *Ex parte* Maulsby, 13 Md. 625.

(*c*) Under the Code, the first step is to file a *petition*, setting forth purely the cause of action, which corresponds to a declaration in law, a bill in chancery, and a libel in admiralty, and must be verified by affidavit. And this petition must be accompanied by a precipe; § 55–60. And see as to Precipe, Coffee *v.* The State, 6 Ohio, 150.

Precipe. A. B. *v.* C. D. } Court of ——— Action of ——— Damages ——— dollars.

The clerk of the court of ——— for ——— county, Ohio, will issue a writ of ——— returnable ———, and indorse that suit is brought to [describe briefly the cause of action]. [Date.] E. F., Atty. for Pltf.

to be issued. This is done by delivering to the clerk a *precipe*, which is a brief written order to him to issue the writ required. It may be made by the plaintiff or his attorney, but usually by the latter. It names the court, the parties, the action, the writ, and the damages, in all which respects the writ and pleadings must correspond with the precipe. The only action, in which no precipe is required, is ejectment, where a copy of the declaration and notice takes the place of a writ. Upon filing the precipe, it is the duty of the clerk to obey it in a reasonable time; and if he fail to do so he is liable in damages on his official bond. The only part of the precipe which is entirely discretionary is the *damages*, as to which the rule is to lay them high enough, to cover all that can by possibility be recovered; since you cannot recover more than you claim, though you may less. If the writ required be a *capias*, *attachment*, or *replevin*, which, by the law of this State, do not issue as a matter of course, at the mere suggestion of the plaintiff, but only when certain facts exist, which are specified in the statute, these facts authorizing the writ must be evidenced by *affidavit* of the plaintiff, his agent, or attorney. An affidavit is a written oath or affirmation, subscribed by the party making it, and certified by some officer qualified to administer oaths. In these cases, the affidavit must accompany the precipe. In describing the parties to the writ, their additions, occupations, or titles need not be stated. If they have a middle name, the initial letter only need be used; but otherwise the full name. In describing partners, the individual names are first stated, and then the partnership name. In describing a corporation, care must be taken to use the exact name mentioned in the charter, since it can only be known by that name. The cause of action must be substantially set forth in the precipe, so that the clerk may indorse it on the writ; otherwise the court will, on motion, quash the writ at the costs of the plaintiff. The writs by which an action is ordinarily commenced are *summons*, *capias*, *attachment*, and *replevin*. But before considering these, I will briefly describe the writs of *scire facias*, *habeas corpus*, *mandamus*, and *quo warranto*, which are resorted to on particular occasions.

Scire Facias. (*a*) This is the name of a writ founded upon some matter of record, as a judgment or recognizance; its purpose being to notify the party against whom it issues, to show cause why some step founded upon such record should not be taken against him. In this State, the cases in which it may be issued are pointed out by statute; and it is sometimes in the nature of a new action, but more generally a consummation of some former action. The cases in which it may be here issued are as follows: 1. To make joint defendants, who were not served with process originally, parties to a judgment already recovered against their co-defendants. 2. To obtain further damages on a

(*a*) 6 Dane's Abr. 462; Wilcox's Forms, 231; Wolf *v.* Poundsford, 4 Ohio, 397.

penal bond, after an original judgment for the whole penalty, in consequence of new breaches of the condition of such bond after such original judgment. 3. To revive a judgment in favor of the executor or administrator of a deceased plaintiff, or against the executor or administrator of a deceased defendant, when the plaintiff or defendant has died after judgment; for if the death took place before judgment, they are made parties to the suit by citation. 4. To revive a dormant judgment, that is, a judgment on which no execution has been issued for five years. 5. To make the sureties of a sheriff parties to a judgment of amercement against him for neglect of duty. 6. To subject real estate to the satisfaction of a judgment rendered by a justice of the peace, when there is no personal property to satisfy such judgment. 7. To obtain satisfaction for any injury arising from the neglect of duty of any executor, administrator, or other officer, after judgment has been recovered on his official bond, in favor of some other person. 8. To compel special bail to satisfy the judgment recovered against their principal. 9. To obtain satisfaction of a judgment against the principal in favor of bail, who have been compelled to pay such judgment. In all these cases, the writ of *scire facias* recites the facts which authorize it to be issued, and then commands the sheriff to make known to the party, against whom it issues, that he appear in court and show cause, if any there be, why the contemplated step should not be taken against him. If he can be found, the sheriff serves him with a copy of the writ, and returns, *scire feci;* if not found, the sheriff returns *nihil;* and in proceedings against special bail, two returns of *nihil* are held equivalent to service. All proceedings by *scire facias* have this peculiarity, that the writ itself operates as a declaration, and may be pleaded or demurred to, as will be explained hereafter.

Habeas Corpus. (*a*) The nature of this writ has already been described. We have seen that it is the great writ of liberty, and that it may be issued in favor of any person unlawfully detained in the custody of another, whether under color of legal process, or the right of a parent, master, or guardian, or any other pretext whatsoever. Application may be made in writing, by the person

(*a*) *Ante*, p. 205. The proceedings on the writ are not affected by the Code, § 604; but are regulated by the statute of 1811. See act of March 27, 1858, restoring section six of the act of Jan. 22, 1811, and section nine of the act of Feb. 8, 1847, and repealing the act of April 5, 1856, which repealed those sections.

The form is as follows: The State of ——, county of ——. To —— [the person detaining the applicant]. We command you that you have the body of ——, said to be detained in your custody, together with the cause of his detention, before [the court or judge], at ——, on the —— [name the day and hour], to abide such order as shall then and there be made in this behalf; and have you then and there this writ with your doings thereon. Given under the seal of said court this [date]. Attest ——, clerk. [Seal of court.]

The return may be as follows: I have the body of said —— before the [court or judge], pursuant to the within order; and do certify that the said —— was by me taken into custody on the ——, and is now detained by virtue of [here set forth the authority for detention]. [Date and signature.]

imprisoned, or any other person in his behalf, to either of the courts in term time, or any judge thereof in vacation. If the cause of detention be legal process, it must be set forth in the application. If not, the truth of the application must be evidenced by affidavit. If the court or judge allow the writ, such allowance is indorsed on the application, and the time is fixed for the return of the writ. The writ is addressed to the person holding the applicant in custody, and directs him to have the body of the applicant, together with the cause of detention, before the court or judge at the time specified. Any disinterested person may serve the writ, by delivering it to the person to whom it is addressed, and retaining a copy to proceed upon in case of default. The writ is returned by bringing the person detained before the court, and setting forth the cause of detention in writing. The court or judge then examines into the cause of detention, and either remands the person back into custody, or discharges him, or holds him to bail, as the facts of the case may warrant.

Mandamus. (*a*) At common law this was a prerogative writ, and not a writ of right. In this State, it is provided for by

(*a*) High, Moses, Wood, Tapping, on Mandamus. Proceedings on *mandamus* are regulated by the Code. The writ may be issued to any inferior tribunal, corporation, board, or person, to compel the performance of a duty prescribed by law to any office, trust, or station, but not so as to control judicial discretion. It may be issued on the information of the party beneficially interested, supported by affidavit. The allowance must be indorsed on the writ by the judge who grants it. The return is made by answer, and there are no other pleadings. Beckel *v.* Union Township, 9 Ohio State, 599; Johnes *v.* Auditor, 4 id. 493; State *v.* Commissioners of Perry Co., 5 id. 497. The issues are tried as in any other civil action. There may be a judgment for damages, § 6753. The law of *mandamus* is very fully discussed in Marbury *v.* Madison, 1 Cranch, 137; Kendall *v.* Stokes, 12 Peters, 524; Decatur *v.* Paulding, 14 id. 497; Brashear *v.* Mason, 6 How. 92; U. S. *v.* Seaman, 17 id. 225; U. S. *v.* Guthrie, 17 id. 284; U. S. *v.* Addison, 22 id. 174. And see State *v.* Trustees, 2 Ohio, 108; State *v.* Com. Pleas, 3 id. 49; State *v.* Todd, 4 id. 351; State *v.* Moffit, 5 id. 358; Cases of Turner & Kazer, 5 id. 542, 544; Universal Church *v.* Trustees, 6 id. 445; Burnet *v.* Auditor, 12 id. 54; Smith *v.* Commissioners, 9 id. 25; State *v.* Treasurer, 17 id. 32, 184; State *v.* Auditor, 19 id. 116, 125; State *v.* Cincinnati, 19 id. 178; State *v.* Commissioners, 19 id. 415; State *v.* Bailey, 7 Clarke (Iowa), 390; Hollister *v.* Judges of District Court, 8 Ohio State, 201; The State *v.* Governor of Ohio, 5 id. 528; City of Zanesville *v.* Auditor of Muskingum Co., id. 589; Shelby *v.* Hoffman, 7 id. 450; Cass Township *v.* Dillon, 16 Ohio State, 39; The State *ex rel.* Anderson *v.* Harris, 17 Ohio State, 608; The State *ex rel.* Hayes *v.* C. & I. R. R. Co., 17 Ohio State, 103; The State *v.* Lewis, 10 Ohio State, 128. The court will not by mandamus compel a party to do what by a subsisting decree of injunction he is prohibited from doing, although the party seeking the remedy by mandamus is not a party to the decree of injunction. Ohio and Indiana R. R. Co. *v.* Commissioners of Wyandot Co., 7 id. 278. Though an inferior board or tribunal failed to perform a ministerial duty at the proper time, a mandamus will not issue to compel its performance if it is no longer consistent with the substantial rights of other parties, or with public interests. Nor will it issue when it must evidently be abortive and fruitless. Ingerson *v.* Berry, 14 Ohio State, 315. Obligations arising upon contract merely, and involving no trust, cannot be enforced by mandamus. Ross Co. *v.* Z. & M. Turnpike Co., 16 Ohio State, 308. It will not lie to compel a judge who has once considered and decided a case to hear it again. *Ex parte* Newman, 14 Wall. 152. Before an officer will be required by mandamus to do an act, the application must show that all the evidence required by the statute upon which he is to act was placed before him. Cincinnati College *v.* La Rue, 22 Ohio State, 469.

statute. Its object is to compel the performance of some public duty, by some public person, when there is no other specific legal remedy. It may be addressed to any public officer, corporation, or inferior court, requiring them to do some specific legal act, agreeably to law. It presupposes a neglect of duty, and never issues for a mere lack of discretion. Its most common purpose is to enforce the admission of a person to an office to which he has been legally elected; or his restoration to an office from which he has been illegally removed. It issues at the instance of the party injured, upon proper showing made to the court, and not as a matter of course. On application for a mandamus, the first step is to issue an alternative mandamus, reciting the facts making out the delinquency, and commanding the delinquent to do the thing required, or show cause for the omission. This is sometimes called a *rule to show cause* why a mandamus should not issue; and the court will hear argument in opposition to this application. If the rule be granted, and the delinquent on being served refuse to make any return, he is in contempt, and may be proceeded against by attachment. If return be made, and the cause shown be not sufficient, it may be demurred to. If not true, it may be pleaded to and the issue tried by a jury. If the verdict be against the delinquent, instead of sending the injured party to his action upon the false return, as was the common-law rule, the court will render judgment for the damages and costs. And in addition thereto, whenever the judgment is against the delinquent, a peremptory mandamus will be ordered forthwith. If the delinquent refuse obedience, he is fined at the discretion of the court.

Quo Warranto. (a) This is the name of a writ which, at common law, might be issued against persons or corporations claiming to exercise any office or franchise, for the purpose of inquiring into their authority, and ousting them from such office or franchise, in case no authority should be shown. But in modern practice an *information*, in the nature of a *quo warranto*, is most frequently resorted to; and such is the practice in this State, as regulated by statute. This information is filed on leave granted by the court in term time, or one of the judges in vacation, by the prosecuting attorney or attorney-general, either on his own relation or that of any individual, or when directed by the governor, general assembly, or supreme court. When the relation is made by an individual, it must be evidenced by his affidavit. The cases provided for are as follows: 1. When any person shall usurp any public office, civil or military, or any franchise, or any office in a private corporation. 2. When any civil or military officer shall

(a) Proceedings on *quo warranto* were not affected by the Code; but regulated by the act of 1838 {until 1880. They now are civil actions under the Code. State *ex rel.* *v.* Thompson, 34 Ohio State, 365}. And see Ohio R. R. Co. *v.* Ohio, 10 Ohio, 360; State *v.* Granville, 11 id. 1; State *v.* Jacobs, 17 id. 143; State *v.* Beecher, 15 id. 753, and 16 id. 358; Bank of Mt. Pleasant, 5 id. 249; State *v.* Moffit, 5 id. 358; State *v.* Bryce, 7 id. 2 pt. 82; Hullman *v.* Honcomp, 5 Ohio State, 237; State *v.* Buckland, 5 id. 216. See *ante*, p. 81, note.

have done or suffered any act which works a forfeiture of his office. 3. When any association of persons shall assume to act as a corporation without being incorporated. 4. When any corporation shall have violated its charter, or forfeited it by non-user, or done any act amounting to a surrender, or misused or usurped any franchise. The information sets forth specifically the facts which form the predicate of the proceeding, and is in the nature of a declaration. On motion for leave to file it, the court may order notice to be given to the opposite party, and hear argument in opposition. When the information has been filed, a summons issues, which is served and returned as in other cases. The defendant may then demur or plead to the information, and the issue is tried as will be described hereafter. When the complaint is for usurping an office claimed by other persons, their claims are set forth in the information, and the judgment will embrace an ouster of the usurper, and an admission of the rightful claimant. (*a*) The latter may also bring his action on the case for damages against the former, at any time within one year after the judgment. When the proceeding is against a corporation to enforce a forfeiture, it must be commenced within five years. Upon judgment of forfeiture, trustees are appointed to wind up its concerns; and an action on the case for damages may be brought against the officers of the corporation, by any person injured, at any time within three years from the judgment. When the proceeding is for usurping a franchise not granted by the charter, it must be commenced within twenty years, and in this case the judgment is that of ouster only. Obedience is enforced, as in other cases, by an attachment for contempt.

Summons. (*b*). This is the name of a writ, *commanding the sheriff to summon the defendant to appear in court on a given day, and answer to the charge of the plaintiff.* If issued in term time, it is made *returnable* forthwith. If in vacation, it is made return-

(*a*) A judgment of ouster may be rendered without passing upon the rights of the claimant who files the application. Gano *v.* The State, 10 Ohio State, 237. {Nor does it affect persons not parties. Society Perun *v.* Cleveland, 43 Ohio State, 481. Nor destroy prior contracts. Gaff *v.* Flesher, 33 id. 107, 115.} Where a specific mode is prescribed for contesting elections, that must be followed. State *v.* Marlow, 15 Ohio State, 114.

(*b*) The Code makes the summons the first process in all cases; requires it to be returnable the second Monday after date, unless to another county, and then the third or fourth Monday at option. R. S. § 5039. The following is the usual form:—

Form of Summons. The State of ——, county of ——. To the sheriff of said county [or coroner if the sheriff cannot act]. We command you to summon —— [the defendant] to appear before our [describe the court] forthwith [or on the first day of the next term, as the case may be], to answer unto —— [the plaintiff], in an action of ——, in damages $——; and have you then and there this writ, with your doings thereon. Given under the seal of said court, this [date]. Attest, ——, clerk. [Seal of court.]

I have omitted the word "*greeting,*" in the address to the sheriff, as superfluous. Sometimes writs have the following *teste:* "Witness the honorable —— [presiding judge of said court]," — then the date, seal, and attestation of the clerk. But as the judge never signs his own name, this adds nothing to the authority of the writ, and may be omitted. The writ is sufficiently authenticated by the seal of the court and the signature of the clerk.

able to the beginning of the next term; that is, the defendant is notified to appear forthwith, or at the next term, as the case may be. This is in pursuance of the rule, that all process must be returned to the court whence it issued, which can only be when the court is in session. The term to which the writ is returnable is called the *appearance term;* and the time specified, the *return-day.* When it becomes necessary to send process to another county, it is directed to the sheriff thereof.

Service. The execution of the command of the writ is denominated *service.* A summons is *served* by leaving a copy thereof with the defendant, which is called *personal service;* or leaving it at his usual residence, which is called *service by copy.* As no writ is valid after the return-day, it must be served before, and the sheriff is bound to use reasonable diligence. The *return* is indorsed on the back of the writ. If the sheriff return the writ "*served*," the defendant, though he makes no appearance either by himself or attorney, is held to be *in court*, and may be proceeded against accordingly. If the return be "*not found*," another may be issued, called an *alias*, and a third called a *pluries*, and so on, indefinitely. If you believe the defendant, though not found, to be still lurking in the county, you may move the court to have *proclamation* made. This is a warning to the defendant to appear, published three successive days at the door of the court-house, and three times in some newspaper, after which you may proceed as if service had been made. If the defendant removed to another county after issuing the writ, and before service, you may have a writ to that county, which is called *testatum summons*, and differs from the common writ only in *stating the fact* of such removal. This is allowed on the ground that a suit has been already *commenced* in the first county before the removal; the general principle being, that suit must be commenced in the county where the defendant is at that time. But if there be more than one defendant, and residing in different counties, you may select the county where either is found; and if your cause of action be founded on a contract, you may issue to all the other counties; otherwise, you can only proceed against those found in the county where you commence, and may be under the necessity of instituting several suits, in different counties, for the same cause of action. In all cases, however, the true course is to name all the defendants in the first *precipe;* and then the sheriff will state in his return those not found; which statement will authorize the requisite proceedings as to them. The writ follows the precipe, in the description of the parties, the kind of action, and the damages; and hence the necessity for accuracy in the specifications of the precipe. On this writ the clerk indorses the cause of action as stated in the precipe; and if the plaintiff be not a resident of the county, the writ must be indorsed by some responsible freeholder of the county, as security for costs. It is then delivered to the sheriff for service. Usually this is done by the clerk as a matter of accommodation; but the clerk discharges his duty by delivering it to the plaintiff or his attorney. The sheriff is bound to make the service in a reasonable time, if the defendant can be found; and if he fail to do so, or make a false return, he is liable in damages on his official bond. There is also a summary proceeding on motion, called *amercement*, to enforce this liability. When the clerk issues a writ, he enters the suit in its order on the *appearance docket*, by substantially copying the precipe; and when the writ is returned, the substance of such return is also there noted. The same is true of all subsequent proceedings, until the issue is made up, when the suit is transferred to the *issue docket*.

Capias. (*a*) This is the name of a writ *commanding the sheriff to take the defendant and have him before the court to answer the charge of the plaintiff.* It is called a *capias ad respondendum*, to distinguish it from another writ, issued after judgment, called a *capias ad satisfaciendum.* In common language, however, we call the former simply a *capias* and the latter a *ca. sa.* It directs that the defendant be *compelled* to appear, while a summons merely directs that he be *notified.* Like that, it is made returnable forthwith, or to the next term, according as it is issued in term time or vacation. There are, however, certain persons who are *privileged from civil arrest* at all times; there are others who are privileged at particular times; and there are certain times and places, when and where all persons are privileged. *First*, in this State, officers and soldiers of the revolution, and females are privileged at all times. *Secondly*, members and officers of the federal and State legislatures; judges, attorneys, officers of court, jurors, witnesses, and suitors; officers and soldiers of the militia, and voters, are severally privileged, while going to their respective places of duty, while remaining there, and while returning. *Thirdly*, all persons are privileged on Sunday and the fourth of July, and in the halls of the legislature and courts of justice, during the sittings therein. Against these classes of persons, therefore, a *capias* would have no more effect than a summons. But with these exceptions of privilege, the plaintiff may have a *capias* whenever he will make affidavit that the defendant is indebted to him in any sum above one hundred dollars, naming the amount; and that he is about to

(*a*) Under the Code an *order of arrest* takes the place of a *capias*, as one of the *provisional remedies*, and may accompany the summons, or be obtained at any time before judgment, on giving security for damages, and making affidavit of one or more of the five following causes: 1. That the defendant has removed, or begun to remove, any of his property, to defraud his creditors. 2. Has begun to convert it into money for that purpose. 3. Fraudulently conceals it. 4. Has disposed of it, or begun to dispose of it, to defraud creditors. 5. Fraudulently contracted the debt. R. S. § 5492. But no order of arrest can go out of the county. The person arrested may be discharged on depositing with the sheriff the amount named in the order of arrest, or may give bail; otherwise he is committed to jail, and the plaintiff may be required to pay jail fees weekly in advance, which shall be part of the costs in the case. There is no distinction between *appearance* and *special* bail, the stipulation being, that if judgment be recovered against the defendant, he shall render himself amenable to the process of the court. This obligation is discharged by his death, imprisonment in a State prison, or surrender to the sheriff, or by a legal discharge. § 149–73.

remove his property out of the jurisdiction, or convert it into money, or conceal it, or otherwise dispose of it with a view to defraud his creditors; or that he fraudulently contracted the debt; or that he is about to remove his person from the jurisdiction; or that he is not a resident of the State. The affidavit, (*a*) as we have seen, must be filed with the precipe. The indorsement on the *capias* is the same as that on the summons; and the same remarks are applicable with respect to an *alias*, *pluries*, or *testatum capias*. A *capias* is *served* by arresting the defendant. Mere words do not constitute an arrest. The sheriff must touch the body of the defendant, or lock the door upon him, or do some other act of like nature. After once touching him, he may break open his house to take him, but not before. For, till then, a man's house is his *castle* against civil arrest. If, however, the outer door be open, the sheriff may enter, even though he have to break an inner door. If the sheriff, having it in his power, fail to make the arrest; or having made it, suffer the party to escape, he becomes liable to an action for damages on his official bond. When the defendant has been thus arrested, he has an option of three things: *to put in bail; to take the benefit of the insolvent act;* or *to go in jail;* in which latter case he may have the *prison limits.* I shall describe these in their order.

Bail. There are two kinds of bail; namely, *appearance bail*, and *special bail;* sometimes called bail below and bail above. *Appearance bail* is only necessary when a *capias* issues in vacation. It is the bail given *to the sheriff*, for his own indemnification; he being held answerable for the appearance of the defendant from the moment of arrest. It consists of a bond, with such sureties as the sheriff shall approve, in double the amount claimed by the plaintiff, conditioned that the defendant shall appear according to the exigency of the writ. Upon giving appearance bail, the defendant is released from custody, and the sheriff returns a copy of the bail-bond. The condition of this bond is complied with, if the defendant appears according to the exigency of the writ, and either puts in special bail in court, or surrenders himself into the custody of the sheriff. If the defendant fails to do either of these things, the plaintiff has an option of two remedies. He may either take an assignment of the bail-bond from the sheriff, and proceed against the sureties; or he may take a rule

(*a*) *Affidavit for a Capias.* A. B., the above plaintiff [or his agent or attorney], makes oath and says, that C. D., the above defendant, is justly indebted to the above plaintiff in the sum of ——— dollars, in manner and form as stated in the above precipe, and that the above defendant is not a citizen or resident of this State [or some other reason specified in the statute]. A. B.

Jurat. Subscribed and sworn to before me a [official character] this ——— day of ———, in the year ———. E. F.

Writ of Capias [omitting the caption and attestation, which are the same as in a summons]. We command you to take ——— [the defendant] and him safely keep, so that you have his body safely before our [describe the court] forthwith [or on the first day of the next term], to answer unto ——— [the plaintiff], in an action of ——— in damages $——— ; and have you then and there this writ with your doings thereon.

upon the sheriff to bring in the body of the defendant during the term, and, on failure, compel him to pay the debt and costs and look to the sureties in the bond. For the law regards the defendant as in the custody of the sheriff from the moment of arrest until special bail is put in. But the sheriff may, for his own indemnity, put in special bail and await the result of the suit. These steps in default of special bail must be taken before filing the declaration; otherwise the right to special bail is waived. (*a*)

Special bail is given in the form of a *recognizance*, (*b*) in which the defendant and his sureties acknowledge themselves indebted to the plaintiff in double the amount of the claim, which they agree to pay, if default be made in the conditions of the recognizance; which are, that if the plaintiff shall prevail in the suit, the defendant shall either pay the judgment and costs, or surrender himself to the sheriff, or the sureties shall pay for him. Upon giving special bail, the clerk makes out a *bail-piece*, (*c*) purporting that the defendant is bailed or delivered to his sureties; which is sufficient authority for them to take their principal, wherever they can find him, if they become apprehensive that he does not mean to be forthcoming. The sufficiency of the sureties is judged of, in the first instance, by the clerk; but the plaintiff has an opportunity of *objecting*, and thereby requiring them to *justify;* that is, to make oath that they are worth the amount named in the recognizance, after their debts are paid. The subject of bail is one of great intricacy; but in this outline I purposely avoid details; it will be seen by the view presented, that the object of taking bail is not to obtain absolute security for the debt; but only security for the forthcoming of the defendant at the final termination of

(*a*) *Bail Bond.* Be it known that [the defendant and his sureties] are held and firmly bound unto [the sheriff] in the sum of $——— [double the amount indorsed on the writ], for the payment of which we do jointly and severally bind ourselves by these presents, sealed with our seals, and dated this [date]. But the condition of this obligation is, that if the above named [defendant] shall appear before the [describe the court], on the first or second day of their next term to answer to the above [plaintiff], in an action of ———, in damages $———, then this obligation is to be void. [Signed and sealed by the defendant and his sureties.]

(*b*) Enos *v.* Aylesworth, 8 Ohio State, 322; Whetstone *v.* Riley, 7 id. 514. Franks *v.* The State, 12 Ohio State, 1; Calvin *v.* The State, id. 60; State *v.* Williams, 14 Ohio State, 140; Bishop & Randolph *v.* The State, 16 Ohio State, 419.

Recognizance of Special Bail. The State of ———, county of ———. Be it remembered that on this [date] ——— and ——— [the sureties], of the county aforesaid, personally appeared before the [describe the court], and severally acknowledged themselves to owe unto the [plaintiff] the sum of $——— [double the amount indorsed on the writ], to be levied upon their several goods and chattels, upon condition, that if ——— [the defendant] shall be condemned in this action, he shall pay the costs and condemnation of the court, or be rendered or render himself into the custody of the sheriff for the same, or that, in case of failure, the said [sureties] will pay the said costs and condemnation for him. Taken and acknowledged the day and year above written before me ——— [judge or clerk, as the case may be].

(*c*) *Bail-Piece.* The State of ———, county of ———, court of ———. Be it known that ——— [the defendant] of said county, was delivered to bail on a *cepi corpus* unto ——— and ——— [the sureties] of said county, at the suit of ——— [the plaintiff] in an action of ———, this [date]. Attest, ———, clerk. [Seal of court.]

the suit. In theory, the defendant is in the custody of the sheriff from the time of giving appearance bail, until that of giving the special bail; after which the sheriff's liability ceases; and the defendant is considered to be in the custody of the special bail sureties. Thus, by means of bail, the plaintiff has as good security for the final forthcoming of the defendant, at the end of the litigation, as if he had been kept during all this time in the actual custody of the sheriff; but if, at any time, the defendant surrender himself, or be surrendered, into the custody of the sheriff, he is then in the same predicament as if he had not given bail; that is, he must either take the benefit of the act or go to prison. When judgment has been recovered against the defendant, if he do not comply with the condition of the recognizance, the first step in order to fix the bail, is to issue a writ of *capias ad satisfaciendum;* and if this writ be returned "not found," an action of *debt* or *scire facias* may be commenced against the bail on their recognizance, giving fifteen days between the service and return day of the writ; and if within that time the principal be not forthcoming, the bail cannot afterwards discharge themselves by surrendering him. But if, in the mean time, the principal die or be imprisoned, so that he cannot be taken on a bail-piece, this will be a discharge.

Benefit of the Insolvent Act. If the defendant, on being arrested, wishes to avoid giving appearance bail, in the first instance, or special bail afterwards; or if, at any time, he wishes to release his bail, he may avail himself of "the act for the relief of insolvent debtors." This act is passed, as we have seen, in pursuance of a declaration in the constitution, "that the person of a debtor, where there is not strong presumption of fraud, shall not be continued in prison, after delivering up his estate for the benefit of his creditors, in such manner as shall be prescribed by law." The design of the act is to exempt insolvent debtors from imprisonment, on account of any debt due by them, at the time they apply for the benefit of it, upon the condition of their honestly surrendering all their property, for the general benefit of all their creditors. As we have already seen, it does not, like a *bankrupt act*, discharge the debtor absolutely from his debts, but only from imprisonment on account of them; for his future acquisitions still remain liable. Two classes of persons may take the benefit of this act; namely, *first*, all persons not under arrest, who have resided two years in the State, and six months in the county; and *secondly*, all persons under arrest in a civil action, whether on mesne or final process, and whether residents in the State or not. An officer appointed by the court of common pleas, and denominated *commissioner of insolvents*, is fully empowered to receive from applicants an assignment of their property, and distribute the proceeds among their creditors. To prevent fraud, the assignment must be made under oath, and severe penalties are annexed to dishonesty or concealment. The proceedings before the commissioner are only preliminary to a final examination in court. But to secure the applicant from imprisonment, in the mean time, the commissioner grants a *certificate*, containing a *schedule* of all the specified debts, which secures him from imprisonment for any of those debts until he can be heard in court. If, after hearing all objections, the court are satisfied that all has been fair and honest, they grant a *final certificate*, containing the same schedule, the effect of which is, for ever to exempt the applicant from imprisonment, within the State, on account of any of these specified debts. The taking of the benefit of this act, therefore, converts a *capias*, for any of these debts, into a summons; for upon producing the certificate, the officer is bound at once to release the person arrested, without bail, and return the fact upon his writ. (*a*) The service, therefore, in such case, only operates as a notification or summons to the defendant.

Prison limits. (*b*) If the defendant when arrested cannot find bail, and will not take the benefit of the act, he must go to jail. But even then he is not necessarily obliged to remain in close confinement. By giving a *bond* to the plaintiff, conditioned for his safe continuance in the custody of the jailer, he may obtain the privilege of *prison limits.* In 1805, these limits extended only four hundred yards from the jail: in 1821, they were so enlarged as to embrace the corporate limits of the township; and in 1833, they were again enlarged so as to embrace the whole county. Now, therefore, the *bond* only requires the debtor to remain within the county. The privilege extends to all persons imprisoned for *debt*, whether on mesne or final process. The defendant must be actually *committed* to prison before the bond can be taken; but when the bond has been executed, his privileges within the limits are the same as those of any other person. He cannot, however, for a moment overstep these limits, without making his sureties liable. The sheriff ceases to be in any manner responsible after the execution of the bond. The sufficiency of the sureties is determined by two judges or justices of the peace; and if they should prove bad, the plaintiff is without remedy. When the defendant takes this course, the sheriff returns the fact, and the plaintiff proceeds against him, as in custody.

Attachment. (*c*) The next writ by which an action may be com-

(*a*) But this does not apply to a *capias* from the federal courts. Duncan *v.* Darst, 1 Howard, 301.

(*b*) See Lucky *v.* Brandon, 1 Ohio, 49; Lytle *v.* Davies, 2 Ohio, 277.

(*c*) On the general subject of attachment, see the treatises of Waples, Kneeland, and Drake. R. S. §§ 5521 to 563 contain the Ohio law upon the subject. An attachment may be had *at* or *after* the commencement of a suit for the recovery of money in nine cases; 1. When one of the defendants is a foreign corporation or a non-resident, the claim being founded on a contract, judgment, or decree. 2. Has absconded with intent to defraud creditors. 3. Has left the county to avoid process. 4. Conceals himself for that purpose. 5. Is about to remove his property to defraud creditors. 6. Is about to convert it into money for that purpose. 7. Has property which he conceals. 8. Has disposed, or is about to dispose, of his property, to defraud creditors. 9. Fraudulently or criminally contracted the debt or incurred the obligation on which menced, is a *writ of attachment.* It may be resorted to whenever the cause of action is founded on a contract, judgment, or decree; and the debtor *absconds*, or is *not a resident* of the State, so that a *capias* or summons cannot reach him. These facts must be evidenced by an *affidavit* (*a*) of the plaintiff or his agent, accompanying the precipe. The writ of attachment *commands the sheriff to attach the property of the defendant of every description within the county.* It must be done in the presence of two disinterested persons, who make out an inventory of the property attached, under oath. If the defendant has no tangible property which can be attached, but has debts due him, or property in the hands of other persons, this is stated in the affidavit; and the debtors or persons

the suit is brought. Amendment of February 16, 1865. Under this amendment an attachment may issue in a suit for damages for an assault and battery. Creasser *v.* Young, 31 Ohio State, 57. Some one of which causes must be shown by affidavit. For the detail of proceedings, I refer to the Code. As to the dissolution of attachments, see act of March 11, 1857; Watson *v.* Sullivan, 5 Ohio State, 42. As to the form of the affidavit, see Harrison *v.* King, 9 Ohio State, 388; Coston *v.* Paige, id. 397. Emmitt *v.* Yeigh, 12 Ohio State, 335. An affidavit merely setting forth a *belief* that ground exists without stating facts is not sufficient. Dunlevy & Co. *v.* Schwartz, 17 Ohio State, 640; Gurner *v.* White, 23 Ohio State, 192. Our first attachment laws were those adopted from Pennsylvania and New Jersey in 1795. Since that time we have always had an attachment law of which the outlines are given in the text. It has been held that jurisdiction attaches from the levy upon the property, so that the subsequent debt of the debtor will not interrupt proceedings. Cochran *v.* Loring, 17 Ohio, 509. {If the property had been sold a garnishment may issue against the buyer on the same writ. Cove *v.* Oil Land Co., 40 Ohio State, 636.} When the record does not show publication of notice, it may be proved by parol. Parker *v.* Miller, 9 Ohio, 108; nor will an imperfect record vitiate the proceedings, where the files show all that was necessary. Mitchel *v.* Eyster, 7 Ohio, 1 pt. 257. The purchaser under attachment obtains a title paramount to that conveyed by a non-resident debtor before the writ issued, but not recorded until after. Parker *v.* Miller, 9 Ohio, 108. Proceedings in attachment under the Code, will reach an equitable interest. Carty *v.* Fenstemaker, 14 Ohio State, 457. {It will reach property in the hands of the plaintiff himself. Norton *v.* Norton, 43 Ohio State, 509.} A purchaser under an attachment takes subject to all equities unless he can protect himself as a *bonâ fide* purchaser with notice. Byers *v.* Wackman, 16 Ohio State, 441. {The order to the garnishee to pay over is not a judgment against him, but an assignment of the debt to the plaintiff, payment of which he can coerce only by action. Secor *v.* Witter, 39 Ohio State, 218.} Where there is no personal service, the judgment, though in form personal, has no effect beyond the property attached in that suit. No general execution can be issued for any balance unpaid after the attached property is exhausted. No suit can be maintained on such judgment in the same court, or any other, nor can it be used as evidence in any other proceeding not affecting the attached property; nor could the costs in that proceeding be collected out of any other property than that attached in the suit. Cooper *v.* Reynolds, 10 Wall. 308 {Wood *v.* Stanberry, 21 Ohio State, 142; Pennoyer *v.* Neff, 95 U. S. 714. For States decreeing the contrary, see dissenting opinion of Harlan, J., in the latter case}.

(*a*) *Affidavit for a Writ of Attachment.* A. B., the above plaintiff, makes oath and says {that the claim sued on is [show the nature of the claim]; that said claim is just. Affiant believes he ought to recover ——— dollars. That the defendant [here state the ground of the attachment]. [Add in case of garnishment] Said A. B. has good reason to believe and does believe that X. Y. has property of said defendant. *Jurat*}.

Writ of Attachment. We command you to attach the lands, tenements, goods, chattels, rights, credits, moneys, and effects of ——— [the defendant] wheresoever they may be found, and the same to keep, or so provide that the same or the value thereof may be forthcoming to answer the judgment of [describe the court] in an action of ———, therein prosecuted by ——— [the plaintiff], in damages $———, on the first day of their next term; and have you then and there this writ with your doings thereon.

having the property may be *garnisheed;* which is done by notifying them of the suit, after which they are held liable for the amount, and may be compelled to answer under oath as to the facts. (*a*) Notice of the suit is given by advertisement, and it must stand three terms before judgment. The defendant may appear at any time before judgment, and by putting in special bail, or surrendering himself into custody, discharge his property. The attaching creditor does not attach for himself alone, but for the equal benefit of all creditors who may file their claims in time. As the defendant, by these proceedings, may be deprived of his property without having what is called *his day in court*, or even *actual notice* of the suit, our court has manifested a disposition to construe the statute strictly. If, therefore, any one of several joint debtors is within the State, the property of the rest cannot be attached. If the sheriff attach personal property, he may return it to the party in possession upon his giving bond in double the appraised value, conditioned for the forthcoming of the said property or its appraised value in money to answer the judgment. If this be not done, the sheriff retains possession. In either case, he returns an inventory and appraisement. If the property be of a perishable nature, the court on motion will order it to be sold. If the sheriff cannot come at the property, he garnishees the person having it in possession, by serving him with a copy of the writ and affidavit; together with a notice to appear at the next term of the court, and answer such questions as may be put to him touching the property or credits in his hands belonging to the defendant. Written interrogatories are thereupon filed, to which the garnishee must put in written answers under oath. Upon proper showing, the garnishee may be compelled to give security for the forthcoming of such property or credits. (*b*) Upon the return of the writ, it is the duty of the clerk, on demand of the plaintiff, to make out an advertisement of the pending of the attachment within thirty days, which must be published for six weeks in some newspaper. The declaration and subsequent proceedings are the same as if the suit had been commenced by a summons or *capias;* except that the defendant, unless he appear and plead, must be called and defaulted at the first and second term; and judgment cannot be had against him until the third term. In the mean time, all other creditors may file their declarations, and thus come in for their share of the proceeds of the property attached.

Replevin. (*c*) The nature of this action, as regulated by our

(*a*) The act of March 17, 1856, repeals section 200 of the Code, and substitutes for it more effective proceedings for securing property in the hands of garnishees.

(*b*) The garnishee is not necessarily exempted from an existing liability to pay interest during the pendency of the proceedings upon his indebtedness to the defendant on attachment. Candee *v.* Webster, 9 Ohio State, 452.

(*c*) This proceeding is regulated by the Code, pursuant to which, the plaintiff may, at the commencement of an action to recover possession of specific personal property, or at any time before answer, obtain an *order of delivery*, upon making affidavit similar to that in the text. And the proceedings of the sheriff are also nearly the same. See Morris on Replevin.

statute, has already been described. The *affidavit* (*a*) accompanying the precipe, after specifying the goods to be replevied, must state that they belong to the plaintiff; that they are wrongfully detained by the defendant, and that they were not taken in execution on any judgment against him; nor for any tax, fine, or amercement assessed against him; nor by virtue of any writ of replevin or other process issued against him. The *writ* (*b*) commands the sheriff to cause the goods mentioned in the affidavit to be replevied to the plaintiff; and also to summon the defendant to appear and answer for the unlawful detention thereof. In executing this writ, the sheriff may break open any building in which the property may be, if peaceable entry be refused. But before the property be delivered to the plaintiff, it must be appraised by two disinterested freeholders, under oath administered by the sheriff; and the plaintiff must give *bond* (*c*) to the defendant in double the appraised value, conditioned to prosecute the suit to effect and abide the judgment. This bond and an inventory of the replevied goods are returned by the sheriff, and the suit proceeds as in other cases.

Appearance. (*d*) We have now traced the proceedings up to the time of the defendant's appearance in court. Anciently, the defendant was required to appear personally, or by attorney, in court, and cause an entry to be made of that fact on the record. This appearance might be enforced by proceeding to *outlawry*, which placed the defendant and his property beyond the protection of the law. But nothing of this kind exists in our practice. Appearance by attorney is generally equivalent to a personal appearance; and as a motive for causing such appearance to be made, we substitute the consequences of *default* in the place of outlawry. The theory of all judicial proceeding is, that after service and return of process, the defendant is to be treated as in

(*a*) *Affidavit for a Writ of Replevin.* A. B., the above plaintiff, makes oath and says, that he {is the owner of the following property [if his interest is not as owner, but is special, it must be described]}: that the same are wrongfully detained by C. D., the above defendant; and that the same were not taken on process issued against the said plaintiff, nor for any tax. [*Jurat* as before.] A. B.

(*b*) *Writ of Replevin* [omitting caption and attestation]. We command you to cause to be replevied unto ——— [the plaintiff], the goods and chattels following, to wit [describe them as in the precipe], which ——— [the defendant] wrongfully detains from [the plaintiff] as is claimed; and also to summon the said [defendant] to appear at the next term of [describe the court] to answer unto [the plaintiff] for the unlawful detention of the said goods and chattels, in damages $———, and have you then and there this writ with your doings thereon.

(*c*) *Replevin Bond.* Be it known that the [plaintiff and his sureties] are held and firmly bound unto [the defendant] in the sum of $——— [double the appraised value], for the payment of which we do jointly and severally bind ourselves by these presents, sealed with our seals and dated this [date]. But the condition of this obligation is, that whereas the said [plaintiff], on the [date of the writ], sued out of the [describe the court], a writ of replevin against the said [defendant], for the following goods and chattels, to wit [describe them], which writ is returnable to the next term of the court; now if the said [plaintiff] shall prosecute the said suit to effect, and pay all costs and damages which shall be awarded against him, then this obligation shall be void. [Signatures and seals.]

(*d*) Steph. on Plead. 29, 34.

court. This is actually true only when the process is a *capias* or *habeas corpus*. In all other cases, where the process does not require the body to be brought into court, but merely a notification to appear, the defendant is either considered to be in court, after service and return of process, so that he may be proceeded against to judgment without any act on his part; or, if necessary to the purposes of justice, as in cases of *mandamus* and *quo warranto*, his actual appearance may be enforced by attachment for contempt. But, otherwise, we substitute a virtual for an actual appearance. It being, however, an established rule, that an appearance cures all defects in process, it becomes important to know what constitutes an appearance for this purpose. When the process is a *capias* the entering of special bail is considered an appearance; and in all other cases, the filing of a plea or demurrer, or doing any other act of record, is considered an appearance; but the entering the attorney's name on the margin of the docket is not. At any time before appearance, as thus described, the defendant may move to have the process quashed for irregularity or informality.

§ 211. **Pleading.** (*a*) Having described the process by which

(*a*) On the subject of pleading, see 3 Black. Com. chap. 20, 21; 1 Swift's Dig. b. 3, chap. 14–21. For the theory of pleading, the best book is that of Stephen, and the next, Gould or Lawes. For the practice, the best work is that of Chitty; the first volume contains the general principles, and the second and third, the forms of pleading.

Pleading under the Code. The code demolishes the immense fabric of special pleading in this summary manner: "The rules of pleading heretofore existing in civil cases are abolished; and hereafter the forms of pleading in civil actions in courts of record, and the rules by which their sufficiency may be determined, are those prescribed by this code." "The only pleadings allowed are: 1. The *petition* by the plaintiff. 2. The *answer* or *demurrer* by the defendant. 3. The *demurrer* or *reply* by the plaintiff." The demurrer to the reply by the defendant, and a cross-petition by the defendant, are added by {R. S. § 5067. As to a rejoinder to the reply to a counter-claim, see Crapster *v.* Williams, 21 Kan. 109, where it was recognized as possible, but not required}. It will thus be seen that the system of the Code very closely resembles those of a chancery and admiralty pleading, to which frequent reference must of course be made in settling doubtful questions. The following is an outline:—

Petition. The petition must contain: 1. The names of the court, county, and parties. 2. A statement of the facts in ordinary and concise language, and without repetition. 3. A demand of the relief claimed. If money, the amount, and time from which interest is to be computed, must be stated. Where there is more than one cause of action, each must be separately stated and numbered. McKinney *v.* McKinney, 8 Ohio State, 423. Where the petition has but one cause of action, the facts cannot be subdivided so as to present fictitiously, as in pleadings at common law, two causes of action. Sturges *v.* Burton, 8 Ohio State, 215. {But it is now believed this can be done where necessary.}

Demurrer. The defendant may demur to the petition for either of eight causes appearing upon its face: 1. Want of jurisdiction. 2. Incapacity of plaintiff to sue. 3. Another action pending. 4. Misjoinder of plaintiff. 5. Defect of parties plaintiff or defendant. 6. Misjoinder of causes of action. {7. Misjoinder of causes of action against several defendants.} 8. No cause of action. {To these the courts have added a ninth, as in fact, however, falling under the eighth, but with a suggestion that it be specially pleaded, viz.: the statute of limitations. Vore *v.* Woodford, 29 Ohio State, 245.} The first seven causes must be stated specially. If the causes do not appear in the petition, they may be set up by answer. If not objected to in either way, they are waived, except the first and last. If there be several causes of action, there may be a demurrer to one, and answer to another. If a demurrer be overruled, leave may be the defendant is brought actually or virtually into court, I am next to consider the proceedings which take place in court. Of these, the first in order are the *pleadings;* by which are meant the formal statements of the complaint and defence, by the counsel of the parties, preliminary to a trial. The professed object of these rules of pleading is to bring the parties to what is called an *issue;* that is, to extract from their allegations the exact matter in controversy, divested of every thing extraneous, and resting upon direct affirmation and negation. At first view, this would seem to be an easy thing. If the plaintiff only state with clearness and precision the nature of his complaint, and the defendant do the same with regard to his defence, one would suppose that an issue might thus be made without any artificial rules; but instead of this, *special pleading* has been wrought up by a series of refinements, into an art so difficult, that it requires years of study and

given to answer, or reply, if there be merits. If sustained, there may be an amendment, if the defect can be remedied. As to demurrer to the answer for insufficiency, see State *v.* Harper, 6 Ohio State, 607.

Answer. The answer must contain: 1. A general or specific denial of each material allegation intended to be controverted. 2. A statement of any new matter constituting a defence, counter-claim, or set-off. This may be either legal or equitable; and if there be several, each must be separately stated and numbered, and must refer intelligibly to the cause of action intended to be answered.

Reply. There is no reply except to a counter-claim or set-off. To this the plaintiff may either demur specially, or reply. In his reply he may deny generally or specifically whatever he controverts, and set up new matter in defence. Or he may demur to part, and answer the rest. See act of April 8, 1857, substituting new provisions for sections 84, 101, and 107, of the Code, and allowing a reply, where new matter is set up in the answer.

General Rules. Every pleading must be subscribed by the party or his attorney. Either party may annex to his pleading, other than a demurrer, pertinent interrogatories to be answered under oath. Act of March 6, 1857. And every pleading of fact must be verified by the affidavit of the party, his agent or attorney, that he believes the facts stated. It is provided, however, that such verification shall not be used against the party in any criminal proceeding, as proof of a fact admitted or alleged; nor shall it make other or greater proof necessary on the part of the adverse party. If the action, counter-claim, or set-off be founded on an account, note, bill, or other writing, as evidence of indebtedness, a copy must be attached to and filed with the pleading, or reason assigned for not so doing. Every material allegation of the petition not controverted by the answer, and of the answer, setting up a counter-claim or set-off, not controverted by the reply, is to be taken as true, except as to value or amount of damage.

Amendments. The Code is very liberal with respect to amendments. They may be made before or after judgment, in furtherance of justice, and on such terms as may be proper, in any pleading, process, or proceeding, provided they do not substantially change the claim or defence. And in every stage of the action, the court must disregard any error or defect in the pleadings or proceedings, which does not affect the substantial rights of the adverse party, and not reverse a judgment by reason thereof. No variance is to be deemed material, unless it has actually misled the adverse party upon the merits. The courts have been extremely liberal in construing this rule; but pleaders have occasionally gone beyond even the limit they have fixed; as in the case of Thatcher *v.* Hersey, 21 Ohio State, 668, where the plaintiff in his petition sued for work done in the construction of a mill-dam, and on the trial proved work done in a harvest field, the court held such evidence wrongly admitted, though the defendant neither alleged nor offered to prove that he had been misled. Facts occurring after petition, answer, or reply, may be set up on leave, by a supplemental pleading. Doty *v.* Rigour, 9 Ohio State, 533.

Such is an outline of pleading according to the Code; and it would be difficult to imagine a system more simple, just, and efficient. Defects will doubtless be discovered, but they can be easily remedied.

practice to master it. Anciently, the pleadings were conducted *orally*, and taken down by the clerk. Up to 1353, the record was in Norman French; from which time to 1730, it was in Latin; and since the latter epoch it has been in English. When the pleadings ceased to be oral, a distinct class of lawyers grew up, called *special pleaders*, who were compensated for their labor in proportion to the number of words employed. From these facts four important consequences have resulted; namely: *First*, the pleadings are still expressed, as if made *orally*, and taken down by the clerk. *Secondly*, the style of pleading is exceedingly clumsy and awkward, being for the most part a very literal translation of the old French or Latin. *Thirdly*, pleadings are redundant beyond all example, being stretched out and amplified, by means of pleonasms, synonymes, and tautologies, to the utmost possible length in order to increase the fees. This abuse, however, has been partially reformed in this country, by abolishing the English rule of compensation, and having no distinct class of special pleaders. *Fourthly*, the system of pleading abounds with exceeding subtlety and technicality. The common observer would be apt to regard it as a wonderfully elaborate monument of the misdirected ingenuity of man. Those, however, who have spent the best part of their lives in exploring its mysteries, hold it to be the perfection of logic. Between these opinions it is not necessary for me to decide. We take the system as it has come down to us from by-gone ages, with now and then an innovation where changes have been most urgently demanded; and it will be my aim in this outline to bring into view some of its leading characteristics, without entering at all into details.

Declaration. The pleadings commence with the plaintiff's statement of his case, which is called the *declaration*, *narration*, or *count*. The *caption* specifies the State, county, court, and term, the name of the parties and of the action. Then follows a full and formal *description* of the cause of action, which forms the main body of the declaration, and, of course, varies according to the circumstances of each case; but the precedents collected in the books of pleading are now so numerous, as to meet almost every case that can arise. The *conclusion* states the *damages* as laid in the precipe and writ. The declaration thus framed, is signed by the plaintiff's attorney, and filed in the clerk's office, where a copy is made out for the other party. The time within which pleadings must be filed, is regulated by certain *rules*, which the courts are authorized to establish; and which become the law of the court establishing them. These rules generally require the pleadings to be closed, and the case brought to issue, during the vacation next after the appearance term; and the consequence of a failure on either side, without good cause, will be a judgment of some kind against the party in default. If for example, the plaintiff neglect to file his declaration within the time required by the rules, it will be in the power of the defendant to have a judgment of *nonsuit*. With these remarks I proceed to lay down some general rules for framing declarations. (*a*)

Fulness. The declaration must contain upon its face a complete cause of action. The omission of any material fact will either occasion a loss of the cause, or expense or delay in *amending* the defective part. The ancient rigor of the law did not permit amendments; but the English *statute of jeofails* first provided for them, and this has been generally imitated in this country. In this State, provision is made for amending any of the proceedings in civil suits, at any time, upon such terms as the court shall prescribe. So that a slip of the pen, or an error in judgment, will not now defeat a meritorious cause. But while every material fact must be stated, care should be taken to avoid *immaterial averments;* because there is an arbitrary rule which requires a party to prove what he alleges, though not necessary to have been alleged. (*b*)

Certainty. The certainty required in pleadings includes both precision and particularity, as opposed to ambiguity and generality. The rule is, that when a pleading admits of two constructions, that shall be taken which operates most against the pleader. You must, therefore, use such definiteness and specification, that any other meaning than that which you intend to convey, would be far-fetched and unnatural. You are to state *facts* only, and not legal inferences; and you are to state them categorically, and not by way of recital or argument. But you need not state matters of evidence nor matters which rest more in the knowledge of your adversary. In describing *written instruments*, you are not generally obliged to set forth more than relates to your case; and you may merely state their substance if you prefer so to do; but if you undertake to give the exact words, you must do it literally; and there is one class of instruments called *specialties*, including matters of record and under seal, which come within an arbitrary rule, requiring a *profert* or full copy to be exhibited upon

(*a*) The merely formal parts of a declaration are the caption and conclusion, which are the same in all declarations. The *caption* is as follows: "The State of ——, county of ——, Court of Common Pleas, —— Term, in the year ——. A. B. by ——, his attorney, complains of C. D. in an action of ——." Then follows the *descriptive part*, beginning: "For that," &c., for which see the specimens annexed to a description of the several actions. The *conclusion* is as follows: "To the damage of the plaintiff —— dollars, and therefor he sues." The following is a specimen of a complete declaration in case for immoderately riding a horse: —

The State of Ohio, Hamilton County, Court of Common Pleas, November Term, in the year 1842.

A. B. by E. F., his attorney, complains of C. D. in an action of case; for that heretofore, to wit, on the first day of January, in the year 1842, to wit, at the county aforesaid, the defendant hired of the plaintiff a certain horse to ride from Cincinnati to Lebanon and back again, for a certain sum of money agreed on between them; and the plaintiff then and there delivered to the defendant the said horse for the purpose aforesaid; and the defendant then and there so immoderately rode the said horse, that by reason thereof, and for want of due care, the said horse afterwards, to wit, on the same day, died, to the damage of the plaintiff one hundred dollars, and therefor he sues.

By E. F., attorney for pl'ff.

(*b*) Conn *v.* Gano, 1 Ohio, 483.

the *oyer* or demand of the adversary. I call this rule arbitrary, because it does not include all writings; for the principle, if it were universal, would perhaps be salutary. Indeed we have a statutory provision which does, though in another way, attain the same end in all cases, by requiring each party, on the demand of the other, to furnish a copy of any writing, or a *bill of particulars* of any matter or claim, which he refers to in the pleading, or intends to prove at the trial, before the other party can be required to plead. If, therefore, a party be taken by surprise, it is his own fault, in not demanding a bill of particulars.

Several Counts. It is a general rule, that no pleading may be *double.* As applied to the declaration, this rule requires that several distinct matters shall not be alleged in *the same count*, to support a single complaint, when either, by itself, would be sufficient; because the object of pleading is to narrow the controversy down to a single specific point. But this does not hinder the plaintiff from joining several *distinct demands* in the same declaration, provided they be of the same nature, by means of *several counts.* This privilege was allowed at common law; but our statute, in affirming it, adds, in order to prevent abuse, that the defendant, before making up the issue, may move to have superfluous counts stricken out. This rule allowing several counts, was manifestly intended for cases, where there were really distinct claims or causes of action. But advantage has been taken of it to set forth the same identical cause of action, in several different shapes, in order that the evidence may be certain to fit some one of them, and thus save the consequence of what is called a *variance* between the allegation and proof. The same motive has also occasioned a departure from the rule of certainty, by introducing what are called the *common counts.* These are, for goods sold and delivered; for work, labor, and materials; for money lent; for money paid; for money had and received; and for balance of account. These counts are expressed in language of the utmost generality; and it is very common to join them all in the same declaration, together with a special count on the actual contract, though there be in reality but a single cause of action. But in order to save appearances, the phraseology of the differents counts is always such as to import distinct causes of action; and damages are only alleged at the end of the declaration. The consequence of this indulgence is, that it is often impossible to decide from the declaration alone, and without recourse to a *bill of particulars*, what the defendant is to be called upon to meet at the trial. It is a general rule, that if a pleading be bad in any part, it is bad altogether; but where there are several counts, this rule only applies to each count by itself. A single good count, therefore, will save the declaration. At common law, if, after a general verdict, one count was found to be bad, the verdict was set aside, because it might possibly have been rendered upon the count. But our statutes enable the plaintiff to avoid this result, if the defect be discovered beforehand, by having the jury instructed to disregard the defective counts.

Common Counts. (*a*) These may be used equally in declarations in debt and assumpsit, and may be joined with any special counts in either of these actions. And as they are of very general use in pleading, I will here state the particular office of each of them. 1. The count *for goods sold and delivered*, may be used whenever the object of the suit is to recover the price of any personal property sold to the defendant, either upon his prior order or subsequent acceptance; and there seems to be no good reason why the price of real property may not be recovered under a similar count for land sold. If the price be not fixed by the parties, the law implies the market price, or *quantum valebant.* If delivery be not necessary to perfect the sale, this count will still be good, because the word *delivered* may be treated as surplusage. 2. The count *for work, labor, and materials* may be used whenever the object of the suit is to recover compensation for any kind of service rendered to the defendant, either upon his prior request or subsequent acceptance, and for any kind of materials furnished by the plaintiff in the course of such service. If the rate of compensation be not fixed by the parties, the law implies a reasonable compensation or *quantum meruit.* 3. The count *for money lent* may be used whenever money has gone directly from the plaintiff to the defendant with the understanding that it should be repaid, whether it were a technical loan or not. 4. The count *for money paid* may be used whenever the plaintiff, by the prior direction or subsequent approval of the defendant, has paid money to any other person on his account or for his use. 5. The count *for money had and received* may be used whenever the defendant has received money in any way which of right belongs to the plaintiff. It is often called the *equitable* count, because the doctrine is, that if the defendant has money which in good conscience the plaintiff ought to have, the defendant holds it for his use, and he

(*a*) *Declaration in Assumpsit on the Common Counts.* For that heretofore, to wit, on ———, at ———, to wit, at the county aforesaid, the said defendant was indebted to the said plaintiff in the sum of $———, for goods, wares, and merchandise, before that time sold and delivered by the said plaintiff to the said defendant at his request.

And in the further sum of $——— for work and labor before that time done, and materials for the same provided, by the said plaintiff for the said defendant at his request.

And in the further sum of $——— for money before that time lent by the said plaintiff to the said defendant at his request.

And in the further sum of $——— for money before that time paid, laid out, and expended by the said plaintiff for the use of the said defendant at his request.

And in the further sum of $——— for money before that time had and received by the said defendant for the use of the said plaintiff.

And in the further sum of $——— for money found to be due by the said defendant to the said plaintiff for the balance of an account then and there stated between them.

And in consideration thereof, the said defendant then and there undertook and promised the said plaintiff to pay him the said several sums of money when thereunto requested; yet though often requested, he has not paid the same nor any part thereof, but refuses so to do.

may recover it under this count. 6. The count *for balance of account* may be used whenever there has been a running account between the parties, and a balance struck in favor of the plaintiff. To constitute such account, there must be both debits and credits, or items on each side. If the defendant has not assented to the balance struck, the plaintiff must prove the correctness of the account. The balance being thus ascertained, the law implies a promise to pay it, and this is the most convenient count to recover it; for it may include matters contained in all the other common counts. Without it, the plaintiff must sue for the whole amount of the debits, and the defendant must bring in the credits by way of set-off.

Description of persons, place, time, quantity, and value. The rule in describing *persons* is, that their full and exact *names* must be given; but in this country there is no law requiring their *additions*, *titles*, or *occupations*. Where the parties have been once accurately named in the introduction, brevity suggests that they be referred to, in future, merely as plaintiff and defendant. The *place* where a thing happened, is technically called its *venue*, from *venire*, because the jurors are required *to come* from that place. Anciently, it was the immediate village, hamlet, or neighborhood; now it never descends below the *county*, where the action is tried. The rule then is, that every material fact must be alleged to have happened within the county, which forms the venue of the action. This is usually done by naming the county in the beginning of the description, and afterwards referring to it by the word "*there*." There are some actions which are called *local*, because they can only be tried in the county where the facts occurred, unless for special reasons the court should permit the venue to be changed. Such are all actions relating to land. In these, therefore, the venue alleged is the true place. But the great majority of actions are *transitory*, and may be brought in any county where the defendant may be found. In these, therefore, the rule must often require a fiction, and sometimes a contradiction in terms. Thus, in declaring upon a contract made in London, you say that it was made "at London, to wit, at the county aforesaid." You must name the true place, because it forms a part of the description of the contract; and then you bring it within the venue of the action by means of a *videlicet*, *scilicet*, or "*to wit*." This *videlicet*, as used in pleading, may be considered as an apology for not stating the exact truth; such being in fact its office, not only with regard to place, but also with regard to time, quantity, and value. For in alleging *time* the rule is that you must allege *some* time for each material fact, but unless the time forms the gist of the action, you need not allege the true time, provided you place it under the salvo of a *videlicet*. The custom is to state a convenient time in the beginning of the description, never descending below days; and afterwards to refer to that time by the word "*then*." Again, in alleging *quantity* and *value*, the rule is similar; you must allege some quantity and value, when the action involves them, and you cannot prove a greater than you allege; but if you have used a *videlicet*, you may prove a less. These rules respecting place, time, quantity, and value, form glaring exceptions to that certainty and truth, which the theory of legal proceedings would seem to require; and which a novice would naturally expect to find in practice. In fact they have the appearance of bordering closely upon absurdity. Why require these matters to be stated at all, if the truth be of no consequence? And if the truth be important, why not require them to be alleged truly? Were men to use fictions in their common transactions, as much as they are allowed to do in their legal proceedings, there would be little confidence between man and man. But so are the precedents.

Demurrer. (*a*) When the plaintiff has thus framed and filed his declaration, the defendant must answer thereto within the time fixed by the rules, or suffer the consequences of *default.* There are two ways of answering the declaration; namely, by *demurrer* and by *plea.* And first by *demurrer.* To *demur* is to *pause.* The party demurring in effect declares that he will proceed no further, until he has the judgment of the court whether the plaintiff, by his own showing, has any cause of action. Thus a demurrer admits the *facts* alleged by the adversary, but denies their *legal sufficiency.* It tenders an *issue in law*, for the decision of the court without a jury. It may be taken upon every pleading whatsoever, except a demurrer and a general issue; and it opens all prior pleadings to the examination of the court, who give judgment against the party committing the first error. Now, a pleading may be defective either in *substance* or *form;* if in substance, the demurrer is *general*, that is, it does not specify wherein the defect consists; but if in form, the demurrer must be *special*, because it is required to point out the defects. A special demurrer, however, is so framed as to include a general demurrer, and thus cover defects in substance. An issue in law being thus tendered, the other party must accept it, or give up his cause. This acceptance is signified by putting in a *joinder* which merely asserts the sufficiency of the pleading demurred to; and the issue being thus made up, the case is ready for argument to the court. I will suppose, for example, that the defendant demurs to the plaintiff's declaration. If on hearing, the court *sustain* the demurrer, this is a decision that the declaration is insufficient, in which case, the plaintiff must either abandon his case or obtain *leave to amend.* On the subject of amendment, as already remarked, our law is very liberal, leaving the matter to the discretion of the court. In the present instance, the conditions of leave would probably be an affidavit of a meritorious cause of action, and the payment of all *costs* since filing the defective pleading. On the other hand, if the demurrer be *over-*

(*a*) Steph. Plead. 65; Parritt *v.* R. R. Co., 3 Ohio State, 330; Burritt *v.* Cowles, 5 id. 87.

ruled, this is a decision that the declaration is sufficient in law; in which case the defendant must either obtain *leave to plead*, on terms similar to the preceding, or suffer a judgment for the plaintiff's claim, to be ascertained by an *inquiry of damages*, if necessary. Should the declaration contain several counts, the defendant must answer them all, either by demurrer or plea, or both; but he cannot demur and *plead* to the same count, at the same time. It follows, then, that if you are willing to admit the *facts* alleged by your adversary, and rest your cause simply upon the question of *law*, you may demur; but this is not always the best course, because almost all *substantial defects* may be taken advantage of at subsequent stages, either on *arrest of judgment* or *writ of error*, as will be explained hereafter. As to *questions of form*, they cannot be raised at subsequent stages. The conclusion is, that unless you are quite sure of succeeding on demurrer, and doubtful on the question of fact, the better course is to try the latter first; and if you fail here, you can afterwards raise the question of law. I will only remark further, that the admission of a general demurrer is another instance of departure from the rule requiring certainty.. Why should not the demurrant be required to point out the substantial, as well as formal defects, upon which he relies? Would not the great object of all pleading, which is information and not concealment, be better promoted? (*a*)

Plea. (*b*) If the defendant does not think proper to demur, his only alternative is to *plead*. A plea raises a *question of fact*, as a demurrer does a question of law. It occurs only in answer to the declaration; but it does not admit the law of the plaintiff's declaration as a demurrer does the facts; for the question of law still remains in reserve. It would seem at first view, that there could only be two kinds of pleas, namely, first, those which simply deny the allegations of the declaration, and which are called *traverses;* and secondly, those which admit these allegations, but evade their legal effect by setting up new matter, and which are called pleas of *confession and avoidance;* and these two classes do, in fact, comprehend the pleas most frequently used. But there is still another class, called *dilatory pleas* or *pleas in abatement*, because they operate merely to delay the proceedings, without touching the merits of the case; in contradistinction to which, all other pleas are called *peremptory pleas* or *pleas in bar*. And since these dilatory pleas can only be pleaded at a preliminary

(*a*) *General Demurrer.* And the said defendant comes and demurs to the said declaration, and says that the matters therein contained are not sufficient in law to maintain the action aforesaid; wherefore he prays that the plaintiff may be barred of his said action.

To make a *special demurrer*, add as follows: And for causes of demurrer the said defendant specifies the following: first, because, &c. [setting forth each cause separately].

Joinder in Demurrer. And the said plaintiff comes and joins in the said demurrer, and says that the matters contained in his declaration are sufficient in law to maintain his action, wherefore he prays judgment and his damages.

(*b*) Steph. Plead. 67, 76.

stage, and then only in a given order, I will first name them in the order in which they must be pleaded.

Dilatory Pleas. (*a*) The *first* is, that the court has no *jurisdiction* of the cause. If this plea be sustained, the plaintiff must seek his remedy elsewhere. If this plea be overruled, or not pleaded, the defendant may plead to the *disability of the plaintiff;* as, that he is an alien enemy, and therefore not entitled to sue at all; or, that he has only a joint interest, and therefore not entitled to sue alone; or that he is not entitled to sue by the name he assumes; or that there is no such person in being. If this plea be overruled, or not pleaded, the defendant may plead to his own *disability*, either to be sued at all, or sued alone, or sued by that particular name. Formerly, though an *infant* might sue by his guardian or next friend, he was not liable to be sued; and he might set up his infancy by a *parol demurrer;* that is, a plea praying that proceedings may be stayed until his majority. But this is altered by our statute, which requires a *guardian ad litem* to be appointed, and the cause to proceed as in other cases Also, the defendant might formerly set up his *joint liability* with another, as ground for abating the suit against him alone. But our statute does not allow the suit to be abated by this plea. The plaintiff is merely required to issue a summons against the other persons named in the plea, and the suit goes on as before. A *misnomer* of the defendant is also good ground for a plea in abatement, because he would otherwise be liable to be sued again by his right name, for the same cause. If this plea be overruled, or not pleaded, the defendant may plead to the *declaration*, as not conforming to the writ, either in reference to the parties, the kind of action, or the amount of damages. The *pendency of a prior suit*, in the same or in another court, between the same parties and for the same cause, is also good ground for a plea in abatement. There are also some other subdivisions of pleas in abatement, but they seem to be of no importance. In general, with the exception of pleas to the jurisdiction, all these pleas are required to show how the plaintiff may correct his mistake in a new suit; or, in technical language, to furnish a better writ. The chief object therefore, is *delay;* and great abuse was formerly practised by the use of these pleas; but our statute goes far to prevent such abuse, by providing that no dilatory plea, other than to the jurisdiction of the court, or where the facts appear of record, shall be received without affidavit of its truth; and that if a plea in abatement be overruled, the defendant shall pay full costs down to the time of overruling it. The ancient form of commencing all pleas was this: "And the defendant comes and *defends*," &c. — which means, comes and *denies;* and a very nice distinction was made between full defence and half defence. But as this distinction is now obsolete, the allegation that the defendant defends is superfluous. These dilatory pleas,

(*a*) Steph. Plead. 68, 75.

like all pleas which set up new matter in defence, conclude with a *verification* — "And this the defendant is ready to verify; wherefore he prays judgment," &c. When the matter pleaded in abatement is not sufficient in law, the plaintiff may demur to the plea, and thus an issue of law will be made up, as before described. But otherwise, he must take issue upon some matter of fact set up in the plea, by filing a replication. For example, if the defendant plead the pendency of a prior suit, which is matter of *record*, the plaintiff may reply that there is no such record — *nul tiel record.* To this the defendant may put in a *rejoinder*, that there is such a record; and thus an issue would be made up, which the court would try by an inspection of the record. (*a*)

Traverse. (*b*) A traverse merely denies the allegations of the plaintiff, without setting up new matter. There are two kinds of traverse, the *special traverse* and the *general traverse* or *general issue.* The one specifically denies one or more of the plaintiff's allegations; while the other, in comprehensive language, denies them altogether. And it being a general rule in pleading that whatever is not denied is admitted, it follows that a special traverse requires the plaintiff to prove only those allegations which are specifically denied; while a general issue requires them all to be proved, because all are denied. For example, if to a declaration in trover the defendant should put in a special traverse, simply denying that the plaintiff owned the goods, this would be all the plaintiff would be required to prove; whereas if the general issue were pleaded, the plaintiff would be required to prove the additional fact that they were converted by the defendant. For this reason the general issue has almost universally taken the place of the special traverse, being more advantageous to the defendant.

General Issue. (*c*) On account of the universal prevalence of

(*a*) As an example of a dilatory plea, the following is the form of a plea of the pendency of a prior suit: And the said defendant comes and pleads to the said declaration, and says that before the commencement of this suit, to wit, on ———, the said plaintiff sued him in the [describe the court], in an action of ———, for the same cause of action set forth in his said declaration, as appears by the record of said suit remaining in said court; which prior suit still remains undetermined; and this he is ready to verify; wherefore he prays judgment, if he ought to answer in this present suit, and for his costs.

(*b*) Steph. Plead. 76.

(*c*) The forms of these general issues, with the *similiter* added, are as follows: —

Non est factum. And the said defendant comes and pleads to the said declaration, and says that the said writing obligatory therein mentioned is not his deed; and of this he puts himself upon the country, and the plaintiff does the like.

Nil debet. And the said defendant comes and pleads to the said declaration, and says that he does not owe the sum of money therein mentioned, or any part thereof, to the said plaintiff; and of this he puts himself upon the country, and the said plaintiff does the like.

Non assumpsit. And the said defendant comes and pleads to the said declaration, and says that he did not undertake and promise in manner and form as the said plaintiff has therein alleged; and of this he puts himself upon the country, and the said plaintiff does the like.

Not guilty. And the said defendant comes and pleads to the said declaration, and says that he is not guilty in manner and form as the said plaintiff has therein this mode of pleading, I shall describe the general issue in each of the actions. 1. The general issue in *debt*, on a sealed instrument, may be *non est factum* — that the said writing obligatory is not the defendant's deed. This, though called a general issue, is in fact very much limited; since it only puts in issue the *execution* and *validity* of the instrument. Under it, the defendant may contend, either that he never executed the instrument, or that it is void; and he can set up no other defence; but another general issue applicable to all actions of debt is *nil debet* — that the defendant does not owe the sums of money alleged by the plaintiff. This issue, being a general denial of indebtedness, is much broader than the other, and authorizes the defendant to set up anything which goes to deny an existing debt; as release, satisfaction, arbitrament, and the like. 2. The general issue in *covenant* is the same as in debt, namely, *non est factum*, and the same remarks apply to it. 3. The general issue in *assumpsit* is *non assumpsit* — that the defendant did not undertake or promise as the plaintiff has alleged. At first view this would seem like *non est factum*, merely to put in issue the making of the promise or its validity; but in practice it is equally comprehensive with *nil debet;* since the defendant, under it, may set up anything tending to deny an existing liability; as a release, performance, and the like. (*a*) 4. The general issue in *trespass* is, *not guilty*. This would seem from the language to be the broadest issue possible, but in practice it merely puts in issue the fact of committing the trespass; and under it the defendant can set up nothing by way of justification. 5. The general issue in *trover* is the same in words, namely, *not guilty;* but in practice it is much broader, since it covers every thing going to deny the plaintiff's right of recovery. 6. The general issue in *detinue* is *non detinet* — that the defendant does not wrongfully detain the goods of the plaintiff. This is comparatively narrow, since it covers only the fact of detaining the goods; and the fact that they belong to the plaintiff. 7. The general issue in *replevin* was formerly *non cepit* — that the defendant did not take the goods of the plaintiff; because a wrongful taking was the gist of the action; but since our statute has made a wrongful detention the gist, it would seem that the general issue ought to be *non detinet*, as in detinue. 8. The general issue in *case* is *not guilty;* and here the words are used as broadly as in trover; since they cover almost every pos-

alleged; and of this he puts himself upon the country, and the said plaintiff does the like.

Non detinet. And the said defendant comes and pleads to the said declaration, and says that he does not wrongfully detain the goods and chattels therein mentioned, or any part thereof; and of this he puts himself upon the country, and the said plaintiff does the like.

(*a*) See 1 Greenl. Ev. § 531; 3 Cowen & Hill's Notes to Phillips's Ev. 538; Henderson *v.* Reeve, 6 Blackf. 101; Inman *v.* Jenkins, 3 Ohio, 271; Reynolds *v.* Stansbury, 20 Ohio, 341. {Not so under the Code; thus under the Code a defence of payment is a confession and avoidance, since it admits and discharges the cause of action sued on; hence it must be pleaded specially and replied to. Fewster *v.* Goddard, 25 Ohio State, 276.}

sible defence. 9. The general issue in ejectment is *not guilty*, because this action is in form trespass; but here the words are more comprehensive than in trespass proper, since they cover every species of defence, even the statute of limitations, which is covered by no other general issue. It is obvious that the extensive prevalence of general issues in pleading, is the result of a great relaxation from its original strictness and particularity. Like the common counts in the declaration, these general issues cease to effect one of the main objects of pleading, which is to notify your adversary fully and particularly upon the points upon which you rely. In fact, *special pleading*, in its original spirit is now almost obsolete; and but for the provision before referred to, authorizing a demand of a *bill of particulars*, each party might be left almost totally in the dark, as to what evidence would be offered at the trial. Another serious objection is found in the perfectly arbitrary character of these general issues, as to their comprehension; some covering almost every thing, and others being narrowed down to one or two points, without any fixed principles of reason or expression to determine the one or the other. These considerations have led many to doubt whether the convenience of this general mode of pleading is not a poor compensation for its want of certainty. If the parties were required in all cases to exhibit specifically their respective grounds, as was the ancient custom, and is still the theory of pleading, perhaps the ends of justice would be better promoted; especially if unnecessary technicalities were dispensed with. At all events, the present mixed system, partly special and partly general, wants harmony and congruity more than almost any other part of the law. But in this connection, it is proper to refer to a provision of our statute which has a salutary effect upon the practice in certain actions of contract; namely, that when the contract is a bond, bill, or note, and the general issue is pleaded, without an affidavit of its truth, the plaintiff shall not be required to prove the execution of the contract by the defendant. This is a highly useful provision; for the plaintiff is thus apprised whether one of the material facts is to be contested or not, and can prepare himself accordingly. All general issues conclude *to the country*, as it is called, — "and of this he puts himself upon the country," — that is, with tendering an issue of fact to be tried by the jury; and this issue, like an issue of law, the plaintiff must accept, or give up his case; for, being a simple denial of the truth of his declaration, it cannot be demurred to. The acceptance of this issue is signified by a replication called a *similiter*, — "and the plaintiff does the like," — that is, he refers his cause in like manner to the jury. In strict practice, the *similiter* should be put in by the plaintiff; but it is usually added by the defendant to his plea, because it is a matter of course.

Pleas of Confession and Avoidance. (*a*) This is the only re-

(*a*) Steph. Plead. 76–87.

maining class of pleas. They are commonly called *special pleas*, and used when the defendant is ready to admit the facts alleged by the plaintiff, but has new matter upon which to rest his defence, as a justification, discharge, or the like. This new matter in avoidance is set forth with the same particularity as in a declaration; and the plea, instead of tendering an issue to the jury as in a traverse, concludes *with a verification*. The plaintiff must then either demur to this plea or put in a *replication*. If he replies, it may either be by a simple traverse of the plea, or by a confession of the new matter of the plea, together with a statement of other new matter to avoid its effect. This last being a replication by confession and avoidance, must conclude with a verification, and not a tender of issue. The defendant, therefore, must either demur to it, or put in a rejoinder. If this rejoinder be a traverse, it brings the cause to issue as before described. If a confession and avoidance, it requires a *surrejoinder* from the plaintiff; and so on, to a *rebutter* and *surrebutter*. But it is very seldom that pleadings extend beyond the rejoinder; for new matter cannot be inexhaustible; and where new matter is not alleged, an issue either in law or fact is always tendered and accepted, which terminates the pleadings. This will be obvious from the following considerations. If the new matter set up in the plea be insufficient in law to constitute a defence, a demurrer and joinder make up the issue. If not true, the replication will be a traverse and the rejoinder by a *similiter* will make up the issue. If both sufficient and true, it can only be met by a replication of confession and avoidance, setting up other new matter, in which case, the defendant must either demur, or rejoin by way of traverse or confession and avoidance, and so on, until an issue be made up either on demurrer or traverse; for to one or the other of these the pleadings must come when there is no longer ground for a confession and avoidance. This may be illustrated by an example. Suppose an action of assumpsit upon a promissory note. The defendant pleads the statute of limitations — that he did not promise within fifteen years. As this is a sufficient defence, if true, it cannot be demurred to. If not true, the plaintiff will reply by way of traverse, — that he did promise within fifteen years, — and then a *similiter* will complete the issue. But though this plea be both true and sufficient of itself, there may be new matter to avoid it, as that the defendant was absent from the State at the time the cause of action accrued; in which case, the time does not begin to run until his return to the State. This, then, may be replied by way of confession and avoidance. The defendant will not demur to this replication, because, if true, it is sufficient. If he rejoin by way of traverse, denying the fact of absence from the State, the surrejoinder will be a *similiter*, which will complete the issue. But this replication may be both sufficient and true, and yet there may be other new matter to avoid its effect. The defendant may have returned to the State more than fifteen years before the commencement of the suit; in which case, he will rejoin by way of confession and avoidance, setting forth this fact. The plaintiff will not demur to this rejoinder, because, if true, it is sufficient. If not true, he will surrejoin, by way of traverse, and the rebutter would be a *similiter*, which will complete the issue. But there may still be other new matter to avoid this rejoinder, though true and sufficient of itself. The return to the State may have been clandestine and not open; in which case, the surrejoinder will be by way of confession and avoidance, setting forth this fact. And here the new matter is exhausted. The issue is reduced to the question whether the return was clandestine or open. The rebutter will therefore be a traverse, and the surrebutter a *similiter*, which will complete the issue. (*a*)

Notice in place of a Special Plea. The kind of special pleading just described is now in a great measure superseded by the practice of pleading the general issue, and appending a *notice* of any special matter, by which is meant such matter as cannot be offered at the trial under the general issue alone. Unfortunately no general rule can be laid down to determine, in all cases, what may and what may not be offered in defence under the general issue. All that can be said is, that when by the arbitrary rules on this subject, any given defence must be particularly set out, it must be done either by a special plea or notice. Our statute authorizes a notice (*b*) in all cases except that of tender, and this exception is probably the result of oversight. This notice is intended to inform the opposite party of the precise nature of the defence, and must therefore be as full and particular as a special plea, from the form of which it differs only in the introduction and conclusion. But the effect of the notice is very different from the special plea in this, that being appended to the general issue, the only replication required is a *similiter*, and the pleadings are always terminated at this stage. The result, therefore, is to do away with special pleadings, strictly so called. And the only matter of regret is, that the requirement of notice is not made universal,

(*a*) As an example of a plea of confession and avoidance, I will give the form of the plea of *son assault demesne* to a declaration in trespass for an assault and battery. And the said defendant comes and pleads to the said declaration, and says that at the time and place when and where the said trespass is supposed to have been committed, to wit, on ———, at ———, the said plaintiff, with force and arms, did assault and beat the said defendant, and would have further injured him, but that he did then and there defend himself; which defence is the trespass complained of; and so the injury, if any was done, was from the assault of the said plaintiff upon the said defendant, and in self-defence; and this he is ready to verify; wherefore he prays judgment, if the said plaintiff ought to maintain his said action.

(*b*) As an example of *notice*, I will take the case of *set-off:* And the said plaintiff will take notice, that on the trial of this suit the said defendant will insist by way of set-off, that before and at the commencement thereof, the said plaintiff was and still is indebted to him in the sum of $———, for [set forth the indebtedness as in a declaration, either specially or by the common counts, or both]: and by reason thereof the said defendant will demand a judgment for such balance as may then and there be found to be due to him, according to the statute in such case provided.

whenever general pleading is resorted to. Let the plaintiff, whenever he uses the common counts, annex a notice of what his claim is, and the defendant, whenever he pleads the general issue, annex a notice of what his defence is, and the system would perhaps be the best possible. But at present we cannot be said to have a system of any sort. It is neither general pleading nor special pleading, but an accidental compound of both.

Several Pleas. At common law, when the declaration contained several counts, the defendant might set up a separate defence to each. Thus, he might demur to one count, traverse another, and confess and avoid a third; or he might plead the same plea to each. But until the statute of Anne, he was not allowed to put in several pleas to the same count. Our statute imitates this, and allows the defendant, with leave of the court, to plead "as many several matters" as he shall deem necessary. But if, on demurrer, any of these pleas be adjudged insufficient, he must pay the costs; accordingly it is common to have several distinct issues in the same suit; but the pleas, however numerous, can only consist of the kinds before described. As to the leave of the court required by the statute, it is seldom in fact asked, because sure to be granted, of course; and yet this privilege, like that of several counts, is very liable to abuse. For we often find the most inconsistent defences set up to the same cause of action; as *not guilty*, and a *release; non est factum*, and *payment; non assumpsit*, the *statute of limitations*, and *infancy*. Indeed it is said that the only pleas that would be objectionable on the ground of inconsistency, are the *general issue* and *a tender;* though for this single exception, there is certainly no good reason, which would not embrace many other cases. When several pleas are pleaded, all after the first are prefaced thus — "and for a further plea, by leave of the court," &c. And for each of the pleas thus pleaded, to each of the counts in the declaration, there must ultimately be a distinct issue; so that it is possible to conceive of an almost infinite number of issues made up in one action. This evil, however, is in a great measure prevented by the rule for avoiding what is called a *departure* in pleading; which is, that neither party can, at any subsequent stage of the pleadings, set up any new matter which is repugnant to that before set up by him, though he may enlarge and render more definite the ground before taken. I will only add, that the consequence of a failure to demur or plead within the time required by the rules is, that the plaintiff may obtain a judgment by default. Such a judgment merely determines the plaintiff's right to recover, but not how much; and the case then stands for inquiry of damages. But the defendant may have his default opened and obtain leave to plead, by making affidavit that he has a meritorious defence, provided he will bring the cause at once to issue. In like manner, the plaintiff must put in his replication within the time required by the rules, or the consequence will be a nonsuit; which, however, may be set aside on like terms; and so on till the issue be made up.

Special Matters of Defence. The foregoing remarks sufficiently explain the general nature of pleading. But for further illustration, I will speak of some of the special matters of defence which occur most frequently.

Set-off. (*a*) At common law, if the plaintiff was indebted to the defendant, the latter had no means of setting off such debt in the suit against him, but was driven to a cross-action. This evil, however, has long been remedied by legislation. By our statute, if the action be on a pecuniary contract, and the defendant at the commencement of the suit held, in the same right, a like claim against the plaintiff, he may bring it in by way of set-off; and if he neglects so to do, he cannot, in a subsequent action for it, recover costs. But unless the set-off amount to an actual payment, it cannot be brought in under the general issue. Set-off, strictly so called, must either be pleaded specially or by way of notice; and the court will render judgment for the party having the balance in his favor. By being due in the same right, is meant, that an individual debt cannot be set off against a partnership debt, nor a debt due to the defendant in his own right against a debt due by him as administrator, and *vice versâ.* And as to the kind of debt which may be set off, it must be strictly a pecuniary claim, and not for consequential damages. Set-off is confined to actions of contract; and the true test is, to inquire whether the defendant could have sued the plaintiff for the subject matter of the set-off, in the same action in which he is now sued. Judgments, however, in all actions, may be set off, because they are liquidated debts. Our practice, on account of the peculiar wording of our statute, is to give notice of set-off instead of pleading it specially; and as there is no replication to the notice except the *similiter*, all objections to it may be taken at the trial, without previous intimation.

Accord and Satisfaction. Where the claim is for a liquidated debt, payment in full need never be pleaded specially, but may be proved under the general issue. But if such claim has been settled by any thing short of full payment, or if it be for unliquidated or consequential damages, and has been settled by the parties,

(*a*) See Montagu on Set-Off; Babington on Set-Off; also Barbour on Set-Off, an American work. By the Code, a set-off, or counter-claim, must be set up in the answer. It may be withdrawn on leave, and made a separate proceeding. It is not affected by the default or discontinuance of the plaintiff. And if it exceed the plaintiff's demand, there may be judgment for the excess. Follett *v.* Buyer, 4 Ohio State, 586; Ernst *v.* Kunkle, 5 id. 520; Hill *v.* Butler, 6 id. 207; Wiswell *v.* First Cong. Church, 14 Ohio State, 31; Allen *v.* Shackleford, 15 Ohio State, 145; Miller *v.* Florer, id. 148. As to recoupment, see Wellsville *v.* Geisse, 3 Ohio State, 333; Timmons *v.* Dunn, 4 id. 680; Upton *v.* Julian, 7 id. 95 {and a set-off may be for unliquidated damages, Needham *v.* Pratt, 40 Ohio State, 186, by the commission followed by the Supreme Court in Elliott *v.* Federal Creek Valley R. R. Co., decided without report or opinion Nov. 20, 1883; so that this is now settled in Ohio. A counter-claim of course may be for unliquidated damages}.

this settlement is technically called *accord and satisfaction*, and is a good defence to a suit, if it be pleaded specially or by notice. But to constitute this defence it is not enough that the parties have agreed upon the terms of settlement, which would be accord only. They must have completed the settlement, so that no further action is required; and such a compromise will be effectual in all cases not criminal. (*a*)

Infancy. (*b*) We have seen that infants sue by their next friend or *prochein ami*, and defend by their guardian *ad litem.* The technical reason is, that an infant cannot appoint an attorney. We have also seen that an infant is not bound by any contract, unless it be for necessaries. But the defence of infancy cannot be offered under the general issue. It must be pleaded specially or by notice. If pleaded, and the contract were for necessaries, this may be replied in confession and avoidance. If notice be given of it, the fact that the contract was for necessaries may be proved at the trial.

Tender. The defendant has the privilege of making a *tender* of what he admits to be due the plaintiff, for the purpose of saving interest and costs. The practice is here regulated by statute; and it so happens that a tender is the only thing which must be pleaded specially, and cannot be proved under the general issue and notice on account of the peculiar wording of our statute. Where the action is on a pecuniary contract, the *money* may be tendered at any time before suit. Where it is on any other contract, *performance* may be tendered at the time and place specified. Also, for a trespass upon real property *sufficient amends* may be tendered. In either case, if the plaintiff refuse the tender and do not recover more, he must lose the interest and costs. There is still another provision, which allows the defendant to bring into court at any time before the trial, without mention of it in the pleadings, the amount which he admits to be due to the plaintiff, with costs up to that time, and if the plaintiff refuse to take it, and do not recover more, he thenceforth loses interest and costs. We have before seen that no State can pass any law making any thing but gold and silver a legal tender. Hence the creditor may object to receiving bank-notes. But unless he makes this objection at the time, he is taken to have waived it, and thus a tender of bank-notes not objected to will be good. (*c*) It is also held that the money need not be actually produced and counted, unless that be insisted on; for it is sufficient to show at the trial, that the defendant was in a condition to substantiate his offer. A tender may be pleaded to part of the amount claimed, and the general issue as to the rest; but no plea of tender either of part

(*a*) Cushing *v.* Wyman, 44 Maine, 121; McGehee *v.* Shafer, 15 Texas, 198; Goff *v.* Mulholland, 28 Mo. 397.

(*b*) By the Code, the suit may be by guardian or next friend; the defence by a guardian for the suit.

(*c*) A tender of a bank check, where all objection to this medium of payment is expressly waived, is good. Jennings *v.* Mendenhall, 7 Ohio State, 257.

or the whole can be united with the general issue as to the whole, because the two are repugnant. The plea of tender must allege that the defendant has been at all times ready to pay the amount tendered; and, therefore, a subsequent demand and refusal is a good replication in confession and avoidance.

Plea puis darrein Continuance. (*a*) By the common law, the parties might at any time ask for an *imparlance*, that is, an opportunity to confer together; but no such practice prevails here. The issue must be made up before the trial term, or the party in default must suffer a judgment against him, if the adversary demand it, unless the court see cause to grant indulgence; and at the trial term, the cause must be called up in its order and disposed of, unless by agreement it be placed at the heel of the docket, or *continued.* A *continuance* is necessary at each term, to keep the cause in court. The reason usually alleged, after issue joined, is the want of testimony. The party wishing a continuance for this cause must make affidavit that he has used due diligence to obtain it; that it is material; and that he expects to obtain it soon; and if he applies a second time, he is usually required to set forth what he expects to prove, that his adversary may admit it, if he choose. This mode of procuring delay is often perverted; but some such provision is necessary for the purposes of justice. And it often happens that a defence may arise after the continuance of a cause, which did not exist when the issue was made up. In such case, the defence must be set up by plea *puis darrein continuance*, which means since the last continuance. For example, a release given before issue joined may be offered in evidence under the general issue; but a subsequent release must be set up by a plea since the last continuance.

Demand of Oyer. (*b*) It has been already stated that the plaintiff in his declaration upon any *specialty* must make *profert* of it. This is done by an averment that the specialty is now in court, or words to that effect. The origin of the rule is this: When the pleadings were oral, and the plaintiff counted on a specialty, the defendant had a right to demand *oyer*, (*c*) that is, to hear it read; and it was then read from beginning to end. Now the same end is obtained in the following manner: The plaintiff makes *profert*, as before stated. This authorizes the defendant to demand a copy, which must be furnished before he can be required to plead. If his defence rest upon matter contained in it, he sets forth the instrument at length in his plea, and then specifies wherein his defence lies. The effect is the same

(*a*) Steph. Plead. 87, 97.

(*b*) Steph. Plead. 92.

(*c*) The form of *demanding oyer* is as follows: "The defendant comes and craves oyer of the said writing obligatory, and it is read to him in these words: [here the instrument is copied]; which being read and heard, the defendant says," &c.

I have already said that there is no good reason why this doctrine of *profert* and oyer should not extend to all written instruments; and that in practice our provision for a bill of particulars does virtually produce this result.

as if it had been fully set forth in the declaration, and after oyer the defendant may either demur or plead.

§ 212. **Trial.** (*a*) When the parties have thus made up an issue, the next step is the trial of that issue. If it be an issue of law, the trial is by the court, who hear the arguments of counsel and then pronounce judgment; but if it be an issue of fact, the court will not try it, unless it be submitted by consent of parties; except in the single case, where the existence of a record is put in issue by the plea of *nul tiel record.* This issue can be decided only by the production of the record denied, for the inspection of the court, who thereupon decide whether it be the alleged record or not. But as to all other questions of fact, there must be a *trial by jury.* Formerly there were other modes of trial, as by *inspection*, by *certificate*, by *witnesses*, by *wager of battle*, and by *wager of law.* But as none of these prevail in this country, I will not waste time by describing them. *The trial by jury* is of high antiquity, and forms the boast of the common law. We have seen that it operates, by a division of the judicial power, as one of our constitutional safeguards. We have also seen, that by the seventh amendment of the *federal* constitution, it extends

(*a*) See 1 Swift's Dig. b. 3, chap. 22; 3 Black. Com. chap. 22, 23; Steph. Plead. 107–13. The Code specifies three issues of fact: 1. Upon a material allegation in the petition denied by the answer. 2. Upon a set-off or counter-claim denied by the reply. 3. Upon material new matter in the answer or reply. Issues of fact in action for money, or for specific, personal, or real property, must be tried by a jury, unless waived, or a reference ordered. All other issues of fact must be tried by the court, with discretion to order a jury or a reference. § 260–4. No change is made in the mode of summoning, impanelling, challenging, or swearing the jury. Each party briefly states his case, and the evidence he expects to offer. The party who would be defeated, if no evidence were offered, must first produce his evidence, and then the adverse party; after which the evidence must be confined to rebutting, unless the court otherwise order. When the evidence is concluded, either party may request instructions on points of law, which shall be given or refused by the court, and must be in writing, if either party require it. The argument follows the order of the evidence, and then the jury may be charged again. The jury may have a *view*, whenever the court think it proper. After the cause is submitted they cannot separate, unless the court permit them, for meals or sleep. They may come into court for further instructions. They may be discharged on account of the sickness of a juror, or other calamity, or by the consent of parties, or when there is no probability of agreeing; in which case there may be another trial at once, or at a future day, as the court may order. The verdict must be in writing and signed by the foreman, and either party may require the jury to be polled, when if one dissents they are to be sent back. § 265–74.

A trial by jury may be waived by the parties in actions of contract and in other actions, with the assent of the court; and it shall not be necessary for the court to state the facts found, unless requested for the purpose of excepting, in which case they must be stated in writing. § 279, 280.

There may be *trial by referees* of all issues, whether of fact or law, when both parties consent, and without such consent a reference may be ordered by the court, when it becomes necessary to examine accounts, or to have an account taken, or to try any question of fact out of the pleadings, arising upon a motion or otherwise. Sect. 282 of the Code is repealed by the act of April 8, 1857, and the court is authorized to direct a reference, in any case in which the parties are not entitled to a trial by jury. See Lawson *v.* Bissell, 7 Ohio State, 129. The referees cannot exceed three, upon whom the parties may agree; if not, the court appoints them. They conduct the trial in the same manner and with the same powers as a court. They state the facts found, and the conclusions of law separately. Their report, unless excepted to, stands as the decision of the court. § 281–9.

"to all suits at common law, where the value in controversy shall exceed twenty dollars." The language of our State constitution is, that "the right to trial by jury shall be inviolate;" and similar expressions are found in all the State constitutions. But these declarations, even where they are unqualified, are not designed, as we have seen, to exclude equity and admiralty jurisdiction, which is exercised without a jury; because the same constitutions recognize both. The right, then, to a trial by jury, is confined to proceedings in courts of law, where *legal rights*, as distinguished from *equitable*, are decided upon. (*a*) Nor are they intended to take away the jurisdiction of justices of the peace, who usually decide without a jury; because the provision of the federal constitution is confined to proceedings in the federal courts; and the State constitutions recognize the ancient powers of justices of the peace. Besides, their decisions being never final, the dissatisfied party may always appeal, and thus have his trial by jury. Lastly, a jury need not necessarily consist of *twelve men*, though this is the usual number required by law. (*b*) But our statutes frequently provide for a less number to determine facts in controversy. Thus three persons appraise the value of property under the law regulating executions, and occupying claimants; six persons form the jury in trials of the right of property, and in forcible entry and detainer; seven, in trials of lunacy; and five in cases arising under the apprentice act. A jury, therefore, may consist of any convenient number of men designated by law. The spirit of the constitutional provisions respecting trial by jury is, that in legal proceedings, the power to decide finally upon law and fact shall not be vested in the same persons; and instead of wasting words in eulogy of this institution, I proceed to show how jurors are designated, and what are their functions. I would previously observe, however, that, admirable as the jury system is admitted to be, it has one feature, which has been the subject of much difference of opinion. I refer to the *entire unanimity* required for their decision. Many have doubted whether it would not be an improvement, at least in civil cases, to dispense with entire unanimity, so difficult to be obtained, when there is room for doubt, and only require a specific majority, say two-thirds or three-fourths, to concur in a verdict.

Jurors. Our jurors are required to have the qualifications of electors, which have been before described. (*c*) The legislature fixes a number sufficient for all the courts in each county, no one

(*a*) This constitutional provision relates to trials of issues of fact, and not mere collateral questions, where no suit is pending. Millyard *v.* Hamilton, 7 Ohio, 111; Hickox *v.* Cleveland, 8 id. 543; Lake Erie R. R. Co. *v.* Heath, 9 Ind. 558. The right of trial by jury may be waived. Gest *v.* Kenner, 7 Ohio State, 75.

(*b*) But where the term is used in the Constitution without any language indicating a different intent, a jury of twelve is presumed to be intended. Lamb *v.* Lane, 4 Ohio State, 167.

(*c*) Eastman *v* Wright, 4 Ohio State, 156.

serving more than one term in each year. These are annually apportioned among the townships, by the clerk of the court of common pleas, according to the number of white male adults. The township trustees *select* the number allotted to their township, and return a list to the clerk of the court; but the mode of selection is not specified. The names thus returned are put into a box, and thirty days before each term of court, the sheriff and clerk draw out twenty-seven. The first fifteen so drawn are *grand jurors* who only act in criminal cases, and need not now be described. The remaining twelve are *petit jurors*, sometimes called *trial* or *traverse jurors*, who serve both in civil and criminal cases. A writ then issues, called a *venire facias*, commanding the sheriff to summon the jurors thus designated, to appear on the first day of the term, which writ is served ten days before the term. The jurors thus summoned are bound to serve unless excused. The number of twelve constitutes the *panel*. If it should not be full, for the trial of any cause, the deficiency is supplied from by-standers, who are called *talesmen*, and are selected by the sheriff. (*a*) When the panel is full, each party may *challenge* two jurors *peremptorily*, that is, without assigning any cause; and *for cause*, each may challenge any number, who are obnoxious, and the court will try the challenge. The principal causes of challenge are, conviction of any crime; interest in the cause; having been an arbitrator, or juror, in the same matter before; being of kin to either party; standing in the relation of master, servant, or attorney; being summoned as a witness; not understanding the language; or any other cause tending to disqualify one from acting intelligently and impartially. Provision is also made for a *struck jury*, at the request of either party. In this case, the clerk draws forty names from those in the box; from this list, the parties proceeding alternately strike out twenty-four, and of the remaining sixteen, the first twelve who are not challenged, form the struck jury. When the panel is thus completed, the oath is administered, by which the jurors bind themselves "to give a true verdict according to the evidence." This oath, (*b*) it may be observed, binds the conscience only, for the violation of it, by giving a false verdict, cannot probably be punished as perjury, under the definition of that offence heretofore given. It is much to be regretted that the organization of our juries cannot be altered with respect to the

(*a*) Provision is made for a special *venire facias* in such cases by the act of March 22, 1860.

(*b*) The following is the form of a *juror's oath:* "You and each of you do solemnly swear in the presence of Almighty God, that you will well and truly try the issue joined between the parties in this cause, wherein ——— is plaintiff, and ——— is defendant, and a true verdict give according to the evidence, unless lawfully discharged therefrom; and this you do as you shall answer to God at the great day." The *affirmation* begins: "You and each of you do solemnly declare and affirm that," &c. — and concludes: "And this you do under the pains and penalties of perjury."

From which it will be seen that the affirmation makes no appeal to God or a future retribution, but relies for its sanction wholly on the temporal consequences of perjury.

talesmen or by-standers. The objection is, that they are selected by the sheriff, and generally from those immediately around the court. This affords an opportunity, at least, for collusion and corruption, by selecting persons who are known to favor one of the parties. Would it not be an improvement to have *supernumeraries* selected in the usual way, to supply probable deficiencies in the panel? This would certainly diminish the present evil, if not remove it entirely.

Evidence. (*a*) The subject of evidence includes all those rules which regulate the procurement and presentation of testimony in courts of justice. Strictly speaking, all evidence consists either of facts proved by *personal testimony*, or of *inferences* drawn from facts so proved. And this leads to a division of evidence into *positive*, *presumptive*, and *circumstantial.* Positive evidence includes all facts directly proved. Presumptive evidence includes all those inferences which the law itself draws from facts directly proved. Circumstantial evidence includes all those inferences which the jury draw, according to their discretion, from facts directly proved. Where evidence is such that it cannot be admitted at all, it is said to be *incompetent*, and where it does not apply to the issue, *irrelevant.* These are questions of law for the court. The *credibility* of testimony is a question of fact for the jury after it has been admitted by the court as both competent and relevant. All evidence is divided into *primary* and *secondary.* Primary evidence in a given case, signifies the highest and best evidence which that case admits of. Secondary evidence, of course, includes all other degrees; and it is a fundamental rule that secondary evidence will not be received, while primary can be had. Thus, the best evidence of the contents of a paper is the production of the paper. The next best evidence is a sworn copy. And the next, the recollection of a witness who had read the paper. And the general rule is, that a lower degree of evidence will not be received, without first showing that a higher degree cannot be had. Again, all evidence is divided into *written* and *unwritten.* Written evidence includes *writings of record* and *writings not of record.* Unwritten or parol evidence includes all other kinds. When written documents are offered in evidence, the first step is to prove their *genuineness;* that is, that they are what they purport to be. The next question is as to their *effect* as evidence. And of the different degrees of written evidence, records are the highest; since the facts they contain cannot be contradicted by any other evidence; and next in order are unrecorded writings which cannot be contradicted by unwritten evidence. Records are either *public* or *private.* Public records are kept in public offices, and not allowed to be removed therefrom; and as they cannot be produced in court, the

(*a*) On the subject of evidence, the principal treatises are those of Wharton, Greenleaf, Swift, Peake, Gilbert, Phillips, Starkie, and Roscoe. The first three are American works, and the edition of Phillips by Cowen and Hill, with its voluminous notes, may be said to be also an American work.

law permits them to be proved by *exemplification.* An exemplification of a record is a copy thereof made and certified by the proper officer, under the proper seal; and this, though in fact secondary evidence, is universally received as primary. Whereas, private records, those of corporations for example, not being confined to one place, must be proved like other writings.

Order of Introducing Testimony. As a general rule, the party having the affirmative of the issue begins by presenting his testimony. It must be such as to make out a *primâ facie case;* that is, it must be sufficient to prove the issue, if nothing come from the other side. Otherwise, the adversary may move the court to overrule the testimony and give judgment accordingly. In making this *primâ facie* case, all the ground must be covered, which it is intended to occupy during the trial; for in strict practice no new matter can be offered at a subsequent stage of the trial. (*a*) The party having the affirmative then *rests*, and the adversary brings forward his counter-proof, the object of which is to assail the case made on the other side. If he bring forward no new matter, the testimony will here close. But if he adduce new matter, the first party may bring evidence to assail such new matter.

Records of this State. (*b*) *Legislative proceedings* are evidenced by the *journal*, which is kept by the clerk of each house. *Statutes*, however, are not set out in this journal, but are preserved in distinct *rolls* in the department of State. They are therefore evidenced by exemplifications, made by the secretary of state under the great seal. (*c*) But as the secretary supervises the publication of these statutes, the printed volume is never objected to within the State. *Judicial proceedings* are evidenced by exemplification of the records thereof, made and certified by the clerk, under the seal of the court. Justices of the peace have no clerk or public seal; but they are required to keep *dockets* of their proceedings; and certified transcripts therefrom, are evidence of such proceedings. *Executive proceedings* are evidenced by exemplifications from the journal thereof, made by the secretary of state under the great seal. In addition to these public records of the State, the law requires *deeds*, *wills*, and *certificates of marriage*, to be recorded, as we have seen, in the public offices; and in the absence of the originals, copies duly certified by the proper officer, are admitted as evidence. These matters, however, being private, the records thereof, although public, do not stand upon the same footing of unques-

(*a*) Graham *v.* Davis, 4 Ohio State, 362.

(*b*) The Code provides that printed copies of statutes of any sister or foreign State or nation, purporting or proved to be published by authority, shall be admitted as presumptive evidence of such statutes; and the unwritten or common law may be proved by parol evidence, or books of reports.

(*c*) An exemplification of the roll thus filed in the office of the secretary of state is the sole and conclusive evidence of the existence and contents of a statute. The journals of the houses are not competent evidence to show that the roll thus filed does not contain the whole of the law, as in point of fact it was enacted. The State *ex rel.* Pangborn *v.* Young, 5 Am. L. Reg. (N. S.) 679 (New Jersey).

tionable verity, as those before spoken of; but only on the footing of their private originals.

Records of the United States. As the federal government extends over the whole Union, its proceedings, whether legislative, judicial, or executive, are proved in the same manner throughout the Union, as the records of a single State are within that State. Nothing, therefore, need be added on this head.

Records of Sister States. In consequence of an express provision of the constitution, which has been remarked upon before, the States, with respect to their public acts and records, have ceased to be foreign to each other: and such acts and records, when proved as directed by the act of Congress, are declared to have the same effect in every other State, as in the State where they belong; but these have been sufficiently described already.

Records of Foreign Nations. As a general rule, our courts are not presumed to know the public offices or public seals of foreign nations; and, accordingly, their public acts and records must be proved in the same way as any other fact. There are instances, however, in which exemplifications under the great seal, accompanied by proof that it is the great seal, have been admitted. But even when proved, these records have not the same absolute and conclusive verity as those of our own country. The facts they contain may be questioned.

Writings not of Record. (*a*) When such writings are produced in court, the first question is, whether they are really the writings they purport to be. But ancient deeds, maps, and histories are usually admitted as such without question, on account of their antiquity. (*b*) Also, the returns of sheriffs and other officers of court, and the notarial acts of notaries public, usually pass unquestioned, because of their official character. But these are exceptions to the general rule, which is, that whenever a writing is offered in evidence, its genuineness or identity must first be proved. If there be a subscribing witness, he must be called; if he cannot be had, his absence must be accounted for, and then his handwriting may be proved, which will be taken as proof of the execution of the writing. If there be no subscribing witness, the handwriting of the maker must be proved. Our statute dispenses with the proof

(*a*) The Code has some excellent provisions relating to documentary evidence. Either party, before trial, may require the other to admit the genuineness of a writing and if he refuses without good reason, he must pay the expense of proof. So either party may demand the inspection or copy of any writing in the possession of the other, and if refused without good reason, may have it excluded on the trial, or if he wishes it as evidence, his affidavit of its contents may be received. This includes all books, papers, or documents. See act of March 6, 1857, amending the Code. As to *handwriting*, see 1 Greenl. Ev. § 576–81, where the subject is exhausted. As to who are *experts*, see same book. Perhaps the best definition is, persons professionally or scientifically acquainted with the subject. And see Hicks *v.* Person, 19 Ohio, 426; Clark *v.* The State, 12 id. 483.

(*b*) {Applegate *v.* Lexington, &c. Mining Co., 117 U. S. 255; Fulkerson *v.* Holmes, id. 389.}

of the execution of bonds, bills, and notes, as we have seen, unless denied under oath. When a witness is offered to prove *handwriting*, the general rule is, that he must have seen the person write. The only exception is where he has become acquainted with the handwriting by a correspondence with the person. It is not allowable to submit to the jury an admitted specimen of handwriting, that they may compare it with the one in dispute. The farthest that courts have gone in the comparison of handwritings, is to call *experts* or men of skill to examine them, and let their opinion go to the jury. But in more recent decisions even this has been denied, unless the persons of skill have seen the person in question write. (*a*) I have thus far supposed the writing to be in the possession of the party offering it. If proved to have been lost or destroyed, its contents may be proved by parol. (*b*) If in the hands of a third person, he may be required to produce it, by notice to that effect in the subpœna, which is thence called a *subpœna duces tecum;* if in the hands of the opposite party, notice must be given him to produce it, and on refusal, the contents may be proved. If the interest of a party require the actual production of books and papers in the possession of the opposite party, our statute empowers the courts of law to enforce their production, whenever a court of chancery would do so. For this purpose, ten days' notice must be given, particularly describing the books or papers required; at the expiration of which a motion may be made for an order that they be produced. If the order be granted upon the plaintiff and he fail to comply, a judgment of nonsuit may be entered against him; if upon the defendant, and he fail, a judgment by default. When a writing is thus made evidence, its effect upon the issue is to be gathered from its contents; and this is partly a question of law for the court and partly a question of fact for the jury. The general rule is, that no extrinsic or parol evidence can be admitted to explain any ambiguity in its contents, or supply any deficiency. But a distinction is made between *latent* and *patent ambiguities*. A patent ambiguity, is one apparent upon the face of the writing, and discoverable on the mere perusal. This cannot be explained by parol evidence, to show the actual meaning, because there would be danger of thus making a writing different from that which was intended. But a latent ambiguity, being discoverable only by reference to extrinsic facts, may be explained by extrinsic evidence. Thus if a writing name one person, and there happen to be two of the same name, the one actually meant may be ascertained by parol evidence.

(*a*) The testimony of experts is admissible, though they have never seen the person in question write, and have no previous knowledge of his handwriting, but found their opinion upon the comparison of the disputed paper with other papers already in the case, and admitted or proved to have been written by the person claimed to have written the disputed paper. Calkins *v.* The State, 14 Ohio State, 222. And see Rogers *v.* Ritter, 12 Wall. 317.

(*b*) As to lost deeds, see Allen *v.* Parish, 3 Ohio, 107; Blackburn *v.* Blackburn, 8 id. 81; Armstrong *v.* M'Coy, 8 id. 128; Starke *v.* Smith, 5 id. 455.

Personal Testimony. (*a*) Personal testimony is that which is

(*a*) The Code has greatly modified the law as to the *competency* of *witnesses*. Neither interest in the event, nor being a party, nor conviction of a crime, is any longer a disqualification, but goes only to the credibility. Each party may testify for himself, and compel his adversary to testify. Nor is color or want of religious belief any longer a criterion of competency. But those who are still incompetent include persons of unsound mind; infants under ten years who appear incapable of testifying intelligently; husband and wife for or against each other, or concerning any communication made by one to the other during the marriage, whether called while the relation subsists, or afterwards; attorneys, as to any professional communication, without the consent of the client; and priests as to confessions made in the course of church discipline, without the consent of the person confessing. R. S. § 5241 provides, "The following persons shall be incompetent to testify: 1. An attorney concerning any communication made to him by his client in that relation or his advice thereon, without the client's express consent, or a physician concerning any communication made to him by his patients in that relation, or his advice thereon, without his patients' consent. 2. A clergyman or priest of any confession made to him in his professional character in the course of discipline enjoined by the church to which he belongs. 3. Husband or wife concerning any communication made by one to the other during coverture, or any act done by either in the presence of the other during coverture, unless such communication was made or such act was done within the known presence, hearing, or knowledge of a third person competent of being a witness, whether the husband or wife be called as a witness while that relation subsists or afterwards. 4. No person who would, if a party, be incompetent to testify under the provision of section 5242, shall become competent by reason of an assignment of his claim. 5. Nor shall any person who would be incompetent to testify under the provisions of section 5242, in an action between himself and any person named therein, become competent by reason of a sale or transfer of any property by said executor, administrator, guardian, trustee, heir, or devisee, concerning which property said action is brought, or in which action the title to the same is involved. By the provisions of the act of July 2, 1864, and of the amendatory act of March 3, 1865, parties may now testify in the courts of the United States, with few exceptions, in civil actions. These provisions apply also to cases in which the United States is a party. Green *v.* The United States, 9 Wall. 655. At common law it has been held in Ohio that a woman, who has been divorced, is not a competent witness against her late husband to prove a contract made by him during coverture. Cook *v.* Grange, 18 Ohio, 526. But a widow is a competent witness against her husband's administrator when her testimony is not a disclosure of her husband's conversations or admissions, or a violation of his confidence or prejudicial to his reputation. Stober *v.* McCarter, 4 Ohio State, 513. R. S. § 5242 excludes the testimony of a party where the adverse party is a guardian, executor, or administrator, except in certain specified cases in which such testimony is admissible. But the section as amended April 15, 1867, does not prevent the administrator from testifying, where he is plaintiff, as to facts occurring prior to the death of his intestate. Doughman's Adm'r *v.* Doughman, 21 Ohio State, 658. A party to a suit is incompetent to testify as against parties claiming through a deceased person, as to facts occurring before the death of such deceased, though his evidence would be admissible against other parties to the suit. If the case be one in which several judgments may be rendered, the testimony may be received as to those against whom it is competent, and excluded from consideration as to the others. Hubbell *v.* Hubbell, 22 Ohio State, 208. It provides also that where the deposition of a party is taken, the notice must state that the deposition to be taken is that of a party. See Myers *v.* Walker, 9 Ohio State, 558. As to the competency of the evidence of husband and wife for or against each other under section 5241, see Bird *v.* Hueston, 10 Ohio State, 418; Nuser *v.* Beach, 15 Ohio State, 172. A court, so far from *requiring* an attorney to disclose the communications of his client, will not *permit* him to do so without his client's consent. But where a party offers himself as a witness, he, under section 315 of the Code, consents to the examination of his attorney. King *v.* Barrett, 11 Ohio State, 261. R. S. § 5242 is in the nature of a statute against frauds and perjuries. The testimony of a party is excluded where it relates to transactions between him and a deceased person whose estate is affected by the suit. It was considered that there would be a temptation in such a case to fraud and perjury against which protection should be given by excluding the testimony. Stevens *v.* Hartley, 13 Ohio State, 525. See also Hoover *v.* Jennings, 11 Ohio State, 624.

The form of the *oath* is as follows: You solemnly swear in the presence of Almighty given under an oath or affirmation. It is either given *orally* in court, or by *depositions*. But in either case, the first question is, who are *competent* to testify? and the law holds the following persons incompetent: 1. For want of requisite understanding, *idiots* and *lunatics* are always excluded; (*a*) and *infants* are excluded whenever, from express interrogation by the court, they are found not to comprehend the nature of an oath. 2. On the ground of *interest*, all persons are excluded who have the least direct *pecuniary interest* in the event of that particular suit; but not those who have an indirect interest, however great, in the question of fact therein disputed. When we reflect that, with the single exception of husband and wife, the nearest friends and relations of the parties are allowed to testify, notwithstanding the strong bias of affection, this absolute exclusion, for any merely pecuniary interest, would seem to be of doubtful expediency, to say the least, yet so the law stands, and the only exceptions made by our statutes, are those of legatees in a will to which they are subscribing witnesses; persons testifying to their own accounts of not more than eighteen months' standing; and mothers of illegitimate children, as to who is the father. 3. On account of *infamy*, all persons are excluded, in this State, who have been convicted of any penitentiary offence, except manslaughter, and duelling, unless afterwards pardoned. If this exclusion proceeds upon the ground that these persons would perjure themselves, and that the jury could not detect their falsehood, it seems unreasonable; and if this be not the ground, it is difficult to conjecture what is, or how a pardon would help the matter. 4. On account of *color*, in this State, all "black and mulatto persons" are excluded from testifying in cases where either party is white. This rule, to say the least, approaches the verge of inhumanity; and hence our courts have decided that they will construe the provision strictly, and admit all persons above the shade of *half black*, which is the meaning of mulatto. (*b*) 5. For want of *religious belief*, (*c*) it has been the rule to exclude all persons who do not believe in the existence of a Supreme Being, and in a future state of retribution. But when our constitution declares "that no human authority can, in any

God [or on the Holy Evangelists], that you will testify the truth, the whole truth, and nothing but the truth, in the case now pending, wherein ——— is plaintiff and ——— is defendant; and this you do as you shall answer to God. The *affirmation* begins: You do solemnly declare and affirm that, &c.; and concludes: And this you do under the pains and penalties of perjury.

It has been doubted whether the phrase, "the whole truth," ought not to be omitted, because the witness may not be interrogated to that extent.

(*a*) {A person whose mind is deranged is admissible as a witness if the court is first satisfied that he sufficiently apprehends an oath, and is capable of correctly recounting the matters he is called on to testify to having seen or heard. District of Columbia *v.* Armes, 107 U. S. 519.}

(*b*) See Medway *v.* Natick, 7 Mass. 88; Gray *v.* Ohio, 4 Ohio, 353. This had ceased to be ground of exclusion before the Code.

(*c*) Hunscom *v.* Hunscom, 15 Mass. 117; Wakefield *v.* Ross, 5 Mason, 16; Kisor *v.* Stanriper, Wright, 323; Easterday *v.* Kilborn, id. 343. The new constitution declares this to be no ground of exclusion.

case whatever, control or interfere with the rights of conscience," it may well be doubted whether this inquiry can properly be made of a *witness*, to say nothing of the absurdity implied in questioning a witness as to his belief, for the purpose of showing that he is not worthy of belief. Besides, the oath of an atheist, though it wants the religious obligation which belongs to the oath of the believer, has yet the same temporal obligation resulting from the pains and penalties of perjury. For these reasons it would seem that the want of religious belief ought not to render a witness incompetent, though the jury may properly take it into consideration in weighing his credibility. These five classes of persons, together with husband and wife, where either is interested, comprehend all the persons who are *excluded* from testifying on the score of incompetency; and the only persons who are *privileged* from testifying, are attorneys, with reference to all matters professionally confided to them by their clients. Efforts have sometimes been made to obtain this privilege for clergymen and physicians, with respect to matters communicated to them in professional confidence; but without success. (*a*) I have often felt a doubt whether the question of competency had not better be altogether dispensed with. From the statements just made, you will readily perceive how often it must happen, that those who know most about the matter before the jury, cannot be heard at all, because incompetent. It is not pretended that all persons are equally entitled to belief; but the question is, whether, with all the sanctions in favor of truth, and all the means of detecting falsehood, which the law so abundantly furnishes, we might not safely hear testimony from every quarter, and credit that which would seem worthy of credit. Equity does not hesitate to receive the testimony of the parties themselves; and why should courts of law be more scrupulous? The question presents a choice of evils. By admitting all persons to testify, we should more frequently have false testimony, which sometimes would escape detection. By excluding certain classes of persons altogether, we often deprive ourselves of the only testimony which could develop the truth. Is not the latter evil the greater? (*b*)

(*a*) Duchess of Kingston's case, 11 State Trials, 243; Du Barre's case, Peake's Cases, 78; 1 M'Nally, 254. But see the case of The People *v.* Phillips, decided in New York in 1813, by the court of sessions, specially reported by Counsellor Sampson, and abridged in 1 Western Law Journal, 109, in which it was held that a Catholic priest was privileged from testifying. De Witt Clinton delivered the opinion. See also a work upon this subject by Anstey, referred to in 5 Law Reporter, 237. The Code privileges clergymen and physicians.

(*b*) By the Code, a witness cannot be compelled to go out of his county, either to testify in court or to give his deposition. At the time of service he may demand his travelling fees, and one day's attendance, and at the commencement of each day after the first, his fee for that day. If he consent to go into another county, he is not liable to be sued therein by being served with process. Prisoners may be produced as witnesses by order of court, or their depositions may be taken in prison. § 316-331.

Form of a Subpœna. To —— [the witness]. We command you, that laying aside all manner of business or excuse, you appear before the court of ——, on the —— [name the day and hour], then and there to testify in a certain action

Attendance and Examination of Witnesses. Every litigant has a right to the personal attendance of witnesses, who are within the jurisdiction of the court, upon tendering the legal fees, if demanded. The first process is a *writ of subpœna*, which in form commands the witnesses to appear and testify under a *penalty* for disobedience; but which in fact is nothing more than a *notice*. If the witness thus notified refuses to appear, he may then be attached and brought in by force, to answer for his *contempt* of the process of the court. He is, likewise, answerable in *damages* to a party who should lose his cause for want of such attendance. When presented at the stand, he may be examined on the *voir dire*, which is a preliminary oath, to answer all questions touching his competency. If no objection be made on this ground, the regular oath or affirmation is administered by the clerk. The party who calls him, first examines him; and this is called the *examination-in-chief*. During this examination no *leading questions* can be asked; that is, no questions so framed as to indicate the answer desired; but the witness may refresh his memory as to names and dates, by consulting his own memoranda. The *cross-examination* by the adversary may be by leading questions, and as searching and particular as he pleases; for this is often the only way to detect a false witness. But cross-examination applies only to the matter brought out in chief. (*a*) As to any new matter, the party makes the witness his own, and becomes an examiner-in-chief. When this examination is closed, the examiner-in-chief may cross-examine as to any new matter brought

wherein ——— is plaintiff and ——— is defendant; and this do under penalty of the law.

In a *subpœna duces tecum*, add: And also that you bring with you a certain [describe the writing or document required].

Sometimes the subpœna is addressed to the sheriff, commanding him to summon the witness; but the above is according to the Code. If the witness has been personally served, and does not appear, a peremptory attachment may be had to bring him in; but if by a copy left at his residence, the practice is to grant a rule in the first instance to show cause why he should not be attached.

The form of the *writ of attachment* is as follows: We command you that without delay you attach ———, so that you have him before our court of ———, to answer touching a contempt which he has committed against said court, as is alleged, and further to abide such order as shall be made in this behalf.

(*a*) The rule as stated in the text is the rule of the federal courts. Phil. & Trenton R. R. *v.* Simpson, 14 Pet. 448, and of some of the States, Helser *v.* McGrath, 52 Penn. State, 531; City of Aurora *v.* Cobb, 21 Ind. 492; Bell *v.* Prewitt, 62 Ill. 362; Congar *v.* Galena, &c. R. R., 17 Wis. 477; Sumner *v.* Blair, 9 Kan. 521; Bassham *v.* State, 38 Tex. 622; People *v.* Miller, 33 Cal. 99. The rule in England is that if a witness has been intentionally called and sworn and is a competent witness, the other party has a right to cross-examine him to the whole case though the party calling him has declined to ask a single question. 2 Taylor Ev. 1216 and cases cited, and p. 1219 and cases cited. The rule in Ohio is that cross-examination is not limited to matters brought out in direct examination, but may extend to all matters bearing on the issue, provided that cross-examination of plaintiff's witnesses cannot be used as a means of introducing any distinct ground of defence. Legg *v.* Drake, 1 Ohio State, 286. The rule held in England, or as limited in Ohio, prevails in some States. Linsley *v.* Lovely, 26 Vt. 123; Beel *v.* Nichols, 2 Gray, 262; Jackson *v.* Varick, 7 Cow. 238; Donelly *v.* State, 2 Dutcher, 463; Lunday *v.* Thomas, 26 Ga. 537; State *v.* Sayres, 58 Mo. 585.

out on the other side. But he can bring out no further new matter himself, because this might make the alternation endless. A party is not permitted to discredit his own witness, because by calling him he has vouched for his credit; but he may disprove facts sworn to by him. Nor is the opposite party permitted to cross-examine as to any collateral or irrelevant matter merely for the purpose of contradicting the witness by other evidence. A witness is allowed to come back and explain any thing he has said before; but he cannot be called back, without consent of counsel or leave of court. The general rule is, that witnesses must testify as to their own *knowledge* only, and not as to their opinion, or as to what they have heard others say. In matters of skill and science, however, *experts* may be called expressly to testify as to their opinion; and there are some few cases, as pedigree, marriage, and character, in which general reputation is sometimes all the evidence that can be had. Each party may give in evidence the admissions of the other, and his own expressions made in the presence of the other; and when part of a conversation has been detailed, he against whom it operates may call for the whole. Witnesses are liable to be impeached, by showing that those who best know their reputation would not believe them under oath; (*a*) but a party cannot fortify the credit of his witnesses, until it has been first assailed on the other side. A witness may for his own protection refuse to answer, when such answer would expose him to a criminal prosecution; but not when it would only expose him to a civil liability, or merely tend to disgrace him.

Depositions. (*b*) When the personal attendance of a witness

(*a*) In impeaching the credit of a witness, the inquiry is restricted to his general reputation for truth and veracity. Craig *v.* The State, 5 Ohio State, 605.

(*b*) The Code does not materially alter the law as stated in the text, except in a few particulars. The time after service is to be sufficient to allow attendance by the usual route of travel, exclusive of Sundays, of the day of service, and one day for preparation. When the adversary is a non-resident of the State, and has no attorney therein, there must be publication for three consecutive weeks. The taking of depositions may be commenced at any time after the suit is commenced. If the officer have an official seal, this shall be a sufficient authentication, though taken out of the State. If not, it may be authenticated as in the text, or by parol evidence in court. The deposition must be filed at least one day before trial. Exceptions for any other cause than incompetency or irrelevancy must be filed before the trial, and the court may be required to decide them before trial. R. S. § 5285. By the act of March 16, 1860, defects in the certificate of the magistrate may be remedied by parol evidence. As to commissioners for the State of Ohio to take affidavits and depositions in other States, R. S. § 124.

As to depositions in the federal courts, see 30th section of the judiciary act of 1789, 1 Stat. at Large, 73, and *note* on page 89. Depositions may be taken when the witness lives or is about to go more than one hundred miles from the place of trial or to sea, or is ancient, or very infirm; and without notice, unless the adverse party is within one hundred miles of the place of taking. In admiralty, *in rem*, this refers to the person in charge of the property.

Form of Notice. A. B. *v.* C. D. Action of ——, in the court of ——. Depositions will be taken in this case by the plaintiff [or defendant], before a competent officer, at —— [giving not only the town, county, and State, but the place in the town], on ——, between the hours of —— ; and will be continued from day to cannot be had, either from infirmity, or from being without the county, the party can take his testimony by *deposition.* A deposition differs from an affidavit, in not being *ex parte.* Before a deposition can be made use of, the opposite party must have had an opportunity to cross-examine. Whereas an affidavit is taken without any notice to the party against whom it is to operate. We have two modes of taking depositions in this State; namely, upon *notice* merely, and by *commission* or *dedimus potestatem.*

Depositions may be taken *upon notice* as follows: The notice must be in writing, naming the time and place; and must be served upon the adverse party or his attorney, at such time as to allow him to attend by travelling twenty miles each day, exclusive of Sundays; and a copy of such notice, together with the proof or acknowledgment of service, must be attached to and returned with the deposition. The officers before whom it may be taken, are, any judge of a State or federal court, chancellor, master in chancery, justice of the peace, mayor, or notary public. The testimony must be reduced to writing in his presence, either by himself, the witness, or some disinterested person; and must be subscribed and sworn to by the witness; all which must be *certified* by the officer. (*a*) The authentication is then made as follows: If taken within the judicial circuit where it is to be used, the certificate of the officer, together with his official seal, if he have one, is sufficient; but if taken elsewhere, and before an officer having no official seal, besides the above certificate, the official character of the officer must be verified, either by parol evidence in court, or by the official certificate and seal of the clerk of the county or district court, or of the secretary of state. The deposition is then sealed up and directed to the clerk of the court where the cause is pending. It will be observed that depositions can be taken in this manner only within the United States; and where the place is very distant, the long notice required by law is often a great inconvenience. (*b*)

day, between the same hours, if necessary {[if the deposition of a party to the suit is to be taken the notice must so specify]}. [Dated and signed.]

Form of the Certificate. I, ——— [giving official character], do hereby certify that ——— [the witnesses before named], were by me sworn or affirmed, to testify the truth, the whole truth, and nothing but the truth; that the foregoing depositions by them respectively subscribed, were truly reduced to writing by me [or by ———, a disinterested person, in my presence]: and that the same were taken at the time and place specified in the enclosed notice. [Dated and signed with official seal, if there be one.]

(*a*) House *v.* Elliott, 6 Ohio State, 497. A waiver of objection to the competency of a witness, so as to allow his deposition to be taken in a cause, is a waiver during the whole progress of the cause. Choteau *v.* Thompson, 3 Ohio State, 424.

(*b*) By the Code, any court, or any judge thereof, may grant a commission to take depositions here or elsewhere; and the deposition must be taken upon written interrogatories, unless the parties otherwise agree.

Form of a Dedimus Potestatem. The State of ———, county of ———, court of ———. To ———. Know ye that we, confiding in your prudence and fidelity, have appointed you to take the depositions of witnesses in a certain cause pending in our said court, wherein ——— is plaintiff, and ——— is defendant; and therefore we command you that at certain times and places to be appointed by you, the said

Depositions may be taken by *dedimus potestatem*, as follows: Upon application to the court in term time, or to the presiding judge in vacation, a *commission* may be had, authorizing *any person* in any part of the world to take depositions in such time, place, and manner as shall be therein directed. The usual course is for the applicant to file his interrogatories with the clerk, and notify the opposite party; who then files cross-interrogatories; and these interrogatories are annexed to the commission. Sometimes, however, a commission issues without interrogatories; provision being made for notice to the opposite party. The *commissioner* thus appointed has all the power of an officer under the preceding method, and proceeds in the same manner. Depositions taken in either of these ways are of course open to all objections on the score of relevancy or competency, which could be made to the witness if present in court; and even when taken, they are not allowed to be read, if the witness can be had in court. There is one peculiar advantage in taking depositions by commission; namely, that by sending interrogatories with the commission, there need be no expense or trouble in employing counsel at a distance. The commissioner has only to take the answers to these interrogatories, in order to do justice to both parties.

Presumptive and Circumstantial Evidence. (*a*) This consists of *inferences* drawn from *facts*, proved in some one of the foregoing ways, that other facts exist. This kind of evidence is often of the most conclusive character. When an act has been done, proof that the defendant was in a condition and had motives to do it, makes it highly probable that he did do it; and if further proof be added, that no other person was in a condition to do it, the conclusion is nearly irresistible. Indeed, there are certain presumptions, which, by reason of their general recognition, have been called *presumptions of law*. Thus a receipt for the rent of the last year, raises a presumption that the rents of the preceding years have been paid. Long and undisputed possession of land raises a presumption of rightful ownership. The omission to produce written evidence within one's power raises a presumption that such evidence if produced would operate unfavorably. The detection of one falsehood in a witness raises a general presumption against his veracity. Good character and sanity are always presumed. The continuance

parties or their agents having ——— days' notice thereof, you cause such witnesses as may be required on either side, to come before you, and then and there examine each of them on oath or affirmation first taken before you; and that you reduce such examination to writing, and return the same, together with this commission, closed up under your seal, into our said court, with all convenient speed. [Conclusion as in writs.]

If interrogatories have been filed, the commission varies from the above, in omitting notice to the parties, and requiring the witnesses to be examined upon such interrogatories. The return or certificate of the commissioner states the time, place, and manner of executing the commission, so as to show that it has been fully obeyed.

(*a*) See Mathew on Presumptions; Wills on Circumstantial Evidence; Best on Presumptions.

of things in their existing state is always presumed. Thus, where there is uncertainty, the life of a person rather than his death is presumed; but this presumption ceases at the end of seven years after he was last heard from. Where parties have long acted as husband and wife, a legal marriage is presumed, and children of the wife are presumed to be children of the husband. In legal proceedings generally, all things are presumed to have been regularly done. These examples sufficiently illustrate the nature of circumstantial or presumptive evidence, as distinguished from positive. When an inference or presumption is thus raised, it makes what is called a *primâ facie* case; that is, such a case as calls upon the adversary for rebutting testimony; the rule is, that the party having the affirmative of the issue, must offer his testimony first, and until he makes a *primâ facie* case, the other party has no occasion to answer him. But I cannot further pursue the subject of evidence; enough has been said to give you some general ideas respecting it, and this is all I proposed to myself. Meantime there are certain incidents, liable to occur during the trial, which require a brief notice.

Incidents during Trial. The more important incidents liable to occur during the trial, are as follows: —

Nonsuit. (*a*) When the plaintiff fails to make out a case, either because his evidence is incompetent, or irrelevant, or insufficient, he must either be nonsuited, or have a verdict rendered against him. If he intends to appeal, it makes little difference which; for in either case, he must pay the costs, and our law allows an appeal in either case; but if not, he will prefer a nonsuit, because this does not hinder him from commencing another action for the same cause. There is, however, an arrangement, by which both consequences may be avoided, and the cause continued in court; and that is, *by withdrawing a juror;* which, by preventing the possibility of a verdict, places the cause back in the same condition as before the trial commenced. It is, of course, a matter of compromise with the parties, under leave of court.

(*a*) The most interesting question as to nonsuit is, whether a court has power to order a peremptory nonsuit, against the will of the plaintiff, after evidence tending to prove his case. On principle, it would seem not, for it virtually abrogates the right of trial by jury, secured by every American Bill of Rights. Nor do the most approved definitions sanction the idea; 3 Black. Com. 316, 376; 3 Bouvier's Law Inst. 530; and it is never allowed in the federal court; Elmore *v.* Grymes, 1 Peters, 469; De Wolf *v.* Rabaud, 1 id. 476; Crane *v.* Morris, 6 id. 598; Foote *v.* Silsby, 1 Blatchord, 445, and 14 How. 218. But in the State courts there is much conflict, though a preponderance against the power. Irving *v.* Taggart, 1 Serg. & R. 360; Girard *v.* Gettig, 2 Binney, 234; Mitchell *v.* N. E. Ins. Co., 6 Pick. 117; French *v.* Smith, 4 Vermont, 363; Smith *v.* Crane, 12 id. 487; Hunt *v.* Stewart, 7 Alabama, 525; Martin *v.* Webb, 5 Pike, 72; Wells *v.* Gaty, 8 Mo. 681; Davis *v.* Hoxey, 1 Scammon, 406; Booe *v.* Davis, 5 Black, 115; Bartow *v.* Brands, 3 Greene (N. J.), 248; Foster *v.* Dixfield, 6 Shepley, 380; Thompson *v.* Dickerson, 12 Barb. 108; Slipher *v.* Fisher, 11 Ohio, 299; Scroggs *v.* Bracken, 4 Yerger, 528; Ross *v.* Gill, 1 Wash. Va. 77; Brown *v.* Frost, 2 Bay, 126. The power is declared in Ellis *v.* Ohio Life Ins. & Trust Co., 4 Ohio State, 628. But under the Code, the court has no such power, if the plaintiff has offered any evidence tending to prove the issue on his part. Byrd *v.* Blessing, 11 Ohio State, 362.

Bill of Exceptions. (*a*) The object of a bill of exceptions is to make that a matter of record which otherwise would not be, for the purpose of a *writ of error*, to be described hereafter. Now the *interlocutory opinions* of the court during the trial, are not regularly recorded. If, therefore, either party thinks the opinion of the court wrong, in admitting or overruling testimony, or directing a nonsuit, or instructing the jury, or allowing or refusing a new trial, he may tender a bill of exceptions, pointing out the facts and error; which bill the court are required to sign and seal; and it thereby becomes a part of the record. This step is only taken for after use, and does not stay the proceedings at the trial.

Demurrer to Evidence. The verdict of a jury may either be *general*, simply finding the issue for one party or the other, and thus concluding both the law and fact; or it may be *special*, setting forth the facts proved, and leaving the law arising thereon to the court. Now the jury cannot be compelled to render the one or the other as may be desired; but may, by our law, have their option. Accordingly, if either party is willing to admit the *truth* of the testimony offered, and wishes to refer its *effect* at once to the court, so as to avoid a general verdict, he may *demur to the evidence;* which is thereupon reduced to writing, and entered like a special verdict, on the minutes of the court for future argument. (*b*)

(*a*) By the Code, an *exception* is defined to be an objection taken to the decision of the court upon a matter of law. It must be taken at the time the decision is made, and reduced to writing during the term. So much of the evidence only must be stated as to explain the exception. When it does not otherwise appear of record, a majority of the court must sign it, if true; and if not, correct it, and then sign it. It is filed as part of the record, but not spread upon the journal. House *v.* Elliott, 6 Ohio State, 497; Coleman *v.* Edwards, 5 id. 51; Hollister *v.* Resnov, 9 id. 9; Gest *v.* Kenner, 7 id. 75; Erwin *v.* Shaffner, 9 id. 43. If a question is asked and objected to, and the objection sustained, in taking an exception there should be a statement made of what it is proposed to prove, which must be something material, the rejection of which is prejudicial to the party excepting. Gandolfo *v.* The State, 11 Ohio State, 114. Mandamus will lie to compel a judge to sign a bill of exceptions. The bill tendered must accompany the application, and if the answer be that the defendant is willing to sign a true bill, but that the bill presented is not a true bill, the writ must be refused. Creager *v.* Meeker, 22 Ohio State, 207.

Form of a Bill of Exceptions. Be it remembered that on the trial of a certain action of ——, wherein —— was plaintiff, and —— was defendant, in the court of ——, at the —— term, the said —— to maintain the issue on his part, offered to prove that [here describe particularly the testimony offered]; to the admission of which testimony the said —— objected; which objection was overruled by the court, and the said testimony was admitted; to which opinion of the court the said —— excepted, and prayed the court to sign and seal this bill of exceptions, which is accordingly done, and the same is ordered to be made part of the record. [Signed and sealed by the judges.]

(*b*) *Form of a Demurrer to Evidence.* This day came the said parties by their attorneys, and thereupon came a jury, to wit [give the names of the jurors], who being impanelled and sworn the truth to speak upon the issue joined between the parties, the said plaintiff to maintain the issue on his part, showed in evidence that [set forth fully the testimony demurred to]; and the said defendant says that the aforesaid matters to the jury shown are not sufficient in law to maintain the issue on the part of the said plaintiff; and this he is ready to verify; wherefore he prays judgment, and that the jury may be discharged from giving any verdict; and that the said plaintiff may be barred of his action. [Signed by the attorney.]

The *joinder* is as follows: And the said plaintiff, because he has shown sufficient

Arguments of Counsel. When the testimony is closed, the cause is argued to the court and jury, by the counsel, not exceeding two on each side. The party on the affirmative of the issue has the opening, the adversary follows, and the opening counsel closes.

Charging the Jury. (*a*) When the arguments are closed on both sides, it is the province of the court to charge or instruct the jury on the points of law presented by the facts of the case. This is done as a matter of course, if there be any dispute about the law; and either party may move for particular instructions; the granting or refusing of which by the court, if erroneous, may be taken advantage of by a bill of exceptions. A sense of propriety does usually, and should always, prevent the court from intimating any opinion upon the weight of evidence; and on the other hand, a similar motive should induce the jury to take the law as laid down to them by the court. The theory of judicial proceedings requires these two functions to be kept entirely distinct. In practice, however, they are liable to be more or less confounded. Judges, in particular, are apt in their charge to sway the minds of the jury, by opinions upon the evidence; but this is as clearly an usurpation, as it would be for the jury to undertake to decide upon the law. In some of the States, the charge of the court is required to be reduced to writing, and read to the jury, who take it with them to their room; and it afterwards remains on file among the papers in the cause. (*b*) Many obvious advantages result from this provision; and perhaps it would be well if it were made universal.

Verdict. (*c*) The jury being thus in possession of the case re-

evidence to maintain the issue on his part, which the said defendant does not deny nor answer unto, prays judgment and his damages. [Signed by the attorney.]

The jury are then instructed to assess the damages, in case the judgment should be for the plaintiff, and return their verdict subject to the opinion of the court on the demurrer.

(*a*) R. S. § 5190 allows counsel before argument to request instructions to the jury on points of law, which the court must give or refuse, and which are to be reduced to writing, if either party require it. After argument, the court is immediately to charge the jury, which charge also is to be reduced to writing, if either party require it, and cannot be orally qualified or explained; and all written charges and instructions are to be taken by the jury in their retirement, and returned with their verdict into court, and filed with the papers of the case. Campbell *v.* Beckett, 8 Ohio State, 210.

(*b*) See Hardy *v.* Turney, 9 Ohio State, 400.

(*c*) See 3 Black. Com. 375. The meaning of verdict is a *true word.* By the Code, in every action for money only, or specific real property, the jury have an option to render a general or a special verdict. In all other cases, the court may require a special verdict, presenting the facts so fully, that the court have only to draw the conclusions of law. R. S. § 5200-3. The right of the court to direct a special verdict is discretionary; and the refusal to do so cannot be assigned as error. C. C. & C. R. R. Co. *v.* Terry, 8 Ohio State, 586. In civil actions at law, verdict is given for the party in whose favor there was a preponderance of evidence, including presumptions as evidence. And it is difficult to see on what ground a court can direct a jury to give verdict for one party when the jury finds the preponderance of evidence is with the other party.

In criminal prosecutions the rule is different. In a prosecution by the sovereign against a subject for crime, the parties being so unequal, and the consequence of conviction being fine or imprisonment or death, the Roman Civil Law as well as the English Common Law, in mercy to the accused required the prosecution to be made out, not merely by a preponderance of evidence, but beyond a reasonable doubt. In Engtire for deliberation, under the charge of an officer, who is sworn not to allow them to hold intercourse with any one, or to take any refreshment without leave of the court. It is a singular provision, and perhaps in civil cases an unwise one, as before observed, that all the jurors must agree in order to find a verdict. Those who reflect how rare it is to find *absolute unanimity* among men on any point of controversy will not wonder that jurors very frequently disagree as to a verdict. When this is the case, and there is no prospect of coming to an agreement by further deliberation, instead of starving them into unanimity, as was formerly done, the court order them to be discharged; and the cause remains for trial at a subsequent term, as if none had taken place. But when, on the other hand, they have agreed upon their verdict, they come into court and declare it, before separation, unless the court, with consent of counsel, give permission to seal it up, and then separate. In this case they either hand it to the clerk or one of the judges, or bring it in themselves at the next opening of the court. We have seen that it may be *general* or *special*, (*a*) at the option of the

land, in 1823, in Thurtell *v.* Beaumont, 1 Bing. 339, it was ruled that where in a civil action on a policy of insurance, the defence was that the plaintiff had wilfully burned the property, this defence must be made out beyond a reasonable doubt. But this case has been ignored and the contrary held in later cases. In civil actions under the Carriers' Act, where it was necessary to allege and prove loss by felonious acts, Voughton *v.* L. & N. W. R. R. Co., 9 L. R. Ex. 93; McQueen *v.* G. W. R. R. Co., L. R. 10 Q. B. 569, and in an action for penalty under the Bribery Act, where it was necessary to aver and prove a crime, Cooper *v.* Slade, 6 H. L. Cases, 746, a preponderance of evidence was held sufficient. One exception is made. Where there is a plea of justification in slander, it is held that the plea must be proved precisely as if the plaintiff were prosecuted for the crime charged. Chalmers *v.* Shackel, 6 C. & P. 478.

Thurtell *v.* Beaumont was followed in some early American cases, but it is now generally rejected. Shaul *v.* Norman, 34 Ohio State, 157; Schmidt *v.* Ins. Co., 1 Gray, 529; Kane *v.* Ins. Co., 38 N. J. L. 441; Ins. Co. *v.* Johnson, 11 Bush, 587; Rothschild *v.* Ins. Co., 62 Mo. 356; Blaeser *v.* Ins. Co., 37 Wis. 31; Hoffman *v.* Ins. Co., 1 La. An. 216; Scott *v.* Ins. Co., 1 Dillon, C. C. 105; Huchberger *v.* Ins. Co., 4 Biss. C. C. 265; 52 Conn. 53; 61 Iowa, 296; 51 Mich. 11. A distinction was made in Sinclair *v.* Jackson, 47 Maine, 102, that where the criminal act must be so set out in the pleadings as to raise the distinct issue of crime before the jury, in such case the criminal act must be proved beyond a reasonable doubt. And this distinction has been often referred to approvingly, as in Strader *v.* Mullane, 17 Ohio State, 624. But even this is disapproved in Gordon *v.* Parmelee, 15 Gray, 413; Jones *v.* Greaves, 26 Ohio State, 2, and Kane *v.* Ins. Co., cited above. And where action was brought for damages for arson of plaintiff's house. Bradish *v.* Bliss, 35 Vt. 326; Mead *v.* Husted, 52 Conn. 53. And for treble damages for a felonious taking, 30 Conn. 102, a preponderance was held sufficient. The exception which once obtained that a plea of justification in slander must be proved beyond a reasonable doubt — see Clark *v.* Dibble, 16 Wend. 601; Steinman *v.* McWilliams, 6 Barr, 170; Mix *v.* Woodward, 12 Conn. 262; Tucker *v.* Call, 45 Ind. 31; Darling *v.* Banks, 14 Ill. 46; Ellis *v.* Lindley, 38 Iowa, 461 — {is not now generally recognized, there being no reason why parties to a civil cause where liberty or life is not involved should not stand on an equality. As to the *quantum* of proof, see Bell *v.* McGinness, 40 Ohio State, 204, and cases cited}.

(*a*) The form of a *special verdict*, as it appears in the final record, is as follows: — This day came the parties by their attorneys, and thereupon came a jury, to wit [names of the jurors], who being impanelled and sworn to speak the truth upon the issue joined between the parties, upon their oaths did say [set forth the facts in their own words]; and if upon this finding the judgment ought to be for the plaintiff, then the jury assess his damages at ——— dollars; but if for the defendant, then they find accordingly.

Thus the question of law is wholly submitted to the court who hear argument thereon.

The form of a *general verdict* must correspond with the issue to be tried, and is jury; and it must assess the damages, if the case require it. The court may correct it in point of form, but cannot change the substance. It is delivered or declared by the foreman, and any juror may then express his dissent, but not afterwards. Sometimes, also, a party is permitted to *poll* the jury, that is, to ask each juror if he assents to the verdict, but this is not a matter of course. Jurors are not now punishable, as formerly, for finding a false or corrupt verdict, unless their misconduct amounts to a contempt. We shall see, however, that there are ways provided for avoiding the effect of a wrong verdict, for which purpose a discretion is lodged in the court; but in the mean time the verdict is entered on the journal of the court, and the jury are discharged, so far as relates to the case in hand.

Incidents after Verdict. In the regular course of proceeding, the next step is to pronounce *judgment.* But between the verdict and the judgment, certain steps may be taken to prevent the judgment, which are now to be described.

New Trial. (*a*) If the party against whom the verdict is, has sufficient cause, he may move for a new trial, and the court will hear argument upon such motion; but not more than two new trials will be granted in the same cause. The reasons of a new trial, which must be filed with the motion, are such as do not appear on the record, unless by a *bill of exception;* namely, where the court misdirect the jury; where evidence has been rejected or admitted contrary to law; where the verdict is against law, or against evidence, or on insufficient evidence, or gives excessive damages; where the jury have behaved improperly; and where a new and material fact has been subsequently discovered, which might change the verdict. Sometimes also a *venire facias de novo* is awarded, which has the same effect. The result is, that the former verdict is set aside, and the cause stands for trial as if none had taken place. (*b*)

commonly in the very words of the issue. Thus on the issue of *nil debet,* after the foregoing introduction: That the defendant does owe to the plaintiff the sum of——— dollars in manner and form as the plaintiff has declared; and they assess his damages by reason of the detention of the said debt to——— dollars.

(*a*) The Code defines a new trial to be, a re-examination in the same court of an issue of fact, after a verdict by a jury, report of a referee, or a decision by the court. Eight causes are specified for granting it. 1. Irregularity in the proceedings of the court, jury, referee, or prevailing party, preventing a fair trial. 2. Misconduct of the jury or prevailing party. 3. Accident or surprise. 4. Excessive damages. Durrell *v.* Carver, 9 Ohio State, 72. {But this may be cured by remittitur. Douglas *v.* Day, 28 Ohio State, 175.} 5. Error in the assessment of the amount of recovery. 6. Where the verdict, report, or decision is not sustained by sufficient evidence, or is contrary to law. Abernethy *v.* Wayne Co. Bank, 5 Ohio State, 266; Breese *v.* The State, 12 Ohio State, 146. 7. Newly discovered material evidence. Loeffner *v.* The State, 10 Ohio State, 598; Moore *v.* Coates, 35 id. 177. 8. Error of law occurring at the trial, and then excepted to. The motion must be made in writing, with the reasons, at the same term, unless the reasons could not then be discovered; and then not later than the second term after discovery. As to the rules governing the granting of new trials, see Waterman on New Trials, Hilliard on New Trials.

(*b*) As to new trial in action for recovery of real property, City of Marietta *v.* Emerson, 5 Ohio State, 288; Singer *v.* Bell, 8 Ohio State, 291. Affidavits of jurors

Arrest of Judgment. The party aggrieved may next make a motion in arrest of judgment, and the court will hear argument upon it. Judgment can only be arrested on account of some error appearing on the face of the record, and which might have been ground for demurrer. It must be an error in substance, and not merely in form, and may occur anywhere in the proceedings. If this motion prevail, no judgment is entered on the verdict, but the party making it has judgment in his favor.

Judgment non obstante. There is one case also in which the proper motion is for judgment notwithstanding the verdict; namely where the defendant has put in a defective plea of confession and avoidance, and yet obtained a verdict. Here the plaintiff's case being confessed by the plea, and the defence or matter in avoidance being insufficient, the verdict must, of course, be wrong; and judgment is properly rendered the other way.

Repleader. It sometimes happens that parties make up an *immaterial issue;* that is, an issue which, being found either way will not decide the cause. Whenever this state of pleading is discovered, the court will direct the parties to plead again, that a proper issue may be made.

§ 213. **Judgment.** (*a*) In the regular course of judicial proceedings, we have now reached the point at which the court pronounce the sentence of law upon the case presented, and which is called the judgment. A judgment is said to be *interlocutory*, when it does not fully terminate the controversy, and *final*, when it does. In general, the judgment is not pronounced in so many words from the bench, but its nature being intimated by the court, the clerk enters it on the journal in due form. From that moment it carries on its face such absolute verity, that while it stands

that they misunderstood the charge of the court will not be received on a motion to set aside the verdict. Holman *v.* Riddle, 8 Ohio State, 384.

(*a*) For the nature and various kinds and forms of judgments, see 3 Black. Com. chap. 24; Steph. on Plead. 138–45. By the common law judgment did not operate as a lien until execution was levied. And the time of being dormant, without execution, was a year and a day, after which it must be revived by *scire facias.* As to *judgment liens,* see an excellent note to 10 Ohio, 74. See provisions of the Code making judgment liens on real estate from the first day of the term at which judgment is rendered, § 5375–6; as to liens of judgments before justices of the peace, see § 5378. As to *questioning judgments collaterally,* see Ludlow *v.* M'Bride, 3 Ohio, 240; Ludlow *v.* Wade, 5 id. 494; Foster *v.* Dugan, 8 id. 87; Adams *v.* Jeffries, 12 id. 253; Douglass *v.* M'Coy, 5 id. 522. As to the power of the same court *to set aside, alter, or amend* a judgment at any subsequent term, unless fraudulently obtained, see Botkin *v.* Commissioners, 1 Ohio, 375; Reed *v.* Hatcher, 1 Bibb, 346; Medford *v.* Dorsey, 2 Wash. C. C. R. 433; Brackenridge *v.* M'Culloch, 7 Blackf. 334; Reynolds *v.* Stansbury, 20 Ohio, 344, and note.

By the Code, the judgment is so shaped as to specify the exact remedy or relief intended; in which respect it resembles a decree in chancery. When it is for a conveyance, release, or acquittance, and is not performed, it is declared to have the same operation and effect as if it had been performed. It is defined to be the final determination of the rights of the parties in an action. R. S. § 5310. And the power of the court which rendered the judgment to reverse, vacate, or modify it, after the term, on motion or petition, is greatly enlarged. R. S. § 5354 *et seq.* The court may in the judgment give the defendant affirmative relief. § 5329. Klonne *v.* Bradstreet, 7 Ohio State, 322.

unreversed, nothing can be received to contradict or gainsay it. To avoid all questions about priority, it takes effect from the first day of the term. Of itself, it is, by our statute, a lien upon all real property of the defendant within the county; and by levy of execution it becomes a lien upon any other property. With the exception of ejectment for reasons before given, it is a conclusive bar to all further litigation between the same parties, touching the same subject-matter. (*a*) Within the State, the plaintiff may take out execution to carry it into effect at any time, unless he suffer an interval of five years to elapse without so doing; in which case the judgment becomes *dormant;* (*b*) that is, it ceases to operate as a lien, or to authorize execution, until revived by an action of *debt* or *scire facias*. If several judgments be recovered against the same debtor, at the same term, and executions be taken out within ten days after the end of the term, there is no preference or priority; but otherwise the first execution has the preference, unless two or more be issued on the same day. If execution be not taken out within one year from the rendition of judgment, it loses its priority of lien with respect to subsequent judgments complying with this rule. If execution have been levied upon so much of the property of the debtor, that two-thirds of the appraised value will satisfy the debt, the lien of that judgment ceases upon the residue of his property, with respect to other judgment creditors. Several decisions have been made upon these provisions, the most important of which are, that if there be several judgments of the same term, and no levy within the year, they all stand upon an equal footing, and the first levy will have the preference; but if of different terms, the elder judgment still retains the preference; that when the title of the debtor was acquired after the judgment, the lien does not attach until levy; and that the lien does not in any case attach to an equitable title. In any other State or territory of the Union, though a judgment neither operates as a lien, nor authorizes execution, yet a mere exemplification of the record, according to the act of Congress, forms the highest possible evidence of debt, because the original merits of the case cannot be called in question; and in the action of debt brought to carry it into effect, the only issue is upon the

(*a*) {Roby *v.* Rainsberger, 27 Ohio State, 674. Ejectment is no longer an exception.} A judgment for or against one of the makers of a joint obligation is a bar to an action afterwards brought against another; but otherwise, if the obligation is joint and several. Clinton Bank *v.* Hart, 5 Ohio State, 33. {A note by a husband and wife is not joint in this sense, however. Avery *v.* Vansickle, 35 Ohio State, 270.}

(*b*) The fact of execution being stayed by injunction will not prevent the judgment from becoming dormant. Tucker *v.* Shade, 25 Ohio State, 355. See Winter *v.* Lightbound, 1 Strange, 301; Mitchell *v.* Cue, 2 Burr, 660. But the statute of limitations does not run against a judgment, though suffered to become dormant. Todd *v.* Crumb, 5 M'Lean, 172. {*Contra* now by R. S. § 5368, limiting the time to 21 years from dormancy. See as to limitations on foreign judgments, Fries *v.* Mack, 33 Ohio State, 52, 58.} As to revivor of dormant judgments, see R. S. § 5367. As to judgment upon a warrant of attorney irregularly entered, see Knox Co. Bank *v.* Doty, 9 Ohio State, 505.

record itself. Such, then, is the effect of a judgment, unless sus pended by an *injunction*, which will be described hereafter, or superseded or reversed by an *appeal* or *writ of error*, which are now to be described. (*a*)

Appeal. The nature of appellate jurisdiction has been already explained. An appeal lies only after the rendition of final judgment in the court below. Notice of intention to appeal must be given during the term, and entered on the journal; and within thirty days after the end of the term, the appeal thus notified must be perfected. This is done as follows: The appellant enters into a bond to the appellee, with such security as the clerk shall approve, in double the amount of the judgment, conditioned for the payment of the judgment and costs in the court above, if the same be against the appellant. The clerk then makes out a transcript of the proceedings, and delivers it, with all the papers in the cause, to the clerk of the court above. The whole case, including questions of law and fact, is thus removed for rehearing, and stands for trial in the court above, in the same manner as if it had been commenced there originally. The judgment, however, in the court below is not absolutely vacated by the appeal, for it still operates as a lien upon the real estate of the judgment debtor; but all proceedings to enforce it are in the mean time suspended; and it becomes finally merged in the judgment rendered above. You will remark that it is often for the interest of the prevailing party that his cause should be appealed; because he thereby obtains absolute security for the satisfaction of the judgment. Moreover, the abuse of the privilege is guarded against by penalties, where the only objection is delay.

Writ of Error. (*b*) This proceeding is designed to bring up

(*a*) Strictly speaking, there are but *two general forms of judgment;* namely, for the plaintiff and for the defendant. For the plaintiff the form is: Therefore it is considered by the court that the plaintiff recover of the defendant the said sum of ——— dollars, his damages aforesaid assessed, and also his costs in this behalf expended, taxed to ——— dollars. For the defendant the form is: Therefore it is considered by the court that the defendant go hence without day, and recover of the plaintiff his costs in this behalf expended, taxed to ——— dollars. But unless these judgments are rendered directly upon a verdict, they are always prefaced by the circumstances under which they are rendered. For example, a *judgment by default* would be entered thus: This day came the plaintiff by his attorney; and the defendant, though solemnly called, came not, but made default; whereupon it was considered by the court that the plaintiff ought to recover his damages by reason of the premises; and no jury being demanded, and the court being fully advised in the premises, did assess the damages to ——— dollars. Therefore it is considered, &c. And *a judgment confessed under a power of attorney* would be entered thus: This day came into court ———, by ———, his attorney, and filed his declaration against ———; and thereupon ———, one of the attorneys of this court, appeared on behalf of the said ———, and by virtue of a power of attorney for that purpose, duly executed by the said ———, and now produced in court and duly proved, did waive the issuing and serving of process, and did acknowledge that the said ——— did owe the said plaintiff [or did assume and promise], in manner and form as the said plaintiff has declared; and did confess that the said plaintiff has sustained damages by reason thereof to $———. Therefore it is considered, &c. And by virtue of the said power of attorney all error is released, and the right of appeal waived. [Signature of the attorney on the journal.]

(*b*) Groves *v.* Stone, 3 Ohio State, 576; Schooner Marinda *v.* Dowlin, 4 id. 500; *Ex parte* Collier, 6 id. 55; Hobbs *v.* Beckworth, 6 id. 254; Steubenville, &c. R. R.

questions of law only, for revision in the court above. At any time within five years after rendition of judgment, if there be substantial errors on the face of the record, a party may apply to the court above, or to one of the judges thereof, for the allowance of a writ of error. For this purpose a certified transcript of the record below is procured from the clerk, and the alleged errors are thereon specifically assigned or pointed out. The allowance of the writ, by the judge or court above, is matter of discretion. If it be allowed, the fact is indorsed by the judge or clerk on the transcript presented. This is handed to the clerk of the court above, who thereupon issues the writ of error, commanding the judges below to certify up the proceedings. At the same time, a *citation* issues to the adverse party that he may appear and attend to his interest. The party applying for the writ is denominated the *plaintiff in error*, and the other, *defendant in error*. If the judgment below is to be *superseded*, the plaintiff in error must give bond, as in case of appeal; and then the judgment below will merely operate as a lien; but, otherwise, it will remain in full force for all purposes until reversed above. Our present law allows proceedings to be amended even after a writ of error. If, therefore, the defect be such as an amendment will cure, there is no use in resorting to a *writ of error*. A writ of *certiorari* is analogous to a writ of error; but it issues from a higher court to any lower court, whether of record or not; and at any stage of the proceedings, as well before as after judgment. The writ of error now described is called a writ *coram vobis*, to distinguish it from one *coram nobis*, by which the highest court revises its own decisions. We have a statutory provision for both these writs. The principle is, that errors are to be corrected whenever discovered. (*a*)

Co. *v.* Patrick, 7 id. 170; Singer *v.* Bell, 8 id. 291; Goode *v.* Wiggins, 12 Ohio State, 341; Smetters *v.* Rainey, 13 Ohio State, 568; s. c. 14 Ohio State, 287; Stewart *v.* Williams, 15 Ohio State, 484; Schaeffer *et al. v.* Marienthal, Lehman, & Co., 17 Ohio State, 183. By the Code, there is no longer a *writ of error* or *certiorari*, but only a *petition in error*, and the time of limitation is two years, instead of five. It lies to the common pleas, to reverse, vacate, or modify any judgment, or final order of any inferior tribunal, board, or officer, and to the district court to do the like with respect to the common pleas, for errors appearing on the record. It also lies to the supreme court in all the preceding cases. The plaintiff in error must file with his petition an authenticated transcript of the proceedings below, whereupon a summons issues, which may be served upon the defendant or his attorney of record. In order to stay execution, security must be given to the satisfaction of the court or clerk; and where the judgment is upon a contract for money only, the plaintiff below may still obtain leave to enforce the judgment, upon giving security for restitution. If the judgment below be reversed, the court may either render the proper judgment or remand the case for that purpose; but the reversing court in no case issues execution. §§ 6707–6734. See *Ex parte* Collier, 6 Ohio State, 55.

(*a*) *Form of a Writ of Error.* To the Judges of the Court of ——— within and for said county. Because in the record and proceedings in a certain action of ———, which was lately in our said court before you, wherein ——— is plaintiff, and ——— is defendant, error has intervened, as is said, to the damage of the said ———, and we being willing that such error, if any there be, should be corrected, and full and speedy justice done in the premises, do command you, that if judgment be thereupon given, then, without delay you send to us, under the seal of your court, an authenticated transcript of the record and proceedings aforesaid, together with this writ; so

§ 214. **Execution.** (*a*) If execution be not prevented in one of the ways before described, it may be ordered out by a *precipe*, at the pleasure of the party interested. Execution may either be against the *person* or *property* of the judgment debtor. 1. The writ against the person is called a *capias ad satisfaciendum* or *ca. sa.* It can only be obtained under the circumstances and by means of the preliminary steps before described for procuring a writ of *capias ad respondendum*, together with the order of the court or judge. It commands the sheriff to take the body of the judgment debtor, and hold him in custody until he satisfies the judgment, or is otherwise legally discharged. Accordingly, when arrested on this writ, he must either pay the judgment, or take the benefit of the insolvent act, or go to jail, where he may have the benefit of prison limits; all of which have been sufficiently described; and the general doctrine is, that an arrest upon this writ, which is the highest remedy known to the law, precludes a resort to the other, whether it result in satisfaction or not. But this is altered by our statute, where one who has property takes the benefit of prison limits. (*b*) 2. The writ against the property is called a *fieri facias et levari facias*, or *fi. fa. et lev. fa.* It is properly a combination of two writs, the *fi. fa.* being directed against personal property, and the *lev. fa.* against real property. It commands the sheriff to cause the amount of the judgment to be made first out of the personalty of the debtor, and for want thereof, out of his realty. Accordingly,

that, the same being inspected, we may, at the next term of our supreme court, to be holden at ———, on ———, cause to be done, what of right ought to be done.

Assignment of Errors. And the said ——— now comes and says that in the record and proceedings aforesaid there is error in this, to wit: 1. That, &c. [specifying each of the errors separately]. Wherefore the said ——— prays that a citation [and a *supersedeas* if bond be given] may issue, that the said judgment may be reversed and that he may be restored to all things which he has lost by reason thereof.

Supersedeas and Citation. We command you that you forbear all further proceedings upon a judgment [describing it], which judgment we have caused to be brought into our supreme court by writ of error; and also that you cite the said ——— to appear before our said court, at ———, on ———, to show cause, if any there be, why the said judgment should not be reversed, and have you then and there this writ with your doings thereon.

Joinder in Error. And the said ——— comes and says that in the record and proceedings aforesaid there is no error; wherefore he prays that the said judgment may be affirmed, and that his costs may be adjudged to him.

If a defective transcript be returned from the court below, upon a suggestion of that fact specifying the defects, the court will issue a *certiorari*, commanding the court below to supply the defects.

(*a*) The Code provides very efficient means *in aid of execution*, when no property can be found to levy upon. An order may be obtained for examining the debtor himself, and any other witnesses, which examination may extend to all the debtor's means, of every description whatsoever; and if any thing be discovered, it must be subjected to the satisfaction of the judgment. R. S. §§ 5472–90. Union Bank of Rochester *v.* Union Bank of Sandusky, 6 Ohio State, 254. For provisions where the goods levied on are claimed by a third person, see § 5444–5.

(*b*) *Form of a ca. sa.* We command you that you take ———, and him safely keep, so that you have his body before our court of ——— on the first day of their next term to satisfy ——— for the sum of $———, which by the judgment [or decree] of our said court at their ——— term, in the year ———, one ——— recovered against the said ———, together with the interest thereon from ——— [date of judgment or decree]; and have you then and there this writ with your doings thereon.

if the sheriff can find no personal property, he indorses on the writ "*no goods*" and proceeds to *levy* upon the land. When goods are levied upon, they are sold at public auction, without appraisement, unless the judgment debtor demands it, on ten days' notice: and there are a few articles of small value, including necessary articles of household furniture, and tools or utensils of trade, which are specially exempted from execution, under all circumstances; but I shall not take up time in enumerating them. When land is levied upon, it must be *appraised* by three disinterested persons under oath; the notice must be thirty days; and the land cannot be sold for less than two-thirds of its appraised value, lest the judgment debtor be injured by a sacrifice. The mode of proceeding in the sale of land has been sufficiently described in a former lecture. If the judgment debtor have no property, personal or real, which can be levied upon, special provision is made for a proceeding in chancery against the debtor's *unleviable* means, which will be described hereafter. (*a*)

Costs. The judges are compensated, as we have seen, by salaries paid out of the public treasury: but the other officers of court, together with the jurors and witnesses, are compensated by specific fees, prescribed by law; and these fees constitute the *costs of court;* which the suitors are required to pay. The theory is, that each party pays his own costs as they accrue, for each particular service rendered; and it would be well to enforce this in practice, because much frivolous litigation would be thereby avoided; but instead of

(*a*) *Form of a fi. fa. et lev. fa.* We command you that you cause to be levied of the goods and chattels of ———, the sum of $———, which by the judgment [or decree] of our court of ———, at their ——— term in the year ———, one ——— recovered against the said ———, with interest thereon from ———; and for want of goods and chattels, that you cause the same to be levied of the lands and tenements of the said ———; and have that money before our court of ———, on the first day of their next term to render under the said ———; and have you then and there this writ with your doings thereon.

If goods or land remain unsold for want of bidders, or other cause, the *venditioni exponas* is as follows: We command you that those goods and chattels [or lands and tenements] of ———, which you, according to our command, lately took into your hands, and which remain unsold, you expose to sale, to satisfy, &c. [describe judgment as above]. In Ohio, a homestead to the value of one thousand dollars is exempted from sale on execution, and the head of a family having no homestead, his personal property to the amount of five hundred dollars in addition to chattel property otherwise exempt, is also exempted from such sale. § 5435-43; Burgess *v.* Everett, 9 Ohio State, 425. As to the notice required in the sale of land, on execution, see § 5393. As to the duty of the officer in making a levy where certain articles are exempted, see Frost *v.* Shaw, 3 Ohio State, 270. As to construction of law securing to married women property of the husband exempt from execution, see Slanker *v.* Beardsley, 9 Ohio State, 589; this act securing to married women the property of their husbands exempt from execution was repealed April 3, 1861. See note at end of chapter on Husband and Wife.

In ejectment, the execution, in addition to the collection of damages and costs, orders the plaintiff to be put in possession of the land. This is called a writ of *haberi facias possessionem*, and is as follows: Whereas, John Doe, on the ———, in our court of ———, recovered, against ——— his term yet to come in [describe the premises], which ——— had demised to the said John Doe, for a term not yet expired; and also the sum of $——— for his damages, and $——— for his costs; therefore we command you, that without delay you cause the said John Doe to have possession of his said term yet to come in the lands and tenements aforesaid: and that you cause to be levied, &c. [as before].

this, costs are seldom paid until the final termination of the suit. In either case, the general rule is, that they ultimately fall upon the losing party, as a regular incident to the judgment. If, therefore, they have been paid as they accrued, the winning party recovers his part back, together with the damages; if not, the whole are collected on execution from the losing party, together with the damages; so that in either case, the loser pays the whole if he has the means; if not, the winner must pay his part, and the officers must lose the rest, as a just punishment for not demanding them on rendering the service. We have seen, however, that in the course of proceedings, divers interlocutory orders are made, in which the payment of certain particular costs by one of the parties, is made the condition upon which some privilege, as amendment, continuance, and the like, is allowed by the court; but these are only exceptions to the general rule before stated.

Complete Record. (*a*) After the final termination of a suit in any court of record, it is the duty of the clerk, during the next vacation, to make a complete record thereof in a book prepared for that purpose, which is signed by the presiding judge at the next term. This record includes the writ, return, recognizance of bail, pleadings, orders, continuances, verdict and judgment, which are copied in the order of proceeding, and furnish a complete history of the cause, with the exception of the evidence: and even the evidence, or some part of it, may be spread upon the record, by means of a bill of exceptions, special verdict, or demurrer to evidence. The object of making this record is to preserve a perpetual

(*a*) *Form of a Record.* Pleas before the court of ——, within and for the county of ——, and State of ——, on the —— [date of the final judgment]. Be it remembered, that heretofore, to wit, on the ——, one —— sued out of the clerk's office of the court aforesaid, the following writ of ——, against one ——, to wit: [here copy the writ]. Upon which writ was the following indorsement, to wit: [here copy the indorsement]. And afterwards, to wit, on the ——, the said writ was returned to the court aforesaid by said sheriff, indorsed as follows, to wit: [here copy the return]. And afterwards, to wit, on the ——, the following recognizance of special bail was entered into, to wit: [here copy the recognizance]. And afterwards, to wit, on the ——, the said —— filed in the said clerk's office the following declaration, to wit: [here copy the declaration]. And afterwards, to wit, on the ——, the said —— filed in the said clerk's office the following plea, to wit: [here copy the plea]. And afterwards, to wit, on the ——, this cause was continued until the next term of said court. And afterwards, to wit, on the ——, before the said court, came as well the said —— as the said ——, by their attorneys aforesaid, and thereupon came a jury, to wit [here give the names of the jurors], who being impannelled and sworn the truth to speak upon the issue joined between the parties aforesaid, upon their oaths did say that [here set forth the verdict]. And thereupon it was considered by the said court that the said —— [here set forth the judgment].

The *certificate of the clerk* is as follows: The State of ——, county of ——. I hereby certify that the foregoing is truly taken and copied from the records of the proceedings of the court of ——, within and for the county aforesaid. In testimony whereof, I do hereto subscribe my name, and affix the seal of said court, this ——. [Signature of clerk and seal of court.]

If this record is to be used in another State, there must be another certificate by the presiding judge, as follows: I, —— [giving his official designation], do hereby certify that —— is clerk of said court, and that his attestation aforesaid is in due form of law; and that to all acts by him so done full faith and credit ought to be given. [Date and signature of Judge.] As to amendment of the record, see Doty *v.* Rigour, 9 Ohio State, 519, 526.

memorial of judicial proceedings, in a form convenient for public inspection. If the record exhibit any thing to show that the judgment is erroneous, we have seen that the error may be corrected by taking the proper course. But the truth of the facts therein contained cannot be called in question; the record itself furnishing the highest possible evidence of verity. We have seen that justices of the peace keep no record, strictly so called, but only a docket. In fact, the proceedings before them are attended with little formality or technical precision; and for this reason I have not thought it worth while to describe them. Here, then, would terminate our imperfect outline of civil proceedings in courts of law, but that there remain two topics, of great practical importance, which I shall discuss briefly, as a proper conclusion to this lecture. I mean the *survivorship of actions* and the *limitation of actions.* I would previously remark, however, that the subjects already discussed in this lecture will necessarily occupy a very wide space in your future inquiries. Perhaps I should be safe in saying that at least one-half of all the learning of a lawyer has reference to practice, pleading, and evidence; three topics, upon which more volumes have been written than I have occupied pages. And I would also remark, that one of the most useful exercises in which a student can engage, is that of making for himself a complete record of all the proceedings in the various actions, and repeating the operation until he becomes perfectly familiar with all its parts.

§ 215. **Survivorship of Actions.** (*a*) This topic, though highly important, is nowhere, so far as I know, made a distinct title in the books of practice. An action or a right of action is said to *survive*, when, upon the death of the original parties, it can be commenced or concluded, by or against their representatives.

As to Actions of Contract. It was a maxim of the civil law, that personal actions die with the person; but by *personal actions* were here meant *actions of tort* only, and not *actions of contract;* and in this sense, the maxim agreed with the ancient common law, which held that actions of contract alone survive. But it is obvious that this ancient doctrine has little foundation in reason. With respect to *crimes*, it is easy to see that the death of the offender must be a bar to punishment; but if a man has done me a *civil injury*, for which the law entitles me to pecuniary damages, why should I not have them out of his property after his death, as well as if the same amount had been due me by contract? It is evident that there is no good reason for the distinction; but we shall be less surprised at this distinction, when we learn that it cost the English courts a struggle of nearly a century to establish the doctrine that any

(*a*) M. E. Church of Dayton *v.* Rench, 7 Ohio State, 369. By the Code, in addition to the causes of action which survive at common law, are causes of action for mesne profits, for an injury to real or personal estate, and for any deceit or fraud. § 4975.

actions of contract survive, except those on contracts under seal, where survivorship both ways is generally one of the express stipulations. At length, however, in 1610, the controversy was finally settled, by a unanimous decision of the house of lords, that simple contracts survive both ways, to the same extent as sealed contracts; though there be no express stipulation with respect to the survivorship. Since that period, it has not been doubted that all actions of contract survive, with respect to both parties; with the single exception of such contracts, as a promise to marry, and the like, which can only be performed by the individuals contracting, and not by their representatives. (*a*)

As to Actions of Tort. The first and leading case, which overthrew the ancient rule as to actions of tort, was that of *Hambly* v. *Trott*, (*b*) decided by Lord Mansfield. The principles there laid down were in substance as follows: Where the cause of action is a tort, which produces no gain to the party committing it, as slander, for example, the action dies on account of the cause; where the form of action is such that the declaration must allege force and arms, as in trespass, or the plea must be that the testator was not guilty, the action dies on account of the form; and all other actions of tort survive. This case relates to the defendant only. With respect to the plaintiff, there was an ancient English statute, giving to the executor an action of trespass for the goods of his testator, carried away in his lifetime. This statute has been generally adopted as common law in this country, and by an equitable construction, has been held to embrace all injuries to personalty. (*c*) But these doctrines with respect to actions of tort, are so far modified by our statute, that here all actions of tort survive both ways, except those for injuries to the person, health, or reputation, which produce no gain to the party committing the tort; and this seems to be the plain good sense of the matter.

At common law, even where a cause of action would itself survive, yet if the action were pending at the death of either of the parties, it would in all cases *abate*, (*d*) and a new action must be

(*a*) See the Year Books, 12 H. 8, p. 11; 27 H. 8, p. 23; 4 Reeves's H. C. L. 383; Narwood *v.* Reed, 1 Plowden, 180; Pinchon's case, 9 Coke's Rep. 86; Chamberlain *v.* Williamson, 2 M. &. S. 408; Stebbins *v.* Palmer, 1 Pick. 71.

(*b*) Cowper, 872.

(*c*) See Berwick *v.* Andrews, 2 Lord Raym. 971; Salk. 314; Wheatly *v.* Lane, 1 Saund. 216; Griswold *v.* Brown, 1 Day's Cases in Error, 180; Holmes *v.* Moore, 5 Pick. 257. At common law, the death of a human being could not be complained of as an injury in a civil action, even by relatives dependent upon him for comfort and support. Baker *v.* Bolton, 1 Camp. 493; Wosley *v.* C. H. & D. R. R. Co., 1 Handy, 481. In several of the States, as in Ohio, acts have been passed making parties by whose wrongful act the death of a person has been caused liable for damages to his near relatives. R. S. § 6134–5; Lyons *v.* Cleveland & Toledo R. R. Co., 7 Ohio State, 336; Woodard *v.* Michigan S. R. R. Co., 10 Ohio State, 272.

(*d*) By the Code, an action does not abate by the death, marriage, or other disability of a party, or by the transfer of any interest therein during its pendency, provided the cause of action survives. § 5012. Nor does an action pending abate by the death of either or both parties, with the exception of libel, slander, malicious prosecution, commenced. This was productive of needless delay and expense; and, accordingly, our statute provides that no action shall abate by the death of either of the parties, except those, the cause of which does not survive. If, therefore, one of the parties die, during the pendency of an action, and his representatives do not of their own accord come in to prosecute or defend such action, a citation issues to bring them in; and if they still neglect to appear, a judgment of nonsuit or default is rendered, as the case may require. Also, if there be two or more plaintiffs and defendants, and one of them die, his death is suggested on the minutes; after which the suit goes on to judgment, and his representatives are made parties thereto by a writ of *scire facias*. The only question then is, who are the representatives of the deceased? In all strictly personal actions, having no reference to the title to realty, the executor or administrator is the legal representative, and is made party to the suit; but in the action of ejectment, and in all actions on covenants real running with land, the heirs or devisees are the legal representatives, and are made parties accordingly. It will thus be seen that on the subject of survivorship, our law is peculiarly simple and reasonable.

§ 216. **Limitation of Actions.** (*a*) Statutes of limitations have

assault, assault and battery, for a nuisance, or against a justice for misconduct in office. § 5144. As to slander, see Alpin *v.* Morton, 21 Ohio State, 536.

(*a*) On the general subject, see the American Treatises of Angell and of Wood. The Code has made important changes, which will be noted. As to courts of equity following the statute, see Bigelow *v.* Bigelow, 6 Ohio, 96; Tuttle *v.* Wilson, 10 id. 24; Ridley *v.* Hettman, 10 id. 524. The federal courts are governed by the statutes of the States. Harpending *v.* Dutch Church, 16 Peters, 455. The *times* of limitation are not materially changed by the Code.

Commencement and Termination of the Time. In general, the time begins when the cause of action actually occurred, and not when the party first knew of it. Williams *v.* Pomeroy Coal Co., 37 Ohio State, 583; Kerns *v.* Schoonmaker, 4 Ohio, 331; Lathrop *v.* Snellbaker, 6 Ohio State, 276. But in the case of fraud, the Code makes it begin with the discovery of it. Moore *v.* Greene, 19 How. 69; Long *v.* Mulford, 17 Ohio State, 485. {This means discovery by the plaintiff; where the wrongdoer was an agent of the defendant, the defendant's ignorance of the fraud does not affect the statute. See Maple *v.* Railroad, 40 Ohio State, 313, 316.} In regard to the public lands, the statute does not begin to run until the Indian title has been extinguished. Thompson *v.* Gotham, 9 Ohio, 170. In the Virginia military district, it does not begin until the emanation of the patent. Wallace *v.* Miner, 6 Ohio, 366; Wallace *v.* Miner, 7 id. 1 pt. 249; Duke *v.* Thompson, 16 id. 34. And where a patent was void on account of the death of the patentee before it was issued, and a curative statute was passed giving the title to his heirs, devisees, or assignees, the statute does not begin to run until the passage of the curative statute. Wood *v.* Ferguson, 7 Ohio State, 288. And see upon the general subject, Williams *v.* Williams, 5 Ohio, 444; Payne *v.* Skinner, 8 id. 159; Abram *v.* Will, 6 Ohio, 164; Fee *v.* Fee, 10 id. 469. An action of ejectment on the demise of husband and wife cannot be maintained during the coverture, after the statute has run for the full period against the husband. Thompson *v.* Green, 4 Ohio State, 216; Ford *v.* Langel, 4 id. 464.

Miscellaneous. The statute does not run against the State, and, consequently, not against a tax-title, because the purchaser succeeds to the State lien. Monroe *v.* Morris, 7 Ohio, 1 pt. 262. But it does run against all corporations created by the State, in the same manner as against individuals. Cincinnati *v.* Presbyterian Church, 8 Ohio, 298. It runs against municipal corporations. City of Cincinnati *v.* Evans, 5 Ohio State, 594. Virginia military district school lands held under a lease for ninety-nine years are subject to the statute. Bently *v.* Newton, 9 id. 489. In a court of equity, the statute does not run against a trust. Gary *v.* May, 16 Ohio, 66. But it does in a been well denominated *statutes of repose.* They proceed upon the maxim that legal rights should be asserted within a reasonable time, and that the law should favor the vigilant, and not the sluggish; but the common law fixed no precise time within which actions must be brought. This is everywhere done by statute; and such statutes are called statutes of limitation. They have been found to be so highly expedient, that courts of chancery, though not always within their letter, have been uniformly governed by their spirit. I shall, of course, confine my remarks to our own statute. But all the American statutes of limitation are much alike, being copies, more or less exact, of the same original; namely, the English statute of limitations. And the federal courts are uniformly governed by the statutes of limitation of the State where the cause of action accrued, and by the constructions thereof given by the courts of such State.

Periods of Limitation. Our statute divides actions with reference to the periods of limitation into seven classes, which are limited as follows: 1. Ejectment, to twenty-one years. There is an exception, however, by our statute, in the case where land has been sold by an executor or administrator under an order of court; in which case no action can be brought by any person claiming under the deceased, after five years from the sale; or in case of disability, five years from the removal thereof. 2. Forcible entry and detainer, to two years. 3. Actions upon any written contract, whether under seal or not, to fifteen years. 4. Actions upon any contract not in writing, and actions on the case for consequential damages, to six years. 5. Actions of trespass upon property, real or personal, and actions of trover, detinue, and replevin, to four years. 6. Actions for personal injuries, including assault and battery, libel, slander, malicious prosecution, and false imprisonment; actions for official misconduct; and *qui tam* actions, or, actions for penalties, where the informer has one-half, to one year. 7. All other actions, not included in the above classes, to four years.

Commencement and Termination of the Time. The limitation begins from the time "*when the cause of action accrued.*" Generally speaking, this means, when the right of action is perfect; and it makes no difference whether the party was then aware of his right of action or not; for it is the happening of the event upon which the right of action is founded, and not the discovery of the right resulting from the act, which fixes the commencement of the limitation. Thus, in ejectment, for example, the cause of action accrues, and the time begins to run, when *adverse possession* commences. So long as the occupant of land acknowledges the right of the owner, there is no cause of action against him; but from the moment when, in word or act, the occupant denies the

court of law. Bigelow *v.* Bigelow, 6 Ohio, 96. The provision as to the removal or non-residence of the defendant, relates to the time when the cause accrued, not after. Coventry *v.* Atherton, 9 Ohio, 34.

owner's title, and claims to hold adversely to him, the cause of action has accrued, and the twenty-one years have commenced running. (*a*) Again, the words of the statute are: "all actions hereinafter mentioned shall be *commenced* within the several times hereinafter limited;" and an action is *commenced* or is *pending*, when the process has been *served*, or if the notice is by publication, when the publication has been completed. If the action be commenced a moment before the limitation expires, it is saved; for the statute provides that if it should abate, or the plaintiff be nonsuited, or judgment be arrested or reversed, the plaintiff shall have one year more within which to commence a new action.

Saving Clause. (*b*) When any cause prevents the statute from operating in a given case, it is said to take the case out of the statute. For example, an agreement to submit a question of boundary to arbitration takes the case out of the statute, because by admitting a doubt in which party the right lies, it negatives the idea of a positively adverse possession. (*c*) But there are certain general causes which, by express provision, take all cases out of the statute, on the ground that the parties affected by them have sufficient reason for not asserting their claims in the usual time. These causes pass under the general name of *disabilities;* and the clause providing for them is called the *saving clause* of the statute. In our statute they are now four; namely, *infancy*, *coverture*, *insanity*, and *imprisonment.* (*d*) These disabilities are personal privileges, and protect only the person laboring under them; so that if one heir be within the saving clause, this does not help his coheirs, who are not within it. In England, and in most of the States, there is a fifth; namely, "*being beyond seas*," which, in this country, means being *out of the State.* (*e*) This was in our statutes of 1804 and 1810; our statute of 1824 substituted the expression, "without the United States;" but the statute of 1831 omits it altogether. In all cases except ejectment, if a party, at the time his cause of action accrued, was under either of the

(*a*) {The exclusive enjoyment by one tenant in common is not deemed to be adverse without unmistakable acts or declarations of which his co-tenants ought to have taken notice; for otherwise his possession is consistent with the character of a tenant in common. Hogg *v.* Beerman, 41 Ohio State, 81.}

(*b*) *Saving Clause.* By the Code, penalties and forfeitures are excepted from the saving clause. It was once held that where one of the parties to a writ of error was within the saving clause, all were saved. Wilkins *v.* Phillips, 3 Ohio, 49. But see to the contrary, Moore *v.* Armstrong, 10 Ohio, 11; Marstellar *v.* M'Clean, 7 Cranch, 156; Perry *v.* Jackson, 4 Term Rep. 516.

(*c*) {Hunt *v.* Guilford, 4 Ohio, 310. So of an agreement not to bring ejectment during a party's lifetime. Dietrick *v.* Noel, 42 Ohio State, 18.}

(*d*) {The immunity of these persons from the operation of the statute is not solely founded on a disability to sue, but also because the power and influence of a husband, parent, or guardian might be such as to render a mere right to sue utterly nugatory, and there ought to be a right to sue after such influence is no longer felt, hence it is that the statutes enabling a married woman to sue alone have not been held to remove her privilege of disability under the statute of limitations. Ashley *v.* Rockwell, 43 Ohio State, 386; Hurlbut *v.* Wade, 40 id. 603.}

(*e*) {Richardson *v.* Richardson, 6 Ohio, 125; Whitney *v.* Webb, 10 Ohio, 513; Smith *v.* Bartram, 11 Ohio State, 690. But this is not a disability under the Code.}

aforementioned disabilities, he has the full period of limitation, after the removal of his disability, within which to commence his action; or, in other words, the statute does not begin to run until the disability is removed: and prior to 1830, this was the case also with respect to ejectment; but now the language of the statute with reference to this action is, "every such person may, after the expiration of twenty-one years from the time his right or title first descended or accrued, bring such action within *ten years* after such disability removed;" and to save existing rights, there is a temporary provision, that when a disability was removed less than eleven years before this act took effect, there shall still be ten years from that time; but if removed more than eleven years before that date, the time shall be just so much less after. It is unfortunate that the permanent provision above quoted was not expressed in clearer language. One would suppose that the legislature, in striking off eleven years from the former period, after the disability removed, would at least have given the remaining ten years as an absolute extension in all cases; but the language above quoted will not bear this construction. The time given, "after the expiration of twenty-one years," must be "within ten years after such disability removed;" accordingly, if the disability ceased at the end of eleven or any less number of years after the statute commenced running, there would be no extension whatever; for the ten years within which the action must be brought, after the removal of the disability, would run out before or with the original twenty-one years; if the disability ceased after more than eleven years of the original limitation, and less than twenty-one, the extension would be so much less than ten years; but if the disability outlasted the original limitation, then, and then only, would there be an absolute addition of ten years. I do not see that the language will admit any other than this singular construction. Its operation will be best illustrated by an example; and we will take the disability of coverture. Suppose that a claim to land descends upon a married woman, and her husband dies ten years after; now without the saving clause, she would still have eleven years, because every one has that; and since these eleven outlast the ten given by the saving clause, she gains nothing by it. But suppose her husband had lived fifteen years after her claim descended to her; here, without the saving clause, she would have only six years left; but with it, she gains four years. Lastly, suppose her husband had lived thirty years after her claim descended; here she would have an absolute gain of ten years after his death, making in all nineteen. (*a*)

Cumulative Disabilities. From the words, "at the time his first title descended or accrued," it follows that the disability, in order to be available, must have been existing at the very time. No subsequent disability can be taken advantage of. (*b*) If but a day

(*a*) This same language is used in the Code.

(*b*) {A disability not occurring until after the statute had begun to run will not intervene, between the accruing of the cause of action and the disability, the statute having once commenced running, will continue to run. And the same is true, when a subsequent disability occurs, while a prior one still exists; for no disability can be taken advantage of, which did not exist when the statute commenced running; but if several concurrent disabilities existed together at that time, advantage may be taken of that which lasts longest. (*a*) Thus, if a title descends upon a single woman of age, and she marries the next day, her coverture is no saving disability. If she were an infant at the time, her infancy may be taken advantage of, but not her subsequent coverture: but if she was both an infant and married, when her title descended, she may take advantage, either of her infancy or coverture, whichsoever continues longest. These points are settled beyond controversy. But the language of our statute raises one question of difficulty. Suppose that adverse possession has been running against an ancestor before his death, can his infant heir take advantage of his infancy? or must he bring his action within twenty-one years after the cause of action accrued to his ancestor? The language of the corresponding provision of the English statute is, "at the time *the said* right first descended or accrued;" and this has been construed, in the case proposed, to preclude the infant from setting up his infancy; because, otherwise, in the language of the books, a right might travel down through minorities for centuries. The same reason exists here; and therefore it has been held that the substitution of "his right," in place of "the said right," especially as the word "first" is still retained, is not to be construed as altering the English rule.

Miscellaneous. In the fluctuating legislation of this State, we have had limitation acts passed or amended, in the years 1804, 1810, 1824, 1826, 1830, and 1831. It is important to bear this in mind, because each new act expressly provides that prior causes of action shall be governed by the prior acts, where the contrary is not specified. (*b*) By a singular omission, the action of *debt on a simple contract* was not limited until the act of 1824. (*c*) Again, until the act of 1830, there was no provision for the case where a contract was made between parties both residing out of the State. But now our statute refers to the law of the place where the

arrest it. Bartlow *v.* Kinnard, 38 Ohio State, 373. Nor can a subsequent additional disability be added to an existing one. Cozzens *v.* Farnan, 30 Ohio State, 491; Granger *v.* Granger, 6 Ohio, 35; Maryland *v.* Shipley, 7 id. 1 pt. 246; Whitney *v.* Webb, 10 id. 513.}

(*a*) There is an exception to this rule where the plaintiff is disabled from suing by the act of a superior power, as by war between his country and that of the defendant. The rebellion was such a war, where the opposite parties resided on different sides of the line of hostilities. The Protector, 9 Wall. 687; Braun *v.* Sauerwein, 10 Wall. 218; Levy *v.* Stewart, 11 Wall. 244; United States *v.* Wiley, 11 Wall. 508; Brown *v.* Hyatt, 15 Wall. 177.

(*b*) Bigelow *v.* Bigelow, 6 Ohio, 96; Hazlett *v.* Critchfield, 7 id. 2 pt. 153; West *v.* Hymer, 7 id. 2 pt. 235.

(*c*) Tupper *v.* Tupper, 3 Ohio, 387; Hazlett *v.* Critchfield, 7 id. 2 pt. 153.

contract was made; and if the action was barred there, it is barred here. (*a*) Whether the reverse would hold, the statute does not say; but as the general rule is, that the courts of one State will not take notice of the limitations of another State, it is probable that the *lex loci* would be noticed here no further than the statute requires. Many statutes contain an exception in favor of *accounts current* between merchants; but ours does not. The act of 1810 limited actions on *book account* to four years; but in the present act accounts are not mentioned. We have elsewhere a provision limiting the time within which a party may swear to his account, to eighteen months; but this only relates to evidence. Consequently, accounts come within the limitation annexed to unwritten contracts; namely, six years. If the account has been closed and balance struck, the six years begin from that date; otherwise it would seem from the date of the last item. (*b*) We have seen that absence from the State is now one of the saving disabilities; but this refers to the absence of the plaintiff; for it is expressly provided, (*c*) that if any person liable to an action resided out of the State at the time the cause of action accrued against him, or removed to any place unknown, during the time limited, the limitation shall begin to run only from the time of his return to the State, or from the time his place of residence within the State becomes known to the plaintiff; and a mere coming into the State clandestinely will not be a *return*, within the meaning of this provision: it must be an open and public return. (*d*) The chief evil intended to be guarded against by the statute of limitations, is that of prosecuting stale demands, after the proof of payment has been lost. But this evil cannot happen when the defendant has acknowledged the existence of the debt; and accordingly courts have held that an acknowledgment of the debt, and a promise to pay it, take the case out of the statute. Prior to the act of 1830, we had a provision that a *mere demand* by the plaintiff should take the case out of the statute. This was unreasonable, because a mere demand is no proof of the existence of a debt. But now the provision is, that in all cases of contract, when there has been a payment of any part of the principal or interest, or an acknowledgment of indebtedness, or a promise to pay *within the time limited*, the limitation shall begin to run anew from the time of such payment, acknowledgment, or promise. (*e*) This provision, you will observe, is confined to the *time limited* by this statute, and thus virtually excludes all beyond that time; otherwise, the effect of a promise made after the time might be a

(*a*) Headington *v.* Neff, 7 Ohio, 229; State of Maryland *v.* Shipley, 7 id. 246.

(*b*) James *v.* Richmond, 5 Ohio, 337.

(*c*) Coventry *v.* Atherton, 9 Ohio, 34.

(*d*) The Code goes still further, and provides, that if the absence or concealment commences after the cause of action accrues, it shall not enter into the computation. § 4989.

(*e*) The Code does not confine the promise to the time limited, but requires it to be in writing. § 4992.

matter of doubt. (*a*) I will only add that where two or more are jointly liable, a payment, acknowledgment, or promise by one, will bind all, with respect to the statute; and this terminates our view of the statute of limitations. There are some special limitations scattered through the statute book; but they have all been mentioned elsewhere in connection with the matters to which they refer.

LECTURE XXXVIII.

CHANCERY PROCEEDINGS. (*b*)

§ 217. **Nature of Equity.** We are now to trace the course of proceedings in courts of chancery; and here, happily, there will not be so much occasion for fault-finding as in the preceding lecture. It would indeed be difficult to devise a system of practice better calculated to answer all the ends of judicial controversy, than the system of chancery practice now in use. It has pre-eminently the merit of reasonableness and simplicity. Though the cases to which its remedies extend, are nearly, if not quite, as numerous and diverse as those of law; yet, instead of nine or ten distinct forms of proceeding, it has but one for all cases; and that is founded, and throughout constructed, upon the principles of nature and reason. Fictions are entirely dispensed with, and truth substituted in their place. The parties tell their stories, as men of common sense would tell them, and the court pronounce their decrees in a corresponding style. There is no occasion for the Procrustean system of torturing forms to meet circumstances. Were this system of procedure extended, as it might easily be, to all the matters of civil controversy, whether in law or equity, even leaving the principles as they now are, the benefits of such a reform could hardly be overrated. This is in fact done to a good degree in Louisiana, where the forms of the civil law prevail, and those of the common law are unknown; and I hope the time is not far distant, when something like an approach to a similar improvement will be made here; when the reign of technicality will end, and that of simplicity begin. Such a change would be similar to that which was effected in philosophy by the overthrow

(*a*) Hill *v.* Henry, 17 Ohio, 9.

(*b*) On the principles of equity, see the fourth book of Swift's Digest; 3 Black. Com. ch. 27; Story's Commentaries on Equity, Pomeroy's Equity, and the English treatises of Jeremy, Fonblanque, and Adams, with American notes by Ludlow and Collins. On Chancery practice, see the works of Mitford, Maddock, Newland, Harrison, Cooper, Barton, Blake, Hoffman, Barbour, and Paine and Duer. The last four are American treatises. To which add Story's Commentaries on Equity Pleading; also Langdale and Heard.

See first note to preceding lecture.

of syllogistic reasoning, and the substitution of the inductive method. The origin and nature of chancery jurisdiction were briefly described in the lecture on divisions and definitions. The constitutional provisions conferring this jurisdiction upon the federal and State courts, were also referred to in their proper place; and will again be noticed as occasion may require. Many of the subjects of equity jurisdiction have necessarily been discussed in the lectures on the law of property. But in order to render this outline as complete as my limits will permit, after describing the general course of proceedings from the commencement to the termination of a suit, I shall close the lecture with a very succinct enumeration of the principal subjects of equity jurisdiction. In the mean time, however, it may aid our future inquiries to indicate the points wherein equity differs from law; and to show how far the English chancery system has been adopted in this country.

We have seen that equity does not differ from law, strictly so called, in being less dependent upon positive regulations. Neither does it differ from law with respect to the subject-matter upon which it operates, except in being confined to a narrow range. It is chiefly conversant with *questions of property*, and rarely, if ever, takes cognizance of *crimes* or *civil injuries* strictly personal. In England, though not in this State, as will be seen hereafter, it does differ from law, in being administered by a different court. But the great and radical difference grows out of the *modes of proceeding;* which are so contrived as to ascertain facts and administer remedies for which the law is incompetent, by reason of the inflexibility of its forms. To illustrate these modes of procedure will be the chief object of this lecture; but it may be well to remark here that in settling disputed facts, there are the following fundamental points of difference: 1. In chancery proceedings the parties themselves are compelled to testify; and thus truth is often reached without difficulty, when by the rules of law it could not be reached at all. This salutary power of putting the parties upon their oaths is the highest recommendation of the chancery system; and to this more than to all other causes is to be ascribed the growth of equity jurisdiction. 2. In chancery proceedings, oral testimony is not allowed. It must be reduced to writing and placed on file. The expediency of this regulation is more questionable. The advantage which results from observing the tone and manner of a witness is lost. But, on the other hand, the testimony is preserved in a durable shape, and can be examined at pleasure. 3. In chancery proceedings, the *facts* as well as the *law*, are submitted to the court without the intervention of a jury. It has been sometimes doubted whether this be not a violation of the constitutional guaranty of the right of trial by jury; but this question cannot arise where the same constitution which declares this right, also recognizes chancery jurisdiction. Besides, we shall see hereafter, that this court has the power to direct an issue to be made up for a jury, whenever a question arises to render it expedient. 4. When we come to describe the manner in which the parties present their case before the court, and the manner in which the court, by their decree, so shape the remedy as exactly to meet all the circumstances of the case, we shall find a still more striking difference between equity and law; and we shall cease to wonder that the two jurisdictions are kept entirely distinct. It will then be manifest, that the great object of equity is to supply the manifold deficiencies of law, and that it is admirably adapted to effect this object, as well on account of the flexibility of its forms, as of its almost entire freedom from the fetters of technicality. But a discussion of these matters would now be premature.

In several of the States, as Pennsylvania and Massachusetts, the general chancery system is not adopted. (*a*) But even there necessity has required some special chancery powers to be conferred on the courts of law, without which the administration of justice would be hardly tolerable. Perhaps the erroneous notion already pointed out, respecting the arbitrary nature of chancery power, has been the cause of this jealous policy. Again, in several other States, as New York and Virginia, the English chancery system is adopted in almost every particular; and full chancery powers are conferred on a single chancellor, who has no common-law jurisdiction. But the constitutions of the United States and of this State adopt a sort of middle course. They admit the existence of chancery powers in their full extent; but instead of creating distinct tribunals to administer them, they require these powers to be conferred, if conferred at all, upon the same tribunals which administer the law. Thus, the same persons officiate both as chancellors and judges; but their modes of proceeding in the two capacities are kept as entirely distinct, as if controlled by different persons. There being a general similarity between these two systems, I shall confine my remarks to the system adopted here. In fact, the principles and practice of equity are nearly the same, wherever it has been adopted; since all systems are copied from the same original; namely, the English chancery system.

By the terms of our constitution, as we have seen, the judicial power "both as to matters of law and equity," is vested in the same courts who are to have "common law and chancery jurisdiction in all cases as shall be directed by law." This language establishes two points: *first*, that equity may or may not be a part of our judicial system, at the option of the legislature; but if adopted, it must be administered by the same tribunals which administer the law; and *secondly*, that our legislature is left entirely free, either to adopt the English chancery doctrines as they are, or to modify them at pleasure. To understand, then, the nature and extent of our equity jurisdiction, we must see what the legislature has actually done; and on referring to the statutes, we find two

(*a*) Full equity powers have been conferred in Massachusetts on the supreme judicial court.

sets of provisions relating to equity jurisdiction. The first set of provisions merely apportions this jurisdiction between the supreme court and the court of common pleas, according to the value in dispute. In general, if this value be between one hundred and one thousand dollars, proceedings must be commenced originally in the common pleas, but may be carried by appeal to the supreme court; but if it exceed one thousand dollars, proceedings may be commenced indifferently in either court. In the single case of injunction, to stay proceedings at law, the common pleas may descend to twenty dollars, and the supreme court to one hundred; and in questions relating to land, either court may exercise original jurisdiction without regard to value. The other set of provisions is designed to fix the limits of chancery jurisdiction, with reference to the subject-matter. This jurisdiction is declared to extend to "all cases properly cognizable by a court of chancery, in which a plain, adequate, and complete remedy cannot be had at law:" and in exercising it, the courts are required "in all things to be governed by the known usages of courts of equity, except where it may be otherwise provided by law." The effect, therefore, of these provisions is, to adopt the English equity system as our own, except where the legislature otherwise directs; and it follows that in order to determine whether a given case is within our chancery jurisdiction, the two following points are to be considered: 1. Is there a plain, adequate, and complete remedy at law? For, equity, as we have said before, is intended only to be subsidiary to law, to supply its deficiencies, and help out its designs. It is neither above law, nor opposed to it. Both are designed to promote the great ends of justice, by the application of established rules. When the law is insufficient, equity steps in; but then only. If, therefore, the law furnishes no remedy, or only a doubtful or inadequate one, we have the first requisite for chancery jurisdiction. 2. Is there any authority either in the statutes or precedents, for entertaining jurisdiction in the given case? For the question must be "properly cognizable by a court of chancery," and one, in deciding which the "known usages" of that court can be followed. Without this restriction, chancery powers would be, as they have been sometimes represented, perfectly arbitrary, and therefore unfit for freemen; but with it they are sufficiently guarded. The proper rule is this: if a case be entirely new *in principle*, the court cannot decide it until the legislature gives authority; for this would be usurping legislative power. But when a case is only new in *the particular instance*, and can be brought within an established principle, by clear expression or analogy, then jurisdiction may be taken. Such, then, are the two predicates of chancery jurisdiction; namely, the absence of a sufficient legal remedy, and the existence of an authority to meet the case. To determine the first, we must know what remedies the law furnishes; and to determine the second, we must consult the statutes and reports. Thus you will observe that a knowledge of equity presupposes a knowledge of law; and this fact justifies the vesting of the two jurisdictions in the same persons.

The general sources of information to which you are referred are: 1. Our *statute* directing the mode of proceeding in chancery. 2. *Rules of court* made in pursuance of the statutory provision. Without such provision, however, courts have the inherent power of making rules for the convenience and despatch of business, not inconsistent with the existing law; which rules become the law of the court, and have the same authority as if made by the legislature. These rules are either *general* or *special*. General rules are those which apply to all cases coming within them; special rules are those adopted for particular cases. General rules are entered upon the journals of the court, and stand for law until rescinded. The general rules of the supreme court run through the State, and are binding upon the common pleas. Those of the common pleas extend only through the circuit in which they are made. Special rules are only obtained on motion of the party desiring them, and expire with the occasion. Our statutory provisions and rules taken together, modify materially those "known usages" of courts of chancery, which would otherwise govern our practice. 3. The "*known usages*" of courts of chancery, not affected by our statutes and rules. These are to be gathered from the books on equity before referred to, which are themselves framed upon the reported decisions.

§ 218. **Bill.** We are now prepared to consider the commencement and progress of a suit in chancery. Our statute declares that all applications to the chancery side of the courts shall be by *petition*, setting forth the nature and grounds of the complaint; which petition shall be filed in the clerk's office. This petition is commonly called a *bill*, and the filing of it is the first step in every chancery suit. I shall give a general description of its form and contents. In England, bills are drawn with extreme formality and redundancy. The books divide a bill into *nine* distinct parts, so framed as to tell the story two or three times over; and each time with all the expletives and tautologies which ingenuity can devise. The reason is, that such service is there paid for according to the number of words. Nor are we wholly exempt from the like abuse in this country; but the profession are beginning to improve in this respect, particularly in this State; and to content themselves with telling their story once in a plain and concise manner. In fact, the only important divisions of a bill are three; namely, the *address*, the *statement*, and the *prayer*. (*a*) 1. The *address* merely designates

(*a*) *Form of a Bill.* To explain more fully the nature of a bill, and show the difference between ancient and modern practice, I shall take the case of a bill to enforce the payment of a legacy, and give its form, first, as divided into nine parts, and then its form as it may be abridged.

1. *The Address.* To the honorable the judges of the court of ———, sitting in chancery, within and for the county of ———, and State of ———.

2. *The Introduction.* Humbly complaining sheweth unto your honors, your orator, ——— of the county aforesaid.

3. *The Premises.* That ———, of the county aforesaid, being seised and possessed

the court to which the application is made. 2. The *statement* must contain a clear and explicit exhibition of the plaintiff's case. In

of a large real and personal estate, on or about the ——, did duly make and publish his last will and testament in writing, and thereby, amongst other things, did devise and bequeath to your orator the sum of $——, by the words following, to wit, [here set forth the words,] as by reference to said will, a copy of which is herewith exhibited as part of this bill, will more fully appear; and that the said testator departed this life on or about the ——, and that on or about the ——, one ——, named as executor in the said will, caused the same to be duly proved, and took upon himself the execution thereof, and took possession of the said real and personal property; and that since the same legacy became due and payable to your orator, he has frequently requested the said executor to pay the same, and had well hoped that he would have complied with such request, as in conscience and equity he ought to have done.

4. *The Confederacy.* But now, so it is, may it please your honors, that the said executor, combining and confederating with divers persons as yet unknown to your orator, but whom, when known, he prays to have made defendants with proper words to charge them with the premises, in order to oppress and injure your orator, does absolutely refuse to pay to your orator the said legacy or any part thereof: and for reason of such refusal, the said confederates sometimes pretend that the said testator made no such will, and at other times that his real and personal estate was not sufficient to pay his debts; and at the same time the said confederates refused to discover and set forth what such real and personal estate really was, or its value, or how the same has been disposed of.

5. *The Charging Part.* Whereas your orator charges the truth to be, that the said real and personal estate was of the value of $——, as he is informed and believes; and that it was more than sufficient to pay all the debts of the said testator, and the legacies mentioned in the said will; and that the said confederates, or one of them, have converted the same to their own use, without satisfying your orator for his said legacy; all which pretences and doings are contrary to equity and good conscience and tend to the manifest injury of your orator.

6. *The Jurisdiction Part.* In tender consideration whereof, and for that your orator is remediless in the premises by the strict rules of the common law, and relievable only in a court of equity, where matters of this sort are properly cognizable.

7. *The Interrogatory Part.* To the end, therefore, that the said confederates may respectively full, true, direct, and perfect answers make, upon their respective corporal oaths, according to the best of their knowledge, information, or belief, to all and singular the matters aforesaid, as fully, in every respect, as if the same were here again repeated; and more especially that they discover and set forth whether the said testator did duly make and execute such a last will and testament as before stated; and did thereby bequeath to your orator such legacy as aforesaid; and that they produce the said will with the probate thereof; and that they state when the said testator died, and who caused the said will to be proved, and undertook the execution thereof; and whether the said legacy has not become due and payable to your orator; and whether he has not requested payment of the same and been refused upon the pretences aforesaid; and that they may discover and set forth the real and personal property belonging to the testator, and its value, and whether the same was not sufficient to pay all the debts and legacies aforesaid, and what has become of the same.

8. *The Prayer for Relief.* And that the said confederates may be compelled by a decree of this honorable court to pay to your orator his said legacy of $——, with interest thereon since the same was due, and that your orator may have such other and further relief in the premises as the nature of the case shall require, and as to your honors shall seem meet.

9. *The Prayer for Process.* May it please your honors to grant unto your orator the most gracious writ of subpœna, to be directed to the said ——, executor, as aforesaid, and the rest of the confederates when discovered, commanding them on a certain day and under a certain penalty therein specified, personally to appear before your honors, and then and there to answer all and singular the premises aforesaid, and abide such order and decree as your honors shall make; and your orator, as in duty bound, will ever pray, &c.

The above bill would be equally effectual in the *abridged form* which follows: To the court of ——, sitting in chancery, within and for the county of ——, and State of ——. Your petitioner ——, of the county aforesaid, respectfully shows, setting it forth, aim first of all at precision, avoiding equally redundancy and ambiguity; and bear this constantly in mind, that the sole object of the bill is to make known the facts material to your claim. The evidence of those facts, and the conclusions of law arising from them, would be out of place. The court wish only to be informed what the facts are; and common sense is the best guide in narrating them. In averring *numbers*, it is safer to use words than figures, but this is not indispensable. *Abbreviations* are to be avoided, because they may not be rightly understood. If your case be connected with *written instruments*, the better practice is to state in the bill only so much of their *substance* as is necessary to make the case intelligible; and to annex *copies* thereof by way of *exhibits*. I say *copies*, because prudence dictates the retention of the *originals*, until the final determination of the cause, when they must of course be produced. You are at liberty, indeed, to copy them out in full in the body of the bill; but it will be seen at once that your case cannot then be so quickly understood as from a judicious abstract. 3. The *prayer* forms the concluding part of the bill; for in obedience to ancient usage, as before explained, you approach the court in the language, not of *demand*, but of *supplication*. The prayer usually includes the four following matters, namely: 1. That all persons supposed to be interested may be made *defendants*, and that a *subpœna* may issue accordingly. It is convenient, though not essential, to name all the defendants together in this clause, though they may have been mentioned before, in order that a single glance may ascertain them; and if their names be not known, their relation to the suit should be stated. 2. That the defendants may answer *under oath* to all the allegations of the bill. This would probably be required without any prayer, being a positive rule of law; but it is customary to insert it. And this is also the place for specific interrogatories, if you think proper to propound them; but as these can only be founded upon the allega-

that on or about the ——, one —— of the county aforesaid, owning a large amount of real and personal property, duly executed his last will and testament, a copy of which is exhibited as part of this bill, and thereby bequeathed to your petitioner a legacy of $——, in the words following, to wit: [here set forth the words;] that the said testator died on or about the ——, and shortly after, on or about the ——, one ——, named in said will as executor, caused the same to be duly proved, and undertook the execution thereof; that the property and effects belonging to the said testator, and taken possession of by the said executor, were more than sufficient to pay all the debts of the said testator and the legacies mentioned in the said will; but the exact description and amount of which your petitioner is unable to state; that since the said legacy has become due and payable to your petitioner, he has often requested the said executor to pay the same, but the said executor has neglected so to do. Being, therefore, without remedy at law, your petitioner prays for relief in chancery; and that a subpœna may issue to the said ——, executor as aforesaid, who is made defendant to this bill, and that the said defendant may answer under oath to all the matters herein alleged; and especially may discover and set forth a copy of the said will and probate, and the nature and value of the property and effects of the testator which came into his hands, and what has become of the same; and that upon a final hearing this court may decree that the said executor pay to your petitioner the legacy of $——, so bequeathed to him; and that your petitioner may have such other and further relief as shall seem equitable.

tions before made, they are seldom of much use, and never indispensable. 3. That the court may grant the *specific relief*, to which you conceive the plaintiff to be entitled, setting it forth particularly. 4. That such other relief may be granted as the court shall deem equitable. This is called the prayer for *general relief*, and should never be omitted; because the plaintiff may be entitled to some relief, when he cannot have the specific relief prayed for. The bill is now signed by counsel. This is the English rule, and the intention is to have security against scandalous or impertinent matter, by holding the solicitor responsible. In common cases the bill is now ready to be filed. But there are two exceptions: namely, *bills of ne exeat*, to prevent persons from departing out of the jurisdiction; and *bills of injunction*, to stay legal or other proceedings. These further require, as will be explained hereafter, an *affidavit* by the plaintiff of their truth; an *allowance* by the court in term time or a single judge in vacation; and *security* to the other party, in such sum as the court or judge shall determine. The bill is now *filed;* that is, deposited with the clerk, who notes the date of filing on the back, and enters the cause on the appearance docket.

§ 219. **Subpœna.** (*a*) The next step is for the clerk to issue the *subpœna.* This is a writ commanding the sheriff, who is the executive officer of this court, as well as of the courts of law, to summon the defendant to appear and answer, under the penalty of a thousand dollars. The form is prescribed by the statute. If the bill be filed in term time, the subpœna is made returnable forthwith, otherwise to the next term; and in either case the term at which the writ is to be returned is called the *appearance term.* We have seen that this writ is usually prayed for in the bill. The statute, however, seems to require a separate application, after filing the bill; and this is usually made in the form of a *precipe* on the back of the bill. The subpœna takes its name from the penalty it threatens in case of disobedience. It was devised, as we have seen, when the foundations of chancery power were not very firmly established; and the threat of a penalty no doubt then had its effect. But it is probable that this penalty could not now be specifically enforced in any way; nor is this necessary in order that the writ may be effectual. For the court has express power, as we have seen, to enforce obedience in all its process, rules, and orders, by *attachment for contempt;* in which proceeding the delinquent may be fined, or imprisoned until he complies, or his property may be sequestrated in certain cases. This, of course, includes disobedience to a subpœna, and supersedes the necessity of a penalty in the writ. Besides, if the defendant disobeys, he is

(*a*) *Form of a Subpœna.* [Omitting the caption and conclusion, which are the same as in all other writs.] We command you to summon ——— to appear before our court of ———, on the ———, to answer a petition in chancery exhibited against him by ———; and this he shall in no wise omit, under the penalty of one thousand dollars; and have you then and there this writ, with your doings thereon.

in general sufficiently punished, as we shall see hereafter, by the consequences of default. The subpœna is delivered to the sheriff to be *served*. If the defendants reside in different counties, within the State, subpœnas may be directed accordingly. *Service* is made anywhere within the State by delivering a copy of the subpœna to the defendant, which is called *personal service:* or by leaving it at his usual place of abode, which is called *service of copy*. The *return* is made by indorsing the time and manner of service upon the original, and returning it to the clerk's office. But if any or all of the defendants reside out of the State, the manner of giving notice is in one of two ways; namely: 1. By personal service of the subpœna, together with a copy of the bill; in which case the return, being made by a person not known to the court, must be verified by affidavit. 2. By a newspaper advertisement published for six consecutive weeks, setting forth the pendency of the suit, with a brief description of the object and prayer of the bill. If there be no newspaper printed in the county, it must be one printed in the State, and which has a general circulation in the county. This is at best a very uncertain mode of notifying non-residents; and, therefore, to prevent hardship, it is provided that, where a decree has been rendered against the defendant under such circumstances, he may, at any time within five years, have the proceedings opened, by giving notice to the plaintiff, making affidavit that actual notice was not received in season to make defence, and paying costs. But if land has been sold in the mean time, under such decree, the purchaser is not to be disturbed. The general principle is, that suit must be commenced in that county where one or more of the defendants reside. But if it relate to *land*, it must be in that county where the land lies; or if it lies in several counties, then in either. In proceedings against *heirs*, whose names or residence are unknown, upon affidavit of that fact the court will allow the suit to go on, and make such order relating to notice as they may deem proper. If any of the defendants be *infants*, as proceedings here are never stayed on that account, the plaintiff must apply to the court to appoint a *guardian ad litem* to conduct the defence, who must be notified of the fact and accept the appointment before the decree will be conclusive against such infants; for although infants may sue by their *next friend*, they can only defend by a *guardian ad litem*.

§ 220. **Appearance and Defence.** Upon the return of the subpœna *served*, or upon due proof of *notice*, as the case may be, the defendant is considered as *in court*, and may be proceeded against accordingly. This is a great departure from the English practice, which requires an *actual appearance* before any final proceedings can be had, but furnishes all possible facilities for enforcing such appearance. Our rule, however, which substitutes a virtual for an actual appearance, is far more beneficial to the plaintiff; since, if he take the requisite steps before mentioned, it is not in the power of the defendant to prevent a decree. When there is an actual appearance, it is usually signified by the counsel for the defendant, usually called *solicitor*, who writes his name in the margin of the appearance docket, opposite to that of his client. He is then entitled to a *copy* of the bill, which is charged among the general costs of the suit. This rule extends to all adversary proceedings, but provides for only one copy, however many opponents there may be. The defendant then has *sixty days*, by our statute, after the end of the appearance term, before he can be placed in default. Within this period he must either *disclaim* or *make defence*, or suffer the consequences of his *default;* and I shall describe the proceedings under each of these aspects.

Our statute justly provides that where a defendant will come in and disclaim all interest in the matter in dispute, the plaintiff shall pay the costs, unless the court otherwise order. In general, such disclaimer need not be under oath; for when a man denies having any interest in that which has value, his word will be taken as sufficient. When, however, the object of the bill is to compel a *discovery of facts* which the defendant may be interested in concealing, his disclaimer of knowledge or interest must be under oath, and takes the form of an *answer*. A disclaimer is signed by the defendant or his counsel; and, on being filed, the bill will be dismissed as to that defendant, at the cost of the plaintiff. In fact, the chief or only motive for putting in a simple disclaimer is to avoid the payment of costs. (*a*) But we will now suppose that the defendant instead of disclaiming, has an interest in the matter of the bill, and wishes to make *defence*. This can only be done in one of three ways; namely, by *demurrer*, *plea*, or *answer*. If the bill, admitting its truth, be insufficient upon its face to entitle the plaintiff to recover, the defendant presents that question to the court by *demurrer:* but if the bill be sufficient upon its face, the defendant must either set up some new matter of defence to obviate its effect, or deny the allegations therein made, or both. If the new matter of defence consists of a single fact, or a single result from several connected facts, it may be presented in the form of a *plea:* but if this be not the case, the defence can only be presented in the form of an *answer*. Whichever course be adopted, the time allowed is sixty days after the end of the appearance term. Would not a shorter time better promote the ends of justice, and redeem the constitutional pledge against delay?

§ 221. **Demurrer.** (*b*) The object of a demurrer in chancery,

(*a*) *Form of a Disclaimer.* The disclaimer of ——— to the bill filed against him by ———. The said ——— comes and disclaims all manner of interest or concern in the matters alleged in the said bill, and prays to be hence dismissed with his costs.

(*b*) *Form of a Demurrer.* The demurrer of ——— to the bill filed against him by ———. The said ———, by protestation, not confessing or acknowledging all or any of the matters or things in the said bill set forth to be true, in manner and form as the same are therein alleged, says he is advised that there is no matter or thing in the after the analogy of a demurrer at law, is merely to present to the court the question of the *sufficiency* of the bill; and it occurs at no other stage of the proceedings. It impliedly admits the facts alleged, but denies the equity claimed. It is signed by counsel, but requires no affidavit, because it alleges no fact. A *special* demurrer differs from a *general* demurrer only in specifying wherein the insufficiency consists. It would seem from the language of the books that a special demurrer may be put in, as at law, for a mere matter of form; but this is in direct opposition to the whole spirit of equity, and is not known in our practice. We demur only for a defect in substance; and though it is always the more liberal course to specify the cause of demurrer for the information of the other party, yet this is regarded as a matter of option, and not of compulsion. The demurrer may be to the entire bill, or to some particular part; and, in the latter case, the part demurred to must be specified, and a plea or answer put in to the rest. But you cannot demur, and at the same time plead or answer to the same part of the bill, for the plea or answer would supersede such demurrer; and when you demur, and plead or answer to different parts, the demurrer must be first disposed of; the manner of doing which I will now describe. Upon filing the demurrer, the cause is at issue without a formal *joinder*, though this is sometimes added. Either party may now "*set the cause for hearing*." This is done by an entry on the office docket thus: "This cause is set for hearing on demurrer," which entry is dated and subscribed by the solicitor. The effect of setting a cause for hearing is to bring it upon the issue docket. By our rules, it may be done either in term or vacation, but the hearing can only take place in term; and at least twelve days must elapse after setting the cause for hearing before it can be called up for hearing, unless by general consent. The language of our rule is that causes shall be entered on the issue docket in the order in which they have been set for hearing; but this, though it seems but reasonable, conflicts with the statutory provision, which requires the order to be the same as on the appearance docket. It now becomes the

said bill contained sufficient in law to call this defendant to answer in this court; and therefore this defendant demurs to the said bill, and for cause of demurrer says that the said bill contains not any matter or thing entitling the complainant to any relief against this defendant; wherefore, and for divers other errors and imperfections in the said bill appearing, this defendant demurs thereunto, and humbly prays judgment of this honorable court, whether he shall be compelled to put in any further answer to the said bill, and that he may be hence dismissed with his reasonable costs, in this behalf most wrongfully sustained.

But this form may be *abridged* as follows. After the caption, as before, say: The said ——— comes and demurs to the said bill, and says that the complainant has not presented such a case as entitles him to relief in equity; wherefore he prays judgment, whether he shall be compelled to make any further answer thereto, and that he may be hence dismissed with his costs.

In case of a *special demurrer*, add the causes thereof immediately before the prayer for judgment. The *joinder* in demurrer merely contradicts the demurrer, by asserting that the bill does present such a case as entitles the complainant to relief in equity. See cases on demurrer. Carl *v.* Iglehard, 3 Ohio State, 457; Gilbert *v.* Sutliff, 3 id. 129.

duty of the counsel demurring to prepare a *brief*, containing an abstract of the case, with the points and authorities relied on; which brief must be presented to the court on the first day of the term, if the cause was set for hearing before that day, otherwise, on the day of setting it for hearing. A neglect to do this may occasion the demurrer to be overruled at the costs of the demurrant; though this penalty is seldom enforced. When the cause comes up for hearing, which must be in its regular order, unless the court assign a particular day, the counsel who furnishes the brief has the opening and close of the argument. The court then pronounces the decree: the nature of which will be considered hereafter. At present, I will merely point out its consequences in the case before us. If the demurrer be allowed, it is a decision against the bill, and the plaintiff must pay the costs; but he may obtain leave to *amend* his bill, if it admits of amendment, and thus put the defendant to his plea or answer. On the subject of *amendments*, the court has unlimited discretion; but when a party obtains leave to amend after hearing, he is required to submit to such terms in regard to *costs*, and to the time and manner of coming to another hearing, as the court deem equitable. Indeed, as to *costs* in chancery, it may be remarked generally that our statute places them entirely at the discretion of the court of chancery, both as to the amount, and the party who shall pay them, except in some few cases where special provision is made; and payment may be forced by any method the court may direct. But if, on the other hand, the demurrer be overruled, the defendant must pay the costs; and no other demurrer will be received. But the defendant may obtain leave to plead or answer, upon making affidavit that he has a meritorious defence, and that the demurrer was not filed for the purpose of delay. Otherwise, a decree will be rendered upon the bill as confessed.

§ 222. **Plea.** (*a*) The second method of making defence is by *plea*. This is the proper course where the defence rests upon a *single point*, as, for example, the statute of frauds, a release, or the like; or upon several matters so connected as to result in a single

(*a*) *Form of a Plea.* The plea of ——— to the bill filed against him by ———. The said ———, by protestation, not confessing or acknowledging all or any of the matters contained in the complainant's bill to be true, in manner and form as the same are therein declared, for plea thereunto says, that before the filing of this present bill, to wit, on or about the ———, the said complainant filed his bill in this court against this defendant, for the same matters and to the same effect, and for the like relief and purpose, as the present bill; to which said first bill this defendant has made answer; and the said first bill is still depending in this court, and the said cause undetermined; wherefore this defendant doth plead the said former bill and proceedings in bar of the present suit; and prays judgment whether he shall be compelled to make any further answer thereunto; and that he may be hence dismissed with his costs.

This form might be *abridged* by leaving out the protestation and commencing thus: The said ——— comes and pleads to the said bill and says, &c. As this plea relies on a matter of record, it requires no affidavit; but when an affidavit is required, its form is the same as that appended to an answer, and will be given hereafter.

point; but two or more distinct matters of defence are not allowed in the same plea, or in different pleas. They can only be presented in an answer. A plea may be either to the whole bill, or to some particular part. In the latter case, the particular part must be specified, and a demurrer or answer put in to the rest. It must be signed by counsel; and as it alleges some fact, it must be verified by affidavit, unless it be founded upon a question of jurisdiction or some matter of record. After stating with precision the matter of defence, and making such denials as the case requires, it concludes with a prayer to be thence dismissed with costs. When the plea has been filed, the plaintiff may contest either its *sufficiency* or its *truth;* and he has *thirty days* after the time of filing the plea within which to make up his mind. If he resolves to contest its *sufficiency*, no demurrer is necessary to present that question, but the cause is simply set for hearing *upon bill and plea.* This may be done by either party, after the thirty days; and the question thus raised being purely a question of law, the course of proceeding, as to brief and argument, is throughout the same as upon demurrer, and need not be here repeated. The consequences, too, are similar. If the plea be held sufficient, the plaintiff will still be permitted to contest its truth upon such terms as the court may prescribe; and if it be held insufficient, the defendant may obtain leave to answer, upon the same terms as when a demurrer has been overruled. But if the plaintiff resolve to contest the *truth* of the plea, he must prepare the way by filing a *replication*, which I will next describe.

§ 223. **Replication.** (*a*) This is the formal method of tendering an issue in fact either to a plea or answer. It is the last stage of chancery pleadings, and opens the door for testimony on both sides. It must be filed, as we have seen, within thirty days. It requires no oath, but is signed by counsel and filed. Our rules then allow *twenty days for the taking of testimony* which will be considered hereafter. Each party may, after that time, set the cause for hearing on bill, plea, replication, and testimony; after which further testimony cannot be taken without special leave; and the subse-

(*a*) *Form of a Replication.* The replication of ——, to the plea (or answer) of ——. This repliant saving and reserving to himself all and all manner of advantage of exception, which may be had and taken to the manifold errors, uncertainties, and insufficiencies of the plea [or answer] of the said defendant, for replication thereunto saith, that he doth and will aver, maintain, and prove his said bill to be true, certain, and sufficient in law, and that the answer is very uncertain, evasive, and insufficient in law to be replied unto by the repliant, without that, that any other matter or thing in the said plea [or answer] contained, material or effectual in law to be replied unto, and therein and hereby well and sufficiently replied unto, confessed or avoided, traversed or denied, is true; all of which matters and things this repliant is ready to aver, maintain, and prove, as this honorable court shall direct, and humbly prays, as in and by his said bill he hath already prayed.

It may be doubted whether the history of judicial proceedings furnishes any thing more inexcusably involved in unmeaning verbiage than this. The following form is entirely sufficient. After the caption, say, The said complainant comes and replies to the said plea [or answer], and says that the matters and things alleged therein are not true; and this he is ready to verify.

quent proceedings, as to brief and argument, are the same as before described on demurrer. If the defendant succeed in proving his plea, this is conclusive; for its efficiency has been admitted by filing the replication. The bill must, therefore, be dismissed at the plaintiff's costs. But if the defendant fail in his proof, the situation of the case is analogous to that of a demurrer overruled; and the court will permit an answer to be filed, upon the terms before stated. This brings us to the consideration of the answer.

§ 224. **Answer.** (*a*) The third and last method of making defence is by *answer*. The answer must respond to all the material allegations in the bill, and may contain any new matter essential

(*a*) *Form of an Answer.* The answer of ——— to the bill filed against him by ———. This defendant, now and at all times hereafter, saving and reserving to himself all manner of benefit and advantage of exception to the many errors and insufficiencies contained in the bill of said complainant, for answer to the same or to so much thereof as this defendant is advised is material to be answered, he answers and says, he admits that ——— did duly make and execute such last will and testament in writing of such date, purport, and effect as is set forth in said bill, and did thereby bequeath to said complainant a legacy of $——— by the words of bequest therein stated; and that this defendant, as executor named in said will, did cause the same to be proved, and took upon himself the execution thereof, and took possession of the real and personal property of the testator, as charged in said bill; and this defendant is ready to produce a certified copy of the said will and probate, as this court shall direct; and this defendant admits that said complainant has repeatedly called upon him for the payment of the said legacy, and that no part of the same has yet been paid. But this defendant denies that the reason for not paying the said legacy is correctly stated in the bill. On the contrary, he avers the truth to be, that the debts due by the said testator amounted to the sum of $——— as nearly as can now be ascertained, a list of which is given in schedule A, annexed to this answer, and made part of it; and that the effects of the said testator, which have come to the hands of this defendant, consist of the *choses in action*, moneys, and chattels returned in the inventory made by this defendant, pursuant to the statute, a copy of which inventory with the appraisement is hereto annexed as exhibit B, and made part of this answer, amounting nominally to ———; and certain real estate described in exhibit C, which is made part of this answer, supposed to be worth $———; and this defendant says, that although he has labored with all diligence to convert the said assets into money, and settle the estate of the said testator, by paying first the debts, and then the legacies; yet up to the present moment it has been and still is doubtful whether there will remain sufficient, after paying the debts, to pay the legacies, as will appear by a statement of the present condition of the estate contained in exhibit D, which is made a part of this answer; and this is the true reason why the legacy of the said complainant has not yet been paid. This defendant denies all unlawful combination and confederacy with which he is charged, without that, that any other matter or thing material to be answered, and not herein sufficiently answered, confessed or avoided, traversed or denied, is true, to the best of his knowledge or belief. All which matters and things this defendant is ready to aver, maintain, and prove, as this honorable court shall direct; and humbly prays to be hence dismissed with his reasonable costs, in this behalf most wrongfully sustained.

Affidavit. The said defendant makes oath and says that the matters and things contained in the above answer, so far as stated from his own knowledge, are true; and so far as stated from information, he believes them to be true. [Signature of defendant.] Sworn to and subscribed before me, a ——— this ———. [Signature of the officer.]

The merely formal parts of the above answer may be omitted without the slightest detriment. They are first, the reservation in the beginning, instead of which, say: This defendant, for answer to the said bill, says, &c.; and secondly, the denial of combination and all which follows it, except the prayer to be dismissed with costs, which is a proper though not a necessary close of the bill. Sometimes, indeed, unlawful combination to defraud is the real matter of the bill, and then its denial is material in the answer; but the clause which follows the awkward phrase, "without that, that," can never be material.

to the defence. The plaintiff has a right to claim a specific admission or denial of every fact he alleges, whether there be specific interrogatories or not; and this without ambiguity or evasion. If the defendant has positive knowledge, he must so answer. If not, he must state his information or belief, or deny having any information or belief; and having thus satisfied the claims of the plaintiff, the answer may go on to make all such statements, by way of explanation or addition, as may be necessary in order to present the whole defence. (*a*) Thus, the answer may include any matter which might have been presented by way of plea; and as its whole effect is to deny the plaintiff's equity, it includes also a demurrer. A defendant, therefore, should never demur or plead, unless he is quite sure there is good cause; for by answering, he may obtain the whole benefit of both, together with much more. Indeed the additional expense and trouble of an answer furnish the only reason for not making it the sole method of defence. In drawing an answer, admit or deny what the bill alleges, and state your own defence, with the same precision, as if you were drawing a bill; and conclude with a prayer that the defendant's interest may be protected, and that he may be thence dismissed with costs. The answer is signed by counsel, and verified by the affidavit of the defendant; which affidavit may be made before the clerk in open court, or before any judge, justice of the peace, or master in chancery. The only case where an oath is not required, is that of a corporation which answers under its corporate seal; and even here an affidavit may be had by making one of the officers a party. If there be several defendants whose defence is the same, they ought to answer jointly and save expense; but this is not imperative. When the answer has been filed, the plaintiff may proceed as in case of a plea; that is, either to contest its *truth* or its *sufficiency:* and he has *thirty days* within which to make up his mind. If within this time he takes no step on the subject, either party may set the cause for hearing *on bill and answer;* in which case the answer will be taken as true in every part; and no evidence will be allowed to contradict it, unless it be matter of record referred to in the answer. The court, however, may, upon good cause and equitable terms, allow the plaintiff still to contest the truth of the answer. This is done, as in the case of a plea, by filing a *replication.* The proceedings are then throughout the same, in every particular, as when a replication is put in to a plea; and therefore need not be here repeated. Our statute provides, that if the defendant wishes to bring *new parties* before the court, he may state this in his answer, and insert *interrogatories* for them to answer; and thereupon a subpœna will issue as in case of a bill. It is further provided that after the answer has been filed, the defendant may file interrog-

(*a*) It is too late for the respondent after answering to the merits and submitting his defence to the court, to object to its jurisdiction on the ground that the complainant had a plain and adequate remedy at law. Nicholson *v.* Pim, 5 Ohio State, 25.

atories to be answered by the plaintiff; and if he neglect to answer them, his bill will be dismissed at his costs. Thus each party is enabled to avail himself to the fullest extent of the other's testimony under oath. There is still another provision of like nature, founded on the English practice, which is, that the defendant may file a *cross-bill*, to which the original plaintiff and any other persons may be made defendants; but the first bill must be answered, before an answer to the cross-bill can be enforced. But it would seem as if the other provisions, allowing the defendant to make new parties by his answer, and compel them to answer interrogatories, and also allowing him to put interrogatories for the plaintiff himself to answer, entirely supersede the necessity of a cross-bill in any case. The object of a cross-bill is, either to bring new parties before the court, when that is essential to the defence; or to set up against the plaintiff some matter of defence, which by the rules of pleading could not be set up in the answer. It is always considered as a defence, and is so connected with the other bill, that they are always considered as but one cause. It can, therefore, effect no purpose, which would not be effected with greater facility and simplicity, by pursuing the course pointed out in the foregoing provisions, which may be regarded as a decided improvement; still a cross-bill may be resorted to because the statute authorizes it.

We have seen that if the defendant undertakes to answer, the plaintiff is entitled to a full and explicit response, by admission or denial, to every material allegation in the bill, without subterfuge or evasion. If, therefore, the answer falls short in this respect, the plaintiff may refer the question to the court by means of *exceptions.* (*a*) The exceptions are signed by counsel, but of course require no affidavit. Upon filing them, it is at the option of the defendant either to supply the deficiency voluntarily by answering further; or to set the cause for hearing on the exceptions, and thus submit the question of the sufficiency of the answer to the court. In the latter case, the exceptions are argued and decided upon as any other question. If they be overruled, the plaintiff must pay the costs; and he may then obtain leave to file a replication; and if they be sustained, the defendant pays the costs, and must put in a further answer within *thirty days*, or such other time as the court shall fix; otherwise, the bill will be taken as confessed. Exceptions may again be filed to this second answer, if it be deemed still insufficient, on which the same course may be taken. And if the answer be held still insufficient, the defendant pays double costs, and cannot put in a further answer; but the bill is taken as confessed. Or, if it be material to the

(*a*) *Form of Exceptions.* The exceptions of ——— to the answer of ———. The said ——— comes and excepts to the answer of the said ———, and for cause of exception says: 1. That, &c. [note all the exceptions in this way and then say]; in all which particulars the said ——— insists that the said answer is evasive, imperfect, and insufficient; wherefore he prays that the said ——— may be compelled to answer further.

plaintiff, as on a bill of discovery, for example, he may have the defendant examined upon interrogatories, and committed until he answers them sufficiently. In like manner, where the defendant under the statutory provision, has put interrogatories to the plaintiff, or to a new defendant, he may take exceptions, if the answer be insufficient. Thus each party has the power of extorting the whole truth from the other, or driving him to imprisonment or perjury.

The only remaining aspect of proceedings is that of *default.* If the defendant does not disclaim, or make defence by demurrer, plea, or answer, within the time limited, he is said to be in default, and the bill is taken as *confessed.* But to provide as far as possible against injustice, when only one party is before the court, the statute and rules provide that even here, proof may be required of the facts alleged in the bill, if the court think proper; and also, that the time of defence may be extended, if good reason be offered. In case of default, the practice is this: the plaintiff, either in term or vacation, files a *decree nisi,* as it is called; that is, a draft of such a decree as he wishes, and makes a memorandum of the fact, with the date upon the office docket. Then, after the lapse of the time fixed by the rules, on any day in term, he moves to have the decree *nisi confirmed.* This is done, of course, unless the defendant had previously entered on the docket notice of his intention to resist such confirmation, and at the time shows sufficient reason to the court for granting leave to make defence; in which case he must submit to such special terms as the court may prescribe. The plaintiff then has his option, to set the cause for hearing at that term, or have it continued.

§ 225. **Hearing.** (*a*) I have thus traced a chancery cause up to the time of hearing, in each of the ways in which it can be presented; namely, on disclaimer, demurrer, plea, answer, and bill confessed. And I think it must have occurred to you, even from this brief sketch, that chancery proceedings are vastly more simple, natural, and rational, than the corresponding legal proceedings by which parties are brought to issue. It would now be in order to speak of the decree which is consequent upon the hearing; but I shall first allude to some prior incidental matters, which could not be mentioned before, without breaking in upon the regular narrative of the proceedings.

1. *Testimony.* The first of these is the taking of *testimony.* It is not intended here to discuss the principles of evidence. The rules which regulate the competency and credibility of witnesses, are, in general, the same in chancery as at law; except, that in chancery, the *parties* are made witnesses. But in the mode of presenting testimony, there is this great difference, that in chancery *oral testimony* is universally excluded. Witnesses are never

(*a*) Upon a hearing upon the bill and answer, the answer will be taken as true in all points. Gwin *v.* Selby, 5 Ohio State, 96.

examined *at the hearing;* the testimony is taken beforehand, and reduced to writing in the form of a *deposition.* If there be a single exception, it is where it becomes necessary at the hearing to identify an exhibit. Depositions, therefore, constitute the only form of presenting personal testimony in chancery. But depositions have been sufficiently discussed in the preceding lecture; there being no difference between those taken in legal and in chancery proceedings.

2. *Issue sent to a Jury.* (*a*) We have already seen that, as a general rule, the court of chancery decide upon the *facts* as well as the law; but as a jury is considered the best tribunal to weigh evidence and decide questions of fact, courts of chancery have always had the power of directing an issue to be tried by a jury, whenever they should deem it expedient. Our statute expressly confers this power, and declares that the verdict shall be entered of record, and made use of at the hearing. But it makes no provision as to the manner in which the issue shall be made up. In England, when the question admits of it, the chancellor directs an action to be brought in a court of law; otherwise, an issue is made up by the master, an officer to be described hereafter; and then a *feigned declaration* is drawn, alleging a *wager* between the plaintiff and defendant on the result of that issue; but this introduction of a wager seems to be as utterly puerile, as it is clearly unnecessary. Indeed, an action could not be sustained upon a wager in this State; but our court has regulated the practice in these cases, in such a manner as to dispense with a wager. According to the precedent reported, when the court order an issue to a jury, they direct the form of the issue, and which party shall have the affirmative. This party then files a declaration simply asserting the affirmative, and the other party files a plea simply denying it. The issue is then tried by a jury in the usual form, and the testimony on file in the cause may be read on such trial, unless the court otherwise order. The verdict is conclusive, unless the court see reason to grant a new trial. In England, it is not uncommon for issues in law to be in like manner referred to the courts of law; but this practice is unnecessary here, because the same judges officiate in both courts. I have before suggested that the forms of chancery procedure might be readily adapted to all cases in law as well as equity; and does not this expedient of making up an issue for a jury whenever such recourse is necessary, and so shaping such issue as exactly to meet the exigency, take away the only plausible objection that could be raised against so immense an improvement; namely, the want of trial by jury?

3. *Master.* (*b*) Our statute empowers each of the courts to appoint such numbers of persons as they think proper, in each county, to act as *master commissioners* in chancery for three years,

(*a*) See Greene *v.* Greene, 5 Ohio, 278; 1 Newland, 350.
(*b*) See 1 Newland, 6.

unless removed for good cause. These officers, who are usually called simply *masters*, have power to take depositions both in law and chancery, and to do all other acts of a ministerial nature, commonly performed by masters in chancery. Their fees are the same as are allowed to other officers for like services, and when not ascertained by law, are fixed by the court. They cannot administer oaths generally, but only to answers in chancery and depositions. The statutory provisions go no further; and for the rest of their duties, we must refer to the usages of chancery. In general, masters act as aids to the chancellor, in stating accounts, estimating damages, taking testimony when more is required, making up issues, examining answers when excepted to, investigating titles to real estate, making sale thereof under decrees, and the like. When the services of a master are required, the court make *an order of reference* to him, with such instructions as the case requires. Having performed the duty, he makes *report* of his proceedings. To this report either party may file *exceptions.* The cause is then sent for hearing on these exceptions, and the proceedings are similar to those upon exceptions to answers. If it be found necessary, the cause may be referred back again for further report; but when the report is not excepted to, it is conclusive of the matter in question. It will be readily seen how much this expedient of referring matters to a master diminishes the labors of the court, and facilitates chancery investigations. Courts of law experience great inconvenience from the want of such an officer. Their most complicated matters must be examined by the jury, and determined upon before separation. Twelve minds unprepared by education or habit, are there required to make the most intricate investigations, in the result of which all must concur, under every disadvantage as to time, place, and convenience; whereas a master in chancery can perform the same duty, under all the advantages of skill, experience, leisure, and singleness of purpose. Here, then, we have another signal instance of the superiority of chancery proceedings.

4. *Receiver.* (*a*) Our statute contains nothing on the subject of *receivers in chancery;* but according to the established *usages* of this court, they are appointed whenever occasion requires; and this happens whenever there is a controversy touching property, which requires some person to take care of it in the mean time, and the parties cannot agree upon that person. In such cases, to prevent waste or deterioration, or perhaps to complete improvements in progress, the court appoint a *receiver*, to take possession of such property, as their officer; and it is thenceforth considered as in custody of the court. The duties of the receiver are specified in the *order* of appointment, and he is required to give bonds for fidelity in such sum as the court shall determine. It will be readily admitted that this power of taking

(*a*) See Edwards on Receivers.

disputed property out of the control of those who claim to own it, is to be exercised with great caution, and only when a strong case is presented, by the party applying; but then the power is found to be a most salutary and beneficial one. For want of something analogous in the courts of law, litigants often suffer great loss and inconvenience; and thus the employment of a receiver, when the case requires it, may be cited as another peculiar advantage of chancery proceedings.

5. *Supplemental Bill.* The object of a supplemental bill is generally to bring before the court any matter material to the plaintiff's interest, which has happened after filing the original bill, and before the rendition of the decree. It states the original bill and proceedings thereon, and the event which makes a supplemental bill necessary. A subpœna issues, as on filing an original bill; but this bill is not confined exclusively to matter which occurred before the decree. It may be founded on matter occurring after the decree; but it is then usually connected with a *bill of review*, or *bill of revivor*, which will be described hereafter; and takes the name of one of these. A supplemental answer may be filed in like manner, on leave of the court, which is usually granted, as a matter of course. In fact, the grand principle which runs through all chancery proceedings, is to give to each party, at all times, every possible facility for bringing the full merits of his case before the court.

§ 226. **Decree.** (*a*) We have now reached that stage in the proceedings, when the court pronounce their decision. This decision is called a *decree*, and corresponds to the judgment in proceedings at law. Decrees are either *interlocutory* or *final*. A decree is *interlocutory*, when some material circumstance is wanting to enable the court to determine finally between the parties; and for that reason some reference is made of the case. Thus, when a cause is referred to a master, or a receiver is appointed, or an issue is directed to a jury, the order made by the court is

(*a*) *Form of a Decree.* When the decree is for the complainant, it must of course adapt itself to the exact relief to which he is found to be entitled, and therefore the form must vary to suit each case. In all cases, however, the following order may be observed. After stating the names of the parties, say: This cause came on for hearing, upon the bill, answer, &c. [stating the condition of the pleadings]; and was argued by counsel; and the court find that, &c. [stating the facts upon which the decree is founded]; and thereupon it is ordered and decreed that, &c. [stating whatever each party is to do, and concluding with the payment of costs].

But when the decree is for the defendant, it is always in the same form, unless with respect to the payment of costs, which, though generally decreed against the complainant, may, for some special reason, be otherwise disposed of. The form is as follows: This cause came on for hearing upon the bill, answer, &c., and was argued by counsel; and the court find the equity of the case to be with the defendant; and thereupon it is ordered and decreed that the complainant's bill be dismissed; and that he pay the costs of this suit within ——— days; and that in default thereof, execution issue therefor, as on judgments at law.

If the bill be dismissed generally, this will be a final bar against further proceedings in another suit. When, therefore, the case is such as to justify such further proceedings, the bill is dismissed *without prejudice.* See Loudenback *v.* Collins, 4 Ohio State, 251.

an interlocutory decree. A decree is *final*, when all the circumstances necessary to a complete explanation of the matters in litigation are brought before the court, and on full consideration, decided upon. In order to determine whether a decree is interlocutory or final, we must look, not to the *stage of the cause* at which it is rendered, but to what the decree itself contains. For a decree may be final as to the subject-matter of it, when it does not put an end to the cause. Thus on a bill of foreclosure, a decree of *sale* of the mortgaged premises is final as to that matter, though a further order remains to be made upon the report of the sale. In practice, the court do not themselves usually frame the decree; but merely indicate its contents in the opinion they deliver. The counsel in whose favor it is rendered then draws up the decree pursuant to the intimations of the court, and submits it to the opposite counsel for approval. If he make no objection, it is *entered in the journal* as a matter of course. If he object, it is submitted to the court, who so correct it as to make it conform to their decision; and it is then entered upon the journal. We have seen that upon a bill confessed, a *decree nisi* must be drawn up and filed beforehand; and would it not be a good practice generally to prepare in advance such a decree as you expect to obtain, and show it to your opponent, that it may be submitted to the court for approval, immediately upon delivery of their opinion, and while the whole case is fresh in the minds of all concerned? Our practice in relation to the entering of the decree is much more simple than the English. We have nothing analogous to their *enrolment*, and of course are not burdened with the distinctions founded thereon. With us a decree is not consummated until its entry in the journal; but then, it can only be altered by the regular action of the court. As the decree must be so shaped as to meet the circumstances of each particular case, no general set of technical forms can be given, answering to all cases, as in judgments at law; but in the books of practice a variety of forms may be found, which can be readily modified to suit any case. In England, the practice is to set forth the facts upon which the decree is made; but in this State, unfortunately, the practice has been to state only the decision of the court, without the facts upon which it is founded; so that the decree contains nothing on its face to show whether it is correct or not; and if it become necessary to review the proceedings, in the manner to be explained hereafter, you have to go behind the decree, and examine the whole case over again. It is much to be regretted that so loose a practice should ever have obtained a footing. A good practitioner will not imitate it; but, on the contrary, will be specially careful to state in the decree all the facts which go to sustain it. Then, a mere inspection of the decree itself will show the principles decided; and the decree will be held to be as conclusive of the facts therein contained, as is the verdict of a jury.

The effect of a decree is declared by statute to be the same as of a judgment at law. (*a*) It is further declared, that a decree for a conveyance, release, or acquittance, if the same be not performed, shall be tantamount thereto. In fact, it is a general and salutary rule that whatever chancery has decreed to be done, shall be considered as done. The court have express authority to *enforce* their decrees, either by *attachment* of the person, or *sequestration* of property; and if necessary, they may issue the same final process of execution as on judgment at law; and the same rules will govern the officer charged with carrying it into effect. If, however, from neglect of parties or any other cause, it becomes impossible to carry a decree into execution without further aid from the court, a bill may be filed for that purpose, and the aid will be given. Such, then, is the effect of a decree, if its natural operation be not prevented; and this, supposing the decree fairly obtained, can only be done in three ways; namely, by a *rehearing*, by *appeal*, and by *review*, which will be described in their order.

Rehearing. (*b*) If a party conceive himself aggrieved by a decree, he may apply for a *rehearing*, which is analogous to a *new trial* at law. The application is by *petition*, which must be filed within *thirty days* after the rendition of the decree. The petition must recite the substance of the original bill and subsequent proceedings, and specify wherein the party considers himself injured, concluding with a prayer that the cause may be *reheard.* It may be *allowed* by any two judges of the common pleas, or any single judge of the supreme court, who made the order objected to. The petition is then filed with the clerk, who issues process as in other cases; and proceedings on the decree are thereby stayed. This is the proper course to be taken, if you wish a decree once entered to be altered in the minutest particular. On a rehearing, the cause is wholly open with respect to the party in whose favor the decree was rendered; but with respect to the other party, it is only open as to those parts of the decree which are complained of in the petition. New evidence on the merits, which might have been had at the hearing, is not admissible at the rehearing; for this would encourage negligence. But evidence duly taken, though not read; or evidence as to *new matter* not then prepared for hearing; or evidence to impeach a former witness, is admissible. If the time for a rehearing be suffered to elapse without application, one of the other methods must be resorted to; for the court has no discretion to enlarge the time. The reason for withholding this discretion is, that the party will not be entirely without remedy, if the thirty days be suffered to pass by; for, as will be seen hereafter, he may still resort to a *bill of review* for nearly all matters which would authorize a rehearing.

(*a*) It is a bar to an action at law. Loudenback *v.* Collins, 4 Ohio State, 251.
(*b*) Myres *v.* Myres, 6 Ohio State, 221.

Appeal. By our statute, an appeal lies of course to the district court from "*any decree*" rendered in the common pleas; and since 1821, this has been the only method of bringing up a chancery cause from one to the other. Prior to that time, there was an anomalous proceeding, *by writ of error*, founded on the language of former statutes, which happened to allow "*final decrees*" as well as *judgments*, to be re-examined upon writ of error. But in the act of 1831, the word "*decrees*" is omitted; and consequently a writ of error, for which there is obviously no occasion, no longer lies to a decree in chancery. The appeal may be from "*any decree.*" This would include interlocutory as well as final decrees. But there is another provision which seems to confine the appeal to a final decree. We have no distinction like that in New York; and it is doubtful, therefore, how far an appeal here from a final decree would open prior interlocutory decrees. The better opinion is, that an appeal opens nothing for the court above but the particular order or decree appealed from. Indeed, our practice allows an appeal from *part of a decree*, when we are satisfied with the rest; and this is not understood to open the whole decree, because both parties often appeal from different parts of the same decree. If, then, an appeal from part of a decree does not open the whole decree, much less would an appeal from a whole decree open prior decrees. It follows therefore that if you are dissatisfied with any interlocutory decision of the court, you must appeal from it at once, and not wait for the final termination of the suit. The course of proceeding to perfect an appeal is the same in chancery as at law. *Notice* of appeal must be given during the term, and entered on the journal; and within *thirty days* after the end of the term the appellant must give *security* in double the amount of the decree appealed from, to abide the event. The appeal being thus perfected, the clerk makes out a transcript of the proceedings, which, together with the original papers, he transmits to the court above. The effect of an appeal is to suspend the operation of the decree, or part appealed from, except as to its lien upon real estate. The cause goes to hearing in the court above, on the pleadings presented to the court below; unless upon terms leave be granted to amend. If the plaintiff be the appellant, and do not recover more than in the court below, exclusive of new costs and interest, he must pay costs. If the defendant appeal, and the plaintiff recovers as much or more than before, exclusive of new costs and interest, the defendant must pay costs. It follows, from what has been said, that if your failure to obtain a satisfactory decree arose from the want of evidence which might have been procured, your only course is to appeal; since you cannot on this ground obtain a rehearing or review; but you may, after appeal, take as much testimony as you deem necessary, without the qualification that it must be newly discovered. The time given for appeal, you will bear in mind, is the same as for a rehearing;

namely, thirty days. If, therefore, you suffer this time to elapse without resorting to either of these, your only recourse will be a bill of review, which I am next to describe.

Review. (*a*) The only remaining method of avoiding the effect of a decree is by a *bill of review.* It is in the nature of a writ of error *coram nobis*, being filed in the same court which renders the decree to procure an alteration or reversal of such decree. It may be filed by any party to the decree, or his representatives, at any time within *five years* from the date of the decree; or in case of disability, five years from the removal thereof. It may be founded either upon errors appearing on the face of the record, or upon new matter discovered since the decree. In the former case, it may be filed as a matter of course; in the latter, by leave of the court. And on application at the term, to which the bill is filed, the court will order proceedings to be stayed upon the original decree. It is at their discretion to require security or not. By the English practice, the court look only to the decree, on a bill of review for error in the record, and will not examine the evidence over again; but in this State, owing to the facts not being inserted in the decree, the court are required to re-examine the whole case. This fact sufficiently demonstrates the incorrectness of our practice in not stating in the decree the facts upon which it is made. The bill of review must carefully recite the substance of all the former proceedings, and specify particularly the matters objected to; for the court will examine no error which is not specified in the bill. All the original parties must be made parties to this proceeding; and they may set up any relevant matter in defence, whether contained in the former proceedings or not. If the bill be founded on *new matter*, it must be such as the party could not have availed himself of when the former decree was rendered; and it will not be sustained after a demurrer allowed to a former bill of review; nor where the original decree was rendered by the consent of parties. You will thus perceive, that in our practice, the chief difference between a rehearing and review is in the time within which they may be prosecuted; for if there be any matters which can be revised in one, and not in the other, they are very few.

Limitation of Suits. (*b*) We have already seen that courts of equity are not within the strict letter of the statute of limitations, though they are uniformly governed by its spirit. Indeed, the general rule is, that a claim which would have been barred by the

(*a*) Gazley *v.* Huber, 3 Ohio State, 399; Longworth *v.* Sturges, 6 id. 143, 4 id. 690. A decree, like a verdict, will not be set aside on the ground of an erroneous finding, unless it is clearly against the weight of evidence or unsupported by it. Medina County Mut. Fire Ins. Co. *v.* Bollmeyer, 5 Ohio State, 107.

(*b*) 1 Story on Equity, § 64 *a*, 529; Bigelow *v.* Bigelow, 6 Ohio, 96; Tuttle *v.* Wilson, 10 id. 24; Fahs *v.* Taylor, 10 id. 104; Ridley *v.* Hetman, 10 id. 524; Kane *v.* Bloodgood, 7 Johns. Ch. 90; Piatt *v.* Vattier, 9 Peters, 405; Hovenden *v.* Annesly, 2 Sch. & Lef. 607; McKnight *v.* Taylor, 1 Howard, 161; Bowman *v.* Wathen, id. 189; Philips *v.* The State, 5 Ohio State, 122.

statute, if sued at law, will equally be barred in equity by lapse of the same time, and *vice versâ*. Thus an equitable title to land will not be enforced, when an action of ejectment would be barred by the statute. So, a court of equity will not compel an account, when the statute has barred the remedy at law. The case of dower in this State furnishes an illustration in point; for it has been held that the petition must be filed within twenty-one years from the death of the husband, because this is the limitation in ejectment. But while the general rule is as above stated, it is not universal. There are cases where equity has held a party barred by lapse of time, when the statute would not have been a bar, because the circumstances evinced gross laches without any excuse. And, on the other hand, there are cases where a much longer time than the statute has not been held a bar, because the party has shown a good excuse for his delay. But a strong case must be made to induce a court of chancery to depart from the statute either way.

Survivorship. Our statute provides that when either party dies, during the pendency of a suit in chancery, the same may be *revived*, for or against the representatives of the deceased, in the same manner as a suit at law. Now, a suit at law does not abate by the death of either party; but such death being suggested, a *citation* issues, if need be to the representatives, and the suit proceeds to judgment. It would seem, therefore, that in this State, the same course may be taken in chancery proceedings. But the usual practice is to file a *bill of revivor*, setting forth the original proceedings and the cause of abatement; and praying that the suit may be revived, and stand in the same condition as if the death had not occurred. If other new matter be set forth, it is then called a bill of *revivor and supplement*, and the books abound with shadowy distinctions on this subject. Thus, they speak of supplemental bills, bills of revivor, bills of revivor and settlement, bills in the nature of a bill of revivor, bills in the nature of a supplemental bill, and so on. But these distinctions serve only to perplex the mind, without any use whatsoever. The general rule is, that in drawing a bill which is not *original*, the proceedings on the original bill must be substantially set forth in the first place; and then any new matter may be added, which has made the subsequent bill necessary, by what name soever the latter may be called. This single direction will be a sufficient guide in the construction of any secondary bill whatsoever.

Complete Record. (*a*) The statute provides that when a chan-

(*a*) *Form of a Complete Record in Chancery.* Proceedings in chancery before the court of ——, within and for the county of ——, and State of ——, on the —— [date of final decree], in a certain cause, wherein —— is plaintiff, and —— is defendant. Be it remembered that heretofore, to wit, on the ——, the said complainant filed in the office of the clerk of said court a certain bill in chancery, in the words and figures following, to wit: [Here copy the bill and exhibits]; and thereupon the following subpœna was issued out of the said clerk's office, to wit: [here copy the subpœna]; and afterwards, to wit, on the ——, the sheriff of said cery cause has been finally determined, the clerk shall enter together in order, the bill, answer, pleadings, exhibits, reports, decretal orders, statement of facts found by a jury or agreed by the parties, and the decree, in a book kept for that purpose, which shall be signed by the court at the next term, as of the day on which such decree was pronounced. Of course this record must be made up in the first vacation after the final decision. But as the purpose and effect of such record are the same as of the record of proceedings at law, no further comment is necessary. I would again, however, repeat the observation that it would be a most useful exercise to make up for yourselves a complete record of all the proceedings in a chancery suit, and repeat the operation until you become perfectly familiar with all its parts.

§ 227. **Subjects of Chancery Jurisdiction.** I have now fulfilled my purpose in relation to chancery practice. I have exhibited an outline of the proceedings in a cause, from its commencement to its final termination. To have entered more into detail would only have perplexed the memory. The sketch now presented is sufficiently full to illustrate the philosophy of chancery practice, and to mark the wide difference between these proceedings and proceedings at law. We are now prepared to understand the reasons why the court of chancery, by a course of gradual usurpation, acquired its present widely extended and most beneficial jurisdiction. The

county returned the said subpœna indorsed as follows, to wit: [here copy the sheriff's return]; and afterwards, to wit, on the ——, the said defendant filed in the said clerk's office a demurrer to said bill, in the words and figures following, to wit: [here copy the demurrer]; and afterwards, to wit, on the ——, the said complainant filed in the said clerk's office a joinder in demurrer, in the words and figures following, to wit: [here copy the joinder]; and afterwards, to wit, at the —— term of said court, on motion of the said —— this cause was continued. And afterwards, to wit, at the —— term of said court, to wit, on the ——, this cause came on to be heard upon the demurrer to the said bill, and was argued by counsel; and the court overruled the said demurrer with costs; and thereupon, the said defendant moved the court for leave to answer the said bill, and filed in the said clerk's office an affidavit, in the words and figures following, to wit: [here copy the affidavit]; and thereupon leave was granted to answer the said bill in —— days, and the cause was continued. And afterwards, to wit, on the ——, the said defendant filed in the said clerk's office an answer to the said bill, in the words and figures following, to wit: [here copy the answer and exhibits]; and afterwards, to wit, on the ——, the said complainant filed in the said clerk's office exceptions to the said answer, in the words and figures following, to wit: [here copy the exceptions]; and afterwards, to wit, at the —— term of said court, to wit, on the ——, this cause came on to be heard upon the exceptions of the said answer, and was argued by counsel, and the court overruled the said exceptions, with costs; and thereupon the said complainant filed in the said clerk's office a replication to the said answer, in the words and figures following, to wit: [here copy the replication]; and afterwards, to wit, on the ——, the said complainant filed in the said clerk's office certain depositions, in the words and figures following, to wit: [here copy the depositions]; and afterwards, to wit, on the ——, the said defendant filed in the said clerk's office certain depositions, in the words and figures following, to wit: [here copy the depositions]; and afterwards, to wit, on the day and year first aforesaid, this cause came on to be heard upon the bill, answer, exhibits, replication, and testimony, and was argued by counsel; and thereupon the court found that, &c. [set forth the facts found by the court]; and thereupon the court ordered and decreed that, &c. [set forth the decree].

The certificates are the same as those appended to the complete record in law; to be found in a preceding note.

two leading principles upon which this jurisdiction depends have already been referred to; namely, the absence of an adequate remedy at law, and the existence of an enactment or precedent suited to the case. But I am now to consider the leading subjects, to which, in conformity with these principles, this jurisdiction extends. These subjects have usually been divided into three classes; namely, *first*, those in which the jurisdiction is *exclusive* of the courts of law; *secondly*, those in which it is *concurrent; thirdly*, those in which it is *assistant*. But I have thought that the most simple course would be, to take up those subjects in some convenient order, without reference to the above classification; and in commenting on each, to specify the character of the jurisdiction exercised over it. To ascertain what subjects are embraced under chancery jurisdiction, we must refer *first* to the *statutes*, which confer special jurisdiction in several cases; and *secondly* to the *precedents*, or *usages*, which settle the question of jurisdiction in all other cases, and I shall take occasion to describe several matters, the proceedings in which are analogous to those in chancery, though not strictly chancery proceedings. In our preceding discussions relating to persons and property, it was inevitable that I should make frequent reference to the subjects which I am here to consider. But we shall now have the advantage of viewing them in connection. I shall first speak of those for which there is special statutory provision, and then of those which depend upon precedent.

1. *When Title is Disturbed.* (*a*) When one person has the *legal title and possession of land* to which another sets up a *claim of title*, by our statute the possessor may file his bill against the claimant, setting forth these facts, and praying that his title may be quieted; and, if he establish his title, the defendant will be decreed to release his claim and pay the costs; or, if the defendant succeed in making good his claim to a better title, the court will decree a conveyance by the plaintiff to him, with costs. If, however, the defendant disclaim any interest, the plaintiff having thus attained his object, must pay the costs. It has been decided that the assertion of a judgment lien upon land in the possession of another is a claim coming within this provision. In cases of this kind, it is clear that the plaintiff is without remedy at law; because being in possession, he cannot bring an ejectment to try his title. A chancery proceeding is, therefore, the only method of quieting his title; and this is sometimes called *a bill of peace*.

(*a*) *Quieting Title.* Actual possession must be alleged and proved. Clark *v.* Hubbard, 8 Ohio, 382. Where a sale on execution would pass no title, but throw a cloud over that of complainant, chancery will interfere. Norton *v.* Beaver, 5 Ohio, 178. The doubt whether an administrator can release an equity of redemption is a ground for quieting title. Bank U. S. *v.* Piatt, 5 Ohio, 540. The remedy by our statute is more extensive than the *quia timet* bill in England. Douglass *v.* Scott, 5 Ohio, 194. An heir, seeking to quiet his title against a void sale by an administrator, must refund taxes, but not purchase-money. Nowler *v.* Coit, 1 Ohio, 519.

2. *When a debtor absconds.* (*a*) When a person has a *suit* at law or in chancery, for the recovery of money or damages, *pending* against a non-resident or absconding defendant, or one who secretes his property, by our statute the plaintiff may file his bill, setting forth these facts, with an affidavit of their truth, against any person who is indebted to the original defendant, or who is in possession of any personal property belonging to him; and the court will *enjoin* such person from paying over such debt, or parting with such property, until the original suit shall have been disposed of; so that if the plaintiff prevail in that suit he will have this fund to satisfy his judgment. The defendant in this suit, from the service of the subpœna, becomes a *trustee* or *garnishee* for the plaintiff, and is responsible to him for the debt or property. This remedy, it will be perceived, differs from the legal remedy by *attachment* in this, that here a suit is already *pending;* whereas an attachment is itself the commencement of a suit. This proceeding can only be resorted to when the original suit would *survive* in case of the death of either party, because in no other case would it be proper to allow the plaintiff to proceed at once against the property of the original defendant; but then it provides for an important case, in which, on account of the pendency of the original suit, there could be no adequate remedy at law. The reason for requiring an affidavit in this case is, that the court are required to act before hearing the other party.

3. *Subjecting Equities: when Execution cannot be levied.* (*b*) When a judgment or decree has been obtained against a debtor who has no real or personal property *subject to execution* at law, by our statute the plaintiff may file his bill by setting forth these facts, and praying to subject to the payment of such judgment or decree any property or effects of the defendant not liable to execution; including, *first*, all equitable interests in real estate, of whatever nature; *secondly*, all shares in joint-stock companies; *thirdly*, all *choses in action*, or debts due or to become due to the defendant; and, *fourthly*, all effects in the hands of third persons belonging to the defendant. These four classes comprehend all kinds of property not liable to execution, with the exception of certain privileged articles before alluded to; and thus the plaintiff has a remedy in equity when he could have none at law.

4. *Ne exeat.* (*c*) When one person wishes to prevent another,

(*a*) The Code, as has been stated, supersedes the necessity of this proceeding.

(*b*) This is commonly called a *creditor's bill.* It is not necessary that execution should be issued where it is shown to be unavailing. Gilmore *v.* Miami, 2 Ohio, 294; Piatt *v.* St. Clair, 6 id. 227. A judgment creditor acquires no lien upon the unleviable property of his debtor, until he files his bill to charge it. Douglass *v.* Huston, 6 Ohio, 156. An occupant, under a parol declaration that he may remain during life, has not such an equity as can be subjected by this proceeding. Waggoner *v.* Speck, 3 Ohio, 292. The bill must distinctly allege the want of unleviable property. Clark *v.* Strong, 16 Ohio, 317.

The Code, by its provisions in aid of execution, supersedes the necessity of this proceeding.

(*c*) See Beames's *Ne Exeat;* Story on Equity, chap. 40; 1 Newland, 234; Wilcox, 318.

who is equitably indebted to him without security, from leaving the State until he shall have given security, by our statute, as well as by general usage, he may file his bill, alleging such indebtedness and intended departure, and praying for a *writ of ne exeat* against the defendant. The bill must be verified by affidavit, because it requires the immediate action of the court. In term time it may be *allowed* by either court, and in vacation by any judge of the supreme court, or by the president judge of the common pleas. The court or judge allowing the writ determines the amount in which *security* shall be given to the plaintiff, and the writ then issues in place of a subpœna. After reciting the cause of complaint, it commands the sheriff to cause the defendant to give him security, in the specified sum, that he will not depart out of the State without leave of the court; and, in default thereof, to commit him to jail, and return his proceedings forthwith. If the defendant, by his answer, satisfy the court that there is no reason for such restraint, or give security to perform the decree, the writ will be discharged. This writ, you will observe, is in the nature of equitable bail, and the general rule is, that it will not be granted when the plaintiff could have bail at law. As it operates in direct restraint of personal liberty, the court will require a very strong case to be made before they will interfere. It would seem that the bill must be explicit as to the *indebtedness* of the defendant; his *intention* soon to leave the State, evinced either by threats or other significant indications; and the *danger* thence resulting to the plaintiff's claim. Nor must the debt be dependent on a contingency; it must be *certain.* If these facts exist, and the debt be an equitable one, there being no remedy at law, this writ may be applied for. And there are two cases in which this writ will be granted upon merely legal claims. The first is the case of alimony decreed to the wife. The second is that of an account, where the defendant admits a balance due the plaintiff, but the plaintiff claims a greater balance.

5. *Injunction.* (*a*) Where one person is in danger of receiving

(*a*) See Eden on Injunctions; Hilliard on Injunctions; Joyce on Injunctions; High on Injunctions; 2 Story on Equity, ch. xxiii.; and the books on chancery practice generally. The Code dispenses with the writ of injunction, and substitutes "a command to refrain from a particular act," which may either be the final judgment in an action, or may be allowed, by interlocutory order, as a provisional remedy, in a case of "*great or irreparable injury,*" or where the act to be restrained would tend to render the judgment sought "ineffectual," or where any statute may specifically provide for such restraining order. § 5571 *et seq.* But the general usages governing injunctions are not essentially altered, unless, perhaps, by enlarging the scope of this preventive remedy. The federal and State courts do not interfere with each other's proceedings by injunction. Rogers *v.* Cincinnati, 5 M'Lean, 337; M'Leod *v.* Duncan, 5 id. 342. As to injunctions to restrain the collection of illegal taxes, see Burnet *v.* Cincinnati, 3 Ohio, 72; M'Coy *v.* Chillicothe, 3 id. 370; Osborn *v.* Bank U. S., 9 Wheaton, 371. An injunction will not be allowed to restrain a trespass, even in respect to a ferry landing, unless the franchise is in question. Ross *v.* Page, 6 Ohio, 166. Execution may be properly stayed where a sale would convey no title. Bank U. S. *v.* Schultz, 2 Ohio, 471. A stay of levy upon chattels is equivalent to setting it aside. Bisbee *v.* Hall, 3 Ohio, 449. As to the liability of a surety on an injunction bond, see Hall *v.* Williamson, 9 Ohio State, 17.

Injunctions are prohibitory or mandatory. They are alike restraining orders in irreparable injury from another, if not prevented by immediate interference, by our statute, as well as by general usage, he may file his bill, praying for an *injunction* against the defendant; and the injunction may be allowed in the following cases: 1. To prevent or stay the commission of *waste*. What waste is has been before considered. In this case, the *allowance* of the injunction may be made by the supreme court, or any judge thereof; and by the common pleas, or any president judge thereof. 2. To stay proceedings of the courts of law, at any stage thereof, either before or after judgment. In this case, the allowance may be made by either of the courts, or any judge thereof; but the supreme court or one of its judges will not allow an injunction in this case,

form. Prohibitory injunctions restrain the doing of an act. Mandatory injunctions ordinarily restrain the continuance of an act, and thereby require the defendant to undo some wrong already committed; for example, to restrain the continuance of a building, wall, or dam which has been constructed, or to restrain the keeping of books away from their proper depositary. It has lately been allowed to restrain a party from failing to perform his covenants, where the court could not grant a decree for specific performance, owing to the impracticability of the court's supervising the performance of the particular covenants. Cook *v.* Chilcott, L. R. 3 Chy. Div. 694.

A provisional injunction will not be granted without notice to the defendant, unless the emergency is such that giving notice would substantially defeat the application. In such case the restraining order is made to last a specified number of days, so that it will expire by its own limitation, and cannot, if wrongfully allowed, be kept alive by appeal from an interlocutory order dissolving it.

Upon an application for a provisional injunction the balance of probable injury to be caused by allowing or refusing it, has weight both in prohibitory and mandatory injunctions. The same is true in final decrees in mandatory injunctions. Senior *v.* Pawson, L. R. 3 Eq. 330; Meyer's Appeal, Penn. State, 164. The right to use discretion as to granting or refusing a prohibitory injunction by final decree, on that ground was declared in England in Flooks *v.* Southwest R. R. Co., 1 Smale & Gif. 142; Graham *v.* Birkenhead R. R. Co., 2 McN. & G. 159; and Hodgson *v.* Earl Powis, 1 De Gex, M. & G. 6. But in practice, an injunction at least in cases of nuisance is never in England refused on the ground of damage that will thereby be caused to the defendant or his employees and dependants by its allowance. Att'y-Gen. *v.* Colney Hatch Asylum, L. R. 4 Eq. 146; Att'y-Gen. *v.* Birmingham, 4 K. & J. 528; Att'y-Gen. *v.* Corporation of Leeds, L. R. 5 Chy. Ap. 587. In such extreme cases the defendant is allowed leave to apply for a stay of the issuing of the order of injunction from time to time. In the United States an injunction to restrain a grievous nuisance has been refused and the complainant left to his action for damages, simply on the ground that its allowance would destroy large and costly works and throw many persons out of employment. Richards's Appeal, 57 Penn. State, 107; Hackenstein's Appeal, 70 Penn. State, 102. On the same ground of overplus of damage, the courts in New Jersey have refused to allow an injunction restraining the running or operating a railway. Torrey *v.* C. & A. R. R. Co., 3 C. E. Green, 293; Hackensack Imp. Co. *v.* N. J. Midl. R. R. Co., 7 C. E. Green, 94; Erie R. R. Co. *v.* Del. & W. R. R. Co., 6 C. E. Green, 283. In England such injunction is allowed. Cossens *v.* Bangor R. R. Co., L. R. 1 Chy. Ap. 594.

It was held that an injunction will not be allowed to restrain the publication of a libel in any case, in Prudential Assurance Co. *v.* Knott, L. R. 10 Chy. App. 142, and Fisher *v.* Apollinaris Co., id., p. 297. These cases overruled Springhead Spinning Co. *v.* Riley, L. R. 6 Eq. 561; Dixon *v.* Holden, L. R. 7 Eq. 494; and Maxwell *v.* Hogg, L. R. 2 Chy. App. 307, and affirmed the earlier case of Clark *v.* Freeman, 11 Beav. 112; but were themselves in turn overruled by Thorley's Cattle Food Co. *v.* Massam, L. R. 6 Chy. Div. 582; and 14 Chy. Div. 763; Dicks *v.* Brooks, L. R. 15 Chy. Div. 22; and Halsey *v.* Brotherhood, L. R. 19 Chy. Div. 386. The rule seems to be that while an injunction will not be allowed to restrain the publication of a personal libel, it will be allowed to restrain the publication of statements concerning the plaintiff's property, provided such statements are not only untrue and injurious, but are known to be untrue, or are made without probable cause and with intent to injure.

unless the matter in dispute be of sufficient value to give original jurisdiction to the common pleas, that is, one hundred dollars; nor will the latter, unless the value amount to twenty dollars. The bill must be verified by affidavit; and the plaintiff must give a bond of *indemnity* to the defendant, in such sum as the court or judge shall determine, to be approved by the clerk before the injunction can take effect. The clerk then indorses on the *subpœna*, "injunction allowed and bail given;" and this is declared to supersede the necessity of a *writ of injunction* in such case. If the effect of the injunction be to stay the collection of money, and it be dissolved in the common pleas, the decree for the defendant will embrace a penalty of five per cent besides the original judgment, interest, and costs; and if the plaintiff appeal therefrom, and fail, the penalty will be doubled. If the money has been actually collected by the officer, but not paid over, he must pay it back again, upon the allowance of the injunction, unless the court otherwise order; and upon refusal so to do he may be *amerced*, as in other cases. 3. In all other cases where it is usual for courts of equity to interfere by injunction. In these cases, the bill must be verified by affidavit, and may be allowed upon such conditions as the court may think proper to annex. The most usual cases coming within this class are: To restrain the infringement of copyrights and patents; to prevent the transfer of negotiable paper or stock; to prevent nuisances, and to prevent irreparable injury of any description. Bills of injunction do not differ in form from other bills except in the additional prayer that the defendant may be enjoined from doing the act complained of. It would seem as if the only case where an affidavit is not required by the statute, is where the injunction is to stay *waste;* and this is probably an accidental omission, for the general principle is, that whenever the immediate action of the court is asked without hearing the other party, the bill must be verified by affidavit. Security is not expressly required, except in case of injunction to stay legal proceedings, but may be ordered whenever the court see proper. The only case where an associate judge of the common pleas can allow an injunction, is to stay legal proceedings. On coming in of the demurrer, plea, or answer to the bill of injunction, the defendant may move to *dissolve* the injunction, and have a hearing at once on that question. If this motion fail, the cause will take the usual course; and if on final hearing the plaintiff prevail, the decree will be that the injunction be perpetual. We have seen how obedience to decrees is generally enforced; but the statute has a special provision in reference to *waste* which authorizes either court in term, or any judge of the supreme court, or president judge of the common pleas, in vacation, to enforce obedience by attachment, fine, and imprisonment. We have seen that the statute does not prohibit the issuing a writ of injunction in any case; but merely supersedes the necessity of it, where security has been given to stay legal proceedings. Accordingly, in all other cases a writ must issue. Its form will be readily imagined without a description. There are two other special cases of injunction authorized by statute: namely, *first*, where a bill has been filed in the second class of cases before mentioned, against the property of a non-resident or absconding debtor; and, *secondly*, to prevent the collection of a school-house tax illegally assessed; but of these there is nothing peculiar to be said. It will be readily perceived that all cases of injunction come clearly within the principle of there being no adequate remedy at law. The law might perhaps give damages for the injury when done, but has no such preventive power as this which a court of chancery exerts. Besides, in many cases, damages would be altogether inadequate, even if they were sure to be recovered; and in all cases, it is better, as a general principle, to prevent the injury from being done, than to run the risk of obtaining compensation after it is done. Indeed, there is no point of view in which the exercise of chancery power appears more beneficial and important, than when it judiciously interferes by injunction to prevent the commission of injuries. It was undoubtedly a very bold movement, on the part of the first chancellor who granted an injunction to stay legal proceedings; and we know, as a matter of history, that this interference met with the most strenuous opposition from the courts of law. A long and exceedingly bitter controversy was carried on between the two courts; but the court of chancery ultimately prevailed; and what was at first a clear and manifest usurpation of power, at last received the sanction of the king and parliament, on account of the obvious utility of its prudent exercise. In fact, were there not a power lodged somewhere to stay legal proceedings, the benign purposes of justice would often be so perverted that remedies would become in themselves injuries.

6. *Contesting of Wills.* (*a*) When the heir of a deceased ancestor or any person interested, wishes to contest the validity of a *will*, after probate, there being no law proceeding for this purpose, our statute allows him to file his bill in chancery; and thereupon an issue is made up for a jury to try whether the writing produced be the last will of the testator, or not. The mode of making up this issue has been determined by the court as we have before seen. The verdict of the jury is final, unless a new trial be granted, or there be an appeal to the district court. We have before seen, when speaking of the *probate* of a will, that the testimony is taken down in writing and filed with the will. On the trial before the jury, this testimony may be used. The time limited for contesting a will is two years from the probate; and in case of *disability*, two years from the removal thereof; and in this one instance, probably from inadvertence, *absence from*

(*a*) See *ante*, lec. 30; 2 Story, Eq. ch. 29; Greene *v.* Greene, 5 Ohio, 278; Hathaway's will, 4 Ohio State, 383. This proceeding is not affected by the Code. See Myres *v.* Myres, 6 Ohio State, 221; Brown *v.* Griffiths, 11 Ohio State, 329; Banning *v.* Banning, 12 Ohio State, 437.

the State is mentioned as one of the disabilities. In all other cases, we have seen that it has ceased to constitute a disability.

7. *Mortgages.* (*a*) The nature of mortgages has been already explained. We have seen that their present legal character is derived from the doctrines established by the court of chancery; and that the most efficient remedies both for mortgagor and mortgagee are in chancery. 1. If the debt be not paid at maturity, the mortgagee may file his bill of foreclosure, setting forth his claim, and making the mortgagor and all persons interested parties; and may thus procure a sale of the land for the payment of his debt, according to its priority. The decree should be so drawn as to give the mortgagor a short time within which to prevent a sale by payment. The sale may be made by the sheriff or master, as the court may direct, and the proceedings are the same as in sales on execution. 2. If the mortgagee have obtained possession of the land in any other way than by foreclosure, the mortgagor may file his bill to redeem the land, by paying the debt and interest; and the court will decree accordingly. The limitation in both cases is the same as in ejectment; namely, twenty-one years. It may be well to remark that the original pretext for chancery interference with respect to mortgagees, was to prevent a penalty or forfeiture, by substituting a fair compensation. Indeed, equity abhors penalties and forfeitures under all circumstances, and, as a general rule, will always interfere to prevent them, in cases admitting of a conscientious adjustment. (*b*)

8. *Dower.* (*c*) Where a widow wishes to obtain an assignment of her dower, which has been before described, our statute requires her to proceed by bill in chancery; and thus virtually does away with proceedings at law. The bill sets forth the grounds of her right, describing the tracts of which she claims to be endowed; and the heirs or assigns of her husband are made defendants. If there be any mortgagees or other encumbrancers, they may set up their rights by a cross-bill. If the lands lie in several counties, the bill must be filed in that county where the principal messuage of her husband was; and the court may, at their discretion, order the whole dower to be assigned, not only in one county, but in one tract where it will not prejudice the rights of others. If the land cannot be conveniently divided, dower may be assigned in a special manner, as one-third of the rents or income. The decree directs the sheriff to cause the dower to be set off by three disinterested men under oath; and if the court approve of their proceedings, a *writ of seisin* is directed to issue, by virtue of which the sheriff delivers possession to her. The great advantage of proceeding in chancery to obtain dower is, that this

(*a*) See *ante*, lec. 25; 2 Story, Eq. ch. 29, 34. The Code embraces proceedings in foreclosure and redemption; and in foreclosure requires a sale in all cases. § 5316. Formerly this was not so. Anonymous, 1 Ohio, 235; Higgins *v.* West, 5 id. 554.

(*b*) See 2 Story on Equity, ch. 34.

(*c*) See *ante*, lec. 28; 1 Story on Equity, ch. 12.

court can take into consideration all the circumstances of the case, and do complete justice between all the parties.

9. *Partition.* (*a*) Where tenants in common wish to obtain a *partition* of the common property, the statute requires the application to be by petition, which is filed in the court of common pleas, if all the land be in one county; but if in several counties, then in either of the courts of either of the counties. The bill sets forth the nature of the petitioner's title, describes the tracts of which partition is claimed, and specifies the name and residence of each of the co-tenants, if known. Also, if there be a widow entitled to dower which is not yet assigned, she must be made a party. If any of the co-tenants be minors, their guardians are empowered to act for them. Thus far the course is the same as in other chancery proceedings; but at this point the statute makes a difference; for no subpœna issues. Their petitioner has his option either to give personal notice in writing of the pendency of the petition, or to advertise the same in some newspaper of general circulation, at least *forty days* before the commencement of the next term; and upon proof of due notice, if no objection be made by the other parties in interest, the court will *order* partition to be made and returned at the next term, and a *writ* will issue accordingly. This writ commands the sheriff to cause the partition to be made by three disinterested freeholders of the vicinity, named by the court, and acting under oath. They are to take into view the improvements, situation, and qualities of the different tracts, if there be more than one; and if they be not all owned by the same proprietors and in the same proportion, a proper portion of each tract must be set off to each of the co-

(*a*) As to partition in chancery, see 1 Story, Eq. ch. 14. The original Code did not affect this proceeding. § 568. Where a partition was reported to the court, but never confirmed, all the heirs, of whom some were minors, took possession and held for seventeen years, equity will not order a new partition unless great unfairness be shown. Piatt *v.* Hubbell, 5 Ohio, 243. Where the facts conferring jurisdiction are not shown by the record, if a long time has elapsed, they will be presumed. Glover *v.* Ruffin, 6 Ohio, 255. The act of 1820 did not require a confirmation, and a purchaser's title will not fail because the proceeds of sale were not brought into court. Goudy *v.* Shank, 8 Ohio, 415. A partition of several tracts, where the petitioner is not a tenant in common as to all, is erroneous. Smith *v.* Pratt, 13 Ohio, 548; Harman *v.* Kelly, 14 id. 502. The husband should be a party to a partition of the wife's land. Pillsbury *v.* Dugan, 9 Ohio, 117. The title of the purchaser is not affected by mere irregularities. Foster *v.* Dugan, 8 Ohio, 87. An appraiser may purchase in the absence of actual fraud. Bohart *v.* Atkinson, 14 Ohio, 228. It is not necessary to divide each tract. Smith *v.* Barber, 7 Ohio, 2 pt. 118. Where one tenant in common has conveyed his undivided share in several tracts, the other must bring separate suit against each purchaser. Prentiss's case, 7 Ohio, 2 pt. 129. As to the effects of partition, see Tabler *v.* Wiseman, 2 Ohio State, 207; Williams *v.* Van Tuyl, id. 336. {Partition is not the creation of a new title, but the dividing of possession, hence does not lie where there is no possession; thus remaindermen cannot partition during the particular estate. Tabler *v.* Wiseman, 2 Ohio State, 207. Doubtless a lease of the premises is not such want of possession, since a tenant's possession is that of his landlord. In Ohio, questions of title and estate between the parties can be settled in the partition case; hence it is held that an answer denying the plaintiff's entire title does not oust the jurisdiction. Hogg *v.* Beerman, 41 Ohio State, 81. In Patton *v.* Patton, 39 id. 590, a suit for partition, it was necessary to construe a will, pronounce the illegality of a bequest, and direct the course of descent.}

tenants. It may happen, however, that the land cannot be divided without great injury to its value; and in this case, the three freeholders return an *appraisement* of its value; and if the court approve of the return, and any one or more of the co-tenants *elect* to take the whole at that appraisement, and pay the rest their proportions, the court will order the sheriff to execute conveyances accordingly; but if no such election be made, the order will order a *sale* at public auction, to be conducted in the same manner as sales on execution. Upon return of sale and approval by the court, they will order the sheriff to execute the deed, and distribute the proceeds among the co-tenants. (*a*) The sale, however, cannot be made for less than two-thirds of the appraisement; unless, after being once offered, the court shall direct otherwise; and if there be a widow entitled to dower, it must be first provided for by the freeholders; who may either include it in one or more of the shares, making them larger in proportion; or may simply divide what remains after setting off dower, and leave that to be divided at a future time. It hardly need be observed, that if the co-tenants can agree among themselves, they may execute deeds of partition, without resorting to the court. In like manner, after the petition is filed, the co-tenants may come into court and agree upon a partition, which, being recorded, will be as valid as any other. As the partition is presumed to be for the benefit of all the co-tenants, the *costs* are usually shared among them; but this rests in the discretion of the court. The order may be that only the share of the petitioner shall be set off, if the rest do not desire partition; in which case he would, of course, pay all the costs. If there be any thing to regret in these provisions, it is, that proceedings in partition are not made in all respects chancery proceedings; for questions may now arise, which will occasion much doubt and difficulty, as not coming within the known usages of chancery, and not specifically provided for by statute.

10. *Execution of real Contracts.* Where one or more persons have entered into a contract for the sale and conveyance of land, and one of them dies before executing the conveyance, our statute authorizes the executor or administrator of the deceased owner, if there be but one owner, or the survivors, if there be more than one owner, to file a petition in the court of common pleas, praying for an order for the execution of the contract. The petition must name all the persons interested in the contract, and describe the land to be conveyed, with all the circumstances. No subpœna issues; but *notice* must be personally served on the parties interested, or published three successive weeks in some newspaper of general circulation; and if, on hearing the case, the court are satisfied that the contract ought to be executed, they order the executor, administrator, or survivor, as the case may be, to execute the deed contracted for. This deed must recite the order,

(*a*) R. S. §§ 5766, 5769.

and when duly executed, conveys as good a title as could have been conveyed, if death had not intervened. At the same time, the court provide that the proportion of money which would have belonged to the deceased shall be secured to his representatives. The same statute provides, in like manner, for the case where the *purchaser* dies before the conveyance is executed. His heirs may file their petition and compel a conveyance to them, in the same manner as their ancestor might have done. It would seem as if this right would have existed without any express provision, on the general doctrines of *specific performance* to be described hereafter. There is another statute which authorizes the guardians of idiots and lunatics, by application to the court of common pleas, to execute the real contracts of such idiots or lunatics, by making the proper conveyances. The importance of these provisions for cases unprovided for at law is at once perceived. But here, again, we have such a departure from the regular course of chancery proceedings, as is likely to create uncertainty; and for which there is no apparent reason.

11. *Applications to sell Land.* When there is not sufficient personal property to pay the debts of a *deceased person;* or when it is necessary for the support, or will be for the advantage, of a *minor* that his real estate shall be sold, our statute authorizes the executor, administrator, or guardian, as the case may be, to file his petition in the court of common pleas, setting forth the facts of the case, and praying for an order of sale. But the course of proceeding in such cases has been sufficiently described before, when treating of executors, administrators, and guardians, and their conveyances. You will again observe, that these applications are not strictly chancery proceedings, although, like them, commenced by petition.

12. *Divorce.*(a) When a husband or wife wishes to be divorced for one of the causes before enumerated, our statute provides that the application shall be by petition, filed in the supreme court, setting forth the particular cause. It also declares that proceedings for divorce shall be "*as in chancery,*" where the contrary is not specified. We have seen that the proceedings under the three preceding heads, though they commence by petition, as in chancery, and are in other respects more analogous to chancery proceedings than to any other, are nevertheless peculiar to those subjects; and the same was true of divorce, until the act of 1834 declared that it should be a chancery proceeding. The petition must distinctly set forth the cause of application. If the adverse party reside in the State, a summons and copy of the petition must

(a) See Page on Divorce; Bishop on Marriage and Divorce. As to allowance, *pendente lite,* see D'Arusmont's case, 8 West. Law Jour. 538. Proceedings in divorce are not affected by the Code. For points of practice, see Lattier *v.* Lattier, 5 Ohio, 538; Tappan *v.* Tappan, 6 Ohio State, 64. A decree from the bonds of matrimony, although sustained by fraud and false testimony, cannot be set aside on an original bill filed at a subsequent term. Parish *v.* Parish, 9 Ohio State, 534. See on the subject of divorce generally, *ante,* § 105.

be personally served at least six weeks before the term. If out of the State, there is an option to make personal service, or give two months' notice by advertisement. On the hearing, the confession of neither party can be received as evidence, for fear of collusion. The facts must be proved by witnesses testifying orally in court, if their attendance can be procured; otherwise, their depositions may be taken. The marriage itself must be first proved; but evidence of cohabitation as reputed man and wife will be sufficient for this purpose. If there be good reason, the court will make an order for the support of the wife during the pendency of the petition; and in the final decree, the support of the wife and the custody of the children are permanently provided for.

13. *Perpetuation of Testimony.* (*a*) Where no suit is pending, but it is apprehended that litigation may arise, and that testimony now accessible may then be lost, our statute authorizes the filing of a bill to perpetuate such testimony. The bill must specially describe the subject-matter to which the testimony relates, and name all the parties interested therein, if known; if not, they must be described as well as the case admits of. They are brought before the court as in other chancery proceedings. The plaintiff then files the names of the witnesses, and the interrogatories to be put to each; and the defendant, or if he has not had actual notice, some attorney appointed by the court and compensated by the plaintiff, files cross-interrogatories. These are forwarded to the person authorized to take the deposition, who must either be a master commissioner of this State, or some person specially authorized by a *dedimus potestatem.* The witnesses are to answer no other questions than those thus filed. If the court are satisfied that the depositions have been properly taken, they order them to be made part of the record in the cause; and thereafter, the originals or certified copies may be used in any suit in law or chancery, between the same parties or privies, touching the same subject-matter; provided the original witnesses cannot be had. It is further provided, that if, after filing the bill, it be made to appear that any witness is old, infirm, or about to leave the State, the court may forthwith, before the appearance of the defendant, order his deposition to be taken *de bene esse;* that is provisionally, to be used if need be. This mode of perpetuating testimony is a chancery proceeding of ancient usage: but it is seldom resorted to in this State, because our statutes provide other methods attended with less trouble, which I will now describe. 1. By the act providing a mode of perpetuating testimony, two associate judges are authorized to take the deposition of any person residing within their county, "to perpetuate the remembrance of any fact, matter, or thing." They are to cause all persons interested in the subject-matter to be "duly notified," that they may attend and cross-examine. The questions and answers must be reduced

(*a*) See 2 Story on Equity, ch. 41. The provisions of the Code are not substantially different. § 5873–9.

to writing. Within sixty days, the deposition, if it relate to land, must be recorded in the recorder's office; if to other property, in the clerk's office: and thereafter, the original or a certified copy may be used "in any cause to which it may relate," if the witness cannot be had. If there be no two associate judges disinterested, two justices of the peace may officiate. If the opposite party was not present at the taking, the deposition is open to all legal objections. 2. By the act enabling landholders to perpetuate testimony, if landmarks be in a "perishable condition," or actually "destroyed," and the owner wishes to plant new ones, he may apply to the county surveyor, who has authority to compel the attendance of witnesses, even from other counties, and take their depositions. All adjoining owners are entitled to twenty days' notice. If non-resident, or unknown, publication must be made. The landmarks are established and a survey made, pursuant to the testimony. The plat and depositions are then recorded; and thereafter, the originals or certified copies may be used as evidence in any subsequent litigation touching the same subject-matter, provided the witnesses cannot then be had.

14. *Discovery.* (*a*) We have already seen that one of the marked peculiarities of chancery proceedings is, that each of the parties is entitled to the testimony of the other under oath. Every bill, therefore, as it requires an answer under oath from the other party, is so far a *bill of discovery;* for while it prays for *relief* as the main object, it calls upon the defendant to discover or disclose the facts upon which the claim for relief rests; but the bill of discovery properly so called, and of which I am now speaking, is that which is resorted to when the discovery is the main object, and no relief is prayed for but what results from the discovery itself. The cases proper for such a bill are the two following: 1. Where the plaintiff is entitled to the production of *deeds* or other *writings* in the custody of the defendant. Formerly, courts of law had no power to compel the production of such things, and a bill of discovery was the only resource. But our statute authorizes our courts, in the trial of actions at law, on motion and ten days' notice, to compel the parties to produce books or writings in their possession, in all cases where courts of chancery would compel their production; and if either party refuses, he may be nonsuited or defaulted, as the case may be. This provision has, in a great measure, superseded bills of discovery to compel the production of books and papers. 2. Where the plaintiff, in a *suit at law,* pending or expected, between him and the defendant, finds it necessary, in order to establish his claim or defence, to avail himself of *facts* resting solely in the knowledge of the defendant. In such case, he files his bill of discovery to aid the jurisdiction of the court of law, which cannot compel a party to testify. This is a strong illustration of what is meant by the *assistant* jurisdiction of chancery. It enables courts of law

(*a*) See 2 Story on Equity, ch. 17 and 41; Hare on Discovery; Wigram on Discovery.

to do justice in cases where it would be otherwise impossible. Numerous business transactions will at once suggest themselves, of which none can have any knowledge but the parties themselves. The payment of money, for example, without taking a receipt, may often render it necessary to put the party who received it to his oath; and our statute against gaming specially authorizes the loser to bring an action against the winner, and file a bill of discovery in aid thereof. In fact, until the arbitrary but inflexible rule, that parties shall not be witnesses in courts of law, shall be abolished, this class of bills of discovery must be frequently resorted to. The form of the bill does not differ materially from other bills. It must state enough to show that the discovery is material, and that the facts cannot be otherwise proved. An affidavit is not necessary, unless the bill prays for relief, in addition to the discovery. If the bill be for discovery merely, and the defendant would avoid answering, he may demur; but if the court think the plaintiff entitled to the discovery, they will enforce an answer by attachment and sequestration. If the answer be insufficient, it may be excepted to, until made sufficient. The whole object of the bill is then attained, and there is no decree except for costs, which are always paid by the plaintiff. The answer is laid before the jury, together with the bill, as if it were a deposition, and both parties may avail themselves of it. The party answering cannot be prohibited from using his own testimony, which has been called out by the other party. The doctrine of our court is thus stated: (*a*) "The bill, if it contain any facts useful to the defendant, is evidence for him against the plaintiff. The answer of the defendant is evidence for him, so far as it is responsive to the call in the bill, or connected necessarily with the responsive matter, or explanatory of it." It will be seen, therefore, that a bill of discovery may be suicidal in its operation; for a dishonest man may thus swear himself clear. It is a well-settled principle in equity, that when a court of chancery have obtained jurisdiction of a cause for any purpose, it may be retained for all purposes, in order to avoid a multiplicity of suits. It follows, therefore, that the party who would be plaintiff in an action at law, may by adding a prayer of relief to that of discovery, avoid the necessity of an action at law; and the consequence is, that bills of discovery in aid of actions at law are chiefly resorted to by defendants, who cannot choose their tribunal in the first instance.

15. *Specific Performance.* (*b*) When a party to a contract re-

(*a*) Methodist Church *v.* Wood, 5 Ohio, 283.

(*b*) Fry on the Specific Performance of Contracts. This question most frequently relates to real contracts. 2 Story, Eq. ch. 18. Real contracts are those which relate to the title, and not contracts to clear land, or to build and repair, or to pay rent. Bridgman *v.* Wells, 13 Ohio, 43. Where money was to have been paid, and a long time has elapsed, without excuse, an offer to pay, with interest, will not be sufficient. Rees *v.* Smith, 1 Ohio, 124; Ludlow *v.* Cooper, 13 id. 552; Hutchinson *v.* M'Nutt, 1 id. 14; Curtis *v.* Cisna, id. 429. In Williams *v.* Campion, 6 Ohio, 169, the court say: "Lapse of time never extinguishes the rights of the parties, merely as lapse of time. It does so when the time for doing an act is fixed, and the party to whom it is to be fuses to comply with his part of it, the other party, in a court of law, can only recover *damages* for the non-performance. The jury will say how much injury he has sustained, and the court will adjudge that he recover so much in money from the delinquent party. This is the only remedy which courts of law can administer. But a court of chancery is empowered to compel a specific performance of the contract according to its terms; and in the opinion of Lord Hardwicke, this is the most useful head of chancery jurisdiction. The leading rules by which chancery is governed in decreeing a specific performance of contracts are these: 1. The contract must be fair and honest in the outset. The man who asks equity must do equity. The court will always relieve against fraud, but never aid in giving it effect. 2. The contract must be to do some particular and specific thing; that is, to execute a deed, remove an encumbrance, or the like. For if the agreement be general, as to pay money or indemnify against loss, or the like, pecuniary damages would be an adequate remedy, and there is no occasion for resorting to chancery. 3. For the same reason, if the contract relate to personal property merely, as to

performed forthwith evinces his intention to put an end to the agreement so soon as the failure to perform has occurred." Time is held to be of the essence of the contract, when the parties have expressly made it so by an agreement to forfeit if not punctual, or something of like nature. Scott *v.* Fields, 7 Ohio, 2 pt. 90; Felter *v.* Weybright, 8 id. 167; Conway *v.* Case, 22 Ill. 127; Steele *v.* Biggs, 22 id. 643. See Emerson *v.* Slater, 22 How. 28. And where there is no such express stipulation, a prompt demand and notice may be equivalent. Rummington *v.* Kelly, 7 Ohio, 2 pt. 97. But where time is not thus made of the essence of the contract, the question of enforcing becomes one of *laches* merely. Wilson *v.* Tappan, 6 Ohio, 172; Ohio *v.* Baum, id. 383; Higby *v.* Whitaker, 8 id. 198; Brewer *v.* Connecticut, 9 id. 189; Brock *v.* Hidy, 13 Ohio State, 306. And the excuse for delay must be a reasonable one. House *v.* Beatty, 7 Ohio, 2 pt. 84; Scott *v.* Barber, 14 Ohio, 547; Henry *v.* Conn, 12 id. 193; Brown *v.* Haines, 12 id. 1; Gibbs *v.* Champion, 3 id. 335. Inadequacy of price is no objection, where each party had equal means of knowledge. Galloway *v.* Barr, 12 Ohio, 354. See Watkins *v.* Collins, 11 id. 31. For other applications of the doctrine of specific performance depending chiefly upon the maxim of doing equity before asking it, see Evans *v.* Strode, 11 Ohio, 480; Williams *v.* Champion, 6 id. 169; Townsend *v.* Alexander, 2 id. 18; Tierman *v.* Beam, id. 383; Edwards *v.* Morris, 1 id. 524; Howard *v.* Babcock, 7 id. 2 pt. 73; Fuller *v.* Perkins, 7 id. 2 pt. 196; Huntington *v.* Rogers, 9 Ohio State, 511. Where the vendor has disabled himself from conveying, the rule of compensation is the value of the land at the contract time of conveying. Dustin *v.* Newcomer, 8 Ohio, 49. {If a vendor's estate is less than what he agreed to convey, if the purchaser did not know it, he can insist on conveyance of what the vendor has and compensation for the deficiency; but if he knew the facts, he can only receive compensation and not conveyance. Hence if a vendor agrees that his own and his wife's interest shall be conveyed, and his wife refuses, the vendee knowing that there was a wife cannot be decreed a conveyance of the husband's interest with a rebate from the price. Lucas *v.* Scott, 41 Ohio State, 636. On the other hand, if a tenant in common contracts to convey the whole to a person ignorant that his interest was partial, such person can require a conveyance of the vendor's share and compensation. Longworth *v.* Mitchell, 26 id. 334.} Where the contract is silent as to taxes, the vendor must pay them until conveyance. Wilson *v.* Tappan, 6 Ohio, 172. As to parties, see Este *v.* Strong, 2 Ohio, 401; Massie *v.* Donaldson, 8 id. 377. A court of general chancery powers may decree specific performance of agreements to convey lands lying out of the State, if all the parties are within its jurisdiction, and have been served with process. Penn *v.* Hayward, 14 Ohio State, 302. But though courts of equity do not ordinarily grant specific performance of contracts for the delivery of articles of personal property, it will be done when the legal remedy is inadequate. Coe *v.* Col., P. & I. R. R. Co., 10 Ohio State, 372.

deliver stock and merchandise, chancery will seldom interfere. Even in such cases, however, if legal damages would be manifestly inadequate, the court will compel a specific performance. 4. The plaintiff must show that he has fully performed his part of the contract, if his performance is to precede that of the other; and if not, that he always has been, and still is, ready to perform, when the other has performed. It may, perhaps, be asked why there should be any restriction upon the power to decree a specific performance of any valid contracts. Why may not the party complaining have his option in all cases, to seek redress in chancery or at law? There is certainly no reason, on principles of natural justice, why every man who makes a binding contract, whatever be the subject-matter, should not be compelled to perform it specifically, instead of paying damages, if the other party should so elect. It would seem reasonable that the option should be with the obligee, rather than with the obligor. But the precedents have established the above distinctions, and in so doing, have only followed up the principle of not granting relief in equity, where relief could be obtained at law.

16. *Accounts.* (*a*) In all matters of account, courts of chancery have concurrent jurisdiction with courts of law. To constitute an account, there must be a series of mutual transactions; for a single dealing will not make an account; nor will several distinct matters all on one side. There must be both *debits* and *credits;* and hence accounts are inconvenient matters to be submitted to a jury. Twelve men cannot investigate such transactions as well as one experienced accountant. And this is the reason why chancery takes jurisdiction. By referring accounts to a master for adjustment, the most complicated transactions are readily unravelled, and the result presented to the court for adjudication. Accordingly, when parties disagree as to matters of account, or when one refuses to render an account to the other, the proper resort is to chancery. But it is a general rule that a *stated* or *settled* account will not be opened, unless upon a distinct allegation of *fraud* or *error.* If you desire to have an account opened on the ground of error, your application, technically speaking, is for leave to *surcharge* and *falsify.* To surcharge is to supply an item which has been omitted; and to falsify, is to strike out or alter a charge which is wrong. All such corrections should be specified in the bill, that the defendant may be prepared to meet them; and the burden of proof falls on the plaintiff. If you reflect how great a variety of controversies may involve matters of account among their details, and then remember that when a court of chancery has obtained jurisdiction of a case for any purpose, it may be retained for all purposes, you will readily perceive that this must be a very prolific source of chancery jurisdiction. We have no statutory provision respecting accounts, except

(*a*) See 1 Story on Equity, chap. 8.

that heretofore mentioned, which authorizes a party to swear to his own accounts of not more than eighteen months' standing.

17. *Partnership Affairs.* (*a*) The ground on which chancery originally assumed jurisdiction of partnership transactions, was, that they usually involve matters of account of a complicated character; but jurisdiction is now exercised on many other grounds. The general principles of partnership have been already stated. I shall here only refer to the leading occasions of chancery interference. 1. If partnership capital be invested in land for the use of the firm, chancery will treat it as personal property, so far as respects the rights of creditors. 2. If a partnership creditor attempt to make his debt out of an individual partner, before the firm property has been exhausted, chancery will prevent him. 3. If a private creditor of one partner attempt to make his debt out of the firm, before all the firm debts have been paid, chancery will prevent him. He can only reach his debtor's distributive share after a final settlement. 4. As one partner cannot sue the firm, and as one firm cannot sue another at law, when the same person is a member of both, chancery will grant relief when such occasions arise. 5. In a very strong case, chancery will restrain an unreasonable dissolution of partnership, though there be no agreement to the contrary. 6. When one of the partners becomes insane, or grossly violates his faith, or the business has become ruinous or impracticable, chancery will enforce a dissolution, though there be an agreement to the contrary; and will appoint a receiver to wind up the concerns. 7. After a dissolution, compulsory or otherwise, chancery will restrain a partner from using the partnership name for any other purpose than to close the concerns. All these points have been before referred to in the lecture on partnerships; but I have recapitulated them here, because they form an important head of chancery jurisdiction.

18. *Accident or Mistake.* (*b*) As no human prudence or sagacity can at all times guard against contingencies, it is right that there should be means of obtaining relief against the hardships they may occasion. Yet courts of law have little latitude in this respect; for their rules are generally inflexible, and must be rigorously enforced; but not so with courts of chancery; one of

(*a*) See *ante*, lec. 13; 1 Story on Equity, chap. 15.

(*b*) On the general subject, see 1 Story, Eq. ch. 4, 5. Where by fraud or mistake a deed is so drawn as not to express the intention of the parties, chancery will correct it. Hunt *v.* Freeman, 1 Ohio, 490; Barr *v.* Hatch, 3 id. 527; Pugh *v.* Cheseldine, 11 id. 109; Shroll *v.* Klinker, 15 id. 152. Parol proof is admissible to establish the mistake. Davenport *v.* Sovil, 6 Ohio State, 459. And a mortgage may be reformed, even after a decree of a sale and the execution of a deed in pursuance of the decree. Id. But while chancery will relieve against the defective execution of a power, it cannot supply the want of power, as where the order of court, for example, was defective. Tierman *v.* Beam, 2 Ohio, 383. Where the mistake was occasioned by ignorance, without fault, it will be corrected, unless the rights of third persons have intervened. Bigelow *v.* Barr, 4 Ohio, 358; Williams *v.* Champion, 6 id. 169. See R. S. §§ 4144–4149, to authorize courts to give effect to the intention of parties and officers by curing defects, omissions, and errors in instruments and proceedings.

their most beneficent functions is to rectify mistakes and relieve against accidents; and I shall refer to the leading occasions of interference. 1. When a written instrument or security has been concealed or lost, chancery will aid in discovering it; and when this cannot be done, will, if possible, supply its place. 2. When the performance of agreements or conditions becomes impossible by the act of God, chancery will relieve against the consequences of non-performance. But, generally speaking, death is not one of the accidents which lay the foundation of such relief. 3. When an instrument or power has been defectively executed or conferred, chancery will supply the deficiency according to the intention of the parties; but this, of course, does not extend to judicial mistakes. 4. When powers created by will cannot be executed literally, chancery will direct them to be executed as nearly as may be. This is technically called the doctrine of *cy pres.* But the mistakes relieved against are chiefly in matters of fact; for chancery seldom relieves against mistakes at law. 5. Chancery will not relieve a person who has mistaken or lost his defence at law, whether it be from negligence or ignorance; it never aids negligence, and seldom ignorance. These rules sufficiently illustrate the limits of chancery jurisdiction over accidents and mistakes. Perhaps they may all be reduced to this one general principle, that chancery will always relieve a person against the consequences of any accident or mistake not occasioned by his own fault, when such relief will not do injustice to third persons.

19. *Fraud.* (*a*) Fraud signifies any kind of artifice, surprise, trick, cunning, dissembling, or misrepresentation, by which another is cheated or deceived, to his pecuniary damage. The law, as before observed, abhors fraud as much as equity does; but chancery possesses by far the most efficient means of detecting and relieving against it. Both its preventive and searching powers are often beneficially exerted for this purpose; and I shall refer to the leading rules established on this subject. 1. Chancery takes special cognizance of all persons in confidential relations, as trustees, guardians, executors, and the like; and prevents them from taking advantage of those whose interests are committed to their keeping. 2. When a person has a right liable to be controverted by different persons in different actions; or where there have been repeated attempts to litigate the same question, as in ejectment, chancery will take jurisdiction, and effect a final adjustment. The bill filed in such case is called a *bill of peace;* (*b*) which may always be resorted to in order to avoid a multiplicity of suits. 3. When two or more persons claim the same debt or duty from a third, and the latter knows not to which of them he ought to render it, chancery will compel the claimants to have their respective rights determined by judicial decision, and the bill filed in such case is

(*a*) See 1 Story on Equity, chap. 6, 7; *ante,* § 177.
(*b*) See 2 Story on Equity, chap. 22.

called a *bill of interpleader.* (*a*) The case of a stake-holder furnishes a familiar illustration. 4. When a person is apprehensive of being subjected to future inconvenience, by the neglect, inadvertence, or culpability of another, he may resort to chancery to have his apprehensions quieted. The bill filed in such case is called a bill *quia timet.* (*b*) The case of a bill to prevent the executor of a deceased debtor from misapplying the assets, is a familiar illustration. 5. Where one creditor has a debt secured by two distinct funds, and another creditor of the same debtor can resort to only one of these funds, chancery will compel the former to resort first to the fund which the latter cannot touch. This is called *marshalling securities.* (*c*) The foregoing rules sufficiently illustrate the power of chancery to prevent fraud. There are others designed to relieve against it when committed. Thus, if an award, verdict, judgment, or decree be fraudulently obtained, chancery will always set it aside; for the doctrine is, that fraud shall have no sure asylum, even in the most solemn determinations known to the law. But fraud most frequently occurs in contracts; and there the general rule is, that fraud vitiates everything it touches. We have already examined the statute for the prevention of frauds; but chancery will relieve against many contracts which do not necessarily infringe that statute; and the following rules apply to such cases: 1. It makes no difference whether the fraud affects the whole contract or only a part. Chancery will not undertake to apportion fraud; the contract will not be sustained in part, and set aside in part. It must stand or fall together. This is the language commonly used; but I see no good reason why in chancery a contract may not be upheld in part and rescinded in part. In law, there is a technical reason; but a decree can rise above technicality. 2. It makes no difference whether the fraud arise from a suppression of truth or assertion of falsehood. If an unfair advantage be obtained in either way, chancery will relieve against it. 3. Chancery will sometimes relieve a party who was ignorant of his rights at the time of contracting, though no fraud was intended by the other party. But mere mental imbecility, whether resulting from old age or intoxication, will not be sufficient to set aside a contract, without some proof of actual imposition. On this point, however, there is some doubt. 4. When one person stands silently by, and sees another purchasing or improving property under a mistaken belief of title, which he might correct, this very silence will be treated as a fraud. (*d*) 5. Mere inadequacy of consideration will not be proof of fraud. It must either be so palpably gross as to create a violent presumption of imposition, or there must be proof of actual imposition. But, as against creditors and subsequent

(*a*) See 2 Story on Equity, chap. 20.
(*b*) See 2 Story on Equity, chap. 21.
(*c*) Fassett *v.* Traber, 20 Ohio, 540; Doyle *v.* Murphy, 22 Ill. 502.
(*d*) Blake *v.* Davis, 20 Ohio, 231; *ante*, p. 460, note.

purchasers, a total want of consideration will avoid any contract. 6. When a contract contains a stipulation by way of *penalty* or *forfeiture* for non-performance, chancery will relieve against it by confining the other party to reasonable damages. But if the stipulation, though in form a penalty, be in fact an agreed liquidation of damages between the parties, chancery will not interfere. Formerly, the only relief in such cases was in chancery; but we have seen that our statute furnishes a complete remedy at law upon all penal contracts, by allowing the party, while he takes judgment for the entire penalty, to have execution for only so much as a jury shall find in their verdict. 7. In sales at auction, where all the bidders except the purchaser are merely puffers employed to enhance the price, the sale will be set aside as fraudulent against the buyer; but if there be real bidders in competition, the mere fact of employing a puffer will not render the sale fraudulent. Also when the bidders enter into a combination not to bid against each other, in order to buy cheap and share the profits, the sale will be treated as fraudulent against the seller. The design of a sale at public auction is to produce fair competition, that property may bring what it is worth; and whatever tends to prevent such competition is treated as a fraud.

20. *Trusts.* The nature of trusts, and of the chancery jurisdiction exercised over them, has already been sufficiently discussed in the lecture on equitable estates. Had we time to go back to the history of uses and trusts, we should find that in the early struggle between law and chancery jurisdiction, the latter sustained itself more on account of its salutary power over trusts than for all other reasons put together. I recur to the subject here merely for the purpose of filling up the enumeration of the subjects of jurisdiction. The proceedings must of course be as various as the nature and objects of the trust may require. The general principle, however, is, that courts of law have no power to superintend the execution of trusts; but all persons acting in the capacity of trustees are amenable to courts of chancery at the instance of any person aggrieved; and it makes no difference whether the trust is express or implied; both being equally and exclusively the subjects of chancery jurisdiction.

21. *Personal Relations.* As a general rule, courts of chancery in this country have very little concern with personal relations, as will be obvious from the view heretofore taken of these relations. There are, however, some exceptions, with respect to infants, idiots, and lunatics, married women, apprentices, and slaves, on account of the comparatively helpless condition in which they are placed either by nature or by law, and the peculiarly confidential relations which they sustain towards other persons; though probably all the occasions of chancery interference, where these relations exist, may be referred to one of the three heads of injunction, fraud, or trust. And the same may be said with respect to the jurisdiction which chancery exercises over corporations, particu-

larly of a charitable kind. I shall not, therefore, take up time with repeating what has been sufficiently explained under preceding heads. Here, then, terminates our view of chancery proceedings. My object has been to place before your minds a general but distinct outline of these proceedings, without perplexing your memory with details. If I have succeeded in this attempt, you are probably ready to concur with me in the remarks with which I commenced, as to the immense superiority of these proceedings over proceedings at law. Not only are they so much more simple, that they may be understood in perhaps one-tenth part of the time required by the latter, but the remedies they furnish are more convenient and efficient, in about the same proportion. What an admirable system of remedial law might, therefore, be formed, by an amalgamation of the two systems together, so as to apply the forms of chancery procedure to the principles of law and equity combined!

LECTURE XXXIX.

ADMIRALTY PROCEEDINGS. (*a*)

§ 228. **Subject of Admiralty Jurisdiction.** In my lecture on the judicial department, I stated that admiralty jurisdiction, so far as locality is concerned, now embraces not only all tide-waters, but also all public navigable rivers and lakes within the United States, without reference to the ebb and flow of tides. (*b*) And in this lecture I propose, first, to speak of the subjects of admiralty jurisdiction, and then to present a very brief outline of the modes of proceeding.

We have seen that the language of the constitution is very comprehensive: "To *all cases* of admiralty and maritime jurisdiction." And as "*admiralty*" and "*maritime*" are nearly synonymous, and mean whatever appertains to the sea; or, as now construed, to any public navigable waters, whether salt or fresh, the language of the constitution is broad enough to include all cases, civil and criminal, appertaining to navigable waters. But the practical construction has not been quite so broad as this; and the precise extent of admiralty jurisdiction, as to subjects, is still involved in much doubt.

(*a*) See on the subject of this lecture, the treatises of Clerke (by Hall), Dunlap, Betts, Benedict, Conkling; Curtis's Admiralty Digest; Curtis on the Rights and Duties of Merchant Seamen; Abbott on Shipping (by Story); Flanders on Maritime Law; Flanders on Shipping; Parsons on Maritime Law; English Admiralty Reports, in nine volumes, published by Little, Brown, & Co., Boston.

(*b*) *Ante*, p. 119.

Criminal Jurisdiction. (*a*) It is well settled, as we have seen, that the federal courts have no common-law jurisdiction as to crimes, but only such as is specially conferred by Congress; and that the trial in all criminal cases must be by jury. There is, then, no criminal jurisdiction in admiralty as such; but only a statutory criminal jurisdiction apportioned between the district and circuit courts, as has been elsewhere described.

Civil Jurisdiction. (*b*) This includes *contracts* and *torts.* As to the classes of contracts, cognizable in admiralty, by reason of their reference to navigable waters, although there is still much controversy, I think the following may safely be set down: contracts between part-owners, charter-parties, affreightments, bottomry, respondentia, insurance, (*c*) supply of materials, wages, salvage, average, jettison, and pilotage. There may be others, but I have little doubt of these.

As to *torts*, if committed upon navigable waters, I am not aware of any exception to the admiralty jurisdiction, although there is, of course, a concurrent State jurisdiction, when committed within the body of a county. Of these torts, that which occupies the largest space in the books, is *collision.* (*d*) At

(*a*) See *ante*, § 49; 9th section of the Judiciary Act of 1789, 1 Stat. at Large, 73; Lindo *v.* Rodney, Doug. 613, n.; Jennings *v.* Carson, 1 Peters, Ad. R. 1; Glass *v.* The Betsy, 3 Dallas, 6; U. S. *v.* M'Gill, 4 Dallas, 426; U. S. *v.* Coolidge, 1 Gallison, 488, and 1 Wheaton, 415; U. S. *v.* Bevans, 3 id. 336. See the act of Congress of March 3, 1857, which provides for the punishment of manslaughter within the admiralty jurisdiction of the United States, and the elaborately considered case of The People *v.* Tyler, 7 Mich. 161.

(*b*) 1 Kent, Com. lec. 17; Curtis on Merch. Seamen, 252; U. S. *v.* Grush, 5 Mason, 290; The Harriet, 1 Story, 259; Thomas *v.* Lane, 2 Sumner, 1; De Lovio *v.* Boit, 2 Gallison, 398; New Jersey Co. *v.* Merch. Bank, 6 Howard, 344; U. S. *v.* New Bedford, 1 Woodbury & M. 401; Steele *v.* Thatcher, 1 Ware, 91; Case *v.* Woolley, 6 Dana, 21; Brittan *v.* Barnaby, 21 How. 527. The jurisdiction of admiralty extends to cases of collision upon navigable waters, although it occurred within the body of a county, and above the flux and reflux of the tide. Jackson *v.* Steamboat Magnolia, 20 How. 296. It extends to petitory as well as to mere possessory actions. Ward *v.* Peck, 18 How. 267. Contracts of affreightment are a lien on the vessel, but contracts for its future employment are not. Vandewater *v.* Mills, 19 id. 82; Schooner Freeman *v.* Buckingham, 18 id. 182. Nor have builders of the vessel a lien for work done and materials found in its construction. People's Ferry Co. *v.* Beers, 20 id. 393.

(*c*) It was for some time a question whether insurance was a maritime contract so as to be a subject of admiralty jurisdiction. It is now settled that it is, and this whenever the vessel insured navigates any of the navigable waters of the United States, or bordering thereon, whether landlocked or open, salt or fresh. Insurance Co. *v.* Dunham, 11 Wall. 1.

(*d*) Story on Bailments, 609–11; 3 Kent, Com. 231; Handaysyde *v.* Wilson, 3 Carr. & Payne, 528; Luxford *v.* Large, 5 id. 421; Pluckwell *v.* Wilson, 5 id. 375; Woolf *v.* Beard, 8 id. 373; Lane *v.* Crombie, 12 Pick. 177; Butterfield *v.* Forrester, 11 East, 61; Harlow *v.* Humiston, 6 Cowen, 191; Smith *v.* Smith, 2 Pick. 621; Clapp *v.* Young, 6 Law Reporter, 111; New Haven *v.* Vanderbilt, 16 Conn. 420; Sills *v.* Brown, 9 Carr. & Payne, 601; The Scioto, Daveis, Rep. 359; Flanders on Mar. Law, 296, 298. As to the rule of damages, see Smith *v.* Condry, 1 Howard, 28; Boyd *v.* Brown, 17 Pick. 453; New Haven *v.* Vanderbilt, 16 Conn. 420; The Anna Maria, 2 Wheat. 327; The Amiable Nancy, 3 id. 546; The Amistad, 5 id. 385; Bell *v.* Cunningham, 3 Peters, 69; Conard *v.* The Pacific, 6 Peters, 262. Vessels propelled by steam, being more under control than others, are required to exercise caution to avoid collisions with sailing vessels. They are liable for injuries to sailing vessels occasioned by not keeping a trustworthy and constant look-out, and exercising other proper precautions, while travcommon law, there can be no apportionment of the damages resulting from a collision, under any circumstances. The sufferer must recover the whole or none. And in order to recover, he must show that the fault which caused the collision was in no part his, but wholly that of the other party. Whereas in admiralty, at least in this country, if there was no fault on either side, or was fault on both sides, or if the case was one of inscrutable fault, the loss may be divided. The rule of computing damages appears to be, full compensation for actual loss at the time and place, but nothing for loss of market, or expected profits.

§ 229. **Origin of Admiralty Forms.** (*a*) These forms and terms are derived wholly from the civil law; and the experience of twenty centuries has not succeeded in devising any essential improvements. Chancery built upon them as models, though with many variations. And all the recent codes of procedure, entirely repudiating common-law forms, have gone back to these, for the outlines of their systems.

The admiralty courts, in the exercise of their functions as such, are either *instance courts*, in which they only try civil causes of a maritime nature; or *prize courts*, in which they exclusively adjudicate upon prizes of war; or *criminal courts*, in which they exercise such criminal jurisdiction as is conferred by Congress, and have a jury for that purpose. In the two former, they have no

ersing waters in which the latter are often met with. The general rule is for a sailing vessel in meeting a steamer to keep its course, while the steamer takes the necessary means to avoid a collision. The steamer is not in fault where the sailing vessel could not with proper effort be seen in time to enable her to change her course. St. John *v.* Paine, 10 How. 557; Propeller Genesee Chief *v.* Fitzhugh, 12 id. 443; Peck *v.* Sanderson, 17 id. 178; Steamboat N. Y. *v.* Rea, 18 id. 223; Steamer Oregon *v.* Rocca, 18 id. 570; Crockett *v.* Steamboat Isaac Newton, 18 id. 581; Ure *v.* Coffman, 19 id. 56; Rogers *v.* Steamer St. Charles, 19 id. 108; N. Y. & Va. Steamship Co. *v.* Calderwood, 19 id. 241; N. Y. & Liverpool U. S. Mail Steamship Co. *v.* Rumball, 21 id. 372; Steamer Louisiana *v.* Fisher, 21 id. 1. By the act of Congress of 1851 (9 Stat. at Large, 635), the liability of shipowners in cases of collision, as well as in cases of injury to cargo, is limited to their interest in the ship or vessel, and her freight then pending. Norwich Co. *v.* Wright, 13 Wall. 104.

{The U. S. courts have jurisdiction over canal boats running on an interstate canal. *Ex parte* Boyer, 109 U. S. 629. They have also jurisdiction of a case of two ships of the same foreign nation colliding on the high seas; for courts of admiralty should not be closed to such cases. The Belgenland, 114 U. S. 355.}

(*a*) The act of 1789, 1 Stat. at Large, 93, expressly declared that admiralty proceedings should be "according to the course of the civil law." The act of 1792, 1 Stat. at Large, 275, declared that they should be "according to the principles, rules, and usages which belong to courts of admiralty, as contradistinguished from courts of common law," subject to future alterations to be made by the federal courts. This provision has been always understood to adopt the admiralty practice of England, at least in its general outlines. The sixth section of the act of 1842, 5 Stat. at Large, 516, authorizes and directs the supreme court to make rules regulating the process and proceedings of the circuit and district courts. This duty was performed in 1844, by the framing of forty-seven admiralty rules, which may be found in the books of admiralty practice. Benedict, 339. The 36th of these rules authorizes each of the circuit and district courts to make its own rules, in cases not provided for by the supreme court rules. Thus, while there may be some diversity in details, the general outlines of admiralty practice are the same in all the American courts, and differ very little from those of the British admiralty.

jury; (*a*) and in this respect, they resemble courts of equity. The forms of criminal procedure have been elsewhere considered. With proceedings in prize cases, we may hope to have no frequent concern. I shall therefore confine myself to the practice "on the instance side of the court," to which the rules referred to in the note are expressly confined.

The counsel are denominated *proctors* instead of attorneys, and *advocates* instead of counsellors, with a corresponding difference of functions, not, however, very rigidly observed.

Suits in admiralty are either *in rem*, or *in personam*, though sometimes the two may be united. Suits *in rem* (*b*) are suits against the thing itself, as a ship, a bale of merchandise, or the like, without reference to the owner; and the relief does not extend beyond the thing sued, unless some person substitutes himself in regard to it, as *claimant* or intervenor. The want of such a proceeding, where it is often so difficult to know, or to serve process upon the owners, was so deeply felt along our lakes and rivers, before the establishment of admiralty jurisdiction over them, that several of the States had attempted to supply the defect by the enactment of what are commonly known as *water-craft laws*, which authorize a suit against the boat or other craft by name. Suits *in personam* are, like ordinary suits, against the person only, without reference to any particular thing.

§ 230. **Libel.** The libel, from *libellus*, a little book, contains a statement of the cause of action, and corresponds to a bill in chancery, or a petition under the Code. Hence the party complaining is called *libellant.* The party defending *in personam*, is called *defendant;* but if intervening *in rem*, he is called *respondent.* There are no technical requisitions in the framing of the libel. All the facts constituting the complaint are to be stated in simple narrative, with appropriate subdivisions, which are numbered consecutively for convenience of reference. The filing of the libel is the first step in the suit. It is usually signed by the party, always by his proctor, and sometimes by an advocate, but this is not essential. If it pray for a seizure, either *in rem* or *in personam*,

(*a*) There was an exception in the act of 1845, 5 Stat. at Large, 726, which extended admiralty jurisdiction over the lakes and the navigable waters connecting them. This act was pronounced constitutional in Propeller Genesee Chief *v.* Fitzhugh, 12 How. 443. See *ante*, p. 119.

(*b*) See Ward *v.* Propeller Ogdensburgh, 5 M'Lean, 622. As to the Ohio watercraft law, see The Monarch *v.* Finley, 10 Ohio, 384; The Huron *v.* Simmons, 11 id. 458; Lewis *v.* The Cleveland, 12 id. 341; The Waverley *v.* Clements, 14 id. 28; Kellogg *v.* Brennan, 14 id. 72; Jones *v.* The Commerce, 14 id. 408; The Ætna *v.* Treat, 15 id. 585; Champion *v.* Jantzen, 16 id. 92; The Aurora *v.* Dobbie, 17 id. 125; Webster *v.* The Andes, 18 id. 187; The Montgomery *v.* Kent, 20 id. 54; Keating *v.* Spink, 3 Ohio State, 105; DeWitt *v.* Sch. St. Lawrence, 3 id. 325; Raymond *v.* Whitney, 5 id. 201; Canal-Boat Housatonic *v.* Kenawha Salt Co., 7 id. 261; Sch. Muskegan *v.* Moss, 7 id. 377; Steamboat Monarch *v.* Potter, 7 id. 457; Steamboat Monarch *v.* Miami Railway Co., 7 id. 478; Thompson *v.* Steamboat J. D. Morton, 8 id. 222. But see The Moses Taylor, and The Ad Hines *v.* Trevor, 4 Wallace, 555, where it is held, that so far as these water-craft laws give an admiralty jurisdiction, they are unconstitutional, and see note on p. 119.

it must be verified by affidavit. In general, security for costs must be given, but this is regulated by the rules of each particular court. This is done by a short writing without seal, called a *stipulation*, and it is usual for the surety to justify, by an affidavit appended to the stipulation, that he is worth twice the amount.

§ 231. **Process.** (*a*) In the theory of admiralty proceedings, the court is always open, not only for the issuing and returning of process, but for all other purposes. But, for the convenience of all concerned in the practice, each court establishes its own *rule days*, and all process is made returnable accordingly. If the process prayed for be a mere notice, like the summons at common law, it is called a *monition*, issues of course, and is served by the marshal as a summons is by the sheriff. If the prayer be for an arrest of the person, and the amount claimed be under five hundred dollars, and the case be one where a *capias* could be issued under the State law, the process is called a *warrant*, and the marshal may take bail upon his own responsibility, not only for appearance, but to abide the event of the suit; there being no distinction like that between appearance bail and special bail at common law. But if the sum exceed five hundred dollars, then, by the seventh rule of the supreme court, the warrant can only issue on the order of the judge. If the warrant contain a clause to attach property, or to garnishee debtors in case the defendant cannot be found, reasonable search should first be made, and then property may be attached to the amount sued for; or if that cannot be found, any person named in the process as a debtor may be garnisheed, by serving him with a copy of the warrant. In either case, the attachment or garnishment will be at once dismissed, upon the defendant appearing and entering into stipulation. If the proceeding be *in rem*, the warrant contains an order to seize the thing described in the libel, and the marshal has no authority to release it on forthcoming bail. In this case the warrant contains a clause of general monition to all persons interested to appear on the return day and show cause why the property should not be condemned as prayed for in the libel, which must be served on the person found in possession. *Advertisement* is also made in such newspapers as the court shall designate by general or special rule. In cases where proceedings *in rem* and *in personam* can be joined, one process may suffice for both; or there may be separate processes, and even at different times, if need be. If property seized be of a *perishable* nature, that is, of a nature to depreciate rapidly

(*a*) Process in the federal courts is regulated by the act of 1789, 1 Stat. at Large, 93, and by the act of 1828, 4 id. 278. These acts provide, in substance, that process in equity and admiralty shall be according to the principles, rules and usages of those courts; and that process in suits at common law shall be the same in each State as is used in the highest courts of that State. See very full and elaborate notes upon this subject, 1 Stat. at Large, 93; 4 id. 278. For leading cases, see Wayman *v.* Southard, 10 Wheat. 1; Ross *v.* Duval, 13 Peters, 45; Beers *v.* Haughton, 9 Peters, 329; Manro *v.* Almeida, 10 Wheat. 473.

in quality or value, or to consume itself by expense in keeping, an order may be procured to sell it, or to have it appraised and delivered to the claimant, upon a deposit of money or a satisfactory stipulation.

§ 232. **Defence.** If the suit be *in personam*, and the defendant do not appear on the return day, a decree of *contumacy* and *default* may be taken, which is similar to a decree *pro confesso* in chancery. In this case, the court either hears the case *ex parte*, or refers it to a commissioner. In all cases, the court requires proof of the allegations in the libel; and great liberality is exercised in allowing the default to be set aside and a defence made, at any time before final decree. If the suit be *in rem*, and no claimant intervene, a similar course is pursued. In like manner, if the libellant be in default, a decree of contumacy may be taken against him as having deserted his case, and it may be dismissed with costs.

If defence be made, it can only be in the form of *exception*, *claim*, or *answer*. There being no demurrer in admiralty proceedings, *exceptions* take its place. They may be taken at any stage in the progress of a case. They are required to state specifically the cause or matter excepted to, as is done in special demurrer. Accordingly, if the libel be insufficient upon its face, granting the allegations to be true, to authorize a decree for the libellant, it should be excepted to for this reason, and the question of sufficiency presented for decision.

A *claim* is interposed, when the suit is *in rem*, by any person interested in the subject-matter. It must set forth specifically in what the claim consists, and be verified by affidavit. The court will take notice of no claim not so presented.

The *answer* performs the same office as in chancery and under the Code. It is the usual form of defence both *in rem* and *in personam*. It must specifically meet every material allegation in the libel, referring to it by number. If the libel contain specific interrogatories, each must be specifically answered. The answer must in all cases be sworn to. It may contain interrogatories to which the libellant must respond. Or either party may file interrogatories, without annexing them to the pleadings, and require an answer from the other party.

If the answer, granting its truth, be insufficient as a defence, or if it contain matter of scandal or impertinence, these questions are all presented by *exceptions*. But if the libellant means to take issue upon the facts set up in the answer, or to set up new matter in avoidance, he files a *replication*. (*a*) If this be a simple denial, as a traverse at common law, it need not be sworn to. But if it make affirmative allegations, they must be verified. And here,

(*a*) By the 52d of the supreme court rules, adopted at the December term, 1854, a replication is dispensed with in all cases. The new matter set up in the answer is considered as denied; and if the libellant desires to meet it by other new matter, he does it by amending the libel.

virtually the pleadings terminate, though the books speak of *duplications*, *triplications*, and so forth.

With regard to *amendments*, the utmost indulgence is given at all stages of a case, even after appeal, provided they be confined to the original subject of controversy. And the same is true as to *defaults*. By the fortieth of the supreme court rules, even after a final decree against the defendant upon default, the court may, within ten days, grant a rehearing upon such terms as may seem just.

§ 233. **Trial.** (*a*) The ninth section of the judiciary act of 1789 declares that "the trial of issues in fact, in the district court, in all causes except civil causes of admiralty and maritime jurisdiction, shall be by jury." The trial of admiralty cases, therefore, is by the court, without a jury; although there is nothing in the constitution to prevent the granting of a trial by jury if it should be deemed expedient. Indeed this was done by the act of 1845, extending admiralty jurisdiction over the lakes.

In the rules of *evidence* there is very little which is peculiar to courts of admiralty. They receive oral or written evidence under the same conditions as courts of law, and observe the same rules as to competency. There is, perhaps, this exception, that parties are permitted to testify when the facts rest in their knowledge alone, and could not be proved in any other way. The maxim that the proofs must correspond, and be confined to the allegations, is observed as strictly as in other courts. With respect to *depositions*, and the notice to be given, we have elsewhere seen that the thirtieth section of the judiciary act of 1789 includes this court. But if depositions are to be taken in a foreign country (*b*) there is a practice peculiar to this court of sending *letters rogatory* to a court of that country, requesting it to have depositions taken in due form of law; and by the comity of nations such a request is always granted. Depositions thus taken are filed in the court taking them, and authenticated copies are received as evidence here.

In the argument of the case, as to opening and closing, and indeed in all other respects, the rules are the same as in other courts.

§ 234. **Decree and Execution.** The decree finely illustrates the flexibility of admiralty proceedings, since it may be so shaped as to meet every possible exigency of the case. If the amount be disputed, the court may ascertain it, or may settle the principles upon which it is to be ascertained, and then refer the case to a commissioner. The *costs* are entirely in the discretion of the court, and the power to adjust them is often used to punish vexatious or frivolous litigation. The *enrolment* of the decree corresponds to a complete record in chancery. It consists in the making up of a full history of the case, including process, pleadings, order stipulations, and evidence; taking the latter, when oral, from the notes

(*a*) 1 Stat. at Large, 73; 5 id. 726; Propeller Genesee Chief *v.* Fitzhugh, 12 How. 443.

(*b*) 1 Greenl. Ev. § 320.

of the judge. As to the effect of the decree, it is a common saying, that the whole world are bound by it, because the whole world are parties. (*a*) This is peculiarly the case when the suit is *in rem;* for then notice is served upon the thing itself by the *seizure*, and this is treated as constructive notice to all persons having an interest in that thing of any kind whatsoever. And to this is added the chance of actual notice from publication.

The enforcement of all decrees in admiralty may be by attachment of the person, when that is practicable. But where the decree is for the payment of money only, the practice is to issue an execution combining the directions of a *fieri facias* and a *capias* at common law; that is a command to levy on property if it can be found, and for want thereof to take the body. When the suit is *in rem*, and the thing is still held by the marshal, the execution takes the form of an order of sale, resembling a *venditioni exponas;* but if it has been delivered upon stipulation to the claimant, an order is made that the stipulators perform the conditions, or, in default thereof, that a summary judgment be entered against them. When the marshal receives money, he has no authority to make distribution. His duty is to pay all moneys to the clerk to be deposited in the *registry* of the court, whence it can only be drawn on the order of the judge, countersigned by the clerk. If there be a *surplus* after satisfying the libellant, the person entitled may obtain it on petition, or motion in writing.

An *appeal* (*b*) lies to the circuit court from all final decrees where the matter in dispute exceeds fifty dollars. As to the libellant, this amount is determined by the claim in the libel; as to the defendant, by the amount of the decree. In either case, it is exclusive of costs; and when there are several claimants, it is the claim of each separately, and not the aggregate. The appeal, which is in writing, must state specifically how much of the case is appealed, and only so much goes up; but as each party aggrieved may appeal, there may be several appeals from the same decree. The time within which an appeal must be taken is determined either by the general rules of the court or by a special order in the particular case. But it must be to the next term of the circuit court, and execution will be stayed to allow time for perfecting the appeal, if written notice of intention be given. On the hearing above no new cause of action can be introduced, but new allegations and proofs are admitted. (*c*) After the appeal, so much of the case as is appealed, is wholly in the circuit court, and does not go back to the district court at all for any purpose. The effect is to suspend the execution below of so much of the decree as is appealed, and leave the residue for execution there. The stipulation is similar to the appeal bond in chancery.

(*a*) But see Thompson *v.* Steamboat J. D. Morton, 8 Ohio State, 222.

(*b*) The 53d of the supreme court rules, adopted December term, 1854, provides how much of the record shall be certified upon appeal.

(*c*) Rice *v.* Minnesota and Northwestern R. R. Co., 21 How. 82.

From the final decree in the circuit court, an appeal lies to the supreme court, in all cases where the matter in dispute exceeds five thousand dollars, and no allowance of the appeal is necessary. The supreme court does not execute its decree, but remands it to the circuit court for execution. The security must be approved by the circuit judge, and remains in his court. The rules furnish minute directions for perfecting appeals.

LECTURE XL.

CRIMINAL PROCEEDINGS. (*a*)

§ 235. **Preliminary Considerations.** We come now to the last division of the law of procedure, which embraces the course of proceeding in criminal prosecutions, from the commencement to the conclusion. The general nature of crimes and punishments, and the offences which are punishable by the State and federal laws, have already been considered. The constitutional limitations of the power of punishment have also been discussed, as immediately connected with personal liberty. It only remains, then, to describe the mode in which criminal justice is administered; and here the distribution of criminal jurisdiction among the federal and State courts would be the first topic; but this has been sufficiently explained in the lecture upon the judicial department. We are, therefore, prepared to turn at once to the commencement of criminal proceedings: but first, I would observe, that although the outlines of these proceedings are marked out by the federal and State constitutions, and the statutes pursuant thereto, (*b*) yet the *terms* usually employed in these provisions, and the *forms* required by them, are chiefly taken from the common law; and their meaning and nature are to be sought in the treatises on criminal law, before referred to. It follows, that criminal proceedings must be much the same in all courts where the common law prevails; and, accordingly, I shall confine myself chiefly to a description of them in this State. Criminal proceedings are much less complicated than civil, as will be evinced by what follows. Meantime, there are some preliminary matters which require a brief notice. When an offence has been committed, the first step is to *secure the offender;* and to this end certain officers are designated to be *conservators of the peace.* By the constitution, judges of the supreme court are conservators of the peace throughout the State; president judges of

(*a*) See Archbold's Criminal Practice; Starkie's Criminal Practice; Davis's Precedents; the works of Chitty and Russell; and Bishop on the Law of Criminal Procedure.

(*b*) A code of Criminal Procedure was enacted in Ohio, in 1869 (66 Ohio Laws, 287), the principal alterations introduced by which will be briefly stated in their proper place.

the common pleas, throughout their circuits; and associate judges of the common pleas, throughout their counties. By statute, it is made the duty of sheriffs to preserve the public peace; to cause all persons guilty of breaking the same, within their knowledge or view, to enter into recognizance to keep the peace, and to appear and answer in court; and to commit to jail in case of refusal. Coroners have the same power when the office of sheriff is vacant, or the sheriff is himself the offender; with the further power of holding inquests over dead bodies, and arresting persons charged by the jury with being concerned in the death. Also, by statute, justices of the peace are declared to be conservators of the peace throughout their counties; and it is made the duty of constables to apprehend and bring to justice felons and disturbers of the peace; to suppress riots and preserve the peace within their counties; and to pursue fugitive offenders into other counties. From all which it appears that judges, justices, sheriffs, coroners, and constables are made the official guardians and protectors of public tranquillity and private security; but the chief burden, as we shall see, falls upon justices and constables, whose functions are, therefore, of the highest importance to the community. (*a*)

§ 236. **Warrant.** In general, before an offender can be *arrested*, or his premises *searched*, the officer must have an official warrant for that purpose; and we have before considered the constitutional guaranty against unreasonable searches and seizures, which is expressed in these words: "the right of the people to be secure in their persons, houses, papers, and effects, against unreasonable searches and seizures, shall not be violated; and no warrants shall issue but upon probable cause, supported by oath or affirmation, and particularly describing the place to be searched, and the persons or things to be seized." For making arrests there are two kinds of warrants, which I will briefly describe.

1. *A Capias upon Indictment.* What an indictment is will be explained hereafter. If the grand jury happen to be in session, when an offence is committed, or before the offender is apprehended, any person may go before them and testify against him; and if upon such testimony an indictment be found, the prosecuting attorney will take out a *capias ad respondendum* for his arrest. This writ may issue in term time or vacation, to any county in the State, commanding the offender to be arrested for trial. If the arrest be made in term time, he is forthwith arraigned. If in vacation, he is either held to bail or committed; all which will be explained hereafter. (*b*)

(*a*) Criminal procedure is concerned only with the punishment of crime, except in the case of binding over to keep the peace, in which a preventive power is exercised. This proceeding consists in bringing the accused before a magistrate, who, if after hearing testimony he is of opinion there is just cause for complaint, puts the accused under bond to keep the peace. The proceedings in Ohio are now governed by §§ 1–12 of the Code of Criminal Procedure.

(*b*) §§ 57, 101, 102 of the Code of Criminal Procedure now provide that the clerk of the court in such cases shall issue a warrant for the accused.

2. *A State Warrant.* (*a*) If the offence be committed under such circumstances that it cannot be laid at once before the grand jury, as is most frequently the case, the course is to procure a warrant, commonly called a *State warrant*, commanding the *arrest* of the offender, and, if need be, a *search* of any suspected premises. The form of these warrants is fixed by the statute. Should there be occasion, they may doubtless be issued by either of the courts in term time, or either of the judges in vacation, in which case they would be called *bench warrants;* but they are usually issued by justices of the peace; and in compliance with the constitutional declaration before referred to, an *affidavit* must first be made, as the predicate of the warrant, that an offence has been committed, and that the deponent either knows or believes that the person named did commit it. Without such a specific affidavit the warrant cannot be issued; and the warrant itself must be equally specific in describing the person and the offence; for human liberty is too dear to be jeoparded upon uncertainties; and the same remarks apply to search warrants. In both of these cases, then, an offence has been already committed, of which oath or affirmation has been made, before the issuing of the *capias* or *warrant.* But it being far better to *prevent* the commission of an offence, if possible, than to wait until it has been committed, and then punish it, provision is made that if any person has just cause to fear, and does fear, that another will kill, wound, beat, or abuse him, or those immediately connected with him, or will burn his buildings or destroy his property, and such person will make affidavit to this effect, a warrant shall thereupon be issued for the

(*a*) *Affidavit.* The State of ———, county of ———. Before me ———, one of the justices of the peace for said county, personally came ———, who being duly sworn according to law, deposeth and saith, that on or about the ———, at ——— [here describe the crime committed and the premises to be searched, if such there be], and that one ——— is guilty of the fact charged; and further saith not.

Warrant for Arrest. The State of ———, county of ———. To any constable of said county. Whereas complaint has been made before me, ——— one of the justices of the peace for the county aforesaid, upon the oath of ———, that ———, late of the county aforesaid, did, on or about the ———, at ———, in the county aforesaid [describe the crime]; these are, therefore to command you to take the said ———, if he be found in your county, or if he shall have fled, to pursue him into any other county within the State, and take and safely keep him, so that you have his body before me or some other justice of the peace forthwith, to answer the said complaint, and be further dealt with according to law. §§ 21–29 of the Code of Criminal Procedure provide for the issuing of warrants before indictment.

Search Warrant. Whereas it appears to me ———, one of the justices of the peace for the county aforesaid, that the following goods and chattels, to wit [here describe them], have been, within ninety days past, by some person or persons, feloniously taken, stolen, and carried away from the premises of ———, of said county, and that the said ——— doth on oath declare that he verily believes that the said goods and chattels are concealed in the [describe the place of concealment] of one ——— of ———, in said county; these are, therefore, to command you, with the necessary and proper assistance, to enter, in the daytime, into the said [describe the place as before] of the said ———, and there diligently search for the said goods and chattels; and if the same or any part thereof be found upon such search, that you bring the goods so found, and also the body of the said ———, forthwith before me, or some other justice of the peace of said county, to be disposed of and dealt with according to law.

arrest of the person complained of; and if, upon investigation, the magistrate shall be of opinion that there was just cause for fear, he will order the accused to enter into a *recognizance* to appear and answer at the next term of the court, and, in the mean time, to keep the peace; and in default of such recognizance, will commit him to jail. This is what is meant by being put under *bonds for good behavior.*

§ 237. **Arrest and Examination.** (*a*) An arrest on a criminal charge is defined to be the apprehending or restraining of a person, in order that he may be forthcoming to answer the charge of an alleged or suspected crime. The act of privilege from arrest, before described, extends to civil arrests only, as we have seen, and not to criminal arrests; which, therefore, may be made upon all persons, and at all times and places. Crime has no asylum but in absolute concealment. Even a man's house is not his castle against criminal arrests, though it is against civil. In general, as we have just seen, the arrest is made by an *officer*, under the authority of a *capias* or warrant, predicated upon the affidavit of some credible person; but there is no question that arrests may be safely made without either. All persons, whether officers or not, must necessarily have the power to arrest offenders committing the offence *in their presence:* and it is their duty so to do; for when they see the act perpetrated, they are in no danger from an act for false imprisonment or malicious prosecution, which is the only hazard they could incur; and it would be wrong to give such offenders a chance of escaping by waiting to take out a warrant. (*b*) The English, and probably the American doctrine, is this: "Conservators of the peace may break open doors to make such arrest; and may command other persons by word only, to assist them, who will be culpable if they refuse so to do; also, if they have *good reason to believe* that an offence has been committed, though not in their presence, and have strong grounds to suspect the individual, they may safely cause the arrest to be made. But a *private person* would not be safe in making the arrest in the latter case; because he would not have the excuse of official duty. The prudent course would be to notify an officer, or go at once to a magistrate, and make the affidavit to obtain a warrant; though if such private person were certain that an offence had been committed, and had reasonable ground for suspicion as to the offender, he might be safe in seizing him without a warrant, for the purpose of carrying him before a magistrate; because, if the suspicion should prove false, probable cause would be a complete defence, and even the good intention would be a shield

(*a*) See 4 Black. Com. 292; Davis *v.* Russell, 5 Bing. 354; Cowles *v.* Dunbar, 12 Com. Law Rep. 265; s. c. 2 Car. & P. 565; Wright *v.* Court, 10 Com. Law Rep. 412; s. c. 4 B. & C. 596; Lawrence *v.* Hedger, 3 Taunton, 14.

(*b*) Derecourt *v.* Corbishley, 5 El. & Black. 188; 32 Eng. L. & Eq. 186. A municipal corporation may authorize an arrest without a warrant in certain cases, for violation of a city ordinance. White *v.* Kent, 11 Ohio State, 550.

against heavy damages. (*a*) So, in regard to arrests to prevent the commission of crime; it is clear that any person seeing another about to commit a crime, may interfere to prevent him; and, if necessary, may detain him, until it may be reasonably presumed that he has altered his mind; but where one thus intervenes to prevent fighting, prudence requires him to declare his purpose beforehand; for, otherwise, he may be confounded with the offender without the means of proving his innocence. Thus, with regard to criminal arrests, the law is wisely framed with a view to protect both parties, those who make, and those who suffer, such arrests.

The accused being thus arrested, the next thing is the *examination* before the magistrate. This must take place immediately, unless some material witness be wanting, or there be some other urgent reason for postponing it; in which case our statute allows the accused to be placed in jail for safe keeping; but not for a period exceeding thirty-six hours, (*b*) lest the power of imprisonment without examination might be abused. In general, this examination is only a *preliminary step*, for the purpose of ascertaining whether there be reasonable cause to hold the accused to abide the inquest of a grand jury. But there are some trivial cases under our statute, in which the proceedings before the magistrate are final. Thus, if a person be arrested on the charge of assault and battery, or an affray at fisticuffs, on the complaint of the party injured, and elect to plead guilty, the magistrate may, at his option, impose a fine within one hundred dollars, or hold him to answer in court; so if a person provoke, or attempt to provoke another to commit a breach of the peace, though the peace be not broken, the magistrate may fine him for this; and there are a few other trifling fines which he may impose. But, with these exceptions, the power of the magistrate is only that of examination without punishment; and according to the result of this examination, the accused will either be entirely discharged, or committed to jail, or held to bail. If not discharged, the witnesses are likewise put under recognizance to appear and testify in court.

§ 238. **Commitment and Bail.** (*c*) If, upon examination, the evi-

(*a*) R. S. § 7129 provides that it shall be the duty of officers to arrest all persons found violating the laws without warrant, and also, § 7130, that any person not an officer may, without a warrant, arrest any person, if a petit larceny or felony has been committed, and there is reasonable ground to believe the person arrested guilty, and may detain him until a legal warrant can be obtained.

(*b*) This period is now four days (Code of Criminal Procedure), and the confinement may be in some other place than the jail if the magistrate so direct. § 7143. §§ 7142–55 now regulate this procedure.

(*c*) *Mittimus.* The State of ———, county of ———. To the keeper of the jail of said county. Whereas ———, late of said county, has been arrested on the oath of ———, for [describe the crime], and has been examined by me ———, one of the justices of the peace of said county, on such charge, and required to give bail in the sum of $———, for his appearance before the court of ———, in said county, on the ———, which requisition he has failed to comply with; therefore, I command dence be such as to convince the magistrate that the accused ought not be discharged; and if the offence charged either be not bailable, or the accused be unable to give bail; the only course is to commit him to jail to await his trial at the next term of the court, if an indictment shall be found against him. The instrument or warrant of commitment is commonly called a *mittimus;* and its form is fixed by the statute. After describing the offence, and the failure to give bail, it commands the jailer to receive and detain the accused, until he shall be discharged by due course of law. Being thus committed, the accused must remain in prison until trial, unless released in one of the ways hereafter to be described. In the mean time, he is entitled to have his situation made as comfortable as the nature of the case will admit of; and any unnecessary severity on the part of the jailer will subject him to punishment; for which provision is made, in conformity with that humane declaration of the constitution, "that no person arrested or confined in jail shall be treated with unnecessary rigor." Both the federal and State constitutions, as we have seen, declare that "excessive bail shall not be required." The actual amount, however, is not fixed by law, except in a few instances, but left to the discretion of the officer who takes bail; and who also decides upon the sufficiency of the sureties. Again, our constitution declares that "all persons shall be bailable by sufficient sureties, unless for capital offences, where the proof is evident, or the presumption great." Thus there can be but one offence in this State which is not bailable, and even that is not absolutely excluded. The federal constitution has no corresponding provision; but under the acts of Congress, all offences are

you to receive the said ——— into your custody, in the jail of said county, there to remain until he shall be discharged by due course of law.

Recognizance. The State of ———, county of ———. Be it remembered, that on the ———, ——— and ——— personally appeared before me, ———, one of the justices of the peace for said county, and jointly and severally acknowledged themselves to owe the State of ——— the sum of $———, to be levied of their goods and chattels, lands and tenements, if default be made in the condition following, to wit: the condition of this recognizance is such, that if the above bound ——— shall personally appear before the court of ——— for said county, on the ———, then and there to answer the charge of [describe the offence], and abide the judgment of the court, and not depart without leave, then this recognizance shall be void. Taken and acknowledged before me on the day and year above written. [Signature of officer.]

If the recognizance be to keep the peace, add to the above condition thus: And in the mean time shall keep the peace, and be of good behavior towards the citizens of the State generally, and especially towards ———, then, &c. The recognizance of a witness differs only in the condition, which is to appear and testify. These recognizances are returned by the justice to the court where the party is to appear; and a memorandum of them being then made on the minutes, they are treated as if taken in that court.

On the subject of bail in criminal cases, see Dewitt's Lessee *v.* Osborn, 5 Ohio, 480; State *v.* Wellman, 3 Ohio, 14; Morris *v.* Marcy, 4 Ohio, 83; State *v.* Dawson, 6 Ohio, 251; Swank *v.* The State, 3 Ohio State, 429; State *v.* West, 3 id. 509; Laws of Ohio, vol. 54, p. 5. As to the power of sureties to arrest the principal within the territory of the United States, see Reese *v.* The United States, 9 Wall. 13. §§ 7159 *et seq.* of the Code of Criminal Procedure now regulate these proceedings; there are no striking alterations introduced by them.

bailable. Thus the accused has abundant provision made for his comfort during the interval between the arrest and trial. The mode of taking bail, in all criminal cases, is by recognizance, the form of which is fixed by the statute, and the nature of which has been already indicated. The occasions of taking bail I will now enumerate: 1. When the sheriff makes the arrest on a *capias* upon indictment, if the offence be below penitentiary, he is specially authorized to take bail in any sum between fifty and two hundred dollars; otherwise, the court, when the indictment is brought in, fix the amount, which is indorsed upon the *capias*, and the sheriff takes bail in that sum. He is also authorized, as we have seen, to take recognizances for appearance and for keeping the peace, in all cases where an offence has been committed within his knowledge or view. 2. The coroner, when he holds an inquest over a dead body, is authorized to recognize the witnesses; but not the accused, for he is not presumed to be yet arrested. 3. The magistrate, whether judge or justice, when he holds the examination, is authorized to recognize both the accused and the witnesses. In certain cases, also, as we have seen, he may recognize persons to keep the peace. 4. The court in passing sentence for any offence enumerated in the act for the punishment of offences, may recognize the offender to keep the peace for two years, if deemed expedient. 5. On *habeas corpus*, a proceeding which has been explained before, the judge, who inquires into the cause of detention, may take bail when he thinks the case justifies it; and this writ may issue for the relief of any prisoner committed for trial, unless it be on a capital charge. 6. Provision is made that the sureties may at any time surrender their principal to any judge, who will thereupon commit him to prison, or take new bail, as the case may require. And this brings us up to the proceedings in court.

§ 239. **Grand Jury**. (*a*) We have already seen that no offender can be put to trial on a criminal charge until a bill of indictment has been found against him by the grand jury. The language of the federal constitution is, "that no person shall be held to answer for a capital or otherwise infamous crime, unless on a presentment or indictment of a grand jury." The language of our State constitution includes "any criminal charge." The sole function, therefore, of a grand jury is to pass upon indictments prepared for them by the prosecuting officer. The term "*presentment*" confers no additional authority. It simply means that they are to present accusations in the form of indictments. The *qualifications* of grand jurors are the same as of electors, which have already been described. (*b*) The mode of *selection*, also, is the

(*a*) See Davis's Precedents, 1-32, 1 Chitty's Crim. Law, chap. 6. A list of the names of the grand jurors need not be furnished to the accused before trial. Fouts *v*. The State, 8 Ohio State, 98.

(*b*) The record need not show that they were so qualified. Parks *v*. The State, 4 Ohio State, 234.

same as for petit jurors, which has before been described. In this State, the number is fifteen; and it has been decided that where the State law fixes the number, the federal courts in that State are governed thereby. Grand jurors are summoned by a writ of *venire facias*, which is served by the sheriff ten days before each term. If, upon impanelling them, a sufficient number be not forthcoming, the panel is filled up with *talesmen* or *by-standers.* I have observed that this course is objectionable, even for petit jurors in civil cases; but the objection is still stronger with respect to grand jurors; for their functions are too important in every respect to justify the giving of a discretion to the sheriff to fill up vacancies with any loiterers who may happen to be about the court. But so stands the law. (*a*) In this State, the right to *challenge* a grand juror seems to be confined by statute to the prosecuting attorney, and it must be for good cause shown. But it has been elsewhere decided, that a prisoner whose case is to come before the grand jury may also challenge for cause before the oath is administered. The principal *causes* of challenge are, the want of any of the prescribed qualifications; irregularity in the mode of selecting, drawing, or summoning; and the having deliberately formed and expressed an opinion. (*b*) When the panel is completed, the *oath* is administered to the *foreman*, who is appointed by the court, and all the rest are sworn to observe the same oath. The form of the oath, as prescribed by our statute, is as follows: "Saving yourself and fellow-jurors, you, as foreman of this grand inquest, shall diligently inquire, and true presentment make, of all such matters and things as shall be given you in charge, or otherwise come to your knowledge, touching the present service: the counsel of the State, your own, and your fellows', you shall keep secret unless called on in a court of justice to make disclosures; you shall present no person through hatred, malice, or ill will, nor leave any person unpresented, through fear, favor, or affection, or for any reward or hope thereof; but in all your presentments you shall present the truth, the whole truth, and nothing but the truth, according to the best of your skill and understanding." The meaning of this language is too plain to need comment. The reason for requiring *secresy* is obvious. If the testimony be not sufficient to justify the finding of an indictment, the reputation of the accused ought not to suffer by having it known that a suspicion had existed. And if sufficient, the accused ought not, by knowing what it is, to be able

(*a*) R. S. § 5171 authorizes the court to issue a special *venire* containing the names of selected persons, to fill the grand jury, and thus remove the ground of the author's criticism.

(*b*) 1 Burr's Trial, 33, 37, 44, 425; Commonwealth *v.* Smith, 9 Mass. 110; Commonwealth *v.* Parker, 2 Pick. 568. It is a good plea in abatement that one or more of the grand jurors who found an indictment had not the legal qualifications of grand jurors. But mere irregularities in selecting and drawing them, which do not affect their personal qualifications, cannot be pleaded in abatement. Doyle *v.* The State, 17 Ohio, 222; Huling *v.* The State, 17 Ohio, 583.

to meet it on the trial by perjury, or avoid its effect by making his escape. After the oath, the presiding judge delivers a *charge*, instructing the jurors in their duties; and in this State, there are several acts relating to elections, auctions, taverns, ferries, gaming, brothels, supervisors, bank-notes, and the like, which are required to be specially mentioned in this charge; but there is no authority for expatiating upon politics, as is frequently done; and one would suppose that a nice sense of judicial propriety would prevent the slightest allusion to such subjects. The grand jury now retire to discharge their duties. If they require other witnesses than those who appear voluntarily, or upon recognizance, the prosecuting officer causes them to be brought in. The witnesses are sworn by the clerk, who gives each a certificate of the fact, and only one is admitted at a time. The rule is, that no testimony ought to be received, which would be incompetent on the trial; and as this is a question of law, the grand jury may take advice of the prosecuting officer, or of the court if they so desire. Another rule is, that they are only to hear evidence against the accused. The meaning is, that they are not to resolve themselves into a traverse jury. They are not to seek evidence in exculpation, nor hear witnesses sent there by the accused for that purpose. But when witnesses are properly before them, they are to receive what tends to exculpate, as well as what tends to inculpate. As to the weight of evidence required, the rule is, that they ought not to find a bill unless the evidence be such as, if uncontradicted, would induce them on the trial to convict. The old rule that a bill ought to be found, if guilt is rendered more probable than innocence, is not adopted in this country. But of the weight of evidence they are the exclusive judges. The prosecuting officer, though sharing in their councils, and entitled to be present in all their deliberations, is not to be consulted on this question. It is for him to prepare the indictments, and answer all questions of law, but not to advise whether an indictment ought to be found. The grand jury are sworn "diligently to inquire." This requires them fairly to investigate all offences brought properly before them or within their own knowledge. But it does not require them to prowl about for matters of accusation out of doors. They are a "grand inquest," but not an inquisition. And they are to observe the most rigorous impartiality. The attribute of mercy belongs elsewhere. If any appear to have violated the law, no matter who or what they are, high or low, rich or poor, informed or ignorant, they are to be indicted, without fear, favor, or affection. The one great aim should be to ascertain the truth, and having done so, to act upon it, regardless of consequences.

Twelve out of the fifteen must concur, in order to sustain an indictment; in which case the foreman indorses it, "*a true bill*," and signs his name by way of authentication, even though his own opinion should be the other way. The indictment is also indorsed by the prosecuting attorney; and, in general, these indorsements are the only authentication it requires; but in our act for the punishment of offences, in order to prevent groundless accusations, the complaining or prosecuting witness is required to indorse the indictment as security for costs; which costs he must pay if the accused be acquitted, unless the court think he had good cause to make the complaint. If twelve do not concur in finding a bill, it is said to be *ignored*, and the accused has a right to be immediately discharged; but this does not prevent a subsequent grand jury from finding a true bill for the same offence. Whenever the grand jury desire instructions from the court, they may come in and receive them; but the accused cannot move for specific instructions beforehand. Indictments when found are brought into court by the foreman, and delivered to the clerk, who dockets them in the order of presentation. Not being included in our statute of *amendments*, they can only be amended in matters of form; nor even then, without the consent of the grand jury. When the grand jury have been discharged unconditionally by the court, they cannot be reconvened. And I may observe that there is no warrant either in law or propriety for an expression of their opinion upon political matters, which is now too much the custom, in imitation of the judge who may have charged them on these subjects.

§ 240. **Indictment.** (*a*) Both our federal and State constitutions declare that the accused shall have a "speedy public trial." And our statute provides that where the offence is capital, so that there can be no bail, the indictment shall be found at the first term after the commitment, or else the prisoner shall be discharged if he require it; unless there be very urgent reasons for postponement. In other cases, the matter is left to the discretion of the court. As to the time within which an indictment may be found, after the commission of the offence, our limitations are these: (*b*)

(*a*) *Form of an Indictment.* I shall here give, by way of illustration, the form of an indictment for murder. I have before given the substantial parts of several indictments for the higher offences, in connection with a description of those offences, to which I now refer.

The State of ——, county of ——, court of ——, —— term, in the year ——. The grand jurors of the county aforesaid, upon their oaths present, that one, ——, heretofore, to wit, on the ——, with force and arms at ——, in the county aforesaid, in and upon one ——, purposely, and of deliberate and premeditated malice, did make an assault; and did then and there discharge, and shoot off, to, against, and upon the said ——, a certain pistol then and there charged with gunpowder and one leaden bullet, which said pistol the said ——, in his right hand then and there held; and with the leaden bullet aforesaid, out of the pistol aforesaid, by force of the gunpowder aforesaid, did then and there purposely, and of deliberate and premeditated malice, strike, penetrate, and wound the said ——, in and upon the right side of the belly of him the said ——, thereby giving to him, the said ——, one mortal wound of the depth of —— inches, and of the breadth of —— inches, of which said mortal wound the said —— then and there instantly died; and so the said ——, in the manner, and by the means aforesaid, did purposely, and of deliberate and premeditated malice, kill and murder the said ——, against the peace and dignity of the said State, and contrary to the form of the statute in such case made and provided.

(*b*) But see now R. S. § 6805.

namely, for all the offences enumerated in the act for the punishment of offences, except petit larceny, one year; for all the offences specified in the act for the punishment of immoral practices, except the neglect of a magistrate to pay over fines, the proceedings must be commenced within ten days; for assault and battery, or affray at fisticuffs, where the defendant pleads guilty before a justice, within three months; and for provoking a quarrel, within ten days. Under the laws of the United States the limitations are these: namely, for all capital offences, except murder and forgery, three years; for all offences against the revenue laws, five years; and for all other offences, not capital, two years. It will thus be seen for the great majority of offences in this State, there is no limitation: and the indictment may be found at any time. I will now make a few remarks upon its form and contents.

1. *Its Form.* In framing an indictment, the highest degree of precision and certainty is required; nothing must be left to inference or implication: the defence must be so described that it cannot be mistaken in any essential particular; but mere clerical or grammatical errors will not vitiate it, unless they render the meaning obscure. (*a*) There must be no figures or abbreviations, except in giving the *fac simile* of a writing; (*b*) and if there be more averments than are necessary, the superfluous ones will merely be rejected as surplusage, and thus do no harm. An indictment properly divides itself into three parts, the *introduction*, *description*, and *conclusion*. The introduction and conclusion being matters of form, are the same in all indictments; but the description varies for each offence. The *introduction* begins with a *caption*, naming the State, county, court, and term. In making up the record, however, the caption contains, in addition, the names of the judges and of the grand jurors, and the date of the commencement of the term. (*c*) And it has been held, that under the law of Congress, requiring the prisoner to be furnished with a copy of the indictment, such copy must contain this full caption. The indictment then proceeds, "the grand jurors of the county aforesaid, upon their oaths present, that," &c.; then follows a description of the offence; and the conclusion is, "against the peace and dignity of the State, and contrary to the form of the statute in such case made and provided." The county stated in the caption is called *the venue.* And by the law of this State, it must be the county in which the offence was committed; for even when the venue is changed for trial, as will be explained hereafter, the change does not take place until the indictment has been found. (*d*) 1. The only difference between

(*a*) Fouts *v.* The State, 8 Ohio State, 98.

(*b*) This is no longer a defect. § 7215.

(*c*) Young *v.* State, 6 Ohio, 435; Mahan *v.* State, 10 id. 232; United States *v.* Insurgents, 2 Dallas, 335.

(*d*) It seems that in some cases a State may punish a citizen for an act committed outside of the limits of the State. Lehman *v.* M'Bride, 15 Ohio State, 573.

indictments in the federal and in the State courts is, that in the former the *district* is named instead of the county, and the United States instead of the State. It was formerly the practice to prefix to the above conclusion words like these: "To the great damage of the person injured; to the evil example of all others in the like case offending; and to the great displeasure of Almighty God;" but these expressions are never necessary.

2. *Description of the Offence.* When the offence is created by statute, as we have seen is the case with all offences punishable by this State or by the United States, the indictment must not only conclude, "contrary to the form of the statute," but must by express words bring the offence substantially within the statutory description; (*a*) and the safest rule, therefore, is to follow the exact words of the statute; but the statute itself, if a public act, need not be recited. If an indictment undertake to set forth a *writing* according to its "*tenor*," the exact words and figures must be copied; for its tenor is held to be synonymous with identity; but if it only undertake to give the "*purport*," a substantial description will be sufficient. (*b*) In describing *persons*, no *addition* is in any case necessary. In England, the necessity was created by statute, and we have not adopted it. When the act must be done with a particular *intent*, in order to render it criminal, that intent must be expressly averred. (*c*) It is doubtful if it be ever essential to say that the act was committed "*with force and arms;*" but when the act was in fact forcible, it is prudent to insert them. (*d*) When *knowledge* constitutes a part of the offence, it must be averred; and this is usually done by the words "*knowingly*," or "*well knowing*." There are certain technical words used in describing particular offences, which are said to be indispensable; thus in treason, "*traitorously;*" in burglary, "*burglariously;*" in larceny, "*feloniously took and carried away;*" (*e*) in robbery, "*feloniously and against the will;*" in rape, "*feloniously ravished and carnally knew;*" in riots, "*riotously;*" and in murder in the first degree, "*purposely and of deliberate and premeditated malice.*" But it is never necessary to use the words, "not having the fear of God before his eyes, but being moved and seduced by the instigation of the devil;" nor the words, "of his own wicked and corrupt mind, being a person

(*a*) See 1 Chit. C. L. 182; United States *v.* Bachelder, 2 Gallison, 15; Williams *v.* State, Wright, 42; Poage *v.* The State, 3 Ohio State, 229; Dillingham *v.* The State, 5 id. 280; Aultfather *v.* The State, 4 id. 467. The words "contrary to the form of the statute" are no longer necessary.

(*b*) Hess *v.* State, 5 Ohio, 1; Pickens *v.* State, 6 id. 274. § 7218–20.

(*c*) Fouts *v.* The State, 8 Ohio State, 98; Kain *v.* The State, 8 id. 306. The purpose or intent to kill must be averred in the indictment for murder. Id. In an indictment for robbery there must be a substantial averment of the intent to steal or rob. Matthews *v.* The State, 4 Ohio State, 539. See Turner *v.* The State, 1 id. 422.

(*d*) They are now expressly dispensed with. § 7215.

(*e*) Under § 7228, in an indictment for larceny of money, it is not necessary to show what kind of money it was, or that it was issued by lawful authority, or that it was intended to pass or circulate as money. McDivit *v.* The State, 20 Ohio State, 231.

of evil disposition." Where *wounds* are mentioned, it is held that their length and depth and the part of the body must be stated; and in murder they must be alleged to be "*mortal.*" But the value of the *weapon* need not be stated; nor the fact that the person slain "was in the peace of God and of the State." The name of the person upon whom the offence was committed, if known, must be stated; but if not known, he may be described as "a certain person to the jurors unknown." It is usual to state the residence of the defendant, but as the place of his residence cannot affect his guilt, there seems to be no good reason for this. A *time* and *place*, however, must be stated for every material fact, but when these have been once stated, they may afterwards be referred to by the words "then and there;" and unless the time enters into the nature of the offence, or the place is out of the county, a different time and place from those alleged may be proved. In the averment of *number* and *quantity*, as well as time and place, it is usual to employ a "videlicet," or "to wit," under the impression that less strict proof will then be required; but it is doubtful if this makes any difference. If *several offenders* be concerned in the same offence, they may all be joined in one indictment, whether principals or accessories; or they may be indicted separately. If joined in the same indictment, it is a matter of discretion with the court to grant them separate trials or not. But if the offence be capital, this is seldom refused, on account of the difficulty, in a joint trial, of giving each his full number of challenges. *Several offences* may also be joined in one indictment, in different counts, although the punishment be different; but the court, in their discretion, may require the prosecuting attorney to elect on which he will proceed, and give up the rest; and the better practice is to have separate indictments for each offence. (*a*) Neither the State nor federal laws contain any provisions varying the common law on the subject of indictments, except in reference to perjury and subornation of perjury. In these cases it was formerly necessary to make the indictment exceedingly voluminous, by setting forth the authority of the person administering the oath, together with all the circumstances of the case. But there are now statutory provisions expressly dispensing with this.

§ 241. **Arraignment.** (*b*) The indictment having been thus found, the next step is to *arraign* the prisoner. Being placed at the bar, he is called upon by name to arise. The indictment is then read to him by the prosecuting attorney or the clerk. Some-

(*a*) Bailey *v.* The State, 4 Ohio State, 440. A judgment on a general verdict is not erroneous where some of the counts are good and others bad. Bailey *v.* The State, 4 Ohio State, 440; Robbins *v.* The State, 8 id. 131.

(*b*) See 3 Black. Com. ch. 25; 1 Chitty's Crim. Law, 337; 2 Swift's Dig. 386. Although a prisoner cannot waive any of the formalities required by law, still, when the record shows that the defendant waived arraignment, the judgment will not be reversed for that cause, if the record subsequently discloses proceedings which constitute an arraignment. Goodin *v.* The State, 16 Ohio State, 344.

times the substance is merely stated, but the whole indictment should be read. The prisoner is then asked whether he is *guilty* or *not guilty*. Before answering he is entitled to have the advice of *counsel*. Formerly, this was not the case in England; but both the federal and State constitutions expressly assert this right by declaring that "in all criminal prosecutions, the accused hath a right to be heard by himself and counsel;" and by our statute, the court are required to assign such counsel, not exceeding two, as the prisoner shall desire, if he be unable to employ counsel; which counsel may have access to him in prison at all reasonable hours. The prisoner may then answer to the arraignment either by himself or counsel. If the indictment be for a capital offence, this is the time to make his election to be tried in the supreme court; in which case, the indictment, plea, and election are recorded in the court of common pleas, and certified under seal to the supreme court. (*a*) If the accused do not so elect, or the offence is not capital, he must plead to the indictment. If he ask time, a reasonable time will be allowed him for preparation; and for this purpose he is entitled to a *copy of the indictment*, as a constitutional right, the declaration being, that he may "demand the nature and cause of the accusation against him, and have a copy thereof." Our statute provides that in capital and penitentiary offences, he shall have this copy at least twelve hours before the trial. (*b*) The act of Congress provides that in treason, he shall have it three entire days before the trial, and in all other capital cases two. As to all other cases, both laws are silent. If, on being arraigned, the prisoner make no answer, but *stand mute*, then, by our statute, a jury is to be impanelled to try whether he stands mute obstinately, or by the act of God. If by the act of God, he is to be remanded to prison until he recovers the use of speech; but if obstinately, the plea of not guilty is to be entered, and the cause goes on to trial; and the same is done when he refuses to plead. This is a singular provision, to say the least. Suppose the prisoner be actually dumb; is he therefore to remain in prison for ever? Or is it seriously believed that he may be miraculously struck dumb by the act of God, and afterwards recover his speech? In England, the course is directly the opposite to this; (*c*) but either course would seem to be entirely unnecessary; and so it is in fact considered by Congress, who have provided that in all cases of standing mute, the prisoner is treated as if he had pleaded not guilty; and this is the common sense of the matter. (*d*) The law presumes every man innocent until

(*a*) State *v.* Turner, Wright, 20.

(*b*) The construction given to this provision is, that if the accused demand a copy of the indictment, he cannot be forced to trial until twelve hours after it is furnished. But if he consents to go to trial without making such demand, he cannot afterwards object that the copy was not furnished. Smith *v.* State, 8 Ohio, 294. He is now entitled to a copy of the indictment a day before he is arraigned or called upon to answer to it. § 7244.

(*c*) 4 Black. Com. 324; 1 Western Law Journal, 162, 415.

(*d*) This is also the provision of R. S. § 7260.

proved guilty; and as the prisoner, by standing mute, does not admit his guilt, the question is properly put to the proof, by entering for him the plea of not guilty, and proceeding to trial. I have just said that every man is presumed to be innocent until proved to be guilty. The meaning is, that such is the *legal presumption*. No doubt the *actual presumption* is, that a man who has been first examined before a magistrate, and afterwards indicted by a grand jury, must be guilty; that is, his guilt is thus rendered more probable than his innocence. But still the law humanely presumes him to be innocent, so far as relates to the *burden of proof*. It is not for the prisoner to prove his innocence, but for the State to prove his guilt; and he need say nothing in defence, until a *primâ facie* case is made out against him. This is all the expression means; and in this connection I will further observe, that as the State has the burden of proof, so it has the opening and closing of the argument, as in other cases. I believe that in France and in Scotland the advantage of closing the argument is given to the prisoner; and would not humanity justify a similar course here? There would certainly be no great danger in giving the prisoner the last word.

§ 242. **Plea and Issue.** (*a*) If, upon being arraigned, the pris-

(*a*) See 4 Black. Com. ch. 26; 1 Chitty's C. L. ch. 9; Davis's Prac. 276; 2 Swift's Dig. 399. The forms of presenting the defence differ very little from the corresponding forms in civil cases, except that the prisoner always pleads in person, as will be seen by the following example:—

1. *Plea to the Jurisdiction.* And the said ——, in his proper person comes into court, and having heard the said indictment read, says that this court ought not to take cognizance of the offence in the said indictment charged, because, protesting that he is not guilty of the same, nevertheless he says that [here state the facts showing the want of jurisdiction]; and this the said —— is ready to verify. Wherefore he prays judgment if this court will take cognizance of the indictment aforesaid, and that he may be permitted to go hence without day.

The *replication* to this plea, which is put in by the prosecuting attorney, states that the court ought not to be precluded from taking cognizance of the indictment, and gives the reasons; and then concludes with a prayer that the prisoner may be held to answer to the indictment.

2. *Demurrer.* And the said —— in his proper person comes into court, and having heard the said indictment read, says that the same, and the matters and things therein contained, in manner and form as the same are therein stated, are not sufficient in law, and that he is not bound by the law of the land to answer the same; wherefore, for want of a sufficient indictment, he prays judgment that he be permitted to go hence without day.

The *joinder* asserts the sufficiency of the indictment, and prays that the prisoner may be convicted.

3. *Plea of a Misnomer.* And now, ——, who in this indictment is called by the name of ——, in his proper person comes into court, and having heard this indictment read, says that his name is ——, by which name he has always hitherto been known and called, without this, that he now is, or hitherto has been called or known by the name of ——, as in the said indictment is supposed; and this he is ready to verify; wherefore he prays judgment of the said indictment, and that the same may be quashed.

The *replication* states that he is, and long has been, known and called, as well by the name mentioned in the indictment, as by that mentioned in the plea; and concludes to the country. It has been decided that a plea of misnomer is the only way of taking advantage of it. After verdict the objection is waived. Smith *v.* State, 8 Ohio, 294. As to what is a misnomer, see Rockville *v.* The State, 12 Ohio State, 427. The criminal code provides that if the defendant pleads misnomer, he must give his oner, instead of standing mute, answer that he is *guilty*, it will only remain for the court to pass sentence; except in the case of murder, where, by special provision, the court are required to hear testimony to determine the degree of murder. But if he deny his guilt, it must be one of the modes pointed out by the common law; for neither the federal nor State laws provide any other way. These modes are as follows: *first*, a plea to the jurisdiction; *secondly*, a demurrer; *thirdly*, a plea in abatement; *fourthly*, a special plea in bar; or *fifthly*, the general issue of not guilty; for we have no such pleas as *sanctuary* or *benefit of clergy;* neither of which absurdities has ever been allowed in this country.

1. *A Plea to the Jurisdiction.* This is the proper course when the indictment is found before a court having no jurisdiction of the offence. We have already considered the distribution of criminal jurisdiction, among the federal and State courts, and nothing further need be said here.

2. *A Demurrer.* This is the proper course, when, admitting the truth of the facts alleged, they do not make out the offence intended. Thus the demurrer here has the same office as in civil cases. If the demurrer should be sustained, it would be the acquittal of the prisoner; for, as we have already seen, there can be no amendment after the discharge of the grand jury. If the demurrer should be overruled, there can be little doubt that the prisoner would still be allowed to make an issue of fact, by putting in a plea. However, as there has been some uncertainty on this point, and as the same question may be raised on the general issue, or in arrest of judgment, or in writ of error, it is generally best not to demur.

3. *A Plea in Abatement.* This is chiefly confined to a *misnomer* of the prisoner. It must be accompanied with an affidavit stating the true name. Of course, delay is the only advantage gained; and this plea is therefore seldom pleaded.

4. *A Special Plea in Bar.* This is the proper course when, admitting the truth and sufficiency of the indictment, the defendant has a reason to offer why he ought not to be tried. The only

true name, which shall be at once substituted, and the proceedings go on. This was held constitutional in Lasure *v.* The State, 19 Ohio State, 43.

4. *Plea of Former Acquittal.* And the said ———, in his proper person comes into court, and having heard the said indictment read, says that the State ought not further to prosecute the same against him, because he says that heretofore, to wit, at the court of ———, holden at ———, on the ——— [here set forth the record of the former verdict, judgment, and acquittal]; as by the record thereof now remaining in said court more fully appears; and the said ——— avers that he is the same person, and the offence in the present indictment charged is the same offence as in the said record and acquittal are contained; and this he is ready to verify; wherefore he prays judgment, and that he may be permitted to go hence without day.

The *replication* is *nul tiel record;* unless the fact of identity of person or offence be denied, in which case it is a traverse concluding to the country. It has been held that this plea must set forth the judgment as well as the verdict, because there is no acquittal until judgment. Hurley *v.* State, 6 Ohio, 399.

pleas in bar which can be pleaded in this country are, a former acquittal; a former conviction; or a pardon. There can be no such plea as a *former attaint*, because attainder is expressly prohibited, as we have seen, by the federal and State constitutions. A *former acquittal*, called *autrefois acquit*, and a *former conviction*, called *autrefois convict*, are both founded upon the fundamental principle, asserted in the federal and State constitutions, as we have already seen, (*a*) that no man "shall be twice put in jeopardy for the same offence." This declaration is general, and includes every offence. If, therefore, the prisoner has been formerly tried, and either acquitted or convicted of the same identical offence, it is a complete defence against the present indictment; but the jeopardy does not exist until there has been a judgment rendered. If the jury were discharged, on the former trial, without rendering a verdict; or if judgment were arrested; or a new trial granted; there has been no jeopardy in the legal sense of the term; and neither of these pleas can be set up to a subsequent indictment, or to the same indictment at a subsequent term, founded on the same cause. (*b*) A *pardon* can only be pleaded in bar, where it is competent to grant a pardon *before conviction*, since, after conviction, there can be no occasion to plead it. This may be done in England. Perhaps it may be done by the constitution of the United States, for the language is not precise; but in the constitution of this State the power to pardon is expressly limited to cases *after conviction*. Consequently, there is no opportunity here for a plea of pardon. If either of these special pleas be decided against the defendant, it does not conclude him; for in favor of life or liberty, he is still permitted to plead the general issue, and require his guilt to be proved.

5. *The General Issue.* (*c*) In all criminal cases the general

(*a*) See 2 Story's Com. § 1787; People *v.* Goodman, 18 Johns. 187; U. S. *v.* Perez, 9 Wheat. 579.

(*b*) The prisoner cannot be tried again for the same offence where the jury, after having retired to consult on their verdict, are discharged without his assent, or any legal cause for such discharge. Poage *v.* The State, 3 Ohio State, 229. But where a jury, after long deliberation in a capital case, cannot agree, they may be discharged by the court, without the assent of the prisoner, and the accused held to a further trial. The record must show the facts. Dobbins *v.* The State, 14 Ohio State, 493. And where a jury has been impanelled, and is afterwards discharged in consequence of the then discovered incompetence of a juror, the prisoner insisting on such incompetence must be held to have assented to such discharge, and a new jury may be impanelled. Stewart *v.* The State, 15 Ohio State, 125.

(*c*) The plea of not guilty traverses the whole of the indictment. The indictment charges an act and a criminal intent, except in the few cases where the law punishes an act without reference to the intent with which it is done. The State is required to prove the offence charged, and hence every material averment in the indictment, beyond a reasonable doubt. Evidence offered to prove the insanity of the accused, is evidence offered to prove that he could not, and therefore did not, have a criminal intent. In some States it is therefore held that if the evidence raises a reasonable doubt of the sanity of the accused, it raises such doubt as to his criminal intent, and he is entitled to an acquittal. State *v.* Jones, 50 N. H. 369; State *v.* Johnson, 40 Conn. 136; Moett *v.* People, 85 N. Y. 374; Dove *v.* State, 3 Heisk. (Tenn.) 348;

issue is simply *not guilty;* and under this issue the defendant may set up every possible defence. It is seldom, therefore, that any other plea is put in. Upon entering this plea, which is by a mere memorandum made by the clerk on the back of the indictment, much of the formality practised in the English courts is dispensed with. There is seldom, if ever, a *joinder* or *similiter* entered at the time, and it is doubtful if the want of it could be objected to even in the final record.

§ 243. **Trial.** (*a*) In all criminal prosecutions, the right "to have a speedy public trial, by an impartial jury of the county or district in which the offence shall have been committed," is expressly secured to the prisoner both by federal and State constitutions; and thus the ancient and absurd methods of trial by *ordeal*, by *corsned*, and by *battle*, as described by Blackstone, are for ever abrogated.

Place of Trial. By the State law, the trial must be had in the *county* where the offence was committed, unless it be shown to the court by affidavit that a fair trial cannot there be had; in which case, the *venue may be changed* to an adjoining county. Whether this can be done at the instance of the prisoner only, or on motion of the prosecuting attorney also, is not specified, and may admit of much doubt. Where poison has been given, or a mortal blow inflicted in one county, and the death takes place in another, there might be some doubt in which the offence could be said to be committed; and to remove this doubt our statute provides that the trial shall be in the former. It may also be made a question, when goods are stolen in one county and carried into another, in which the trial shall be. Probably in the former, though I am not aware that the point has been decided with re-

Cunningham *v.* State, 56 Miss. 272; Gueting *v.* State, 66 Ind. 94; Chase *v.* People, 40 Ill. 352; People *v.* Garbutt, 17 Mich. 9; State *v.* Crawford, 11 Kan. 32; Wright *v.* People, 4 Neb. 408.

But a greater number of States hold that the defence of insanity must be made out by a preponderance of evidence. State *v.* Lawrence, 57 Me. 574; Commonwealth *v.* Heath, 11 Gray, 303; apparently in State *v.* Hoyt, 46 Conn. 330; in State *v.* Spencer, 1 Zab. 201; Sayres *v.* Commonwealth, 88 Pa. St. 301; Baccigalupo *v.* State, 33 Gratt. 807; State *v.* Strauder, 11 W. Va. 745, 823; Boswell *v.* State, 63 Ala. 307; State *v.* Coleman, 27 La. Ann. 691; Johnson *v.* State, 10 Tex. App. 571; McKenzie *v.* State, 26 Ark. 334; Kriel *v.* Commonwealth, 5 Bush, 587; Bergin *v.* State, 31 Ohio State, 115; State *v.* Felter, 32 Iowa, 50; State *v.* Redemeier, 71 Mo. 173; People *v.* Wilson, 49 Cal. 14. In Delaware the accused is bound to prove his insanity beyond a reasonable doubt. State *v.* Pratt, 1 Houston, Crim. Cas. 269.

The claim of self-defence being a denial of the malice which the State is bound to prove beyond a reasonable doubt, it is held in some States that the defendant is entitled to an acquittal if, upon the evidence, it is doubtful whether the homicide or assault was malicious or was in self-defence. State *v.* People, 53 N. Y. 164; State *v.* Porter, 34 Iowa, 131; State *v.* Wingo, 66 Mo. 181. So held in cases of assault and battery in Massachusetts. Commonwealth *v.* McKie, 1 Gray, 61. It is held that the accused must establish the fact of self-defence by a preponderance of evidence. People *v.* Shroyer, 42 N. Y. 1; Weaver *v.* State, 24 Ohio State, 584.

As to shifting the burden of proof in cases of larceny and forgery. State *v.* Merrick, 19 Me. 401; State *v.* Flye, 26 Me. 312.

(*a*) See 4 Black. Com. chap. 27; 1 Chitty's Crim. Law, chap. 12; 2 Swift's Dig. 403; *ante* p. 202.

spect to counties. (*a*) With respect to *States*, (*b*) there have been contradictory decisions. In Massachusetts it has been held that a thief who stole goods in another State, and brought them there, might be tried and punished there, as for a continued larceny; but in New York the contrary has been held, and this would seem to be the better opinion. By the federal constitution, the trial must be in the *State or district* where the offence was committed; and if not committed within any district, then where Congress shall appoint; and Congress has provided that it shall be in the district where the offender is apprehended, or into which he is first brought; also, that in capital cases the trial shall be had in the county where the offence was committed, unless it would be attended with great inconvenience; in which case, at least twelve of the petit jurors shall be from that county; but there is no provision in any case for a change of venue.

Time of Trial. We have already seen that the trial must be at the same term in which the indictment is found, unless there be good reason for postponement; (*c*) and by our statute the prisoner, in capital cases, is entitled to a *copy of the panel of the jury* twelve hours before the trial. Nothing is said as to other offences, or as to a list of the witnesses. By the act of Congress, in case of treason, the prisoner is entitled to a list of the jury and witnesses against him, three days before the trial; and to a list of the jury, in all other capital cases, two days before the trial.

Petit Jury. The trial or traverse jury is so called, to distinguish it from the grand jury. These jurors must have the same qualifications, and are selected, drawn, and summoned in the same way as grand jurors. In all but capital cases, twelve only are summoned. In capital cases, our statute requires thirty-six. The act of Congress is silent respecting the number, and it is left to the discretion of the court. If the requisite number be not at hand, the panel may be filled as in other cases, with *talesmen* from the by-standers. In all criminal trials, our statute allows the State and the prisoner each to *challenge* (*d*) two jurors

(*a*) Where the poison is prescribed and furnished in one county to a person who carried it into another county, and there took it and died thereof, the crime of homicide in *administering* poison is committed in the latter county, and must be tried there. Robbins *v.* The State, 8 Ohio State, 131.

(*b*) See Commonwealth *v.* Andrews, 2 Mass. 14; People *v.* Gardner, 2 Johns. 477.

(*c*) By §§ 7309–11 the prisoner is entitled to his discharge if not brought to trial before the end of the second term of the court having jurisdiction of the offence held after the indictment is found, or if bailed, of the third term, unless the court are satisfied that reasonable exertions have been made, and that there is just ground to believe that the evidence can be had at the succeeding term.

(*d*) Where several offenders are tried together, each has his full number of challenges, but the State only has two. Mahan *v.* State, 10 Ohio, 232. And see on the subject of challenge, Hooker *v.* State, 4 Ohio, 348; Bixby *v.* State, 6 id. 86; Doyle *v.* State, 17 id. 222; Fouts *v.* The State, 8 Ohio State, 98; People *v.* Rathbun, 21 Wend. 509; People *v.* Mather, 4 id. 229; People *v.* Vermilyea, 6 Cowen, 555, and 7 Cowen, 108; People *v.* Bodine, 1 Denio, 281; Commonwealth *v.* Knapp, 9 Pick. 495; Webster's Trial, 6.

peremptorily, that is, without assigning cause: and in capital cases, the prisoner may challenge twenty-three peremptorily. (*a*) The act of Congress allows no peremptory challenge by government; but in treason the prisoner may challenge thirty-five peremptorily: in the other capital offences mentioned in the act of 1790, he may challenge twenty; and in all capital offences created since that act, thirty-five, as at common law; but in offences not capital, there is no peremptory challenge. (*b*) *Challenges for cause* must, of course, be without limit as to number. These challenges may be *to the whole array*, if not summoned according to law; otherwise, to the individuals as they are called. The causes of challenge are, *first*, a want of any of the prescribed qualifications; and *secondly*, some presumed or actual bias, founded on relationship or enmity to the prisoner, or the having formed or expressed an opinion. (*c*) The panel must be full before the challenge begins; and no challenge can be made to the array after challenging individuals. All the objections to a juror must be stated at once. If a juror be challenged by one side without success, he may still be challenged by the other; and if first challenged for cause without success, he may still be challenged peremptorily. By the act of Congress, if the prisoner challenge peremptorily more than his number, he is treated as standing mute, and the trial proceeds; but we have no such provision. When a *panel* of twelve has thus been completed, the *oath* or *affirmation* is administered, "well and truly to try, and true deliverance make between the State of Ohio and the prisoner at the bar, and a true verdict to give, according to the evidence." (*d*) The oath says nothing about the *law*, yet there is

(*a*) The act of Feb. 25, 1859, amending the act of Feb. 9, 1831, determines the causes of challenge, and the mode of trying them. The act of March 30, 1860, provides that an opinion formed as to the guilt or innocence of the accused, from rumor or newspaper statements, shall not disqualify a juror, if he states, and the court is satisfied, that he can render an impartial verdict upon the law and evidence. This act was held constitutional in Cooper *v.* The State, 16 Ohio State, 328. This act is substantially re-enacted by § 134 of the Criminal Code as amended February 10, 1872 (69 Ohio Laws, 11), except that a distinction is now taken between opinions formed on mere reports, and those formed on conversations with witnesses, or reading their testimony, or hearing them testify.

(*b*) Under the act of July 20, 1840, 5 Stat. at Large, 394, the courts may regulate the challenges of jurors, except that they cannot take from the prisoner his right of peremptory challenge in cases of treason and other crimes punishable with death. United States *v.* Shackleford, 18 How. 588.

(*c*) Parks *v.* The State, 4 Ohio State, 234. The expression of a juror before trial of a hypothetical opinion as to the guilt of a prisoner, dependent upon a certain state of facts, without any expression of opinion as to the existence of those facts, is not a ground for a new trial. Lœffner *v.* The State, 10 Ohio State, 598. If no inquiry is made of the jury as to causes of challenge until after verdict, the prisoner will not necessarily be entitled to a new trial, though the cause was unknown to the prisoner. So held in a case where one of the jurors had been on the grand jury that found the indictment. Beek *v.* The State, 20 Ohio State, 228.

(*d*) A prisoner is not entitled to reserve his peremptory challenges until a full panel of twelve not liable to successful challenge for cause shall be selected. He may be required by the court to make his peremptory challenge, after having exhausted challenges for cause, to each juror as called, and upon failure to make a valid challenge the juror called may be at once sworn. Schufflin *v.* The State, 20 Ohio State, 233.

an opinion very prevalent in this State, that in criminal cases jurors are judges both of *law and fact.* This absurd idea is, perhaps, founded upon an expression in the constitution on the subject of libels, "that in all indictments for libels, the jury shall have a right to determine the law and the facts, under the direction of the court, as in other cases." But this, if it means any thing, which may well be doubted, does not by any means sustain the inference just mentioned; on the contrary, it indicates that the jury are to take the law in all cases from the court; for the very sufficient reason that they do not of themselves know what the law is. Again, the language of our statute has been thought to favor the same opinion. But this merely asserts the right of the jury in all cases to render a *general* or *special* verdict at their pleasure. And although a general verdict of guilty or not guilty does decide both law and fact, yet if this verdict be against the law as laid down by the court, it will, as a matter of course, be set aside on application; though we have no means, as in England, of punishing jurors for so doing. In no sense, therefore, are jurors judges of the law in criminal cases, more than in civil. (*a*)

Witnesses. (*b*) Both the federal and State constitutions, as we have seen, declare that the prisoner "shall have compulsory process for obtaining witnesses in his favor;" or, in other words, that he shall have the same means of compelling the attendance of his witnesses as can be had on the other side, except that he cannot have them *recognized;* and the statutory provisions carry out this principle. Subpœnas are first issued, and if the witnesses refuse to obey them, they may be brought in by attachment; but the general rules of evidence are nearly the same as in civil cases, and have been already stated. There are, however, some peculiar provisions respecting evidence in criminal cases, which require to be noticed. In the first place, no man can be forced "to give evidence against himself." There can be no such thing as *torture* to extort confessions. This is prohibited by both constitutions. Again, every prisoner has a right to "meet his witness face to face." (*c*) This excludes the evidence of *depositions*, except with

(*a*) And so it has been decided in Ohio. Robbins *v.* The State, 8 Ohio State, 131. See *ante*, p. 203, note (*c*). *Contra* in Vermont. State *v.* McDonnell, 8 Am. Law Register (Aug. 1860), p. 609.

(*b*) See, on the general subject of evidence in criminal cases, M'Nally's Criminal Evidence, Roscoe's Criminal Evidence, and the third volume of Greenleaf's Evidence. By the act of April 17, 1867, 64 Ohio Laws, 260, all criminals are made competent witnesses on their own behalf, at their own request. But if they do not testify, it is not to create any presumption against them, nor shall any reference be made to or any comment upon their not testifying. This provision is repeated in § 7286, and is now found in the statutes of most of the States. When the accused testifies on his own behalf, his cross-examination can be carried to the same extent, and is subject to the same limitations, as the cross-examination of any other witness. Commonwealth *v.* Mullen, 97 Mass. 545; Hanoff *v.* State, 37 Ohio State, 178; Farley *v.* State, 57 Ind. 321; State *v.* Cohn, 9 Nev. 179; People *v.* McGunnigill, 41 Cal. 429.

(*c*) This provision does not exclude evidence of the statements of a deceased witness under oath at a former trial between the same parties. Summons *v.* The State, 5 Ohio the consent of the prisoner. In treason, as we have seen, there must be "at least two witnesses to the same overt act, or a confession made in open court." To prevent witnesses from being tampered with, it is made penal, as we have seen, to bribe them, and for them to accept a bribe. That they may not be prevented from attending court, they are privileged from arrest for civil matters, while going, attending, and returning; and that they may not refuse to testify, when before the court, such refusal is made penal. The subpœna in criminal cases runs throughout the State; and that witnesses may be assured of receiving their fees, they are paid by the county. By the acts of Congress, subpœnas in criminal cases run throughout the United States; and the witnesses are held to be privileged, without express provision.

The Verdict. (*a*) When the testimony has been closed, and the cause argued by the counsel on each side, it is given to the jury, under instructions from the court as to matters of law. (*b*) The jury then retire for deliberation, under the charge of an officer, who is sworn to see that no person has access to them, or communication with them, unless by permission of the court. They cannot separate until they agree upon a verdict, or are discharged by the court. Formerly, they could not be discharged until they came to an agreement one way or the other; and if it became necessary for the court to remove, the jury were carried after them in a cart; nor could they in the mean time take any nourishment of any description; in order, it would seem, that starvation might produce unanimity; but both these absurdities are now done away. The jury may take nourishment under permission from the court; and whenever the court are satisfied that there is no prospect of their agreeing upon a verdict, they may be discharged, and the cause tried over again, as if no trial had taken place. But the principle is still retained, that the jury cannot separate, unless by agreement of counsel, after the trial commences, until their verdict be rendered, or they be discharged. If, therefore, the court adjourn during the trial, from day to day, the jury, unless by consent, must remain together under the charge

State, 325. Or of dying declarations. Robbins *v.* The State, 8 id. 131. See State *v.* Gillick, 7 Clarke (Iowa), 287. Acts and declarations of a conspirator, when a part of the *res gestæ*, are admissible, after proof of the conspiracy, to charge a fellow-conspirator. Patton *v.* The State, 6 Ohio State, 467. A full and liberal cross-examination of accomplices should be permitted, and it will be error to restrict it too closely. Lee *v.* The State, 21 Ohio State, 151. Evidence of voluntary confession is admissible. Fouts *v.* The State, 8 id. 98. In prosecutions for rape, the declarations of the prosecutrix, made immediately after the commission of the offence, are admissible to corroborate her testimony. M'Combs *v.* The State, 8 id. 643. As to incompetency as a witness caused by conviction for forgery, see Poage *v.* The State, 3 Ohio State, 229.

(*a*) See 4 Black. Com. chap. 27; 1 Chitty's Crim. Law, 636; Hurley *v.* State, 6 Ohio, 399.

(*b*) The order of proceedings on trial is regulated in § 7300. Under the provisions of this section it has been held that the court is not bound to reduce a charge to writing, unless requested so to do before the argument of the case to the jury; nor to deliver a written charge until after the close of the argument, if any argument is made. Blackburn *v.* The State, 23 Ohio State, 146.

of the officer. (*a*) Should one of the jurors be taken ill, or die, his place cannot be supplied; but the rest must be discharged, and a new jury called; and it is on this principle that a juror is sometimes withdrawn by agreement, in order to effect a continuance of the cause. We have seen that the verdict may be general or special, at the option of the jury. It cannot be sealed up and sent into court, as in civil cases; but must be delivered personally in open court, all the jurors being present; and in capital cases, at least, the verdict must be delivered in the presence of the prisoner. (*b*) If it be manifestly an improper verdict, the court may at once send the jury back to reconsider it; but when it has been once recorded, it must stand unaltered, and a juror cannot himself contradict it. But a request by the prisoner that the jury be *polled* is never refused. This consists in calling upon each juror to say whether the verdict reported by the foreman is his verdict, and can only be done at the time the verdict is brought in. If any juror then dissents, it is no verdict. Should it be an acquittal, the prisoner is entitled to an immediate discharge; for proceedings are at an end. The government cannot move for a new trial, or an arrest of judgment, or have a writ of error. (*c*) But if the verdict be against the prisoner, he may take either or all of those steps, as his counsel may advise; the two first before judgment, the last after judgment. He cannot appeal: for our law allows no appeal in criminal cases. Perhaps it would have been well to allow an appeal in capital cases; but instead of this, our law gives the prisoner his option in these cases, upon being arraigned, to choose the court in which he will be tried. (*d*) After the verdict, sentence will follow, unless prevented in some one of the ways now to be described.

New Trial. (*e*) Both the federal and State courts have power to grant new trials, for reasons for which new trials have usually been granted in courts of law; and the power extends to all offences; but not more than two new trials can be allowed in the same cause. The motion must be made and disposed of at the

(*a*) Under the original § 164 of the Code of Criminal Procedure, the jury in cases of felonies were not permitted to separate after being sworn. This provision was held mandatory. Cantwell *v.* The State, 18 Ohio State, 477. This was changed by the amendment of January 5, 1871, R. S. § 7312, and they may now be permitted to separate before the final submission of the case to them, but not afterwards. After final submission, the separation of one of the jurors from his fellows, for the purpose of getting and drinking intoxicating liquor, if unexplained, or shown to be excusable, will entitle the prisoner to a new trial. Weis *v.* The State, 22 Ohio State, 486.

(*b*) But it has been held that where the accused, who has given bail, absconds during the trial, the verdict may be rendered in his absence. Fight *v.* State, 7 Ohio, 1 part, 180.

(*c*) By § 7305, the prosecuting attorney can except to the ruling of the court, and take a writ of error to such ruling to the supreme court, but the decision shall not affect the decision of the court in the case in which the error is claimed to occur, but only determine the law for similar cases afterwards.

(*d*) All criminal cases are now tried in the court of common pleas, except some minor ones of which the magistrates, police courts, and probate courts have jurisdiction, and the criminal has no choice of courts.

(*e*) See 1 Chitty's Crim. Law, 654.

same term with the trial; and it cannot be made after the hearing of a motion in arrest of judgment. The grounds for a new trial are the same as in civil cases; and only need to be recapitulated. 1. Misbehavior of the jury. 2. Improper instructions by the court. 3. The verdict being contrary to law or evidence. 4. The improper admission or rejection of evidence. 5. The discovery of new and material evidence since the trial. These are all matters of fact, which do not appear of record, and which cannot, therefore, be taken advantage of in any other way, unless made part of the record by a *bill of exceptions*, as before explained. The allowance of a new trial vacates the proceedings on the first trial; (*a*) and the cause is continued, as if no jury had been impanelled. A *venire facias de novo* may also be resorted to, which is the same as a new trial; except that it is allowed only on a special verdict, and for the purpose of curing some defect in such verdict.

Arrest of Judgment. (*b*) The motion in arrest of judgment must be founded on some substantial error apparent on the record, which error may have occurred at any stage of the proceedings; for as no defects can be amended, so none are cured by the verdict. Whenever a demurrer would have been sustained, judgment will be arrested. The motion ought to be made before sentence is pronounced; and if notice be given of it, sentence will be stayed; but as the court have control over their judgments during the term, the motion may be heard even after sentence. The effect of arresting the judgment, is to vacate all the proceedings, and set the prisoner at large; but this is no bar to a new indictment for the same cause, as we have seen before; for the jeopardy has not existed until the rendition of the judgment.

§ 244. **Judgment.** (*c*) As we allow no compromise between the prosecutor and offender after verdict, and no benefit of clergy, it follows, that unless a new trial be granted, or the judgment be arrested, it must be rendered during the term. This judgment is the sentence of the law upon the verdict, and the terms judgment and sentence are synonymous. The form of the judgment of course varies to suit the punishment annexed to each offence; as we have seen, the court usually exercises a discretion as to the amount of punishment, with certain fixed limits. When the offence is below capital, the judgment must include costs against the defendant; and in this State, as we have seen, for certain minor offences, if the defendant be acquitted, there must be a judgment for costs against the prosecuting witness who has indorsed the indictment, unless the court should think he had good cause for instituting the prosecution. But if the defendant be

(*a*) In some of the States it has been held that it vacates it only as to the verdict of conviction on one count or of one grade of offence, and not as to the corresponding verdicts of acquittal on the other counts or for the other grades. In this State, however, it is held to vacate the whole verdict, and that the case stands just as if it had never been tried. State *v.* Behimer, 20 Ohio State, 572.

(*b*) See 1 Chitty's Crim. Law, 661.

(*c*) See Chitty's Crim. Law, chap. 16.

convicted, the judgment may require him to give security for good behavior. If the sentence be death, it can only be by hanging; and in case of murder, the federal courts may add that the body be given up for dissection. When the sentence has been pronounced, it must be carried into execution, unless prevented by a *writ of error*, *pardon*, *reprieve*, or *commutation*, which are next to be considered.

1. *Writ of Error.* (*a*) In this State no writ of error was allowed in criminal cases until 1831. But now it may be allowed in all criminal cases, upon application on behalf of the defendant.(*b*) In capital cases, the application must be made to two judges of the supreme court; in other cases to one judge. The error must be a substantial one, appearing on the record itself, or made part of it by a bill of exceptions. The course of proceeding is nearly the same as in civil cases, before explained. In capital and penitentiary offences, the writ is either made returnable forthwith to the supreme court wherever it may be sitting, or to the next court in bank; and in the mean time an order is made for the suspension of the sentence. In other cases, the writ is made returnable to the next term of the court in the proper county; and a recognizance to prosecute it to effect is required before suspending the sentence. On hearing the writ of error, if the judgment be reversed, the court may either order a new trial, or an absolute discharge, according to the nature of the case. If the prisoner be already in the penitentiary, it is made the duty of the keeper to transport and deliver him to the sheriff of the county. If the

(*a*) This writ is the same in form as that used in civil cases, of which an example has been given. The *record* is as follows: At a court of ——, for the county of ——, and the State of ——, begun and holden at ——, by and before [name the judges], the grand jurors for the said county, to wit [name the jurors], returned to the said court an indictment against ——, in the words and figures following, to wit: [copy the indictment and indorsements thereon]; and afterwards, to wit, on the ——, by order of the prosecuting attorney aforesaid, the following writ of *capias ad respondendum* was issued out of the clerk's office of the court aforesaid, to wit: [copy the writ and indorsements]; and afterwards, to wit, on the ——, at the term aforesaid, the said writ was returned to the court aforesaid by the said sheriff, indorsed as follows, to wit: [copy the return]; and the said sheriff also returned with the said writ the following recognizance of bail, to wit: [copy the recognizance]; and afterwards, to wit, on the ——, at the term aforesaid, the said —— in proper person comes into court; and being arraigned upon the said indictment, and having heard the same read, says: [copy the plea, replication, &c., making up the issue]; and afterwards, to wit, on the ——, at the term aforesaid, came as well the said prosecuting attorney as the said ——, together with —— and —— his counsel, and thereupon came a jury, to wit [give their names], who being impanelled and sworn the truth to speak upon the issue joined between the State aforesaid and —— aforesaid, upon their oaths did say: [copy the verdict]; and thereupon the said —— moved the court to grant him a new trial, and assigned the following reasons, to wit: [copy the reasons]; which motion, after argument heard thereon, the court overruled; and thereupon it was considered by the court that [copy the judgment].

On the subject of a writ of error in criminal cases, see Baldwin *v.* State, 6 Ohio, 15; Kazer's case, 5 id. 544; Kinsley *v.* The State, 3 Ohio State, 508; Gerhard *v.* The State, 3 id. 508; Montgomery *v.* The State, 7 id. 107.

(*b*) By the provisions of the Code of Criminal Procedure the prosecuting attorney may take exceptions to the ruling of the court, and take them to the supreme court; but the decision is not to affect the judgment in the case below, but merely to settle the law in future cases. §§ 7305-8.

judgment below be affirmed, the only hope of the convict is to obtain a pardon.

2. *Pardon.* (*a*) By our constitution the governor has power to grant reprieves, commutations, and pardons *after conviction* in all cases except treason and impeachment. The president has a similar power by the federal constitution; but it is not specified whether before or after conviction. The propriety of this disposition of the pardoning power has been already considered. The effect of a pardon in this State is to restore a convict to all his civil capacities. The acts of Congress say nothing on this subject. The governor is required to communicate to the general assembly each case in which he exercises this power, with his reasons. Since 1852, notice is required to be given to the prosecuting attorney, and also to be published, of every application for a pardon, at least three weeks previous to the application. In capital cases a reprieve may be granted upon conditions, to be accepted in writing by the convict, upon breach of which the original sentence may be enforced.

§ 245. **Execution.** (*b*) If the effect of the judgment be not prevented in one of these ways, it must be carried into execution. If the judgment be death, the sheriff, or in his absence, the coroner, must be the executioner; for the language of the statute is such that a deputy sheriff cannot act in this case. Under the laws of the United States the marshal is the executioner. If the judgment be imprisonment in the penitentiary, the sheriff, with such assistance as may be necessary, must transport the convict, within thirty days, to the penitentiary, and deliver him, together with a copy of the sentence and bill of costs, to the warden; who thereupon pays the costs; and then deals with the convict according to the directions of the law governing the penitentiary. If the judgment be imprisonment in jail, the prisoner is forthwith remanded; and the jailer, under a penalty for disobedience, must see the sentence strictly performed. Finally, if the judgment be a fine, the convict must either pay it at once, or be committed until payment; or, if not committed, execution may issue as in civil cases.

From the view now presented of criminal proceedings, it will be obvious that the most jealous precautions have been taken to prevent the power of punishment from being abused. No important matter has been left even to legislative discretion; but from the arrest to the execution, the rights of the accused are carefully guarded by constitutional declarations. First, an oath must be made against him, before he can be arrested; then, he must be examined before a magistrate before he can be committed; then, he may give bail, and the bail cannot be excessive; then, between commitment and trial he may have his case reheard on *habeas cor-*

(*a*) See State *v.* Gardiner, Wright, 404–6; 4 Black. Com. ch. 32; 1 Chit. C. L. ch. 20.

(*b*) 2 Black. Com. ch. 32; 1 Chitty's Crim. Law, ch. 20.

pus, or before a single judge, or before the examining court; then, twelve impartial men must concur in finding an indictment against him; then, he may have counsel and witnesses, and every other means of making his defence; then, he may apply for a new trial, or an arrest of judgment, or for a writ of error, or pardon, after judgment; and, finally his punishment, if it cannot be avoided, can be neither cruel nor unusual. So far, therefore, as the offender is concerned, the security against being improperly punished is all that can be asked for. And, on the other hand, the public are sufficiently provided for, in the certainty that the punishment prescribed will be inflicted. The simplicity of all the proceedings is such, that the prosecuting attorney is inexcusable if he fail to procure a conviction from not complying with the requisite forms. In this respect criminal proceedings compare very advantageously with civil; and this very fact serves to prove, that there is nothing in the nature of the case to prevent civil proceedings from being simplified in the manner heretofore proposed.

PART VII.

INTERNATIONAL LAW.

LECTURE XLI.

PUBLIC INTERNATIONAL LAW.

§ 246. **Preliminary Considerations.** We have now completed such a survey as our plan would permit, of our internal or domestic law, comprehending whatever is ordained by our own government for the regulation of persons and property within our own jurisdiction. But the operation of law is not confined to these limits. We constitute one of the great family of nations, our relations with each of which as much require to be regulated by law as do the relations between individuals composing one nation; and this law no one nation can prescribe or administer for itself alone. Accordingly, there yet remains another division of law, which we denominate *international.* This has usually been made the first part of a course of legal study. Instead of adopting the synthetic method, as I have, and commencing with the simplest elements of municipal organization, writers have generally preferred to begin where this process would end, and to pursue the inverse order of analysis. Accordingly, they have commenced with the aggregate of human beings inhabiting the whole earth, and made a primary division of them into those great communities which we call *nations.* They have then proceeded to treat of these nations as a kind of complex persons, possessing a collective unity, though composed of associated millions; and have expounded their rights and obligations in advance as constituting the first and highest branch of law. In this way, they have introduced us to international law, before they have informed us how nations are constituted. In other words, they have exhibited the external relations of nations before explaining their internal organization. But for reasons which appear to me sufficient, I have preferred the opposite course. Certainly, the most simple and natural method is to begin at home, and gradually widen the circle of inquiry. Besides, there is an important part of international law which cannot well be understood until domestic law has been first explored.

I shall consider this subject under two distinct subdivisions, devoting a lecture to each. Of course, I can only exhibit the most general outlines. In the present lecture, I shall present a concise epitome of the *public law of nations*, strictly so called, comprehending that system of rules by which nations are governed in their intercourse with each other, as well in peace as in war. In the next lecture, I shall consider the *private law of nations*, having for its object to ascertain in what cases of conflict between the domestic and foreign law, respecting private rights, one nation is bound to recognize and enforce the laws of another.

You will readily perceive, that if these inquiries are not as practical as those which have hitherto occupied us, they more than make up in dignity what they lack in every-day utility. They contemplate mankind from a loftier eminence, and embrace in their scope a far wider horizon, than any of the subjects before discussed. The law we have been considering rests upon direct and positive sanctions. The same power which ordains it enforces obedience. But international law relies upon moral sanctions alone. The sublime spirit which animates the whole system is submission to the right. Nations stand, not upon legal compulsion, but upon their own honor and integrity. Their grand maxim is, *fides est servanda* — good faith is to be preserved. By this title they hold their domains, and on this basis they frame their contracts. Acknowledging no allegiance to any human power, they fear not the sentence of any human tribunal. Their profession is to demand nothing that is not right, and submit to nothing that is wrong; and when their rights are violated, there being no power to grant them redress, they redress themselves. These and similar considerations give to international law a grandeur and dignity which belong to hardly any other subject of investigation.

But here the question arises, how and by whom is this law ordained? There being no great international legislature, no general congress or common government of nations, whence originates the law which controls them? Dispensing with much unprofitable discussion, I briefly answer that nations, like individuals, are bound to observe the immutable and eternal principles of natural justice; and these, accordingly, form the professed basis of the international code. Hence the law of nature and the law of nations are sometimes spoken of as synonymous. But in point of fact, as nations might not in all cases concur in the application of these abstract principles to their own concerns; and as, in case of difference of opinion, there is no common umpire to adjust such controversy, recourse is necessarily had to the binding authority of *usage;* and the fundamental doctrine is that nations are bound by what custom has settled. The law of nations, therefore, belongs to the department of *unwritten law;* and may be described as a collection of usages and precedents, dating as far back as the earliest histories, and gradually accumulating with the progress of ages, until the aggregate, by general, though tacit adoption among civilized nations, has become a comprehensive body of established law, whose sanctions are, the public opinion of mankind on the one hand, and the countless evils of war on the other. The original source of information, therefore, is history, in which the doings of nations are recorded. But the student is relieved from traversing the wide field of history, by the splendid labors of distinguished writers, such as Grotius, Puffendorf, Bynkershoeck, Burlamaquy, Vattel, Wheaton, and many others, who have collected and arranged the original elements, and thrown around them the light of their own luminous reasonings. (*a*)

Of the history of international law I have not room to speak. Suffice it to say, that whatever is most valuable is of comparatively modern date. There could be little sense of obligation among nations, so long as it was held a maxim that nations are natural enemies, and that war is their congenial element. But in recent times, a mighty change has taken place in public sentiment upon this subject. Nations are now regarded as natural friends, and peace their proper condition. The dictates of humanity have been listened to by governments; and they hold that war is only to be resorted to when all other means of adjusting controversies fail, and then is to be conducted with all possible clemency. In fact, philanthropy can derive from history no subject of more gratifying contemplation, than the improved state of international intercourse.

§ 247. **First Principles.** Our subsequent inquiries will be greatly facilitated by attending, at the outset, to those leading ideas or first principles which lie at the foundation of the law of nations. And first, what constitutes a nation? By a nation in the sense in which I am now using the term, I understand a society of people so organized as to govern themselves independently of foreign powers. The elements of such organization have been before considered. The particular form of government is not here material. It may be a democracy, aristocracy, monarchy, or despotism, or a combination of these; it may be either consolidated or federative; and it may or not have colonies, or other dependencies. These are considerations which do not enter into the definition. The simple criterion is independent self-government in some form or other. What that form shall be, is a question for the people of each nation to determine for themselves. Other nations look only to the fact of independent self-government. Hence it follows that if a community be in any way dependent upon or subordinate to another community, it is not of itself a nation, but only a part of a nation on which it depends. Thus the American colonies, before the

(*a*) The student is advised to read the first nine lectures of Kent, and Wheaton's Elements of International Law, the sixth edition of which is enlarged by W. B. Lawrence. See also 4 Black. Com. 66. There are late editions of Wheaton by Lawrence and R. H. Dana, Jr.

revolution, were only parts of the British nation. And, in like manner, the States of this union are not nations, because they have parted with many of the attributes of independent self-government, but only parts of that one and entire nation, known and recognized by other nations as the United States, and comprehending the people of all the States and territories bound together under one supreme federal government. Accordingly, we are relieved from the necessity of inquiring into the various and complex forms under which nations may exist, internally considered; since their external relations are not thereby affected. In fact, the simplest method of arriving at the general nature of these relations, is to consider each nation as a kind of complex human being, and then to compare nations to individuals existing in a state of nature. In this way, we readily arrive at those fundamental principles upon which the system of international law is constructed.

The first of these principles is a *perfect equality of rights.* We have seen that individuals, before entering into the social compact, are absolutely equal in their rights, however unequal in other respects. In like manner, and for the same reason, nations, however unequal in numbers or resources, and however diverse in their forms of government, are altogether equal in their rights. This equality among nations might be deduced from the consideration, that no one nation can have derived originally from nature any rights which all other nations have not also derived from the same common source. But it results directly from the idea of sovereignty, the very essence of which is, that it acknowledges no earthly superior. Rights and obligations are reciprocal between nations as between individuals. What one nation has a right to demand, all other nations are bound to concede. If, therefore, one nation could claim rights which another could not, the latter would be subordinate to the former; or, in other words, would cease to be sovereign. In short, sovereigns can only be conceived of as equals. This original equality may, indeed, be forcibly disturbed by superior might, or voluntarily modified by compact; but still it must form the basis of all reasoning upon national rights. Attempts have been sometimes made to classify nations with respect to dignity, and thus give to some precedence over others. But this relates only to ceremonial observances, and does not in the least affect the doctrine of a perfect equality of rights.

Another principle, nearly allied to the preceding, is that of *absolute independence.* This, as we have seen, enters into the very definition of a nation. The doctrine is, that every nation has a perfect right to do what it pleases; provided it does not interfere with the same right in all other nations. Subject to this single qualification, every nation has supreme and exclusive control within its own limits, and other nations have no right whatever to interfere with its internal concerns. Thus national independence is the result of equality and sovereignty combined, and the rightful power of each nation is qualified and measured by corresponding rights in all other nations.

But equality and independence, though recognized in theory, would be practically of no avail without the *right of self-defence.* This, therefore, is the paramount right of nations, as of individuals; serving as the shield and protection of all other rights. We must be careful, however, to distinguish between the right of self-defence and the right of retaliation. Self-defence, by the very import of the terms, is purely preventive in its operation. It authorizes any measures necessary to prevent the violation of any rights; but it goes no further. Whereas retaliation avenges wrongs actually committed, with a view to prevent their repetition. On this ground, and this alone, can retaliation be justified between nations, though not allowed between individuals. Nations are compelled to take vengeance into their own hands, because there is no criminal tribunal to punish for them; and aggressors must be taught that they cannot do wrong with impunity.

Next follows the *right of redress.* This, like retaliation, presupposes a wrong actually committed; but its aim is indemnity, and not punishment. And here, again, nations are under the necessity of taking the matter into their own hands. Of the mode as well as measure of redress, they are obliged to be the exclusive judges, there being no superior power to determine for them.

Finally, on these three fundamental rights, self-defence, retaliation, and redress, depends the justifiableness of war. Without some one or all of these grounds, war is in itself the greatest possible wrong. But when they exist, it is permitted as a necessary evil. Accordingly, in the law of nations, the rights and usages of war occupy a place as important as those of peace, since without the former, the latter would have no effectual sanction. I proceed, therefore, to consider, first, the rights of nations in time of peace, and next, those which result from war. For the sake of convenience, I shall endeavor to arrange them under the several heads of jurisdictional, proprietary, diplomatic, commercial, belligerent, and neutral rights.

§ 248. **Jurisdictional Rights.** We have just seen that each nation has the fundamental right of regulating its internal concerns according to its own pleasure, this being the very essence of sovereignty. Efforts have, indeed, been made among some of the leading powers of Europe to qualify this right to some extent, by asserting what they call the *right of intervention.* They base this right of intervention upon the principle of self-defence, and claim to interfere with the internal transactions of other nations, whenever such interference appears to be necessary for their own security. To this end, the most formidable alliances have been formed, and the most destructive wars carried on. Nor can it be doubted that, to the extent here claimed, the right of intervention exists; because self-defence is the first and highest of all rights. And if nations would confine their interference to extreme cases, manifestly endangering their own security, the right of intervention might safely be admitted, as a qualification of the right of sovereignty. But the serious danger is, that under this pretext, the stronger will make aggressions upon the weaker, and that self-defence will thus be made to authorize uncalled-for intermeddling. At any rate, subject to this rare exception, the right of supreme internal jurisdiction is absolute and unqualified. And this includes, of course, the right of revolution, which, as we have already seen, must exist as an ultimate right among all people. Of the emergency which may call for a change of government, the subjects of each nation are the exclusive judges. But it is important to observe that such a change does not affect existing rights and obligations with respect to other nations. These rights and obligations survive in full force, in favor of and against the succeeding government. This is true even when a nation has been divided into distinct governments; in which case, unless apportioned by special agreement, pre-existing rights and obligations attach to all the parts in common, so far as other nations are concerned. But here the question arises, how far may foreign aid be given to either of the contending factions in a civil contest? It is very clear that one nation may not invite or induce the subjects of another to rebel against the constituted authorities. But when a state of revolution or insurrection actually exists, it is held that foreign interposition may lawfully take place. Writers usually annex to the granting of aid to the insurgent party, the condition that the revolution must be for a justifiable cause; and no doubt this consideration would furnish the strongest ground for appeal to foreign sympathy. But in practice, nations usually view the question as one of mere expediency. The end of a successful revolution being to establish a new government, the right to aid the struggling party, in anticipation of this event, is merely a consequence of the right to form alliances. And on the same ground rests the right to acknowledge the independence of the new government. In either case, the question is one of expediency only. If the revolution be in progress, or the new government established, other nations may grant or refuse assistance or recognition, as they deem proper, without inquiring into the justifiableness of the revolution. Acting upon this principle, France did not hesitate to lend her aid to our early struggles, and we did not hesitate to recognize the independence of the South American States and of Texas. (*a*)

With these qualifications of the general right of jurisdiction, it may be laid down as a broad proposition, that each government has complete and absolute control over all persons and things within its territorial limits, exclusive of every other government. How far the accommodating principle of national comity has been admitted to modify the strict exercise of this imperative power, will

(*a*) The European nations claimed that these principles applied to the so-called Confederate States, and some of them recognized that government as a *de facto* government for the time being, and as belligerents.

be seen in the next lecture. It is sufficient here to say, that with the single exception of immunities conceded to diplomatic agents, to be mentioned hereafter, this absolute control over all persons and things within its dominions, is universally acknowledged to appertain to every government. As to persons, the jurisdiction embraces foreigners as much as natives; and as to things, it makes no difference whose property they are. Every nation has a right, either to prohibit altogether the entrance of foreigners or their property into its dominions, or to prescribe the conditions upon which they shall be admitted; and one of these conditions, always implied if not expressed, is a full and entire submission to the laws, while they remain. Nor does this jurisdiction terminate with the territorial limits of each nation. It follows the persons and property of its subjects over the ocean, on which, as common ground, every government may regulate and protect its own citizens and their effects. In short, it follows them until they come within the jurisdiction of some other government; and is resumed again, the moment they are free from such foreign jurisdiction. It hardly needs to be added, that on the same broad principle of power, each nation may prohibit the persons or property once within its jurisdiction from being removed out of it, or prescribe the conditions of such removal. With respect to property, all nations freely exercise this right. But with respect to persons, it is seldom exercised, except upon citizens. In fact, the right of admission and detention, as well of persons as things, has been so far modified by the commercial spirit of modern times, that the ancient doctrines above announced, exist only in theory. And even the right of regulating foreign persons and things, while within our own limits, is now seldom exerted in its original rigor. The convenience of national intercourse, ever increasing with the progress of civilization, has almost revolutionized this part of international law.

§ 249. **Proprietary Rights.** Every nation has a perfect right of property, to the exclusion of all other nations, in every thing within its territorial limits, including not only the public property of the nation, but also the private property of individuals. With respect to public property, it is the right of ownership strictly so called, of which our public lands furnish an example. With respect to private property, it is called the right of *eminent domain*, and includes the right of regulating, taxing, appropriating to public use, taking by escheat, and the like. We have seen, that, according to the ancient feudal theory, the absolute ownership of all real property was vested in the lord paramount, or supreme governor, of whom it was held on certain conditions of tenure. This right, whether of absolute ownership or eminent domain, is equally exclusive with respect to other nations; and it not only embraces those possessions which a nation may now have, but also such new possessions as may be afterwards acquired. Such acquisitions may be made in three ways; namely, by *discovery* of vacant territory, which we have seen to be the source of European title to the American continent; and by *purchase* or *conquest* of territory not vacant. Thus we have seen that the United States acquired Louisiana and Florida by purchase from France and Spain, and the rest of their dominions by conquest from Great Britain. It would seem, however, according to strict ethics, that purchase is the only rightful source of title to occupied territory; and accordingly, we profess to extinguish the Indian title to our territory by purchase only, and never by conquest. The truth is, that the right of conquest being only the right of the stronger, can never comport with natural justice, as against the conquered. But in the law of nations, this is held to be a question between victors and vanquished only, with which other nations have no concern; and therefore, with respect to them, conquest is regarded as a valid source of title. *Prescription* is sometimes mentioned as another source of title; but it is only the presumption of right arising from long possession, and is not so much a source of title as an evidence of it. Among civilized nations at this day, there is little occasion to resort to this kind of evidence, because the limits of nations are usually ascertained by treaty. As a general rule, there is no limit to the right of acquiring new possessions in either of the ways before mentioned. The only qualification grows out of the right of self-defence in other nations. If the enlargement of its possessions by one nation would injuriously affect the rights, or endanger the existence of another, the latter may lawfully interpose to prevent such enlargement. But this pretext for interposition is always a doubtful and dangerous one. It presupposes that a nation will cease to be just, in proportion as it becomes able to practise injustice. It is, therefore, only to be resorted to in those extreme cases where there is a moral certainty that new acquisitions will be made the means of injuring other nations. Vague fears respecting a change in the balance of power can never justify such interposition.

What has now been said relates to property lying wholly within the territorial limits of a nation. It would, therefore, embrace lakes and navigable rivers thus situated. But when a lake or river lies between two nations, instead of being the exclusive property of either, each nation is owner to the middle of the stream or channel, subject to a common use for fishing and navigation. This, at least, is the general rule of public law, though there are said to be cases in which prescription has given to one of the bordering proprietors an exclusive right to the whole. But suppose a navigable river to flow through more nations than one. In this case, may one of the nations prohibit the other from using that part of the river lying within the dominions of the former? This question arose in this country, when the lower part of the Mississippi was under the control of Spain; and it was then claimed to be our right, under the law of nations, to use that part of the river for navigation, and, consequently, its banks for mooring our boats, subject only to such conditions as Spain might reasonably impose for her own security or fiscal accommodation, not amounting to an absolute or virtual prohibition. Questions of this sort, however, are usually adjusted by treaty between all the nations interested in the river.

With respect to the ocean, the general rule is, that it is the common property of all nations, for the purposes of navigation and fishing; and no part of it can ever become the exclusive property of any one nation. It is held, however, that each nation bordering on the ocean may exercise exclusive dominion to the distance of a cannon shot from its own shore, as well for the sake of its own security, as because, to this extent, it may command the neighboring sea by means of its fortifications. And as the distance of a cannon shot would be a vague designation, the modern usage is to substitute a marine league, as the limit of such exclusive control. The rest of the ocean, therefore, is the common highway of all nations; though, as we have seen, each nation there exercises exclusive jurisdiction over its own citizens and their property. Thus far, then, notwithstanding the ancient controversy respecting free navigation, the law of nations is now clear and definite. But with respect to those branches of the sea which come under the name of bays, gulfs, straits, friths, estuaries, arms of the sea, or narrow seas, there is more difficulty. According to the foregoing rule, the criterion would be the distance across from one cape or headland to the other; and if this were less than two leagues, a nation owning both the capes or headlands would have exclusive dominion over the included waters; if otherwise, they would be common like the rest of the ocean. Claims have, indeed, been set up to exclusive dominion in some cases where the distance across is much greater; sometimes on the ground of national security, and sometimes of prescription; but in these claims there has been no such general acquiescence as to establish an exception to the limit of a marine league before mentioned.

§ 250. **Diplomatic Rights.** (*a*) The term diplomacy is used to designate the political intercourse carried on between nations, through their recognized agents. Of the ceremony and etiquette which belong to this intercourse, my plan will not permit me to speak. Every nation has a right to send diplomatic agents to every other nation; and the usage is to reciprocate, by sending to each nation one of the same rank as is received from that nation. On extraordinary occasions such agent is denominated an *ambassador* or *envoy*, who is charged with the execution of some specific trust. But the ordinary intercourse of nations is conducted by resident agents, called *ministers* or *chargés d' affaires*, according to their

(*a*) In addition to the works on the law of nations, see Diplomacy of the United States, a work in two volumes, comprising an interesting history of our foreign relations. See *ante*, p. 596. An important act of Congress was approved March 1, 1833, which regulates the duties, compensation, and titles of persons appointed in the diplomatic and consular service. 10 U. S. Stat. at Large, 619.

rank. The mode of designating such agents depends upon the constitution of each nation. In this country, as we have before seen, they are appointed by the president, with the assent of the senate. Every diplomatic agent carries a letter of credence from his government, stating the general object of his mission, and requesting that full faith and credit may be given to his acts. If the object of the mission be special, the requisite powers may be contained either in the letters of credence or in a separate letter. In time of peace, a public minister requires no other protection on his way than a passport from his own government; but during war, he requires, in addition, a passport from the government to which he is sent. If it be necessary to travel through intermediate nations, his public character is respected by them, though not to the extent of absolute inviolability. (*a*) On arriving at the post of destination, his first duty is to present his credentials, and be formally received in his diplomatic capacity. We have seen that the receiving of foreign ministers is one of the functions devolved upon our president; but this is nowhere a peremptory duty. Every government exercises its discretion upon the question of receiving or not; and when the nation sending is in a state of civil war, this question is often one of exceeding delicacy; because the reception or rejection is almost sure to give umbrage to one or the other of the contending factions.

During his official residence, a public minister is as completely exempt from the local jurisdiction, both civil and criminal, as if he were not within the territory. This absolute immunity is secured to him, not only because he is the representative of sovereignty, but in order that he may discharge the high duties of his mission without fear. And that he may be as independent of bias from favor as from fear, our constitution forbids an American minister to receive even a present from a foreign government. Nor is the immunity, thus held sacred among all nations, confined to the person of the minister. It also embraces his family, suite, servants, house, and furniture; but in order to secure it to his servants, the usage of nations and our act of Congress require the minister to furnish an official list of them for that purpose. When speaking of offences against the law of nations, we have seen that a violation of the immunity here spoken of is one of the principal. And a similar immunity is secured to messengers sent with despatches to or from foreign legations, providing they carry passports attesting their official character; for the violation of such passports is another offence against the law of nations. It hardly need be added, that while public ministers and their families are thus exempted from foreign jurisdiction, they remain as amenable to the jurisdiction of their own government as if they had continued at home.

After the first formal reception of a minister, all diplomatic

(*a*) Holbrook *v.* Henderson, 4 Sandf. 619.

intercourse, saving that of mere ceremony, is conducted through the officer having charge of foreign affairs. Here, this officer is the secretary of state, who transmits the instructions of this government to our ministers abroad, and negotiates with the foreign ministers resident here. It is to be observed that the instructions here spoken of, are for the private guidance of the minister; and the government to which he is sent has no right to demand an exhibition of them. When negotiations upon any subject have been concluded, the result usually takes the form of a treaty; but however ample the powers of the negotiators may be, treaties are not usually regarded as consummated until they have been ratified by the respective governments. To remove all doubt on a question so important, a provision to this effect is usually inserted in the treaty itself; but even if this were omitted, a treaty with this government could not be claimed to be binding until such ratification, because all nations may be presumed to know that our constitution requires such ratification by the senate before a treaty can be recognized by us as the supreme law of the land. After ratification thus made, should legislation be necessary to carry the treaty into effect, we have seen that the national faith is considered as pledged to pass the requisite laws.

A diplomatic mission is usually terminated by a letter of recall. If the minister be recalled because the object of the mission has been accomplished, or for any other reason not affecting the friendly relations of the two governments, the minister presents his letter of recall, and takes a ceremonious leave. In case of misconduct in a minister, the government to which he is sent usually demands his recall, which is of course complied with. But, on the other hand, if a minister be so treated by the government where he is stationed, as, in his opinion, to justify the step, he may assume the responsibility of demanding his passport, and terminate the mission without a recall. In any event, however, be the cause or form of terminating the mission what it may, the minister retains all the privileges of his public character until his return to his own country.

In past times the term diplomacy has had a meaning almost sinister annexed to it, being associated in the mind with every form of cunning, intrigue, stratagem, and overreaching. But the history of our diplomacy bears no such reproach. Thus far the subjects of negotiation between this government and other nations have been chiefly those of commerce and boundary, requiring the exercise of no diplomatic arts, but simply intelligence, firmness, and a sense of justice. It has been our wise and settled policy to keep aloof from those complicated political alliances which have rendered European diplomacy so intricate and embarrassing. And it may be observed generally that the spirit of diplomatic intercourse has been improving. The frequent mediation of friendly powers, when the parties in controversy have been unable to adjust their differences, is one of the most gratifying features in the history of the times. Sanguine philanthropists have even been encouraged to hope, that, at no distant day, the civilized nations of the earth may be able to agree upon a permanent tribunal to settle all disputes. This may prove to be a visionary dream; but the very fact that it is cherished at all, is a high compliment to the diplomacy of the age.

§ 251. **Commercial Rights.** It follows from what has before been said, that every nation has a right to decline all commercial intercourse with other nations in the same manner as an individual may decline all society with his fellow-creatures; but the one would be deemed as blind to its best interests as the other. Nature herself, by assigning different products to different climes, has ordained that nations should interchange them with each other; and, accordingly, except in time of war, no civilized nation adopts the selfish and barbarian policy of consuming only its own products. We have already seen that commerce with foreign nations is one of the great national objects provided for in our constitution; and that a very large proportion of the acts of Congress are commercial regulations. But whence the necessity of so much local regulation? If commerce be a matter of such universal interest, why is it not governed by the universal law? I answer that, to a great extent, this is the case. There are no rules of law so universal in their operation among all nations, as those which form the body of commercial law. But hitherto the doctrines of free trade, however inviting in their theory, have never been adopted in practice. Could they meet the assent of all nations, perhaps a happier condition of the human race would be the consequence. But so long as any one nation chooses to impose restrictions upon commerce, self-defence will prompt other nations to adopt countervailing regulations; and the result is, that hitherto all nations have exercised the undoubted right of placing their commerce with other nations upon such terms as they deem most conducive to their own interests. Accordingly, in the absence of free trade, the first step towards establishing commercial relations between nations is to have them ascertained by treaty; and the grand principle which runs through all our commercial treaties is that of entire reciprocity. In other words, we grant to each nation the same privileges, and impose upon each the same limitations, which that nation grants to or imposes upon us. And when the outlines of commercial intercourse have thus been defined by treaty, the numberless details are supplied from the vast body of commercial law before referred to.

Much of the next lecture will be occupied with matters growing out of commerce between nations; and in this connection, I shall only advert to certain officers recognized by the law of nations in all commercial affairs. I have already mentioned *notaries public*, and it is sufficient here to say, that full faith and credit are everywhere given to their acts connected with commerce, from the simple verification of their official seals. But the most important officers connected with foreign commerce are *consuls*, who are strictly commercial, and not diplomatic agents. Every nation appoints them to reside in foreign seaports, and watch over the commercial interests of its citizens who traffic there. We have already seen that our consuls are appointed by the president and senate. Before a consul can act in his official capacity, he must present his credentials to the government under which he is to reside, and be formally recognized. In some instances consuls have been invested with judicial power to decide controversies between their own countrymen; but this can only be done by treaty, and is not usual. Nor is it necessary; for a foreign tribunal would act impartially in such cases; or if not, the dispute could be adjourned until their return home. The principal duties of our consuls have been prescribed by Congress in the acts of 1792 and 1803. In the absence of the master, owner, or consignee, they take charge of the effects of stranded vessels. They receive protests in relation to all commercial matters where protests are required; and our courts give full faith and credit to their certificates and seals. They provide for our destitute seamen within their consulates, and send them home, if necessary, at the public expense. If our citizens die there, leaving no legal representatives, they administer upon their estates, unless prohibited by the local law. In general, they are admitted to prosecute and defend suits for their countrymen, without any special authority for that purpose. But being merely commercial agents, they have none of the immunities attached to public ministers. (*a*) They are subject to the jurisdiction of the government where they are stationed, to the same extent as private persons travelling under a safe-conduct or passport. If guilty of misconduct, their recognition as consuls is liable to be withdrawn; and they may either be punished where they are, or sent home for punishment.

§ 252. **Belligerent Rights.** I have thus far considered the rights of nations at peace. Let us now turn to those that result from war. Here we have one class of rights for those nations actually engaged in war, and thence called *belligerent;* and another class of rights for those who take no part in the war, and thence called *neutral.* I shall consider these two classes in the order above named. I have already said that war can only be justified on one of the three grounds of self-defence, retaliation, or redress; all of which ultimately resolve themselves into the one grand principle of self-defence. But theorize as we may, each nation must determine

(*a*) By the Judiciary Act of 1789, now chap. 12, Revised Statutes, the jurisdiction of the courts of the United States is exclusive of the courts of the several States in "all suits or proceedings" against consuls or vice-consuls. The defect of jurisdiction of a State court in an action against a consul, may be suggested after the defendant has pleaded to the merits, and may be suggested as error in fact after judgment against him. Davis *v.* Packard, 6 Pet. 41, 7 Pet. 276; Griffin *v.* Dominguez, 2 Duer, 656; Valarino *v.* Thompson, 7 N. Y. 576; Manhardt *v.* Soderstrom, 1 Binn. 138; Sartori *v.* Hamilton, 1 Green (N. J.), 107. Hence a consul cannot be prosecuted for crime in a State court. Commonwealth *v.* Kosloff, 5 S. & R. 545; *contra,* State *v.* De la Foret, 2 N. & M. 217.

for itself, under the sanction of the public opinion of the world, what reasons are sufficient for embarking in war. Waiving, therefore, this preliminary question, let us attend to the rules by which war is to be conducted, and the effects which it produces upon pre-existing rights.

We have before seen that, in this country, Congress has the sole power of declaring war, and making all the provisions required for prosecuting it; while the president and senate are empowered to negotiate the terms of peace. This makes it unnecessary here to inquire what amounts to a declaration of war, or whether a formal declaration must precede the commencement of hostilities; for here war exists the moment that Congress has so declared, and not before. And the theory is, that when two nations are at war, all the individuals of these two nations are personally at war, each with the other; because government speaks the voice and expresses the sentiments of the whole community. How different is the fact, I need not say; but the laws of war are framed upon this theory. Each citizen, therefore, is presumed to espouse personally the cause of his own government, right or wrong, and becomes a traitor by adhering to the other side. Hence all pre-existing contracts between citizens of the two nations are suspended, because neither can sue the other during war; and all contracts made during war are absolutely void, with the single exception of contracts of ransom to be mentioned hereafter. It has also been held, as a matter of strict right, that each nation may confiscate the debts due from its citizens to enemies, and may seize not only the property but the persons of enemies, wherever they may be found, except within neutral jurisdiction. This savage right, however, is seldom asserted in its full rigor, in modern warfare; and with respect to persons and property within each other's jurisdiction, it is not unusual to provide beforehand, by treaty, that each nation shall give to the citizens of the other a reasonable time for removal. Even without such a stipulation, our courts have decided that no seizure or confiscation can here take place without a special provision of Congress to that effect. This of itself is an important security to alien enemies in case of a war with us: and the cause of humanity is also everywhere promoted by the granting of licenses, passports, and safe-conducts, for the protection of alien enemies and their property; the violation of which is an offence against the law of nations. But with these exceptions and modifications, the theory of individual hostility and responsibility is fully carried out in the practice of war. All commercial, as well as diplomatic, intercourse is broken off; and even partnerships existing between belligerents are held to be dissolved. Nor is this all; for property may sometimes be liable to seizure as hostile, when the owner himself is not an alien enemy. Thus the produce of hostile soil is liable to capture, whoever may be the owner; and the same is true of property found in a hostile country belonging to a person having his domicile, or a commercial establishment, there; though not a subject of that government. The test of domicile, in such cases, is residence in the hostile country, with the intention of remaining; or, in case of temporary absence, the intention of returning. Again, according to the rule asserted by some of the European nations in 1756, but not universally acquiesced in, if a neutral be engaged in the colonial or coasting trade of the enemy, which trade was not open to foreigners in time of peace, such employment takes away his neutral protection, and subjects his property to capture. Lastly, if property be found under the flag and protection of the enemy, that circumstance alone gives it a hostile character. And it may be observed generally, that where property has a hostile character at the commencement of a voyage, it cannot avoid that character by transfer during the voyage. On the whole, then, it appears, that from the moment war breaks out, as a matter of stern right, both the persons and property of the enemy are subject to seizure wherever they can be found, except within neutral jurisdiction; and that property may be seized, when it does not actually belong to an enemy, if it have either of the foregoing characteristics of hostile property. These harsh doctrines spring legitimately from the ancient spirit of war, which was to do the enemy as much harm as possible, by every means whatsoever. But the modern practice of nations, under a more humane spirit, has rendered such doctrines rather mementos of the past than guides for the present. This will be evident by a reference to some of the prevailing usages of war.

One of the acts which frequently precedes the breaking out of hostilities is, the imposition of an *embargo*. This we have seen to be one of the incidental powers of Congress. An embargo may have one of two objects: either to prevent the ships of the nation declaring it from leaving the port and becoming a prey to the enemy; or to detain the ships of the enemy in pledge, until subsequent events determine whether they shall be condemned or not, as hostile property. The result, in such case, will greatly depend upon the course pursued by the enemy; for in war the rule is, not to do as you would be done by, but to do as you are done by. In other words retaliation is deemed admissible and often practised.

Another measure which may either precede or accompany open war, is the authorizing of *reprisals*. We have seen that Congress is expressly empowered to grant letters of marque and reprisal; and the law of nations authorizes such a step, whenever the subjects of one nation have been injured by those of another, and a demand of redress has not been complied with. Reprisals may extend to the persons as well as property of the offending nation, though usually to the latter; and they are for the most part confined to the high seas. The persons seized are sometimes held by way of hostage, and the property by way of pledge, until the conduct of the offender shall determine the disposition to be made of them.

I have said that the ancient spirit of war was to do the enemy as much harm as possible. But the modern rule is to use no more violence than is necessary to accomplish the purposes of the war. Hence, even in ravaging the territory of the enemy, it is usual not to molest any persons not actually engaged in hostility, unless they be found violating some of the usages of war. To take captive or put to death the members of the municipal government, women and children, or any other persons pursuing the ordinary avocations of civil life, would, therefore, be regarded as a barbarous outrage upon the usages of modern warfare. And a similar change has taken place in the treatment of prisoners of war. Once it was deemed right to put them to death. Now this fate is reserved for spies only. Nor are prisoners now reduced to slavery as in ancient times, when slavery or death was the only alternative of capture. But, on the contrary, often during the war, and always at the termination of it, the prisoners are either exchanged or ransomed. In fact, it is a part of the discretionary power, as it must be the grateful duty, of the chief officers in command, to alleviate, as far as practicable, the evils of war, by negotiating cartels for the exchange of prisoners, truces for the suspension of hostilities, and capitulations for the surrender of posts.

With respect to hostile property, a similar, though not quite so extensive, amelioration has taken place. Property on land, whether public or private, is now seldom seized or destroyed, unless for the sustenance of the invading army, or by way of retaliation, or when such seizure is absolutely necessary to accomplish the object of the war. But with respect to hostile property at sea, the ancient spirit still prevails in full vigor; and such property is always liable to capture and confiscation. The reason alleged for this difference is, that it is the only effectual method of humbling the maritime power of the enemy, or prosecuting a maritime war to the intended issue. Yet even this right of making captures at sea is subject to several regulations tending to moderate the evils naturally resulting from licensed plunder. Private individuals who rob the enemy without authority from government, are not indeed liable to be treated as pirates; but the main inducement to commit such depredation is taken away by the doctrine that the captures so made belong not to the captors themselves, but to their government, being technically called *rights of admiralty*. To avoid the effect of this doctrine, and transfer the ownership from the government to the captors, a commission for making prizes is necessary from the government; and this is the case with respect to those private armed vessels called *privateers*, which are commissioned to cruise against the floating commerce of the enemy. In order to stimulate individual zeal against the enemy, by invoking avarice to the aid of patriotism, the owners of privateers are permitted to retain for themselves the prizes they make; but at the same time they are required to give security to government, that they will respect neutral rights, and conform to the usages of war. Under all possible safeguards, however, the practice of privateering is subject to manifold abuses. It is, in fact, only one step removed from lawless depredation. Efforts have more than once been made to abolish it by treaty; and there is good reason to hope that public sentiment will ere long be too powerful against it to be resisted. We have already seen that in this country privateering is confined to our own wars; it being highly penal for any person within our jurisdiction, and for our own citizens elsewhere, to be concerned in fitting out privateers to cruise against powers with whom we are at peace. It therefore wants but one step more to rid ourselves altogether of this reproach to modern civilization.

When property has been lawfully captured from the enemy, the title, strictly speaking, is changed the moment the capture is completed. It remains, however, subject to recapture or rescue by the former owner or his countrymen. And in the latter case, the right of *postliminy* intervenes, and the property recaptured, instead of being a new prize belonging to the recapturer, is restored to its original owner, that fellow-countrymen may not thrive upon the misfortunes of each other. But this right of postliminy is subject to many qualifications. In case of captures on land, it does not exist, if the property has been in possession of the captor for twenty-four hours, or has been transferred in good faith to a neutral; and in cases of maritime captures, it does not exist after a regular sentence of condemnation by a prize court. In fact, by the modern usage of nations, there can be no security of title to maritime captures, until such sentence has been pronounced; this being considered the only sure way of furnishing satisfactory proof that the capture was lawful, and not an infringement of neutral rights. By the law of nations, the prize court must be constituted by the government of the captor, and must sit within the dominions of that government or of its ally, and not within the dominions of a neutral power. But it is now held that the condemnation may take place while the prize itself is in a neutral port, and out of the jurisdiction of the court. Further than this, a neutral port cannot be made the theatre of hostile operations. In this country, the district court, by virtue of its admiralty jurisdiction, discharges the functions of a prize court. Such courts professedly administer the law of nations, and their decision is conclusive upon the question of property. If neutral rights be thereby violated, the nation becomes responsible for the injury, but the property passes pursuant to the sentence. A purchaser, therefore, of condemned property is secure in his title against everything but a recapture by the enemy; and a neutral purchaser is secure even against that. The recaptor is secure against the claim of postliminy, unless there be some internal regulation of his government to the contrary. But it sometimes happens that a prize cannot be sent into port; in which case, the captor may either destroy it or permit the former owner to ransom it. Contracts of ransom are highly favored by the law of nations, and the ransom is held equivalent to a safe-conduct of the ransomer. But the ransom bill is as liable to recapture as the prize itself would have been. With respect to real property in the hands of the captor, the title by conquest is not conclusive, until the treaty of peace. In the event of reconquest, it returns again to the original proprietor by the right of postliminy, notwithstanding intermediate transfers. But if ultimately ceded to the conqueror, the transfers are valid. Finally, with respect to all captures, if the treaty of peace makes no provision concerning them, the right of postliminy is at an end, and the title remains confirmed in the possessor.

§ 253. **Neutral Rights.** A neutral nation, as the term imports, is one that takes neither side in an impending war. Our natural position with respect to other nations has been eminently favorable to the observance of a strict neutrality; and this has accordingly been our steadfast policy from the commencement of our national existence. Thus far we have entirely avoided those entangling alliances so common among the nations of Europe, which would have required us to embark in war, at the will of others, in order to redeem a pledge. To us, therefore, attached to neutrality both from principle and expediency, the subject of neutral rights is especially interesting.

The grand principle of neutrality is neither to aid nor hinder either of the belligerents, but to stand entirely indifferent between them; and in return for this strict impartiality, not to be in any way molested by them. With some slight exceptions, which will be adverted to, this principle forms the basis of all neutral rights and obligations.

In the first place, neutral territory is not to be made the theatre of hostile operations. This operates as well for the protection of belligerents as neutrals. But the persons and property of each of the belligerents on neutral ground are exempt from liability to seizure by the other; and if a neutral permit such seizure, he is bound to make restitution. But it is no departure from neutrality to permit belligerent forces to pass through neutral territory provided no acts of hostility be allowed; though a neutral is under no obligation to grant this privilege. When prizes are brought within neutral jurisdiction, which were made in violation of neutral rights, the neutral government may reverse the sentence of condemnation and restore the property for the purpose of vindicating its neutrality; and still more may it reclaim the property of its own citizens illegally captured. We have already seen that prize courts may not sit within neutral jurisdiction, though the prizes themselves may be brought there to await the adjudication of the proper tribunal. Public ships of war may also be received into a neutral port, provided there be no hostile object, and the same favor be granted to both belligerents; but they may not be built, armed, or equipped there, for the purposes of war. (*a*) And to

(*a*) This was the principle at issue in the Alabama case, lately settled by arbitration, between the United States and England.

give the highest possible sanction to these rules within our jurisdiction, we have seen that Congress has made it highly penal for any person within our jurisdiction to set on foot any military expedition, or enlist troops or seamen, or fit out ships, or augment the force of foreign ships, in violation of the obligations of neutrality.

In the next place, neutrality is to be observed and respected upon the ocean. On the one hand, the neutral is not to be disturbed in the prosecution of his ordinary commerce as well with the belligerents as with other nations; and on the other hand, he is not to favor either of the belligerents in his hostile operations at the expense of the other. It is a general rule that neutral property is exempt from seizure, even when found in hostile ships; and also that neutral ships carrying hostile property are themselves exempt from seizure, though the hostile property in them is not. Efforts have been made to establish the maxim that free ships make free goods; or in other words, to render the neutral flag a protection even to hostile property. This was the object of the celebrated armed neutrality. But there has been no general acquiescence in this maxim; and the rule still is, that hostile property in neutral ships, out of neutral jurisdiction, is liable to capture. To these general rights of neutrals there are, however, two exceptions, one relating to contraband goods, and the other to blockaded ports.

Without attempting a detailed description of the articles which are held to be *contraband of war*, it is sufficient here to say that they include not only implements and munitions of war, but all other articles which are directly auxiliary to hostile operations. Provisions are not generally contraband, but may become so from the special circumstances under which they are supplied. Sometimes treaties stipulate what shall, and what shall not, be contraband as between the contracting parties. But the question of contraband or not, being once settled, the rule is universal that neutrals may not furnish contraband articles to either of the belligerents, under the penalty of confiscation not only of the contraband articles themselves, but also of the whole cargo of which they form a part; and formerly the ship itself suffered the same fate.

The rights of *blockade and siege* are among those well settled belligerent rights, which neutrals are bound to respect. Each nation at war has a right to blockade the ports, or besiege the fortifications of the other. But it is not sufficient simply to declare a port under blockade or a place under siege. There must be an actual force on the spot to constitute a blockade or siege; for otherwise a mere proclamation might shut up the commerce of the world. But when a blockade or siege actually exists, neutrals cannot knowingly maintain any commerce whatever with the places thus invested, under the penalty of confiscation of the ship destined to or coming from such places; and also of the cargo, unless it can be shown that its owners had no concern in the matter. This rule is vindicated upon the ground that blockades and sieges are legitimate measures of war, which would be rendered of no avail if neutrals were permitted to relieve against them.

There is still a third exception to neutral intercourse, analogous to the preceding, which is, that neutrals may not be concerned in bearing *hostile despatches*, under the penalty of confiscation of the vehicle, and of the cargo also, unless it can be shown that its owners had no knowledge of the offence.

Such being the rights and obligations of neutrals, it is incumbent on them to see that their ships are furnished with the documents requisite to sustain their neutral character. Mere custom-house documents, as we have seen, are not sufficient for this purpose, not being known to the law of nations. The only evidence of national character is a passport or sea-letter, duly authenticated. But still the question arises, how are belligerents to know what ships are in fact neutral? The answer is that they have the right of search, for the purpose of ascertaining. However inconvenient and vexatious the exercise of this right may be to neutrals, they are bound to submit to it; and resistance may involve a confiscation of the ship and cargo. No other rule could prevent the neutral flag from being made a pretext for violating the rights of belligerents.

LECTURE XLII.

PRIVATE INTERNATIONAL LAW. (*a*)

§ 254. **Preliminary Considerations.** This branch of international law is usually discussed under the title of *conflict of laws*, its object being to determine in what cases of conflict between the laws of different nations the domestic law shall give place to the foreign law. But as questions of this kind chiefly concern the private relations of individuals, depending upon the law of different nations, and not the political relations existing between those nations, I prefer the title of private international law; in contradistinction to that of public international law, which has just been considered. We have already seen that each nation of right possesses an exclusive sovereignty and jurisdiction within its own territory, but none whatever beyond it, except upon the ocean. Hence it follows that the laws of one nation can have no *intrinsic* authority in any other nation. Whenever, therefore, any nation, within its own limits, gives effect to the laws of another nation, it is to be regarded as a matter of concession. The disposition to

(*a*) On the subject of this lecture, I need make no other reference than to Story's Commentaries on the Conflict of Laws, a lucid and comprehensive treatise, which scarcely leaves anything to be desired in this department of jurisprudence.

make such concession is denominated *comity;* and hence we say that comity is the foundation of private international law. But comity, which is but another name for the spirit of accommodation, if left to the control of an arbitrary or capricious will, would be but a dubious and unstable guide. To render it a safe criterion of rights, it must be exercised according to established rules; and hence the original suggestions of comity, founded on a sense of mutual convenience, have been clothed with the sanctions of positive law. Accordingly, it is no longer optional with the tribunals of one nation to recognize, or not, the laws of another, as the disposition of the moment may incline them; but the question is to be settled, as in all other cases, either by legislative enactments or by judicial precedents. In one or the other of these ways each nation prescribes for itself the limits of its comity; and hence we may naturally look for more diversity in this branch of law than in the public law of nations. The prevailing practice has formerly been to apply the rule of reciprocity; that is, to give effect to the law of other nations only when they, under similar circumstances, give effect to our law. But this rule is gradually giving way to the higher considerations of abstract justice and the universal welfare; and just in proportion as these exalted motives shall operate upon legislators and judges throughout the world, will this branch of law approximate to general uniformity. In the brief outline which I propose to exhibit, I shall confine myself to the doctrines held in this country, and to a very general view even of them. I shall arrange my remarks under four general heads: namely, *persons*, *property*, *crimes*, and *procedure*.

§ 255. **As to the Law of Persons.** In the view I am now taking, the law which determines the capacity, state, and condition of persons, is called *personal law*, as to which there is no universal rule admitted by all nations. But the rule prevailing in this country is, that as to acts done, rights acquired, and obligations incurred, in the place of domicile, the law of such domicile will govern everywhere; but, otherwise, the law of the place of the transaction will govern. This general rule will determine the capacities and incapacities incident to infancy, coverture, idiocy, and lunacy, and all other personal abilities and disabilities, founded in the law of nature, and not in derogation of common right. But foreign nations will not regard disqualifications created by penal laws, or laws authorizing slavery, unless there be some express compact on the subject, like that existing between the States of this Union. Moreover, each nation may make an exception to the above rule with respect to its own subjects; for as to them there can be no question of comity, and, therefore, they will not be permitted to evade their own law, by resorting to countries where a different law prevails. Such, then, being the general rule, I shall first consider what constitutes domicile, and then apply the rule to the various classes of persons heretofore mentioned.

1. *Domicile.* In the common acceptation, domicile means the place where a person resides; but in a legal sense domicile means the place where a person has his fixed and permanent home or establishment. Two things must concur to constitute domicile, namely, actual residence, and the intention of remaining; or, in case of temporary absence, the intention of returning; and as there must be this concurrence of fact and intention, the question of domicile is often a difficult one. The most general rules on the subject are these: the place where one is born is his domicile, if it was the domicile of his parents; if not, their domicile is his during minority, unless changed by the parents. A married woman has the domicile of her husband. Residence is *primâ facie* evidence of domicile; but no length of time is essential; and, therefore, if an adult person removes to a new residence, with the intention of remaining, it becomes his domicile immediately. The place where the family of a married man reside is considered his domicile, though he may do business in another place; and if the family have different places of residence for different periods of the year, that place will be the domicile in which the head of the family exercises the rights of citizenship; but the domicile of a single man is usually the place where he transacts his permanent business. Every person must have a domicile somewhere; and, therefore, when a domicile has once been acquired, it continues until a new one is acquired. These are the leading rules of local domicile, and they apply, for the most part, to national domicile. When a person has acquired a foreign domicile, and abandons it to return to his native domicile, the latter is reacquired the moment the former is left. Diplomatic agents do not acquire a foreign domicile by residence abroad, but consuls and commercial agents generally do. It will thus be seen that domicile and citizenship have no necessary connection. Our citizens may have their domicile abroad; and aliens may have their domicile here.

2. *Corporations.* The general rule is, that the existence of foreign corporations is recognized for all purposes and in all respects, except those specially prohibited by the domestic law. Subject to this exception they may make contracts, sue and be sued, establish agencies, and do any other acts to which they would be competent in the place of their domicile. They must dwell in the place of their creation, and cannot migrate elsewhere; but this does not hinder their rights from being recognized and protected elsewhere. (*a*)

3. *Husband and Wife.* The general rule is, that the validity of a marriage depends upon the law of the place where it is celebrated. If valid there, it is valid everywhere; and if invalid there, it is invalid everywhere. The reason of this rule is found in the disastrous consequences which would follow from any other doctrine;

(*a*) This subject is very fully discussed in the case of the Bank of Augusta *v.* Earle, 13 Peters, 519. See also Day *v.* Newark Co., Blatchford, 628.

and so strong is this reason, that the rule prevails even when persons have gone to a foreign country to marry, for the express purpose of evading the domestic law. The exceptions are with respect to incestuous marriages and polygamy; which though lawful where they take place are not recognized elsewhere. Some nations also expressly prohibit their own subjects from marrying anywhere unless according to their own laws, and, therefore, will not recognize other marriages. And the necessity of the case sometimes requires a resort to the law of the domicile, for want of a local law suited to the condition of the parties. With respect to the property acquired by marriage, the rule, so far as any is settled, seems to be this. When there is no change of domicile, the law of the place of the marriage will determine the rights of the parties as to personalty everywhere; but their rights as to realty will depend upon the law of the place where it is situated. When there is a change of domicile after marriage, the law of the new domicile will govern future acquired personalty everywhere, but realty will still depend upon the law of its place. In either case, however, if there be a special contract on the subject of property, that contract will everywhere govern personalty, and to some extent realty. Finally, when parties marry in one place with the intention of immediately settling in another, the law of the latter will govern their rights, because they are presumed to marry with that understanding. As to divorces, the rule is, that a divorce lawfully obtained, in the place where the parties were married and had their domicile, will be valid everywhere. It has also been held in this country, that if the parties have changed their domicile after marriage, a divorce granted in their new domicile for a cause occurring there is valid everywhere, even in States where that cause would not have authorized a divorce. But when a party goes to another State for the express purpose of procuring a divorce, which he could not procure at home, such divorce, being in fraud of the law of the domicile, will not be recognized there. Whether it would be recognized elsewhere, is an unsettled question. It is also held in this country, that in determining what cause shall be sufficient for a divorce, the law of the forum and not of the marriage is to govern; and that one State will not grant a divorce for a cause which occurred in another, unless there be express legislation to that effect, as is the case in this State.

4. *Parent and Child.* The only important question under this head is that of legitimacy, which is generally determined by the law of the place of the marriage. If by that law the issue be legitimate, they will be held legitimate everywhere else, at least with respect to heirship. But the converse is not always true. The law of Ohio, for example, makes children legitimate here, who would not be so by the law of the place of the marriage.

5. *Guardian and Ward.* The general rule is, that the rights and powers of guardians are strictly local, and they can exercise

no power over the persons or property of their wards, beyond the jurisdiction appointing them, and to which they are amenable. Our statute makes an exception with respect to the real estate of minors living out of this State, by allowing their guardians to sell it under the same regulations as guardians appointed here. But with this exception, it follows that if the guardian change the domicile of his ward, as he may for good cause, he requires a new appointment or confirmation under the law of the new domicile; and the same is generally true, where the ward has property in different jurisdictions. The question who are minors, or otherwise subject to guardianship, depends upon the law of the place where they are when the question arises; and their capacities or incapacities depend upon the same law.

6. *Master and Servant.* Under this head we need notice only slaves and apprentices; for the relation of principal and agent is nearly the same everywhere. With respect to slaves, the general rule is, that slavery will not be recognized in any country whose laws prohibit slavery. And this is the doctrine held in the non-slaveholding States of this Union, except so far as affected by the federal compact respecting fugitive slaves, which has before been commented upon. With respect to apprentices, the general rule is, that foreign indentures of apprenticeship are of no binding force, unless the nature of the service, or the express provision of the indenture, contemplated a change of domicile.

7. *Executors and Administrators.* By our statute, authenticated copies of wills made and proved in any part of the world, according to the law of the place, are admitted to record here, and have the same effect as if made here. And if a person die intestate out of this State, leaving rights or credits here, administration may be granted here. So if an executor or administrator be duly appointed elsewhere within the United States, he may sue here, and may sell real estate here, in the same manner as if appointed here. But these latter provisions do not extend to foreign nations; and, therefore, no foreign executor or administrator can sue or be sued, or otherwise judicially recognized here, by reason of his foreign appointment. New letters of administration must be taken out here according to our laws, and a settlement must be made of the assets found here; and all debts or legacies due here must be paid out of such assets, before any thing is transmitted abroad, even though the estate were insolvent there. But the better opinion is, that he is not liable to be sued here for assets received abroad. The next question relates to descent and distribution. With respect to real property, the rule is that the rights of dower, curtesy, and descent, depend exclusively upon the law of the place where it is situated. But with respect to personal property, the rule is, that it is to be distributed according to the law of the intestate's domicile, at the time of his death, wherever such property be situated. With respect to a will of personalty, the rule is, that if made according to the law of the testator's actual domicile,

it will pass personalty wherever it may be; but if not made according to the law of the domicile, it is not valid anywhere. With respect to a will of realty, its validity and effect must depend wholly upon the law of the place where the property is.

§ 256. **As to the Law of Property.** I shall consider this subject under three points of view; namely, as to real property, personal property, and contracts.

1. *Real Property.* We have seen that immobility is the distinguishing characteristic of realty. Its *situs* never changes; and therefore if the soil of a nation could be subject to foreign domination, the very foundation of national independence would be taken away. Hence the general rule is, that real property is governed exclusively by the law of the place where it is situated. This may be illustrated in several particulars. First, the capacity of persons to take or transfer real estate, depends, not as in other cases, upon the law of their domicile, but upon the law of the place of the real estate. To this there is no exception in England or in this country. Secondly, the forms and solemnities of passing the title are governed exclusively by the law of the place. We have seen, however, that the law of Ohio, in relation to deeds, expressly recognizes any foreign deed executed according to the law of the place where it is executed; and in relation to wills, expressly recognizes a will, made and proved in any part of the world, according to the law of the place where it is made and proved; and it would be a great convenience if all the States would make similar provisions. Thirdly, the law of the place governs with respect to descent, dower, and curtesy. Lastly, the law of the place governs with respect to what shall be considered real estate, and all restrictions upon alienation or encumbrance. In a word, therefore, real property is wholly governed by the domestic law.

2. *Personal Property.* The general rule is, that personal property has no *situs*, but follows the person of the owner; and consequently the law which governs it is the law of the owner's domicile, and not the law of the place where it happens to be. Accordingly, any transfer or disposition of personal property which is valid by the law of the owner's domicile, is valid everywhere, unless, perhaps, in the place where it was at the time, by reason of some prohibitory law of that place. The only kinds of personalty excepted, are such stocks or funds as are local in their nature, and require a particular mode of transfer by the local law; and perhaps some other things to which the same reason applies. But it does not follow, from the above rule, that a transfer not made according to the law of the domicile, but according to the law of the place where it is, would be invalid. For the benefit of commerce, such transfers will be sustained even in the courts of the domicile.

3. *Contracts.* Real contracts, or those which relate to real property, are exclusively governed by the law of the place where the property is situated, as we have already seen. Personal contracts

include those which relate to persons only, or to personal property, or debts; and the general rule is, that the law of the place where a personal contract is made, everywhere governs the contract, as to the capacity of the parties to make it; as to its validity or invalidity; as to the formalities, proofs, and authentications of it; and as to its nature, obligation, interpretation, and consequences. There is, however, this general exception, that no nation will give effect to foreign contracts which violate the law of nature or the law of God, or which contravene its own fundamental policy. And the rule itself presupposes that the parties have not stipulated for the law of a different place. For if the contract is either expressly or impliedly to be performed in a different place from that where it is made, the law of the place of performance will govern, as to the validity, nature, obligation, and interpretation of the contract. As between merchants residing in different countries and keeping accounts with each other, the rule in adjusting balances is, that each transaction is to be governed by the law of the place where it originated. As to interest, the rule is, that it is to be governed by the law of the place where the contract is made, unless the parties had in view a different place of payment; in which case the latter will govern. As to damages on protested bills, the place where each party contracts will govern the amount he is to pay. Where money is payable by contract in one place, and is sued for in another, the creditor is entitled to recover an amount sufficient to pay for its remittance to the place of payment; and exchange is to be added or deducted accordingly. Days of grace are governed by the law of the place of payment. Contracts which stipulate no particular place of performance, are performable everywhere. A defence to or discharge from a contract, which is good by the law of the place where the contract is made or is to be performed, is good everywhere else. But with respect to discharges under the insolvent laws of the different States, we have seen, that owing to the peculiar relations of the States, this rule is so far modified that such discharges are only valid with respect to contracts made between citizens of the same State authorizing the discharge. And the converse of the rule also prevails, that a discharge by the law of any other place than that where the contract was made, will not, on that account, be valid elsewhere.

§ 257. **As to the Law of Crimes.** The general rule is, to consider crimes as altogether local, that is, exclusively cognizable and punishable within the jurisdiction where they are committed. Accordingly, one country does not take cognizance of the penal laws of another, for any purpose whatsoever. This doctrine is carried out so strictly, that conviction of an infamous crime in one of the States of this Union does not render a witness incompetent in another State, unless by express provision, such as we have in this State; nor do the consequences of attainder in one nation attach to the attainted person in another. In short, no nation pays any respect whatever to foreign criminal laws, except in surrendering up fugitives from justice. This is sometimes stipulated for by treaty (*a*) and sometimes left to comity alone. In the absence of any positive compact, it is a subject of much controversy whether there is any binding obligation among nations to surrender a fugitive in any case whatever. In this country, the weight of authority is against the obligation. Such surrenders have been frequently made, and as frequently refused; and the result is, that unless the case is a very strong one, our tribunals would refuse to order the surrender, and such refusal is no just cause of offence to the nation making the demand. But in this respect, the States of this Union, as we have seen, have ceased to be foreign with reference to each other, under an express compact in the federal constitution; and Congress has provided the manner in which the demand and surrender shall be made. (*b*)

§ 258. **As to the Law of Procedure.** The general rule is, that the law governing the remedy is the law of the place where the remedy is sought. Even where the right is determined by recourse to foreign law, the redress must be obtained according to the domestic law, for the obvious reason that our courts cannot be presumed to be acquainted with foreign modes of procedure; and also because the adoption of them would introduce endless confusion and uncertainty into our practice. But I shall consider the subject under several aspects.

1. *Jurisdiction.* Upon the question of jurisdiction, the rule is, that it can only be rightfully exercised, when either the person or thing is within the territory; for as judicial process cannot go beyond the territory, the attempt to exercise an extra-territorial jurisdiction would be a nullity. But, on the other hand, the right of jurisdiction extends to all persons and things within the territory, except foreign ministers and their families and effects. In our tribunals, foreigners may sue and be sued, in like manner as citizens, with the single exception of alien enemies; and to give them every assurance of an impartial hearing, we allow them to select the federal tribunals. Where the person only, and not his property, is within the jurisdiction, the judgment or decree can-

(*a*) For example, the Ashburton treaty.

(*b*) The leading cases on the subject of surrendering fugitives are, the case of Washburn, 4 Johns. Ch. 106; Commonwealth *v.* Green, 17 Mass. 515; Commonwealth *v.* Deacon, 10 Serg. & Rawle, 123; and Rex *v.* Ball, 1 Amer. Jur. 297; 22 id. 330. See *ante*, § 64; see act of State of Ohio, March 24, 1860. In Kentucky *v.* Dennison, 24 How. 66, the State of Kentucky applied to the Supreme Court of the United States for a mandamus to compel the Governor of Ohio to deliver up a person who had been indicted for some offence connected with the slave laws of Kentucky. The court held that the clause in the constitution gave a right to the executive of one State to *demand* and imposed an obligation on the other to deliver up the fugitive, without any reference to the character of the crime charged, or to the policy or laws of the State to which the fugitive is fled, and that the governor cannot look behind or inquire into the certificates required by the statute. But they further held that the constitution provided no means of enforcing this duty, though merely ministerial, and on this ground alone refused the mandamus.

not of course operate directly upon such property; but where the property is within the jurisdiction, though the person is not, the judgment or decree will bind the property. In such case, however, our statute requires notice to be given by publication, and if the person affected did not receive this notice, time is given him to open the judgment or decree and have a hearing.

2. *Limitation of Actions.* With respect to the limitation of actions, the universal rule is, that statutes of limitation belong to the remedy, and the law of the forum must govern. Courts, therefore, will not take notice of the statute of limitations of the foreign place where the cause of action accrued, but will be governed wholly by their own statute. We have seen, however, that Ohio has made an exception to this rule, in the case of foreign contracts, by providing, that if the right of action is barred by the law of the place where the contract is made, it shall be barred here.

3. *Discharges by Bankruptcy or Insolvency.* With respect to bankrupt or insolvent laws, the American rule differs from the English. The English rule is, that proceedings under the bankrupt law have a universal operation everywhere. We hold this doctrine only to a partial extent. Where no other rights intervene, the assignment under a foreign bankrupt or insolvent law passes the title of personalty to the assignees or commissioners; but such assignment is not good as against a subsequent attaching creditor here. And realty does not pass by such foreign assignment, unless the domestic law so provide. As to the discharge under a foreign bankrupt or insolvent law, the rule seems to be, that if the effect of the discharge be to extinguish the debt, by the law of the place of the contract, such discharge will be valid everywhere. But where the effect is only to take away some portion of the remedy, as the arrest of the debtor, such exemption from arrest is not elsewhere recognized. Such is the general principle of international law. But between the States of this Union, since no State can pass any law impairing the obligation of contracts, it is held that State bankrupt and insolvent laws can only operate upon contracts made between citizens of the State which enacts the law. (*a*)

4. *Evidence.* The general rule respecting evidence is, that its competency must depend upon the law of the forum. But in the case of deeds, wills, and other instruments of writing, it would seem to be almost a matter of necessity, that the evidence which would be sufficient to prove their execution in the place where made, should be held sufficient everywhere. With respect to foreign laws, their existence must be proved like any other facts, before the court will take notice of them. And the same is true of foreign judgments. The mode of proof varies according to the nature of the case. The great seal of a nation is sufficient to authenticate a foreign written law or judgment, but not the seal

(*a*) See *ante*, § 55, n.

of a court, except it be a court of admiralty. So a copy sworn to be a true copy will be held sufficient. But the unwritten laws and usages of foreign nations are proved, either by the exhibition of printed reports, or by the oaths of persons having the means of knowing, or sometimes by the certificates of persons in high authority.

5. *Foreign Judgments.* With respect to foreign judgments, we have already seen that the States, by a compact in the federal constitution, have ceased to be foreign to each other. The general rule is, that foreign judgments, except in courts of admiralty, are not elsewhere held conclusive even upon the merits; (*a*) but the original cause of action may again be investigated. As between the States, however, the rule is changed, and a judgment rendered in one State, when duly authenticated according to the act of Congress, must be held conclusive upon the merits in every other State. It does not, however, have the full efficacy of a domestic judgment; for execution cannot issue upon it until it has been converted into a domestic judgment by an action of debt. And the statute of limitations will operate upon this action as upon any other. (*b*)

LECTURE XLIII.

CONCLUDING REFLECTIONS.

§ 259. **Present Condition of our Jurisprudence.** We have now reached the end of this course of lectures; but before we part, let us indulge in a few reflections, which arise naturally from a retrospect of our past labors. And in the first place, you can now form some faint conception of the vast compass of the law; for without any very important omissions that I am aware of, I have called your attention to all the prominent subjects about which the law is conversant; and pointed out their general bearings, relations, and dependencies. In no instance, however, have I attempted to descend to particulars; but while I have necessarily confined my sketches to the most general outline, I have at the same time referred you to the sources of more detailed information. These sources you will hereafter consult; and you will find volumes written upon topics for which my plan would scarcely allow pages. As yet, therefore, you have only caught transient glimmerings of

(*a*) Where the record of a foreign judgment shows no service of process on him, nor any notice of the suit other than a personal one given in another country than that where the judgment was rendered, it is not even *primâ facie* evidence, but is simply null. Bischoff *v.* Wethered, 9 Wall. 813.

(*b*) This subject has been fully discussed in the case of McElmoyle *v.* Cohen, 13 Peters, 312.

the light which is to beam upon you hereafter. You have been preparing for the study of the law, but you have not yet fairly commenced it. You will devote months and perhaps years to subjects for which I could not spare hours; and if I have left no other durable impression upon your minds, I shall assuredly leave this, that a general course of lectures, like those to which you have been now listening, will not make you lawyers. In fact, these lectures have had no such pretension. If they serve you for a guide-book, they will have fulfilled their design. I stated in the outset, that I should only undertake to *introduce* you to the study of the law; and while I trust I have done thus much, I am sure that I have done no more. The acquaintance which is to result from this introduction, you must make for yourselves; and it will be the work of no short time. If any of you have selected this profession, under the expectation that the learning required for it is of easy acquisition, it is well to have the error corrected now, while you are yet upon the threshold; for be assured that nothing but days and nights of patient toil, unremittingly persevered in for years, can make any man, whatever may be his natural capacity, a consummate lawyer; and they who cannot or will not undergo such toil, will do wisely to betake themselves forthwith to some other vocation. To skim over the surface as we have now done, is comparatively nothing; you are to penetrate far into the depths; and even then still lower deeps will remain to be explored.

But in our rapid sketch of the structure of the federal and State governments, we have found the two so nicely adjusted to each other, as to form beautifully harmonious parts of one stupendous whole. I cannot use language too strong on this subject. When you come to examine with more leisure and attention, as you assuredly will, the department of constitutional law, I am persuaded you will do so with a growing sentiment of inexpressible admiration at the almost unerring wisdom and sagacity which framed a system at once so complicated and so complete, without the aid of pre-existing models. From the commencement of civilization, the grand problem in politics has been, to attain the exact medium between anarchy on the one hand and despotism on the other; and a convincing proof of the matchless excellence achieved by our American sages at a single effort, may be found in the fact that, after half a century of trial, it is even now a debated question, whether the tendency of our system be more toward the one or the other of these two extremes of political evil. Of course the fair conclusion is, that we enjoy that golden mean so long looked for, but never before discovered. In fact, the wondrous fable of Minerva's birth here finds almost an actual parallel. There is no doubt that the most sanguine anticipations of those who framed this system have been more than realized. They expected that time and trial would disclose deficiencies, and demand amendments; and they wisely made provision therefor. It is one of the transcendent beauties of the work they have left us that it admits of *reform*, without revolution. We can *amend* it at any time, without first demolishing it. As the light of experience accumulates, we can take the full advantage of it, without even a temporary inconvenience. The stately machine continues to move on, though its parts be undergoing repairs; and this crowning excellence of our organic law belongs equally to the subordinate departments; for while our people can peacefully convene and amend their constitutions, our annual legislatures stand ever ready to supply defects in the rest of the system. Time has but to make known an error or deficiency in either, and abundant provision is made to correct or supply it. Let us then glance for a moment, by way of recapitulation, at some of the more prominent changes suggested by our past observations.

§ 260. **Proposed Constitutional Amendments.** Of these I shall indicate but three, (*a*) about which I presume there cannot be much difference of opinion.

1. The exact *relations* between the federal and State governments ought to be definitely ascertained. The *nature of our Union* ought not to be matter of controversy. The deeply agitating questions of State rights, secession, nullification, and the like, ought to be put forever at rest. If the States be in fact bound together effectually, as with an adamantine chain, we ought to know it, that we may enjoy the confidence thereby inspired; if with a mere rope of sand, still we ought to know it, that we may be prepared for the worst. One way or the other, these high questions should be settled, by the most solemn and explicit declarations of the people, in the form of a constitutional amendment. I may indeed be told, as I in fact believe, that no reasonable doubt ought to exist upon these points, as the constitution now stands; but the truth is, that a wide and radical difference of opinion does exist; and whether reasonably or not, is of no consequence to the proposition; for such topics are too momentous even for plausible cavil. (*b*)

2. The extent of *incidental powers* ought to be more exactly ascertained by the constitution itself. Many indeed may think with me, that there is room for doubt at present; but as a matter of fact, we know that there is doubt. These powers have been a fruitful theme of contention ever since the first organization of the government; and there is no prospect that the controversy will cease until the people shall speak their will definitively, through the constitution itself. I would particularly mention three of the incidental powers, which pre-eminently deserve attention, on

(*a*) At the last election of president, attention was forcibly called to the dangers, in case of contested elections, growing out of our present mode of electing a president. Various modes have been suggested to remedy it, and the matter is now under consideration by a committee of the senate. It is to be hoped that some feasible change may be suggested by them and adopted, as it is an evil which certainly calls loudly for a remedy.

(*b*) The late war has settled this question, though at the expense of vast amounts of treasure, money, and blood.

account of their vast importance; namely, the power of acquiring new territory, of making internal improvements, and of protecting domestic industry. Powers of such magnitude as these ought not to be left to inference. They should be declared to exist, or not to exist, to be granted or withheld, in a manner which cannot be misunderstood. Certainly, either way would be better than the present uncertainty.

3. The vast *patronage* of government ought to be placed under the most jealous control. On this point it would seem as if there could not be two opinions. Surely corruption will find its way into our politics rapidly enough, without the resistless allurements of bribery, under the name of patronage. On this subject the lessons of history are not to be mistaken. It may indeed be said, that Congress already has the power so to regulate *appointments* and *salaries*, as to prevent all danger from this quarter. No doubt much might be done under the existing provisions of the constitution, by a different course of legislation. But unquestionably the most effectual corrective of the present evil would be so to amend the constitution as to make the president eligible for one term only. Under any possible arrangement, a tremendous patronage must be at his disposal; and by this amendment, all temptation to employ this patronage during the first term, in securing suffrages for the second, would be taken away. Having once reached the highest eminence to which political ambition can aspire, and having nothing more to gain, but everything to lose, by disgrace or dishonor, we may reasonably presume that his sole study, even on selfish principles, would be to fill and leave with honor a place he could not fill again. But time will not permit me to dwell on these topics; and I pass to the other departments of law. (*a*)

§ 261. **Proposed Extension of the Civil Code.** The important subject of legal reform has been frequently alluded to, both in general and in detail. I now propose merely to recapitulate and bring together some of the more important suggestions heretofore made. And, at the outset, there is one primary measure of reform which is capable of being so conducted as to include all others. I refer to the project of *enlarging our civil code*, which has already been discussed under the head of codification: and lest I may be misapprehended in the views before expressed, let me here say, that I do not suppose a perfect code can at once, if ever, be produced; but I cannot be mistaken in believing that a gradual approximation to a complete code may be effected; and that every effort towards such a result must produce great good. Our criminal law has been codified, though with not much systematic skill: but the other divisions of law, except here and there an isolated provision, have never received a legislative sanction. And let us suppose that

(*a*) It is the aim of the civil service bill, which has lately been discussed in Congress, to effect this object.

a philosophic stranger from a distant land, having read and admired the theory of our social system, should visit us for the purpose of becoming a citizen, if he should find our theory realized in practice. He would naturally apply to some eminent jurist for a reference to the books in which he might find the law regulating his personal and proprietary rights. And what would this jurist be obliged to tell him? Instead of pointing to an American code, the result of American legislation, and in harmony with the rest of the system, he must refer the stranger to an immense law library, composed, more than two-thirds, of English books, which it would require years to read; and must tell him to search through that library for the knowledge he wanted. But how could he satisfactorily account to such a stranger for the fact, that with the most ample provision for all needful legislation, our statute-book as yet contained only a few disconnected provisions, scattered here and there over the wide surface of the law, to fill up chasms, but furnishing no complete view of our law on any single subject? This illustration of the importance of enlarging our civil code has always struck my mind with great force. The limits of written law ought certainly to be much extended, even though unwritten law should not be wholly superseded. The great point is to introduce positive enactments in place of judicial decisions. At present judicial discretion is of two kinds: the one consists in applying fixed principles to new cases; the other in overruling former principles, and substituting new ones. Now this latter kind of discretion always produces evil; this is what a code would supersede, so far as it should extend. Judges who do not scruple to overrule precedents, would not think of questioning positive enactments. As to the other kind of discretion which applies settled principles to new cases, it must always exist, whether we have a code or not; but it would be diminished in exact proportion to the completeness of the code. At all events, it could not be increased; for the common law might still prevail, where the code should be silent. But I cannot pursue the argument, though I feel deeply impressed with the importance of the subject. Unless I greatly mistake the tendency of the times, this great enterprise is destined to occupy a wide space in the minds of the generation in which you are to be the actors; (*a*) and as the extension of our civil code will furnish the most favorable opportunity for reforming the existing law, I will now recapitulate some of the changes which our past inquiries have suggested as expedient.

§ 262. **Proposed Changes in the Law of Persons.** In the *law of persons* we have found some evils which undoubtedly admit of remedy, and some which may justly excite apprehension, without much hope of remedy.

1. *As to Slaves.* The wide prevalence of slavery is a subject

(*a*) We have seen how much of this anticipation has already become reality; and the work still advances.

upon which conjecture is utterly at fault. Like the national debt of Great Britain, its extinction baffles all calculation. One thing is certain, that the federal government cannot interfere with it, in the States where it exists, without violating a compact of peculiar sacredness, without which the Union could not have been formed, and cannot now be preserved; but all else is doubtful. Whichever way we turn, shadows, clouds, and darkness rest upon the prospect. Can the Union survive the strife which threatens to be carried on with increasing violence, between the advocates and opponents of slavery? This is a fearful question, which time only can answer.

2. *As to Aliens.* We have an immense vacant territory, which is fertile beyond example, and sold so cheap that almost every man is able to buy it. To the foreigner, therefore, we hold out every temptation to quit the crowded settlements of the Old World, and seek ease and abundance here. Upon his first arrival, we extend to him the privilege of a freeholder; and in five years, by taking the proper steps, we admit him to all the privileges of an American citizen. The natural consequence is, that Europe is annually pouring her thousands into our rushing stream of population. They come for the most part uneducated, at least in the great lessons of republicanism; and who can tell what is to be the ultimate consequence to our institutions? Will they always be safe in the hands of a population, so large a portion of whom are not born and bred to understand and love them, and who owe to them at best only a divided allegiance? Would not a longer probation for citizenship have been wiser in the first instance? Is it now too late to make the experiment? These are questions of deep moment, upon which all of us should have our minds definitively made up.

3. *As to Indians.* The condition of the Indians is a cause of sorrow rather than apprehension. Whose fault is it, that the original occupants of the American soil are dwindling away by their contact with civilization? Would a different policy have left them in as good a condition as that in which the Europeans first found them? Can any thing be done now to save them from that utter extinction, towards which they seem to be fast hastening? I state these questions, because they are of deep and mournful import. Our country must one day answer them to the enlightened world; and it is our individual duty to examine them with care, that we may form our own opinions understandingly.

4. *As to Married Women.* On this subject reform is loudly called for. There is no foundation, in reason or expediency, for the absolute and slavish subjection of the wife to the husband, which forms the foundation of her present legal relations. The law ought to furnish some means by which, in case of emergency, she can protect herself from the utter ruin in which he now has the power to involve her. Were woman, in point of fact, the abject

thing which the law in theory considers her to be when married, she would not be worthy of the companionship of man. But I have before enlarged sufficiently upon this topic.

5. *As to Debtor and Creditor.* Humanity requires that the person of a debtor should not be at the mercy of his creditor; and the law has in most places met this demand, by abolishing or qualifying imprisonment for debt. But on the other hand, justice requires that all a debtor's property should be scrupulously subjected to the payment of his debts; and that every facility should be furnished to the creditor for securing payment when there is property out of which to make it. This cannot be done, unless the utmost precaution be taken to prevent insolvent debtors from concealing their means of payment; and in this respect, our law stands greatly in need of modification.

§ 263. **Proposed Changes in the Law of Property.** In the *law of property* there are also some topics of strong interest to the friend of reform; among which are the following: —

1. *As to the Public Domain.* This is in every point of view a subject of deep anxiety. The first difficulty is to determine upon the best scheme for disposing of it; and upon this opinions are widely different. Another more serious difficulty may grow out of the exclusive claims advanced by some of the States, to the portions situated within their respective limits, in violation of the fundamental condition, upon which the whole was ceded to the United States. But the gravest question relates to the rapid formation of new States, which are extending the limits of the Union far beyond what was originally contemplated. Whether the effect of this extension will be to make us the greatest nation on the face of the globe, or to break our Union asunder by its own increasing weight, is an awful problem, which a few generations must determine one way or the other.

2. *As to the Law of Remainders.* We have seen that this immense fabric has been built upon reasons which no longer exist. It is perhaps well to allow men to make future limitations of their property, within the boundaries prescribed by the statute against perpetuities; and if so, it is certainly desirable that this should be done in the most simple and certain manner; whereas, the present law of remainders is, beyond any other branch of law, complicated and uncertain. Now a single enactment would, in a great measure, remove this objection. It is only necessary to apply to remainders created by deed, the present doctrines of executory devises, or, in other words, to give to deeds the same capacity of future operations that wills already have, and to this there can be no inherent objection. The main prop of the present fabric, as we have heretofore seen, is the particular estate which precedes the remainder. By the reform proposed, this prop being withdrawn, the fabric itself would be dispensed with. While at the same time, the object of creating remainders would be equally well attained, and in a far simpler manner.

3. *As to Mortgages.* We have seen that the design of a mortgage is to give the mortgagee a lien upon the property of the mortgagor, to secure the payment of a debt; but that when the time arrives, if the debt is not paid, the mortgagee can sue for the debt, bring ejectment for the land, and foreclose the mortgage in chancery, all at the same time, or either first, at his option. Now, this makes the nature of a mortgage much more complicated than its object requires it to be; while it gives the mortgagee the power of unnecessarily harassing the mortgagor. If the form of a mortgage were changed so as to give it no other effect than that of a common lien, the law would be greatly simplified without injury to either party. The mortgagee's security would be equally good, his remedy even more speedy, and the rights of the mortgagor would be equally well protected. Whereas, at present, owing to the fact that the equitable construction put upon a mortgage, is entirely different from its original legal effect, the law of mortgages is greatly wanting in symmetry and simplicity. (*a*)

4. *As to Descents.* In prescribing the rules by which property shall descend, the law proposes to effectuate the presumed wishes of the deceased. On this ground, as we have seen, it makes *ancestral property* descend in the blood of the ancestor from whom it came, though in so doing it should pass into hands very remote from the last owner. The expediency of this arrangement may perhaps be doubted; but I mention it here, to show how much regard the law professes to pay to the presumed wishes of the deceased. And now, I ask, why it does not carry the principle through the whole law of descent? We have seen that husband and wife are the very last persons to inherit to each other, being postponed to the most remote relative that can be found. This certainly cannot be the presumed wish of the deceased in any supposable case. Next to children, and perhaps equally with them, the husband or wife should be provided for on the principle assumed; and it seems to me that the law ought to be so changed as to make this provision. (*b*) I would further suggest, that the rule in *Shelley's case* ought to be abolished, with respect to deeds as well as wills. It professes to be a rule of construction designed to effectuate the intentions of those who make settlements of property; and yet no one can doubt that in nine cases out of ten, it directly frustrates their intentions by attaching to their language a meaning not deducible from its natural import. It gives a fee-simple where a life-estate only was intended; and thus cuts off the heirs from the limitation expressly made for them. They may perchance take by descent; but it is only a chance, and not that certainty which must have been intended by the person making the settlement.

(*a*) This evil is now remedied by the Code.
(*b*) This alteration has been made. See the last note to Lecture XXIX.

5. *As to Conveyances.* The simplicity which prevails in the transfer of personalty is perhaps all that can be desired; but it would be a great improvement, if there were some specific provision, as to what shall constitute a contract of sale. In like manner, our conveyances of realty are so much more simple and expeditious than the ancient common-law conveyances, that we have little room for complaint. But the inexcusable redundancy and surplusage of deeds, is an abuse which ought not to be tolerated. The mere statement of this proposition must carry conviction of its truth.

6. *As to Contracts.* The principal objection to the present law of contracts is found in the distinction between sealed and unsealed contracts. Abolish this, and the law of contracts would be as simple as could be desired. I am unable to conceive of a single argument in favor of continuing the use of private seals. They perpetuate a thousand distinctions without any corresponding benefits. Perhaps another improvement would be, to extend the doctrines of negotiability to a greater number of contracts. At all events, there is no reasonable foundation for the present doctrine that contracts in general cannot be assigned. They can be assigned in equity, and indirectly in law; and why not remove the restraint entirely? I can perceive no evil which would counterbalance the benefit of simplicity. Credit and traffic are now so widely extended, that such restraints are often very serious inconveniences.

§ 264. **Proposed Changes in the Law of Crimes.** In the law of crimes, the grand improvement has already been made by superseding the common law, in the definition of crimes and punishments. Our criminal enactments are pre-eminently characterized by simplicity and humanity. But even here, some improvements may be suggested.

1. *As to Definitions.* The present system is to make the definitions of crimes as specific as possible. This has been illustrated by the examples of perjury, forgery, burglary, arson, and the like. Now, the danger in such cases is, that some particulars will be omitted; whereas, there could be no danger in using general terms sufficiently comprehensive to include all possible particulars. And the brevity thereby attained would be an additional motive for the change.

2. *As to Punishments.* Whether capital punishment ought to be abolished, and solitary imprisonment for life substituted in its place, is a question of great interest, which I shall not here discuss. All agree, however, that if executions are to continue, they ought to take place *in secret.* In like manner, public opinion is strongly inclining in favor of *solitary*, instead of promiscuous, confinement. But the *abolition of fines* seems to be the reformation most required, as well on the ground of their inequality as their inefficiency. If they do not actually encourage crimes, they certainly do very little to prevent them; and they look too much like

a sale of criminal license. Lastly, the *repetition* of offences ought to be provided against by increased penalties. When an offender repeats an offence, this is proof that the former punishment was not sufficient; and the law should be imperative, in increasing the punishment.

§ 265. **Proposed Changes in the Law of Procedure.** In the law of procedure there is abundant room for improvement, particularly in common-law proceedings; for as to chancery and criminal proceedings, they are perhaps as simple and certain as we can expect to make them. The only prominent objection is to their length and redundancy, a common fault of all judicial proceedings; but the English forms have been so much pruned and corrected even in this respect, that we ought to congratulate ourselves, rather than find fault. Our common-law proceedings, however, are complicated, burdensome, and unwieldy, beyond all reason. The leading improvements suggested are as follows:

1. *As to the Forms of Action.* (*a*) We now have three distinct *actions of contract;* while in reason there can be no imaginable necessity for more than one. Indeed, by abolishing seals, as before suggested, the action of covenant would at once be dispensed with; and then debt and assumpsit could be readily consolidated. Again, there are five distinct *actions of tort*, while there can be no occasion for more than two; one to recover the specific thing, as in replevin, and the other to recover damages for injury or detention. Again, though we have gained much by extending the scope of *ejectment*, so as to supply the place of all real actions, yet that action would itself be greatly improved by striking out all the fictions, and adapting the language of the proceedings to the object they are now intended to effect. By these three measures, the law of remedies would be immensely simplified. But this is not the limit of improvement. The grandest step of all would be, to adopt the forms of *chancery proceedings* in all civil cases, leaving the principles of law as they now are. These forms are as simple and rational as we can ever hope to devise; and they are abundantly adequate to all civil remedies.

2. *As to the Pleadings.* To say nothing of the style and language of pleading, which are wholly destitute of neatness and elegance, there is a still more substantial objection to the present system. I refer to the wide prevalence of *general pleadings* as distinguished from *special.* The object of all pleading is to apprise each party accurately of the grounds assumed by the other. Special pleading effects this; general pleading does not. The *common counts* and *general issues* convey no intimation of the matters to be relied on at the trial. They may be convenient for counsel, but the ends of justice would be far better attained by requiring each party to disclose his case fully.

(*a*) These reforms have all been effected by the Code.

3. *As to Evidence.* The object of all the rules of evidence should be to establish the truth; and, in order to effect this object, and thus to complete justice between the parties, it is necessary to obtain all the light which can be had from every available source. Against false swearing, we have the restraints of moral and religious obligation, and the penalties of perjury; moreover, the jurors are competent to determine whether, under all the circumstances, a witness is to be believed or not. Is there, then, any occasion for allowing the question of *competency* to be raised? I can see no good end that it answers. On the contrary, I believe that in the average of cases, the ends of justice would be far better attained by admitting all persons, the parties themselves, persons interested, and even convicts, if they know anything relevant to the matter in issue, to give in their testimony and let it pass for what it is worth. The wide latitude of cross-examination, the astuteness of counsel, and the good sense of jurors, make it highly improbable that a false witness would escape detection. At all events the evil would be less than that which now results from the frequent exclusion of testimony which may be indispensable. (*a*)

I have thus recapitulated some of the more prominent points, in which our law, though in the main so excellent, may admit of improvement; and I commend them to your serious and deliberate consideration. During the period in which you are to be actors on the public stage, the topics I have been suggesting will be among those of the most absorbing interest. Even the existence of our Union, if not of free government itself, may be involved in some of them. It is the part of wisdom, therefore, to examine them in all their bearings, that your opinions may be fully made up when the time comes for action.

§ 266. **Ways and Means of Professional Success.** It would seem appropriate that I should close this lecture with some suggestions respecting professional success. I presume you have not selected the law as a road to great wealth; for, if so, you are almost sure to be disappointed. No lawyer in this country can become very rich in the strict pursuit of his profession. If great and rapid gains be your object, there are many vocations to be chosen before this. But if properly pursued, it will lead to independence, which is all a wise man need desire. And as to reputation, it opens an ample field. Tastes may differ on this subject; but for myself, had I the most burning thirst for fame, I would rather be a great jurist than a great statesman or hero. To answer, therefore, the question, what is included in the idea of professional success, I would say that it embraces moderate emolument and high reputation; or, in other words, that he who, at the end of his career, has acquired a reasonable independence and an honored name, has been a successful lawyer. The

(*a*) This has all been accomplished by the Code.

question then is, what are the conditions of success as thus defined? Undoubtedly, the first condition of all success is to deserve it. And this is pre-eminently true of success at the bar, which cannot be the result of luck or chance. Accident has made many a hero, and many a king, but never a Mansfield or a Marshall. And, on the other hand, there is a moral certainty of success, if you do but deserve it. You will not have it suddenly, for it is a plant of slow growth. You must take not days or months, but years, into the account. And as certainly as those years come round, so certainly will success come with them, if it be deserved. Indolence may excuse itself by the miserable plea of fatalism, that merit is not sure to meet its reward. But this is an error as pernicious as it is stale. Every observer knows that there is a sure retribution, even in this world. Public opinion may err for the moment, but in the long run it always comes out right. The question, then, is reduced to this: How are you to deserve success in your profession?

The first requisite, certainly, is a competent knowledge of the law. This has been sufficiently dwelt upon already. But I will add, that it is not enough to know and have the precise books, in which this knowledge can be had. It must be ready, available knowledge. You must have it at your tongue's end, or it may come too late for use. At first, this condition is hard to be complied with; but it will become easier as you advance. Every case will be a lesson. Your whole professional life will be one of progressive improvement. Item after item will be daily added to the sum of knowledge, until you find yourselves accomplished at all points. Prepare your first case thoroughly, and this will not only gain you a second, but enable you the more easily to master it. Thus every step you take will prepare you, with less effort to step still higher, until you reach that eminence where toil is at an end.

But a competent knowledge of the law, although the first, is not the only condition of success. The most learned of lawyers would not get business if he did not attend to it. The question with the client is, who will manage his cause the best? And other things being equal, he will manage a cause the best, who devotes most attention to it. Next to legal knowledge, therefore, the most important condition of success is, a habit of strict attention to business. Your clients must know where to find you and when to find you. Once establish a reputation for attending faithfully to whatever you undertake, and this alone will secure you a good share of business. But in order to do this, you must make the law your exclusive pursuit. You cannot be men of all work and lawyers besides. In this country, the temptation is strong to diverge from the profession, either for the sake of speculation or politics. Our young men are anxious to make money faster than by fees, and therefore enter upon a course of speculation; or, to gain notoriety faster than by regular practice, and therefore plunge into politics. But either course is fatal to distinguished professional success. The law cannot be put on and taken off like a garment. It requires all the energies you can command; and just in proportion as you direct them to other pursuits, you discourage clients from employing you, because you disqualify yourselves for attending faithfully to their interests.

Supposing, then, that you have a competent knowledge of the law, and that you attend strictly to business, is any thing more required? Undoubtedly one thing more, and that the greatest of all; I mean professional integrity. Be not misled by the false idea that cunning can be successfully substituted in its place. Now or then a trick or stratagem may succeed; but in the end chicanery always ruins him who practises it. Be as acute and discriminating as you please, but by all means avoid artifice. It never yet raised a man to honorable distinction. A cunning lawyer, if not a knave, is very likely to be mistaken for one; whereas, uncompromising probity is sure to win confidence in every quarter. You will find it as true in your practice, as in geometry, that the straight line is always the shortest distance between two points; and that the most adroit manœuvring or finesse can never prove a match for downright integrity. The rule I would inculcate not only excludes all indirection in doing business, but in obtaining it. Were I to concentrate in a single word whatever I can conceive of despicable in our profession, it would be pettifogging. I would have you feel that it is infinitely better to wait years for a case, than to obtain it by fomenting litigation. Dig or beg, if necessity drive you to it, and it will be respectable; but resolve to starve, sooner than prowl about courts for human victims. I am the more anxious to dwell upon the necessity of professional integrity, because the moral character which should belong to our profession is often egregiously misconceived or misrepresented. The vulgar notion is, that lawyers are seldom honest men. Because the profession abounds with opportunities for the practice of dishonesty, and because, occasionally, lawyers have been found who have no scruples on this score, the exceptions are perversely mistaken for the general rule, and the more ignorant part of the community seem really to believe that the conscience of every lawyer can be bought and sold. They also affect to find Scripture authority for this prejudice, in the woe so emphatically denounced upon lawyers; not knowing that a very different sort of lawyers are there anathematized. But the most efficient cause of this wholesale libel upon the profession, is to be found in the fact, that, with very few exceptions, wherever you find a lawyer introduced into the popular fictions of the day, you find him represented as an arrant knave. I need not refer to instances, for hundreds will suggest themselves. You can scarcely call to mind a novel or a drama, where a lawyer figures at all, in which he is not made use of to help out some infamous scheme of villany. In fact, I have heard this very circumstance adduced to prove that rascality must be a prominent attribute of the profession. But be the cause of the misconception what it may, we know the fact to be, that popular sentiment is greatly against us, insomuch that the question is often asked, whether the world would not be better off if there were no lawyers. No doubt it would be a happy state of society in which lawyers could be entirely dispensed with; for it would be that perfect state in which laws themselves would be superfluous; and it may also be admitted that just in proportion as laws become simple and certain, the demand for lawyers will grow less, because litigation, which is their aliment, will be correspondingly diminished. But so long as the litigious spirit exists among mankind, and the uncertainty which belongs to all human affairs furnishes occasion for its exercise the principle which requires a division of labor in all other cases will require it also in this; and we may safely conclude that a distinct class of men will always be required to conduct the litigation of their fellow men. Indeed, those who join in the obloquy so generally cast upon us, seem to forget that in so doing they reproach mankind in the mass. Let the demand for lawyers be diminished, and the supply will correspond. Let men cease to be contentious, and be always ready to do right without compulsion, and lawyers will not trouble them. But while it is evident that without dishonest clients there would be no dishonest lawyers; and that as a profession we are grossly belied by this indiscriminate censure; yet it may perhaps be safely admitted, that the standard of professional ethics is not always as elevated as the honor of the profession requires it should be. In fact, it is by no means easy to fix a precise standard. There is not, perhaps, a more difficult question in casuistry, than that which every lawyer has to decide in determining the nature and extent of his professional obligations. We are, however, to remember at the outset, that in becoming attorneys, we do not cease to be moral agents; that in pledging ourselves to our clients, we do not also pledge to them our consciences; and therefore, that no principle can justify us in doing, or our clients in requiring us to do for them, what we should blush to think of doing for ourselves. It is also obvious that even on selfish principles, honesty is the best policy for us, as it is for all other men; and, therefore, that in consultations with clients, we are not only morally bound to tell them frankly our real opinions, but it is manifestly our interest so to do, because otherwise we shall soon cease to be consulted. Again, it is clear that in conducting proceedings through the various stages of litigation, we can never be justified in attempting to mislead either the court or jury, by wilfully misrepresenting the law or the facts. Thus far there can be no room for hesitation. But if we believe that our client has the wrong side, and have candidly told him so, are we then justified in undertaking his cause, if he should persist in having it litigated? This is a question of no small difficulty, and it arises in two classes of cases; namely, *first*, when we believe the law to be against our client; and *secondly*, when, though the law may be with him, the abstract justice of the case appears to be against him. With regard to the first, when we think the law to be against him, it would seem that after so informing him, if he should still persist, we need not hesitate to act for him; because we are not infallible, and peradventure the law may turn out to be the other way; or he may have justice on his side, though the law may seem against him; and in either case, he ought not to be cut off from the chances of litigation. The chief difficulty then arises in the second class of cases, where we believe right and justice to be against our client, though the law may be with him. But even here, I have come to the conclusion, that no principle of moral obligation prohibits me from prosecuting his cause. In the first place, I am not an infallible judge of right and wrong, and possibly I may be mistaken; but at all events, I am not his conscience keeper. I undertake only to assert his legal rights; and if, in so doing, I make use of no chicanery or deception, I come out of the cause with clean hands. The question of abstract justice is with him, and not with me; and I am as much justified in conducting his cause, as the judge is in deciding it for him. But there is another more comprehensive view conducting to the same result. Every man, as a general condition of the social compact, has a right to have his case fairly presented before the court; and it is the province of counsel to assist him in so doing. Now, although there may be particular cases, which, considered by themselves, ought not to be prosecuted, yet as no line of demarcation can be drawn beforehand, to indicate which these are; if it were the duty of counsel to decide in each case, the preliminary moral question, whether they ought to undertake it, their decision against any case would be a prejudging of its merits, which might operate prejudicially upon the final result; and on this account it is a good general rule, that counsel are not to be held responsible for the moral character of the cause they advocate, but only for the manner in which they discharge their duty. This reasoning may be fallacious, but it has satisfied my own mind. I desire, however, to be distinctly understood. I abhor, as much as any one, the rascally maxim that everything is fair in litigation. I hold that the greatest fee ever offered is no justification for attempting to gain a cause by dishonest means; and I look upon that lawyer as essentially a knave, who practises upon such a doctrine. Such then are my views of professional integrity, as indispensable to professional success. I have considered the question chiefly in a worldly point of view. And the result is, that if there were no such thing as religious or moral obligation, it would still be true, that the strictest honesty is the lawyer's wisest policy. Confidence and trust are the life-blood of his being; and the All-wise Creator has ordained that integrity alone can inspire confidence and trust. Set out, then, with the unwavering purpose, that, come what may, you will hold fast to your integrity; and that the world may always know where to find you, by simply considering where you ought to be found. Let this unbending integrity co-operate with a daily increasing knowledge of the law, and a faithful attention to the business committed to you, and your success is as certain as any thing future can be. (*a*)

(*a*) There is an excellent article on The Rights and Duties of Advocates, in the Edinburgh Review, for October, 1836, No. CXXIX. p. 82.

INDEX

TO THE PRINCIPAL MATTERS.

A.

B.

C.

J.

O.

P.

T.

Y.

University Press: John Wilson & Son, Cambridge.